PDF Forms Using Acrobat® and LiveCycle® Designer Bible

PDF Forms Using Acrobat® and LiveCycle® Designer Bible

Ted Padova and Angie Okamoto

WILEY

Wiley Publishing, Inc.

PDF Forms Using Acrobat® and LiveCycle® Designer Bible

Published by
Wiley Publishing, Inc.
10475 Crosspoint Boulevard
Indianapolis, IN 46256
www.wiley.com

Copyright © 2009 by Wiley Publishing, Inc., Indianapolis, Indiana

Published simultaneously in Canada

ISBN: 978-0-470-40017-3

Manufactured in the United States of America

10 9 8 7 6 5 4 3 2 1

Ted Padova:

For Arnie.

Angie Okamoto:

For my family, who put up with me while I tried to figure out how to become an author.

About the Authors

Ted Padova is the former chief executive officer and managing partner of The Image Source Digital Imaging and Photo Finishing Centers of Ventura and Thousand Oaks, California. He has been involved in digital imaging since founding a service bureau in 1990. He retired from his company in 2005 and now spends his time writing and speaking on Acrobat, PDF forms, and LiveCycle Designer forms.

For more than 17 years, Ted taught university and higher education classes in graphic design applications and digital prepress at the University of California, Santa Barbara, and the University of California at Los Angeles. He has been, and continues to be, a conference speaker nationally and internationally at PDF conferences.

Currently he lives in the Philippines where he serves as President/CEO of his company ApoVisions, Inc. — a company working with third-world nations to develop electronic document workflows and forms routing.

Ted has written more than 30 computer books and is one of the world's leading authors on Adobe Acrobat. He has written books on Adobe Acrobat, Adobe Photoshop, Adobe Photoshop Elements, Adobe Reader, Microsoft PowerPoint, and Adobe Illustrator. Recent books published by Wiley Publishing include *Adobe Acrobat PDF Bible* (versions 4, 5, 6, 7, 8, and 9), *Adobe Creative Suite Bible* (versions CS, CS2, CS3, and CS4), *Color Correction for Digital Photographers Only, Color Mangement for Digital Photographers For Dummies, Microsoft PowerPoint 2007 For Dummies — Just the Steps, Creating Adobe Acrobat PDF Forms, Teach Yourself Visually Acrobat 5,* and *Adobe Acrobat 6.0 Complete Course*. He also co-authored *Adobe Illustrator Master Class — Illustrator Illuminated* and wrote *Adobe Reader Revealed* for Peachpit/Adobe Press.

Angie Okamoto works as the Director of Enterprise Development for Easel Solutions in Lincoln, Nebraska. She has been in the technology training industry for more than nine years. Angie is an Adobe Certified Expert, an Adobe Certified Instructor and a Master Level Microsoft Office Specialist. She currently specializes in Adobe Acrobat, Adobe LiveCycle Enterprise Suite, and PDF forms. Angie enjoys presenting at business associations and conferences on PDFs, Acrobat forms, and LiveCycle Designer forms. Teaching is her passion, getting excited about each of the new features released in the new versions of the software, and sharing them with her students.

Credits

Senior Acquisitions Editor
Stephanie McComb

Project Editor
Martin V. Minner

Technical Editor
Lori DeFurio

Copy Editor
Gwenette Gaddis Goshert

Editorial Manager
Robyn Siesky

Business Manager
Amy Knies

Senior Marketing Manager
Sandy Smith

Vice President and Executive Group Publisher
Richard Swadley

Vice President and Executive Publisher
Barry Pruett

Project Coordinator
Erin Smith

Graphics and Production Specialists
Andrea Hornberger, Nikki Gately,
Jennifer Mayberry, Sarah Philippart,
Ronald Terry

Quality Control Technician
Caitie Kelly

Proofreading
Christine Sabooni

Indexing
Broccoli Information Management

Media Development Project Manager
Laura Moss

Media Development Assistant Project Manager
Jenny Swisher

Media Development Associate Producer
Kit Malone

Contents at a Glance

Preface xxv
Acknowledgments xxxii
Introduction xxxiv

Part I: Getting Familiar with Forms 1
Chapter 1: Taking a Tour of Acrobat Forms 3
Chapter 2: Getting Started with Acrobat Forms 15
Chapter 3: Knowing Form Design Standards 33
Chapter 4: Creating Form Designs 41

Part II: Using Acrobat Forms Tools and Properties 79
Chapter 5: Creating Simple Office Forms 81
Chapter 6: Scanning Office Forms 113
Chapter 7: Working with Form Fields 137
Chapter 8: Working with Tables 181
Chapter 9: Working with Field Properties 207

Part III: Preparing Forms for Deployment 265
Chapter 10: Enabling PDF Forms for Adobe Reader 267
Chapter 11: Making Forms Accessible 291
Chapter 12: Using Signatures and Security 321
Chapter 13: Working with PDF Portfolios and Layers 367

Part IV: Managing Form Data 401
Chapter 14: Working with Data 403
Chapter 15: Working with Field Calculations 457

Part V: Working with JavaScript 487
Chapter 16: Introducing JavaScript 489
Chapter 17: Creating Simple JavaScripts 517
Chapter 18: Working with Advanced JavaScripts 547
Chapter 19: Creating JavaScripts for Acrobat Users 585

Part VI: Getting Started with LiveCycle Designer 629
Chapter 20: Using LiveCycle Designer on the Macintosh 631
Chapter 21: Introducing LiveCycle Designer 639
Chapter 22: Getting Familiar with the Designer Workspace 655

Part VII: Creating XML Forms 695

Chapter 23: Designing Forms in LiveCycle Designer ES 697
Chapter 24: Working with Designer's Form Fields and Objects...................................743
Chapter 25: Working with Objects..789

Part VIII: Creating Dynamic Forms with LiveCycle Designer 821

Chapter 26: Creating Dynamic XML Forms...823
Chapter 27: Working with Tables..833
Chapter 28: Working with Subforms..873

Part IX: Working with Data and Scripts 925

Chapter 29: Introducing LiveCycle Designer Scripting...927
Chapter 30: Deploying Forms...971
Chapter 31: Working with Data...993
Chapter 32: Examining Some Dynamic Forms..1027
Chapter 33: Working with Databases 1055
Chapter 34: Introducing LiveCycle Enterprise Suite 1071
Chapter 35: Getting More Help with LiveCycle Designer..1109

Appendix: Using the CD-ROM 1125
Index 1129
End-User License Agreement 1185

Contents

Preface . . . . **xxv**

About This Book xxv
Staying Connected xxix
Contacting Us xxxi

Acknowledgments . . . . **xxxii**

Introduction . . . .**xxxiv**

Part I: Getting Familiar with Forms   1

Chapter 1: Taking a Tour of Acrobat Forms 3

Starting with a PDF Document.. 3
Populating a Form with Field Objects 5
Editing a Form 7
Adding Special Features to PDF Documents 10
Aggregating Form Data 11
Moving On 13
Summary 13

Chapter 2: Getting Started with Acrobat Forms 15

Understanding the Forms Industry 15
    Comparing costs 16
    Why Acrobat forms are cost effective 17
What Are PDF Forms? 18
    Scanned paper forms... 18
    Static forms... 18
    Fillable forms 20
Looking at Forms Hosted on Web Servers 21
Understanding the Acrobat Viewers 29
    Acrobat viewers... 29
    Using different versions of Acrobat 30
Summary 32

Contents

Chapter 3: Knowing Form Design Standards 33

Looking at Some Forms Standards...33

BFMA standards...35

W3C standards 36

Individual standards...36

Designing Forms for the Form Recipient...36

Rules for PDF Forms Designs..38

Summary 40

Chapter 4: Creating Form Designs 41

Designing PDF Forms 41

Using Tools for Form Designs..43

Using Microsoft Word to design forms..44

Using Microsoft Excel to design forms..54

Using Microsoft PowerPoint as a forms designer 55

Using OpenOffice.org Writer as a forms designer.......................................56

Using layout programs for form design 57

Using illustration programs to design forms..58

Using other programs to create forms...58

Creating PDF Files 59

Using PDFMaker to convert to PDF documents (Windows only) 59

Using Acrobat to convert to PDF..62

Exporting to PDF 64

Using Acrobat Distiller 65

Modifying Forms 67

Editing text 68

Editing objects 70

Editing images..72

Replacing pages..73

Setting Initial Views 75

Adjusting Layout and Magnification..76

Using Window Options..77

User Interface Options 77

Summary 78

Part II: Using Acrobat Forms Tools and Properties   **79**

Chapter 5: Creating Simple Office Forms 81

Understanding Form Editing Mode..81

Getting Familiar with the Form Editing interface 82

Toggling views 88

Editing fields in Viewer mode 92

Using the Wizards to Create PDF Forms 94
    Converting a native file to a PDF form (Windows) 95
    Creating a form from a PDF file..99
    Setting properties 99
Adding Field Objects 101
    Adding fields..101
    Adding essential buttons 103
Overcoming Auto Field Detection Problems 109
Saving Forms 110
Summary 111

Chapter 6: Scanning Office Forms 113
Setting Up Acrobat Scan 113
    Understanding scanner drivers...114
    Creating presets (WIA scanners on Windows)..............................116
    Setting scanner options 120
Recognizing Text Using OCR 120
    Understanding Acrobat's text recognition features.........................121
    Converting image files to text (in Windows) 123
    Converting image files to text (on a Macintosh)..........................125
    Recognizing text in multiple files.......................................126
Converting Paper Forms to PDF Forms...128
    Converting a paper form to a fillable form...............................131
    Scanning forms for Adobe LiveCycle Designer (Acrobat Pro/Pro Extended for
        Windows only)..133
Using Batch Sequences...134
Summary 136

Chapter 7: Working with Form Fields 137
Understanding the Field Types 137
    Loading the Form tools..138
    Working with text fields..139
    Using some common features for Form tools 140
    Working with button fields..142
    Working with check box fields...143
    Working with radio button fields 144
    Working with list boxes 145
    Working with combo boxes 146
    Working with digital signature fields.....................................147
    Working with barcode fields...148
    Getting familiar with the Form tools.....................................149
Naming Fields...150
    Auto field naming in Acrobat 151
    Editing field names...151
    Using hierarchical names..154

Contents

Managing Fields...155
    Organizing fields...155
    Creating multiple copies of fields 161
    Creating forms in Viewer mode 163
Using Rulers, Guides, and Grids 165
    Using Rulers 165
    Working with grids 166
Filling in Forms 169
    Using the Typewriter tool.......................................169
    Navigating form fields 171
Setting Field Tab Orders 176
Summary 179

Chapter 8: Working with Tables 181

Creating Tables in PDF Forms 181
    Auto-detecting fields in tables 183
    Adding fields manually to tables.............................190
Converting Tables to Application Documents 199
    Exporting tables to Microsoft Excel 200
    Exporting tables to Microsoft Word 202
Exporting Table Data 204
Summary 205

Chapter 9: Working with Field Properties 207

Getting to Know the Properties Window..........................207
    Using default views 208
    Using tab options 209
Understanding Field Properties Options 211
    Working with General properties 211
    Assigning appearances to fields 213
    Setting Options properties......................................217
    Using Actions properties 230
    Using the Format properties....................................236
    Using Validate properties 238
    Understanding the Calculate properties....................239
    Using Selection Change properties 240
    Setting digital signature fields properties 240
    Using the barcode properties..................................241
    Using the Properties bar 243
Editing Multiple Fields Properties 244
Using Field Properties..245
    Setting text field properties....................................246
    Setting check box properties for mutually exclusive fields...255
    Setting button field properties 257
Summary 263

Part III: Preparing Forms for Deployment   265

Chapter 10: Enabling PDF Forms for Adobe Reader 267

Understanding Reader Enablement 267
    Knowing the licensing limitations 268
    Using form servers 269
Adding Permissions for Adobe Reader Users...270
    Enabling PDFs for form save and digital signatures 270
    Enabling PDFs for commenting..272
    Using wizards to enable files 277
    Enabling LiveCycle Designer forms 278
Editing Enabled Forms 278
    Keeping backups of forms prior to enabling..278
    Editing enabled PDF files 279
    Working with enabled files and PDF Portfolios 280
Using Batch Sequences...281
    Using preset sequences for PDF forms..284
    Creating custom sequences 287
Summary 289

Chapter 11: Making Forms Accessible 291

Understanding Accessibility...292
    Understanding assistive devices...293
    Creating a workflow for authoring accessible PDF forms......................296
Tagging PDF Files 297
    Checking the status of tagged PDF files 297
    Creating tags in untagged documents...302
Designing Forms for Accessibility 305
    Designing an accessible form 308
    Choosing a language 310
    Setting up form fields..311
    Editing form elements 312
Summary 319

Chapter 12: Using Signatures and Security. 321

Understanding Digital Signatures..321
    Using third-party signature handlers 323
    Using wet signatures 323
Creating Digital Signatures..331
    Exploring digital ID and security menu commands...............................332
    Creating a digital ID 334
    Using signature fields 341
    Locking fields...342
    Applying multiple signatures on a form..345
    Validating signatures 346

Contents

Using Password Security 354
    Understanding the security settings options 355
    Using a security policy 359
Summary 364

Chapter 13: Working with PDF Portfolios and Layers 367

Creating PDF Portfolios 368
    Creating a new PDF Portfolio 368
    Working with details 376
    Navigating PDF Portfolios 381
    Enabling forms in PDF Portfolios 390
    Submitting forms from PDF Portfolios 390
Working with Layers...391
    Using layered PDF forms...391
    Adding new layers to a form...393
Summary 399

Part IV: Managing Form Data   401

Chapter 14: Working with Data 403

Deploying Forms 404
    Hosting forms on Web sites 404
    Distributing forms via e-mail..406
    E-mailing forms using Acrobat 412
    Participating in an e-mail form distribution..413
    Hacking the Submit Form button..416
Working with Network Servers..422
Using Acrobat.com 424
    Logging into Acrobat.com 425
    Using Acrobat.com services..427
    Submitting forms to Acrobat.com..429
    Viewing files on Acrobat.com 432
Managing Data...434
    Using the Tracker..434
    Managing responses from distributed forms.......................................437
    Managing manually distributed forms 450
Summary 456

Chapter 15: Working with Field Calculations 457

Using Acrobat's Preset Formulas 457
    Formatting fields...458
    Getting familiar with calculation formulas..460
    Averaging data 462
    Calculating a product 466

Summing data 469
Summing and averaging data 470
Setting field calculations orders 479
Using Simplified Field Notation 480
Naming fields for SFN 481
Performing math calculations with SFN 481
Calculating Time 482
Designing a form using time calculations 483
Creating time calculations 484
Summary 485

Part V: Working with JavaScript   487

Chapter 16: Introducing JavaScript 489

Getting Started with Acrobat JavaScript 490
Finding JavaScripts 490
Using the JavaScript Debugger 498
Using the JavaScript Console 500
Writing a script in the console 500
Copying and pasting scripts 502
Changing editors 504
Learning JavaScript 505
Searching for JavaScripts 505
Reviewing manuals 505
Using online services 511
Filing Scripts 512
Summary 516

Chapter 17: Creating Simple JavaScripts 517

Creating Application Alerts 518
Creating a message alert 518
Assessing viewer versions 520
Assessing viewer types 522
Adding alerts to document actions 523
Adding application beeps 524
Managing Field Behaviors 525
Showing and hiding fields 525
Locking fields 529
Changing highlight color 530
Changing text colors 531
Check box and radio button behaviors 536
Creating Form Submission Scripts 539
Submitting a form 539
Submitting form data 540

Contents

Using Scripts for Printing..541
    Printing a document...541
    Printing a page...541
    Eliminating fields from print 541
Creating Document Viewing Scripts..542
    Resetting fields 542
    Zooming views...544
    Navigating pages 545
    Full Screen scripts 545
Summary 546

Chapter 18: Working with Advanced JavaScripts 547

Adding Annotations 547
    Assessing coordinates 548
    Adding a text box comment 550
Writing Calculation Scripts..553
    Summing columns and rows 553
    Calculating a sales tax 556
    Calculating a shipping charge..559
    Date stamping a form 561
Custom Formatting Fields...564
    Eliminating zeros 564
    Creating fixed response options 569
    Moving items between lists...573
Creating Application Response Dialog Boxes....................................577
    Using an application response dialog box for a name field 577
    Using an application response dialog box for a credit card number........580
Working with Optional Content Groups..582
Summary 584

Chapter 19: Creating JavaScripts for Acrobat Users 585

Adding Fields via JavaScript...586
    Designing the form...586
    Using the addField Object...594
    Deleting fields 598
Spawning Pages from Templates 598
    Creating page templates 599
    Appending pages to a document 600
    Overlaying templates on form pages...602
    Working with scanned forms 603
Sending Data to Secondary Forms...613
    Setting up secondary forms 614
    Sending data to summary forms 615
    Summarizing data with paper forms..617

Adding Menu Commands 623
    Adding functions to menus 624
    Adding URLs to menus 627
Summary 628

Part VI: Getting Started with LiveCycle Designer   629

Chapter 20: Using LiveCycle Designer on the Macintosh 631

Understanding Designer's Development...632
Setting Up Designer on the Macintosh 633
    Using virtualization software 633
    Installing Acrobat on Windows 634
    Justifying the costs 635
Editing XML Files in Acrobat 636
Summary 638

Chapter 21: Introducing LiveCycle Designer 639

Why LiveCycle Designer?..640
    Creating dynamic forms 640
    Understanding system requirements 642
Knowing Designer Advantages and Limitations....................................643
    What you can do with LiveCycle Designer 643
    What you cannot do with LiveCycle Designer 644
Using LiveCycle Designer and Acrobat..645
    Editing XML forms in Acrobat...646
    Enabling XML forms in Acrobat 647
    Distributing XML forms in Acrobat 648
Looking at the Installed Files 648
    Examining the sample files 648
    Using the scripting references...652
Summary 653

Chapter 22: Getting Familiar with the Designer Workspace 655

Getting Familiar with the LiveCycle Designer Environment 655
    Navigating the welcome window...656
    Creating forms with the New Form Assistant 657
    Examining the workspace 661
    Examining the Fields palettes..669
    Working with the tabs..679
Customizing the Workspace 681
    Using the Window menu 681
    Changing palette views..687
    Using the View menu 692
Summary 694

Contents

Part VII: Creating XML Forms   695

Chapter 23: Designing Forms in LiveCycle Designer ES 697

Creating New Forms from Blank Pages 698
    Setting up the environment 700
    Creating blank new forms 704
    Using the New Form Assistant wizard 705
    Adding objects to a blank page 706
    Using Microsoft Word documents 725
    Using Microsoft Excel spreadsheets 730
Creating a Form Based on a Template 732
    Examining the templates 732
    Creating a form from a template 733
    Creating a custom template 734
Importing a PDF Document 741
Summary 742

Chapter 24: Working with Designer's Form Fields and Objects 743

Adding Fields and Objects to a Form 743
    Using the drag and drop metaphor 744
    Stamping fields and objects 746
    Drawing fields and objects 748
    Copying fields and objects 749
    Using the Insert menu to add objects 750
    Using the Tools toolbar to add objects 750
    Duplicating fields and objects 752
    Using Copy Multiple 753
    Selecting and aligning objects 755
    Grouping fields and objects 762
Examining the Object Library Palette 763
    Working with object types and default settings 763
    Exploring the Standard Group 766
    Exploring the My Favorites group 767
    Exploring the Custom Group 768
    Exploring the Barcodes Group 769
Creating Custom Library Objects 771
    Creating a new library group 771
    Adding a new library object 773
    Managing custom library objects 774
    Sharing a custom library 775
Form Fragments 778
    Creating form fragments 778
    Creating fragment library groups 780
    Using form fragments 780
    Updating form fragments 783

Adding Fields and Objects to Master Pages 784
Using the Object Editor 785
Summary 786

Chapter 25: Working with Objects 789

Formatting Field Objects Appearances... 789
Changing Appearance properties... 790
Changing object attributes.. 795
Changing font attributes... 797
Setting paragraph attributes... 799
Editing strokes and fills.. 801
Setting Field Object Properties... 805
Changing field attributes... 805
Binding data to fields.. 807
Understanding pattern types... 812
Setting Tab Orders... 817
Reordering fields... 817
Changing the views... 818
Returning to normal edit mode 819
Summary 820

Part VIII: Creating Dynamic Forms with LiveCycle Designer 821

Chapter 26: Creating Dynamic XML Forms 823

Comparing Static and Dynamic Forms... 823
Creating dynamic forms in Acrobat... 828
Using dynamic elements in Designer 829
Understanding data binding.. 829
Understanding Runtime... 830
Using the Hierarchy Palette.. 830
Understanding Dynamic Properties.. 831
Summary 832

Chapter 27: Working with Tables 833

Creating Tables in LiveCycle Designer ES 834
Creating a static table in Designer.. 836
Creating static tables using Insert Table.. 843
Working with dynamic tables.. 845
Working with Table Data... 851
Creating an XML file 852
Adding field objects from a data source file 856
Creating Sections in Tables... 860
Designing the form.. 861
Adding fields... 865
Summary 872

Contents

Chapter 28: Working with Subforms **873**

Creating Subforms 874

   Setting subform properties 878

   Adding headers (overflow leaders) and footers (overflow trailers) to subforms 888

   Previewing a dynamic form 892

   Nesting subforms 894

   Using tables for dynamic subforms..901

   Creating dynamic expanding text fields..903

Creating User-Controlled Dynamic Forms...915

   Understanding the Instance Manager 916

   Creating buttons to call the Instance Manager 916

Testing Forms and Previewing XML Data in Dynamic Forms............................919

   Creating some sample XML data 920

   Importing sample XML data 922

Summary 924

Part IX: Working with Data and Scripts   925

Chapter 29: Introducing LiveCycle Designer Scripting **927**

Scripting Advantages..928

Using the Script Editor..930

Setting Scripting Language Preferences 932

Writing Scripts...934

   Referencing objects 939

   Choosing the right scripting event...944

   Using FormCalc 946

   Using JavaScript 955

Debugging Scripts..961

Getting Help 965

   Using the FormCalc user reference 966

   Using the LiveCycle Designer Scripting Reference 967

Comparing Scripting Languages...968

Summary 969

Chapter 30: Deploying Forms **971**

Preparing for Deployment...971

Saving LiveCycle Designer Forms..974

   Saving static forms 977

   Saving dynamic forms 978

   Setting the target version 979

   Saving XDP forms 981

   Rendering HTML forms...981

   Rendering form guides 982

Adding Security 985
Distributing Forms 989
Summary 991

Chapter 31: Working with Data **993**

Creating an XML File 994
    Understanding XML structure 996
    Using XML editors 999
Creating New Data Connection 1001
    Binding to an XML schema 1003
    Binding to an XML sample file 1005
    Binding to an OLEDB database 1007
    Binding to a WSDL file 1015
Setting Field Data Bindings 1022
    Setting bindings to existing fields 1022
    Setting bindings while creating new fields 1025
Summary 1026

Chapter 32: Examining Some Dynamic Forms **1027**

Working with Designer's Tutorials 1027
Examining the Sample Forms 1029
    Copying the Sample files 1030
    Examining the Dunning Notice form 1030
    Examining the E-ticket form 1033
    Examining the Form Guide 1035
    Examining the Grant Application form 1039
    Examining the Purchase Order form 1041
    Examining the Scripting form 1043
    Examining the SubformSet forms 1047
    Examining the Tax Receipt form 1049
Exploring Sample Forms Online 1053
Summary 1054

Chapter 33: Working with Databases **1055**

Working with a Database 1056
    Exploring a database design 1057
    Importing data into an Access database 1061
    Exporting data from the Access database 1063
Importing Data from a Database 1064
    Testing the exported database data in the original form 1065
    Modifying a form for importing data 1067
Summary 1070

Contents

Chapter 34: Introducing LiveCycle Enterprise Suite **1071**

    Examining a Process 1072
        Looking at the paper workflow 1072
        Comparing a paper process to the LiveCycle ES workflow 1073
        Justifying the need for electronic processes 1073
        Exploring the LiveCycle ES solution...1074
    Getting an Overview of LiveCycle ES 1080
        LiveCycle ES clients 1081
        LiveCycle ES Foundation 1082
        LiveCycle ES solution components...1086
        LiveCycle ES development tools...1088
    Taking a Tour of LiveCycle Workspace ES...1094
        What is the Workspace?...1095
        Overview of the interface...1095
    Optimizing Designer Forms–Server Deployment 1102
        Scripting considerations 1104
        File type considerations...1105
        Additional server-required objects...1106
    Summary 1107

Chapter 35: Getting More Help with LiveCycle Designer **1109**

    Using Some Help Guidelines...1109
    Using Internet Resources..1111
    Using the Reference Manuals 1114
        LiveCycle Designer Help Guide...1115
        Using scripting guides...1120
    Monitoring RSS Feeds...1121
    Summary 1124

Appendix: Using the CD-ROM. **1125**

    System Requirements...1125
    Installation Instructions 1125
    Contents 1126
        Adobe Reader 9.0...1126
        PDF version of the book..1126
        Author-created PDF documents 1126
        PDF forms eBook 1127
    Troubleshooting...1127
    Customer Care...1127

Index **1129**

End-User License Agreement **1185**

PDF Forms Using Acrobat and LiveCycle Designer Bible is written for a cross-platform audience. Users of Microsoft Windows XP Professional or Home Edition, Windows Vista Professional and Home Editions, Tablet PC Edition, and Apple Macintosh computers running OS X v10.2.8, 10.3, 10.5 and later will find references to these operating systems.

About This Book

This book is like having two books in one. The first half of the book is devoted to working with Adobe Acrobat on both Windows and the Macintosh. The second half of the book is devoted entirely to LiveCycle Designer ES, which is a Windows-only program. In Chapter 20 we provide some guidance for using LiveCycle Designer ES on an Intel Macintosh computer using virtual desktop software, the Windows operating system, and the Windows version of Acrobat Pro.

Most of the chapters in the first part of the book include screenshots from Acrobat running under Windows. The user interface is closely matched between Windows and the Macintosh; therefore, Macintosh users will find the same options in dialog boxes and menu commands as found in the screenshots taken on a Windows machine. Where significant differences occur, you'll find additional screenshots taken on a Macintosh to distinguish the differences.

With the exception of Chapter 20, the second half of the book shows screen shots take on Windows only. Because LiveCycle Designer ES is a Windows application, you'll fine no images taken on the Macintosh.

How to read this book

This book is designed for the novice forms author as well as intermediate and advanced users of Acrobat Standard, Acrobat Pro, Acrobat Pro Extended, and Adobe LiveCycle Designer ES. We created a publication that's like having two books in one. Because LiveCycle Designer ES ships with Acrobat for Windows users, we broke the book up to cover in the first half all you need to know about PDF forms using Acrobat Standard or one of the Pro applications. The second part of the book is for Windows-only users who want to know how to create dynamic forms using Adobe LiveCycle Designer ES.

To begin with, you need to think about what application you have access to. If you're a Windows user you need to decide what application you want to work with — either Acrobat or LiveCycle Designer ES. If you're a Macintosh user and you want to create dynamic forms using LiveCycle Designer ES, your first stop should be Chapter 20 where we talk about how you can install LiveCycle Designer ES on an Intel Mac.

If PDF forms are of interest to you then Chapters 1 through 19 are where you want to spend your time reading pages related to Acrobat forms. If you're interest is in LiveCycle Designer you'll want to look at Chapter 3 where we talk about forms standards that apply to all forms authors, and then move on to Chapter 21 where we begin talking about LiveCycle Designer.

Although we made our best effort to develop this work to read in a nonlinear fashion, there are some basics that all forms authors need to know respective to the programs. You'll find some of the essentials for Acrobat forms in Chapters 1 through 5. For LiveCycle Designer, you'll find the basics covered in Chapters 21 through 25.

We made an effort to support key concepts liberally with exercises through most of the chapters. This design affords you an opportunity to jump into a chapter, step through an exercise and get right to the point where you can apply what you learn to a real world form creation task. Included in the chapters you'll find many Cross-Ref icons that refer you to other chapters where you can find information to amplify a concept or description of a program feature.

Throughout several chapters related to working with Acrobat Forms we included URL resources where you can learn some more information. You can go beyond the material in this book for more in-depth learning on specific topics like using JavaScript or creating accessible forms.

For readers interested in LiveCycle Designer, we know that using this program is not easy. It takes some hard work and dedicated study to become proficient with the program. In Chapter 35 we provide some recommendations for learning more and we included URL links to a wealth of resources.

You will find exercises in most of the chapters, and we loaded up the CD-ROM with sample files that correspond to almost every series of steps. In some chapters we provide you with sample files in different stages to help you follow steps in a chapter. We included PDF documents for all sample files so the Acrobat users can see the results of the files we created in LiveCycle Designer. We recommend looking over the example files to see the results of various editing jobs. Each file related to the exercises is contained in folders respective to the chapters. Therefore, you can easily find a chapter that describes steps to create a form from a given chapter folder on the CD-ROM.

Icons

The use of icons throughout the book offers you an at-a-glance hint of what content is being addressed. You can jump to this text to get extra information, be warned of a potential problem, or amplify the concept being addressed in the text. In this book you'll find icons for the following:

CAUTION A Caution icon alerts you to a potential problem in using Acrobat or LiveCycle Designer, any tools or menus, or any supporting application that may be the origination of a document to be converted to PDF. Pay close attention to these caution messages to avoid potential problems.

CROSS-REF The Cross-Ref icon indicates a cross-reference to another area in the book where more information can be found on a topic. It is almost impossible to walk you through creating a form for a given purpose in a linear fashion because there may be many interrelated features. Covering all aspects of a single feature in a contiguous section of the book just doesn't work. Therefore, some common features for a command, a tool, an action, or task may be spread out and discussed in different chapters. When the information is divided between different sections of the book, you'll find a Cross-Ref icon that cross-references the current passage to another part of the book covering related information.

NOTE A Note icon signifies a message that may add more clarity to a text passage or help you deal with a feature more effectively.

ON the CD-ROM This icon directs you to related material on the CD-ROM.

TIP Tips are handy shortcuts. They help you to more quickly produce results or work through a series of steps to complete a task. Some tips provide information that may not be documented in the Help files accompanying Acrobat Professional.

The book's contents

This book is about creating forms using Adobe Acrobat Standard (on Windows), Adobe Acrobat Pro on Windows and the Macintosh, Adobe Acrobat Pro Extended on Windows, and Adobe LiveCycle Designer ES on Windows. All the content related to Acrobat Forms in Chapters 1 through 19 in the book applies to Acrobat Standard, unless you see a reference that a specific section applies only to Acrobat Pro or Pro Extended. Acrobat Pro features are clearly marked throughout the book so you know when Acrobat Standard doesn't support a particular feature. In many instances we refer to Acrobat Pro to include both Pro and Pro Extended. When a feature is unique to Acrobat Pro Extended (and there are few of these), you'll find a specific mention of this difference.

Just about everything you need to know to create PDF and XML forms is contained in this book. This book is *not* about using the many different features of Acrobat and all the options you have available for PDF creation. We stick to working with forms tools and converting documents most often used to create forms designs.

To simplify your journey through working with the two programs covered in this book, we broke up the chapters into nine separate parts. A total of 35 chapters address Acrobat and LiveCycle Designer features best used by forms authors. The nine parts include the following:

Part I: Getting Familiar with Forms. To start off, we begin with taking a tour of Acrobat Forms in Chapter 1. This chapter gets you involved in creating a form before we explain anything else about authoring forms in Acrobat. By the time you finish this chapter you can create forms for a number of purposes for your company. In Chapters 2 through 4 we cover information that should be of interest to all forms authors. We cover designing forms, following standards, and show examples of what we consider to be good form designs and some not so good form designs.

Part II: Using Acrobat Forms Tools and Properties. You have a number of different tools in Acrobat designed for creating forms and you have a variety of file formats that can be used to create PDF forms. In Chapter 5 we start this part discussing simple office forms, the purpose for these kinds of forms, and easy methods you can employ to create the forms. In Chapter 6 we talk about converting paper forms to electronic forms using Acrobat's built-in scanning and Optical Character Recognition (OCR) features. Tables are a fundamental design element in many forms and we devoted two chapters in the book to creating tables on forms. The first chapter appears in this part where we talk about creating tables in Acrobat. To finish up this part we cover the vast number of forms properties you can assign to all the field types.

Part III: Preparing Forms for Deployment. After you complete a form in Acrobat, you'll want to add some additional edits to prepare a form for distribution. This part relates to many of the things you'll want to handle before you actually deploy a form. In Chapter 10 we talk about adding special features to a PDF form for Adobe Reader users. In Chapter 11 we talk about making forms accessible to meet U.S. government standards for document accessibility. We move on to Chapter 12 where we talk about adding security to forms and using digital signatures. We finish up this part talking about some of the benefits for using forms with PDF Portfolios and creating forms with layers.

Part IV: Managing Form Data. When you've prepared your forms and are ready to distribute the form to recipients, you'll want to learn some of the ways you can handle the form data when forms are returned to you. In Chapter 14 we talk about distributing forms and collecting data from recipients. In Chapter 15 we talk about calculating field data.

Part V: Working with JavaScript. We often refer to many forms created in LiveCycle Designer as dynamic forms where the form recipient interacts with a form and the form is modified according to user input. These dynamic characteristics of a form can be applied to Acrobat Forms through the use of JavaScript. We realize many novice users may be unskilled at writing scripts so we begin this part with an introduction to JavaScript that any user can understand. In Chapter 17 we extend the knowledge from Chapter 16 and provide a number of code examples with two lines of JavaScript code that any user can comprehend. In Chapter 18 we move on to more advanced JavaScripting and in Chapter 19 we finish up the chapters related to Acrobat Forms by covering more in-depth JavaScripts designed to work only with Acrobat.

Part VI: Getting Started with LiveCycle Designer. This section begins the part of the book devoted to LiveCycle Designer. In Chapter 20 we talk about how Macintosh users can install LiveCycle Designer on Intel Macs. In Chapter 21 we put the Mac to rest and for the remainder of the book we stick to working with LiveCycle Designer on Windows. Chapter 21 is an introduction to LiveCycle Designer and Chapter 22 gives you an in-depth look at the Designer workspace.

Part VII: Creating XML Forms. This part covers some essentials related to designing forms in LiveCycle Designer from new blank pages, converting Word and Excel documents to Designer forms, using PDF Backgrounds, and creating Designer templates. The chapter is designed to take you on a tour of forms development in Designer before we look in-depth at all the assets you have for adding objects to a form. We add the definitions for the many different objects and objects properties in Chapters 24 and 25.

Part VIII: Creating Dynamic Forms with LiveCycle Designer. What makes a form dynamic in Designer is handled through subforms and scripts. We leave the static forms designs from Part VII and begin this part by talking about creating XML forms. In Chapter 27 we cover tables and in Chapter 28 we cover using subforms and how to add dynamic features to forms.

Part IX: Working with Data and Scripts. This part addresses working with data from XML forms. We begin this part by talking about scripting using FormCalc and JavaScript then move on to deploying forms in Chapter 30. Chapter 31 covers a number of ways to work with XML data and in Chapter 32 we look at sample files designed to add dynamic features to forms and manipulate data. In Chapter 34 we talk about working with servers to manage data. We finish up the sections on LiveCycle Designer by covering many methods you can use to learn the program in more depth in Chapter 35.

Staying Connected

Acrobat and LiveCycle Designer are on fierce upgrade programs with a new revision appearing every 18–24 months. When the first release of a new version is made, you may find a bug in the program. Adobe engineers are constantly working to make all their products efficient and stable. During some releases you may find a maintenance upgrade that is provided free to registered users. You should stay in constant contact with Adobe's Web site to learn about any program fixes, new features, and new versions.

Internet connection

With newer releases of computer software, an Internet connection is now essential. Programs, including Acrobat and LiveCycle Designer, prompt you routinely to check for updates over the Internet. To optimize your performance with Acrobat and Designer, you should run the software on a computer that has an Internet connection.

Registration

Regardless of whether you purchase Acrobat Pro Extended, Acrobat Pro, Acrobat Standard, or download the free Adobe Reader software, Adobe Systems has made it possible to register the product. You can register on the Web or mail a registration form to Adobe. You will find great advantage in being a registered user. First, update information will be sent to you, so you'll know when a product revision occurs. Second, information can be distributed to help you achieve the most out of using Acrobat and/or LiveCycle Designer. By all means, complete the registration. It will be to your benefit.

Web sites to contact

Obviously, the first Web site to frequent is Adobe's Web site. When Acrobat and the Acrobat plugins are revised, downloads for updates will become available. You can also find tips, information, and problem solutions. Visit Adobe's Web site at `www.adobe.com`. Also make use of the Help➪Adobe Expert Support menu command in all Acrobat viewers. This command opens a Web page where you can order technical support for a nominal fee. To acquire plug-ins for Acrobat visit the Adobe Store where you can find a comprehensive list of plug-ins and demonstration software that works with Acrobat. Visit the Adobe Store at: `www.store.adobe.com/store`.

For LiveCycle Designer, you have a number of different resources available to help you learning the program, downloading sample files, and information on all the LiveCycle products that work together in concert with Designer. Look over the information in Chapter 25 where we included a number of URL links to help you find more information on using Designer.

A wealth of information is available on the Acrobat Users Community Web site at `www.acrobat users.com`. Here you can find tips, techniques, blogs hosted by some of the world's leading Acrobat professionals, and support for starting and maintaining a local Acrobat User Group. Be certain to routinely check Acrobat Users for up-to-date information and assistance. You can e-mail leading professionals who can help you solve problems.

Acrobat and LiveCycle Designer tips are available on many Web sites — all you need to do is search the Internet for Acrobat or LiveCycle Designer information.

If learning more about Acrobat and/or LiveCycle Designer is your interest, you can find regional conferences sponsored by Mogo Media. If you want to meet and discuss PDF issues and dynamic forms with some of the world's experts, look for a conference in your area. You can find information at `www.mogo-media.com/`.

If JavaScript is what you want to learn, you can find information on Thom Parker's Acrobat Users blog site. Log on to `www.acrobatusers.com/tech_corners/javascript_corner/` to see Thom's JavaScript Corner, which contains a number of blog posts on using Acrobat JavaScript. Thom also hosts the `www.pdfscripting.com` Web site where you'll find hours and hours of video tutorials, easy copy/paste JavaScripts, a generous library of PDF example forms, automation tools, and the most comprehensive single source of information on using Acrobat JavaScript. When we're in trouble with getting our code debugged, Thom is always the person who bails us out and helps us correct our errors.

A new conference has popped up in the Midwestern part of the U.S.A. in Minneapolis/St. Paul. To find out more about the Acrobat Central Conference log on to `www.pdfcentral conference.com`.

In Japan try out the PDF Conference held in Tokyo. Visit `www.pdfconf.gr.jp` for more information.

Whatever you may desire can usually be found on some Web site. New sites are developed continually so be certain to make frequent searches.

Contacting Us

If, after reviewing this publication, you feel some important information was overlooked or you have any questions concerning Acrobat or LiveCycle Designer, you can contact us and let us know your views, opinions, hoorahs, complaints, or provide information that might get included in the next revision. (If it's good enough, you might even get a credit line in the acknowledgments!) By all means, send us a note.

For Ted, send your e-mail inquiries to: `ted@west.net`.

For Angie, send your e-mail inquiries to: `angie.okamoto@gmail.com`.

Chances are that if you have a problem or question about Acrobat or Designer, you're not alone and many others might be interested in your question and a response to the question. Send your questions directly to Ted's blog on Acrobat Users at: `www.acrobatusers.com/blogs/ted padova`. You also can visit the Acrobat Users Forum at: `www.acrobatusers.com/forums/aucbb/`. In addition to Ted's blog, some very talented friends who are skilled in both programs host blogs on Acrobat Users. Visit `www.acrobatusers.com/blogs` to see a complete list of the blog hosts.

If you happen to have some problems with Acrobat or Designer, keep in mind that we didn't engineer the program. Inquiries for technical support should be directed to the software developer(s) of any products you use. This is one more good reason to complete your registration form.

Acknowledgments

We would like to acknowledge some of the people who have contributed in one way or another to make this edition possible. Barry Pruett, executive publisher at Wiley, who gave us much support for moving forward with this project. A special thank you goes to our acquisitions editor Stephanie McComb and equally to Martin V. Minner, our project editor. Both Stephanie and Marty were a great support for us and helped keep us on pace and focused. Additional gratitude is extended to other Wiley people: copy editor Gwenette Gaddis Goshert and editorial manager Robyn Siesky, as well as the rest of the Wiley crew who participated in the project.

There's probably no single individual on the planet who does more for evangelizing Acrobat, PDF, and LiveCycle Designer than our good friend and colleague Lori DeFurio who served as our technical editor. Lori travels all over the world helping Acrobat and LiveCycle Designer users in every imaginable way. When she doesn't have an answer, she's one of the most connected people at Adobe Systems who can get to the right person fast to answer a question. Lori's vast knowledge of Acrobat and LiveCycle Designer helped us so much in making sure what we had to say was technically correct. Thank you Lori for another fine job.

A close second to Lori and also a good friend and colleague is Ali Hanyaloglu, another Adobe employee who equally spends his time sharing his vast knowledge of Acrobat and LiveCycle Designer with users worldwide. Thank you Ali for your continued support and assistance in this work.

A very special thank you goes to our good friend Thom Parker — author and host of www.windjack.com and www.pdfscripting.com. Without Thom's generous assistance and expert help we would still be working through some JavaScript routines to get them right. When it comes to JavaScript debugging in Acrobat and LiveCycle Designer, Thom is our first and only contact to help us work through code errors.

We feel very fortunate in having so much support from many people at Adobe Systems who were continually available for comments, suggestions, and favors over a five-month period of time while this work was in development. A hearty thank you is extended to Rick Brown, senior Acrobat product manager (and Chief Acrobatist), for his continued support in all our endeavors.

Other Adobe employees who were very helpful include David Stromfeld, product manager, who provided continual support for Acrobat forms authoring and data handling; Greg Pisocky for adding some pointers on Acrobat and accessibility; Amy Wang who helped us out with PDF Portfolios and connecting us to additional resources; Robert Goldberg, Paul Michniewicz, Paul Foster, and Mike Bessuille in the LiveCycle Designer team who helped us keep Designer working strong and steady; Leonard Rosenthol who jumped in to clarify some things on a variety of Acrobat-related questions; Ashu Mittal for constant assistance for getting things going with Acrobat and connecting us to more Adobe personnel; and many other Adobe employees in the engineering and marketing divisions who graciously offered feedback and advice.

We would also like to thank Carlo M. Arellano for contributing an excellent example of a dynamic form found in the SampleForm folder on the book's CD-ROM. We liked this form so much we asked Carlo for permission to include it on the CD-ROM.

Ted's acknowledgments

Above all, I'd like to thank my coauthor Angie Okamoto for her willingness to engage in this project and for all the fine work she did in developing some of the content.

I'd also like to thank Kurt Foss, editor of Acrobat Users Community; Stephanie Baartz-Bowman and Lori Kassuba of Adobe Systems; my colleagues on Acrobat Users, Duff Johnson, Dimitri Munkirs, Douglas Hanna, and Patty-Bing-You for much support in keeping up-to-date in formation available on the Acrobat Users Community Web site and for their willingness to help when we needed it. And in my local Davao City Philippines Acrobat User Group, thanks to Chris Cubos, Blogie Robillo, Rodney C. Jao, Severino "Bong" Domingo, John Grant, Ian Fredericks, and MiGs for all their generous assistance in helping organize Acrobat users in our area. And in Manila, a special thank you to the Director General of the National Computer Center, Angelo Timoteo Diaz de Rivera, for all his generous assistance in helping promote fillable forms in Philippine Government offices.

Last, but certainly some of the most valuable contibutors, I'd like to thank the many readers of my previous works who through the years have sent me direct mails with questions, kudos, and helpful remarks that has helped me develop this work. My labors as an author, alone behind a computer writing daily, is really very dull during the project period. What makes it all worthwhile is hearing from people about real world applications for forms created in Acrobat or LiveCycle Designer and interacting with all of you — that's the real treasure and the reward for me spending many hours putting this thing together over a three-to-four month period.

Angie's acknowledgments

How can I possibly begin to thank Ted Padova for the opportunity he provided with this book? Without him I would not have ventured into the world of publishing. He provided encouragement when I thought I was crazy for trying to write, and he always found the time to answer my endless questions.

I'd like to thank Stacey Sell and Nicole Sell, my long time colleagues at Easel Solutions (formerly known as Tech Ed Solutions) for their support and encouragement over the years; the entire Easel Solutions Team in the St. Paul, MN office; the Partner Enablement Group at Adobe Systems, Bob Bailey, Matt Boles, Sue Hove, and Leo Schuman for their continued efforts to provide up to date courseware for the LiveCycle products.

I would also like to thank all of my students. They have taught me as much as I have taught them by challenging me with inquiries I could never dreamt up and giving me the opportunity to look at the products from alternate perspectives. To the readers of this work, for without each of you there would be no reason to write at all. Thank you.

Introduction

Several years ago, in the mid-nineties, I wrote a book called *Creating Adobe Acrobat PDF Forms* (Wiley Publishing) that covered forms authoring in Adobe Acrobat 5. In those days we had no LiveCycle Designer application and PDF forms was in an infancy state of development. Yet the book sold well and users continued to purchase the book through Acrobat versions 6, 7, 8, and even up to this writing. It seems as though the Acrobat user community was hungry for any kind of information that could be found related to creating PDF forms.

For several years readers asked me if I would write a book covering new forms features in Acrobat and when I might want to look at including LiveCycle Designer. Although many other publications and various work prevented me from tackling this job, one of the important reasons I postponed the project was because I wanted to bring on a coauthor to help create this massive work you're holding.

I wasn't content working with just any author but wanted someone more special, one who lives with Acrobat and LiveCycle forms on a daily basis. For almost a decade I searched, somewhat passively, for just the right person to help with writing this book.

It wasn't until 2005 that I met Angie Okamoto at a PDF conference. From the first day I met Angie I knew I had the right person to help me create a comprehensive book on Acrobat and LiveCycle Designer forms. Angie conducts training for many companies weekly on using both Acrobat and LiveCycle Designer, and her knowledge of both programs is exceptional. After just a few days working together at a conference I was confident that I found the right individual who *lives* in the programs and one who could help create this publication.

I'm very pleased with the result, not because I have another Acrobat book to distribute, but because it gives me an opportunity to introduce you to Angie Okamoto. I sincerely hope you will find, as I have, that many contributions in this work by Angie have made the publication that much better. And if you have an opportunity to contact Angie, I'm sure you will find an exceptionally talented individual who knows just about everything one needs to know about creating PDF and LiveCycle Designer forms.

—*Ted Padova*

Nomenclature

The official name for the products discussed in this book are: Adobe® Acrobat® Standard, Adobe® Acrobat® Pro, Adobe® Acrobat® 9.0 Pro Extended and Adobe® LiveCycle® Designer ES. You'll notice the registered marks appearing in the names. For the sake of ease and clarity, as you read through the book and see a reference to Acrobat, Adobe Acrobat, Standard, Acrobat Pro, Acrobat Pro Extended, LiveCycle Designer, and Designer please realize that the reference is to Adobe Acrobat Standard, Adobe Acrobat Pro, Adobe Acrobat Pro Extended, or Adobe LiveCycle Designer ES. For purposes of clarity, when we refer to Acrobat, we'll be talking about Acrobat Standard, Acrobat Pro and Acrobat Pro Extended. When referring to Adobe LiveCycle Designer ES we may use terms like LiveCycle Designer or simply Designer.

For Windows users, Acrobat Pro and Adobe Acrobat Pro Extended also ship with Adobe LiveCycle Designer ES. Designer is a separate executable application that is installed in the Designer 8.2 folder inside the Acrobat 9.0 folder.

Adobe Systems' View on Forms

The very first introduction of Forms tools in Acrobat appeared in Acrobat 3.0. In Acrobat 3.2 Adobe implemented JavaScript in the program. LiveCycle Designer originated from a company known as Delrina and was later purchased by Symantec. A year later the product was purchased by JetForms that later changed the company name to Accelio. Adobe acquired Accelio and with it the program we now know as LiveCycle Designer.

Adobe didn't originally engineer Designer, but for several generations of Acrobat dating back to Acrobat 6, Adobe has added features and refinements to the program.

At times some users are confused and perhaps concerned about the lifespan for either Acrobat forms or LiveCycle Designer forms and some wonder what product will emerge and bury the other. We don't have any *inside* information on whether this may occur, but our confidence in seeing both products thrive in the years ahead is supported by a glimpse at Adobe's development history.

Adobe has continued adding new features and improvements to Acrobat forms for several generations of Acrobat. In Acrobat 6 we experienced a complete change in the user interface for Acrobat and enhancements with forms authoring. In Acrobat 8 Adobe provided us with PDF Packages and methods for distributing forms and aggregating form data. In Acrobat 9 Adobe completely changed the way we work with Acrobat forms by introducing the new Form Editing Mode. With LiveCycle Designer, Adobe has introduced new features in the program and support for other LiveCycle products since it acquired the program from Accelio.

In short, we believe Adobe has demonstrated a commitment to the user community that both products will be continually upgraded and refined.

Each product serves a different audience and some distinctions exist for what tool is best used for some different purposes. With Acrobat forms you have a set of features that enable you to create simple forms from many different original document file formats. However, Acrobat is not limited to simple forms and adding sophistication to forms authoring is well defined in the program. You can create complex forms using Acrobat and it's suited to work in a cross-platform environment.

LiveCycle Designer excels at creating complex and dynamic forms to support industrial strength forms needs. However, Designer also offers you tools to create simple static forms. Because Adobe didn't have control of the original development of the program and other factors related to the operating system, the program is exclusive to Windows.

Based on our confidence that both products will move ahead with the same commitment and development resources, we believe that the serious forms author is best served by being proficient in both Acrobat and LiveCycle Designer. In the chapters ahead we provide examples where one product may serve as a better form development tool than the other. Hopefully when you finish reading this book you'll understand more about what product to use for what purpose and develop your own personal set of rules for when to use Acrobat or LiveCycle Designer.

Part I

Getting Familiar with Forms

This section begins with an overview of forms, forms designs, and how to convert original designs from authoring application documents to PDF. We start in Chapter 1 by walking you through steps to create and deploy a form. Remaining chapters in this part cover forms design issues and standards. Much of the content in this section applies to both Acrobat Forms and LiveCycle Designer XML forms.

IN THIS PART

Chapter 1
Taking a Tour of Acrobat Forms

Chapter 2
Getting Started with Acrobat Forms

Chapter 3
Knowing Form Design Standards

Chapter 4
Creating Form Designs

Chapter 1

Taking a Tour of Acrobat Forms

T he chapters ahead cover many things you need to know to become a real PDF forms specialist. But now it's 4:45 p.m. on a Wednesday afternoon, and the boss wants you to hand over a fillable form to the IT department for hosting on the company's Web site. You have 15 minutes before jumping in the car, speeding home to make dinner, and trying to get a little recreational time before you face another day's work. Can you do it?

Fortunately, you've picked just the right tool whether it be Adobe Acrobat Standard, Acrobat Professional, or Acrobat Professional Extended on Windows or Adobe Acrobat Professional on the Macintosh. You also picked the right book because we'll show you how to create that form in just 15 minutes with time to spare.

IN THIS CHAPTER

Converting documents to PDF

Adding form fields

Modifying forms

Enabling special features in PDF documents

Merging data

Looking ahead

Starting with a PDF Document

The first thing you need to do to begin your tour of Acrobat Forms is to start with a PDF file. All documents you open in any Acrobat viewer, including the free Adobe Reader software, begin with an authoring application document that is converted to a PDF file. Your favorite authoring tool can be used to construct the layout and look of your form designs, and from there you convert your file to a PDF document.

If you're starting with a Microsoft Office program, the process of converting the original Office document to a PDF file is made very easy after you install Adobe Acrobat. All Office programs include a button, installed by Adobe Acrobat, to convert your Office document to a PDF file.

If you're using Office 2007, click the Acrobat tab in the Ribbon, and the Ribbon changes to show all the options you have for working with PDF documents, as shown in Figure 1.1.

FIGURE 1.1

Click the Acrobat tab in the Ribbon, and the Ribbon displays options for creating Adobe PDF files.

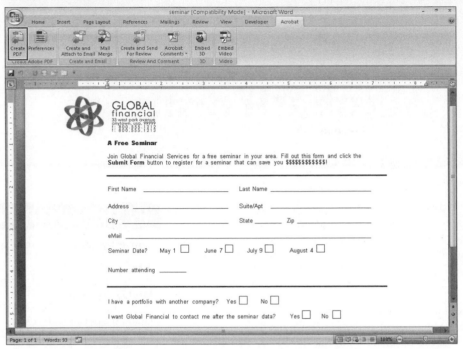

To convert to PDF, click the Create PDF button on the far left side of the Ribbon. The Save Adobe PDF File As dialog box opens. Locate the target folder where you want to save your PDF document, and click Save.

If you're using Office 2003, you have similar options using a Create Adobe PDF button. Just click the button, and save the file as a PDF document.

NOTE Windows users don't need to convert Office documents to PDF when creating a form. You can use Acrobat's Start Form Wizard command and convert native file documents when creating a PDF form. On the Macintosh, you need to start with a PDF document.

On the Macintosh, choose File ➪ Print in Microsoft Word. In the Print dialog box, choose Save as PDF from the PDF pull-down menu.

Populating a Form with Field Objects

After you convert a document to a PDF document, it's time to add form fields in Adobe Acrobat. Acrobat enables you to add form fields automatically via a menu command or add fields by manually drawing field objects on a page. In Acrobat 9, you perform all your form editing work in the new Acrobat 9 Form Editing mode.

To open Form Editing mode and add fields to your form, follow these steps.

ON the CD-ROM The book's CD-ROM contains all the files you need to follow the steps in this book. Open the Chapters folder, and inside the Chapters folder, open the Chapter01 folder. To follow the steps here, open the *seminar.pdf* file.

STEPS: Adding Field Objects to a Form

1. Open the form in Acrobat (Standard, Pro, or Pro Extended).

NOTE Windows users can select a native Office document and choose the Start Form Wizard command to convert to PDF and edit a new form.

2. **Open the PDF in Form Editing mode.** Choose Forms ➪ Add or Edit Fields, as shown in Figure 1.2.

FIGURE 1.2

Choose Forms ➪ Add or Edit Fields to open the form in Form Editing mode.

3. **Auto Field Detection.** As the form opens in Form Editing mode, a dialog box prompts you to have Acrobat automatically detect fields on your form. Click Yes, and Acrobat detects areas on your form and adds appropriate fields.

4. **Review the field objects created by Acrobat.** A Welcome to Form Editing Mode dialog box opens, providing some information about form editing. Click OK in the dialog box, and look over the field objects created by Acrobat. In our example, Acrobat created all field objects perfectly. However, two fields added to the form were non-usable, as you can see in Figure 1.3.

5. **Delete all unwanted field objects.** In our example, two fields on the form need to be deleted. Click the fields (refer to Figure 1.3), and press the Delete/Backspace key.

FIGURE 1.3

All field objects were created perfectly, but with two extra fields not needed on the form.

Extra fields

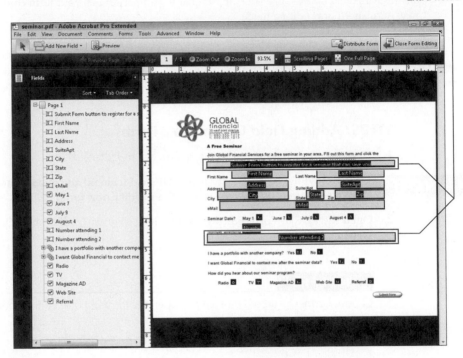

6. **View the form in Viewer mode.** When you edit a form, you enter Form Editing mode. All other work you perform in Acrobat is handled in a mode we refer to in this book as Viewer mode. To exit the Form Editing mode and change to the Viewer mode, click the Close Form Editing button in the top-right corner of the Form Editing mode workspace.

7. **Save the form.** Choose File ➪ Save to update the form.

CROSS-REF There's an art to using Acrobat's auto-field detection features, knowing when to use them and when not to use them. For more information, look over Chapters 5 through 8.

Editing a Form

One field object still needs to be added to our example form: a button for a user to click to submit form data. Although you create forms in Form Editing Mode, you don't need to return to the mode if you want to add a button field. You can remain in Viewer mode when you need to add a button field to a form. To add a button field, do the following.

STEPS: Adding a Submit Form Button to a Form

1. **Open the Advanced Editing toolbar while in Viewer mode.** If the Advanced Editing toolbar is not open, open a context menu on the Toolbar Well and choose Advanced Editing or open the Tools menu, choose Advanced Editing, and choose Show Advanced Editing Toolbar.

2. **Select the Button tool.** Open the Add New Field pull-down menu, and choose Button. The cursor is loaded with the Button tool.

 **If you don't have the Advanced Editing toolbar open and you want to select one of the tools such as the Button tool, you can choose Tools ➪ Advanced Editing ➪ Button.**

3. **Add a button to the form.** Move the cursor to the Submit Form button design on the page, and click in the top-left corner of the button graphic.

4. **Name the field.** A mini Properties window opens. Type a name for the button field in the Field Name text box, as shown in Figure 1.4.

5. **Open the Properties dialog box.** Click Properties in the window shown in Figure 1.4. The Button Properties dialog box opens. The default tab in the Button Properties dialog box is General.

FIGURE 1.4

Drag the handles on the rectangle in and out to size the button field.

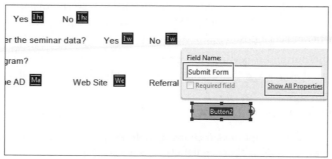

6. **Change the button appearance.** By default, button fields have a gray fill. Because our form design has a graphic for the Submit Form button, we don't need to add any appearance properties such as a border or fill color to the field. Click the Appearance tab, and click the Fill swatch. From the pop-up color palette, click No Color, as shown in Figure 1.5.

FIGURE 1.5

Set the button appearance to No Fill in the Appearance tab.

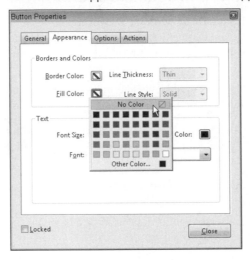

7. **Add an Action.** The purpose of this button is so users can submit data back to you. For this, we need to assign an action to the button. Click the Actions tab, and choose Submit a form from the Select Action pull-down menu, as shown in Figure 1.6. Click the Add button to add the action.

8. **Define the Submit Form attributes.** When you click the Add button, the Submit Form Selections dialog box opens. At the top of the dialog box, enter *mailto:* followed by your e-mail address, as shown in Figure 1.7. Click the radio button beside PDF The complete document, and click OK to set the action to submit the form back to you.

9. **Close the Button Properties dialog box.** After clicking OK in the Submit Form Selections dialog box, you are returned to the Button Properties dialog box. Click Close in this dialog box.

10. **Save the form.**

 You have many options for changing field Properties. For an in-depth look at all the properties options for each field type, see Chapter 9.

FIGURE 1.6

Choose Submit a form from the Select Action pull-down menu, and click the Add button.

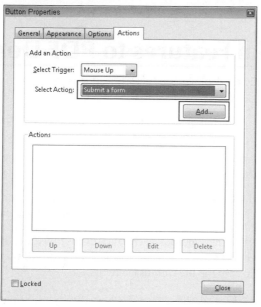

FIGURE 1.7

Add *mailto:* followed by your e-mail address, and click the PDF The complete document radio button.

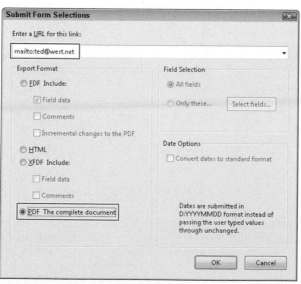

After saving the form, be sure to test the form by filling in the field objects with data. Fill in the form like a form recipient would populate your form, and test it to be certain that all field objects are properly formatted.

Adding Special Features to PDF Documents

Our sample form is almost ready for deployment, but one feature is still needed if your forms are to be filled in by an Adobe Reader user.

An ordinary PDF document cannot be edited in Adobe Reader, and form data, by default, cannot be saved by the form recipient using Adobe Reader. Furthermore, a PDF document cannot be submitted back to you with data from an Adobe Reader user without adding special features to the PDF document.

Using Acrobat viewers, you add special features to a PDF file that permit an Adobe Reader user to save form data, add a digital signature, and submit the entire PDF document back to you.

To add special features to a PDF for these purposes, choose Advanced ⇨ Extend Features in Adobe Reader. Selecting this command opens the Enable Usage Rights in Adobe Reader dialog box shown in Figure 1.8. Click Save Now to save the file with usage rights.

FIGURE 1.8

Click Save Now to enable the PDF form with special features for Adobe Reader users.

TIP When you click Save Now in the Enable Usage Rights in Adobe Reader dialog box, a Save As dialog box opens that enables you to modify the filename and locate a target folder for your saved file. We like to add an extension to the filename to keep the enabled file separate from the original form—something like: seminar_enabled.pdf where _enabled_ is added to our original filename. If you need to edit a form later, you can't edit an enabled file, and Acrobat prompts you to save a copy of the form before editing it. By keeping the original file unenabled, you can always return to it, edit the form, and re-enable the form.

Aggregating Form Data

If you followed the steps throughout this chapter and create a form, form recipients would be e-mailing the form back to you. As you collect forms from your e-mail attachments, save the forms to a common folder. After you collect all the returned forms, you may want to assemble the data in a more appropriate format, such as a Microsoft Excel spreadsheet.

To aggregate data from several forms, follow these steps.

 To follow these steps, use the files in the *completedForms* folder inside the Chapter 01 folder on the book's CD-ROM.

STEPS: Merging Data into Spreadsheets

1. **Save all collected forms to a common folder with each filename having a unique name.** When you collect the forms from your e-mail attachments, you need to rename the forms so each form has a unique name.

2. **Add files to merge.** Choose Forms ⇨ Manage Form Data ⇨ Merge Data Files into Spreadsheet. The Export Data From Multiple Forms wizard opens, as shown in Figure 1.9. Click the Add Files button, and add all the files you want to merge in the Select File Containing Form Data dialog box. In our example, we use the forms located in the *completedForms* folder inside the Chapter01 folder on the book's CD-ROM.

FIGURE 1.9

Use the Export Data From Multiple Forms wizard to merge data into a spreadsheet.

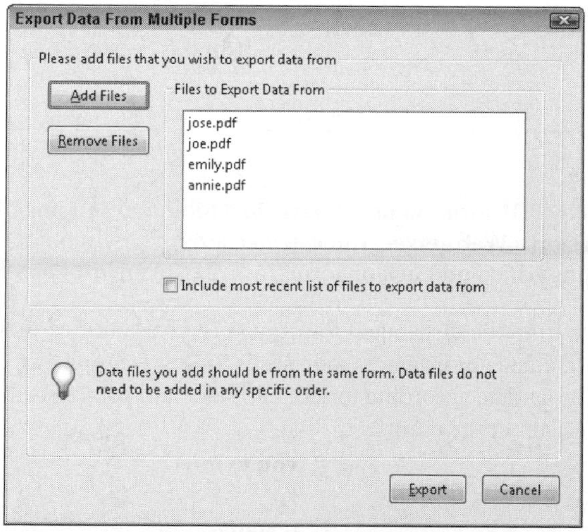

> **Export Data From Multiple Forms**
>
> Please add files that you wish to export data from
>
> [Add Files]   Files to Export Data From
>
> [Remove Files]   jose.pdf
>   joe.pdf
>   emily.pdf
>   annie.pdf
>
> ☐ Include most recent list of files to export data from
>
> 💡 Data files you add should be from the same form. Data files do not need to be added in any specific order.
>
> [Export]   [Cancel]

3. **Export the data.** After adding the files for the data merge, click Export. Pause a moment for Acrobat to complete the export. The Export Progress dialog box displays the progress and reports Done when finished, as shown in Figure 1.10.

FIGURE 1.10

The Export Progress dialog box notifies you when the export is finished.

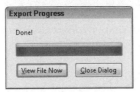

4. **View the data in a spreadsheet.** Click View File Now, and your aggregated data appear in a new Excel worksheet window, as shown in Figure 1.11.

FIGURE 1.11

The exported data open in a new Excel worksheet.

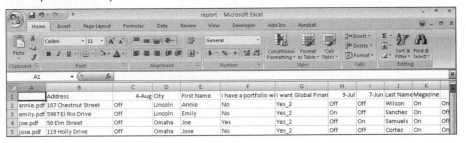

CROSS-REF You can deploy PDF forms in many ways. In addition to sending files via e-mail and hosting forms on a Web server, you can take advantage of the Acrobat.com service for hosting forms, collecting data, and tracking forms, as we explain in Chapter 15.

After you combine the data from the distributed forms, you can sort and rearrange columns and rows in Excel to organize the data according to your needs. In our example, we created a form for a free seminar. We can sort the data according to seminar dates and print lists that we can use to check off people as they register at the event.

Moving On

It's now 4:55 p.m. and you have 5 minutes to spare. Your form is ready for deployment. Hand it over to the IT department, and you've finished your work for the day.

If all you want to do is to create simple forms, use Acrobat's automatic field recognition capabilities, and aggregate data into Excel worksheets, you're finished with this book. The rest of the pages can be used as a paperweight.

However, if you're willing to travel on a journey with us and experience all the possibilities that Adobe Acrobat and Adobe LiveCycle Designer offer you for creating dynamic interactive forms, add scripts for enhancing your forms, merge data to back-end databases, and so much more, then read on. After all, this is a Wiley Bible. It's complete, it's comprehensive, and it's your ultimate resource for working with Acrobat Forms and LiveCycle Designer XML forms.

Go home now. Come back in the morning to talk to Miyagi.

Summary

- PDF forms begin with a document created in an authoring program. The original authoring documents are converted to PDF and edited in Adobe Acrobat to populate forms with field objects.

- You can open many forms in Acrobat and use Acrobat's automatic field recognition features to populate a form with field objects.

- Forms are edited in Form Editing mode. Other Acrobat editing occurs in Viewer mode.

- You add fields manually in Form Editing mode by choosing form tools from the Add New Field pull-down menu.

- Form recipients using Adobe Reader need to work with forms that carry special features for Adobe Reader. Enabling a PDF file with special features is handled via a menu command in Acrobat.

- Data from populated forms can be aggregated into spreadsheet applications.

Chapter 2

Getting Started with Acrobat Forms

IN THIS CHAPTER

Understanding the forms industry

Understanding PDF forms

Comparing forms hosted on government Web servers

Understanding the Acrobat viewers

efore we jump into forms design and use Adobe software to create forms, let's first look at the forms industry and try to develop an understanding for why electronic forms, and in particular Acrobat forms, are a viable resource for any business.

We know we're probably preaching to the choir. After all, if you purchased this book, you probably know the value of creating electronic forms and collecting form data electronically.

We want to start this chapter with a little foundation to help put things in perspective, in case you need to fight any battles at the office. Although we all understand the value of electronic forms, we know that our opinions are not shared by everyone. Therefore, a little analysis of the forms industry and where we are today with paper versus electronic forms can be useful information.

Understanding the Forms Industry

Over the past four decades, people have commented about the *paperless office* with some notion that we may eventually experience this phenomenon. What is much more common among office workers is the belief that we are producing more paper in businesses than before the computer revolution. Today, people in the business and government sectors believe we have seen quantum leaps in paper production to sustain office operations.

About a decade ago, we looked at the forms industry and found that according to the U.S. Department of Commerce Census of Manufacturers Report of

1992, American manufacturing of business forms has actually declined as compared to the prior report in 1982. In both domestic production and import/export markets, office forms have declined in total sales and the labor force has decreased by more than 10 percent. The manufacturing, shipping, and related costs of distributing business forms was estimated by the U.S. Department of Commerce at $7.4 billion annually almost 20 years ago.

Where are we today? Well, we still see a decline in the manufacturing of paper forms and the reduction in the workforce related to printing forms. Manifold business forms total production in the U.S. was more than $8 billion as reported by the U.S. Department of Commerce. In 2002, the total was reduced to a little over $6.5 billion. The same holds true for many other types of business forms. The U.S. Census Bureau's Economic Report of 2002 shows that bound business forms reached valued shipment levels of 1.5 billion in 1997 and was reduced to 1.2 billion in 2002.

The figures aren't remarkable when you compare the numbers. However, given the fact that more people are entering business and consumption levels for all products are higher, the numbers are definitely showing a strong decline. Although we don't have statistical evidence to support our claim, our assumption is that electronic file exchanges are growing while paper exchanges are declining in U.S. businesses.

Comparing costs

Let us offer but one small example of how analog forms' routing and distribution costs can affect a company's bottom line. Let's look at the computer publishing world. Authors writing books like the one you're reading receive monthly reports on their individual sales figures. Many of these figures are related to royalty payments to be distributed to authors. A given monthly report is generated by an office worker who prints a copy of the report for an author, keeps a copy for an internal file, and routes another copy to the publisher's accounting office.

Costs associated with producing the form are a few cents to print each copy, the cost of a printed envelope, and the cost of a stamp to mail the author's copy. Each report runs about $.64 including printing and mailing. If 5,000 titles are in print from a large publishing firm, the total monthly costs result in $3,200. In a year, the amount would be $38,400. In a decade, the total amount would cost the publisher more than one-third of a million dollars.

As a comparison, let's examine the cost of distributing electronic forms. In the above example, all computer book authors are required to submit manuscript and images via the Internet. Therefore, all authors have access to e-mail. The cost of distributing a PDF form from the publisher, notwithstanding labor costs, is $0.00. That's Zero with a capital Z. Because anyone can obtain the free Adobe Reader software to view a PDF file, no hidden cost is incurred by the recipient of the form.

Let's take another look at a real-world cost analysis. Assume you work in a large corporation with more than 1,000 employees. On any given day, 50 employees are away from the office buildings. Some may be on sick leave, some on vacation, some on business trips, and so on. If every employee needs to complete a request for leave form, then 50 forms a day could conceivably be produced.

Let's assume a form is duplicated at a copy machine, the employee contacts a supervisor, the supervisor signs the form and routes it to accounting, and an accounting clerk enters the data in a computer. Let's further assume it costs a few cents for the photocopy and about 10 minutes for all employee time for routing the form and keying the data.

The costs for copying and labor at a fixed labor rate of $12.00 per hour would be $2.02 per each request. The daily costs would be $101 and an annual cost would be $26,260. For 10 forms related to various company procedures, distribution costs would be over $260,000 per year!

Assuming that you can cut the labor by 70 percent through electronic routing and elimination of a need for keying in data, the $260,000 figure would be reduced to $78,000. The end result is $182,000 in annual savings. That's a savings for only 10 forms in a company of 1,000 employees. Imagine what kinds of savings we might see in the U.S. Federal Government, large educational institutions, and industry-wide enterprises.

Obviously, it is difficult to factor all variables to isolate costs for routing individual forms. But as a broad generalization, we think it is safe to assume that many different forms used in organizations routed through analog means are often much more costly than electronic forms usage, especially if form data input is redundant between workgroups.

Why Acrobat forms are cost effective

When you analyze the analog form workflow, you see that you can create a form on a computer, print it on a desktop printer (or commercial print shop), mail or fax it to a form recipient who completes the form, signs it, and returns it via fax or mail. The form data are then keyed into a computer.

The electronic workflow cuts out several steps in the workflow and allows you to perform them much more efficiently. You create a form on a computer, send it via e-mail or make it available on a Web server, to be downloaded by the form recipient who keys in the data and clicks a submit button to send the form back to you. The form never touches paper because you have it in electronic form and the form recipient has the same completed form on his/her personal workstation. The cost savings for this workflow should be obvious.

The other cost consideration in electronic forms over analog forms is the tool that produces, views, and/or prints the form. With regard to Adobe Acrobat 9 as a tool, Adobe Systems offers employers a few different solutions. You can purchase Adobe Acrobat Pro (or Acrobat Standard in version 9—for Windows only) and create PDF forms using tools in Acrobat. Additionally, along with an Acrobat 9 Pro or Acrobat 9 Pro Extended installation on Windows, you also get Adobe LiveCycle Designer. Either tool can create electronic forms that can meet your needs, and the purchase price of the software is likely to be earned back within a few months for businesses that produce many forms.

The freely downloadable Adobe Reader software can be installed on any computer system without cost to the end user. Adobe Reader has the capability to view, fill in, and print any PDF form. And since Acrobat 8, users also can save form data and add digital signatures to forms that were created in Adobe Acrobat 8 or above or in Adobe LiveCycle Designer.

What Are PDF Forms?

The definition of a PDF form varies greatly among many users. The universal common ingredient is that all documents are in fact Portable Document Format (PDF) files. If you explore the World Wide Web and seek out PDF forms, you find documents in one of four categories. Analog forms are sometimes scanned and saved in PDF format as scanned images. These forms are static and intended for the end user to print, complete, and fax back to the forms provider or route them through an organization. The second type of PDF form is a document authored in some application, then converted to PDF file. The appearance of the form is often better than a scanned document, but the means of completion and routing are the same as above. The third and fourth kinds of forms are much more dynamic. An authoring application document is converted to PDF documents and forms content such as field boxes, menus, signature fields, and more are created from within Adobe Acrobat. Or a form is created in Adobe LiveCycle Designer with live form fields and distributed as a PDF form. These latter two forms enable users to electronically fill in and route data.

Of the four types of forms described above, the PDF forms edited in Acrobat or created in Adobe LiveCycle Designer are much more efficient and more purposeful for any organization. Creating smart forms eases the burden of forms completion for users and optimizes electronic data workflows for any company using forms for almost any purpose. It is the creation of these forms that will be the subject of all the following chapters.

Scanned paper forms

Oddly, some companies often print an electronic file to an office printer, scan the printed document back into digital form, and save the file as a PDF document. The PDF document may then be distributed electronically via e-mail, hosted on a network server, or hosted on a Web server.

Among the four kinds of forms described above, the scanned document is the least efficient. If a file already resides on a computer, there is no need to print and scan it. Any file of any type can be converted to a PDF document. If scanned documents are used, as shown in Figure 2.1, the appearance of the form can be much more degraded than the original and the file size will always be much larger.

You may need to scan forms at some point. If a printed form isn't available in digital form, you may want to scan a paper form rather than re-create the form in an authoring program. However, once scanned, you can add form fields in Acrobat to make the form a fillable form.

CROSS-REF   To learn about adding form fields, see Chapter 5.

Static forms

From an authoring application, a form is designed and then converted to a PDF document. The form appearance is much better than the scanned form, and the file size is much smaller; however, the end user must print the form and manually fill in the form fields such as the form shown in Figure 2.2.

FIGURE 2.1

A form printed then scanned on a flatbed scanner features text that is obviously jagged and less attractive than the original authored document.

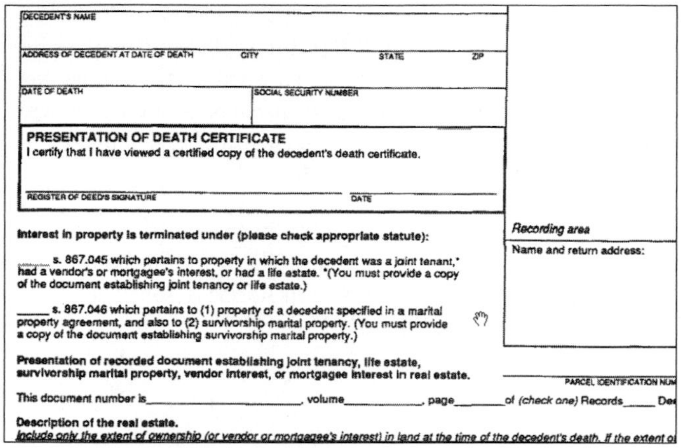

DECEDENT'S NAME

ADDRESS OF DECEDENT AT DATE OF DEATH | CITY | STATE | ZIP

DATE OF DEATH | SOCIAL SECURITY NUMBER

PRESENTATION OF DEATH CERTIFICATE
I certify that I have viewed a certified copy of the decedent's death certificate.

REGISTER OF DEED'S SIGNATURE | DATE

Interest in property is terminated under (please check appropriate statute):

_____ **s. 867.045 which pertains to property in which the decedent was a joint tenant,* had a vendor's or mortgagee's interest, or had a life estate. *(You must provide a copy of the document establishing joint tenancy or life estate.)**

_____ **s. 867.046 which pertains to (1) property of a decedent specified in a marital property agreement, and also to (2) survivorship marital property. (You must provide a copy of the document establishing survivorship marital property.)**

Presentation of recorded document establishing joint tenancy, life estate, survivorship marital property, vendor interest, or mortgagee interest in real estate.

This document number is_____________, volume_________, page_______of *(check one)* Records_____ De

Description of the real estate.
Include only the extent of ownership (or vendor or mortgagee's interest) in land at the time of the decedent's death. If the extent o

Recording area

Name and return address:

PARCEL IDENTIFICATION NUM

FIGURE 2.2

An authoring application document converted to a PDF document with no form fields

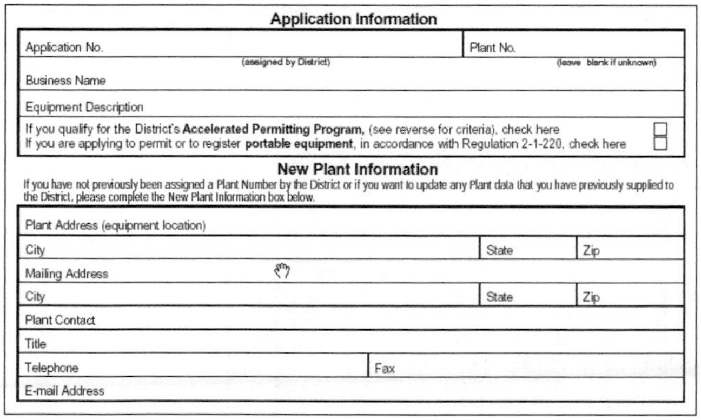

Application Information

Application No. (assigned by District) | Plant No. (leave blank if unknown)

Business Name

Equipment Description

If you qualify for the District's **Accelerated Permitting Program**, (see reverse for criteria), check here
If you are applying to permit or to register **portable equipment**, in accordance with Regulation 2-1-220, check here

New Plant Information

If you have not previously been assigned a Plant Number by the District or if you want to update any Plant data that you have previously supplied to the District, please complete the New Plant Information box below.

Plant Address (equipment location)

City | State | Zip

Mailing Address

City | State | Zip

Plant Contact

Title

Telephone | Fax

E-mail Address

Redundancy and extra labor costs are evident with static forms. When a user completes an analog form, the data are handwritten on the form or perhaps the Typewriter tool is used in an Acrobat viewer to type text on the form. When the form is received by the form author, the data then must be keyed in a computer by a technician or office worker. If the end user keys the data electronically when filling out a form, the redundancy and extra labor costs are eliminated.

Most PDF forms found on Web sites are static forms. Users are quick to convert authored documents to PDF documents, but often little effort is used to make the forms more efficient. This was the case over a decade ago when people began to use Acrobat extensively to create forms and it still is true today. Many more unpopulated forms exist on the Web than forms populated with fields.

Fillable forms

Fillable forms are one step above static forms. We use the term *fillable* throughout this book to differentiate forms that have no fields for user input versus forms populated with fields. At times we make a reference to PDF forms having some *dynamic* features. The term *dynamic* is often used with Adobe LiveCycle Designer forms; dynamic as it relates to LiveCycle Designer forms is defined in Chapter 26.

Fillable forms are forms that contain form fields formatted for user input in an Acrobat viewer. Creating fillable forms requires some extra effort for the forms provider. The workflow consists of first converting a form design to a PDF document and then opening it in Adobe Acrobat. In Acrobat, form fields are added to the PDF file as shown in Figure 2.3.

FIGURE 2.3

Fillable forms include form fields where data are added electronically by the end user. When the Select Object tool is selected, all the form fields appear as shown in the figure.

NOTE If you are using Acrobat 9.0 you may find a little bug in the program when viewing field objects. Many times when you click the Select Object tool, the form field objects are not shown on the form. If you want to see the field objects, press Ctrl/⌘ + A to select all fields. The fields are then shown as in Figure 2.3.

Fillable forms also can be created as *smart forms*. A smart form might include fields where automatic calculations and field completion help prevent user entry errors. Calculations such as total amounts, sales tax, and item costs can be programmed on a form. Taking unnecessary calculations away from the end user can help eliminate potential errors and more efficiently process transactions.

Looking at Forms Hosted on Web Servers

The U.S. Census Bureau reports that the number of printed business forms has declined in the U.S. over the past decade, and we've made the assumption that the reason for the reduction in printed forms is due to more electronic forms in use today. If you read the preceding section, you also know that static and fillable PDF forms are in circulation on the Web.

We're moving slowly to converting static forms to fillable forms, but hopefully we are moving forward. The next question that comes to mind is this: How good are the PDF forms that we find hosted on Web servers? If indeed we are seeing more electronic forms, are the forms fillable and are they properly designed and suited for a true electronic workflow?

We were curious about this question and decided to do a little study. One very good example of forms hosting services is income tax reporting in the United States The U.S. Federal Government has led the way with forms hosting to make it easy for citizens to download income tax forms and file them electronically. For several years, the Internal Revenue Service has hosted fillable forms that can be downloaded and completed with an Acrobat viewer.

All but seven of the 50 U.S. states also have income tax forms that the residents of those states need to file annually. We thought it would be interesting to look at all 50 states and examine the income tax reporting forms that each state hosts on its Web servers. Since seven states don't require income tax reporting, we looked at comparable forms for reporting inheritance taxes, sales and use taxes, or a similar type of tax reporting form that those seven states use.

In our research, we looked at some aspects of what we would define as a form that's designed properly. We compared all 50 states, the District of Columbia (Washington, D.C.), and the U.S. Federal IRS Form 1040, resulting in a sample size of 52 comparisons. We used the most recent forms hosted by all samples for the 2007 tax year where available or the 2006 tax year for states not hosting the 2007 forms as of this writing.

Our first question was: Are the forms fillable? In other words, do the forms have fields where an Acrobat or Adobe Reader user can type in the form data? As far as the file type goes, all states host PDF documents. Of the 52 samples, 31 had fillable forms (60%), while 21 states (40%) hosted forms that were not fillable. We find 40 percent to be a significant number. Because the IRS has served as an example for income tax forms hosting, we expected more states to host fillable forms. Yet the results show that much work still needs to be done to make these forms true PDF forms.

We had to toss out 21 samples for our comparison because no form fields were added to those forms. For the remaining 31 forms, we looked at the following:

- **State:** In Table 2.1, the first column identifies the state by name. We added the U.S. Federal Form 1040 at the top of the table.

- **Type:** Column two shows the type of PDF form hosted by the individual states. The types are either PDF forms created in Adobe Acrobat or forms created in Adobe LiveCycle Designer (LCD).

- **Creator:** The Creator column identifies the original authoring document. In one sample, we were unable to determine the file creator.

- **DP:** We looked at Document Properties for each form. The Document Property metadata is especially helpful when searching PDF documents. We recommend all users completely fill in the Document Property items for Title, Author, Subject, and Keywords fields. The columns show Y for Yes, indicating that Document Property Information is properly added to the form; P for Partial, indicating that the Document Property information is partially filled in; and N for No, meaning that no Document Property information was added to the form.

CROSS-REF For more information in setting Document Properties, see Chapter 4.

- **IV:** Next we looked at the Initial View settings. Were the Initial View settings edited to open the PDF document in a standard view that the PDF document authors wanted all users to see when the file opens? Users can set opening views to different preferences, so a form can open at different zoom levels and different page layouts on different computers. We recommend editing these settings to force a default override, so forms open at the same zoom and page layout view on every user's computer. Of the 31 sample forms we examined, only four forms had Initial View settings prescribed in the form.

CROSS-REF For more information in setting Initial Views, see Chapter 4.

- **FS:** We looked at file size for each form. A few things affect the file size. If the PDF file is not properly created with an acceptable PDF creator such as Acrobat Distiller or exported using an export feature from an Adobe Application or the PDFMaker from an Office program, the file size can grow. Additionally, the more fields you add to a form and the more pages added to your form, the more the file size increases. The thing we were most interested in was comparing forms with similar attributes. For example, if you look at the form for New Jersey, you see that the four-page form has 752 fields and the file size is 443K. Compare the New Jersey form to the Hawaii form, and you see that the Hawaii form is almost twice the size of the New Jersey form. Yet the Hawaii form has the same number of pages and almost half the number of fields.

- **PP:** This column reports the total pages on the form.

- **FLDS:** This column reports the total number of fields. Look at the form for Georgia. The form has 1131 fields for a four-page form! Compare the Georgia form to the Ohio form, where you see a four-page form with 141 fields. When we looked at the Georgia form, we noticed that form fields were used as design elements, and nested within the design elements were the data fields. This form has twice as many fields as needed because you can assign appearance attributes such as border styles and colors to the data fields. There's no need to create separate fields for design appearances as was used on the Georgia form.

- **RB:** The RB column shows results for how radio buttons and check boxes were configured on the sample forms. We looked at mutually exclusive fields where the form recipient needs to make a decision for one choice or another. Were these fields properly configured so a user could click on one field while the remaining fields in the same group were turned off? Were the fields named properly such as the same name for the field with different export values? When we compared the forms, we found more than half the forms had radio buttons/check boxes improperly configured. In most cases, the forms with improper radio button/check box assignments had individual fields with actions assigned to clear other fields within the same groups.

CROSS-REF For more information on configuring radio buttons and check boxes, see Chapter 7.

- **CMB:** This column looks at comb fields. You find comb fields on many U.S. government forms where a single field such as a name field is designed with boxes or vertical lines to separate individual characters such as what you see in Figure 2.4. A properly configured comb field is a single field with an option switch in Acrobat that spaces the data to fit within the field box. Users who improperly configure comb fields generally add separate fields for each box. This results in creating larger file sizes and more work to handle the data exported from a form. Not all forms we examined had comb fields. Of the 15 forms that used comb fields, only the Federal IRS form and the states of Alaska and Texas properly configured these fields.

FIGURE 2.4

Comb fields are designed with boxes or lines to separate characters in fields.

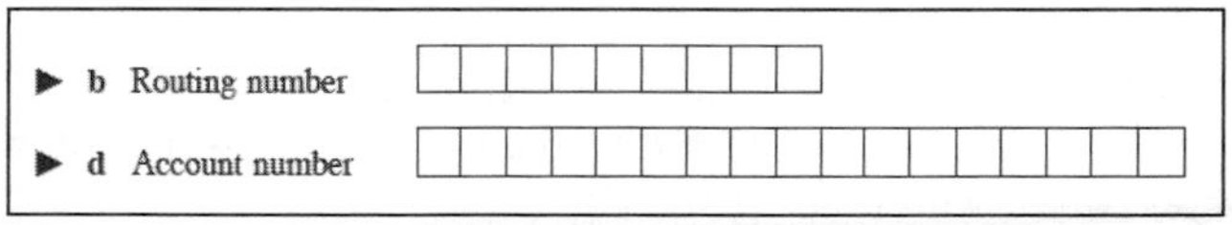

▶ b Routing number

▶ d Account number

CROSS-REF

- **SEC:** Were the forms protected with password security? If a form is not secured, users can edit the background and the fields. At a glance, a tax specialist may not notice a form that was edited. For the purpose of tax reporting, we thought it was important for all states to secure the forms. Of all the samples (including the non-fillable forms), we found only six states had added security to the forms. The state of Montana (denoted as Y**) added security to protect a document from page extractions but didn't bother to secure the file against editing the form. We therefore tossed this form into the batch that weren't secured. Interestingly enough, we also found that the most recent IRS Form 1040 is not a secure form. In past years, these forms were secure documents, but the IRS is now using a forms service (Amgraf One Plus) to create the forms and manage the data. The forms are now being produced without security.

CROSS-REF   For more information on securing forms, see Chapter 12.

- **FD:** This column reports the results of the field designs. We looked at how well fields are assigned attributes and how well the fields are configured. Was it clear to the user where form data needed to be added? Did the form make use of proper configurations for naming conventions, number formatting, dates, social security numbers, and so on? We could have categorized this column in several subdivisions for above average, good, below average, and poor. However, we decided to simply use G for good and B for bad. If fields were obviously designed improperly, we gave a hit to the form and placed it in the B category. As you can see in Table 2.1, we found more than half the forms, in our estimation, poorly designed in terms of field attribute assignments.

  We also included consideration for the overall design appearance. Of the worst among our sample for overall form design was the state of Utah, whose form is shown in Figure 2.5. Inasmuch as the form displays a message for turning on the field Highlight option in Adobe Reader, this form is very poorly designed and a form recipient can easily become frustrated in completing the form.

- **CLC:** This column reports whether fields are calculated on forms. With all tax reporting forms in our sample, some fields needed to be calculated. Did the form authors add calculation scripts to remove the possibility of error from the form recipient or were the fields added without formulas? As you can see in Table 2.1, only seven forms made use of calculation formulas.

CROSS-REF   For more information on creating calculation formulas, see Chapters 15 and 18.

- **E:** Were the forms enabled with Adobe Reader usage rights so the Adobe Reader users could save the form data after completing the form? Our research showed only seven forms were enabled with Reader usage rights.

CROSS-REF   For more information on enabling forms with Adobe Reader usage rights, see Chapter 10.

FIGURE 2.5

Among the 52 samples, the state of Utah had the worst form design.

TABLE 2.1

Comparing Fillable Income Tax Reporting Forms Hosted by U.S. States

State	Type	Creator	DP	IV	FS	PP	FLDS	RB	CMB	SEC	FD	CLC	E
U.S. IRS 1040	PDF	Amgraf	Y	N	438	2	252	Y	Y	N	G	N	Y
Alabama	PDF	QuarkXPress	P	N	682	1	98	N	NA	N	G	N	N
Alaska	PDF	Amgraf	Y	N	239	1	73	Y	Y	N	G	N	Y
Arizona	PDF	UltraForms*	N	N	428	9	406	Y	N	Y	G	Y	N
Arkansas	PDF	InDesign	N	N	233	2	134	Y	NA	N	G	N	N
California	PDF	InDesign	Y	N	378	2	219	N	N	N	B	N	Y
Delaware	PDF	PageMaker	P	N	124	3	211	Y	N	Y	G	N	N
Georgia	PDF	PageMaker	Y	N	691	4	1131	N	N	N	B	N	N
Hawaii	PDF	Distiller	Y	N	808	4	301	N	NA	N	G	N	N
Idaho	PDF	PageMaker	Y	N	180	2	161	N	N	N	B	N	N
Illinois	PDF	Distiller	P	N	128	2	109	N	N	N	B	N	Y
Iowa	PDF	PageMaker	P	N	372	2	208	Y	NA	N	B	N	N
Louisiana	PDF	Distiller	N	N	921	5	754	N	N	N	B	N	N
Maryland	PDF	UltraForms*	P	N	274	2	253	N	N	N	B	N	N
Michigan	PDF	Distiller	Y	N	250	2	174	N	NA	N	B	N	N
Minnesota	PDF	InDesign	N	N	838	4	399	N	NA	N	B	N	N
Missouri	PDF	UltraForms*	P	N	214	2	143	N	NA	Y	G	Y	N
Montana	PDF	InDesign	Y	N	573	2	230	Y	N	Y**	G	N	N
Nevada	LCD	Designer	--	--	1019	2	167	NA	NA	N	G	Y	N
New Jersey	PDF	Distiller	Y	Y	443	4	752	Y	N	N	G	N	N
New York	PDF	InDesign	Y	N	161	2	188	NA	NA	N	B	N	Y
North Dakota	PDF	Distiller	Y	Y	324	2	76	N	NA	N	B	N	Y

State	Type	Creator	DP	IV	FS	PP	FLDS	RB	CMB	SEC	FD	CLC	E
Ohio	LCD	Designer	--	--	424	4	141	Y	NA	Y	G	Y	Y
Oklahoma	PDF	UltraForms*	Y	N	488	6	395	Y	N	Y	G	Y	N
Oregon	PDF	InDesign	N	N	172	2	108	N	N	N	B	N	N
Pennsylvania	PDF	QuarkXPress	Y	N	292	2	87	Y	NA	N	B	N	N
South Dakota	PDF	PageMaker	Y	N	113	1	107	NA	NA	N	B	Y	N
Tennessee	PDF	PageMaker	Y	Y	145	3	135	Y	NA	N	B	N	N
Texas	PDF	Undetermined	Y	N	137	1	63	Y	Y	N	B	Y	N
Utah	PDF	Distiller	N	N	62	2	106	N	NA	N	B	N	N
Wisconsin	PDF	PageMaker	Y	Y	182	4	192	Y	NA	N	B	N	N

* UltraForms was the final PDF producer. The original authoring program could not be determined.

** Security was limited to protecting against page extractions only.

What form was the best overall? Hands down, our vote goes to the state of Ohio, whose form is shown in Figure 2.6. The form was created in Adobe LiveCycle Designer, so the Document Properties and Initial View settings couldn't be changed because Designer 8.1 and earlier doesn't support editing these properties. The file size is 424K for a four-page form with 141 fields. The form has properly configured radio button/check boxes, security is added to the form, overall field design is excellent with the use of drop-down lists for restricting responses and masks for formatting fields such as dates and social security numbers, calculation formulas are added to the form, a 2D barcode is included on the form, and the form is enabled with Adobe Reader usage rights.

FIGURE 2.6

In our opinion, the best form design among the samples comes from the state of Ohio.

If we can assume that federal and state tax reporting forms should be among the most advanced form designs available on Web servers, you can easily see that there is much work to do to create properly designed forms.

Understanding the Acrobat Viewers

The line of Acrobat products represents almost an entire division within Adobe Systems, Inc. There are products designed as standalone applications, enterprise solutions, online hosting services, and add-ons in the form of Acrobat plug-ins. These products are intended to be used with files converted to PDF documents.

Acrobat viewers

For the forms designer, the products of most interest are the Acrobat viewer products. There are four Acrobat viewers you should become familiar with to help guide users for viewing, printing, and completing your forms.

Adobe Reader

At the low end of the Acrobat viewers is the Adobe Reader software. Reader is a freely distributed application intended for users who need to view, print, and search PDF files. Reader users can fill in form fields and print a populated PDF form. When PDF authors add special features to forms by enabling a PDF document with Adobe Reader usage rights, the Adobe Reader users can save edited forms and add digital signatures.

Adobe estimates more than 750,000 million computer users have Adobe Reader program installed. The number of copies of Reader installed by users makes it one of the most popular computer programs (including operating systems) in existence today.

Adobe Acrobat 9 Standard (Windows only)

Acrobat Standard prior to version 9 had no Forms tools, and forms authoring, editing, and modification was not possible in this viewer. In Acrobat 9 Standard has all the form editing options you find in Acrobat Pro and Acrobat Pro Extended.

Adobe Acrobat 9 Pro (Macintosh and Windows)

When users purchase the Adobe Acrobat 9 Pro software (both Windows and Macintosh), they can add form fields to populate a form. Adobe Acrobat Pro has more editing features than Acrobat Standard (Windows only), and although Acrobat 9 Standard offers forms editing features, the more serious forms author is best off using Acrobat Pro.

Acrobat supports a plug-in architecture whereby third-party software manufacturers can develop tools and add-ons designed for special editing purposes. If Acrobat cannot perform a given task, chances are good that you can find a third-party plug-in to support your needs. You can find many plug-ins that work with Acrobat by doing a Web search or looking at the products available at the Adobe Store (http://store.adobe.com/store/).

Adobe Acrobat 9 Pro Extended (Windows only)

Adobe Acrobat 9 Pro Extended is more robust in features such as transcoding Adobe Flash files and offering Adobe Presenter as a PowerPoint add-in and includes many of the 3D and CAD conversion options that were available in Acrobat 8 3D. All the forms features you find in Acrobat Pro are included in Acrobat Pro Extended.

Using different versions of Acrobat

We're certain that everyone reading this book and everyone creating PDF forms is not using the most recent version of Acrobat. In every version of Acrobat from version 6 to the current version, we've seen many new features added related to forms authoring. A major overhaul of the forms editing features was introduced in Acrobat 6 and extended greatly in Acrobat 8. In Acrobat 9, we find many additional forms editing features and improvements.

To help you understand some of the differences in features among the various Acrobat viewer versions, look over Table 2.2 and bookmark this page for future reference.

TABLE 2.2

Forms-Related Features by Acrobat Versions

Feature	Acrobat 6	Acrobat 7	Acrobat 8	Acrobat 9
Acrobat Standard on Mac	X	X		
Acrobat Standard Forms Editing (Windows only)				X
Arbitrary Mask	X	X	X	X
Assemble Forms in PDF Collections (PDF Packages in Acrobat 8 and PDF Portfolios in Acrobat 9)			X	X
Auto Tab Order via Page Properties	X	X	X	X
Barcode Fields		*	X	X
Create Dataset File			X	X
Collect/Distribute Data via Acrobat.com				X
Collect/Distribute Data via Internal Server				X
Comb Fields	X	X	X	X
Create Multiple Copies (creating tables)	X	X	X	X
Create Spreadsheet from Data Files		X	X	X
Customize Toolbars		X	X	X**
Digital Signatures - Adobe Reader			X	X

Feature	Acrobat 6	Acrobat 7	Acrobat 8	Acrobat 9
Distribute Form			X	X
Document Message Bar		X	X	X
Document Message Bar - Always Hide			X	X
Drag and Drop Tab Order in Fields Panel				X
Form Editing Mode (change interface for form editing)				X
Enable for Commenting in Adobe Reader		X	X	X
Enable for Forms Saving and Digital Signatures in Adobe Reader			X	X
Export Data Tool			X	X
Flash-based Interactive PDF Portfolios				X
Fill in LCD Dynamic Forms in Adobe Reader		X	X	X
Flatten Form Fields (via PDF Optimizer)			X	X
Forms Menu (a separate menu in the menu bar)			X	X
Forms Toolbar (floating)	X	X	X	
JavaScript	X	X	X	X
Limited Execute Menu Items			X	X
Properties Bar	X	X	X	X
Quick Access to Forms Toolbar (Tools Menu)			X	
Restricting Some Features via JavaScript			X	X
Simplified Field Notation	X	X	X	X
Track Forms		X	X	X
Typewriter Tool		X	X	X
XML Data Exports	X	X	X	X

* Barcodes were available in Acrobat 7 via a plug-in distributed by Adobe.

** Can customize toolbars but no Forms tools.

Inasmuch as you can create forms in Acrobat 6 and even earlier back to Acrobat 3, as shown in Table 2.2, there's a huge difference in forms features between Acrobat 6 and 7. Additionally, you see many more options available for forms authoring between Acrobat 7 and 8. Our recommendation is that serious forms authors should consider upgrading to Acrobat 9.0 or greater. If that doesn't fit your budget, then at the very least you should consider using Acrobat 8 Professional.

NOTE Forms editing was available in Acrobat 6, 7, and 8 Professional only. In Acrobat 9, forms editing is supported in Acrobat Standard (Windows only), Acrobat Pro (Windows and Mac), and Acrobat Pro Extended (Windows only).

Summary

- The U.S. forms industry is a multi-billion dollar economy. Recent reports from the U.S. Census Bureau indicate that printing of business forms is declining.

- Several types of PDF forms are hosted on Web servers today. Static forms are forms that are either scanned paper documents with no form fields or electronic form designs converted to a PDF document with no form fields. Dynamic forms include PDF forms that contain form fields and can be filled in by a user of an Acrobat viewer.

- A comparison of income tax reporting forms from U.S. states shows that although the number of dynamic forms is increasing on government Web servers, many forms are not properly designed.

- Acrobat viewers include the free Adobe Reader software, Adobe Acrobat Standard, Adobe Acrobat Pro, and Adobe Acrobat Pro Extended. Forms can be filled in using any one of the Acrobat viewers. Forms authoring can be accomplished in all versions of Acrobat 9.

Chapter 3

Knowing Form Design Standards

Several efforts have been made by different governing bodies to create a set of standards for form elements and form designs. Having common form elements and overall design appearances makes it much easier for form recipients to understand your forms and easily fill them in.

Form design is an important consideration for a forms author. Where to place objects, text, and fields on a form and creating a visually appealing document is part of your form design process.

In this chapter, we look at some efforts made to bring a set of standards to forms designers and offer some basic rules to guide you in designing better forms.

IN THIS CHAPTER

Getting familiar with forms standards

Designing for the form recipient

Understanding form design basics

Looking at Some Forms Standards

In a nutshell, no global standards have yet been adopted for designing forms. When you consider different industries such as real estate, law, banking, healthcare, and so on, each industry attempts to set its own standards. Add to the large industries various enterprises, small businesses, education, and government, and you find institutions wanting to set standards for their own unique reporting mechanisms.

Another factor influencing form design in recent times is the development of Web page design. We can deploy forms for print and online processing. Printed forms are designed for standard page sizes, while forms that never see a printer can be designed at an infinite number of page sizes. Traditional black-and-white paper forms are suited for printing. However, the businesses that devote time and money to create visually appealing Web page designs aren't likely to be content with an appearance similar to a plain paper form.

As an example of a form that might be designed for a company investing much time and expense in its Web image, consider the company Global Financial. Because Global is very much interested in the layout and appearance of all Global branded documents, the people at Global just won't be satisfied with a traditional black-and-white form that might appear on its Web site. Rather, you might see an online form something like Figure 3.1.

The form in Figure 3.1 is a bogus design, but it illustrates how a more contemporary form's look might be influenced by a company's Web page designs. This type of form design is not likely to fit into standards for printed forms that are established by a governing body.

Does this mean that all forms can't be standardized? Not necessarily. Some rules and standards can be applied to various types of forms, such as forms for print, forms hosted on Web servers intended to be routed electronically, and XML type forms that need to adhere to certain data compilation standards.

A bogus form we created to match design appearances similar to Web pages

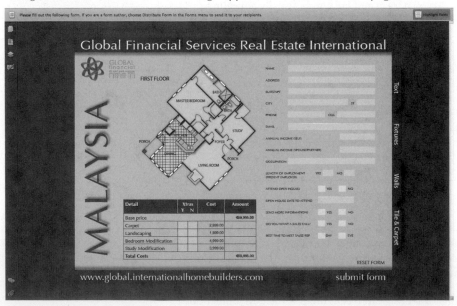

BFMA standards

The Business Forms Management Association (www.bfma.org/) has been around for 45 years. For some time, BFMA has been working on prescribing standards for printed forms; in recent years, it has added electronic forms to its standards recommendations.

All of the standards the BFMA recommends for paper forms design are extensive and beyond the scope of inclusion here. These topics are among the important considerations the BFMA recommends for an acceptable form:

- **Positioning:** A company logo should be placed at the top-left corner of a form. The form title should be at the top-right corner. Form numbers should be in the lower-left corner and page numbers at the bottom-right corner.

- **Grouping Form Elements:** Identifying information should be grouped together. Table data should be displayed in table formats, and totals for calculated fields should appear at the bottom of the form.

- **Fonts and Rules:** Use serif fonts for instructions and help. Use sans serif fonts for captions. Form titles should be at 20 point, and captions should be at 7–10-point type. Rules should be .5 to 1 point. Screened boxes can be used in lieu of rules.

- **Use of White Space:** Forms should be made easy to read and fill in. Adding ample white space can help break up the design to facilitate easier reading and form filling. In Figure 3.2, compare the design of the form on the left to the one on the right. A little white space between columns, as shown on the right, can help form recipients accurately complete a form.

FIGURE 3.2

Adding some white space can help break up a form, aiding the form recipient in accurately completing the form.

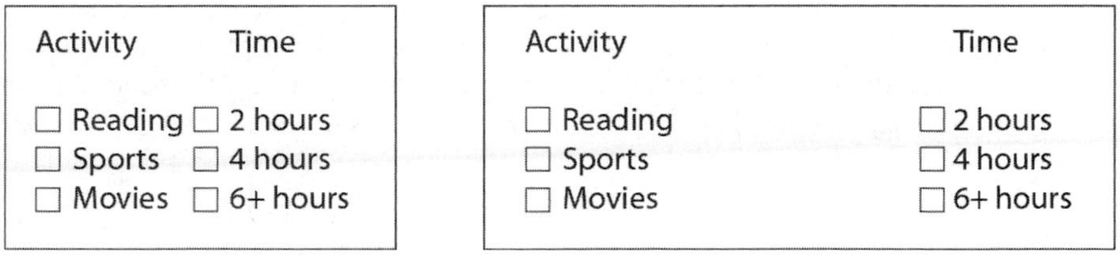

Activity	Time		Activity		Time
☐ Reading	☐ 2 hours		☐ Reading		☐ 2 hours
☐ Sports	☐ 4 hours		☐ Sports		☐ 4 hours
☐ Movies	☐ 6+ hours		☐ Movies		☐ 6+ hours

- **Language:** The BFMA recommends writing for a third-grade reading level. Form recipients may be filling out a form where the form language is a second language.

- **Check Boxes/Radio Buttons:** The BFMA recommends positioning check boxes and radio buttons to the left of the choice caption. If you deviate from this convention, what's most important is to be consistent on all your forms. Don't position radio buttons and check boxes to the left of some captions and to the right of other captions on the same form.

- **Flow:** The flow of the form should be left to right and top to bottom on roman text forms.
- **Signatures/Buttons:** Signatures, reset buttons, and submit buttons should be placed at the bottom of a form.

The BFMA has many more recommendations for designing forms. The preceding list is merely a short compilation of some of the more salient points to consider when designing a form.

For more information on form design, visit the BFMA Web site at `www.bfma.org/`.

W3C standards

The World Wide Web Consortium is a standards body that governs some Internet protocols. Among the interests of the W3C is developing a specification for Web forms. For several years, W3C has been working on the XForms specification that standardizes XML forms across various devices such as PCs, handheld devices, cell phones, and other systems.

As of this writing, the specification has not yet been accepted by an international body. W3C is working to promote the XForms standard, and we may see the specification eventually adopted. For more information on W3C, visit `www.w3.org/`.

Individual standards

If you're a forms designer in a small company, you may not give a hoot about adopting a standard dictated by a governing body. You may have constraints imposed by your own organization that require you to break some rules recommended by the authorities. What's important is to first become aware of various standards being proposed by influential groups and try to adopt the standards that fit within the scope of your company's form design framework.

What's required here is a study of the different proposed standards. First look at BFMA, and try to adopt as many rules as possible that fit your company's own design standards. Look over the proposed standards from W3C, and look at the XForms specification when you design Web forms, particularly in the area of handling XML data. Use the resources at hand to guide you in designing forms that make sense and are easy to read by the completed form recipients as well as the form recipients.

Designing Forms for the Form Recipient

When it comes to PDF forms, you need to ask yourself a few questions about the way your form is viewed and how data are handled when you receive the forms. Taking a few moments to think through the form routing process will help guide you in designing a form.

You may want to look at these important considerations when designing a PDF form:

- **Initial View:** Do you want the form to open in Full Screen mode or the standard editing mode in an Acrobat viewer? If you choose to have your forms open in Full Screen mode, the form recipient won't have access to menu commands or the Navigation panel. Therefore, you'll need to add buttons for printing a form, e-mailing/submitting a form, pop-up menus in lieu of bookmarks when required, and an exit button to make it easy for the form recipient to bail out of Full Screen mode.

- **Viewer Requirements:** Will the form be filled out by an Adobe Reader user? What version of a viewer can a form recipient complete your form? If you design forms for Adobe Reader users, you must pay attention to all JavaScripts added to your form. Some scripts won't work in Adobe Reader, such as spawning pages from templates, adding fields, deleting fields, and other actions that add objects or delete them from a form.

CROSS-REF For more information on JavaScript for Acrobat Forms, see Chapters 16 through Chapter 19. For information on JavaScript in LiveCycle Designer, see Chapter 29.

Viewer version is an important consideration. If a form can be filled out only with Acrobat/Reader version 7 or above, for example, you should include a JavaScript that assesses the viewer version when the file opens. Form recipients who take time filling out a form only to find that they can't submit the form are likely to abandon a potential sale.

- **Usage Rights:** If Adobe Reader users are to fill in the forms, the form should be enabled with Adobe Reader usage rights. Does the collection of the form data fit within the EULA (End User License Agreement) you agreed to when you installed Acrobat? If you collect data on more than 500 forms, you should add a message to your form telling users they can't save the form data, because collecting data on more than 500 forms would clearly violate the license agreement.

- **Distribution:** Will the form data be returned to you via e-mail? If yes, then you need to add a properly configured submit button or use the Distribute Form tool in Acrobat. It adds the submit button automatically for you.

- **Signatures:** Does the form need to be signed by the form recipient? If yes, then the form may need to be faxed back to you with a wet signature. Unless you deploy forms to an audience of people who are used to using digital signatures, you may not be able to retrieve forms from form recipients who don't understand how to create a digital ID.

NOTE We use the term *wet signature* to define an analog signature that you normally use when signing a document with a pen. A wet signature might be a graphic of your analog signature for an electronic form or a signature added to a paper form. This type of signature is much different from a digital signature you can use with all Acrobat viewers. For more information on using signatures (both wet and digital), see Chapter 12.

Rules for PDF Forms Designs

You need to follow a few basic rules in designing most types of PDF forms. These rules help the form recipient more easily fill out your form and help you in protecting the form integrity:

- **Naming Conventions:** Perhaps one of the most important design issues to consider is how you name fields. Don't use the default names Acrobat provides when you add fields to a page. Unless you use auto field detection to permit Acrobat to auto-detect form fields on a simple form, you should manually rename all fields. It is particularly important to use hierarchical names if you create calculations; copy formatted fields and paste them into other forms, reset form fields, show/hide form fields, or use JavaScripts.

CROSS-REF For more information on using hierarchical names, see Chapter 7.

- **Security:** If the background content and the form field properties are not to be tampered with by the form recipient, you must add security to your form. You can protect a form from editing page content as well as modifying field attributes, as we explain in Chapter 12.

- **Calculations:** Take all calculation errors away from the form recipient. The fields retaining calculations should be read-only fields, so a user cannot override the calculation formula. Fixed-price items should likewise be read-only fields to prevent form recipients from editing price values. When creating reset buttons, be sure to eliminate the fixed-price items from the reset action.

- **Field Configuration:** Be certain to configure fields properly. Text fields with numbers should be formatted as numbers. Radio buttons and check boxes for mutually exclusive choices should be formatted so that only one choice within a common group can be selected. Comb fields, as shown in Figure 3.3, should be formatted so that only a single field holds the comb field data. Dates, masks, and special formatted fields should be properly formatted using options in the Format tab in the field properties.

- **Design Elements:** Other than occasional button faces, avoid using form fields as design elements. Create the overall look and appearance in an authoring program, and add only those fields that are necessary to hold data or execute actions.

- **Tab Order:** Be certain to check the tab order as one of the last steps in designing a form. Striking the Tab key when a form opens should take the user to the top-left field on the form. Pressing the Tab key thereafter should take the form recipient to the next field in logical order and so on. If the tab order deviates from a logical order, you may need to manually reset the tab order.

- **Field Visibility:** It should be obvious where a field exists on a form. Don't rely on showing field highlights by the form recipient. Some users may not know how to turn on the highlight. Fields should appear within boxes, above lines, or in other design elements that clearly indicate where a field exists on a form.

FIGURE 3.3

This simple form has comb fields, proper field configurations, and good use of white space to break up sections on the form.

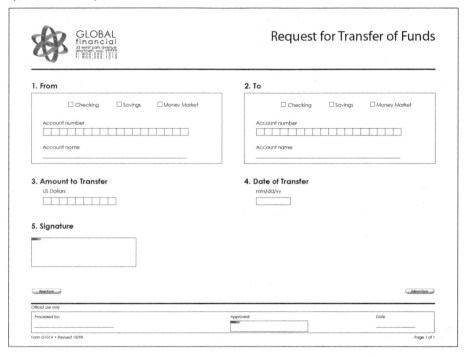

■ **Document Properties:** Be certain to take the time to complete the document property information, especially if you have an abundant number of forms circulating in your workplace. Document Property information facilitates searching for PDF files and makes finding forms infinitely easier.

■ **Save the Form:** As a last step in designing a form, choose File ➪ Save As and overwrite the saved form. When you use Save As to rewrite the document, the file size is optimized, which results in a much smaller file size.

Using the recommendations for designing for the form recipient and adding the items listed here will help you design better forms and make the job of completing a form much easier on the form recipient.

CROSS-REF If you started this book reading Chapters 1 and 2 and you don't understand some of the terms listed in this chapter, don't worry. We explain most of this material in detail in Chapters 5 and 6.

Summary

- No clear set of standards exists that encompass all forms in use today.

- The Business Forms Management Association has been working extensively on proposing a set of standards for use with paper and electronic forms. Many rules and standards advocated by the BFMA can be helpful to you when designing forms.

- W3C has been working for more than two years to develop standards for Web forms.

- When designing a form, you need to carefully examine several considerations for the form recipient.

- Employing a few rules can help you create forms that are easy for form recipients to complete and help you in processing the form data more efficiently.

Chapter 4

Creating Form Designs

P DF forms begin with a design. The background text, rules, boxes, graphic images, and design elements are assembled together in an authoring program. This is the first stage for designing PDF forms.

After you complete the form design, the file must be converted to a PDF document. Once converted to PDF, you then open the file in Acrobat and add the form elements that make your form a fillable form.

In this chapter, we look at some tools available to you for creating PDF forms, and we talk about getting your original authoring files to PDF.

IN THIS CHAPTER

Understanding design for PDF forms

Using authoring tools

Exporting to PDF

Modifying form designs

Setting Initial Views

Designing PDF Forms

For those who are novice forms designers, the most important thing for you to remember is that Acrobat is *not* a program where you begin a layout—forms or otherwise. Acrobat was never intended to be an original authoring program. As a matter of fact, Acrobat doesn't have a File ➪ New command to start a new design—something that almost all authoring applications provide you. It's only in recent releases of Acrobat that you could create a blank new page. When you create a blank page, that's precisely what you get—a blank document, and there are no tools available in Acrobat for adding text and elements in a layout.

Acrobat does provide a few tools that can aid you with minor touchups for text and image editing, but for the most part, it would be a convoluted task to try to create a form or other layout from scratch in Acrobat.

When creating a new form, you must begin with a file you have already assembled in another program. Just about any program you feel comfortable using for a form design is perfectly acceptable. Virtually any program file can be converted to a PDF document. And that's really what you need to begin creating a fillable form—a document designed in another program and converted to a PDF file.

To Convert or Not to Convert to PDF

Acrobat forms designers on Windows using Microsoft Office programs can avoid converting documents to PDF before launching Acrobat. Acrobat provides Windows users a one-step operation for converting Office files to PDF, auto-detecting fields, and opening a form in Form Editing mode where additional fields can be added and the newly created field objects can be modified.

To convert a Microsoft Office form to a PDF document, use the Forms ➪ Start Forms Wizard menu command. The Create or Edit Form wizard opens. The default radio button choice in the Create or Edit Form wizard is set to open an existing electronic document. On Windows, you can choose a native Office document to open. The file is converted to a PDF document and automatically opens in Form Editing mode.

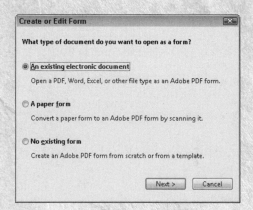

Macintosh users don't have the same options in the Create or Edit Form wizard, and they cannot open a native file on the Macintosh when using the wizard. Macintosh users must first create a PDF document and then open the PDF document in Form Editing mode in order to populate a form with field objects. When using Office programs on the Macintosh, use the Print dialog box and choose the Adobe PDF 9 Printer. From the PDF pull-down menu, choose Save as PDF and save the file.

After converting to a PDF document, open the form in Acrobat and choose Add or Edit Fields instead of using the Start Form Wizard command.

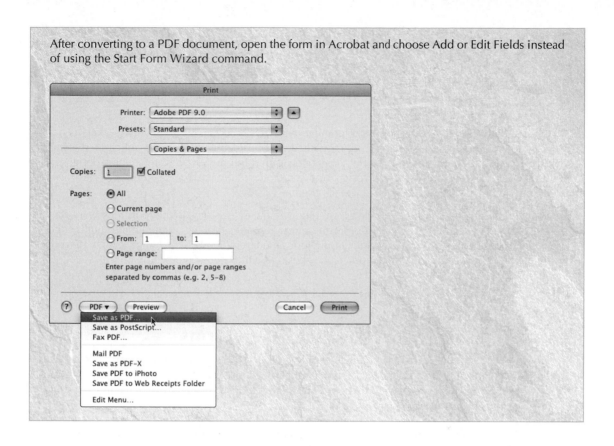

Using Tools for Form Designs

Like we said, any program file can be converted to a PDF document. The tool you choose to create your form largely depends on the complexity of your form. Although you can finesse a number of design elements in a word processing program like Microsoft Word, a complex design might be better assembled in a program like Adobe InDesign or perhaps Microsoft Publisher.

Likewise, you can create some impressive form designs in programs like Microsoft PowerPoint and Microsoft Excel, but again other programs like the page layout applications can provide you more freedom for laying out design elements when it comes to forms.

The best program is really a matter of personal taste. If your designs are relatively simple to moderately complex, using the table features and graphics options in Microsoft Word can get the job done. If you feel comfortable using the Office programs and your tools are capable of creating the form designs you want, then, by all means, use the program that you are familiar with to create designs in the fastest and easiest way possible.

Forms Designs in Enterprises

Independent forms designers and small businesses have a luxury for choosing the tool that works best within the comfort level of existing staff. The program you feel most familiar with for creating designs that work is a personal choice.

In a large enterprise, leaving choices for original authoring programs to individual workers is not something we recommend. A large company needs to consider staff turnover, anticipated forms needs, data processing needs, and similar kinds of decisions. If some workers are creating designs in Office programs, others in Adobe InDesign, and some others in QuarkXPress, then you may have difficulty finding new people with skills in all programs.

A company is best advised to assemble a committee to make decisions on the tools they want staff to use and the program they want to use for the forms authoring. Taking a little time to outline the conversion of existing paper forms to electronic forms, determine how the data are to be managed, and set company standards for what applications best serve the needs of the company can save lots of time and money.

Using Microsoft Word to design forms

More PDF forms were originally designed in Microsoft Word than any other program. When you look at bank and finance forms, legal forms, real estate forms, health care forms, education forms, a good number of government forms, and many other industry-wide forms, you'll find the lion's share of these forms were originally created in Microsoft Word.

MS Word is an excellent program for creating simple forms. Figure 4.1 shows a simple form designed for internal use within an organization. Designing this kind of form doesn't require a sophisticated layout program, and a tool such as MS Word works well for the job.

Moving to more complex form designs, Figure 4.2 shows another form designed in Microsoft Word. With Word's table and layout features, the proficient MS Word user can easily create forms similar to the document shown in Figure 4.2.

A simple internal form designed in Microsoft Word

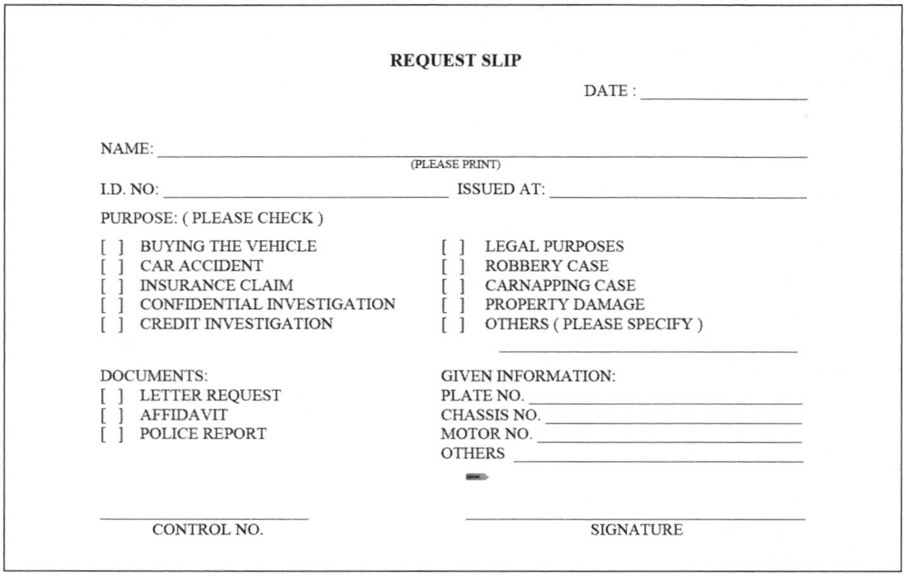

REQUEST SLIP

DATE : _____

NAME: _____
(PLEASE PRINT)

I.D. NO: _____ ISSUED AT: _____

PURPOSE: (PLEASE CHECK)

[ ] BUYING THE VEHICLE   [ ] LEGAL PURPOSES
[ ] CAR ACCIDENT   [ ] ROBBERY CASE
[ ] INSURANCE CLAIM   [ ] CARNAPPING CASE
[ ] CONFIDENTIAL INVESTIGATION   [ ] PROPERTY DAMAGE
[ ] CREDIT INVESTIGATION   [ ] OTHERS (PLEASE SPECIFY)

_____

DOCUMENTS: GIVEN INFORMATION:
[ ] LETTER REQUEST   PLATE NO. _____
[ ] AFFIDAVIT   CHASSIS NO. _____
[ ] POLICE REPORT   MOTOR NO. _____
     OTHERS _____

_____   _____
CONTROL NO.   SIGNATURE

Using proper design elements

Acrobat provides you an automated feature for populating a form with fields. Using a menu command, Acrobat can assess the form elements and presto, your form is populated with fields. We discuss using auto field detection in Chapter 5. For now, it's important to understand how to design a form that optimizes your chances for Acrobat to automatically detect fields.

CROSS-REF For more information on using auto field detection, see Chapters 5 through 7.

Compare the forms in Figure 4.1 and 4.2. In Figure 4.1 you see brackets appearing where the form recipient is supposed to add a check mark for one of the options in the *Purpose* and *Documents* categories. In Figure 4.2, you see boxes for similar options choices.

If we run Acrobat's automated command to detect fields, no check boxes will be picked up on the form shown in Figure 4.1. On Figure 4.2, virtually all fields are detected when a user chooses to permit Acrobat to auto detect fields. Therefore, when using MS Word or any other application to author your form design, be certain to use boxes where you want radio button and check box fields.

FIGURE 4.2

A complex design created in Microsoft Word

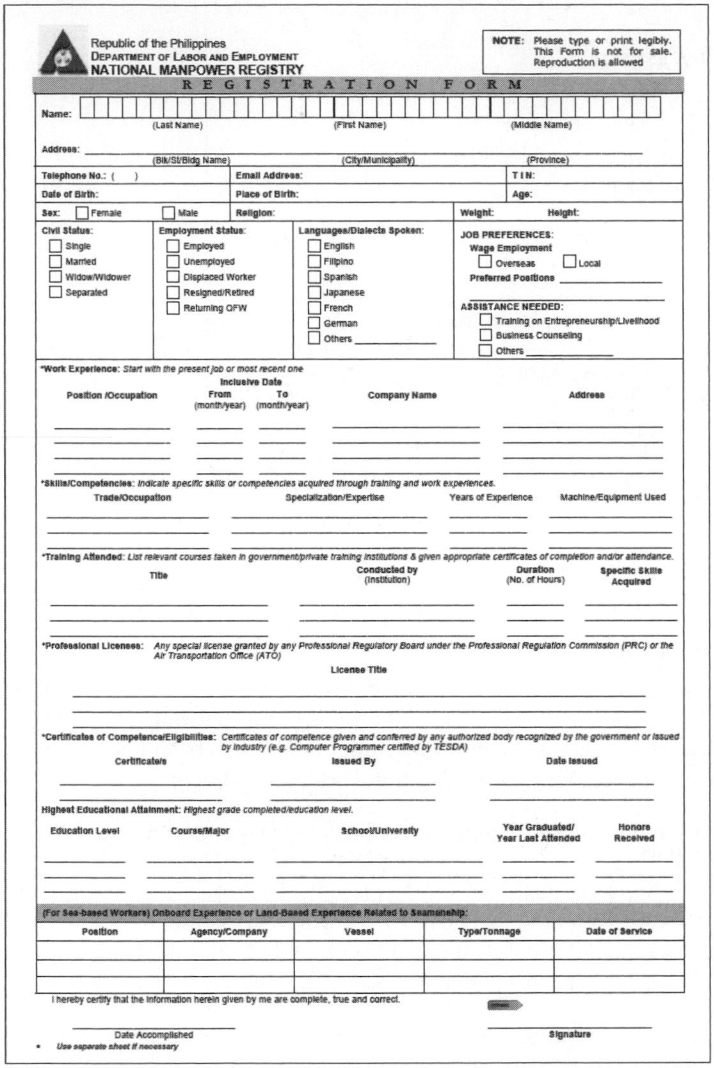

Republic of the Philippines
DEPARTMENT OF LABOR AND EMPLOYMENT
NATIONAL MANPOWER REGISTRY

NOTE: Please type or print legibly. This Form is not for sale. Reproduction is allowed

R E G I S T R A T I O N F O R M

Name: (Last Name) (First Name) (Middle Name)

Address: (Blk/St/Bldg Name) (City/Municipality) (Province)

Telephone No.: ( ) | Email Address: | T I N:

Date of Birth: | Place of Birth: | Age:

Sex: ☐ Female ☐ Male | Religion: | Weight: Height:

Civil Status: ☐ Single ☐ Married ☐ Widow/Widower ☐ Separated

Employment Status: ☐ Employed ☐ Unemployed ☐ Displaced Worker ☐ Resigned/Retired ☐ Returning OFW

Languages/Dialects Spoken: ☐ English ☐ Filipino ☐ Spanish ☐ Japanese ☐ French ☐ German ☐ Others ______

JOB PREFERENCES:
Wage Employment ☐ Overseas ☐ Local
Preferred Positions ______

ASSISTANCE NEEDED:
☐ Training on Entrepreneurship/Livelihood
☐ Business Counseling
☐ Others ______

*Work Experience: *Start with the present job or most recent one*

Position /Occupation | Inclusive Date From (month/year) To (month/year) | Company Name | Address

*Skills/Competencies: *Indicate specific skills or competencies acquired through training and work experiences.*

Trade/Occupation | Specialization/Expertise | Years of Experience | Machine/Equipment Used

*Training Attended: *List relevant courses taken in government/private training institutions & given appropriate certificates of completion and/or attendance.*

Title | Conducted by (Institution) | Duration (No. of Hours) | Specific Skills Acquired

*Professional Licenses: *Any special license granted by any Professional Regulatory Board under the Professional Regulation Commission (PRC) or the Air Transportation Office (ATO)*

License Title

*Certificates of Competence/Eligibilities: *Certificates of competence given and conferred by any authorized body recognized by the government or issued by industry (e.g. Computer Programmer certified by TESDA)*

Certificate/s | Issued By | Date Issued

Highest Educational Attainment: *Highest grade completed/education level.*

Education Level | Course/Major | School/University | Year Graduated/ Year Last Attended | Honors Received

(For Sea-based Workers) Onboard Experience or Land-Based Experience Related to Seamanship:

Position	Agency/Company	Vessel	Type/Tonnage	Date of Service

I hereby certify that the information herein given by me are complete, true and correct.

Date Accomplished

Signature

• *Use separate sheet if necessary*

TIP Acrobat's auto field detection feature doesn't detect all text characters as form fields. Some characters used with fonts such as Zapf Dignbats and Wingdings convert the characters to form fields such as check boxes and radio buttons. But all characters are not recognized, so you need to exercise a little caution. When you need check boxes on a form, you can use a rectangle drawing tool in your authoring program and avoid fonts that have box characters such as Wingdings, Symbol, Carta, and other fonts that use text characters for boxes for more reliability.

In Figure 4.2, take a close look at the comb field appearing at the top of the form. Figure 4.3 shows a zoomed view of the comb fields. In Figure 4.3, notice a slight difference in the line weight to the right side of the second box.

FIGURE 4.3

A slight difference in the stroke weight is shown to the right of the second box in the comb field.

When you use the auto field detection, Acrobat will create two comb fields if the design includes these kinds of fields. However, even the slightest difference in stroke weights signifies an end and a beginning of comb fields when auto detecting fields. This is a good thing because you can intentionally indicate where one comb field ends and another begins. When designing comb fields be certain to keep stroke weights identical until you reach the end of a field. When you want to start a new comb field on the same line, you can change the stoke weight.

Signature fields are also recognized by Acrobat's auto field detection. You must use the word *signature* in the field caption for Acrobat to create a signature field. However, any form of caption identifying a signature can be used such as Customer Signature, Approval Signature, Signature, and so on.

Using custom page sizes

If you design forms for print, standard page sizes such as US Letter, US Legal, A3, A4, and so on are page options choices you find by default in MS Word and most other authoring programs. Set up your Word document using one of the standard page sizes, and design your form. After you populate the form with fields, it's ready to be filled in and printed.

Forms designed for an electronic workflow, on the other hand, don't necessarily adhere to a standard size. You might use a landscape 10x7-inch design that's well suited for a computer monitor. If you intend to use non-standard page sizes, you have to do a little work in Word to create the custom page sizes.

Understanding Auto Field Detection

Acrobat 8 includes a menu command for Run Form Field Recognition. When you open a form without any fields, you can choose Forms ⇨ Run Form Field Recognition, and Acrobat uses an auto-detection algorithm to analyze a form for where field objects need to be created. Acrobat looks for clear design elements such as underlines, boxes, comb field grids, well-constructed tables with line borders on the cells, and signatures to create field objects on a form. The text descriptions adjacent to the form design elements are used for field names.

In Acrobat 9 and later viewers, you use a different command for Acrobat to auto-detect fields. Choose Forms ⇨ Add or Edit Fields, and Acrobat changes the interface view from a normal Viewer mode to Form Editing Mode. A dialog box opens prompting you to decide whether you want to auto detect fields. If you click Yes, the auto-detection feature is used, and Acrobat creates form field objects the same way with much improvement as it did in Acrobat 8.

Although you don't have a direct command for Run Form Field Recognition, we refer to the process of auto-field detection in Acrobat 9 as using Acrobat to auto detect field objects.

The following steps describe how to create a custom page size in Microsoft Word 2007 on Windows XP and Vista.

STEPS: Creating Custom Page Sizes in Word 2007 (Windows)

1. **Create a new blank document in Word.** Click the Office button, and click Blank Document in the New Document window.

2. **Click the Page Layout tab in the Ribbon.**

3. **Click Size to open the Size menu, and choose More Paper Sizes, as shown in Figure 4.4.** The Page Setup dialog box opens.

4. **Add a new page size.** Type the width and height of your new page size in the Width and Height text boxes, as shown in Figure 4.5. If you want the new page size to default to the custom page size, click the Default button in the Page Setup dialog box.

5. **Click OK.** You may see a dialog box reporting a problem with the margins. Click Fix, and the margins are adjusted to your new page size. When you return to the document window, the new blank page is adjusted according to your settings in the Page Setup dialog box.

FIGURE 4.4

Click More Page Options on the Size drop-down menu.

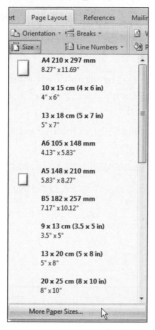

FIGURE 4.5

Edit the Width and Height text boxes to create a new custom page size.

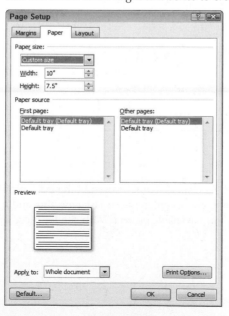

On the Macintosh, the steps are a little different. Using Microsoft Word, do the following to create a custom page size.

STEPS: Creating Custom Page Sizes in Microsoft Word (Macintosh)

1. **Open Word, and choose File ⇨ Page Setup.**

2. **In the Page Setup dialog box, open the Paper Size drop-down menu and choose Manage Custom Sizes at the bottom of the menu.** The Custom Page Sizes dialog box, shown in Figure 4.6, opens.

3. **Click the plus (+) button on the lower-left side of the dialog box.** The word *Untitled* appears in the list of custom page sizes.

4. **Add the page size.** Type the new page size in the Width and Height text boxes.

5. **Name the custom page.** Double-click *Untitled,* and type a descriptive name, as shown in Figure 4.6.

6. **Click OK, and your page is formatted to the new page size.**

FIGURE 4.6

Click the plus button, and edit the page size and name the new custom page in the Custom Page Sizes dialog box.

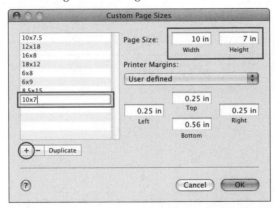

Preparing forms for print

At times you may have a need to create a form that will be used both electronically and as a printed document. As an example, you might attend a conference or large meeting and hand out paper forms, and then later make the same form available on your Web site for those individuals who couldn't attend the meeting.

If you prepare forms at standard page sizes (US Letter, US Legal, A4, and so on.), you can easily submit PDF files to your local commercial printer or copy shop for printing without a need to prepare the files in any special manner. However, if you create forms at custom page sizes and you want your forms printed at a commercial print shop, you need to add one more step in your workflow.

Commercial presses print non-standard sized forms and other documents on oversized papers—especially when the design bleeds off the edge of the paper. For layout and illustration programs, the printer can receive your native files and print direct to press or to film any custom page size you create. At the time the files are printed, the printer adds crop and trim marks to the output. These marks tell the printer where to cut the paper to the custom page size. If you submit PDF files to your printer, you can add trim marks from a layout or illustration program at the time you create the PDF document, thereby minimizing the work for your print shop.

Office applications were not designed for commercial printing and hence provide you no means for adding trim marks either at print time or to PDF exports. Additionally, the local print shop generally curses the documents they receive when the files are from MS Office applications. This is due to the potential problems the printer can encounter with the Office documents and the fact that they need to add extra steps to print the files on commercial equipment. Among the potential problems that can arise is a complete document reflow when a file like an MS Word document is formatted for a PostScript device. The extra work comes in when the printer has to find a way to add crop and trim marks to the file.

You can make the job much easier for your printer by adding crop and trim marks to the PDF files you submit for printing. If you submit any Office document of any size to a commercial printer, follow these steps before placing an order.

STEPS: Adding Crop and Trim Marks to Office Documents (Acrobat Pro and Pro Extended only)

1. **Create a form on a custom page size.** In this example, we use a landscape form 10 inches wide by 7.5 inches high. To easily create a non-standard PDF page size, you can open MS Word, create a blank page at a non-standard size, and convert to a PDF document.

2. **Open the Print Production tools.** Right-click (Control-click on the Mac) the Toolbar Well to open a context menu. Choose Print Production from the menu commands to open the Print Production toolbar, shown in Figure 4.7.

Open the Print Production toolbar.

Add Printer Marks tool   Crop Pages tool

The two tools we'll use for these steps are the Add Printer Marks tool and the Crop Pages tool. The sequence of using the tools is critical. You must first add printer's marks and then crop the page. In Figure 4.7, you'll notice that the Add Printer Marks tool appears first followed by the Crop Pages tool. The order of the tools in the toolbar can help you remember what tool you use first.

3. **Click the Add Printer Marks tool.** The Add Printer Marks dialog box opens, as shown in Figure 4.8.

FIGURE 4.8

Click the Add Printer Marks tool to open the Add Printer Marks dialog box.

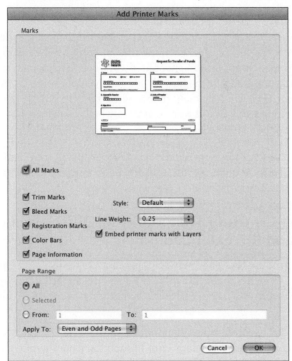

4. **Add printer's marks.** Click the All Marks check box to add all printer's marks. In many cases, you won't need all marks. Black and white forms, for example, won't need the color bars. If you have no bleeds or color separations, you won't need the Bleed or Registration Marks. However, just to observe all the marks available to you, click All Marks and then click OK.

You won't see any marks on the page after you click OK in the Add Printer Marks dialog box. To reveal the marks, you need to address the next two steps.

5. **Open the Crop Pages dialog box.** Click the Crop Pages tool in the Print Production toolbar. The Crop Pages dialog box opens, as shown in Figure 4.9.

FIGURE 4.9

Click the Crop Pages tool to open the Crop Pages dialog box.

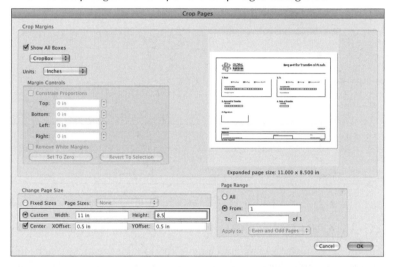

6. **Change the Page Size.** Edit the Custom Width and Height text boxes by adding one inch to your page size. One inch added to the page provides one-half inch on either side of the page. When the page is sized larger, the printer's marks will appear on the page.

7. **Click OK.** When you return to the Document pane, your document displays the printer's marks, as shown in Figure 4.10.

FIGURE 4.10

Printer's marks are added to a custom page in Acrobat.

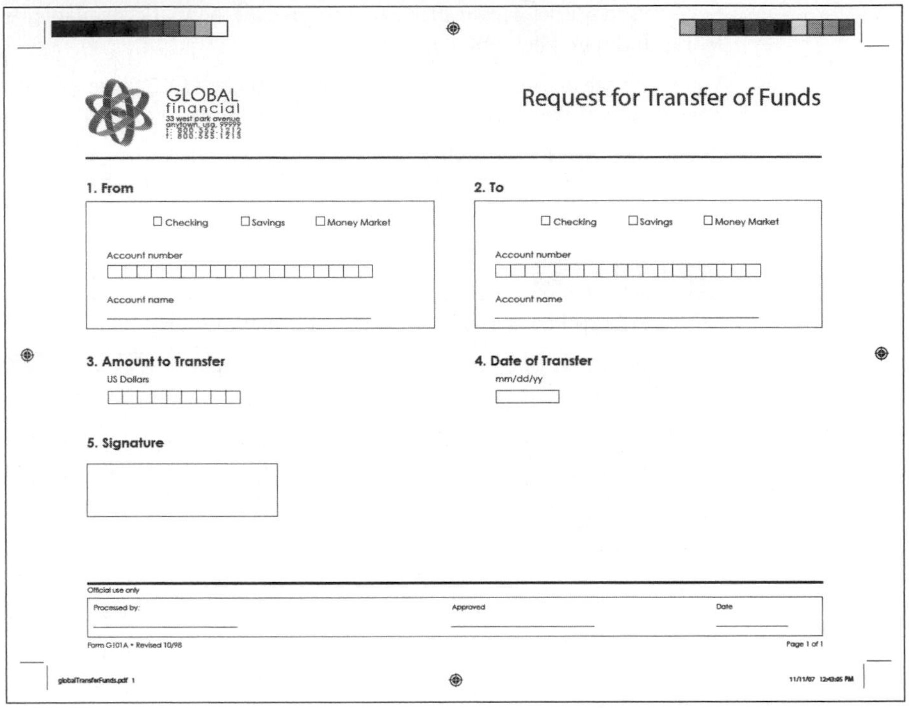
GLOBAL
financial

Request for Transfer of Funds

1. From

☐ Checking ☐ Savings ☐ Money Market

Account number

Account name

2. To

☐ Checking ☐ Savings ☐ Money Market

Account number

Account name

3. Amount to Transfer

US Dollars

4. Date of Transfer

mm/dd/yy

5. Signature

Official use only

Processed by: Approved Date

Form G101A • Revised 10/98

Page 1 of 1

Using Microsoft Excel to design forms

The Microsoft Excel power user might be more comfortable creating designs in Excel. Although Excel isn't our first choice for a forms authoring program, the sophisticated Excel user can create complex forms using Excel's tools for formatting, adding border and fill appearances, and importing graphics. Figure 4.11 shows a form that was originally designed in Microsoft Excel.

When we chose auto field detection on the form shown in Figure 4.11, all the comb fields were perfectly recognized. There were problems with the check box fields, but the reason check boxes were not recognized is because they weren't formatted properly in the original design. We cover tips for designing forms for auto field detection in Chapters 5 through 7.

Cropping Pages

Acrobat provides two Crop tools. The Crop tool is located in the Advanced Editing toolbar. The Crop Pages tool appears in the Print Production toolbar. The Crop tool in the Advanced Editing toolbar can crop pages down, and you can increase additional page area in the Crop Pages dialog box. That is to say, you can change the page size as it appears in Acrobat.

The physical page size in Acrobat terms is called the MediaBox. Regardless of what tool you use, the MediaBox does not really change. What changes is what you see in the Document pane. The page appears to be cropped but the data are not eliminated from the document.

In Acrobat 9 you can permanently remove the page area outside a crop region using the Preflight tool. Because this kind of task is not typically something forms authors are likely to do, we don't go into detail about using the Preflight tool and eliminating page data. If you need to perform this kind of task, see the Acrobat Help document or look at the *Acrobat 9 PDF Bible* (Padova, Wiley Publishing).

The Crop Pages tool in the Print Production toolbar is used only to add page area to your document. When you click the tool, the Crop Pages dialog box opens. There is no provision for dragging open a rectangle to define a crop region. If you attempt to set the page size smaller in the Crop Pages dialog box, an error dialog opens informing you that page size cannot be reduced.

The Print Production tool is handy when you design a form and want to send the form to press for printing. If you designed the form without showing crop marks, you can add crop marks in Acrobat using the Print Production tools, and then use the Crop Pages tool to upsize the page to show the crop marks and send the file off for printing.

Using Microsoft PowerPoint as a forms designer

PowerPoint is another program many users are comfortable with and use for much more than the program was designed to do. People create layouts, oversized banners and large format prints, and a host of other documents. You can design forms in PowerPoint and convert the files to PDF files. Our choice isn't PowerPoint as a primary authoring program for forms designs, but if it works for you, you can use the program to design PDF forms.

For the Mac user, PowerPoint for any kind of document is much less desirable than the Windows version if you want to convert PowerPoint files to PDF files. The PDF Maker in Acrobat 9 isn't supported with Microsoft Office programs including PowerPoint on the Mac, and you may struggle with page sizes if you use the Print to PDF options in the Print dialog box. If we were going to recommend one program not to use for forms design, it would be PowerPoint on the Mac.

FIGURE 4.11

You can create complex form designs in Microsoft Excel.

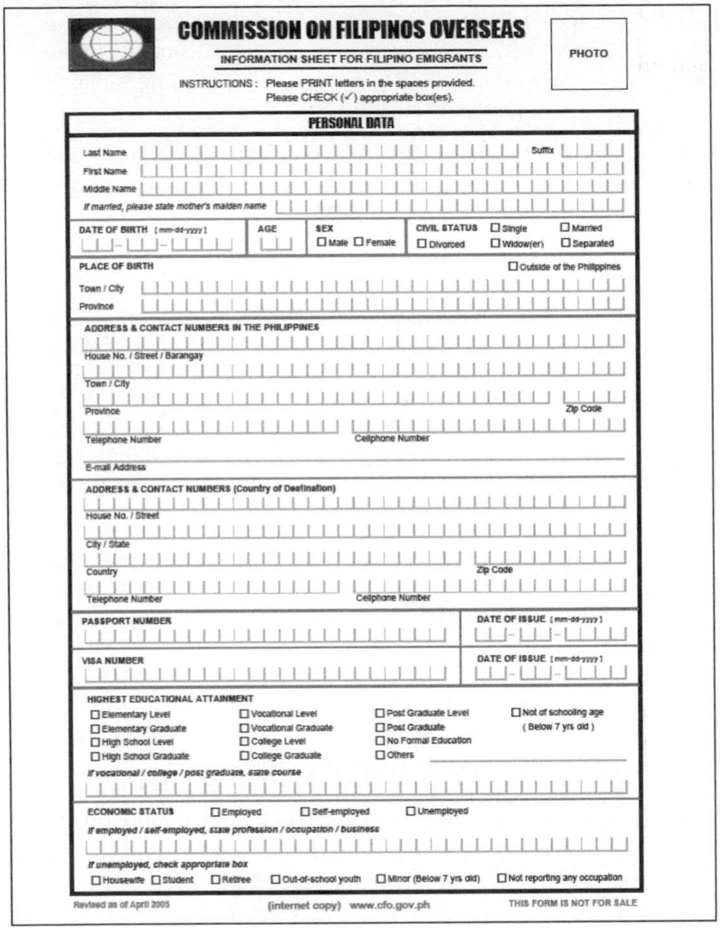

COMMISSION ON FILIPINOS OVERSEAS

INFORMATION SHEET FOR FILIPINO EMIGRANTS

PHOTO

INSTRUCTIONS : Please PRINT letters in the spaces provided.
Please CHECK (✓) appropriate box(es).

PERSONAL DATA

Last Name — Suffix
First Name
Middle Name
If married, please state mother's maiden name

DATE OF BIRTH [mm-dd-yyyy] — AGE — SEX ☐ Male ☐ Female — CIVIL STATUS ☐ Single ☐ Married ☐ Divorced ☐ Widow(er) ☐ Separated

PLACE OF BIRTH — ☐ Outside of the Philippines
Town / City
Province

ADDRESS & CONTACT NUMBERS IN THE PHILIPPINES
House No. / Street / Barangay
Town / City
Province — Zip Code
Telephone Number — Cellphone Number
E-mail Address

ADDRESS & CONTACT NUMBERS (Country of Destination)
House No. / Street
City / State
Country — Zip Code
Telephone Number — Cellphone Number

PASSPORT NUMBER — DATE OF ISSUE [mm-dd-yyyy]

VISA NUMBER — DATE OF ISSUE [mm-dd-yyyy]

HIGHEST EDUCATIONAL ATTAINMENT
☐ Elementary Level ☐ Vocational Level ☐ Post Graduate Level ☐ Not of schooling age (Below 7 yrs old)
☐ Elementary Graduate ☐ Vocational Graduate ☐ Post Graduate
☐ High School Level ☐ College Level ☐ No Formal Education
☐ High School Graduate ☐ College Graduate ☐ Others
If vocational / college / post graduate, state course

ECONOMIC STATUS ☐ Employed ☐ Self-employed ☐ Unemployed
If employed / self-employed, state profession / occupation / business
If unemployed, check appropriate box
☐ Housewife ☐ Student ☐ Retiree ☐ Out-of-school youth ☐ Minor (Below 7 yrs old) ☐ Not reporting any occupation

Revised as of April 2005 — (internet copy) www.cfo.gov.ph — THIS FORM IS NOT FOR SALE

Using OpenOffice.org Writer as a forms designer

OpenOffice.org Writer is a perfectly acceptable tool for authoring forms. Writer has an advantage over Microsoft Word in that Writer offers you form design tools, support for calculation formulas, and XML-based documents, and it exports directly to a PDF document. Writer is similar in many ways to Adobe LiveCycle Designer, where subforms are used to create dynamic forms.

Writer is available for Macintosh, Windows, and Linux. The advantage you have with Writer over LiveCycle Designer is that the forms you create in Writer can be completely edited in Acrobat. LiveCycle Designer forms cannot be edited in Acrobat, as we explain in Chapter 21.

Using layout programs for form design

Page layout programs are the most ideal authoring tools for creating form designs. You have much more freedom in moving objects, formatting type, creating tables, and working with images.

If you look back in Chapter 2 and browse Table 2.1, you'll see that 15 (almost half of the 31 fillable forms) for tax forms by U.S. states were originally authored in a layout program while only one form was created in an Office application.

Among the most popular layout programs are Adobe InDesign, Adobe PageMaker, QuarkXPress, and Microsoft Publisher. InDesign offers one extra benefit over the other layout programs. You can create button fields in InDesign, and the button properties are editable in Acrobat after converting to a PDF document. Buttons not only invoke actions, but you can add design elements that aren't available with other programs. Figure 4.12 shows a layout converted to a PDF document from InDesign.

In Figure 4.12, the discount coupon extends beyond the page border. This type of design element can be added only using InDesign. Additionally, InDesign, as well as some other layout programs, offers you options for exporting to a PDF document with Adobe PDF layers. Layers can be useful in many ways for forms designers, as we explain in Chapter 13.

FIGURE 4.12

InDesign offers some design features not available in other programs.

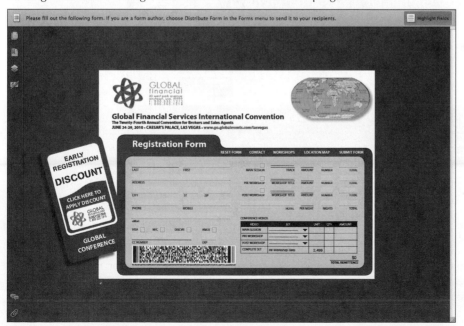

Using illustration programs to design forms

Programs like Adobe Illustrator and CorelDraw can be used to create forms. Typically, you don't find as many options for handling type in illustration programs as you do in layout programs, but impressive type control features such as creating character and paragraph styles have been added to more recent versions of illustration software.

If you have a need for creating layered PDF documents, adding gradients, and using vector objects in a form design, then an illustration program could be used. Our preference would be to stick to the layout programs, as these same features can be used in a layout program. However, a design like you see in Figure 4.13 is just as easily created in a program like Adobe Illustrator.

FIGURE 4.13

Illustration programs like Adobe Illustrator can be used to create visually appealing form designs.

Using other programs to create forms

It doesn't matter what program you use, the original authoring document can be converted to a PDF document. It's not likely that you'll use Windows Notepad or WordPad or TextEdit on the Mac to create a form design. You could convert the files to PDF files, but formatting text and design elements would be much more challenging using a text editor.

Vertical market applications documents, off-the-shelf software documents, accounting programs documents, and so on can be converted to a PDF document via Acrobat Distiller. If a file can print, you can convert it to a PDF document. Of course, once converted to a PDF document, you can add form fields in Acrobat to make the form a fillable form.

 **CROSS-REF** For more information on Acrobat Distiller, see "Using Acrobat Distiller" later in this chapter.

Creating PDF Files

After you create your form design in an authoring program, you need to convert the document to a PDF file. Acrobat provides you with a number of different ways to convert application documents to PDF documents, and many application programs offer support for direct exports to PDF documents.

Using PDFMaker to convert to PDF documents (Windows only)

The PDFMaker is a macro installed with the Microsoft Office programs and several other applications such as Autodesk AutoCAD, Lotus Notes, Microsoft Visio, and some others (a total of 11 different PDFMakers) when you install Acrobat on Windows. The PDFMaker offers you an easy and straightforward means for exporting your application documents to a PDF file.

PDFMaker on Windows

In regard to the Office applications, you'll find a new Acrobat tab in the Ribbon in Office 2007 programs after you install Acrobat on your computer. Click the Acrobat tab, and the Ribbon changes to display items specific to creating Acrobat PDF files. Figure 4.14 shows options available to you from Microsoft Word after clicking the Acrobat tab.

FIGURE 4.14

Click the Acrobat tab in the Ribbon to display options for converting to a PDF document.

As shown in Figure 4.14, you have several choices in the Acrobat tab for creating PDF files. We won't bother explaining the Create and Email, Review and Comment, and categories you see in the Ribbon. For forms designers, your work is with the two items you see to the far left for Create PDF and Preferences. In most cases, you can bypass the Preferences button and just click the Create PDF button that appears first in the Ribbon.

Click Create PDF, and the Save Adobe PDF File As dialog box opens. Click the Options button, and the Acrobat PDF Maker dialog box opens, as shown in Figure 4.15.

FIGURE 4.15

Click Adobe PDF conversion options in the Save Adobe PDF File As dialog box to open the PDF Options dialog box.

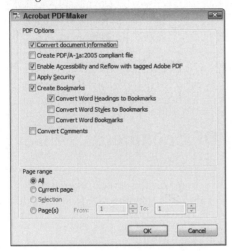

Unless you have a need for creating bookmarks for multi-page forms, uncheck the Create bookmarks check box. Most forms you create are not likely to use bookmarks. If you add document properties, such as Title, Author, and Subject in Word, be certain to check the Convert document information check box. Additionally, you'll want to be certain the Create Accessible (Tagged) PDF file check box is checked. This item serves a dual purpose. You can make your forms accessible for users with screen readers for the vision and motion challenged form recipient, and you can add structure to your document. Adding structure to the document can help if you need to get the background content out of a PDF file and back to a Word document. We recommend always tagging your files by keeping this check box checked as a default.

CROSS-REF   **For more information on creating structured and tagged PDF documents, see Chapter 11.**

Click OK, and you return to the Save Adobe PDF File As dialog box. When you click Save, the document is converted to a PDF file and opens in Acrobat.

If you're new to Acrobat and PDF forms, walking through steps in the PDFMaker will be a snap after you've converted a few files. Practice a few times creating blank pages using different custom page sizes, and your PDF conversion steps from any Office application will become commonplace.

Converting to PDF on the Macintosh

On the Macintosh, the PDFMaker was installed with Acrobat versions 8 and below. The PDFMaker was not included on the Macintosh in Acrobat 9.

To convert Office files to PDF files, you use the Print command. Choose File ➪ Print to open the Print dialog box. In the Printer drop-down menu, choose Adobe PDF 9.0. Open the PDF drop-down menu, and choose Save as PDF. The Save dialog box shown opens, in Figure 4.16.

After choosing Save as PDF, the first of two Save dialog boxes open. Click Save in the first dialog box and a second Save dialog box opens. In OSX Leopard, when the second Save dialog box opens, you'll see options for adding document property information. Now's a good time to add the document properties information. Type descriptive information in the field boxes, and click Save. Your form is converted to a PDF form.

FIGURE 4.16

Choose File ➪ Print in an Office application, and select the Adobe PDF 9.0 Printer. Open the PDF drop-down menu, and choose Save as PDF.

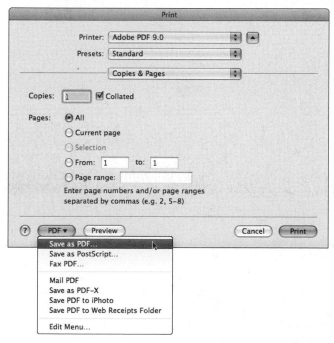

Using Acrobat to convert to PDF

If you are working in Acrobat, you don't need to switch to an authoring program to convert a file to a PDF file for a good many different file types. Presuming you've already created a form in an authoring program, you can convert your document to a PDF document from within Acrobat.

File types supported by Acrobat for PDF creation

To check out the file types that Acrobat supports for direct conversion to PDF, open the Preferences dialog box by pressing Ctrl/⌘+K. In the Preferences dialog box, click Convert to PDF in the left panel. The right panel changes to display all the file types acceptable to Acrobat for PDF conversion in a scrollable window, as shown in Figure 4.17.

FIGURE 4.17

File types supported by Acrobat for conversion to PDF appear in the Preferences dialog box.

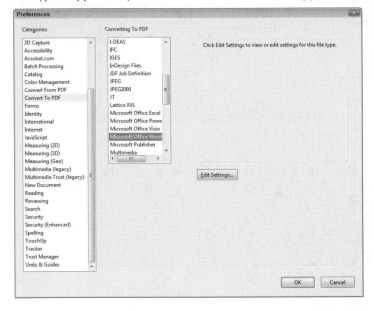

On the Macintosh, you'll find fewer file types supported for PDF conversion, as shown in Figure 4.18. Office documents, for example, are not supported by Acrobat on the Mac. If you need to convert Office files to PDF, use the method described earlier for printing a document to the Adobe PDF 9.0 printer.

FIGURE 4.18

Fewer file types are supported for PDF conversion on the Macintosh.

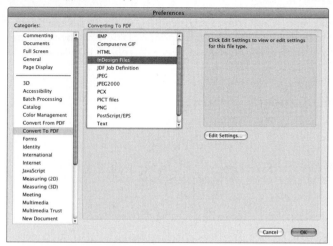

For many file types, you have an option for changing the PDF conversion settings. Select a file type in the scrollable window, and click Edit Settings. The Adobe PDF Settings for supported documents dialog box opens, as shown in Figure 4.19.

FIGURE 4.19

Click Edit Settings to open the Adobe PDF Settings for supported documents dialog box.

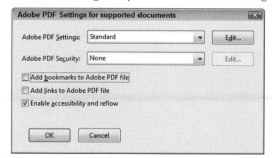

Notice the Adobe PDF Settings drop-down menu. The default choice for the Adobe PDF Settings is Standard. For almost any form you create for electronic processing, the Standard option works well. You can make changes by selecting other menu options; choose High Quality for printing higher-quality documents or Press Quality for forms that go to press. Additionally, you have some options for choosing a PDF subset such as PDF/X and PDF/A. To keep it simple, just keep the Standard choice active and you'll be fine for producing PDF forms that can be used for electronic processing and printing to desktop printers.

NOTE   If you prepare forms for prepress and commercial printing, you have several things to consider. Delving into the world of prepress and printing is beyond the scope of this book. For information related to professional printing, see *Adobe Acrobat 9 PDF Bible* (Wiley Publishing).

Converting files to PDF using Acrobat

After checking conversion options in the Preferences dialog box, click OK to return to the Acrobat window. At this point, you can convert files to PDF in a number of ways.

- **Open a document:** Choose File ➪ Open, and select a file Acrobat supports for PDF creation. In the Files of type (Windows) or Show (Macintosh) drop-down menu, choose All Files. Select the file you want to convert, and click Open.

- **Drag and drop:** From the desktop, drag a file to the Acrobat window to convert to PDF.

- **Drag and drop to the Pages panel:** Open the Pages panel, and drag a file from the desktop to a page location in the Pages panel. This action appends a page to the existing PDF document.

- **Combine Files:** If you have a page to append to a form, drag a file to the Pages panel or click the Combine Files task button. In the Combine Files dialog box, click the Add Files button and select the files you want to append to your form. Note that in Windows the Office applications native files are supported, so you can select a native document file and the file is converted to PDF and appended to the document in one step. On the Mac, Office files are not supported in the Combine Files wizard.

- **Context menu on the Desktop (Windows only):** From the desktop, right-click a file and choose Convert to Adobe PDF.

- **Using QuickLook on the Mac:** Although you cannot convert to PDF from the desktop on the Mac, OSX Leopard provides an easy way to examine file content. Open a folder of files, and press the spacebar on the first file listed in a folder. Press the down arrow key to scroll through the files. QuickLook shows the file contents without launching an application. Locate the file you want to convert to PDF, and double-click to open it in the Original authoring program. Use the Print command to convert to PDF.

Exporting to PDF

Many programs today export directly to PDF. The Adobe Creative Suite programs, QuarkXPress, CorelDraw, OpenOffice.org Writer, and many other others you might use to create a form support PDF creation via a menu command in the program. For example, look at the file export options for Adobe InDesign by choosing File ➪ Export. Choose Adobe PDF from the Format menu, and click Save. The Export Adobe PDF dialog box opens.

Depending on your authoring program, you may have different conversion options than in Office PDF exports. For example, InDesign supports creating layers and adding button fields when designing a form. If you want layers converted to Adobe PDF Layers and you want the buttons active in the PDF document, options in the Export Adobe PDF dialog box can enable these items during the PDF conversion.

Figure 4.20 shows the Export Adobe PDF dialog box options for enabling layers and buttons. Check Create Acrobat Layers and Interactive Elements to ensure that layers are preserved and the button fields are recognized.

FIGURE 4.20

Check Create Acrobat Layers and Interactive Elements in Adobe InDesign if you want layers and buttons converted in the PDF file.

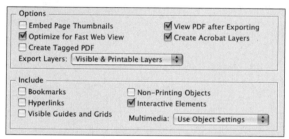

Adobe Illustrator files can be saved from Illustrator and opened in Acrobat as long as you save an Illustrator `.ai` file with the option checked for Create PDF Compatible File. Illustrator also supports saving as a PDF. In the Save As dialog box, choose Adobe PDF (pdf), and you can make choices for the Adobe PDF Settings after clicking the Save button.

If you use non-Adobe programs to export to PDF, look over options in the File menu for saving and exporting a document. If a direct export is supported in the application, you'll find an option most likely under the File menu.

Using Acrobat Distiller

If conversion to PDF is not supported from within Acrobat and your authoring program does not support a direct export to PDF, you can still convert your form to a PDF document using Adobe Acrobat Distiller. Distiller is a separate executable program installed with Acrobat. Although you may not be aware of it, Distiller often works in the background when you use some of the methods described earlier for converting to PDF.

To use Acrobat Distiller, you first need to create a PostScript file.

Printing PostScript on Windows

From any authoring program, choose File ⇨ Print. In the Print dialog box, choose the Adobe PDF printer from the Name drop-down menu. Check the box where you see Print to file, as shown in Figure 4.21, and click OK. (Note that in some applications, you may see a Print button instead of an OK button.) Click Print after choosing Print to file to obtain the same result.

Check Print to file in the Print dialog box.

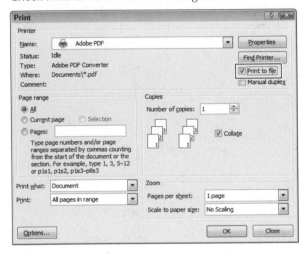

After clicking OK (or Print), a dialog box opens prompting you for a filename. Type a name for your file, and click OK. The file is then printed to disk as a PostScript file. Remember that this produces a file saved to disk and does not send your file to any printer.

Printing PostScript on the Macintosh

You can print a PostScript file to disk on the Macintosh, but it's really not necessary. For any program on the Mac, you can simply choose File ⇨ Print, choose the Adobe PDF 9.0 printer driver, and choose Save as PDF from the PDF drop-down menu. This action prints a file to disk as a temporary file and uses Acrobat Distiller in the background to produce the PDF document. On the Mac, the PDF conversion is handled in a single step.

Converting PostScript to PDF

In Windows, after you have a file converted to PostScript, launch Acrobat and choose Advanced ⇨ Print Production ⇨ Acrobat Distiller. Acrobat Distiller, shown in Figure 4.22, opens on top of the Acrobat window.

FIGURE 4.22

In Acrobat, choose Advanced⇨Print Production⇨Acrobat Distiller to launch the Acrobat Distiller application.

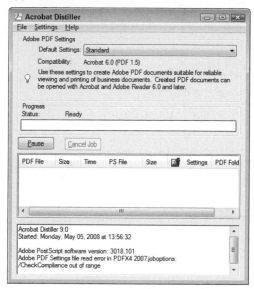

 **You also can launch Acrobat Distiller via the Start⇨Programs submenu.**

In the Distiller window, choose a Default Setting. As we stated earlier, the Standard settings work well for PDF forms. If Standard is not selected, open the Default Settings drop-down menu and choose Standard. Choose File⇨Open, and open the PostScript file you want to convert to PDF. Acrobat Distiller shows a progress bar as the file is being distilled and when finished reports the successful conversion to PDF.

If you want Distiller to prompt you for a file destination, choose File⇨Preferences and check the box for Ask for PDF file destination.

 **You also can drag and drop a number of PostScript files to the Acrobat Distiller window to convert multiple PostScript files to PDF.**

Modifying Forms

Beginning in Chapter 5, we talk about adding form fields to PDF documents. As you read through subsequent chapters, you'll quickly become aware that adding form fields can take some editing time on complex forms. If you need to make changes to the design, you don't want to recreate all your steps to produce a PDF document and then to add form fields.

Although Acrobat is not intended to be an original authoring program, you can make changes to background designs on forms that have been populated with form fields. Making minor edits to a PDF in Acrobat can save time when you need to modify the form design.

Editing text

Acrobat isn't designed for editing text in a PDF document. Some tools can perform minor text edits, but editing paragraphs and bodies of type can be troublesome if not impossible. On PDF forms, you might have lines of type that need some minor edits. A misspelled word, adding punctuation, or changing a word might be some of the edits you need to make. For these edits, you have a tool that might handle text changes.

Using the TouchUp Text tool

We say the TouchUp Text tool *might* handle some text changes because it has some limitations. Its most prominent feature is the ability to edit embedded fonts and overcoming licensing restrictions related to fonts in a PDF document.

To determine whether you can edit a font, click the TouchUp Text tool in the Advanced Editing toolbar, as shown in Figure 4.23.

FIGURE 4.23

Click the TouchUp Text tool in the Advanced Editing toolbar.

Drag the tool across a word to highlight it, and open a context menu (right-click in Windows, Control-click on the Mac). Choose Properties from the menu options to open the TouchUp Properties dialog box. If the font can't be edited, the Permissions item in the TouchUp Properties dialog box will report No system font available, as shown in Figure 4.24.

If the font permissions do not restrict your editing, use the TouchUp Text tool by dragging across text you want to edit and type the new text to replace the highlighted text. Remember that using the TouchUp Text tool to edit text on a form works for minor type changes. Editing a paragraph of text in most cases isn't possible. Your best solution for making text changes on a form is to return to the original authoring document and make your edits in the program that produced the PDF file.

What happens if you don't have the original authoring document and you need to make a minor text change? Let's say you need to change a phone number or a URL or some other minor text change. Are you stuck? Not necessarily. A little workaround is available that can make some minor text changes when you don't have the original authoring application document and the font restrictions prevent you from editing the text. To do so, follow the steps below.

FIGURE 4.24

The TouchUp Properties dialog box informs you if text cannot be edited.

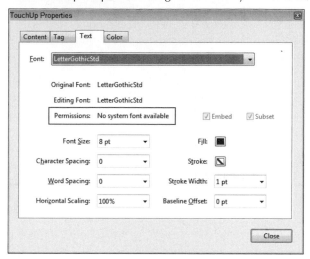

STEPS: Editing Text When a Font Is Not Available

1. **Drag the TouchUp Text tool across a word or few words on a form.** If you don't have a form handy that restricts editing permissions, you can still follow the steps here to get an idea for how to edit text when font restrictions prevent editing.

2. **Open the TouchUp Properties.** Open a context menu, and choose Properties.

3. **Change the font.** Open the Font drop-down menu, and choose a font that closely resembles the font you want to edit. When you open the Font drop-down menu, you'll see a line dividing several fonts at the top of the menu and a long list of fonts appearing below the line. Those fonts below the line are fonts available to your system. Choose one of the fonts below the separator line.

4. **Click OK.**

5. **Type new text.** The text you type replaces the old font with the new font selected in the TouchUp Properties dialog box. If the new font appears significantly different, it will be obvious on the form. However, if you find a close match when changing to a new font, the text change can be unnoticed by the form recipient.

In a perfect world, you would return to the original document to make text edits. However, the more you work with forms, the more you'll discover that you're not working in a perfect world. Using these steps for a minor text edit can save you much time when some text changes need to be made on your forms.

Editing objects

Text on a form is comprised of vector objects. Vector objects are created in programs like Adobe Illustrator, CorelDraw, and some other vector-type illustration programs. If your form needs some text changes and the TouchUp Text tool won't handle the job, another workaround is available. This workaround requires you to have Adobe Illustrator or another vector art illustration program such as CorelDraw installed on your computer.

Presume you have a form like Figure 4.25. You want to make several edits such as eliminating the border, replacing the logo, replacing the check box items at the bottom of the form with two list boxes, and adding some text to the photo placeholder. If you don't have the original application document, redesigning this form will take quite a bit of time.

FIGURE 4.25

This form needs some design adjustments.

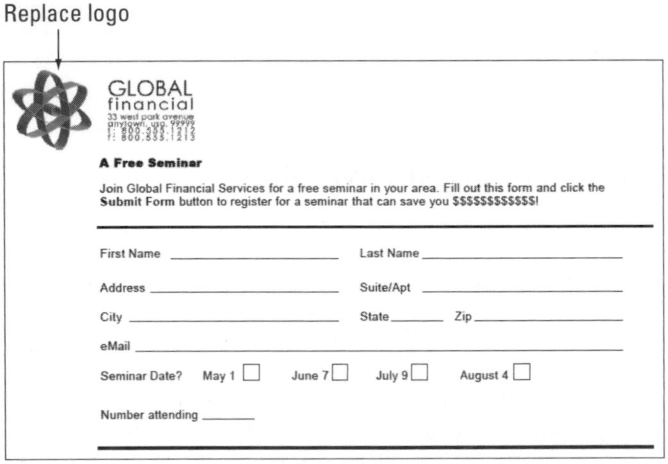

Replace logo

With the help of an illustration program such as Adobe Illustrator, you can cut the time to redesign the form down to a few minutes. The following steps are used to make changes on a form when you use Adobe Illustrator together with Acrobat.

STEPS: Editing Objects Using Adobe Illustrator

1. **Open a form you want to edit in Acrobat Pro Or Pro Extended.** The following steps cannot be performed in Acrobat Standard.

2. **Click the TouchUp Object tool in the Advanced Editing toolbar, as shown in Figure 4.26.**

Click the TouchUp Object tool in the Advanced Editing toolbar.

3. **Select all objects.** With the TouchUp Object tool selected, choose Edit ⇨ Select All or press Ctrl/⌘+A. All objects on the form are selected, including text objects.

4. **Open the file in Adobe Illustrator.** Open a context menu on one of the selected objects, and choose Edit Objects from the menu commands. If you have Adobe Illustrator installed on your computer, the document opens in Illustrator.

5. **Edit the objects.** Make your edits in Adobe Illustrator. You can type new text or bodies of text, delete objects, draw new objects, and replace objects.

6. **Save the file.** Choose File ⇨ Save. Be certain to use the Save command and not Save As. When you save the file, the edits you made in Adobe Illustrator are dynamically updated in the Acrobat PDF.

7. **Return to Acrobat.** Quit Adobe Illustrator, and view your edited file in Acrobat. The edits made to the form are shown in the Document pane. If your original form had field objects, the fields are retained while the background design is changed, as shown in Figure 4.27.

FIGURE 4.27

Edits made in Adobe Illustrator are dynamically updated in the PDF file.

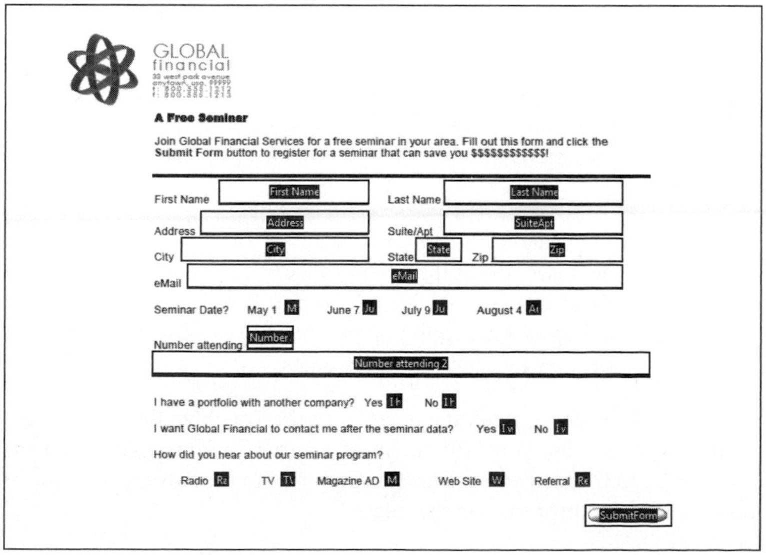

TIP If you want to edit paragraphs of text, click a body of text with the TouchUp Object tool and open a context menu. Choose Edit Object to open the text in Adobe Illustrator. When you click the text with the Direct Selection tool, you'll see the lines broken into several separate lines of type. To reform the paragraph into a single body of type, select all the type and press Ctrl/⌘+X to cut the text. Click the Type tool, and drag open a rectangle sized to the original size of the body of type. Press Ctrl/⌘+V to paste the type. The text is now pasted as one body of text and can be edited using normal paragraph editing features. Click Save when you're finished, and the text is dynamically updated in the PDF document.

When you use Adobe Illustrator to edit a form via the Edit Object(s) command, you will find font problems when fonts are not available in your system fonts. If you edit all objects, you can globally change the font in Adobe Illustrator. If you edit a paragraph on a form, you may need to use a substitution font.

Editing images

To edit an image, you need to have an image editor such as Adobe Photoshop or Adobe Photoshop Elements installed on your computer. Editing images is similar to editing objects. You use the TouchUp Object tool to click an image, and from a context menu, choose Edit Image. The file opens in your default image editor, where you can make changes and save the file. After you save the edited file, the image is dynamically updated in the PDF document.

TIP Click the TouchUp Object tool, and press the Ctrl/Option key. Double-click, and an object or image opens in an external editor.

If you want to introduce an image on a form such as a logo or other graphic image, click the TouchUp Object tool in the Advanced Editing toolbar. Open a context menu in a blank area on the form (but don't click on text or other objects). From the menu command, choose Place image. In the Open dialog box that appears, locate the image you want to place and click it. Click Open, and the image is placed on your form.

TIP Acrobat supports importing images of a variety of file types when you use the Place Image command. In the Open dialog box, click the Files of type (Windows) or Show (Macintosh) drop-down menu. Choose a file format for the image file you want to import from the menu choices.

After you place an image on a form, use the TouchUp Object tool to scale and crop the image, if necessary. To scale the image, move the cursor to a corner and wait until you see the cursor change to two opposing diagonal arrowheads. Drag the corner handles in or out to size down or up, respectively. When scaling an image, don't press the Shift key. Acrobat automatically keeps the image sizing in proportion when moving the handles.

If you need to crop an image, click the image with the TouchUp Object tool. Open a context menu, and choose Set Clip. Move the cursor to a corner handle, and wait for the cursor to change to an icon similar to the icon you see for the Crop tool in the Advanced Editing toolbar. Drag corner handles with this cursor to crop the image.

Replacing pages

If you return to the original document to change the design in any way after you have added form fields to your form, then you won't want to convert the edited form to PDF and start over with adding form fields. Fortunately, Acrobat offers you a brilliant method for modifying a form design while retaining form field objects: the Replace Pages command. This command is perhaps one of the most frequent steps we perform when creating PDF forms in Acrobat.

Unless you are very precise about designing a form, you'll always find minor edits you need to make on the form design after you've spent considerable time adding field objects. The Replace Pages command lets you keep all the field objects, comments, and other elements you added with Acrobat and just change the background design.

To use the Replace Pages command, create a form and modify the original design. When you save the file, be certain to save the file with a new filename. Open your form with the field objects, and choose Document ➪ Replace Pages. In the Select File to Replace Pages dialog box, select the file you saved after making edits and click the Select button. The new design replaces the old background while retaining all the field objects you added to your form.

> **TIP** When renaming files, use the same filename with a number preceding the old file-name. For example, if you have a form named *jobApplication.pdf,* save the new edited file as *1.jobApplication.pdf.* When you use the Replace Pages command, there's no question about what form needs to be selected in the Select Files to Replace Pages dialog box to replace the page on the original form.

As an alternative, you also can use the Pages panel to replace pages. Click the Pages panel button to open the panel, and from a context menu you open on the page, choose Replace Pages. Follow the same steps as when using the top-level menu command to replace pages.

If you have a multi-page form and you want a more visual approach to replacing pages, do the following.

> **ON the CD-ROM** You can follow these steps using the files *globalApplicationRawPopulated.pdf* and *globalApplicationDesign.pdf* found in the Chapter04 folder on the book's CD-ROM.

STEPS: Replacing Pages Using the Pages Panel

1. **Open a form you created in Acrobat with field objects, and open a second form where you edited the background design.** Note that when you edit a design in an original authoring program, you need to export the file to PDF using a different filename. In our example, we use the *globalApplicationRawPopulated.pdf* for the form that has fields and the *globalApplicationDesign.pdf* file for the redesigned form.

2. **Tile the view.** With both files open in Acrobat, choose Window ➪ Tile ➪ Vertically.

3. **View the Pages panels.** Click the Pages panel button in each document to open the Pages panels.

4. **Replace the page.** Click the page number appearing below the document thumbnail in the new design, press Ctrl/⌘+Alt/Option, and drag the page to the old form with field objects. Drag to the number the page thumbnail, wait until you see the page highlighted (as shown in Figure 4.28), and then release the mouse button. The page is replaced in the old document with your modified design. If you have field objects on the original form, the fields are retained in the file.

FIGURE 4.28

Drag a page thumbnail while pressing the Ctrl/⌘+Alt/Option keys to the target document, and wait until the page in the Pages panel highlights before releasing the mouse button.

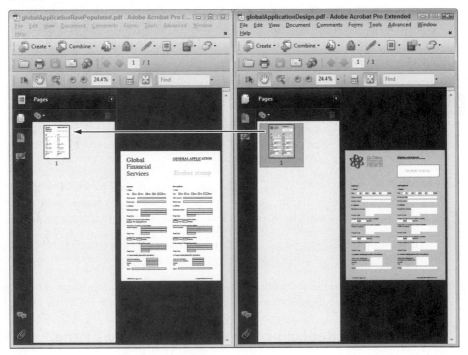

NOTE   You cannot drag a file from the desktop to replace a page. Dragging files from the desktop to the Pages panel only inserts pages in a document. You must open both files in Acrobat in order to replace pages using the Pages panel.

Setting Initial Views

Individual users can determine the initial view of a form that opens in Acrobat by adjusting Preferences. Open Acrobat Preferences by pressing Ctrl/⌘+K and clicking Page Display in the left pane. Under the Default Layout and Zoom section, shown in Figure 4.29, you find two drop-down menus that offer options for the page layout view and the default zoom view. The views set in the Page Display preferences prevail when a PDF author leaves the Initial View settings at the Default settings.

FIGURE 4.29

Initial View settings can be adjusted in the Document Properties dialog box for PDF documents saved with default views.

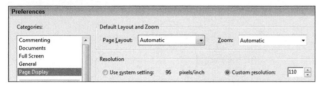

You can override the individual user's preferences by setting the Initial View within your form and saving the settings when you save the file from Acrobat. Any adjustments you make to the Initial View will always override the end user's view when your forms are opened in any Acrobat viewer.

We think setting the Initial View is important when you create forms. Most users of Acrobat viewers either won't take time to make adjustments in the preferences or they won't know how to set the Initial View. By saving the Initial View settings with your document, you can help the form recipient prepare to fill in your form by standardizing an opening view that will be shown identically on all monitors.

The Initial View settings are handled in the Document Properties dialog box. Press Ctrl/⌘+D to open the Document Properties, and click the Initial View tab to see the settings choices, as shown in Figure 4.30.

FIGURE 4.30

Open the Document Properties dialog box, and click the Initial View tab.

Adjusting Layout and Magnification

Under the Layout and Magnification category, you have several choices for the opening view:

■ **Navigation tabs:** For PDF forms, especially single-page forms, you don't need to set the view to open a Navigation panel. Bookmarks, Pages, and so on are useless to the form recipient. If you have a multi-page PDF form that's bookmarked, you might choose Bookmarks Panel and Page from the Navigation tab's drop-down menu, so the PDF opens showing the Bookmarks panel. This is rare, but on occasion you may use this option.

■ **Page Layout:** The Page Layout drop-down menu offers you choices for viewing a Single Page, Single Page Continuous, and various choices for Two-Up. For single-page forms, choose Single Page from the menu commands. If you have multi-page forms, you may want to choose Single Page Continuous, especially if you want a form recipient to view a previous section at the bottom of one page on a form when filling out the top of the next page. If

Single Page is selected, the pages snap to the next page in view, and the form recipient can't see the bottom of the previous page when working on the top of the next page.

■ **Magnification:** Making a choice for the zoom magnification requires you to address a few questions. If the form is viewed in a Fit Page view, can the form recipient clearly see all the fields and text on the page? Certainly, if you create a form that's sized to an A4 page size and a form recipient is working on a 15-inch monitor, the view is likely to be difficult for the form recipient to comfortably read text on your form. On the other hand, if your form is a non-standard page 10 inches wide by 7 inches high, and the user has the Acrobat Preferences set to 800% view, then the zoom view would be too high to comfortably fill out the form. For custom landscape views, the Fit Page view might work best. The determination for setting the Magnification should be appropriate for the form and a 15-inch monitor. Ask yourself what view is likely to be advantageous for most form recipients working on a 15-inch monitor, and make choices accordingly from the Magnification drop-down menu.

■ **Open to page:** In most cases, your choice would be to open the form on page one. You may have a form designed for both e-mail and Web hosting. If your form is designed so page one provides instructions for the form recipient followed by the actual form on page two, you may want to e-mail the form with the opening view set to page one. If a form is Web hosted and a Web page details the instructions, you may want a URL link to open page two.

Using Window Options

Window Options control how the PDF is displayed in an Acrobat viewer. The Resize window to initial page and Center window on screen options are not likely to be choices you want to make for form filling. Sizing the window might be a little confusing for the form recipient because some forms will be shown in a smaller view with the desktop in the background.

The Open in Full Screen mode option may be a frequent choice for you. This view hides the toolbars and menu bar from view. The form is shown at the largest possible view when in Full Screen mode and can make large forms on small monitors much easier to fill out.

User Interface Options

If you choose to hide all options by checking the three boxes, you may as well choose the Open in Full Screen mode in the Window Options. If you want the form recipient to access menu commands, you might think about checking the Hide window controls box and leaving the other two boxes unchecked. Checking the Hide window controls box hides the Navigation panel and provides the form recipient with a little more real estate when filling in your form. When it comes to filling in single-page forms, there's really no need to display the Bookmarks panel, the Pages panel, or any other Navigation panel. As a default, you may want to hide the window controls for all your single-page forms.

> **TIP** When you're in an authoring mode, you may want the Navigation panels to be in view especially if you use the Fields panel. If you save a form with the Hide window controls option checked and open the file to edit the form, you won't see the Navigation panel buttons. You can easily bring them in view by moving the cursor to the far left side of the Acrobat window and opening a context menu. From the menu options, choose Show Navigation Panel Buttons. This action gives you temporary control over the Navigation panels and won't change the window controls view when you save to update your form.

Summary

- Form designs can be created in Microsoft Office applications, page layout programs, and any other program where design elements easily can be added to a layout.

- The Adobe PDFMaker is installed with all Microsoft Office applications and several other programs for an easy one-button click to convert native files to PDF. (This is true only for computers running Windows.)

- Any program document can be converted to PDF using either a direct export to PDF or by printing a file as PostScript and converting the PostScript file to PDF using Acrobat Distiller.

- Editing form designs in Acrobat can be for minor edits made using the TouchUp Text and TouchUp Object tools in the Advanced Editing toolbar.

- Editing a form design is always best performed in the original authoring application.

- When editing a design that has been populated with field objects, create a new PDF document and use the Replace Pages command.

- Initial Views can be set and saved with a PDF file so the opening view overrides a user's default page layout and magnification views.

Part II

Using Acrobat Forms Tools and Properties

We start this section by working through several exercises for creating simple office forms and then move on to Chapter 6 where we cover converting paper forms to electronic forms using Acrobat's scanning and OCR features. In Chapter 7 we cover all the field types you can add to a form in Acrobat, and we cover all the field properties associated with the field types in Chapter 9. In Chapter 8 we cover creating and editing tables in Acrobat.

IN THIS PART

Chapter 5
Creating Simple Office Forms

Chapter 6
Scanning Office Forms

Chapter 7
Working with Form Fields

Chapter 8
Working with Tables

Chapter 9
Working with Field Properties

Chapter 5

Creating Simple Office Forms

This chapter deals with simple forms—not just a file converted to a PDF document; but rather a fillable form that can be completed by form recipients. In a way, a simple form as we define it here, is one that won't require much work to prepare for deployment.

Acrobat provides you with features that can help you add field objects to forms automatically. Auto field detection can be used on many documents to quickly prepare a form and make it ready for distribution.

In this chapter we cover working in the Form Editing Mode, adding field objects through Acrobat's automation features, tweaking a form, and saving it for optimum performance.

IN THIS CHAPTER

Using Form Editing Mode

Using the Create or Edit Form wizard

Adding field objects

Saving a form

Understanding Form Editing Mode

Prior to Acrobat 9, you used the Forms toolbar in Acrobat Professional to add field objects to a document. The eight form tools found in Acrobat 8 were used to create field objects on a page in the normal Viewer mode.

Acrobat 9 introduced a new user interface called Form Editing Mode. When you create field objects on a page, you enter Form Editing Mode where you can add fields, preview your work, and complete a form. When you're finished with form editing, you return to Viewer mode with the click of a button.

If you're using Acrobat Professional below version 9, you can follow much of what is contained in this chapter. The difference for you is that you need to open the Forms toolbar and stay in Viewer mode to add field objects.

One other addition was made to Acrobat 9. You can now create field objects and perform most of the form editing that was once reserved for Acrobat Pro in Acrobat Standard (Windows only) in version 9 and above. Acrobat 9 also introduced Acrobat 9 Pro Extended (Windows only). Hence, you can create PDF forms using most of what we cover in Parts I through V in any one of the commercial Acrobat 9 products. There are very few distinctions between these products when it comes to form editing. If a particular feature is implemented in only one viewer such as Acrobat Pro Extended, we make the point of clarification as you read through the chapters.

Getting Familiar with the Form Editing interface

You enter Form Editing Mode via menu commands in the Forms menu. The Forms menu has two commands that take you into Form Editing Mode. At the top of the menu, Start Form Wizard appears as the first command. The second command is Add or Edit Fields. To choose this command, you must have a document open in Acrobat's Document pane.

In this section, we explain the menu commands and the differences between the two options that eventually get you into Form Editing Mode. For more detail on using one command or another, see the section "Using the wizards to create PDF forms" later in this chapter.

Using the Start Forms Wizard menu command

When you choose Forms ➪ Start Form Wizard, the Create or Edit Form wizard opens. Depending on your platform, you have different options, as shown in Figure 5.1. Your choices in the wizard include:

FIGURE 5.1

Choose Forms ➪ Start Form Wizard to open the Create or Edit Form wizard. You have different options in Windows (left) and Macintosh (right).

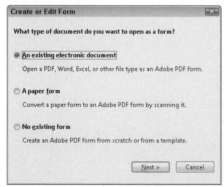
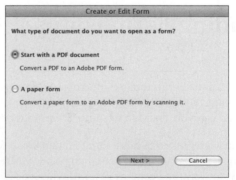

- **An existing electronic document (Windows)/Start with a PDF Document (Macintosh):** On Windows, you can choose a PDF document, a Word document, an Excel document, or many other native documents. When you open the document, Acrobat converts the file to PDF and opens the document in Form Editing Mode.

  On the Macintosh, the same thing happens, but you are restricted to opening only PDF files. If you're a Mac user, you need to first convert your native files to PDF and then use the Create or Edit Form wizard.

- **A paper form:** As you can see in Figure 5.1, a paper form is an option for both Windows and Macs. Choosing this option performs three steps. A paper form is scanned using Acrobat Scan, the form is converted to text using Acrobat's Recognize Text Using OCR (form fields are automatically applied), and the form opens in Form Editing Mode.

CROSS-REF For more information on scanning paper forms, see Chapter 6.

- **No existing form:** This option is available only in Acrobat Pro and Pro Extended. When you choose No existing form and click Next, the Adobe LiveCycle Designer New Form Assistant wizard opens, as shown in Figure 5.2. Note that if you don't have Designer open in the background, Acrobat launches Adobe LiveCycle Designer and your computer pauses a moment while Designer opens.

FIGURE 5.2

When you click No existing form (Pro and Pro Extended only), the New Assistant Form wizard opens.

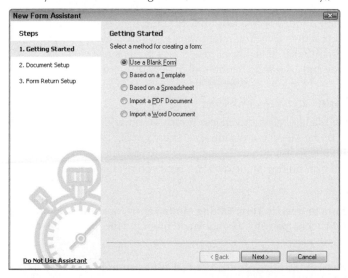

CROSS-REF For more information on LiveCycle Designer, see Parts VI through IX.

Using the Add or Edit Fields menu command

To use the Forms⇨Add or Edit Fields menu command, you need to have a file open in the Document pane. This command is grayed out if a document is not open. If you have multiple documents open in the Document pane, the foreground document is the one that opens in Form Editing Mode.

You can enter this mode using one of several different kinds of PDF files. Here are some examples of the files you can use to edit in Form Editing Mode:

- **Form designs:** The most frequent use you'll have for entering Form Editing Mode is to add field objects to populate a form.

- **Editing a form:** If you have an existing PDF form and you want to edit your form, choose Forms⇨Add or Edit Fields. Additional fields can be added to the form after you enter Form Editing Mode.

- **Non-PDF form:** Any document you convert to PDF that was not originally designed as a form can be opened in Form Editing Mode. If you want to add a series of text boxes containing a URL for your company's Web address and copy the field across multiple pages, that's a reason for using Form Editing Mode. The only way to access the Text Field tool is through Form Editing Mode.

TIP You have one workaround available for adding different field objects while remaining in Viewer mode. You can add a Button field from the Advanced Editing toolbar and open a context menu on the button field. From the menu choose Add New Field. A submenu opens where you can choose from all the field types and add a new field while remaining in Viewer mode.

- **Flash videos:** If you convert Adobe Flash videos to PDF, you can enter Form Editing Mode and add fields on top of the video. You might want to add text fields that appear on top of a video playing in Acrobat. If you want to add play buttons to a video file, you can remain in Viewer mode and access the Button tool in the Advanced Editing toolbar.

Browsing Form Editing Mode

If you open a PDF form that contains field objects and choose Forms⇨Add or Edit Fields, Acrobat immediately takes you into Form Editing Mode and the interface shown in Figure 5.3. The tools, fields panel, and menu commands are important to understand. Be sure to earmark this page so you can come back and review the Form Editing Mode interface until you're familiar with all the options at your disposal.

ON the CD-ROM If you don't have a form to open in Form Editing Mode handy, open the Chapter05 folder on the CD-ROM accompanying this book and open the file *globalCommitteeMembership.pdf*.

TIP Press Ctrl/⌘+7 to enter Form Editing Mode. As a PDF forms author, you'll use this keyboard shortcut frequently.

FIGURE 5.3

Open a PDF form, and choose Forms ⇨ Add or Edit Fields.

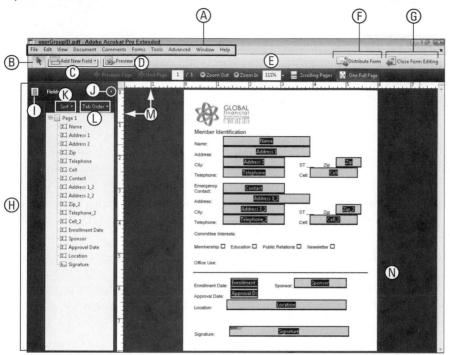

The view you see in Figure 5.3 applies to all commercial Acrobat viewers. The options include:

NOTE When we talk about the commercial Acrobat viewers, we're talking about Acrobat 9 Standard, Acrobat 9 Pro, and Acrobat 9 Pro Extended. In other words, we mean the Acrobat products you need to purchase. The interface and editing features are not available in the free Adobe Reader software.

A. **Menu bar:** The same menu bar that appears in Viewer mode appears at the top of the interface. Many menu commands are not available in Form Editing Mode. For example, open the Comments menu, and most commands are grayed out.

B. **Select Object tool:** Acrobat's toolbars are not accessible in Form Editing Mode. Because the Select Object tool is frequently used when editing PDF forms, the Advanced Editing tool appears in the toolbar row.

C. **Add New Field pull-down menu:** Open the Add New Field pull-down menu, and you can select from eight forms tools. You also can choose to have the tools appear in the toolbar. Choose Show Tools on Toolbar from the menu commands, and the tools are displayed in the Form Editing toolbar, as shown in Figure 5.4. When the toolbar is expanded on the Form Editing toolbar, the Add New Field menu disappears. You can collapse the tools and display the menu again by clicking the Collapse button on the tool-bar (see item J).

FIGURE 5.4

Open the Add New Field pull-down menu and choose Show Tools on Toolbar to display the form tools on the toolbar.

CROSS-REF For more information on the eight form tools, see Chapter 7.

TIP If you manually add several fields of the same type on a form, such as a number of text fields, check the Keep tool selected box and the tool remains selected until you click another tool.

D. **Preview:** Click the Preview tool, and the display in Form Editing Mode changes to preview your form. While in Form Editing Mode, you cannot edit fields and test them for data entry. The Preview button enables you to remain in Form Editing Mode, but the editing options disappear, and you can add field data to your forms and test buttons and JavaScripts.

E. **Viewing toolbar:** Following the form tools are several tools used for viewing a form while remaining in Form Editing Mode, including:

- **Previous Page:** Click Previous Page to view the previous page on a multi-page form.

- **Next Page:** Click Next Page to view the next page on a multi-page form.

- **[1]/1:** The number denotes the page number (of *x* pages) on a form that's in view in the Document pane. In multi-page forms, you see the current page number followed by the total number of pages in the document. The first value is editable. For example, if you have a ten-page document and you want to open page 5, type 5 in the text box and press the Enter key to move to that page.

- **Zoom Out:** Click to zoom out at fixed zoom levels.

- **Zoom In:** Click to zoom in at fixed zoom levels.

- **Magnification:** Type a value in the text box and press Enter to zoom to a percentage value. Adjacent to the text box is a pull-down menu with fixed page magnifications.

- **Scrolling Pages:** Click the tool to display a form in a continuous view. When you scroll pages, you can see the bottom of one page as the top of the next page comes into view.

- **One Full Page:** One Full Page displays a whole page in view in the Document pane (see item N). As you drag the scroll bar, a mini page thumbnail displays the current page in view, as shown in Figure 5.5. The page thumbnail appears because as you scroll pages swiftly in Acrobat, the page view in the Document pane doesn't change. You see the thumbnail as you scroll pages and when you arrive at the page you want to edit, release the mouse button and the page snaps into place in the Document pane. This interface design enables you to scroll through long documents swiftly because each page in the document pane isn't refreshed on your monitor as you scroll the pages.

FIGURE 5.5

Scrolling pages in the One Full Page view shows a pop-up thumbnail of pages as you move the scrollbar. This design for displaying page views helps speed up Acrobat editing because the screen refresh takes place when you release the mouse button.

F. **Distribute Form:** Click the Distribute Form button, and the Distribute Form wizard opens. In the wizard, you make a choice for how you want to distribute a form.

CROSS-REF For more information on distributing forms, see Chapter 15.

G. **Close Form Editing:** Click this button to return to Viewer mode. All the menu commands are available when you return to Viewer mode.

H. **Fields panel:** In Acrobat 8 and below, the Fields panel is available in Viewer mode and can be docked in the Navigation pane. In Acrobat 9 and above, the Fields panel is available only in Form Editing Mode. As you add fields to a form, the panel dynamically updates to display the field objects added to a form.

I. **Collapse/Expand Fields panel:** Click the Fields panel icon, and you collapse the Fields panel, but the icon remains in view. Click the icon again, and the panel is expanded.

J. **Collapse:** This button also collapses the Fields panel. The same button appears in the Toolbar when the form tools are in view (refer to item C). Click the button, and the form tools disappear.

K. **Sort pull-down menu:** Open the pull-down menu, and you find two options for sorting fields in the Fields panel. Choose Alphabetical Order to display the fields alphabetically by field name. When you sort alphabetically, the Tab Order (see item L) disappears. Choose the Tab Order menu command from the Sort pull-down menu, and the fields are sorted according to tab order.

TIP **Fields in the Fields panel can be moved to rearrange the field tab order. Click a field and drag up or down to reorder the fields.**

L. **Tab Order pull-down menu:** The Tab Order pull-down menu provides several commands for setting the field tab order.

CROSS-REF **For more information on setting tab orders, see Chapter 7.**

M. **Rulers:** By default, rulers appear in the Document pane. You can hide the rulers using the keyboard shortcut Ctrl/⌘+R.

N. **Document pane:** The space where your form pages appear is the Form Editing Mode Document pane.

Toggling views

Getting in and out of Form Editing Mode and changing views are common tasks you'll perform as a forms author. It's important to commit to memory how you navigate the different interfaces when you edit forms.

 When you enter Form Editing Mode, you don't have access to the Hand tool. The Hand tool is needed when you fill in a form field, such as typing text in a text field or clicking a check box or radio button. As you work in Form Editing Mode, you may want to test fields to be certain that field formats such as dates, numbers, values, and calculations are working properly.

You can leave Form Editing Mode to test your fields by clicking the Close Form Editing button in the Form Editing Mode toolbar. Doing so, however, takes you out of Form Editing Mode. If you click the Preview button in the Form Editing toolbar, you stay in Form Editing Mode, but your view changes to a Preview mode; think of it like nested views. Click Preview, and you see the view shown in Figure 5.6.

In Preview mode, you see the Acrobat Message Bar. On the Message Bar, you find some tools not available when in Edit mode. The Highlight Fields tool, which is selected in Figure 5.6, highlights the fields on the form with a light blue highlight. Adjacent to the Highlight Fields button is the Submit Form button. This button appears on forms designed in Acrobat 9 and above.

CROSS-REF **For more information on creating Submit Form buttons, see Chapter 15.**

Click Preview in Form Editing Mode to test field objects for form completion.

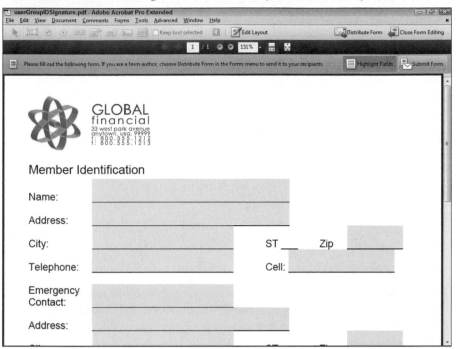

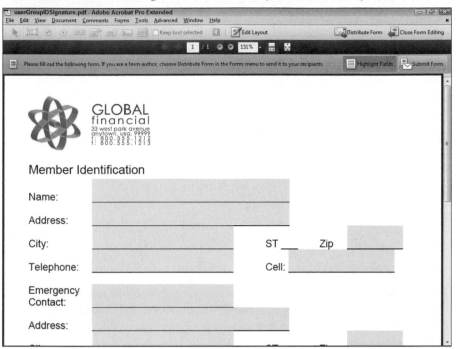 To return to Form Editing Mode, click the Edit Layout button. Notice this button appears only when you click the Preview button to move to Preview mode.

 Closing Form Editing Mode can be accomplished using several methods. You can click the Close Form Editing button in the Form Editing toolbar, open the Forms menu and choose Close Form Editing, or use the keyboard shortcut Ctrl/⌘+7. Any of these choices takes you back to Viewer mode.

TIP How you work as a forms author is a matter of personal taste. There are some things you must do, such as enter Form Editing Mode when adding fields to a form. After fields have been added, you can either choose to stay in Form Editing Mode or return to Viewer mode. In both modes, you have access to the Select Object tool. Using this tool, you can select fields, manage fields, and open field Properties dialog boxes, and you have full access to the menu commands for adding JavaScripts. Therefore, your workflow for editing fields is a matter of personal taste.

When you examine the Forms menu in both Form Editing Mode and Viewer mode, you will notice that some commands are not accessible when in Form Editing Mode. In Figure 5.7, the Forms menu commands are shown when opening the menu in Viewer mode. Some of the commands do not appear in the Forms menu when you open the same menu in Form Editing Mode.

FIGURE 5.7

The Forms menu commands available in Viewer mode.

The commands not available to you while working in Form Editing Mode include:

- **Start Form Wizard:** Why this command is not available in Form Editing Mode should be obvious. If you're in an edit mode, choosing this command takes you to the Create or Edit Form wizard that eventually takes you to Form Editing Mode. Likewise, the Add or Edit Fields command is not available in Form Editing Mode because you're already in the mode.

- **Compile Returned Forms:** This command is used to aggregate form data in a PDF Responses file from forms that have been e-mailed to you. The command is not available when in Form Editing Mode.

CROSS-REF For more information on compiling returned forms, see Chapter 15. For more information on forms and PDF Responses files, see Chapter 13.

- **Manage Form Data:** The Forms ⇨ Manage Form Data menu command opens a submenu where you find the commands Import Data, Export Data, and Merge Data Files into Spreadsheets. Handling data is available only when viewing the form in Viewer mode.

CROSS-REF For more information on working with form data, see Chapter 15.

- **QuickBooks:** You can integrate data with Intuit QuickBooks and have several menu commands for preparing and editing QuickBooks templates. These commands are available only when working in Viewer mode.

When in Form Editing Mode, you find a few additional menu commands not available in Viewer mode. In Form Editing Mode, open the Forms menu and you find the commands shown in Figure 5.8. Commands not available in Viewer mode include:

FIGURE 5.8

The Forms menu commands available in Form Editing Mode.

- **Form Tools:** This menu lists all the Form tools. Because you need to be in Form Editing Mode to use the tools, the command and submenu choices are not available in Viewer mode.

- **Edit Fields:** The Edit Fields submenu items include Duplicate, Place Multiple Fields, Show Tab Numbers, and Set Field Calculation Order. The menu is not available in Viewer mode, but the Duplicate and Place Multiple Fields commands are accessible in Viewer mode via a context menu.

CROSS-REF For more information on managing, duplicating, and placing multiple fields, see Chapter 7.

A few other menu commands that are used frequently by forms authors appear in the Advanced menu. For a summary of what's available in one mode or the other and the Advanced menu commands that are accessible according to the interface mode, look over Table 5.1.

TABLE 5.1

Menu Commands Accessible According to Interface Mode

Menu Commands	Viewer Mode	Form Editing Mode
Start Form Wizard	X	
Add or Edit Fields	X	
Close Form Editing		X
Distribute Form	X	X
Compile Returned Forms	X	
Form Tools	*	X

continued

TABLE 5.1 (continued)		
Menu Commands	**Viewer Mode**	**Form Editing Mode**
Edit Fields		X
Show Field Properties	X	X
Manage Form Data (submenu commands)	X	
Track Forms	X	X
Highlight Fields	X	X
Clear Form	X	X
QuickBooks (submenu commands)**	X	
Advanced Menu (extend features in Adobe Reader)	X	
Advanced Menu (JavaScript commands)	X	X
Advanced Menu (page templates)	X	

* The Button tool is available in the Advanced Editing toolbar in Viewer mode.

** The QuickBooks submenu is available in the English version only.

CROSS-REF For more information on enabling Adobe Reader features, see Chapter 10. For more information on page templates, see Chapter 19. For more information on JavaScript, see Part V.

Editing fields in Viewer mode

As we stated earlier in the section "Toggling views," you can choose to edit fields in either Form Editing Mode or Viewer mode. To edit fields in Viewer mode, you first need to open the Advanced Editing toolbar. This toolbar should be loaded in the Acrobat Toolbar Well when you are engaged in a form editing session in Acrobat.

To open the Advanced Editing toolbar, open a context menu on the Toolbar Well and choose Advanced Editing from the menu commands. Alternately, you can choose Tools ➪ Advanced Editing ➪ Show Advanced Editing Toolbar. Either method opens the Advanced Editing toolbar shown in Figure 5.9.

FIGURE 5.9

The Advanced Editing toolbar contains the Select Object tool.

Select Object tool

Additionally, you can select the Select Object tool by using a keyboard shortcut. Before you use keyboard shortcuts in Acrobat, you need to adjust one preference setting. Open the Preferences dialog box by pressing Ctrl/⌘+K or choosing Edit ⇨ Preferences (Windows) or Acrobat ⇨ Preferences (Macintosh). Either action opens the Preferences dialog box.

In the Preferences dialog box, click General in the left pane, as shown in Figure 5.10. In the right pane, check the box beside Use single-key accelerators to access tools. Click OK in the Preferences dialog box, and Acrobat is set up for you to strike keys on your keyboard to access tools. The preference change is dynamic, and you don't need to quit Acrobat to use keyboard shortcuts.

FIGURE 5.10

Open the General Preferences and check Use single-key accelerators to access tools.

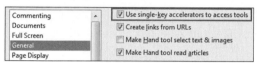

After you enable the preference to use single-key accelerators to access tools, press the R key on your keyboard and the Select Object tool becomes the active tool.

> **TIP** When in Form Editing Mode, you can access the Form tools using a keyboard shortcut. Press F on your keyboard and Shift+F to toggle the form tools. Pressing F in Viewer mode accesses the Button tool.

After you have the Select Object tool as your active tool, you can click form fields to select them in Viewer mode. Click a field and open a context menu, and you find a number of commands that aren't available from the Forms menu for editing fields, as shown in Figure 5.11.

FIGURE 5.11

Click the Select Object tool in Viewer mode and open a context menu to see additional options, features, and commands.

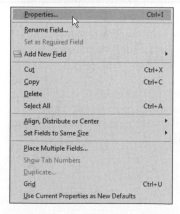

Using Context Menus

Context menus are used liberally in Acrobat and when designing forms. Throughout this book, we make reference to opening context menus. If you're a Windows user, press the right mouse button on an object such as a form field and a context menu opens. If you're a Macintosh user and you have a two-button mouse, press the right mouse button and you open a context menu just like Windows users. For Mac users with a single button mouse, press the Control key on your keyboard and click to open a context menu.

Context menus can be opened on objects or in many cases outside an object such as the form page, the Document pane, the navigation panels, and so on. When you open a context menu in an empty area (in other words when not selecting an object), you find different menu choices than you have when opening context menus on objects.

Adobe has introduced context menus in all its products. In many cases, you can intuitively discover how to make edits by exploring context menu commands. If in doubt about a particular edit, open a context menu, and more often than not you're likely to find the command you want to use.

For the remainder of this book, we'll simply suggest you open a context menu and assume henceforward that you know how to open context menus on your computer. When we say something like "open a context menu on a text field," we assume you know that you need to click the Select Object tool, move the cursor over a text field, and right-click/Control-click to open a context menu.

If you choose Properties from the menu commands, you have access to all field properties where you can change field names, edit appearances, edit options, change field formatting, and add actions. In other words, you don't need to work in Form Editing Mode to handle all the properties changes you want to make on fields.

Using the Wizards to Create PDF Forms

Thus far in this chapter, we've talked about starting with a populated form and looking at options we have for making edits on forms. The area of focus so far has been for us to point out the differences you have between the Viewer mode, which is the default view when you open a PDF document in Acrobat, and Form Editing Mode, which is used for adding fields to a form. You should be clear on the differences of the two modes and what can and cannot be accomplished in one mode versus another.

Assuming you're clear on the different modes and the editing tasks you can complete in each mode, it's now time to look at creating forms in Acrobat. As we said in the introduction of this chapter, our emphasis is on creating simple forms where you don't have to perform lots of editing, such as adding calculations, JavaScripts, and special field formatting.

Converting a native file to a PDF form (Windows)

If you're a Mac user, you need to first convert native documents to PDF, and then open the PDF document in Acrobat and choose Forms⇨Add or Edit Fields. Windows users can start with a native authoring application document that's supported for PDF conversion by choosing File⇨Create PDF ⇨From File.

 For Mac users, if you work with Adobe InDesign you can convert InDesign files directly to PDF files from within Acrobat.

In addition to converting native files to PDF, Windows users can apply a one-step operation to convert to PDF and open the PDF document, run Acrobat's auto field detection, and open the form in From Editing Mode. To see how to convert a native document to PDF on Windows, do the following.

ON the CD-ROM To follow the steps below, use the *seminarGlobal.doc* file in the Chapter 5 folder on the book's CD-ROM.

STEPS: Converting a Native Microsoft Word Document to a PDF Form on Windows

1. **Choose Forms⇨Start Forms Wizard.** You don't need a file open in Acrobat to access this menu command. The Create or Edit Form wizard opens.

2. **Select the An existing electronic document radio button.** Choose the first radio button option in the Create or Edit Form wizard and click the Next button.

3. **Import a file.** Click the Import a file from file system radio button. The Browse button becomes active. Click the Browse button and locate a native Microsoft Office document. In our example we use the *seminarGlobal.doc* file from the book's CD-ROM. Click the file-name and click Next in the Create or Edit Form wizard.

4. **Click OK in the Welcome to Form Editing Mode dialog box.** The document is automatically converted to PDF, Acrobat automatically detects fields, and the Welcome to Form Editing Mode dialog box opens. Click OK and you can make any necessary edits to the field objects.

TIP For a quick look into file formats supported by Acrobat for PDF conversion, open the Preferences dialog box (Ctrl/⌘+K) and click Convert To PDF in the left pane. In the right pane you'll see the file formats that your Acrobat viewer can convert directly to PDF.

If you're a Mac user and you want to populate a form, you need to first convert the native document to a PDF file. On Windows, you may have several MS Office files that you want to convert to PDF and later add field objects. To convert a PDF file to a PDF form with field objects on either platform, do the following.

ON the CD-ROM To follow the steps below use the *seminarGlobal.pdf* file from the Chapter 5 folder on the book's CD-ROM.

STEPS: Converting a Microsoft Word Document to a PDF Form

1. **Open a PDF file in Acrobat.** Click the Open tool or choose File ⇨ Open to open a PDF document.

2. **Choose Forms Add or Edit Fields.** Acrobat opens a dialog box asking you if you want to run auto field detection. Click Yes and the form opens in Form Editing Mode.

3. **Review the Welcome to Form Editing Mode window.** When you use auto field detection, Acrobat recognizes locations for field objects and creates the fields.

CROSS-REF Acrobat recognizes fields on a form through a field recognition algorithm that was introduced in Acrobat 8. For more information on using auto field detection, see the sidebar "Using Auto Field Detection" later in this chapter.

When you enter Form Editing Mode, a help Welcome window appears, as shown in Figure 5.12. In this window, you find some helpful hints concerning form editing. Look over the information to learn how Acrobat identifies a field name and a field object. Click OK, and you see the form in Form Editing Mode populated with field objects.

FIGURE 5.12

When you enter Form Editing Mode and permit Acrobat to auto detect fields, the Welcome to Form Editing Mode dialog box opens.

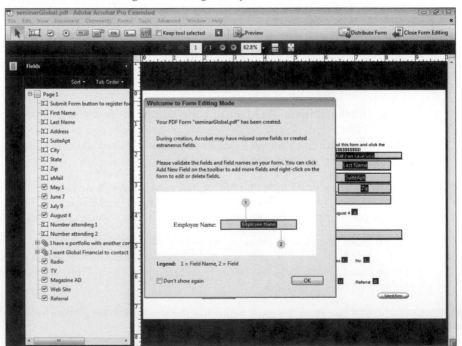

4. **Review the form.** Our form has a few extra fields that are not supposed to be on the form. Acrobat looked over the document and created two fields over separator lines we used as design elements in the file. These two extra fields need to be deleted. To delete a field, click the field in question and press the Delete/Del key.

5. **Preview the form.** Click the Preview button, and click the Highlight Fields button when you switch to Preview mode. Look over the fields on the form to be certain that all fields appear per the form design.

6. **Test the fields.** Fill in the form as a form recipient would complete your form. In our example form, Acrobat did an excellent job of recognizing the form fields. The only problem we have on this form is that the check boxes are not designed as mutually exclusive fields, so that a form recipient can make only a single choice in a row of common fields. For the moment, we'll leave the form as it appears in Figure 5.13.

FIGURE 5.13

Fill in the form to test the fields.

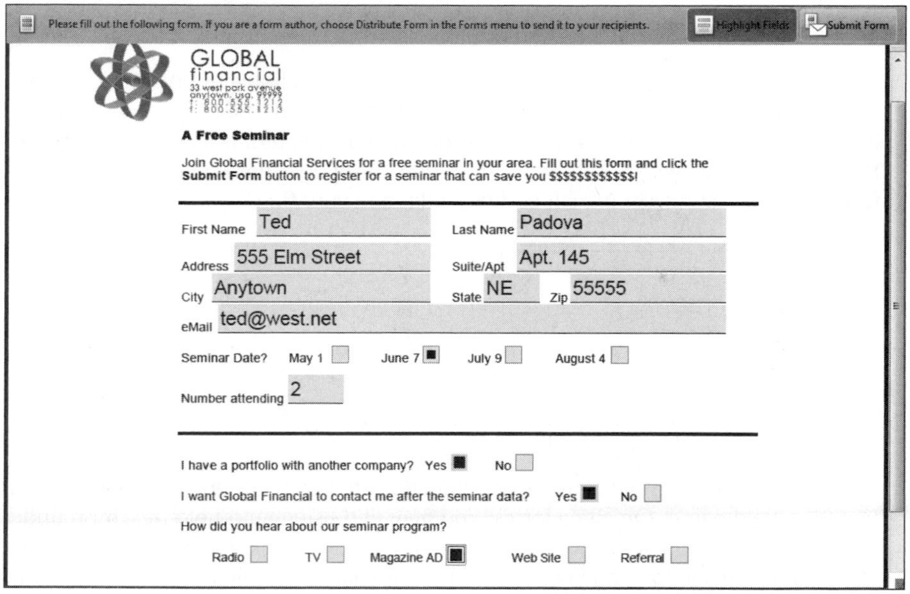

CROSS-REF For more information on working with mutually exclusive radio buttons and check boxes, see Chapter 8.

7. **Return to Form Editing Mode.** After testing the fields, click the Edit Layout tool in the Form Editing toolbar and you return to Form Editing Mode.

8. **Clear the form.** Open the Forms menu and choose Clear Form. You'll find this menu command handy when creating forms and testing the fields. For the final file, you'll want to clear all data before saving the form.

TIP   If you forget to clear fields on a form and use the Distribute Form button in Acrobat, you are warned that the fields are not cleared. Acrobat offers you a choice to clear fields in a warning dialog box. Click Yes and the fields are all cleared before the form is deployed. For more information on deploying forms, see Chapter 14.

9. **Save the form.** If you converted an authoring application document to PDF, a Save As dialog box opens. Type a name for you file, and click Save to save the form.

Using Auto Field Detection

Adobe added a very impressive feature called Run Form Field Recognition to Acrobat 8. Quite often we refer to the feature simply as auto field detection. In Acrobat 8, you visited the Forms menu and chose Run Form Field Recognition. Acrobat inspected your form, detected areas where fields belonged, and added the fields automatically to the form.

Acrobat 9 has the same feature, but it's much improved; however, there is no separate menu command to use RFFR. When you choose Forms ⇨ Add or Edit Fields, Acrobat opens the Add or Edit Fields dialog box. If you click Yes in this dialog box, you are instructing Acrobat to Run Form Field Recognition; however in Acrobat 9 terms, we call it auto field detection. Clicking No opens your form in Form Editing Mode with no fields added to your form.

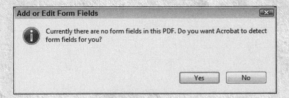

When Acrobat creates fields using auto field detection, it picks up caption text and adds the caption text for a field name. On some forms, you may find using auto field detection undesirable because you may want to add your own field names. If you need to manually name fields, you can choose to use auto field detection and later change the field names, or click No in the Add or Edit Fields dialog box and manually add fields using the Form tools.

Open the MS Word file *seminarGlobal.doc* on the CD-ROM in the Chapter05 folder in Microsoft Word and examine it. You'll notice that the boxes on the form are not type characters. In order for Acrobat to accurately identify check boxes as form fields, you may need to draw geometric shapes. In some cases certain characters from the Wingdings and Zapf Dingbats fonts work fine for check boxes and radio buttons and some characters won't work. To be safe, you can use geometric shapes for more reliability. If using Acrobat 8, you must use geometric shapes. Acrobat 8 doesn't recognize any text characters for radio buttons and check box fields.

The form used in the steps here is a rather simple form. However, you can see that converting a number of forms—especially forms designed for HR departments and in-house use—can be accomplished easily with little or no editing.

Creating a form from a PDF file

If you use tools such as the PDFMaker in MS Office programs and convert to PDF or you're a Macintosh user working with PDF documents, you can use auto field detection on the PDF files. When you open a file in Acrobat and choose Add or Edit Fields, Acrobat opens the Add or Edit Form Fields dialog box. If you click Yes, then auto field detection populates your form with field objects in the areas where Acrobat recognizes the location for a potential form field.

Not all your designs can successfully be populated with fields using auto field detection. Form designs with gradients and field locations not clearly identified with lines and boxes that appear with stroke values are often a problem for auto field detection. Figure 5.14 is a form designed in Adobe Illustrator. When we select Forms⇨Add or edit Fields and attempt to detect fields on this form, Acrobat is unable to create any field objects.

Setting properties

Field Properties appear in a particular field type's Properties dialog box. When you click a field with the Select Object tool in either Form Editing Mode or Viewer mode and choose Properties from a context menu, double-click a field with the Select Object tool, or select a field in Form Editing Mode and choose Forms⇨Show Field Properties, the Properties dialog box opens.

The easiest method for opening a field's Properties dialog box is to click the Select Object tool in either Form Editing Mode or Viewer mode and double-click the field object. Using this method enables you to open the field's Properties dialog box in either mode during an editing session.

FIGURE 5.14

Auto field detection can't recognize field objects on a form that doesn't have design elements such as lines and boxes with stroke values.

Each field type has different properties that can be assigned to fields. With text fields, you have options for calculating fields; with buttons you have options for adding button face images; with combo and list box fields, you can add lists of items for user-selected choices. Some properties are common to all the field types, such as naming fields, setting appearances, and assigning actions, as well as the unique choices according to the field type you use.

Figure 5.15 shows the Text Field Properties dialog box, with the Options tab selected. On our sample form created in the section "Converting a native file to a PDF form," we might want to right-align the text field for the *Number attending* field. To do so, we open the field's Properties dialog box, click Options, and choose Right from the Alignment pull-down menu.

As you browse through different properties, many options choices are self-explanatory. In other cases, you may need help deciphering the choices. For now, we want to introduce the Properties dialog box. Later in Chapter 7, we cover all you need to know about field properties.

Click the Select Object tool, and double-click a field to open the field's Properties dialog box.

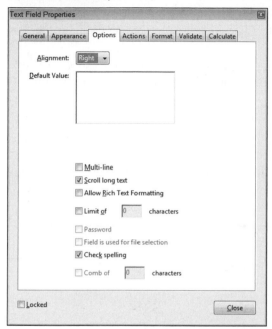

Adding Field Objects

You'll eventually need to add a field to a form. When fields are added, you typically need to open the field properties to customize some attribute settings. In some cases, you'll need to create some essential fields that aren't part of the original form design.

Adding fields

You use the Form tools in Form Editing Mode to add fields to a form. If you use auto field detection and populate a form, you may want additional fields on your form. Certainly if you create fields manually, you'll need to use the Form tools to add fields.

For a brief look at adding a field to a form, follow these steps.

ON the CD-ROM For these steps we use the file *seminarGlobalPopulated.pdf* found in the Chapter05 folder on the book's CD-ROM.

STEPS: Adding a Field to a Form

1. **Open a form in Acrobat.** For this example, we use the *seminarGlobalPopulated.pdf* form. This form has been populated with fields using auto field detection.

2. **Open the form in Form Editing Mode.** Choose Forms ➪ Add or Edit Fields, and the form opens in Form Editing Mode.

3. **Select the Text Field tool.** Open the Add New Field pull-down menu, and select Text Field. (If you chose to show the tools on the Form Editing Toolbar, you can click the Text Field tool.)

4. **Click the cursor on the form page.** In this example, we add a text field to the top-right corner of the page. We'll use this field to add a form number to the form.

5. **Name the field.** When the field is added to the form, a help window opens as shown in Figure 5.16. Type a name for the field. In our example, we use *formNumber* for the name.

FIGURE 5.16

Type a field name in the Field Name text box, and click Show All Properties.

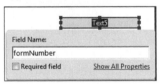

CROSS-REF There are some considerations to take into account regarding naming fields. Look over Chapter 7 for some important issues related to field naming conventions.

6. **Open the Properties dialog box.** Click the blue text where you see Show All Properties, and the Text Field Properties dialog box opens.

7. **Set the text point size.** Click the Appearance tab in the Text Field Properties dialog box, and change the Font Size from the default Auto to 8 point, as shown in Figure 5.17. Note that you can choose a font size from the Font Size pull-down menu or type a value in the Font Size text box.

8. **Set the Alignment.** For this text box, we want the text to be right-aligned. Click the Options tab, and choose Right from the Alignment pull-down menu.

9. **Close the Text Field Properties dialog box.** Click the Close button, and all the attribute choices you made are applied to the field.

10. **Type a value in the text box.** Click the Preview button, and type text in the new text field. In our example, we typed *GL-101* to create a form number.

FIGURE 5.17

Choose 8 for the Font Size from the pull-down menu, or type 8 in the Font Size text box.

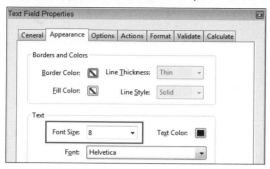

11. **Set the field to Read Only.** This field contains data that we don't want edited on the form. Therefore, we'll lock out the possibility for a form recipient to inadvertently type text in the text field. Click the Edit Layout button, and double-click the field to open the Text Field Properties dialog box. In the General tab, check the Read Only check box, as shown in Figure 5.18. When a field is marked for Read Only, the field cannot be edited unless a user opens the Text Field Properties dialog box and removes the Read Only check mark.

FIGURE 5.18

Check Read Only in the General Properties.

12. **Click Close.** When you close the Text Field Properties, all changes are assigned to the field properties.

Adding essential buttons

Many forms have two essential buttons that you prepare for form recipients. One button is used to clear a form. Although Acrobat users have a menu command to clear a form, Adobe Reader users do not have such a command. Having a button on a form designed for clearing the form data is great for a user who wants to start over. This type of button is optional when creating forms, but is usually added to help form recipients complete your forms.

Another button that you need on many forms is a submit button. If your forms are distributed to using the Distribute Form button, a Submit Form button automatically is added to the forms Document Message Bar. If you e-mail a form or someone downloads a form from your Web site, you'll need a Submit Form button so the form recipient can return the form to you.

 **CROSS-REF** For more information on Acrobat.com and distributing forms, see Chapter 15.

Adding a reset form button

Buttons are often used to execute an action on a form. For clearing form data, we use a button field and assign an action to reset the form. Here's how it's done.

STEPS: Creating a Reset Form Button

1. **Open a form in Form Editing Mode.** We'll continue with the form we used earlier in this chapter. While the form remains in Viewer mode, you can add buttons to your form. There is no need to enter Form Editing Mode.

2. **Open the Advanced Editing toolbar.** If the toolbar is not open, choose Tools ⇨ Advanced Editing ⇨ Show Advanced Editing Toolbar.

3. **Select the Button tool.** Click the Button tool in the Advanced Editing toolbar.

4. **Click in the document where you want the button placed.** Our form has some graphic objects identifying the Reset Form button and the Submit Form button. We clicked the Button cursor over the Reset Form graphic image, as shown in Figure 5.19.

CROSS-REF See the sidebar later in this chapter, "Using Loaded Cursors," to understand the meaning of terms such as Button cursor.

FIGURE 5.19

Click the mouse button, and the field drops on the form with the mini Properties window open.

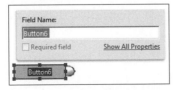

5. **Resize the field.** Drag any one of the eight handles on the rectangle to reshape the object.

6. **Type a name.** Type a name for the field in the Field Name text box. In our example, we use *resetForm* for the field name.

7. **Click Properties to open the Button Field Properties.**

8. **Change the appearance.** By default Buttons have a dark gray fill. Since we have a graphic on the page that clearly identifies the existence of a button, we want our button field to appear transparent. When the button field object is transparent, the background graphic is not obstructed from view. In the Appearance tab, click the Fill Color swatch and choose No Color in the palette, as shown in Figure 5.20.

FIGURE 5.20

Click the Fill Color swatch to open the pop-up color palette, and choose No Color.

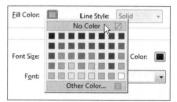

9. **Open the Actions tab.** Click the Actions tab in the Button Properties dialog box. Open the Select Action pull-down menu, and choose Reset a form, as shown in Figure 5.21.

FIGURE 5.21

Choose Reset a form from the Select Action pull-down menu.

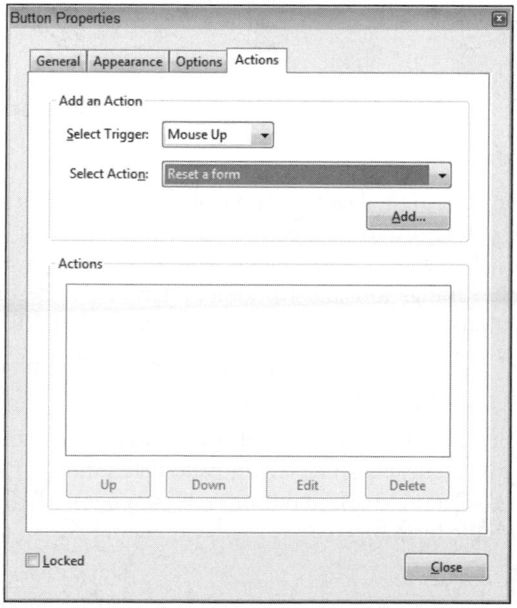

10. **Add the action.** After choosing the option you want from the Select Action pull-down menu, click the Add button in the Actions tab to add the action. When adding the Reset a form action, the Reset a Form dialog box opens, as shown in Figure 5.22.

11. **Select the Fields to Reset.** In our example, we created a field in the section "Adding fields" earlier in this chapter that was added to the form so we could add a form number. After we added the form number, we marked it as Read Only. That field isn't one we want to clear. If we reset all fields on our form, the form number will disappear. Therefore, when the Reset a Form dialog box opens, we scroll down to the field we don't want cleared and deselect the check box. By default, all boxes are checked, so you need to remove check marks from those boxes for fields you don't want cleared of data.

FIGURE 5.22

Remove check marks from all fields you don't want to be reset.

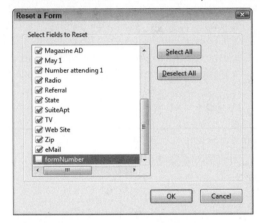

12. **Set new defaults.** Click OK in the Reset a Form dialog box, and click Close in the Button Properties dialog box; you return to the Document page. At this point, your field is set for clearing data on the form. If you want to add more buttons to a form, you may want to use the new appearance settings you adjusted for a button field to become a new default. When you create additional buttons, you won't need to bother with the Appearance tab.

To set the current appearance as a new default, open a context menu on the button field and choose Use Current Properties as New Defaults.

13. **Test the button.** If you're in Viewer mode, click the Hand tool and add data to the form. If you're in Form Editing Mode, click Preview and add data. After adding data to the fields, click the Reset button (in Viewer mode or Preview mode). All data but the Read Only field is cleared on the form.

Using Loaded Cursors

When you choose any one of the eight field types from the Add New Field pull-down menu, the cursor changes to reflect a visual of the type of field you have selected. We refer to the cursor as being *loaded* with the field type after you select a field from the Add New Field pull-down menu. A loaded Text Field cursor, therefore, is one that contains the Text Field object.

Text Field   Radio Button/Check Box

List Box   Combo Box

Button   Digital Signature

Bar Code

When you select a tool from the Add New Field menu, the cursor remains loaded until you click the mouse button. You can move the cursor around a form page, and the cursor displays guidelines to help you position the field in the right location before clicking the mouse button.

When you click the mouse button, the field drops down on your form. Precise alignment is not necessary because you can click and drag a field after it has been dropped on the form.

You also can click and drag a rectangle to shape a form field before dropping the field on the form page. In this manner, you can estimate a size for a field before actually creating the field.

Adding a Submit Form button

Submit Form buttons are used to submit forms and/or form data to you or a location you identify when setting up the button properties. To create a Submit Form button, follow these steps.

STEPS: Creating a Submit Form Button

1. **Open a form in Acrobat.** In this example we'll continue with the form to which we added a Reset Form button.

2. **Add a button field.** We can create a new button using the Button tool, or we can use an easier method: duplicating the Reset Form button and changing the properties. To duplicate a field, press the Ctrl/Option key and click+drag with the Select Object tool. Drag the new button to position on the form.

CROSS-REF For more information on duplicating fields, see Chapter 7.

3. **Rename the field.** At this point, we have a duplicate of the Reset Form button. To rename the field, double-click the duplicate button with the Select Object tool to open the General tab in the Button Properties dialog box. Type a new name in the Name text box.

4. **Delete the action.** Click the Actions tab. The current action is to reset the form. Click the Mouse Up text in the actions list, and click the Delete button to remove the action.

5. **Add a new action.** Open the Select Action pull-down menu, and choose Submit a form. Click the Add button, and the Submit Form Selections dialog box opens, as shown in Figure 5.23.

6. **Add a URL link.** In our example, we want the form e-mailed back to us. Type *mailto:<your email address>* in the Enter a URL for this link text box, as shown in Figure 5.23.

7. **Choose an export format.** For our example, we want the complete PDF document sent back to us, so we click the PDF The complete document radio button.

8. **Click OK in the Submit Form Selection dialog box, and click Close in the Button Properties dialog box.** Your form is now set up with a submit form button.

FIGURE 5.23

Type **mailto:** followed by your e-mail address in the Enter a URL for this link text box, and click the PDF The complete document radio button.

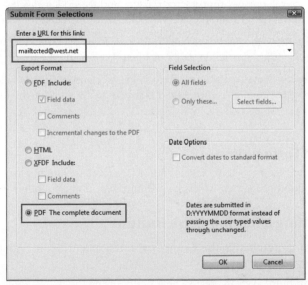

> **CAUTION** If you intend to have Adobe Reader users fill in the form and send it back to you, you must enable the form with Adobe Reader usage rights. For more information on enabling forms with Adobe Reader usage rights, see Chapter 10.

Overcoming Auto Field Detection Problems

There may be times when fields should be auto-detected, but it doesn't happen. You look at a form seeing a clear indication where field objects should be placed, but when you choose Forms ⇨ Add or Edit Fields, Acrobat opens your form in Form Editing Mode without prompting you to use auto field detection.

Some forms just don't work because of design issues, forms that have been enabled with Adobe Reader usage rights, and forms that have security applied that prevent editing the PDF file. These conditions are logical, and we can easily understand why Acrobat can't auto-detect fields.

> **CROSS-REF** For more information on enabling forms for Adobe Reader users, see Chapter 10. For more information on securing forms, see Chapter 12.

If you already have at least one form field on the document, auto field detection won't work. If you want to use auto field detection, you must delete all fields, save the form, and open it in Form Editing Mode. You should be prompted by Acrobat to auto-detect fields on the modified form.

Sometimes, you may have a form with no fields, and Acrobat still doesn't prompt you to auto-detect fields. Look at Figure 5.24 as an example. This form seems like a good candidate for Acrobat to prompt us to auto-detect fields when opening the form in Form Editing Mode. When using this form and opening it in Form Editing Mode, the form opens without Acrobat auto-detecting any fields.

Some files may have certain metadata or something in the document structure that prevents Acrobat from auto-detecting fields. Even if you use the PDF Optimizer and optimize the document, strip away metadata, and change the Acrobat compatibility, Acrobat may still not be able to auto-detect fields.

> **CROSS-REF** For more information on using the PDF Optimizer, see Chapter 13.

> **ON the CD-ROM** To examine a form where auto field detection doesn't work, look at the *employee-ApplicationExtract.pdf* document in the Chapter05 folder on the book's CD-ROM.

FIGURE 5.24

Although this form has some color in the design, field locations are clearly identified and we would presume by looking at the form that Acrobat should be able to auto-detect fields.

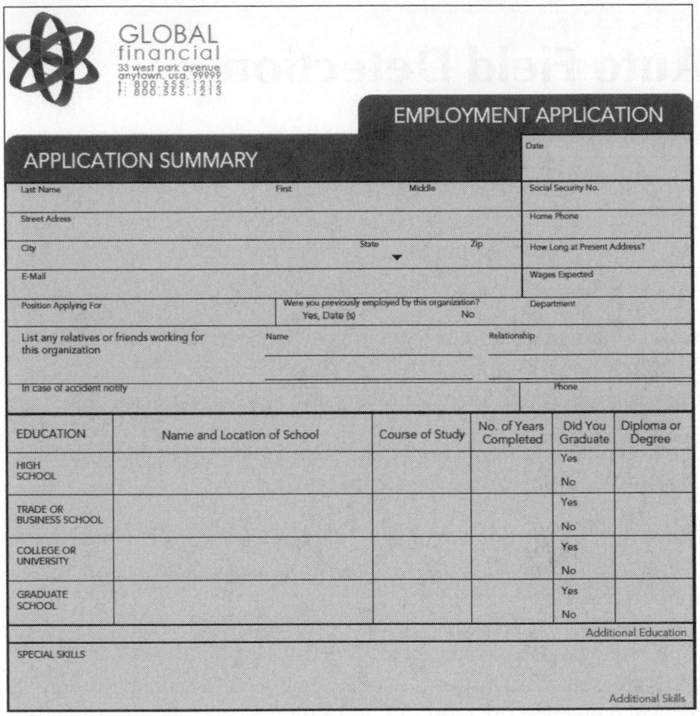

As a workaround, try extracting a form page. You can use the Document ⇨ Extract Pages command on a single-page form or on multiple pages. Use the *employeeApplicationExtract.pdf* on the book's CD-ROM to perform the steps. After the page is extracted, save the form and open the document in Form Editing Mode. In many cases, you'll find auto field detection working after extracting a page such as is the case with the *employeeApplicationExtract.pdf* form.

Saving Forms

We're certain you intuitively know how to save documents from Acrobat and other applications. The Save commands are found under the File menu in most applications. In Microsoft Office 2007, the Save command is found under the Office menu.

As you work on a form in Acrobat, you should plan on saving frequently. Opening Properties dialog boxes can, on occasion, cause a hiccup in the program, and you might experience a program crash. This is particularly true of applications when first released. When we see maintenance upgrades appear like 9.1, 9.05, 9.2, and so on, the programs tend to be more stable.

After you complete a form, your last step should be choosing File ⇨ Save As and rewriting the form to disk. Adding fields, removing fields, changing properties, and so on can create some overhead in your forms. When you use Save As, Acrobat completely rewrites the file and you end up with a file much smaller than the one you worked on with multiple Saves.

Summary

- Form fields are added in Form Editing Mode in Acrobat 9.

- All commercial Acrobat viewers in version 9 support creating PDF forms, including Acrobat 9 Standard (Windows).

- Forms can be tested and filled in while in Form Editing Mode by clicking the Preview button.

- While in Form Editing Mode, you do not have access to many Acrobat tools. You need to click the Close Form Editing button to return to Viewer mode to access all of Acrobat's tools and menu commands.

- The Fields panel is available only while in Form Editing Mode. The Fields panel cannot be opened when in Viewer mode.

- A field's Properties dialog box can be opened in both Form Editing Mode and Viewer mode. The easiest way to open a field's Properties dialog box is to click the Select Object tool and double-click a field object.

- Native file formats can be opened in Windows directly from within Acrobat. When a native file designed as a form is opened in Acrobat, the file is converted to PDF, automatic field detection is performed, and the form opens in Form Editing Mode.

- When opening a file in Form Editing Mode, you are prompted to use auto field detection. If you click Yes, Acrobat makes its best effort to automatically populate a form with field objects.

- Two frequently used buttons on forms are reset form and submit form buttons.

- Forms need to be enabled with Adobe Reader usage rights in order for an Adobe Reader user to return a PDF form to a form author.

- If auto field detection doesn't work on a form, use the Document ⇨ Extract Pages command and open the file in Form Editing Mode to see if Acrobat can auto-detect fields.

- As a last step in creating forms, you should use the Save As command to rewrite the file. Rewriting a file optimizes it and reduces the file size.

Chapter 6

Scanning Office Forms

I n Chapter 5, we talked about creating simple forms from original authoring application documents converted to PDF. Adobe has invested much development time to help novice users create rich, intelligent fillable forms. Using the Acrobat 9 features for editing a form in Form Editing mode and using auto field detection are two things that help all Acrobat users create forms with a minimal amount of work.

Adobe has received much feedback from users who have a need to convert legacy analog forms to electronic forms. In response to users' requests, Adobe has introduced in Acrobat 9 superb features for scanning paper forms and converting the scanned documents into rich intelligent forms.

With the introduction of ClearScan technology and support for Windows Imaging Architecture scanner drivers, scanning a paper form is as easy as converting original authoring documents to PDF forms. In this chapter, we cover scanning paper forms, using Acrobat's built-in Optical Character Recognition (OCR) features, and converting the scanned documents to fillable forms.

IN THIS CHAPTER

Configuring your scanner

Using OCR to recognize text

Creating forms from scanned documents

Setting Up Acrobat Scan

Acrobat Scan is a feature available in all commercial Acrobat viewers. While in Acrobat, you can trigger your scanner to perform a scan, and the scanned document opens in the Acrobat Document pane. In essence, the scanned image file is immediately converted to PDF when the scan is completed.

Configuring a scanner requires you to know some things about the scanner drivers supported by Acrobat and the tools you use to perform the scan.

Understanding scanner drivers

Before you can scan a page in Acrobat, you need to configure your scanner and be certain it functions properly. After you complete your installation of Acrobat, it should recognize your scanner immediately. If all the scanner hardware is in place and operational and Acrobat still does not recognize your scanner, the next step is to be certain the scanner's software is recognized by Acrobat. If Acrobat doesn't see your scanner, you may need to relocate software to another location on your hard drive or acquire a software update from your scanner developer.

You can access your scanner in Acrobat through three methods: TWAIN drivers, Acquire plug-ins, or WIA-compliant drivers.

TWAIN software

TWAIN (Technology With An Important Name) software is developer-supplied and should be available on the CD-ROM you receive with your scanner. In Windows, the TWAIN files are stored in the \Windows\twain_32 folder. When you install scanner software, the TWAIN driver should find the proper folder through the installer routine. On a Macintosh, you'll find TWAIN resources in the System\Library\Image Capture\TWAIN Data Sources folder.

Many scanner developers produce the equipment but use third-party developers to write the software. Adobe has certainly not tested the Scan plug-in with all scanner developers and all software developers, but many of the popular brands have been thoroughly tested to work seamlessly with Acrobat. Theoretically, the TWAIN software should work for scanners using TWAIN resources. If you have problems accessing your scanner from within Acrobat, but can perform scans in other applications, then you most likely have a problem with the TWAIN driver. If this is the case, contact your scanner manufacturer and see whether it has an upgrade or whether you can get some technical support. In many cases, you can download upgrades for registered software on the Internet.

When you scan a paper form using a TWAIN driver, your scanner's interface is used to perform the scan. In your scanner's interface, you make choices for paper size and resolution, create previews, and so on. You also use the Scan button or menu command in your scanner's interface to initiate the scan. As the progress of a scan is reported in your scanner's interface, you watch the scan process until the scan is completed. After a scan is completed, the resultant document opens in Acrobat and your scanner's interface is no longer used.

Adobe Photoshop plug-in software

Acrobat 9.0 supports Acquire plug-ins used with Adobe Photoshop. More prevalent than TWAIN drivers, Photoshop plug-ins are available from almost every scanner developer. If you use Adobe Photoshop or Adobe Photoshop Elements, you may need to copy your Photoshop Acquire plug-in to your Acrobat plug-ins folder. On Windows, copy the Photoshop Acquire plug-in, open the Acrobat\plug_ins\PaperCapture folder, and paste your Acquire plug-in.

Mac OS X requires you to expand the Acrobat 9.0 Professional package in order to paste your Photoshop Acquire plug-in. To do so, follow these steps.

STEPS: Setting Up the Photoshop Plug-in in Mac OS X

1. **Open your Applications/Adobe Acrobat 9.0 Pro folder and select (not double-click) Adobe Acrobat 9.0 Pro.**

2. **Ctrl-click to open a context menu, and select Show Package Contents.** The Contents folder appears in the Adobe Acrobat 9.0 Pro folder.

3. **Double-click the Contents folder, and double-click the Plug-ins folder that comes into view.**

4. **Double-click the PaperCapture.acroplugin folder, and drag your Photoshop Acquire plug-in into this folder.** (Option+click+drag to copy the plug-in to the target folder.) When you close the folders, the package is restored.

If your scanner doesn't support scanning directly via a plug-in in Acrobat, you need to scan a paper form in Photoshop, Photoshop Elements, or your native scanning application supplied by your scanner developer. If you do scan using one of these applications, you need to save your file to disk and then choose File ⇨ Create PDF ⇨ From File and open the scan in Acrobat.

NOTE When saving files from programs like Photoshop and Photoshop Elements, you need to save files using Photoshop PDF, TIFF, JPEG, or PNG in order to open the files in Acrobat. Native file formats such as .PSD are not supported in Acrobat.

Configuring Windows Imaging Architecture (WIA) scan drivers (Windows only)

TWAIN drivers have been around for a long time, and many developers are still supporting TWAIN drivers, but many newer scanners now support a more recent driver technology called Windows Imaging Architecture (WIA). WIA is a Microsoft-developed technology that provides developers with a relatively easy way to write support for scanners. Developers such as Acer, Compaq, Epson, Fujitsu, HP, Kodak, Microtek, Ricoh, and UMAX have all embraced WIA in many of their newer models.

The good news from Adobe is that if you have a WIA-supported scanner, you can configure your scanner's Scan button with Acrobat. To do so, open the Start Menu and choose Control Panels/Scanners and cameras/<scanner name>. The Scanners and Cameras dialog box opens. Click your scanner name, and click the Properties button to open the scanner properties.

The WIA scanner Properties dialog box opens, as shown in Figure 6.1. Select your scanner's Scan, Copy, Photo, or other button you want to activate. When using scanners with a button to initiate a scan, choose the Scan button. Click the Start the Program radio button, and choose Adobe Acrobat from the options in the pull-down menu. Click OK, and the next time you press your scanner's Scan button, the scan is opened in Adobe Acrobat.

Scanners and PDF

PDF is so popular that almost every developer in one market or another is supporting the Portable Document Format. Today, you find the support for PDF broadening with scanner developers. Many new scanner models support hardware buttons on the scanners for scanning to a PDF file. Additionally, you can find scanner proprietary software supporting scanning to PDF.

In some cases, you can find scanners that are great at scanning to PDF files, but they don't support WIA architecture or TWAIN drivers; such is the case with the Fujitsu Scansnap 510 scanner. In these cases, you can use the scanner's button or the software to scan to PDF. After the file is scanned to PDF, it typically opens in Acrobat where you can recognize text and populate forms with form fields.

FIGURE 6.1

Choose an Event, and choose Adobe Acrobat from the pull-down menu.

Creating presets (WIA scanners on Windows)

If you have a WIA-compliant scanner, your options for scanning from within Acrobat are much more plentiful than using Acrobat Scan and a TWAIN driver. Acrobat Scan has been greatly simplified in Acrobat 9, and you have far fewer options than when using Scan to PDF on a WIA-compliant scanner.

Working with presets

Presets are settings that you can configure and retain to perform scans with a set of options defined by you or created by Adobe as a series of defaults.

Acrobat 9 provides you with several presets that are used with black and white documents, grayscale documents, color documents, and color images. The settings for scanning each of these types of documents are preset for you. You can use them *out of the box,* or you can configure each preset for your own personal needs.

Adobe's intent is to help you simplify your scanning and OCR recognition by setting up some general options that apply for scanning a range of original document types. However, you may have some special needs. For example, you may be scanning a different paper size than the default choice for one of the scanning presets, or you may want to scan at a different resolution than the choice in a given preset. If this is the case, you'll want to change a preset to suit your own personal scanning needs.

Look at some of the options available when you first start a scan. Choose Document ⇨ Scan to PDF, and the submenu opens, as shown in Figure 6.2. From the menu choices, you have the four preset choices, a choice for Custom Scan, and a choice for Configure Presets. The Custom Choice is provided in case you want to deviate from all the presets and choose your options prior to a scan; this is like a one-time use. The last item in the submenu is Configure Presets. Choose this option, and you can configure any of the first four presets listed in the menu.

FIGURE 6.2

Choose Document ⇨ Scan to PDF to open the submenu where the preset commands are listed.

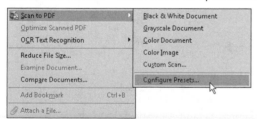

To edit a preset, follow these steps.

STEPS: Editing a Preset

1. **Choose Document ⇨ Scan to PDF ⇨ Configure Presets.** The Configure Presets dialog box opens, as shown in Figure 6.3.
2. **Choose your scanner.** Open the Scanner pull-down menu, and choose the scanner you want to use. If you have multiple scanners, all scanners configured properly appear in the menu.

3. **Choose the preset you want to edit.** From the Presets pull-down menu, choose the preset you want to edit, as shown in Figure 6.3.

FIGURE 6.3

Choose Document ➪ Scan to PDF ➪ Configure Presets to open the Configure Preset dialog box. From the Preset pull-down menu, choose the preset you want to edit.

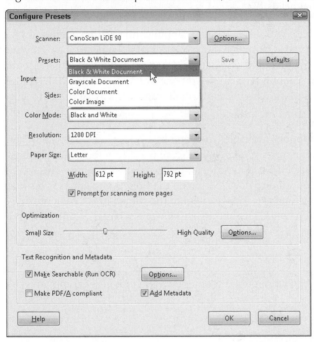

4. **Change the attributes.** From the options shown in the Configure Presets dialog box, use the menus and text boxes to make the changes you want for the preset. In our example, we edited Resolution and changed our scanner's default A4 paper size to US Letter.

5. **Save the settings.** Click the Save button, and your new settings are applied to the preset. The next time you want to scan a document with the new preset, choose Document ➪ Scan to PDF ➪ *<preset choice>*.

TIP When setting up the paper size, notice that you have an option for Custom from the Paper Size pull-down menu. Click Custom, and edit the Width and Height text boxes to scan custom size pages.

If you change a preset but find that the settings have all been configured improperly and you want to start over, simply open the Configure Presets dialog box and choose your edited preset. Click the Defaults button, and the options change back to the originally installed preset choices.

Creating a custom scan

For an occasional scan where options don't exist in one of your presets, you may want to use the Document ⇨ Scan to PDF ⇨ Custom Scan command. Choosing this option opens the Custom Scan dialog box, as shown in Figure 6.4.

When you perform a scan using the Custom Scan dialog box, you need to address the choices in the dialog box before clicking the Scan button. Your first choice is selecting your scanner from the Scanner pull-down menu. Next, choose the number of sides, the color mode, resolution, and paper size. Other choices for quality and activating the OCR engine also are choices you'll make for custom scans.

When you use the Custom Scan dialog box, your options choices become new defaults. Therefore, you can perform several scans using the same settings in a given editing session.

FIGURE 6.4

Choose Document ⇨ Scan to PDF ⇨ Custom Scan to open the Custom Scan dialog box.

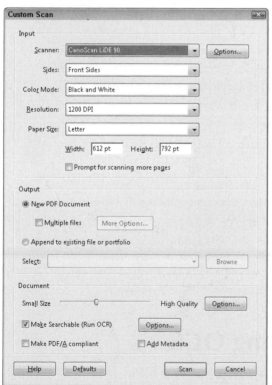

CROSS-REF For more information on using the OCR engine, see the section "Recognizing Text Using OCR" later in this chapter.

Setting scanner options

In both the Configure Preset dialog box and the Custom Scan dialog box, you find an Options button adjacent to the Scanner pull-down menu. Click this button, and the Scanner Options dialog box opens, as shown in Figure 6.5, where you can make some choices for the transfer method and user interface.

FIGURE 6.5

Click the Options button adjacent to the Scanner pull-down menu to open the Scanner Options dialog box.

For the Transfer Method, you can choose Native Mode or Memory Mode from the pull-down menu. Both modes prompt you to save your file in a Save dialog box. For faster scanning of multiple pages, choose the Memory Mode option.

For User Interface, choose between options in Acrobat for your scanner's interface. To use the options in the presets and the Custom Scan dialog box, you'll want to choose Hide Scanner's Native Interface. If the pull-down menu is grayed out, you are forced to use your scanner's interface.

NOTE Using the scanner's interface provides the same options you find when scanning a paper form using a TWAIN driver.

The Invert Black and White Images check box is used for scanning white text on a black background. This option is a likely candidate for using the Custom Scan menu choice if you have an occasional piece of artwork designed with white text on a black background. You wouldn't want to change a preset if this type of artwork is used infrequently when scanning.

Recognizing Text Using OCR

All paper forms you scan should be converted from the image file to recognizable text. You could keep a scan as an image file, but doing so defeats the purpose of using Acrobat's auto field detection command. Working with an image file would require you to manually create form fields.

After a file is converted from an image file to recognizable text, auto field detection automatically populates form fields when you enter Form Editing mode (discussed in Chapter 5) when converting to PDF native documents designed as forms.

Although in this chapter, we explain scanning, using OCR, and opening files in Form Editing mode, Acrobat can perform all these steps automatically when you scan a paper form.

CROSS-REF For more information on using the one-step operation for scanning a paper form, converting text using OCR, and adding form fields with auto field detection, see "Converting Paper Forms to PDF Forms" later in this chapter.

Understanding Acrobat's text recognition features

You can use Acrobat's OCR engine in a few ways. If you have image files scanned in another program, such as Photoshop or Photoshop Elements, and convert the image files to PDF, you might want to use the Document ⇨ OCR Text Recognition ⇨ Recognize Text Using OCR command. If your document is a form and you want to convert the form using auto field detection, you must first use the OCR engine.

The other way you can use the OCR engine is to activate it at the time you perform the scan. When you open either the Configure Presets dialog box (refer to Figure 6.3) or the Custom Scan dialog box (refer to Figure 6.4), you find a check box for Make Searchable (Run OCR). When the box is checked, the paper form is scanned and the text is recognized using OCR.

In both the Configure Presets and Custom Scan dialog boxes, you find an Options button. Click Options, and the Recognize Text – Settings dialog box opens, as shown in Figure 6.6. You have three choices for PDF Output style, which determines how the text recognition is performed:

FIGURE 6.6

Click Options in either the Configure Presets dialog box or the Custom Scan dialog box, and the Recognize Text – Settings dialog box opens.

- **Primary OCR Language:** By default, Acrobat installs 42 language dictionaries available for OCR. If you scan documents from any of the supported languages, select the appropriate language in the pull-down menu in the Recognize Text – Settings dialog box.

■ **PDF Output Style:** From the pull-down menu shown in Figure 6.6, your options are as follows:

   ▪ **ClearScan:** In earlier versions of Acrobat, this item was called Formatted Text and Graphics. When using the legacy format or the ClearScan technology introduced in Acrobat 9, the bitmapped image is discarded and replaced with searchable text and graphics. If there is an instance where the OCR engine does not have confidence, the original bitmap is left in place and the best guess is placed behind, mimicking the "Searchable Image" style.

   Formatted Text and Graphics had some problems related to color images in Acrobat 8 and earlier viewers. The newer ClearScan technology does a much better job of converting scanned images to text. In addition, pseudo fonts are created when you use ClearScan and the scan file sizes are significantly reduced.

   ▪ **Searchable Image:** Text is placed behind the original image, preserving the integrity of the original documents. The image scan is compressed to reduce file size. Some of the quality of the original scan is lost. However, when scanning forms, this option is your best choice because auto field detection works well on Searchable Image PDF outputs.

   ▪ **Searchable Image (Exact):** This option keeps the image scan in the foreground with text placed in the background. The appearance of the scanned image does not change. Text is added on a hidden layer that gives you the capability of creating indexes and performing searches. Use this option when you don't want to change a document's appearance, but you do want to be able to search the text of that document. Something on the order of a legal document or a certificate might be an example of such a document.

NOTE See the "PDF Image versus ClearScan" sidebar in this chapter for more detail on the differences among the PDF Output Styles.

■ **Downsample Images:** This option enables you to downsample images or keep them at the original scanned resolution. If None is selected, no downsampling is applied to images. The remaining options offer downsampling values at 600 dots per inch (dpi), 300 dpi, 150 dpi, and 72 dpi.

After you make choices in the Recognize Text – Settings dialog box and click OK, you return to the dialog box where you selected the Options button. When you click Scan or choose Document ⇨ OCR Text Recognition ⇨ Recognize Text Using OCR, the last settings you made in the Recognize Text – Settings dialog box are used by the OCR engine.

CROSS-REF The options for choosing PDF output style also are available to Macintosh users. For more information recognizing text using OCR on the Macintosh, see "Converting image files to text (on a Macintosh)" later in this chapter.

PDF Image versus ClearScan

When you search OCR pages with either Searchable Image (Exact) or Searchable Image, the pages are image files with searchable text. The original file is an image file produced from your scan designed to be viewed as an original, unaltered document. This option enables you to electronically archive documents for legal purposes or when unaltered originals need to be preserved.

When you convert a document with Recognize Text Using OCR, the OCR conversion places text behind the scan. The intent is for you to be able to archive files and search them either by using the Search panel to search files on your hard disk or by searching an index where these documents have been cataloged.

The text behind PDF Image is not editable with Acrobat. If Recognize Text Using OCR misinterprets a word, you cannot make corrections to the text. The text is selectable, and you can copy the text and paste it into a word processor or text editor. If you want to examine the OCR suspects, paste the text into a word processor and review the document.

If you want to scan a form and redesign it in an original authoring program, you can copy text from a PDF Image format using the Select tool. Click the cursor anywhere in the text, and choose Edit ➪ Select All (Ctrl/⌘+A). Choose Edit ➪ Copy File to Clipboard. Open a word processor, and choose Edit ➪ Paste. You may find the number of suspects to be too many to be usable. If you want to improve the OCR conversion, return to the Create PDF From Scanner dialog box and rescan the file with a higher resolution or different scanning mode.

ClearScan files (previously referred to as Formatted Text & Graphics in Acrobat 6 through 8) are scanned documents converted to text. When you select ClearScan in the Recognize Text – Settings dialog box, the file conversion is made to a PDF with formatted text and graphics. Recognize Text reads the bitmap configuration of words and converts them to text. This text can be edited and altered on a page. When you make text corrections, you see the changes reflected on the document page.

When scanning paper forms, use the Searchable Image PDF Output Style. Using the other options may not work with auto field detection. If you want to redesign a form in an authoring program, use ClearScan for your PDF Output Style.

Converting image files to text (in Windows)

You may have a number of scanned forms saved as image files that you want to convert using OCR. You can convert forms using OCR and open the forms in Form Editing mode to populate the documents with field objects.

TIP   **In some workflows, it may be more efficient to set up scanners to produce image scans on some computers and use Acrobat's OCR to convert to text and edit forms on other computers. If you have a great number of paper forms to convert to PDF, creating such a workflow might be more efficient.**

Assuming you have a scanned form saved as an image file and you want to convert the image file to recognizable text, follow these steps.

STEPS: Converting Image Files to Searchable Text

1. **Open a scanned form in Acrobat.** Use the Create ➪ PDF From File menu command or the Create PDF ➪ Merge Files into a Single PDF menu command to convert image files to PDF.

2. **Recognize text.** Select Document ➪ OCR Text Recognition ➪ Recognize Text Using OCR to open the Recognize Text dialog box, as shown in Figure 6.7.

3. **Set the PDF Output Style.** Click the Edit button in the Recognize Text dialog box to open the Recognize Text – Settings dialog box (refer to Figure 6.6). From the PDF Output Style pull-down menu, select Searchable Image. If you don't make this selection, auto field detection may not work and may result in no form fields being detected. Click OK, and you return to the Recognize Text dialog box.

4. **Run the OCR engine.** Click OK, and Acrobat starts the OCR engine to convert the image file to recognizable text.

FIGURE 6.7

Choose Document ➪ OCR Text Recognition ➪ Recognize Text Using OCR to open the Recognize Text dialog box. Choose Searchable Image for your PDF Output Style.

5. **Save the PDF.** Select File ➪ Save As to optimize the file and update your corrections.

Converting image files to text (on a Macintosh)

Some of the features related to setting up scanning presets are not available to Macintosh users. In addition, you don't have WIA support on the Macintosh. All your scanning occurs using a TWAIN driver and making choices for scan attributes in your scanner's software. To create a scan in Acrobat on the Macintosh and recognize text, follow these steps.

STEPS: Scanning a Text Document on a Mac

1. **Place a document on the scanner platen.** Be certain your scanner is configured and operational.

2. **Select Document ⇨ Scan to PDF.** The Acrobat Scan dialog box opens, as shown in Figure 6.8.

3. **Choose your scanner.** Open the Scanner pull-down menu, and choose your scanner.

4. **Set the OCR Settings.** Be certain the Make Searchable (Run OCR) box is checked, and click the Options button adjacent to the text to open the Recognize Text – Settings dialog box.

FIGURE 6.8

Choose Scan to PDF to open the Acrobat Scan dialog box.

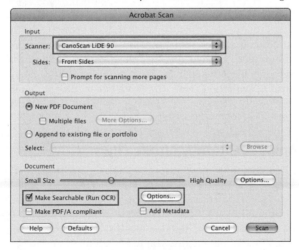

5. **Choose Searchable Image.** Open the PDF Output Style, and choose Searchable Image from the menu items, as shown in Figure 6.9. Click OK to return to the Acrobat Scan dialog box.

FIGURE 6.9

Choose Searchable Image.

6. **Set attributes in your scanner application.** Click Scan, and your scanner application interface opens. Make choices for resolution and paper size, and preview the scan. Click Scan to start the scan.

7. **Make text corrections on the document.** If you find any errors, type corrections in the Find Element dialog box. Click Accept and Find to find additional suspects.

8. **Save the file.** Select File ⇨ Save As to optimize the file and update your corrections.

Recognizing text in multiple files

If you set up a workflow where you perform scans on multiple scanners and save files as PDFs or an image format compatible with the Create PDF From File command, you can recognize text in multiple files.

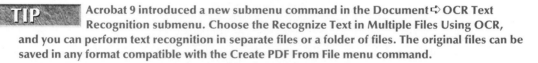

TIP Acrobat 9 introduced a new submenu command in the Document ⇨ OCR Text Recognition submenu. Choose the Recognize Text in Multiple Files Using OCR, and you can perform text recognition in separate files or a folder of files. The original files can be saved in any format compatible with the Create PDF From File menu command.

To recognize text in multiple files, follow these steps.

STEPS: Performing OCR on Multiple Files

1. **Choose Document ⇨ OCR Text Recognition ⇨ Recognize Text in Multiple Files Using OCR.** The Paper Capture Multiple Files dialog box opens.

2. **Add files.** Open the Add Files pull-down menu, and choose from three menu commands. Add Files enables you to add individual files. Add Folders enables you to add a folder of scans. Add Open Files enables you to add all files open in the Document pane.

You can combine choices in the Paper Capture Multiple Files dialog box. For example, you can add individual files, add a folder, and add some files open in Acrobat and list them in the Paper Capture Multiple Files dialog box, as shown in Figure 6.10.

FIGURE 6.10

Open the Add Files pull-down menu, and choose files to a list for OCR conversion.

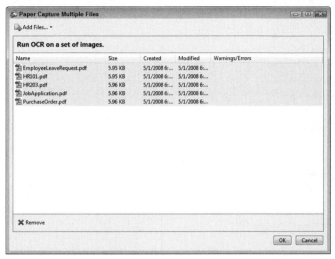

3. **Set the Output Options.** Click OK in the Paper Capture Multiple Files dialog box, and the Output Options dialog box opens, as shown in Figure 6.11. Click the Browse button to make choices for the folder where you want to save the files, add text to the filename, and select an output format. You also can open the PDF Optimizer and choose optimization settings for the saved files.

4. **Click OK to start the OCR process and save the files.**

CROSS-REF For more information on using the PDF Optimizer, see Chapter 10.

FIGURE 6.11

Make choices in the Output Options dialog box, and click OK.

Converting Paper Forms to PDF Forms

If you scan paper forms that you want populated with form fields in Acrobat or Adobe LiveCycle Designer and you want to use auto field detection in Acrobat, you need to start with a form that has sufficient resolution for the form fields to be recognized by Acrobat. If the resolution and image contrast aren't sufficient for Acrobat to recognize form fields, Acrobat will create few fields on low-resolution scans, and your results will be disappointing.

CROSS-REF For more information on using auto field detection in Acrobat, see Chapter 5. For more information on creating forms in Adobe LiveCycle Designer, see Parts VI through IX.

Developing a workflow for scanning forms using your scanner and Acrobat requires some practice and testing. Scanners vary considerably with quality, options, and resolution choices. The first thing you need to do is run a series of tests to determine what settings are optimal for recognizing fields automatically in Acrobat. Some considerations include:

■ **Resolution:** More is generally better when it comes to scanning forms. Most desktop scanners support two resolutions. Optical resolution is the true resolution of your scanner. You may have a 600 ppi (pixels per inch) scanner that supports an optical resolution of 600 ppi. Your scanner also supports an interpolated resolution. For the 600 ppi scanner, the interpolated resolution is likely to be 1200 ppi. A 1200 ppi optical resolution scanner often supports an interpolated resolution of 2400 ppi, and so on.

Interpolated resolution is best suited for line art drawings. Because most office forms are black and white, your scan resolution for forms at the highest interpolated resolution (up to 1200 ppi) of your scanner usually produces the best results when it comes to recognizing form fields. In Figure 6.12, you can see three scans we created using Scan to PDF. The form on the left is a 150 ppi scan, the one in the middle is a 300 ppi scan, and on the right is a 1200 ppi scan. Although auto field detection isn't perfect, you can see that the 1200 ppi scan produced the best results. In the 150 ppi scan, fields were created in areas where we don't want fields and some fields were not detected. In the 300 ppi scan, several fields were missed. In the 1200 ppi scan, Acrobat recognized the fields almost perfectly. Only one extra field was added between the second and third sections.

■ **Color Mode:** Black and white art is generally scanned in a line art (bitmap) color mode. However, when it comes to OCR Text Recognition and ultimately using auto field detection, the anti-aliasing of grayscale scans often provides you with better results.

■ **Make Searchable (Run OCR):** When you use Scan to PDF for scanning forms on which you want to use the auto field detection command, be certain to check the box for Make Searchable (Run OCR) in the Acrobat Scan dialog box (refer to Figure 6.3). Using auto field detection produces no results if you attempt to run the command on a scan that hasn't been converted with the OCR Engine.

TIP Note that ClearScan works well for documents you intend to view in Acrobat. However, forms, and especially forms with check boxes and ones on which you've used auto field detection, are best scanned using the Searchable Image PDF Output Style.

■ **Clean Up:** Ideally, you're best off using Scan to PDF and you'll achieve optimal results using the controls in your scanner software for brightness, contrast, color mode choices, and scanning resolution. However, if your scanner software doesn't produce good results when recognizing form fields on your scans, you may be able to do a little image editing to adjust brightness and contrast. You'll need a program like Adobe Photoshop or Adobe Photoshop Elements to adjust Levels (in Photoshop and Elements) and Curves (in Photoshop only).

If you do plan to do some image editing to adjust your scans' brightness and contrast, turn off Make Searchable (Run OCR) if using Scan to PDF. After editing a scan in Photoshop or Photoshop Elements, save as a Photoshop PDF file, open in Acrobat, and choose Document ➪ OCR Text Recognition ➪ Recognize Text Using OCR. After running the OCR Engine, you can then choose Forms ➪ Add or Edit Fields.

FIGURE 6.12

Three scans after selecting Forms ⇨ Add or Edit Fields and using auto field detection. On the left is a 150 ppi scan, in the middle is a 300 ppi scan, and on the right is a 1200 ppi scan. The scans were performed on a scanner with an optical resolution of 1200 ppi and an interpolated resolution of 2400 ppi.

150 ppi   300 ppi   1200 ppi

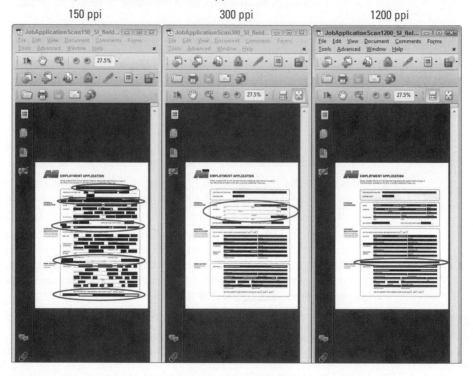

TIP If the quality of your original form is poor and you can't adjust contrast in Photoshop or Elements sufficiently to convert text with the OCR Engine and ultimately recognize fields, you can use Photoshop or Photoshop Elements to improve image brightness. Duplicate the Background layer in the Layers palette in either program. For the layers blending mode, change the default Normal to Multiply. Add more duplicate layers using the Multiply blending mode until you see enough brightness in areas such as text, lines, boxes, and so on. Flatten the layers and make your final adjustments in the Levels dialog box.

Plan to do lots of testing if you need to scan many forms and populate them with form fields in Acrobat or Adobe LiveCycle Designer. Try scanning forms with different resolutions to pinpoint the resolution setting that works best for your forms. After you find the settings that work best, go about scanning the forms you need to prepare in Acrobat.

Converting a paper form to a fillable form

When scanning forms, you can use a one-button action to perform three steps in your paper form conversion to a PDF fillable form. When you choose Forms ⇨ Start Form Wizard, the Create or Edit Form wizard provides a choice for creating a form from a paper form. When you make the choice, Acrobat Scan is used to scan the form, the scan is recognized using the OCR engine, and the form is automatically populated with form fields using Acrobat's auto field detection feature.

 **The steps to convert a paper form can be completed in Acrobat Standard, Pro, and Pro Extended.**

To convert a paper form to a fillable form, follow these steps.

STEPS: Scanning a Form in Acrobat

1. **Choose Forms ⇨ Start Form Wizard.** The Create or Edit Form Wizard opens, as shown in Figure 6.13.

2. **Choose A paper form.** From the radio button choices, click A paper form and click Next.

FIGURE 6.13

Select A paper form, and click Next.

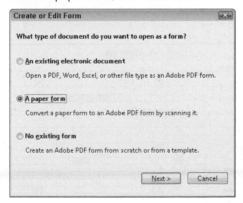

3. **Choose a preset or custom option (WIA-compliant scanners).** When you click Next in the Create or Edit Form Wizard, an Acrobat Scan dialog box opens, as shown in Figure 6.14. If you have a preset already created for scanning forms, click the option (Black and White or Grayscale). If you want to adjust scan options, click Custom. In the Custom Scan dialog box, choose scan options.

FIGURE 6.14

Click a preset, or click Custom.

If scanning using a TWAIN driver, your scanner software opens where you make your scan adjustments.

4. **Click Scan.** If you choose a preset, your scan commences and you don't need this step. If using a TWAIN driver, click the Scan button in the scanner's interface to start the scan.

5. **Edit the form.** The scan finishes, and the OCR engine recognizes text. The document is then moved to Form Editing mode where Acrobat automatically starts auto field recognition and populates the form. In many cases, you may need to edit a form such as the form shown in Figure 6.15. In this form, Acrobat missed a few check box fields. The fields are added while you stay in Form Editing mode.

6. **Save the form.** Preview the form by clicking the Preview button, and test the fields. When all fields appear on the form, choose File ⇨ Save to save the form.

FIGURE 6.15

Auto field detection picks up most of the form fields, but the check boxes were missed.

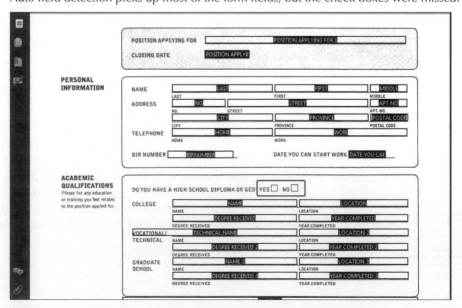

NOTE When you open a scan in Form Editing mode, Acrobat prompts you in a dialog box to use auto field detection. Click Yes in the Add or Edit Form Fields dialog box, and Acrobat searches the document for the placement of field objects on the form.

CROSS-REF For more information on Form Editing mode and adding fields to forms, see Chapter 5.

Scanning forms for Adobe LiveCycle Designer (Acrobat Pro/Pro Extended for Windows only)

In earlier versions of Acrobat and LiveCycle Designer, the duties of scanning a form and Running Form Field Recognition were the responsibility of LiveCycle Designer. In Acrobat 9, Acrobat takes control of the scanning, OCR recognition, and populating a form.

NOTE Adobe LiveCycle Designer is available only in Acrobat Pro and Acrobat Pro Extended for Windows.

When you open the Create or Edit Form wizard, the only option that takes you to LiveCycle Designer is No existing form. Click this radio button and then click Next, and the New Form Assistant wizard opens, as shown in Figure 6.16. Notice that this wizard doesn't have a choice for scanning a paper form.

If you want to edit a form in LiveCycle Designer and use a form where you let Acrobat populate the form with fields using auto field detection, you need to scan from within Acrobat following the steps outlined earlier in the section "Converting a paper form to a fillable form." Exit the Form Editing mode after adding all the fields by clicking the Close Form Editing button shown in Figure 6.15. Save the form, and choose Forms ⇨ Start Form Wizard.

In the Create or Edit Form wizard, choose No existing form and click Next. This choice opens LiveCycle Designer and the New Form Assistant Wizard shown in Figure 6.16. Click Import a PDF Document, and click Next. Add the Submit and Print buttons in the next pane, and click Finish. The form with the fields added in Acrobat opens in LiveCycle Designer. From here, you can use Designer to add additional fields and modify the form.

CROSS-REF For more information on using the New Form Assistant in Adobe LiveCycle Designer, see Chapter 22.

FIGURE 6.16

Click Import a PDF Document, and click Next to proceed with editing a PDF form in LiveCycle Designer.

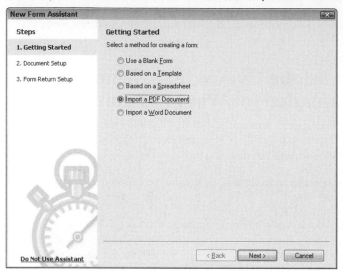

Using Batch Sequences

If you want to scan a number of forms from paper and convert to either Acrobat PDF forms or Adobe LiveCycle Designer XML forms, you use a Batch Sequence command to convert the text using OCR and using auto field detection in one step.

Two things need to be accomplished for preparing forms for editing in Acrobat or Adobe LiveCycle Designer. You need to Recognize Text Using OCR and Detect Form Fields. Open the Batch Sequences dialog box (Advanced ⇨ Document Processing ⇨ Batch Sequences), and create a new sequence. Select Recognize Text Using OCR, and add it to the right pane in the Edit Sequence dialog box. Next, select Detect Form Fields in the Edit Sequence dialog box, and click the Add button to add the item as a second sequence, as shown in Figure 6.17.

When you finish creating the sequence, the new sequence appears in the Batch Sequences dialog box, as shown in Figure 6.18. Select the sequence, and click Run Sequence. You can run the sequence on a folder of forms, and the files are converted with the OCR Engine and form fields are added to the documents. You can open the resultant files in either Acrobat or Adobe LiveCycle Designer for editing.

FIGURE 6.17

Create a batch sequence for Recognize Text Using OCR and Detect Form Fields on files you save in an image format.

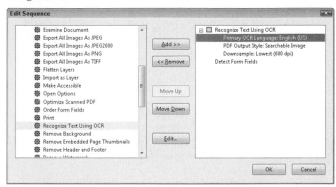

FIGURE 6.18

Select the sequence in the Batch Sequences dialog box, and click Run Sequence.

NOTE You can use Document ⇨ OCR Text Recognition ⇨ Recognize Text in Multiple Files Using OCR to batch process the OCR function. However, using this command only gets you half way. You still need to set up a Batch Sequence to use auto field detection to populate the scanned forms.

Summary

- Acrobat Scan provides choices for using presets and customizing presets with WIA-compliant scanners on Windows.

- TWAIN drivers or Adobe Photoshop Acquire plug-ins are needed when you use the Create PDF From Scanner command on Macintosh and when you use non-compliant WIA scanners.

- Acrobat 9 uses a new technology called ClearScan that replaces the Formatted Text & Graphics PDF Output Style used with earlier versions of Acrobat.

- Text can be converted and saved as a PDF ClearScan Output Style, where you can edit text and change the appearance of the original scan. Text can be converted with Optical Character Recognition and saved using the Searchable Image option, which preserves the original document appearance and adds a text layer behind the image.

- For optimum results with auto field detection, use the Searchable Image Output Style when using Recognize Text Using OCR.

- A new feature introduced in Acrobat 9 enables you to perform OCR text recognition on multiple scanned documents saved in any format compatible with the Create PDF From File command.

- OCR suspects are marked when the OCR Engine does not find an exact word match in its dictionary. Text editing is performed in the Find Element dialog box.

- Scanned paper forms can be populated with form fields when you enter Form Editing mode. Acrobat automatically uses auto field detection to place field objects on a page when you enter Form Editing mode.

- You can convert a paper form to a fillable PDF form using a single menu command in Acrobat.

- You can set up a batch sequence to Recognize Text Using OCR and Detect Form Fields that can be run on a folder of image files.

Chapter 7

Working with Form Fields

U p to this point, we've covered many different uses for auto detecting fields using auto field detection. When you need to quickly create a simple form and convert an application document to PDF and then use auto field detection as discussed in Chapter 5, you may not need to manually create new fields or edit fields on a form. When you scan a paper form using Acrobat's OCR engine as discussed in Chapter 6 and then auto field detection, you may not need to perform much manual editing.

In some cases, however, detecting fields won't work for all fields on a form. In other cases, you may need to start from scratch adding fields manually when auto field detection doesn't detect any fields. In these cases, you need to use Acrobat's Form tools, draw fields on a form, and make various changes to the fields' properties.

In this chapter, we leave Acrobat's auto-detection features and talk about the Form tools, how to manage fields on a form, use some design assistants, and set up tab orders. Even though you may often use auto field detection, you'll typically encounter instances in which you need some help using the methods described here.

IN THIS CHAPTER

Knowing the field types

Using proper field names

Arranging fields

Using design aids

Tabbing through fields

Understanding the Field Types

Fields are added to a form in Form Editing Mode in Acrobat 9 and in Viewer mode in all earlier versions of Acrobat. In Acrobat 9, you have access to eight Form tools via a pull-down menu or after loading the tools in the Form Editing toolbar.

In earlier versions of Acrobat, you opened the Forms toolbar, docked the toolbar in the Toolbar Well, and accessed the Form tools. In all viewer versions back to Acrobat 6, the Form tools appeared as separate tools in the Forms toolbar. In Acrobat 8, the Barcode tool was added to Acrobat. Earlier versions of Acrobat had the remaining seven Form tools you find in Acrobat 9 loaded in the Forms toolbar. Prior to Acrobat 6 and dating back as far as Acrobat 3, you could use the primary seven Form tools to create fields on a PDF form. We've seen some changes in the Field Properties dialog boxes, but if you happen to be working in an earlier version of Acrobat, much of what you find in this chapter can be used in Acrobat versions 3 through 9.

Loading the Form tools

When you enter Form Editing Mode by selecting Forms ➪ Add or Edit Fields, the first thing to do is make the Form tools visible in the Form Editing Mode toolbar. Having the tools visible in the toolbar is handier than using the Add New Field pull-down menu to select a tool.

To display the Form tools in the Form Editing toolbar, enter Form Editing Mode and from the Add New Field pull-down menu, choose Show Tools on Toolbar, as shown in Figure 7.1. When you select the command, the Form tools appear in a row in the Form Editing toolbar.

FIGURE 7.1

Choose Show Tools on Toolbar from the Add New Field pull-down menu to display tools on the Form Editing toolbar.

> **NOTE** In Chapters 7 through 19, we assume you have the Form tools visible to follow instructions. When we say, "click the Text Field tool," we assume the Form tools are visible in the Forms toolbar on your monitor. If you don't open the toolbar, remember that the instruction requires you to open the Add New Field menu and choose the respective Form tool.

> **ON the CD-ROM** For this section, we use the *globalCreditApp.pdf* document in the Chapter 07 folder on the book's CD-ROM.

Working with text fields

The first Form tool appearing in the Form Editing toolbar when you load the Form tools is the Text Field tool. Text fields are a bit misleading because they handle both text and numeric data. If you want to create fields where numbers are used, you use a text field.

 Text fields can be created for text data entered on a single line or for large passages of text. Text can be scrolled in a field and can be justified left, right, or centered. Numbers can assume different formats and symbols like currency, percentages, time formats, and date formats. Additionally, text fields are used when you perform data calculations using built-in formulas, using Simplified Field Notation, or writing JavaScripts.

CROSS-REF   For more information on calculations using built-in formulas, Simplified Field Notation, and JavaScripts, see Chapters 15 through 19.

Dropping fields on a form

To add a text field to a form, click the Text Field tool and the cursor is loaded with the Text Field. Move the cursor to a location on a form, and click. A text field is dropped on the form at the cursor location. When you use Form tools in Acrobat 9, a small Properties window opens, as shown in Figure 7.2. We refer to this window as the *mini Properties window* to distinguish it from the Properties dialog box.

FIGURE 7.2

After dropping a field on a form, the mini Properties window opens.

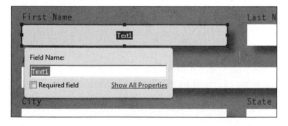

TIP   You also can select the Text Field tool by pressing the F key on your keyboard. Pressing the F key loads the text field by default. Using keystrokes to change tools requires you to open the Preferences dialog box (Ctrl/⌘+K) and click the General item in the left pane. In the right pane, you need to check Use single-key accelerators to access tools. Clicking OK in the Preferences dialog box and striking keys on your keyboard respective to tool selections enables you to change tools.

In the mini Properties window, you have three options:

■ **Field Name:** By default, Acrobat adds a name to the field for you. You can pick a name of your choosing and type the name in the Field Name text box. Notice that when you add a field to a form, the Name Field text (Text2 in Figure 7.2) is highlighted. Type a new name, and the highlighted text is deleted while the new name you type is added for the field name. Pressing Enter on your keyboard or clicking outside the mini Properties window registers the name you type in the Field Name text box.

CROSS-REF   For more on naming fields, see "Naming Fields" later in this chapter.

■ **Required field:** Click the check box, and the field becomes a required field for the form recipient to complete before submitting data. If a required field is not filled in, the form won't be submitted.

CROSS-REF   For more information on submitting forms, see Chapter 15.

■ **Show All Properties:** What you have available in the mini Properties window is a few property assignments you add to a field's properties (field name and required field). A field's properties are extensive for all field types. When you want to edit field properties, click Show All Properties and the Text Field (or other field types) Properties dialog box opens.

CROSS-REF   For more information on using field Properties dialog boxes, see Chapter 9.

Using some common features for Form tools

Some common views, assignments, and methods are common to all Form tools. You can set defaults for field sizes and appearances, set up tools to display tool labels, and assign tooltips to fields. This section helps you to understand some issues related to all the Form tools and how to adjust these settings.

Sizing fields as you add them to a form

Each field type has a fixed size. When you zoom in on a document, the loaded cursor displaying a field zooms its view at the same magnification as your zoom view.

If the default size for a field is not the same size as the field location on a form design, you can click a loaded cursor and drag to shape the size of a field. You begin drawing a field in the top-left corner of the field location and drag to the lower-right corner. All fields you add to a form appear with rectangle bounding boxes. As the cursor reaches the lower-left corner, release the mouse button and the field is drawn to a custom size.

When you draw fields on a form, the same mini Properties window opens where you can name a field, check it for a required field, and open the Properties dialog box.

Unloading the cursor

When you click a Form tool in the Form Editing toolbar, the cursor is loaded with the respective field type. If you decide to change your mind and want to add a different field type, press the Escape (Esc) key and the cursor is cleared of the selected field.

You also can click the Select Object tool or any other Form tool to remove a field from the cursor. If you click the Select Object tool, the cursor is cleared of all fields. If you have a loaded cursor and click another tool, the next tool replaces the loaded cursor tool.

Using labels

The Form tools in the Form Editing toolbar appear as icons and don't provide you an immediate clue as to what the tools are. Until you're familiar with the icons, you'll need a little help in discerning the differences between the tools such as displaying labels or names for the tools in addition to the icons shown in the toolbar.

In Viewer mode, when you open a context menu on the Toolbar Well, you have some choices for button label appearances. Buttons, per the Toolbar Well context menu command, refer to the tool buttons in the Acrobat toolbars.

Open a context menu in Viewer mode on the Toolbar Well, and choose Button Labels ➪ All Labels. The tools in the Toolbar Well appear with label names. Acrobat displays as many labels as it can within the space in the Toolbar Well. If toolbars stretch across the Acrobat window, some tools won't display the labels.

After choosing All Labels from the Button Labels submenu, open Form Editing Mode. When you look at the Form tools in the Form Editing toolbar, you'll see the Digital Signature tool and the Barcode tool appearing with labels, as shown in Figure 7.3.

FIGURE 7.3

You can have Acrobat show button labels on the toolbar—it's sort of like creating a cheat sheet on the toolbar.

While in Form Editing Mode, you don't have access to a context menu on the Form Editing toolbar. You need to toggle the view, make your Button Label choice, and return to Form Editing Mode to make changes in the toolbar appearances.

Using tooltips

Another way to distinguish the Form tools while in Form Editing Mode is to open tooltips. When you start creating forms in Acrobat, you may be confused by the similar appearance of the Text Field tool icon and the Digital Signature tool icon. Likewise, the List Box tool and Combo Box tool can be confused.

To know what tool you are selecting when moving the cursor to the Form Editing toolbar, place the cursor over a tool and pause. A tooltip opens with a description of the tool. In Figure 7.4, the cursor rests over the Combo Box tool.

FIGURE 7.4

Place the cursor over a tool in the Form Editing toolbar, and pause a moment to view a tooltip describing a tool's use.

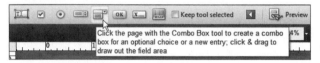

Working with button fields

Buttons are used commonly on forms and other PDF documents. PDF authors frequently use buttons to invoke actions for interactivity such as navigating pages, opening pop-up menus, navigating Web pages, and more. Because button fields are used for these kinds of interactive actions, the tool is made available in both Viewer mode and Form Editing Mode.

If you are in Viewer mode and press the F key, the Button tool is the default tool loaded in the cursor. No other Form tools can be accessed by a keyboard shortcut when in Viewer mode. Press F and click to drop a button field on a document, as shown in Figure 7.5.

 Likewise, you can add buttons in Form Editing Mode. Pressing the F key, however, won't load the Button tool. You need to click the Button tool in Form Editing Mode and drop the field, or click+drag the cursor to add a button field to a form.

Using Keyboard Shortcuts to Access Tools

In Acrobat versions 8 and earlier, you could access a Form tool by pressing F on your keyboard. The default tool that was selected was the Text Field tool. If you pressed Shift+F, you could toggle all Form tools without having to use the Forms toolbar.

In Acrobat 9, pressing the F tool in Viewer mode loads the Button tool in the cursor. Pressing Shift+F does nothing, and you cannot select other Form tools while you remain in Viewer mode. When in Form Editing Mode, pressing the F key loads the Text Field tool. If you press Shift+F, the keystrokes do nothing and you're stuck with the Text Field tool. Unfortunately, Acrobat doesn't provide you a means for selecting all the Form tools using keyboard shortcuts.

Button fields can be dropped on a document when working in Viewer mode.

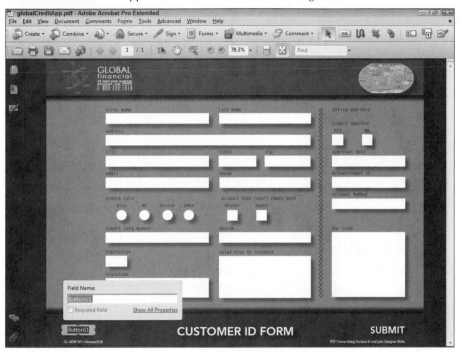

Working with check box fields

Check boxes are used for selecting items within a group. Check boxes can be designed as mutually exclusive fields where only one box can be checked within a group, or as independent boxes where one or more boxes are checked within a group.

As an example, you might use a check box field for identifying gender. In this example, you would design the fields as mutually exclusive fields where only male or female can be selected. Another group of fields might ask a form recipient to select favorite recreational activities from within a group of several options. All activities that meet the form recipient's interests would be checked. In this example, the fields are designed as independent check boxes.

 To use the Check Box tool, click the tool in the Form Editing toolbar. The cursor is loaded with the Check Box tool. Move the cursor to the location on the form where you want to add the field, and click to add the field to the form, as shown in Figure 7.6.

FIGURE 7.6

Click the Check Box tool, and click on the form to add a check box field.

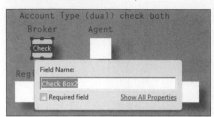

Notice that the options you have for this field type are identical to text fields where you can name the field, mark it as a required field, and open the Properties dialog box.

CROSS-REF For information on creating mutually exclusive and independent check boxes, see Chapter 9.

Working with radio button fields

By default, Acrobat assumes that when you add radio button fields, you want mutually exclusive fields within a group. Offering a choice of credit cards is a typical use of radio buttons.

Notice that when you select the Radio Button tool and drop the field on a form, you see additional options in the mini Properties window, as shown in Figure 7.7. Options for radio button fields include:

FIGURE 7.7

Radio button fields offer some additional options, such as for Button Value and for adding another button to the same group.

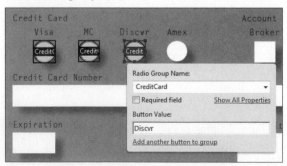

■ **Radio Group Name:** Type the name for the group in this text box. In our example, we typed CreditCard for the Radio Group Name.

■ **Required field:** Check this box, and at least one button in the group must be selected by the form recipient in order to submit the form.

■ **Button Value:** Each button in the group has the same name as it is defined in the Radio Group Name. However, each radio button must have a different value in order for the radio buttons to select a single choice from within the group. It doesn't matter what you type in the Button Value text box. You just need to be certain that no two radio buttons within a group have the same value.

■ **Add another button to group:** Click the blue text, and the cursor is immediately loaded with another radio button field. When you drop the field on the form, the Radio Group Name appears in the mini Properties window.

You may have several Radio Group Names on a form. Each time you select Add another button to group, Acrobat picks up the name for the current group and places the group name in the Radio Group Name text box. If you work on a form and come back to a group where you want to add another field to a given group, you select the Radio Button tool and from the Radio Group Name pull-down menu, you choose the group you want the new radio button added to, as shown in Figure 7.8.

FIGURE 7.8

When adding more buttons to a group, select the group you want to add the button to from the Radio Group Name pull-down menu.

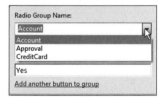

> **CROSS-REF** By design, Adobe assumes you want to create check boxes as independent fields and radio buttons as mutually exclusive fields. However, the reality of using one field type for another for either use is virtually the same, as explained in Chapter 9.

Working with list boxes

List boxes are used for scrollable windows where a form recipient has an option to choose one or more choices from among a list you compile in the List Box Properties dialog box. List boxes are handy when you have limited space on a form and a long list of options from which the form recipient chooses. Because the box is fixed to a size, you can add a huge number of options in a small space on your form.

Click the List Box tool in the Form Editing toolbar and the cursor is loaded with the field type. The fixed size of this cursor is not likely to match the space on most of your form designs, so you may want to click and drag with the loaded cursor to the size you've allocated on the form for the list box.

When you release the mouse button, the mini Properties window opens, as shown in Figure 7.9. Your choices in the window are the same as for text fields. Whereas you might get by with leaving the default properties set up for fields like text fields, check boxes, and radio buttons, list boxes always require you to open the List Box Properties dialog box, where you assemble the options for the scrollable window choices.

FIGURE 7.9

List Box options are the same as you find with text fields.

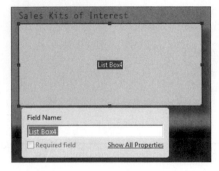

CROSS-REF   For more information on setting up list box properties, see Chapter 9.

Working with combo boxes

With the exception of appearance and some different Properties choices, combo boxes are very similar to list boxes. Instead of a scrollable window to choose from among many different options, a combo box appears with a pull-down menu where choices are listed. Again, this type of field can be added to a form within a limited space to offer the form recipient a large number of options from which to choose. A good example of a combo box is one that lists U.S. state names or country names. In an address block where identifying information is added, a combo box can list all the countries in the world while fitting within a section of a form used for identifying information.

 To create a combo box field, select the Combo Box tool in the Form Editing toolbar and click in a form where you want the field added. Like list boxes, you have a limited set of attribute choices when dropping the field on a form, as shown in Figure 7.10.

FIGURE 7.10

Combo Box options are the same as you find with list boxes.

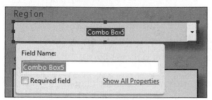

Like list boxes, combo boxes require you to click the Show All Properties button to add a list for the combo box choices. This is another field type that you can't leave at default values without making changes in the Properties dialog box.

Working with digital signature fields

Digital signature fields enable a form recipient to add a digital signature to a form. Adobe Reader users can create and add digital signatures to forms, as can Acrobat users.

 To drop a digital signature field on a form, click the Digital Signature tool in the Form Editing toolbar and move the cursor to the area where you want the field added to your form. Like list boxes, you'll often find clicking and dragging a better solution than clicking to drop the field. When you release the mouse button, the Digital Signature mini Properties window opens, as shown in Figure 7.11.

FIGURE 7.11

Options for a digital signature field

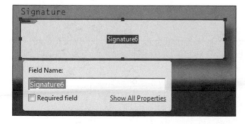

Unlike combo boxes and list boxes, you can leave digital signatures at default values. You do have a number of options to choose from in the Digital Signature Properties dialog box, but without making any options choices, a signature field does work on a form.

Working with barcode fields

Barcode fields dynamically assemble barcode data as a form recipient completes a form. In order to read the barcode on a PDF form, the form must be printed and a barcode reader is needed to read the data. For best results when working with barcodes, fill in a form in Preview mode, and then return to Edit Layout mode and add the barcode after all your fields are populated with data. The barcode needs to estimate the amount of space required to encode the data typed on a form.

 When you click the Barcode tool in the Form Editing toolbar, and either click or click+drag the cursor and release the mouse button, a dialog box opens informing you that using a barcode field requires you to acquire Adobe LiveCycle Barcoded Forms ES in order to read the data. Click OK in the dialog box shown in Figure 7.12, and a second dialog box opens, as shown in Figure 7.13.

FIGURE 7.12

When you drop a barcode field on a form, a dialog box opens informing you of what's needed to read barcodes.

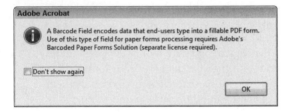

This dialog box informs you that you need to fill in all fields in order for the barcode to be created. This dialog box opens only when you have data missing from fields. If all fields are filled in, this dialog box doesn't appear.

FIGURE 7.13

Be sure to complete all the barcode fields, or you'll be scolded by Acrobat.

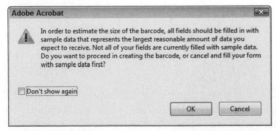

If the second dialog box appears, click Cancel and fill in your form with sample data. Try to use the maximum number of characters for any given field, such as a last name field. You should plan on the maximum amount of data any given form recipient will use to make the field usable. Acrobat estimates the amount of room needed for the barcode field to encode the data.

When you drop the field on the form, you see options in the mini Properties window similar to many other field types, as shown in Figure 7.14. Click the Show All Properties link to configure the barcode field with your barcode reader.

FIGURE 7.14

Options for a barcode field

Getting familiar with the Form tools

We introduce the Form tools in this chapter for readers who are new to creating forms in Acrobat. You can make a huge number of choices in the various Properties dialog boxes, but we don't want to overwhelm the novices quite yet, so we cover all the Properties descriptions in Chapter 9.

If you're new to Acrobat forms and you're following this book in a linear read, we encourage you to open the CD-ROM file *globalCreditApp.pdf* and practice a little using the different Form tools. By the time you get to Chapter 9, you'll have a good idea of how to add fields to a PDF form.

If you attempt to auto-detect fields on the CD-ROM file used for this section of the book, you'll find that Acrobat cannot populate the form with fields. The design of the form shown in Figure 7.15 isn't Run-Form-Field-Recognition-friendly and no fields are recognized.

FIGURE 7.15

The *globalCreditApp.pdf* form on the book's CD-ROM is designed for using all the eight field types. Use this form to practice adding fields manually to a form.

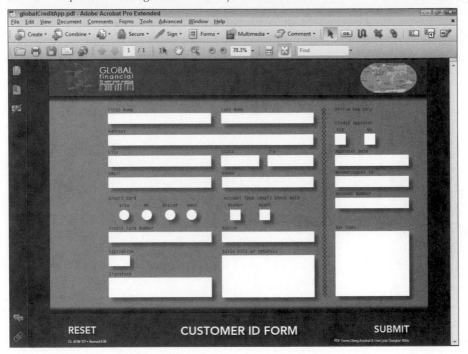

Naming Fields

If there's a single section in the parts related to Acrobat Forms, it's this one. If you don't commit to memory anything else in the first half of this book, be certain to understand the importance of field naming and how field names are developed in Acrobat.

What you have control over is naming fields you create using manual methods of adding fields in Form Editing Mode. What you don't have control over is the way Acrobat automatically names fields. However, you have the option to rename any fields created by you or by Acrobat. When you create or rename form fields, you need to take a few general considerations into account.

Setting up proper field names can save you much time when calculating field data, renaming fields, and working with JavaScript. A little attention to naming fields can save you much time if field names are creating using hierarchical naming conventions.

Auto field naming in Acrobat

When you use auto field detection, Acrobat names fields according to text adjacent to where a given field is detected and plotted. You have no control over how fields are named by Acrobat using auto field detection.

With auto field detection, Acrobat might name one field *Signature* and another field *Position Applying For*. If two fields appear with the same name, such as Position Applying For, Acrobat will name the fields *Position Applying For 1* and *Position Applying For 2* when auto-detecting fields. Field naming depends on the text Acrobat finds adjacent to where a field is added to a form.

When you manually add fields with the Form tools, Acrobat again offers an auto name for fields. When you launch Acrobat and add a text field in Form Editing Mode, Acrobat names the field *Text1*. Add another field, and the field name used is *Text2*. If you switch to the Check Box tool, the next field added to the form is *Check Box3*. Change to the Combo Box tool, and the next field added is *Combo Box4*. Acrobat numbers each field sequentially, regardless of the field type, and adds a prefix relative to the type of field created.

When you quit Acrobat and later return to a form and add a new field, Acrobat picks up the field type and adds a new field in sequential order. For example, suppose you have three text fields named *Text1, Text2,* and *Text3*. You also have *Combo Box1, Check Box1,* and *Check Box2*. Add a new text field, and the field is named by Acrobat *Text4*. Add a new combo box, and the field is named *Combo Box2*. Add a new check box, and the check box is named *Check Box3*.

The important thing to remember is that each field requires a unique name. If two fields of a common type are named with identical names, the data added to one field is duplicated in the remaining fields with the same name. For example, suppose we add a text field on a form and name the field *Name*, and then add a second field and name the field *Name*. Typing *Angie* in field 1 adds *Angie* to field 2. If we edit field 2 and type *Ted*, field 1 reads as *Ted* too.

Editing field names

Assume you want to edit field names that have been added with auto field detection or names of fields you manually add to a form. After you create a field in Acrobat or when you edit a form that's been populated with field objects, you can use the Fields panel in Form Editing Mode, the mini Properties window in Viewer mode, or the field Properties dialog box to edit names in either mode.

ON the CD-ROM For renaming fields, use the *jobApplication.pdf* document in the Chapter07 folder on the book's CD-ROM.

Editing field names in the Fields panel

After fields are added to a form, you can easily rename fields in the Fields panel. By default the Fields panel is open when you enter Form Editing Mode. If you use auto field detection and you want to change some names or if you've added some fields manually and want to edit names, follow these steps.

STEPS: Renaming Fields in the Fields Panel

1. **Open a form containing fields in Acrobat, and choose Forms⇨Add or Edit Fields.** Alternately, you can open a form in Acrobat, choose Add or Edit Fields, and let Acrobat's auto field detection feature populate a form.

2. **Open a context menu on a field you want to rename.**

3. **Choose Rename Field from the context menu, as shown in Figure 7.16.** Alternately, you can click once on a field name and click again and the name is ready to edit.

FIGURE 7.16

The right-click context menu lets you rename a field.

| TIP | You also can rename fields using the Fields panel while in Form Editing Mode. Locate a field in the Fields panel and double-click the field name. The name is highlighted and ready for you to type a new name. |

4. **Type a new name for the field.** In our example, the first field name in the Fields panel is POSITION APPLYING FOR 1. The second field in the Fields panel is POSITION APPLYING FOR 2. We typed *position* for the first new field name.

5. **Press Enter on your keyboard.** When you press Enter, the field name is recorded and the next field in the Fields panel is highlighted. Click once on the field, and it's ready to edit. In our example, field 2 in the Fields panel is named POSITION APPLYING FOR 2. Acrobat picked up the text from the first field caption, duplicated it for the field name, and then added 2 after the name to keep the field as a unique name. However, the field is designed to enter a closing date. Therefore, we named this field *closeDate*.

6. **Press the Num Pad Enter key (or Ctrl + Enter).** When you press the Num Pad Enter key, the field name is recorded but the field highlight does not jump to the next field.

Using acceptable field names

Acrobat recognizes almost any character or combination of characters for field names. You can use wildcard characters such as / ? > @ ! *, but we don't recommend using symbols and characters that don't have literal meanings. The more complex your forms, the more you'll need to use descriptive names for fields.

Case sensitivity is also an issue. If you name a field Last Name, last name, or last NAME, Acrobat sees these fields as three different fields. If you want data repeated on a form, be sure to use the same field name including case sensitivity for each occurrence of the data.

Length of field names can be a problem if you're writing JavaScripts and need to use field names in the scripts. If you have a field named *The first order item in the shopping cart,* Acrobat accepts the name, but having to retype a name like this is awkward and time consuming.

So what are the best field names to use? Programmers tend to use field names that are descriptive, short, without spaces between words, and lowercase with the exception of when a new word is introduced in the name. Names like *item, quantity, amount, salesItem, creditCard, amountTotal,* and so on are common field names used by programmers. Sometimes you find a little more description for the field names, but generally field names are written in similar fashion by JavaScript programmers.

What's most important when naming fields in Acrobat is to be consistent. If you use lowercase for field names, ALWAYS use lowercase. If you use uppercase/lowercase (*Name, Item, Amount*), be certain to ALWAYS use uppercase/lowercase. When it comes time to use field names in scripts, you'll find it very difficult to remember field names if you use different syntax among the field names on a form.

Editing field names in Viewer mode

In Viewer mode, select a field with the Select Object tool, open a context menu, and choose Rename Field. When you choose this menu command, the mini Properties window opens the same as when creating fields in Form Editing Mode. Click the Field Name text, and type a new name. Press Enter on your keyboard, and the name is changed.

Editing field names in the Properties dialog box

You also can edit fields using the Properties dialog box. Changing field names in the Properties dialog box is handy when you want to edit additional properties for a field. After populating a form in Form Editing Mode, you can open the Properties for a field in either Viewer mode or Form Editing Mode.

 In either Form Editing or Viewer mode, click the Select Object tool and move the cursor to a field you want to edit. Double-click the field, and the Properties dialog box opens. By default, the General pane in the Text Field Properties (when changing Text Field names) dialog box opens.

When you open the Properties dialog box, you'll see the Name text box containing the name that Acrobat supplied for the field name. If you use auto field detection, you'll also find the name duplicated in the tooltip text box. If you add fields manually on a form and Acrobat supplies the name, the tooltip field is left blank. In Figure 7.17, we edited the field name on the *jobApplication.pdf* form on the CD-ROM. You can see the tooltip Acrobat added when we used auto field detection.

Open the properties dialog box to edit a field name in either Form Editing Mode or Viewer mode.

Tooltips are where you want to add descriptions for form recipients. You might use a field with a field name such as *item*, and in the tooltip you might use a description such as *Item Product Description*. The tooltip pops up when a form recipient moves the cursor over a field. With regard to using tooltips, the names you use to describe a field in a tooltip do not need to follow any particular nomenclature. You can use long word descriptions, spaces, uppercase/lowercase, and so on. Tooltips aren't used in scripts so you don't need to have the same concern for these names as you do with field names.

The important thing to remember regarding tooltips is that they are designed for legibility. Avoid using all uppercase text because it's more difficult to read than lowercase or a mixture of uppercase and lowercase.

Something else that's important with tooltips is when you make your forms accessible for screen readers used by the visually and motion challenged form recipients. The tooltip content is read aloud by a screen reader.

CROSS-REF   For more on making forms accessible, see Chapter 11.

Using hierarchical names

Hierarchical names are a beneficial when it comes to calculating field data, and use of hierarchical names is perhaps the most important part of this section on naming fields. Hierarchical names are written like *item.0, item.1, item.2; customer.first.name, customer.last.name, customer.emailAddress; lineTotal.0, lineTotal.1, lineTotal.2,* and so on. In these examples, the names have parent/child relationships. The parent items in these sample names are *item, customer,* and *lineTotal*.

The first part of a hierarchical name is the parent. The parent is separated from the child names with a period (.). When it comes time to perform calculations, you can calculate fields using a parent name. If you have a form with a table, for example, and the number of rows are 15 separate data fields, you can write a script that can calculate the 15 rows in two lines of code. If you use individual field names for the same 15 rows of data, the code to perform a calculation will exceed more than 30 lines of code.

Hierarchical names have many uses. Simplicity in calculating formulas is the obvious advantage for using hierarchical names, but you'll also find great advantages for copying and pasting fields, duplicating fields, and renaming fields.

CROSS-REF For more information on using hierarchical names, see Chapter 8.

Managing Fields

We use the term *managing fields* to mean dealing with field duplication, deleting fields, and modifying field attributes. After you create a field on a PDF page, you may want to alter its size, position, or attributes. Editing form fields in Acrobat is made possible by using one of several menu commands or returning to the respective field's Properties window.

Organizing fields

To edit a form field's properties, use the Select Object tool and double-click the field rectangle. The Properties window opens after you double-click the field object. You also can use a context-sensitive menu opened from the Select Object tool and click the form field to be edited. At the top of the context-sensitive menu, select the Properties command. Also, you can select Forms ⇨ Show Field Properties. Using any one of the menu commands opens the Properties dialog box.

To select multiple fields of different types, you must use the Select Object tool. Because you cannot use a Form tool in Acrobat 9 to select a field, all field selections are made with the Select Object tool. In earlier versions of Acrobat, you can use the individual Form tools to select fields respective to the Form tool you're using. For example, you can select all text fields with the Text Field tool.

When you select multiple fields and choose Properties from the context-sensitive menu, options in the General tab, the Appearance tab, and the Actions tab are available for editing. Specific options for each different field type require that you select only common field types. For example, you can edit the Appearance settings for a group of fields where the field types are different. However, to edit something like radio button field options for check mark style, you need to select only radio button fields in order to gain access to the Options tab.

TIP If the fields you want to select are located next to each other or you want to select many fields, use the Select Object tool and drag a marquee through the fields to be selected. When you release the mouse button, the fields inside the marquee and any fields intersected by the marquee are selected. The marquee does not need to completely surround fields for selection; just include a part of the field box within the marquee.

All of the editing you perform using the Select Object tool and context menu commands can be performed in either Form Editing Mode or Viewer mode.

Copying and pasting fields

Fields can be copied and pasted on a PDF page, between PDF pages, and between PDF documents. Select a field or multiple fields, and choose Edit ➪ Copy. Move to another page or open another PDF document, and choose Edit ➪ Paste. The field names and attributes are pasted together on a new page.

> **TIP**   To ensure that field names are an exact match between forms, create one form with all the fields used on other forms. Copy the fields from the original form, and open the target document in Form Editing Mode. Choose Edit ➪ Paste to paste the fields in the target document. By pasting the fields, you ensure that all field names are identical between forms and can easily swap data between them.

When you're in Form Editing Mode, the top-level menu commands for Edit ➪ Cut, Edit ➪ Copy, and Edit ➪ Paste are accessible.

> **TIP**   You can duplicate a field by selecting it and holding down the Ctrl/Option key while clicking and dragging the field box.

Placing multiple fields

Using the Place Multiple Fields command from a context menu enables you to create table arrays or individual columns or rows only on a single page. If you want to duplicate fields on a page, you use the Place Multiple Fields command. If you want to duplicate fields across pages, you use the Duplicate command.

> **CROSS-REF**   For more information on using Place Multiple Fields, see "Creating multiple copies of fields" later in this chapter.

Pasting Fields

When pasting fields in Viewer mode, be certain to click the Select Object tool when pasting. If you have the Hand tool selected the fields are pasted, but the pasted fields are immediately deselected. If you want to paste a number of fields on a form containing existing fields, the pasted fields could be a problem to reselect and move into position.

If the Select Object tool is active, the pasted fields remain selected and you can easily drag them into position. When dragging fields, be careful to place the cursor well within a field bounding box to be sure you don't deselect the fields before dragging them into position.

If pasting fields in Form Editing Mode, the Select Object tool is active by default. You can paste fields on a form, and the fields remain selected after pasting. If you click the Close Form Editing tool and switch to Viewer mode, the selected fields are deselected. When pasting fields in Form Editing Mode, be certain to move the fields into position before changing modes.

To duplicate a field on a page, you can use the copy/paste commands in the top-level Edit menu or from context menus. For a fast method for duplicating fields, press the Ctrl/⌘ key and click+drag a field with the Select Object tool. If you duplicate a field and you want the field to hold unique data, you need to change the field name.

You also find a Duplicate context menu command. This command is inactive on single page forms. You use Duplicate from a context menu opened on a field with the Select Object tool to duplicate a field across multiple pages. You might have a navigation button set up with an action to open the next page in a PDF Document containing multiple pages. To easily duplicate the field, choose Duplicate from a context menu. When you choose Duplicate, the Duplicate Field dialog box shown in Figure 17.18 opens. You specify the page range and click OK, and the fields are duplicated at the same position on the page across all pages chosen in the Duplicate Fields dialog box.

FIGURE 7.18

Select a field with the Select Object tool on a multi-page PDF document, and choose Duplicate from a context menu to open the Duplicate Fields dialog box.

Moving fields

You can relocate fields on a PDF form by selecting the Select Object tool and then clicking and dragging the field to a new location. To constrain the angle of movement (horizontal or vertical), select a field with the Select Object tool, press the Shift key, and drag a field to a new location. You can use the arrow keys on your keyboard to move fields and perform some other actions when using modifier keys. You have these options with the arrow keys:

- **Left, Right, Up, Down (arrow keys):** Select a field(s) with the Select Object tool, and press the arrow keys. Fields move in the direction of the arrow key you press (up, down, left, and right) one-pixel at a time.

- **Shift+Left, Right, Up, Down (arrow keys):** This key combination moves the selected field(s) 10 pixels in the direction of the arrow key you press.

- **Ctrl/Option+Left Arrow:** This sizes the field object 1 pixel smaller in width moving the right side of the field object inward.

- **Ctrl/Option+Right Arrow:** This sizes the field object 1 pixel larger in width moving the right side of the field object inward.

- **Ctrl/Option+Up Arrow:** This sizes the field object 1 pixel smaller in height moving the bottom side of the field object upward.

- **Ctrl/Option+Down Arrow:** This sizes the field object 1 pixel larger in height moving the bottom side of the field object downward.

- **Ctrl/Option+Shift+Arrow:** This sizes the field object 10 pixels in width/height according to the arrow key you press.

Deleting fields

You delete fields from PDF forms in three ways:

- Select the field, and press the Backspace key (Windows) or Delete key (Macintosh) or Del key (Windows/Macintosh).

- Select the field, and choose Edit ⇨ Delete.

- Open a context menu and choose Edit ⇨ Delete.

In all cases, Acrobat removes the field without warning. If you inadvertently delete a field, you can Undo the operation by choosing Edit ⇨ Undo or pressing Ctrl/⌘+Z.

> **TIP** If you cannot delete a field, open the field's Properties dialog box and check to see if the Locked check box is checked. You need to unlock any locked fields in order to delete them.

Aligning fields

Even when you view the grids on a PDF form, aligning fields can sometimes be challenging. Acrobat simplifies field alignment by offering menu commands for aligning the field rectangles at the left, right, top, and bottom sides, as well as for specifying horizontal and vertical alignment on the form. To align fields, select two or more fields, open a context menu, and select Align, Distribute, or Center, as shown in Figure 7.19. The alignment options for Left, Right, Top, Bottom, Horizontally, and Vertically appear in a submenu.

Acrobat aligns fields according to the first field selected (the anchor field appearing with handles). In other words, the first field's vertical position is used to align all selected fields to the same vertical position. The same holds true for left, right, and top alignment positions. When you use the horizontal and vertical alignments, the first field selected determines the center alignment position for all selected fields. All fields are center aligned either vertically or horizontally to the anchor field. (See the sidebar "Selecting Fields" for more information about changing the anchor field.)

You can distribute fields on a PDF form by selecting multiple fields and choosing Distribute from a context menu. Select either Horizontally or Vertically for the distribution type. The first and last fields in the group determine the beginning and end of the field distribution. All fields within the two extremes are distributed equidistant between the first and last fields.

> **CROSS-REF** For an example of how to use the Distribute command, see "Creating multiple copies of fields" later in this chapter.

FIGURE 7.19

Open a context menu using the Select Object tool on one field in a group of selected fields, and choose Align, Distribute, or Center from the menu.

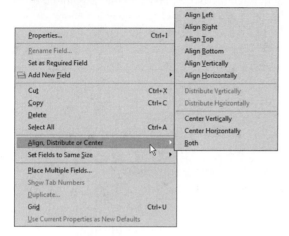

Sizing fields

Field rectangles can be sized to a common physical size. Again, the anchor field determines the size attributes for the remaining fields selected. To size fields, select multiple field boxes, open a context menu, and choose Set Fields to Same Size ⇨ Height, Width, or Both. Size changes are made horizontally, vertically, or both horizontally and vertically, depending on which menu option you choose. To size field boxes individually in small increments, hold down the Shift key and move the arrow keys. The left and right arrow keys size field boxes horizontally, whereas the up and down arrow keys size field boxes vertically. (See "Moving fields" earlier in this chapter for information on using keystrokes to size fields.)

Setting attribute defaults

If you spend time formatting attributes for field appearances, options, and actions, you may want to assign a new default for all subsequent fields created with the same Form tool. After creating a field with the attributes you want, open a context menu and select Use Current Properties as New Defaults. The properties options used for the field selected, when you choose the menu command, become a new default for that field type. As you change Form tools and create different fields, you can assign different defaults to different field types.

If you quit Acrobat and re-launch Acrobat in another editing session, the new defaults you last established prevail each time you use the respective Form tool on additional forms.

Selecting Fields

When you click the Select Object tool and drag through a group of fields, all fields within the marquee area of the Select Object tool are selected. The anchor field appears with handles (or tiny squares at the corners and middle points) on the field rectangle. All the selected fields appear with blue text for the field name but without the handles.

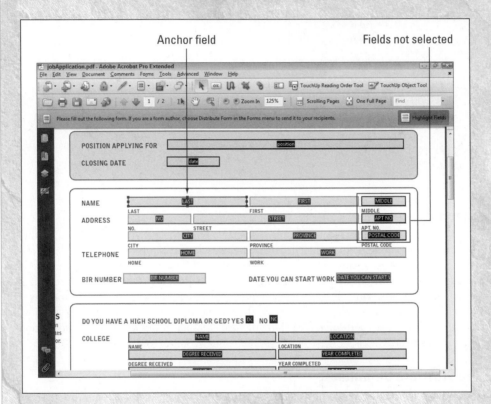

An anchor field is used for field alignment. When you choose Align, Distribute, or Center ⇨ Align Left, all the selected fields are aligned to the left side of the anchor field.

If you want to change the anchor field among the group of selected fields, press the Ctrl/⌘ key and click the field you want to select as the new anchor. If you press the Shift key and click a selected field, the field becomes deselected while other fields in the group remain selected.

If you want to add a deselected field to the group of selected fields, press the Ctrl/⌘ key and click the field with the Select Object tool. If you press the Shift key to add a field to a selected group, you may add additional fields within a zone that you may not want as part of your selected group.

Creating multiple copies of fields

If you want to duplicate fields on a single page form, you cannot use the Duplicate command from a context menu. However, Acrobat provides another command for duplicating fields on a page. The Place Multiple Fields context menu command is commonly used for creating tables on forms. You can use the command for creating multiple fields in a column or row or when you want to populate a table having several columns and/or rows.

To understand how the Place Multiple Fields command is used, follow these steps.

 For the steps following, we use the *purchaseOrder.pdf* file found on the book's CD-ROM in the Chapter07 folder.

STEPS: Creating Multiple Fields on a Form

1. **Open a form in Acrobat.** In this example, we use the *purchaseOrder.pdf* file from the book's CD-ROM found in Chapter07. This form is populated with fields in the first four columns. A single field appears in the Total column. This field needs to be duplicated down the column. Because we have fields on the form, we don't need to enter Form Editing Mode to perform our edits.

2. **Open a context menu on a field.** Use the Select Object tool to select the *total* field, and open a context menu. From the menu selections, choose Place Multiple Fields, as shown in Figure 7.20. When you release the mouse button, the Create Multiple Copies of Fields dialog box opens.

FIGURE 7.20

Click a field with the Select Object tool, and choose Place Multiple Fields.

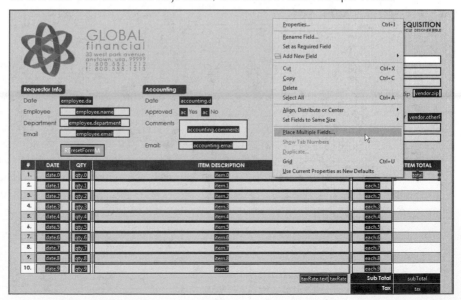

3. **Set the attributes for placing multiple fields.** In the Create Multiple Copies of Fields dialog box, shown in Figure 7.21, type the number of fields down and across that you want to create. In our example, we need 10 copies down and only 1 field across. Therefore, we type **10** in the Copy selected fields down text box and **1** in the Copy selected fields across text box. The remaining options in the dialog box we leave at the default values and click OK.

FIGURE 7.21

Make choices about how many columns or rows to create in the Create Multiple Copies of Fields dialog box.

4. **Move the last field into position.** When you arrive back at the Document pane, the fields are plotted on the form. But the location of the fields needs to be adjusted so they fit within the cells on the form design. To begin the alignment, click the last field in the column with the Select Object tool, press the Shift key to constrain the movement, and drag down to the bottom cell.

5. **Distribute the fields.** All fields between the first and last fields can be spaced equidistant from the others using a simple menu command. With the Select Object tool, select all fields in the column. Open a context menu, and choose Align, Distribute, or Center ⇨ Distribute Vertically, as shown in Figure 7.22. When you release the mouse button, the fields are aligned to the cells for each row in the form design.

FIGURE 7.22

Open a context menu on the selected fields, and choose Align, Distribute, or Center ⇨ Vertically to distribute the column of fields.

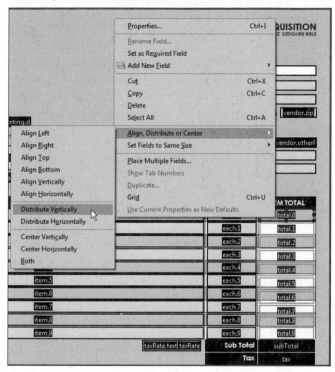

When using the Distribute command, you can only distribute single rows or columns. If you attempt to select all fields in a table containing multiple columns and distribute several rows or columns at once, the results produce a cascaded arrangement.

CROSS-REF There's much more to creating tables on PDF forms than we covered in this chapter. For an in-depth look at working with tables, see Chapter 8.

Creating forms in Viewer mode

If you're a seasoned Acrobat forms developer, you may find the Form Editing Mode in Acrobat 9 a bit too simplistic for your taste. You might prefer to create forms in Viewer mode and visit the Form Editing Mode only when needed.

To stay in Viewer mode while you create a PDF form, you need a little workaround that you can use by following these steps.

> **ON the CD-ROM**   We created a blank page with all the field types and saved the file as *blankPage.pdf* that you can review on the CD-ROM in the Chapter07 folder.

STEPS: Creating Forms in Viewer Mode

1. **Create a blank new page.** Choose File ➪ Create PDF ➪ From Blank Page.

2. **Save the file.** When you create a blank new page, Acrobat assumes you want to type a memo. To dismiss the text tools and eliminate the text frame on the blank page, choose File ➪ Save and save the file using a name like *fieldsTemplate.pdf*. After saving the file, close the document.

3. **Reopen the blank page.** After closing the file, open the File menu (Windows) and choose blankPage.pdf (or whatever name you chose for your file) to reopen the document without the text frame and text tools appearing in the Acrobat toolbar. On the Macintosh, choose File ➪ Open Recent File and select the file to reopen it.

4. **Add one form field for each field type.** Open Form Editing Mode by choosing Forms ➪ Add or Edit Fields. Click No in the dialog box that opens, and you enter Form Editing Mode. Use the individual Form tools to create one field for each field type. When creating the fields, you may want to click Show All Properties to adjust any field properties for common settings used on most of your forms.

5. **Save the form.** Your form should look something like Figure 7.23. Choose File ➪ Save, and update the last save.

FIGURE 7.23

A template form is created with each field type.

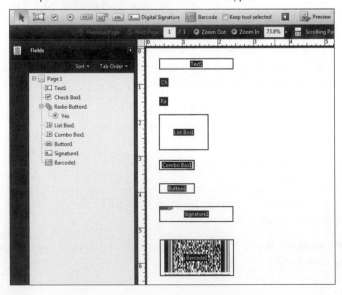

---

6. **Copy/paste fields.** When you want to create a new form, open the template file, click the Select Object tool, and select all fields (Ctrl/⌘+A). Open your new form, and select Edit ⇨ Paste or press Ctrl/⌘+V. All the fields are pasted in Viewer mode. You can click a field with the Select Object tool and press Ctrl/⌘ to drag fields to duplicate them. You can use Place Multiple fields, and rename fields by opening a context menu and choosing Rename Field. In short, all the form editing features are available to you in Viewer mode except using the Fields panel.

If it's not inconvenient, you can always open Form Editing Mode and create individual field types for a form you work on, and then switch to Viewer mode and copy/paste fields, set properties, and make all the edits in Viewer mode. The benefit of a template file is that you can set up the field properties used most often on your forms without having to open the Properties dialog box when adding fields in Form Editing Mode.

Using Rulers, Guides, and Grids

When you're in Form Edit Mode, a cursor loaded with a form tool helps you align field objects as you drop them on a form. For a number of different form designs, the design of the cursor when using Form tools is all you need to assemble field objects on a page. Together with the context menus for alignment, you may find that you don't need any additional tools for precisely positioning fields on a page.

In other cases, you want more assistance for field placement. Acrobat offers you a number of different design assistants in the form of rulers, grids, and guides.

Using Rulers

By default, rulers are turned on when you enter Form Editing Mode. Rulers also are available in Viewer mode. You can toggle rulers on and off by pressing Ctrl/⌘+R in either mode or by opening the View menu and choosing Rulers. With rulers in view, you can make some choices by opening a context menu on a ruler, as shown in Figure 7.24. You have these menu choices:

FIGURE 7.24

Move the cursor to a ruler, and open a context menu.

- **Units of measure:** Choose from the items in the first section of the context menu to set your unit of measure to Points, Picas, Millimeters, Centimeters, or Inches.

- **Show Guides:** You can draw guidelines on each page on a form. Guidelines are used to help you with a form design. The guidelines added to a form are not shown in printed documents. When you want the guides to be hidden, remove the check mark adjacent to Show Guides in the context menu. To display the guides, select this command from the menu.

- **Clear Guides on Page:** After drawing guides, use this command to clear guides on the page in view.

- **Clear all Guides:** If you have more than one page for a form and you draw guides on separate pages, use this command to eliminate all guides in the document.

- **Hide Rulers:** This option hides the horizontal and vertical rulers. To show the rulers after hiding them, open the top level View menu and choose Rulers or press Ctrl/⌘+R.

Drawing guidelines

The rulers contain an inexhaustible well of guides that you can add to a form page. You draw guidelines by selecting any tool in Viewer mode, clicking on a ruler, and dragging down (or right) to add a new guideline to a form page. If you have the cursor loaded with a Form tool in Form Editing Mode, you can move the cursor to a ruler and drag a new guide to the document, and the cursor remains loaded with the selected Form tool.

To relocate a guideline after you've added one to a form page, click the Select Object tool and drag the guideline to a new position. You also can eliminate a guideline by dragging a guideline to a ruler well.

Snapping fields to guidelines

Field objects can be snapped to guides you draw on a page. After creating the guidelines you want, you can load the cursor in Form Editing Mode and move the cursor to a guideline. As you approach a guideline, move the cursor slowly. If you move too fast, Acrobat won't sense the guideline and you'll move past it. As you slowly move a loaded cursor to a guideline, you'll see the field object bounding box snap to the guideline. Click to drop the field, and the field object is aligned to the guideline.

You also can snap field objects while in Viewer mode. Click a field with the select object tool (this works in both modes), and drag a field toward a guideline. You follow the same principles as when creating new fields that you want to align to a guideline. Drag slowly until you see an edge of the field object bounding box snap to a guideline.

Working with grids

Grids provide you with a series of horizontal and vertical guidelines that are divided in major and minor subdivisions. When you show a grid by choosing View ➪ Grid or pressing Ctrl/⌘+U in either mode, a grid is displayed. Showing grids is an application-level function. When you open additional files after selecting the View ➪ Grid command, grids stay visible for all documents you work with until you turn the grid off. When the grid is in view, you can snap field objects to the grid.

Setting up a grid

By default, grids are set up with 1-inch major divisions having three minor divisions. Major and minor divisions are customizable, and you can define the units of measure, major divisions and minor divisions in the Preferences dialog box.

Open Preferences (Ctrl/⌘+K), and click Units & Guides in the left pane. The right pane opens displaying the choices you have for creating a custom grid, as shown in Figure 7.25. You have these options:

FIGURE 7.25

Open the Preferences dialog box and click Units & Guides to display options for creating a custom grid.

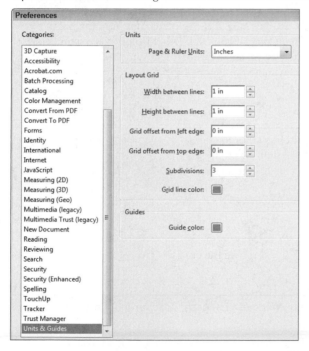

- **Page & Ruler Units:** Five choices are available from the pull-down menu. You can choose Points, Picas, Millimeters, Centimeters, or Inches.

- **Width between lines:** The horizontal distance between the major gridlines is determined in the field box for this setting. You can click the arrows, enter a number between 0.028 and 138.888 in the field (when inches are selected for the unit of measurement), or press the up-arrow key or down-arrow key to change the values.

NOTE The limit of 138.888 relates to inches. If you change the units of measure, the limits are roughly the same as the 138.888-inch limit. In points, the range measures between 2 and 10,000.

■ **Height between lines:** You can change the major gridlines appearing vertically with this field. Use the same methods of changing the values here as for the lines for the Width option.

■ **Grid offset from left edge:** Each grid has x and y coordinates indicating where the grid begins on a page. You set the x-axis (offset left) in this field.

■ **Grid offset from top edge:** Use this field to set the starting point of the y-axis (offset down).

■ **Subdivisions:** The number of gridlines appearing between the major gridlines is determined in this field. The acceptable values range between 0 and 10,000 (when units are set to points).

■ **Grid line color:** By default, the color for the gridlines is blue. You can change the grid color by clicking the color swatch. When you click the blue swatch for Grid line color, a pop-up color palette opens, as shown in Figure 7.26. Select a color from the preset color choices in the palette, or click Other Color. If you click Other Color, the system color palette opens, where you can make custom color choices. The Windows and Macintosh system color palettes vary slightly, as shown in Figure 7.27.

FIGURE 7.26

Click the color swatch for the Grid line color to choose from a selection of preset colors, or select Other Color to open the system color palette.

FIGURE 7.27

When you select Other Color, the Windows (left) or the Macintosh (right) system color palette opens.

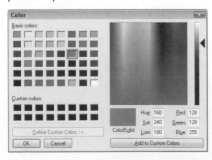

■ **Guide color:** Guides are added from ruler wells, and you can manually position them in the Document pane. If you have ruler guides and a grid, you'll want to change one color to easily distinguish the guides from the grid. Both default to the same blue. To change the guide color, click the Guide color swatch in the Units & Guides Preferences and follow the same steps as described for Grid line color.

Snapping to a grid

Grids are viewable in both the Form Editing Mode and Viewer mode. Setting up a custom grid doesn't snap field objects to a grid in either mode unless you turn on the Snap to Grid menu command. To snap field objects to a grid, choose View ⇨ Snap to Grid in either Form Editing Mode or Viewer mode or press Shift+Ctrl/⌘+U.

When Snap to Grid is turned on, field objects are snapped to the major and minor gridlines. It doesn't matter whether you view a grid, the Snap to Grid feature snaps field objects to the grid with or without gridlines visible.

Dragging field objects to a grid works the same as when dragging fields to guidelines. You need to slowly approach the grid for a field to snap to one of the gridlines.

If you want to disable the Snap to Grid feature momentarily, so you can add a field not aligned to the grid, you need to turn off Snap to Grid by choosing View ⇨ Snap to Grid and remove the check mark adjacent to the menu command or press Shift+Ctrl/⌘+U again. No modifier key is available to press while dragging a field that permits you to freely move a field object without aligning to a grid or guide line.

Filling in Forms

Forms authors should be familiar with filling in forms in Adobe Reader and Acrobat viewers to help guide the form recipients receiving your forms or by adding help messages on forms to ease the completion process for the form recipients.

A little practice with filling in forms in Adobe Reader helps you understand the limitations that a Reader user may face when completing your forms.

Using the Typewriter tool

As a PDF form author, you won't be using the Typewriter tools, but you may need to guide form recipients in filling in forms and, occasionally, using the Typewriter tools on forms created by other PDF form authors. Ideally your forms have all the necessary fields that a form recipient needs to complete your form, but there may be times when you receive a form that doesn't have field objects and you need to complete the form yourself.

You want to discourage the use of the Typewriter tool if you're processing data from your forms. Any data added with the Typewriter tool is not going to flow into a database or be exported to a spreadsheet. As a matter of practice, you should secure your forms with Acrobat Security to prevent the Typewriter tool from being accessed by a form recipient completing one of your forms.

CROSS-REF   For more information on processing data, see Chapter 15. Form more on securing forms with Acrobat Security, see Chapter 12.

Typewriter   To use the Typewriter tools, open a document in an Acrobat viewer and select Tools ➪ Typewriter ➪ Show Typewriter toolbar. You can open the Typewriter toolbar only in Viewer mode. Note that the Typewriter tools also are accessible to Adobe Reader users only when a form is Reader enabled. After the Typewriter tools are in view, you can dock the toolbar in the Toolbar Well by opening a context menu on the Toolbar Well and choosing Dock Toolbars.

NOTE   If you don't see the Typewriter appearing in the Toolbar Well context menu, the form you opened in Acrobat is secured with password security and permissions for using the Typewriter tool have been denied. (For more on Acrobat Security and preventing the Typewriter tool from being accessed by a form recipient, see Chapter 12). If you're using Adobe Reader, the Typewriter is not available unless the form is not secured and is enabled with Adobe Reader usage rights.

Click on the page where you want to type text, and an I-beam cursor appears. Type the text on a line. You'll notice right away that the default font is Courier, and you don't have much paragraph formatting control. In Acrobat versions prior to version 9, your font choices were limited to Courier. In Acrobat 9, you have options for changing fonts and some font attributes.

If you want to stop typing on one block of text and start a new block, press the Escape (Esc) key. Then click the Typewriter tool and click again on the page in an area where you want to start a new block of text.

The Typewriter tools in the Typewriter toolbar from left to right, as shown in Figure 7.28, include the Typewriter tool, the Text Smaller tool, the Text Larger tool, the Decrease Line Spacing tool, the Increase Line Spacing tool, the Text Color pop-up palette, the Font Pull-down menu, and the Font Size pull-down menu. If you want to move a text block after typing, use the Select Object tool.

FIGURE 7.28

Click the Typewriter tool, and click on a page to type text. The text defaults to Courier font.

You'll often find that you can't quite get the line spacing right for the form you fill in using the Typewriter tool. However, when a form recipient needs to fill in a form where no form fields appear on a document, using this tool saves some time over printing, completing by hand, and then faxing the form back to the form author.

Typewriter Tool Avoidances

All text typed with the Typewriter tool appears as comment notes on a form. You can check to see if the Typewriter tool was used on a form by clicking the Comments panel icon to expand the Comments panel.

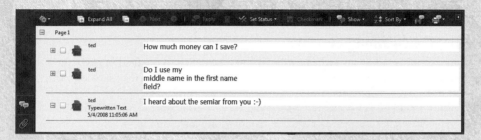

When designing PDF forms, always avoid using the Typewriter tool for text used as part of your form design. Adding text with the Typewriter tool makes your form appear sloppy, and form recipients can get confused by seeing a list of comments in the Comments panel. If you need to add more text to a form, do so in the original authoring program and recreate the PDF file.

If you populated a form with fields and you need to make changes to text on a form, you can use the Document ⇨ Replace Pages command and replace the old background design with a newly created PDF. (For more information on using the Replace Pages command, see Chapter 4.)

Navigating form fields

To fill out a text field, select the Hand tool, place the cursor over the field, and click the mouse button. When you click, a blinking I-beam cursor appears, indicating that you can add text by typing on your keyboard.

TIP To begin filling in a form, press the Tab key on your keyboard. When the Hand tool is selected and the cursor is not active in any field, pressing the Tab key places the cursor in the first field on the form.

To navigate to the next field for more text entry, you can make one of two choices: Click in the next field, or press the Tab key on your keyboard. When you press the Tab key, the cursor jumps to the next field, according to an order the PDF author specified in Acrobat when the form was designed. Be certain the Hand tool is selected, and a cursor appears in a field box when you press the Tab key. If you have any other tool selected, you can tab through the fields and type data in the field boxes; however, if you click with the mouse when another tool is selected, you make edits according to the active tool.

When selecting from choices in radio button or check box fields, click in the radio button or check box. The display changes to show a small solid circle or check mark within a box or other kind of user-defined symbol from options you select for button/check box styles. When using a combo box, click the down-pointing arrow in the field and select from the pull-down menu choices. List boxes are scrollable fields. Scroll to the choice you want to make using the up and down arrows.

CROSS-REF   **For more information on field object appearances, see Chapter 9.**

Form field navigation keystrokes

As mentioned earlier, to move to the next field, you either click in the field or press the Tab key. Following is a list of other keystrokes that can help you move through forms to complete them:

- **Shift+Tab:** Moves to the previous field.
- **Esc:** Ends text entry.
- **Return:** Ends text entry for single line entries or adds a carriage return for multi-line fields.
- **Double-click a word in a field:** Selects the word.
- **Ctrl/⌘+A:** Selects all the text in a field.
- **Left/right arrow keys:** Moves the cursor one character at a time left or right.
- **Up arrow:** Fielding combo and list boxes moves up the list.
- **Down arrow:** Fielding combo and list boxes moves down the list.
- **Up/down arrow with combo and list boxes selected:** Moves up and down the list. When the list is collapsed, pressing the down-arrow key opens the list.
- **Ctrl/⌘+Tab:** Accepts new entry and exits all fields. The next tab places the cursor in the first field.

Viewing fields

You may open a form in Acrobat where the fields are not clearly visible. Creating form fields on white backgrounds for fields with no border or fill color makes a field invisible when opened in an Acrobat viewer.

If you start to fill in a form and can't see the form fields, click the Highlight Fields button on the Forms Document Message bar. All fields are highlighted with a color specified in the Forms Preferences. In Figure 7.29, the fields are white in the form design but highlighted with the default blue highlight color. Some of the lines indicating where data needs to be typed are drawn across the form without separations indicating where one field ends and another begins. When we click the Highlight Fields button in the top-right corner of the Forms Document Message bar, the fields are highlighted, making it easy to see where each field appears in the form.

FIGURE 7.29

Click Highlight Fields in the Forms Document Message bar to display fields with highlights.

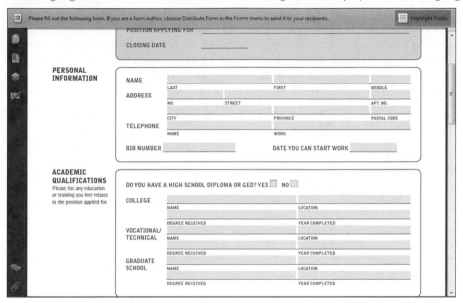

If you don't see the Forms Document Message bar, you need to adjust a preference setting. Press Ctrl/⌘+K to open the Preferences dialog box. Click Forms in the left pane, and uncheck the Always hide forms document message bar option, as shown in Figure 7.30.

FIGURE 7.30

Uncheck the Always hide forms document message bar box to display the message bar in the Document pane.

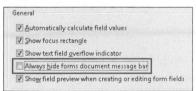

Understanding the Document Message Bar

The Document Message bar can be made visible or hidden from view by form recipients. If you open the Preferences dialog box (Ctrl/⌘+K) and click Forms, under the General items in the right pane the Always hide forms document message bar check box is disabled by default. If a form recipient checks the box, the form recipient won't have access for toggling on and off the field highlight colors.

General

- ☑ Automatically calculate field values
- ☑ Show focus rectangle
- ☑ Show text field overflow indicator
- ☐ Always hide forms document message bar
- ☑ Show field preview when creating or editing form fields

Highlight Color

- ☑ Show border hover color for fields

Fields highlight color: ☐

Required fields highlight color: ◼

You have no control over preventing a user from hiding the Document Message bar and other preference choices for Forms in the Preferences dialog box. There is no JavaScript you can write to prevent these Preferences changes.

When designing forms, you should try to avoid creating forms where users cannot intuitively know where form fields exist. For example, form fields on white backgrounds with no fills, no borders, and no design elements to clearly indicate where a field exists can be confusing for form recipients if they choose to hide the Document Message bar.

As a forms author, you need to anticipate all the controls that can be changed in Acrobat by unknowing users and try to create forms that are functional regardless of what preference options are changed by the form recipients.

Using Auto-Complete features

While filling in a form, you can enable Acrobat to record common responses you supply in form fields. After recording responses, each time you return to similar fields, the fields are automatically filled in or a list is offered to you for selecting an option for auto-completing fields.

To turn the recording mechanism on, you need to address the Forms preference settings. Open the Preferences dialog box by pressing Ctrl/⌘+K, and select Forms in the left pane. In the right-hand pane, open the pull-down menu under the Auto-Complete section of the Forms preferences. You can make menu choices from Off, Basic, and Advanced, as shown in Figure 7.31. Selecting Off turns the Auto-Complete feature off. Selecting Basic stores information entered in fields and uses the entries to make relevant suggestions. Select Advanced from the pull-down menu to receive suggestions from the stored list as you Tab into a field. If a probability matches the list, using the Advanced option automatically fills in the field when you tab into it.

By default, numeric data are eliminated from the data stored for the suggestions. If you want to include numeric data for telephone numbers, addresses, and the like, check the Remember numerical data check box.

Click Forms in the Preferences dialog box, and select Basic or Advanced from the Auto-Complete pull-down menu to use the auto-completion feature.

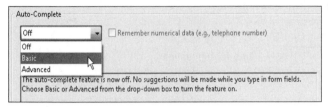

The list grows as you complete forms when either the Basic or Advanced choice is enabled in the pull-down menu. You can examine the list of stored entries by clicking the Edit Entry List button; the Auto-Complete Entry List dialog box opens, as shown in Figure 7.32. To remove an item from the list, select it and click the Remove button. To remove all entries, click the Remove All button.

FIGURE 7.32

To remove entries from your suggestion list, click the Edit Entry List button in the Forms preferences. Select items in the Auto-Complete Entry List, and click the Remove button.

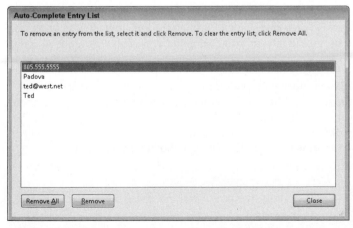

In order to record entries, you need to first make the selection for using either the Basic or Advanced Auto-Complete feature. To have suggestions for entries submitted as you type in fields, one of the two menu options must be enabled. When you select Off in the pull-down menu, both recording entered data and offering suggestions is turned off.

After selecting either Basic or Advanced in the Forms preferences and editing entries, fill out a form. If you recorded data after filling out one form, the next time you fill out another form you'll see suggestions, as shown in Figure 7.33. The cursor appears just below City, and the suggestion (Fairways) is derived from recorded data supplied on another form.

FIGURE 7.33

Enter a field, and a data suggestion appears in a drop-down menu.

How good is the Auto-Fill feature in Acrobat? When the feature was first introduced several generations ago, it was pretty clumsy. There wasn't much sophistication in controlling what data are recorded and what data are suggested when filling in a form. After several Acrobat revisions, there remain no changes in the Auto-Fill feature. It's still quite clumsy, and you'll find sometimes it may work well for you and in other cases, you'll find turning off the Auto-Fill option less distractive when completing a form. As a general rule, you might guide form recipients to not use the Auto-Fill features in Adobe Reader.

Setting Field Tab Orders

This is one item you should address before saving your final edited form. You should be able to press the Tab key to enter the first field on a page and tab through the remaining fields in a logical order to make it easy for the end user to fill in your form. Before deploying your form, be sure to check the tab order.

You can set tab orders in either Viewer mode or Form Editing Mode. How you approach setting tab orders varies a bit between the modes. When in Viewer mode, open the Pages panel and open a context menu on the page where you want to set tab order. Select Properties from the menu options, and the page Properties dialog box opens, as shown in Figure 7.34. By default, the Tab Order pane opens with options for setting tab order by making radio button selections.

FIGURE 7.34

To set tab order, open the Pages panel and open a context menu on the page where you want to edit the tab order. Select Properties from the menu choices, and click Tab Order in the Pages Properties dialog box.

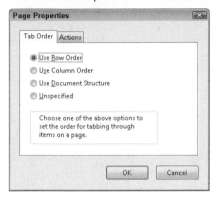

The options for setting tab order include the following:

- **Use Row Order:** Tabs through rows from left to right. If you want to change the direction for tabbing through fields, choose File ➪ Properties. Click Advanced in the left pane, and select Right Edge from the Binding pull-down menu. When you select Use Row Order and the document binding is set to Right Edge, the tab order moves from right to left.

- **Use Column Order:** Tabs through columns from left to right, or right to left if you change the binding as described in the preceding bullet.

- **Use Document Structure:** When selecting this option, you first need to use a PDF document with structure and tags. The tab order is determined by the structure tree created by the original authoring application when the file was exported to PDF.

CROSS-REF For more information on structured PDFs and tags, see Chapter 11.

- **Unspecified:** All documents you created in earlier versions of Acrobat that you open in Acrobat 6 through 9 have the Unspecified option selected by default. Unless you physically change the tab order to one of the preceding options, the tab order remains true to the order set in Acrobat 5 or earlier.

The order in which you create fields and add them to a page is recorded. If you happen to create a row of fields, and then change your mind and want to add a new field in the middle of the row, Acrobat tabs to the last field in the row from the last field created. Changing the tab orders in the Page Properties won't help you fix the problem when the fields need to be reordered.

Fortunately, you do have more options for setting tab orders, and the ideal method for changing tab orders is available only in Form Editing Mode. Switch to Form Editing Mode, and from the Sort menu in the Fields panel, be certain that Tab Order is selected. Open the Tab Order, and you find several menu commands, as shown in Figure 7.35.

FIGURE 7.35

Open the Tab order pull-down menu to display options for setting tab order when working in Form Editing Mode.

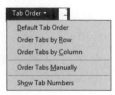

You have these options available in the Fields panel Tab Order pull-down menu:

- **Default Tab Order:** This order is determined by the order in which you create fields on a form.

- **Order Tabs by Row:** This option is the same as selecting Use Row Order in the Page Properties dialog box.

- **Order Tabs by Column:** This option is the same as selecting Use Column Order in the Page Properties dialog box.

- **Order Tabs Manually:** This option is automatically selected if you reorder fields in the Fields panel by dragging them up or down. If you make the selection here in the Tab Order pull-down menu, you can click and drag fields to change an order in the Fields panel, but it's not necessary to first select the menu command. The check box in the menu merely lets you know that the order has been set manually.

- **Show Tab Numbers:** Choose this menu item, and each field on a form displays the tab order number, as shown in Figure 7.36. You also can choose Forms ➪ Edit Fields ➪ Show Tab Numbers to display the tab order number on each field. Viewing the tab order number shows you at a quick glance how the tab order is defined on a form. If you want the order changed, drag fields up or down in the Fields panel to rearrange the order.

TIP When you want to change the order of a field on a form, click the field object and the field name is highlighted in the Fields panel. After you've identified the field in the Fields panel, you can easily move it up or down to reorder the tabs.

Prior to Acrobat 9, you had to set tab orders manually by clicking a field using a modifier key (Ctrl/Option) on the field preceding the field you wanted to reorder. You then had to click the next field in the order you wanted and click all subsequent fields following the first field you changed.

In Acrobat 9, you have the ability to rearrange fields by dragging them in the Fields panel. Click a field in the Fields panel, and drag up or down to move to the location you want to reorder the field tab order. As you move a field in the Fields panel, you see a right-pointing arrow and dashed line between two fields. Drag to the position, be certain the line appears after the field you want in the order, and release the mouse button.

FIGURE 7.36

Numbers on each field show you the current tab order.

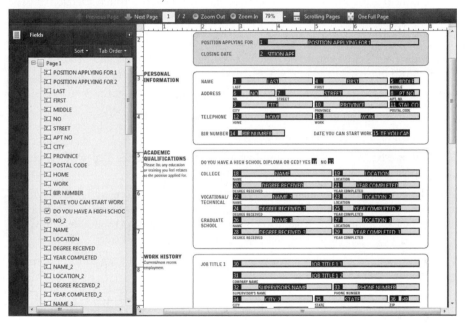

Summary

- Eight different Form tools can be used to create form field objects in Form Editing Mode.
- When you click a Form tool in the Form Editing toolbar, the cursor is loaded with the respective field type.
- Forms are added by clicking a loaded cursor on a form in Form Editing Mode.
- When a form field is added to a form, you can name the field and select from a few options in the mini Properties window.
- The field Properties dialog box can be opened in ether Viewer mode or Form Editing Mode.

- Acrobat automatically names fields when using auto field detection and when adding fields with the Form tools.

- Fields can be renamed in the Properties dialog box and the Fields panel.

- When creating tables, columns, or rows of fields, use hierarchical names.

- When naming fields, always be consistent with naming conventions.

- You can organize fields by aligning, sizing, and distributing them from context menu commands in either Viewer mode or Form Editing Mode.

- An anchor field is the one where all fields are aligned and sized within a selection of fields.

- You can duplicate fields across multiple pages.

- You can duplicate fields on a single page by opening a context menu and choosing Place Multiple Fields.

- You can add guidelines to a form by dragging them from a ruler well.

- Custom grids are set up in the Units & Guides Preferences dialog box.

- You can snap fields to guidelines and grids.

- Form authors should be familiar with filling in PDF forms, using the Typewriter tool, and setting up the auto completion options.

- When designing forms, avoid using the Typewriter tool as a replacement for modifying a form. You should return to the original authoring application, make changes, and then recreate the PDF form. If you have field objects on a form and need to modify a design, you can use the Document ➪ Replace Pages command.

- Tab orders can be set in the Pages panel in Viewer mode and the Fields panel in Form Editing Mode.

- You can reorder fields in the Fields panel by dragging them up or down.

Chapter 8

Working with Tables

Tables are part of many PDF forms. Tables are commonly set up with columns and rows having a header at the top that describes the content for each column and two or more rows of data following the header.

You find tables in a variety of forms. You might have a job application form where tables are used for work and education history. You see many tables in point of sale purchase forms where you find columns of descriptions, quantity, price, and totals across each row. In other forms, you see tables that make data entry and exporting data intuitive and easy for form fillers.

Tables can be as small as a few rows of data following a header or many pages of data all within a tabular format. In Acrobat, you need to design a table for the maximum anticipated rows of data that a form recipient is likely to use on your form. In LiveCycle Designer, you can create dynamic forms that spawn new rows based on user input or data flowing into a form.

In this chapter, we talk exclusively about creating and editing tables in Acrobat. If you want to know more about dynamic tables created in LiveCycle Designer, see Chapter 28.

IN THIS CHAPTER

Creating tables

Opening tables in other programs

Exporting data

Creating Tables in PDF Forms

When designing tables, you should use a table feature in an authoring application. Programs like Microsoft Word and Adobe InDesign both have table features that support formatting tables, such as adding columns and rows, adding headers, and alternating fills for cells according to rows; Figure 8.1 shows an example of such a table. Authoring programs like Word and InDesign also allow you to format text within cells and perform many more formatting tasks.

FIGURE 8.1

This table contains rows with alternating fills. With the calculations added to this form and the column of combo box fields, this form isn't a good candidate for using auto field detection.

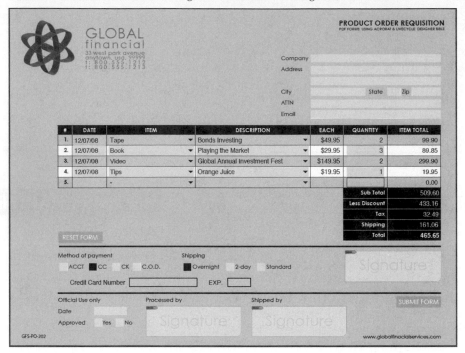

If you have to get the data from a table in a PDF form out to an authoring program, Acrobat recognizes the structure of a table and can easily export data to a spreadsheet application. If you use other authoring programs and use tables and indents, you might find more challenges when attempting to export data. As a general rule, try to use table features in programs to design your original forms that have tables.

After you convert your original authoring application documents to PDF, you can add fields in Acrobat to populate the forms with form field objects. Tables often require you to avoid using auto field detection when you open a form containing a table in Form Editing Mode. You might get away with populating a table that has no calculation fields such as a job application form; but when you have calculations to perform on a form, you most often are best served by adding fields manually.

Knowing when to use auto field detection and when to avoid it is helpful when you create PDF forms containing tables.

Auto-detecting fields in tables

You can always open a file in Form Editing Mode, populate the form, check over the fields, and delete fields that you feel are better designed by adding field objects manually on a form. This method works if fields are recognized for areas where you don't need some special properties such as calculation formulas for the fields.

Regardless of whether you use auto field detection or open a form and decide to manually add form fields, you'll want to know some standards in regard to adding fields in a table where auto field detection isn't your best solution. The forms that you should plan on manually populate with field objects contain fields such as:

- **Calculation formulas:** If you have to write JavaScripts to calculate row totals, discounts, sales tax, shipping costs, and grand total fields, then you'll want to use hierarchical names in a table, as explained in Chapter 7. Using auto field detection won't help you when hierarchical names are needed.

- **Radio buttons and/or check box columns:** If you have several columns containing radio buttons and check boxes, using hierarchical names will speed up your form editing by ten to one over using auto field detection and using independent field names.

- **Combo box and list box fields:** You might choose to auto-detect fields on a form as a partial solution when adding combo box and list box fields; however, the combo boxes and list boxes should be created manually. If you have long lists of options for each combo/list box, you're better off creating one field for each column/row manually and then placing multiple fields that duplicate the responses while changing field names for the remaining columns/rows. If you rely totally on auto field detection, you'll have to edit properties for each of these field types on the table.

- **Duplicating text fields:** This issue is not related exclusively to forms with tables. If you have a block of text fields that need to be replicated on a form, it's best to use hierarchical field names especially when populating several forms with the same types of fields. For example, suppose you have identifying information for one block of fields and another group of fields designed for emergency contact information. The fields are identical in the two blocks but they need separate field names for each block. You can easily copy one block, change the parent names, and paste the changed name fields back to your form. Using auto field detection requires you to set properties on each field separately.

- **When auto field detection doesn't detect fields:** Quite obviously as explained in Chapter 5, some form designs are not auto field detection-friendly. If Acrobat cannot detect fields on a form, then you need to add fields manually. With many different forms, Acrobat may recognize fields in many areas outside a table. If you find this to be true with some of your forms, you may only need to add the table fields to complete your form editing.

Creating tables by auto-detecting fields

For forms that don't meet the criteria for low-optimum results when using auto field detection, you can open the form in Acrobat and choose Forms ⇨ Add or Edit Fields. If the fields can be detected on the form, you're prompted in a dialog box to permit Acrobat to use auto field detection as described in Chapter 5.

To see the results of creating a form with a table where auto field detection is used, follow these steps.

 To follow the steps, use the *globalEmploymentApplicationRaw.pdf* in the Chapter08 folder on the book's CD-ROM.

STEPS: Using Auto Field Detection with Tables

1. **Open a form containing a table in Acrobat.** In our example, we use the *globalEmploymentApplicationRaw.pdf* document found in the Chapter08 folder on the book's CD-ROM.

2. **Choose Forms ⇨ Add or Edit Fields.** Acrobat prompts you in a dialog box for auto-detecting fields on the form. Click Yes, and the form opens in Form Editing Mode populated with fields, as shown in Figure 8.2.

3. **Examine the form.** In this example, the table in the Education area of the form was successfully populated with field objects. Acrobat did not pick up the Yes/No boxes/radio button fields needed to complete the form because no geometric shapes were added to the form design.

4. **Save the form.** The form needs some editing. Before proceeding, save the file by choosing File ⇨ Save As to rewrite the file with a new filename.

The form in Figure 8.2 is a good candidate for using auto-detection of fields. The form requires no calculation fields, only a few radio button/check boxes need to be added, and the form has no combo/list boxes. With a few edits, we can finalize this form and distribute it.

Adding fields to a table

Partial auto-detection of fields is most common with many forms and especially on forms with tables. That is to say, you let Acrobat detect fields, and some fields are missed when using auto field detection. You can expect to modify a form with manual edits using the Form tools in Form Editing Mode.

FIGURE 8.2

When you open the form in Form Editing Mode, you see the table in the Education area populated with fields.

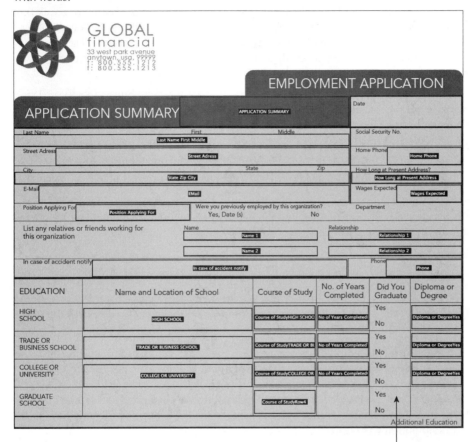

Auto field detection didn't
pick up the check box fields

For the form in Figure 8.2, we need to add some radio button or check box fields for the Yes/No responses. To see how this form would be edited in Form Editing Mode, follow these steps.

STEPS: Editing a Table with Auto-detected Fields

1. **Open a form with a table where you need to add more fields after Acrobat has auto-detected fields.** In our example, we use the form shown in Figure 8.2.

2. **Zoom in to the target area on the form where you want to add fields.** Click the Zoom In tool several times to zoom into the area where you want to add fields.

 Form Editing Mode doesn't provide you with a Zoom tool in the Form Editing Mode toolbar. To access the Zoom tool, press Ctrl/⌘+spacebar on your keyboard. Click+drag a marquee in the area you want to increase the magnification.

3. **Add a radio button field.** The Yes/No responses can be either radio button or check box fields. We'll use radio buttons to easily create mutually exclusive fields. In Form Editing Mode, click the Radio Button tool in the toolbar. Make certain the Keep tool selected in the toolbar check box is not checked. Doing so won't open the mini Properties window where you can choose the Radio Group Name.

   Click the loaded cursor in the first row where you want the radio button to appear. Don't worry about the size of the field for now. We'll take care of sizing fields after adding all the radio button fields.

4. **Name the fields.** In the mini Properties window, name the field. In our example, the first two radio buttons are used for Yes/No responses for graduating high school. We named our first radio button field *highSchool*. Type a field name, and press Enter.

 When naming fields, you don't have to press Enter. You can click a tool in the toolbar or click outside the field, and the name you last typed for the field name is recorded for the field.

5. **Add another radio button.** Click the Radio Button tool again, and click below the first field. By default, the second radio button is added to the same Radio Group Name. Type No in the Button Value text box, as shown in Figure 8.3.

 When creating a mutually exclusive set of radio buttons you can also click the Add another button to group check box to add another radio button field.

6. **Add an additional Radio Group Name.** Click the Radio Button tool again, and click the loaded cursor in position to add another field. In our example, the next row asks about receiving a trade or business diploma. We typed a new name for the field and called it *businessDiploma*. Then we added a second radio button to this group and set the Button Value to No. By default, Acrobat adds the name of the last group you identified when the last radio button was created.

7. **Add all the fields needed for the form.** In our example, we need two more groups of radio buttons. We named the next two groups *college* and *graduateSchool*, as shown in Figure 8.4. We changed the Button Value for the second radio button in each group to No and left the default value Yes for the first button in each group.

8. **Resize an anchor field.** In our example, the radio button sizes are too large. We want to reduce the size of each field. To do so, click the top radio button, press the Shift key, and drag one of the corner handles inward to size the field down. We'll use this field as an anchor field and size the remaining radio buttons to the same size. If the field is not positioned carefully within the area where you want the field to appear, click with the Select Object tool and drag it into position. This field will be used for alignment and positioning of the remaining radio button fields.

FIGURE 8.3

Type No for the Button Value for the second radio button field.

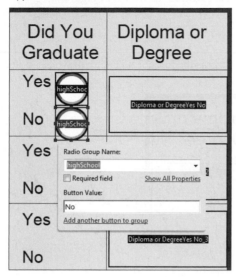

FIGURE 8.4

All the radio buttons are added to the form.

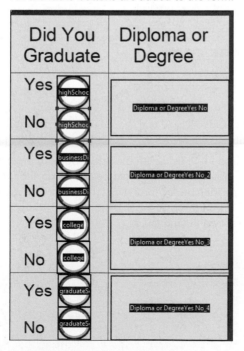

9. **Resize all the radio buttons.** Drag the Select Object tool through the fields you want to resize. Open a context menu after selecting the fields, and choose Set Fields to Same Size ⇨ Both (for both height and width), as shown in Figure 8.5.

FIGURE 8.5

Size the fields to the same size as the anchor field shown with handles on the field rectangle.

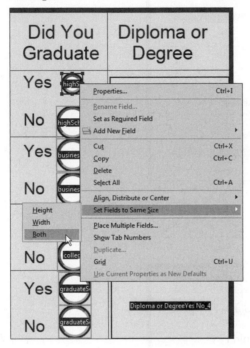

10. **Align the fields.** With the fields selected and the handles appearing on the top anchor field, open a context menu and choose Align, Distribute, or Center ⇨ Align Left.

11. **Distribute fields.** Click the bottom field with the Select Object tool, press Shift, and drag down (or up) to vertically place the field in proper position. You should have the top and bottom fields in the right position on the form. Drag the Select Object tool through the fields, and choose Align, Distribute, or Center ⇨ Distribute Vertically. The fields should nicely fit into position, as shown in Figure 8.6.

FIGURE 8.6

After sizing, aligning, and distributing the fields, they fall into the proper position on the form.

Did You Graduate	Diploma or Degree
Yes highSc	
No highSc	Diploma or DegreeYes No
Yes busine	
No busine	Diploma or DegreeYes No_2
Yes colleg	
No colleg	Diploma or DegreeYes No_3
Yes gradu	
No gradu	Diploma or DegreeYes No_4

The appearance of the radio buttons doesn't match the design of the form in Figure 8.6. We'll hold off for now on changing Appearance Properties and cover the options you have for appearances in Chapter 9. At this point, you should have an idea for some of the kinds of edits you need to make on forms where auto field detection doesn't pick up all fields in a table.

Notice that we first added the fields to our form and didn't worry about sizing and alignment. You could add fields with a guideline in place and snap fields to a guideline as discussed in Chapter 7. You could size them by sizing a field to the correct size and then choosing Use Current Properties as New Defaults. All subsequent radio buttons fields would then be created at the same size. However, you still need to use the context menu command to Distribute the fields. If you try to visually position fields in vertical or horizontal alignment, you'll rarely get it right the first time. Because we had to visit a context menu command for distributing fields, we found it just as easy to size and align fields using the menu commands.

Adding fields manually to tables

When creating tables on forms, you not only have to decide what tables work with auto field detection, but also what's the easiest way to populate a table. If you read the preceding section, you should have an idea for the complexity of making edits to prepare a single column of fields in a table.

Modifying fields created with auto field detection can sometimes take more time than starting from scratch and adding all fields manually. If you have to edit a few columns, you may as well populate the entire form manually and make edits to all columns and rows. Creating fields manually can sometimes take less time by populating the entire form than using auto-detection for partial field creation.

Creating tables with radio buttons and check boxes

Figure 8.7 shows a table with several columns and rows. This type of form is just as easy to create manually as it is by letting Acrobat auto-detect fields. If we open the form in Form Editing Mode and use auto field detection, Acrobat misses the first column. The Meeting Days column is designed for a Combo box so this column needs to be created manually. The remaining six columns are designed for check box fields. If Acrobat adds fields via auto field detection, the fields won't be mutually exclusive for the Yes/No columns following the Meeting Days columns. Therefore the last six columns will be unusable. The only usable fields we end up with after auto field detection are the second, third, and fourth columns where we won't need to rename fields.

FIGURE 8.7

A table such as this one is created more easily using manual methods than using auto field detection.

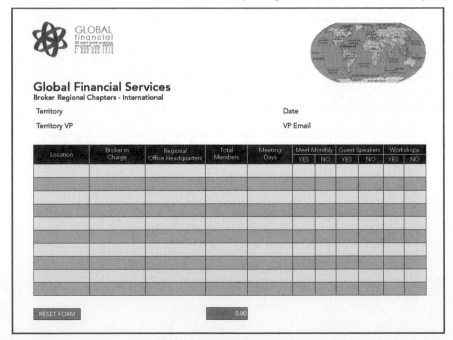

Adding the first row of fields

The first order of business for populating the form shown in Figure 8.7 is to add a row of fields in the top row. When you choose Add or Edit Fields, be certain to click No when prompted for auto-detecting fields.

After entering Form Editing Mode, add fields and set the properties appropriately for each field. The Meeting Days column is designed as a combo box with options for days of the week. The last five columns do not need to be populated. We'll just add one check box field for the first column where Yes/No responses are needed. The first two Yes/No columns appear under the Meet Monthly heading. The No column under this heading is intentionally left empty. The form, with the fields added to the top row, appears in Figure 8.8.

FIGURE 8.8

Fields needed to populate the table are added in the first row. The last five columns are left empty intentionally.

Location	Broker in Charge	Regional Office Headquarters	Total Members	Meeting Days	Meet Monthly		Guest Speakers		Workshops	
					YES	NO	YES	NO	YES	NO
location	brokerLeader.0	-------regionalOffice-- ▼	members	--------days------- ▼	monthly					

ON the CD-ROM We added the first row of fields and two fields at the bottom of the form to the *globalBrokerChaptersFirst.pdf* file found in the Chapter08 folder on the book's CD-ROM. You can use the file to follow steps in this chapter.

Adding the first columns of fields

Beginning with the column heading *Location* and ending with the column heading *Monthly Meetings,* we can use the Place Multiple Fields command to populate the rows below the first row. The Yes/No columns under the *Meet Monthly* heading need some special treatment that we'll use later to populate the last five columns, but we'll use the first Yes field under this heading.

To populate the first six columns, follow these steps.

STEPS: Manually Populating Rows in a Table

1. **Select the fields to be populated.** Click the Select Object tool, and draw a marquee around the fields in the first row. All fields on the form in the table are selected.

2. **Open the Create Multiple Copies of Fields dialog box.** Open a context menu and choose Place Multiple Fields to open the Create Multiple Copies of Fields dialog box. There are ten rows on our form. Type **10** in the Copy selected fields down text box, as shown in Figure 8.9, and click OK to populate all rows with the first five fields.

NOTE When you use Place Multiple Fields, Acrobat doesn't count the first field you created on a form. Inasmuch as you might think Acrobat is copying the first field and pasting nine copies for a column of ten rows, Acrobat is actually replacing the first field and giving it a hierarchical name. Therefore, you need to type the total columns/rows on your form in the Number of Fields text box in the Create Multiple Copies of Fields dialog box.

FIGURE 8.9

Type **10** in the Copy selected fields down text box to add a total of ten fields for each column.

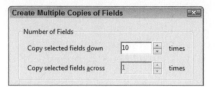

3. **Move the bottom row to fit within the last row in the table.** Click the Select Object tool, and drag through the bottom row of fields to select them. Drag the fields to the correct position in the bottom row.

4. **Distribute the fields.** You must distribute fields individually for each column. Select the first column of fields, and open a context menu. Choose Align, Distribute, or Center ➪ Distribute ➪ Distribute Vertically, as shown in Figure 8.10. Repeat these steps for the remaining five columns.

FIGURE 8.10

Select the first column of fields and distribute them.

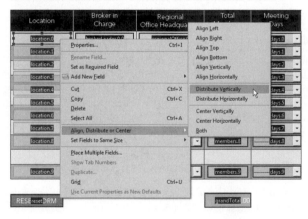

5. **Save the file.** The fields added thus far are shown in Figure 8.11. You can use the saved file to follow additional steps later in this chapter.

FIGURE 8.11

The first six columns of fields are populated in all ten rows.

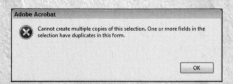

The first five columns are set up for the form. For the remaining columns, we have to use some different methods for the check box fields and use a little shortcut to easily populate the rest of the form.

Using Place Multiple Fields with Radio Buttons and Check Boxes

When you use the Create Multiple Fields command, all fields you want to duplicate need to have unique field names. If you try to duplicate fields with the same name, Acrobat opens a dialog box informing you that you cannot create multiple copies from the selected fields.

> **Adobe Acrobat**
>
> Cannot create multiple copies of this selection. One or more fields in the selection have duplicates in this form.
>
> OK

When you create radio buttons and check boxes designed to be mutually exclusive fields, you must use the same field name and choose different export values in the field Options Properties dialog box. Having fields with different names and different export values ensures that when one field is clicked in a common row of fields with the same field name, all other fields having the same field name are turned off as the target field is turned on.

The dilemma facing you is that you must use the same field names, but Acrobat won't let you place multiple fields if you do use the same field names. The way you get around the problem is to create one column (or row) of fields using the Place Multiple Fields command, duplicate the fields, and change the export value in the duplicated fields.

Adding mutually exclusive fields to a table

In Figure 8.10, we created ten fields for the first five columns and one field for the *Monthly Meeting* Yes column. This field is a check box field with an export value of Yes. Our next task to complete this form is to add the remaining check box fields to the form for the last five columns.

To get a better understanding of how to add radio button/check box fields to a table, follow these steps.

STEPS: Adding Mutually Exclusive Check Boxes to a Table

1. **Open a form with a table in Acrobat designed for several columns of check boxes used for mutually exclusive choices.** For this example, we continue with the form shown in Figure 8.11. This form has one column of check boxes formatted for our use.

2. **Duplicate a column.** Click the Select Object tool, and drag through the column of check box fields to select them. Press Ctrl/⌘+Shift, and duplicate the fields by dragging to the next column. Using the Shift key constrains the movement so your vertical alignment remains intact.

3. **Change the Export value.** Open a context menu on the selected fields, and choose Properties. Be careful not to deselect any of the fields. When the Check Box Properties dialog box opens, click the Options tab. Note that when you have multiple check box or radio buttons selected and you open the Properties dialog box, you can change the Export Value for all the selected fields. Type No in the Export Value text box as shown in Figure 8.12. Click Close after editing the Export Value.

FIGURE 8.12

Select a column of check box fields, and open the Options tab in the Check Box Properties dialog box. Change the Export Value, and you can apply a new export value to all the selected fields.

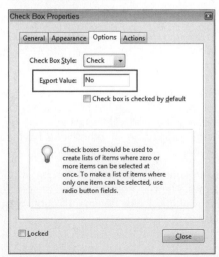

4. **Save the form.** Click File ⇨ Save to update your edits. This step is critical at this point. From here we're going to make some temporary changes, and we'll want to revert our file to this saved version.

5. **Open the Fields panel.** If you're not in Form Editing Mode, choose Forms ⇨ Add or Edit Fields. Be certain the Fields panel is open, and open the Sort pull-down menu. From the menu options, choose Alphabetic Order.

6. **Select the field parent name you want to edit.** Scroll the Fields panel to locate the *monthly* field. The parent name for the check box fields is *monthly*. We need to change this name, and all the child names nested below the parent name will change too. Open a context menu on the parent name, and choose Rename Field, as shown in Figure 8.13.

FIGURE 8.13

Select the parent name you want to edit, and choose Rename Field from a context menu.

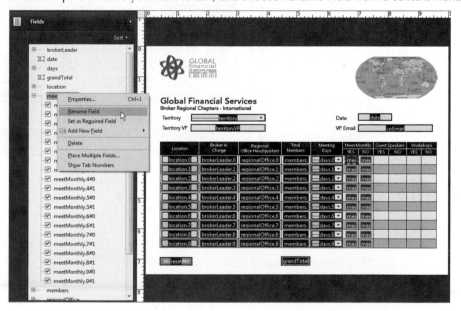

7. **Type a new name for the parent name.** When you choose Rename Field, the name for the field in the Fields panel becomes highlighted and ready to accept new text. In our example, we type *xxx* for the new parent name, as shown in Figure 8.14. This is a bogus name that we'll use temporarily.

8. **Copy the fields with the new parent name.** Drag the Select Object tool through all fields having the same root name. You should see both the Yes and No check box fields appearing with new parent/child names. When selected, choose Edit ⇨ Copy.

9. **Select Edit ⇨ Undo.** At this point, the copied fields on the clipboard have the parent name *xxx*. It does us no good to paste the same names on a form. We cannot change

parent names in the Fields panel for a partial list of names. Therefore, we need to undo the renaming the fields to return the first column back to the original field names—*Monthly*—while keeping the clipboard names at *xxx*.

10. **Paste the fields on the clipboard into your form.** Choose Edit ➪ Paste (or press Ctrl/ ⌘+V) to paste the fields in the document. By default, the Select Object tool is active. Click one of the selected fields, and drag them to position on the form.

FIGURE 8.14
_____

Type a new name for the parent name in the Fields panel, and all children nested below the parent likewise change names.

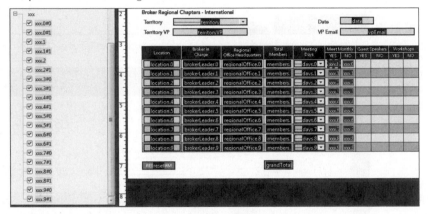

11. **Edit the parent name.** The fields are pasted with *xxx* as the parent name. In the Fields panel again, choose Alphabetic from the Sort pull-down menu and locate the *xxx* field's parent name. Open a context menu, and rename the parent. In our example, we renamed the field *Guest Speakers*.

12. **Add another group of fields.** The *xxx* fields are still on your clipboard. Press Ctrl/⌘+V to paste another group, and rename the fields in the Fields panel. We named our third group of fields *Workshops,* as shown in Figure 8.15.

13. **Save the final form.** Choose File Save As, and rewrite the form to optimize it.

The first time you follow the steps outlined here, it may seem a little lengthy and cumbersome. However, after you perform these steps a few times and can rely on memory to complete them, you'll find populating tables with mutually exclusive fields to be efficient and much faster than trying to edit field names and properties after Acrobat has recognized them with auto field detection.

Copying and pasting non-table data

Changing parent names and pasting fields back to a form is not something you need to reserve for columns and rows in tables. Even some of the simplest forms can take advantage of creating fields quickly and efficiently using similar methods you use for tables.

FIGURE 8.15

After you've pasted all three sets of columns, the form contains mutually exclusive check box fields.

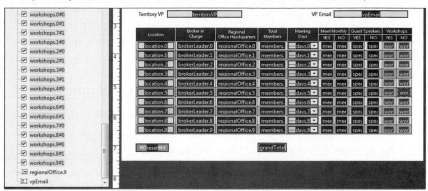

For example, in the form in Figure 8.16, we have a block of fields set up for employee identification, including name, address, phone, email, and so on. Some of the fields require special formatting, such as the state combo box field, the zip code field, and the phone number field.

FIGURE 8.16

This form has two sections with virtually identical fields. You can easily copy and paste fields in this type of form.

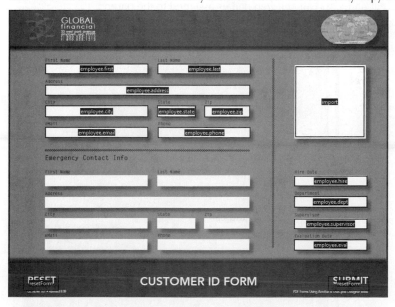

Below the employee ID section is another section for emergency contact information. The emergency contact fields are identical to the employee ID fields. On this form, you can easily format all the fields in the first section and then copy and paste the fields for the emergency contact fields. To see how easy it is to perform the task, follow these steps.

ON the CD-ROM To follow the steps here, you can use the *globalCreditApp.pdf* form in the Chapter08 folder on the book's CD-ROM.

STEPS: Copying and Pasting Fields with Hierarchical Names

1. **Open a file that requires setting up two identical blocks of fields.** In our example, we use the *globalCreditApp.pdf* form on the CD-ROM.

2. **Open the form in Form Editing Mode.** Choose Forms ⇨ Add or Edit Fields.

3. **Rename the parent name for the employee ID fields.** Choose Alphabetic from the Sort pull-down menu, and click the *employee* parent name as shown in Figure 8.17. If you click again on the parent name, the name is highlighted and ready to accept new text. Type *emergency* for the parent name.

4. **Select the renamed fields.** Drag the Select Object tool through the *emergency* fields, and press Ctrl/⌘+C to copy the fields to the clipboard.

FIGURE 8.17

Click once on a parent name, and click again to highlight the text. Type a new name to change the parent name and all children names assigned to the parent.

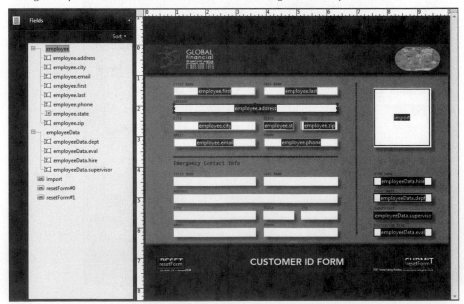

5. **Choose Edit ⇨ Undo.** The employee fields return to the default parent names when you opened the file while the fields on the clipboard remain with the *emergency* parent name.

6. **Paste the fields.** You don't need to open the fields panel and change names on this form, so you can use either Form Editing Mode or Viewer mode and paste the fields. If using Viewer mode, click the Select Object tool and then press Ctrl/⌘+V. The final result is shown in Figure 8.18.

FIGURE 8.18

You can paste the fields on the clipboard while in Viewer mode.

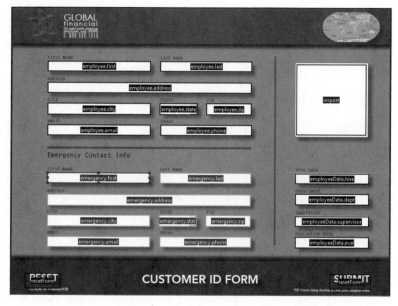

Converting Tables to Application Documents

At best, a table exported to another format requires lots of revision if you need it re-edited in an authoring application. A Microsoft Word file, Excel file, or Adobe InDesign file converted to PDF won't get converted back to the authoring program with the original look and design elements created in the native application document as a completely editable table. Still, you can obtain some interesting results when exporting PDFs as tables for purposes of redesigning forms and using tables for other layout uses.

The primary thing to keep in mind is that you have two completely different types of data to work with when exporting PDF files to other file formats. You have the background design that comprises one form of data, and you have the form fields (if populated) with another set of data. In their original state, you cannot export both background data and form data together in another file format.

You can flatten form fields to eliminate the field objects while retaining any data contained in form fields and then export the layout and the data together to another format. After you flatten the form fields, however, you lose all field attributes, and the document is no longer a PDF form.

 For more information on flattening fields, see Chapter 13.

If you're concerned with the data only, then exporting table data is perhaps the most successful thing you can do regarding table data exports. Fortunately, Acrobat provides some impressive options for exporting table data.

Exporting tables to Microsoft Excel

In terms of background design, exporting to Microsoft Excel format sends data to individual cells without retaining any design elements. Only the text is exported when you select background text and export to a spreadsheet.

To export a background layout to Excel, select text on a form with the Select tool. If you want the entire form exported in addition to any tables on the form, press Ctrl/⌘+A to select all text. With the text selected, open a context menu and choose Open Table in Spreadsheet, as shown in Figure 8.19.

As you might expect, data are exported to a spreadsheet with data appearing in individual cells. As you can see in Figure 8.20, this type of file is fairly useless for redesign purposes when the data appears in a Microsoft Excel spreadsheet.

When it comes to table exports to spreadsheets, the only real use you'll find worthwhile is when exporting field data.

CROSS-REF For information related to exporting field data, see "Exporting Table Data" later in this chapter.

FIGURE 8.19

Select text with the Select tool, and from a context menu, choose Open Table in Spreadsheet.

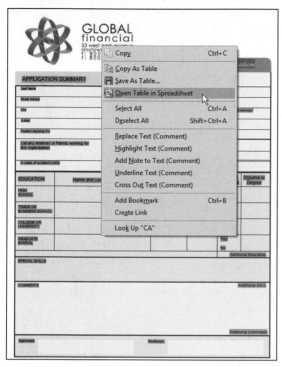

FIGURE 8.20

Data are exported to a spreadsheet as text only and without any design elements.

	A	B	C	D	E
1	NAMICMARINE" SUPPDynamic Marine Supply 555 Spinnaker	CA 93003 800-555-1234 "			
2	DYLYhttp://www.dynamicMarine.com "				
3	APPLICATION SUMMARY	Date			
4	Last Name	First	Middle	Social Security No.	
5	Street Adress			Home Phone	
6	City	State	Zip	How Long at Present Ad	
7	E-Mail			Wages Expected	
8	Position Applying For		Were you previously	Department	
9	List any relatives or friends working for this organization	Name	Relationship		
10					
11					
12	In case of accident notify			Phone	
13	EDUCATION	Name and Location of School	Course of Study	No. of Years Completed	Did You Gradua
14	HIGH SCHOOL				Yes No
15	TRADE OR BUSINESS SCHOOL				Yes No
16	COLLEGE OR UNIVERSITY				Yes No
17	GRADUATE SCHOOL				Yes No
18		Additional Education			
19	SPECIAL SKILLS				
20	COMMENTS	Additional Skills			
21		Additional Comments			
22	Approved:	Reviewed:			

Exporting tables to Microsoft Word

When editing a form design for forms containing tables, you'll find tables exported to Microsoft Word a better solution than exporting to Microsoft Excel. Word can retain formatting from PDF exports much better than Excel, and you have several options for getting PDF content into Word.

Using the Export command

Open a PDF file in Acrobat, and choose File ➪ Export ➪ Word Document. When the Save As dialog box opens, click the Settings button; the Save As DOC Settings dialog box opens, as shown in Figure 8.21. In this dialog box, you have some options choices.

FIGURE 8.21

Choose File ➪ Export ➪ Word Document, and click the Settings button in the Save As dialog box to open the Save As DOC Settings dialog box.

If you want to retain the original format of the form design, choose the Retain Page Layout radio button. Other options appear for tags, comments, and image settings. Make your choices, and click OK. Word does a nice job in converting the PDF content back to a Word .doc file. Not all designs will work for you, but you might get away with copying and pasting tables to new layouts. In Figure 8.22, the tables look fine as converted and are editable in Word.

FIGURE 8.22

The form exported to Microsoft Word.

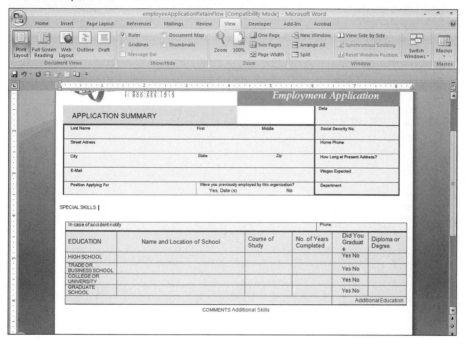

Using Copy as Table

Another option you have for exports to Word is to use a context menu command to copy a background design as a table and paste the copied content into Word. When exporting to Excel, we used the Open Table in Spreadsheet command from a context menu. When exporting to Word, use the Select tool to select text and open a context menu on the selected text. From the menu options shown earlier (refer to Figure 8.19), choose Copy as Table.

After the data are copied to the clipboard, open Word and press Ctrl/⌘+V to paste the clipboard contents. The result you get is text pasted as a table. You won't get any graphic elements when copying a table and pasting into Word. What you wind up with is simply text added to a table.

Ideally, you should return to an original document that was converted to PDF to make any design changes on forms. The methods discussed here are intended for those who need to at least get part of the data in a design application for forms where you don't have the original files that were converted to PDF. In a pinch, you can rescue some parts of a form. However, you should plan of doing lots of revision work when you get to either Excel or Word.

Exporting Table Data

Whereas Microsoft Word is best used for exporting PDF content to an authoring application, when it comes to field data, Microsoft Excel is the program to use. You can export field data to a spreadsheet from one form or many forms having the same data fields.

In Acrobat, choose Forms ➪ Manage Form Data ➪ Merge Data Files into Spreadsheet. Note that this command is available only in Viewer mode. When you select the command, the Export Data From Multiple Forms dialog box opens, as shown in Figure 8.23.

Click the Add button, and locate files on your hard drive to import. Select the files, and click Select; the files are listed in the Files to Export Data From list, as shown in Figure 8.23.

FIGURE 8.23

Choose Forms ➪ Manage Form Data ➪ Merge Data Files into Spreadsheet to open the Export Data From Multiple Forms dialog box.

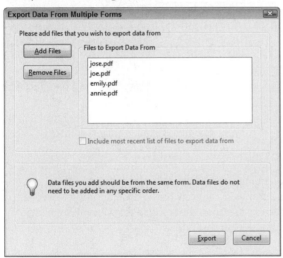

After adding files to the list, click the Export button; Acrobat aggregates the data and opens a spreadsheet in Microsoft Excel. In Excel, you can sort columns and rows, add new columns and rows, and delete any unwanted columns and rows.

CROSS-REF You have many more options for handling form data. For more on managing Acrobat forms data, see Chapter 15. For more on managing LiveCycle Designer data, see Chapters 31 through 34.

Summary

- You can use auto field detection with tables; however, in many instances tables can be populated with field objects more efficiently using manual methods for adding field objects.

- When manually creating fields on a table, you can use the Place Multiple Fields command only when applying it to fields all having unique field names. The command doesn't work when attempting to create multiple fields having the same name.

- When creating radio buttons, you can set Export Values at the time the radio button is created in the mini Properties window.

- You can edit a parent name for a row or column of fields, copy the fields, undo the edits, and paste a column or row on a form.

- Fields can be aligned and sized to an anchor field via a context menu command.

- After placing multiple fields, select a row or column of fields with the Select Object tool and choose the Distribute (Vertically or Horizontally) command to space the fields equidistant from each other.

- The Distribute command works only when distributing single columns or rows. If you distribute multiple columns or rows, the fields are distributed in a cascaded arrangement.

- You can export table design content to Microsoft Excel as a table. In Excel, the data are placed in individual cells and are not well suited for redesigning a form.

- You can export any PDF file to Microsoft Word format while retaining the layout of the form. Microsoft Word recognizes tables and enables you to edit the tables in Word.

- You can export form data from a single PDF form or multiple PDF forms directly to a spreadsheet.

Chapter 9

Working with Field Properties

S etting field properties is an important part of creating forms that are
fillable and work properly. So far, though, we've only had a glimpse of
the numerous field properties available to you for preparing fields to
accept data from form recipients.

As you'll discover in this chapter, you have numerous choices available for
setting appearances, options, formatting, and actions properties. As you turn
through the pages in this chapter, you'll find descriptions you'll want to use
as references and make some frequent returns to review items we discuss relative to properties. You'll find what you need to know to set up fields properly for optimizing your results.

Read through this chapter, and keep it bookmarked for future reference when
you need a short description for assigning different form fields properties.

IN THIS CHAPTER

Understanding properties

Knowing the field properties

**Setting properties for multiple
fields**

Working with field properties

Getting to Know the Properties Window

The process of manually adding form fields to a form is the same for all
fields. Click a Form tool in the Form Editing mode, click or click+drag open
a rectangle on a form, and release the mouse button, and a mini Properties
window opens. Some choices vary a little, depending on the field type created in the mini Properties window, but all fields drawn on a form have limited choices that you can make for field properties in the mini Properties
window. For a much larger set of choices for properties settings, you need to
open the Properties window.

If you use auto field detection and Acrobat has populated a form with fields, you can open a field's Properties window using the Select Object tool and double-clicking a field object.

Yet another way to open the Properties window is to select a field with the Select Object tool in either Form Editing Mode or Viewer mode and open a context menu. From the menu commands, choose Properties at the top of the context menu.

One last method for opening Properties is to select a field in Form Editing Mode and choose Forms ⇨ Show Field Properties. Regardless of the method you use and regardless of what field you choose to address Properties, the Properties window opens.

Using default views

When you first open the Properties window in a new Acrobat session, the General tab shown in Figure 9.1 is selected, showing the settings identified as General properties. The General tab also opens for all field types when you open a field's Properties window.

FIGURE 9.1

By default, a field's General Properties open when you start a new Acrobat session.

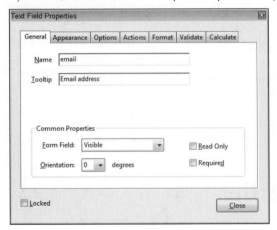

If you work with text fields and open the Properties window and click on another tab, such as Appearance, all subsequent text fields in the current Acrobat session open the Appearance tab when you open the Text Field Properties window.

If you open a radio button's properties and click the Options tab, all subsequent radio buttons opened in the current Acrobat session open to the Options tab. Click another field, such as a digital signature field, and open the properties, and the default General tab opens. Change the view to the Signed tab and all subsequent digital signature fields open to the Signed tab.

In essence, Acrobat changes the default to the last tab for each field individually that you viewed in the current session only. If you quit Acrobat, opening any field's properties defaults to the General tab. If you change from the Appearance tab to the Calculate tab in a session for a text field, all subsequent views of the Text Field Properties window default to the Calculate view. The new defaults you establish remain in effect until you change a view in the Properties window.

Using tab options

There are eight different field types in Acrobat 8 and 9. Acrobat 7 and earlier had only seven different field types. The barcode field was added as a plug-in during the Acrobat 7 life cycle so Acrobat 7 users could make use of all eight different field types. In Acrobat 8 and 9, the barcode tool exists among the Form tools.

Each field type has various options in the different tabs respective to the field type's Properties window. The most tabs belong to the combo box and text fields. Only two tabs are common for all fields. The General tab and the Actions tab, where you can assign actions such as JavaScripts to the fields, are common to all fields. Other tabs hold various options specific to a given field type.

For a quick glance and resource to visit regularly, look over Table 9.1, which displays all tabs contained for all the field types. In the next section, we talk about each tab and all the options available for defining field properties.

TABLE 9.1

Tab Options for Field Types in the Field Properties Window

Field Type	General	Appearance	Options	Actions	Format	Validate	Calculate	Selection Change	Signed	Value
Button	X	X	X	X						
Check Box	X	X	X	X						
Combo Box	X	X	X	X	X	X	X			
List Box	X	X	X	X				X		
Radio Button	X	X	X	X						
Text	X	X	X	X	X	X	X			
Digital Signature	X	X		X					X	
Barcode	X		X	X						X

Understanding Field Properties Options

Table 9.1 shows the different fields listed in the first column. Across the top of the table are all the individual tabs you find in the Properties windows. The tab titles give you a general idea of what to expect for options choices in the individual tabs, but a clear understanding for all the toggles and controls in each tab is required for all Acrobat forms authors.

Working with General properties

The General properties tab (refer to Figure 9.1) is the default tab where general properties are assigned. These properties are common to all field types. The properties include:

- **Name:** By default, Acrobat adds a name in the Name field. As a matter of practice, you should type a descriptive name in the Name text box. Don't use spaces in names, and try to use parent/child names for fields in common groups, as discussed in Chapter 7.

- **Tooltip:** Type a name, and when the cursor is placed over the field in Preview mode or Viewer mode, the text appears as a tooltip below the Hand tool cursor.

- **Form Field:** From the pull-down menu, you have four choices:

  - **Visible:** The default is Visible, which simply means your field is visible to form recipients.

  - **Hidden:** When the field is hidden, the field object and the data contained in the field are hidden to the form recipient. You might use a hidden field to hold a calculation that's not necessary for the form recipient to use when filling in the form. You also might use a hidden field to be displayed on a particular action. For example, suppose you have a form that asks a user to make a choice in a check box for a shipping address. If the mailing address and the shipping address are the same, the form recipient clicks No, indicating there is no difference between mailing and shipping address. The hidden shipping fields remain invisible. If the form recipient clicks Yes, indicating that mailing and shipping addresses are different, the shipping addresses are made visible. In Figure 9.2, you can see an example for this kind of use for hiding fields.

  - **Visible but doesn't print:** You might have some buttons on a form used for actions such as printing a form, resetting a form, submitting a form, and so on. When you mark the fields for Visible but doesn't print, the buttons won't print, thereby reducing the clutter on the printed form.

  - **Hidden but printable:** You might have a watermark, symbol, or other type of graphic as a button face that you want printed on the output but perhaps the graphic is too distracting when visible. If you encounter a situation like this, choose Hidden but printable.

FIGURE 9.2

The top view shows a form with fields hidden. When the form recipient clicks the Yes
check box, indicating the shipping address is different from the mailing address, the
shipping address fields are made visible.

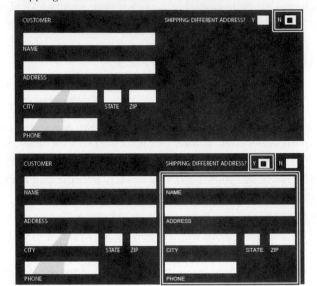

- **Orientation:** A field and a field's contents can be rotated in 90-degree rotations. By
  default, fields are at a 0 (zero)-degree rotation. Select from 90, 180, and 270 to rotate
  fields in fixed rotations. You might use an orientation other than the default 0 (zero) setting when adding buttons fields with icon images or text labels. Perhaps you might want
  the button to read vertically on a form to save some space at the bottom on a tight form
  for a digital signature.

- **Read Only:** When a field is marked as Read Only, the field is not editable. The form
  recipient is locked out of the field. A Read Only field might be something you use to
  show fixed price costs in a table where you don't want users changing a fixed purchase
  price on an order form. Another example is a value that is pre-populated from a database
  or with fields that show results of calculated data.

- **Required:** If a field needs to be filled in before the data are submitted, select the Required
  box. Note that Required is also an option you can choose in Form Editing Mode when
  you drop a field on a form.

- **Locked:** Locking a field prevents the field from being moved. You can still type data in
  the field or make a choice from options for other fields. This item might be used to fix
  fields in position as you edit a form. The Locked check box is visible in all tabs.

■ **Close:** The Close button is visible in all tabs. If you make a change in any properties tab and click the Close button, the property changes take effect. Also, if you click the features button (the X in the top-right corner for Windows, the top-left circle for Macintosh) to close the window, any changes made in the Properties also take effect. There is no way to cancel out of a field's Properties window to revert to the settings that were in place when you opened the Properties.

All the options you have in the General properties are available for all field types.

Assigning appearances to fields

The Appearance tab relates to form field appearances. The rectangles you draw can be assigned border colors and content fills. The text added to a field box or default text you use for a field can be assigned different fonts, font sizes, and font colors. These options exist in the Appearance properties for all field types except barcode fields, because barcode fields don't have an Appearance tab. In regard to radio buttons and check box fields, you have all options available except changing the font. These fields use a special font for symbols used as check marks. Figure 9.3 shows the Appearance properties for a selected text field.

FIGURE 9.3

Click the Appearance tab for any field properties, and make choices for the appearance of fields and text.

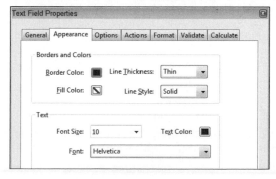

The Appearance options include the following:

■ **Border Color:** The keyline created for a field is made visible with a rectangular border assigned by clicking the Border Color swatch and choosing a color.

■ **Fill Color:** The field box can be assigned a fill color. If you want the field box displayed in a color, enable this option, click the color swatch next to it, and choose a color the same way you do for the borders. When the check box is disabled, the field contents appear transparent.

- **Line Thickness:** Select the pull-down menu, and choose from Thin, Medium, or Thick. The pull-down menu is grayed out unless you first select a Border Color.

- **Line Style:** You can choose from five style types from the pull-down menu shown in Figure 9.4. The Solid option shows the border as a keyline at the width specified in the Width setting. Dashed shows a dashed line; Beveled appears as a box with a beveled edge; Inset makes the field look recessed; and Underline eliminates the keyline and shows an underline for the text across the width of the field box.

FIGURE 9.4

The Appearance tab offers five choices for border style in the Line Style pull-down menu.

- **Font Size:** Depending on the size of the form fields you create, you may need to choose a different point size for the text. The default is Auto, which automatically adjusts point sizes according to the height of the field box. You want to exercise some care in examining your forms after using auto field detection and creating fields manually—especially large text boxes designed for comments.

  Acrobat sets the fields to an Auto Font Size by default. In some cases, the font size may look awkward on a form if the captions appear with text much smaller than the field text. You can make adjustments for the point size ranging from 2 to 300 points. If you want to use a custom point size for all fields on a form as you create them, add one field, set the Properties, and choose Use Current Properties as New Defaults. For more on setting type in the Appearance tab, see the nearby sidebar "Setting Font Attributes."

- **Text Color:** If you identify a color for text by selecting the swatch adjacent to Text Color, the field contents supplied by the end user change to the selected color.

- **Font:** From the pull-down menu, select a font for the field data. All the fonts installed in your system are accessible from the pull-down menu. When designing forms for screen displays, try to use sans serif fonts for better screen views.

Setting Font Attributes

When you want to determine a point size for the type in a field, click either the Preview button or the Close Form Editing button in Form Editing Mode. Type some text in a field, and then open the Text Field Properties. As you make selections in the Appearance tab for Font Size, the text is sized dynamically on the form field.

If you choose Auto for the font size and then move to the Options tab and check Multi-line for large text fields, the point size for the type is fixed to 12 points. If you remove the check mark for Multi-line in the Options tab, Auto font sizes expand to the height of the text field.

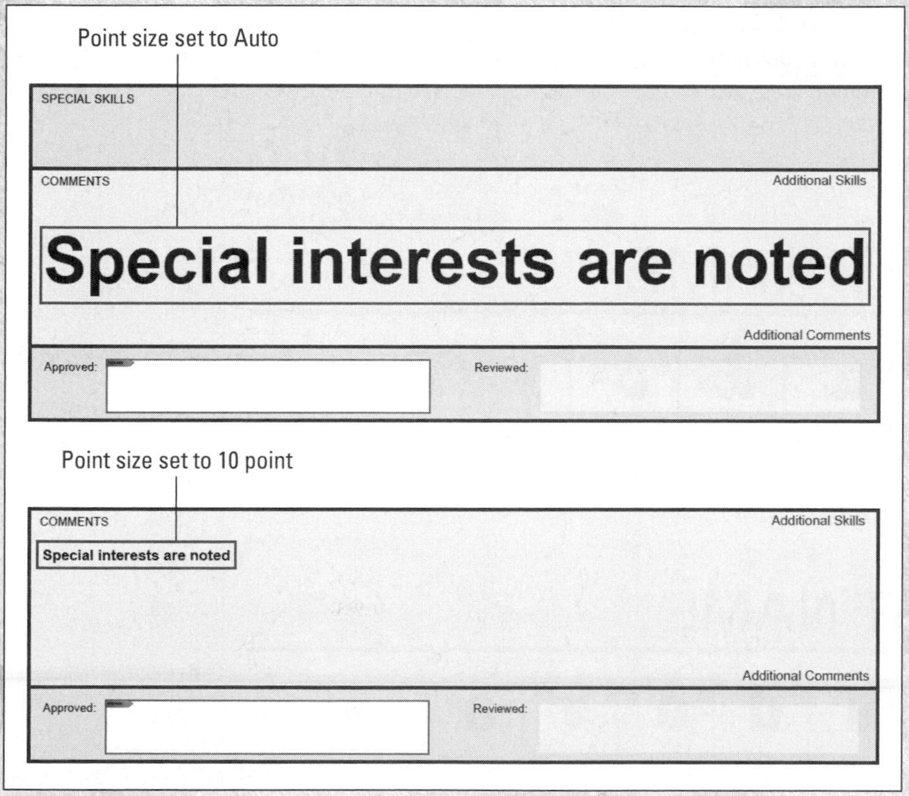

Point size set to Auto

SPECIAL SKILLS	
COMMENTS	Additional Skills

Special interests are noted

Additional Comments

Approved: Reviewed:

Point size set to 10 point

COMMENTS	Additional Skills
Special interests are noted	

Additional Comments

Approved: Reviewed:

When you choose a font from the Font pull-down menu, any font that cannot be embedded in your form is prohibited from use. Acrobat opens a warning dialog box and informs you that there are licensing restrictions. Fonts that can be embedded can be seen on other computers where the operating system has no access to the original font. If you want to check your forms for embedded fonts, open the Document Properties window (Ctrl/⌘+D) and click the Fonts tab. Scroll the list of fonts, and you'll see that every font embedded in your system is denoted as Embedded.

continued

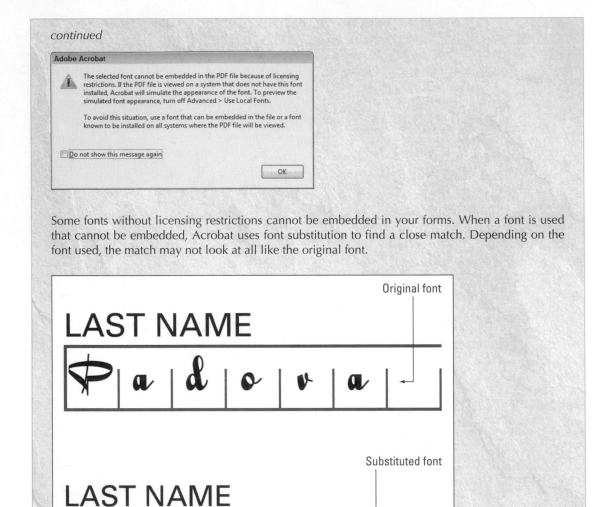

continued

Adobe Acrobat

⚠ The selected font cannot be embedded in the PDF file because of licensing restrictions. If the PDF file is viewed on a system that does not have this font installed, Acrobat will simulate the appearance of the font. To preview the simulated font appearance, turn off Advanced > Use Local Fonts.

To avoid this situation, use a font that can be embedded in the file or a font known to be installed on all systems where the PDF file will be viewed.

☐ Do not show this message again

[OK]

Some fonts without licensing restrictions cannot be embedded in your forms. When a font is used that cannot be embedded, Acrobat uses font substitution to find a close match. Depending on the font used, the match may not look at all like the original font.

Original font

LAST NAME

Substituted font

LAST NAME

The Appearance settings are identical for all field types except digital signature fields, radio button fields, check box fields, and barcode fields. The radio button and check box fields use fixed fonts for displaying characters in the field box. You choose what characters to use in the Options tab. When creating radio button and check box fields, you don't have a choice for Font in the Appearance properties. By default, the Adobe Pi font is used. Remember, barcode fields do not have an Appearance tab in the Properties window.

Setting Options properties

The Options tab provides selections for specific attributes according to the type of fields you add to a page. Options are available for all fields except the digital signatures field. Options tab attributes for the other seven field types include settings for text, radio buttons, combo boxes, list boxes, buttons, and barcodes.

Setting text options

When you use the Text Field tool to create a field and click the Options tab, the Properties window appears, as shown in Figure 9.5.

FIGURE 9.5

The Options settings in the Text Field Properties window

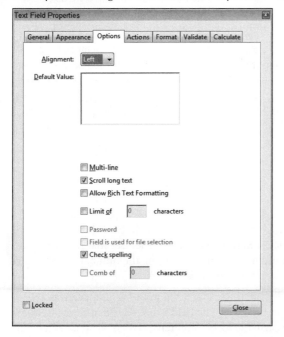

Each of the following attribute settings is optional when creating text fields:

- **Alignment:** The Alignment pull-down menu has two functions. First, any text entered in the Default field is aligned according to the option you specify from the pull-down menu choices. Alignment choices include Left, Center, and Right. Second, regardless of whether text is used in the Default field, when the end user fills out the form, the cursor is positioned at the alignment selected from the pull-down menu choices. Therefore, if you select Center from the Alignment options, the text entered when filling out the form is centered within the field box.

■ **Default Value:** You can leave the Default Value field blank, or you can enter text that appears in the field when a form recipient views the form. The Default item has nothing to do with the name of the field. This option is used to provide helpful information when the user fills out the form data. If no text is entered in the Default field, the field appears empty. If you enter text in the Default field, the text you enter appears inside the field box and can be deleted, edited, or replaced.

One use you may have for default text is to add a country name in a field designed for specifying a country of residence. If most of the form recipients come from Botswana, you type Botswana in the Default Value text box. The form opens with the text appearing in the field as a default. When a form recipient from Zambia fills in the form, the user needs to delete the text from the field and add the new Zambia text to the field.

■ **Multi-line:** If your text field contains more than one line of text, select the Multi-line option. When you press the Enter key after entering a line of text, the cursor jumps to the second line where additional text is added to the same field. Multi-line text fields might be used, for example, as an address field to accommodate a second address line or a comment box where several lines of text would be used to add a message.

■ **Scrolling long text:** If Multi-line is selected and text entries exceed the height of the field, you may want to add scroll bars to the field. Enable the check box to permit users to scroll lines of text. If this check box is disabled, from recipients won't be able to scroll, but as text is added, automatic scrolling accommodates the amount of text typed in the field. To see text without scroll bars, use the down arrow key. As you move the cursor down the text field, the text automatically scrolls up.

■ **Allow Rich Text Formatting:** When you check this box, users can style text with bold, italic, and bold italic font styles. Enable the check box if you want users to be able to emphasize a field's contents.

■ **Limit of [ ] characters:** The box for this option provides for user character limits for a given field. If you want the user to use a two-letter abbreviation for a U.S. state (CA, TX, MA, and so on), for example, check the box and type 2 in the field box. If the user attempts to go beyond the limit, a system warning beep alerts the user that no more text can be added to the field. You might use this option for limiting the number of characters in a postal code or limit names to a given number of characters.

■ **Password:** When this option is enabled, all the text entered in the field appears as a series of asterisks when the user fills in the form. The field is not secure in the sense that you must provide a password to complete the form; it merely protects the data entry from being seen by an onlooker.

■ **Field is used for file selection:** This option permits you to specify a file path as part of the field's value. The file is submitted along with the form data.

■ **Check spelling:** Spell-checking is available for comments and form fields. When the check box is selected, the field is included in a spell-check. Disabling this check box for many fields can be helpful so the spell-checker doesn't get caught up with stopping at proper names, unique identifiers, and abbreviations that may be used in some fields.

- **Comb of [ ] characters:** When you create a text field box and check this box, Acrobat automatically creates a text field box so characters are spaced equidistant from each other to the value you supply in the Characters text box. Comb fields are most often designed with separator lines or individual boxes in the form design. When you add comb fields to a form, one character fits in each separator box or between two separator lines.

  Be certain to deselect all other check boxes. If any other check box in the list is selected, the Comb of [ ] check box is inactive. You can set the alignment of the characters by making a choice from the alignment pull-down menu, but all other check boxes need to be disabled to access the Comb of [ ] check box.

NOTE Comb fields are limited to single characters. If you need to create comb fields where two characters are contained in each subdivision, you need to create separate field boxes for each pair of characters.

Working with check box and radio button options

Check boxes and radio buttons have similar Options choices. When you select either field type and click the Options tab, the settings common to both field types include:

- **Radio Button/Check Box Style:** If a radio button is selected, the title is Button Style, as shown in Figure 9.6. If the field is a check box, the title is listed as Check Box Style. From the pull-down menu, you select the style you want to use for the check mark inside the radio button or check box field.

FIGURE 9.6

You can choose various options for radio buttons and check boxes, including those for the style of the check marks or radio buttons.

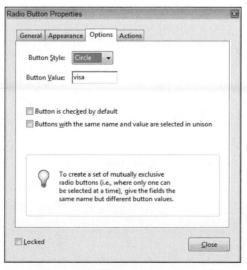

■ **Button/Export Value:** When a radio button is used, the next value you need to set is Button Value in the Options tab. When check boxes are used, the second setting in the Options tab is listed as Export Value. Both these items are essentially the same.

When creating either a check box or radio button to create mutually exclusive fields, use the same field name for all fields in a common group. To distinguish the fields from each other, add a Button Value/Export Value that differs in each field box. You can use export values such as Yes and No or other text, or number values such as 1, 2, 3, 4, and so on.

■ The creation of radio buttons and check boxes on Acrobat forms has been confusing to many users, and users often inappropriately create workarounds for check boxes and radio buttons to toggle them on and off. To help eliminate confusion, notice that the Options properties in Figure 9.6 include a help message informing you to name fields the same name but use different export values.

■ To further help PDF forms authors, radio buttons offer options in the mini Properties window for naming fields with a common group name (Radio Group Name) while adding different button values. You don't have to open the Properties window when adding radio buttons on a form to create mutually exclusive fields. If you want mutually exclusive check box fields, you need to make edits in the Options tab.

■ **Button/Check box is checked by default:** If you want a default value to be applied for either field type (for example, Yes), enter the export value and select this box to make the value the default. One distinction appears in the Options window between radio buttons and check boxes. The second check box with the circle shown in Figure 9.7 in the radio button properties is unique to radio buttons.

■ **Buttons with the same name and value are selected in unison (applies to radio buttons only):** For data export purposes, you'll want to add a different export value for each radio button and check box when designing mutually exclusive fields. If you don't need to export data to a database with unique export values for each radio button, you can add radio buttons to a page with the same export values, and by default, when a user clicks one radio button, all other radio buttons are unchecked. If you want all radio buttons to be checked when clicking one button in a group having the same name and export value, check this check box.

The Button/Check Box Style selection from the pull-down menu in both field types provides almost identical appearances. The single difference is that radio buttons appear with a circle when using the Circle Button Style, while check boxes appear with a rectangle, as shown in Figure 9.7.

FIGURE 9.7

Six icon options are available for check boxes and radio buttons. The appearances are virtually the same with the exception of the Circle Button Style.

Radio Button/Check Box Styles

	CHECK	CIRCLE	CROSS	DIAMOND	SQUARE	STAR
CHECK BOXES	✓	●	⊠	◆	■	★
RADIO BUTTONS	✓	◉	⊠	◆	■	★

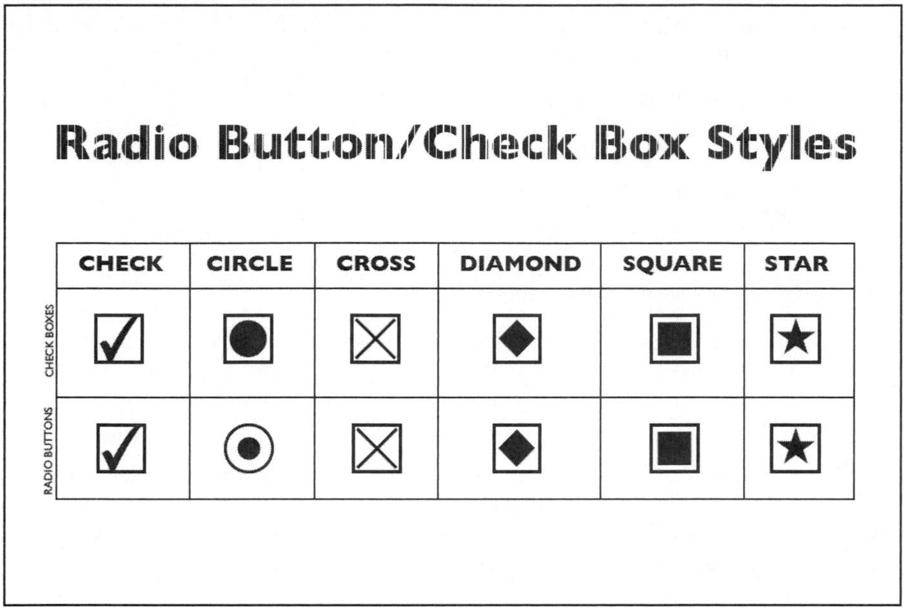

When to Use Radio Buttons and Check Boxes

Adobe designed the Radio Button and Check Box tools and attributes assigned to them to encourage you to create radio buttons when you need mutually exclusive field choices and check boxes when you want to use nonexclusive field choices. The idea is that if you have a credit card question on a form and ask a form recipient to choose a credit card option from several choices (Visa, M/C, AmEx, and Discover, for example), you would always use a radio button. If you have a section on a form where you want form recipients to select all the choices that apply for something like recreational interests, the check boxes would be designed in the group so a form recipient could make multiple choices.

There are two differences between radio buttons and check boxes. Radio buttons have one appearance difference when selecting the Circle Button Style, and radio button fields cannot be unmarked by a form recipient. If you use a check box, the form recipient can click to mark the field and click again to remove the check mark. With radio buttons, once a form recipient clicks a field, s/he cannot toggle the field again to remove the check mark.

continued

continued

Suppose you have a form that has radio buttons in a group to make a choice, but the choice within the group is not necessary. For example, suppose you ask a question about marketing and where the form recipient heard about your company. A response is something the marketing department wants to know, but checking a field in this group is not necessary to process an order.

Further suppose that a form recipient clicks a radio button for Magazine Ad to indicate how your company was discovered by the customer. Then later the form recipient decides that this answer is not accurate and wants to leave all radio buttons in this group unmarked. That may seem like a bit of a stretch, but these types of decisions by form recipients do occur.

If you use radio buttons, the form recipient has no option to uncheck a radio button field. After a field is clicked, she cannot remove a mark from the group. Some form recipients will actually reset a form and start over if they need to clear a radio button field.

As a guideline, you might think of using radio buttons for all fields in a group where a choice is required to fill in a form and use check boxes for all fields where choices are not required and when setting up fields that are not mutually exclusive. In terms of appearances, there is no difference between a radio button and check box unless you use the Circle Button Style.

Also be aware that both check boxes and radio buttons can be created without borders. You can use the background design of your form for the field appearances. For example, if you want circles for check box fields to appear on the form, you can create circles in your authoring application. When you create the check boxes, choose No Color for the Border Color and Fill Color.

Setting combo box and list box options

Combo boxes enable you to create form fields with a list of selections appearing in a pull-down menu. The form recipient makes a selection from the menu items. If all items are not visible, the menu contains scroll bars made visible after selecting the down-pointing arrow to open the menu. A list box is designed as a scrollable window with an elevator bar and arrows as you see in authoring application documents, as shown in Figure 9.8.

The two field types differ in several ways. First, combo boxes require less space for the form field. The combo box menu drops down from a narrow field height where the menu options are shown. List boxes require more height to make them functional to the point where at least two or three options are in view before the user attempts to scroll the window. Second, you can select only one menu option from a combo box. List boxes enable users to select multiple items. Finally, combo boxes can be designed for users to add text for a custom choice by editing any of the menu items. List boxes provide no option for users to type text in the field box, and the menu items are not editable.

FIGURE 9.8

View the combo box items by clicking the down arrow. After you open the menu, the scroll bars become visible. List boxes enable users to select multiple items in the scrollable window.

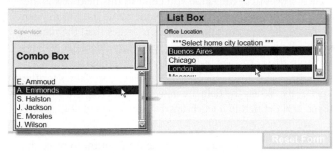

The data exported with the file include the selected item from the combo boxes and all selected items for list boxes. The item choices and menu designs for the field types are created in the Options tab for the respective field type. Choices for list boxes shown in Figure 9.9, with the exception of the Multiple Selection, are identical for combo boxes.

FIGURE 9.9

The Options settings for list boxes have common properties also found in combo boxes.

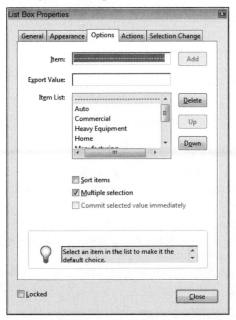

The options include:

- **Item:** Enter the name of an entry you want to appear in the scrollable list in this field.

- **Export Value:** When the data are exported, the name you enter in this field box is the exported value. If the field is left blank, the exported value is the name used in the item description typed in the Item field. If you want different export values than the name descriptions, type a value in this field box. As an example, suppose you created a consumer satisfaction survey form. In that form, the user can choose from list items such as Very Satisfied, Satisfied, and Unsatisfied, and you've specified the export values for these items to be 1, 2, and 3, respectively. When the data are analyzed, the frequency of the three items would be tabulated and defined in a legend as 1=Very Satisfied, 2=Satisfied, and 3=Unsatisfied.

- **Add:** After you type an Item name and Export Value, click the Add button to place the item in the Item List. After adding an item, you return to the Item field and type a new item in the text box, type a new export value in the Export Value text box, and click Add again to add the item to the list.

- **Item List:** As you add items, the items appear in a scrollable list window. To edit a name in the list window, delete the item, type a new name in the Item text box, and then click the Add button to add the newly edited item back in the list.

- **Delete:** If an item has been added to the list and you want to delete it, first select the item in the list and click the Delete button to remove it from the list.

- **Up/Down:** Items are placed in the list according to the order in which they are entered. The order displayed in the list is shown in the combo box or list box when you return to the document page. If you want to reorganize items, select an item in the list and click the Up or Down button to move one level up or down, respectively. To enable the Up and Down buttons, the Sort Items option must be disabled. Note that only one item in the list can be moved up or down. Acrobat does not provide a means for selecting multiple items in the list and reordering them in unison.

- **Sort items:** When checked, the list is alphabetically sorted in ascending order. As new items are added to the list, the new fields are dynamically sorted while the option is enabled.

- **Multiple selection (list box only):** When a form recipient completes your form, multiple items can be selected. The form recipient uses Shift+click (Windows) for contiguous selections and Ctrl/⌘+click (Mac) for noncontiguous selections. This option applies only to list boxes.

- **Commit selected value immediately:** The choice made in the field box is saved immediately. If the check box is disabled, the choice is saved after the user exits the field by tabbing out or clicking the mouse cursor on another field or outside the field.

With the exception of the multiple selection item, the preceding options also are available for combo boxes, as shown in Figure 9.10. In addition to the List Box options, combo boxes offer two more items:

- **Allow user to enter custom text:** The items listed in the Options tab are fixed in the combo box on the Acrobat form by default. If this check box is enabled, the user can create a custom value. Acrobat locks out some items from being edited.

- **Check spelling:** Spell-checking is performed when a user types a custom value. As text is typed, the spelling is checked. Found spelling errors are underlined in red text as the user types data into the field.

FIGURE 9.10

The Options tab for combo boxes also includes choices for Allow user to enter custom text and for Check spelling.

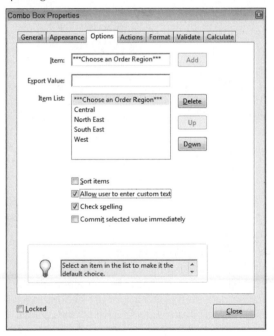

Setting Combo Box and List Box Defaults

When you create combo boxes and list boxes, the item selected in the Item list is the default choice that appears on your form. If you select one of the options in the list and exit the respective field properties, the selected item becomes the default. A form recipient may pass by this field, and the default choice will be exported when you export the data or it will appear as a choice a form recipient made when viewing the PDF document.

For a better solution, add an item to a list by typing a series of spaces created with the spacebar, a series of asterisks (*) or other character, or a description such as ***Please Choose Your Favorite Ice Cream Flavor***. You can sort your list alphabetically and then uncheck the Sort items check box. Your list still remains sorted. Next, click the item you want to use as a default and click the Up button in the Options tab to move the item to the top of the list. Select this item before closing the Properties window, and your selected item becomes the new default.

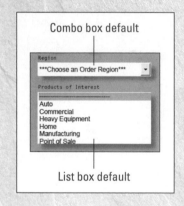

Using button options

Buttons differ from all other fields when it comes to appearance. You can create and use custom icons for button displays from PDF documents or file types compatible with Convert to PDF from File. Rather than entering data or toggling a data field, buttons typically execute an action. You might use a button to clear a form, export data, import data from a data file, or use buttons as navigation links. When you add a button to a page, the Options tab attributes change to those shown in Figure 9.11.

FIGURE 9.11

The Options tab for the Button field properties includes options for button face displays and several different mouse behaviors.

When you create a button, you make choices from the Options tab for the highlight view of the button, the behavior of the mouse cursor, and the text and icon views. The Options attributes for buttons are as follows:

- **Layout:** Several views are available for displaying a button with or without a label, which you add in the Label field described later in this list. The choices from the pull-down menu for Layout provide choices for displaying a button icon with text appearing at the top, bottom, left, or right side of the icon, or over the icon. Figure 9.12 shows the different Layout options you can set in the Options tab of the Button Field Properties window.

- **Behavior:** The Behavior options affect the appearance of the button when the button is clicked. The None option specifies no highlight when the button is clicked. Invert momentarily inverts the colors of the button when clicked. Outline displays a keyline border around the button, and Push makes the button appear to move in on Mouse Down and out on Mouse Up.

- **Icon and Label State:** Three choices are available in the list when you select Push in the Behavior pull-down menu. Up displays the highlight action when the mouse button is released. Down displays the highlight action when the mouse button is pressed. Rollover changes the icon when a second icon has been added to the rollover option. When the user moves the mouse cursor over the button without clicking, the image changes to the second icon you choose—this behavior was designed to replicate the same effects used in HTML buttons on Web pages.

FIGURE 9.12

The Layout options include Label only; Icon only; Icon top, label bottom; Label top, icon bottom; Icon left, label right; Label left, icon right; and Label over icon.

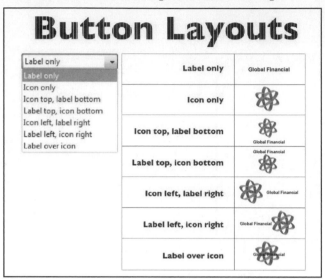

- **Label:** If you've selected a layout that includes a label, type text in the Label text box for the label you want to use. Labels are shown when one of the options for the layout includes a label view with or without the icon. You might frequently use labels such as Reset Form, Submit Form, Print Form, and so on when your design doesn't provide the text for setting buttons for these actions.

- **Choose Icon:** When you use an icon for a button face, click Choose Icon to open the Select Icon window. In the Select Icon window, use a Browse button to open a navigation window where you locate a file for the button face. The file can be a PDF document or a file compatible with converting to PDF from within Acrobat. The size of the file can be as small as the actual icon size or as large as a letter-size page or larger. Acrobat automatically scales the image to fit within the form field rectangle drawn with the Button tool. When you select an icon, it is displayed as a thumbnail in the Select Icon dialog box.

- **Clear:** You can eliminate a button face by clicking the Clear button. Clear eliminates the icon without affecting any text you added in the Label field box.

■ **Advanced:** Notice the Advanced button at the top of the Options tab. Clicking the Advanced button opens the Icon Placement dialog box where you select attributes related to scaling an icon as shown in Figure 9.13. You can choose from icon scaling for Always, Never, Icon is Too Big, Icon is Too Small to fit in the form field. The Scale option offers choices between Proportional and Non-proportional scaling. Click Fit to bounds to ensure the icon fits to the bounds of the field rectangle. Sliders provide a visual scaling reference for positioning the icon within a field rectangle.

FIGURE 9.13

Click the Advanced button in the Button Options tab and the Icon Placement dialog box opens.

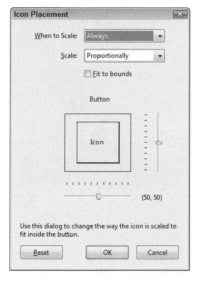

Looking at barcode options

Barcode fields have unique options designed to work with barcode scanners. You have options from pull-down menus and pop-up dialog boxes opened from buttons, as shown in Figure 9.14. In order to make choices for the items in the Options tab in the Barcode Field Properties window, you need to know what parameters are used by your barcode scanner, fax server, or document scanner. Setting the options requires reviewing the documentation supplied by the hardware you use to scan barcodes.

The Options tab for the Barcodes requires setting options conforming to the tools you use to scan barcodes.

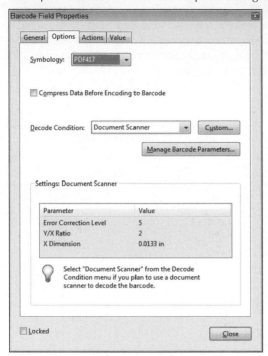

Using Actions properties

The Actions tab enables you to set an action for any one of the eight field types; the attribute choices are identical for all fields. Sixteen action items are available from the Select Action pull-down menu in any field's Properties window. The same action items also can be added to bookmarks, links, and page actions. Click the Actions tab, and the pane changes, as shown in Figure 9.15.

FIGURE 9.15

Click the Actions tab in any field Properties window, and the actions you have available are identical to all fields.

When you open the Actions tab in any field Properties window, you have these choices:

- **Select Trigger:** From the Select Trigger pull-down menu, you make choices for different mouse behaviors that are assigned to invoke the action. From the menu options, you have choices for:
  - **Mouse Up:** When the user releases the mouse button, the action is invoked.
  - **Mouse Down:** When the user presses the mouse button, the action is invoked.
  - **Mouse Enter:** When the user moves the mouse cursor over the field, the action is invoked.
  - **Mouse Exit:** When the user moves the mouse cursor away from the field, the action is invoked.

- **On Focus:** This specifies moving into the field boundaries through mouse movement or by tabbing to the field. As the cursor enters the field, the action is invoked.

- **On Blur:** This specifies moving away from the field boundaries through mouse movement or by tabbing out of the field. As the cursor exits the field, the action is invoked.

The most common trigger used by forms authors is the Mouse Up trigger. This behavior is consistent with users' experiences in working with computer applications and browsing the Web. You might use behaviors like On Focus and On Blur to open a field with a help message for a form recipient to move the mouse cursor over text indicating that a help message exists.

- **Select Action:** From the pull-down menu, you choose from one of the 16 action items in the menu. Although not likely to be part of every field type for every action, all Actions are available for all fields.

- **Add:** You first select a Mouse Trigger, then select an action from the Select Action pull-down menu, and finally click the Add button. Clicking the Add button does two things. For the action item you select, a dialog box opens where you define attributes for the action. For example, if you select Open a file, after clicking Add a Select File to Open, a dialog box opens where you can browse your computer and select the file you want to open. Choose Reset a form from the menu, and the Reset a Form dialog box opens where you can choose what fields on your form to reset. Each action item has a corresponding dialog box where you set up the action parameters.

  The second thing the Add button does is add the action item in the Actions list. After you click OK in a dialog box, the action is added to the list.

- **Actions:** The Actions window displays all actions you assign to a field. You can nest actions to perform multiple tasks. For example, you might Show a field on a Mouse Enter trigger and hide the field on a Mouse Exit trigger. When the cursor enters a field, another field is made visible. When you move the mouse away from a field, the field that was made visible is now hidden from view. To perform these actions you would add two actions to the same field.

- **Up/Down:** Two buttons enable you to sort the order of multiple actions. You must select an action in the Actions list and then click either the Up or Down button to move the selected action up or down in the list. All actions are performed in the ascending order you see appearing in the Actions list.

- **Edit:** If you want to change the attributes of an action, select the action in the Actions list and click the Edit button. You would use this button frequently when writing JavaScripts while debugging a script. If you have a Run a JavaScript action in the Actions list, clicking the Edit button opens the JavaScript Editor where you make changes to the code.

- **Delete:** Select an action in the Actions list, and click this button to delete the action.

Not all actions are items that a PDF forms author might use in constructing forms. Those action items that are more often used appear listed here first.

Go to a page view

The Go to a page view action might be used with forms when you want other documents associated with a form. For example, you might have a product catalog and a form as separate PDF documents. The documents could be independent of each other or assembled together in a PDF Portfolio. Assuming you have a cover page followed by a contents page, you might want a button on a form to link to the contents page. To do so, you would need to use the Go to a page view action.

 For more information on working with PDF Portfolios, see Chapter 13.

Execute a menu item

This action executes a menu item just like you would open a top-level menu and select a command. Not all menu items are available, but you do have choices for zooming views, closing a file, toggling Full Screen view, navigating pages, printing forms, and more. One common use for this action might be choosing the File ⇨ Print command for a form recipient to print a form.

Import form data

You can set up this action on a Page Action so that when a form recipient opens a PDF document, data are imported on the form, or you could use a button, link, or bookmark to execute the same action. This action might be helpful if you have something like a purchase order that needs to be filled in. All the identifying information such as company, employee name, company address, phone, e-mail, and so on could be a data file that gets imported on the form each time you open the document or click a button. The same data could be added to other forms such as a vacation request, an employee evaluation, or a travel reimbursement form, for example.

 For more information on working with data, see Chapter 15.

Multimedia Operation (Acrobat 9 and later)

Standard office forms that are simple and designed in a traditional manner won't make much use of this action. However, if you create more dynamic forms where multimedia is used for instructions on forms completion, displaying maps, charts, or other information, or some other animated event, you might use this action to play, stop, pause, or resume a media clip or Adobe Flash animation.

Open a file

This action is similar to the Go to a page view action discussed earlier. If you want to open a file accompanying a form on the first page in the document, use the Open a file action.

Open a Web link

You might have instructions that are updated routinely on a Web site. You can add a URL link for a form recipient to visit a Web page for obtaining the most up-to-date information on completing a form. This action might be used with very complex forms that need to be filled in such as income tax forms, real estate forms, healthcare forms, and so on.

Play a sound

Although you may not use this action frequently, if you decide to add some audio to a form for the purposes of helping a form recipient walk through the completion process, you can use this action to play the audio.

Run a JavaScript

This is the action you're likely to use the most as a PDF forms author. JavaScript adds great opportunity for making PDF documents interactive and dynamic. When you select Run a JavaScript and click the Add button, the JavaScript Editor dialog box opens. You type JavaScript code in the dialog box, or copy and paste code from a text editor to the JavaScript Editor. Click OK to commit the JavaScript.

CROSS-REF For more information on writing JavaScripts, see Chapters 16 through 19.

Set layer visibility

You can create forms as layered documents in programs such as Adobe InDesign. You might use layers for multiple language versions of your forms, to display some graphic such as a seating chart in an auditorium for an event, or playing a Flash video on a separate layer. When the form recipient needs to change layer views, this action assigned to a button changes the layer state.

CROSS-REF For more information on using layers on forms, see Chapter 13.

Show/hide a field

The Show/hide a field action is particularly useful when you want to display help messages or show fields that are filled out based on user responses. In the latter case, you might design a form that shows all the fields required to complete a form. If a form recipient responds to a question in one way or another, you might show additional fields that were hidden when the form opened in an Acrobat viewer to amplify a response.

Reset a form

Not all forms require a Reset a form action. Some simple office forms may not be good candidates for resetting a form, but complex forms might make use of this action routinely. You can add a single button to clear a form of form data or set up several buttons that you design to clear data in sections. If you create forms having several pages, try to avoid clearing the entire form with a single reset button. Items such as identifying information are less likely to be cleared by a form recipient than other parts of the form. Setting up reset buttons on a complex form requires you to think through the task of when it's best to add buttons for what parts of a form that need be cleared of data.

Submit a form

Unless you're working primarily on in-house forms stored on a company network server, the Submit a form action is perhaps the one action you'll use more than the other actions. You use this action to e-mail a form back to you, host the form on Acrobat.com or on your own Web server. When the form is completed by a form recipient the form is sent back to you via an e-mail attachment or directly to a server.

Remaining actions you find in the Select Action pull-down menu include Go to a 3D View, Play media (Acrobat 5 compatible), Play media (Acrobat 6 and Later Compatible), and Read an article. These action types are not likely to show up in many of your forms. If you want to use media and you prepare files for legacy viewers, you might use the play actions for playing Acrobat 5 and Acrobat 6 media.

As a general rule, several action items are used frequently to moderately for PDF forms authors, while several items are infrequently to rarely used by forms designers. Table 9.2 shows a quick glance at the use of actions in terms of how often the various actions are used by most PDF forms authors today.

TABLE 9.2

Action Items Frequency of Use by Form Designers

Acton Item	Frequent	Moderate	Infrequent	Rare
Execute a menu item		X		
Go to a page view			X	
Import form data		X		
Multimedia Operation (Acrobat 9 and later)*				X
Open a file			X	
Open a web link			X	
Play a sound				X
Run a JavaScript	X			
Set layer visibility				X
Show/hide a field		X		
Reset a form	X			
Submit a form	X			

* Adobe made many advances in Acrobat 9 for integrating Adobe Flash in PDFs. We expect to see forms authors increasingly more interested in including Flash video and Flash widgets in PDF forms.

Using the Format properties

The General, Appearance, and Actions tabs are available for almost all field types. Option attributes are available for all field types except digital signatures. The Format, Validate, and Calculate tab options are available only for combo box and text field types. To access the Format tab, select either of these field types. The Format options are the same for both field types.

When you click the Format tab, you'll find a pull-down menu for selecting a format category. To define a format, open the Select format category and choose from the menu choices the format you want to assign to the text field or combo box field. As each item is selected, various options pertaining to the selected category appear directly below the pull-down menu. When you select Number from the menu choices, the Number Options appear, as shown in Figure 9.16.

FIGURE 9.16

When you choose either combo box or text field as the field type, you can select data format options from the Format tab.

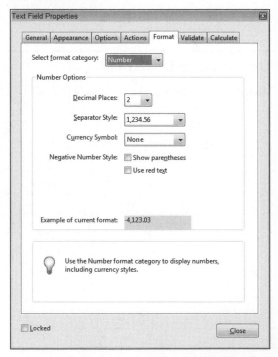

The Select format category menu options include:

- **None:** No options are available when None is selected. Select this item if no formatting is needed for the field. An example of where None applies is a text field where you want text data such as name, address, and so on.

- **Number:** When you select Number, the Number Options choices appear below the Select format category pull-down menu. The options for displaying numeric fields include defining the number of decimal places, indicating how the digits are separated (for example, by commas or by decimal points), and specifying any currency symbols. The Negative Number Style check boxes enable you to display negative numbers with parentheses and/or red text. When you design forms that use calculation formulas, you must format your number fields with a number format.

- **Percentage:** The number of decimal places you want to display for percentages is available when you select Percentage from the pull-down menu. The options are listed for number of decimal places and the separator style.

- **Date:** The date choices offer different selections for month, day, year, and time formats in various combinations.

- **Time:** If you want to eliminate the date and identify only time, the Time category enables you to do so, offering choices to express time in standard and 24-hour units and a custom setting where custom formats are user-prescribed in a field box.

- **Special:** The Special category offers formatting selections for U.S. social security numbers, Zip codes, extended Zip codes, phone numbers, and an arbitrary mask. When you select Arbitrary Mask, a field box is added where you define the mask. The acceptable values for setting up an arbitrary mask include:

  - **A:** Add *A* to the arbitrary mask field box, and only the alphabetical characters A–Z and a–z are acceptable for user input.

  - **X:** When you add *X* to the arbitrary mask field box, most printable characters from an alphanumeric character set are acceptable. ANSI values between 32–166 and 128–255 are permitted. (To learn more about what ANSI character values 32–166 and 128–255 are translated to, search the Internet for ANSI character tables. You can capture Web pages and use the tables as reference guides.)

  - **O:** The letter *O* accepts all alphanumeric characters (A–Z, a–z, and 0–9).

  - **9:** If you want the user to be limited to filling in numbers only, enter *9* in the Arbitrary Mask field box.

  - **Example:** As an example for an Arbitrary mask, a mask defined as A-BFM-9999 means that the form recipient can type any alphabetic character for the first character (*A*) and four numbers (*9999*). The result would be something like Z-BFM-1234. The characters *BFM* are part of the mask definition, and the form recipient cannot change these characters. To fill in a form designed with this mask, the form recipient would type Z1234. Typing more than one alpha character or more or less numeric characters would be rejected by Acrobat.

    When a form recipient fills in an arbitrary mask field, the form recipient needs some clue as to how to type in the data. You might add such a clue on the form itself if you use an arbitrary mask. Usually these kinds of fields are added in an *Official Use Only* area on your form, where employees in a company might use an arbitrary mask for a client or account number. Under these circumstances, the employees are likely to know what characters needed to be typed in the arbitrary mask field(s).

■ **Custom:** Custom formatting is available using a JavaScript. To edit the JavaScript code, click the Edit button and create a custom format script. The JavaScript Editor dialog box opens where you type the code. As an example of using a custom JavaScript, assume that you want to add leading zeros to field numbers. You might create a JavaScript with the following code:

```
event.value = "000" + event.value;
```

The preceding code adds three leading zeros to all values supplied by the form recipient. If you want to add different characters as a suffix or prefix, enter the values you want within the quotation marks. To add a suffix, use this:

```
event.value = event.value + "000";
```

Using Validate properties

The Validate tab helps ensure that proper information is added on the form. If a value must be within a certain minimum and maximum range, select the radio button for validating the data within the accepted values, as shown in Figure 9.17. The field boxes are used to enter the minimum and maximum values. If the user attempts to enter a value outside the specified range, a warning dialog box opens, informing the user that the values entered on the form are unacceptable.

FIGURE 9.17

Validate is used with combo box and text field types to ensure acceptable responses from user-supplied values.

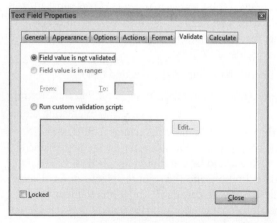

Selecting the Run custom validation script radio button and clicking the Edit button enables you to add a JavaScript. Scripts that you may want to include in this window are those for validating comparative data fields. A password, for example, may need to be validated. If the response does not meet the condition, the user is denied access to supplying information in the field.

Understanding the Calculate properties

The Calculate tab (supported in text fields and combo box fields) in the Properties window enables you to add calculation formulas. You can choose from preset calculation formulas or add a custom JavaScript for calculating fields, as shown in Figure 9.18.

FIGURE 9.18

The Calculate tab offers built-in formula options for calculating fields for summing data, multiplying data, and finding the average, minimum, and maximum values for selected fields. In addition, you can add custom calculations by writing Simplified Field Notation scripts and JavaScripts.

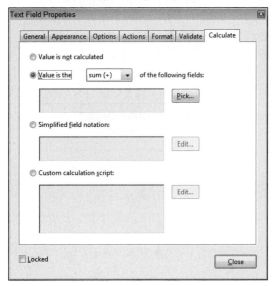

The preset calculation formulas are limited to addition, multiplication, averaging, calculating the minimum in a range of fields, and calculating the maximum in a range of fields. For all other calculations, you need to select the Simplified Field Notation or Custom calculation script radio button and click the Edit button. In the JavaScript Editor, you write JavaScripts to perform other calculations not available from the preset formulas. Writing scripts in the JavaScript Editor requires you to know JavaScript as it is supported in Acrobat. Simplified Field Notation is written in the JavaScript editor and follows syntax similar to writing formulas in spreadsheets.

NOTE Understanding JavaScript or Simplified Field Notation is essential. Even the simplest math functions, such as subtraction and division, are not available as preset formulas and require scripting to perform these calculations.

CROSS-REF For more information on calculating data, see Chapter 15. For more information on using Simplified Field Notation, see Chapter 15. For more information on JavaScript, see Chapters 16 through 19.

Using Selection Change properties

The Selection Change tab, shown in Figure 9.19, is available for list box fields only. If a list box item is selected and then a new item from the list is selected, JavaScript code can be programmed to execute an action when the change is made. As with the other dialog boxes, clicking the Edit button opens the JavaScript Editor, where you write the JavaScript code.

A variety of uses exist for the Selection Change option. You might want to create a form for consumer responses for a given product—something such as an automobile. Depending on information preceding the list box selection, some options may not be available. For example, a user specifies "four-door automobile" as one of the form choices, and then from a list, the user selects "convertible." If the manufacturer does not offer a convertible for four-door automobiles, then through use of a JavaScript in the Selection Change tab, the user is informed that this selection cannot be made based on previous information supplied in the form. The warning message could include information on alternative selections that the user could make.

FIGURE 9.19

The Selection Change tab is available only for list box fields. When using a Selection Change option, you'll need to program JavaScript code to reflect the action when a change in selection occurs.

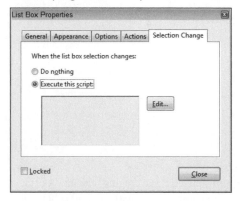

Setting digital signature fields properties

The Digital Signature tool enables you to create a field used for electronically signing a document with a digital signature. The Signed tab, shown in Figure 9.20, offers these options for digital signature behaviors:

- **Nothing happens when signed:** As the item description suggests, the field is signed but no action takes place upon signing.

- **Mark as read-only:** When signed, the selected fields are changed to read-only fields, locking them against further edits. You can mark all fields by selecting the radio button and choosing All fields from the pull-down menu. Choose All fields except these to isolate a few fields not marked for read-only, or select Just these fields to mark a few fields for read-only.

■ **This script executes when the field is signed:** Select the radio button, and click the Edit button to open the JavaScript Editor. Write a script in the JavaScript Editor that executes when the field is signed. An example of a JavaScript you might use with a digital signature is date-stamping a document when it is signed. You can write a JavaScript that adds a date in a text field marked as Read Only. When the form recipient signs the document, a text field is populated with the current date from the user's system clock, using a JavaScript. Because a user's system clock is not the most secure form of creating a date-stamp, you have to use a form server or a Web-based clock if you want the utmost security on sensitive forms.

CROSS-REF   For more information on using servers, see Chapter 34.

FIGURE 9.20

For custom actions when a user signs a form, use a JavaScript.

Using the barcode properties

The unique property settings in the barcode field are located in the Value tab. Options in this tab are available only with barcode fields, as shown in Figure 9.21. You have options for Encoding from a pull-down menu offering a choice between XML and Tab Delimited data.

Click the Pick button, and the Field Selection dialog box opens, as shown in Figure 9.22. You use this dialog box to determine what field data are added to the barcode. Uncheck those items you don't want added, such as buttons that invoke actions, temporary calculation fields, and so on. The Include field names text box offers an option to include field names along with the data in the barcode.

FIGURE 9.21

The Value tab appears only in barcode fields.

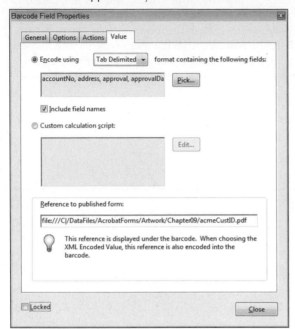

FIGURE 9.22

Click Pick, and check the items you want to appear as data in the barcode.

An additional box appears for adding a Custom calculation script. Click the radio button, and click Edit to open the JavaScript Editor.

Note that when you design forms with barcodes, you must pre-populate a form with data. After all the field data have been added to the form, you create a barcode. If there's too much data for the barcode to form, you'll see a message in the barcode field indicating that too much data exists on your form, as shown in Figure 9.23.

FIGURE 9.23

If the barcode can't create the data field, an error is reported in the field object.

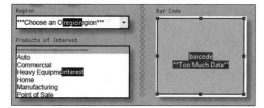

You have one of two choices to make the barcode functional. You can resize the barcode and make it larger until you see a barcode in the field, or you must remove data fields in the Field Selection dialog box shown in Figure 9.22 by unchecking fields. When the barcode can be successfully drawn on the form, you'll see a barcode appear whether you have the Hand tool or the Select Object tool selected.

Using the Properties bar

Many of the appearance attributes you apply in the Field Properties Appearance tab also can be applied by making selections in the Properties bar shown in Figure 9.24. The Properties bar is visible only in Viewer mode. You don't have access to the Properties bar while in Form Editing Mode.

FIGURE 9.24

Use the Properties bar to make changes to field appearances while in Viewer mode.

The Properties bar offers you the following choices:

- **Fill Color:** Click Fill Color, and the same color palette that opens in the Appearance tab appears for choosing a color fill for the selected field object.

- **Line Color:** This choice is the same as using Border Color in the Appearance tab for a field's Properties. Click the Line Color item, and a color palette pops up for making a color choice for the field border.

- **Text Color:** Again, a pop-up color palette opens where you can make a color choice for the text added to a field object. You might use a blue color for text added with the Label Only option for a Button Layout Style. If nothing but text appears for a button face, form recipients are more inclined to recognize blue text as a button or link.

- **No Line:** Click this button on the Properties bar, and the choice is the same as making the No Color Choice in the Appearance tab.

- **Line Style:** Again, the options are the same as you find in the Appearance tab for line styles of Solid, Dashed, Beveled, Inset, and Underlined.

- **Line Thickness:** This item also matches choices in the Appearance tab for choosing Thin, Medium, or Thick lines.

- **Font:** Choose a font from the pull-down menu.

- **Size:** Open the pull-down menu, and choose a preset font size or type a value ranging between 2 and 300.

- **More:** Click More, and the Properties dialog box opens.

Editing Multiple Fields Properties

In Chapters 5 through 7, we talked about modifying properties for single fields. You know that you have several options to return to the Properties window such as using the Select Object tool and double-clicking a field object.

You can make some changes to multiple fields by changing properties when several fields are selected and you open the Properties dialog box. If you have fields of different types and you select all fields and from a context menu you choose Properties, only the General, Appearance, and Actions tab open, as shown in Figure 9.25. In the General tab, the options available are the Locked check box, Read Only, and Required. You can select all fields, no matter what types of fields are selected, and adjust settings for these three areas.

FIGURE 9.25

When multiple fields are selected and you open the Properties window, the General, Appearance, and Actions tabs are accessible.

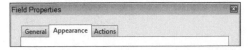

In the Appearance tab, when you select all fields on a form of varying types, you can make changes for most of the options. The one thing you cannot do is change the font if you select other fields along with radio buttons and check boxes. Because these fields are limited to using the Adobe Pi font, you cannot make font changes to these fields. If you select all fields on a form while excluding radio buttons and check boxes, you can make all settings changes in the Appearance tab.

The Actions tab is active when you select multiple fields of different types. You can globally assign actions to all fields on a form using the Actions tab.

When you have multiple fields within a common type, you have some additional choices for making some global settings choices. In addition to the options you have when selecting all fields on a form, you can make changes to common field types as follows:

- **Text fields:** Options choices are available when multiple text fields are selected. Any and all of the options choices you have for text fields can be applied to multiple fields.

- **Radio buttons/check boxes:** If you select both radio buttons and check boxes, the Properties options are the same as when selecting all fields on a form. If you select a group of check box fields or a group of radio button fields, the Options tab opens. In the Options tab, you can globally change the Button/Check Box Style for all selected radio buttons or check boxes. The Button Value/Export Value items are not available when selecting multiple fields.

- **Combo boxes/list boxes:** Although the Options tab opens, you don't have any more choices to make other than when selecting all fields of varying types. No changes can be made to Options if selecting both field types or a group of common field types.

- **Button fields:** You can change Options for multiple button fields. When selecting several buttons, the Options tab is visible where button faces, labels, and button behaviors can be globally changed for all selected buttons.

- **Signature fields:** Your only choice for Properties changes with multiple signature fields is to select all field types of varying fields.

- **Barcode fields:** Because barcode fields don't have an Appearance tab, opening the Properties window for multiple barcode fields shows only the General and Actions tabs. You can make changes to these settings the same as when selecting all fields of varying types.

Using Field Properties

All the preceding content in this chapter should be thought of as a reference guide to assigning properties to fields. You can glance over the content and refer to this chapter and the preceding section when you have specific issues related to a given field type and the properties adjustments you can make to them.

Assuming you have a general idea of the kinds of properties available for each field type, we're going to deviate from reference mode to learning mode and try to provide some real-world examples for making properties selections for a variety of fields.

Setting text field properties

In Chapters 5 through 7, we talked about naming fields when creating them manually. In Chapter 8, we talked about naming fields using hierarchical names in tables. We traveled through a few text field properties in earlier chapters, but we haven't yet applied any property settings for real-world conditions.

Just about every form you create in Acrobat requires addressing properties settings for some fields. If you use auto field detection, you still need to add some buttons to the file for distributing your forms, change field names in tables, format some text fields for a more polished form completion experience, or set up radio buttons and check boxes properly. In short, working in the Properties window will be a common editing task you'll perform on most forms edited in Acrobat.

Naming fields

In Figure 9.26, you see a form where auto field detection couldn't successfully detect form fields. The only fields detected on the two-page form were the table fields. We could use the fields Acrobat created for this form, but our work for formatting fields and setting up a calculation formula would be much greater than manually populating the table.

FIGURE 9.26

This form wasn't successfully populated with field objects when using auto field detection. The only fields on the form that were detected by Acrobat were the fields in the table.

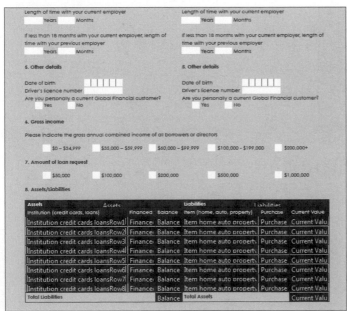

Because field objects appear on the form, we can use the first row of fields Acrobat created, delete the fields below the first row, and format the first row's fields. After formatting the fields, we can easily populate the table using Place Multiple Fields and prepare the calculation formulas for the last two fields.

To prepare the table properly, use the following steps.

ON the CD-ROM   To follow the steps here, use the *generalApplication.pdf* file found in the Chapter09 folder on the book's CD-ROM.

STEPS: Formatting Fields in a Table

1. **Open a form in Form Editing Mode.** Open the *generalApplication.pdf* file found in the Chapter09 folder on the book's CD-ROM, and choose Forms ⇨ Add or Edit Fields. The only fields recognized on this form are the table fields on page 2.

2. **Delete all fields below the first row.** Drag the Select Object tool through the fields below the first row, and press the Delete (or Del) key. Two additional fields were added in the header on this form. Delete the Assets and Liabilities fields in the header.

3. **Change the names of the fields in the row.** You can rename fields using a number of different methods. Perhaps the easiest way to rename fields quickly is to rename them in the Fields panel. Double-click the first field in the Fields panel, and the field name is highlighted. Type a new name, and press Enter/Return. When you press Enter/Return, the field name is changed and you move to the next field in the Fields panel. Double-click the field name, type a new name, and then press Return. Follow the same steps to rename all fields. In our example, we renamed fields *institution, financed, balance, item, purchasePrice,* and *currentValue,* as shown in Figure 9.27

TIP   When you click a field name in the Fields panel, the respective field on the form is highlighted. Take a quick glance at your form, and you can be certain the field you are renaming is the correct field to accept the new name.

4. **Format the number fields.** Four columns contain number fields (*financed, balanced, purchasePrice,* and *currentValue*). We need to format these fields as numbers before populating the table. Double-click the Select Object tool on the *financed* field to open the Text Field Properties dialog box. Click the Format tab, and choose Number from the Select format category pull-down menu to format the field as a number. From the Decimal Places pull-down menu, choose 0 for zero decimal places, as shown in Figure 9.28. Click OK, and repeat these steps for the remaining three fields (*balance, purchasePrice,* and *currentValue*).

5. **Populate the table.** After all the fields are formatted properly, it's time to populate the table. Drag through the fields, and open a context menu. From the menu options, choose Place Multiple Fields. Eight rows need to be populated. Type 8 in the Copy selected fields down text box, and click OK. If you leave the remaining items at the default values, the fields are added nicely to the cells in the table without having to use any align and distribute commands.

6. **Save the form.** Choose File ⇨ Save to save your edits.

FIGURE 9.27

Rename fields in the Fields panel by double-clicking a name, typing a new name, and pressing Enter/Return.

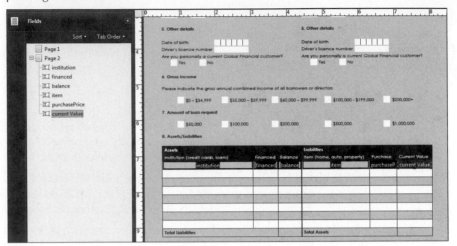

FIGURE 9.28

Choose Number from the Select format category and 0 (zero) from the Decimal Places pull-down menu.

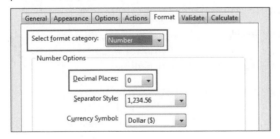

Notice that after formatting fields, the duplicated fields created with the Place Multiple Fields command created new fields with the same Format properties. As a matter of rule, you'll always want to format fields before duplicating them. This workflow saves you a huge amount of time when you need to duplicate many fields on a form.

NOTE You might ask "Why didn't we use the fields Acrobat created and format the number fields globally by selecting all fields requiring a number format and changing the Format properties?" In the section "Editing Multiple Fields Properties" earlier in this chapter, we stated that Format properties options are not available when selecting two or more text fields. The only way to change the format for text fields is to individually change the properties or follow the steps to edit the number format and create multiple copies of fields.

Calculating fields

A more important reason for renaming fields and letting Acrobat create the hierarchical names for fields when populating a table is when you want to add a calculation formula. In Figure 9.29, we need four fields at the bottom of the table to calculate the totals for the respective four columns of data.

We explain much more in Chapter 14 about using calculation formulas; for a first look, follow these steps to add fields for calculations to a table.

ON the CD-ROM If you saved the file from the steps on formatting fields in a table earlier in this chapter, use the saved file. If you didn't save the file, use the *generalApplication. pdf* file found in the Chapter09 folder on the book's CD-ROM. You'll need to return to the "Formatting Fields in a Table" steps to follow the steps for adding calculation formulas.

STEPS: Adding Calculations Formulas

1. **Duplicate the last fields in the four columns you want to calculate.** The easiest way to duplicate the fields is to press Ctrl/⌘ and click the fields that you want to duplicate to create a non-contiguous selection. When the fields are selected, press Ctrl/Option and drag down to position them properly in the last row in the table.

2. **Rename the fields.** You can use the Fields panel for changing the field names, but the panel is getting cluttered with lots of fields. An easier way to change the field names is to select a field with the Select Object tool and open a context menu. From the menu options, choose Rename Field. The mini Properties window opens, as shown in Figure 9.29. Type a new name for the field, and press Enter. You can quickly rename the four duplicated fields using this method. In our example, we named the four fields *financed-Total, balanceTotal, purchasePriceTotal,* and *currentValueTotal.*

3. **Add a calculation formula.** Double-click a field, and click the Calculate tab in the Text Field Properties window. Click the radio button beside Value is the. By default, sum (+) is selected. Leave the setting at the default to sum a column of data, as shown in Figure 9.31.

FIGURE 9.29

Select a field with the Select Object tool, and choose Rename Field from a context menu. Type a new name in the Field Name text box.

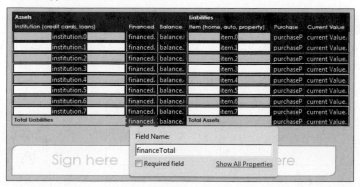

---

4. **Pick fields to add to the formula.** Click the Pick button, and the Field Selection dialog box opens. Scroll the dialog box, and check the parent name for the fields in the column you want to sum. In our example, we checked the *financed* field in the list, as shown in Figure 9.30.

   Note that because Acrobat created fields in the table with hierarchical names, the field names in our first column where we need a calculation are named *financed.0, financed.1, financed.2,* and so on. When we want to calculate the sum for this column, we choose *financed* in the Field Selection dialog box. All fields using the same parent name are added to the formula.

5. **Click OK in the Field Selection dialog box.** When you click OK, you return to the Calculate tab in the Text Field Properties dialog box. Below the formula used for the calculation, you'll see the field(s) used as part of the formula, as shown in Figure 9.31.

6. **Follow these steps to add the same formula using different parent names respective to the columns you want to calculate.**

FIGURE 9.30

Open the Field Selection dialog box, and check a parent name to sum a column.

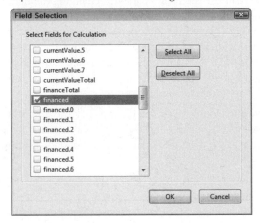

FIGURE 9.31

When you return to the Calculate tab in the Text Field Properties window, the fields used in the formula are shown below the formula selection.

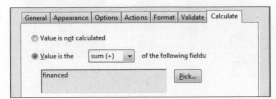

Hopefully, the steps used to perform a calculation help you understand the importance for naming fields in hierarchical order when calculations need to be made. If Acrobat didn't create a name hierarchy in the table, we would need to individually choose each field for the calculation. If your field names are dissimilar, you'd have to scroll through the Field Selection dialog box and try to locate all fields in a column or row while running the risk of missing critical fields that need to be part of the formula.

Creating comb fields

You find comb fields on many government and education forms. A comb field is typically designed with separator lines to mark areas on a form design where individual characters need to fall in place. We've seen lots of forms created with what should be comb fields created in the most bizarre manners. You can find forms on the Web where forms authors have created individual fields for each character requiring the form recipient to tab to each field individually. You also can find forms where the form designs have the separator lines but the fields are not formatted properly. When the form recipient types data, the data appear over the lines, not equally spaced in the comb fields.

Fortunately, Acrobat provides a solution for easily creating comb fields. To see how easy setting up comb fields is, follow these steps.

 Use the *generalApplication.pdf* file found in the Chapter09 folder on the book's CD-ROM to follow these steps.

STEPS: Formatting Comb Fields

1. **Open a form that contains at least one comb field.** On page 2 in the *generalApplication.pdf* file found in the Chapter09 folder on the book's CD-ROM are two fields designed for comb fields. Zoom in to the Date of Birth area in the "5. Other details category" on the form.

2. **Open the form in Form Editing Mode.** Choose Forms⇨Add or Edit Fields. Note that if you open the form the first time, Acrobat populates the table below the comb fields, but no other fields are recognized on this form.

3. **Add a text field.** Click the Text Field tool, and click+drag to shape the field precisely in the area on the design where the field needs to be added.

4. **Type a name for the field.** As shown in Figure 9.32, we used *dob* for the field name.

FIGURE 9.32

Draw a text field object to fit the design, and type a name for the field. Click Properties to open the Text Field Properties window.

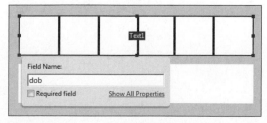

5. **Open the Text Field Properties window.** Click Properties after typing a field name in the mini Properties window to open the Text Field Properties.

6. **Set the comb field attributes.** Click the Options tab, and remove all check marks below the Default Value text box. Check the Comb of [ ] check box, and type 6 for the number of characters, as shown in Figure 9.33. Note that the Comb of [ ] check box is not active until you remove all the check marks in the Options tab. Adding 6 to the characters text box means we'll use a total of six characters for the comb field.

7. **Add text to the field.** Click Preview, and type a birth date using only six characters. The comb field appears, as shown in Figure 9.34, when text is added to the field.

FIGURE 9.33

Remove all check marks, and type 6 in the Comb of [ ] characters text box.

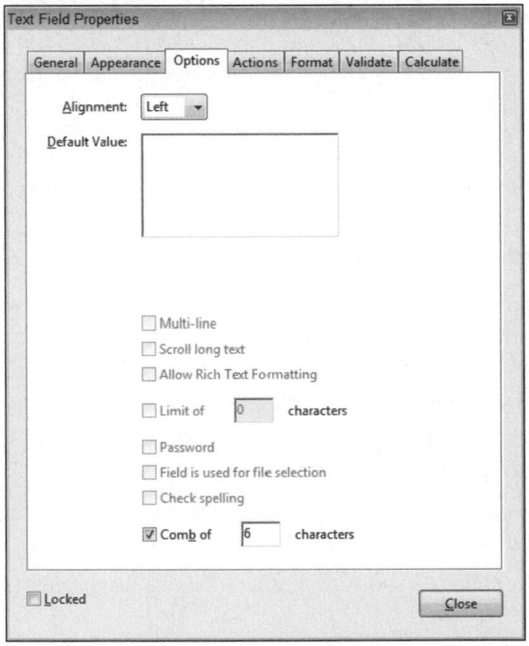

FIGURE 9.34

When comb fields are set up properly, the data appear evenly spaced within the hash marks.

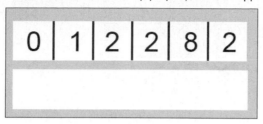

ON the CD-ROM Use the file *applicationDetail.pdf* in the Chapter09 folder on the book's CD-ROM for these steps.

STEPS: Formatting an Arbitrary Mask

1. **Open a file where you want an arbitrary mask field on your form.** We used the *applicationDetails.pdf* document in the Chapter09 folder on the book's CD-ROM. At the top of this form is an account number. We'll use this area to create a field with an arbitrary mask.

2. **Open the form in Form Editing Mode.** When you choose Forms➪Add or Edit Fields, Acrobat opens the form in Form Editing Mode without recognizing any fields. All fields must be added to this form manually.

3. **Create a text field.** Click the Text Field tool, and draw a rectangle around the design for the Account Number field. When you release the mouse button, you can type a field name and open the Text Field Properties window.

4. **Name the field.** Type a name for the field, and click Properties to open the Text Field Properties window.

5. **Open the Format tab, and choose Special from the Select format category pull-down menu.**

6. **Format an arbitrary mask.** In the Format tab, click Arbitrary Mask in the Special Options list, as shown in Figure 9.35. Type the mask in the text box below the Special Options list. In our example, we use GFS-487-9999-AAA. The form recipient would need to type four numeric characters (9 is the wildcard where the form recipient can type any numeric character in the field) and three alpha characters (A is the wildcard for using alpha characters). The first part of the mask is fixed (GFS-487) and cannot be edited by the form recipient. Click Close in the Format Properties tab, and you return to the Document pane.

7. **Test the field.** Click Preview in Form Editing Mode, and type four number characters and three alpha characters to fill in the field. Our example appears as shown in Figure 9.36 after we typed 5666GHT.

FIGURE 9.35

Choose Special from the Select format category pull-down menu, click Arbitrary Mask, and type a mask in the text box.

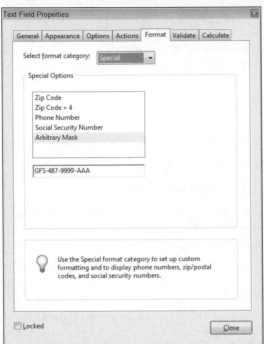

FIGURE 9.36

After filling in the field, the contents appear with the mask elements.

You have a number of other options for setting properties for text fields, We touched on a few in this chapter. When you get to later chapters dealing with calculations and JavaScripts, you'll find many more formatting options in a Text Fields Properties' Format, Validate, and Calculate tabs.

Many of the options for formatting dates, times, social security numbers, phone numbers, percentages, and zip codes should be easy to handle after stepping through some exercises in this chapter.

Setting check box properties for mutually exclusive fields

We covered quite a bit on radio buttons and check boxes in this chapter in the section "Understanding Field Properties Options." If you read through that section, you should have a good idea of how mutually exclusive fields are created.

To help clarify creating mutually exclusive check box fields and solidify your understanding for how they are created, follow these steps.

 **To follow these steps, use the** *applicationDetail.pdf* **file in the Chapter09 folder on the book's CD-ROM.**

STEPS: Creating Mutually Exclusive Check Box Fields

1. **Open the file** *applicationDetail.pdf* **from the Chapter09 folder on the book's CD-ROM.** This file illustrates a good example for using mutually exclusive check box fields. If you look at the Title row of fields, you find choices for *Mr, Mrs, Miss, Ms,* and *Other*.

   We could use radio buttons, but we would have to go through some extra steps to clear the radio button fields if a form recipient decided to use Other after clicking another radio button. Remember: After you click a radio button, you cannot remove the check mark unless you clear the form.

   Suppose a form recipient clicked Ms and then decided that a better choice is to type Dr in the Other field. We would have to prevent a potential error by adding a JavaScript or field action to the Other field to clear all radio buttons in the group if a form recipient types data in the Other field.

   By using check boxes, we can leave it up to the form recipient to unmark a check box if the user decides to make a choice for the Other field after clicking a check box. Unlike radio buttons, check boxes can be toggled on and off by the form recipient.

2. **Add a check box field to the form.** Open the form in Form Editing Mode, and click the Check Box tool. Click and drag the cursor to shape the rectangle for the first field in a row of check boxes. Type a name for the check box field. As shown in Figure 9.37, we typed *title* for our field name.

FIGURE 9.37

Open Form Editing Mode, and create a check box. Name the field by typing a field name in the Field Name text box.

3. **Open the Check Box Properties window.** Click Properties, and the Check Box Properties window opens.

4. **Edit the appearances.** By default, check box fields are created with a black border and a white fill. Our design takes care of the appearances for the fields, so we need to remove the border and fill. Click the Appearance tab, and choose No Color for the Border Color and Fill Color.

5. **Set the Export value for the first check box field in the group.** Click the Options tab, and type an Export Value. In our example, we typed *Mr* for the first field.

6. **Duplicate the field.** While the Check Box Properties window is open and the Options tab is in view, drag the Properties window aside so you can clearly see the area where the field objects need to be created, as shown in Figure 9.38. Move the cursor to the first field you created, press Ctrl/Option+Shift, and drag the field to duplicate it. Position the field in the area for the next check box.

   When you duplicate the field, the same attributes for the field are also duplicated. The same field name is used for the duplicate, the same field appearances, and the same export value. The only item we need to change is the export value. All other properties need to remain the same.

7. **Change the Export Value in the duplicated field.** In the Options tab, type a new export value. In our example, we used *Mrs* for the second field.

8. **Repeat Steps 6 and 7 for the remaining fields.** In our example, we used *Miss* for the third field export value, as shown in Figure 9.38.

9. **Click Close in the Check Box Properties window.** The check boxes are mutually exclusive fields. When checking one box, all other check boxes are cleared of data. Clicking a marked box removes the check mark.

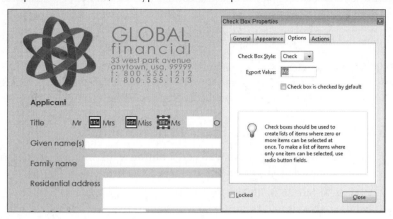

FIGURE 9.38

Duplicate the fields, and type a different export value for each field in the Options tab.

Setting button field properties

Button fields can be used for a number of different actions you want form recipients to perform when completing your forms. The possibilities for button uses are limitless. One of the many uses you may find interesting for buttons is adding help information for a form recipient to easily work through your form.

With analog forms, we need to add instructions to help form recipients complete complicated areas of a form. Adding instructions to a form takes up space and reduces the amount of area on a form for the most important elements that are the fields.

With electronic forms, you can use buttons to show and hide information, tips, and help guides without taking up valuable space on a form.

Creating a button face

Button faces are graphic icons and images that appear within a button field. You can add button faces from any native file format that's supported by using the File ➪ Create PDF ➪ From File menu command. A Word file, an Excel file, an image file such as JPEG, PNG, TIFF, and so on can be used to create a button face. Additionally, any PDF file can be used to create a button face.

Typically, you'll find creating PDF files to be the best option for creating button faces. After a file is converted to PDF, you can see if the document will work well for a button face. If you use a native file directly in Acrobat and need to go back to the authoring application to make some edits, you have to interrupt your form editing to make the changes and then come back later to populate the form.

Most often, you'll have two issues to deal with when working with button faces. First, you need to create a button and choose a button face. Second, you need to set an action for something that will happen when the form recipient clicks the button. The second item isn't essential if you want to add an icon or graphic to a form, but typically you add graphics when you lay out your form.

To understand how button faces are added to button fields, follow these steps.

ON the CD-ROM   Button faces we'll add in this chapter are the *guidelinesButton.pdf* and the *guidelinesMessage.pdf* files in the Chapter09 folder on the book's CD-ROM. Additionally, we'll use the *generalApplication.pdf* document from the same folder.

STEPS: Adding Button Faces to Button Fields

1. **Open a file where you want to add a button field.** In our example, we used the *generalApplication.pdf* document from the Chapter09 folder on the book's CD-ROM.

2. **Create a button field.** You can work in either Viewer mode or Form Editing Mode when adding buttons to PDF documents. If you work in Viewer mode, click the Button tool in the Advanced Editing toolbar. If you work in Form Editing Mode, click the Button tool in the Form Edit toolbar. When the cursor is loaded with a Button field, click+drag a button field above the Applicant text in the top-left side of the form, as shown in Figure 9.39. Type a name for the field, and click Properties. In our example, we used *help* as the field name.

3. **Set the appearances.** By default, the button has a gray fill color. Open the Appearance tab, and choose No Color for the fill.

4. **Set the Options attributes.** Click the Options tab, and choose Icon only, as shown in Figure 9.39. Click the Advanced button to open the Icon Placement dialog box, and check Fit to Bounds. Click OK in the Icon Placement dialog box to return to the Button Properties window.

5. **Choose a button face.** Click the Choose Icon button to open the Select Icon dialog box. Click the Browse button in the Select Icon dialog box, and browse your computer to locate a button to use as the button face. In our example, we used the *guidelinesButton.pdf* file from the Chapter09 folder on the book's CD-ROM.

   Select the file and click Select in the Open dialog box, and you return to the Select Icon dialog box. The button icon you chose appears in the dialog box, as shown in Figure 9.40.

6. **Click OK.** You return to the Button Properties dialog box. Normally, you would click the Actions tab to define an action for the button. But in our example, we'll use this button to show/hide another button that has not yet been added to our form. We'll postpone the actions options until after we add another button field.

FIGURE 9.39

Choose Icon only, and click Advanced to adjust the icon placement.

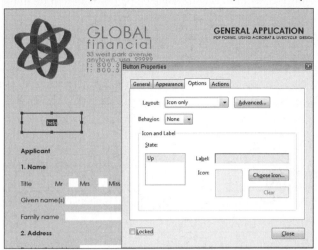

FIGURE 9.40

Click Browse in the Select Icon dialog box to locate the file you want to use as a button face.

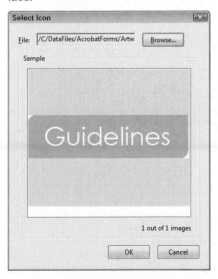

7. **Set the button visibility.** Before leaving the Button Properties, click the General tab. From the Form Field pull-down menu, choose Visible but doesn't print. This button is used for a form recipient to acquire some help information to fill in the form. The button has no significance when the form is printed.

8. **Define new defaults for the button fields.** Click Close in the Button Properties dialog box. Click the Select Object tool on the button, and open a context menu. From the menu commands, choose Use Current Properties as New Defaults. When you create additional buttons, you won't need to change the Appearance for the buttons.

9. **Create another button.** Follow Steps 2 through 7 to add another button. In our example, we used the file *guidelinesMessage.pdf* for the second button face. We named this button *helpMessage*. The second button is a sizeable field, as shown in Figure 9.41.

FIGURE 9.41

Add a sizable second button, and use the *guidelinesMessage.pdf* document for the button face.

10. **Add a third button.** On the message button face is an area designated for a Close button. We need to add another button here, but because the graphic shows the form recipient what will happen when the action is executed, we don't need a button face. Click the Button tool, and try to draw the field rectangle carefully to the same size as the item denoted as Close on the second button image.

11. **Name the button.** We named our third button *helpClose*. Notice that we named the three buttons *help, helpMessage,* and *helpClose*. When it comes time to find these buttons in a list of fields, we can easily scroll a dialog box to locate the three buttons listed together.

12. **Close the Button Properties and save the file.** Because we don't need any edits for the third button, click Close in the Button Properties window. Choose File ⇨ Save to update the file.

Adding actions to buttons

If you followed the steps in the steps section "Adding Button Faces to Button Fields," you should have three buttons on the *generalApplication.pdf* document. After all the buttons are created, you can now apply actions to show/hide the button fields.

To add actions to the buttons, do the following.

STEPS: Adding Actions to Buttons

1. **Set the attributes for the help message to Read Only.** The only two buttons that require an action are the *help* button and the *close* button. These buttons are used to show/hide the message button. Because the message button won't have an action assigned to it, you can lock it as a read-only field. Double-click the large message button, and click the General tab. In the General Properties, check Read Only.

    When you mark a field as read only, the mouse cursor won't appear with the index finger on hand pointing upward. This cursor shape denotes a button that is assigned an action. Because the cursor doesn't display a clue that the button is used for an action, it results in less confusion for the form recipient.

2. **Select an action for the Close button.** Double-click the *helpClose* button to open the Button Properties. Click the Actions tab, and leave the Mouse trigger set at the default Mouse Up trigger. Open the Select Action pull-down menu, and choose Show/hide a field. Click the Add button to open the Show/Hide Field dialog box.

3. **Choose Show/Hide Options.** When the Close button is clicked by the form recipient, we want both the *helpMessage* button and the *helpClose* button to disappear. In the Show/Hide Field dialog box, select helpMessage and be certain the Hide radio button is selected, as shown in Figure 9.42. Click OK, and you return to the Button Properties Actions tab.

FIGURE 9.42

Click a button to hide in the Show/Hide Field dialog box, and click the Hide radio button.

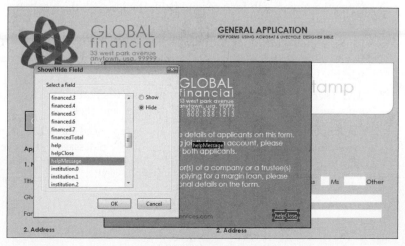

4. **Define a second action.** The Select Action menu choice is still active with the Show/hide a field action type. Click the Add button again. When the Show/Hide Field dialog box opens, click helpClose in the list and be certain the Hide radio button is selected. Click OK, and you finish setting the actions for this button. When you return to the Actions tab, both actions appear listed in the Actions list, as shown in Figure 9.43

FIGURE 9.43

After adding multiple actions to a field, all actions are listed in the Actions list.

5. **Open the Actions tab for a second field.** Double-click the *help* button to open the Button Properties. Click Actions to open the Actions tab.

6. **Choose Show/hide a field from the Select Action pull-down menu.** Click the Add button to open the Show/Hide Field dialog box. Scroll to the helpMessage item, and select it. Click the Show button, and click OK.

7. **Add a second action to the help button field.** Click Add again, scroll to the helpClose item, and select it. Click the Show radio button, and click OK.

8. **Test the buttons.** At this point, all the actions you need should be properly assigned to the buttons. Click the Close button to close the helpMessage and the helpClose buttons. Click the help button, and the other two buttons should appear.

You can assign many more actions to fields in the Properties windows. We introduced a few in this chapter to get you started on the methods for assigning actions to fields. The most robust of the action types are JavaScripts that provide forms authors almost limitless opportunities for creating more dynamic interactive PDF forms. In the chapters remaining where we cover Acrobat Forms, we introduce more field properties and more actions.

Summary

- Each of the eight form field types have associated Properties windows where a field's attributes are defined.

- Many fields have some common properties, and many fields have properties settings exclusive to a given field type.

- Properties adjustments can be made in Form Editing Mode or Viewer mode.

- The Properties bar is available only in Viewer mode, where appearance properties can be assigned in the toolbar.

- Each field's Properties window has multiple panes selected by clicking the tabs in the window.

- All field types have a General tab where filenames and tooltips are edited, choices for making fields read only, and choices for displaying and hiding fields.

- All fields have an Actions tab where all the actions options can be assigned to any field.

- Check box fields can be set up to be mutually exclusive fields using choices for export values in the Options tab in the Check Box Properties window.

- Text and combo fields have identical properties options. These two fields offer the most choices you have when making properties changes.

- Text fields can accept alpha and numeric data. Calculations are made in the Text Field Properties Calculate tab.

- Buttons can be used to display icons, images, and help files. All fields including buttons can be made visible or hidden.

- Comb fields are used to separate characters in a single field equidistant from each other. A comb field typically uses separator lines or boxes to mark the character divisions.

- Arbitrary masks are used to create alphanumeric codes for items such as account numbers, client numbers, file numbers, and so on. You can define a mask for accepting user input for alpha and numeric values as well as format fixed values.

- Numbers should be properly formatted as number values when fields are used to perform calculations.

- Calculations are made much easier when using hierarchical names.

Part III

Preparing Forms for Deployment

Before you distribute a form you need to understand some preparation tasks common to many forms. We start this part covering special features in forms for Adobe Reader users, how to add them, and how to edit enabled files. We move on in Chapter 11 to discuss how to make forms accessible for visually and motion challenged readers using assistive devices. In Chapter 12 we talk about securing forms and adding digital signatures and we finish up this part by working with form examples containing layers and contained in PDF Portfolios.

IN THIS PART

Chapter 10
Enabling PDF Forms for Adobe Reader

Chapter 11
Making Forms Accessible

Chapter 12
Using Signatures and Security

Chapter 13
Working with PDF Portfolios and Layers

Chapter 10

Enabling PDF Forms for Adobe Reader

Enabling features for Adobe Reader or adding special features for Reader users is a means whereby certain features not appearing in the default Adobe Reader program can be added to PDF documents. This enabling function can be handled by one of two applications. You can use a server product such as the Adobe LiveCycle Reader Extensions Server (LCRE) or Adobe Acrobat 9 Standard, Pro, and Pro Extended.

Prior to Acrobat 9, Acrobat Standard users were left out of the enabling arena. Using Acrobat 9 and greater, you have one of two available enabling features. Acrobat 9 Standard can enable forms for saving form data and signing documents with digital signatures. Acrobat Pro and ProExtended can enable forms for saving data and signing documents with digital signatures and enable PDF documents for commenting.

In this chapter, you discover some of the issues related to enabling files for Adobe Reader users and some reasons why you might extend enabling for comments.

IN THIS CHAPTER

Getting familiar with Adobe Reader usage rights

Adding usage rights to PDF forms

Editing forms that have been enabled with usage rights

Automating Acrobat tasks

Understanding Reader Enablement

We refer to enabled forms as forms that have special features that were added in Acrobat 9 Standard and above or Acrobat Professional 7.0 and above. Adobe Readers users can add the following special features to a PDF file:

- Save form data.
- Apply digital signatures.

267

- Use comment and markup tools, and save the comment marks.
- Sign an existing signature field.
- Digitally sign a document anywhere on a page.

There are some limitations to the programs that can enable files and the kinds of files that can be used by different viewer versions. The following applies to enabled files and the viewers:

- **Acrobat Professional 7:** You can only enable PDFs for comment and markup.
- **Acrobat Professional 8 and above:** You have all enabling features available.
- **Acrobat 9 Standard:** You can only enable files for saving edits related to adding data in form fields and apply digital signatures with Acrobat Standard version 9.0 and above.
- **Adobe Reader 7.0:** You can add comments and markups.
- **Adobe Reader 7.05:** Adobe Reader 7.05 and above is required for using enabled forms.
- **Adobe Reader 8.0 and above:** You can digitally sign a document anywhere on a page requires Acrobat 8.0 or greater.
- **Adobe Designer XML Forms:** All enabling features are available except digitally signing a document anywhere on a page when using a dynamic XML form. When using a static XML form, digital signatures can be used anywhere on the form.
- **Submitting entire PDFs:** One of the options you have available when setting up a submission button is to permit the form recipient to send the entire PDF back to you. Adobe Reader users version 7.05 and greater can return a PDF file to you when the PDF has been enabled.

PDF forms authors should plan on enabling all forms that are used within the Adobe's licensing restrictions. As a matter of course, you should plan on enabling PDF forms as the last task you perform in your editing session.

Knowing the licensing limitations

You must obey some limitations when enabling PDF documents for Adobe Reader users for forms enabling rights. Enabling forms for comment and markup do not carry the same limitations as do enabling forms for forms rights.

The limitations imposed on forms enabling features are defined in the End User License Agreement (EULA) you agree to when installing Acrobat. Just in case you are confused about language in the agreement after reading it, let us paraphrase the licensing agreement and amplify some of the conditions. In addition to what is covered in this chapter, you should carefully read the agreement and understand the limitations of use.

The language in the EULA suggests that you can enable PDF forms with forms saving and digital signatures for Adobe Reader users for up to 500 instances of returning form data back to you for a given document. The document usage can be done one of two ways. You can distribute an unlimited number of enabled forms, but you can only aggregate up to 500 responses per form template/

design; this is useful when you're hosting a form on your Web site or on Acrobat.com where you might get fewer than 500 registrants for, say, a conference. The other instance is distributing forms to 500 named individuals, and you can aggregate any number of those forms. This is useful for something like expense accounts that people fill out and return monthly for an organization of fewer than 500 employees.

To help clarify the issues, let's say I'm going to distribute a form to a limited number of known people. For example, suppose I work at a small company of fewer than 500 employees. There is no limit to the number of times that form is submitted—ever—because it is coming from only 500 known persons. Think of an expense report form that is sent in monthly, or the annual benefits signup.

In another scenario, I'm going to distribute a form to an unknown number of people. For example, I'm posting it on my Web site. I can collect only 500 responses from that single form—ever. However, I can have five forms on my Web site (one for the East Coast, one for the West Coast, one for Canada, and so on), and I can collect 500 responses from each of those forms. Think of a conference registration or a one-time survey.

You can create an unlimited number of form templates with Adobe Acrobat. You can distribute these forms anywhere, anyhow. The data collection itself is what is limited:

- I have only 500 people in my "circle of trust," and I can collect from those people as much as necessary, or
- I need to collect feedback from some people (known/unknown), and I can collect only 500 responses in the lifetime of that single form.

NOTE For an up-to-date description of the Acrobat EULA or any other Adobe product, visit `www.adobe.com/products/eulas`. On the opening Web page, you'll find links to Acrobat and other Adobe products specifying the conditions of the license agreements.

Adobe uses no special coding or technology to ensure that users are complying with the licensing agreement. Adobe believes that the enforcement for restricting users to the limitations is vested in the amount of work people need to perform. For limited use, the enabling features in Acrobat 9 serve a need for many PDF authors. However, enterprise uses require using a form server product for more robust forms processing and data collection.

Using form servers

When you use Acrobat to enable forms, you are limited to the enabling features that Acrobat provides. You may have some other types of enabling features that you would like to include for Adobe Reader users. For example, you may want to spawn new pages on a PDF form. In a sense, LiveCycle Designer can spawn new pages as data flow into a document; however, Acrobat PDF forms don't have this type of dynamic feature. Using a form server from Adobe or Adobe partners, you can add additional rights such as spawning pages on your forms that can be handled by Adobe Reader users.

In the area of data collection, the Acrobat EULA limits you to collecting 500 responses per form template. Even if the EULA provided you unlimited use of enabled forms, the practicality for using Acrobat would be useless for more than about 300 responses. Acrobat would take forever to aggregate data on more than 500 form responses. To manage form data for great numbers of forms, you need a server product.

When it comes to enabling features not found in Acrobat and managing volumes of PDF forms, a forms server product is what you need. You can use Adobe's product LCRE (`http://www.adobe.com/products/livecycle/readerextensions/`) or third-party form servers such as FormRouter (`www.formrouter.com`), or other products designed to collect and route data as well as enable PDF files.

One thing to be certain of is that you won't want to let the job of routing form data be a task for your IT department. IT departments won't be able to enable forms unless they are licensed by Adobe to offer enabling features, and they won't provide you with the robust options you have with commercial products for handling data. The easiest way for you to tackle industrial jobs is to use a server product provided by Adobe or an authorized Adobe partner.

CROSS-REF For more information on form servers and LCRE, see Chapter 34.

Adding Permissions for Adobe Reader Users

In Acrobat 9 Standard, Pro, and Pro Extended, you can enable PDF documents with special usage rights for Adobe Reader users to save form data from forms created in Acrobat or LiveCycle Designer and apply digital signatures to those forms. Adding comments in Adobe Reader is possible if the forms are enabled in the Acrobat products, with the exception of Acrobat Standard.

NOTE When enabling PDF forms for Adobe Reader users with Acrobat Standard, you must have a signature field on the form in order for a Reader user to digitally sign the form. When using Acrobat Pro or Pro Extended, you can enable a form so a Reader user can apply a signature anywhere on the form without needing a signature field.

How you go about enabling files from Acrobat is handled through menu commands or through a wizard when you distribute forms. You choose one of several methods for adding special features to PDF documents for Adobe Reader users.

NOTE Adding usage rights is also handled when setting up shared reviews via a wizard.

Enabling PDFs for form save and digital signatures

Enabling a file for Adobe Reader users is handled via a simple menu command. In any Acrobat 9 or greater commercial viewer, select Advanced ➪ Extend Features in Adobe Reader, and the Enable Usage Rights in Adobe Reader dialog box opens, as shown in Figure 10.1.

FIGURE 10.1

Select Advanced ⇨ Extend Features in Adobe Reader, and a dialog box opens informing you of the features that you can enable.

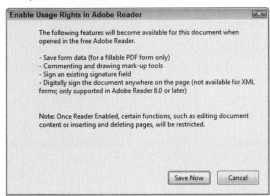

 **If you're an Acrobat Standard user, you choose Advanced ⇨ Extend Forms Fill-in & Save in Adobe Reader.**

Click Save Now, and all the features listed in the dialog box are enabled in the PDF file for Adobe Reader users. This option provides a complete set of enabling features, including the following:

■ **Save form data (for fillable PDF form only):** Adobe Reader users can add data to PDF forms containing form fields and save the edited file.

■ **Commenting and drawing mark-up tools:** The same comment and markup tools are available to Adobe Reader users as when enabling files for Comment & Markup and Review & Comment. All comments can be saved (Acrobat 9 Pro/Pro Extended).

■ **Sign an existing signature field:** Adobe Reader users can add a digital signature to a signature field on a form and save the edits.

■ **Digitally sign the document on the page (supported in Adobe Reader 8 only):** This feature, available only to users of Adobe Reader 8 and above, allows users to sign a document without the appearance of a signature file and save the edits (Acrobat 9 Pro/Pro Extended).

When you click Save Now, the file is enabled with the usage rights. Forms authors might use this menu command to e-mail a form to a client, to use a form for in-house usage such as HR or accounting forms, or to add a form to a PDF Portfolio.

If you want to distribute forms and collect data from form recipients, you can waive this step in your editing workflow. When you set up forms for distribution, the wizards you use in Acrobat add the enabling features when you distribute a form.

Enabling PDFs for commenting

It's not very likely that you'll use the enabling for commenting feature often as a PDF author. Enabling forms for commenting cannot be performed in Acrobat Standard, and you don't need to enable files separately for commenting and for form saves. Using the Advanced ➪ Extend features in Adobe Reader takes care of everything, including enabling forms for commenting.

You may have some isolated needs for enabling a form for commenting. If you need to have approval for a form design from other departments or coworkers in your company, but you don't want any Reader users to save the data from, you could send a form out for a comment review. However, if a form needs to be tested before deployment, you'll want all the enabling features for forms added to a document before sending it out for review.

If a rare occasion exists when you want only commenting enabled for Adobe Reader users, then choose Comments ➪ Enable for Commenting and Analysis in Adobe Reader. The Reader Enable Document for Commenting dialog box opens, as shown in Figure 10.2.

FIGURE 10.2

Choose Comments ➪ Enable for Commenting and Analysis in Adobe Reader to open the Reader Enable Document for Commenting dialog box.

Click OK in the application alert dialog box, and a Save As dialog box opens. Type a new name for your file to avoid overwriting the original, and click Save. The PDF is now enabled with Adobe Reader usage rights for commenting and markup.

When an Adobe Reader user opens the enabled PDF document, the Comment & Markup tools are accessible. You can add the same kinds of comments as you can with either Acrobat Standard or Acrobat Pro. After adding comments, the Reader user also has access to a File ➪ Save command. This command is not available unless a file has been enabled. Selecting File ➪ Save permits the Reader user the opportunity to save all comments added to the PDF.

Using comments with forms

As a general rule, messages and notes can be used in application alert dialog boxes rather than using comment notes. Notes and comments can clutter a form, and they add a little more to the file size. But sometimes you may want to have comment tools available to users. One good example is using a Stamp comment. You can use a variety of comment stamps that Acrobat provides, or you can create custom stamps to suit your own needs. If you want Adobe Reader users to add stamp comments to a form, all Reader users of Adobe Reader 7.5 and above can add stamp comments to forms enabled with Reader usage rights.

Creating a custom stamp

Custom stamps can add a little benefit to form approvals. A quick glance at a form immediately tells you if a form has been approved or meets some other condition. Acrobat has a number of preset stamps that can be used for approval, signing, initialing, marking completed, for public release, and so on.

To view stamps, you need to open the Comment & Markup toolbar. Choose Tools ⇨ Comment & Markup, and select Show Comment & Markup Toolbar from the submenu. When the Comment & Markup toolbar opens, click the down arrow on the Stamps tool and select one of the menu items. From the choices you have in the Stamps pull-down menu, submenus display various stamp comment icons. In Figure 10.3, we selected Dynamic stamps; the submenu displays the choices you have for these stamps.

FIGURE 10.3

Open the Stamps pull-down menu, and choose a category. A submenu displays stamps available from the selected category.

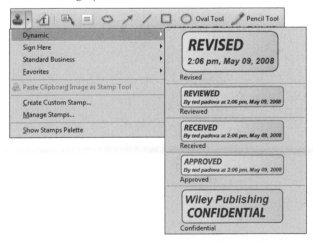

If one of the preset stamps from the different menus doesn't meet your needs, you can create a custom stamp. Custom stamps can be created from any file you can convert to PDF using the File ⇨ Create PDF ⇨ From File command.

To create a custom stamp, try following these steps.

STEPS: Creating a Custom Stamp

1. **Open the Comment & Markup toolbar in Acrobat.** Choose Tools ⇨ Comment & Markup ⇨ Show Comment & Markup Toolbar to open the Comment & Markup tools.

2. **Select an image for the custom stamp.** From the Stamp tool pull-down menu, choose Create Custom Stamp. The Select Image for Custom Stamp dialog box opens. Click the Browse button, and locate a file you want to use as a custom stamp. You can choose any file that Acrobat can convert to PDF. When you select the file and click Select, you return to the Select Image for Custom Stamp dialog box. A preview of your stamp appears in the Sample window in the Select Image for Custom Stamp dialog box, as shown in Figure 10.4.

FIGURE 10.4

Choose a file you want to use for a custom stamp, and when you return to the Select Image for Custom Stamp dialog box a preview of the selected image appears in the Sample window.

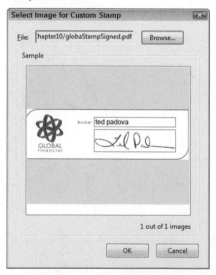

3. **Select a category for the new stamp.** Click OK in the Select Image for Custom Stamp dialog box, and the Create Custom Stamp dialog box opens. Here you can choose a category to organize your custom stamps or create a new category. If you want a new category to store the stamp in, type a name for the category in the Category text box. In our

example, we added a new category name, and typed My Stamps in the Category text box, as shown in Figure 10.5. If you want to use an existing category, open the pull-down menu adjacent to the Category text box and choose one of the existing categories.

4. **Name the stamp.** Type a name for the new stamp in the Name text box. In our example, we typed Global Stamp in the Name text box, as shown in Figure 10.5. Click OK, and you return to the document pane.

FIGURE 10.5

Type a category and name for the new custom stamp.

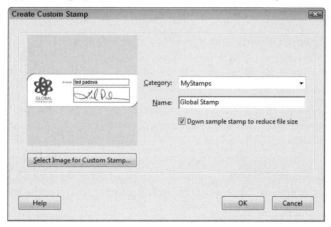

At this point, your new stamp is available from the Stamp tool pull-down menu. If you added a new category, the stamp appears in a submenu off the category name, as shown in Figure 10.6. You click the stamp from the submenu, and the cursor is loaded with the selected stamp. Click anywhere on the page, and the stamp is added to your form.

FIGURE 10.6

After adding a new category, the category is listed in the Stamp pull-down menu. The stamp name appears in the new category submenu.

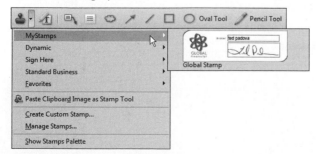

Adding custom stamps to forms

After you add a custom stamp to the Stamp pull-down menu, it's a matter of selecting the stamp and clicking on a form. If you followed the steps to add a custom stamp, do the following to apply your new stamp to a form.

 For these steps, we use the *generalApplication.pdf* file in the Chapter 10 folder on the book's CD-ROM.

STEPS: Adding a Stamp to a Form

1. **Open a file where you want to add a custom stamp.** In our example, we use the *generalApplication.pdf* file on the book's CD-ROM. The design of this form displays an area at the top-right of the first page where a stamp should be applied.

2. **Select a stamp.** Open the Stamp pull-down menu, and choose the category where the stamp is stored that you want to add to the form. In our example, we opened the My Stamps custom category we added to the Stamps menu. From the submenu, click the stamp you want to use. In our example, we clicked the Global Stamp.

3. **Add the stamp to the form.** When you select a stamp, the cursor is loaded with the selected stamp, much like you load the cursor with Form tools in Form Editing Mode. Move the cursor to the area where you want to add the stamp, and click to drop it on the form.

4. **Resize the stamp.** When a stamp is added to your form, the stamp appears with handles on the bounding box. Click a handle, and drag in or out to size the stamp.

5. **Add a comment note.** Stamps are comments. Each stamp has an associated comment note. To open the note pop-up window, double-click the stamp. When the note pop-up opens, type a message in the window, as shown in Figure 10.7.

FIGURE 10.7

Double-click the stamp to open a pop-up note window. Click the cursor in the note window, and type a message.

When you create custom stamps, try using vector art files such as those you can create in Adobe Illustrator. If you want to size a stamp after adding it to a form, vector art files appear crisp and without any resolution loss at any size. If you want to use raster images such as Adobe Photoshop files for photographic images, sizing the stamps up eventually pixelates the image. If you want to use raster images, try to anticipate the largest size you might size the stamp up. Use a resolution that won't fall below 72 pixels per inch (ppi) for screen displays. For example, if you intend to size a stamp up 400 percent, you need to create a stamp at 288-ppi. As you size the stamp up, the resolution drops. Hence, a 288-ppi stamp sized up to 400 percent renders a 72-ppi image (288/4 = 72).

Using wizards to enable files

Another menu command you can use to enable PDF documents is the Distribute Form command found in either Form Editing Mode or in Viewer mode. Choose Forms from either menu, and choose Distribute Form. Additionally, you have a button for Distribute Form in the Form Edit toolbar. Choose either menu option or click the Distribute Form button, and the Distribute Form wizard opens, as shown in Figure 10.8.

FIGURE 10.8

Choose a command or click the Distribute Form button in Form Editing Mode to open the Distribute Form wizard.

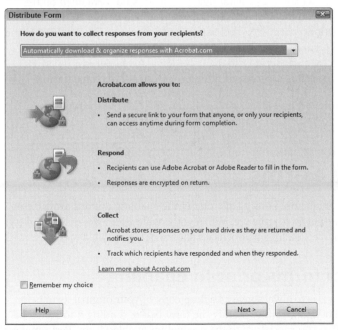

If you use Acrobat 8, you also can distribute a form via a menu command in the Forms menu or by clicking the Distribute Form tool in the Forms toolbar. Users of Acrobat earlier than version 8 do not have the same choices for distributing forms.

You have several options for distributing forms. Regardless of the option you choose, the form is enabled for Adobe Reader users when you complete the last step in the wizard.

CROSS-REF We cover more on distributing forms in Chapter 15. For now, be aware that you have the option for enabling forms for Adobe Reader users when choosing the Distribute Form command.

Enabling LiveCycle Designer forms

When you open an Adobe LiveCycle Designer form in Acrobat, you have very limited editing opportunities. However, adding Reader extensions via the Comments menu and the Advanced menu is not restricted in Acrobat. You can enable forms, and you can distribute forms. You cannot enable a form with Reader Extensions directly in Adobe LiveCycle Designer, per se. You can select File ⇨ Distribute Form in Adobe LiveCycle Designer, but doing so launches Acrobat and opens the Distribute Form wizard. All enabling features of Designer forms are handled within Acrobat Pro.

When you enable a form using the Comments ⇨ Enable Commenting in Adobe Reader command, you don't have an option for enabling form save and commenting in the same file. Likewise, you don't have an option to add a digital signature if a digital signature field is not contained on the form. When you use the Advanced menu for Enable Usage Rights in Adobe Reader or the Distribute Form command, commenting, form save, and using digital signatures are enabled in the form for Reader users (only Pro/Pro Extended). The only limitation you have with Designer XML *dynamic* forms is that adding rights for a Reader user to digitally sign a document is not permitted. Form recipients need to use signature fields to electronically sign a Designer dynamic form.

CROSS-REF For more information on Adobe LiveCycle Designer, see Parts VI through IX. For more information on using digital signatures, see Chapter 12.

Editing Enabled Forms

Occasionally, you may enable a PDF document using any one of the enabling options available in Acrobat and then later decide you want to edit the file. When you enable a PDF document and try to edit it in Acrobat, an application alert dialog box opens, as shown in Figure 10.9.

Keeping backups of forms prior to enabling

The best way to handle editing forms is to always save a backup copy of your original form before deployment. If you enable a PDF and later want to modify the form before sending it to recipients or hosting the form on a Web server, you can return to the original un-enabled form. Perform your edits and save the original, and then enable the final form while saving under a new filename.

FIGURE 10.9

If you try to edit an enabled file in Acrobat, an alert dialog box opens informing you that you can't edit the file.

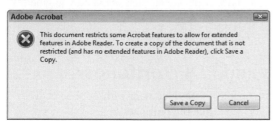

At times, the dialog box shown in Figure 10.9 that opens when you try to edit an enabled form becomes annoying when modifying the form. Additionally, sometimes you can find some problems associated with files that have been saved as copies after enablement. To guard against potential problems and save yourself some aggravation, always keep a backup of the original form.

Editing enabled PDF files

To edit an enabled file in Acrobat you first need to save a copy of the document. When you open non-enabled forms, the File menu lists commands for Save and Save As. When you open an enabled file in Acrobat, you find the commands Save, Save As, and Save a Copy. The addition of the Save a Copy command is unique to enabled forms, and only this command will remove the restrictions applied when the PDF was enabled. The usage rights are removed when you save a copy, so after editing you need to re-enable the form.

Select File ⇨ Save a Copy, and the Save a Copy dialog box opens, as shown in Figure 10.10. Click the Save a Copy button, and a second Save a Copy dialog box opens where you can name the copy and select a folder where you want to save it. After you save a copy, your copy file is not opened in the Acrobat Document pane. It's merely saved to disk. Your original file remains open, and it's still not editable. Close the open file, and select File ⇨ Open or click the Open tool in the Toolbar Well. When the Open dialog box appears, select the copy file and open it in Acrobat. You can edit this file and enable it after you complete your editing tasks.

FIGURE 10.10

Click the Save a Copy button to save an editable copy of the enabled PDF document.

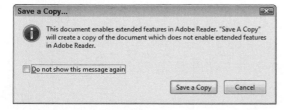

You'll find that most of the kinds of editing you typically perform on a form aren't available with enabled documents. Items such as changing any of the Document Properties (Description, Security, Initial View, Custom, and Advanced), adding headers and footers, changing backgrounds, adding comments, editing form fields, and changing JavaScripts are all unavailable to you when working on an enabled PDF form. To edit any of these items, select File ➪ Save a Copy and open the copy file.

Working with enabled files and PDF Portfolios

When you create PDF Portfolios, you may want to enable a PDF document with Adobe Reader usage rights or edit an enabled PDF document after you create the portfolio.

PDF Portfolios are available in Acrobat 9 and take the place of PDF Packages introduced in Acrobat 8. In Acrobat 8, you worked within the Acrobat User Interface (UI) to edit and manage files within a PDF Package. In Acrobat 9, the UI changes, and you lose access to many of Acrobat's tools and menus when viewing files in the basic layout interface.

To change the view of a file from the layout view to a document view within the PDF Portfolio interface, double-click the file. The form opens, but it's still within the PDF Portfolio in a Preview mode interface shown in Figure 10.11. When you view files outside the layout view, you have access to the menu commands for enabling the file. Acrobat makes it easy for you to enable files within the PDF Portfolio. When you choose an enabling command from either the Comments menu or the Advanced menu and save your file, you're not prompted to type a name or browse your hard drive. The file is enabled without any fuss.

If you use Acrobat 8 and PDF Packages, you need to enable a file and then replace the original file with the enabled file. Unlike PDF Portfolios, Acrobat opens a Save As dialog box when enabling forms within PDF Packages. When you click Save, the file is saved as a new file while the original file within the PDF Package remains unaltered. You then need to choose Document ➪ Replace Pages to replace the original file with the enabled file or delete the original from the PDF Package and insert the new enabled file. In short, using PDF Portfolios is much easier when you want to enable a file after the portfolio has been created.

CROSS-REF For more information on replacing pages, see Chapter 4. For more information on using PDF Portfolios, see Chapter 13.

FIGURE 10.11

To enable forms within a PDF Portfolio, double-click the file in the layout view, and then you have access to the enabling commands.

Using Batch Sequences

Using batch sequences provides you a means for automating certain editing tasks. Several batch sequences are available from preset options that you can use with forms, and you can create custom sequences by writing JavaScripts. Although you don't have a batch sequence for enabling forms, we tossed in using batch sequences in this chapter as it relates to comments and several other batch sequence commands available for working with forms.

Batch sequences are available only in the Acrobat Pro and Pro Extended products. You won't find batch sequences in Acrobat Standard.

You set up a batch sequence by choosing Advanced ➪ Document Processing ➪ Batch Processing. Selecting the command opens the Batch Sequences dialog box shown in Figure 10.12. In the Batch Sequences dialog box, you can choose to create a new sequence, edit an existing sequence, rename a sequence, delete a sequence, and run a sequence by clicking the respective buttons on the left side of the dialog box.

FIGURE 10.12

Choose Advanced ⇨ Document Processing ⇨ Batch Processing to open the Batch Sequences dialog box.

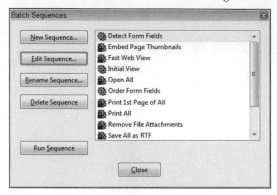

In this chapter, we talked about adding comments to forms. If you add comments and later want to delete comments from forms, you can use a batch sequence to delete all comments on forms within a folder on your hard drive. The batch sequence is run without the files open in Acrobat, thereby saving you much editing time. To see how a batch sequence is created for the purpose of deleting comments, do the following.

STEPS: Creating a New Batch Sequence

1. **Choose Advanced ⇨ Document Processing ⇨ Batch Processing.** The Batch Sequences dialog box opens.

2. **Create a new sequence.** Click New Sequence in the Batch Sequences dialog box. The Name Sequence dialog box opens. Type a name for your sequence, and click OK. In our example, we typed Delete Comments in the Name Sequence dialog box.

3. **Select commands.** The next dialog box that opens is the Edit Batch Sequence – (*name of sequence*) dialog box. In our example, the title of the dialog box is Edit Batch Sequence – Delete Comments. The last part of the dialog box title uses the name you typed in the Name Sequence dialog box.

   Click the Select Commands button, and the Edit Sequence dialog box opens. In this dialog box, you select from the list of preset commands in the list window on the left. In our example, we choose Delete All Comments, as shown in Figure 10.13. After a command is selected in the left list window, click the Add button to move the command to the right window.

FIGURE 10.13

Click the command you want to be part of your sequence in the scrollable list window, and click the Add button to move the command to the right window.

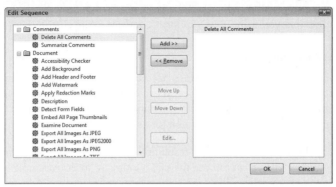

4. **Define the run conditions.** Click OK, and you return to the Edit Batch Sequence – (*name of sequence*) dialog box. You have two more choices to make. From the Run commands on the pull-down menu, choose a menu item to run the sequence. Your choices are to run the sequence on Selected Files, Selected Folder, Ask When Sequence Is Run, and Files Open in Acrobat. These choices should be self-explanatory.

   The second item to address is selecting the output options. From the Select output location options pull-down menu, choose Specific Folder, Ask When Sequence Is Run, Same folder as originals, or Don't Save Changes. The last item among these choices is one you might choose if you run a sequence on files open in Acrobat and want to check the files after running the sequence before saving them.

5. **Choose Output Options.** In the Output Options dialog box, you have choices for file naming, using the PDF Optimizer, and export formats. Make choices in this dialog box, and click OK.

When you click OK, you return to the Batch Sequences dialog box, and your sequence is ready to run. Click the Run Sequence button, and the sequence is run on the files you selected and saved according to the options you chose for the output. In terms of deleting comments, we could delete comments from an entire folder of files without having to open each file separately.

CROSS-REF For more information on using the PDF Optimizer, see the section "Using the PDF Optimizer" later in this chapter.

Using preset sequences for PDF forms

Deleting comments is but one of several sequences you might choose to use on PDF forms. Other presets help you perform some automated tasks that can help you batch process folders of files. You find the preset options all listed in the Edit Sequence list window. If you don't find a sequence listed in the window that you want to use on forms, you can write custom JavaScripts.

Using the PDF Optimizer

The PDF Optimizer enables you to reduce files sizes and clean up documents by eliminating unnecessary information to reduce file sizes. You can downsample images, remove hidden text, and perform cleanups on forms to get the file sizes smaller. PDF forms authors might use the PDF Optimizer to repurpose files that were prepared for commercial printing.

Whereas commercial printing requires high-resolution image files, viewing forms onscreen requires much lower resolution images. You can use the PDF Optimizer to downsample high-resolution images that can significantly reduce file sizes. If your form recipients will be downloading forms from Web sites, you'll want to minimize the download time by keeping your forms small in file size.

A built-in preset for optimizing files is handled by clicking the Output Options button in the Edit Sequence – (*name of sequence*) dialog box. Click Output Options, and the Output Options dialog box opens. In this dialog box, you find a direct link to the PDF Optimizer. Check the PDF Optimizer box, and click Settings to open the PDF Optimizer, as shown in Figure 10.14.

FIGURE 10.14

Click the Settings button in the Output Options dialog box to open the PDF Optimizer.

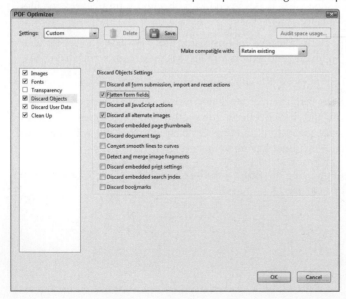

NOTE You also can open the PDF Optimizer by choosing Advanced ⇨ PDF Optimizer. Choosing this command allows you to optimize a file you have open in the Document pane.

The PDF Optimizer has a list of items on the left side of the dialog box similar to the Preferences dialog box. Click an item in the left list, and the pane on the right changes. In Figure 10.14, the Discard Objects pane is open. One item you find in this pane is the Flatten form fields option. If Flatten form fields is checked and you run the PDF Optimizer, the form fields are removed from the file while the data contained in the form fields are retained. You might use this feature to get rid of form fields on a form with many columns and rows to post results on a Web page.

When form fields are eliminated from a form, the file size can be reduced considerably. However, if you repurpose a form to reduce the file size or use other settings in the PDF Optimizer, be certain to disable the check mark for forms you intend to distribute. If you lose the field objects, form recipients can't fill in your forms.

Another item you find in the PDF Optimizer is the Make compatible with pull-down menu. The default is Retain existing, which is used to preserve the compatibility of the files you optimize. From this menu, you have choices to change the Acrobat compatibility to versions 4 through 9.

When a form recipient opens your Acrobat 9 forms in a version of Acrobat earlier than 9.0, a dialog box opens informing the user that the form was created in a newer format than the version used that opens the file. Also in the application alert dialog box is a recommendation that the user upgrade to a newer version of Acrobat, as shown in Figure 10.15. This warning is a good thing because it informs users that they should look into upgrading to newer versions of Acrobat/Reader that can take advantage of features in newer viewers.

FIGURE 10.15

When form recipients open PDF documents that were created in versions later than the form recipient's version of Acrobat, a dialog box recommends the user upgrade to a newer version of Acrobat.

In some enterprises, users are at the mercy of IT departments and decision makers who control the versions of the software you use. Employees may not have the luxury to routinely upgrade software until approved by management. If you know that form recipients need to work in an earlier version of Acrobat than the version you use, you can change the compatibility in the PDF Optimizer. When you save the file from the PDF Optimizer in an older format compatibility, the dialog box won't appear when form recipients use a version of Acrobat or Adobe Reader equal to or greater than the compatibility settings you chose when you optimized the file.

You must thoroughly test any forms you optimize in earlier versions of Acrobat/Reader to be certain everything on your form works. There are settings and edits you can make in one version of Acrobat that won't be accessible in earlier versions.

Optimizing scanned files

Another built-in batch sequence you find in the Edit Batch Sequence dialog box is the Optimize Scanned PDF setting. Choose this option, and add it to the list on the right in the Edit Sequence dialog box. When you double-click the item after adding it to the right pane, the Optimize Scanned PDF dialog box opens. Here you can make some adjustments to improve scanned forms, such as adjusting file size, removing halos, de-skewing the scans, removing edge shadow, and more, as shown in Figure 10.16.

FIGURE 10.16

You have a number of options to choose from when optimizing scanned forms.

Detecting fields and using OCR

Another preset found in the Batch Sequences dialog box is the Detect Form Fields item. This choice is the same as opening a file in Form Editing Mode, where Acrobat uses auto field detection to populate a form.

You could set up a workflow where you add the Optimize Scanned PDF item, add another item also found in Batch Sequences – Recognize Text Using OCR, and then add the Detect Form Fields item. The order of the options should follow the same order noted here. You first polish up a scanned image, then use Acrobat's OCR engine, and finally detect fields.

NOTE Using Detect Form Fields requires PDF forms to have text in the document. If you scan a form, the scanned document is an image file. You always need to use Recognize Text Using OCR if you want the Detect Form Fields command run on a scanned form. Be certain to add the Recognize Text Using OCR first, followed by Detect Form Fields if you are converting scanned image files to PDF forms.

As you create sequences, note that you can nest the settings in a list order in the right window in the Edit Sequence dialog box. The order you see in the list window is the same order in which the actions are run.

CROSS-REF For more information on using auto field detection, see Chapters 5 through 7. For more information on scanning paper forms and using OCR, see Chapter 6.

Ordering fields

The last item pertaining to form editing in batch sequences is the Order Form Fields item. Use this option to change the tab order on multiple files. If you know ahead of time that the tab orders are scrambled, run a sequence for changing the tab order.

CROSS-REF For more information on setting tab orders, see Chapter 7.

Creating custom sequences

The preset sequences can be a huge help to forms authors when a sequence exists to help you speed up your form editing. However, sometimes you won't find a preset listed in the batch sequences that serves your needs. If this is the case, you might be able to write a JavaScript to perform the action you want run on multiple files in a folder.

As an example, let's look at adding a stamp comment to a folder of files. For this kind of action, you need to create a custom sequence command using a JavaScript. To add a custom JavaScript to a batch sequence, follow these steps.

STEPS: Creating a Custom Batch Sequence

1. **Chose Advanced ➪ Document Processing ➪ Batch Processing.** The Batch Sequences dialog box opens.
2. **Add a new sequence.** Click New Sequence, and name the sequence when the Name Sequence dialog box opens. Click OK, and the Edit Batch Sequence dialog box opens.
3. **Select a command.** Click Select Commands to open the Edit Sequence dialog box.

4. **Add the Execute JavaScript command.** Scroll the list of commands, and click Execute JavaScript. Click the Add button to move the command to the right window.

5. **Write a JavaScript.** Double-click the Execute JavaScript command in the right window, and the JavaScript Editor opens. Type the following code in the JavaScript Editor.

```
1. /* adds a stamp to the first page */
2. var annot = this.addAnnot ({
3.   page:0,
4.   type: "Stamp",
5.   author: "Your Name",
6.   name: "Standard",
7.   rect: [400, 700, 600, 790],
8.   popupOpen: false,
9.   contents: "First Approval",
10. AP: "Approved"});
```

6. **Exit the JavaScript Editor.** Click OK to return to the Edit Sequence dialog box. Click OK and OK again to return to the Batch Sequences dialog box.

Note that the line numbers in the code are not used when you write a JavaScript. The script should be written similar to what you see in Figure 10.17. The code in this script uses a Stamp comment and adds the Approved stamp from the Standard Business stamps. The *contents* item adds the text within the quote marks in a pop-up note. When you run the script on a folder of files, you add the same stamp to all files in the folder. The location of the stamp on the form is defined by the coordinates described in line 7.

FIGURE 10.17

Write the JavaScript without the line numbers in the JavaScript Editor.

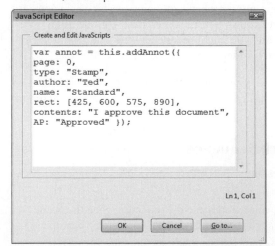

288

If you want to use a custom stamp in a batch sequence, your easiest way to handle it is to open your Acrobat folder and locate the Standard Business Stamps file. On Windows, the path is Acrobat 9.0/Acrobat/plug_ins/Annotations/Stamps/ENU/ (where ENU is the English installation of Acrobat).

On the Macintosh, you need to open a context menu on the Adobe Acrobat Pro application icon found in the Adobe Acrobat 9 Pro folder in your Applications folder. From the context menu commands, choose Show Package Contents. The path you follow to open the Stamps folder is Contents/Plug-ins/Comments.acroplugin/Stamps/ENU (for English language installations).

Be sure to back up this file on your hard drive. Move the file out of the folder, and open it in Acrobat. You have 14 stamps in this file. Choose a stamp that you're not likely to use, and choose Document ⇨ Replace Pages. Replace the existing stamp page with your custom design. Copy the folder back to the original folder in your Acrobat folder.

When you write a JavaScript, use the original name for the stamp. For example, if you replace the Approved stamp, use Approved in the JavaScript code as we described in the steps for creating a custom batch sequence. When you run the sequence, your custom stamp is added to the selected files.

CROSS-REF For more information on JavaScript, see Part V and Chapter 29.

Summary

- PDF documents can be enabled with special features for Adobe Reader users in version 9 of Acrobat Standard, Acrobat Pro, and Acrobat Pro Extended that enable Adobe Reader users to save form data and add digital signatures.

- Only Acrobat Pro and Pro Extended can enable files for comment and review.

- Adobe LiveCycle Designer forms are enabled in Acrobat.

- When you distribute a form, Acrobat enables the form with Reader usage rights in a wizard.

- Licensing restrictions do apply with adding special features to PDF files for Adobe Reader users.

- Form servers are used to add more features to PDF forms and aggregate data on more than 500 responses.

- In order to edit an enabled form, you need to save a copy and edit the copy that has been stripped of the enabling rights.

- PDF files can be enabled for Reader usage rights from within PDF Portfolios.

- Some commenting features can be used by forms authors. One of the more useful comment tools for forms authors is the Stamp tool.

- You can create custom stamps from any file supported by Acrobat for PDF creation.

- Batch sequences are helpful for automating tasks for forms authors.

- You can change Acrobat compatibility and save forms in earlier compatible versions of Acrobat from the PDF Optimizer.

- You can choose from a number of preset commands designed to work with forms to create batch sequences.

- Custom batch sequences are created with JavaScripts.

Chapter 11

Making Forms Accessible

Making a form or any other type of document accessible is to prepare a file with logical structure and tags that can be interpreted by a screen reader and other assistive devices. A screen reader is most commonly a software product that reads a document aloud for people who cannot see the text or have motion limitations that prohibit navigating a document.

The preparation of an accessible document begins with exporting a file to Adobe PDF from an authoring program that supports creating tagged documents. Programs such as the Microsoft Office applications and Adobe InDesign are examples of applications that can export tagged PDF documents. Be aware that the more complex the file in terms of design and page geometry, the more editing you may need to perform to make a document truly accessible.

Fortunately, Acrobat Pro and Pro Extended provide all the tools you need to create tagged PDF documents for accessibility and other tools to polish documents for defining logical reading orders and adding alternate text descriptions for page elements.

In this chapter, we cover creating accessible forms using Acrobat Pro and Pro Extended, adding alternate text for objects, creating tags, and organizing logical reading orders. In addition, we show you how to test your files for accessible features within Acrobat.

> **NOTE** All the content in this chapter applies only to Acrobat Pro and Pro Extended. Making documents accessible and using the Accessibility commands you find in Acrobat Pro and Pro Extended are not supported in Acrobat Standard.

IN THIS CHAPTER

Getting familiar with accessibility

Creating tagged PDF files

Creating accessible forms

Understanding Accessibility

U.S. Census reports on Americans with disabilities include a wide range of areas that are difficult to categorize within the scope of disabilities that affect one's ability to work on a computer and complete forms.

According to a 1997 U.S. Census report, almost 20 percent of the American population had one form of disability or another. Not all the disabilities included in the report would prevent a form recipient from completing and submitting a PDF form. For example, individuals with limited mobility may have sufficient sensory, visual, and motor skills to work on keyboards and manipulate a mouse.

Further investigation shows that more than 12 percent of the American population, as reported by the U.S. Census, are categorized as having severe disabilities. Again, these may include disabilities that do not affect one's ability to complete a form on a computer.

Table 11.1 shows the data accumulated by the U.S. Census Bureau in 1997 for Americans with disabilities. Although we cannot calculate with confidence the number of individuals within the American population that may need assistive devices to work on computers, we are confident that, of the 52 million people reported as having a disability, sufficient numbers need some form of assistive device to complete online forms.

TABLE 11.1

Americans with Disabilities—1997 U.S. Census Report

	Total	All Severities		Severe		Needs Assistance	
		Number	Percent	Number	Percent	Number	Percent
All ages	267,665,000	52,596,000	19.7	32,970,000	12.3	10,076,000	3.8
Under 15 years	59,606,000	4,661,000	7.8	2,256,000	3.8	224,000	0.4
15 to 24 years	36,897,000	3,961,000	10.7	1,942,000	5.3	372,000	1
25 to 44 years	83,887,000	11,200,000	13.4	6,793,000	8.1	1,635,000	1.9
45 to 54 years	33,620,000	7,585,000	22.6	4,674,000	13.9	1,225,000	3.6
55 to 64 years	21,591,000	7,708,000	35.7	5,233,000	24.2	1,280,000	5.9
65 to 69 years	9,555,000	4,291,000	44.9	2,930,000	30.7	777,000	8.1
70 to 74 years	8,514,000	3,967,000	46.6	2,407,000	28.3	898,000	10.5
75 to 79 years	6,758,000	3,897,000	57.7	2,565,000	38	1,140,000	16.9
80 years and over	7,237,000	5,325,000	73.6	4,170,000	57.6	2,525,000	34.9

Source: U.S. Census report 1997

Understanding assistive devices

For individuals with visual and motion challenges, a number of devices and applications are available for people with certain disabilities to effectively manipulate a computer and fill in PDF forms. Several software packages for the visually challenged, such as the JAWS screen reader and Window-Eyes, have internal speech synthesizers that read aloud content on pages. These applications also permit the user to read text character by character for optimal comprehension.

Setting accessibility preferences

For individuals with less severe disabilities, Acrobat itself has a number of settings you can control for displaying PDF files that enhance views for people with limited vision. For example, people in the early stages of a condition such as retinitis pigmentosa might be able to see large text and contrasting colors at higher zoom levels. You can make a number of changes to the display of PDF files by choosing Edit ⇨ Preferences (Windows) or Acrobat ⇨ Preferences (Mac) or pressing Ctrl/⌘+K to open the Preferences dialog box. Click Accessibility in the left pane, and the right pane changes as shown in Figure 11.1.

FIGURE 11.1

Open the Preferences dialog box, and click Accessibility in the left pane.

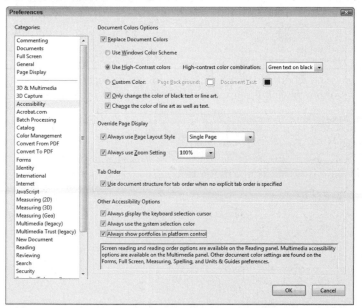

A number of preference options enable you to change the document colors and page display, including these:

- **Replace Document Colors:** Check the boxes and define colors for appearances of text and backgrounds. The default high-contrast setting uses green text on a black background. You can change the colors of text and backgrounds by clicking the color swatches adjacent to the high-contrast color combination text, or add your own custom colors for background and text.

- **Override Page Display:** If a PDF forms author creates an Initial View for displaying pages in Single Page-continuous layout and Fit Page view, you can change the page layout and the zoom level by making choices from the pull-down menus.

- **Tab Order:** Typically this option won't be critical for forms since you'll want to set tab orders properly for logical movement of the cursor to complete a form. If the user reads additional documents, the user may want to check this box for viewing PDFs without document structure.

- **Other Accessibility Options:** Enable options for keyboard selection cursor and system selection colors here. If you create PDF Portfolios, users can display a portfolio similar to the way PDF Packages were shown in Acrobat 8 and earlier viewers. In Figure 11.2, a PDF Portfolio is shown when the Always show portfolios in platform control check box is enabled. This view permits a user to use the keyboard arrow keys to navigate the files in a PDF Portfolio.

FIGURE 11.2

When you check Always show portfolios in platform control in the Accessibility preferences, PDF Portfolios are shown with files listed for easy navigation using keystrokes.

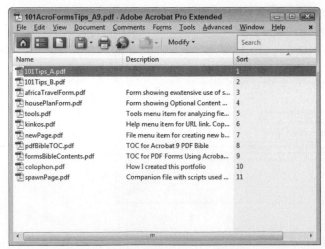

Using the Accessibility Setup Assistant

In addition to preference options, individual users can work with a setup assistant wizard to configure Acrobat for optimal viewing and interacting with accessible forms. To open the Accessibility Setup Assistant, choose Advanced ➪ Accessibility ➪ Setup Assistant. The Accessibility Setup Assistant opens, as shown in Figure 11.3.

FIGURE 11.3

Choose Advanced ➪ Accessibility ➪ Setup Assistant to open the Accessibility Setup Assistant.

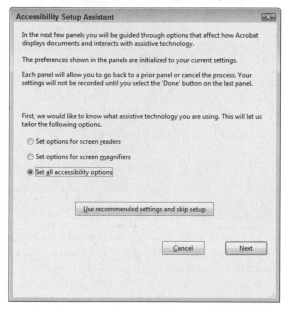

The Accessibility Setup Assistant has five panes that you move through to configure Acrobat for working with accessible documents. Some of the settings are not necessarily applicable to PDF forms, but making choices for handling all PDF documents won't adversely affect working with forms.

For an easy configuration, choose one of the three radio button options in the opening pane in the Accessibility Setup Assistant, and click the Use recommended settings and skip setup button. Acrobat configures your viewer to work with accessible documents as recommended by Adobe.

If you want to override some settings, step through the panes by clicking the Next button. The panes offer you choices for establishing reading order, tagging documents, handling large documents, overriding initial views, setting zoom levels, and setting some other displays. Many of the options you choose in the Accessibility Setup Assistant also are available in the Accessibility preferences.

Creating a workflow for authoring accessible PDF forms

Acrobat and LiveCycle Designer forms have some essential ingredients that need to be considered to make the forms accessible. Each of the following items must be addressed when creating forms that are truly accessible and can be read using assistive devices:

- **The document contains searchable text.** Some assistive devices can read image file formats such as TIFF. Image files, however, are not forms and cannot be used for form filling. You must be certain a form has text that can be interpreted by an assistive device. If you start with a scanned document, you need to use an OCR application such as Acrobat's Document ➪ OCR Text Recognition ➪ Recognize Text Using OCR menu command to convert the image file to a file with rich text. From there, you go add form fields as explained in Chapter 6.

- **Form Fields must be accessible.** Field descriptions are critical and must be added to form fields when making forms accessible. Field descriptions can be added in both Acrobat and LiveCycle Designer.

- **Forms must be structured and include tags.** All structural elements must be clearly identified in a form through the use of tagging elements. A tagged PDF file can be created when a file is exported from some original authoring programs and from within Acrobat.

- **Reading order must be logical.** Tagging a PDF file does not necessarily ensure that the reading order of the structural elements is properly set. You may need to manually order elements in Acrobat and spend some time preparing a file for accessibility.

- **Alternate text must be added for images and objects.** This is another manual operation you need to perform. Acrobat cannot interpret objects and images and deliver the content to a screen reader with descriptive text. Logos, drawings, illustrations, images, and so on must have alternate text added to each element to give the form recipient using an assistive device a text description for what exists on a form.

- **Navigational links must be described.** Form field navigation is determined by setting proper tab orders for fields. If you have URL links, page navigation links, bookmarks, and so on, these link items must have descriptive text associated with the links so a form recipient using an assistive device fully comprehends the action associated with each link.

- **A document language needs to be defined.** Some screen readers are designed for multiple language use. You need to specify a default language for accessible files for users who can switch languages with their devices. Specifying a language can be handled directly within Acrobat.

- **Documents must use type fonts that can be extracted.** Fonts need to carry enough information so the text can be extracted by a screen reader for proper interpretation. If you use fonts that are substituted by Acrobat, certain characters may not be properly interpreted by the screen reader.

- **Security settings must permit text extraction.** You must be certain that secure forms do not prohibit text extraction by screen readers. Acrobat's security options offer you options for securing documents while making them accessible.

CROSS-REF For more information on securing files, see Chapter 12.

By applying these nine criteria you can create accessible forms that can be filled in by Adobe Reader and Acrobat users working with screen readers. Each criterion is significant and requires both attention and verification that all the elements are properly added to a form to make it accessible. Unfortunately, you cannot completely automate creating accessible forms. Depending on the complexity of a form, you should plan on devoting more time to making a form accessible than the time required to create a form.

Tagging PDF Files

Forms must be structured and tagged to make them accessible for users of assistive technology so they may navigate and read the forms easily in programs like Adobe Reader and Acrobat. Many users depend on assistive devices to properly read documents in an order similar to the way people not needing such devices may fill out a form. For example, reading forms and filling in fields from top to bottom in sections might be the most logical way to fill in a form. If a document is unstructured and without tags, an assistive device might read the same form from left to right across the page, ignoring columns and divisions and making the task for the form recipient more complicated.

Creating tags and adding structure to forms is best achieved by starting with an authoring program that exports PDFs with tags and structure. Programs like Microsoft Office applications and Adobe InDesign are the best candidates for creating tagged PDF files.

Checking the status of tagged PDF files

The easiest way to check a PDF file for tags is to open the Document Properties dialog box; choose File ➪ Properties or press Ctrl/⌘+D. Click the General tab in the Document Properties dialog box. In the Advanced section in the lower-left corner of the dialog box, document tagging is reported, as shown in Figure 11.4.

FIGURE 11.4

Open the Document Properties dialog box by pressing Ctrl/⌘+D, and click the General tab to check a document for tagging.

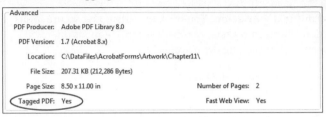

Advanced			
PDF Producer:	Adobe PDF Library 8.0		
PDF Version:	1.7 (Acrobat 8.x)		
Location:	C:\DataFiles\AcrobatForms\Artwork\Chapter11\		
File Size:	207.31 KB (212,286 Bytes)		
Page Size:	8.50 x 11.00 in	Number of Pages:	2
Tagged PDF:	Yes	Fast Web View:	Yes

Running a quick accessibility check

You also can check a document's structure and reading order via the Advanced ⇨ Accessibility ⇨ Quick Check menu command (keyboard shortcut: Shift+Ctrl/⌘+6). Acrobat checks the document for structure and reports findings in a dialog box like the one shown in Figure 11.5.

FIGURE 11.5

Choose Advanced ⇨ Accessibility ⇨ Quick Check to perform an accessibility quick check.

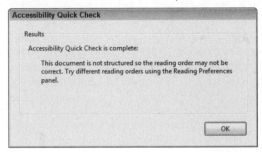

Accessibility Quick Check

Results

Accessibility Quick Check is complete:

This document is not structured so the reading order may not be correct. Try different reading orders using the Reading Preferences panel.

OK

For a quick glance at a document's structure and tags, open the Order panel by opening a context menu in the Navigation pane and choosing Order or by selecting View ⇨ Navigation Panels ⇨ Order.

The Order panel displays tags in the document in a hierarchical order and bounding boxes on a document page where the page elements are located according to the tag order, as shown in Figure 11.6.

FIGURE 11.6

Open a context menu on the Navigation pane, and choose Order to open the Order panel.

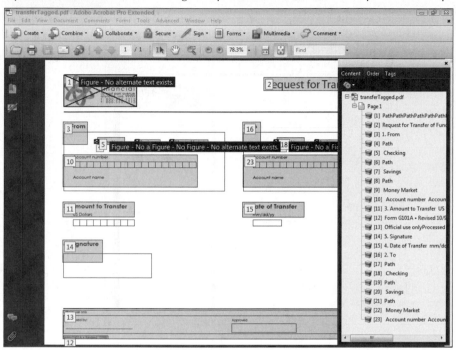

If you open the same file without tags and display the Order panel, you find no structural elements on the page and no list of page elements in the Order panel, as shown in Figure 11.7. The document shown in Figure 11.6 was exported from Adobe InDesign with tags. The document shown in Figure 11.7 is the same form exported from Adobe InDesign without tags.

When you open the Order panel on an untagged PDF document, the document displays no structural elements and no tags appear in the Order panel.

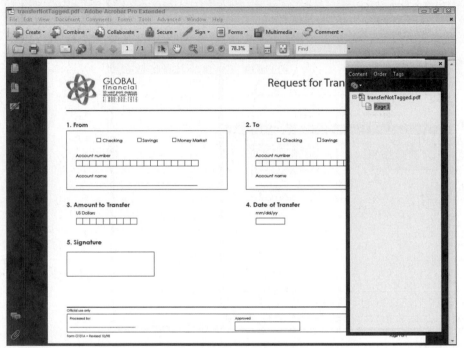

Running a full accessibility check

The quick accessibility check provides you a report in a dialog box informing you of the status for document accessibility. The description is brief and provides no information on how to overcome problems with an untagged document.

For a more comprehensive report and suggestions that offer you information on how to resolve problems with an untagged PDF document, you can run the Accessibility Full Check. To do so, choose Advanced ➪ Accessibility ➪ Full Check. The Accessibility Full Check dialog box opens, as shown in Figure 11.8.

For the most comprehensive report, check all boxes. By default, the Create comments in document check box is disabled. Check this box to add comment notes to the document. For the Name checking options, Adobe PDF is the default. If you want to create accessible documents that conform to standards such as U.S. Section 508 laws or Web Content Accessibility Guidelines, open the pull-down menu and make a choice for the standard you want to work with.

FIGURE 11.8

Choose Advanced ➪ Accessibility ➪ Full Check to open the Accessibility Full Check dialog box.

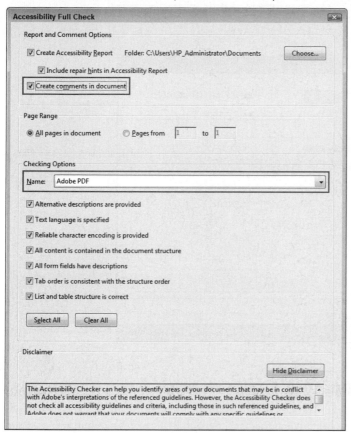

After making choices for assessment options in the Accessibility Full Check dialog box, click OK and Acrobat performs a more comprehensive check than when using the Quick Check. If you checked Create comments in document, comment notes are added to the document and the Accessibility Report opens in the Navigation pane, as shown in Figure 11.9.

Scroll the Accessibility Report panel to review the status of the document. In the panel you'll find hints and suggestions for making the document more accessible. Note that one suggestion you find always appearing when checking untagged PDF files is a recommendation to return to the original authoring program and recreate the PDF file with tagging enabled.

After running a full check, Acrobat displays a report in the Navigation pane.

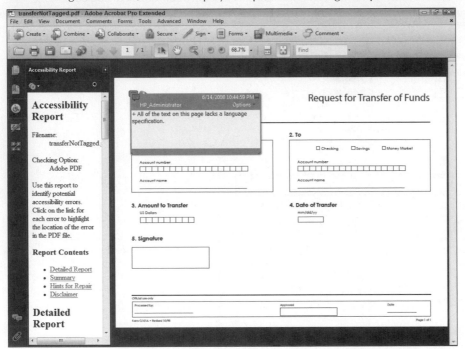

Creating tags in untagged documents

Again, we reiterate the fact that you're best served by starting with a tagged document where tags are supported in an authoring application and the conversion to PDF creates tags and retains document structure. If your work requires you to consistently create accessible forms, you must seriously consider using programs that produce tagged PDF files. Using manual methods to create tags is not only more timely, but the results are most often less desirable than when creating tagged PDF files by exporting from authoring programs supporting tags.

Adding tags and document structure after PDF creation typically results in a structured document with less conformity to the original document structure. As an example, look at Figures 11.10 and 11.11. Figure 11.10 shows a document where tags were added in the original authoring applications and preserved when converted to PDF. In Figure 11.11, the tags were added after PDF creation.

FIGURE 11.10

Document structure shown on a file where tags were added in the original authoring program.

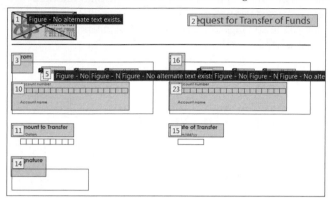

FIGURE 11.11

Tags added to a document after PDF creation.

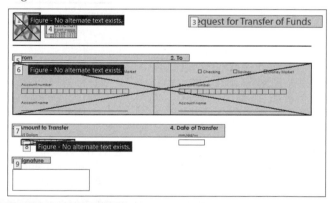

ON the CD-ROM You can compare an untagged PDF file with a tagged PDF file by opening the *transferTagged.pdf* and *transferNotTagged.pdf* files on the book's CD-ROM in the Chapter 11 folder. Open the Order panel, and compare the two files.

In some cases you may have no other alternative than to create tags after a file has been converted to PDF. If you plan to add tags to a PDF in Acrobat, you should try to anticipate the time needed to completely redesign a form in an authoring program supporting tags versus the time you need to manually structure the PDF to make it accessible. If you must tag a document after PDF creation, Acrobat provides tools that enable you to add tags to untagged PDF documents. To add tags to an untagged PDF document, follow these steps.

 You can follow the steps using the *transferNotTagged.pdf* file on the book's CD-ROM in the Chapter 11 folder.

STEPS: Adding Tags to an Untagged PDF Document

1. **Open an untagged PDF document.** In our example, we use the *transferNotTagged.pdf* file in the Chapter 11 folder on the book's CD-ROM.

2. **Add tags to the document.** Choose Advanced ➪ Accessibility ➪ Add Tags to Document. Alternately, you can open the Tags panel, and from a context menu opened on the text that reads *No Tags available,* choose Add Tags to Document, as shown in Figure 11.12.

Open a context menu in the Tags panel, and choose Add Tags to Document.

3. **Review the document structure.** Open the Order panel, and look over the document structure. If the structure of the document is such that it would make the job of creating an accessible form difficult, you'll want to redesign the form and add tags when you export to PDF.

4. **Review the Accessibility Report.** When you add tags to a document, the Accessibility Report panel opens in the Navigation pane, as shown in Figure 11.13. Scroll the report and read all the information to help you determine what needs to be done to make the document accessible.

FIGURE 11.13

The Accessibility Report panel details what you must do to make the document accessible.

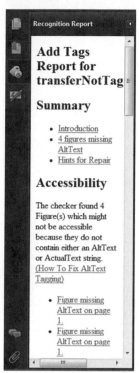

Designing Forms for Accessibility

Designing forms for accessibility requires some different considerations than you might have for forms that are not accessible. Among other things, you'll want to keep the number of form elements at a minimum. For example, boxes, lines, and graphic dividers on a form should be minimal. When the time comes to add alternate text and change properties for form objects, the fewer items you have to work with, the easier your editing tasks will be.

As an example, look at the form design in Figure 11.14. For a non-accessible form, this form is simple and works well. Creating the field objects is easy, and finishing the form design for form recipients to complete and submit back to you is an easy editing task.

FIGURE 11.14

This form is a simple design that can be used for a non-accessible form.

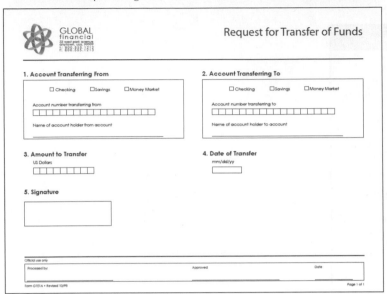

Now look at the elements on this form in Figure 11.15. It's not overbearing, but quite a few document elements must be modified when adding alternate text and changing elements' properties.

FIGURE 11.15

When the Order panel is open, you see the form elements.

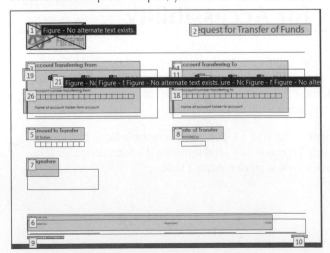

Compare Figure 11.14 with Figure 11.16; both figures show the same form, but there are fewer objects on the form designer than in Figure 11.14. By using the Document Message Bar to highlight fields, certain objects such as boxes and lines are unnecessary. If you look over the form elements when you open the Order panel, you can see that the form shown in Figure 11.16 has less than half the document elements as the form in Figure 11.14.

FIGURE 11.16

The same form as shown in Figure 11.14, with fewer document elements.

There is one caveat to designing a form like the one shown in Figures 11.16 and 11.17. You need all the elements in the first form shown in Figure 11.14 to use Acrobat's auto field detection when you add fields to a form. Without all the form objects, Acrobat won't be able to automatically detect fields. The problem then becomes how to create the form shown in Figure 11.16 using all the objects for auto field detection from those shown in Figure 11.14.

FIGURE 11.17

When the Order panel is open, this form shows less than half the document elements as the form shown in Figure 11.15.

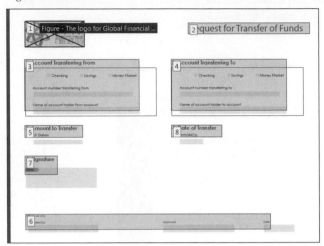

Designing an accessible form

Many of the design principles we covered in Chapter 4 apply to forms you design for accessibility. Above all, remember to not use text for objects. As discussed in Chapter 4, you need to use geometric shapes for boxes rather than text characters for Acrobat's auto field detection to pick up check boxes.

You also need to avoid using text for lines. If you use a series of underscores for a line, the screen reader may pick up the text and read aloud *underscore, underscore, underscore* for each keystroke used to create the line. If you draw a line using a shape tool in your authoring program, the lines won't be picked up by the screen reader unless you add alternate text to the objects.

To minimize the number of objects you add to an accessible form, you have two choices. You can design two forms in authoring programs that don't support exporting to PDF with Adobe PDF Layers. One design must have all the elements you want to use for auto field detection, and the other design is the final form with a minimal number of objects.

You export both files to PDF and open the file with all the objects in Acrobat. Choose Forms ➪ Add or Edit Fields, and let Acrobat auto detect fields when you enter Form Editing Mode. After adding the fields, exit Form Editing Mode, choose Document ➪ Replace Pages, and replace the page of the original design with the second file you exported from the authoring application that contains a minimal number of objects.

CROSS-REF For more information on replacing pages, see Chapter 4.

Your second option (and our preference) is to use an application that supports exporting Adobe PDF Layers and creates a tagged PDF document. The only choice you have for the authoring application is Adobe InDesign. In Figure 11.18, you can see a form layout in Adobe InDesign CS4 that contains two layers. The Objects layer contains all non-essential objects for the final form except those objects needed to take advantage of using Acrobat's auto field detection. The Accessible layer is the layer that contains the elements needed for the final form appearance.

A layered form design is created in Adobe InDesign CS4.

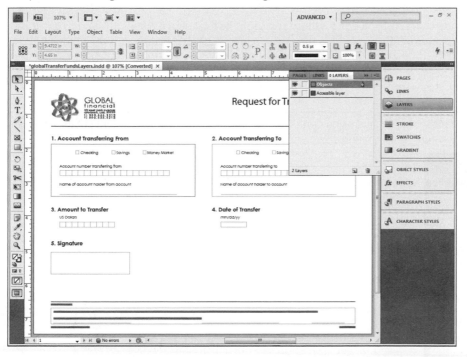

When we export the form from Adobe InDesign, we make certain the Create Acrobat Layers check box is checked in the Export Adobe PDF dialog box. When the file opens in Acrobat, we choose Forms ➪ Add or Edit Fields and let Acrobat auto detect fields on the form. We exit Form Editing mode and open the layers panel.

To eliminate a layer, hide the layer in the Layers panel by clicking the eye icon. When the eye icon is not visible, the layer is hidden, as shown in Figure 11.19.

FIGURE 11.19

Click the Layers panel icon to open the Layers panel, and click an eye icon to hide a layer.

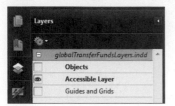

After you hide layers that you don't want to appear in the final design, choose Flatten Layers from the Layers panel drop-down menu, as shown in Figure 11.20. Acrobat discards the hidden layers and you're left with the final form design.

FIGURE 11.20

After auto detecting fields, hide all layers you don't want to appear in the final design and choose Flatten Layers from the Options drop-down menu.

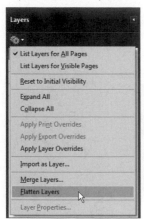

ON the CD-ROM To practice working with layered PDF files, open the *globalTransferFundsLayers.pdf* file from the Chapter 11 folder on the book's CD-ROM.

Choosing a language

Accessible forms should have a primary language identified for the form. To select a language, open the Document Properties dialog box by choosing File ➪ Properties or pressing Ctrl/⌘+D. Click the Advanced tab in the Document Properties dialog box, and from the Language drop-down menu, choose the primary language form recipients will use to complete your form, as shown in Figure 11.21.

FIGURE 11.21

Click the Advanced tab in the Document Properties window, and choose a primary language from the Language drop-down menu.

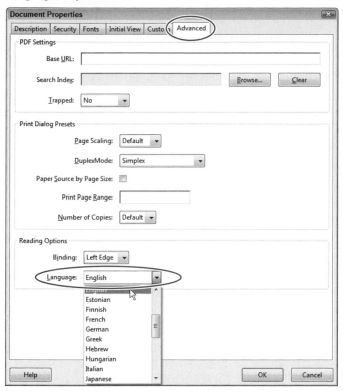

Setting up form fields

Ideally, you first start working with a PDF form that has been tagged when converted to PDF. If you have to manually tag a document, first add the tags and then create the PDF form.

Creating a form follows the steps we outlined in Chapters 5 through 9. You can use Acrobat's auto field detection by choosing Forms ➪ Add or Edit Fields to entering Form Editing mode. If additional fields need to be added to a form, use the Form tools in Form Editing mode to add additional fields and open the Properties window to adjust field properties.

Each field should have a tooltip description for the respective field. In the field Properties dialog box, type a tooltip in the General tab. Tooltips are not read when you read a form aloud, but they are read by screen readers when a form recipient tabs into a field.

In Figure 11.22, you can see a tooltip added to a check box field. When the form recipient tabs into the field, the tooltip text is read by the screen reader. In addition, the screen reader reports the status of check boxes as being *Unchecked* or *Checked*.

FIGURE 11.22

Screen readers read aloud tooltips when a form recipient tabs into a form field.

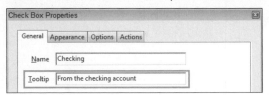

After creating fields, exit Form Editing mode by clicking the Close Form Editing button and use Viewer mode to perform edits to structural elements such as adding alternate text to document elements.

CROSS-REF For more information on using Form Editing mode, see Chapters 5 through 7.

Another item that needs attention is setting tab orders. Although you ideally want to set tab orders for all forms, you can get away with not paying attention to tab orders when preparing forms for the general population. When it comes to accessible forms, setting tab orders carries a different level of importance and it's critical that you set the tab orders properly to follow the document structure.

CROSS-REF For more information on setting tab orders, see Chapter 7.

Editing form elements

Presuming you've spent some time creating a form design in an original authoring program, exported to PDF, and then added form fields to your form, your work is less than half finished. Quite often the most work you need to do to create an accessible form is related to organizing the reading order of a form, adding alternate text, and testing the form with a screen reader to be certain the form reads aloud intelligently.

Setting the reading order

The tab order you set up in the Fields panel in Form Editing mode determines the order for tabbing into form fields. You'll want to be certain that the tab order matches the reading order on a form. To order form elements, follow these steps.

ON the CD-ROM To follow these steps, you can use the *globalTransferFundsFields.pdf* on the book's CD-ROM in the Chapter 11 folder.

STEPS: Setting the Reading Order of a Form

1. **Open a form in Acrobat Pro or Pro Extended.** For our example, we use the *global-TransferFundsFields.pdf* file in the Chapter 11 folder on the book's CD-ROM.

2. **Open the Order panel.** Choose View ⇨ Navigation Panels ⇨ Order to open the Order panel, or open a context menu on the Navigation pane and choose Order.

3. **Dock the Order panel in the Navigation pane.** This step is optional. You can leave the Order panel as a floating panel in the Acrobat window or dock the panel in the Navigation pane. Docking the panel provides a little more uncluttered viewing area if you're working on a smaller monitor.

4. **Examine the reading order of the form.** Each element on the form contains a number. The reading order of the document follows a sequential order according to the numbers displayed when the Order panel is in view. In Figure 11.23, we have a few items that need to be reordered. Notice that item 6 appears at the bottom of the form. The reading order follows a top to bottom order, and we want this form to read left to right for each row.

FIGURE 11.23

Examine the reading order by opening the Order panel.

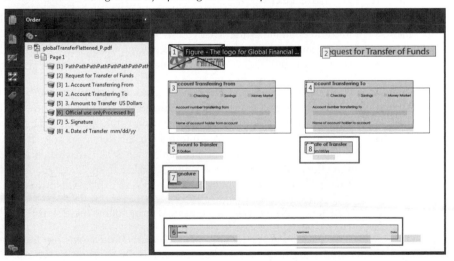

5. **Reorder elements.** Just like reordering fields in the Fields panel, you can reorder elements on a form in the Order panel. Click an item such as item 8 in the Order panel, and drag it to the bottom of the panel to make this item the last element in the reading order. Click the date of transfer item, and move it below item 5 in the Order panel. The final order is shown in Figure 11.24.

6. **Save the file after reordering the elements.**

FIGURE 11.24

The form shown after reordering elements

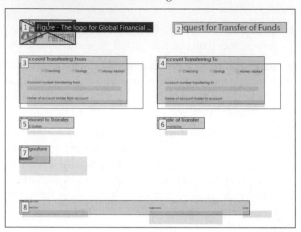

Adding alternate text

Perhaps the most time-consuming aspect of creating accessible forms is adding alternate text to elements on a form. Keep in mind that what you see graphically on a form needs to be spelled out in text for a screen reader to read aloud a description of your form. Any objects such as images, logos, diagrams, Flash videos, and similar items need alternate text descriptions.

In addition to objects, you need to think about the various sections on your form. Looking back at Figure 11.16, there are five different sections on the form. The first item deals with money to be transferred from an account. As a visual form recipient, you can quickly glance over this form and see that item 1 identifies the *from* account information and item 2 specifies the *to* account information. Unfortunately form recipients using a screen reader don't have the advantage of quickly glancing at a form to understand the various sections that relate to specific form data. In this regard, you might want to introduce each section with alternate text to explain the purpose of each section.

To add alternate text to objects and elements on a form, follow these steps.

ON the CD-ROM We continue with the form *globalTransferFundsFields.pdf* found in the Chapter 11 folder on the book's CD-ROM. Use this file to follow the steps.

STEPS: Adding Alternate Text to Objects

1. **Open a form in Acrobat Pro or Pro Extended.** For the steps used here, we work with the *globalTransferFundsFields.pdf* found in the Chapter 11 folder on the book's CD-ROM.

2. **Open the Tags panel.** Choose View ➪ Navigation Panels ➪ Tags, or open a context menu on the Navigation pane and choose Tags.

3. **Dock the Tags panel.** Drag the Tags tab to the Navigation pane to dock it. Again, this step is optional. You can leave the panel as a floating panel or dock it in the Navigation pane.

4. **Expand the tags.** If the tags are collapsed so only the Tags item is visible in the Tags panel, click the plus symbol to expand the tags.

5. **Turn the Highlight on.** Open a context menu on a tag, and choose Highlight Content. When Highlight Content is active, the tags you select in the Tags panel displays the corresponding objects on the form with a keyline border.

6. **Locate the logo on the form.** Click items in the Tags panel, and observe the highlights on the form. Expand the Figure item in the Tags panel, and click the item marked PathPathPath, and so on. The logo in the top-left corner of the form is highlighted, as shown in Figure 11.25.

7. **Open the Properties dialog box.** Open a context menu on a tag where you want to add alternate text.

FIGURE 11.25

Turn Highlight Content on, and choose Properties when you select an object where you want to add alternate text.

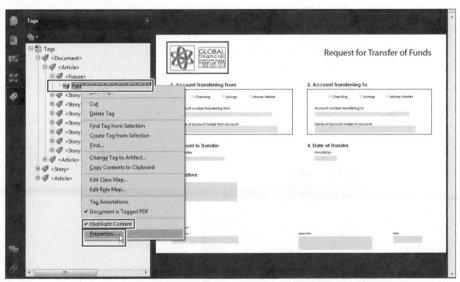

8. **Add text to the Alternate Text box.** When you click Properties from a selected tag context menu, the TouchUp Properties dialog box opens, as shown in Figure 11.26. Type the alternate text you want read aloud by a screen reader in the Alternate Text box.

FIGURE 11.26

Type alternate text in the Alternate Text box.

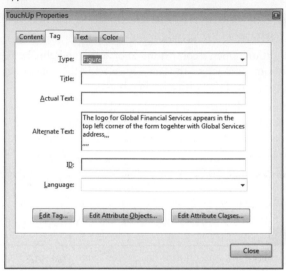

9. **Click Close.**
10. **Select a text object on the form.** With the Tags panel in view, open the Tags panel and locate the check boxes for the 1. Account Transferring From section, as shown in Figure 11.27. You may need to expand tags and click several tags to highlight the tag you want to edit.
11. **Open the Properties dialog box.** Open a context menu, and choose Properties on the item selected in the Tags panel.

FIGURE 11.27

Locate a text object in the Tags panel.

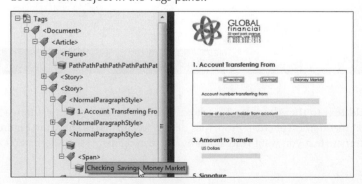

12. **Add alternate text to the object.** Type text in the Alternate Text box for the selected object. In our example, we want the screen reader to inform the form recipient that three check boxes are in the group and what each check box is used for, as shown in Figure 11.28.

Type alternate text for the selected object.

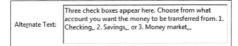

Alternate Text: Three check boxes appear here. Choose from what account you want the money to be transferred from. 1. Checking,, 2. Savings,, or 3. Money market,,,

13. **Continue finding objects that need alternate text, and add text to the TouchUp Properties Alternate Text box.**

ON the CD-ROM You can find alternate text added to all the elements on a final form we created in the Chapter 11 folder on the book's CD-ROM. Open the *globalTransferAltText.pdf* file, and look over the alternate text we added to this file.

Setting reading preferences

Ideally, you should have a screen reader or several screen readers from different developers to test your form after making edits. However, you may be a forms author who doesn't have a screen reader and you are engaged in creating accessible forms. If you don't have a screen reader to test the final results, you can use Adobe Reader or any Acrobat viewer to read aloud a form. Using Acrobat, you can test your results to be certain that all the elements have proper alternate text to make the form intelligible for people using screen readers.

Before you begin reading a document, you can make some preferences adjustments in the Reading Preferences. Choose Edit ➪ Preferences (Windows) or Acrobat ➪ Preferences (Macintosh) or press Ctrl/⌘+K to open the Preferences dialog box. Click Reading in the left pane, and the right pane changes as shown in Figure 11.29.

Open the Preferences dialog box and click Reading in the left pane to display Reading preferences in the right pane.

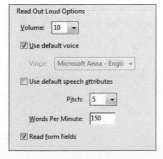

The Read Out Loud section in the Reading Preferences has some options that are used with the Read Out Loud commands. The options include:

- **Volume:** Adjust the volume from selections in the drop-down menu, or type a value from 1 to 10 in the text box.

- **Use default voice:** Check this box to use the default text to speech voice supported by your operating system. If you uncheck the box, you can choose another voice listed in the drop-down menu.

- **Pitch:** Change the pitch value from 1 to 10. Some experimenting may be needed here to find the best pitch value.

- **Words per minute:** The lowest value you can choose is 150 words per minute. Set the value to 150 to slow down the reading.

- **Read form fields:** Check this box to read form fields on your forms.

Reading a form aloud

Open a form in any Acrobat viewer. The form *globalTransferAltText.pdf* file on the book's CD-ROM in the Chapter 11 folder contains alternate text. You can use this form to test the read aloud feature in Acrobat.

From the View menu, choose Read Out Loud. The submenu contains several commands to read a document aloud, as shown in Figure 11.30.

FIGURE 11.30

Choose View ➪ Read Out Loud to open the Read Out Loud submenu.

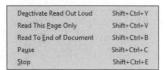

When you first open the submenu, all items are grayed out and the first command in the submenu is listed as Activate Read Out Loud. Selecting this command loads the Read Out Loud routine used in Acrobat viewers. The first item then changes to the Deactivate Read Out Loud command you see listed in Figure 11.28. From the submenu, you have these additional commands:

- **Read this page only:** Choose this item to read out loud the page in view in the Document pane. Be certain your computer speakers are working properly before activating Read Out Loud.

- **Read to End of Document:** If you have a form with several pages and want all pages read, choose this command.

- **Pause:** Try to remember the keyboard shortcuts listed adjacent to the commands. You can temporarily pause the reading by choosing this command or pressing Shift+Ctrl/⌘+C. When you pause the reading, the Pause command changes to Resume. Use the same keyboard shortcut to resume reading.

- **Stop:** Clicking Stop stops the reading, but Read Out Loud remains activated. You can choose the Read This Page Only or Read to End of Document commands or use the keyboard shortcuts to read the document again.

After you review the form from the Chapter 11 folder on the book's CD-ROM, activate Read Out Loud and press the Tab key to tab through fields. As you tab to new fields, the tooltips are read aloud by your Acrobat viewer.

Read Out Loud is a nice feature in Acrobat to test accessible forms you edit. However, one of the main limitations you have is that the reading cannot be controlled to read character by character text for better comprehension and the reading speed cannot be lower than 150 words per minute. Screen Readers provide many more options for controlling reading.

Summary

- Accessible forms are used with screen reading devices and assistive devices for persons with disabilities.

- In the U.S., almost 20 percent or more than 50 million people are categorized as having some form of disability.

- All Acrobat viewers have preferences options to change the interface to accommodate certain visual appearances that can help individuals with limited vision.

- In order to make forms accessible, the forms must be tagged.

- Tagging forms is best handled in authoring applications supporting tagging when converting to PDF.

- You can add tags to untagged documents using commands in Acrobat Pro and Pro Extended.

- Forms are easier to make accessible when you have fewer document elements. You can create layered files containing all elements needed for auto field detection in Adobe InDesign and flatten and discard layers in Acrobat after using auto field detection.

- When designing forms for accessibility, avoid using text characters for graphic objects such as underscores for lines.

- Forms can be read aloud using commands in all Acrobat viewers.

- When a document is activated for Read Out Loud, tabbing into fields reads the tooltips for the fields.

Chapter 12

Using Signatures and Security

We lightly touched on adding digital signatures to forms in Chapters 5 through 7, and in several other earlier chapters we also mentioned securing files. We combine these two topics in this chapter because signing a form provides a form recipient with one level of security. Anyone signing a form can be assured that additional edits on a form will invalidate a signature.

All users of all Acrobat viewers can create digital signature ID files that are necessary to sign a form, and all Acrobat users are subject to the same limitations for permissions when files have been secured.

You should be aware of the steps needed to create digital IDs so you can create your own digital IDs for signing forms and coach Adobe Reader users when the need arises on how to create and use digital IDs. You also should know the various options you have for securing a document and preventing your forms from being edited by others. Knowing when to secure a form and what permissions you need to lock out of forms is critical. In this chapter, we talk about the issues related to digital signatures and security options that are important for PDF forms authors.

IN THIS CHAPTER

Getting familiar with digital signatures

Creating a digital ID

Adding security to forms

Understanding Digital Signatures

A digital ID can be created in all Acrobat viewers. Adobe Reader and Acrobat users can create and use digital IDs. For Adobe Reader users, forms must be enabled with Reader usage rights before the Reader user can sign a document.

CROSS-REF For more information on enabling PDFs with Adobe Reader usage rights, see Chapter 10.

To sign a form, you need a digital ID. Digital IDs are created in an Acrobat viewer and saved as a file. The IDs you create are displayed in the Security Settings dialog box shown in Figure 12.1. As you sign forms, you use your digital ID. Typically you don't need to locate your digital ID file to sign a document, but if your Acrobat viewer looses the file location on your hard drive, you may need to browse your drive to find the file.

FIGURE 12.1

Digital IDs are displayed in the Security Settings dialog box.

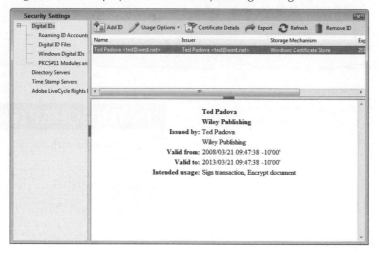

Digital IDs have two important components—your personal or private digital ID and your public certificate. When you create a digital ID with Acrobat, you are creating your private ID and your public certificate. The public certificate is a file you share with other users so they can authenticate your signature.

Digital IDs can be created in all Acrobat viewers. However, more industrial-strength digital IDs can be acquired and used through services provided by third-party vendors. A digital ID you create from within an Acrobat viewer is stored locally on your computer. If you use a third-party product for signature handling, IDs are stored on a vendor's server.

Using Acrobat viewers to create digital IDs or choosing to use a third-party signature handler largely depends on the level of security you need for your company. Individuals, small businesses, and companies not dealing with sensitive information can confidently use an Acrobat viewer to create a digital ID. If you work with government offices and large enterprises dealing with sensitive information, then using a third-party product might be the best choice. Organizations dealing with the most sensitive data such as the U.S. National Security Agency or the Homeland Security Office are likely to develop their own in-house signature handlers running on their secure servers.

Using third-party signature handlers

For the purposes of the Acrobat Forms section of this book, we don't delve into the world of third-party signature handlers. Rather, we try to focus on what you can do with digital signatures right out of the box when you install Acrobat and for signatures added by Adobe Reader users.

You can research an abundant amount of information related to digital signatures and third-party signature handlers on the Web. Adobe's Web site is full of great information. See `http://www.adobe.com/devnet/acrobat/security.html` for information related to security and `http://www.adobe.com/security/digsig.html` for more information on third-party signature handlers.

For some third-party signature handlers, look at some of the products provided by Entrust `http://www.entrust.com/` and VeriSign `http://www.verisign.com`.

Using wet signatures

A wet signature on an electronic form might be a scanned image of your analog signature. If you use a wet signature that's not part of a digital ID, the signature carries no validity, verification, security, or authenticity. In this regard, a wet signature might just be an imported graphic, and you cannot add a level of security to graphic imports used as wet signatures.

Wet signatures, however, do have their place. You might be working on internal forms within a company and need to sign a vacation leave request, maternity leave form, memo, or some such document that does not require authentication of your signature and needs no security.

Unfortunately, Acrobat viewers do not have an option for applying wet signatures to documents unless you create an appearance for a digital ID. The downside for using digital IDs, particularly for the Adobe Reader audience, is that creating an ID and using it is complicated. Novice users often find creating IDs and verifying signatures to be a difficult task.

As an alternative to using digital IDs for signing documents where merely a scan of your analog signature is acceptable to a host organization, you can create some workarounds using Acrobat Pro, Pro Extended, or Adobe LiveCycle Designer to prepare files for applying a wet signature.

Scanning an analog signature

To use a graphic for a wet signature, you need to scan your signature and save the scan as an image file compatible with conversion to PDF from within Acrobat or save as a PDF file. Adobe Reader users would need a scan saved as a PDF file.

Depending on whether form recipients are using Acrobat or Adobe Reader, you may want to polish up your scan a bit in a program like Adobe Photoshop. If a graphic can be imported with transparency like you see in Figure 12.2, the signature looks a little more authentic than importing a signature without transparency, as shown in Figure 12.3.

FIGURE 12.2

A graphic imported into a PDF document with transparency

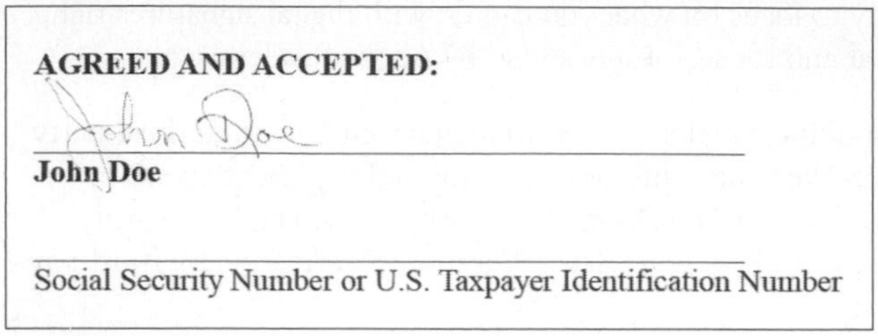

FIGURE 12.3

Without transparency, the background white area knocks out background objects and text.

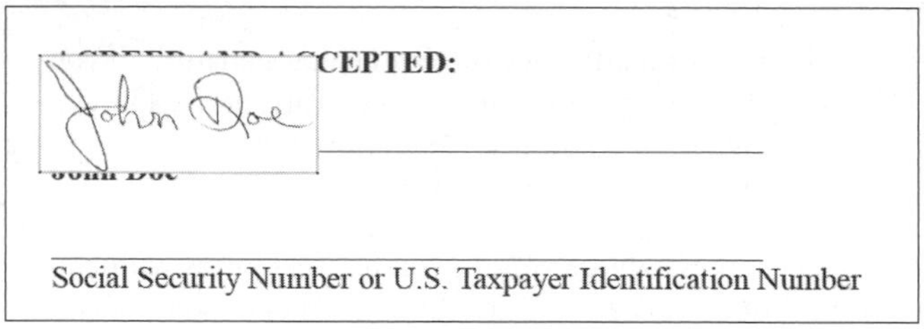

Adding wet signatures in Adobe Reader

Unfortunately, you cannot import the graphic in Figure 12.2 in Adobe Reader. Reader users are stuck with importing graphics with solid white backgrounds, as shown in Figure 12.3. Such imports demonstrate an obvious manipulation of the digital file when the signature appears over text or objects rather than appearing like an authentic signature.

If using a wet signature with the appearance shown in Figure 12.3 works for your needs, the following steps are needed for the Reader user to import a scan into a PDF document.

ON the CD-ROM For the following steps, you can use the *leaveRequestEnabled.pdf* and *johnDoe-Solid.pdf* files found on the book's CD-ROM in the Chapter 12 folder.

STEPS: Applying a Wet Signature in Adobe Reader

1. **Scan an analog signature.** All users applying a wet signature need to scan a signature and save the scan as an Adobe PDF file. Use a high-resolution scan such as 1200 dpi, and size the image to about three inches without resampling in a program like Adobe Photoshop.

2. **Open a PDF document needing a signature.** For Adobe Reader users, the PDF documents must be enabled with Adobe Reader usage rights for commenting from either Acrobat Pro or Pro Extended.

3. **Open the scanned signature file.** In our example, we use the *johnDoeSolid.pdf* file in the Chapter 12 folder on the book's CD-ROM.

4. **Load the Snapshot tool.** Open a context menu on the Adobe Reader Toolbar Well, and choose More Tools to open the More Tools window. Scroll down to the Select & Zoom Toolbar, and click the check box adjacent to the Snapshot tool. Click OK, and the Snapshot tool is added to the Toolbar Well, as shown in Figure 12.4.

FIGURE 12.4

Use the More Tools window, and load the Snapshot tool.

5. **Take a snapshot of the signature.** Place the file with the signature in the Document pane, and click the document page. A dialog box opens confirming that a snapshot has been taken.

6. **Bring the form to the foreground.** Choose Window ⇨ *<document name>*. Open the Window menu, and you'll find the form document listed at the bottom of the menu. In our example, we use the *leaveReaquestEnabled.pdf* file from the Chapter 12 folder on the book's CD-ROM.

7. **Open the Comment & Markup toolbar.** Because the files you work with need to be enabled for Comment & Markup, the Comment & Markup toolbar is accessible in Adobe Reader. Choose Tools ⇨ Comment & Markup ⇨ Show Comment & Markup Toolbar.

8. **Paste the image as a stamp comment.** Open the Stamps drop-down menu, and choose Paste Clipboard Image as Stamp Tool. This action loads the cursor with the Stamp tool.

9. **Place the image on the form.** Drag open a rectangle with the Stamp tool in the area where you want the wet signature, as shown in Figure 12.5. Although the image is now an annotation, the appearance of the graphic looks very much like the document has been signed.

FIGURE 12.5

Drag open a rectangle to place the copied image as a Stamp comment.

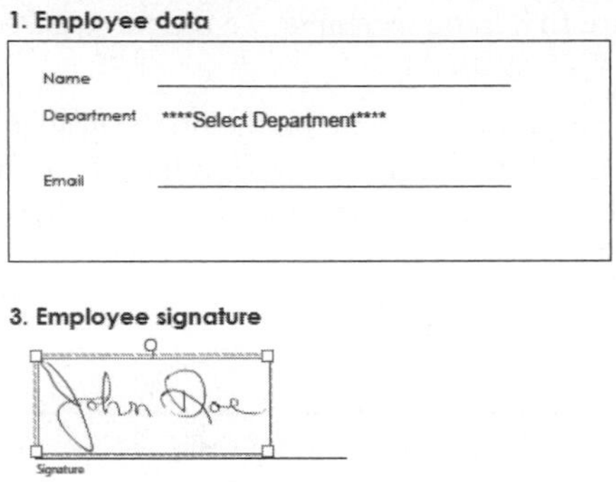

1. Employee data

Name _____

Department ****Select Department****

Email _____

3. Employee signature

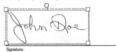

Signature

Using wet signatures with an Acrobat Audience

For those form recipients using Acrobat, you have some alternative options for applying a wet signature. You can add transparency to a signature in a program like Adobe Photoshop and then paste the graphic as a transparent object in a PDF file.

To create a transparent image, scan an analog signature, again using a high-resolution scan, and open the file in Photoshop. Choose Image ➪ Image Size and size the image to about 3 inches horizontally without resampling.

 If you scan a file as line art, you need to choose Image ➪ Mode ➪ Grayscale in order to proceed.

Click the Magic Wand tool, and set the Tolerance to 1 pixel, as shown in Figure 12.8. Click in the white area around the signature to select all the white background on the outside of the signature. Choose Select ➪ Similar to select all the white inside the signature such as characters like *a* or *e*.

Inverse the selection by choosing Select ➪ Inverse or press Shift+Ctrl/⌘+I. Copy the selection to a new layer by pressing Ctrl/⌘+J. Delete the background by dragging the Background layer to the Trash icon in the Layers panel, as shown in Figure 12.6.

You need to save the file with transparency. Choose File ➪ Save for Web and Devices, and choose either PNG-24 or GIF for the file format. Be certain the Transparency check box is checked, and click Save.

After you've prepared a transparent file, follow these steps in Acrobat.

 The following steps can be performed only in Acrobat Pro and Acrobat Standard.

FIGURE 12.6

Select all the white background, and inverse the selection. Copy the selection to a new layer, and delete the Background layer.

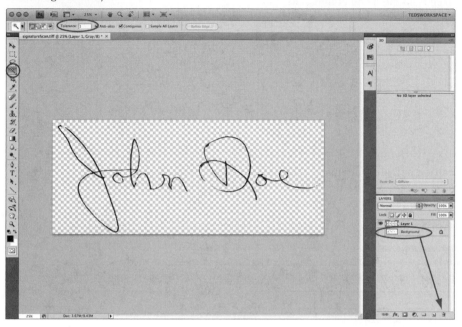

ON the CD-ROM To follow these steps, you can use the *leaveRequest.pdf* and the *johnDoeTrans.png* files in the Chapter 12 folder on the book's CD-ROM. The form is not enabled with Adobe Reader usage rights.

STEPS: Adding a Transparent Wet Signature in Acrobat

1. **Open a form in Acrobat.** The form you open in Acrobat *must not* be enabled with Adobe Reader usage rights to work through these steps.

2. **Place the scan on the form.** Click the TouchUp Object tool in the Advanced Editing toolbar. Open a context menu, and choose Place Image, as shown in Figure 12.7. Choose a file format for the image you're placing when the Open dialog box appears. In our example, we used a PNG image, so we chose PNG (*.png) from the Files of type (Format on the Macintosh) drop-down menu. When the file appears in the Open dialog box, double-click the file to import it.

FIGURE 12.7

Click the TouchUp Object tool, and open a context menu on the form. Choose Place Image from the menu commands.

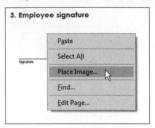

3. **Position and size the image**. Keep the TouchUp Object tool active, and drag the placed image to position. You can resize the image by dragging in or out with any of the four corner handles, shown in Figure 12.8.

FIGURE 12.8

Drag to position and resize by dragging the corner handles in or out.

 When you resize an image imported to a form in Acrobat, don't press the Shift key when dragging the handles. Dragging a handle without any modifier key constrains the scaling.

Preparing files for wet signatures using Adobe LiveCycle Designer

The easiest way to add a wet signature requires a little help from Adobe LiveCycle Designer. You can create a new form using LiveCycle Designer or open a form created in Acrobat in LiveCycle Designer for some additional editing. If you do use an Acrobat form, you need to use forms that don't have JavaScript calculations or be prepared to edit JavaScripts in Designer.

Because we cover creating forms in LiveCycle Designer beginning in Chapter 20, we limit this discussion to editing a PDF form initially created in Acrobat.

To prepare a file for image imports using Adobe LiveCycle Designer (for Windows only users), follow these steps.

ON the CD-ROM **For the following steps, we use the *leaveRequest.pdf* and *johnDoeTrans.png* files in the Chapter 12 folder on the book's CD-ROM. The final file we created is the *leaveRequestLCDenabled.pdf* file, which you can find in the Chapter 12 folder.**

STEPS: Preparing Forms for Wet Signatures Using LiveCycle Designer

1. **Open a PDF form in Adobe LiveCycle Designer.** In our example, we used the *leaveRequest.pdf* form in the Chapter 12 folder on the book's CD-ROM. When you open the form, the New Form Assistant wizard appears. Do the following in the wizard panes:

   Leave the default Create an Interactive form with Fixed Pages radio button active, and click Next.

   The next pane prompts you to add e-mail and print buttons to your form. Uncheck the boxes, as shown in Figure 12.9. Click Finish, and the form opens in LiveCycle Designer.

FIGURE 12.9

Remove the check boxes for Add an email button and Add a print button, and click Finish to open the form in LiveCycle Designer.

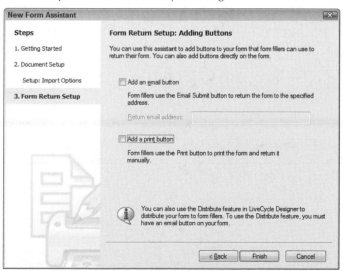

2. **Locate the Image Field.** Scroll the Object Library, and locate the Image Field shown in Figure 12.10.

3. **Add an image field to the form.** Drag the Image Field to the form, as shown in Figure 12.10. You can size the field after adding it to the form by dragging corner handles in or out.

4. **Save the form.** Choose File ➪ Save to save the form. Leave the file format at the default Acrobat (Static) PDF Form (*.pdf) for the Save as type item, and click Save.

5. **Enable the form with Adobe Reader usage rights.** Open the form in Acrobat, and choose Advanced ➪ Extend Features in Adobe Reader. Click Save Now when the Extend Usage Rights in Adobe Reader dialog box opens.

FIGURE 12.10

Add an image field to the form.

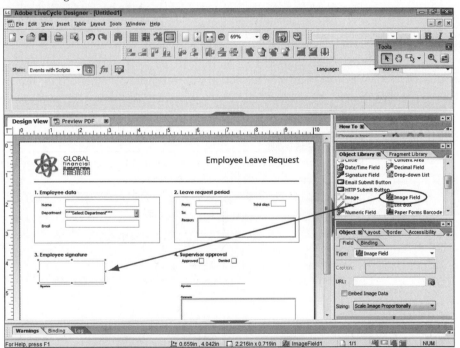

The form is now ready for deployment. Any user of an Acrobat viewer, including Adobe Reader users, can add a wet signature by clicking the image field button added to the form. To test the form, click the image field button in Adobe Reader or Acrobat, and the Select Image File dialog box opens. As you can see in the Files of type (Windows) or Format (Macintosh) drop-down menu, the file formats supported are .jpg, .gif, .png, and .tif.

Choose PNG (*.png) for the file type, click the *johnDoeTrans.png* file, and click Select. The transparent wet signature is placed in the button field, as shown in Figure 12.11.

FIGURE 12.11

Click the Image Field button, and import an image file.

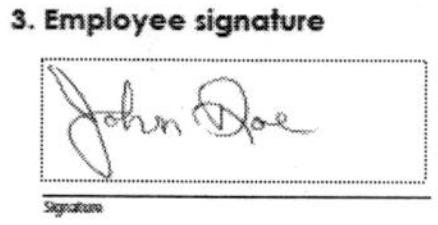

This method of preparing a form for adding a wet signature permits Adobe Reader users, as well as Acrobat users, to add a graphic to a form. The only issue the end user needs to handle is scanning a signature and adding transparency. Unfortunately, Macintosh users need to send the form off to a Windows user to work with LiveCycle Designer or install Windows and Adobe LiveCycle Designer on your Intel Macintosh as we explain in Chapter 20.

Creating Digital Signatures

To begin understanding creating and using digital IDs, look at the Advanced menu. As shown in Figure 12.12, you have four menu items that in one way or another relate to digital IDs and security.

Also two task buttons in the Acrobat Toolbar Well are loaded by default that relate to security. The Secure task button relates to security items, and the Sign task button relates to applying digital signatures, as shown in Figure 12.13. In addition to these menu commands, you have a Security tab in the Document Properties dialog box and security options in the Preferences window. All these locations for accessing commands for security and digital signatures make it a bit confusing for novice users, and it's often difficult to determine where you need to start when creating a digital ID. The menu commands are not intuitive when you first begin creating new digital IDs.

FIGURE 12.12

The Advanced menu has four menu items that relate to digital IDs and security.

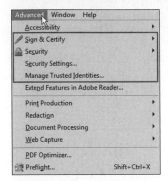

FIGURE 12.13

The Secure and Sign task buttons provide different options.

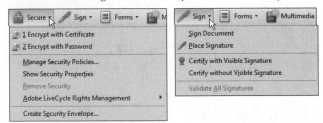

Exploring digital ID and security menu commands

Because you don't have an intuitive menu description or a hint for where to start when creating a digital ID, you need to commit to memory one command that takes care of creating a new ID. Digital IDs are created using the Advanced menu and selecting Security Settings. This is the only command available from all the menu items used with signatures and security that permits you to create a new digital ID.

When you choose Advanced ➪ Security Settings, the Security Settings window opens, as shown in Figure 12.14.

In the Security Settings window, you choose from options listed in the left pane of the window. As shown in the Security Settings window, you have these options for working with digital IDs and configuring server access:

- **Digital IDs:** Four options for working with Digital IDs are available:
  - **A file:** Available on Windows and Macintosh, this form of ID is similar to what you had available in earlier versions of Acrobat when using Acrobat Certificate Security. You can select Add ID, which opens the Add Digital ID dialog box to find an existing digital ID, create a new Acrobat Self-Sign ID, or get a third-party certificate.
  - **A roaming ID stored on a server:** This option permits you to host your ID on a Web server. You can access your ID anywhere in the world by logging on to the server that contains your roaming ID and digitally sign documents using any one of your IDs available on the server. Roaming ID accounts are available to both Windows and Macintosh users.
  - **A device connected to this computer:** Use this option if you have a hardware device such as a token connected to your computer.
  - **A new digital ID I want to create now:** You use this option when you want to create your own personal ID that will be stored locally on your computer.

- **Directory Servers:** This option is used to locate specific digital ID certificates from network servers for encrypting documents using Certificate Security. Directory Servers can be added by importing a configuration supplied by a system administrator or by entering the parameters required to configure the server.

- **Time Stamp Servers:** This option is used if you will be adding time stamps to documents. As with Directory Servers, Time Stamp Servers are added by importing a configuration from a system administrator or by adding parameters required to configure the server.

- **Adobe LiveCycle Rights Management Servers:** Adobe LiveCycle Rights Management Server (`www.adobe.com/products/server/policy/main.html`) is a Web server–based security solution provided by Adobe Systems that provides dynamic control over PDF documents. Policies created with Acrobat or Adobe LiveCycle Rights Management Server are stored on the server and can be refreshed from the server. After you've configured an Adobe LiveCycle Rights Management Server, all polices maintained on this server are available to you. You must log in to Adobe LiveCycle Rights Management Server to use these policies. This option also requires that you access a URL provided by a system administrator and add the server to your list of Adobe LiveCycle Rights Management Servers.

CROSS-REF   For more information on LiveCycle Rights Management Server, see Chapter 34.

FIGURE 12.14

Choose Advanced⇨Security Settings to open the Security Settings window where digital IDs are created.

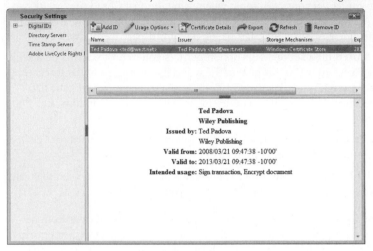

Creating a digital ID

Digital IDs can be created with or without custom appearance settings. The appearance of your signature has no effect on the kind of security you add to a signature. If you want to create a custom signature appearance such as a scanned analog signature, it's usually best to first create the appearance and then create the digital ID.

Custom appearances such as a scanned image of an analog signature are very different than the wet signatures we talked about earlier in this chapter. When you add a wet signature to a form, you simply add a graphic to the form. When you use a graphic associated with a digital signature, you configure the appearance of a signature as it is shown on the form, but behind that appearance is data using a key that describes the signature. This data can be verified and authenticated. A wet signature cannot be verified or authenticated.

Creating a custom appearance

Appearances for your digital IDs are created in the Security preferences. Open the Preferences dialog box (Ctrl/⌘+K), and click Security in the left pane. The right pane changes as shown in Figure 12.15.

FIGURE 12.15

Click Security in the left pane in the Preferences dialog box, and the right pane changes where you can add a new appearance for a digital ID.

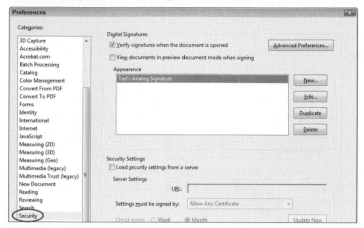

Two preferences dialog boxes are used for creating an appearance and setting some attributes for your signatures:

- **Security Preferences:** You use the Security Preferences to create digital ID appearances for your personal digital IDs. If you want to add a logo, analog signature, symbol, or some text to an ID, you can do so by clicking the New button and choosing from various settings in the Configure Security Appearance dialog box.

- **Advanced Preferences:** If you have an ID configured such as the one shown in Figure 12.18, the ID(s) appears listed in the Appearance list in the Security Preferences dialog box. Select an ID, and click Advanced Preferences to open another dialog box where a number of options exist for verifying signatures, creating them, and (in Windows) selecting settings for Windows Integration. A number of different options exist in three tabs in Windows or two tabs on the Macintosh. For a detailed description of each item, consult the Acrobat Help document.

NOTE If you have not created a digital ID yet, you will see nothing listed in this box, but you still can create appearances that can later be used with a digital ID.

To understand how to create a custom appearance for a digital ID, follow these steps.

ON the CD-ROM If you don't have a scan of your analog signature available you can use the *johnDoe-Trans.png* file in the Chapter 12 folder on the book's CD-ROM.

STEPS: Creating a Custom Digital ID Appearance

1. **Open the Security preferences.** Press Ctrl/⌘+K. Click the Security item in the left pane.

2. **Click the New button in the right pane to open the Configure Signature Appearance dialog box.**

3. **Configure the appearance.** Type a title in the Title text box. This title will appear as the name for your appearance, and you'll select it when configuring a digital ID. If you want to use a graphic, click the Imported graphic radio button and click File to open the Select Picture dialog box. Locate and select the graphic you want to use for the appearance. (The file can be any file type supported by the File ➪ Create PDF ➪ From File command.)

   Select the text items you want to display on your signature by checking boxes in the Configure Text area of the Configure Signature Appearance dialog box. In our example, we removed all check boxes, as shown in Figure 12.16.

4. **Click OK in the Configure Signature Appearance dialog box.** The signature is listed by Title in the Security preferences. Click OK in the Preference dialog box, and your appearance for a signature is now configured.

FIGURE 12.16

Type a title in the Title text box, import a graphic, and check the boxes you want to use for text appearances.

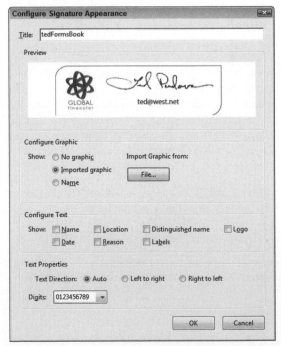

Creating a new digital ID

The steps used to create a signature appearance are optional. You don't need to use a custom appearance when creating a digital ID. If you do create a signature appearance, you can use it when creating a new ID.

To understand how digital IDs are created, follow these steps.

STEPS: Creating a Digital ID and Appearance

1. **Open the Security Settings dialog box.** Click Advanced ➪ Security Settings. The Security Settings wizard opens, as shown in Figure 12.17. When the wizard opens, click Digital IDs in the left pane.

2. **Create a Self-Signed digital ID.** Click Add ID in the Security Settings dialog box. The Add Digital ID wizard opens, as shown in Figure 12.18. Select A new digital ID I want to create now, and click Next.

3. **Choose an option for your ID.** The next pane has two options for locating or creating an ID. The first radio button assumes you have an ID available either as a file, a roaming ID on a server, or a hardware device.

   The second option enables you to create a new ID. Select the second radio button (A new digital ID I want to create now), and click Next to open the second pane in the wizard.

FIGURE 12.17

Choose Advanced ➪ Security Settings to open the Security Settings dialog box.

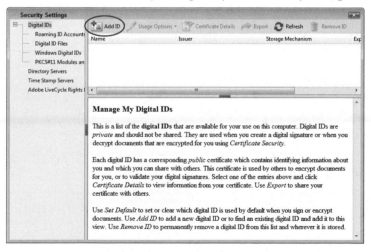

FIGURE 12.18

Click Add ID in the Security Settings dialog box, and the Add Digital ID dialog box opens.

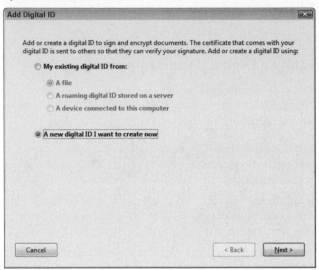

4. **Choose a location to store your ID.** Click the first radio button to create a password-protected ID using Acrobat, as shown in Figure 12.19—this option works best for cross-platform compliance. Click Next to move to the next pane in the wizard.

FIGURE 12.19

Click the first radio button, and then click Next.

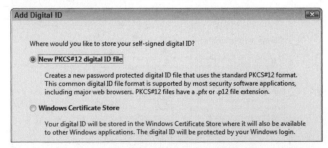

5. **Add identity information.** The next pane opens with text boxes for you to supply identity information. If you added identity information in the Identity preferences, the information is transposed to the pane shown in Figure 12.20. If you want to use special characters, non-Roman languages, or non-ASCII characters, check the box for Enable Unicode Support.

FIGURE 12.20

Fill in the text fields, choose a key algorithm, and a use for the ID.

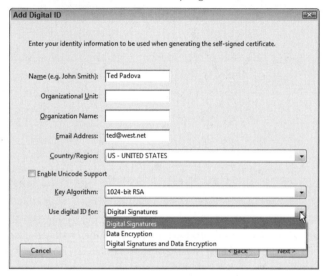

6. **Choose a key algorithm.** The default is 1024-bit encryption. If you expect users of Acrobat prior to 9.0 to work with your files, leave this default alone. If you use Acrobat 9.0 or above exclusively, you can choose 2048-bit encryption.

7. **Choose a use for the ID.** If you use your digital ID exclusively for digital signatures, choose Digital Signature from the drop-down menu. If you anticipate using your ID for encrypting documents, choose Digital Signatures and Data Encryption.

8. **Choose where you want to store the ID and type a password.** Click Next in the wizard, and click the Browse button to locate a folder where you want to save the ID (for New PKCS#12 digital ID files). Type a password in the Password text box, and type the password again in the Confirm Password text box, as shown in Figure 12.21.

9. **Click Finish.** Click Finish in the Add Digital ID dialog box and you return to the Security Settings dialog box. Your new digital ID is now ready to use.

FIGURE 12.21

Specify a target location, and type a password. Confirm the password, and click Finish.

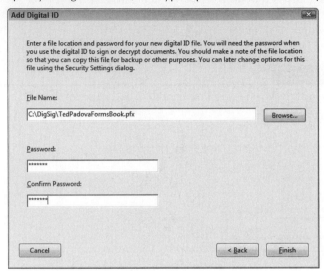

After you click Finish, your ID appears listed in the Security Settings dialog box, as shown in Figure 12.22. The Security Settings dialog box offers some options for managing your IDs. You can choose usage options from the Usage Options drop-down menu, examine certificate details, export your ID to a new location on your hard drive, and click Refresh to update any changes to IDs and locations.

FIGURE 12.22

After creating a new ID, the ID is listed in the Security Settings dialog box.

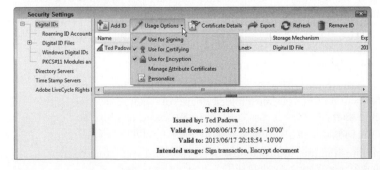

Notice that we have not selected an appearance for the digital ID. You can store multiple appearances in the Security preferences, and each time you sign a document, you can choose which appearance you want to use for your signature. You might, for example, sign documents internally in your company using one appearance and with the same ID sign documents coming from other sources outside your company with another appearance.

Using signature fields

After you have an ID created, you can use it to sign signature fields using any Acrobat viewer. You also can sign documents without signature fields. Forms authors are most likely to use signature fields rather than asking form recipients to sign documents without signature fields, so we'll limit our discussion on digital IDs to forms containing form fields.

To sign a document, follow these steps.

 You can use the *leaveSignaturesLock.pdf* file in the Chapter 12 folder on the book's CD-ROM for these steps.

STEPS: Signing a Form

1. **Open a form with a signature field.** In our example, we opened the *leaveSignaturesLock. pdf* file in the Chapter 12 folder on the book's CD-ROM.

2. **Fill in the form.** The form used in our example has some fields designed for an employee of a company to fill in. Fill in the items in sections 1 and 2.

3. **Click the signature field.** With the hand tool active, click the signature field below item 3, Employee signature. To proceed, you must have created a digital ID.

4. **Add your password, and choose an appearance.** The Sign Document dialog box opens, as shown in Figure 12.23. Type your password in the Password text box. Your password is the same password you used when you created your digital ID.

    From the Appearance drop-down menu, choose an appearance. The appearances listed in this menu are the appearances you created in the Security preferences. If you created multiple appearances, they all are listed in the drop-down menu.

5. **Sign the document.** Click the Sign button, and the Save As dialog box opens. Save the file with a new name, such as adding a *_signed* extension on the original filename.

Creating Appearances when Signing Documents

You have another choice when creating signature appearances. Rather than use the Security Preferences to add a new signature appearance, you can create a new appearance by opening the Appearance drop-down menu in the Sign Document dialog box and selecting Create New Appearance. The Configure Signature Appearance dialog opens where you can import a graphic and make choices for the text items you want shown on the signature.

FIGURE 12.23

Click a signature field with the hand tool, and the Sign Document dialog box opens.

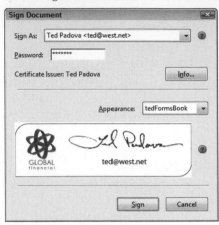

When you click Sign, you are prompted to save your file. Locate the folder where you want to save the file, and click Save. The document is signed as shown in Figure 12.24 using the Usage Options assigned to the signature.

FIGURE 12.24

A signature field shows the signature after signing a document with your digital ID.

3. Employee signature

Locking fields

Signatures in and of themselves provide a level of security on forms. If anything is changed on a form, the signature won't be validated. If you add additional security as explained in the "Using Password Security" section coming up next, you can prevent form recipients from tampering with the form fields. When signatures are added to a document, you can configure the signature fields to lock fields. Therefore, if your file is secured against editing form fields and signatures lock fields, then you have a high level of security applied to your form preventing any alterations to the field data.

To configure signature fields for locking fields on your forms, follow these steps.

ON the CD-ROM On the book's CD-ROM in the Chapter 12 folder, you'll find two forms with signature fields. The *leaveSignaturesNoLock.pdf* has three signature fields with no settings applied for locking fields. The *leaveSignaturesLock.pdf* file has three signature fields configured for locking fields when the form is signed. You can use the file with no locks assigned to the signature fields to follow these steps and use the file with locks to compare your results.

STEPS: Configuring Signature Fields for Locking Fields

1. **Open a form with a digital signature field.** In our example, we used the *leaveSignaturesNoLock.pdf* file found in the Chapter 12 folder on the book's CD-ROM.

2. **Open a signature field's Properties window.** Click the Select Object tool while in Viewer mode, and double-click a signature field to open the Signature Field Properties window. In our example, we opened the *employee.signature* field on the *leaveSignaturesNoLock.pdf* form.

3. **Click the Signed tab in the Properties window.** The Signed tab contains options that are unique to signature fields.

4. **Check Mark as read-only.** With the Signed tab in view, click the Mark as read-only radio button, as shown in Figure 12.25.

5. **Choose the fields to mark.** If you look at the form shown later in Figure 12.27, you can see that the form has three signature fields. Each signature is intended to be filled in by different parties after adding data to the form. For the first signature field, items 1, 2, and 3 are to be completed by an employee. Therefore, we want to lock fields related only to the employee's data fields.

   If you want all fields locked when a form recipient signs a form, you can choose All fields from the drop-down menu. If you find it easier to choose all fields but a few, choose the All fields except these menu item from the drop-down menu. As a third option, you have a choice to choose Just these fields when it's easier to mark just the fields you want to lock.

   In our example, it's easiest to choose All fields except these from the drop-down menu. To choose what fields to *not* mark, click the Pick button. The Field Selection dialog box opens, as shown in Figure 12.26.

6. **Select fields to eliminate from locking.** Because we chose to *lock all fields except these*, we need to mark the fields that we don't want to lock. In the Field Selection dialog box, check the fields you want to remain unlocked. In our example, we chose the fields shown in Figure 12.26.

7. **Click OK in the Field Selection dialog box.** Then click Close to close the Signature Fields Properties window, and the fields are marked for locking when a form recipient signs the form.

FIGURE 12.25

Click Mark as read-only in the Digital Signatures Properties Signed tab.

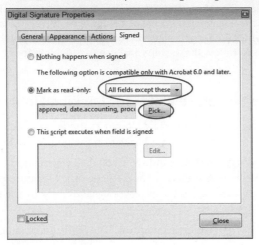

FIGURE 12.26

Check the fields you want to remain unlocked when the form recipient signs a document.

Notice in Figure 12.26 that we chose the fields to remain unlocked that will be filled in by a supervisor and an accounting clerk. All fields the employee fills in will be locked. The remaining fields will not be affected when the employee signs the form.

To complete this form, we would choose fields to lock respective to the supervisor signature and the accounting clerk signature. Each signature field would be configured to lock fields appropriate for the person signing the form.

ON the CD-ROM To examine a form where the signature fields are configured for locking different fields, open the *leaveSignaturesLock.pdf* file on the book's CD-ROM in the Chapter 12 folder.

Applying multiple signatures on a form

You can add multiple signature fields to a form. A signature field, unlike all other field types, cannot be duplicated either by Ctrl/Option+clicking and dragging or by copying the field and pasting into the same form. Signature fields require you to enter Form Editing mode and create additional signature fields on the same form using the Digital Signature tool.

To sign a document with multiple signatures, follow these steps.

ON the CD-ROM To follow these steps, use the *leaveSignaturesLock.pdf* file on the book's CD-ROM in the Chapter 12 folder.

STEPS: Signing a Form with Multiple Signatures

1. **Open a form with multiple signatures.** In our example, we used the *leaveSignaturesLock.pdf* file on the book's CD-ROM in the Chapter 12 folder.

2. **Fill in the data related to the first signature.** On the form used in our example, we filled in the employee-related data.

3. **Sign the form.** Sign the form by clicking the first signature field with the Hand tool. Supply your password, choose an appearance, and click Sign. Save the file with a new filename—something like 01 for the extension of the original filename (*leaveSignaturesLock_01.pdf*).

4. **Check the locked fields.** Move the hand tool over the fields related to the first signature. These fields should be locked and should not accept any new data or modifications.

5. **Fill in the data related to the second signature field, and sign the form.** You can use your same digital ID to sign the form again if you don't have a second ID. When you click Sign in the Sign Document dialog box, use another extension such as 02 for the second save.

6. **Fill in data, and sign the third signature field.** Follow the same steps, and save the file with a 03 extension added to the filename.

After signing the form with three signatures, click the Signatures panel icon to open the Signatures panel. Notice that all three signatures appear in the panel along with the signatures you see on the form, as shown in Figure 12.27.

FIGURE 12.27

The form contains three different signatures.

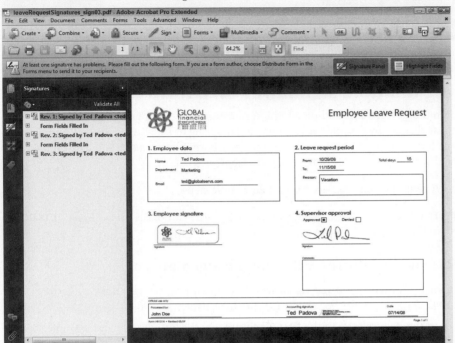

If you check the form by moving the Hand tool around the fields (other than the Signature fields), you'll notice that all the fields are locked and can't be modified. If you click a Signature field, the Signature Properties dialog box opens, where you can obtain information about the respective signature. However, like the other fields, you cannot modify the signature. In Figure 12.29, notice that the Advanced Editing tools are grayed out to ensure you that, indeed, the form cannot be modified.

Validating signatures

When a form recipient completes a form, signs a document, and then sends the form back to you, you'll want to validate signatures on the form. Validating signatures is handled by obtaining a public certificate from a form recipient. A public certificate is created at the time a user creates a digital ID. The ID itself is stored on the user's computer when creating an Acrobat digital ID, and the public certificate that's created along with the ID is intended to be distributed to people receiving a signed document.

Typically, you acquire public certificates from form recipients in two ways: Either the certificate is sent to you by a form recipient as a separate file, or you acquire a certificate from within a signed document.

Acquiring certificates via e-mail attachments

A form recipient can use the Security Settings dialog box to export a public certificate as a file and send the file to a forms author via an e-mail attachment. After the forms author receives the certificate, forms are validated using the certificate.

To export a public certificate to a file, follow these steps.

STEPS: Exporting Public Certificates to Files

1. **Create a digital ID.** In order to export a public certificate to a file, you need to have a digital ID. If you don't have a digital ID, follow the steps outlined earlier in this chapter in the section "Creating a digital ID."

2. **Open the Security Settings dialog box.** Choose Advanced ⇨ Security Settings to open the Security Settings dialog box.

3. **Click the Export button.** At the top of the Security Settings dialog box, locate the Export button shown in Figure 12.28.

4. **Choose Save the data to a file.** When you click the Export button, the Data Exchange File – Export Options dialog box opens. The default selection is Save the data as a file, as shown in Figure 12.28. Accept the default selection by clicking Next.

5. **Save the file.** Clicking Next opens the Export Data As dialog box. Navigate to a target location on your hard drive, and click Save. Your public certificate is saved to a file and ready for e-mailing to other users.

FIGURE 12.28

Open the Security Settings dialog box, and click the Export button.

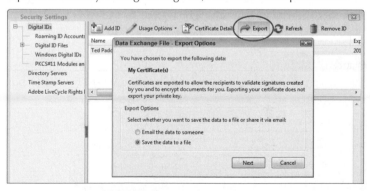

> **TIP** If you create several IDs and many public certificates, you may want to create a folder on your hard drive and save all files to the same folder. At the root C drive (Windows) or Macintosh HD (Macintosh), create a new folder and name it DigSigs or some descriptive name. Copy all your files to this folder for easy access, particularly if you uninstall Acrobat and reinstall at a later time and happen to lose some Acrobat settings.

When you export a public certificate, realize that the certificate does not compromise the security added to your digital ID. Select information in the public certificate is merely used to verify your signature each time a forms author receives your signed forms.

Exporting certificates from signed documents

When you receive a certificate via e-mail, the certificate is sent to you apart from a signed document. You also can export certificates directly from within a signed document. Which method you choose depends on the level of security you want to associate with public certificates.

If you export a certificate from a signed document, you are assuming that the form was signed by the person you distributed the form to. This carries a fairly low level of security, because anyone can sign a form pretending to be the intended form recipient. If you receive a public certificate and a signed form, you receive two documents. This method offers you a bit more security knowing that the form recipient had to receive your file and an e-mail request for sending you a public certificate. It's a slight difference, but it does offer you a bit more confidence knowing that the certificate you receive is indeed from the individual you expect to return a completed form.

If your level of confidence is high that a signed document is received from authentic form recipients, you can use the following steps to export a public certificate.

 To follow these steps, you can use the *leaveRequestSignatures.pdf* file on the book's CD-ROM in the Chapter 12 folder.

STEPS: Exporting Public Certificates from Signed Documents

1. **Open a signed document.** In our example, we used the *leaveRequestSignatures.pdf* file on the book's CD-ROM in the Chapter 12 folder.

2. **Click a signed signature field.** Using the Hand tool, click a signed signature field. The Signature Validation Status dialog box opens, as shown in Figure 12.29.

FIGURE 12.29

Click a signed signature field, and the Signature Validation dialog box opens.

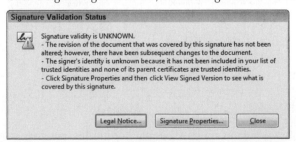

3. **Click Signature Properties.** Click the Signature Properties button in the Signature Validation dialog box, and the Signature Properties dialog box opens, as shown in Figure 12.30.

FIGURE 12.30

Click Signature Properties to open the Signature Properties dialog box.

4. **Click the Show Certificate button.** Click Show Certificate in the Signature Properties dialog box, and the Certificate Viewer dialog box opens, as shown in Figure 12.31.

FIGURE 12.31

Click Show Certificate in the Signature Properties dialog box to open the Certificate Viewer.

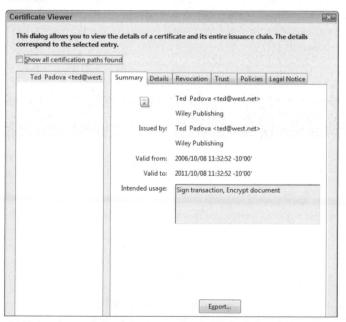

5. **Click the Export button.** At the bottom of the Certificate Viewer, you find the Export button. Click the button, and the Data Exchange File – Exporting Certificate dialog box opens. The first pane in the dialog box offers choices for Export Options, as shown in Figure 12.32.

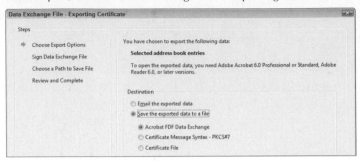

FIGURE 12.32

Click Export, and the Data Exchange File – Exporting Certificate dialog box opens.

6. **Choose a destination.** From the radio button choices, you can choose to save the certificate to a file, e-mail the exported data, and choose from other destinations. To export to a file, choose Save the exported data to a file and click Next. The next pane offers you an option to Sign the document adding your signature. Bypass this option, and click Next again.

7. **Save the file.** When you make a destination choice and click Next, the Choose a Path to Save File dialog box opens. Navigate your hard drive to locate a target destination, and click Save to save the file. Another pane opens after you save the file. Click Finish to complete the steps.

Adding levels of trust to certificates

Up to this point, we've saved public certificates to files. Saving a certificate to a file does nothing more than add a public certificate to your hard drive. The next step is to use the certificate you saved as a file to validate a signature.

Trusted Identities is like an address book. You add certificates to your Trusted Identities for easy management for all the signatures you acquire from signed documents. To add a new certificate to your list of Trusted Identities, follow these steps.

ON the CD-ROM You can export a certificate from the *leaveRequestSignatures.pdf* file on the book's CD-ROM in the Chapter 12 folder. After you have a certificate exported, you can follow the steps here.

STEPS: Managing Trusted Identities

1. **Know the location of at least one exported certificate.** Be certain you have a certificate file on your hard drive and know the folder location where you can find the file.

2. **Open the Trusted Identities.** Choose Advanced ⇨ Manage Trusted Identities to open the Manage Trusted Identities dialog box.

3. **Display the certificates.** From the Display drop-down menu, choose Certificates to display your existing certificates. We have several certificates loaded in our Trusted Identities, as shown in Figure 12.33. You may not have any certificates added to your Trusted Identities.

FIGURE 12.33

Choose Certificates from the Display drop-down menu.

4. **Add a new certificate.** Click the Add Contacts button to add a new certificate, and the Choose Contacts to Import dialog box opens, as shown in Figure 12.34.

5. **Browse for a contact.** Click the Browse button, and locate an exported certificate file. Select the file, and click Open.

6. **Add a level of trust to the contact.** Click the name in the list of contacts in the top list, and the certificate name is added to the bottom list. Select this name, and the Trust button becomes active. Click Trust to open the Import Contact Settings dialog box.

7. **Check the boxes for the items you want to trust from the contact.** For forms with signatures, you may need only the default selection for Signed documents or data. The check box is selected when you open the Import Contacts dialog box, as shown in Figure 12.35. You can add more trust items by checking additional boxes. Leaving the default and clicking OK trusts the certificate for all signed form fields on a form. Leave the default as is, and click OK.

FIGURE 12.34

Click the certificate in the second list, and click Trust to set the level of trust for the respective contact.

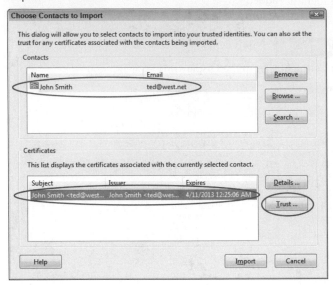

FIGURE 12.35

Leave the default as shown, and click OK to trust the certificate for signing forms.

8. **Import the contact.** After you click OK in the Import Contact Settings dialog box, you return to the Choose Contacts to Import dialog box. Click the Import button to import the trusted certificate, and the Import Complete dialog box opens. Click OK, and your certificate is now added to your Trusted Identities and trusted for accepting signatures from the respective form recipient.

9. **Click Close in the Manage Trusted Identities dialog box.**

Adding Certificates to Trusted Identities

Another way to add a certificate to a trusted identity is to use the Certificate Viewer. In this case you don't need to export a file from a signed document nor do you need to acquire a public certificate from the form recipient.

In the Certificate Viewer click the Trust tab and click Add to Trusted Identities. The certificate is added to your certificate list without any need for managing certificate files.

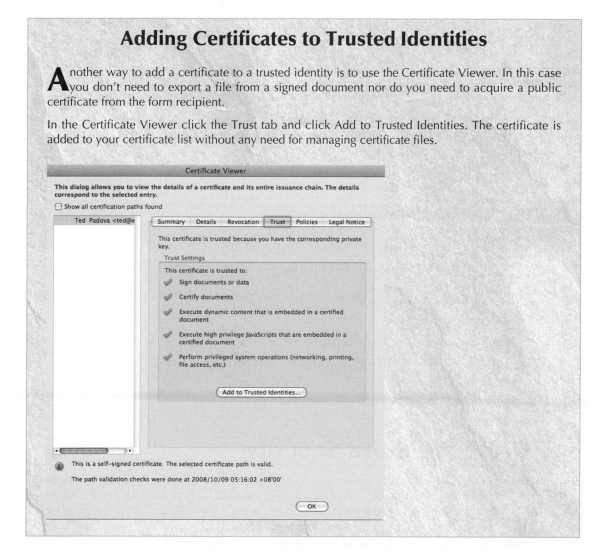

Using a Trusted Identity to validate a signature

After you have a trusted certificate added to your Trusted Identities and determined a level of trust for the certificate, you can use the certificate to validate a signature. In the Signatures panel, select individual signatures, and from the Signatures panel drop-down menu, choose Validate Signature. If the certificate was added to your Trusted Identities with a specified level of trust, the signature is validated.

If you have multiple signatures on a form, you can validate all signatures by clicking the Validate All button in the Signatures panel. When the signatures are validated, the Document message bar reports the validation, as shown in Figure 12.36.

FIGURE 12.36

Click Validate All in the Signatures panel, and the signatures are validated.

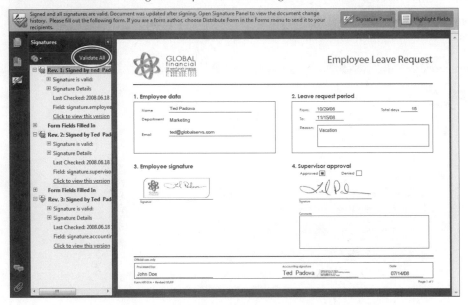

Using Password Security

You apply security to forms to prevent form recipients from changing your form and altering field objects in Acrobat. Securing forms is particularly important if you have fixed data on a form that you do not want a form recipient to change. As an example, look at Figure 12.37. The form contains some fields with fixed prices. If the form is not secured to prevent users from editing the fields, form recipients can change the fixed amounts and/or the calculation formulas.

Understanding the security settings options

Fortunately, Acrobat provides an easy way to secure forms with an elaborate set of options to prevent editing and changing forms. To secure an open document, choose File ⇨ Properties. Click the Security tab in the Document Properties window shown in Figure 12.38.

Notice the Security Method drop-down menu shown in Figure 12.38. Four menu items are listed that relate to different security methods. Below the drop-down menu, you see a list of different permissions and the status of the items. When no security has been added to a document, the status of all items is *Allowed*.

FIGURE 12.37

The form contains fixed unit prices and calculation formulas that need to be protected against editing.

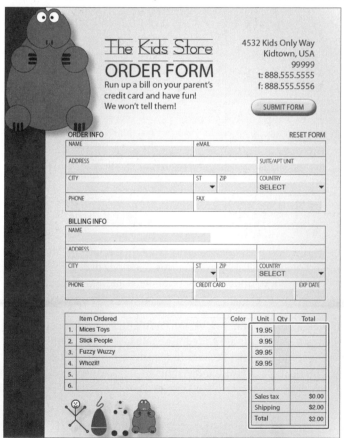

FIGURE 12.38

Open the Document Properties (Ctrl/⌘+K), and click the Security tab.

To add password security to a form, you choose Password Security from the Security Method drop-down menu. Choosing this option opens the Password Security – Settings dialog box, shown in Figure 12.39. As a forms author, you'll want to understand several items and use them when you secure forms, and they're all contained in the Password Security – Settings dialog box.

You add Password Security via this dialog box anytime you want to restrict users from opening a file and/or making changes to the content. Passwords are added to require a user to supply the password when opening the file and/or editing the file. Because forms authors typically design forms for many users, you're unlikely to use a password to open a file.

FIGURE 12.39

Choose Password Security in the Security tab in the Document Properties, and the Password Security – Settings dialog box opens.

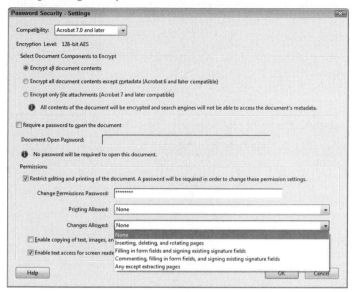

In the Password Security – Settings dialog box, you have these options available to secure a PDF form:

- **Compatibility:** The options from this pull-down menu include Acrobat 3.0, Acrobat 5.0, Acrobat 6.0, Acrobat 7.0, and Acrobat 9.0 compatibility. The more recent compatibility settings offer you higher levels of encryption. At a minimum, you should choose Acrobat 7 compatibility for your forms.

- **Encryption level:** Below the Compatibility pull-down menu, Acrobat informs you what level of encryption is applied to the document based on the compatibility choice made in the pull-down menu. If you select Acrobat 3 from the Compatibility pull-down menu, the encryption level is 40-bit encryption. Acrobat 5 and Acrobat 6 compatibility are encrypted with 128-bit RC4 encryption. Acrobat 7 and Acrobat 8 support 128-bit AES. Acrobat 9.0 supports 256-bit AES. All the higher encryption levels offer you more options for restricting printing and editing.

  - **Encrypt all document contents:** This option applies encryption to all document contents.

  - **Encrypt all document contents except metadata (Acrobat 6 and later compatible):** Use this option to apply encryption to all document contents except document metadata. As the item name implies, this level of security is compatible with Acrobat 6 and later. This is a good selection if you want to have the metadata in your secure documents available for a search engine.

■ **Encrypt only file attachments (Acrobat 7 and later compatible):** Use this option to encrypt file attachments but not the PDF document. This option is compatible only with Acrobat 7 and above. For forms authors, you're unlikely to use this option often.

■ **Require a password to open the document:** Select this check box if you want a user to supply a password to open the PDF document. Again, this option is one that you're unlikely to use when distributing forms.

■ **Restrict editing and printing of the document. A password will be required in order to change these permission settings:** This option is critically important for forms authors. You first check this box and then choose the items you want to secure against editing.

■ **Change Permissions Password:** Fill in the text box with a password.

■ **Printing Allowed:** If you want forms to be submitted electronically and don't want form recipients to print a form, you can choose to prevent printing by choosing the None option from the drop-down menu.

■ **Changes Allowed:** From this pull-down menu, you make choices for the kinds of changes you allow users to perform on the document. When compatibility is set to Acrobat 7 or above, the options include the following:

▪ **None:** This option prevents a user from any kind of editing and content extraction. This choice is one you must not use as a forms author. If you use None, form recipients won't be able to fill in the form fields.

▪ **Inserting, deleting, and rotating pages:** For forms, you probably don't want this option available to form recipients. Inserting pages on your forms can lead to confusion and problems with data collection.

▪ **Filling in form fields and signing existing signature fields:** For forms authors who do not want form recipients to add any comment notes or add markups to a document, this is your best choice. All the document content is protected and fields cannot be edited in Form Editing mode, but form recipients can fill in the form and submit the form to you.

▪ **Commenting, filling in form fields, and signing existing signature fields:** If for some reason you want to add commenting opportunities for form recipients, you can choose this option.

▪ **Any except extracting pages:** With this option, all the permissions are available to users except extracting pages from the document and creating separate PDFs from selected pages. This setting is one you should avoid using for forms.

■ **Enable copying of text, images, and other content:** If you want to prevent users from copying text and images in your forms, leave the box unchecked.

■ **Enable text access for screen reader devices for the visually impaired:** As explained in Chapter 11, screen readers need access to text on a form when using assistive devices. By default, you should keep this box checked.

CROSS-REF For more information on screen readers and accessibility, see Chapter 11.

After you make choices for the password permissions, click OK. A password confirmation dialog box opens and prompts you to type your password again. Type the same password added to the Change Permissions Password text box and click OK, and you return to the Document Properties dialog box. Click OK again in the Document Properties dialog box, and then save your file to apply the security. If you close the document without saving, the security settings are not applied.

Using a security policy

Security policies are settings you save that are used later when securing documents—similar to creating style sheets in word processors or layout programs. Three different options for creating a security policy are available:

■ **Use passwords:** This option is the same as applying a password to a document via the Document Properties Security pane. The difference between applying password security in the Password Security – Settings dialog box, shown in Figure 12.43, and adding a security policy is that the latter is more efficient when you're applying the same security settings repeatedly to multiple forms. If you use the Password Security – Settings dialog box, you need to set options each time you secure a form by selecting check boxes and making choices from pull-down menus. When you use a security policy, the options you choose are captured and saved as part of the policy; you just use the policy each time you want to encrypt documents with the same settings.

■ **Use public key certificates:** Use this option to share files with users who have sent you a public certificate. These certificates include ones you've added to your Trusted Identities list or by searching directories you have access to. You can create a policy that applies different permissions to different users. Using this policy encrypts the same document with choices for granting different permissions for different recipients. As a forms author, you might use this option when you have in-house forms and want to grant different permissions to different people in the organization.

■ **Use the Adobe LiveCycle Rights Management:** If you have access to an Adobe LiveCycle Rights Management Server, you can create a security policy that is enforced by connecting to the Adobe LiveCycle Rights Management Server. PDF forms and attachments can be secured for a selected group of users or for a period of time you determine when creating the policy. When a policy changes or expires on the server, the forms tied to the policy respect these changes as well.

> **CROSS-REF**   **For more information on the Adobe LiveCycle Rights Management Server, see Chapter 34.**

To make the process of creating a security policy a little more clear, try the following steps to create a policy using password security.

> **ON the CD-ROM**   **Creating a security policy does not require having a form open in Acrobat. If you want to apply the security to a form after creating it, use the *leaveRequest.pdf* form in the Chapter 12 folder on the book's CD-ROM.**

STEPS: Creating a Password Security Policy

1. **Open the Managing Security Policies wizard.** You open the Managing Securities Policy wizard by selecting Manage Security Policies from the Secure task button pull-down menu or choosing Advanced ⇨ Security ⇨ Manage Security Policies. You can access the wizard with or without a file open in the Document pane. When you choose one of the menu commands, the Managing Security Policies dialog box opens, as shown in Figure 12.40.

FIGURE 12.40

Choose Manage Security policies from the Secure task button drop-down menu to open the Managing Security Policies dialog box.

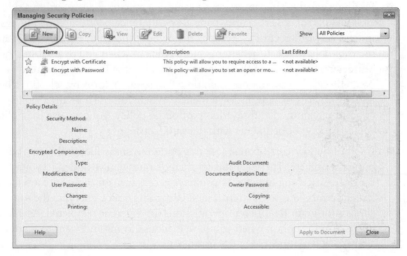

2. **Create a new policy.** In the Managing Security Policies wizard, click the New button to open the New Security Policy wizard pane, as shown in Figure 12.41. You have three options from which to choose. The default is Use passwords, as shown in Figure 12.41. For these steps, we used the Passwords option to create a policy where we secured documents using Acrobat Security. Select Next.

3. **Add a name and description for the new policy.** Type a Policy name and Description in the respective field boxes in the General settings panel of the New Security Policy wizard, as shown in Figure 12.42. Select the box for Save passwords with the policy. The name and description you add in the second pane appear when you access the Managing Security Policies dialog box. Try to add information in the field boxes that describe the settings you use when creating the policy.

If you want to periodically change passwords, leave the box unchecked. Each time you use the policy, Acrobat prompts you for a new password.

FIGURE 12.41

Click New in the Managing Security Policies wizard to open the New Security Policy wizard.

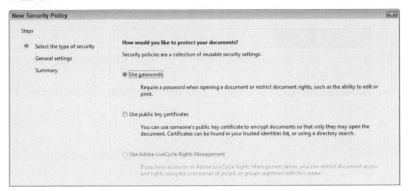

FIGURE 12.42

Name the policy, and add a text description.

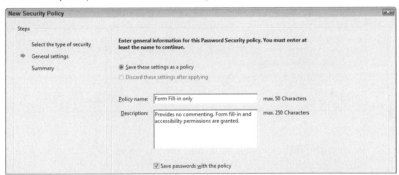

4. **Add the security settings.** Click Next, and you arrive at the Password Security – Settings dialog box. This is the same dialog box you see in the Password Security – Settings dialog box shown earlier in Figure 12.43. Here, you set the attributes for the security to be applied when using the policy. In our example, we did the following:

 ▪ Selected Acrobat 7 compatibility.

 ▪ Checked the box for Restrict editing and printing of the document. A password will be required in order to change these permission settings.

 ▪ Added a password.

 ▪ Selected None from the Print allowed pull-down menu.

- Selected Filling in form fields and signing existing digital signatures from the Changes Allowed drop-down menu.

- Checked the last box in the dialog box, as shown in Figure 12.43.

FIGURE 12.43

Security settings applied to our new policy are shown in the Password Security – Settings dialog box.

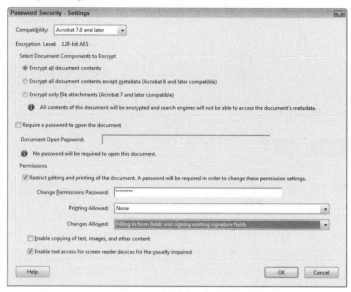

5. **Review the policy.** Click Next, and the last pane (Summary) appears with a Finish button, as shown in Figure 12.44. Click Finish to create the policy. You are returned to the Managing Security Policies dialog box, where your new policy is listed in the policy list window, as shown in Figure 12.45. Notice that the name and description you added when creating the policy now appear in the Name and Description headings. Additionally, you see a description of the policy details and encryption components for the policy you created. If creating multiple policies, select a policy name in the top window, and the policy details and encryption components in the lower half of the dialog box change to reflect attributes for the selected policy.

6. **Secure a document.** By default the Managing Security Policies dialog box opens, as shown in Figure 12.45. Your new policy is listed in this dialog box. If you have a document open in the Document pane, you can apply the policy to the open document. If not, open the *leaveRequest.pdf* form in the Chapter 12 folder on the book's CD-ROM.

Select the policy you created, and click the Apply to Document button. Acrobat opens a dialog box informing you that you need to save your file after applying the policy to complete the security. Click OK, and save the file. Your file is now secure using the permissions you identified for the policy.

FIGURE 12.44

Review the policy in the Summary pane.

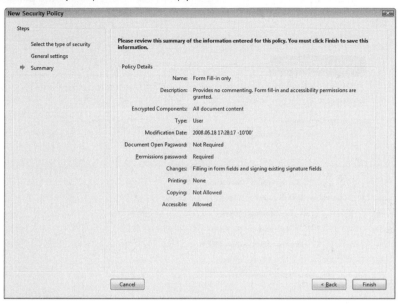

FIGURE 12.45

Select the policy you want to use for securing a document, and click Apply to Document.

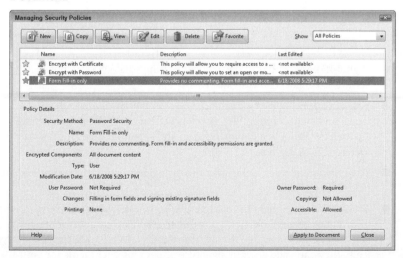

7. **Review the security applied to the document.** After saving the form using a security policy, press Ctrl/⌘+D to open the Document Properties dialog box. Click the Security tab, and note the permissions allowed. In our example using the policy described here, you can see the allowed items in Figure 12.46.

FIGURE 12.46

Open the Security tab in the Document Properties to review the Document Restrictions Summary.

Document Restrictions Summary

Printing:	Not Allowed
Changing the Document:	Not Allowed
Document Assembly:	Not Allowed
Content Copying:	Not Allowed
Content Copying for Accessibility:	Allowed
Page Extraction:	Allowed
Commenting:	Not Allowed
Filling of form fields:	Allowed
Signing:	Allowed
Creation of Template Pages:	Allowed

Summary

■ To digitally sign a document, you need to create a digital ID. You create and manage digital IDs via several menu commands and menu options found in the Secure Task Button pull-down menu.

■ Digital IDs are created in the Security Settings dialog box. Choose Advanced ➪ Security Settings to create a new digital ID.

■ You can apply appearance settings to your signatures in the form of scanned documents, icons, and symbols from files saved as PDF or other file formats compatible with the Create PDF From File command. You add signature appearances via the Security Preferences dialog box.

■ You can digitally sign a document by using an existing signature field and clicking the field with the Hand tool.

■ Trusted Identities are a list of digital ID certificates from people with whom you share information. You can export your public certificate to a file or attach your public certificate to an e-mail message from within Acrobat. When other users have your public certificate, they can validate your signature or encrypt documents for your use.

- In order to validate a signature, the public certificate for that digital ID needs to be loaded into your Trusted Identities list.

- PDF forms can be secured with built-in Acrobat Self-Signed Security and security handlers acquired from third-party developers. Files can be secured from users opening documents, editing documents, or for both.

- Securing forms prevents form recipients from changing things on your forms like fields and calculation formulas.

- Security policies are created to apply the same security settings to multiple files.

Chapter 13

Working with PDF Portfolios and Layers

Until now, we've talked about flat forms that include all the directions, help information, and content needed to help form fillers complete forms.

PDF forms provide more opportunities to combine additional content for descriptions, help information, or any similar information that may be needed to help form fillers more clearly understand how to complete a form.

As a PDF author, you are interested in receiving data back from form fillers. However, the form fillers may need much more than a form to guide them through completing a form. Complex forms that you find in the health care industry, real estate industry, and income tax reporting agencies are examples of where you may need to add extensive help and descriptions for form fillers to complete forms.

When a form filler receives a package containing both a form and all the related documents to help individuals complete forms, your only interest is in receiving back the populated form. All the other associated documents are of no interest to you. Through the use of PDF Portfolios, you can compile all the documents you need to help the form filler complete forms, and when data are submitted back to you, only the forms are returned.

Likewise, you may have some type of description that appears apart from a form. You can create multiple page forms, but another option you have with Acrobat is to create layered forms where you can separate the form containing field objects from ancillary content.

In this chapter, we look at creating PDF Portfolios for the complex form author and add some discussion on using Adobe PDF Layers.

IN THIS CHAPTER

Assembling files in portfolios

Using layers on forms

Creating PDF Portfolios

In Acrobat 8, Adobe offered PDF Packages as a means for assembling files together. You could add LiveCycle Designer forms, secure documents, signed forms, native application documents, and aggregate data from multiple forms with the same form fields.

In Acrobat 9, Adobe introduced PDF Portfolios. A PDF Portfolio has all the advantages of PDF Packages along with an Adobe Flash-based interface and a focus on the package design. Forms authors can use PDF Portfolios with forms that require companion files for providing instructions, additional information about completing a form, or any other content pertinent for form fillers to complete a form accurately.

Creating a new PDF Portfolio

In Acrobat 9.0 and later, you have several menu commands to create a PDF Portfolio. You start by adding files to a portfolio and then you can customize the appearance in many ways.

To create a PDF Portfolio, follow these steps.

ON the CD-ROM In the Chapter13 folder on the book's CD-ROM, you'll find several files. For these steps, you can use the *generalApplication_populated.pdf, applicationGuidelines.pdf, powerAttorney.pdf,* and *riskDisclosure.pdf* files.

STEPS: Creating a New Portfolio

1. **Open Acrobat and choose File ➪ Create PDF Portfolio.** Note that you can alternately choose several other commands to create a PDF Portfolio. For example, you can choose File ➪ Create PDF from the submenu or choose Assemble PDF. You also can choose the File ➪ Combine menu command, and from the submenu, choose Assemble PDF Portfolio or Merge Files into a Single PDF. When you use the Merge Files into a Single PDF command, the Combine Files wizard opens with options to create either a single PDF document or a PDF Portfolio. Choosing any one of the commands opens the PDF Portfolio interface shown in Figure 13.1.

2. **Add files.** You can add individual files or a folder of files to a PDF Portfolio. We have additional files in the Chapter13 folder on the book's CD-ROM, so we used the Add Files button in the lower-left corner of the PDF Portfolio window. Click this button, and the Add Files dialog box opens. Locate the Chapter13 folder on the book's CD-ROM, and select these files: *generalApplication_populated.pdf, applicationGuidelines.pdf, powerAttorney.pdf,* and *riskDisclosure.pdf.*

FIGURE 13.1

Choose File ⇨ Create PDF Portfolio to open the PDF Portfolio interface.

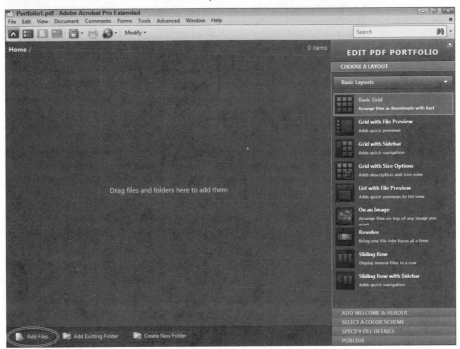

> **TIP** To select files in the Add Files dialog box in a noncontiguous order, press the Ctrl/⌘ key and click the individual filenames.

3. **Click OK in the Add Files dialog box.**

4. **Change the layout.** When you first add files to a new PDF Portfolio, the default layout is the Basic Grid you find in the Edit PDF Portfolio panel on the right side of the PDF Portfolio window. You can change the layout view by making selections in the Edit PDF Portfolio panel when the Basic Layouts panel is in view, as shown in Figure 13.2. For our example, we used the Sliding Row layout. Click Sliding Row to change the layout.

FIGURE 13.2

Click Sliding Row in the Edit PDF Portfolio panel.

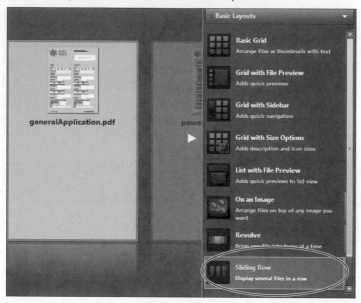

5. **Add some file descriptions.** In the Sliding Row layout, a text box appears below each document thumbnail. Click below the filename, and type a description, as shown in Figure 13.3.

6. **Save the Portfolio.** Choose File ➪ Save Portfolio to save your edits. Keep this file handy to follow additional steps in this chapter.

FIGURE 13.3

Type a description below each page thumbnail.

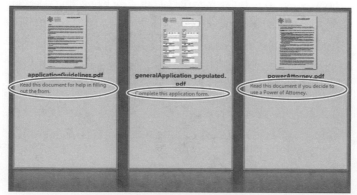

Files added to the new portfolio include a general application form, a document to assist form fillers completing a form, a document specifying risk conditions, and a document explaining some details for a power of attorney. The only file that would be of interest to the form author to get back from the form filler is the application form with data. The additional documents are not needed to process the application form because no fields appear on the other three documents and no signatures are required.

Add a welcome page

Welcome pages in PDF Portfolios can be instructive and provide form fillers an idea of what's contained in the portfolio. Welcome pages can contain text, images, both text and images, and Adobe Flash animations. As a general rule, you might want to consider avoiding Flash files for distributing portfolios with forms. Having large files in the portfolio makes the download times longer for the form fillers. Keeping the welcome page simple is best advised for packages containing forms.

To add a welcome page to a portfolio, follow these steps.

ON the CD-ROM Use the same portfolio file created in the preceding set of steps. In the Chapter13 folder on the book's CD-ROM, you'll find a file titled *globalLogo.jpg*. Use this image file for these steps.

STEPS: Adding a Welcome Page to a PDF Portfolio

1. **Open a PDF Portfolio.** We continue with the portfolio created in the steps "Creating a New Portfolio."

2. **Click Add Welcome & Header in the Edit PDF Portfolio panel.** If the Edit PDF Portfolio panel is not open, select Modify ➪ Edit Portfolio. Click the Add Welcome & Header panel name, and then click Welcome Page.

3. **Make a choice for the layout.** In the Add Welcome & Header panel, you have several options for the design of the Welcome page. The items shown in Figure 13.4 should be self-explanatory. For our example, we chose the Image & Text layout. This option provides us an opportunity to use a graphic for the company logo and a text description.

4. **Add an image.** You find two boxes in the left pane when you click Image and Text in the Welcome Page panel. One frame is used for placing images, and the other is used for typing text in the frame. Click the Add an image frame, and the Browse for Image dialog box opens. File formats supported for importing images on a Welcome page include .jpg, .gif, and .png.

   Locate the *globalLogo.jpg* file on the book's CD-ROM in the Chapter13 folder, and select it. Click Open to place the image in the frame. When the image is placed, you can change the frame border by dragging the corner and midpoint handles on the frame edges.

5. **Add text.** Type text in the Add text frame. Notice the Text palette at the bottom of the window. You can set type attributes for font, font size, bold, italic, and underline, specify type color and background color, and choose from left, center, and right paragraph justification.

6. **Position the image and text frames.** The image and text frames can be moved and sized to any position. In our example, we swapped the default text left and image right to image left and text right by dragging the frames in the window, as shown in Figure 13.5.

FIGURE 13.4

Click Image & Text in the Welcome panel.

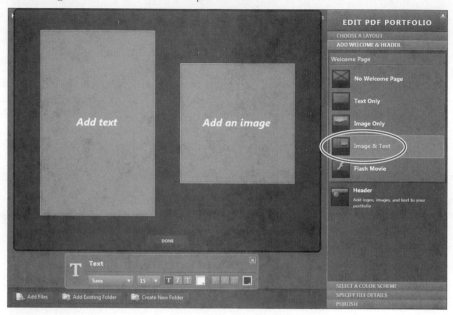

FIGURE 13.5

Drag the image and text frames into the positions you want them for the Welcome page.

7. **Close the Edit PDF Portfolio panel.** Click the close button (X) in the top-right corner of the Edit PDF Portfolio panel, or choose Modify ⇨ Close Edit Portfolio.

8. **Preview the Welcome page.** Click the Open the Welcome Page button shown in Figure 13.6 to preview the Welcome page.

9. **Save the file.** We use the same file for additional steps in this chapter, so save the file to your hard drive and keep it handy to use again.

FIGURE 13.6

Click the Open the Welcome Page button to preview the Welcome page.

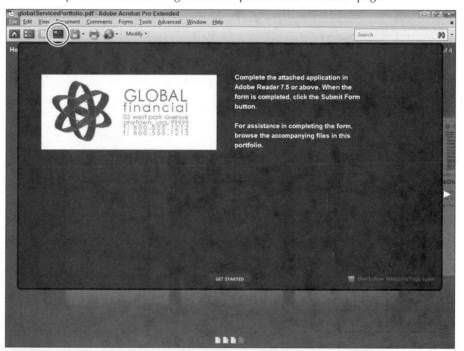

Add a header

A Welcome page in a PDF portfolio can be dismissed by a form filler at any time and never appear again if a user clicks the Don't show Welcome Page again check box shown in Figure 13.6. If you want some pertinent information or your company logo to be in view as a form filler explores the files in a portfolio, you can add information to a header. A header in a portfolio appears on the welcome page and in all the page layouts when users navigate documents in the Home view.

To add a header to a PDF Portfolio, follow these steps.

ON the CD-ROM We continue using the same file created in previous steps in this chapter. In addition, we reuse the *globalLogo.jpg* file from the Chapter13 folder on the book's CD-ROM.

STEPS: Adding a Header to a PDF Portfolio

1. **Open the file saved from previous steps in this chapter.**

2. **Enter Portfolio Editing mode.** Choose Modify ⇨ Edit Portfolio. The Edit PDF Portfolio panel opens.

3. **Click Add Welcome & Header.** In the Edit PDF Portfolio panel, click Add Welcome & Header.

4. **Click Header in the Edit PDF Portfolio panel.**

5. **Choose a header style.** When the Header panel opens, choose a header style from the list shown in Figure 13.7. In our example, we used the Logo & Structured Text style shown in Figure 13.8.

6. **Fill in the header data.** When you choose Logo & Structured Text, the header place-holders permit you to add an image, a title, and three lines of text for contact into, e-mail address, and a URL, as shown in Figure 13.8.

   ■ Click Add an image, and select the *globalLogo.jpg* file to import the image.

   ■ Click the cursor in the Add a title frame, and type a title.

   ■ Click the cursor in each of the three frames, and type contact info, an e-mail address, and a URL.

   The results of the edits we made are shown in Figure 13.9.

FIGURE 13.7

Click Header in the Add Welcome & Header panel to open the Header style options.

FIGURE 13.8

We chose the Logo & Structured Text style.

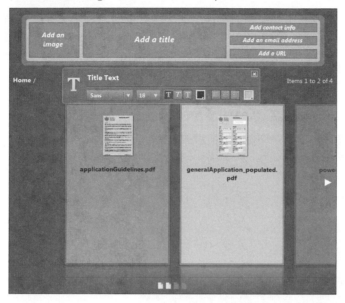

FIGURE 13.9

We added an image and title and filled in the three text frames adding contact info, an e-mail address, and a URL.

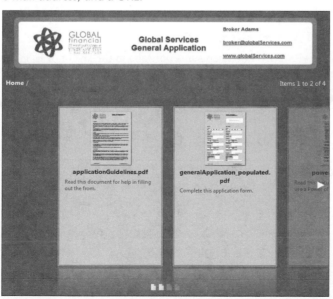

The header information appears when any file is brought forward in the portfolio as well as on the Welcome page. In Figure 13.10, the Welcome page is in view together with the new header we added to the portfolio.

FIGURE 13.10

Headers appear on all layout views and on the Welcome page.

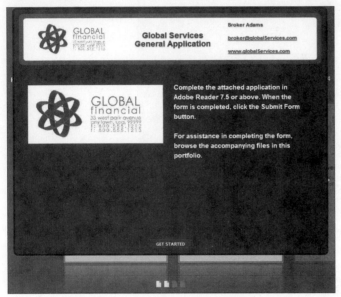

Working with details

Up to this point, we've viewed documents in a portfolio in the layout or *Home* view. In the PDF Portfolio toolbar, the first icon with a house image is the Home view. The second icon is the File Details view. You also have a few other icons that display a Preview and the Welcome page, as shown in Figure 13.11.

FIGURE 13.11

The PDF Portfolio tools that are used to change views

When you click the File Details button, the files in your portfolio are displayed in a list similar to list views you see when files in folders are viewed as a list from your operating system. Click the File Details tool, and the portfolio display changes as shown in Figure 13.12.

FIGURE 13.12

Portfolio files shown in a Details view

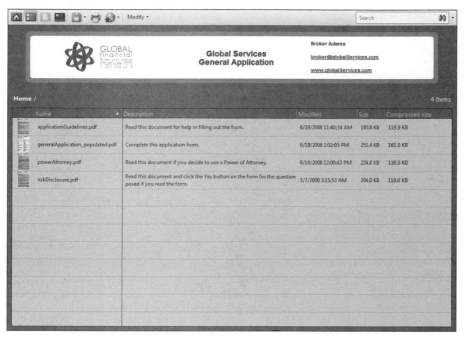

Examining the File Details view

In the File Detail view, you see columns with information. By default, a PDF Portfolio displays the filename, file descriptions, date modified, file size, and compressed file size. The columns can be toggled on or off in the Specify File Details panel when you enter Edit Portfolio mode. When you choose Modify ➪ Edit Portfolio and click Specify File Details, the Specify File Details panel opens. In the panel, you find check boxes for items that can be displayed or hidden, as shown in Figure 13.13.

Check one of the checked boxes, and you hide the column from the list when viewing the portfolio in Details view. Conversely, check an unchecked box to display the column. You can adjust column sizes in either the Edit Portfolio mode or File Details mode by dragging the column separator bars at the top of the list.

The fixed list of columns you see in Figure 13.14 cannot be removed from the panel. You can hide the views, but the items cannot be deleted. At the top of the Specify File Details panel, you find a text box where you can type a name for a new column, a drop-down menu with the default listed as text, and a plus (+) icon. The drop-down menu offers choices for text, number, and date. Clicking the plus (+) icon adds a new column to the File Details. Any custom columns you add to the File Details view can be deleted by clicking a custom column to select it and clicking the Trash icon.

FIGURE 13.13

Click Specify File Details in the Edit PDF Portfolio panel, and the Specify File Details panel opens.

At the bottom of the Specify File Details panel, you find another drop-down menu with the default Name label. You use this menu to sort files according to the column you choose from the list. As new columns are added, they are dynamically added to the Sort menu. Adjacent to the drop-down menu are two icons. The first icon (A/Z) is used to sort in ascending order. The second icon is used to sort in descending order.

Adding new columns to the File Details view

If you look back at Figure 13.12, you'll notice that the files added to the portfolio we created in earlier steps are sorted in an ascending alpha order by filename. This is the default for PDF Portfolios when you create them.

In many cases, you may want to sort your PDF Portfolio files in an order other than the default alpha order for filenames. You cannot drag files to new locations in the File Details view, and no up/down buttons are available to reorder the files. Reordering requires you to create a new column and sort files according to the column criteria.

NOTE As of this writing, we're using the first release of Acrobat 9. We've been informed that the Acrobat 9.1 maintenance upgrade may take care of many issues related to PDF Portfolios such as reordering files in the List view mode. If you're using Acrobat 9.1 or above, you may not need to add a sort column in List view.

To create a new column for a custom sort order, follow these steps.

STEPS: Creating a New Column to Sort Files

1. **Open a PDF Portfolio.** In our example we use the file saved from earlier steps in this chapter.

2. **Click the File Details tool to view the portfolio in a File Details view.**

3. **Open the Edit Portfolio view.** Choose Modify ⇨ Edit Portfolio.

4. **Open the Specify File Details panel.** Click Specify File Details in the Edit PDF Portfolio panel.

5. **Add a new column.** Type a name for the new column in the Add a column text box. From the drop-down menu, choose Number. To add the column, click the plus (+) button. In our example, we created a new column named Sort, as shown in Figure 13.14.

FIGURE 13.14

Type a name, choose a selection from the drop-down menu, and click the plus (+) button.

6. **Add column data.** If the column is not in view, scroll horizontally to bring the new column in view. Double-click the mouse button in the first row in the new column, and type the data you want for the value for the selected cell. In our example, we wanted the *applicationGuidelines.pdf* document to be the second file in the file order, so we typed 2 in the column for this file. Subsequent values are 1, 4, and 3, as shown in Figure 13.15.

7. **Sort the columns.** As yet, the sort order hasn't changed. Open the Sort drop-down menu, and choose Sort from the list. The File Details view now shows the files sorted in the new order, as shown in Figure 13.16.

8. **Choose File ⇨ Save Portfolio to update your edits.**

FIGURE 13.15

Type a number for the sort order you want for each file shown in the File Details view.

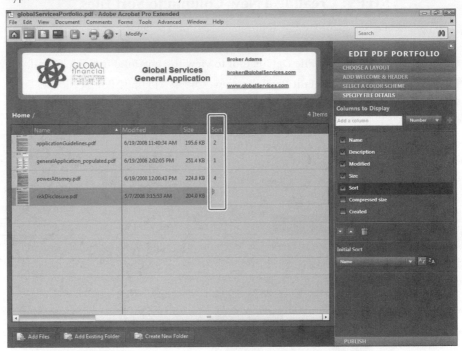

FIGURE 13.16

Choose Sort from the Sort drop-down menu to change the sort order to a custom order.

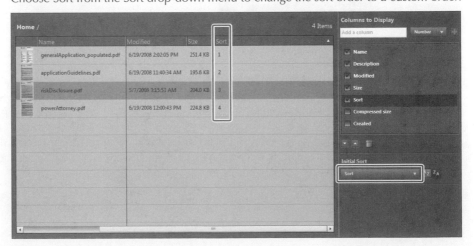

In this particular case, we want the most important document, the PDF form, to appear first when the form filler opens the portfolio. The second document is the detail for instructions for filling in the form, followed by two other informational documents.

Navigating PDF Portfolios

Form fillers can easily navigate documents in the Home view by clicking arrows to scroll documents and clicking the Preview tool to preview a file. For many files added to portfolios, this method of navigation works well. However, if a form filler is completing a form and wants to look up some help information, closing one document, searching for another document that contains the needed description, and then returning to complete the form is awkward and can be frustrating. A simpler solution for the form filler is to click link buttons that open other files in a portfolio and a return button to take the form filler back to the area on the form where the editing can be resumed.

Understanding different preview options

Before we jump into creating navigation links, you should be aware of the different views you can preview a file and the kinds of editing you can perform while in one view or another. If you double-click a file in Home view or File Details view, the file opens in Preview mode in the portfolio interface. You also can click the Preview tool, and the view is the same as double-clicking a file.

When you enter Preview mode, the portfolio toolbar displays an Open button, as shown in Figure 13.17. Click this button, and the file opens in a New Window view.

When you're in Preview mode, you have a limited set of menu commands available and no Acrobat toolbars are in view. If you open the Tools menu and select Advanced Editing, you find that the Link tool is the only tool you can access, as shown in Figure 13.18. While in the Preview mode, you can add links using the Link tool.

FIGURE 13.17

Double-click a file or click the Preview tool to open a file in Preview mode. When in Preview mode, the portfolio toolbar displays an Open button.

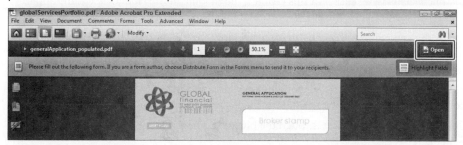

FIGURE 13.18

Choose Tools ⇨ Advanced Editing, and the only tool accessible is the Link tool when you're in Preview mode in a PDF Portfolio.

If you want to add buttons for navigational links, you need to click the Open button when in Preview mode. Clicking Open opens a file in a New Window view. When in this view, you have access to all Acrobat commands and toolbars.

To exit the New Window view, click the close box (X) in the top-right corner of the window or press Ctrl/⌘+W. Either action simply closes the New Window view. The PDF Portfolio remains open. If you make an edit in a New Window view, you can choose File ⇨ Save to update your edits, and the edits are reflected in the file in the PDF Portfolio. You also can close the New Window view without saving. If you don't save the edits and you choose File ⇨ Save PDF Portfolio, any edits made in New Window views are updated.

Adding navigation links to files in a portfolio

In the example portfolio we used in this chapter, a few items on the second page of the application form need to be linked to other documents in the portfolio. To create these links, we use the Link tool.

To add navigational links in a PDF Portfolio using the Link tool, follow these steps.

STEPS: Creating Navigation Links in a PDF Portfolio

1. **Open a PDF Portfolio.** For these steps, we use the portfolio saved from earlier steps in this chapter.

2. **Double-click the *generalApplcation_populated.pdf* file to open it in Preview mode.** If you followed the steps to sort files as described in the section "Adding new columns to the File Details view" earlier in this chapter, the first file in the Home view is the application form. Double-click this file to open it in Preview mode, or click the Preview tool.

3. **Open the second page.** At the top of the window, you find up/down arrows that are used for page navigation for a file in Preview mode. Click the down arrow to open page 2 of the application form, and scroll to the bottom of the page.

4. **Click the Select tool.** Right-click (Windows) or Control+click (Macintosh) to open a context menu. From the menu options, choose Select Tool.

5. **Select text.** Drag the cursor through the blue text where you see Risk Disclosure Statement to select the text.

6. **Create a link.** Open a context menu on the selected text, and choose Create Link, as shown in Figure 13.19.

7. **Set the link attributes.** Choose Invisible Rectangle from the Link Type drop-down menu, and choose None for the Highlight Style, as shown in Figure 13.20. Leave the default radio button selection at Go to a page view, and click Next.

8. **Set the link.** The Create Go to View dialog box opens when you click Next in the Create Link dialog box. Leave the Create Go to View dialog box open, and click the Home tool in the PDF Portfolio toolbar. Click the right-pointing arrows in the Home view until the *riskDisclosure.pdf* document moves to the foreground. Double-click the file or click the Preview tool to open the file in Preview mode. Set the view you want using the zoom tools in the PDF Portfolio toolbar, and click Set Link, as shown in Figure 13.21.

FIGURE 13.19

Select text, and open a context menu. From the menu options, choose Create Link.

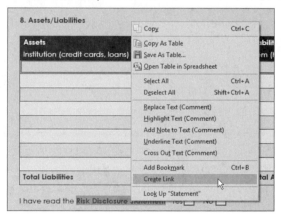

FIGURE 13.20

Choose Invisible Rectangle for the Link Type and None for the Highlight Style, and click Next.

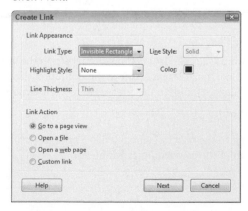

FIGURE 13.21

Click Set Link when the target view is in place.

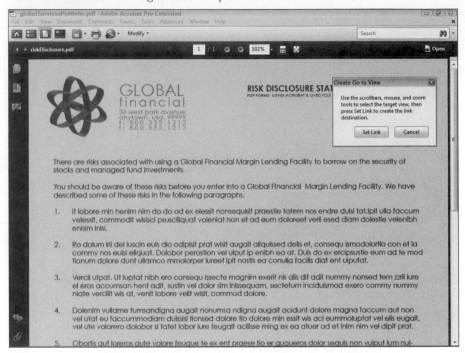

9. **Create a return link.** The link we created leaves the form and opens another document in Preview mode in the PDF Portfolio. After a form filler reviews the document, we need another link to take the form filler back to the view last shown on the application form.

   Open the *riskDisclosure.pdf* file in Preview mode, and scroll to the bottom of the page where you see Return. Choose Tools ➪ Advanced Editing ➪ Link tool. Draw a link rectangle around the Return item, as shown in Figure 13.22. When the Create Link dialog box opens, follow the same steps for setting the link attributes, and click Next to open the Create Go to View dialog box.

10. **Open the target destination.** Click the Home tool, and return to the application form; open it in Preview mode. Open page 2, and scroll to the bottom of the page where the original link was created. Click Set Link in the Create Go to View dialog box.

11. **Choose File ➪ Save Portfolio.**

We created one series of steps to link to the *riskDisclosure.pdf* file. Try to step through the same procedure to create a link and return to the *powerAttorney.pdf* file.

FIGURE 13.22

Draw a link rectangle around the Return button, and click Next in the Create Link dialog box to open the Create Go to View dialog box.

Adding buttons for navigational links in a portfolio

At times you may want to have links to actions that are visible on a form, but when a form is printed you don't want any evidence of the link. In this case, you need to use a button. Links don't provide options for adding text or a graphic to the link appearance. Other than a border and fill color, a form filler won't know where a link is located or what it does. With buttons, you can use a graphic icon, text, or both text and an icon that gives the form filler an idea for what a button does. Furthermore, because buttons are form fields, you can configure a button to be visible on a form and hidden when printed.

Using the same portfolio we worked on in this chapter, we want to add a button to submit a form. Ideally, you would create the button before assembling the portfolio. However, if you find after creating a portfolio that you need to add buttons, you can add them to documents within a portfolio.

To see how we approach adding buttons to documents in a PDF Portfolio, follow these steps.

ON the CD-ROM We continue using the portfolio created in steps throughout this chapter. In addition, we use the *submitFormButton.pdf* file in the Chapter13 folder on the book's CD-ROM. You'll also find the *resetForm.pdf* file in the same folder, which you can use to add a second button to the form.

STEPS: Adding Buttons to Documents within a Portfolio

1. **Open a PDF Portfolio.** In our example, we used the portfolio created in earlier steps in this chapter.

2. **Open the application form in Preview mode.** If you followed steps to reorder the files, the application form is the first file shown in Home view. Double-click the file to open it in Preview mode.

3. **Open the file in a New Window view.** Click the Open button when you arrive in the Preview mode to open the file in the New Window view. Creating buttons requires access to the Advanced Editing toolbar (or entering Form Editing mode). Because the Advanced Editing toolbar isn't accessible in Preview mode and you can't enter Form Editing mode, you need to open the form in the New Window view where you have access to all tools and menu commands.

4. **Scroll to the bottom of page 2.** We want to add a Submit Form button at the bottom of the last page on the form.

5. **Open the Advanced Editing toolbar.** Choose Tools ⇨ Advanced Editing ⇨ Show Advanced Editing Toolbar.

6. **Add a Button field.** Click the Button tool in the Advanced Editing toolbar, and click the cursor in an open area on the lower-right corner of the form, as shown in Figure 13.23.

7. **Name the field.** Type a name for the field in the default Properties mini window. In our example, we used *submitForm* for the field name.

8. **Show all Properties.** Click Show All Properties to open the Button Properties window.

FIGURE 13.23

Click the Button tool in the Advanced Editing toolbar, and click the cursor on the form to add a button field. Click Show All Properties to open the Button Properties window.

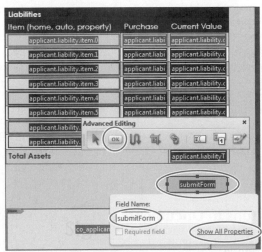

9. **Set the button value to Visible but doesn't print.** By default, the General tab opens in the Button Properties window. From the Form Field drop-down menu, choose Visible but doesn't print, as shown in Figure 13.24.

FIGURE 13.24

Choose Visible but doesn't print from the Form Field drop-down menu.

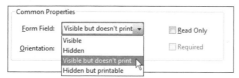

10. **Add an icon to the button face.** Click the Options tab in the Button Properties window, and then choose Icon only from the Layout drop-down menu and None from the Behavior drop-down menu, as shown in Figure 13.25. Click Choose Icon to open the Select Icon dialog box, where you can identify the button face you want to use for this field.

FIGURE 13.25

Choose Icon only, choose None for the Behavior, and click Choose Icon to open the Select Icon dialog box.

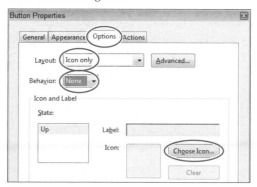

11. **Browse for a file to add for the button face.** Click Browse in the Select Icon dialog box shown in Figure 13.26. Locate the *submitFormButton.pdf* file from the Chapter13 folder on the book's CD-ROM, and select it. Click Select and OK in the Open dialog box. When you return to the Select Icon dialog box, the file you selected is shown in the Sample window, as shown in Figure 13.26.

387

FIGURE 13.26

Select a file, and open it. When you return to the Select Icon dialog box, an image preview is displayed in the Sample window.

12. **Click OK.** Click OK in the Select Icon dialog box, and you return to the Button Properties Options tab.

13. **Fit the icon to the field bounds.** Click Advanced in the Options tab, and the Icon Placement dialog box opens. Click Fit to Bounds so the icon fills the button field rectangle, and click OK to return to the Options tab.

14. **Choose an action.** Click the Actions tab. From the Select Action drop-down menu, choose Submit a form, as shown in Figure 13.27. After making the choice for the action type, click the Add button, and the Submit Form Selections dialog box opens.

15. **Enter a URL.** Type **mailto:** and *<your email address>* in the Enter a URL for this link text box, as shown in Figure 13.28.

16. **Choose an export format.** Click PDF The complete document, as shown in Figure 13.28, and click OK.

17. **Click Close in the Button Properties window.**

18. **Choose File ⇨ Save.** This step is optional. You can close the New Window without saving and save the portfolio when finished editing.

You can practice adding another button by opening the form in a New Window and adding a Reset Form button at the top of the page. Follow the same steps to add the button, and use the Reset a form Action. You'll find the *resetForm.pdf* file in the Chapter13 folder on the book's CD-ROM to use for the button face.

FIGURE 13.27

Select the Submit a form action and click the Add button to open the Submit Form Selections dialog box.

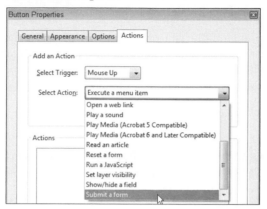

FIGURE 13.28

Type a URL for the link, and click PDF The complete document.

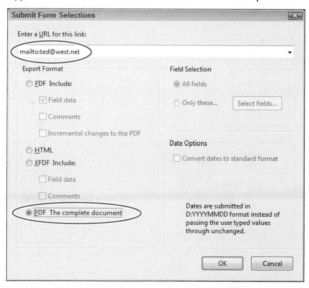

ON the CD-ROM The completed portfolio with all the steps outlined in this chapter is included in the Chapter13 folder on the book's CD-ROM. Open the file *globalServicesPortfolio.pdf* to examine all the edits we made to create the PDF Portfolio.

Enabling forms in PDF Portfolios

When you choose to submit the PDF The complete document in the Submit Form Selections dialog box, you need to be certain that the PDF is enabled with Adobe Reader usage rights before Adobe Reader users can submit the complete document back to you.

Again, ideally you might prepare a form with all required assets before assembling a portfolio. However, if you forget to properly prepare a file before creating a portfolio, Acrobat offers you the flexibility to make edits from within the portfolio. You can add security to the portfolio, and you can enable forms for Adobe Reader users to extend rights to the Reader users.

CROSS-REF For information related to securing files, see Chapter 12.

To add Adobe Reader usage rights for Reader form fillers, place the form in view in Preview mode. Choose Advanced ⇨ Extend Features in Adobe Reader, and the Enable Usage Rights in Adobe Reader dialog box opens, as shown in Figure 13.29.

FIGURE 13.29

Open a form in a PDF Portfolio in Preview mode, and choose Advanced ⇨ Extend Features in Adobe Reader.

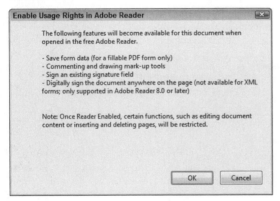

Click OK in the dialog box, and your file is saved so Adobe Reader users can save form data, add digital signatures, and return the complete PDF back to you.

Submitting forms from PDF Portfolios

The nice thing about using a PDF Portfolio is that when a form filler clicks a submit button on a form, only the document where the button is located is submitted to you. Using our example of the portfolio we created in steps throughout this chapter, the submit form button on the application form sends just the form. The description file, power of attorney statement, and risk disclosure statement are not submitted, thus requiring less upload time for the form filler.

Working with Layers

Layered files offer you another dimension for showing data apart from the necessary form fields. Whereas PDF Portfolios enable form fillers to send back just essential data to you, layered files cannot be separated and the forms you receive from form fillers contain the form as well as the additional layers on the form.

You can find a number of ways to use layers with forms. You might have a form designed as a program event registration. On a second layer, you might have a seating chart where form fillers can make choices for seating preferences. Another use might be showing diagrams such as a house plan where different layers can show different structural elements. Of course, the most obvious use for layered files is when designing multi-lingual forms.

Using layered PDF forms

To create a layered PDF document, you need an authoring program capable of producing Adobe PDF Layers. Programs like Adobe InDesign, Adobe Illustrator, and a few other vector art applications can create layers and export to PDF with the layers intact.

Typically, layered forms require two action items that are most often triggered by buttons. You need an action to change layer visibility; with forms, you need actions to hide form fields.

The form in Figure 13.30 is a layered document with several fields on the layer in view. In Figure 13.31, you see the layer visibility changed to display the second layer (*Seating*). The numbers on the seating diagram are buttons that are used to place a value in a field on the first layer. If all the fields are visible from the first layer when looking at the second layer, the form would be difficult to work with. Therefore, when changing the layer visibility, we also hide the form fields on the first layer. When the layer visibility is changed back to the first layer, the fields on the second layer are hidden and the fields on the first layer are placed in view.

In the Actions tab for field properties, you have an action to set layer visibility. Changing layer visibility is similar to creating bookmarks. You first display the layer visibility you want for the target view and then set the layer visibility in the Actions tab. Always remember to set the target view and then add the action to set the visibility.

Hiding fields is another matter. You have an action to show/hide form fields. However, the form fields need to be individually hidden/shown using the Show/hide a field action. Individually selecting fields and adding an action to hide each field becomes a laborious task when you have many fields on a form such as the form shown in Figures 13.30 and 13.31. Rather than using the Show/hide a field action, write a simple JavaScript to do the job.

We save the detail for using JavaScripts for showing/hiding fields in later chapters when we talk about JavaScript. For now, you can look at the sample form on the CD-ROM to see how we change layer visibility and show/hide fields.

FIGURE 13.30

A form shown with two layers

FIGURE 13.31

When the second layer is made visible, the fields on the first layer are hidden from view.

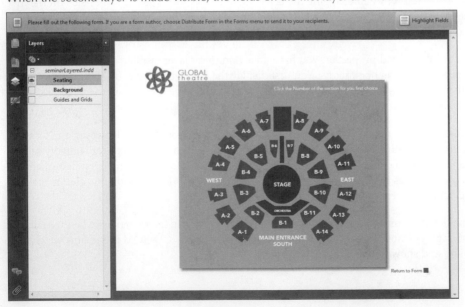

ON the CD-ROM To see an example of a form using buttons to show/hide layer visibility, see the *seminarLayered.pdf* file in the Chapter13 folder on the book's CD-ROM.

CROSS-REF For more information on using JavaScript to show/hide fields, see Chapter 17.

Adding new layers to a form

If you use Microsoft Office or other applications that do not create Adobe PDF Layers, Acrobat 9 and above supports adding layers in Acrobat. You have two methods for creating layers in Acrobat 9 and above. Use the Preflight window to create layers from an existing PDF document, or use the Layers panel to import new content in a PDF file as a new layer.

Again, you can use layers in a variety of ways. Suppose you want to add an agreement to a form that specifies terms and conditions. Rather than create a PDF Portfolio and add the terms along with a form to a PDF Portfolio, you can add the terms and conditions statement as a new layer. You also can create an action to display the terms and conditions statement based on a field that a form filler completes, tabs into, or exits.

To add new layers to a PDF and create a scenario where you might use a terms and conditions statement on a form, follow these steps.

ON the CD-ROM On the book's CD-ROM in the Chapter13 folder, you'll file the following files we use for these steps: *globalTransferFields.pdf, globalTransferTerms.pdf, globalTransferAgree.pdf,* and *agreeButton.pdf.*

STEPS: Adding New Layers to a PDF Form

1. **Open a form in Acrobat Pro or Pro Extended.** Adding new layers to PDFs can be performed only in Acrobat Pro or Pro Extended. In our example, we used the *globalTransferFields.pdf* document. Open this file from the Chapter13 folder on the book's CD-ROM.

2. **Import a new layer.** Open the Layers panel, and from the Options menu, choose Import as Layer. The Import as Layer dialog box opens.

3. **Choose a file to import as a new layer.** Click the Browse button in the Import as Layer dialog box. When the Select Source File dialog box opens, select the file you want to import as a new layer, and click Select. In our example, we used the *globalTransferAgree. pdf* file from the Chapter13 folder on the book's CD-ROM. This document contains an opaque background, and when added to the form, it hides the background data.

4. **Name the Layer.** You must provide a name for the new layer. Type a name in the Create new layer text box, and click OK. For this layer, we used the name *agree.*

5. **Add a second layer.** Repeat the same steps to add another layer, and use the *global TransferTerms.pdf* document. Name the new layer *terms,* as shown in Figure 13.32.

6. **View the layers.** In the Layers panel, you should see both layers added to the list of layers with both layers visible in the document, as show in Figure 13.33. The layer state you see in the Layers panel is the default view when the file is opened.

7. **Save the file.** We'll use the saved file for the remaining steps in this chapter. Save the file to a location where you can easily access it for following additional steps.

FIGURE 13.32

Import and name a new layer in the Import as Layer dialog box.

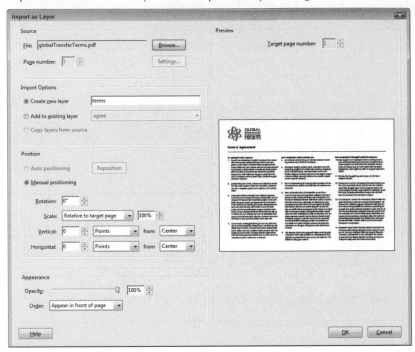

FIGURE 13.33

The layer view shown in the Layers panel is the default view when the file is saved and reopened.

Creating Opaque Backgrounds

If you use a program like Microsoft Word and import a PDF converted from Word as a new layer, the background of the imported document is transparent. In order to create opaque backgrounds, you need to create opaque objects in applications that do not support direct exports to PDF with Adobe PDF Layers and place text on top of the opaque objects.

Programs like QuarkXPress and Microsoft Publisher easily support creating opaque backgrounds. You can draw rectangles and fill with white either on document pages or master pages and set type over the backgrounds. In MS Word, you can import pictures from photo images or create graphic objects and format the text to be on top of the objects.

You can use blank white image files to create opaque backgrounds, and you can use multiple layers for background and text. In short, regardless of the program you use to author forms, you can typically find a way to add text on an opaque background that hides layers below the imported layers.

Changing layer visibility

One of the new layers added to the file in the steps "Adding New Layers to a PDF Form" has an opaque background. This layer is intended for a temporary view for the form filler to read the terms of agreement and dismiss the layer after reading the content. Therefore, we need a button to hide the layer from view. The second layer added to the form is where the form filler confirms that he has read the agreement. This layer needs to remain in view when the file is saved.

Several actions need to be added to the form to change the layer visibility. To learn more about changing layer visibility, follow these steps.

ON the CD-ROM We continue with the file saved after adding new layers to the *globalTransferFields. pdf* form. Additionally, we create a button face from the *agreeButton.pdf* file found in the Chapter13 folder on the book's CD-ROM.

STEPS: Changing Layer Visibility

1. Open the *globalTransferFields.pdf* form with the two new layers.

2. **Add a button.** Click the button tool in the Advanced Editing toolbar, and add a new button in the lower-right corner of the form. Name the button *agree*.

3. **Set the button properties.** Add a button face for the button field using the *agreeButton. pdf* file from the Chapter13 folder on the book's CD-ROM. Follow the same steps for adding a button face as covered earlier in this chapter in the steps "Adding Buttons to Documents within a Portfolio."

4. **Set the layer visibility.** When the form filler clicks the *agree* button, we want to hide the *terms* layer and show the *agree* layer. We also want to hide the *agree* button. If you added a button face, the Button Properties window should be open. Click the Actions tab in the button Properties.

While the Actions tab is in view in the Button Properties, click the eye icon in the Layers panel adjacent to *terms* to hide the layer. In the background, you should see the layer disappear. When you click the eye icon, the button field is deselected. Select the button, and choose Set layer visibility from the Select Action drop-down menu, as shown in Figure 13.34. Click the Add button, and click OK in the warning dialog box that opens.

Open the Select Action drop-down menu, and choose Show/hide a field. Click Add, and the Show/Hide Field dialog box opens. Scroll down to the *agree* item in the Select a field list, and select it. The default action is to hide the field, which is what we want to happen when the form filler clicks this button. Click OK, and you return to the Button Properties window.

FIGURE 13.34

Hide the *terms* layer, set the layer visibility, and hide the *agree* button.

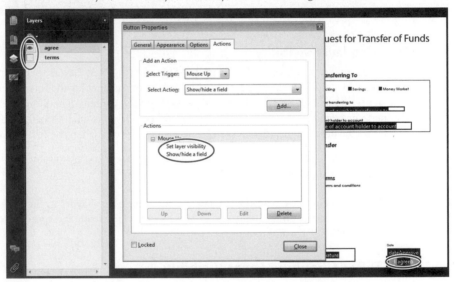

5. **Set layer visibility to open the terms statement.** When a form filler works on the form, we need a trigger to open the terms statement. The best location for the action is the Date of Transfer field (*transferDate*). Open the Text Field Properties dialog box by double-clicking the field with the Select Object tool, and click the Actions tab.

Choose On Blur from the Select Trigger drop-down menu. On Blur invokes the action when the form filler tabs out of the field. Because all fields are filled in prior to this field, the last action the form filler does before signing the form is to read the terms of agreement.

Set the layer visibility to show the *terms* and hide the *agree* layers by clicking the eye icons, as shown in Figure 13.35. Choose Set layer visibility from the Select Action drop-down menu, and click Add. Click OK in the warning dialog box to add the action.

FIGURE 13.35

Set the layer visibility to show the *terms* layer and hide the *agree* layer.

6. **Show the agree button.** When the *terms* layer is in view, we want the *agree* button to be in view also. Add another action using the On Blur mouse trigger, and add the Show/hide field action. Locate the *agree* item, click Show in the Show/Hide Field dialog box, and click OK. Both actions should appear in the Actions tab for the *transferDate* field, as shown in Figure 13.36.

FIGURE 13.36

Both the set layer visibility and show/hide fields actions are visible in the Actions list.

7. **Hide the agree button.** One last item you need to deal with is hiding the *agree* button. By default, the button is visible, but when the form filler works on the form, the button should be visible only when tabbing out of the *transferDate* field. Open the Button Properties Window for the *agree* button, and in the General tab, choose Hidden from the Form Field drop-down menu.

8. **Save the form to update it.**

Changing default layer states

Two more items need attention on our form with layers. The default layer state is set for both the new layers added to our form to be in view when the file opens. We need to change the default state to hide the layers when the file is opened. Additionally, a form filer could conceivably use the Layers panel to place layers in view and hide them, which would defeat the purpose of having the form filler agree to the terms of the agreement. We need to lock the layers so a form filler won't be able to change the layer states without executing the actions we added to the form.

To change the default layer state and lock the layers, follow these steps.

STEPS: Changing Layer Default States and Locking Layers

1. **Open the form created in the steps in this section.** We continue with the form we used for adding new layers.

2. **Open the Layers panel.** Click the Layer panel icon to open the panel.

3. **Select the first layer.** Select the *agree* layer in the Layers panel.

4. **Open the Layer Properties dialog box.** With the first layer selected, choose Layer Properties from the Layer Options drop-down menu. Alternately, you can open a context menu on the layer, and choose Properties.

5. **Change the default state.** Open the Default state drop-down menu, and choose Off.

6. **Lock the layer.** Click the Locked check box in the Layer Properties dialog box, as shown in Figure 13.37.

FIGURE 13.37

Choose Off from the Default state drop-down menu, and check the Locked box.

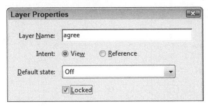

7. **Repeat these steps for the second layer to change the default state to Off and lock the layer.**

8. **Save the file.**

ON the CD-ROM You can open the *globalTrasferFinal.pdf* document in the Chapter13 folder on the book's CD-ROM to browse the form we created by following all the steps in this section.

As a final step, you'll want to secure the form with Acrobat security to prevent a user from unlocking fields and changing the layer states.

CROSS-REF To learn more on adding document security, see Chapter 12.

What we've accomplished working through the steps in this section was to add new layers to an existing form. Both layers are off by default after changing the default layer state. When a form filler tabs out of the *transferDate* data field, the terms of agreement opens and hides all the content on the form. Because we locked the layers (and subsequently secured the form), the form filler cannot change the layer state. The only way to return to the form to sign the document is to click the agree button. Clicking the agree button hides the *terms* layer and displays the *agree* layer that adds a simple statement to the form indicating the form filler agrees to the terms.

You can add one more level of confidence to the form by hiding the Signature field and showing the field only after the form filler clicks the agree button. In this regard, a form cannot be signed unless a form filler agrees to the terms of the agreement.

Something else we might do to the form is hide all the form fields when the *terms* layer is placed in view and show the fields when the form filler clicks the agree button. Again, showing and hiding fields is much better handled using JavaScripts, so we'll defer the steps to hide fields using JavaScripts until we get to the chapters on using JavaScript.

CROSS-REF For more information on using JavaScripts to show/hide fields, see Chapter 17.

Summary

- PDF Portfolios provide you opportunities to add companion documents helpful for form fillers to understand how to complete complex forms.

- Forms can be submitted from PDF Portfolios without sending all the files back to you for processing data.

- Forms can be enabled easily with Adobe Reader usage rights from within a portfolio.

- Links can be added to open documents in a portfolio while in Preview mode.

- In order to access Acrobat toolbars and menu commands in PDF Portfolios, you need to open the New Window view.

- You can create welcome pages and headers in PDF Portfolios; headers are displayed in Home view and when the welcome page is in view.

- In the Detail view, you can add new columns. A custom sort column can be created to sort the file order different than the default filename sort order.

- Layer views can be changed in the Layers panel and through actions added to fields.

- You can import layers in non-layered as well as layered PDFs using the Layers panel Options menu or the context menu only in Acrobat Pro and Pro Extended.

- Layer default states can be changed in the Layer Properties dialog box.

- You can lock layers and secure files so form fillers cannot change layer views in the Layers panel.

Part IV

Managing Form Data

Electronic forms aren't much good if you don't know how to work with the form data. Chapter 14 handles precisely that—managing form data. We cover distributing forms, collecting form data, and exporting data to databases and spreadsheets. In Chapter 15 we look at creating calculations for fields within PDF forms.

IN THIS PART

Chapter 14
Working with Data

Chapter 15
Working with Field Calculations

Chapter 14

Working with Data

IN THIS CHAPTER

Distributing forms

Using servers

Working with Acrobat.com

Importing and exporting data

What is missed by many forms authors, small companies, and large enterprises in regard to PDF forms is handling the form data. A PDF form is great for the form recipient who can type data on a form without having to fill in the form by hand-writing responses—then later return to a saved form to modify the data. But for the form distributor, receiving a faxed form that was printed by a form recipient isn't much better than distributing forms that are not fillable. A form recipient can use the Typewriter tool to complete a form so at least a form is legible when returned to you, but it does nothing for saving you time or making your job more efficient.

Working with data is the real value in creating fillable forms. Among other things, you don't have to type data in a data management system—you leave the task of data entry to the form recipient. And, if you use a server product to collect and route data, you are miles ahead of those who are distributing forms needing to be faxed back to the forms authors.

Acrobat provides you with several options for collecting and managing data. If you work within the licensing restrictions for enabling forms for Adobe Reader users, you're limited to collecting data on up to 500 responses per form. In real-world use, collecting data from 500 responses without using a server product is quite a bit burdensome and impractical. However, if you have events for smaller groups of people filling out forms, you have marvelous options provided by Acrobat and Adobe services for managing data.

If you need industrial-strength data processing, you have options for managing PDF data through the use of several server products that you can purchase or license to handle these needs. In short, Acrobat provides much flexibility for managing data, and your work needs to include this very important function to make your forms development and deployment effective.

In this chapter, we focus primarily on managing form data for smaller groups and using the tools Acrobat provides when you install the program. Later in Part IX, we talk about using servers and other methods for managing data.

Deploying Forms

Acrobat 9.0 and later provides you with several methods for deploying forms via the Distribute Form command from within either Form Editing Mode or Viewer mode. Additionally, you can deploy forms without using the Distribute Form command either by directly hosting a form on your company's Web site or by e-mailing a form to recipients.

When you use the Distribute Form command, Acrobat creates a data responses file where the form data are collected. If you elect to bypass the Distribute Form command, no data responses file is created for you to aggregate the form data.

Hosting forms on Web sites

Web site form hosting comes in several flavors. You can add a form to a Web site and have form recipients download the form. If the form is not intended to be part of a server that collects responses, you typically add a submit form button and the form is returned to you. In this regard, the data are not routed by a server product. This type of form is generally used for something like a utility form as we discuss in Chapter 19 or a process that doesn't need to have the data manipulated or managed. Perhaps something like an internal human resources form might be an example of this type of form.

If the form is not a fillable form, you can host a PDF file on a server and the recipient completes the form and gets it back to you either by fax or hand delivery. If the form is filled out using the Typewriter tool in Acrobat or Adobe Reader, the form can be e-mailed back to the host company. Obviously, we've avoided talking about these types of forms throughout this book because this is the least efficient way to handle PDF forms.

Another type of hosting for a form would be one that uses a server product to collect responses and possibly route the data. This task can be accomplished in several ways. You can use a network folder on an internal company server or your own internal server to collect responses via the Distribute Form wizard or have the forms submitted to a URL. If you use a URL, then you need an IT department to program the server for collecting the responses. Another option is to use a form server product from Adobe Systems or a third-party vendor to collect (and route) data. This option eliminates your need to program a server to collect responses data.

The last method for hosting forms on a server is to let Adobe handle the responses collection process through the use of Acrobat.com. In this regard, you don't need to worry about server programming, but you are limited to collecting data on up to 500 responses.

Setting up the Web site design

One of the big problems we find with Web hosted forms, particularly on government Web sites, is that a potential form recipient often has a hard time finding forms. When you consider the fact that the very first point of interaction a constituent has with a government office is most often a form, one would think that the priority for the Web site architecture should be for form recipients to easily locate and download forms. Unfortunately, most government Web sites were first developed to disseminate information. Adding forms to many government Web sites was an afterthought as more and more offices engaged in creating PDF forms.

If forms are a critical area for your Web site, whether it be government, rendering services, or selling products, access to forms and easily finding them should be a top priority. For Web sites hosting a number of forms, you should consider developing Web pages completely devoted to forms hosting and information related to working with forms. This Web site arrangement is much easier for the form recipient who wants to grab a form quickly to download, fill out, and submit responses back to you.

Adding instructions for downloading forms

If you navigate to a location where a PDF is hosted on a Web site and the recipient clicks the link to download a form, by default the form opens inline in a Web browser. (Go to the Internet Preferences by pressing Ctrl/⌘+K, and check the box for Display PDF in Browser.)

As a download progress occurs, no progress bar indicates how long the download will take. However, an indication in the lower-left corner of the Acrobat window shows how large the PDF document is and the status of the download.

Users can set up preferences to download forms either as inline PDFs inside a browser window or a file saved to the recipient's hard drive. Unfortunately, most Adobe Reader users won't know that they can toggle the download between display in a Web browser or saving the file to disk—especially if they do not download many PDF forms. Typically, users are more inclined to wait for a download if they see a progress bar than finding the download progress in the lower-left corner of the viewer window.

On a Web page where you host forms, inform users that opening a context menu on a download link provides them the option to download the file to disk. Ideally, you should show screen shots similar to Figure 14.1.

When this option is selected on a Web page and the download commences, a progress bar reports the download progress, as shown in Figure 14.2. Even if the form is a large file, you'll find more success for users completing downloads when they are informed how long they need to anticipate the download to finish.

FIGURE 14.1

Open a context menu on a URL link to a PDF file, and choose Save Target As (Windows) or Download Linked File As (Macintosh).

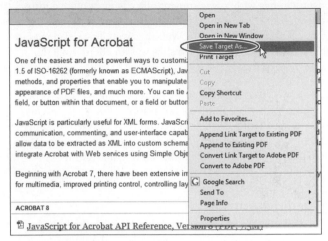

FIGURE 14.2

When saving a PDF file to disk from a URL link, a progress bar displays the download status.

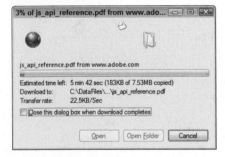

Distributing forms via e-mail

If you distribute a form, the most likely method of communicating with potential recipients is to send either an e-mail with a form attachment or an e-mail with a URL address for where your form can be downloaded. If you use Acrobat to collect responses data, you use the Distribute Form wizard to send a form or a URL.

In this section, we'll stick to sending forms via e-mail. Later in the section "Working with Network Servers," we'll talk about using a network folder and downloading a form from a Web server.

Using Submit Form buttons

If you choose to send a form as an e-mail attachment without using a wizard in Acrobat, make certain a form recipient can return the form via a button action. This is optional because any recipient can attach a form to an e-mail message, but it makes it easier for the recipient if a button is added to the form to submit the completed form back to you.

When using Submit Form buttons, you need to know a few things. If you send a form via e-mail to a form recipient, you need to add a button on the form if you want the form sent back to you via a button action. If you send a form to Adobe Reader users, you need to enable the form with Reader usage rights so the PDF with the data can be returned to you. All these tasks are required when you don't use the Distribute Form wizard in Acrobat.

If you use the Distribute Form wizard to send a form, the wizard automatically adds a Submit Form button that appears in the document message bar, as shown in Figure 14.3. When the form recipient opens an e-mail attachment or downloads the form from a server, this button is made visible on the form. Additionally, when you use the Distribute Form wizard, the form is automatically enabled with Reader usage rights.

FIGURE 14.3

When you use the Distribute Form wizard, a Submit Form button appears in the document message bar.

Manually collecting responses in an e-mail inbox

With Acrobat 8 and above, you have an easy method for distributing forms via e-mail. You use the Distribute Form wizard to e-mail a form, and Acrobat does several things when working with the wizard. Your form is enabled with special features for Adobe Reader users so the Reader users can save the form after filling it out, add digital signatures, and submit the entire PDF file back to you. In addition, Acrobat creates a responses file so when forms are sent back to you, the form data are collected in a single responses file.

When you elect to distribute a form via e-mail, you can select from several methods to distribute your form. You can choose to Send it automatically using Adobe Acrobat which attaches it to an e-mail, or Save a local copy and manually send it later which saves it to your computer. A third option is to send the file to Acrobat.com in which case your e-mail client is bypassed and Acrobat serves as the e-mail client.

To distribute a form using the Distribute Form wizard, we use a form on the CD-ROM.

ON the CD-ROM **For the steps that follow, we used the *globalPicnicRaw.pdf* file from the Chapter14 folder on the book's CD-ROM. You can use this file or any form you have handy to follow the steps.**

The form we want to distribute is a request for employees to indicate how many people will attend the annual company picnic and what dishes the individuals will bring. In addition, because some employees work out of town at satellite offices, a few questions on the form pertain to lodging needs, arrival time, and departure date. The form shown in Figure 14.4 is an ideal form for e-mailing to employees and collecting responses in a responses file.

FIGURE 14.4

A form used for collecting responses from employees regarding participation in the company annual picnic

Notice in Figure 14.4 that the form doesn't have a Submit Form button. We'll use the Distribute Form wizard to distribute the form, create the Submit Form button, enable the file with Adobe Reader usage rights, and create a data responses file. Follow these steps to accomplish all these tasks easily.

STEPS: Distributing a Form for Manual E-mail Responses Collection

1. **Open a PDF form with form fields in Acrobat.** In these steps, we set up the *globalPicnic Raw.pdf* form for e-mail collection. Because we are using a wizard to distribute the form, we don't need a Submit Form button.

2. **Distribute the form.** Choose Forms ⇨ Distribute Form in either normal Viewer mode or Form Editing mode. The Distribute Form wizard opens, as shown in Figure 14.5.

3. **Choose a collection method for acquiring the form data.** From the pull-down menu in the wizard, choose the form collection method you want to use. For this example, we used Manually collect responses in my e-mail inbox, as shown in Figure 14.5.

FIGURE 14.5

Choose a collection method from the pull-down menu at the top of the Distribute Form wizard.

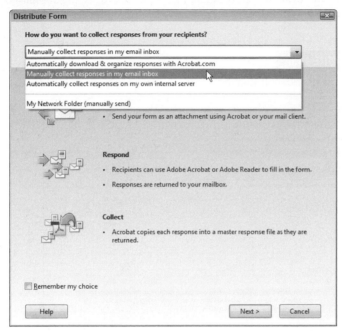

4. **Click Next.** The second pane in the wizard opens, as shown in Figure 14.6.

5. **Choose a method for distributing the form.** When you choose to collect data in your e-mail inbox, you have two options for distributing the form, as shown in Figure 14.6. You can choose to send the form automatically using Acrobat, which requires you to have an MAPI-compliant e-mail application—see the sidebar "Checking for MAPI Compliance"—or to save a local copy and manually send the form later. In this example, we chose Save a local copy and manually send it later.

6. **Click Next.** You arrive at the last pane in the wizard. At the bottom of the wizard window, a check box is checked by default, as shown in Figure 14.7. If you keep the box checked, e-mail addresses of recipients are added to the Tracker to help you track the responses. If you don't want to collect the recipient e-mail addresses, uncheck the box. Doing so means the form recipient will be prompted to add your e-mail address when the form is submitted to you. Make sure the box is checked.

7. **Click Finish.** Click the Finish button in the last wizard pane, and the Tracker opens in Acrobat.

8. **Open the original form.** When the Tracker opens, click the blue text where you see Open Original Form, as shown in Figure 14.8.

9. **Review the form.** In the document message bar, you see the Submit Form button, as shown in Figure 14.9, that was automatically added by Acrobat.

FIGURE 14.6

Choose a distribution method.

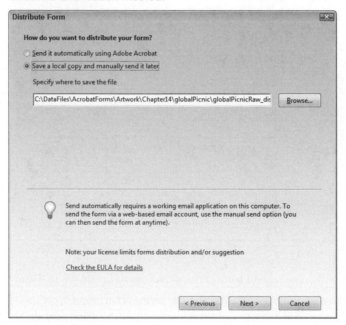

FIGURE 14.7

Click Finish after completing all the steps to distribute the form.

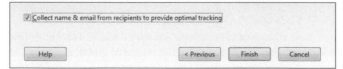

FIGURE 14.8

Click Open Original Form in the Tracker to review the form.

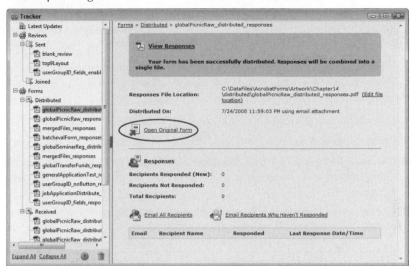

FIGURE 14.9

When you open the form, you find the Submit Form button in the document message bar.

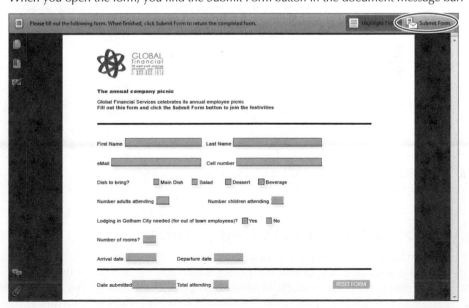

Checking for MAPI Compliance

MAPI (Messaging Application Programming Interface) allows various messaging and workgroup applications such as e-mail, voice mail, and fax to work through a single client. Mail clients such as Microsoft Outlook, Microsoft Outlook Express, and Apple Mail are all MAPI compliant.

If you use an e-mail client and you're not certain if the application is MAPI compliant, you can easily check the compliance in Microsoft Word. Do the following to test your e-mail client application for MAPI compliance:

- Launch Microsoft Word on Windows or the Macintosh.

- Create a blank new document, and type a few characters on the blank page.

- Choose File⇨Send To⇨Mail Recipients (as Attachment). If you use Word 2007, click the Office button and choose Send. In the panel to the right of the Send command, click E-mail.

- If your e-mail client is MAPI compliant, a new message window opens in your default e-mail client with the Word document attached.

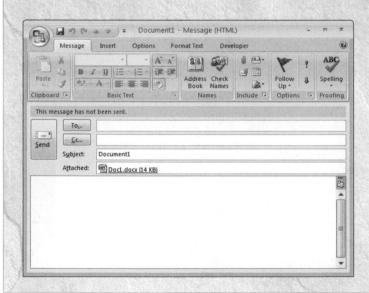

E-mailing forms using Acrobat

In Figure 14.6, you see two choices for manually distributing forms. The first radio button choice is to send an e-mail automatically using Adobe Acrobat. You follow the same steps in the Distribute Form wizard to use Acrobat to automatically create an e-mail for you. Click the first radio button choice in the third pane in the Distribute Form wizard, and a new e-mail message window opens, as shown in Figure 14.10.

FIGURE 14.10

When you choose to let Acrobat send an e-mail, your form is attached to a new e-mail message in Acrobat if you use a MAPI compliant e-mail application.

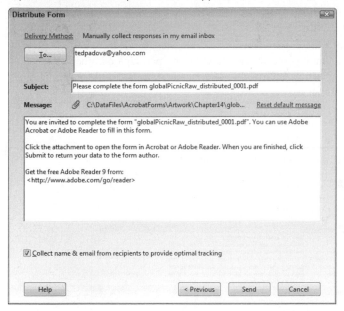

Figure 14.10 shows Distribute Form at the top of the window. The new message that appears is created by Acrobat, not your e-mail client. When you make the choice to let Acrobat send the e-mail, Acrobat then becomes your e-mail client and sends the mail without having to open your e-mail program.

Letting Acrobat serve as your e-mail client is particularly helpful for those who use Web browser e-mail clients, other applications that are not MAPI compliant, and when you're away from the office and want to use another computer to submit a form.

Participating in an e-mail form distribution

A form recipient follows an easy process for completing and returning a form to you. By default, Acrobat adds a message in the Message window when you e-mail a form to a recipient. The form recipient is instructed via the message how to proceed.

To participate in a form distribution session, follow these steps.

STEPS: Receiving and Filling in a Distributed Form

1. **Open your default e-mail client, and retrieve a form.** To follow these steps, you need to distribute a form to an e-mail address. If you have more than one e-mail address, distribute a form to a second address. If you have a single address, send a form to your own address and when your form is returned to your e-mail inbox, you're at this step.

2. **Open the file attachment.** First, look at the e-mail message. The default message provided by Acrobat instructs the form recipient what to do to participate in the form distribution, as shown in Figure 14.11. After reading the message, open the file attachment by double-clicking the attachment icon.

Read the default message, and open the file attachment.

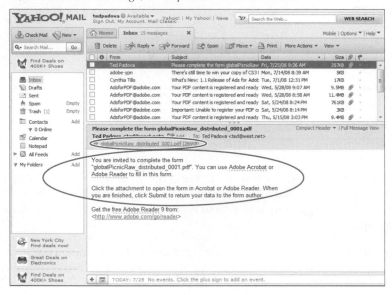

3. **Fill in the form.** Fill in the data fields on the form.

4. **Click the Submit Form button.** If you distributed a form via the Distribute Form wizard, a Submit Form button appears in the document message bar. Click the button.

5. **Check your e-mail address.** By default, your e-mail address and name appear in the Send Form dialog box that opens after you click the Submit Form button. If the address or name is not correct, make any edits needed to the two text boxes shown in Figure 14.12.

FIGURE 14.12

If your e-mail address and/or name is not correct, make edits in the two text boxes.

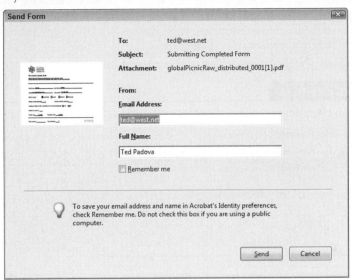

6. **Send the form.** Click Send in the Send Form dialog box.

7. **Choose an e-mail client.** After clicking the Send Form button, the Select Email Client dialog box opens, as shown in Figure 14.13. Choose either a Desktop Email Application or an Internet Email application from the radio button choices.

FIGURE 14.13

Choose your e-mail application.

8. **Click OK.** If you choose Internet Email and click OK, Acrobat prompts you to save the form. Choose a target location you can remember, and save the form. After saving the form, you need to manually create a new e-mail message, attach the saved file, and then send the form to the form author. After you choose this option, Acrobat opens an application alert dialog box instructing you what you need to do to e-mail the form back to the form author, as shown in Figure 14.14.

FIGURE 14.14

If you choose Internet Email, Acrobat informs you how to proceed after saving the form.

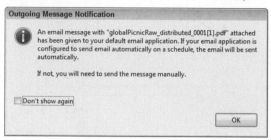

If you have a MAPI-compliant application, click Desktop Email Application in the Select Email Client dialog box and click OK. The form is attached to a new message in your default e-mail client. If the new message window doesn't open, you may need to open your e-mail client and click the Send (or Send/Receive) button to send the form back to the form author.

Hacking the Submit Form button

Advanced forms authors may want some more flexibility than what Acrobat provides when distributing forms via the auto-generated Submit Form button. For example, in Figure 14.9 on our example form used in this chapter, you see a form field in the lower-left corner designed for a date stamp for when a form is submitted. For the form responses collector, the date a form is received appears in the responses file when you collect the data. But there is no indication on the form itself for when a form is submitted.

What if you want a submitted date to appear on a form just in case you need to send the form back to the recipient to prove that a form was submitted on a given date? You don't want to send the responses file with the data from all the collected forms, but you want a recipient to review a form and verify when the form was submitted. If you want to send a copy of the completed form back to the recipient to support your claim, it would be nice to have the form date stamped in a locked field. In other cases, you may want to add a field, add a comment note, perform a calculation, or do any number of other routines you can add with JavaScript to a Submit Form button.

CROSS-REF There are issues related to the reliability of date stamps generated from the computer system clock. For a detailed explanation of date stamping forms, see Chapter 18.

We offer a warning in this section to those who may not be sophisticated in using JavaScript and editing functions and field scripts. You'll want to keep a backup copy of your original form in case you need to set up a new Distribute Form session using an unedited form if you fail at editing the distributed form. Be certain you practice a little and test all JavaScripts before using the techniques we describe in this section.

Understanding the Submit Form button and distributed forms

When you distribute a form using the Distribute Form wizard and Acrobat adds the Submit Form button in the document message bar, the button is not a field button and it has no properties other than executing a script on another button that Acrobat adds to a form. The button Acrobat adds to a form is hidden, so you won't see it when distributing forms.

If you choose to manually submit a form via e-mail and choose the option to save a local copy and manually send it later in the Distribute Form wizard, as shown in Figure 14.6, you end up with a form saved to your hard disk. This form has some special properties. The form is enabled with Adobe Reader usage rights, so you cannot edit the form as is and a responses file has been created so you can collect the returned form data in a PDF Portfolio. The original form by default is saved as *form name_distributed.pdf,* and the responses file is saved as *form name_responses.pdf.*

The *form name_distributed.pdf* file is the one you distribute to form recipients, and the *form name_responses.pdf* is the file you use to collect the responses data. When the files are created, a link is established between the two files so that when you double-click the distributed file, data are automatically added to the responses file. If you edit the distributed file, you break the link.

Adobe didn't intend for you to make edits on the *distributed.pdf* form, so there are no recommended methods for editing the file. However, just because it wasn't intended doesn't mean we can't create a little workaround to customize a form to suit our needs. The one thing you need to keep in mind is that if you make edits to a *distributed.pdf* file, you need to manually add data collected from the forms to the responses file.

Editing the Submit Form button properties

Going back to the Submit Form button, you can make edits to the real button Acrobat adds to a distributed form. If you do make edits to the button properties, you need to remove the special features added to the *distributed.pdf* file, which breaks the link to the *responses.pdf* file. Be aware of this before you proceed.

To edit the Submit Form field properties on a button added by Acrobat when a form is distributed, follow these steps.

ON the CD-ROM We use the same *globalPicnicRaw.pdf* file found in the Chapter14 folder on the book's CD-ROM for these steps. If you wish, you can use any other form to follow the steps.

STEPS: Customizing the Submit Form Button

1. **Open a form in Acrobat.** For our example, we use the *globalPicnicRaw.pdf* file from the book's CD-ROM.

2. **Distribute the form.** Use the Distribute Form wizard, and manually send the form via e-mail while choosing Save a local copy and manually send it later in the wizard.

3. **Save the form.** When the Distribute Form wizard prompts you to save the form, save to a target folder you can easily remember.

4. **Open the form.** You can open the form from the Tracker or open the target folder and select the file you saved and open it. If you elect to use the Tracker, choose Forms ⇨ Track Forms in Viewer mode. Click Open Original Form when the Tracker opens in Acrobat.

5. **Save a copy.** The form has been enabled with Adobe Reader usage rights. You cannot edit the form when the special features have been added. Choose File ⇨ Save a Copy, and you can edit the saved copy.

6. **Open the saved copy.** When you save a copy of a form, the original form remains in view in the Document pane, and the saved copy appears in the target folder as yet unopened in Acrobat. Close the original form, and choose File ⇨ Open to open the copy of the original form. This form has the special features removed and can be edited.

7. **Locate the button field.** Click the Select Object tool in the Advanced Editing toolbar. You'll find the button added by Acrobat in the top-right corner on the form, as shown in Figure 14.15. By default, the button field name is SubmitForm2.

FIGURE 14.15

The SubmitButton2 field is located in the top-right corner of the form. Double-click the button field with the Select Object tool to open the Button Field Properties window.

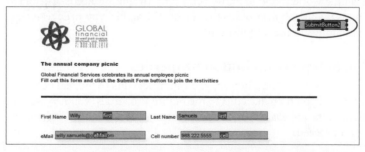

8. **Open the Button Field Properties window.** Double-click the button field with the Select Object tool to open the Button Field Properties window.

9. **Open the JavaScript editor.** Click the Actions tab, and click Run a JavaScript in the Actions list. Click Edit to open the script in the JavaScript Editor.

10. **Edit the JavaScript.** For this example, we want to add a date stamp to a field that exists on the form. We need to locate the routine in the JavaScript that submits the form and add our JavaScript in this area. We presume all form recipients are using Acrobat 9 or above, so we'll scroll the code and locate the comment where you see //*submit the form*. We want to add our JavaScript just before this area in the code. Preceding this comment, add the following script, as shown in Figure 14.16:

```
1. // before submitting we'll add the date to the Date received
   field
2. var f = this.getField("Date received");
3. f.value = util.printd ("mmm, dd, yyyy", new Date());
```

FIGURE 14.16

Add a script preceding the // *submit a form* line of code.

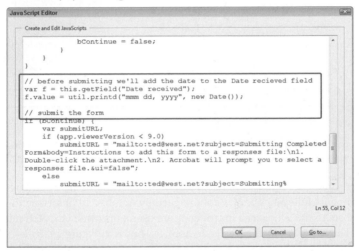

11. **Click OK in the JavaScript Editor, and click Close in the Button Field Properties window.**

12. **Save the form.**

13. **Enable the form with Adobe Reader usage rights.** The current form lost the special features for Adobe Reader users. Choose Advanced ➪ Extend Features in Adobe Reader. Save the form when prompted by Acrobat. Use the same name for the file to overwrite the file you opened.

14. **Send the form to recipients.** You can attach the form to an e-mail message or host the form on Acrobat.com for recipients to acquire. When recipients submit the form, the form is date stamped, as shown in Figure 14.17.

FIGURE 14.17

When a recipient clicks the Submit Form button in the document message bar, the form is date stamped.

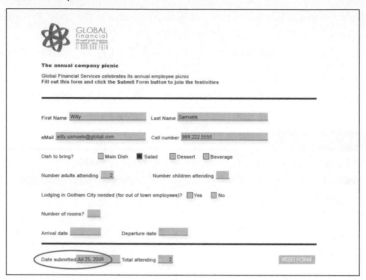

CROSS-REF For information on hosting forms on Acrobat.com, see the section "Working with Network Servers" later in this chapter.

In the JavaScript we use to date stamp the form, we begin the routine by adding a programmer's comment. Anything following the // is not executed by Acrobat. In observing the script, be aware that the numbers to the left of each line of code are used to provide you with information related to each line. They are not typed in the code itself, as shown in Figure 14.16.

In line 2, we assign the variable *f* to the *Date received* field, which is the field name for the field we want to add our date stamp. Line 3 sets the value of *f* to the current date derived from the form recipient's computer system clock.

CROSS-REF For more information on writing JavaScripts in Acrobat, see Part V.

Examining JavaScript functions

The JavaScript assigned to the SubmitButton2 field is not the only JavaScript added to a *distributed. pdf* file. Another script handles all the processing for setting up the *responses.pdf* file and opening an application response dialog box where a recipient adds a name and e-mail address. This script also assesses viewer versions so that the SubmitForm2 button is made visible for any user of an Acrobat viewer less than 9.0 and hidden when using Acrobat 9.0 or greater. If you wonder how the button is shown when your form opens in an earlier version of Acrobat, you find the answer in this JavaScript function.

You can edit the script by choosing Advanced ➪ Document Processing ➪ Document JavaScripts. The JavaScript Functions dialog box opens, as shown in Figure 14.18.

FIGURE 14.18

Chose Advanced ➪ Document Processing ➪ Document JavaScripts to open the JavaScript Functions dialog box.

To edit the JavaScript, click the Edit button and the script opens in the JavaScript Editor. To make any edits on this script, you need to have an advanced level of understanding for JavaScript. We show you the way to access the script so you know how the events are executed when a form is distributed, but we don't recommend you make any changes to the script unless you have an advanced understanding for writing and debugging JavaScripts.

Later in this chapter, we talk about aggregating data in the *responses.pdf* file. The data we use as an example to illustrate the methods was created from bogus e-mail accounts. You may wonder how we collected forms without using real e-mail addresses. The way we were able to set up a series of forms to explain the responses collection process was by editing the JavaScript Function and the SubmitButton2 two-field script. Instead of submitting the form on the button action, we recoded it to save the form using bogus e-mail addresses and names. When we collected the data in the responses file, we manually added the forms to compile the data.

We won't go into the scripts to recode them for producing a similar outcome here because you're not likely to use forms with example data. As a matter of information, we wanted you to know how the files were created.

CROSS-REF For more information on compiling data, see "Managing Data" later in this chapter.

Working with Network Servers

Up to this point, we have talked about e-mailing forms from your e-mail client, your Internet e-mail application, and through Adobe Acrobat. Distributing forms works well when you want to distribute a form to a limited number of people who need to complete and return a form, and you know who these people are. When you distribute forms via any form of e-mail, you need to know each recipient's e-mail address. If you have a few hundred forms to distribute and don't have all the addresses in an address book, distributing forms this way can be overwhelming.

A better option for you is to host a form on a server where form recipients can acquire a form. When you distribute a form, you have several options to choose for server hosting, as discussed in the section "Hosting forms on Web sites" earlier in this chapter. For hosting forms on your own internal Web server, we refer you to the Acrobat Help document and information Adobe has hosted on Adobe.com. In this chapter, we'll stick to using network folders on an internal server and using services provided by Acrobat.com.

CROSS-REF This chapter is related to working with Acrobat forms and distributing and collecting data for forms that are managed by Acrobat. In Chapter 34, we cover much more related to using servers as it relates to Adobe LiveCycle Designer forms.

If you work in a large company and use internal networks, you may want to have a variety of internal forms hosted in a shared folder on a company server. Employees can access the forms and submit responses in a way very similar to submitting e-mail responses.

To set up a shared folder, you begin by opening the form you want to share in Acrobat and choosing Forms ➪ Distribute Form. The Distribute Form wizard opens the same as when distributing forms for e-mail responses. In the Distribute Form wizard, you choose Automatically collect responses on my own internal server, as shown in Figure 14.19.

FIGURE 14.19

Choose Automatically collect responses on my own internal server in the Distribute Form wizard.

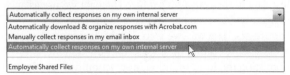

Click Next, and you arrive at the pane where you make choices for where to host the form and attributes associated with the server location, as shown in Figure 14.20. If you use a SharePoint Workspace server, you set up a new folder on the server to collect responses. Your other choice is to use a network folder that doesn't require anything more than a network connection to a server. If you choose Network folder in the Distribute Form wizard, click the Browse button to locate a directory on the server where you want to create a new folder to collect responses and host the form for employees to complete.

FIGURE 14.20

Check an option in the Distribute Form wizard, and click Browse to locate a target folder where you want to save the *distributed.pdf* form and the *responses.pdf* files.

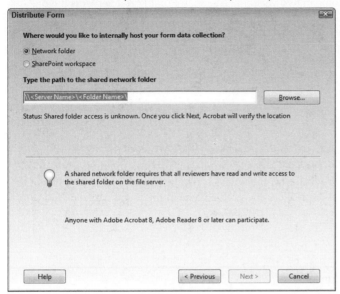

Click Next, and you arrive at the pane where you determine how to distribute a form. You have the same choices available as when e-mailing forms. Make a choice, and click the Browse button to locate the server location where the *distributed.pdf* file will be located.

Click Next, and you are prompted to specify a name for the server profile, as shown in Figure 14.21. Type a descriptive name, and click Next. Click Finish in the last pane, and your file is ready for users to complete. When you send an e-mail to recipients, the folder location is contained in the e-mail message. As recipients fill in a form, the responses are collected in the *responses.pdf* file.

FIGURE 14.21

Type a name for the new Profile in the text box.

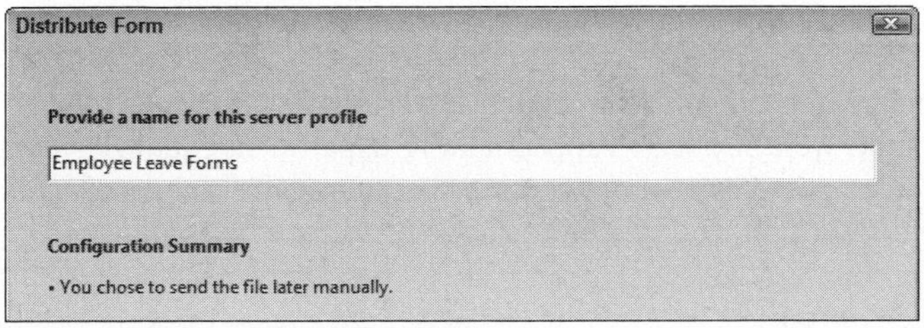

Microsoft SharePoint Workspaces

Microsoft SharePoint Workspaces come in two versions. The SharePoint Portal Server is the bigger and more robust product, and the SharePoint Team server is the smaller, less expensive and more easily manageable product. SharePoint workspaces enable you to work together with colleagues on the same document, save different versions of documents, inform users of document changes, and leverage security with Windows. If you have a SharePoint server designed to collaborate on documents with colleagues, you can use the server to share PDF forms and collect responses.

Each location you add to servers is listed in the Tracker Preferences. To view the locations, open the Preferences dialog box (Ctrl/⌘+K) and click Tracker in the left pane. In the right pane, open the Remove Custom Server Locations drop-down menu, as shown in Figure 14.22. If you want to remove a server location from the Tracker, select the profile name in the menu and click Remove Server Profile.

FIGURE 14.22

All server locations are listed in the Tracker preferences.

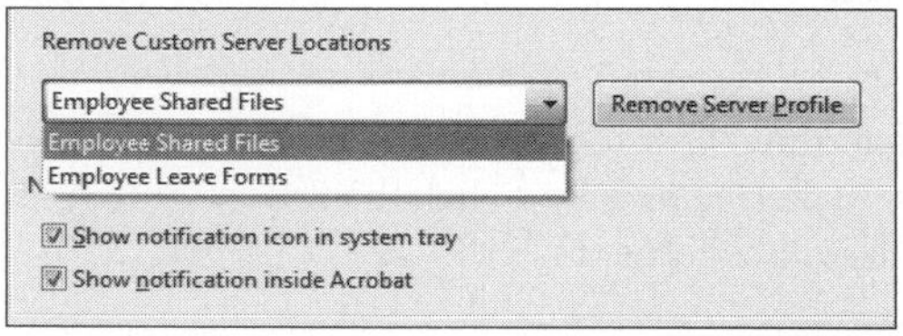

Using Acrobat.com

Those who work in large companies with sophisticated IT departments often have the advantage of accessing a variety of servers and a number of server services. Until the introduction of the Acrobat.com, individual users and smaller companies had no real opportunity to share forms on servers. The likelihood for individuals to engage in complex programming to distribute a form was beyond the reach of most individual users and small companies without IT departments.

Users in large companies who needed to depend on IT departments to set up new server locations and perform various programming tasks were also handicapped if an IT department couldn't get a server configured within the timeframe desired by an employee. Certainly a social event sponsored by a company is in a lower priority than critical work that needs to be performed by employees.

With the introduction of Acrobat.com that coincided with the release of Acrobat 9, Adobe has provided a solution for the individual users, small companies, and large enterprises that need some immediate action for distributing forms and collecting responses.

Logging into Acrobat.com

Acrobat.com is a free service provided by Adobe Systems. Any user can access Acrobat.com regardless of the Adobe product one uses. However, Acrobat.com is much more in tune with Acrobat and LiveCycle Designer experiences than with any other Adobe product. Although the applications and the Acrobat.com services are separate entities, Acrobat 9 and above has many menu commands that facilitate your interaction with Acrobat.com.

You need only look at the File ➪ Collaborate submenu or the Comments menu, and you find many commands that utilize Acrobat.com services.

Creating an Adobe ID

All the work you do with Acrobat.com requires you to create an Adobe ID. Each time you submit a form to Acrobat.com, you need to log in with your ID (e-mail address) and password. If you don't have an Adobe ID, you need to create one. If your first effort is to Distribute a form on Acrobat.com from within the Distribute Form wizard, you are immediately prompted to sign into Acrobat.com. On the Distribute Form logon dialog box, shown in Figure 14.23, you find a link to another dialog box where you can apply for an Adobe ID.

FIGURE 14.23

When you attempt to distribute a form on Acrobat.com, a logon dialog box opens. If you don't have an Adobe ID, click the Create Adobe ID blue text.

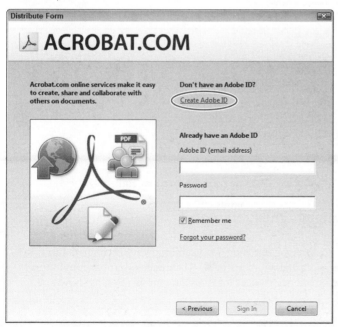

Click the blue text where you see Create Adobe ID, and the Distribute Form panel changes to what you see in Figure 14.24. In this panel, fill in the text boxes, select the country where you live, and check the box for I have read and agree to the following. To review the license agreement, click Acrobat.com Services Agreement and look over the Web pages specifying the terms of the agreement. After reviewing the services agreement, click Next and the information is sent to Adobe. You are informed that an e-mail message has been sent to your e-mail inbox, and you need to click the link to complete setting up your ID.

FIGURE 14.24

Fill in the form, and click Next to send the application information to Adobe Systems.

After you create an Adobe ID, you're ready to distribute forms to Acrobat.com.

Adding the log-on information to the Preferences

If you use a personal computer that doesn't have public access, you may want to have your ID and password set up so you can bypass the logon dialog box each time you distribute a form. In any Acrobat viewer, open the Preferences dialog box (Ctrl/⌘+K) and click Acrobat.com in the left pane; in the right pane, you see preference choices for Acrobat.com services, as shown in Figure 14.25.

FIGURE 14.25

Open the Preferences dialog box, and click Acrobat.com in the left pane to display options for using the service appearing in the right pane.

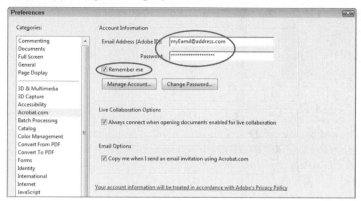

Fill in the e-mail address you used for your Adobe ID. Check the Remember me check box, and type your password; your password cannot be typed until you check the Remember me check box. Also check Always connect when opening documents enabled for live collaboration if you intend to engage in live collaboration services on Acrobat.com. Setting up the Acrobat.com preferences in this manner eliminates the need to type your ID and password each time you log onto the service.

NOTE Setting the Acrobat.com preferences is optional. If you use your computer in a workgroup where others have access to your computer, you may want to avoid filling in the Acrobat.com preferences and use a manual logon each time you access the Acrobat. com Web site. If you are confident that no one can access your computer, go ahead and set up the preferences so you can use an automatic logon each time you visit Acrobat.com.

Before you read farther in this chapter, be certain to have your Adobe ID confirmed and ready to go. Make sure you can log onto Acrobat.com by choosing File ➪ Collaborate ➪ Go to Acrobat.com.

Using Acrobat.com services

As a forms author, your primary use for Acrobat.com is distributing forms and collecting responses using the service. But Acrobat.com services offer much more than distributing forms and collecting responses. Some of the additional services can be helpful when designing forms, gathering input from coworkers, and conducting online collaboration sessions to discuss forms designs and deployment. To get a feel for what's available on Acrobat.com, choose File ➪ Collaborate ➪ Go to Acrobat.com or open your Web browser and visit www.acrobat.com.

When you arrive at Acrobat.com, you find five icons on the welcome page. Clicking any one of the icons shown in Figure 14.26 first prompts you for your Adobe ID logon and then takes you to the respective service. The services include:

When you arrive at www.acrobat.com, the welcome page displays five icons representing access to various services.

- **Adobe Buzzword:** Adobe Buzzword is an Adobe Flash-based word processor. You can write documents online, and the files are stored in your Acrobat.com library. You don't need to be concerned about saving files on a flash drive and copying to a laptop when you're on the road. You can access your Buzzword documents wherever you have an Internet connection.

- **Acrobat ConnectNow:** This version of Acrobat Connect is a free service for Web conferencing where you can have up to three people (two others plus yourself) in a meeting room complete with VOIP and screen sharing.

- **Create PDF:** This option enables you to convert up to five native files to PDF. The service is intended for Adobe Reader users who do not have PDF creation opportunities using the free Reader software. A maximum of five (lifetime) conversions are available. After a user has converted five files, additional conversions are available on a subscription basis. When we say *lifetime*, we mean that the total conversions are five from Acrobat 9 through Acrobat 100 or more until Adobe changes the policy. Forms authors are not likely to use the service, but you may recommend it for Adobe Reader users.

- **Share:** You use Share for sharing files with colleagues, coworkers, and clients. In addition to sharing files, you can conduct shared reviews (available only with the Acrobat Pro products). A shared review might entail sharing a new form design with coworkers. If you're an Acrobat Pro or Pro Extended user, you can initiate a review and users of the Adobe Reader software can add comments to the form design.

- **My Files:** Click My Files, and you are taken to your Acrobat.com online library. Here you find all the files you shared, forms you distributed, Buzzword documents you created, and files others have shared with you, and you have access to all the other services provided by Acrobat.com.

Like we said, the primary interest for forms authors is using Acrobat.com for distributing forms and collecting data. However, if you work in an enterprise environment, government office, medium-sized company, or you're an independent forms author, you'll find several other services available on Acrobat.com very useful. All but the Create PDF (after a user converts five files to PDF) are free through this service.

Submitting forms to Acrobat.com

Let's focus on the one huge use you'll find with Acrobat.com services: distributing forms. Up to this point, we've talked about distributing forms via e-mail and network servers. When you distribute a form to Acrobat.com, you follow the same initial steps using the Distribute Form wizard. Files are enabled automatically with Adobe Reader usage rights and a *responses.pdf* file is created on your hard drive.

The process for using Acrobat.com is that the form file you distribute (*filename_distributed.pdf*) is sent to Acrobat.com. Form recipients go to Acrobat.com to download the hosted form. When a recipient fills in a form and submits data using the Submit Form button in the document message bar, the data are uploaded to Acrobat.com. You use the Tracker to download the recipient responses to your computer's *filename_responses.pdf* file, where you aggregate the data.

CROSS-REF For more information on using the Tracker to download responses, see "Using the Tracker" later in this chapter.

To understand more clearly the process for distributing forms to Acrobat.com, follow these steps.

ON the CD-ROM We continue using the same *globalPicnicRaw.pdf* file from the Chapter14 folder on the book's CD-ROM for these steps.

STEPS: Distributing Forms on Acrobat.com

1. **Set up the Acrobat.com Preferences.** In order to proceed through these steps, you need an Adobe ID as explained in the section "Logging onto Acrobat.com." Make sure you have a valid Adobe ID, and open the Preferences dialog box by pressing Ctrl/⌘+K. Click Acrobat.com, and add your e-mail address and password in the right pane. This step is optional. If you prefer to manually log on, you can do so when prompted in the Distribute Form wizard.

2. **Open a form in Acrobat.** For these steps, we used the *globalPicnicRaw.pdf* file from the book's CD-ROM.

3. **Open the Distribute Form wizard.** Choose Forms ⇨ Distribute Form in either Viewer mode or Form Editing mode to open the Distribute Form wizard.

4. **Choose Automatically download & organize responses with Acrobat.com from the drop-down menu at the top of the Distribute Form wizard, as shown in Figure 14.27.**

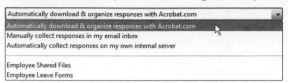

FIGURE 14.27

Choose Automatically download & organize responses with Acrobat.com.

5. **Click Next.** If you didn't add your logon information in the Preferences dialog box, the Distribute Form wizard displays a panel for your logon information. Type your e-mail address and password, and click OK. If you added your logon information in the preferences, your logon is automatic.

6. **Wait while Acrobat authenticates your ID.** Your computer will pause a moment while the authentication takes place. Wait until you see a new e-mail message window appear before proceeding.

7. **Add recipient addresses to the e-mail message.** An e-mail message window opens, as shown in Figure 14.28. Type recipient e-mail addresses in the To field. You don't need to know all the recipients at the time you upload the file. Just adding one e-mail in the To field enables you to upload the file.

8. **Choose an Access Level.** Notice the drop-down menu at the bottom of the Distribute Form wizard where you see Access Level. The options in the menu are available only when distributing forms to Acrobat.com. You have a choice for Limited access or Open access. If you choose Limited access, form recipients can download and complete the form only if you personally invite them with an e-mail message and the URL specified for where to download the form. (The URL is automatically added to an e-mail message when you distribute the form and when you invite additional recipients from the Tracker.)

   If you choose Open access, then anyone arriving at your Acrobat.com library can download and fill out the form. If you intend to post a URL link from a Web site or communicate a URL link via other means, you'll want to choose Open access from the menu. Make a choice, and click Send.

9. **Review the file in the Tracker.** After clicking Send, Acrobat serves as your mail client and uploads the form to your Acrobat.com workspace. When the upload completes, the Tracker opens and reports the successful upload, as shown in Figure 14.29.

CROSS-REF For information regarding using the Tracker, see "Using the Tracker" later in this chapter.

FIGURE 14.28

Fill in recipient e-mail addresses, and choose an Access Level.

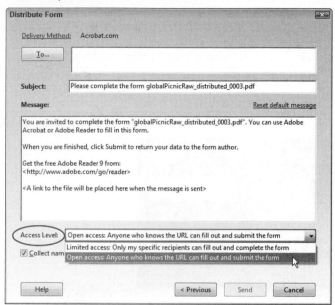

FIGURE 14.29

After Acrobat uploads the file, the Tracker opens reporting the upload status.

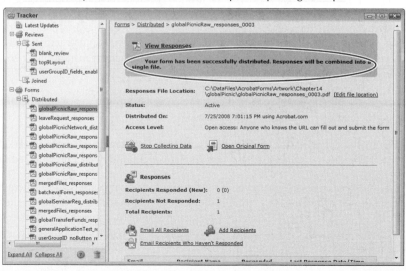

Viewing files on Acrobat.com

To quickly access Acrobat.com from within any Acrobat viewer, choose File ⇨ Collaborate ⇨ Go to Acrobat.com. When you arrive at Acrobat.com, you see the five buttons shown earlier (refer to Figure 14.26) on the opening page. Click the last button in the row where you see My Files listed, and the My Files logon pop-up window opens, as shown in Figure 14.30. Type your Adobe ID and password, and click Sign in to open your Acrobat.com library.

FIGURE 14.30

Type your e-mail address and password, and click Sign in to open your Acrobat.com library.

Your Acrobat.com library displays all the files you have uploaded to the workspace. Among the files are your distributed forms. If you want to copy the URL where your form is hosted, click the form you want to use, and a down-pointing arrow appears on the page thumbnail. Click the arrow, and a drop-down menu opens, as shown in Figure 14.31. From the menu options, choose Copy Link.

After you copy the link, a pop-up message box opens informing you that the link has been copied to the clipboard, as shown in Figure 14.32. You also find some instructive information telling you that you can paste the copied link into an e-mail, Web page, or instant message to share the file with others.

When you paste the code, you see the link text similar to what's shown in Figure 14.33 when we pasted the text into a Sticky Note in Acrobat.

In Figure 14.30, notice that you also have an option for copying the embedded code. The embedded code is HTML that you can paste in your Web-page-authoring program when editing Web pages.

We want to reiterate that when you have a group of known users with recipient e-mail addresses, you can invite recipients at the time you distribute a form or later via the Tracker. When you have a group of unknown form recipients—for example, when posting a registration for a workshop on a Web site—you can copy the URL link or HTML code in Acrobat.com and paste the link text/code in an HTML-editing program.

FIGURE 14.31

Click a form page thumbnail, and from the drop-down menu, choose Copy Link.

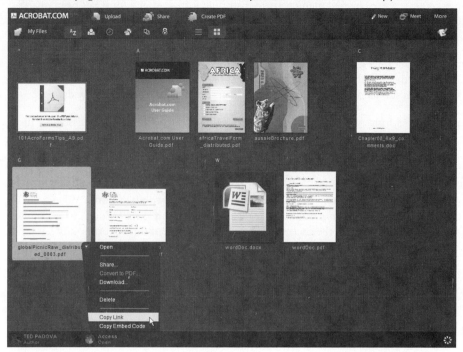

FIGURE 14.32

After you copy text, a pop-up message informs you that the data have been copied to the clipboard and where you can paste the clipboard data.

FIGURE 14.33

The code copied from a form uploaded to Acrobat.com and pasted into a Sticky Note

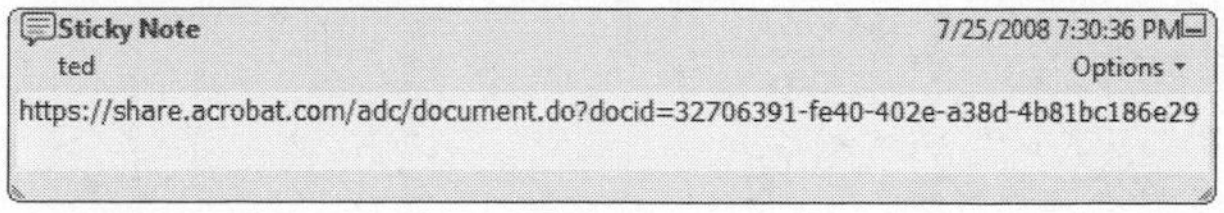

Sticky Note	7/25/2008 7:30:36 PM
ted	Options ▾
https://share.acrobat.com/adc/document.do?docid=32706391-fe40-402e-a38d-4b81bc186e29	

Managing Data

In preceding sections, we've covered many ways to distribute forms. After a form has been distributed and form recipients have submitted data, it's time to review the data and possibly pass the data to another application for further analysis.

When aggregating data from recipient responses, you have a couple ways to handle viewing the data. When you use the Distribute Form wizard and send forms to recipients, a *responses.pdf* file is created. As recipients submit data back to you, the responses file is updated with new data.

If you manually collect forms without having a responses file, you need to manually assemble the data by exporting to another application such as a spreadsheet program to analyze the data.

Using the Tracker

The Tracker is like a personal assistant when it comes to handling distributed forms. When you submit a form, the Tracker opens in Acrobat as shown earlier in Figure 14.29. Your first encounter with the Tracker is when it reports the successful form submission. But this report is only a fraction of what you can expect from the Tracker.

In Figure 14.34, we show a different view of the Tracker. This view shows a form selected in the left pane and the responses collected from recipients. In the Tracker you see options for:

FIGURE 14.34

The Tracker shows a list of recipients for forms collected.

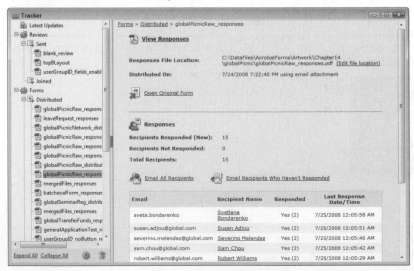

- **Reviews:** The list of reviews shows any files you have sent or joined for shared reviews.

- **Forms:** Below the Forms heading in the left panel, you find a list of subheadings. In Figure 14.34, you cannot see the other subheadings in the scrollable list. The items include:

  - **Distributed:** The list pertains to all forms you have distributed and remain in the list until you delete them.

  - **Received:** If you are a form recipient, you see a list of forms you have received from a forms author.

  - **Server Status:** Files you distribute on network servers, SharePoint Workspaces, internal servers, and Acrobat.com appear listed under this subheading.

- **View Responses:** Click a form in the left panel and then click View Responses, and the responses file respective to the selected form opens in Acrobat. (See "Managing Responses" later in this section.)

- **Open Original Form:** Click the text, and the distributed form opens in Acrobat. When you distribute a form, a copy of the form is saved as *filename_distributed.pdf*. The original form is never overwritten, and you can always return to it for editing and redistribution. In the Tracker where you see Original form, this means the original distributed form that has been enabled with Reader usage rights and a Submit Form button appears in the document message bar.

- **Responses:** This section of the Tracker reports the responses activity. You see some data regarding the number of respondents, recipients who have not responded, and the total recipients.

- **Email All Recipients:** Click the text, and a new message window appears in your default e-mail client with the recipient names automatically added in the To text box, as shown in Figure 14.35. Type a message, and you can send it to all the form recipients.

- **Email Recipients Who Haven't Responded:** Click the text, and a similar e-mail message as the one shown in Figure 14.35 opens with the e-mail addresses of recipients who have been invited to fill out the form but haven't yet responded.

- **Recipient list:** Below the text links, you find a list of recipients who have responded with the responses dates.

FIGURE 14.35

Click Email All Recipients, and all the form recipient e-mail addresses are added to a new message window in your default e-mail client.

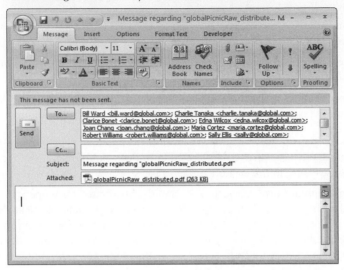

The form selected in the Tracker in Figure 14.34 was a form that was manually distributed. When you distribute a form and ask users to return the form using the Submit Form button in the document message bar, you see a Tracker window similar to the one in Figure 14.29, shown earlier in this chapter. In addition to the Tracker items discussed thus far, you also have a text link to Stop Collecting Data. Click this link when you are finished collecting responses.

NOTE The Tracker has one more feature that is disabled by default. If you open the Tracker Preferences and check the Enable RSS feeds in Tracker check box, you'll see another topic heading in the Tracker's left panel. You can add RSS feeds to the Tracker and monitor updates as they are added for any RSS feed you choose to add to the Tracker. You also can export a feed to PDF and read a blog or other type of feed while on the road on your laptop computer. If you're engaged in lots of forms distribution and use another RSS reader, you may want to keep this option disabled. Loading up more data slows down the interaction you have with the Tracker.

If you open a context menu on a file listed in the left panel of the Tracker, you see many menu commands the same as the text links in the Tracker window. One additional command that you don't have in the Tracker window is the Create PDF From Tracker Details. Open a context menu on a file and choose this command, and a PDF is created as shown in Figure 14.36.

In addition to this menu command, you have some other commands to create folders and send files to folders. Using these commands, you can organize the files in a nested hierarchy list in the left panel.

Choose Create PDF From Tracker Details, and a PDF document is created with the Tracker information related to the respective file.

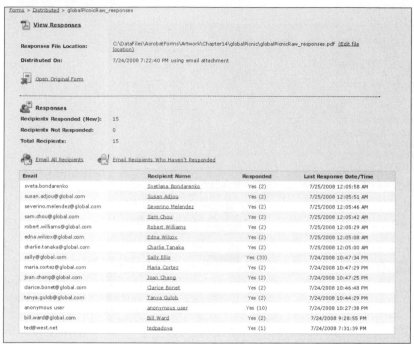

Managing responses from distributed forms

We talked quite a bit about the responses file, but up to this point, we haven't yet shown an image of what the file looks like. As we said earlier, the responses file is a single file that collects recipient responses. Actually, the file is a PDF Portfolio with a special customized interface. You can't break apart the forms because the original forms don't exist in the file. You can't edit the layout view because the layout is fixed to the view you see when you open the file. You can't edit the Welcome Page because the page is a custom design that displays some information regarding what tools you can use once inside the portfolio.

ON the CD-ROM To look over various options you have when examining a responses file, you can use the *globalPicnic_responses.pdf* from the Chapter14 folder on the book's CD-ROM.

The responses file can be opened from within the Tracker by clicking the View Responses text link, or you can navigate to the location where the file is stored and choose File ➪ Open to open the file. When you open a responses file, you see the Welcome Page, as shown in Figure 14.37.

When you open a responses file, you see a Welcome Page in a PDF Portfolio interface.

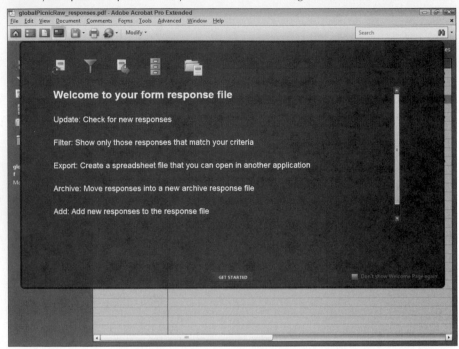

The Welcome Page has a list of items with descriptions. When you open the responses file, a special set of tools is added to the left side of the document pane. The tasks you can perform with data collected from forms are shown in Table 14.1

Options Available for Data Collection and Management

Icon	Item	Description
	Update	Click Update, and Acrobat checks for new updates to the responses file.
	Filter	Choose Filter, and a side panel opens where you can filter data on any field name on a form.
	Export	From a pull-down menu, choose Sort All or Selected. If you choose Export All or Export Selected, the data are exported as a CSV or XML file that can be opened in Microsoft Excel or a database.

Icon	Item	Description
	Archive	You can archive selected responses data or all responses data. The archive can overwrite the existing dataset file or create a new dataset file. Note that when you archive, the data are removed from your responses file.
	Add	Click Add, and you can add new responses to the responses file.
	Delete	Click a row, and click the Delete tool to remove the data from the responses file.
	Form thumbnail preview	A mini thumbnail preview of the selected row item respective to the form is shown below the tools.

Click the Get Started button on the Welcome Page, and you see the files shown in a table view in the PDF Portfolio, as shown in Figure 14.38. This view is the Home view with a special layout designed for the responses file.

Click the Get Started button on the Welcome Page, and the data table is shown in the PDF Portfolio document pane.

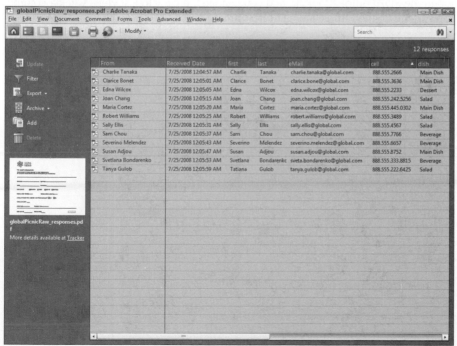

TIP If you frequently return to a responses file, click the Don't show Welcome Page again check box. When you open the document again, the Welcome Page won't appear and you won't have to continually dismiss it to get to the data view. If you want to review the Welcome Page when it is hidden, click the Open the Welcome Page tool in the PDF Portfolio toolbar.

Viewing the responses data

While in the responses file, you can view the data in a number of ways. The default view of the data is shown in the Home view in a PDF Portfolio, as shown earlier in Figure 14.38. You also can show the data in a List view, as shown in Figure 14.39. In either view, you can sort a given column in ascending or descending order. In Figure 14.39, we sorted the *dish* column in ascending order. Notice the tiny up-pointing arrow you see when sorting a column in ascending order. Click the arrow, and the sort changes to descending order; the arrow changes to a down-pointing arrow.

Column widths are sized by moving the vertical separator bar between the column title names to the left to size a column smaller and to the right to size a column larger. You cannot collapse a column completely, and if you have lots of data on a form, you'll scroll the window sideways frequently to view and examine different columns.

FIGURE 14.39

Click the List view icon in the PDF Portfolio toolbar, and you change the view to List view. Click a column title name, and you can sort the column in ascending or descending order.

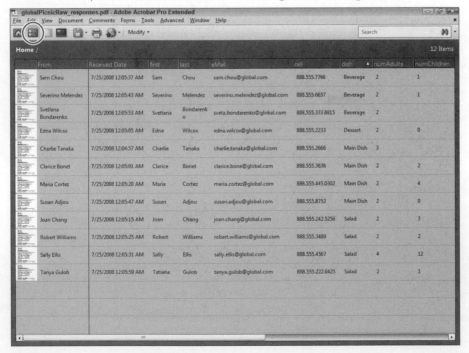

Filtering data

In the Home view, you can sort data according to a number of different options when using the Filter tool. Click Filter, and the left panel changes where you can choose from a number of different filter options for fields in the responses file. For example, you may want to examine responses from a given state or country or look at all the Yes responses for a given check box field.

In the Filter panel, you can sort up to a maximum of six different fields concurrently. For example, you might want to filter for geographic location, age range, civil status including married people only, income above a certain amount, education over a certain grade level, and you might exclude all monolingual people. The rows in the responses file would display the data according to the filter choices. In Figure 14.40, you see selections made in the Filter panel, and the filtered columns to the right of the panel are shown with highlights indicating that the columns have been selected for filtering.

To filter data, you make a choice for the field in a drop-down menu, and from a second drop-down menu, you can choose from a number of different filter options. Below the second drop-down menu, you add the criteria depending on the choice made from the second menu item. For example, if you have a Name field and select Name in the first drop-down menu and choose Begins with from the second drop-down menu, a text box opens where you type the characters you want to define what text a name begins with such as *Mc*. All fields meeting the criteria are shown in the data table to the right of the Filter panel.

By default, when you open the Filter Settings panel, no fields are selected for filtering. You begin filtering data by selecting a field from the drop-down menu labeled Select field name, as shown in Figure 14.41.

FIGURE 14.40

The Filter panel provides options for filtering up to six fields.

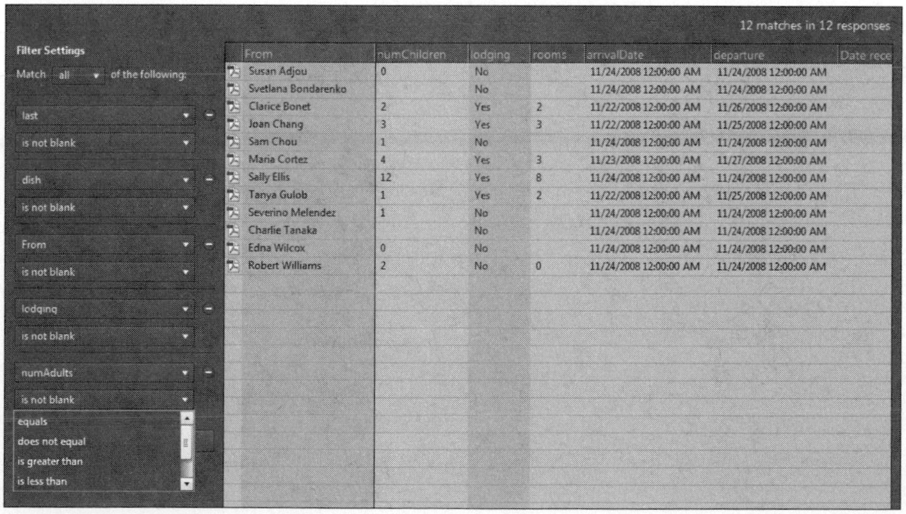

FIGURE 14.41

By default, no items are selected for filtering. Click Select field names to open a drop-down menu where all field names in the responses file are listed.

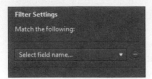

After selecting a field name, you make a choice for the filter action and type text in a text box to define the filter criteria. After you have one field filtered, the Filter Settings panel appears as shown in Figure 14.42. As you can see, several items are added to the Filter Settings panel after filtering an item. Your options include:

FIGURE 14.42

Select a field, choose a filter definition, and then type the criteria in the text box.

A. **Fields drop-down menu:** Click to open the menu, and choose a field name from the fields in the responses file.

B. **Filter definition:** Chose from options in the drop-down menu to define the filter option.

C. **Filter criteria:** In the text box, type the criteria for the filter.

D. **Add Filter:** Click the button to add a new group containing a Fields menu, Filter definition menu, and Filter criteria text box.

E. **Delete the filter item:** Click the minus (-) symbol to delete the filter item.

F. **Calendar pop-up window button:** For date fields only, click the icon to open a pop-up calendar used for selecting dates.

G. **Clear all:** This option removes all filter items in the panel and returns to the default shown in Figure 14.41.

To add an additional filter option, click the + Add Filter button. After adding filter options, you can remove an item by clicking the minus (-) symbol to the right of the field name.

The options choices you have in the Filter definition drop-down menu include:

- **equals:** For numeric data only. Type text in the text box for an exact match.

- **does not equal:** For numeric data only. Type text for the criteria to be excluded, such as for a City field *does not equal, Los Angeles*.

- **is greater than:** For numeric data only. Type a value, and the results show values greater than what you type in the text box.

- **is less than:** For numeric data only. Opposite of *is greater than.*

- **contains:** For text data only. Type characters where you want to search for text contained in a field. You might type MA for Master of Arts degree when the field includes BA, MA, MS, PhD responses.

- **does not contain:** For text data only. Excludes items such as the example shown for *contains.*

- **begins with:** For text data only. Type characters a field begins with.

- **ends with:** For text data only. Type characters a field ends with.

- **is:** For text data only. Same as *equals* for numeric fields.

- **is not:** For text data only. Same as *does not equal* for numeric fields.

- **is blank:** Used for all field types. When you want to exclude all fields not containing data for a given field, use this choice.

- **is not blank:** Used for all field types. When you want to include all fields containing data for a given field, use this choice.

- **is before:** Date fields only. Type the date for all data you want displayed prior to the date you specify. You can click the icon appearing to the right of the text field when you make this choice, and a calendar opens, as shown in Figure 14.43. Click a date on the calendar, and the date is added to the text field.

FIGURE 14.43

Click the icon adjacent to the text field when you choose a date field, and a pop-up calendar opens.

- **is after:** Date fields only. Type the date for all data you want displayed after to the date you specify.

- **is exactly:** Date fields only. Type the date for all data you want displayed to match the date you specify.

- **is today:** Date fields only. Filters the data for the system clock reading of the current date.

- **is yesterday:** Date fields only. Filters the data for the system clock current date minus one (yesterday).

- **is within last 7 days:** Date fields only. Filters the data for the past week.

- **is within last 30 days:** Date fields only. Filters the data for the past 30 days.

Filtering fields provides an at-a-glance view for analyzing data. You might use the filter options to double-check forms that have been filled in properly, and when you find incomplete forms, you might use the Tracker to send an e-mail to a recipient asking for more complete information.

In terms of data analysis, the responses file and filtering options are not designed to provide the flexibility to thoroughly analyze data and build summaries like you have available with database managers and spreadsheet applications. For example, you cannot delete or hide data columns, perform complex sorts such as sorting multiple columns in ascending/descending order, add new data fields, manually move rows up or down, export a data summary as PDF, perform calculations in new fields, and so on. For these kinds of tasks, you need to export the data in a file format that can be read in a database management system or spreadsheet application.

Exporting data

Exporting data from the responses file can be saved as CSV or XML data. You can export all data from the file, or you can select individual rows (or *records*) of data and export the selected data only. To select rows, you can click one row, move down the list, and Shift+click another row to select a contiguous range of rows. If you want to select noncontiguous rows, press Ctrl/⌘ and click the rows you want to select.

To export data from a responses file, click the Export tool, and a drop-down menu opens, as shown in Figure 14.44. If you want the selected data to be exported, click Export selected. If you want all the data to be exported, click the first option for Export All. Assuming you want to export all the data, make the choice in the Export drop-down menu and a Select Folder to Save File dialog box opens. Navigate your hard drive to a target folder, and from the Save as type (Windows) or Format (Macintosh) drop-down menu, choose either CSV (Comma delimited) (*.csv) or XML Files (*.xml). If you want to open the file in Microsoft Excel, choose CSV for the format and click Save.

To view the data, open the program where you want to analyze the data. If using Microsoft Excel and saving the data as CSV, open the CSV file in Excel, and your data appears in a spreadsheet like the one shown in Figure 14.45. In this figure, we deleted some columns and added some totals at the bottom of the spreadsheet. These tasks cannot be performed in Acrobat in the responses file.

FIGURE 14.44

Click the Export tool to open a drop-down menu where you can choose to export all data or selected data.

FIGURE 14.45

CSV data exports can be opened directly in Microsoft Excel.

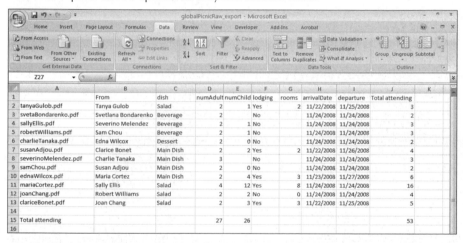

Creating a summary file

In Chapter 19, we talk about creating summary files using JavaScript and exporting PDF data from one file to a summary form. The responses file isn't as easily managed for taking data from one form and introducing the data in another form. Your simplest option is to export the data to Microsoft Excel and create a PDF file from Excel.

A little workaround is available if you want to create a summary PDF form. You need a workaround because the XML (or CSV) data you export from the responses file cannot be introduced in another PDF form. However, XML data is what LiveCycle Designer is all about, so to create our workaround, we need a little help from Designer.

ON the CD-ROM In the Chapter14 folder on the book's CD-ROM, you'll find the *globalPicnic Summary.pdf* form. This form was created in LiveCycle Designer. Use this form to follow steps and explanations in this section.

To begin the process for creating a summary PDF form to introduce data exported from a responses file, we create the summary document in Adobe LiveCycle Designer. We first created a design in Adobe InDesign, exported to PDF, and opened the PDF file in Designer to use it as a PDF background. Using the XML data export file, we created a data connection, brought the fields in the Hierarchy panel, and then duplicated the fields to create the table shown in Figure 14.46.

CROSS-REF The specifics for creating a data connection and adding fields to a LiveCycle Designer form are covered in Chapter 24. For now, don't be concerned about the construction of the LiveCycle Designer form; focus more on understanding how to handle the data.

We added a few fields on the form to calculate results for three different columns. The calculation formula in FormCalc was simple enough using the following formula:

```
sum(numAdults).[*]*)
```

In the above formula, *numAdults* is the parent name for fields in one column. The formula is shown in Figure 14.47. Note that the text appearing above the calculation formula is default text added by Designer. We added a similar formula to the two remaining total fields on the form.

FIGURE 14.46

A PDF document was opened in LiveCycle Designer where fields were added to the form.

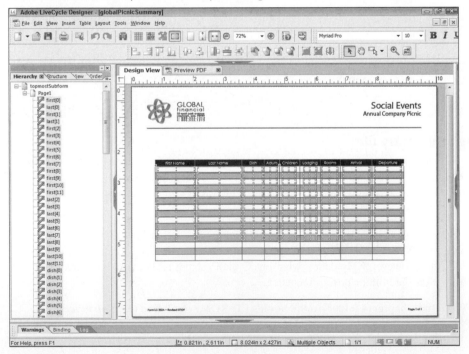

FIGURE 14.47

Formulas were typed in the Script Editor at the top of the Designer window.

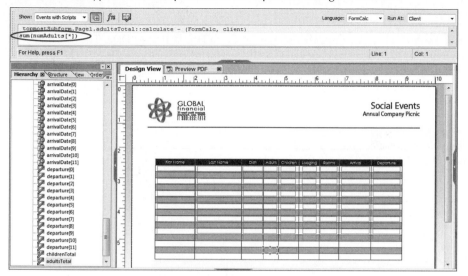

NOTE The form shown in Figures 14.46 and 14.47 is a static form. Because we know the number of records in the data file, we created the form with a table populated with fields only to demonstrate introducing data from a responses file without making it too complicated. If you create summary forms for forms distributed regularly and the number of respondents varies with each new form distribution, a better solution is to create a dynamic form that spawns fields to accommodate the amount of data introduced in the form. For this type of solution and more understanding for working with dynamic forms, see Chapter 27.

ON the CD-ROM The *globalPicnicSummary.pdf* form in the Chapter14 folder on the book's CD-ROM is the final summary form we created in LiveCycle Designer. Use this form to follow the steps here.

To see how we export the responses file data to XML and import the data in a PDF form, follow these steps.

STEPS: Importing XML Data in PDF Forms

1. **Open a responses file.** In our example, we used the *globalPicnic_responses.pdf* file from the book's CD-ROM. Click get Started on the Welcome Page to view the data.

2. **Export the data.** The responses file is populated with 12 records. To export the data, click the Export tool in the left panel and choose Export All from the menu options. In the Select Folder to Save File dialog box, select a folder for the data export and choose XML Files (*.xml) from the Files of type (Windows) or Format (Macintosh) drop-down menu. Click Save to export the data. Make a note of the target folder where you save the data.

3. **Close the responses file.**

4. **Open a summary file.** For our example, we used the *globalPicnicSummary.pdf* file from the book's CD-ROM.

5. **Import the data.** You must be in Viewer mode to access the command to import the data. From the Forms menu, choose Manage Form Data ⇨ Import Data. The Select File Containing Data dialog box opens. Navigate your hard drive, locate the XML file you exported from the responses file, select it, and click Select. The data are imported, as shown in Figure 14.48.

Import the XML data in the summary file.

We want to emphasize again that the best option you have is to create a dynamic form in LiveCycle Designer. You can filter a responses file, export selected data, and introduce the data in a dynamic form that automatically creates new fields as the data flow into the form. You can use the same form many times to display data according to the filter options you choose in the responses file, and the form appearance neatly shows a table accommodating the precise number of records imported into the form.

What's important to know at this point is that if you don't get some help with Designer, you don't have options for importing responses data into forms designed in Acrobat.

Archiving data

The Archive tool in the responses file enables you to archive all records in a file, filtered data, and selected data. If you wish to archive filtered data, you need to first filter fields for at least one field. When you click the Archive tool and choose an option such as Archive All or select rows of data and choose Archive selected, the Archive Data dialog box opens, as shown in Figure 14.49.

Choose an option in the Archive drop-down menu, and the Archive Data dialog box opens.

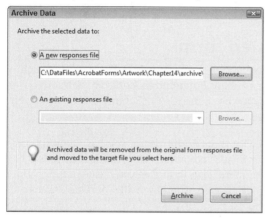

You have two choices in the Archive Data dialog box. You can create a new archive file, or you can append data to an existing responses file. When you click the Archive button, all the data selected from the option you choose in the Archive drop-down menu are deleted from the current responses file as they are added to the target responses file.

One thing to be absolutely sure of is that you don't use the Archive all option if you intend to archive to additional files. Acrobat treats all data exported to a new responses file as an Archive file, and you are limited in what you can do in the file compared to the original responses file, such as archiving to additional files. If you do attempt to create an archive from an archive file, Acrobat informs you in an application alert dialog box, shown in Figure 14.50, that you cannot complete the operation.

Data archiving is helpful when you want to filter fields. You can choose from among all the filter options you have and archive the filtered data. If you choose an option such as *is not blank,* you can eliminate all the records in a file where no responses were added to a given field. Because the records are deleted from the original responses file, you end up with a responses file containing only records with complete data.

FIGURE 14.50

If you attempt to archive data in an archive file, Acrobat opens an application alert dialog box informing you that you cannot complete the operation.

Managing manually distributed forms

If you collect forms other than when forms are submitted to you via e-mail or Acrobat.com, such as forms copied to a network server without using a Submit From button, copied to a flash drive or other media source, or e-mailed to you by a recipient who didn't use the Submit Form button, you have a file that ultimately needs to be added to a responses file.

If you distribute forms manually without using the Distribute Form wizard, you have no responses file where you can aggregate the data, and Acrobat provides no options for creating a responses file to support adding forms collected manually. Furthermore, PDF Portfolios you create in Acrobat do not support the same data views and data management options you have when Acrobat creates a custom PDF Portfolio responses file.

In order to aggregate data from files collected manually when a responses file does exist and when collecting forms manually when a responses file does not exist, you need to use other methods than what we covered earlier in the section "Managing responses from distributed forms."

Manually adding data to a responses file

Assuming you used the Distribute Form wizard to deploy forms to recipients, you have a responses file that the Distribute Form wizard created when the form was distributed. If you collect forms other than when a recipient uses the Submit Forms button, such as forms copied to external media, you use the Compile Returned Forms command.

If a responses file does exist, you can open the responses file, click the Add tool, and add files in the Add Returned Forms dialog box.

Another option you have is using a menu command in Acrobat. While in Viewer mode, choose Forms ➪ Compile Returned Forms. Note that you do not need a file open to use the command and you cannot compile returned forms while in Form Editing mode. After you choose the menu command, the Compile Data dialog box opens, as shown in Figure 14.51.

FIGURE 14.51

Choose Forms ⇨ Compile Returned Forms in Viewer mode, and the Compile Data dialog box opens.

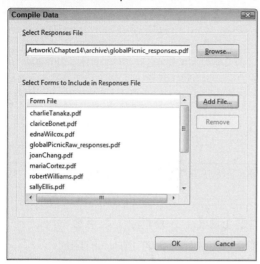

The first thing you need to do is locate the responses file. Click the Browse button, and open the responses file for which the returned form(s) match. If you attempt to choose a responses file that doesn't belong to the forms you're trying to assemble, Acrobat opens an alert dialog box and informs you that you cannot add the data to the selected file.

After opening the responses file, click the Add File button, again making sure that the forms belong to the responses file, and click OK. The files are added to the existing responses file.

Compiling data from legacy files

Using the Compile Returned Forms menu command also works great with legacy forms that weren't distributed from Acrobat 9. Remember all those PDF forms you had returned from recipients and didn't know how to extract the data? In Acrobat 9 you can copy them to a folder and choose Forms ⇨ Compile Returned Forms to extract all the data. This command is a great feature when you need to aggregate data from legacy forms. However, you need to first create a Responses file before you can collect the data.

Follow these steps to collect data from legacy forms or when you distributed forms without creating a Responses file.

ON the CD-ROM To follow these steps, use the files in the *distribute_colllectForms* folder inside the Chapter14 folder on the book's CD-ROM. In this folder you find a blank unpopulated form titled: *globalBlankForm.pdf*. The remaining files in the folder are the same form, each with different data.

STEPS: Aggregating Data from Legacy Files

1. **Copy the folder *distribute_collectForms* from the Chapter14 folder on the book's CD-ROM to your hard drive.**
2. **Open a blank form used for the responses you want to collect.** In our example we open the *globalBlankForm.pdf* document from the Chapter14 folder inside the *distribute_collectForms* folder that we copied to our hard drive. The blank form is shown in Figure 14.52. The other forms in the *distribute_collectForms folder* were completed in Adobe Reader 8 and originally distributed via e-mail to recipients. Our goal is to aggregate these legacy files into an Acrobat 9 responses file.

FIGURE 14.52

Open the *globalBlankForm.pdf* file from the *distrubute_collectForms* folder that you copied to your hard drive

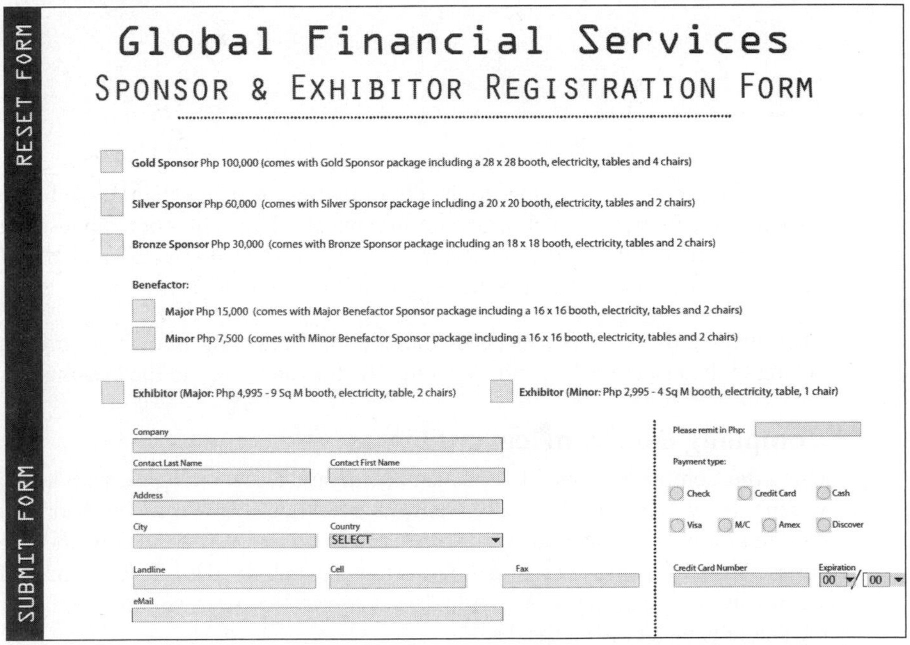
RESET FORM
SUBMIT FORM

Global Financial Services
SPONSOR & EXHIBITOR REGISTRATION FORM

Gold Sponsor Php 100,000 (comes with Gold Sponsor package including a 28 x 28 booth, electricity, tables and 4 chairs)

Silver Sponsor Php 60,000 (comes with Silver Sponsor package including a 20 x 20 booth, electricity, tables and 2 chairs)

Bronze Sponsor Php 30,000 (comes with Bronze Sponsor package including an 18 x 18 booth, electricity, tables and 2 chairs)

Benefactor:

Major Php 15,000 (comes with Major Benefactor Sponsor package including a 16 x 16 booth, electricity, tables and 2 chairs)

Minor Php 7,500 (comes with Minor Benefactor Sponsor package including a 16 x 16 booth, electricity, tables and 2 chairs)

Exhibitor (Major: Php 4,995 - 9 Sq M booth, electricity, table, 2 chairs)

Exhibitor (Minor: Php 2,995 - 4 Sq M booth, electricity, table, 1 chair)

Company
Contact Last Name
Contact First Name
Address
City
Country SELECT
Landline
Cell
Fax
eMail

Please remit in Php:
Payment type:
Check
Credit Card
Cash
Visa
M/C
Amex
Discover
Credit Card Number
Expiration 00 / 00

3. **Distribute the form.** Our first task is to create a responses file. In order to create the file we need to use the Forms ➪ Distribute command. Choose the command to open the Distribute Forms wizard.
4. **Submit the form via e-mail.** Choose Manually collect responses in my email inbox from the drop-down menu at the top of the wizard and click Next.

5. **Save a local copy of the form.** In the next wizard pane click the Save a local copy and manually send later radio button. The default directory for the saved file is the same as the folder where you opened the *globalBlankForm.pdf*. Leave the location at the default and click Next.

6. **Click Finish in the last pane in the Distribute Form wizard.** The Tracker opens with the Responses file listed in the left pane in the Tracker and highlighted. Close the Tracker window.

7. **Select the Responses file.** Choose Forms ⇨ Compile Returned Forms to open the Compile Data dialog box.

8. **Select the Responses file.** Click Browse in the Compile Data dialog box and select *globalBlankForm_responses.pdf*. This file was created for you when you clicked Finish in Step 6.

9. **Add files.** Click the Add File button in the Compile Data dialog box. When the Add Returned Forms dialog box opens, select all the forms in the *distribute_collectForms* folder. Avoid selecting the *globalBlankForm.pdf, the globalBlankForm_distributed.pdf,* and the *globalBlankForm_responses.pdf* files that also appear in this folder. You can eliminate these three files by first selecting all files in the folder then pressing Ctrl/⌘ and clicking each of those files you want to eliminate from adding to the Responses file.

10. **Click Open in the Compile Data dialog box.** You return to the Compile Data dialog box with the selected files appearing in a list as shown in Figure 14.53.

11. **Click OK in the Compile Data Dialog box.** Wait for a moment as Acrobat adds the data to the Responses file. A progress bar displays the loading progress and the Responses file opens after all data are added to the file.

12. **Click Get Started.** The Responses file opens with a help menu displayed. Click the Get Started button on the menu and the data are shown in the Responses file as you see in Figure 14.54.

FIGURE 14.53

Files are shown that will be added to the Responses file.

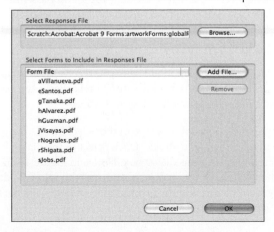

FIGURE 14.54

The data are collected in the Responses file.

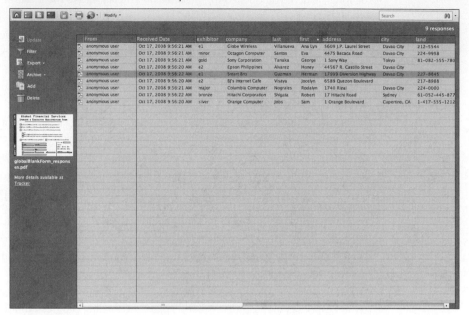

The important thing to remember when you want to aggregate data from returned forms that were not distributed using the Distribute command in Acrobat is that you must first create the Responses file by using the Forms ⇨ Distribute command. Once you create the Responses file, you can then add data from forms and have the data displayed as you see in Figure 14.54.

Aggregating data when a responses file does not exist

If you receive forms when no responses file has been created, you cannot assemble the files in a PDF Portfolio to analyze the data. Files added to a new portfolio lose the data characteristics you find with responses files. The best you can hope for is viewing each form in a portfolio without options to assemble the data in a table for analysis.

However, one option is available for any collection of forms you receive from recipients. In Viewer mode, choose Forms ⇨ Manage Form Data ⇨ Merge Files into Spreadsheet. Acrobat opens the Export Data From Multiple Files dialog box shown in Figure 14.55.

Click Add files, and select all the files you want to merge in the Select File Containing Form Data dialog box that opens after you make the menu choice. Click Select in the dialog box, and you return to the Export Data From Multiple Forms dialog box. Notice in Figure 14.52 that we added a number of files to the dialog box. Click Export, and Acrobat opens the Select Folder to Save File dialog box where you can target a folder to save the exported file and type a name for the file. By default, the name appears as *report*.

FIGURE 14.55

Choose Forms ➪ Manage Form Data ➪ Merge Files into Spreadsheet to open the Export Data From Multiple Files dialog box.

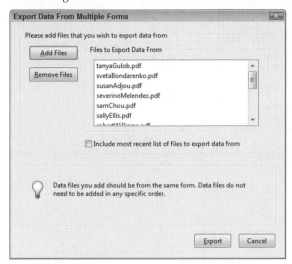

From the Files of type (Windows) or Format (Macintosh) drop-down menu, you can choose to export the data as either CSV or XML. If you choose CSV, you can immediately open the file in Microsoft Excel. Click Save, and wait a moment for Acrobat to complete the export. When finished exporting, Acrobat opens the Export Progress dialog box shown in Figure 14.56.

FIGURE 14.56

After the export finishes exporting data, the Export Progress dialog box opens.

If you chose CSV as the export file format and you click the View File Now button in the Export Progress dialog box, your data open in Microsoft Excel similar to the file we opened earlier in Figure 14.45. If you chose XML as the file format and click the View File Now button in the Export Progress dialog box, the XML data open in a browser window, as shown in Figure 14.57.

The XML file you export using the Merge Files into Spreadsheet command can also be imported in a LiveCycle Designer form similar to what you see earlier in Figure 14.47.

FIGURE 14.57

If you export as XML and view the file, the file opens in a Web browser window.

Summary

- When you deploy forms using the Distribute Form command, Acrobat automatically creates a responses file, enables the PDF with Adobe Reader usage rights, and adds a Submit Form button in the document message bar.

- Forms can be deployed via e-mail, on internal servers, and on Acrobat.com.

- When forms are deployed via e-mail, Acrobat automatically creates a new e-mail message for MAPI-compliant e-mail clients and submits the form. You also can choose to let Acrobat serve as your e-mail client.

- Acrobat.com is a service offered free to users of any Adobe products. The services include hosting distributed forms, sharing files, holding online collaboration conferences, and using Adobe's online word processor, Buzzword.

- You can copy URLs and HTML links to distributed forms hosted on Acrobat.com and e-mail the links to recipients or use the HTML code in Web-authoring programs.

- The Tracker keeps updated information on reviews and distributed forms. You can collect responses, e-mail recipients, send reminders, and update responses files from within the Tracker.

- Responses files are assembled together in a custom-designed PDF Portfolio where you have a number of tools to view and analyze data.

- Data can be exported from responses files as CSV data that can be opened in Microsoft Excel or XML data that can be imported in XML-compliant databases and LiveCycle Designer forms.

- You can aggregate data and export to spreadsheets forms that do not have a companion responses file.

- You can manually add data to a responses file when recipients do not use the Submit Form button and the files are collected on servers and external media.

Chapter 15

Working with Field Calculations

IN THIS CHAPTER

Working with preset formulas

Scripting with Simplified Field Notation

Working with time calculations

Calculating field values is a common function for many types of forms. You may have product sales forms that need calculations for sums, sales tax, shipping charges, and so on, or you might want to calculate employee time on HR forms or average responses on customer satisfaction surveys. Other than simple office forms, calculating values is commonplace with many PDF and LiveCycle Designer forms.

Acrobat provides several methods for performing calculations. You can use some preset built-in formulas, use a simple scripting language known as Simplified Field Notation, or use a more robust scripting language like Acrobat JavaScript.

In this chapter, we begin with simplicity covering preset formulas built into Acrobat and explore scripting formulas using Simplified Field Notation. To create some basic field calculations, you can follow steps in this chapter. However, when you need more sophisticated formulas, you'll need to look ahead at Part V where we cover JavaScript.

Using Acrobat's Preset Formulas

As a forms-authoring application, Acrobat is the ideal program that permits you to create very impressive and utilitarian forms. Tools and features enable you to create just about any kind of form you need for whatever purpose you desire. Adobe has worked hard on making Acrobat a simple but very powerful forms-authoring program for several years, and each year new features are added to the program to support PDF forms authors.

Unfortunately, Acrobat is not without fault. Forms features were added in Acrobat 3 and, as of this writing, have been upgraded six times. Yet, in seven generations of Acrobat, we haven't seen any development in Acrobat's preset formulas that permits you to easily subtract values or produce dividends. The basic preset formulas remain the same in Acrobat 9 as we had available in Acrobat 3 with virtually no changes.

Unless all your calculations are performed for sums and products, you'll need to use a scripting language when you want to perform other simple math operations.

If you have no experience with writing scripts, be assured that using scripting languages can be very easy when performing simple calculations. Inasmuch as Adobe hasn't provided us with more preset formulas, some easy methods are at hand to assist you in adding scripts to perform those math functions not available via the preset calculations.

Formatting fields

Before we address any method for adding calculations to fields, it is critically important for you to format fields properly before adding preset math functions or writing scripts. In Acrobat, we use the Text Field tool in Form Editing Mode to add text fields to forms. The Text Field object is used to hold both numeric and alpha characters. Unlike LiveCycle Designer, where you have a number of different field objects to hold data (either numeric or alpha), Acrobat requires you to format fields for numbers in the same field object as when using text if calculating data.

This means, of course, that if you use Acrobat's auto field detection, you need to open the Text Field Properties window and format text fields in the Format tab. If you intend to add a number of data fields that are designed to hold numeric data, you can format one text field and from a context menu choose Use Current Properties as New Defaults. All subsequent text fields added with the Text Field tool hold the same properties as your new assigned defaults.

CROSS-REF For more information on setting new defaults for field properties, see Chapters 5 and 7.

To format a field for number values, open a Text Field Properties window and click the Format tab. As shown in Figure 15.1, you have several choices for formatting text fields, including these:

FIGURE 15.1

Open the Text Field Properties window, and click the Format tab.

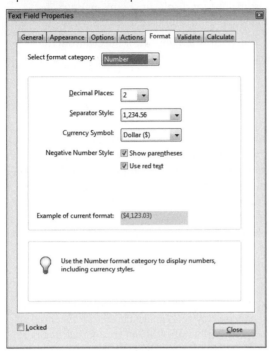

- **Select format category:** From the drop-down menu choose from these options:
  - **None:** The default for text fields is None, which means no special formatting is applied to the field properties. By default, if you add a number to a field formatted as None, the field contains zero decimal places. Additionally, you cannot perform calculations on fields when the format is set to None.
  - **Number:** Choose Number as shown in Figure 15.1, and you have several choices for formatting numbers, such as number of decimal places, separator styles (including format styles used by many countries outside the U.S.), currency symbols for a variety of different countries, and choices for displaying negative numbers using parentheses and/or red text.

■ **Date:** Choose Date, and several different date formats appear in a scrollable list. You also can add custom dates by typing a date format in the text box below the scrollable list.

■ **Time:** Several preset time options exist in a list for displaying hours, minutes, seconds, or choose Custom for typing a custom format in the text box below the list.

■ **Special:** Several special formats appear in a list when you select Special from the drop-down menu. Zip codes, phone numbers, U.S. social security numbers, and an Arbitrary Mask option are listed.

CROSS-REF For more on creating arbitrary masks, see Chapter 7.

■ **Custom:** When you choose Custom from the menu, two text boxes appear. Adjacent to each box is an Edit button. Click Edit, and the JavaScript Editor opens where you type JavaScript code for creating Custom Format Scripts or Custom Keystroke Scripts. JavaScripts afford you an infinite number of formatting options. You might want to eliminate default zeros from fields by using a Custom Format Script, or you might want to auto tab the cursor to subsequent fields after a form recipient types data in a field. To create the auto tab action, you would use a Custom Keystroke Script.

CROSS-REF For more on creating Custom Format and Custom Keystroke Scripts, see Chapter 18.

■ **Choosing options:** When you make a choice for a format type from the Select format category drop-down menu, the items below the menu change to reflect choices for the respective menu option. In Figure 15.1, you see the options for Number. When creating calculations, most often you'll use Number for the format. Other options such as percentage, date, and time are used with calculations, but Number is typically the most frequent choice you'll make for the format type.

Realize that when you create fields by duplicating them on a page, the format characteristics follow the new field addition. If, for example, you press Ctrl/Option and click+drag a field to copy it, formatting for the field is preserved. Be certain to exercise care in duplicating fields. If you copy a date field to an area where you expect the form recipient to type text for a name, the formatting must be changed for the duplicated field.

Getting familiar with calculation formulas

Almost all calculations are made in the Calculations tab in either a Text Field Properties window or a Combo Box Properties window. Only these two field types support the Calculate tab.

Open a Text Field Properties (or Combo Box Properties) window, and click the Calculate tab. In this tab you find all the calculation options available in Acrobat. The options, as shown in Figure 15.2, include the following:

FIGURE 15.2

Field calculations are assigned in the Calculate tab for text fields and combo boxes.

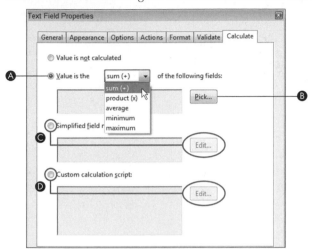

A. **Value is the:** Click this radio button, and the drop-down menu becomes active. The drop-down menu contains all the preset calculations provided by Acrobat, including:

- **sum (+):** Choose this menu command when you want to sum two or more values.

- **product (x):** Choose this item when you want to calculate the product of two or more values.

- **average:** Choose this item to average two or more values.

- **minimum:** Choose this option to return the minimum of two or more values.

- **maximum:** Choose this option to return the maximum of two or more values.

B. **Pick:** After making a choice from the Value in the drop-down menu, click the Pick button, and the Field Selection dialog box opens, as shown in Figure 15.3. You must choose fields from this dialog box for the fields to be considered in a calculation. Acrobat 6 and above makes no provision for typing names of fields in the text box below the Value drop-down menu. After you check the boxes for the fields you want to use in the calculation, Acrobat adds the names of the fields to the text box.

C. **Simplified Field Notation:** As mentioned earlier in this chapter, two scripting languages are available for performing custom calculations. The first listed in the Calculations tab is Simplified Field Notation (SFN). To create an SFN script, click the radio button and then click the Edit button. The JavaScript Editor window opens where you type a script.

D. **Custom calculation script:** Click the radio button and then click the Edit button, and the same JavaScript Editor window opens. You type JavaScript code in the editor to create custom calculation JavaScripts.

FIGURE 15.3

Click Pick to open the Field Selection dialog box.

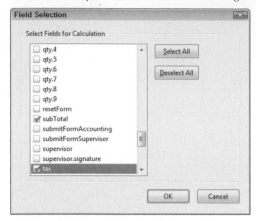

 In this chapter, we limit our discussion to preset formulas and Simplified Field Notation scripts. To learn how to write JavaScripts, look over Part V for Acrobat forms and Part IX for JavaScripts used in LiveCycle Designer.

Averaging data

Up to this point, we've provided the background for the preliminaries you need to consider when creating calculations on a PDF form. It's now time to take a look at the preset formulas and see how they are used on a form. The first item we deal with is averaging data.

Using the average preset

You might use the *average* preset to average responses on a survey. Something like a consumer satisfaction survey is an ideal candidate for using the average preset. To understand how averaging data is handled in Acrobat, follow these steps.

ON the CD-ROM For these steps, we used the *customerSatisfactionSimplePopulated.pdf* form on the book's CD-ROM in the Chapter15 folder.

STEPS: Averaging Data Fields

1. **Open a file that contains fields needing averaging.** In our example, we used the *customerSatisfactionSimplePopulated.pdf* found on the book's CD-ROM. Note that this form is fully populated with form fields, as shown in Figure 15.4.

   The objective for calculations on this form is to average data in the first column with the result placed in the *Broker score* text field and averaging data in the second column with the result placed in the *Company score* text field.

This form has fields where averaging data is calculated in two fields.

2. **Open the first result field Properties window.** In our example, we wanted to format the *Broker score* text field for a number. To edit the format, open the Text Field Properties window by clicking the Select Object tool, and double-clicking the text field; alternately, you can select the field and from a context menu choose Properties.

NOTE You can work in Form Editing Mode or Viewer mode to edit field properties. Typically, after fields have been added to a form, you may find it easier to work in Viewer mode.

3. **Format the field.** Click the Format tab, and choose Number from the Select format category drop-down menu (refer to Figure 15.1). The default for decimal places is 2. Leave the setting at the default.

4. **Open the Calculate tab.** Click Calculate to open the Calculate tab.

5. **Choose average for the preset formula.** Click the Value is the radio button, and choose average from the drop-down menu.

6. **Pick the fields to average.** Our first calculation is performed using the fields in the first column on the example form. Be sure to select the exact fields you want to use in the calculation. If you view the form in a Fit Page zoom level, you can't see the field names. You have two choices to see what field names appear in the first column of fields. Either zoom in on the form until the fields display the field names, or place the cursor over a field name to display a tooltip. The names contained in the tooltips on this form are the same as the field names.

For the first column of fields on the example form, the fields to be used in the calculation are *Score* and *Score_2* through *Score_10*.

Click the Pick button to open the Field Selection dialog box, and check the corresponding fields from the scrollable list, as shown in Figure 15.5.

FIGURE 15.5

Check the boxes adjacent to the names of the fields you want included in the calculation.

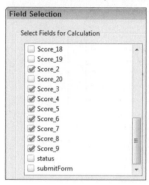

7. **Click OK in the Field Selection dialog box.**

8. **Repeat these steps to calculate the second column of fields.** Open the *Company score* Text Field Properties window, and format the field. Open the Calculate tab, and choose average from the Value drop-down menu. Click Pick, and check fields *Score_11* through *Score_20*.

9. **Save the file.**

10. **Test the form.** Type values for all the Score text boxes. You'll see the value change as each field is populated with data.

TIP If a form recipient skips a field when answering questions, the data are skewed. Acrobat doesn't take into consideration fields with no responses when averaging data. To be sure a form recipient adds data to each field, select the Required check box in the General Properties tab. Alternately, you can check Required if you manually create fields in Form Editing Mode.

Averaging with check boxes and radio buttons

When designing forms, you'll want to take into consideration the amount of time you have for completing and distributing a form and the complexity you want in your form design. You might make forms more attractive, but you may need to spend more time during the form creation process.

If you look back at Figure 15.4 or open the *customerSatisfactionSimplePopulated.pdf* form from the Chapter15 folder on the book's CD-ROM, you find a simple form edited in Acrobat in a matter of minutes. This form took more time laying out in Adobe InDesign than populating the form in Acrobat. By using Acrobat's auto field detection, we needed to make only a few edits in the result fields and add two buttons to the form.

Using Auto Field Detection with Columns of Data

The *customerSatisfactionSimplePopulated.pdf* sample form on the book's CD-ROM in the Chapter15 folder was populated with fields using Acrobat's auto field detection. We opened the PDF file in Acrobat, chose Forms ➪ Add or Edit Fields, and clicked OK to let Acrobat auto detect fields. None of the fields on the form were edited for field names or properties. The only manual editing we performed was adding the Reset and Submit Form buttons.

For the example form, auto field detection worked about as well as creating a form manually while editing field names and properties. Notice on this form that we did not format the columns of fields for a number format and we left the default format None as it was created by Acrobat. In this case, formatting the columns of fields was not critical to producing the averages for the result fields.

Occasionally, you can get by using Acrobat's auto field detection when designing forms containing columns and rows. However, in most cases, you'll want to manually create tables as explained in Chapter 8. Things become more complicated when you have an abundant number of fields in columns and rows, and you have to check each individual field name in the Field Selection dialog box. In the sample form, we checked each field we wanted included in the calculation. Checking 10 fields wasn't much of a problem. However, if the number of fields were 50, 100, or more, the task of checking field names and getting it right becomes more complicated.

The alternative is to create hierarchical names such as *score.1, score.2, score.3*, and so on for the first column and perhaps names like *scoreTwo.1, scoreTwo.2, scoreTwo.3*, and so on for the second column. When you arrive at the Field Selection dialog box, you need only check *score* for the first column and *scoreTwo* for the second column. Acrobat lists all the parent names in the Field Selection dialog box followed by each child name. This alternative not only makes finding the fields in the Field Selection dialog box easier, but it also minimizes your chances for errors.

To create tables in Acrobat, you would create the first row of fields in a table and supply all the formatting options in the Format tab. You then select the fields and from a context menu choose Place Multiple Fields, as explained in Chapter 8. Acrobat automatically adds the hierarchical naming structure when the fields are created.

The tradeoff is that creating fields in Acrobat using auto field detection is faster to add fields on a form, but editing all the individual fields for changing field names and formatting field objects is much longer than manually creating fields. In many cases, you'll find manually creating fields to be a faster solution for populating a form that needs calculations and field formatting.

Compare Figure 15.4 with Figure 15.6. The form in Figure 15.6 has the same questions and solicits the same responses from the form recipient. In Figure 15.6, we still want to use the average preset to average the responses in two groups and place the results in the same two fields at the bottom of the form. But to do so, we have many more calculations to perform.

FIGURE 15.6

This form uses the average preset but requires more calculations to create the results.

Each check box needs to be assigned a value. The value of the checked box then needs to be calculated as a sum of all fields in a given row and then the average taken from the sums for each row. In Figure 15.4, we were able to produce the correct results by formatting two fields and adding a calculation to two fields. In Figure 15.6, we needed to format 100 fields, and unless we created a complex JavaScript, we needed to add 22 calculations to produce the same results.

The bottom line is this: If the form shown in Figure 15.4 gets the job done, you save lots of editing time and can distribute your form much faster. However, if you need to conform to certain design standards for your company or client, you need to invest some more editing time.

CROSS-REF To see how the calculations are added to Figure 15.6, see the section "Summing and averaging data" later in this chapter.

Calculating a product

The most frequently used preset calculation formulas are no doubt sum (+) and product (x). Simple math calculations for addition and multiplication are used on forms much more often than any of the other formulas.

We cover creating a product first, and later in the section "Summing data" we talk about summing values. If you look at Figure 15.7, you'll see that we need to first create a product for the *amount* fields before we can sum the Item Total column.

On this Purchase Order Requisition form, a product needs to be created for the amount fields before the subTotal field in the Item Total column can be calculated.

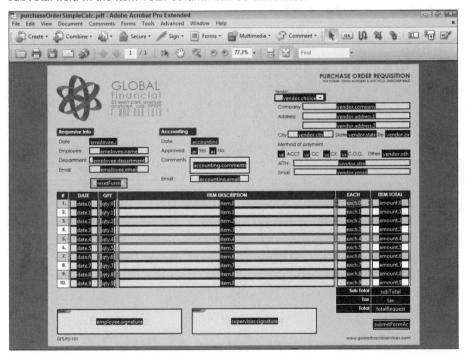

Designing the form

Before we look at adding calculation formulas to the form shown in Figure 15.7, let's review the design process. When we opened this form in Form Editing Mode, no fields were auto detected by Acrobat. For this form, it's just as well that Acrobat didn't pick up any fields because most fields on the form need to be added manually, particularly the fields in the table.

We created the table by adding the first row of fields and formatted the number fields with Number values. We then used the Place Multiple Fields command to populate the remaining rows in the table. Unfortunately, the calculation for each *amount* field in the Item Total column needs to be assigned a calculation formula individually. Acrobat makes no provision for looping through a column to create formulas respective to each field automatically.

Adding the calculation formulas

In the Item Total column, each *amount* field needs to calculate the product of the *qty* * *each* for the individual rows. The following steps show you how to set up the calculations for the fields in the Item Total column.

 To follow these steps, use the *purchaseOrderSimpleCalc.pdf* file from the Chapter15 folder on the book's CD-ROM.

STEPS: Calculating a Product

1. **Open a form with fields needing calculations for a product.** In our example, we used the *purchaseOrderSimpleCalc.pdf* file from the Chapter15 folder on the book's CD-ROM.

2. **Open the Text Field Properties window.** With the Select Object tool, double-click the *amount.0* field in the Item Total column in the first row.

3. **Choose the calculation.** Click the Calculate tab, and from the Value is the drop-down menu, choose product (x), as shown in Figure 15.8.

FIGURE 15.8

Select product (x) from the Value is the drop-down menu.

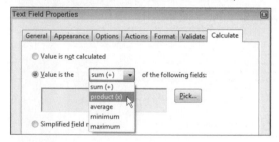

---

4. **Choose the fields to calculate.** Click the Pick button, and the Field Selection dialog box opens. Scroll to the *each.0* field, and select the check box. Scroll to the *qty.0* field, and select the check box. Click OK to dismiss the Field Selection dialog box.

5. **Repeat the steps for choosing the formula for each row respective to the *amount* field where the formula is assigned.** This part of your work to assign calculation formulas is tedious. You need to be patient and be certain to check the proper fields in the Field Selection dialog box that match the field where the formula is assigned.

6. **Save the form after adding a formula to each *amount* field.**

TIP Because the fields in the table in this example use hierarchical names, you can easily keep track of what fields need to be checked in the Field Selection dialog box. Move the Text Field Properties window aside so you can see the column where you add formulas to the fields. When you open the Field Selection dialog box, move it out of the way so you can see the column of fields you are editing. When you select a field, the field is highlighted—for example, *amount.5*. In the Field Selection dialog box, you know what fields need to be checked by observing the highlighted field. In this case, you would check *qty.5* and *each.5*. Because all fields have matching child names, you can easily keep track of the fields that need to be added to a given calculation.

Eliminating default zeros

One annoying problem you find when adding calculations is that, by default, you find fields appearing with zeros where data has not yet been added to a result field. After adding calculations to the Purchase Order Requisition form, you find the default zeros appearing in the Item Total column, as shown in Figure 15.9.

FIGURE 15.9

After you add calculation formulas, the fields display zeros by default.

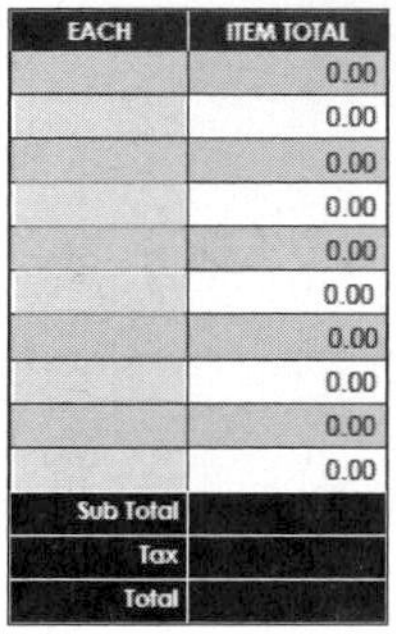

EACH	ITEM TOTAL
	0.00
	0.00
	0.00
	0.00
	0.00
	0.00
	0.00
	0.00
	0.00
	0.00
Sub Total	
Tax	
Total	

The downside for using the preset calculation formulas is that there is no way to eliminate the default zeros from the fields containing calculations. In order to eliminate zeros, you need to use JavaScript.

CROSS-REF For sample code used to eliminate zeros for calculated fields, see Chapter 18.

Summing data

If you followed the steps to produce a product in the "Calculating a product" section of this chapter, you should have a handle on how to sum data. For adding individual fields, you choose the sum (+) menu item in the Value drop-down menu in a field's Calculate tab and click the Pick button to open the Field Selection dialog box. Check all fields you want to include in the sum amount.

Using the *purchaseOrderSimpleCalc.pdf* form from the Chapter15 folder on the book's CD-ROM, you see that we need to sum a column of data. To sum a column on this form, follow these steps.

ON the CD-ROM We continue using the *purchaseOrderSimpleCalc.pdf* form from the Chapter15 folder on the book's CD-ROM. If you saved the form from earlier steps in this chapter, use the saved form.

STEPS: Summing Data in Columns

1. **Open a file with a column of data that needs to be added.** In our example, we used the form we saved from the steps in "Calculating a product" earlier in this chapter.

2. **Open the Text Field Properties on the field where you want the sum result to appear.** In our example, we clicked the Select Object tool and double-clicked the *subtotal* field.

3. **Choose the formula.** Click the Calculate tab, and choose sum (+) from the Value drop-down menu.

4. **Choose the fields to sum.** Click Pick to open the Field Selection dialog box. Locate *amount,* and check the box adjacent to the name, as shown in Figure 15.10. Notice that you find the amount field name followed by child names. In addition, the parent name (amount) appears above the first child. You need only check the parent name, and Acrobat sums all fields having the same parent name.

FIGURE 15.10
_____

Check the box adjacent to the parent name.

5. Click OK, and save the form.

Summing and averaging data

Let's return to Figure 15.6 shown earlier in this chapter. The Customer Satisfaction Survey that contains check boxes for form recipient responses needs both the sum (+) and the average calculations to complete the form.

Locking Calculated Fields

When we formatted the fields in the first row of the table on the *purchaseOrderSimpleCalc.pdf* form, we opened the General Properties for the *amount* field. In the General Properties window, we checked Read Only to lock the field and prevent any user entry in this field.

The amount field is where we calculated a product for of the *qty* and *each* fields. Because Acrobat populates the amount fields with data derived from calculations, you don't need to keep this field unlocked and available for a form recipient to enter data. As a security measure, you can lock calculated fields so form recipients cannot tamper with the calculated amounts.

We used Acrobat's auto field detection to populate the form, but the check boxes for sections 3 and 4 on the form all need reformatting. The best way to complete the design is to delete all the check boxes in these sections and manually create fields in Form Editing Mode.

Designing the form

To prepare the form for calculating an average value, we need to assign a numeric value to each check box and calculate the form recipient's response in a new field. When all the responses are calculated, we can then average the fields. To see how this form needs to be prepared for calculating an average, follow these steps.

ON the CD-ROM To follow these steps, use the *customerSatisfactionFieldsAuto.pdf* file in the Chapter15 folder on the book's CD-ROM.

STEPS: Preparing Check Boxes for Averaging Data

1. **Open a form with a table of check box fields to be used for averaging data.** In our example, we used the *customerSatisfactionFieldsAuto.pdf* file in the Chapter15 folder on the book's CD-ROM. This form has check box fields created with Acrobat's auto field detection.

2. **Delete the check box fields.** Draw a marquee with the Select Object tool around the check box fields on the form, and press Delete (or Del). Be sure to leave one check box on the form and delete all others in sections 3 and 4. By leaving one check box on the form, you can stay in Viewer mode and don't need to enter Form Editing Mode to populate sections 3 and 4.

3. **Open the Check Box Properties window.** Click the Select Object tool, and double-click the one check box field remaining in section 3 on the form.

4. **Rename the field.** Click the General tab, and type a new name for the field. In our example, we used *broker,* as shown in Figure 15.11, because the questions for section 3 relate to satisfaction with a client's broker.

FIGURE 15.11

Rename the field in the General tab in the Check Box Properties window.

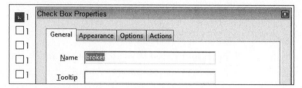

5. **Edit the Export Value.** Click the Options tab, and edit the Export Value text box. This first column of check boxes is for responses for a value of 1. Therefore, we typed 1 in the Export Value text box, as shown in Figure 15.12.

FIGURE 15.12

Click Options can change the Export Value to 1.

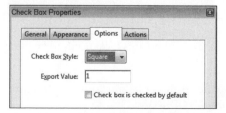

6. **Populate the first column with check box fields.** To create mutually exclusive fields, we need to use identical field names across each row with each check box having a different Export Value. Unfortunately, to populate a table with multiple columns and rows, we cannot use the Place Multiple Fields menu command when fields have the same name. Therefore, each column must be created individually.

To populate the first column, open a context menu on the check box field you renamed. From the menu items, choose Place Multiple Fields to open the Create Multiple Copies of Fields dialog box. Type **10** in the Copy selected fields down text box and **1** in the Copy selected fields across text box, as shown in Figure 15.13. Click OK, and the fields are created with each field having the same Export Value.

FIGURE 15.13

From a context menu, choose Place Multiple Fields to open the Create Multiple Copies of Fields dialog box.

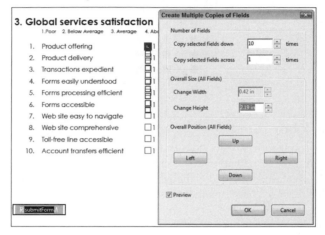

7. **Position the fields.** Drag the bottom field to position. Select all fields in the column with the Select Object tool, and open a context menu. Choose Align, Distribute, or Center⇨ Distribute Vertically to distribute the fields.

8. **Duplicate the first column.** Select the first column of fields with the Select Object tool, and press Ctrl/Option and drag to the right to position the duplicated fields in the second column.

9. **Open the Check Box Properties window.** With the second column of fields selected, open a context menu and choose Properties.

10. **Change the Export Value.** You can change Export Value for multiple fields. Click the Options tab, and edit the Export Value text box. For the second column of fields, type **2** in the text box.

11. **Repeat duplicating fields and changing export values for each column.** In Figure 15.14, you can see column 4 duplicated and the Export Value edited.

12. **Repeat these steps to populate section 4.**

13. **Save the file.** After duplicating columns and changing Export Values, save the form and keep it handy for following additional steps in this chapter.

FIGURE 15.14

Duplicate fields, and change the Export Value for each column.

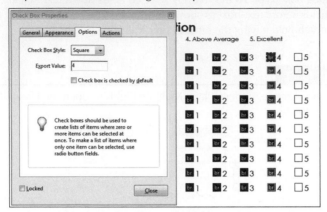

Calculating check box sums

Continuing with the sample form we used to create check box fields with different Export Values in the section "Designing the form" earlier in this chapter, we now need to calculate values. You could write a complicated JavaScript to loop though fields and increment values when a form recipient clicks each check box, but using the preset formulas keeps it simple.

You can use two approaches to calculate an average. Which method you use depends on the names used for the check box fields—either individual names or hierarchical names. The methods are:

- If you use hierarchical names for all the check box fields such as *broker.0, broker.1, broker.2,* and so on. then you can calculate an average using the parent name *broker*.

- Most often you'll have a column of names like *broker1.0, broker1.1, broker1.2,* and so on. and the second column will use a different parent name such as *broker2.0, broker2.1, broker2.2,* and so on. If you use auto field detection then all fields will have unique names.

Using field names like those described in the second bullet point, the first order of business is to create fields that hold values for each row. We can create fields as temporary placeholders and keep the fields out of view for the form recipients. These fields are nothing more than temporary placeholders to be used when averaging the responses.

To calculate rows from check box fields with different Export Values, follow these steps.

ON the CD-ROM **We continue using the *customerSatisfactionFieldsAuto.pdf* file in the Chapter15 folder on the book's CD-ROM. You should have a file saved after following steps to populate the form with check box fields.**

Duplicating Tables

In Figure 15.14, four columns are created on the form. After adding the final column, you end up with a table. On the example form, two tables need to be added that are virtually identical. The only difference between the tables is that the parent names for the tables need to be different. You can easily duplicate tables on a form by editing the parent name. However, editing the parent name on a duplicated table isn't something you can do without a little workaround.

The easiest way to duplicate a table is to open Form Editing Mode and edit the parent name of a column of fields. Type something like *xxx* for the parent name. Copy the fields to the clipboard, and then press Ctrl/⌘+Z to Undo. The undo action reverts the edited name back to the original name of a column while the clipboard retains the copied fields (*xxx* in this case). Paste the column of fields on the form and edit the parent name. Repeat the process until all columns are populated.

Location	Broker in Charge	Regional Office Headquarters	Total Members	Meeting Days	Meet Monthly		Guest Speakers		Workshops	
					YES	NO	YES	NO	YES	NO
location.0	brokerLeader.0	regionalOffice.0	members.0	days.0	meetMon	meetMon	speakers	speakers	workshop	workshop
location.1	brokerLeader.1	regionalOffice.1	members.1	days.1	meetMon	meetMon	speakers	speakers	workshop	workshop
location.2	brokerLeader.2	regionalOffice.2	members.2	days.2	meetMon	meetMon	speakers	speakers	workshop	workshop
location.3	brokerLeader.3	regionalOffice.3	members.3	days.3	meetMon	meetMon	speakers	speakers	workshop	workshop
location.4	brokerLeader.4	regionalOffice.4	members.4	days.4	meetMon	meetMon	speakers	speakers	workshop	workshop
location.5	brokerLeader.5	regionalOffice.5	members.5	days.5	meetMon	meetMon	speakers	speakers	workshop	workshop
location.6	brokerLeader.6	regionalOffice.6	members.6	days.6	meetMon	meetMon	speakers	speakers	workshop	workshop
location.7	brokerLeader.7	regionalOffice.7	members.7	days.7	meetMon	meetMon	speakers	speakers	workshop	workshop
location.8	brokerLeader.8	regionalOffice.8	members.8	days.8	meetMon	meetMon	speakers	speakers	workshop	workshop
location.9	brokerLeader.9	regionalOffice.9	members.9	days.9	meetMon	meetMon	speakers	speakers	workshop	workshop

NOTE On our sample form, auto field detection was used to populate the form. Ideally, it would be best to delete all the check box fields and use the Place Multiple Fields command to create a hierarchy of field names. However, we'll proceed with the steps to demonstrate how to calculate an average using the existing field names. There are many different names that were created with auto field detection so you need to be certain to double-check the field names as you create calculations for each row.

STEPS: Calculating Sums for Check Box Fields

1. **Open a form containing check box fields.** We continue using the form saved after following steps in "Preparing Check Boxes for Averaging Data" earlier in this chapter.

2. **Add a text field.** Choose Forms ⇨ Add or Edit Fields to enter Form Editing Mode. Click the Text Field tool, and create a text field to the right of the last check box in the first column in section 3 on the form. Type a name for the field in the mini Properties window. In our example, we named the field *brokerSum*.

3. **Format the field.** Click Show All Properties to open the Text Field Properties window. Click Format, and choose Number from the Select format category drop-down menu. Choose 0 (zero) for the number of decimal places.

4. **Check the export values for all check box fields.** Auto field detection didn't assign proper export values to the fields. You need to manually add the correct export values. For the first column in both tables you need to set the export value to 1. Set the second column to 2, and so on.

5. **Add a calculation.** Click Calculate, and choose sum(+) from the Value drop-down menu. Click Pick, and choose the first row field names. In our example, the first row field names are: *1_2, 2_2, 3, 4,* and *5.* Unfortunately, we need to pick each field individually because auto field detection created all the fields with unique field names.

   Each check box has a default value of zero when the box is unchecked. Therefore, if we click the check box with the Export Value of 3, then the sum of the row is 3. Because only one check box can be checked in a row, the placeholder text field you add to the row contains only the value of the Export Value respective to the box checked.

6. **Duplicate the placeholder text field.** Open a context menu on the text field, and choose Place Multiple Fields. Copy ten fields in a single row, and distribute the fields to align them adjacent to each row in section 3.

7. **Edit the calculations.** The first calculation is duplicated for all fields. You need to change the calculation for each row after the first row. Open each row's text field, and change the sum to the fields respective for each row. The last row calculates the sum for *brokerSum.9,* as shown in Figure 15.15.

8. **Save the file.** Before you hide the fields, it's a good idea to test your form. We'll continue with further steps on this sample form, and as the final step, we hide the fields.

FIGURE 15.15

Change the field to be summed respective to each row.

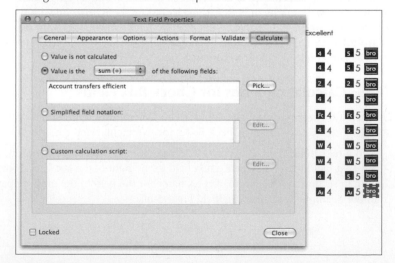

NOTE In Figure 15.15 you see the field name for the last row in the first table was named *Account transfer efficient* by Acrobat when auto field detection was employed. This row did not have individual names for the fields in each column; therefore the sum of the fields is simply set to the sum of the field name used for all fields in this row.

Averaging check box values

Following the example from the steps in "Calculating Sums for Check Box Fields" earlier in this chapter, we now have a form that provides a value for each row based on a form recipient's responses. The last step to complete the form is to average the data from the placeholder fields. To perform the final steps, follow these steps.

STEPS: Averaging Data from Placeholder Fields

1. To follow these steps, we continue with the form saved from the steps "Calculating Sums for Check Box Fields."

2. Open the *Broker score* Text Field Properties window by double-clicking the field at the bottom of the form.

3. **Add an average calculation.** Click the Calculate tab, and choose average from the Value drop-down menu.

4. **Pick the fields to calculate.** Click Pick to open the Field Selection dialog box. The place-holder fields we created use the parent name *brokerSum*. Scroll the list of fields, and click the check box adjacent to *brokerSum*. Be certain to click the parent name check box and not one of the fields with a child name. Click OK, and click Close in the Text Field Properties window.

5. **Repeat these steps to create calculations for the table in section 4.**

6. **Test the form.** While the placeholder fields are in view, check the boxes in the first table. The placeholder fields should calculate the values, and the broker score should reflect the average of the placeholder fields, as shown in Figure 15.16.

7. **Test the second table by clicking check boxes and observing the average calculation. Be certain all calculations are correctly producing the results.**

8. **Reset the form.** A Reset Form button appears on our sample form. Click the button to reset the form.

9. **Hide the placeholder fields.** Select the placeholder fields in section 3, and open a context menu. From the menu options, choose Properties. Click the General tab, and choose Hidden from the Form Field drop-down menu, as shown in Figure 15.17. Note that when you select multiple fields, you can hide all selected fields in the same Properties window.

10. **Repeat the same steps to hide the section 4 placeholder fields.**

11. **Save the form.** The final form contains the hidden fields, as shown in Figure 15.18. Inasmuch as the fields are hidden, they still hold values when the form recipient selects the check box fields in the tables.

FIGURE 15.16

Test the calculations by checking boxes in the first table.

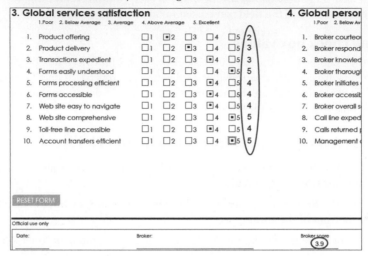

FIGURE 15.17

Select multiple fields, and open the General Properties. Choose Hidden from the Form Field drop-down menu.

FIGURE 15.18

The final form appears with the placeholder fields hidden.

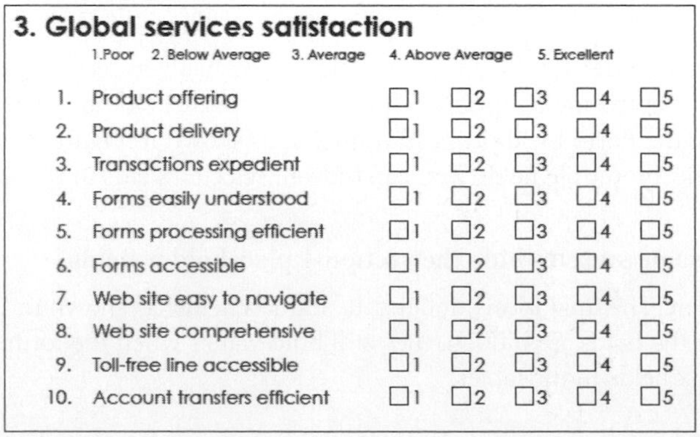

3. Global services satisfaction

1.Poor   2. Below Average   3. Average   4. Above Average   5. Excellent

		1	2	3	4	5
1.	Product offering	☐1	☐2	☐3	☐4	☐5
2.	Product delivery	☐1	☐2	☐3	☐4	☐5
3.	Transactions expedient	☐1	☐2	☐3	☐4	☐5
4.	Forms easily understood	☐1	☐2	☐3	☐4	☐5
5.	Forms processing efficient	☐1	☐2	☐3	☐4	☐5
6.	Forms accessible	☐1	☐2	☐3	☐4	☐5
7.	Web site easy to navigate	☐1	☐2	☐3	☐4	☐5
8.	Web site comprehensive	☐1	☐2	☐3	☐4	☐5
9.	Toll-free line accessible	☐1	☐2	☐3	☐4	☐5
10.	Account transfers efficient	☐1	☐2	☐3	☐4	☐5

The steps illustrate how difficult it is to keep the field names unedited when auto field detection is used. If you use the same parent name for all fields such as *broker.rowOne* (+child values) for the first row, *broker.rowTwo* (+child values) for the second row, and so on, there is no need to create temporary fields to calculate an average. You simply use the root name *broker* to calculate the average. We went through the elaborate sets of steps here to demonstrate the process if you don't create tables manually on your forms.

These steps show you how you can use placeholder fields when you need to calculate fields with complex calculations. Until you get up to speed with JavaScript, you can break down complex calculations by using placeholder fields that remain hidden from view when a form recipient completes a form.

The creation of temporary fields, however, has much value in many instances. For example, you might have a form that calculates a total and a sales tax in one field. If you're not familiar with JavaScript, you can create a placeholder field that sums data in a column. You can then use preset formulas or Simplified Field Notation to calculate a sales tax in another placeholder field using results from the column sum field. The final result field can be the sum of the two placeholder fields. In this regard, a form recipient has no idea that multiple fields are used to perform the calculations, and because the fields are hidden, no clutter appears on the form.

Setting field calculations orders

In many cases, the order in which calculations are established in Acrobat won't have an effect for properly obtaining calculation results. However, sometimes one calculation depends on the result of another calculation that won't yield the correct result if it's out of sequential order. It is rare that calculation orders can affect obtaining correct results, but it does happen. As a matter of practice, you should review the calculation order for each form you create where calculations are present. A quick review can help you prevent potential errors when calculating fields.

To manually adjust calculation orders, you need to be in Form Editing Mode. In Viewer mode, you don't have access to a command that can open the Calculated Fields dialog box where calculation orders are organized.

Choose Forms ⇨ Add or Edit Fields to enter Form Editing Mode. From the Forms menu, choose Edit Fields ⇨ Set Field Calculation Order. The Calculated Fields dialog box opens, as shown in Figure 15.19. Observe the order of the calculations from top to bottom. The first field appearing in the dialog box is calculated first followed by the fields appearing in the list from top to bottom.

In Figure 15.19, notice that the *amount.9* field appears after the *subTotal* field. The subTotal field is a sum of the amount fields. Therefore, the calculation order is a little scrambled. To reorder fields in the Calculated Fields dialog box, click the field to be reordered and click the Up or Down button. In Figure 15.19, we want to move the *amount.9* field up so it appears before the *subTotal* field.

After you reorder fields, click OK and the new order is established.

Choose Forms ➪ Edit Fields ➪ Set Field Calculation Order in Form Editing Mode to open the Calculated Fields dialog box.

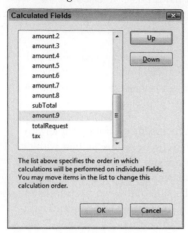

> **TIP** You can use the Calculated Fields dialog box as a diagnostic tool. If at first glance you see fields where you expect calculation results appearing empty, you can open the Calculated Fields dialog box to be certain all the fields you expect to have formulas are listed in the dialog box. You won't see any errors in calculations, but the dialog box lists only fields that have been assigned a calculation formula.

Using Simplified Field Notation

If you haven't written a single line of code in an Acrobat PDF form, then using Simplified Field Notation is a good place to start. It's much less complex than JavaScript, and if you have any experience adding calculations to spreadsheet cells, then you're already familiar with the basic structure of this scripting language. It uses a syntax very similar to spreadsheet formulas.

If you want to stay completely away from scripting, then you need to stay away from forms where simple math functions such as subtraction and division are used. You have no alternatives other than scripting either by using SFN or JavaScript to create these calculations.

Anyone who can create a form using tools in Acrobat can learn some simple scripting. You can copy and paste fields containing scripts and modify some code sections to fit your form. You can view text written on a page and copy the text in a script editor. You may not understand the fundamentals behind the code when you start writing some scripts, but you can add scripts that work when your form needs them.

As you peruse the remaining pages in this chapter and delve into the chapters ahead where we talk about JavaScript, realize that you *can* write some scripts. As you begin, you start with the very simple scripts using SFN, and the more you explore, study, and copy and paste scripts, the more you'll learn.

Naming fields for SFN

Before we type a script using SFN, you need to be aware of one simple issue related to field naming conventions. In several chapters, we've repeated many times the fact that you'll want to use hierarchical names when creating forms. This is true especially for those forms that contain calculations and JavaScripts.

The exception to the rule is when you intend to add an SFN script to your form. You cannot use hierarchical names with SFN. Fields like *amount.0, item.1, total.5,* and so on cannot be used with SFN. You must avoid using these names and use something like *item, amount, subtotal, My first field,* and the like. In short, forget the periods in field names when you intend to use SFN.

Performing math calculations with SFN

You add scripts for calculations using SFN in the Calculate tab in Text Box Field or Combo Box Field properties windows. Figure 15.20 shows a form that uses a placeholder field called *sub*. This field holds the sum of amounts in a column of fields. The orderTax field is used to calculate a sales tax based on a fixed tax rate.

FIGURE 15.20

This form has a placeholder field for holding a sum of a column of fields and a field for calculating sales tax.

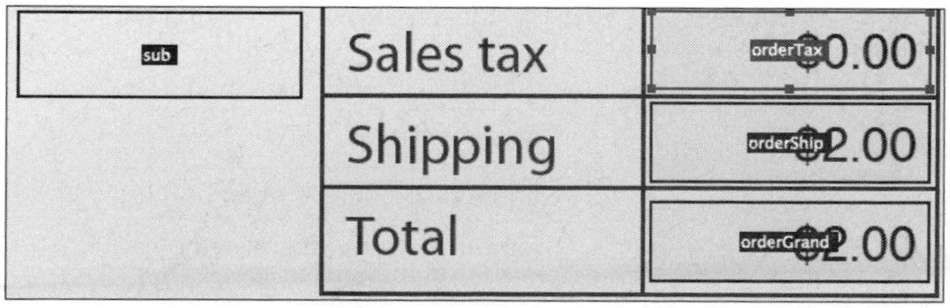

Using SFN, we would open the Calculate tab on the orderTax field and click the Simplified Field Notation radio button. When we click the Edit button, the JavaScript Editor opens. To calculate the sales tax for the sub field amount with a fixed rate of 7.5 percent, we would type *sub * .075*. When you click OK and return to the Calculate tab in the Text Field Properties window, the script appears in the Simplified Field Notation text box, as shown in Figure 15.21.

FIGURE 15.21

After typing an SFN script in the JavaScript Editor, click OK and the script appears in the Calculate tab.

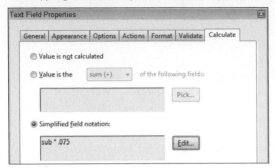

Although you can calculate a product using a preset formula, preset formulas are limited to calculating fields contained on a form. Using the example in Figure 15.21, you would need to create a separate field to hold the tax rate (.075) if you use the product (x) preset formula. Using SFN, you are not confined to using data fields on a form. You can add values in the formulas.

SFN follows basic algebraic notation. For some sample scripts, look over Table 15.1.

TABLE 15.1

Some Sample Simplified Field Notation Scripts

Field Name	Field Name	Field Name	Operation	SFN Script
qty	each		Multiply	qty * each
amount	discount		Subtract	amount – discount
amount	items		Divide	amount / items
apples	oranges	mangos	Add	apples + oranges + mangos
amount	commission	bonus	(A – B) + C	(amount – commission) + bonus
amount	discount		(A * (A – B))	(amount * (amount – discount))

Calculating Time

Calculating time is something you might want for time and billing worksheets, HR forms such as employee timesheets, or other types of forms that need calculations for the amount of time devoted to tasks. In Figure 15.22, you can see a time and charges worksheet for a legal department.

Under the Time heading, you see two fields for a beginning time and an ending time. The Total Time column calculates the amount of time for each row where the In and Out entries are made.

FIGURE 15.22

A time and charges worksheet that contains calculations for amount of time devoted to tasks

Designing a form using time calculations

Creating the form shown in Figure 15.22 requires lots of manual editing. We began working on this form in Acrobat by using Acrobat's auto field detection when we chose Forms ⇨ Add or Edit Fields. Acrobat populated the form nicely, but a considerable amount of field formatting was needed to finish the editing job.

The Location and Personnel fields are combo boxes. Therefore, we deleted the default fields and manually added combo boxes in Form Editing Mode. After configuring the first field in the Personnel column, we used Place Multiple Fields to populate the rows in this column. All the options for the first combo box field were duplicated for each field in the column.

The Date, In, Out, and Rate columns each needed number formatting. Unfortunately, Acrobat doesn't allow format multiple fields, so we had to open the field Properties window and individually format each one of these fields.

Acrobat named the fields in the table using unique names such as In1, Out1, Rate1, and so on. No hierarchical names were used, which is fine if you want to use Simplified Field Notation to perform calculations. For the Amount column, we deleted the fields Acrobat created and added our own field, named *amount,* to the first row. After formatting the field, we chose Place Multiple Fields and created 16 copies of the fields.

There are only 15 rows, but we created an extra row for the Amount column. We then deleted the *amount.0* field and moved the remaining fields up. This enabled us to use the same values for the field names that match the fields Acrobat created. For example, in row one, we had field names such as Rate1, In1, Out1, and so on. By deleting the *amount.0* field and moving the fields in the Amount column up, we matched the *amount.1* field with the same value as the other fields in the row. This made it much easier to keep track of field names we used in the SFN scripts. The Total Charges field at the bottom of the form was easy to calculate when we chose sum (+) for the formula and the *amount* parent name in the Field Selection dialog box.

> **NOTE**   As we mentioned earlier, you cannot use a hierarchical name when performing calculations with SFN. You'll also note that we added fields such as *amount.1, amount.2,* and so on. These fields are the result fields holding SFN calculations. The result fields themselves are not used in SFN calculations. By using a hierarchical order for the result fields, it was easy to create a sum for the total amount simply by adding *amount* in the Value is the sum (+) text box in the Calculate tab.

Creating time calculations

The In and Out columns required us to format the fields for Time values. When you open the Format tab, you have several choices for formatting time, as shown in Figure 15.23. We chose the HH:MM format that formats time on a 24-hour clock. This made the calculation in the fields in the Total Time column easy to calculate.

FIGURE 15.23

Open the Format tab, and choose Time from the Select format category drop-down menu. Choose a time format from the list window.

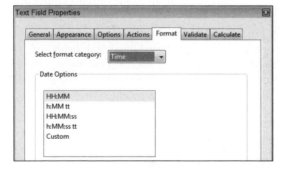

After formatting all the In and Out fields, we then began to work on the fields in the Total Time column. The formula for calculating the total time based on the values in the In and Out columns was easy enough using Simplified Field Notation. Figure 15.24 shows the formula used to calculate the total time for the fields in the first row.

FIGURE 15.24

The first row formula to calculate the total time is shown in the Simplified Field Notation text box.

Again, we had to add the calculation formula for each field in the Total Time column. For the formatting for these fields, we used a Number format with two decimal places. Be aware that you need the value here set to Number and not a Time format.

The easiest way to perform this repetitive task is to add the SFN formula to the first field. Test the field to make sure it works, and then open the field containing the formula and copy it to the clipboard. As you add formulas to additional fields, press Ctrl/⌘+V to paste the clipboard data in the JavaScript Editor window. Just edit the value at the end of the field name. For example, if adding the formula to the row two total time field, paste the copied text from the first field calculation (*Out1 – In1*). Change the number values so the formula appears as *Out2 – In2*.

NOTE The calculations on the sample form require you to use *Out1 – In1, Out2 – In2, Out3 – In3,* and so on. Be certain to place the Out value first in the formula.

The Rate fields are intended for user input, but the Amount fields require calculations. Again, using Simplified Field Notation, you can easily calculate the amount by adding *Rate1 * totalTime1* in the JavaScript window for an SFN calculation. Also, after you create the formula for the first row, you can copy and paste and just change the number values when you add the formula to additional fields.

ON the CD-ROM On the book's CD-ROM in the Chapter15 folder, open the *globalAttorneyTime.pdf* file. This form is fully populated with the fields shown in Figure 15.22. You can practice formatting and adding calculations by deleting the fields and repopulating the form.

Summary

- When calculating data fields, format text (or combo box) fields as numbers.

- Acrobat has a limited number of built-in preset formulas. For some simple math operations and complex formulas, you need to use a scripting language.

- Averaging fields and summing two or more fields is available using preset formulas.

- When designing forms requiring many calculations, Acrobat's auto field detection has limited value, and you often need to add form fields manually.

- Adding a placeholder field and hiding the field can help break down complex calculations and help you simplify writing scripts.

- Summing data in columns or rows within tables is made much easier when you name fields with hierarchical names.

- Be sure to review the calculation order on forms containing calculations to ensure that all fields are calculated in the proper order.

- Simplified Field Notation is a scripting language where formulas are written similar to the way you write spreadsheet formulas.

- When using SFN, you cannot use field names with parent/child relationships for all fields that are used as part of a calculation.

- Time calculations are helpful when creating forms for time and service charges and human resource forms such as employee timesheets.

Part V

Working with JavaScript

T his part is devoted entirely to working with JavaScripts on
Acrobat PDF forms. Realizing many readers may not have
a programming background, we begin this part with some
fundamentals for understanding JavaScript used in Acrobat. We
move on in Chapter 17 to introduce many JavaScripts having
only two lines of code so anyone without programming knowledge can add some refinements to forms using simple scripts. In
Chapter 18 we proceed to adding complex JavaScripts in forms to
show you the results of adding some dynamic features to Acrobat
Forms. In Chapter 19 we cover several JavaScripts that can be
executed only in Acrobat.

IN THIS PART

Chapter 16
Introducing JavaScript

Chapter 17
Creating Simple JavaScripts

Chapter 18
Creating Advanced JavaScripts

Chapter 19
**Creating JavaScripts for Acrobat
Users**

Chapter 16

Introducing JavaScript

In Chapter 15, we introduced field calculations using preset formulas and Simplified Field Notation (SFN). If you read Chapter 15, you'll notice we didn't devote much time to SFN. When you compare the flexibility of SFN to JavaScript, SFN is child's play. JavaScript opens a world of possibilities when creating PDF forms, and some of the dynamic characteristics you find with LiveCycle Designer forms can be applied to Acrobat forms through the use of JavaScript.

If you're not a programmer, don't be concerned about the mere mention of programming or scripting. As we explain in this chapter and the remaining chapters in Part V, you can duplicate many scripts we use in this book and those you find on forms on the book's CD-ROM.

What's most important for non-programmers is knowing that you can write scripts, modify scripts, and implement them in your forms. You may not be interested in becoming a JavaScript programmer, but you can add some scripts to forms quite easily with a little help—and, that's what we hope to do for you in this chapter.

We start this chapter by informing you where to find JavaScripts on forms. You might acquire forms from others that contain scripts, or you might download forms from the Internet that contain scripts. Where to look for scripts to copy and paste into your own forms is the beginning of your JavaScript education.

We also cover in this chapter some easy learning methods and some tips on collecting and reusing scripts. We hope that, after you read this chapter, you'll discover that you can begin using JavaScript in many ways on your forms.

IN THIS CHAPTER

Getting familiar with the basics of JavaScript

Knowing how to learn JavaScript

Organizing scripts

Getting Started with Acrobat JavaScript

If you are not inclined to become involved in an intense study of JavaScript and learn the language and programming model, perhaps the easiest way to jump into learning about JavaScript is by examining scripts written by other users. You can find a number of forms on the Internet that contain JavaScripts and download the forms.

Try searching in your Web browser for *PDF forms, JavaScript,* or similar search criteria. You'll find links to many different forms containing scripts. Some forms may be old, but a good number of scripts written for PDF forms way back in Acrobat 3 can still be used with the current version of Acrobat.

You also can find blogs and Web sites that cover many aspects of writing scripts and sample code. We mention some sites for you to explore in the section "Learning JavaScript." You also can search the Web for *Acrobat JavaScript* and look over links to various sites where more information can be found on writing scripts.

Keep in mind that the Acrobat implementation of JavaScript is different than JavaScripts written in HTML code. When you perform searches to find more information, be certain to include Acrobat and/or PDF in your search criteria.

Finding JavaScripts

As you peruse documents searching for JavaScripts either to paste into your own designs or to learn more about using JavaScript in Acrobat, you need to know where scripts are contained in PDF files. You might copy and paste a script and find that the script doesn't execute properly. One reason is that the script relies on a function contained in another area in the document. Therefore, to gain a complete understanding of how a form works, you need to examine all the potential containers for scripts. As a matter of practice, you'll want to examine several areas in a form where JavaScripts are found.

TIP   If you want a quick glance at JavaScripts contained in a document, select Advanced ➪ Document Processing ➪ Edit All JavaScripts. The JavaScript Editor opens and displays all JavaScripts in the document in a scrollable window.

JavaScripts can be contained in the following areas in a PDF document:

NOTE   You can examine scripts in an Acrobat form by opening fields and other locations where scripts may be found. If you acquire forms created with Adobe LiveCycle Designer, you need to open the files in Designer to examine the scripts.

- **Field scripts:** Depending on the field type, you'll find JavaScripts in various tabs in the Field Properties dialog box. For text fields and combo box fields, you can find scripts in the Format, Validate, and Calculate tabs. Other field types can have scripts contained in tabs specific to the field type.

- **Bookmarks:** JavaScripts can be contained in the bookmarks properties in the Actions tab. If you have a multi-page form and you want to execute an action such as browsing different pages, spawning a page from a template, or performing a calculation, you could use bookmarks to trigger the action. By adding the action to a bookmark, you can access the bookmark from any page, thereby eliminating the need to add form fields or links with JavaScripts to every page.

- **Links:** Links can hold JavaScripts in the link properties in the Actions tab, but you're not likely to use link actions with forms. Links can execute actions such as resetting a form, distributing a form, triggering a calculation, and more. Forms authors are much more limited when using links to trigger actions than using button fields. With button fields, you find the fields listed in the Fields panel in Form Editing mode, you can duplicate buttons across multiple pages, use icons for appearances, set the buttons to read only, make them visible but hidden when printing, and more. For the most part, forms authors should forget about using links to execute actions. However, if you acquire forms from other users, you may find JavaScripts added to links. Therefore, you'll want to examine link properties when analyzing a form.

- **Page actions:** JavaScripts can be added to Page Open and Page Close actions. You might use a page action to execute a script when a form filler opens another page or closes the current page in a multi-page form. JavaScripts can be executed when a document opens, but the better choice for running a script when a file opens is to use a document-level JavaScript. When you download forms created by other users, some authors may have used a JavaScript on the first page of a form to execute an action when a form opens. Therefore, you'll want to check page actions when you look over a form.

- **Document-level JavaScripts:** JavaScript functions can be added at the document level. You've probably seen some document-level scripts at work. A dialog box appearing when you open a form is one example of a document-level JavaScript. A message, an alert dialog box, a response dialog box prompting you to answer yes or no, and similar types of dialog boxes are some examples of when document-level JavaScripts are used.

- **Document actions:** Document actions such as saving a file or printing a file can have JavaScripts applied when the action is invoked. You might want to open a message box to inform the form filler what to do with a form after it has been saved or printed. This type of action would best be handled as a document action.

> **TIP** If you have form fields on a PDF form, you don't need to enter Form Editing mode to add or change a JavaScript on form field objects. Use the Select Object tool, double-click or open a context menu on a field, and choose Properties. The form object's Properties dialog box can be opened where you can edit a JavaScript without entering Form Editing mode.

Examining field scripts

The most frequent use of JavaScript in Acrobat forms is when scripts are written for field actions. To examine JavaScripts associated with fields, click the Select Object tool and open the field Properties window. Depending on the field type, you may find several places where a script can be located. The first logical place to look is the Actions tab unless you're looking at a text field or combo box that is calculating data. Actions can contain JavaScripts for all field types. Click the Actions tab to see what actions are assigned to the field, as shown in Figure 16.1.

CROSS-REF For more information on the different field types in Acrobat, see Chapter 7.

FIGURE 16.1

Click the Actions tab to see whether a JavaScript action has been added to the field.

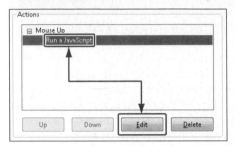

If you see JavaScript assigned to a mouse behavior, click Run a JavaScript in the Actions list and click the Edit button. Acrobat opens the JavaScript Editor and displays the code written for the script, as shown in Figure 16.2. The code in the JavaScript Editor can be copied from one field and pasted into the editor when you assign a script to another field. In addition, the field can be copied and pasted into another form. When you paste fields with JavaScript associated with a field, the code is preserved in the pasted field.

FIGURE 16.2

Select JavaScript in the Actions tab, and click the Edit button. The JavaScript Editor dialog box opens, displaying the code.

With text and combo box fields, you can find JavaScripts in the Actions properties as well as the Format, Validate, and Calculate properties. If you are examining a form to understand how the field actions are executed, be certain to select each of these tabs to see whether any custom formatting or validation is used. Click the Format tab, and look for Custom selected in the Select format category pull-down menu, as shown in Figure 16.3. If a JavaScript appears in either the Custom Format Script window or the Custom Keystroke Script window, click the Edit button adjacent to where the script is written. The JavaScript Editor opens, where you can edit the script or copy the text.

FIGURE 16.3

Select the Format tab, and click Edit to see a script appear in the JavaScript Editor.

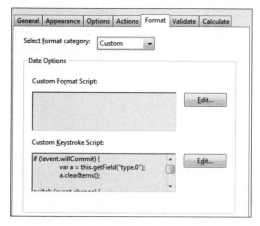

The Validate properties offer the same options. Follow the same procedures for finding JavaScripts as described earlier in this section by clicking the Validate tab and clicking Edit where you see a JavaScript in the Run custom validation script window to open the JavaScript Editor.

Field calculations are most often handled in the Calculate properties. When JavaScript produces data calculations, be certain to examine the Calculate properties, as shown in Figure 16.4. However, not all field calculations are assigned to the Calculate properties, so be certain to check the Actions properties as well as Calculate if a calculation is performed on an action.

List boxes offer different properties. If a list box is used, click the Selection Change tab. A JavaScript can execute when a selection in the list box changes. If a script appears in the dialog box, click the Edit button to open the JavaScript Editor.

Digital signatures also can be assigned custom JavaScripts. Click the Signed tab for a Digital Signature field, and examine the dialog box for a custom script. In Figure 16.5, you see a script appearing in the Signed tab for a digital signature field.

FIGURE 16.4

Click the Calculate tab to see whether a custom calculation script has been added to a field. If a script appears in the dialog box, click Edit to open the JavaScript Editor.

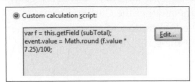

FIGURE 16.5

JavaScripts are written in the Signed tab for digital signature fields.

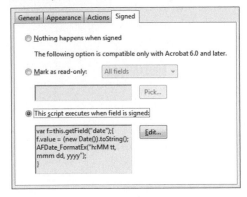

Buttons, radio buttons, and check boxes can have JavaScripts added only to the Actions properties. When opening these field types, click the Actions tab.

Barcode fields also can contain JavaScripts. The Value tab in the barcode properties contains an area where you can add custom JavaScripts similar to scripts you add in the Format and Validate tabs.

Bookmarks and links

Both bookmarks and links use the same action types as form fields. You might use a bookmark for navigating documents rather than creating form field buttons or links on every page to open and close files. When the Bookmarks tab is open, users can click a bookmark to open secondary files or perform other actions such as spawning pages from templates.

CROSS-REF For more information on button field properties, see Chapter 7. For information on spawning pages from templates, see Chapter 19.

To check for JavaScripts contained in bookmark actions, open the Bookmark Properties dialog box and click the Actions tab. JavaScripts are listed the same as when examining actions for form fields (described in the preceding section). Likewise, when you open the Link Properties dialog box, you can check to see whether a JavaScript has been added as a link action.

Examining document-level JavaScripts

You may copy a field and paste it into another document and find an error reported when executing the JavaScript action. Notwithstanding variable names differences, you can experience problems like this because the routine in the JavaScript might be calling a JavaScript function or global action that was contained in the original document as a document-level JavaScript. Among your tasks in dissecting a form should be an examination of any document-level JavaScripts. To find document-level JavaScript functions contained in a form, choose Advanced ⇨ Document Processing ⇨ Document JavaScripts. The JavaScript Functions dialog box opens, as shown in Figure 16.6.

In the JavaScript Functions dialog box, search for any names in the box below the Script Name box. All document-level functions are listed in this dialog box. To examine a script, select the script name and click the Edit button. The JavaScript Editor window opens, where you can examine, copy, and paste a script.

Writing functions and accessing them in JavaScript code written for field actions is much more complex. If you are new to JavaScript, you may want to start with simple scripts in form fields until you learn more about how JavaScript is coded and implemented in Acrobat. As you learn more, you can develop more sophisticated routines that include functions.

FIGURE 16.6

Open the JavaScript Functions dialog box by choosing Advanced ⇨ JavaScript ⇨ Document JavaScripts.

Examining page actions

Page actions execute when a user opens or closes a PDF page. You can assign any action type available from the Select Action types for field actions, including Run a JavaScript. When examining forms, open the Page Properties dialog box by opening a context menu in the Pages tab and selecting Properties. Click Actions when the Page Properties dialog box opens. If a JavaScript or any other page action is assigned to either the Page Open or the Page Close action, the action types are listed in the Actions window. Notice in Figure 16.7 that a Page Open action appears in the Actions window showing Run a JavaScript.

FIGURE 16.7

When you open the Page Properties dialog box and click the Actions tab, a Page Open action is shown in the Actions window for this file.

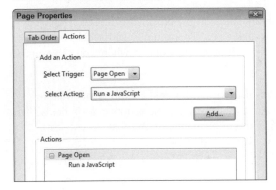

As with the other dialog boxes described earlier in this chapter, click Run a JavaScript and click the Edit button. The JavaScript Editor opens where you can view, edit, copy, and paste JavaScript code.

Examining document actions

Document actions execute JavaScripts for any one of five different Acrobat functions. On a document close, during a save, after a save, during a print, or after a print, a JavaScript action can be executed. To view any document actions assigned to a PDF document, choose Advanced ⇨ Document Processing ⇨ Set Document Actions.

The Document Actions dialog box opens. If a JavaScript is assigned to a document action, an icon appears adjacent to the action type. You can view a script in the dialog box, as shown in Figure 16.8, or you can open the JavaScript Editor by selecting the action name and clicking the Edit button.

Searching for page templates

Although not a JavaScript action, page templates can be called upon by JavaScript routines or additional fields can be created from template pages. Because templates can be hidden, the only way to examine JavaScripts on template pages is to first display a hidden template. As a matter of routine, you should search for page templates when examining forms.

CROSS-REF Creating new pages from templates is available only to Acrobat users. You cannot create new pages in Adobe Reader on forms that were authored in Acrobat. In Chapter 19, we cover JavaScripts that can be executed only using Acrobat. Look at Chapter 19 for more information on spawning new pages from templates.

To display a hidden template, choose Advanced ⇨ Document Processing ⇨ Page Templates. If a Page Template is used in the PDF file, a template name appears in a list box in the Page Templates dialog box. If the Page Template is hidden, the square adjacent to the template name appears empty. To show the template page, click the square adjacent to the template name. The icon changes to an eye icon inside the square. In Figure 16.9, you see four templates listed in the Page Templates dialog box. Two templates are visible, and two templates are hidden.

FIGURE 16.8

Any document actions assigned to the PDF document are displayed with a green circle adjacent to an action type in the Document Actions dialog box.

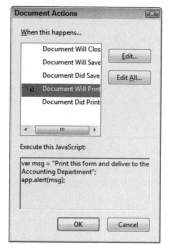

FIGURE 16.9

Clicking the square to the left of a template name for hidden templates makes the template visible in the PDF.

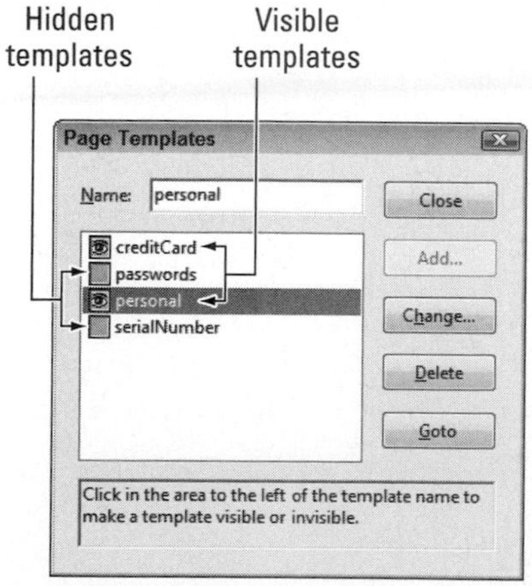

Hidden templates   Visible templates

The template most often appears at the end of the document. After you make a template visible, click the Goto button to navigate to that page. If form fields or links are on the page, you can open them and examine them for JavaScripts.

Using the JavaScript Debugger

All of the aforementioned JavaScript locations can also be found in the JavaScript Debugger. The JavaScript Debugger dialog box enables you to examine JavaScripts from a list in the Scripts window.

Setting the Debugger preferences

Before you can view JavaScripts in the JavaScript Debugger, you need to modify some preferences. By default, the preferences for enabling the interactive console are off. To set JavaScript preferences, open the Preferences dialog box by choosing Edit ➪ Preferences (Windows) or Acrobat ➪ Preferences (Macintosh). Alternately, you can use the keyboard shortcut Ctrl/⌘+K. Either the menu command or the keyboard shortcut opens the Preferences dialog box. In the left pane, click JavaScript, and the right pane displays the preference options you have for JavaScript, as shown in Figure 16.10.

Press Ctrl/⌘+K to open the Preferences dialog box. Click JavaScript in the left pane, and the right pane changes to display preference choices for JavaScript.

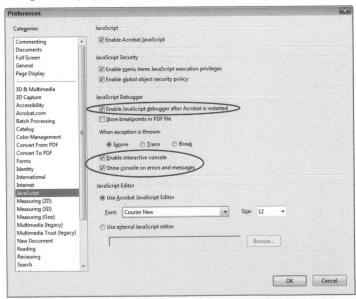

A couple of preference options are important when you want to use JavaScript and when you want to examine files containing JavaScripts. By default, the Enable JavaScript debugger after Acrobat is restarted check box is unchecked. You need to check this box for the scripts in a PDF document to be shown in the Debugger window. After you check the box, you need to restart Acrobat.

The other item to deal with is Enable interactive console. You want this box checked when writing JavaScripts. Also, be certain to check Show console on errors and messages. When you write scripts and execute them, if an error is encountered, the console window opens reporting an error.

Opening the Debugger window

Press Ctrl/⌘+J or select Advanced ➪ Document Processing ➪ JavaScript Debugger to open the Debugger window shown in Figure 16.11. When your preferences are set for enabling the JavaScript Debugger, you'll find a list of scripts in the Scripts window. As you scroll the window, you see all the scripts added to a form.

Click the right-pointing arrows to expand a list, and click a script in the Scripts window. When you select a script, the script is displayed in the larger window at the bottom of the JavaScript Debugger window, as shown in Figure 16.11. If you are viewing a script as shown in Figure 16.11, you cannot edit the code in the widow. Click the Pencil icon, and the JavaScript Editor opens where you can modify the code, copy and paste code, and write new code.

The JavaScript Debugger also helps you debug scripts you write. You can set break points that halt routines to help narrow down bugs in your code. To set a break point, click the left side of each line of code where you want a break to occur. A red circle appears after you set a break point.

FIGURE 16.11

Press Ctrl/⌘+J to open the JavaScript Debugger.

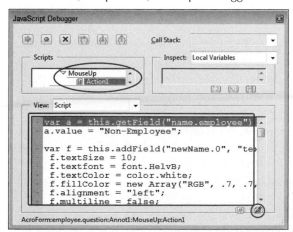

The Debugger window has three views you can toggle by choosing options from the View drop-down menu. The view shown in Figure 16.11 is the Script view that permits you to view a script selected in the scripts window. From the menu, you also can choose Console or Scripts and Console.

Using the JavaScript Console

The JavaScript Console is part of the same dialog box where you find the JavaScript Debugger. In the console window, you can type a line of code to test it for errors, or you can copy code from a field and paste it into the console window. To execute a segment in a routine, select the segment to be tested and press the Num Pad Enter key (or Ctrl+Enter).

You also can execute a statement by placing the cursor at the beginning of the line to be executed. Press the Enter key on the Num Pad (or Ctrl+Enter), and the routine runs.

CAUTION When testing code in the JavaScript Console, click in a line of code or select several lines of code and press the Num Pad Enter key (or Ctrl+Enter). If you press the Enter/Return key, you'll add a paragraph return in the console window. If text is selected, the text is deleted when pressing Enter/Return.

Writing a script in the console

Even if you haven't written a single line of code, we guarantee this section will be very easy for you. Let's look at writing a JavaScript and executing it using just the Console window. To write and execute a script, follow these steps.

STEPS: Writing and Executing a Script in the JavaScript Console

1. **Set the Preferences for enabling JavaScript.** Open the Preferences dialog box (Ctrl/⌘+K), and click JavaScript in the left pane. Check Enable Acrobat JavaScript at the top of the right pane, and click OK.

2. **Open the JavaScript Console.** Press Ctrl/⌘+J. From the View drop-down menu in the JavaScript Debugger, choose Console.

3. **Clear the default text.** When you open the Console, some default text appears in the Console window, as shown in Figure 16.12. To clear the text, click the Trash icon in the lower-right corner of the window.

4. **Type a JavaScript in the Console window.** For your first JavaScript, we keep this simple. We type two lines of code to display a message in a dialog box. The code to type in the JavaScript Console is as follows and appears in Figure 16.13:

```
var msg = "This is my first JavaScript";
app.alert(msg);
```

5. **Execute the script.** Select both lines of text by dragging the cursor through the text to highlight it, and press the Num Pad Enter key (or Ctrl+Enter). The code is executed, and you should see a dialog box open, as shown in Figure 16.14.

FIGURE 16.12

Choose Console from the View menu, and click the Trash icon to clear the default text.

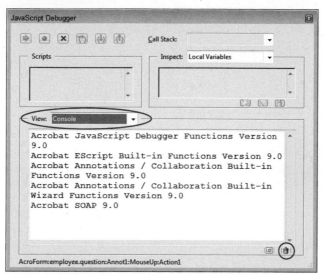

FIGURE 16.13

Type these two lines of code in the JavaScript Console.

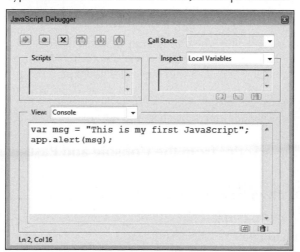

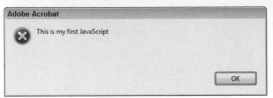

FIGURE 16.14

Select the code in the JavaScript Console, and press the Num Pad Enter key (or Ctrl+Enter). A dialog box opens displaying the message you typed in the Console.

The first step in writing the preceding JavaScript was to assign a variable to a value. The variable name we used was *msg*. You could easily use *x, y, myvariable, message,* or any other text you want for the variable name. We chose *msg* because this is a common variable name used by programmers to assign values to a message. The second line of code opens an application alert dialog box, and the *(msg)* at the end of the line of code tells Acrobat to display the message. Note that the message in the first line of code is within quotes. Whatever you type between the quotes will be shown in the application alert dialog box when you use the same code shown in Figure 16.13.

For anyone who has not yet written any code in JavaScript, this is a huge step forward. At this point, you can create application alert dialog boxes to be shown on a number of different action items we've discussed in this chapter such as buttons, bookmarks, page actions, document-level JavaScripts, and document actions.

Copying and pasting scripts

You can copy JavaScripts in any editor where you can select a script, such as the JavaScript Editor, the JavaScript Console, any comment note, or from a text file. Additionally, when you copy and paste a field on a form, any script associated with the field is also pasted.

As an example for copying and pasting JavaScript, let's look at copying a script from the JavaScript Console to a button action. The following steps show you how to do it.

STEPS: Copying a Script from the Console and Pasting into a Button Action

1. **Open any PDF document in Acrobat.**
2. **Open the JavaScript Console.** Press Ctrl/⌘+J.
3. **Click the Trash icon to clear the default text.**
4. **Type the same text as shown in Figure 16.13 in the Console window.**
5. **Select the text, and press Ctrl/⌘+C to copy it.**

6. **Create a button field on a page.** Click the Button tool in the Advanced Editing toolbar, and click on the page to drop the button field.

7. **Show All Properties.** Click Show All Properties in the mini Properties window.

8. **Add a JavaScript action.** Click the Actions tab in the Button Field Properties window, and open the Select Action drop-down menu. Choose Run a JavaScript from the menu options, and click the Add button to open the JavaScript Editor, shown in Figure 16.15.

FIGURE 16.15

Choose Run a JavaScript from the Select Action drop-down menu, and click the Add button to open the JavaScript Editor.

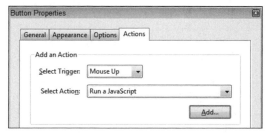

9. **Paste the text.** Press Ctrl/⌘+V to paste the text you copied earlier from the JavaScript Console. The same script appears in the JavaScript Editor, as shown in Figure 16.16.

FIGURE 16.16

Press Ctrl/⌘+V to paste the text on the clipboard into the JavaScript Editor window.

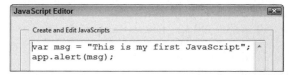

10. **Dismiss the windows.** Click OK in the JavaScript Editor, and click Close in the Button Field Properties window.

11. **Execute the script.** Click the button where you added the script. The same dialog box as shown earlier in Figure 16.14 should open.

As you move on to other chapters where we offer much more related to JavaScript, realize that the process outlined in these steps is routinely used to copy and edit JavaScripts. After you locate the Run a JavaScript action and click Add when adding a new script or Edit for editing an existing script, you open the JavaScript Editor. Here is where your scripts are written and edited.

Changing editors

By default, when you choose the Run a JavaScript action and click Add (for writing a new script) or Edit (for editing an existing script), Acrobat's built-in JavaScript Editor opens.

The Acrobat JavaScript Editor is limited in functionality. You can copy and paste text in the editor, but you have no real formatting controls or any text-editing features, such as searching and replacing text. To be able to use more text-editing power, you need to use an external editor.

Acrobat provides you an option to choose any editor you want to use by making a simple preference choice. Open the Preferences dialog box (Ctrl/⌘+K), and click JavaScript in the left pane. When the JavaScript options appear in the right pane, click the Use external JavaScript editor radio button, as shown in Figure 16.17. After you click the radio button, the Browse button becomes active. Click Browse, and navigate your Program Files (Windows) or Applications (Macintosh) directory to locate a text editor.

FIGURE 16.17

Open the JavaScript Preferences, and click Use external JavaScript editor. Click the Browse button to locate an editor.

CAUTION Do not use a word-processing program for your JavaScript editor. Programs like Microsoft Word can present problems when executing JavaScript code. You need to use a plain text editor or tool specifically designed for writing code.

Choose a text editor or program editor, and click OK. The editor name appears in the Preferences dialog box in the text field adjacent to the Browse button. In Windows, you can use Notepad, WordPad, or a text editor you acquire from various Internet downloads. On the Mac, you can use TextEdit or BBEdit. These types of editors offer you many more features for editing code than you have with Acrobat's JavaScript Editor. In Figure 16.18, you can see some code written in TextPad. Notice the menu commands provide many more options than Acrobat's JavaScript Editor.

For simple scripts, using Acrobat's JavaScript Editor works well. Novice users may want to stay with the default editor. Programmers are more likely to work with an external editor. To keep things simple, we use Acrobat's JavaScript Editor to show code examples in this book. If you use an external editor, the code will be identical, but your editor window will appear different than the screen shots we show throughout this book.

FIGURE 16.18

A text editor such as TextPad has many more editing features than Acrobat's JavaScript Editor.

Learning JavaScript

As we mentioned earlier in this chapter, one method for learning JavaScript is by examining files that contain JavaScripts. Through analyzing code written by other users, you can begin to get a feel for JavaScript and observe lines of code that execute different actions. Other sources for learning JavaScripts include reading manuals and searching online blogs and Web sites devoted to Acrobat JavaScript programming.

Searching for JavaScripts

When you search the Internet for keywords such as *Acrobat JavaScript, PDF, Forms*, your search engine returns lots of links listed as wikis, blogs, and Web sites. Click a link, and you find information on Acrobat JavaScript and quite often sample code such as the code shown in Figure 16.19.

Plan to make some routine searches and locate different sites that provide you with code examples and descriptions for using JavaScripts. When you find sites that provide the kind of information you can easily understand, bookmark the sites and make some frequent visits.

Reviewing manuals

Manuals and documentation on Acrobat JavaScript are a bit scarce. You won't find an abundance of manuals and books written on Acrobat JavaScript, but a few very important documents do exist. Among the most valuable are those provided by Adobe Systems.

Acquiring the JavaScript for Acrobat API Reference

Adobe provides a number of documents that you can download free from the Adobe Development Center. Among the documents you find on Adobe's Web site is the JavaScript for Acrobat API Reference. You should download this file and add it to your Organizer so you can easily access the document when writing scripts.

Search the Internet to find many sites containing information and sample code using JavaScript.

To set up a JavaScript library on your hard drive, follow these steps.

STEPS: Adding the JavaScript Manual to Your Organizer

1. **Create a folder on your hard drive where you want to organize files for JavaScript documents.** When you upgrade Acrobat, you'll lose some folders you add to your Acrobat folder in your Program Files directory (Windows) or Applications directory (Macintosh). Be certain to create a folder outside the Acrobat application folder. The root on your startup drive is a good location to create a new folder. Name the folder *JavaScripts*.

2. **Log on to Adobe's Development Center.** Open your Web browser and go to www. adobe.com/devnet/acrobat/javascript.html.

3. **Locate the reference manual.** Scroll the Web page, and locate the file *JavaScript for Acrobat API Reference <version>*. Depending on when you visit the site, the version

number may change. Typically the reference manual appears long after a program release, so you may find only the manual designed for the previous version of Acrobat. Most of what is contained in the manual is applicable to the recent release of Acrobat, so download the most current version you see on the Web page.

4. **Download the manual.** The manual is a PDF document. Right-click (Windows) or Control-click (Macintosh with one-button mouse), and choose Save Target As (Windows) or Download File As (Macintosh). Figure 16.20 shows the download page for the manual on a Windows machine.

5. **Locate your JavaScripts folder.** If you created a JavaScripts folder on the root of your boot drive as specified in Step 1, locate the folder and select it, as shown in Figure 16.21. Click Open, and click Save to save the file to this directory.

6. **Open the File.** Launch Acrobat, and open the downloaded file.

7. **Load the Organizer tool.** Right-click the File toolbar to open a context menu, and select Organizer, as shown in Figure 16.22. By default, the Organizer does not appear loaded in the File toolbar.

FIGURE 16.20

Open a context menu, and save the file link.

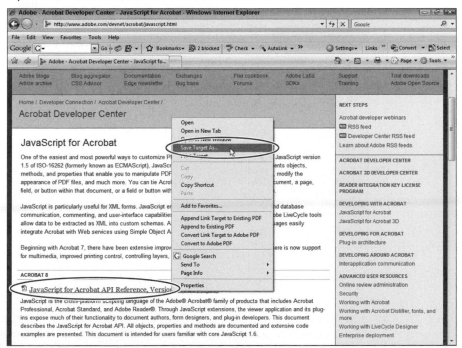

FIGURE 16.21

Save the file to your JavaScripts folder.

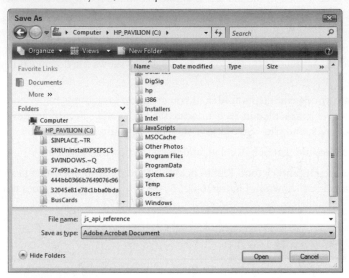

FIGURE 16.22

Load the Organizer tool in the File toolbar.

8. **Add the open file to a collection.** Open the Organizer drop-down menu, and choose Add to Collection, as shown in Figure 16.23. In Figure 16.23, you can see the reference manual in the background. You must have a file open for the Add to Collection menu command to be active. When you select the menu command, the Add to a Collection dialog box opens.

9. **Create a new collection.** By default, you have three collections in the Organizer labeled Collection1, Collection2, and Collection3. To create a new collection, click the New Collection button when the Add to a Collection dialog box opens, as shown in Figure 16.24.

10. **Name the Collection.** When you click the New Collection button, the Create New Collection dialog box opens, as shown in Figure 16.25. Type **JavaScripts** for the collection name, and click Create.

FIGURE 16.23

Add the open file to a collection.

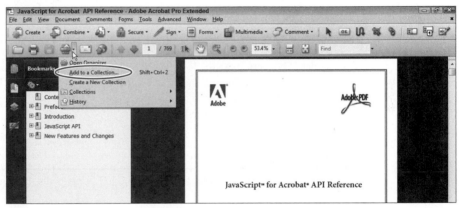

FIGURE 16.24

Click the New Collection button to create a new collection.

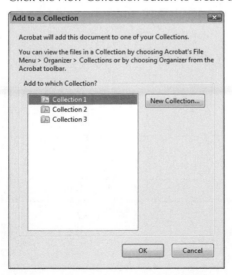

FIGURE 16.25

Type **JavaScripts** for your collection name.

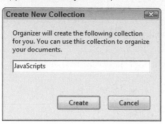

11. **Click the Organizer tool.** The open file is added to the new collection you created. When you want to open the file, click the Organizer tool to open the Organizer window. From the list of collections in the lower-left corner of the window, you see your collection names. Click JavaScripts, as shown in Figure 16.26, and the files added to your JavaScripts collection appear listed in the center pane. When you want to open a file listed in the pane, double-click the file.

FIGURE 16.26

Open the Organizer, and click JavaScripts in the left pane to display files added to the JavaScripts folder.

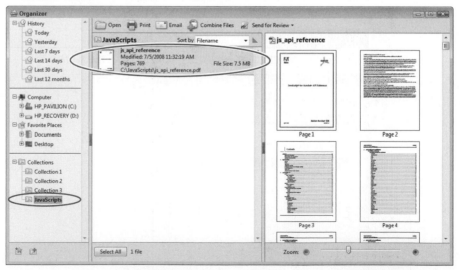

The JavaScripts folder you created on your hard drive and the collection added to the Organizer can be used for a library of documents containing sample code and documentation related to JavaScript.

Using the 101AcroFormsTips_A9.pdf document

We included an eBook type document on the book's CD-ROM. This file contains tips for creating forms in Acrobat, and a number of those tips relate to Acrobat JavaScript.

ON the CD-ROM **Look in the Chapter16 folder on the book's CD-ROM to find the *101AcroFormsTips_ A9.pdf* file.**

Copy this file to your JavaScripts folder, and add the file to your JavaScripts collection in the Organizer.

Using online services

In addition to the files and Web sites you can search for on the Internet, some sites you'll want to bookmark in your Web browser. Many sites are available that are unsubscribed, and the information is provided free. Some sites that may also be of value to you are available as subscription services.

Using non-subscription fee services

Articles are written by several Acrobat gurus on JavaScript, and some individuals host blogs dedicated entirely or in part to JavaScript in Acrobat. You'll want to bookmark these sites:

- **Acrobat Users:** Visit www.acrobatusers.com and register on the Acrobat Users Community Web site. At this site, you'll find many articles related to JavaScript with sample code and sample files. Several individuals host blogs on the Acrobat Users Web site and frequently write articles related to JavaScript. Thom Parker's *JavaScript Corner* (www.acrobatusers.com/blogs/thomp) is a blog completely devoted to Acrobat JavaScript.

- **Acrobat Users Forum:** The Acrobat Users Forum at www.acrobatusers.com/ forums/aucbb/ is a place where you can post questions and receive responses from various people monitoring the forums. On the Forums Web page, you'll find categories for different Acrobat functions. You'll want to visit the Forms:Acrobat, Forms:LiveCycle Designer, and JavaScript categories. You can review questions and responses on the forums and post your own questions after you register for participating in the Acrobat Community.

- **Acumen Journal:** John Deubert, a well-known PostScript and JavaScript programmer, writes a journal and distributes it free to the user community. Each journal contains a sample script in Acrobat JavaScript and another sample script using Adobe PostScript. You can subscribe to John's service and receive announcements for when a new journal is available for download by visiting www.acumentraining.com/AcumenJournal.html.

- **USC Google Groups:** The University of Southern California hosts a Google group where you can find information related to Acrobat, PDF, and JavaScript. Browse the group topics at http://groups.google.com/group/usc.list.pdf-1/topics.

- **Planet PDF:** Planet PDF hosts a number of articles related to Acrobat JavaScript. Log on to www.planetpdf.com and search for JavaScripts.

Subscription services

Few Web sites provide Acrobat JavaScript information as a paid subscription service. As a matter of fact, we know of only one such service. Thom Parker is one of the world's leading authorities on the Acrobat implementation of JavaScript, and he hosts a subscription service for providing information on Acrobat JavaScript.

Log on to www.pdfscripting.com and browse the contents and services found on this site. If what you find meets your needs, be sure to sign up for the service. You'll find these things, among others, on Thom's Web site:

- **Training videos:** This is one of the few places where you'll find training videos on Acrobat JavaScript. The videos cover Acrobat JavaScript Core Language Basics, Beginning Acrobat JavaScript, and Forms Scripting.

- **Library of JavaScripts:** A huge library of JavaScripts you can copy and paste into your forms are all ready to use with explanations on their usage.

- **Library of forms:** The download library contains working, scripted PDF forms and documents. The code is useful for examination and reuse in other PDF documents/forms.

- **Automation tools:** A number of JavaScripts provide you with tools that are useful for automation and common tasks you may perform when creating forms. You'll find scripts to add tools to the toolbars, custom menu additions, and routines that can be used regularly with Acrobat.

Filing Scripts

Looking over all the documentation and browsing Web sites can help you learn some JavaScript programming, but when you create a PDF form that needs a script, you'll want to get the script fast if you cannot program from memory. You may have many forms that all use some similar scripts. To access commonly used scripts, you can create your own reference document and quickly find those scripts you use routinely on your forms.

To create a reference document for cataloging your frequently used scripts, follow these steps.

ON the CD-ROM   In these steps, we copied a JavaScript from a form. The form we used is the *travel ExpenseSample.pdf* file found in the Chapter16 folder on the book's CD-ROM.

STEPS: Creating a Personal JavaScript Reference Document

1. **Create a blank new page in Acrobat.** Choose File ➪ Create PDF ➪ From Blank Page.

2. **Save the file.** When you create a blank new page in Acrobat, the page contains a default text box. You won't need the text box, so the easiest way to eliminate it is to save your file. Save the file as *formulas*. Close the file, and then reopen it. When you reopen the document, the New Document toolbar is eliminated from the toolbar well. Leave this file open as you follow the steps here.

NOTE If you intend to use this file as one where you catalog a number of scripts, be sure to save the file to the JavaScripts folder you created on your root drive as explained in the steps "Adding the JavaScript Manual to Your Organizer."

3. **Open a file containing a JavaScript you want to archive.** You might have written a script on a form or acquired a form containing a script you intend to use frequently. In our example, we wanted to copy a script from the *travelExpenseSample.pdf* file on the book's CD-ROM. The script for the *total* field at the bottom of the form sums the column of the amount fields. If no values are contained in the amount fields, the script also eliminates the default zeros in the total field. At this point, don't be concerned about the JavaScript code. Just follow the steps to add the script to a new document.

4. **Copy the fields needed to execute the script.** Copy all the fields in the amount column on the sample form as well as the total field that contains the script in order to make sense of what this script does. Drag the Select Object tool through the fields, as shown in Figure 16.27, and choose Edit ➪ Copy to copy the fields to the clipboard.

5. **Paste the fields in the new document.** Close the source document containing the fields, and you should see the blank (*formulas*) document in the foreground. Click the Select Object tool, and choose Edit ➪ Paste. Move the pasted fields to a position, as shown in Figure 16.28.

TIP When you paste fields, be certain to click the Select Object tool before pasting. If you have another tool selected, such as the Hand tool, the pasted fields are deselected when you click the Select Object tool. If you have the Select Object tool active, pasting the fields keeps them selected, and they are ready to move around the document by dragging with the Select Object tool.

6. **Add a label to the fields group.** Click the TouchUp Object tool, press Ctrl/Option, and click above the field group. This action opens a new text box where you can type text without using a form field or comment note. As shown in Figure 16.29, we typed **sum a column, delete default zeros.** Be sure to add text that adequately describes the script action. The text you type is searchable, so you can easily find the right script if you have many scripts and a number of pages added to your formulas file.

FIGURE 16.27

Select the fields related to the script, and choose Edit⇨Copy.

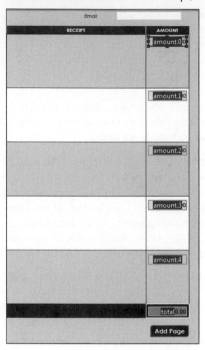

7. **Add the file to the Organizer.** Open the Organizer tool drop-down menu, and choose Add to a Collection; the Organizer tool should be loaded in the toolbar if you followed steps in the section "Reviewing manuals" earlier in this chapter. Click JavaScripts in the lower-left corner of the Organizer, and click OK in the Add to a Collection dialog box. When you open the Organizer, the file is shown in the center panel when you click the JavaScripts collection, as shown in Figure 16.30.

Keep this file handy in your JavaScripts folder, and when you want to add more scripts, open the Organizer, double-click the file to open it, and paste new fields containing scripts into the document. You can copy fields from the formulas document and paste them into new forms.

TIP If you intend to add several pages to the formulas document, after creating a blank new page and saving the file, open the Pages panel by clicking the Pages panel icon. Press Ctrl/Option, click the page appearing in the panel, and drag to the right of the default page. You'll duplicate the page and end up with two blank pages. As you exhaust the space on the first page, open the Pages panel again and duplicate the second page before adding new scripts to the page.

FIGURE 16.28

Choose Edit ➪ Paste to paste the fields on the blank page.

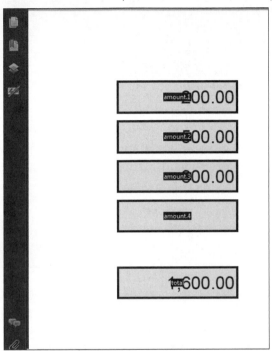

FIGURE 16.29

We added a script that uses code to calculate a column of values.

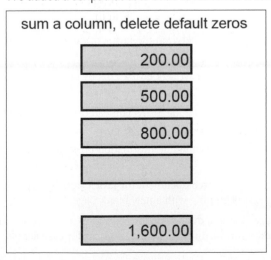

FIGURE 16.30

Add the formulas file to the Organizer.

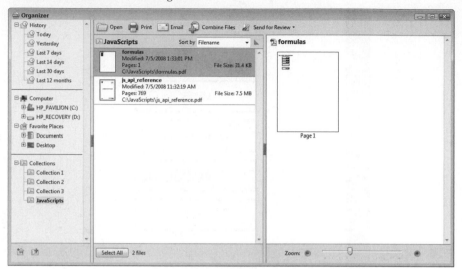

Summary

- JavaScripts can be found in many locations in a PDF file, including fields, bookmarks, page actions, document level scripts, and document actions scripts.

- The JavaScript Console contains two windows—the Debugger window and the Console. You examine scripts in the Debugger Scripts window and write scripts in the Console.

- Before using the JavaScript Console, you should enable JavaScript in the JavaScript preferences.

- Scripts can be copied and pasted between the JavaScript Console and the JavaScript Editor.

- You can use an external editor for writing JavaScripts by choosing an editor in the JavaScript preferences.

- Sources for learning JavaScripts include forms you can download from the Internet and manuals you can acquire from Adobe Systems.

- One of the premier sources for obtaining information on JavaScript is found on www. acrobatusers.com.

- You can create a personal resource document for JavaScripts by copying and pasting fields to a file you create beginning with a new blank page.

- You can easily manage resource documents by setting up a new collection for JavaScript in the Organizer. Add your documents to the Organizer for easy access.

Chapter 17

Creating Simple JavaScripts

IN THIS CHAPTER

Creating alert messages

Changing field properties

Submitting forms

Using JavaScript for printing

Changing page views

I n Chapter 16, we started off this part on JavaScript with some basic fundamentals for the novice programmer. We're going to take this entire Part V on JavaScript slow and easy and continue the pace we started in Chapter 16.

We get to more advanced JavaScripting in Chapters 18 and 19. For now, let's look at some sample code. In this chapter, we cover writing JavaScript code with just a few lines to create some scripts that can be used by all forms designers and can help you polish your Acrobat forms before deploying them. Most of the scripts in this chapter are written with just two lines of code that anyone at any level of programming expertise can duplicate.

We won't get too complicated here, so again, if you're not inclined to become a programmer, you'll find some useful lines of code that you can simply copy and paste without having to completely understand JavaScript. If you're more interested in results without the theory, this chapter is for you.

ON the CD-ROM All the scripts involved in steps in this chapter can be added on the two forms you find in the Chapter17 folder on the book's CD-ROM. We added comments on the forms containing the JavaScript code referred to in the text in this chapter. When you follow the steps in this chapter, try to write the code by duplicating the text in the JavaScript Editor. If you get into trouble and find the code you write is not working, copy the text from the Sticky Note pop-up windows and paste the code in the JavaScript Editor window.

Creating Application Alerts

In Chapter 16, we introduced you to application alerts by writing two lines of code in the JavaScript Console and adding the script to a button action. The *Hello World* message is something you see for every example that illustrates some programming steps but has no practical application.

Creating a message alert

Let's apply this theory now to a real-world event that might be used on one of your forms. As you may remember in Chapter 16, we talked about document-level JavaScripts. A JavaScript written at the document level is executed when a file opens.

To write a JavaScript to open an application alert dialog box when a file opens, follow these steps.

ON the CD-ROM For the following steps, we used the *globalTransferFields.pdf* form from the Chapter17 folder on the book's CD-ROM. This file contains comments with scripts added to the note pop-up windows for all scripts discussed in this section.

STEPS: Adding an Alert Message to a Document-Level JavaScript

1. **Open a PDF form.** You can use any form you like for these steps. We used the *global TransferFields.pdf* file from the book's CD-ROM.

2. **Open the JavaScript Functions dialog box.** Choose Advanced ⇨ Document Processing ⇨ Document JavaScripts to open the JavaScript Functions dialog box. All document-level JavaScripts are added via this dialog box.

NOTE You can work in either Viewer mode or Form Editing Mode to add document-level JavaScripts.

3. **Type a name for the function.** Type a name for the script in the Script Name text box in the JavaScript Functions dialog box. In our example, we used *openAlert* for the script name, as shown in Figure 17.1.

4. **Click Add.** Click Add to open the JavaScript Editor.

FIGURE 17.1

Type a name for the script in the Script Name text box.

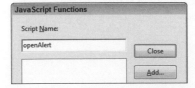

5. **Clear the default text in the JavaScript Editor, and add the following script:**

```
1. var msg = "Please allow three business days to complete
      transaction after submitting the form.";
2. app.alert(msg);
```

CAUTION All code listings appear with numbers in the text for easy reference to the lines of code. When typing JavaScripts in the JavaScript Editor, do not add the numbers preceding the lines.

6. **Click OK in the JavaScript Editor, and you return to the JavaScript Functions dialog box.**

7. **Review the script, and close the JavaScript Functions dialog box.** As shown in Figure 17.2, the code appears when you return to the JavaScript Functions dialog box. Look over the code, and click Close to dismiss the dialog box.

FIGURE 17.2

Look over the code to be sure it's correct, and click Close.

8. **Click OK in the alert dialog box.** When you close the JavaScript Functions dialog box, the alert message you created with the JavaScript opens. Look over the message to be certain it appears as you designed it, and click OK.

9. **Save the file.** Save the file, and close it. Open the file after closing, and the alert dialog box should open.

Assessing viewer versions

Perhaps one of the most important application alert messages you'll add to a form is one that examines the form recipient's version of Acrobat or Adobe Reader. Many forms you create in Acrobat 8 and above won't work properly for users of Acrobat or Adobe Reader less than version 7.5. This is especially true for forms that have been enabled with Adobe Reader usage rights.

Before a form recipient begins to work on your form, check the Acrobat viewer and determine if the version is 7.5 or above. If the version is 7.5 or above, nothing happens. If the version is lower than version 7.5, an application alert dialog box opens informing the form recipient that the Acrobat viewer needs to be updated.

The following steps show you how to add a script that looks at the viewer version and opens a dialog box if the version is lower than 7.5.

 We continue to use the same *globalTransferFields.pdf* form from the Chapter17 folder on the book's CD-ROM.

STEPS: Assessing a Viewer Version with a Document-Level JavaScript

1. **Open a PDF form.** In our example, we continued using the *globalTransferFields.pdf* form on the book's CD-ROM.

2. **Open the JavaScript Functions dialog box.** Choose Advanced ➪ Document Processing ➪ Document JavaScripts.

3. **Type a name, and open the JavaScript Editor.** Type a name for the script, and click the Add button to open the JavaScript Editor. Clear the text in the Editor window. In our example, we used *viewerVersion* for the script name.

4. **Type the following code in the JavaScript Editor.** Figure 17.3 shows this snippet of code.

```
1. if (app.viewerVersion <7.5)
2. {
3.    var msg = "You must use Adobe Acrobat or Adobe Reader version
          7.5 or above to complete this form.";
4.    app.alert(msg);
5. }
```

5. **Click OK in the JavaScript Editor, and click Close in the JavaScript Functions dialog box.**

6. **Save the file.**

In the script for these steps, the first line of code assesses the viewer that opens the form. Line 1 begins with an *if* statement. If the assessment is true, lines 3 and 4 are executed. If the assessment is not true, nothing happens.

FIGURE 17.3

Type the JavaScript code in the JavaScript Editor.

```
Java Script Editor                                    [_][□][X]
 ┌ Create and Edit JavaScripts ───────────────────────
 │ if (app.viewerVersion <7.5)                      ▲
 │ {
 │     var msg = "You must use Adobe Acrobat or Adobe Reader
 │ version 7.5 or above to complete this form.";
 │     app.alert(msg);
 │ }
 │
 │
 │
 │
 │                                                  ▼
                                          Ln 1, Col 1
              [  OK  ]   [ Cancel ]   [ Go to... ]
```

Testing Application Alert Dialog Boxes

You'll notice that when you dismiss the JavaScript Functions dialog box, the application alert does not open. Furthermore, if you close the file and reopen it, the application alert dialog box won't open if you're working with Acrobat 7.5 or above.

You should test application alert dialog boxes when you create them with JavaScripts. You may see misspelled words or find code errors when opening an alert dialog box.

To test the code, copy the code you write in the JavaScript Editor and close the Editor. Close the JavaScript Functions dialog box, and press Ctrl/⌘+J to open the JavaScript Console. Paste the code in the JavaScript Console, and select the text.

When you select the text, just select the lines of code beginning with *var msg* through *app. alert(msg)*—lines 3 and 4 in Figure 17.3. If you select the first line of code shown in Figure 17.3, the alert dialog box won't open if you're using Acrobat 7.5 and above. After selecting the code, press the Num Pad Enter key, and the dialog box should open.

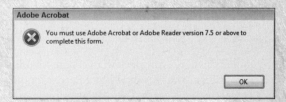

If the alert dialog box does not open, you need to examine the code. Common errors are usually found by leaving off a quotation mark, a closing brace, a parenthesis mark, and other punctuation items. Also be sure to double-check spelling and case sensitivity for JavaScript objects such as *viewerVersion*.

Assessing viewer types

Another type of application alert you may want to consider using on forms assesses a viewer type. Is the type of viewer Adobe Reader or Adobe Acrobat? This alert is one you may use much less frequently than assessing a viewer version since most of your forms are likely to be designed for users of both Acrobat and Adobe Reader.

In Chapter 19, we cover JavaScripts that can be used only by Acrobat users. You can do some things in Acrobat relative to forms that cannot be done in Adobe Reader, such as adding new pages to a form, exchanging data between forms, adding and/or deleting fields, and more. Although these functions may not be something you regularly add to forms, occasionally you may design forms for Acrobat users only. When you design such forms, you'll want to let the form recipient know that Acrobat and not Reader must be used to complete the form.

To assess the viewer type in a document-level JavaScript, follow these steps.

 **You can use any file to follow these steps. If you don't have a file handy, use the** *globalTransferFields.pdf* **file in the Chapter17 folder on the book's CD-ROM.**

STEPS: Assessing Viewer Types

1. **Open a form in Acrobat.** Use any form you like to follow the steps.

2. **Open the JavaScript Functions dialog box.** Choose Advanced ➪ Document Processing ➪ Document JavaScripts.

3. **Type a name for the script, and click Add.** For the name of this script, we used *viewerType*.

4. **Type the following code in the JavaScript Editor:**

```
1. if (app.viewerType == "Reader")
2. {
3.   var msg = "You must use Acrobat Standard, Acrobat Pro, or
         Acrobat Pro Extended to complete this form.";
4.   app.alert(msg);
5. }
```

5. **Click OK in the JavaScript Editor, and click Close in the JavaScript Functions dialog box.**

6. **Save the file.**

We added a similar routine as when assessing a viewer version. Line 1 checks the viewer, and if the viewer is Reader, the script is executed. If the view is not Reader, nothing happens. The *msg* statement and application alert are the same as used with code examples in earlier scripts in this chapter. Because the script is added at the document level, the script is executed when the file opens.

To test the script, copy the text and paste it into the JavaScript Console. Select the text (in lines 3 and 4), and press the Num Pad Enter key. You should see the dialog box open. Again, if the dialog box does not open, you need to carefully look over the code for errors.

Adding alerts to document actions

In Chapter 16, we talked about the actions associated with saving and printing files. You may want to add a message window in the form of an application alert when the form recipient prints a document. Something on the order of filling in a vacation request and handing the form to a supervisor or accounting office might be one example for displaying a message to alert the form recipient what to do with the form when it's printed.

These kinds of alerts are added as document actions. The trigger for opening the alert is when a file is about to close, when it's about to be saved, after it's been saved, when it's about to be printed, or after it's been printed. You make a choice from the five options and add a JavaScript to that action in the Document Actions dialog box.

To add a document action JavaScript, follow these steps.

 We continue using the *globalTransferFields.pdf* form from the Chapter17 folder on the book's CD-ROM to complete these steps.

STEPS: Adding a Document Action JavaScript

1. **Open a PDF file.** In our example, we used the *globalTransferFields.pdf* form from the book's CD-ROM.

2. **Open the Document Actions dialog box.** Choose Advanced ⇨ Document Processing ⇨ Set Document Actions. The Document Actions dialog box opens, as shown in Figure 17.4.

3. **Click Document Did Print, and click the Edit button to open the JavaScript Editor.**

4. **Type the following code in the JavaScript Editor.**

```
1. var msg = "Please allow 3 business days for processing your
        transaction after faxing this form."
2. app.alert(msg);
```

5. **Click OK in the JavaScript Editor.** The script appears in the Document Actions dialog box. Review the script, and click OK.

6. **Save the file.**

If you read over the sections earlier in this chapter, by now you should have a good idea for how to check the script and know what results you can expect.

FIGURE 17.4

Click Edit to open the JavaScript Editor, type the code, and click OK to return to the Document Actions dialog box. The code appears in the Execute this JavaScript window.

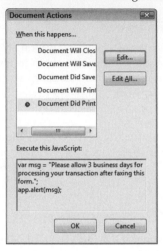

Adding application beeps

If you've worked on a computer in any application, you've heard an application beep. These beeps are audio sounds that tell you something cannot be done. Perhaps you are trying to choose a menu item while a dialog box is open or choose a tool from a tools panel when a current tool hasn't completed a task. Rather than opening alert dialog boxes, programmers offer you a polite little beep to get your attention and remind you to look over your work. Generally, you become immediately aware that a task cannot be performed until you finish doing something else.

You can add application beeps to your forms with a simple JavaScript. Use beeps conservatively and only when necessary. A form with continual beeping sounds can be annoying for a form recipient.

Beeps can be added to any field action with or without an accompanying application alert dialog box. You might trigger a sound and open a dialog box to get the attention of the form recipient for items that need more definition than just adding an audio sound. You also can add a beep to a field without opening an application alert. These additions should be added only when a form recipient logically knows how to overcome the beep action by filling in a field or doing something to avoid hearing the beep again.

Ideally, you might add an application beep by first assessing a field value, such as a form recipient using a wrong field date, not completing a required field before a form is submitted, or a similar type of assessment. If the date format or a field is not filled in, you might trigger a beep. These types of actions also might require adding an application alert dialog box to further explain the error in completing the form.

Rather than going into a more complex script that assesses field values, here's the one line of code that you can add to trigger a sound:

```
app.beep();
```

You can vary the audio using different system sounds by adding a value within the parentheses such as:

```
app.beep(1);
```

Experiment a little by changing the value from 1 to 0, 3, 4, and so on to get an idea for the different sounds you can trigger. Note that 2 is silent and anything greater than 4 is the same as 4.

Managing Field Behaviors

We use the term *field behaviors* in this section to cover viewing fields, changing properties, and changing field attributes. A number of different types of changes made to field behaviors help you polish your forms, can often prevent user errors, or may be essential for a form recipient to adequately work with your form.

Showing and hiding fields

We can suggest a number of uses for showing and hiding fields on a form. You might want one form recipient to be restricted to filling in certain fields and signing the form, and another user might need to complete additional fields and sign the form. Rather than showing all fields for the first form recipient, you can keep all the fields hidden that the first form recipient should not fill in. When the second form recipient works on the form, you'll want the respective fields for that form recipient to be visible.

You also can show/hide fields when changing layers, as discussed in Chapter 13; make fields visible only when necessary, such as showing shipping address fields when a form recipient indicates the shipping address is different than the billing address; show fields based on other field responses such as a form recipient's age where all those over the age of 18 fill in additional fields; and many more uses.

Let's use the first set of criteria as an example for when one form recipient needs to be restricted to filling in certain fields and then the form is routed to a second form recipient to complete additional fields. In Figure 17.5, you can see the first page in a ten-page form designed for an employee review. It appears that the first block of fields are populated on the form, but the block of fields for the supervisor data are not populated. In actuality, the supervisor fields are hidden when the form opens.

Inasmuch as the directions ask the employee to fill in only employee-related fields, some form recipients may not carefully read and follow the directions. We can prevent user error for employees filling in this form by making only those fields the employee should address visible. The remaining fields on the form are hidden, and the employee cannot display the fields if the form is secured.

FIGURE 17.5

A form showing visible fields, with the fields for the supervisor data hidden

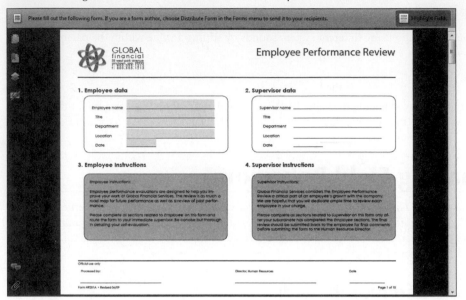

CROSS-REF For more information on securing forms, see Chapter 12.

After an employee fills in the form, we need some way to display the supervisor fields so the supervisor can then complete the form. One way to handle this is to use a submit button. When the form is submitted to the supervisor, the fields become visible.

We also can add multiple submit buttons to the form. When the employee fills in and submits the form, the employee submit button is hidden and the supervisor submit button is made visible. When the supervisor submits the form to the Human Resources department, the HR fields are made visible on the supervisor submit form button action.

To see how all this is accomplished, follow these steps.

ON the CD-ROM To follow these steps, use the *globalPerformanceReview.pdf* form from the Chapter17 folder on the book's CD-ROM.

STEPS: Showing Hidden Fields on a Form

1. **Open a PDF file.** Be certain to use the *globalPerformanceReview.pdf* form on the book's CD-ROM.

2. **Scroll through the pages on the form.** As you scroll the ten-page form, notice that all the fields for the employee to fill in are visible and no fields appear for those items for the supervisor or HR department to fill in.

3. **Open page 10 on the form.** The last page on the form has a submit button. This is the field we use to add our JavaScript.

4. **Open the Submit Form Button Field Properties window.** With the Select Object tool, double-click the Submit Form button shown in Figure 17.6. Note that you can stay in Viewer mode to change the field properties.

FIGURE 17.6

With the Select Object tool, double-click the submitForm button field.

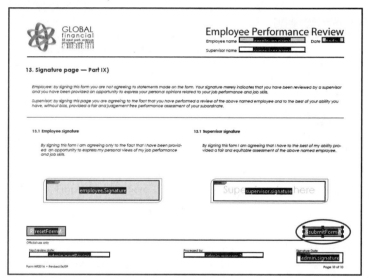

5. **Open the Actions tab.** Click Actions in the Button Field Properties window.

6. **Run a JavaScript.** Open the Select Action drop-down menu, and choose Run a JavaScript.

7. **Open the JavaScript Editor.** Click the Add button in the Actions tab, and the JavaScript Editor opens.

8. **Type the code in the JavaScript Editor.** Type the following code in the JavaScript Editor, as shown in Figure 17.7:

```
1. var f = this.getField("supervisor");
2. f.hidden = false;
```

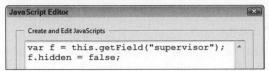

FIGURE 17.7

Type the code in the JavaScript Editor.

```
var f = this.getField("supervisor");
f.hidden = false;
```

9. **Click OK in the JavaScript Editor.** When you return to the Button Field Properties window, you should see your JavaScript added to the actions list following the Submit a form action, as shown in Figure 17.8.

FIGURE 17.8

After you add the Run a JavaScript action, the action appears at the bottom of the Actions list.

10. **Change the order of the actions.** In our example, we want the JavaScript to run before the form is sent to the supervisor so the supervisor sees all the supervisor fields when the form is received. To change the order, click the Run a JavaScript action to select it and click the Up button to move the action above the Submit a form action.

11. **Close the Button Field Properties window.**

12. **Save the file.**

NOTE   The Submit a form action on this form is shown to clarify setting the order of the actions. If you click the Submit Form button, the form has no place to go because we added a bogus e-mail address to the Submit Form Actions tab. If you want to test the JavaScript, open the Submit Form Button Field Properties and delete the Submit a form action. Close the properties window, and click the button to show the supervisor fields.

We were able to hide fields on the sample form because all the supervisor fields were named with hierarchical names. We used names like *supervisor.name*, *supervisor.date*, *supervisor.department*, and so on. Line 1 in our code assigns the variable *f* to the parent name *supervisor*. In line 2, we instruct Acrobat to hide all fields assigned to variable *f*.

With just two lines of JavaScript code, we were able to show all the supervisor fields spread over the ten-page form. If you used manual methods for picking the supervisor fields in a dialog box, it would take considerably more time than writing these two lines of code.

To finish the form, we could add another submit button that might be named *supervisor.submitForm*. Because the field uses the same parent name, the button would be shown when the form is submitted by the employee. On the supervisor submit button, we would add a similar script to show the fields for the Human Resources department when the form is submitted by the supervisor. All these fields have a parent name of *admin*.

We also would have to modify the script used by the employee submit button. We would need to hide the employee's submit button when the form is submitted so the supervisor button (if the button appears at the same location as the employee submit button) can be selected. This is the code we would use in the JavaScript Editor:

```
1. var f = this getField("supervisor");
2. var g = this getField("employee.submitForm");
3. f.hidden = false;
4. g.hidden = true;
```

In this script, we assign the *employee.submitForm* field to variable *g*. In line 4, we hide the field. Notice that it's important to add the entire name of this field to the script. If you use *employee* in line 2, all the employee fields would be hidden, so the form would be useless to the HR department.

Locking fields

Using the same form we discussed in the preceding steps, we want to ensure that all data added to the employee fields cannot be tampered with. In order to do so, we need to lock the fields so additional reviewers cannot change the data.

Because all the employee fields need to remain visible, we need to use something other than hiding fields to guard against tampering with the data. The following steps show you how to lock field data.

ON the CD-ROM **You can use the *globalPerformanceReview.pdf* form from the Chapter17 folder on the book's CD-ROM or the file saved from the steps in "Showing Hidden Fields on a Form" to follow these steps.**

STEPS: Locking Fields

1. **Open a form in Acrobat.** For these steps, we used the *globalPerformanceReview.pdf* form on the book's CD-ROM.

2. **Open page 10 on the form.**

3. **Open the *employee.signature* field properties.** Click the Select Object tool, and double-click the *employee.signature* field to open the Digital Signature Properties window.

4. **Click the Signed tab.**

5. **Open the JavaScript Editor.** Click the radio button beside This script executes when field is signed, and click Edit to open the JavaScript Editor.

6. **Type the following script in the JavaScript Editor:**

```
1. var f = this.getField("employee");
2. f.readonly = true;
```

7. **Click OK in the JavaScript Editor.** You return to the Digital Signatures Properties Signed tab where the script appears as shown in Figure 17.9.

8. **Click Close, and save the file.**

After you add a JavaScript, the script is displayed in the Digital Signatures Properties Signed tab.

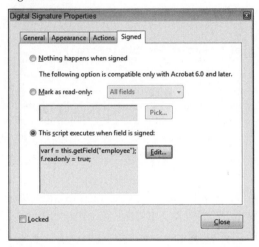

Notice in the Signed tab that if you click the Mark as read-only, select Just these fields, and click the Pick button, you don't have an option to select a parent name in the Field Selection dialog box. Choosing what fields to mark as read-only requires you to check each field individually that you want to lock.

As with showing and hiding fields, with just two lines of JavaScript you can lock all fields having the same parent name. When the employee signs the form, the fields are locked and cannot be edited if the file is secured.

Changing highlight color

You might decide that a form doesn't need the default blue highlight color when a form recipient works on one of your forms. In other cases, the design of your form may contain colors similar to the highlight color, and you may want to change the highlight color to a different color that adds more contrast between the fields and the background design.

With a simple one-line JavaScript, you can change the highlight color. Open the JavaScript Functions dialog box by choosing Advanced ➪ Document Processing ➪ Document JavaScripts, and add the following script in the JavaScript Editor:

```
app.runtimeHighlightColor = color.white;
```

This line of code changes the highlight color from the default color to white. You also can change the color to a number of other colors and to custom colors.

Changing text colors

You can change text colors for field data to emphasize text, make the text appear more subtle, or use colors of text for design changes. You could set the text color to a light color where you want default text to appear on a form and change the color as form recipients add data. Precisely how you use text colors we leave up to you. In this section, we provide you with the essentials to know how to change colors for text fields.

Changing colors

Figure 17.10 shows the same *globalTransferFields.pdf* form we've used in many steps earlier in this chapter; it shows an amount field for transferring funds. This form is a good example of where we might want to emphasize a field's contents. Assume that you want to change the field text color for the amount to transfer to another color if the amount is in excess of a certain figure—say, $10,000. By changing text color, anyone quickly looking at the form can see the amount that exceeds a value that the host agency may want to look into.

FIGURE 17.10

The US Dollars field below Amount to Transfer is the field where we want to add a custom format script.

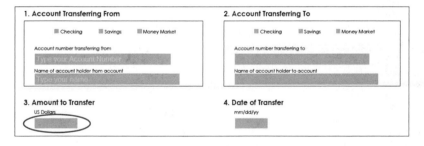

To format the field for changing text color, we use the text field's Format tab and write a custom JavaScript. Here's how to do it.

 For these steps, use the *globalTransferFields.pdf* form found in the Chapter 17 folder on the book's CD-ROM.

STEPS: Changing Text Colors

1. **Open a form in Acrobat.** In our example, we used the *globalTransferFields.pdf* form from the book's CD-ROM.

2. **Open the *US Dollars* Text Field Properties window.** Using the Select Object tool, double-click the US Dollars text field.

3. **Open the Format tab.** Click Format in the Text Field Properties window.

4. **Open the Custom Format options.** Choose Custom from the Select format category drop-down menu.

5. **Open the JavaScript Editor.** In the Custom Options of the Format tab, you have two areas where you can use a JavaScript. The top item is the Custom Format Script area. We want to use this option to add our script for custom formatting. Click the first Edit button adjacent to the Custom Format Script window shown in Figure 17.11 to open the JavaScript Editor.

6. **Add the following script in the JavaScript Editor:**
   ```
   1. var f = event.target;
   2.    if (f.value > 10000)
   3.    f.textColor = color.red;
   4. else
   5.    f.textColor = color.black;
   ```

7. **Click OK in the JavaScript Editor.** You return to the Format tab in the Text Field Properties window. When you return to the Format tab, the script appears in a scrollable window, as shown in Figure 17.11.

8. **Click Close, and save the file.**

FIGURE 17.11

Add a JavaScript to the Custom Format Script area in the Format tab.

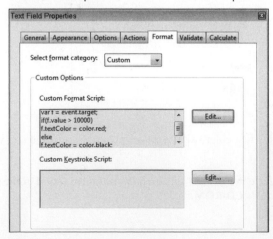

This script introduces a few new things not yet covered in this chapter. Notice the script is not added as an action or in the Calculate tab. The script is added to the Format tab and more specifically to the Custom Format Script item in the Format tab.

In line 1, we introduce the *event.target* object. Typically, you target fields by using *this.getField("field name")*. This is the most common code used to add a field to a script for assigning variables. However, in our example, we aren't targeting another field; we want to use the field where the script is written. We use *event.target* to inform Acrobat that we'll change the results of the field where the script is written.

In line 2, we examine the target field and see if the value is over 10000. If it is, we change the text color to red. If the value is 10000 or less, the text color is set to black.

Defining custom colors

If you're used to working with an image-editing program like Photoshop, Photoshop Elements, Corel Photo-Paint, or any other paint type program, you know that color is specified in values from 0 to 255 for RGB color for each of the RGB channels and CMYK color is specified for various percentages of the CMYK inks from 0 to 100%.

Figure 17.12 shows the Photoshop Color Picker dialog box where such values are typed or when clicking a color in the Color Picker.

FIGURE 17.12

The Adobe Photoshop Color Picker

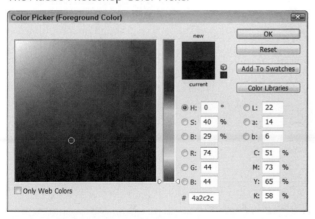

Additionally, illustration programs, layout programs, and Office programs all use the same model for specifying color. Acrobat JavaScript, however, uses a different numbering schema for color specification. If you want to add a custom color using JavaScript, you need to be familiar with how JavaScript defines color.

Instead of using RGB values from 0 to 255, JavaScript uses values from 0 to 1. You might see an RGB color defined as .334, .546, and .978. Because Acrobat doesn't have a color wheel where you can easily see colors and their associated values when using JavaScript, you need to use a little workaround to easily convert RGB color values to JavaScript color values.

The easiest way to pick a color you want to code in JavaScript is to open an image editor like Photoshop and open the Color Picker shown in Figure 17.12. Choose a color by clicking in the large color swatch, and read the RGB values. You take each of these three values and divide by 255. Therefore, a color defined as 74, 44, 192 in an image editor would be .290, .172, .753 in JavaScript code.

To change a text color to a custom color, you might use this line of code in your script:

```
f.textColor = new array ("RGB", .290, .172, .753);
```

Let's suppose you have a form and you want some default text to appear in fields for something like help information or guiding the user through the fields with hints. Tooltips work for this kind of help information, but the cursor needs to be placed above a field to display the tip, and only one tip at a time can be displayed. If you want the form recipient to see all the helpful tips at a glance, you might type values in each field to indicate what's needed for each field's contents.

We've seen quite a few forms designed with two sets of fields. One field appears on top of another or adjacent to a field showing some information about what needs to be typed for a given field. This way of designing a form is overkill and can cost you lots of storage space. Each field added to a form adds more memory to the file size. A much better way to handle the problem is to use only one set of fields and add a little finesse to your form design.

To more clearly understand our point here, look at Figure 17.13. This section of the form contains two fields marked as shown in Figure 17.13. The default text is ghosted back (lightened) with a light gray custom color. We don't want the text to appear black because that might confuse the form recipient. Where the text appears light, the form recipient has an easy clue that the field needs to be filled in with data.

FIGURE 17.13

Two fields are shown with default text using a light gray custom color.

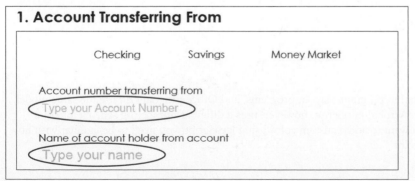

To create a form with this kind of help text for fields, follow these steps.

STEPS: Defining Custom Colors with JavaScript

1. **Open a form in Acrobat.** Any form with fields will do. In our example, we used the *globalTransferFields.pdf* from the book's CD-ROM.

2. **Define some custom color values you want for your field's text color.** Open an image-editing program, or obtain some RGB values for a light color. In our example, we used RGB values of 215, 215, 215. This color is a light gray. To convert the color values to the equivalents used by JavaScript, we divided 215 ÷ 255. The result is .843.

3. **Open a field's properties where you want to add some default text for a help item.** In our example, we double-clicked the Select Object tool on the *Account number transferring from* field to open the Text Field Properties dialog box. This form was created using Acrobat's auto field detection operation, and we left the field names as Acrobat created them.

4. **Open the Format tab.** Click the Format tab in the Text Field Properties window.

5. **Add a Custom Format Script.** Choose Custom from the Select format category drop-down menu, and click the Edit button for Custom Format Script to open the JavaScript Editor. Type the following code in the JavaScript Editor:

```
1. var f = event.target;
2. if (f.value != "Type your Account Number")
3.    f.textColor = color.black;
4. else
5.    f.textColor = new Array ("RGB", .843, .843, .843);
```

6. **Click OK in the JavaScript Editor.** You return to the Format tab in the Text Field Properties window, as shown in Figure 17.14.

7. **Click Close, and save the file.**

FIGURE 17.14

The code is listed in a scrollable window in the Format tab.

This script is similar to the script written in "Changing colors" earlier in this chapter. The only differences are line 2 where we used text as a value to assess and line 5 where we used a custom color.

Check box and radio button behaviors

In a way, radio button and check box fields are similar to button fields. The field Properties window has an Actions tab, and JavaScripts are written by choosing the Run a JavaScript action from the Select Action drop-down menu in this tab. That's the same way you add JavaScripts to buttons.

When a form recipient clicks a radio button or check box field, the JavaScript associated with the field is executed. Executing JavaScripts when a user clicks radio button fields or check boxes offers you a wealth of opportunity for your form designs. You might use a radio button/check box to show or hide fields such as showing a shipping address if a form recipient clicks a Yes box to indicate the shipping address is different than the mailing address. On the form, you would show only the mailing address fields unless a form recipient indicates the shipping address is a different address. You can use radio buttons and check boxes to confirm actions such as if clicking *yes,* something happens, or if clicking *no,* something else happens.

The *globalTransferFields.pdf* file we've used in many steps throughout this chapter offers us an opportunity to add some JavaScripts that can help prevent user error, which is another condition where you might add a JavaScript to a radio button or check box field. In Figure 17.15, you see the check box fields in two sections on the form.

FIGURE 17.15

Two sections on the form contain a row of check box fields.

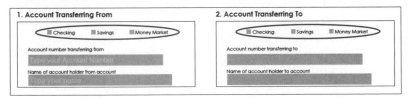

Although it's not critical to add JavaScripts to the check box fields for a form recipient to complete this form, you can save lots of aggravation when processing form data if you guard against some potential errors.

One potential error on the form shown in Figure 17.15 is that a form recipient may click the *Checking* check box field to transfer money from and, without thinking, click the same respective field in Section 2. When the form is submitted, this error creates lots of aggravation because you likely won't permit a form recipient to transfer money from and to the same account.

An account representative may have to call the customer to report the error and ask that the form be resubmitted, or the representative may need to obtain the proper information to change the form on behalf of the customer. This is time consuming and delays processing the form.

By adding some JavaScript to the check box fields in Section 2, we can prevent an error when a customer checks one of these fields. If the customer wants to transfer money from savings to checking and clicks Savings in Section 1 but inadvertently clicks Savings in Section 2, we can instruct Acrobat to not accept the value in Section 2. This means a customer needs to select one check box in Section 1 and cannot select the same check box in Section 2.

Designing check box fields

Before we look at the JavaScript to prevent errors on the form shown in Figure 17.15, we need to point out a few issues related to the design of the check box fields. When we created this form, we let Acrobat populate the fields by using auto field detection.

CROSS-REF For more information on using auto field detection, see Chapters 5 through 7.

Acrobat created the check box fields on the form, but the fields are not mutually exclusive. So we modified the fields in Section 1 to create a row of mutually exclusive fields. We deleted the Savings and Money Market fields and renamed the Checking field to *from* for the field name. We added the export value *checking* to the first field and duplicated the field twice adding *savings* and *mm* for the export values for the other two fields in this group.

CROSS-REF For more information on creating mutually exclusive fields, see Chapter 7.

We had to modify the Section 1 check box fields so a form recipient couldn't check two fields in this group. By making the fields mutually exclusive, one check box is enabled when the form recipient clicks the check box and all other check boxes in the group are turned off. We didn't worry about the check box fields in Section 2 because the JavaScripts we add to these fields takes care of clearing the fields, as you can see in the next section where we talk about adding the JavaScripts.

Adding JavaScripts to check box fields

Using the *globalTransferFields.pdf* form shown in Figure 17.15, we need to add a JavaScript to the three check box fields in Section 2. The JavaScript needs to look at the check box fields in Section 1 and check to see if the field value matches the target value where we write the JavaScript. For example, the Checking_2 field in Section 2 needs a JavaScript that looks at the check box fields in Section 1. If the export value is *checking,* we don't want the value to be accepted because the from recipient cannot transfer money from checking to checking. In this example we'll assume that the same account number is used in the From and To account number fields to illustrate our point. Obviously, if the form recipient has two account numbers, than a transfer from checking to checking is possible. If the export value in Section 1 is either *savings* or *mm* (for Money Market), then the value can be accepted.

To understand more clearly, follow these steps.

ON the CD-ROM   Use the *globalTransferFields.pdfl* file in the Chapter17 folder on the book's CD-ROM, or use the modified version of this file that you saved by following steps earlier in this chapter.

STEPS: Adding a JavaScript to a Check Box Field

1. **Open a form containing check box fields in Acrobat.** The JavaScript we add in these steps makes more sense when using the *globalTransferFields.pdf* file on the book's CD-ROM. Be certain to use this file to follow these steps.

2. **Open the check box field Properties.** We started these steps by opening the *to* field in Section 2 on the *globalTransferFields.pdf* form by double-clicking the field with the Select Object tool. The check box fields are all properly formatted on this form, so you don't need to worry about modifying the check box fields in Section 1.

3. **Open the Actions tab.** Click Actions in the Check Box Properties window.

4. **Open the JavaScript Editor.** Choose Run a JavaScript from the Select Action drop-down menu, and click the Add button to open the JavaScript Editor.

5. **Type a JavaScript in the JavaScript Editor.** Add the following code in the JavaScript Editor, as shown in Figure 17.16:

```
1. var f = this.getField("from");
2. var g = event.target;
3. var msg = "You cannot transfer funds from Checking to Checking"
4.
5. if (f.value == "checking"){
6.    app.alert(msg);
7.    f.value = "";
8.    g.value = "";
9. }
```

6. **Click OK in the JavaScript Editor, and click Close in the Check Box Properties window.**

7. **Save the file.**

The script in Step 5 begins with assigning variables in the first three lines of code. We start with assigning variable f to the *from* check box fields. The field name is *from* for the three check boxes in Section 1, and they all have different export values. Variable g is assigned to the target for where the script is written. In line 3, we have the message text that is shown in an application alert.

We use a blank line in line 4 just to break up the code visually for you. It's not necessary and has no effect on executing the script. We just wanted to separate the code for assigning variables from the routine that examines the fields and executes an action.

In line 5, we look at the export value for the *from* field (f). If the export value is *checking,* lines 6 through line 8 are executed. Keep in mind we're writing this script for the *to* field on the form. Therefore, we don't want to accept the checking export value in the *from* field for the *to* field.

FIGURE 17.16

Type the code in the JavaScript Editor.

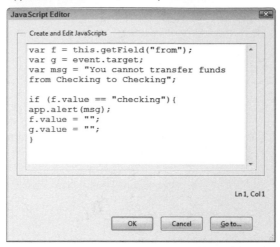

If the form recipient attempts to transfer funds from checking to checking, line 6 opens an application alert dialog box and reports the message in line 3. In line 7, the *f.value,* which is the check box checked in Section 1, is cleared. In line 8, the target value (*to*) is cleared.

In line 5, you see two equals signs (=). In line 7, you see one equals sign. Using two equals signs is an equality operator. It is used only for value comparisons and not for assignments. A single = sign is used only for value assignments.

To add the JavaScript to the remaining two fields in Section 2, you can copy the script from the *to* field and paste into the JavaScript Editor for the other fields. The only changes you need to make are in line 3 where you change *Checking* to *Savings (or Money Market)* and line 5 where you change *checking* to *savings (or mm)*.

Creating Form Submission Scripts

Acrobat provides a number of options for submitting form data using the Submit a form action in the Actions tab. You can simply add an action to submit a form via e-mail, to a URL, or to Acrobat. com. In addition to using the Submit Form Selections dialog box, you also can write JavaScripts for button actions to submit forms and form data.

Submitting a form

You can submit the full PDF file with Acrobat; however, if your end users use Adobe Reader, then you need to enable the file with reader extensions. However, before you enable the file, you'll want to add a submit button and write the JavaScript.

To submit a form using JavaScript, use the following code:

```
1.  this.mailDoc({
2.    bUI: true,
3.    cTo: "your email address",
4.    cCC: "cc",
5.    cBCC: "bcc",
6.    cSubject: "The Latest News",
7.    });
```

The script triggers Acrobat to submit the entire PDF document *this.mailDoc*. The *true* item tells Acrobat to submit the entire form followed by the e-mail address for where to submit the form, the *cc* address, and the *bcc* address. If you don't want a send copies to cc or bcc addresses, use "". The last item in the code is a subject line.

An abbreviated real-world example of the code might appear something like this:

```
1.  this.mailDoc (true, "sally@company.com", "henry@company.com", "",
        "Mileage Claim Form");
```

When a form recipient clicks the submit button where the script is added, the default e-mail client opens with the form attached and the fields for the To, CC, and Subject text boxes populated with the data described in the script.

Submitting form data

If you have a form with a file size of several megabytes, you might want to submit just the data and not the entire PDF file. To send data instead of a complete PDF file, use the following code:

```
1.  this.mailForm ({
2.  bUI: true,
3.  cTo: "email address",
4.  cCC: "cc",
5.  cBCC: "bcc",
6.  cSubject: "Subject"
7.  });
```

By using JavaScript, you can add a number of conditions to the submit form action. For example, you may want to check a field for a value and open an alert dialog box if the value is not what you want returned on the form, add an e-mail address from a field's contents, or any number of different circumstances you encounter with submitting a form.

As an abbreviated example, look over the following code:

```
1.  var f = this getField("emailAddress");
2.  this.mailDoc (true, "your email address", f.value, "", "Subject").
```

In line 1, we assign the variable *f* to a field on the form. The field is intended for the form recipient to add an e-mail address so a copy can be sent to the form recipient when the form is submitted. In line 2, the value of the field is denoted by *f.value* that appears for where a cc would be placed in the script.

Using Scripts for Printing

You can use JavaScripts for printing forms for a number of different conditions. You may want a form to open in Full Screen mode where the form recipient won't see tools and menus. While in Full Screen mode, you can make it easier for the form recipient to print a form using a button action that executes a print command. You also might want certain conditions to apply when printing a form. For example, if a field contains something, print the form or open a dialog box informing the form recipient that something else needs to be added to a field in order to print the form. Additionally, you can eliminate fields from printing using JavaScript and choose different print attributes and page ranges.

Printing a document

When you use JavaScript to print a form, you have a number of different toggles you can set in the script, such as showing or not showing the Print dialog box, printing annotations, shrinking a page to fit a paper size, and more.

```
this.print ({bUI: false, bShrinkToFit: true, bReverse: true});
```

In the above script, the print action is set to print a form without the Print dialog box opening (*bUI: false*), shrink the page to fit the paper (*bShrinkToFit: true*), and print from the end of the document to the start of the document (*bReverse: true*).

Printing a page

If you have a form with several pages used for directions and you want to set up a print button to print just the form appearing on the current in a multi-page document, use the following script:

```
this.print ({this.pageNum, bUI: false});
```

The above code prints the current page (*this.pageNum*) and prevents the Print dialog box from opening (*bUI: false*).

Eliminating fields from print

If you set up fields for being visible in the General properties, all fields will print when a form is printed. You may want a condition where a field prints under certain circumstances and doesn't print based on some field criteria. If you set the General properties to Visible, but doesn't print, the field won't print under any circumstances. Therefore, you need to set the field properties to Visible for all fields and control the fields you don't want to print using JavaScript.

The following code targets a field for not printing:

```
1. var f = this.getField("fieldNotToPrint");
2. f.print = false;
```

In the above script, we set the variable *f* to the field we don't want to print. In line 2, we instruct Acrobat to not print the field. Of course, you would add this script to a larger routine that examines field data, and you might use an *if* statement in the code to determine whether the field should or should not print.

Creating Document Viewing Scripts

We've added a number of different scripts to demonstrate various viewing options. We started out with resetting fields using JavaScript. In this regard, we're talking about viewing the field data or not seeing the data by choosing to clear data from a form, so we added the description in this section. We continue with looking at zoom views, page navigation for multiple-page documents, and controlling Full Screen mode.

Resetting fields

Although not something that you generally think of when viewing a form, we tossed resetting a form in this section. As you may recall from Chapter 5, we can use an action to reset a form, which essentially means clearing the data from the field objects. When you use the Reset a form action, you need to either use the Select All button in the Reset a Form dialog box or individually check each field in a group that you want to reset.

For forms where you want to reset all fields, the Reset a Form action is all you need. However, if you use a form like the *globalPerformanceReview.pdf* form we've used several times in this chapter, you have a ten-page form with fields on every page. The form is designed for three different parties to complete the form (an employee, a supervisor, and an HR representative). If you use a reset button on the form to clear data, you'll want to add three buttons designed for use by each individual clearing fields respective to the party responsible for filling in the fields.

If you browse the *globalPerformanceReview.pdf* form and look at the fields, you find a number of fields that makes it difficult to individually select fields in the Reset a Form dialog box. An easier way to set the Reset Form attributes is to use a JavaScript.

Creating separate fields for resetting a form

When you have multiple users filling in a form, you should set up several reset buttons so each form recipient clears only those fields pertaining to the user's responsibility for completing the form.

ON the CD-ROM   **For this example, we used the *globalPerformanceReview.pdf* form from the Chapter17 folder on the book's CD-ROM.**

On the *globalPerformanceReview.pdf* form, we have one reset button currently on the form. Since three individual form recipients will complete the form, we need to add two more reset buttons. The default button on the form is named *resetForm*. The first order of business is to rename the field. If you followed steps earlier in "Showing Hidden Fields on a Form," you know that we used hierarchical names on the form with the parent names being *employee, supervisor,* and *admin.* The first field name we want to use is a field name containing the *employee* parent name.

To rename the field, open a context menu using the Select Object tool and choose Rename Field. Change the name to *employee.resetForm.* Duplicate the field by clicking with the Select Object tool, pressing Ctrl/⌘, and dragging to a new location. The field is duplicated.

Choose Rename Field from a context menu, and rename the second field using *supervisor.resetForm* for the field name. Follow the same steps to duplicate and rename the field using *admin.resetForm* for the third field, as shown in Figure 17.17.

FIGURE 17.17

Rename the *resetForm* button field using *employee.resetForm* for the field name, and duplicate the field twice using *supervisor.resetForm* and *admin.resetForm* for the second and third field names.

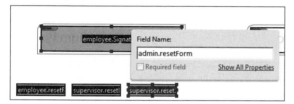

One more thing you need to do is to hide the second and third fields. In "Showing Hidden Fields on a Form," we created JavaScripts to display fields that were hidden based on a form submission action. When you use the same parent names, the fields are made visible by executing the scripts discussed earlier in this chapter.

To set the field attributes for Hidden, select the *supervisor.resetForm* and *admin.resetForm* fields with the Select Object tool and choose Properties from a context menu. Click the General tab, and choose Hidden from the Form Field drop-down menu.

Save the form, and use it to follow steps for adding a JavaScript to reset a form.

Using JavaScript to reset a form

Just like JavaScripts that you use to show/hide fields and lock fields, resetting a form using JavaScript is handled with just a few lines of code. To reset a group of fields, follow these steps.

STEPS: Resetting Fields Using JavaScript

1. **Open a form in Acrobat.** We continue using the *globalPerformanceReview.pdf* form edited in the last section, "Creating separate fields for resetting a form."

2. **Open the *employee.resetForm* Button Field Properties window.** Use the Select Object tool, and double-click the field.

3. **Open the Actions tab.** Click Actions in the Button Field Properties window.

4. **Add a JavaScript.** Choose Run a JavaScript from the Select Action drop-down menu, and click Add. In the JavaScript Editor, type the following code:

```
1. var f = this getField("employee");
2. this.resetForm(f);
```

5. **Click OK.**

6. **Repeat the same steps for the supervisor reset button using "supervisor" in place of employee in the code in line 4.**

7. **Click Close in the Button Field Properties.**

8. **Save the form.**

Quite simply, the code assigns the parent name to variable *f,* and in line 2, the form is reset for the *f* value, which is all fields having a parent name of *employee.*

Preserving default values

When you reset fields, all the data are cleared from the fields, even if you click Locked in the General properties. At times, you may want to have data assigned to a field. For example, a form that has a fixed cost for an item is something you don't want cleared from the form. If you look back to Figure 17.10, you may remember we added default text to form fields and used a custom color for the text. We want the text to appear on the form and don't want the data cleared when resetting the form.

The way to handle the problem is to set up the fields with different parent names. For all fields where you want to preserve data in a field, use a parent name common for all the fields. For the remaining fields, use a different parent name. When it comes time to use a JavaScript to reset the form, you use the name for the fields you want to clear.

Zooming views

You can set fixed zoom levels in the Initial View tab in the Document Properties. You can choose from a number of fixed preset views. Typically, you might choose the Default choice to let each form recipient keep the zoom level at his preferred choice, set the zoom to 100 percent for easily completing a form, or use a Fit Page view to fit the form within the document pane on any monitor displaying a form. The Fit Page view conforms to each monitor size and shows the whole page in the document pane.

If you demonstrate filling out a form on a laptop computer in front of an audience, you may find that you want to set a custom zoom level for a form that doesn't have a zoom view among the preset zoom levels in the Initial View properties.

CROSS-REF For more information on setting Initial View properties, see Chapter 3.

By adding a document-level JavaScript, you can set zoom levels to custom zoom views. Open the JavaScript Functions dialog box (Advanced ⇨ Document Processing ⇨ Document JavaScripts), and add the following script in the JavaScript Editor:

```
this.zoom=89;
```

The above script sets the zoom level to 89 percent.

Navigating pages

Multi-page forms, such as the *globalPerformanceReview.pdf* form used throughout this chapter, might benefit from adding navigation buttons if you decide to have the form open in Full Screen mode. You can add buttons with button faces to indicate clicking a button opens the next or previous page. Something like right and left arrows are one button face you might use for navigation buttons.

You do have options in the Actions tab for controlling page navigation by using the Execute a menu item action and choosing page navigation menu commands. If you want to add JavaScripts for navigating pages, use the following scripts:

- **this.pageNum++:** Opens the next page.
- **this.pageNum--:** Opens the previous page.
- **this.pageNum=1:** Opens page 2 in a document. JavaScript is zero-based, so the first page is page 0.
- **this.pageNum:** The current page number. This doesn't navigate to a page, but the value can be used in calculations.
- **this.numPages:** Returns the value of the total number of pages in a document. Again, no navigation is associated with the script, but you might use it with calculations.

Full Screen scripts

In Chapter 3, we talked about setting the Initial View to open a file in Full Screen mode using the Initial View tab in the Document Properties. You can use a number of different JavaScripts to control Full Screen behaviors when you want to display forms in Full Screen mode.

You can use a number of scripts to set the looping and timer for viewing pages in Full Screen mode. We'll skip these because you're not very likely to use the scripts with forms. The more frequent scripts you might use for controlling Full Screen viewing with forms include:

- **app.fs.cursor = cursor.visible:** The switch is *visible* or *hidden*. You can choose to show or hide the cursor.
- **app.fs.clickAdvances = false:** The switch is *true* or *false*. This script is a good one to turn off the automatic page advancement when a form recipient clicks the cursor. If you have buttons, check boxes, and radio buttons in addition to text fields, a user that accidentally misses a field object and clicks the page will be taken to the next page in the document. Set the switch to *false,* and you can eliminate auto page advancement.

- **app.fs.escapeExits = true:** The switch is *true* or *false*. Most users know that pressing the Esc key exits Full Screen mode. You also have the Ctrl/⌘+L keyboard shortcut to switch between viewing in Full Screen mode and Viewer mode. If you want to keep the form recipient in Full Screen mode, you can set the switch to *false*. Most Adobe Reader users won't know how to exit Full Screen mode by using the keyboard shortcut. If you do set the switch to *false,* be certain to add buttons for the form recipient to print and exit the form.

- **app.fs.backgroundColor = color.ltGray:** This script changes the background color of the Full Screen window appearing outside the page area. You can use preset colors or custom colors as described earlier in "Defining custom colors."

- **app.fs.isFullScreen = true:** The switch is either *true* or *false*. If you add a button to a form, you can let the form recipient click the button to enter Full Screen mode (*true*) or exit Full Screen mode (*false*).

Summary

- Application alerts are used to open dialog boxes with messages.

- You can create JavaScripts that assess an Acrobat viewer version and viewer type when a form opens.

- An application alert added to a document action can inform a user what to do with a form when it is printed or saved.

- Audio beeps can be created with JavaScript to alert form recipients of potential problems when completing a form.

- Using JavaScript, you can more easily show and hide field objects, lock fields, and reset form fields than when using the respective actions in the Actions tab.

- Using JavaScript, you can change the field highlight color and field text color using preset colors or custom colors.

- Executing JavaScripts added to radio buttons and check boxes is similar to executing scripts added to button fields.

- You can use JavaScript to submit PDF forms and PDF form data.

- JavaScripts used for printing can be particularly helpful when viewing forms in Full Screen mode.

- A number of different JavaScripts can be used for controlling zoom levels and page navigation.

Chapter 18

Creating Advanced JavaScripts

We hope this book provides you an exposure to scripting in Acrobat and LiveCycle Designer. To be completely thorough, we would have to write a book equal to this size covering just Acrobat JavaScript and a separate book for JavaScript and FormCalc in LiveCycle Designer.

This book is not a JavaScript book; as such, we offer you only some samples that we hope guide you into looking at more opportunities for adding scripts to your forms.

In this chapter, we provide some different examples of JavaScript routines to demonstrate how JavaScript is used for adding content to forms, calculating data, formatting fields, working with functions, working with dialog boxes, and changing views. In essence, we use examples for a variety of conditions that can be used on your forms.

Scripting for conditions more specific to your forms will require you to understand what we cover in this chapter and use additional JavaScript objects you learn from the manuals and resources you can find on Adobe's Web site.

All the scripts we talk about in this chapter work with Adobe Reader and Acrobat. We leave scripts unique to working with Acrobat to Chapter 19.

IN THIS CHAPTER

Creating scripts for annotations

Calculating data

Formatting data

Working with response dialog boxes

Changing layer views

Adding Annotations

A variety of JavaScripts can be used to add new content to a form. You can add fields using JavaScript, add new pages using JavaScript, add bookmarks using JavaScript, and add a number of other items as new content to a form.

Unfortunately, most of the new content you add to a form can be performed only using Acrobat. You cannot add new content to a form using Adobe Reader. However, there is one exception. If you enable a form with Adobe Reader usage rights, you can add annotations via executing JavaScript routines.

CROSS-REF   For more information on enabling forms with Adobe Reader usage rights, see Chapter 10.

You may want to provide a form recipient an option for adding a comment note or markup on a document. Rather than use design space on a form, you can add a button with a button field to dynamically create a comment if the user decides to amplify a response with a comment message.

Assessing coordinates

Comment note pop-ups and text box comments locations are defined in JavaScripts using x,y coordinates on a page. You need to define the bounding area for a comment in the JavaScript code to inform Acrobat where the comment appears on a form. Therefore, before you write a JavaScript to add comments, you need to determine the coordinates for where the comment note (or text box) is to be placed on the form. The code for specifying the location of a comment note might be written as follows:

```
[200, 100, 300, 400]
```

In the above code, we are defining the coordinates on a page beginning with 200 points from the left and 100 points from the bottom for the lower-left corner coordinates of a note. The top-right corner of the comment note rectangle appears 300 points from the left and 400 points from the bottom of the form.

Understanding User Space

Annotations always appear in what we refer to as *Default User Space* while field objects always appear in *Rotated User Space*. If the two spaces are the same, you can easily move annotations around a form and use the JavaScript shown in Figure 18.2 without any modification.

A Default User Space and the Rotated User Space are the same if a form is neither rotated nor cropped. Additionally, the PDF was created without transversing the media. Media can be transversed in programs like QuarkXPress and Adobe InDesign where a portrait document prints landscape to save media on roll-fed devices.

If you find that when you use a JavaScript with coordinates reported back in the JavaScript Console not matching the annotation object you add to a form, the Default User Space and the Rotated User Space are different. You can convert one space to another using JavaScript, but the code is much more complicated.

To learn more about converting User Spaces, consult the JavaScript for Acrobat API Reference mentioned in Chapter 16.

To take the guesswork out of finding coordinates, you can let JavaScript return coordinate locations to you in the JavaScript Console. The following steps show you how.

STEPS: Using JavaScript to Locate Annotation Comment Coordinates

1. **Open a form in Acrobat.** For our example, we used the *productOrder.pdf* form from the book's CD-ROM.

2. **Open the Comment & Markup toolbar.** Click the Comment task button, and choose Show Comment & Markup Toolbar.

3. **Draw a rectangle comment precisely in the area where you want a comment to be drawn when a JavaScript is executed.** Click the Rectangle tool in the Comment & Markup toolbar, and draw a rectangle, as shown in Figure 18.1.

FIGURE 18.1

Draw a rectangle with the Rectangle tool from the Comment & Markup toolbar on the form in the location where you want to add a comment note.

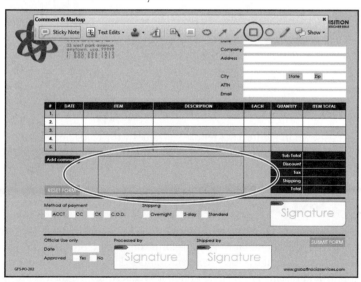

4. **Open the JavaScript Console.** Press Ctrl/⌘+J to open the JavaScript Console.

5. **Clear the default text in the JavaScript Console.** Click the Trash icon to clear the text.

6. **Type the following code in the JavaScript Console:**

   ```
   this.getAnnots()[0].rect
   ```

7. **Press the Num Pad Enter key.** The JavaScript Console reports the annotation coordinates, as shown in Figure 18.2.

FIGURE 18.2

Type the code, and press the Num Pad Enter key to display the coordinates for the Rectangle comment in the JavaScript Console.

The coordinates shown in Figure 18.2 report x,y values with 13 decimal places. You can copy the code as it appears and paste into a script in the JavaScript Editor or simply use the integers (187, 168, 487, and 243) to add to the code.

Adding a text box comment

In Figure 18.1, we defined an area where we want to add a comment note. The form is straightforward and easy enough to fill out. However, this form contains no provisions to advise the host company when to ship the order if the form recipient wants a delayed shipment, no way of dealing with different shipping and mailing address, no option for requesting an e-mail confirmation that an order has been successfully processed, or some other information that a form recipient may want to know.

Rather than add a text box field to the form, we decided to let the form recipient add a comment note if some additional comments need to be added to the order. Because some Adobe Reader users may not be familiar with using the Comment & Markup tools, we use JavaScript to create a new text box comment when the form recipient clicks a button.

 **In order to add a comment in Adobe Reader, the form must be enabled with Adobe Reader usage rights using Acrobat Pro or Pro Extended.**

To create a button action that adds a new comment to a form, follow these steps.

ON the CD-ROM Use the *productOrder.pdf* form in the Chapter18 folder on the book's CD-ROM to follow these steps.

STEPS: Adding a Button Action to Create a Comment Text Box

1. **Open a form in Acrobat.** In our example, we used the *productOrder.pdf* form from the book's CD-ROM.

2. **Assess the coordinates for the comment text box.** Use the same method for assessing coordinates as shown in Figure 18.2. Generally, it's a good idea to open a text editor to paste the coordinates and keep it open while writing the JavaScript. When you come to the line of code for adding coordinates, you can copy from the text editor document and paste into the JavaScript Editor.

3. **Delete the Rectangle comment.** If you created a Rectangle comment to display coordinates in the JavaScript Console, click the Rectangle comment with the Select Object tool and press Delete to remove it from the form.

4. **Create a button field.** Add a button field where you see *Add comment* on the form shown in Figure 18.1. We used *addComment* for the field name and set the appearances for the button field to no border and no color fill in the Button Field Appearance Properties.

5. **Add a JavaScript.** Click the Actions tab, and choose Run a JavaScript from the Select Action drop-down menu. Click the Add button to open the JavaScript Editor.

6. **Write the code.** Type the following code in the JavaScript Editor, as shown in Figure 18.3:

```
1. var annot = this.addAnnot({
2.    page: this.pageNum,
3.    type: "FreeText",
4.    rect: [187, 168, 487, 243],
5.    strokeColor: ["RGB", .270, .270, .270],
6.    fillColor: color.white
7. });
```

7. **Click OK in the JavaScript Editor, and save the file.**

Click the button, and the text box comment note is added. Type some text in the text box shown in Figure 18.4 to test it.

FIGURE 18.3

Type the code in the JavaScript Editor.

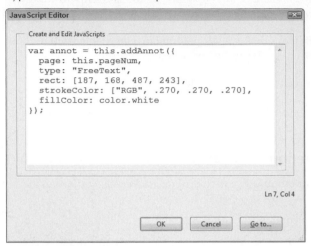

FIGURE 18.4

Click the button to add a text box comment, and type text in the comment window to test it.

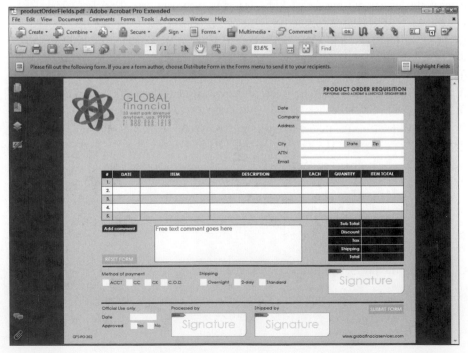

In line 1 in our script, we use the addAnnot object to add an annotation. Lines 2 through 6 set the attributes for the annotation. Line 2 targets the current page for the annotation. Line 3 defines the type of annotation to be added when the script is executed. If we want to add a Sticky Note, we would use "Text" instead of "FreeText." Line 4 contains the coordinates we obtained in Figure 18.2 earlier in this chapter. Lines 5 and 6 set the stroke and fill colors. In Line 5, we used a custom color.

CROSS-REF For more information on creating custom colors with JavaScript, see Chapter 17.

Writing Calculation Scripts

Calculation scripts are among the most frequent types of scripts you'll use. As discussed in Chapter 15, you need to use a scripting language to perform some of the most basic math functions. Using Simplified Field Notation offers you an easy method for creating simple math calculation formulas, but it is much more limiting than using JavaScript. When you need to use functions, write complex scripts, and perform calculations based on conditions, JavaScript is what you need to use.

CROSS-REF For more information on using Simplified Field Notation, see Chapter 15.

Summing columns and rows

In Chapter 15, we learned that summing rows and columns of data can be performed easily when you use hierarchical names and Acrobat's preset sum + formula. You name a column of fields *total.0, total.1, total.3,* and so on, and pick the parent name *total* in the Field Selection dialog box when you choose sum + from the Value drop-down menu in the Calculate tab.

CROSS-REF For more information on using preset formulas, see Chapters 8 and 9.

Using Acrobat's preset formula works for a number of different forms where all you need to do is sum a row or column. However, if you have to do something else with the result, such as add a sales tax after summing a column, then you need to use a JavaScript. Because SFN cannot be used with hierarchical names, you don't have any option other than JavaScript to perform the calculation.

ON the CD-ROM For descriptions and steps in this section, we used the *purchaseOrder.pdf* form from the Chapter18 folder on the book's CD-ROM.

Designing the form

Figure 18.5 shows the *purchaseOrder.pdf* form from the book's CD-ROM. Acrobat's auto field detection didn't recognize any fields on the form, so we had to add all the fields manually. As you can see in Figure 18.5, the Item Total column contains ten fields using hierarchical names. The first field below the tenth row is used to calculate a subtotal.

FIGURE 18.5

An Item Total column contains fields using hierarchical names. Below the last row, a total of the *amount* fields needs to be calculated.

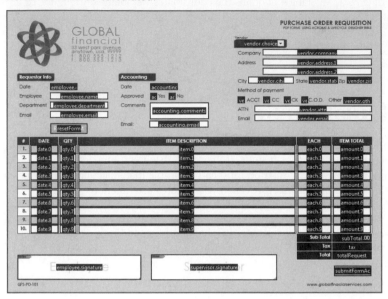

We use this form as an example to keep the scripting simple. For purchase order forms, any taxable items generally contain sales tax in each row total, so you may not need a separate field for tax on purchase order forms you design for your company. We broke this form up to illustrate different formulas you may need to use on forms, so focus on the process we describe in this chapter and not so much on the design of the sample form.

On some forms, you might not have a separate tax field like the one shown in Figure 18.5. For any form where sales tax is added to an amount total using a single calculation, you need to use JavaScript.

For the example form, we can use the preset sum + formula in the *subtotal* field to calculate the total for the Item Total column; but because we're talking about JavaScript, we'll use a script to total the column. Later, we talk about why we use JavaScript when we come to "Hiding zeros" later in this chapter.

Calculating a column of fields

Although the calculation to sum a column or row using JavaScript involves several lines of code, copying and pasting the code into additional forms is very easy. To create a JavaScript to sum a column, follow these steps.

STEPS: Summing a Column of Fields Using JavaScript

1. **Open a form in Acrobat having a column of fields that need to be summed.** In our example, we used the *purchaseOrder.pdf* file shown in Figure 18.5 from the book's CD-ROM.

2. **Open the Text Field Properties window for the field used to sum a column.** In our example, we used the Select Object tool and double-click the *subTotal* field while in Viewer mode. All the fields on this form have been properly formatted. If you use another form to follow these steps, be certain to format the fields you use in the calculation as numbers.

3. **Click the Calculate tab in the Text Field Properties window.**

4. **Add a JavaScript.** Click the Custom calculation script radio button in the Calculate properties, and click the Edit button to open the JavaScript Editor.

5. **Add a JavaScript.** Type the following code in the JavaScript Editor window:

```
1. var f = this.getField("amount");
2. var a = f.getArray();
3.    var sum = 0;
4.    for (i = 0; i < a.length; i ++)
5.    sum += a[i].value;
6. event.value = sum;
```

The code as you should type it in the JavaScript Editor appears in Figure 18.6.

FIGURE 18.6

The JavaScript code added in the JavaScript Editor.

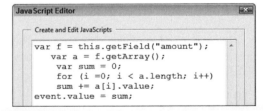

6. **Click OK, and click Close in the Text Field Properties window.**

7. **Save the file.** We'll use this file in more steps in this chapter. Keep the file handy to follow additional steps.

We introduce a few new routines in the script shown in Figure 18.6. We start the routine by assigning the parent name *amount* to variable *f*. If you followed other steps in Chapter 17 and this chapter, this assignment should be familiar to you.

In line 2, you find a new object. We set up an array and assign the array to variable *a*. Another item that's new is the loop we introduce in line 4. We first set the counter *i* to zero. The *i < a.length* item tells Acrobat to run the loop until the value *i* is less than the total number of rows. But we need to increment the *i* value through each pass in the loop, which is what the i++ item does.

In line 3, we set a variable *sum* to zero. In line 5, you see the sum value incremented with each pass in the loop. As the first row value is acquired, the *a* item is the field value and the *i* item is the counter. The last line of code (line 6) is the total sum we place as the *event.value*.

What's especially nice about this script is that you can add the script to a document where you collect an assortment of scripts as explained in Chapter 16 and paste the script into a document you use to collect various scripts. When it comes time to use the script, copy it from your template file and paste it in any form needing a similar calculation.

The only concern you have is just making sure you use the correct parent name for a row or column of fields. It you use the Place Multiple Fields command, Acrobat names the fields in hierarchical order. If you use a name like *total,* just replace *amount* in the first line of code with *total.* Every other line of code remains the same.

At the end of the script, you have a value *sum*. If you want to add a sales tax with a fixed tax rate, you would add a line 7 to the code, such as:

```
sum = sum + (sum * .075)
```

The above line of code adds a sales tax of 7.5 percent to the total. If you want a discount applied to the total, you might add a line 7 as follows:

```
sum = sum - (sum * .15)
```

This line of code creates a total less 15 percent.

The important thing to remember is that you have lots of flexibility for using the script shown in Figure 18.6 and can add just one more line of code for calculating various totals.

Calculating a sales tax

You can handle calculating a sales tax in several ways. You can use a fixed tax rate in a calculation formula as one method. Using such a method for calculating a sales tax, however, means that when a tax rate is changed, you need to modify your form and change the formula to reflect the new rate.

Another method is to add a field to a form for a form recipient to supply the tax rate. This option works well for sales to areas where tax rates differ, such as selling products to various U.S. states or when international sales require adding sales tax.

An alternative to adding a field for a user-supplied tax rate is to create an application response dialog box where a user is prompted to add a tax rate in a dialog box. The value added to the dialog box is then used in the calculation for the sales tax amount.

Calculating sales tax using fixed tax rates

Using a tax rate in a field calculation for a fixed rate is nothing more than adding the formulas as:

```
1. var f = this.getField("amountFld");
2. event.value = f.value * .085;
```

The simple two-line script assigns variable *f* to a subtotal field or an amount field (*"amountFld"*) you want to use for taxable items. Line 2 contains the fixed rate. In this example, the tax rate is 8.5 percent.

If you use a script like this on your forms, any change in tax rate requires you to edit the calculation script and change the rate to a new rate value.

Calculating sales tax from user-supplied tax rates

Tax rates can vary among U.S. states and among different counties within a state. If you use forms that require calculating tax for each individual location where products are purchased, adding a user-supplied tax rate field might be the best way to calculate the tax. The formula uses the tax rate input to calculate the result.

In Figure 18.7, a tax rate field is used for a user-supplied tax rate. The Tax field is calculated based on the rate entered for this field.

FIGURE 18.7

A user-supplied tax rate field is used in the tax amount calculation formula.

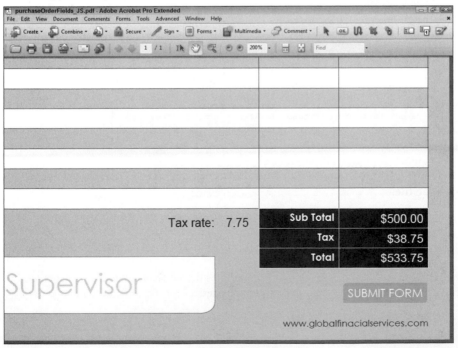

To calculate a tax rate based on user input for the rate amount, follow these steps.

ON the CD-ROM For these steps, we used the *purchaseOrder.pdf* file from the Chapter18 folder on the book's CD-ROM.

STEPS: Calculating Sales Tax Based on User Input Rate Values

1. **Open a form having a field used for user-supplied tax rates.** In our example, we used the *purchaseOrder.pdf* file from the Chapter18 folder. On this form, the field is added for the user-supplied tax rate data, and the fields are formatted as numbers.

2. **Open the *tax* Text Field Properties.** Double-click the *tax* field with the Select Object tool where the tax result is calculated.

3. **Click the Calculate tab.**

4. **Add a JavaScript.** Click the Custom calculation script radio button, and click Edit to open the JavaScript Editor. Type the following code in the JavaScript Editor, as shown in Figure 18.8:

```
1. var f = this.getField("subTotal");
2. if (f.value !=0){
3.   var j = this.getField("taxRate.amount")
4.   event.value = Math.round (f.value * j.value)/100;
5. }
```

FIGURE 18.8

Type the code in the JavaScript Editor.

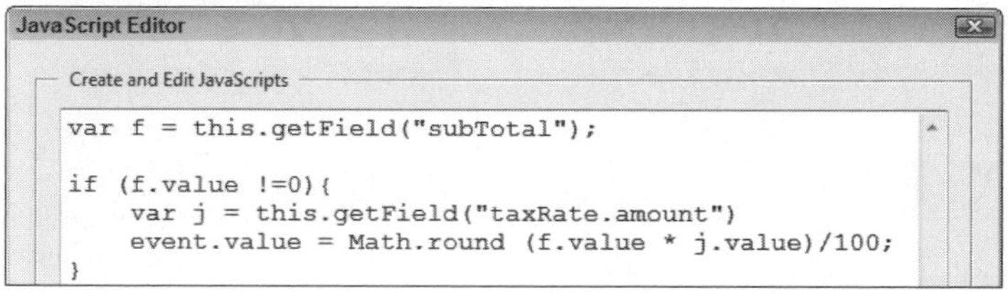

5. **Click OK, and click Close in the Text Field Properties window.**

6. **Save the file.**

We start the script off in line 1 in Figure 18.8 by looking at the *subTotal* field. If the field is not yet populated with data, the calculation script is not run. This line prevents a calculation on zero error. If the value is greater than zero, the script is executed.

In line 2, we get the user-supplied tax rate. Line 3 multiples the *subTotal* value times the *taxRate.amount* value and rounds off the result to two decimal places.

Calculating a shipping charge

Shipping charges often offer a form recipient a few options for the shipping service. As an example, you might design a form that offers overnight shipping, two-day shipping, and standard shipping. Shipping charges are then calculated according to the shipping preference made by the form recipient.

In Figure 18.9, you can see three check box fields used for choosing a shipping preference. Below the tax field on the right side of the form, you see an amount calculated for the shipping fees.

FIGURE 18.9

A form with three check box fields used to choose a shipping preference

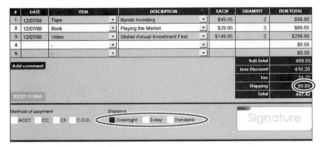

Shipping fees can be calculated in a number of ways. You can use fixed rates for different shipping options, use a percentage value based on total purchase price, or create a number of different other custom calculations.

ON the CD-ROM For calculating a shipping fee, we used the *productOrder.pdf* form from the Chapter18 folder on the book's CD-ROM. This form has many JavaScripts we explain in this chapter. Because many scripts are dependent on other scripts in the document, we added the JavaScripts to the document level and various fields rather than adding them to comment notes. You can delete the scripts from the document level and fields and save the file under a new name to step through examples in this chapter or review the scripts contained in the document as you follow steps.

Designing the form

We created two fields for calculating a subtotal. One field is the sum of the Item Total fields, and the other field is the same value less a discount amount. We used the subtotal (or discount) amount for calculating a shipping fee and sales tax.

The Sub Total field sums the data in the Item Total column. The Less Discount field is the Sub Total less 15 percent for an amount exceeding $200. If the amount is less than $200, we use the Sub Total value to calculate the shipping fee and sales tax. If the amount is equal to or greater than $200, we use the Less Discount field to calculate the shipping fee and sales tax.

The three check box fields in the Shipping area of the form contain the JavaScripts for calculating the shipping fee. We used rates based on the total purchase price (from either the Sub Total field or the Less Discount field) to determine the shipping fee. The three check boxes are mutually exclusive fields with separate JavaScripts to calculate the shipping fee.

Calculating a shipping fee using check box JavaScripts

Using the *productOrder.pdf* file from the Chapter18 folder on the book's CD-ROM, we add three different scripts to the check box fields for calculating a shipping fee. To understand how to create the calculations, follow these steps.

STEPS: Calculating a Shipping Fee

1. **Open a form where a shipping fee needs to be calculated.** In our example, we continued with the *productOrder.pdf* file from the book's CD-ROM.

2. **Open the first *shipMethod* Check Box Properties window.** The Shipping area on the example form contains three check boxes. Double-click the Select Object tool on the first check box field to open the Check Box Properties window.

3. **Click the Actions tab.**

4. **Add a JavaScript.** Leave the default Mouse Trigger at Mouse Up, and choose Run a JavaScript from the Select Action drop-down menu. Click Add to open the JavaScript Editor, and type the following script in the editor window, as shown in Figure 18.10.

```
1. var oShip = this.getField("shipping");
2. var oSub = this.getField("subTotal");
3. var oDiscount = this.getField("discount");
4.
5. if (oSub.value <200)
6.    var oRate = oSub.value * .24;
7. else
8.    var oRate = oDiscount.value * .24;
9.    oShip.value = oRate;
```

5. **Click OK, and click Close in the Check Box Properties window.**

6. **Save the form.**

FIGURE 18.10

Type the JavaScript in the JavaScript Editor.

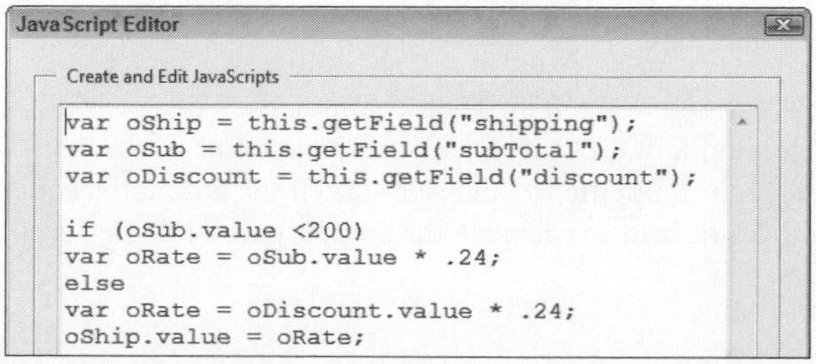

In lines 1 to 3, we assign the variables. We need the Sub Total and Less Discount fields used in this calculation. If the Sub Total field is less than 200 (line 5), we use the subTotal value. If the amount is 200 or more, we use the discount value to calculate the shipping fee.

The shipping fee is calculated as 24 percent of the total value (line 6 or line 8 depending on the total purchase price).

For the next check box, we copied the script from the first check box and pasted it into the JavaScript Editor we opened from the second check box field. The only change needed is the fixed rate (.24). We changed this value to .18. In the third check box, we changed the rate to .12.

When the form recipient completes the form, clicking a check box shows the amount of shipping costs. Click a second check box, and the shipping cost changes to reflect the respective calculation. This way, a form recipient can view how much one shipping method varies from another before clicking the submit button.

Date stamping a form

Unless you use a server product, the reliability of a date stamp is dependent on the date being accurate on a user's computer. If you have a controlled environment in an enterprise with an IT department responsible for configuring computers and implementing security, date stamps can be reliable when using a computer system clock.

Date stamps can be used for a variety of conditions. Perhaps you want a document to be stamped when a user submits or signs a form. You can easily add a date to the form when the action is invoked. In Figure 18.11 you see the JavaScript code that adds a date stamp to a field.

FIGURE 18.11

JavaScript code used to date stamp a field on a form

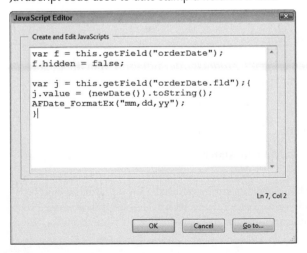

The easiest way to use a date stamp for something like a submit form action is to create a text field. You don't want the field to be displayed on a form while a form recipient is completing the form because the user will wonder what data to add to the form field. So keep it hidden until you are ready to display it on a submit form action.

Designing the form

On the *productOrder.pdf* form, we added a field above the identifying information fields and named the field *orderDate.fld,* as shown in Figure 18.12. We set the field properties to Read Only and Hidden in the General field properties window. We formatted the field as *None* in the Format tab.

FIGURE 18.12

We added a field to the purchaseOrder.pdf form and named the field *orderDate.fld*.

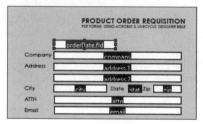

Adding a date stamp using JavaScript

Using JavaScript, you can add the current time based on the computer system clock to populate the field as well as add a title such as *Date:*. If you set the field properties to Read Only, the field cannot be edited if the file is secured after the field is shown on the form.

CROSS-REF For more information on securing forms, see Chapter 12.

To add a date stamp to a form, follow these steps.

ON the CD-ROM For these steps, we continued using the *productOrder.pdf* form from the Chapter18 folder on the book's CD-ROM. If you saved the form from earlier steps, use the saved version.

STEPS: Date Stamping a Form

1. **Open a form where you want to add a date stamp.** In our example, we used the *productOrder.pdf* form from the book's CD-ROM.

2. **Add a field to hold the date value.** In our example, we used a form that has a field formatted properly for holding a date value that we'll add with a JavaScript. If you use another form, add a text field and leave the formatting at the default None from the Select

format category drop-down menu in the Format tab. While testing the JavaScript code, leave the field visible and do not mark it for Read Only. After you check the code to be sure it works properly, clear the data and set the General properties for the field to Read Only and Hidden.

3. **Open the Button Properties for the Submit Form button.** In our example, we have a button field to be used for submitting the form. We use the Select Object tool and double-click this field to open the Button Field Properties window.

4. **Add a JavaScript.** Click Actions, and add a JavaScript action to open the JavaScript Editor. Type the following code in the JavaScript Editor, as shown in Figure 18.13.

```
1. var f = this.getField("orderDate.fld");
2. f.hidden = false;
3. f.value = "Date: " + util.printd("mmm dd, yyyy", new Date());
```

FIGURE 18.13

The code added in the JavaScript Editor.

5. **Click OK in the JavaScript Editor.**

6. **Move the JavaScript action above the Submit a form action.** We didn't add a Submit a form action to the example form. However, if you have a form with a Submit a form action, be sure to move the JavaScript action above the Submit a form action in the Actions tab. You want the date field to be visible to the recipient of the submitted form, and you need to show the field before submitting it to make the field visible.

7. **Click Close to close the Button Field Properties.**

8. **Click the button.** If the script was added correctly to the button action, you should see the field appear with the current date from your system clock after clicking the button with the Hand tool.

9. **Clear the field, and change the General properties.** If the field works properly, clear the field data, open the General properties, click the Read Only check box, and choose Hidden from the Form Field drop-down menu.

10. **Save the file.**

The script shown in Figure 18.13 is a simple three-line code script. We assign variable *f* to the field where we want to add a new date. We show the field in line 2, and we add the date in line 3. After clicking the button to add a date, the form appears as shown in Figure 18.14.

After clicking the Submit button, the date from the system clock is added to a field and the field as made visible.

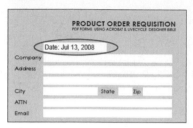

Custom Formatting Fields

You have a variety of formatting options when using the Format tab and writing scripts to create custom field formatting, as well as writing scripts to format fields when using calculation formulas. You might want to eliminate zeros that appear as defaults for calculated fields, add fixed responses to combo and list fields, format fields for accepting defined values, limit responses to fixed character lengths, and more.

Generally, scripts handling field formatting issues are written as Custom Format Script or Custom Calculation Scripts in the Format tab. Additionally, you can add some formatting to calculation scripts in the Calculate tab.

Eliminating zeros

Many forms authors want to eliminate default zeros from calculation formulas. Rather than have a field with no result appear as *0.00*, forms authors generally prefer having a null value in a field so the field appears empty.

Adding null values to fields

The *purchaseOrder.pdf* form we used in several examples in this chapter contains a combo box field at the top of the form, as shown in Figure 18.15. In this example, when the form recipient chooses an approved vendor from the combo box list the vendor name is added to the Company field appearing below the combo box.

We could add addresses in a JavaScript so when a vendor is selected, not only the vendor name is added to the Company field, but all the identifying information shown in Figure 18.15 is also added. We kept it simple to illustrate a point here, so we didn't add the additional information. For now, just be aware that additional lines of code can populate the remaining fields in this section on the form.

FIGURE 18.15

A form with a combo box is used to add a name to a text field.

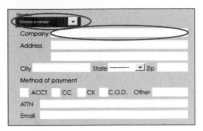

The combo box has a default value of *Choose a vendor*. For the Company field, you'll notice in Figure 18.15 that nothing appears in this field. The reason for this is that we added a null value to the Company field if the combo box value is *Choose a vendor*. Here's how we do it.

ON the CD-ROM To follow these steps, use the *purchaseOrder.pdf* form from the Chapter18 folder on the book's CD-ROM.

STEPS: Adding a Null Value to a Field

1. **Open a form in Acrobat having a combo box.** In our example, we used the *purchase Order.pdf* form from the book's CD-ROM.

2. **Open the *vendor.company* Text Field Properties window.** The Customer item field is the *vendor.company* field. Click the Select Object tool, and double-click this field to open the Text Field Properties window.

3. **Click the Calculate tab.**

4. **Add a JavaScript.** Click the Custom calculation script radio button, and click the Edit button to open the JavaScript Editor. Type the following code in the JavaScript Editor window, as shown in Figure 18.16:

```
1. var f = this.getField("vendor.choice");
2. if (f.value != "Choose a vendor")
3.    event.value = f.value;
4. else
5.    event.value = "";
```

5. **Click OK in the JavaScript Editor, and click Close in the Text Field Properties window.**

6. **Save the file.**

FIGURE 18.16

Type the code in the JavaScript Editor.

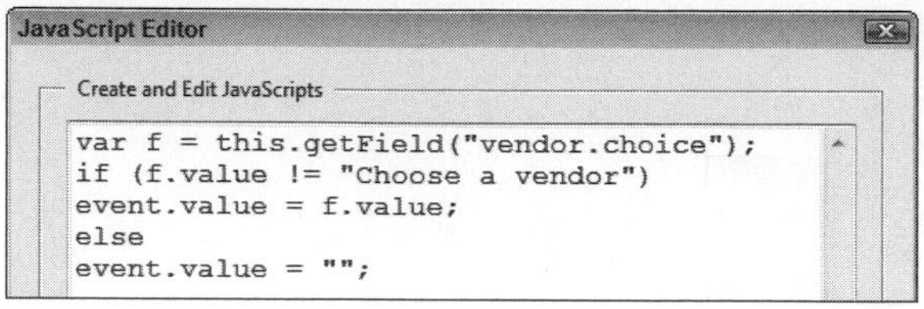

```
JavaScript Editor

Create and Edit JavaScripts

var f = this.getField("vendor.choice");
if (f.value != "Choose a vendor")
event.value = f.value;
else
event.value = "";
```

In the first line of code, we assign variable *f* to the combo box field. The default value for the field is *Choose a vendor*. In line 2, we set up an *if* condition. If the value of the combo box field is not *Choose a vendor,* line 3 in the script is executed where we get the value of the combo box and place it in the field where this script is written (the *vendor.company* field).

If the *f.value* is *Choose a vendor,* line 5 is executed. We place the value "" (a null value) in the field. If any item in the combo box other than the default value is chosen, the value shown in the combo box is added to the Company field, as shown in Figure 18.17.

FIGURE 18.17

If the form recipient selects any item other than the default value, the respective item is added to the Company field.

Replacing zeros with null values

A similar kind of script is used for eliminating zeros from calculated fields. You can handle this in a number of ways. You can add a custom format script in the Format tab, add a script in the Calculate tab, or add a Function at the document level and call the function from a format script. What you do, where you put it, and for what type of fields are important to know.

If you have a form that contains an integer, something like a quantity field, you format the field differently than when you format a field containing a calculation, something like (quantify * amount). As an example, look at the table in the *purchaseOrder.pdf* form we've worked with in this chapter and shown in Figure 18.18.

Notice that all the fields are empty and devoid of default zeros. In the Qty column, we use a custom format script to eliminate the zeros. In the Each, Item Total, and calculation fields at the bottom of the form, we add some code to the calculation formulas to eliminate zeros.

FIGURE 18.18

The table is shown from the *purchaseOrder.pdf* form.

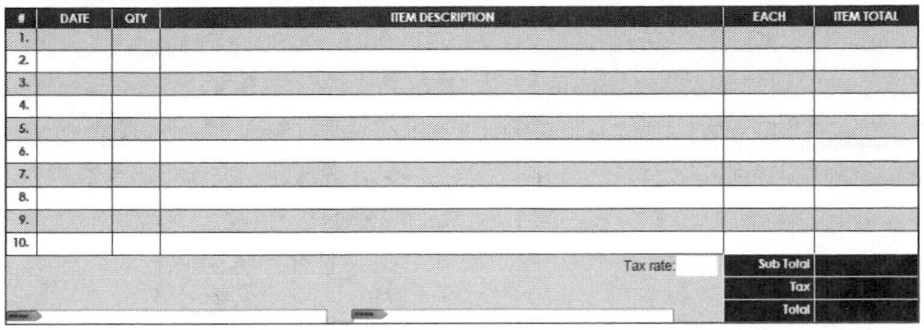

Why do we have two formatting controls on this form? The reason is that the Qty fields are not calcu-lated, so we cannot use a calculation script on these fields. When we add a custom format script to the fields, we're not formatting the fields for a number. In the remaining fields, we definitely need to format the fields as a number. If we do, we cannot add a custom format script in the Format tab. The Format tab permits only format fields using either a custom script or number formatting.

To make this clearer, follow these steps to add both formulas to the form.

ON the CD-ROM To follow these steps, use the *purchaseOrder.pdf* form from the Chapter18 folder on the book's CD-ROM.

STEPS: Eliminating Zeros Using Format and Calculation Scripts

1. **Open a form in Acrobat.** For the steps here, use the *purchaseOrder.pdf* form from the book's CD-ROM.

2. **Open the *qty.0* Text Field Properties.** This form contains all the scripts we cover in these steps. If you begin creating a new form, you'll want to add the format scripts before you create a table. The script will be duplicated when you use the Place Multiple Field command to populate a table without needing to modify the script for each field. To open the Text Field Properties window, double-click the field with the Select Object tool.

3. **Click the Format tab.**

4. **Add a Custom Format Script.** Click the Edit button for a Custom Format Script, and the JavaScript Editor opens. Type the following code:
   ```
   1. event.rc =/\d*/.test(event.change);
   ```

5. **Click OK in the JavaScript Editor.**

6. **Add a Custom Keystroke Script.** Click the Edit button for Custom Keystroke Script, and type the following code in the JavaScript Editor:
   ```
   1. event.value =event.value?event.value: "";
   ```

7. **Click OK in the JavaScript Editor.** You return to the Format tab with the scripts appearing as shown in Figure 18.19.

FIGURE 18.19

Click OK in the JavaScript Editor to return to the Format tab.

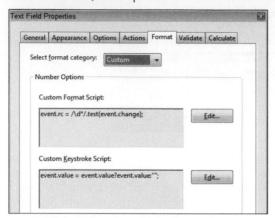

8. **Open the *each.0* Text Field Properties window.** Double-click the first field in the Each column with the Select Object tool to open the Text Field Properties window.

9. **Click the Calculate tab.**

10. **Add a JavaScript.** Click the Custom calculation script radio button, and click Edit to open the JavaScript Editor. Type the following code:

```
1. var f = this.getField("qty.0");
2. if (f.value == 0)
3. event.value ="";
```

11. **Click OK.**

12. **Add a JavaScript to the first field (*amount.0*) in the Item Total column.** Follow the same steps to add a Custom calculation script in the Calculate tab, and type the following code in the JavaScript Editor, as shown in Figure 18.20:

```
1. var f = this.getField("qty.0");
2. var g = this.getField("each.0");
3.
4. if (f.value != 0)
5.   event.value = f.value * g.value
6. else
7.   event.value = "";
```

13. **Click OK in the JavaScript Editor, and click Close in the Text Field Properties window.**

14. **Save the file.**

FIGURE 18.20

Type the JavaScript code for the *amount.0* field.

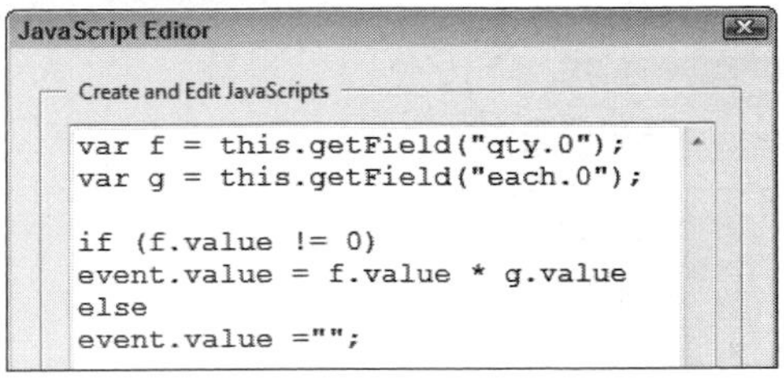

```
JavaScript Editor

Create and Edit JavaScripts

var f = this.getField("qty.0");
var g = this.getField("each.0");

if (f.value != 0)
event.value = f.value * g.value
else
event.value ="";
```

In the first script, we set the formatting for a non-calculated field having an integer value. If a formatted number needed to be added to this field, we couldn't use the format scripts used in the first set of JavaScripts.

In the second script, we look at the first field in the Quantity column (*qty.0*). If the value is zero, a null value is placed in the *each.0* field. We cannot use the same script for the *qty.0* field because we need to format the *each.0* field as a number with two decimal places.

In the third script for the *amount.0* field, we have similar conditions as the *each.0* field. This field also needs to have the field formatted as a number. Therefore, we add the script in the Calculate tab to look at the *qty.0* field. If the value is not zero, we execute a calculation formula to multiple *qty.0* times *each.0*. If the value *f* is zero, we add a null value to the *amount.0* field.

Unfortunately, the scripts you write for the Each column fields and the Item Total fields require you to add scripts individually to each field. You need to open the field's properties for each field in the respective rows (*each.1, each.2, amount.1, amount.2*) and add a JavaScript in the JavaScript Editor.

Creating fixed response options

We use the term *creating fixed response options* here to mean that when you make a selection from one combo box, a second combo box offers you fixed responses from the menu options. For example, if you have a list of choices in a combo box such as books, shirts, and pens, your response options for books might be a variety of titles, for shirts a variety of sizes, and for pens a variety of ink colors. When a choice is made for something like books, only book titles appear in a second combo box. Likewise, if you make a choice for shirts, only shirt sizes appear as choices for the same second combo box.

Using the *productOrder.pdf* form we've used in many steps in this chapter, you can see an example of fixed responses in combo boxes shown in Figure 18.21.

FIGURE 18.21

This form has two combo box fields. The second combo box field displays fixed responses according to the menu choice made in the first combo box field.

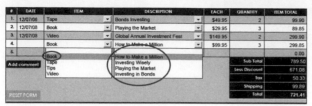

This type of setup for fixed responses has a number of applications for your forms. It's particularly useful when creating point of sale purchase forms. As you look over Figure 18.21, there are only four different sets of fields the form recipient can interact with.

The date fields are open for a form recipient to supply a date. The Item combo box fields are open for the form recipient to choose an item. The Description combo box fields are confined to choices based on the first combo box fields, and the form recipient selects an option from the list of fixed responses. The Quantity fields are open for the form recipient to indicate how many items to order. All the remaining fields in the table are marked Read Only. Prices are fixed, and calculations are performed by JavaScripts. This type of form limits user error through limited choices that a form recipient needs to make to complete the form.

Adding programmer's notes

Up to this point, we've dealt with scripts having fewer than ten lines of code. Simple scripts are easy to review and understand. However, when you write a substantial amount of code, when you plan to come back later to the scripts, or when other forms authors work with the forms, you'll want to add comments within the code to understand the routines.

We haven't added notes to the code in this chapter to try to keep the amount of text down so you can easily duplicate the routines. However, in the real world when you add JavaScripts to fields and functions, you'll want to make a habit out of adding programmer's comments.

To add comments to JavaScript code, you add two forward slashes where you want a comment to appear in the code such as:

```
// This routine calculates sales tax.
```

Or add code to a line such as:

```
var f = this.getField("tax"); //get the text field
```

When a routine is executed, the lines of code following // are ignored by JavaScript.

Creating a function

On the form shown in Figure 18.21, we created three separate functions. You can use multiple functions in a single script, but we broke this example down to three scripts to make it a bit easier to follow.

For the combo box fields on the *productOrder.pdf* file, we created two functions for formatting the fields. We also needed a third function for the Item Total fields.

Preceding the first function, we set up an array for the combo box fields. We opened the JavaScript Functions dialog box by choosing Advanced ➡ Document Processing ➡ Document JavaScripts. We typed *addItems* in the Script Name text box, and clicked the Edit button to open the JavaScript Editor. In the Editor, we added the following code for our array and first function:

```
1.  var oArray = {
    Book: [ ["-","None"], ["How to Make a Million",99.95],
    ["Investing Wisely",69.95], ["Playing the Market",29.95],
    ["Investing in Bonds",34.95]],
2.  Tape: [ ["-","None"], ["Stocks Investing",69.95], ["Bonds
    Investing",49.95], ["Commodities Investing",79.95],["Property
    Investing",139.95]],
3.  Video:  [ ["-","None"], ["Global Annual Investment Fest",149.95],
    ["Investing Wisely",159.95], ["Playing the Market",219.95],
    ["Staying Ahead of Inflation",139.95]],
4.  Tips:[ ["-","None"], ["Gold",39.95], ["Silver",29.95], ["Orange
    Juice",19.95],["Coffee",9.95]]
5.  };
6.  function SetDescriptionEntries()
7.  {
8.    if(event.willCommit)
9.    {
10.     var cRowName = event.target.name.split(".").shift();
11.     var list = oArray[event.value];
12.     if( (list != null) && (list.length > 0) )
13.       this.getField(cRowName + ".Description").setItems(list);
14.     else
15.     {
16.      this.getField(cRowName + ".Description").clearItems();
17.     }
18.     this.getField(cRowName + ".Each").value = 0;
19.    }
20. }
```

With 20 lines of code, you obviously want to add some programmer's comments if you create a script like this. We show you just the lines of code that are executed without any notation to simplify the demonstration.

In lines 1 through 4, we set up an array. The first item in each of the four lines of code is the name that appears in the first combo box fields. Therefore, the first combo box contains *Book, Tape, Video,* and *Tips*. Making a choice from the first combo box provides the options respective to the item you choose in the second combo box in the Description column. For example, if you choose *Book* in the Item combo box field in row one, the combo box for the Description row 1 options are *"How to Make a Million", 99.95, "Investing Wisely", 69.95,* and so on. The value after the name is the price that is placed in the Each column.

In line 6, we added a function named *SetDescriptionEntries()*. In line 10, we split the name of the field so we can use a loop to loop through the items beginning in line 11. Field names were added such as *Row1.Item, Row2.Item, Row3.Item,* and so on. Because the names aren't hierarchical, we needed to split the name to gain access to the number following *Row* for each field.

In line 12, we set the value of the *Each* column to zero to clear out any data that may have been there from another choice.

The second function we added was named *addDescription* for the Script Name in the JavaScript Functions dialog box, and we used *SetEachValue()* for the function name. This function sets the value for the *Each* column and was written as follows:

```
1. function SetEachValue()
2.  {
3.    if(!event.willCommit)
4.    {
5.      var cRowName = event.target.name.split(".").shift();
6.      var nSelection = 0;
7.      if(!isNaN(event.changeEx))
8.      nSelection = event.changeEx
9.      this.getField(cRowName + ".Each").value = nSelection;
10.   }
11. }
```

This script is set up to run using the Change Event of the previous function. It will not run on other events because the *event.willCommit* and *event.changeEx* parameters are used.

The third function we named *calculateTotal* in the JavaScript Functions dialog box, and we used *CalculateTotal()* for the function name. We use this function to calculate the totals for the Item Total column. The script was written as:

```
1. function CalculateTotal()
2.  {
3.    var cRowName = event.target.name.split(".").shift();
4.    event.value = this.getField(cRowName + ".Each").value * this.
   getField(cRowName + ".Qty").value;
5.  }
```

ON the CD-ROM The code is available in the *productOrder.pdf* file in the Chapter18 folder on the book's CD-ROM.

The code for the functions is contained in three separate document-level JavaScripts. Rather than analyze the code here, you can open the Advanced ➪ Document Processing ➪ Document JavaScripts menu command and click Edit for each of the individual functions.

Formatting the fields is easy after you add the functions. For the Item fields, we added a Custom Keystroke Script in the Format tab and used the first function name. The code was written as:

```
SetDescriptionEntries();
```

NOTE The name of the function is used in the JavaScript in the code samples. The name you use for the Script Name in the JavaScript Functions dialog box has nothing to do with the name of the function you address in the field properties.

The second field to format is the second combo box fields in the Description column. Again, a Custom keystroke Script was added in the Format properties. The Script was written as:

```
SetEachValue();
```

The last field where we used a function was the Item Total fields. We opened the Calculate tab on the fields in the Item Total column and added the following code as a Custom calculation script:

```
CalculateTotal();
```

Obviously, writing the functions is much more complex than the other scripts we've discussed in this chapter. It will take a bit of doing to duplicate the scripts on another form, especially if you're a novice programmer. You can copy the Item, Description, Each, Quantity, and Item Total Fields and the document-level JavaScripts and paste into a new form. Everything will work if you leave the field names and code unmodified.

The one item you can change is the array names. Just be certain to use the same syntax when you change the names. After you get some experience and study the scripts, you can begin to change variable names and values.

Moving items between lists

In Figure 18.22, you see a form with two list box fields. The master list on the left contains a list of personal attributes for an employee to list in the list box on the right. The list on the right is intended to be populated in a rank order, so a few buttons are added to move items in the right list up or down, delete an item, or clear all items to start over.

To make the buttons functional on this form, we added a simple function as a document-level JavaScript and a script for each button action.

ON the CD-ROM A modified version name *globalPerformanceList.pdf* of the *globalPerformance Review.pdf* form used in earlier chapters is found in the Chapter18 folder on the book's CD-ROM. Open the *globalPerformanceList.pdf* file from this folder to review the scripts found on page 4 of the form.

FIGURE 18.22

A form with two list boxes designed for swapping data

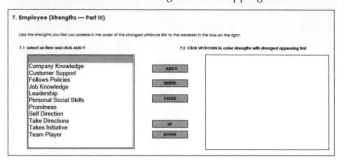

We started with a function added to a document-level JavaScript that we use in the Add button action. The script was written as follows:

```
1. function addToRankList(cEntry)
2.   {
3.     var oFld = this.getField("rankList");
4.     var bFound = false;
5.     for(var i=0;i<oFld.numItems;i++)
6.       {
7.         if(oFld.getItemAt(i,false) == cEntry)
8.           {
9.             bFound = true;
10.            break;
11.          }
12.      }
13.
14.    if(!bFound)
15.    {
16.      oFld.insertItemAt({cName:cEntry, nIdx:-1});
17.    }
18.  }
```

The script to add a selected item in the list box on the left to the list box on the right was written as a button field action as:

```
1. var oFld = this.getField("attributeList");
2. if(oFld)
3.   {
4.     var cEntry = oFld.getItemAt(oFld.currentValueIndices,false);
5.     addToRankList(cEntry);
6.   }
```

The Delete button action was scripted as:

```
1.  var oFld = this.getField("rankList");
2.  var prev = oFld.currentValueIndices;
3.  if(oFld.currentValueIndices > -1)
4.    {
5.      oFld.deleteItemAt(oFld.currentValueIndices);
6.      if(oFld.numItems > prev)
7.        oFld.currentValueIndices = prev;
8.      else if(oFld.numItems > 0)
9.        oFld.currentValueIndices = prev-1;
10.   }
```

To clear all items from the list box on the left, we added a single line of code on the Clear button action as:

```
1.  this.getField("rankList").clearItems();
```

To move a selected item up in the list on the right, we added the following script to the Up button action:

```
1.  oFld = this.getField("rankList");
2.  if(oFld)
3.  {
4.    var prevIdx = oFld.currentValueIndices;
5.    if(prevIdx > 0)
6.    {
7.      var curVal = oFld.getItemAt(prevIdx);
8.      oFld.deleteItemAt(prevIdx);
9.     oFld.insertItemAt({cName:curVal, nIdx:prevIdx-1});
10.     oFld.currentValueIndices = prevIdx - 1;
11.   }
12. }
```

The final script was added to the Down button action and written as:

```
1.  oFld = this.getField("rankList");
2.  if(oFld)
3.  {
4.    var prevIdx = oFld.currentValueIndices;
5.    if( (prevIdx >= 0) && (prevIdx < (oFld.numItems -1)) )
6.    {
7.      var curVal = oFld.getItemAt(prevIdx);
8.      oFld.deleteItemAt(prevIdx);
9.      oFld.insertItemAt({cName:curVal, nIdx:prevIdx+1});
10.     oFld.currentValueIndices = prevIdx + 1;
11.   }
12. }
```

Although fairly extensive, these scripts can be easily copied and pasted into your forms. If you change field names or values, you need to modify the code. If you copy the document-level script, add a function with the same name we used *addToRankList(cEntry)*, and copy the fields, the only edits you need to make are in the *attributeList* list box field.

Unlike the scripts used for creating fixed responses (see the section "Creating fixed response options" earlier in this chapter), you don't need to create an array. Open the first list box shown in Figure 18.22, and edit the Options tab shown in Figure 18.23.

FIGURE 18.23

To change the items list in the first list box, edit the List Box Properties Options tab items.

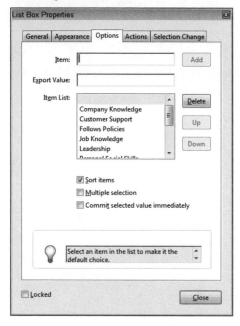

Delete the existing items, and add new items to the list. Be certain to select the item you want to appear as a default before closing the List Box Properties window.

CROSS-REF For more information on creating list boxes, see Chapter 7.

When you click an item in the left list box on the *globalPerformanceList.pdf* form, the item is added to the list on the right side of the page, as shown in Figure 18.24.

FIGURE 18.24

Click an item in the box on the left, and click the Add button to copy the item to the list on the right.

Creating Application Response Dialog Boxes

An application response dialog box prompts a form recipient for a response in a dialog box. After the user types a response, you can add the data to a field or perform an action based on the response data. You might use an application response dialog box for a form recipient to add a social security number or credit card number, type a date or name, or enter some other kind of data. In the response dialog box, you can display the format you want the form recipient to use.

Fields for credit card numbers are good candidates for adding this kind of action to a form. People are not always certain whether to type nnnn-nnnn-nnnn-nnnn or nnnnnnnnnnnnnnnn for a credit card number. You can display the format you want the form recipient to use in the application response dialog box to make it clear whether dashes are used in the number or not. Additionally, JavaScript can evaluate the response, and if it doesn't meet an acceptable response, the form recipient can be alerted and prompted again to fill in the field properly.

Using an application response dialog box for a name field

Assume you want a form recipient to type a name as last, first. We'll use a simple application response to set up the conditions for adding a name to a text field. To see how an application response dialog box is added to a form, follow these steps.

577

For the following steps, we used the *globalPerformanceList.pdf* form that you can find in the Chapter18 folder on the book's CD-ROM.

STEPS: Adding an Application Response Dialog Box to a Form

1. **Open a form in Acrobat.** You can use any form you like to follow these steps. In our example, we used the *globalPerformanceList.pdf* form on the book's CD-ROM.

2. **Open the Text Field Properties window.** On page 1 in the sample form, we used the employee name field to add our JavaScript. The design of the form does not inform the form recipient whether the name should be typed as first and last or last, first. We use an application response dialog box for the form recipient to add the name and show a message in the dialog box for how the name should be added to the field. Double-click the *employee.name* field with the Select Object tool to open the Text Field Properties window.

3. **Click the Actions tab.** We add the JavaScript in the Actions tab.

4. **Choose On Focus from the Select Trigger drop-down menu.** We want the script to be executed when the form recipient tabs into the field (or clicks the mouse cursor in the field). Using the On Focus trigger executes the JavaScript when a form recipient enters the field.

5. **Add a JavaScript.** Choose Run a JavaScript from the Select Action drop-down menu, and click the Add button to open the JavaScript Editor. Type the following code as shown in Figure 18.25:

```
1. var t = event.target; // the target field
2. var cResponse = app.response({
3.    cQuestion: "Type your name Last, First",
4.    cTitle: "Name",
5.    cDefault: "Name not added",
6.    cLabel: "Type your name"});
7.    {
8.       if ( cResponse == null){ // if Cancel is selected
9.       app.alert ("You cancelled adding your name?");
10.      cResponse = "";
11.   }
12.      else
13.
      app.alert("You typed your name as: \""+cResponse+"\" \n\n Tab
      out of the field to register your name",2);
14.   }
15. t.value = cResponse; // places the data from the dialog to the
      target field
```

6. **Click OK in the JavaScript Editor, and click Close in the Text Field Properties window.**

7. **Save the form.**

We begin this script by assigning the target value (the *employee.name* field) to variable *t*. Lines 2 through 6 set up the application response dialog box formatting. The application response dialog box appears as shown in Figure 18.26. The default text defined in line 5 appears when the dialog box opens.

In line 8, we check to see if the form recipient clicked Cancel. If true, the alert message in line 9 opens in an application alert dialog box, as shown in Figure 18.27.

FIGURE 18.25

Type the code in the JavaScript Editor.

```
Java Script Editor
  Create and Edit JavaScripts
  var t = event.target; // the target field
  var cResponse = app.response({
  cQuestion: "Type your name Last, First",
  cTitle: "Name",
  cDefault: "Name not added",
  cLabel: "Type your name"});
  {
  if ( cResponse == null){ // if Cancel is selected
      app.alert ("You cancelled adding your name?");
      cResponse = "";
  }
  else
    app.alert("You typed your name as: \""+cResponse+"\" \n\n Tab
  out of the field to register your name",2);
  }
  t.value = cResponse; // places the data from the dialog to the
  target field
```

FIGURE 18.26

The application response dialog box as it appears from the code used to format the dialog box

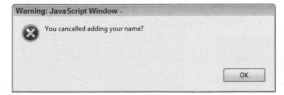

Warning: JavaScript Window - Name

Type your name Last, First

Type your name | Name not added

OK   Cancel

Warning: JavaScript Window

FIGURE 18.27

If the form recipient clicks Cancel in the application response dialog box, an application alert dialog box opens.

Warning: JavaScript Window -

You cancelled adding your name?

OK

If the form recipient doesn't click Cancel, line 13 is executed. In line 13, another application alert dialog box opens confirming the form recipient action, as shown in Figure 18.28. Notice the item \n\n in line 13. This addition to the code is a switch that forces a carriage return so the second line appears as shown in Figure 18.28. The last line of code takes the value typed in the application response dialog box and copies it to the target field.

FIGURE 18.28

After the form recipient clicks OK, another dialog box opens confirming the action.

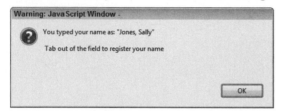

Using an application response dialog box for a credit card number

We'll use a script similar to the application response dialog box for a name field to demonstrate how a credit card number might be formatted. For this script, we evaluate the response and if the response doesn't meet the text string length, we instruct JavaScript to place a null value in the target field.

Follow these steps to script a field meeting these conditions.

ON the CD-ROM Use the *productOrder.pdf* form from the Chapter18 folder on the book's CD-ROM to follow these steps.

STEPS: Using an Application Response for a Credit Card Number

1. **Open a form in Acrobat.** Use a form where you need a credit card number filled in by a form recipient. In our example, we used the *productOrder.pdf* form from the book's CD-ROM.

2. **Open the Text Field Properties window for the Credit Card field.** In our example, we double-clicked the Credit Card number field on the *productOrder.pdf* form shown in Figure 18.29.

FIGURE 18.29

Locate a credit card field, and open the Text Field Properties window.

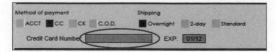

3. **Add a JavaScript in the Actions tab, and use an On Focus Mouse Trigger.** Follow the same steps as used in the section "Using an application response dialog box for a name field" earlier in this chapter. Type the following script in the JavaScript Editor, as shown in Figure 18.30:

```
1. var t = event.target; // the target field
2. var cResponse = app.response({
3.   cQuestion: "Type your credit card number using numbers only
   and without dashes",
4.   cTitle: "Credit Card",
5.   cLabel: "Type your credit card number"});
6.   {
7.     if ( cResponse == null){ // if Cancel is selected
8.     app.alert ("You cancelled adding your number?");
9.     cResponse = "";
10.  }
11.    else {
12.    if (cResponse.length != 16){
13.    app.alert("Type the complete number without dashes.");
14.    cResponse = "";}
15.    else
16.    app.alert("You typed your card number as: \""+cResponse+"\"
   \n\n Tab out of the field to register the card number",2);}
17.  }
18. t.value = cResponse; // places the data from the dialog to the
   target field
```

4. **Exit the windows, and save the file.**

FIGURE 18.30

Type the code in the JavaScript Editor.

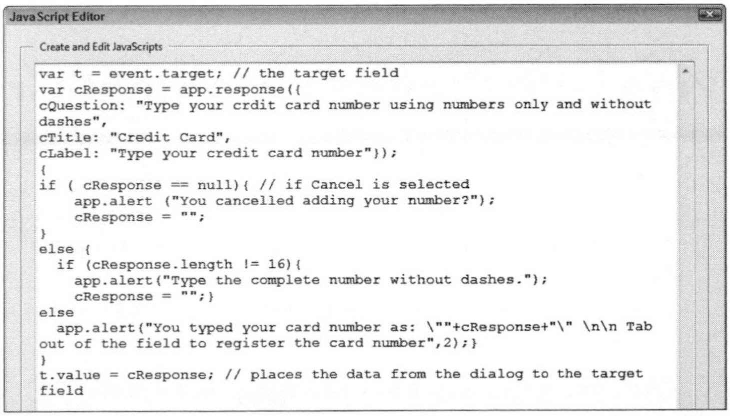

Setting up the application response dialog box is the same as the code we used to create the application response dialog shown in Figure 18.25 earlier in this chapter. Beginning in line 12, we have a little twist in the script shown in Figure 18.30. When the script is executed, the application response dialog box opens, as shown in Figure 18.31.

FIGURE 18.31

The application response dialog box opens and prompts the form recipient to add a credit card number.

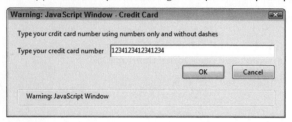

In Figure 18.31, the message in the dialog box asks the form recipient to type numbers without dashes. In line 12 of our code, we simply check to see if the number of characters are not equal to 16 (total numbers needed for the credit card without dashes). If a form recipient leaves off a number or types the number with dashes, the value in the response dialog box is different than 16. We use line 13 to inform the form recipient in an application dialog box that the number needs to be without dashes, and line 14 clears the target field.

If the numbers total 16 for the text string, line 16 is executed confirming adding 16 numbers and the response value is added to the target field in line 18.

This example demonstrates one method for evaluating responses and the kind of flexibility you have with data handling using application response dialog boxes.

Working with Optional Content Groups

In Chapter 13, we talked about creating forms with Adobe PDF Layers. We discussed a number of different types of forms you may create having layers, and we used the form shown in Figure 18.32 as one example for a form benefiting from layers. The form is designed for an inquiry for a potential homebuyer. The buttons on the right side of the form are used to display the house diagram in a number of different views by showing and hiding individual layers. For example, a potential buyer may be interested in looking at the house plan without the fixtures. By clicking a button, the layer containing fixtures is hidden.

In the Actions tab for field properties, you have an action to show and hide layers using the Set layer visibility action. Generally, this action takes care of showing and hiding layers. However, if you create interactive elements in a program like Adobe InDesign, the button field objects are displayed only on the layers where they were added in InDesign, making it impossible to use the Set layer visibility action. In other situations, you may want to execute different actions based on the choice of a layer's visibility. With these types of conditions, you need to use JavaScript to show/hide layers.

ON the CD-ROM We use the *housePlan.pdf* file in the Chapter18 folder on the book's CD-ROM to demonstrate some uses for working with forms having layers and JavaScripts needed to change layer views.

The Button.6.Page.1 field contains a JavaScript to toggle on and off the text layer. When you open the Actions tab, select Run a JavaScript and click the Edit button, you find the following code displayed in the JavaScript Editor:

```
1. var docOCGs = this.getOCGs();
2. for (var i=0; i < docOCGs.length; i++)
3.    {
4.      if(docOCGs[i].name == "Text")
5.      {
6.        docOCGs[i].state = !docOCGs[i].state;
7.      }
8.    }
```

FIGURE 18.32

A form used for a potential homebuyer where the house plan can be viewed in different ways by showing and hiding layers

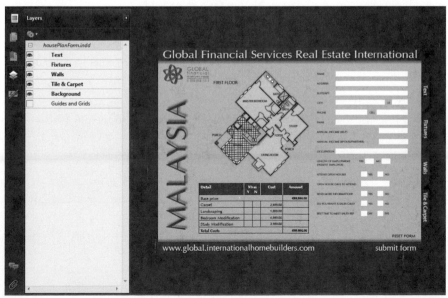

The remaining buttons use the same code with a single change in line 4 where we use a name respective to the layer we want to hide. When you want to display a hidden layer, you click the button again, and line 6 changes the state. Therefore, if a layer is hidden, changing the state makes the layer visible.

This code is relatively easy to copy and paste into your forms. Just make a single change to line 4 using the names of the layers you use on your form. As discussed in Chapter 13, you can create multi-lingual forms, add Adobe Flash animations for displaying diagrams and showing instructions, add help information on separate layers, and use this method in a number of other ways.

Summary

- When forms are enabled with Adobe Reader usage rights, you can use JavaScript to create new annotations in a document.

- Using a simple JavaScript in the JavaScript Console, you can obtain coordinates of annotations added to a form.

- Summing columns and rows using JavaScript enables you to perform multiple calculations for the same event and eliminate zeros from calculated fields.

- You can date stamp a form from a submit form action that uses the form recipient's computer system clock to add a date for when a form is submitted.

- Fixed response options provide you with a means for reducing user error in filling in a form and limiting responses to options chosen for a given field.

- When writing JavaScripts, be sure to add programmer's comments to explain each routine with notes.

- Functions provide you an option for accessing routines from multiple fields without having to write the same routine for each field.

- Using JavaScript, you can add data from one list box to another.

- Application response dialog boxes let you help clarify proper data formatting when a form recipient completes a form.

- You can use JavaScript to change layer visibility.

Chapter 19

Creating JavaScripts for Acrobat Users

When you design forms for distribution to an unknown audience of users, you'll want to be certain your forms use program features and JavaScripts that can be performed by users of Acrobat and Adobe Reader.

If you have a known audience of Acrobat only users such as coworkers in an enterprise environment, you can add JavaScripts for a number of different actions with more dynamic features on forms that can be used only with Acrobat.

You may work in an accounting office where you need to create calculation tapes to show values calculated for auditing purposes, or need to create additional pages on a time and billing form, or perhaps you want to send data from one form to another form for summarizing data.

If all your form recipients use Acrobat, you have some more options for adding these features that can be performed only by the Acrobat users. The real power for dynamic interactivity that can be used by both Adobe Reader users and Acrobat users rests with Adobe LiveCycle Designer. But, if you're an Acrobat Forms author, you still have some opportunities for creating some dynamic type of interactive forms using Acrobat.

Beginning in Chapter 20 we introduce Adobe LiveCycle Designer, where you find the best in regard to dynamic forms. To end this part of the book on Acrobat Forms, we talk about creating JavaScripts that can be used only with Acrobat users.

IN THIS CHAPTER

Adding new fields to forms

Working with page templates

Sending data to summary forms

Customizing menus

Adding Fields via JavaScript

As we explained in Chapter 18, almost all new content added to a PDF file cannot be performed in Adobe Reader. We talked about adding comments in Adobe Reader via JavaScripts, but other items such as adding fields, creating bookmarks, and adding new pages are accomplished only in Acrobat unless a PDF document is enabled with Adobe Reader usage rights.

When working with an Acrobat only audience you may find adding new fields to a form based on certain actions to be a welcome opportunity. Adding new content that can be used by Adobe Reader users is something you can do with Adobe LiveCycle Designer as we explain in Chapters 26 and 27. When creating Acrobat Forms, you need to limit your forms distribution to Acrobat users if you add JavaScripts to add new fields on a form.

You might work in or serve clients in an accounting office, a law office, an engineering firm, an advertising and marketing agency, or other professional group of users who work with Acrobat Standard or one of the Pro products. Rather than distribute forms to these users for form fill in and returns, you might create forms for utilitarian purposes such as time and billing sheets, day planners, appointment calendars, tracking client histories, or any number of different forms for similar uses.

As an example, look at Figure 19.1. This form was designed for a law office to accumulate time and billing information. The form has an *In* time and an *Out* time for each row, a total time field to calculate the row total time, a combo box for choosing the individual working on an aspect of the case, an open field for the form user to type the rate that corresponds to the individual selected in the combo box, a description field for typing the service description, and an amount column for calculating the product of the time and rate.

Designing the form

The form contains seven rows for calculating time and billing for a given client for the time period which is one month. Obviously, most law offices need more than seven lines of billing information. Therefore, a button exists on the form to create new pages as needed.

> **CROSS-REF**   To add more pages to a form, see the section "Spawning Pages from Templates" later in this chapter.

When an attorney completes page one of this form, the *New Page* button action creates a new page on the form. When a new page is created we're going to do some things with the buttons on the bottom of the page shown in Figure 19.2. The *Create Summary* button exports data from the form to a summary document. We want to keep this button on all pages on the form so we can export data per client to a summary form.

> **CROSS-REF**   For information on exporting data from this form to a summary form, see the section "Sending Data to Secondary Forms" later in this chapter.

The *New Page* button creates a new page in the document. The next page added to the file is identical to page one including the buttons. Therefore, we don't need the Next Page button on subsequent pages.

FIGURE 19.1

A worksheet form used for calculating time and billing for a law office professional.

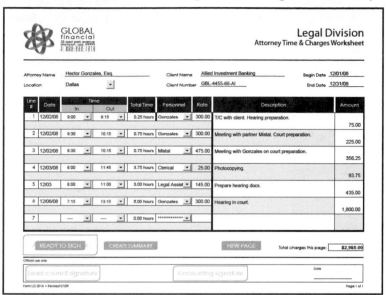

FIGURE 19.2

The Next Page and Ready to Sign buttons on the first page are no longer necessary when a new page is created.

Create a Digital Signature field   Delete fields

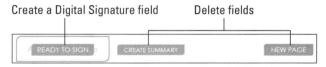

The *Ready to Sign* button adds a digital signature to the document. We didn't want to create a digital signature field on the form and have that field duplicated with each new page added to the form. We want only a single digital signature field to appear on the form. Therefore we use JavaScript to create the signature field, but the field is created only when the form user clicks the Ready to Sign button. When the form user clicks this button a new signature field is added on the last page of the form and the button action also deletes the *Ready to Sign* button. After the form is signed, the form user clicks the Submit Form button to submit the form to the law office accounting department.

Quite a few JavaScripts are added to this form. Some of the scripts work in Adobe Reader such as the calculation scripts in the table and, if the form is enabled with Adobe Reader usage rights, the JavaScripts used to delete fields work. The two things you cannot do in Adobe Reader are adding new fields and creating new pages. You need Acrobat Standard Pro or Pro Extended to perform these tasks.

Understanding spawned fields

When you create a new page on a form you use the *spawnPageFromTemplate* object. As new pages are spawned, you can make a choice for renaming fields or keeping the field names the same on each new page. For a form where you need to add unique data for the data fields, such as our form shown in Figure 19.1, you must instruct JavaScript to rename the fields when new pages are created.

CROSS-REF To write JavaScripts to spawn pages from templates and understand how templates are created, see the section "Spawning Pages from Templates" later in this chapter.

In terms of preparing a form for spawning new pages, you need to understand how JavaScript renames fields before you write and test routines that spawn new pages. Hence, we'll tackle the job of working with the calculations formulas and other routines on the example form before we start talking about spawning new pages.

When a new page is spawned from a template and fields on the page are renamed, JavaScript needs a way to easily rename fields. If you have a field such as *total* on page one and create a new page without renaming the field, the new page contains a second field named *total*. Any data you add to either field is duplicated in the second field. Therefore it's critical to rename fields when new pages are added to a form.

When JavaScript renames fields you'll see a field name such as *P0.newPage.totalField*. The first character in the field name is a constant. *P* appears on all field names when a page is spawned from a template. The *0* is derived from the page number. Since JavaScript is zero based, the first page would have a zero following the constant. The *newPage* item in the example field name is the name of the template. When you create templates you provide template names. You can use any name you like and the name used for the template is used for part of the field name. The last part of the example name is *totalField*. This is a field name. Therefore all fields on a page using a similar example would be named *P0.newPage.* followed by the individual field names.

Calculating fields using field names from spawned pages

Let's say you have a field called *item* and another field called *quantity*. In a total column you want the product of *item* and *quantity* for the event.value. Let's further presume you have a template you named as *myTemplate*.

When a page is spawned, the *item* name is changed to *P1.myTemplate.item* and the *quantity* name is changed to *P1.myTemplate.quantity* for page one (this follows page zero). On page two, the names would appear as *P2.myTemplate.item* and *P2.myTemplate.quantity*. As each new page is added to the form, the unique identifier is the page number. Therefore you need to write a calculation JavaScript that takes into account the page number in order to write a formula that works on each new spawned page.

The code you would use to calculate a product, might appear as:

```
1. var oPage = this.pageNum;
2. var oItem = this.getField("P" + oPage + ".mytemplate.item";
3. var oQuantity = this.getField("P" + oPage + ".mytemplate.
   quantity";
4. event.value = oItem.value * oQuantity.value;
```

In the first line of code we set the variable *oPage* to the current page number (*this.pageNum*). In line 2 we get the field *P1.myTemplate.item* (if the page number is 1) and in line 3 we get the field *P1.my Template.quantity* (again if the page number is 1). The fourth line of code puts the product value in the target field. As each page is spawned the variable oPage is used to identify the unique page numbers.

You have a bit of a challenge when designing a form like the one shown earlier in Figure 19.1. When you add fields to a form, you can't use a field name like *P0.mytemplate.item*. Yet the formulas you write need to use such names for the calculations to work. You need to create a little work-around to set up the form properly. Generally, you design a form as follows:

STEPS: Creating a Form for Spawning Pages

1. **Create fields on a form.** Your first step is to create a form like you would any other form. You use field names such as *item, quantity, total, employee.name, employee.address,* and so on. When you create tables you create them the same way as creating any other form. You may have fields with names like *total.0, total.1, total.2,* and so on.

2. **Write the formulas and button actions.** This is the most difficult task because you can't test the formulas. You have to use the field names JavaScript will create when a page is spawned. Try to do the best you can, realizing that you'll make some modifications to the code later.

3. **Add a blank page.** Insert a page preceding the page where your fields appear. You can use the File ⇨ Create PDF ⇨ From Blank Page command and drag the page thumbnail to the pages panel in your form. Make sure the page is the first page on the form.

4. **Copy the button that spawns a new page and paste on the blank page.** You can bypass pasting a button into a blank page by using the JavaScript Console to use the same code to spawn a new page. However, adding the button to a new page keeps the JavaScript code accessible in case you use the Console to test other scripts.

5. **Create a template.** Navigate to page 2 and create a template from the page containing the form fields. To create a template choose Advanced ⇨ Document Processing ⇨ Page Templates. When the Page Templates dialog box opens, type a name for your template and click the Add button.

6. **Hide the template.** Later in this chapter in the section "Spawning Pages from Templates" we cover creating templates. For now, realize that this step needs to be performed in the order shown here. You needed to create a blank new page because you cannot hide all pages on a form. At least one page must be visible. To hide the template click the eye icon in the Page Templates dialog box and click OK.

7. **Spawn a page.** Click the button or execute a script that spawns a new page while renaming fields. At this point you have two pages on the form—the blank page and the second page that was spawned from a template.

8. **Delete the blank page.** You'll see that there are two pages on the form. When templates are hidden they don't show up as part of the total pages on the form. Open the Pages panel and from a context menu opened on the blank page, choose Delete Pages. Click OK when a dialog box opens to confirm the action.

9. **Rename the fields.** Because you had a blank page on the form, the spawned page became page 1 (following page zero). The field names for the page appear as *P1.myTemplate.myField*. You want to change the *P1* to a *P0* as shown in Figure 19.3 because you have only one page on the form and the page number is zero. Choose Forms⇨Add or Edit Fields to open Form Editing Mode. In the Fields panel, choose Sort⇨Alphabetical Order. When the order is sorted the top of the Filed panel shows *P1* for the parent name. Click this name and change it to *P0*.

FIGURE 19.3

Change the parent name from *P0* to *P1* in the Fields panel in Form Editing Mode.

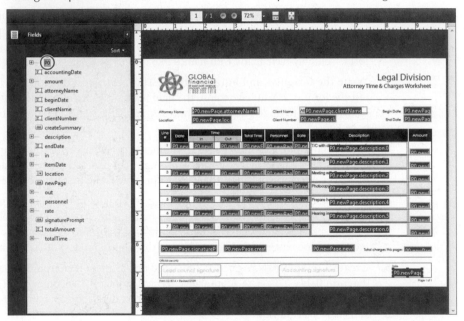

10. **Test the formulas.** Any changes in the formulas must be duplicated on the page template. You can copy/paste fields after showing the template and rename the fields to the original field names you have on the template page.

NOTE Renaming fields to *P0* in the Fields panel is an optional step. You can leave the fields at *P1* but things get more complicated if you do. If the page number is zero and the fields are *P1* fields, you have a mismatch and need to compensate by subtracting one from the *this.pageNum* object. With just a quick change to the parent name you can simplify getting the page number and keeping things straight as you write the JavaScript code.

TIP You can create all your calculations on page 0 (zero). Show the template page and delete all the fields on this page. When ready to duplicate the fields on page 0 you can select all fields and from a context menu choose Duplicate. The fields are duplicated in the exact same position on the target page. You then need to rename the template fields back to the root names.

Calculating time

On our example form shown in Figure 19.1 we have two columns of combo box fields with options for choosing time in 15-minute increments as shown in Figure 19.4. The time begins at 5:00AM and ends at midnight on a 24-hour clock. In the *Total Time* column we calculate the amount of time between the *In* and *Out* choices. The field formatting and calculation results work the same in Adobe Reader as they do in Acrobat.

FIGURE 19.4

The *Total Time* column calculates the amount of time from selections made in the *In* and *Out* combo boxes.

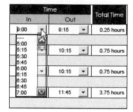

ON the CD-ROM The *globalAttorneySpawnRaw.pdf* file shown in Figure 19.1 is contained in the Chapter 19 folder on the book's CD-ROM. Use this file to view the field formatting and calculation formulas discussed in this chapter.

The *In* and *Out* fields are formatted as None and there are no calculations in these fields. In the *Total Time* column, we use a Custom Format in the Text Field Properties Format tab. The script we added to the fields in this column was written as:

```
event.value = util.printf("%.2f", event.value) + "hours"
```

This script is used to format the number with a decimal place and two decimal values. You can add whatever you like between the quotes in the text string. For combo box fields, *printf("%.2f"* formats a value to a string and sets the face value for combo box fields. We added *hours* because we're calculating hours and fractions of hours in the fields in this column.

For the *Total Time* fields we used the following script in a JavaScript Function:

```
1. function doCalculate()
2. {
3.    var aNameParts = event.targetName.split(".");
4.    var cPostFix = aNameParts.pop();
5.    var cPage = aNameParts.shift();
6.
7. // Test for valid Page. i.e. Skip calculation from raw template
8. if(/^P\d/.test(cPage))
9.    {
10.     var aIn = this.getField(cPage + ".newPage.in." + cPostFix);
11.     var aOut = this.getField(cPage + ".newPage.out." + cPostFix);
12.     event.value = (aOut.currentValueIndices -
            aIn.currentValueIndices)/4;
13.  }
14. }
```

What you see in the first eight lines of code is not needed to calculate the template fields. If we didn't add these lines of code an error would be reported in the JavaScript Console and the calculations for additional pages would duplicate values when we come to calculating the Amount column.

In lines 10 and 11 we get the In and Out times on the current page. The *currentValueIndices* object returns the options-array indices of the strings that are the value of a list box or combo box. The fields in the combo box are listed as 0, 1, 2, 3, and so on. The *currentValueIndices* object passes an integer that is the 0-based index of the string in the options array. The actual value is the value assigned to the index position. Therefore, if line 2 in the first combo box is 5:15 and line 7 in the second combo box is 6:45 we can easily subtract the values using the *currentValueIndices* object without converting the time values to date objects and converting the result to a number. In line 12 we use the *currentValueIndices* object and since we want to report time in 15-minute intervals, we divide by 4.

In the Total Time fields on the template page we simply called the JavaScript function by adding to the Calculate tab the following:

```
doCalculate();
```

Over in the *Amount* column we set up a function to calculate the product of the *Rate* times the *Total Time*. Open the Document Level JavaScripts and click Edit on the doAmountCalcs name. The function name is *doAmountCalcs* and the script for the function was written as:

```
1. function doAmountCalcs()
2. {
3.     var aNameParts = event.targetName.split(".");
```

```
4.      var cPostFix = aNameParts.pop();
5.      var cPage = aNameParts.shift();
6.
7.// Test for valid Page. i.e. Skip calculation from raw template
8.      if(/^P\d/.test(cPage))
9.       {
10.          var aRate = this.getField(cPage + ".newPage.rate." +
                 cPostFix);
11.         var aTime = this.getField(cPage + ".newPage.totalTime." +
                 cPostFix);
12.         event.value = (aRate.value * aTime.value);
13.      }
14.    }
```

We begin by setting up this function to again split the field names and skip calculations on the first page in lines 1 through 8. In lines 9 through line 12 we calculate the product of the rate and total time fields.

At the bottom of the page use again another function. Look in the JavaScript Functions dialog box and click Edit on the *doAmountTotals* name in the list. The function name we used in the Calculate tab is *doAmountTotals()*; The script was written as:

```
1. function doAmountTotals()
2. {
3.   var aNameParts = event.targetName.split(".");
4.   var cPostFix = aNameParts.pop();
5.   var cPage = aNameParts.shift();
6.
7.// Test for valid Page. i.e. Skip calculation from raw template
8. if(/^P\d/.test(cPage))
9.   {
10.     var a = this.getField(cPage + ".newPage.amount").getArray();
11.     var total = 0;
12.     for (i = 0; i < a.length; i++)
13.        total += a[i].value;
14.     event.value = total;
15.   }
16. }
```

This script is similar to the scripts we talked about in Chapter 18 where we set up an array to calculate fields in a column. The only difference here is using the same initial lines of code we used in the preceding scripts to bypass calculating the template page.

By using three functions to make our calculations for the time, time and rate products, and total time values we can easily add the functions to the fields on the first page and the template page. If we have to do any debugging or editing, the functions are assigned to the fields and changes to the functions are immediately updated on all the fields where the functions are assigned.

CROSS-REF **For more information on using arrays to sum columns of data, see Chapter 18.**

A few miscellaneous items remain on the *globalAttorneySpawnRaw.pdf* form on the book's CD-ROM. The attorney name and the location fields at the top of the form would typically use the same input values from the given form user. Therefore on the template page we simply took the value typed on the first page and used it as an *event.value* for the remaining fields for attorney name and location for all spawned pages. We used the following script as a custom calculation script in the Calculate tab on the template page for the attorney name field:

```
1. var attorneyName = this.getField("P0.newPage.attorneyName");
2. event.value = attorneyName.value;
```

Notice in line 1 we get the precise field name for the first page field and take the value of the field in line 2 and use it for the *event.value*. The location field combo box field on the template page was created using the same script. In the first line of code we set the *attorneyName* variable to the combo box field on the first page.

Using the addField Object

All the scripts up to this point work with Adobe Reader. Some of the next few scripts don't work with Adobe Reader—particularly the script we use to add a new field to the form. In Figure 19.5 you see a place on the form for a digital signature and in the top-right corner of the form we want a date added when the form is signed. Atop the area where we need to add a signature is a button. This button is used to hold the JavaScripts to add new fields on the form. Since this form may have many pages, we want the digital signature and date fields added to just the last page in the file.

We could add these fields to the template page and delete the fields on pages when new pages are spawned so only the last page in the file would contain the two fields. Deleting and adding fields works for Adobe Reader users if the file is enabled with Adobe Reader usage rights. But, because the Reader user cannot spawn new pages, it's just as easy to add the fields when a form recipient is ready to sign the form.

To understand more on how to add fields to a form, do the following.

ON the CD-ROM **For these steps we use the *globalAttorneySpawnRaw.pdf* file in the Chapter19 folder on the book's CD-ROM. There's another file on the CD-ROM named *globalAttorneySpawnPopulated.pdf*. This form is used later in this chapter in the section "Sending Data to Secondary Forms." To follow these steps use the *globalAttorneySpawnRaw.pdf* file. The *Ready to Sign* button field on this form has all the JavaScripts we explain in this section. You can delete the button and add a new button to follow the steps.**

FIGURE 19.5

The form shows an area where a field is needed.

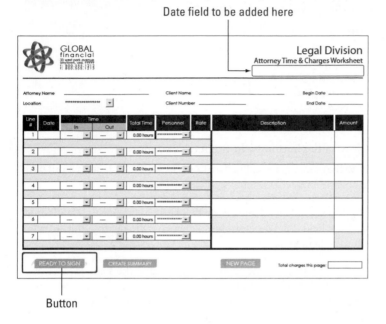

Date field to be added here

Button

STEPS: Adding Fields to a Form Using JavaScript

1. **Open a form in Acrobat.** For these steps we use the *globalAttorneySpawnRaw.pdf* file from the book's CD-ROM.

2. **Add a button field to the form.** On the example form a button exists. If you want to follow the steps here, you can delete the *Ready to Sign* button at the bottom of the form and create a new button. We'll use a button on the first page in the form to walk through the steps. To make the form more functional you'd have to add the button on both the template page and the page in view.

3. **Get the coordinates for the digital signature field.** Open the Comment & Markup toolbar and draw a rectangle with the Rectangle Comment tool where you want a signature field to be added on the form. Open the JavaScript Console (Ctrl/⌘+J) and type the following script to get the rectangle coordinates. Keep the JavaScript Console open as you write the button action script in Step 5. Press the Num Pad Enter key to execute the script in the JavaScript Console.

   ```
   this.getAnnots()[0].rect;
   ```

4. **Delete the Rectangle comment.** Click the Rectangle comment with the Select Object tool and press Delete.

5. **Create a button and open the Button Field Properties and add a new JavaScript action in the Actions tab.** Choose Run a JavaScript from the Select Action drop-down menu and click Add to open the JavaScript Editor. For line 5 look at the JavaScript Console and add the coordinates you see in the Console.

6. **Add the following script:**

```
1. var c = this.addField({
2.    cName: "attorneySignature",
3.    cFieldType: "signature",
4.    nPageNum: this.pageNum,
5.    oCoords: [35,74,176,112]
6. })
```

7. **Click OK and click Close in the Button Field Properties window.**

8. **Save the file with a new filename.** Choose File Save As and save the file with a different filename. Keep the file open to follow additional steps in this section.

In line 1 we use the addField object to add a field. In line 2 we define the name for the field. Line 3 sets the field type to a digital signature field. Line 4 determines what page the field is added to and in line 5 we get the coordinates for the field rectangle.

We took care of the digital signature field in the previous steps. We'll add to the same JavaScript by continuing steps to create the text field in the top-right corner of the form. Once again you need to get the coordinates for the text field rectangle. Use Step 3 in the previous steps to determine the coordinates shown where the field appears in Figure 19.6.

9. **Get coordinates for the second field.** We use the same steps as line 3 to get new coordinates for the second field. Delete the Rectangle comment after getting the coordinates.

10. **Type the following code after Step 5 from the previous steps.** We add the following code in the JavaScript Editor to create a text field. Open the Actions tab, click Run a JavaScript and click Edit to open the script in the JavaScript Editor. Add the following code after line 6:

```
7.
8. //script that creates the text field
9.    {
10.    var r = [427, 445, 683, 460];
11.    var i = this.pageNum;
12.    var f = this.addField(String("completeDate."+i),"text",i,
   r);
13.       f.textSize = 10;
14.       f.alignment = "right";
15.       f.textColor = color.blue;
16.       f.fillColor = color.transparent;
17.       f.textfont = font.HelvB;
18.       f.strokeColor = color.transparent;
19.       f.value = String("This page completed on: " +
          util.printd("mmm dd, yyyy", new Date()));
20.    }
```

11. **Close the JavaScript Editor and close the Button Field Properties Window.**

12. **Save the form.** Be sure to save the file at this point to follow additional steps later in this chapter.

13. **Click the button.** You should see the text field similar to Figure 19.6.

14. **Revert the file.** After you click the button and observe the results, chose File ⇨ Revert. It's important you save the file in Step 11 to revert to the script you just added. Keep the file open to follow steps in the section "Deleting fields."

In line 10 we assign the new coordinates to the variable *r* and in line 12 we assign the current page number to variable *i*. In line 13 we use the addField object and define the field name *"complete-Date."* After the field name we add a child value to the field name so the name of the field would appear as *completeDate.2* if there were three pages in the file (remember, JavaScript is zero based). Following the field name in line 13 the *"text"* item defines the field type and we use the *i* value which adds the field to the current page and the *r* value which is the coordinates for the rectangle.

Lines 14 through 19 define attributes for the field appearance such as type font, type color, fill color of the field, and stroke color. In line 20 we add the field contents. The field displays the text *This page completed on:* and the date the field was created.

One problem exists after you click the button to add the two fields to a page as shown in Figure 19.6.

The button field containing the JavaScript appears on top of the signature field. We need to delete this field from the form.

FIGURE 19.6

After you click the button, the two fields are added to the page in view.

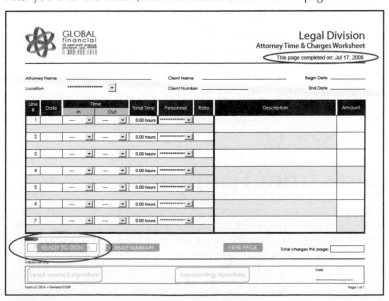

Deleting fields

When the form is ready to sign, the form recipient clicks the *Ready to Sign* button that adds the digital signature field and the text field containing the date the form was completed. At this point we no longer need the button field and the *New Page* button field. The *Create Summary* button produces a summary from each page, so we need to keep this button on the form.

To delete fields from a form, follow these steps.

STEPS: Deleting Fields on a Form

1. **Open the JavaScript Editor.** We continue using the same form from the last series of steps. We'll add code after item 20 in the JavaScript we created to add fields to the form.

2. **At the end of the code listing, add the following code in the JavaScript Editor:**

```
21. var oPage = this.pageNum;
22. this.removeField("P" + oPage + ".newPage.signaturePrompt");
23. this.removeField("P" + oPage + ".newPage.newPage");
```

3. **Exit the JavaScript Editor and the Button Field Properties Window and click File ⇨ Save to update your edits.**

In line 21 we assign the current page number to the variable *oPage*. Note that in the scripts used to add fields we didn't need to use this variable. But now we need to get the fields that were spawned from a template and named using the page numbers. Line 22 deletes the button when the form is ready to sign. We use the *removeField* object followed by the field name. In line 23 we use a similar script to delete the *New Page* button.

A few more *removeField* scripts are used on this form. When a form recipient clicks the *New Page* button, the *Ready to Sign* and *New Page* buttons are no longer needed on the previous page after a new page is added to the form. Rather than keep these buttons on the form we can delete them from the previous page. If a form recipient needs to use the buttons, they appear on the last page in the document because we'll only delete the buttons on the previous page when a new page is spawned.

The script used to delete these buttons is part of the script used to spawn new pages in the document so we'll hold off on explaining the code until we look at creating a button action to spawn new pages.

Spawning Pages from Templates

Up to this point we talked about creating the *globalAttorneySpawnRaw.pdf* form while taking into account that new pages are added to the file via button action. We've talked about spawning pages from templates quite a bit in the preceding sections, but as yet we haven't looked at creating templates and the code needed to create new pages from a template.

Creating page templates

The first thing you need to do when spawning pages from a template is to create a template on your form. In the section "Creating a form for spawning pages" earlier in this chapter we talked about adding a blank page to a form and creating a template from the second page that contains all the field objects and form design.

You can create a template on a single page PDF form but you cannot hide a template unless you have at least two pages in a document. Generally, it's a good idea to hide template pages so a form recipient doesn't inadvertently add data to the templates.

When creating a new template, you navigate to the page you want to use for the template page. The page must be in view in the Document pane. When the page is in view, choose Advanced ➪ Document Processing ➪ Page Templates. The dialog box shown in Figure 19.7 opens. In this dialog box you type a name for the template. The name you use is used in the scripts you write to perform actions when new pages are added to the form, so be sure to type a simple name you can easily remember.

FIGURE 19.7

Choose Advanced ➪ Document Processing ➪ Page Templates to open the Page Templates dialog box.

NOTE   **Page templates can only be added while in Viewer mode. You cannot add page templates while in Form Editing Mode.**

When you type a name for the template, click the Add button and a dialog box opens prompting you to confirm the action as shown in Figure 19.8. Click OK in the dialog box and the page is added as a template.

FIGURE 19.8

Click OK in the alert dialog box to create a template.

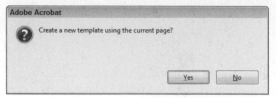

Notice in Figure 19.7 you see an eye icon adjacent to the template name after you click the Add button. The template name appears in the list after you click OK in the alert dialog box. By default templates are visible. If you want to hide the template click the eye icon and the eye icon is removed from the box adjacent to the template name as shown in Figure 19.9. Click the Close button after hiding a template and you'll notice that the total number of pages in the document does not include templates as pages if you elect to hide a template. If templates are visible they are counted in the total number of pages in the document.

FIGURE 19.9

When the eye icon is not visible, the template is hidden.

Appending pages to a document

Once you have a template, you can write the code and execute an action to spawn a new page from a template. Essentially, Acrobat duplicates the template page and adds it to the document as a visible page. You have a number of options when spawning pages from templates. One of the most important decisions you need to make when spawning pages on forms is whether to rename fields or not.

Using the *globalAttorneySpawnRaw.pdf* document we've used in many steps in this chapter, do the following to write a JavaScript to spawn a page from a template.

STEPS: Spawning a New Page from a Template

1. **Open a form in Acrobat.** In our example we continue using the *globalAttorneySpawnRaw.pdf* from the book's CD-ROM. You can use the saved file from earlier steps in this chapter or open the file from the Chapter19 folder on the CD-ROM.

2. **Create a page template.** In our example the *globalAttorneySpawnRaw.pdf* form already contains a template. If you start with a new form you need to create a template and you need to be certain all the field calculations will work on spawned pages as we described in the section "Calculating fields using field names from spawned pages" earlier in this chapter. For now, we're concerned with adding the JavaScript on a form that already has a page template.

3. **Create a button field.** On our example form we have a *New Page* button on the form. You can delete this button and create a new button to follow these steps or examine the JavaScript added to the button action.

4. **Add a JavaScript to the button action and type the following code in the JavaScript Editor.**

```
1. var oPage = this.pageNum;
2. var a = this.getTemplate("newPage"); //newPage is the template
        name
3. a.spawn ({
4.    nPage: this.numPages+1,
5.    bRename:true,
6.    bOverlay:false
7.    });
8. //move to the next page after spawning a new page
9. this.pageNum++;
10. //delete unnecessary buttons from the previous page
11. this.removeField("P" + oPage + ".newPage.signaturePrompt");
12. this.removeField("P" + oPage + ".newPage.newPage");
```

5. **Exit the JavaScript Editor and the Button Properties window.**

6. **Save the file.**

The lines of code that relate to spawning a page from a template are lines 2 through 7. Other lines of code do some other things we'll explain after we cover spawning pages. In line 2 we set the variable *a* to the page template name. This is the name we used in the Page Templates dialog box when we created the template. Line 2 uses the *spawn* object and we're using the template assigned to variable *a*. In line 4 we tell Acrobat where the new page will be added to the document. We get the current page number, and *+1* means that the new page will follow the current page. In line 5 we tell Acrobat to rename the fields when a page is spawned. The *bRename* flag can be *true* or *false*. In line 6 we tell Acrobat to create a new page as opposed to overlaying the spawned page on top of another page. The *bOverlay* flag also accepts either *true* or *false*.

In line 1 we assign the current page number to the variable *oPage* so we can use the value in lines 11 through 13. Because the oPage value is the previous page number, what we delete from the form will be deleted from that page. These last two lines of code delete the *Ready to Sign* and the *New Page* buttons from the previous page. Because these buttons are part of the template and are added to the new spawned page, we no longer need them on other pages.

When you create new pages from templates, be sure to place the new page in view. When a form recipient clicks a button to spawn a new page, most likely the form recipient wants to interact with the new page. Line 9 in the script takes care of this. Using the code in line 9 advances the page view to the next page.

Overlaying templates on form pages

In the preceding series of steps we talked about spawning pages from templates to append pages to a form. You also can spawn pages from templates and have the data added to page as an overlay by setting the *bOverlay* flag to *true*. In a number of circumstances you might want to overlay data on an existing page. You may have a form where you want to add a watermark via a button action, add fields based on conditions, or add a temporary work series of fields to a page for calculating additional results.

In Figure 19.10 we added a calculator tape to the *globalAttorneySpawnRaw.pdf* form we've used in this chapter for earlier steps. The idea behind this addition to the page is that if an attorney fills in the form the total amount is recorded for all personnel billing time but there's no way to break down the billing for additional personnel performing work on the case. If an attorney wants to check the amount billed by a given individual, a calculator tape is added to the form and the attorney can discuss the amount that a colleague billed for a given time period.

A form using a spawn page from template action where the data are overlaid on an existing page.

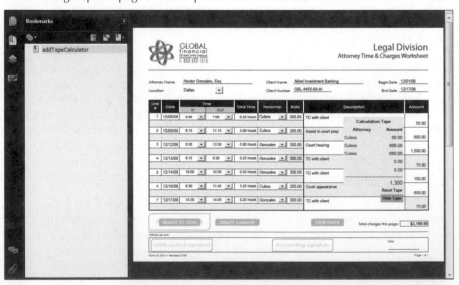

ON the CD-ROM The JavaScript to perform the calculations in the tape are extensive with several functions added to the document. You can view the scripts added to the form by opening the *globalAttorneySpawnCalcTape.pdf* file from the Chapter19 folder on the book's CD-ROM.

We won't go into all the scripts to create the fields added to the form to create the calculator tape. You can review the Document Level JavaScript functions and the template page where the calculation scripts are written. There are many on this form used to calculate a total, hide the tape from view, and show the tape.

The action we wrote to spawn a page from a template was written on a bookmark action. Rather than adding buttons to the form, we used a bookmark property. In the Bookmarks panel we created a bookmark and opened a context menu on the new bookmark and chose Properties. When the Bookmark Properties dialog box opened, we clicked the Actions tab and deleted the default action that was added when we created the bookmark. We then added a JavaScript action and typed the following code in the JavaScript Editor:

```
1. var a = this.getTemplate("5lineTape");
2. a. spawn ({
3.    nPage:this.pageNum,
4.    bRename:true,
5.    bOverlay:true,
6.    })
```

This script is very similar to the script used for spawning pages from templates when appending new pages. Notice in line 1 we used the name of another template. The only other difference is line 4 where we set the *bOverlay* flag to *true*. This line tells Acrobat to add the content from the template (*"5lineTape"*) on the current page in view (line 3).

The Hide Tape button shown in Figure 19.10 hides the tape and all the buttons and shows an invisible button named *Show Tape* at the top of the page. After using the calculator tape, the form user can hide the tape to view the content behind the tape.

Working with scanned forms

Sometimes you can't get away from paper forms. If you hold an event and want participants to fill out a form while in attendance, you may not be able to set up computer systems for them. Suppose you hold a class or a workshop and you want the attendees to fill in an evaluation form before the class or workshop adjourns. Typically you need to pass out paper forms and ask the attendees to fill in the forms by hand.

You can't circumvent some manual labor in accumulating data. You can type data in a spreadsheet or you can add data in PDF forms. Either method requires you or a staff of people to manually key in the responses.

Many forms have some open-ended questions for comments. If you hold an event and have a number of different speakers, you may want to accumulate the data and keep the forms handy in electronic form to review comments. If you add comments to a spreadsheet, the amount of time to record the data would be much more than recording responses from multiple-choice answers. In this regard, working with PDF forms may be the best solution because you can keep the responses in an electronic file without having to type the comments in a spreadsheet.

As an example, take a look at Figure 19.11. This form is designed for conference attendees to fill out after attending workshop sessions. The form provides choices for the session attended and responses to evaluate the quality of the session. At the bottom of the form is an area for the form user to add open-ended comments.

FIGURE 19.11

A paper form used to evaluate conference workshops

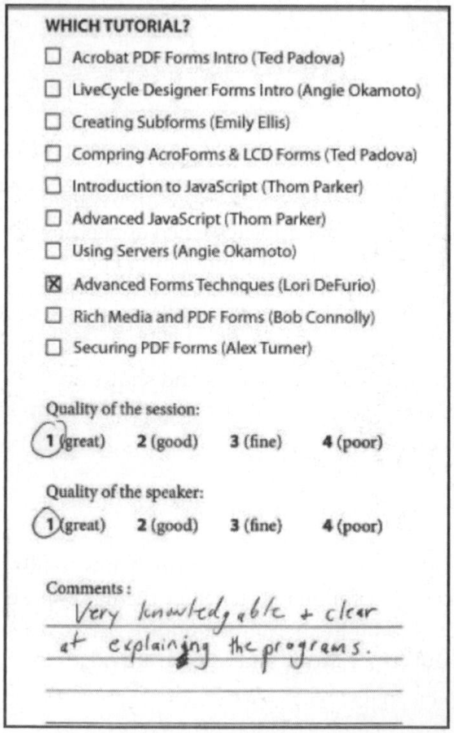

WHICH TUTORIAL?

- ☐ Acrobat PDF Forms Intro (Ted Padova)
- ☐ LiveCycle Designer Forms Intro (Angie Okamoto)
- ☐ Creating Subforms (Emily Ellis)
- ☐ Compring AcroForms & LCD Forms (Ted Padova)
- ☐ Introduction to JavaScript (Thom Parker)
- ☐ Advanced JavaScript (Thom Parker)
- ☐ Using Servers (Angie Okamoto)
- ☒ Advanced Forms Technques (Lori DeFurio)
- ☐ Rich Media and PDF Forms (Bob Connolly)
- ☐ Securing PDF Forms (Alex Turner)

Quality of the session:

1 (great) 2 (good) 3 (fine) 4 (poor)

Quality of the speaker:

1 (great) 2 (good) 3 (fine) 4 (poor)

Comments:

Very knowledgable + clear at explaining the programs.

To convert the paper forms to PDF forms, begin by scanning them. You can use a low-cost scanner with a document feeder that scans directly to PDF such as the Fujitsu ScanSnap S510 (Windows) or 510 (Macintosh) scanner. If you have lots of forms, you can walk away from the scanner and let the document feeder do the work.

The sample form shown in Figure 19.11 won't work with Acrobat's auto field detection because the second set of questions require a form recipient to circle numbers. The form has no recognizable areas where fields can be auto detected in this area. Therefore you need to add fields to the forms. Once you have the forms scanned you have two options for adding data to the forms. You can add fields to a single file or to individual files. Each method has advantages and disadvantages.

Using scanned forms in a single file

If you scan forms into a single document and add form fields, populating the form is easier than when using individual forms because you don't have to open, save, and close multiple forms. The downside to using a single document is that when you export the data to a spreadsheet program, the data isn't as neatly organized as when you create a spreadsheet from multiple forms.

We'll take a look at using both methods. For the first method where we use a single PDF document from merged forms, do the following.

 For these steps we use the *mergedFiles.pdf* document and the *template.pdf* document in the Chapter19 folder inside the *scannedForms* folder on the book's CD-ROM.

STEPS: Populating Scanned Forms in a Single File with Fields

1. **Assemble scanned forms in a single PDF file.** In our example the *mergedFiles.pdf* document on the book's CD-ROM contains 12 pages of individually scanned forms.

2. **Create a blank page for use as a page template.** The easiest way to create a page template is to duplicate one of the pages in the document by opening the Pages panel and pressing Ctrl/Option while you drag to another area in the panel. The page is duplicated when you release the mouse button. To create a blank page, click the TouchUp Object tool and press Ctrl/⌘+A to Select All. Press Delete to delete all the content and you end up with a blank page.

3. **Populate the blank page with fields.** You want the fields to be precisely located on the page template so that when spawned, the fields fall into place on the form. The easiest way to do it is to navigate to one of the form pages and create the fields. After the fields are created, select all fields and open a context menu. From the menu choices select Duplicate as shown in Figure 19.12. When the Duplicate Field dialog box opens, choose the page number where the blank page is found. Typically you'll find it best to add the blank page at the end of the document to keep track of the page order. In Figure 19.13 we duplicated the fields on the last page in the document.

4. **Delete the fields on the form page.** After duplicating the fields, delete the original fields you added to one of the form pages.

FIGURE 19.12

Select fields added to a form page and from a context menu choose Duplicate.

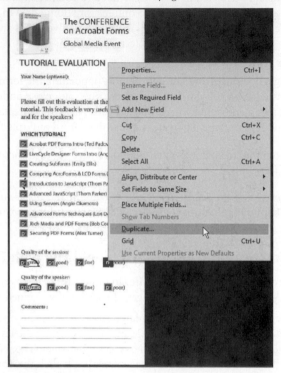

FIGURE 19.13

Duplicate the fields to the blank page in the document.

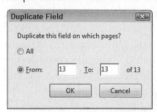

5. **Add a button with a JavaScript to spawn pages from a template to the template page.** If you'll use the same form for many events, you can set up the template page with a button containing the JavaScript and add only the template page and button to additional scanned forms. On a button action, write the following script:

```
1. var a = this.getTemplate("template");
2. for (var i=0; i < this.numPages; i++)
3.    a.spawn({
4.    nPage:i,
5.    bRename:true,
6.    bOverlay:true,
7.    });
8. this.removeField("spawnPage");
```

6. **Extract the page.** If you intend to use the template on other forms, show the template in the Document pane and choose Document ➪ Extract Pages. Extract the blank page with the button and JavaScript. Save the file and you can insert the page in any other identical forms you scan and merge together.

7. **Cut and paste the button.** For the document at hand, we'll cut the button from the template page and paste it on the first page in the document. This way, when we hide the template we have access to the button and JavaScript.

8. **Create a page template.** Open the blank page and choose Advanced ➪ Document Processing ➪ Page Templates. Type a name for the template, click Add and click the eye icon to hide the template.

9. **Click the button on the first page.** The fields are added to all pages in the document.

The JavaScript used in these steps is very similar to the scripts we've used for spawning pages from templates in other exercises. We added a loop in this script in line 2 to loop through the total number of pages (*this.numPages*). We turned the *bRename* and *bOverlay* flags on (*true*) to rename fields and overlay the fields on each page. The button we created we named *spawnPage*. In line 8 we remove the button field from the file.

Next, go through each page and click the check boxes to match the marks on the scanned forms. After checking all the fields choose Forms ➪ Manage Form Data ➪ Merge Data Into Spreadsheet to export a CSV file that you can open in Microsoft Excel. The data unfortunately won't be easy to read because you can't sort the data. All the field values appear on a single row in Excel.

You need to get the files back to single page forms for a better export to a spreadsheet. To do so, you can split the file as we describe later in the section "Splitting files."

Using individual scanned forms

Adding fields to a single form is much more work than you'll want to do to analyze data for an event. You have a few options if you need to add fields individually to single forms. You can paste the script to create the fields in the JavaScript Console and run the script when you open each form. This is a bit time consuming and not the best way to handle adding fields to individual forms

The other option you have is to create a batch sequence and run the sequence on a folder of forms. A batch sequence is not limited to running the sequence on multiple forms however. Rather than creating page templates and messing around with button fields, you can use a batch sequence on a single document that has merged forms.

We'll address creating a batch sequence in the next section of this chapter. For now, let's take a look at the JavaScript needed to populate the same form we used in the last exercise.

ON the CD-ROM The *1.pdf* file you can find in the *scannedForms* folder that's inside the Chapter19 folder on the book's CD-ROM contains a field with the JavaScript used to add fields to the example forms also in the same folder. The example forms are named *1.pdf* through *12.pdf*.

The script we·used to add fields to the individual sample forms was written as follows:

```
1.  // add the check box fields for the workshop attended
2.  var f = this.addField("workshop","checkbox",0, [25, 486, 36,
    497]);
3.    this.addField("workshop","checkbox",0, [25, 463, 36, 474]);
4.    this.addField("workshop","checkbox",0, [25, 441, 36, 452]);
5.    this.addField("workshop","checkbox",0, [25, 419, 36, 430]);
6.    this.addField("workshop","checkbox",0, [25, 397, 36, 408]);
7.    this.addField("workshop","checkbox",0, [25, 375, 36, 386]);
8.    this.addField("workshop","checkbox",0, [25, 353, 36, 363]);
9.    this.addField("workshop","checkbox",0, [25, 331, 36, 341]);
10.   this.addField("workshop","checkbox",0, [25, 309, 36, 319]);
11.   this.addField("workshop","checkbox",0, [25, 287, 36, 298]);
12.     f.style = style.sq;
13.     f.textSize = 18;
14.     f.strokeColor = color.black;
15.
16. // add the check box fields for Quality of Session
17. var g = this.addField("session","checkbox",0, [25, 223, 36,
    233]);
18.   this.addField("session","checkbox",0, [87, 223, 97, 233]);
19.   this.addField("session","checkbox",0, [152, 223, 163, 233]);
20.   this.addField("session","checkbox",0, [214, 223, 224, 233]);
21.   this.addField("speaker","checkbox",0, [25, 166, 36, 177]);
22.     g.strokeColor = color.black;
23.     g.style = style.sq;
24.     g.textSize = 18;
25.
26. //add the checkbox fields for the Quality of speaker
27. var j = this.addField("speaker","checkbox",0, [87, 166, 97,
    177]);
28.   this.addField("speaker","checkbox",0, [152, 166, 163, 177]);
29.   this.addField("speaker","checkbox",0, [214, 166, 224, 177]);
30.     j.style = style.sq;
31.     j.textSize = 18;
32.     j.strokeColor = color.black;
33.
34. // now give each check box field an export value
35. f.exportValues = ["introAcro", "introLCD", "subforms", "acro_
    LCD",
        "JS_Intro", "JS_Adv", "servers", "advTech", "richMedia",
                    "security"];
```

```
36. g.exportValues = ["4", "3", "2", "1"];
37. j.exportValues = ["4", "3", "2", "1"];
```

We start this script by using the addField object to add the ten check box fields under the Which Tutorial? heading shown in Figure 19.14. We needed to get all the coordinates for the check box fields individually by drawing comment rectangles and using the script we discussed earlier in this chapter in the section "Using the addField object."

The first set of fields added in the script are the ten check box fields in the Which Tutorial? heading.

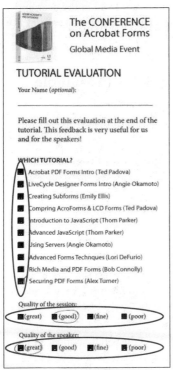

In line 12 we set the check box style to a square and in line 13 we set the text size for the check box mark to 18 points. The larger size check box style hides the mark on the paper form to make the choice stand out a bit more. We then added a stroke to the check box fields in line 14.

In lines 16 through 24 we added similar lines of code to create the first four check boxes in the Quality of session section, and lines 26 through 32 add the check boxes for the second row of four check box fields.

In lines 35 through 37 we set the export values for each of the check box fields. All the check boxes in the three respective groups are mutually exclusive fields.

To execute the JavaScript action either via buttons or from the JavaScript Console is not the best way to handle it. A better option is to use this script in a batch sequence.

Setting up a batch sequence

The script described in the last section can be added to a batch sequence and run on a folder of files. As a batch sequence, the code is available to you at any time in Acrobat once you add it as a new sequence. This eliminates a need for saving template files with code to run on the same forms collected at different times.

To create a batch sequence to add fields to multiple forms, do the following.

ON the CD-ROM For these steps we use the button script you find on the *1.pdf* form in the scanned-Forms folder inside the Chapter19 folder on the book's CD-ROM. When we run the batch sequence we use the *1.pdf* though the *12.pdf* forms also found in the same folder on the book's CD-ROM.

STEPS: Creating a Batch Sequence for Adding Fields to Multiple Forms

1. **Open the *1.pdf* file.** We'll copy the JavaScript to create the fields for the forms in the *scannedForms* folder on the book's CD-ROM.

2. **Open the *addFields* button and open the Actions tab in the Button Properties window.**

3. **Copy the JavaScript.** Click Run a JavaScript and click Edit in the Actions tab to open the JavaScript Editor. Select all the text and press Ctrl/⌘+C to copy the text.

4. **Close the *1.pdf* form.**

5. **Choose Advanced ⇨ Document Processing ⇨ Batch Processing.**

6. **Type a name for a new sequence.** Click the New Sequence button and the Name Sequence dialog box opens. Type a name for the sequence. In our example we use *add-Field* for the sequence name. Click OK and the Edit Batch Sequence (– addField) dialog box opens as shown in Figure 19.15.

7. **Select Commands.** Click the Select Commands button in the Edit Batch Sequence dialog box. The Edit Sequence dialog box opens. Scroll the list until you see JavaScript and below JavaScript you find Execute JavaScript shown in the left panel. Click Execute JavaScript and click Add to move Execute JavaScript to the right panel as you see in Figure 19.16.

8. **Add a JavaScript.** Double-click the Execute JavaScript text in the right panel to open the JavaScript Editor.

9. **Paste the text copied in Step 3.** Press Ctrl/⌘+V to paste the text from the clipboard.

10. **Click OK in the Edit Sequence dialog box.** You return to the Edit batch Sequence dialog box shown earlier in Figure 19.15.

11. **Set the Output options.** Chose Ask when Sequence is Run from the two drop-down menus in the Edit Batch Sequence dialog box. Click Output Options to open the Output Options dialog box. Here you can make selections for naming conventions and choose to overwrite files or not. Make your choices and click OK.

FIGURE 19.15

Type a name and click OK to open the Edit Batch Sequence dialog box.

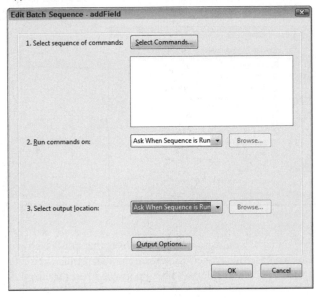

FIGURE 19.16

Double-click Execute JavaScript in the right panel to open the JavaScript Editor.

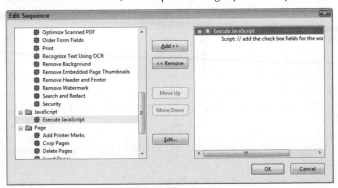

12. **Click OK in the Edit Batch Sequence dialog box.** Your new sequence is shown in the Batch Sequences dialog box as shown in Figure 19.17.

13. **Run the Sequence. Click Run Sequence in the Batch Sequences dialog box.** Make choices for the files to include in the sequence and target location for the saved files.

FIGURE 19.17

Click OK in the Edit Batch Sequence dialog box and you return to the Batch Sequences dialog box.

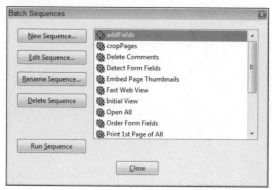

The main disadvantage you have with using scanned forms is that you have no way to use the scanned form and create a dataset file. When you create the dataset file from a form you have to use the form that you used to create the dataset file to populate the other forms. You can't edit the form after a dataset file has been created because the form has been enabled with Adobe Reader usage rights. Therefore you can't use a PDF Portfolio to aggregate the data the same as when distributing forms.

CROSS-REF   For more information on creating datasets and aggregating data, see Chapter 14.

Splitting files

If you followed steps in the last section, you have a file that has all the fields needed to fill in the form. If you add all the data or you use the same method we described in the section "Using scanned forms in a single file" you end up with all the data added in a single document. As we explained earlier, getting data to a spreadsheet from a single file isn't as attractive as exporting data from multiple files.

You can create single files from the merged forms after adding data to each form using the Split Document command. After filling in the data on the file, choose Document ⇨ Split Document to open the Split Document dialog box shown in Figure 19.18.

FIGURE 19.18

Choose Document ⇨ Split Document to open the Split Document dialog box.

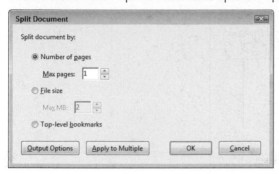

Enter 1 for the maximum number of pages. You have some attributes you can control that are found by clicking Output Options. In the Output Options dialog box make choices for file naming and overwriting switches. Click OK in the Output Options and OK again in the Split Document dialog box and the file is split into separate PDF files.

When you have separate files you can use the Merge Data into Spreadsheet command to add the data to a spreadsheet. The data arrangement is much more manageable than when sending data to a spreadsheet from a merged file.

Sending Data to Secondary Forms

Another function available to Acrobat only users is the ability to export data to other forms. If you turn back to Figure 19.1 and revisit the *globalAttorneySpawnRaw.pdf* file we used in several exercises in this chapter, you see the first page in a document populated with data. This form is intended for the form user to create individual pages for calculating time and billing for each client on separate pages. This provides the form user the opportunity to extract a given page and send it to a client to summarize a given month's billing information. Rather than mixing up clients on the same page, each page is used for a single client.

If the form user wants to summarize an entire month showing total billing hours and amounts charged to a client, a summary on the original form isn't practical. Because we want the flexibility to send billing information for a given client, we don't want to mix other data on a client's page. The best solution is to create a separate PDF file that holds summarized information for total billing hours and charges for all clients in a given billing period. We can create a summary form and send the data from the original billing form to calculate summary data for the billing period as you can see in Figure 19.19.

FIGURE 19.19

A separate form used to calculate a summary from data in another form

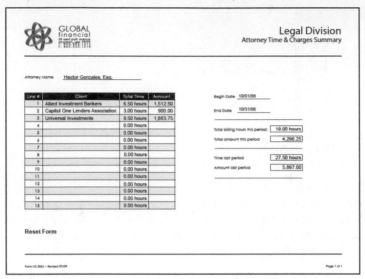

Because an attorney may have several cases in a given month, each individual client page can be reopened after once spawning a page from a template and additional data can be added to the page. The button at the bottom of the original billing form sends the summary data to the summary form at precisely the same location to update the totals. If additional data are later added to the billing form, the summary page can be updated to reflect additional billing by overwriting the same line on the summary form.

The original billing form provides for identifying various individuals participating on a case. We could break out individual billing for the attorney, but we'll keep it simple so you can copy and paste a less complicated routine.

Setting up secondary forms

We set up a summary form with a table of fields with columns for the client name, the total billing time. and the total charges as shown in Figure 19.20. The data are derived from the original billing form as well as the data for the attorney name, begin date, and end date for the billing period. The total billing hours for the period and the total amount for the period are calculated fields on the summary form. The fields for containing data from the last period are open entry fields for user-supplied data.

ON the CD-ROM You can examine the *globalAttorneySummary.pdf* file found in the Chapter19 folder on the book's CD-ROM. We also use the *globalAttorneySpawnPopulated.pdf* form from the book's CD-ROM to send data to the summary form.

FIGURE 19.20

A summary form with the data fields

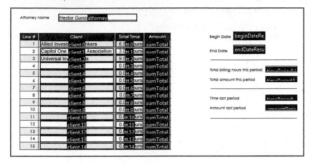

After we created the summary form, we added one document level JavaScript to the form. In the JavaScript functions dialog box we added the following script:

```
this.disclosed = true;
```

This one line of code is necessary to open the form from a JavaScript action used on the original form.

Another important issue is the location of the forms. Both the original billing form and the summary form need to be contained in the same folder. If the files are in different folders you'll get an error message and Acrobat won't be able to populate the summary form with data from the billing form.

Sending data to summary forms

On the original billing form we added a Calculate button to the form on the page template. When new pages are spawned from a template, the Calculate button is added to each page. This makes it easy to script the routine to send data from the current page to the summary form.

ON the CD-ROM The *globalAttorneySpawnPopulated.pdf* file in the Chapter19 folder on the book's CD-ROM is a file with data used to populate the summary form. The Calculate Summary button contains the JavaScript to send data to the summary form.

You may recall from the earlier exercise in the section "Appending pages to a document" that we removed the buttons on the previous page for spawning new pages. We also removed the button we used when the form user is ready to sign and submit the form. We don't want these two buttons on any page but the last page in the document. In regard to the Calculate button we assign properties to hide the field when printed. It's used on each page in the form to update the summary form, but we don't need to display it when a form is printed.

To populate the summary form with data from a given page on the billing form we used the following JavaScript on the Calculate button:

```
1. this.slave = app.openDoc("globalAttorneySummary.pdf",this);
2. this.bringToFront();
```

```
3. var oPage = this.pageNum;
4.
5. // send attorney name to slave
6. var oAttorney = this.getField("P0.newPage.attorneyName");
7. var sAttorney = this.slave.getField("attorney");
8. sAttorney.value = oAttorney.value;
9.
10. // send the client name to the slave
11. var oClient = this.getField("P" + oPage + ".newPage.clientName");
12. var sClient = this.slave.getField("client." + oPage);
13. sClient.value = oClient.value;
14.
15. // send amount to slave
16. var oAmount = this.getField("P" + oPage + ".newPage.
    totalAmount");
17. var sAmount = this.slave.getField("sumTotal." + oPage);
18. sAmount.value = oAmount.value;
19.
20. // calculate total time & send to slave
21. var oTime = this.getField("P" + oPage + ".newPage.totalTime");
22. var a = oTime.getArray();
23.    var sum = 0;
24.    for (i =0; i < a.length; i++)
25.    sum += a[i].value;
26.    var sTime = this.slave.getField("tt." + oPage);
27. sTime.value = sum;
28.
29. // send begin date to slave
30. var oBegin = this.getField ("P0.newPage.beginDate");
31. var sBegin = this.slave.getField("beginDateResult");
32. sBegin.value = oBegin.value;
33.
34. // send end date to slave
35. var oEnd = this.getField ("P0.newPage.endDate");
36. var sEnd = this.slave.getField("endDateResult");
37. sEnd.value = oEnd.value;
```

Although this script is a bit long, it's broken up into very short routines. Beginning in line 1 we set a variable *slave* to the openDoc() object that's used to open our summary data file. In our example the file is *globalAttorneySummary.pdf*. In line 2 we bring the target file to the front of the Document pane where it stays as data are added to the form. In line 3 we get the current page number. As the button is duplicated across pages, the oPage value is always the page number of the current page.

In lines 5 through 13 we send the attorney name and the client name to the target file. Notice we get the current attorney name on page 1 ("P0.newPage.attorneyName") only. Each page that is spawned from the template uses the attorney name from the first page so the form user doesn't have to retype a constant value. We use the same treatment in lines 29 through line 37 for the begin date and the end date. These three values are constant so we don't need to loop through fields picking up the same name. In line 7 we get the attorney field name on the summary form. Notice how the variable *slave* is used in this line of code. In line 8 we simply say that the target value is equal to the current value from the billing form.

Beginning in line 20 we need to do a little calculation to sum the total time. The billing form has no field that sums the time in a separate field, so we leave that task to the button action. We set up an array to calculate the total time for the current page only *a[i].value*. In line 26, as we do for all the data sent to the summary form, we get the target field *"tt." + oPage*. This means that we use the current page number that is the oPage value and use that value for the child name in the target field. For example, if we're on page 1, the *tt* value is *tt.0*. Because there is only one target field named *tt.0*, the data from the zero page is sent to that field. When we move to page 2 in the billing form we send the time data to *tt.1* and so on. All the summary data fields on the billing form use the current page number, and the target form table fields have child values matching the page numbers up to 15 pages.

Summarizing data with paper forms

Let's again roll back to an earlier section in this chapter and revisit the section "Working with scanned forms." We can create a summary form for the scanned forms assembled in a single PDF document after populating fields spawned from a template page. Of course, this only makes sense if you work routinely with a similar form where you need to scan the form and add data using Acrobat. The process is complex, but once you've set up the JavaScripts it's a simple matter of copying and pasting the scripts to new scanned forms assembled in a single PDF document.

Earlier in Figure 19.12 we looked at creating fields on a template page and spawning the template using the *bOverlay* flag to create form fields on pages created from scanned paper forms. If you want to create a summary form where data are sent from the original scanned forms to a summary document we need to add several new scripts to the form.

ON the CD-ROM In this section we use three files to follow the detailed explanation of what we need to add to the forms. Look in the Chapter19 folder on the book's CD-ROM and find the *workshopForms.pdf* file. This file has additional JavaScripts to send data to a summary file. The *workshopFormsPopulated.pdf* is the same form after we spawned pages from a template and filled in the form fields. The *workshopSummary.pdf* form is the target file where we'll send the data from the populated form.

Adding new fields to the scanned forms document

The first step in setting up the original forms document is add a few new fields on the template page and modify the script in the check box fields. In Figure 19.21 you can see one page of the form we used in Figure 19.12. On this form we added a few text fields. One text field holds the value of the workshop session full name. In our earlier script we used abbreviated names for the workshop names as export values in the check box fields where the form user checks the workshop attended. The first new field added to the form holds the full workshop name. Adjacent to the workshop name are two more text fields. These two fields hold the export value for the Quality of the session and the Quality of the speaker export values.

FIGURE 19.21

We added a few text fields on the form.

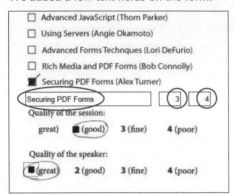

For the workshop field we added it on the template page and then edited each check box script on the template page. The code we used for the first check box is as follows:

```
1. var oPage = this.pageNum;
2.
3. var f = this.getField("P" + oPage + ".template.tutorialName");
4. f.value = "Introduction to Acrobat";
```

We simply get the workshop field (line 3) and add the full workshop name to the field (line 4). For each check box we changed the name in line 4. If you reuse a similar form for a variety of different classes or workshops, you have to edit the check box fields on the template page if you change workshop names when holding new conferences.

The two text fields that hold the values of the check box fields use a JavaScript Function to calculate the values of the export values of the session and speaker assessments. For the Quality of the session fields we added the following JavaScript at the Document Level:

```
1. function doSession()
2. {
3.    var aNameParts = event.targetName.split(".");
4.    var cPage = aNameParts.shift();
5.
6. // Test for valid Page. i.e. Skip calculation from raw template
7. if(/^P\d+/.test(cPage))
8.    {
9.    // Get the ID of the Session
10.      var oSesIDFld = this.getField(cPage + ".template.tutorial");
11.   // Get the score for the Session
12.      var oSesScoreFld = this.getField(cPage +
            ".template.qualitySession");
```

```
13.
14.    // Only do calculation if session ID and Score are set
15.
16.      if(!isNaN(oSesScoreFld.value) && !isNaN(oSesIDFld.value))
17.        { // Write evaluation score to field on individual
                evaluation sheet
18.           event.value = oSesScoreFld.value;
19.         }
20.      else
21.           event.value = "";
22.    }
23. }
```

In this script we split the name parts so we don't need to use the *("P" + oPage + ".templateName. fieldname")* convention we used in many other scripts in this chapter. We split the name and use line 7 to identify the different field names. The /^P\d+/ part of the line of code takes the P + the page number. If the page numbers were fewer than ten we would use /^P\d/ without the + in the code. Adding the + means we have more than nine potential fields to calculate. cPage takes care of everything else and we use it in the remaining code.

In line 10 we get the tutorial name. If the name is not checked, then the calculation is not per-formed (line 16). If it is checked, the value we assign to the variable *oSessScroreFld* becomes the event.value for this field.

We added *doSession()*; (the function name you find in line 1) as a custom calculation script in the Calculate tab in the Text Field Properties window for the session score field. We then copied this script and pasted into a new function we called *doSpeaker()*; and just changed the *oSess* items to *oSpkr*. In line 12 we retrieved the speaker check box fields. Then we added the function to the text field where we calculate the speaker values.

These two functions place the export value of 4, 3, 2, or 1 in the respective fields. This made it easier to sum the total values and average the data per speaker when we send the data to the summary form.

To make this form easy to reuse, you would add the fields and functions to a blank page and save the file as a template. When you scan new forms, use the File ⇨ Combine ⇨ Merge Files into a Single PDF. In the Combine Files wizard you add the scanned forms and the template page. When the template page is added to the scanned forms the JavaScript function and all the fields are added. You would then use the Advanced ⇨ Document Processing ⇨ Page Templates command to create a page template from the blank page.

Sending data to the summary file

On the *workshopForms.pdf* file you find two buttons. One button is used to spawn pages from the template. The code for this button is identical to the code we used in the section "Working with scanned forms."

The second button contains the script used to perform several calculations. We need to sum the quality of the session and the quality of the speaker fields and calculate the average for the values. We then need to send the workshop name and the average values to the summary form. This script is very complicated so we'll break it down into several subroutines.

On the *Send data to summary form* button, we added the following script:

```
1.  //export data to summary form
2.  // loop through tutorial name and send to slave doc
3.  // First we have to collect all the data for each session
4.  var aSesNames = [];
5.  var aSesScores = [];
6.  var aSpkrScores = [];
7.
8.  for(var i=0;i<this.numPages;i++)
9.  {
10. // Setup Session Names
11.    var oSesIDFld = this.getField("P" + i + ".template.tutorial");
12.    var oSesNameFld = this.getField("P" + i +
           ".template.tutorialName");
13.    if(!isNaN(oSesIDFld.value))
14.    {
15.      aSesNames[oSesIDFld.value] = oSesNameFld.value;
16.      var oSesScoreFld = this.getField("P" + i +
             ".template.sessionTotal");
17.      if(aSesScores[oSesIDFld.value] == null)
18.        aSesScores[oSesIDFld.value] = {Count:1,
             Total:oSesScoreFld.value};
19.      else
20.      {
21.        aSesScores[oSesIDFld.value].Count++;
22.        aSesScores[oSesIDFld.value].Total += oSesScoreFld.value;
23.      }
24.
```

In lines 4 to 6 we set up variable names for the session name, the quality of the session, and the quality of the speaker fields. In line 8 we loop through all pages in the document. In lines 11 and 12 we get the workshop name check box (*tutorial name*) and the workshop name field and set them to the variables shown in these lines of code. In line 13 we check to see if the value for the check box is zero. If it is not we proceed with the calculations. In lines 15 through line 22 we count the instances of each workshop identical name.

```
25.      var oSpkrScoreFld = this.getField("P" + i +
             ".template.speakerTotal");
26.    if(aSpkrScores[oSesIDFld.value] == null)
27.      aSpkrScores[oSesIDFld.value] = {Count:1,
             Total:oSpkrScoreFld.value};
28.    else
29.    {
30.      aSpkrScores[oSesIDFld.value].Count++;
31.      aSpkrScores[oSesIDFld.value].Total += oSpkrScoreFld.value;
```

```
32.    }
33.   }
34. }
```

The preceding routine counts the number of instances per workshop for the session values and the speaker values.

```
35. // Now it's time to loop through these and calculate the averages
36. for(var i=0;i<aSesScores.length;i++)
37. {
38.   if(aSesScores[i] != null)
39.   aSesScores[i].average = aSesScores[i].Total/aSesScores[i].
    Count;
40. }
41.
42. for(var i=0;i<aSpkrScores.length;i++)
43. {
44.   if(aSpkrScores[i] != null)
45.   aSpkrScores[i].average =
        aSpkrScores[i].Total/aSpkrScores[i].Count;
46. }
```

The preceding routine then calculates the averages for each session quality and each speaker quality.

```
47. // Now Open up the summary document and enter the data
48. this.slave = app.openDoc("workshopSummary.pdf",this);
49.
50. var dstFld;
51. var dstID = 0;
52. var len = Math.max(aSesScores.length,aSpkrScores.length);
53. for(var i=0;i<len;i++)
54. {
55.   if(aSesNames[i] != null)
56.   {
57.     dstFld = this.slave.getField("workshop." + dstID);
58.     dstFld.value = aSesNames[i];
59.
60.     if(aSesScores[i] != null)
61.     {
62.       dstFld = this.slave.getField("qualitySession." + dstID);
63.       dstFld.value = aSesScores[i].average;
64.     }
65.
66.     if(aSpkrScores[i] != null)
67.     {
68.       dstFld = this.slave.getField("qualitySpeaker." + dstID);
69.       dstFld.value = aSpkrScores[i].average;
70.     }
71.
72.     dstID++;
73.   }
```

```
74. }
75.
76. this.slave.bringToFront();
```

The last part of the script takes the values calculated for the workshop names, the session quality averages, and the speaker quality averages and sends the data to the summary form shown in Figure 19.22. The last line of code brings the slave document to the front of the Document pane.

FIGURE 19.22

The summary form after data has been introduced from the original scanned forms file

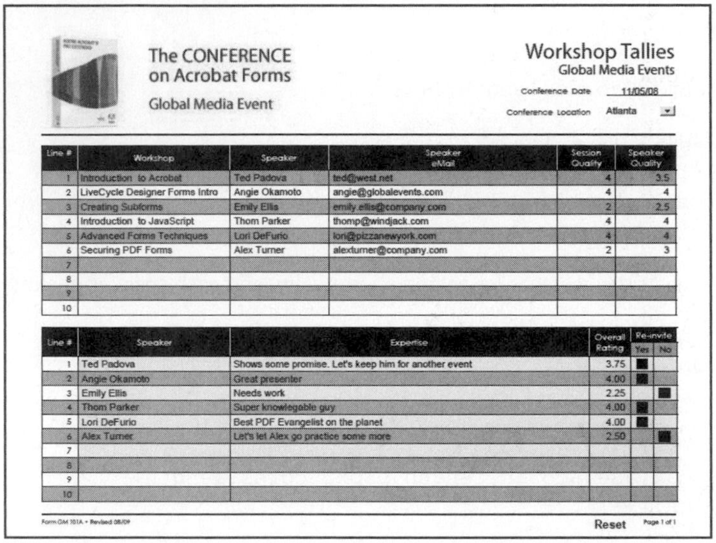

Remember from our earlier calculation for the attorney summary form in the section "Setting up summary forms" we need to add a Document Level JavaScript to the summary form. Again, the code is:

```
this.disclosed = true;
```

The summary form shown in Figure 19.22 shows data collected from six workshop evaluations. Additional lines are available for calculating summaries for up to ten workshops. But notice that you don't have to calculate data for the maximum. Nothing is added to the summary form when there are fewer than ten workshop evaluations to calculate.

To make the form more functional for repeated events, the Speaker and Speaker email columns are not added to the JavaScript when populating the form. Because speakers may change along with the e-mail addresses, these fields are open and available for the form user to type in the data. Because we need only up to ten entries for each column, there's no reason to edit the code each time you want to calculate a summary.

The bottom half of the form is for evaluations by the event's producers. This table contains fields for subjective information; therefore no additions were made when the data were exported from the forms file. The speaker column on the bottom of the form gets the same values from the speaker column on the top of the form. The overall rating is a calculation of the average of the session and speaker values. The remaining fields are open-ended for the form user to fill in. The calculation we used for the Overall Rating fields was as follows:

```
1. var f = this.getField("qualitySession.0");
2. var g = this.getField("qualitySpeaker.0");
3. if (f.value !=0)
4.   event.value = (f.value + g.value)/2;
5. else
6.   event.value = "";
```

We've used a similar script many times in this chapter and Chapter 18. For each of the ten fields in the Overall Rating column we changed the child name to reflect the names for the respective fields in the top table. In line 4 we average the session quality and speaker quality values.

Reusing the JavaScripts

Obviously going through all the steps to create a summary report is not advantageous if you have only one event where you want to calculate similar data. This approach makes more sense when you have a series of events and want to use the same scripts for repeated evaluations.

To make the procedure easy, all you need to do is to add the template file and assemble the forms as we described in the previous section. You need to add the two button fields to a new form. One button spawns the fields from the template and the other button creates the summary file.

The only edit you need to make in the JavaScript is to make changes on the template for the check box export values and check box JavaScripts if the workshop titles change. The JavaScript for these fields is only three lines of code with the workshop name appearing in the fourth line of code. Just make these changes and you can use the same form repeatedly for many events.

If you have to add more evaluation questions, you'll have to edit the JavaScripts in more depth. This requires carefully reviewing the routines and making edits to assign variables, calculate results, and send the data to the summary form.

Adding Menu Commands

Hundreds of plug-ins are available for Acrobat that can help you with various editing jobs. A limited number of them are helpful with JavaScripting. You can find a few great tools for creating dialog boxes and custom buttons at WindJack Solutions (`http://windjack.com`). These plug-ins write the JavaScript for you from selections you make in dialog boxes. You also can find a number of tools at `www.pdfscripting.com` that are ready made to help you with various forms editing tasks all based on JavaScript.

In addition to purchasing third-party developer tools you can customize your Acrobat workspace by adding buttons and menu commands that are helpful when creating forms. Adding buttons for tools in Acrobat is a bit more complex, but adding menu commands is a relatively easy task you can do, and you can easily copy/paste scripts that add new commands to any menu you want.

Adding functions to menus

Menu items are added with the *addMenuItem* object in JavaScript. You can easily view menu names in the JavaScript Console by typing the following code in the JavaScript Console and pressing the Num Pad Enter key or Ctrl + Enter for laptop computers:

```
app.listMenuItems();
```

After you press the Num Pad/Ctrl Enter key, a list of menu names is reported in the JavaScript Console. You can add new menu commands to the parent menu names and the submenu names you see reported back in the JavaScript Console.

We find a couple of commands particularly helpful and use them regularly when designing forms in Acrobat. These include:

- **Total Fields:** Counting the total fields on a form is helpful especially if there's a chance that fields are placed on top of other fields. If you expect your form to contain 50 fields and you have 65 fields on a form, you can use a simple script to calculate the total number of fields on a form open in the Document pane.

- **Total Templates:** You can easily find the total templates with the Advanced ➪ Document Processing ➪ Page Templates command. However, if you examine a form that is secured, you don't have access to this menu command. Using a simple JavaScript you can count page templates on any form whether secured or not.

- **List Field Names:** You can easily view field names in the Fields panel when in Form Editing Mode, but this requires you to toggle views between Form Editing Mode and normal Viewer Mode. If working in the JavaScript Console and adding scripts to fields, you can stay in Viewer mode and easily view field names in the JavaScript Console while editing scripts.

- **Get Annots Coordinates:** In Chapter 18 we talked about adding comments via JavaScript and in this chapter we covered adding fields using JavaScript. In both cases we need to find the coordinates for where the annotations and/or the fields are added to a form. With a simple menu command, you can easily view coordinates in the JavaScript Console.

ON the CD-ROM You can copy the file *tools.js* found in the Chapter19 folder inside the *placeJS_ Folder* on the book's CD-ROM to your Acrobat JavaScript folder. For the directory path, see the end of this section.

Here's the code you'll find in the *tools.js* text file:

```
1. // add the functions
2. function totalFields(){
```

```
3.   app.alert("Total Fields: " + this.numFields);
4. }
5.
6. function totalTemplates(){
7.   app.alert("Total Page Templates: " + this.numTemplates);
8. }
9.
10. function fldNames(){
11.   for(var i=0; i<this.numFields; i++)
12.   {
13.     var fName = this.getNthFieldName(i);
14.     var f = this.getField(fName);
15.     console.println("Name: " + f.name + ", Value: " + f.value);
16.   }
17. }
18.
19. function getCoordinates(){
21.   console.println(this.getAnnots()[0].rect);
22. }
23.
24. // add the menu items
25. app.addMenuItem ({cName: "Number of Fields",
26. cParent: "Tools", cExec: "totalFields()"
27. });
28.
29. app.addMenuItem ({cName: "Number of Page Templates",
30. cParent: "Tools", cExec: "totalTemplates()"
31. });
32.
33. app.addMenuItem ({cName: "Get Field Names",
34. cParent: "Tools", cExec: "fldNames()"
35. });
36.
37. app.addMenuItem ({cName: "Get Annotation Coordinates",
38. cParent: "Tools", cExec: "getCoordinates()"
39. });
```

In lines 2 through 22 we set up the functions for four menu commands. The names listed in each function should be self-descriptive. In lines 24 through 39 we add the menu items for the four functions. The *cParent* item tells Acrobat in what menu to place the new commands. The *cExec* item executes the function from the list in lines 2 through 22.

We could add menu items in a submenu using the *app.addSubMenu* item, but the Tools menu is such a short menu, adding only four items keeps the menu short and makes the commands easily accessible.

When you save the file, you must use a *.js* extension for the filename. Again, we reiterate that you need to use a text editor. Do not use a word processor to write the code. Doing so places unwanted characters in the text file and the script won't work properly.

After saving the file you need to copy the file to your Acrobat JavaScripts folder. On Windows the directory path is: `C:/Program Files/Adobe/Acrobat 9.0/Acrobat/Javascripts`.

On the Macintosh you need to copy the script to the Acrobat JavaScript folder inside your application package. If you use the Acrobat User Data folder inside the log-on Library folder the script won't be loaded by Acrobat. On Macintosh, do the following.

STEPS: Adding a Folder Level JavaScript on the Macintosh

1. **Open the Applications folder.** Open the Macintosh HD or whatever name you use for your hard drive name.

2. **Open the Applications folder.**

3. **Open the Adobe Acrobat 9 Pro folder.**

4. **Show the application package contents.** Control + click on the Adobe Acrobat Pro file name to open a context menu. From the menu commands, choose Show Package Contents. You'll then see a folder named *Contents*.

5. **Open the Contents folder.**

6. **Open the MacOS folder.**

7. **Copy the file to the JavaScripts folder.** Inside the MacOS folder you'll find the JavaScripts folder. Copy the file to this folder.

Once you copy the file to the Javascripts (Windows) or JavaScripts (Macintosh) folder, quit Acrobat if the program is open. Relaunch the program and wait a few moments. The JavaScript may take a moment to load in Acrobat. Click the Tools menu and you should see the new menu commands added to the menu as shown in Figure 19.23.

Each of the four menu items in Figure 19.23 requires you to have a file open in the Document pane to report the findings of each function. For the Get Field Names and Get Annotation Coordinates menu commands you need to open the JavaScript Console (Ctrl/⌘ + J) to view the reported information.

FIGURE 19.23

After adding the .js file to your JavaScript folder, the new menu commands are available in Acrobat.

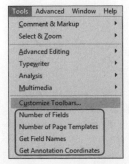

Adding URLs to menus

Another menu item you'll find helpful is adding a URL or several URLs as commands. If you frequently want to search the Internet for forms information or JavaScript, you can stay in Acrobat and launch a URL from a menu command.

We follow the same process as described in the previous section for writing the JavaScript and copying the *.js* file to the JavaScripts folder. The following script is added to the Help menu, and when selected, launches the URL specified in line 4 in your default Web browser.

ON the CD-ROM In the Chapter19 folder inside the place_JS folder you'll find the *helpMenu.js* file. Copy this file to your Acrobat JavaScripts folder to see the menu command appear in the Help menu.

```
1. app.addMenuItem({
2.    cName: "JavaScript Development Center",
3.    cParent: "Help",
4.    cExec: "app.launchURL('http://www.adobe.com/devnet/
          acrobat/javascript.html');",
5.    nPos: 16
6. });
```

In line 5 you see *nPos: 16*. This line of code specifies the placement of the menu command in the Help menu. After copying the file to your Acrobat JavaScripts folder and launching Acrobat the menu command appears as shown in Figure 19.24.

FIGURE 19.24

A new custom menu item added to the Help menu launches a URL.

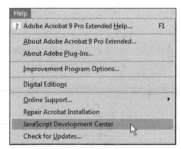

TIP If you want a custom menu command to appear in the first position on a menu use nPos: 0.

This script opens a Web page on Adobe's Web site (see Figure 19.25) where you can find information on JavaScript and download the most recent version of the JavaScript for Acrobat API Reference document. Typically the latest version of the document is released some time after a new Acrobat version release. Check this site frequently after you upgrade Acrobat and download the latest document when it becomes available.

FIGURE 19.25

Selecting the custom menu command opens the specified URL in your default Web browser.

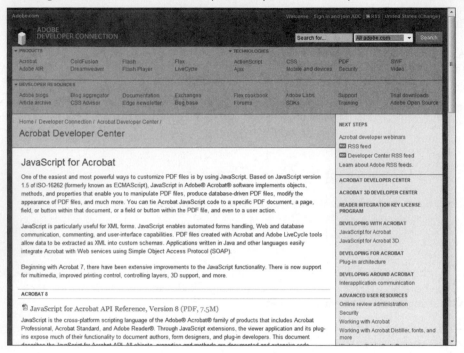

Summary

- You can use JavaScript to add and delete fields on a form. Adding fields requires using Acrobat or Adobe Reader when forms are enabled with Adobe Reader usage rights.

- You can append new pages to a document from page templates only in Acrobat.

- You can spawn new pages to overlay data on existing pages using JavaScript.

- You can write JavaScripts and add the scripts to a Batch Sequence to add fields to a folder of forms. This is particularly helpful when using scanned paper forms.

- Using JavaScript you can add data from one form to a secondary form.

- You can use JavaScript to add custom menu commands to Acrobat.

Part VI

Getting Started with LiveCycle Designer

This part leaves Acrobat Forms and begins our journey through LiveCycle Designer. Because Designer is a Windows-only application, in Chapter 20 we talk about how Macintosh users can install Designer on an Intel Mac. In Chapter 21 we start covering the basics of learning Designer and some of the differences you'll find between Designer forms and Acrobat Forms. In Chapter 22 we explore the Designer workspace and talk about tools, menu commands, and palettes.

IN THIS PART

Chapter 20
Using LiveCycle Designer on the Macintosh

Chapter 21
Introducing LiveCycle Designer

Chapter 22
Getting Familiar with the Designer Workspace

Chapter 20

Using LiveCycle Designer on the Macintosh

I f you used PostScript fonts back in 1985, you were an Adobe customer and a Macintosh user. If you used Adobe Illustrator back in 1986, you used Illustrator on a Macintosh. If you were one of the first to purchase Adobe Photoshop in 1989, you definitely used a Macintosh computer.

Adobe began its life serving Macintosh users. Nothing appeared on Windows until Windows 3 was released much later in the 1990s. When Adobe began developing cross-platform software, the initial incarnations of the Windows versions took a backseat to their Macintosh counterparts. Using Illustrator 4 on Windows was clunky and very slow, and Photoshop didn't appear on Windows until Aldus Photostyler on Windows went into retirement.

As Adobe evolved with much more sophistication and support for Windows applications, Macintosh users at times felt a little betrayed seeing more support and more features available for Windows applications than Mac applications. This is most evident when looking at Acrobat Pro on the Mac compared to Acrobat Pro Extended on Windows. Of course, when it comes to LiveCycle Designer, the Mac community feels completely left out, and the continual cry from the Mac audience is "when will we see LiveCycle Designer appear on the Macintosh?"

Despite what some users may think, Adobe is committed to serving a cross-platform audience. This is most evident when you look at the Creative Suite 4 applications. In just about all the CS4 programs, you can equally perform the same tasks in each individual program on either platform.

Adobe's development decisions are not based on any particular bias or influences in market share. The most important decision is how well a product performs within an operating system. Unfortunately, some things work on one system that don't work on another. In addition, you have to look at the

IN THIS CHAPTER

Getting familiar with Designer

Using Windows on the Mac

Converting Designer forms to Acrobat forms

history of a product's development. Those programs initially engineered by Adobe over the past two decades were all designed for cross-platform performance. With other products, Adobe acquired many from developers that didn't have a focus on delivering cross-platform applications.

Adobe LiveCycle Designer falls into this last category: The issue of what you can do on one platform versus another is related to the fact that Designer was not a program originally engineered by Adobe. As of this writing, if you want to use Designer, you need to use the product on Windows. For the Mac user, you are fortunate if you have an Intel Mac, because using Designer on the Mac with Windows installed and Acrobat and LiveCycle Designer for Windows, you have the same benefits at hand as the Windows-only users.

In this chapter, we offer some suggestions and recommendations for the Macintosh users who want to use Adobe LiveCycle Designer on their Macs.

Understanding Designer's Development

If you're curious about why Designer is not a product that can be installed on Mac OSX, understanding a little development history can help ease the curiosity.

Adobe Acrobat was developed and engineered internally by Adobe Systems and first appeared in 1993 as a cross-platform product. In 1996, Acrobat 3 was introduced with the first inclusion of the Forms tools, and in version 3.02, Acrobat JavaScript was added to the program. From 1996 through the current date, Acrobat has been upgraded by Adobe supporting both the Mac OS and Windows operating systems.

LiveCycle Designer was originally developed by Delrina in 1995 as a Windows-only product (under a different product name). Later that year, the product was purchased by Symantec. A year later, Designer was purchased by JetForm, which later changed the company name to Accelio. In 2002, Adobe acquired Accelio and with it the product we now know as Adobe LiveCycle Designer ES.

Through the early development stages, the product was engineered by several companies without having any thought for fitting into a much larger product inventory such as the Adobe LiveCycle products. In 2004, Adobe ended its support for the Accelio product and seriously looked at developing Designer. Later that year, we saw the introduction of Adobe Designer 6.0, and with this release, Adobe included support for creating dynamic forms with data propagated with what was then known as the Adobe Form Server.

Since 2004, Adobe has seriously looked at Designer as a rich tool to create dynamic forms while maintaining its commitment to Acrobat forms for cross-platform Acrobat users. If we could roll back the clock and put the initial engineering of Designer into Adobe's hands, we might have a cross-platform version of Designer today. Still, it's only a dream, because of the restrictions imposed by operating systems.

For the Adobe user, Designer looks like a visitor from a foreign land. The interface and methods for using the program don't quite fit into the Adobe culture we see when using the Creative Suite applications. The tools, palettes, and menu commands look and feel a little different than when using other Adobe products. And the reason is primarily because Designer is an inherited product and not an Adobe original product.

As Designer matures, we expect to see much improvement and perhaps one day we'll see the product released as a cross-platform application. Until then, if you're a Mac user, you must be content with using Designer on Windows that you can install on your Intel Macs.

Setting Up Designer on the Macintosh

Although products have been released for the Macintosh to support installing Windows, the real advantage for running Windows on a Mac is on Intel Macintosh computers. If you're a Mac user working with a PowerPC, you should forget about reading this chapter, tear the book in half at this page, and give the chapters that follow to a Windows buddy.

For Intel Macintosh users, you need several things to run Designer on your Mac. First, we talk about using Designer on Windows using Mac OSX Leopard or greater. Be sure to upgrade your Mac OSX software to the latest release.

Using virtualization software

In addition to your Mac OSX operating system, you must acquire a virtual machine application that will allow you to install Windows on your Mac. Several products are available to create virtual machines. The most popular products include:

- **Apple's Boot Camp:** Boot Camp supports most of the 32-bit releases of Windows XP and Vista. When running Windows applications, they run at native speeds. As a matter of fact, most Windows users who have purchased Intel Macs claim that running Windows applications on a Mac with Boot Camp has noticeable speed performance increases. We haven't tested Boot Camp on an Intel machine, so we cannot confirm this. However, you can browse numerous reports on the Internet to find the claims made from users.

    When you install Windows under Boot Camp, you have full access to multiple processors, accelerated 3D graphics, and high-speed connections such as USB, Firewire, Wi-Fi, and Gigabit Ethernet. The difference between Boot Camp and other virtual machines we talk about in this chapter is that you have to reboot your computer to use one operating system or another. You cannot run Mac OSX and Windows concurrently on your computer. For more information on Boot Camp, visit `www.apple.com/macosx/features/bootcamp.html`.

- **CrossOver Mac:** CrossOver Mac enables you to install Windows applications without installing Windows. Once installed, the applications integrate with Mac OSX. A huge range of Windows applications can be installed with CrossOver Mac, but we haven't tried installing LiveCycle Designer with this application. It may not be supported in the latest version as of this writing, but you may want to make frequent visits to www.codeweavers.com/. You can download a trial version from the developer's Web site.

- **Parallels Desktop:** Parallels Desktop is a virtual machine that allows you to run Mac OSX and Windows side-by-side; as of this writing, it has over 1 million installed users. Parallels provides near native speed and full access to dual core processors. You can find out more about Parallels Desktop at www.parallels.com.

- **VirtualBox:** VirtualBox is the only OpenSource application for virtualization that we know of. The product was acquired by and as of this writing is currently owned by Sun Microsystems. Because it is in continual development, you'll want to make frequent visits to www.virtualbox.org/ to check on the development progress.

- **VMWare Fusion:** VMWare Fusion is a product similar to Parallels, and although the installed user base isn't as great as Parallels, this product is our first choice. Like Parallels, Fusion enables you to run Windows and Mac OSX side-by-side, and you can easily exchange files between Mac and Windows applications via a folder visible while in either operating system. To learn more about VMWare Fusion, visit www.vmware.com.

Installing Acrobat on Windows

After you have an application installed to permit using Windows applications, you need to install Windows. Most of the products we talk about in this chapter enable you to install Windows XP or Vista. As of this writing, Windows XP is a much more stable operating system than Windows Vista SP1. The Internet is loaded with reports from Vista users about problems encountered with Microsoft's latest operating system release. You might check articles, blogs, and reports on the Internet before purchasing a Windows operating system. If you find many reports of problems with Vista when you do your search, choose Windows XP as your operating system.

You must install Windows when using the products we discuss in this chapter. This requires a separate purchase of Microsoft Windows over and above the virtualization software.

After installing Windows, you need to install Adobe Acrobat Pro or Adobe Acrobat Pro Extended for Windows. This again requires an additional purchase. If you are a current licensed user of Acrobat for the Macintosh, you can't use any upgrade path to purchase the Windows version of Acrobat. You need to purchase the full Acrobat Pro product in order to run Acrobat and LiveCycle Designer on the Mac.

Installation is very easy after you have your computer configured for running Windows. You open Windows on your Mac through one of the virtual desktop applications and insert the Acrobat Pro installer CD or purchase and download the application from Adobe's Web site. Open the Setup application, and follow the directions for installing Acrobat. The installer sees Windows on your computer the same as a dedicated Windows machine. When you complete the install process, LiveCycle Designer also is installed and runs the same as when using the program on a Windows-only machine.

In Figure 20.1, you can see a form opened in LiveCycle Designer on the Macintosh using VMWare's Fusion, Microsoft Vista, and Adobe Acrobat Pro Extended. At the top of the screen, you can see the Macintosh menu bar.

FIGURE 20.1

Adobe LiveCycle Designer running on a Macintosh Intel computer

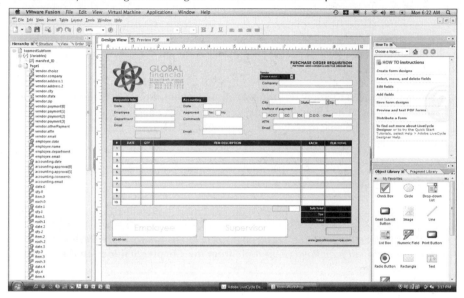

Justifying the costs

We assume you purchased this book because you're a serious forms author. If a good amount of the work you do is to create forms and handle form data, then you need to invest in the tools that enable you to do all the work required in your job. For some forms authors, you can get by using Acrobat forms exclusively. For others, you might be able to get by using LiveCycle Designer exclusively. For most serious forms authors, however, the best of all worlds is to use both programs and let the needs of your forms and data handling dictate what program to use for any given form.

Considering the price of the software versus a new computer system, not to mention the tasks of setting up a network to exchange files back and forth, installing the applications on your current system makes good sense and can provide you with the best affordable solution. If you're a Mac Intel computer user, you'll find using LiveCycle Designer to be flawless when you purchase the right tools to run Windows on your machine.

Editing XML Files in Acrobat

You may be a Macintosh user who works exclusively with Acrobat forms on your Macintosh. On occasion, you may receive a file that was created in Adobe LiveCycle Designer. By default, you cannot edit the Designer XML form in Acrobat.

You do have one workaround to convert an XML form to an Acrobat form. For Acrobat users on the Macintosh, you may want to convert a LiveCycle Designer form to edit form fields, add new fields, or edit the background of the form design. If this is your task, you need to weigh the time it would take to create a new form or to convert a form and edit the converted form. If the redesign of a form would take much more time than converting and editing the form, you can use a workaround to convert some forms.

Before we move ahead, you need to know one thing about Designer forms. You can save forms in Designer as dynamic forms or static forms. If you try to convert a dynamic form as we explain in the steps following, you won't be able to convert the form. Only static forms can be converted using the method we describe here.

> **CROSS-REF**   For more understanding of static forms and dynamic forms, see Chapters 24 and 26.

To convert a Designer XML form to a form you can edit in Acrobat, follow these steps.

> **ON the CD-ROM**   To follow these steps, you need a static form saved from LiveCycle Designer. You can use the *globalPicnicRawLCD.pdf* file from the Chapter20 folder on the book's CD-ROM to follow these steps.

STEPS: Converting a LiveCycle Designer Static Form to an Acrobat Form

1. **Open a form in Acrobat.** For these steps, we use the *globalPicnicRawLCD.pdf* from the book's CD-ROM.

2. **Open the Document menu.** A quick look at the Document menu tells you whether the form you want to convert is a dynamic form or a static form. If Extract Pages is grayed out, you cannot convert the form in Acrobat because it's a dynamic form. If the Extract Pages command is accessible, the form is a static form.

3. **Choose Extract Pages.** Our example form is a static form, so we can convert the form. Choose Document ➪ Extract Pages, as shown in Figure 20.2.

4. **Edit and save form.** You have a few options to choose from. You can delete all fields, save the form, and open the form in Form Editing mode. When Acrobat prompts you to use auto field detection, you can add fields on the form. If running auto field detection on the form doesn't adequately populate the form with field objects, you can modify the fields on the page. Figure 20.3 shows the form converted in Acrobat. All the field names inherited the subform root names, and the names are quite long. If the long names present a problem when analyzing the data, you can edit field names on the form.

FIGURE 20.2

If the Extract pages command in the Document menu is accessible, you can convert a Designer-created XML form to a form that can be edited in Acrobat.

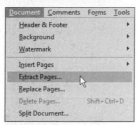

FIGURE 20.3

After you convert the form, the field objects have long field names inherited from Designer.

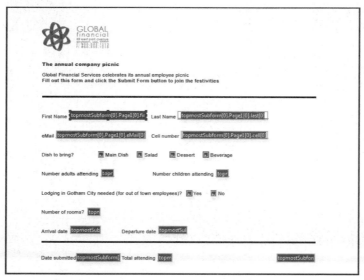

One thing to remember when you convert XML forms to Acrobat forms is that any scripts either with FormCalc or JavaScript won't work on the form you convert. Any scripting on the original form needs to be rescripted using JavaScript in Acrobat.

If you need to convert dynamic forms to Acrobat forms, your best solution is to edit the form in LiveCycle Designer and forget about converting the form. When you convert a dynamic form, you lose all the dynamic characteristics of the form. If the form is really a static form that was saved as a dynamic form, you can ask the form author to save the form from LiveCycle Designer and then convert the form using the Extract Pages command in Acrobat.

If you absolutely must convert a dynamic form to an Acrobat form and you don't know the form author to request conversion of the form from dynamic to static, you can convert the form using another workaround. However, doing so requires you to go back to Acrobat 7, open the form in a Web browser, and save the form from the Web browser. It would be a rare circumstance for you to convert forms in this manner, so we won't go into any detail about it. It's there if you want it, but your best option is to visit a Windows machine and edit the form in LiveCycle Designer.

Summary

- Macintosh Intel computer users can run LiveCycle Designer on their Macs by installing a virtual desktop application, either Windows XP or Vista and Acrobat Pro or Pro Extended for Windows.

- You can convert static XML forms to forms you can edit in Acrobat by using the Extract Pages command.

Chapter 21

Introducing LiveCycle Designer

Welcome to the section on LiveCycle Designer (LCD). We have covered lots of information relating to Acrobat forms in the preceding chapters. Now we begin to focus on the additional form design tool available to PDF form designers, LiveCycle Designer. In this chapter, we explore the differences between Acrobat Forms and LiveCycle Designer Forms. It is important to understand the advantages and limitations in the two programs. If you are unsure which program you want to use to design your PDF forms, reading this chapter should help shed some light on which tool is better for you and the project you're working on.

Both Acrobat and LiveCycle Designer are capable of creating great PDF forms. We feel that one product is not better than the other; each has its strengths and weaknesses. This topic can cause very heated debates between PDF forms designers. Many designers do have a strong preference when designing their forms. We hope to provide you with enough unbiased information that you are able to make your decision an educated one. You also may need to consider what happens if you started creating a form in one product and then realize you want to work in the other application? Keep reading—we'll cover these topics and much more.

Keep in mind, as we've said many times in earlier chapters that using Adobe LiveCycle Designer is a Windows-only experience. Unless you have a virtual desktop installed on an Intel Mac along with either Windows XP or Windows Vista and Acrobat Pro or Acrobat Pro Extended—Windows version, you won't have LiveCycle Designer on your Acrobat installer CD-ROM. This territory is restricted for Windows users only.

IN THIS CHAPTER

Using LiveCycle Designer

Knowing Designer advantages and limitations

LiveCycle Designer and Acrobat

Looking at the installed files

Why LiveCycle Designer?

LiveCycle Designer began shipping with Acrobat Professional (Windows only) version 7 and has been included in each Acrobat Professional release since. Now, why does Adobe just give you another program when you simply purchase Acrobat? Form designs are frequently being used to collect data electronically. The inefficient workflows where paper forms are entered by data entry workers who have to decipher illegible writing are becoming a thing of the past. We need a way to exchange form data with a variety of database systems.

Extensible Markup Language (XML) is an open source industry standard format used to exchange data. XML was designed to structure, store, and transport data. Because LiveCycle Designer forms are based on XML, sharing data with other sources is easier to manage.

LiveCycle Designer is a graphical environment that writes XML for you. When you save your Designer form in the native XML format, it is stored as an XML Data Package (XDP). If you double-click the file, it opens in LiveCycle Designer. Saving in XDP format is recommended when you are still in the design phase, or if you leverage the other Adobe LiveCycle Enterprise Suite Products to process your forms. LiveCycle Designer Forms are sometimes called XFA forms, because LiveCycle Designer creates a form based on the XML Form Architecture (XFA). For additional information on XML or XFA, see the World Wide Web Consortium at `http://www.w3.org/`, or the Adobe Developer site at `http://partners.adobe.com/public/developer/xml/index_arch.html`.

> **NOTE** LiveCycle Designer Forms are called by a variety of names including XML forms, XFA forms, and Designer Forms.

How do XML and PDF work together? When you save a LiveCycle Designer form as a PDF, the XML is essentially placed in a PDF wrapper. This allows all Acrobat viewers, including the free Adobe Reader, to interact with the document. When an Acrobat viewer opens the PDF file, the XML is rendered to the screen. This ability for including Adobe Reader to utilize the XML file also gives us the capability to create truly dynamic forms.

Creating dynamic forms

Dynamic forms grow or shrink based on the form recipient's input or the quantity of the data being merged with the document. The document has a flowing layout that continues to adjust as more or less information becomes available.

Consider a purchase order form design with ten rows, a fixed number. Not all purchase orders need ten rows of data, and yet other purchase orders need more than ten rows. This often causes the form recipient to submit two copies of the form, or find some other workaround to add the additional data. Imagine that a form recipient chooses to handwrite two additional rows of information on the back of the original form, yet he forgets some of the requested information. What if each person filling out the purchase order comes up with her own way to add that additional data? This presents a problem for the person trying to collect the data, because the data now arrives in an inconsistent and incomplete manner. Having a breakdown in the workflow process is both costly for the company and frustrating for the individuals involved.

What if we could design that same purchase order form in such a way that it contained five rows for most users and gave them the ability to add additional rows if needed? It could even generate additional pages in the document if necessary. This method allows us to control the data collection process, without the form recipient needing to find a workaround solution. The time savings associated with having all the necessary information consistently is significant.

To help clarify our message here, look at Figure 21.1. This form is an AcroForm created in Adobe Acrobat. We anticipate all the rows that are needed for a form recipient to complete the form before deploying the form.

FIGURE 21.1

An Acrobat Form created with a fixed number of rows

Compare Figures 21.1 and 21.2. We designed the form in Figure 21.2 with only a single row for ordering items. On the form, notice that we have a button marked *Add Row*. When a form recipient clicks this button using any Acrobat viewer, a new row is spawned on the form. The form is dynamic and designed to accommodate needs of the form recipient as the form is populated with data. In Figure 21.2 you can see a form completed by an Adobe Reader user where several rows were dynamically added per the form recipient's needs.

CROSS-REF For more information on creating or using dynamic forms, see Chapters 26, 27, and 32.

LiveCycle Designer Form with a button to control the adjustable layout

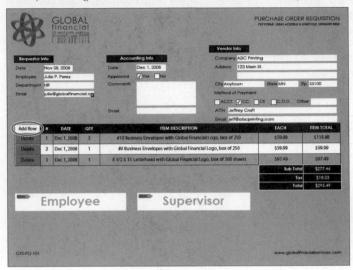

Understanding system requirements

Adobe Reader has been around since the early 1990s. However, LiveCycle Designer and XML have not. This is important to understand, because it affects the version of Adobe Reader the form recipient must have in order to interact with your LiveCycle Designer form. Acrobat and Reader 6.02 are the first versions that are XML aware. This means that if you attempt to open a LiveCycle Designer form with a version prior to 6.02, it won't understand the XML format it contains, and the form won't open. The dynamic capabilities of LiveCycle Designer forms also place dependencies in the Reader version, as shown in Table 21.1. Dynamic documents require a minimum of Acrobat or Reader version 7.05 or higher.

Acrobat/Reader Minimum Version Requirements

Document Type	Minimum Acrobat / Reader Version Required	Notes
Static LiveCycle Designer Document	6.02	If any prior version is used the document does not open.
Dynamic LiveCycle Designer Document	7.0.5	Version 6.0.2 through 7.0.3 open this file, but with errors. (Note: Adobe skipped 7.0.4)

We recommend that the newest version of Acrobat or Reader be utilized, so that all the new features deployed are supported. When the intended audience is a broad spectrum of users, you cannot enforce the Acrobat/Reader version you want them to use, and that can be a big hurdle for you as a form designer. Of course, you can encourage users to download the newest version; even Reader prompts them to do so. However, you cannot guarantee that they will download or that they are able to install it. Many IT departments restrict program installation to someone with an administrative role.

Knowing Designer Advantages and Limitations

Because LiveCycle Designer forms are not PostScript-based PDFs like AcroForms, some of the features we really like in AcroForms are not available in Designer forms. Likewise, because AcroForms are not based on XML, they don't have the same abilities as LiveCycle Designer forms. Understanding that these two document types are completely different helps clarify when and why you may want to use one over the other.

What you can do with LiveCycle Designer

The following is a partial list of Designer features:

- **Create dynamic forms:** These forms adjust based on input or quantity of data merged with the form (refer to Figures 21.1. and 21.2). A flowing layout continually adjusts as information changes. Dynamic forms allow additional pages to be added to the document if desired.

- **Templates:** LiveCycle Designer includes a template library with a variety of forms to choose from. You can create additional templates of your own to add to the library.

- **Field hierarchy structure:** Designer offers a hierarchical view of the data in the form, complete with nested data nodes that can easily be collapsed or expanded while working.

- **Data binding:** When you bind the fields in your form design to a data source, you create an association between them. This allows you to collect data, process it, and present data associated with fields in the data source.

- **Object library:** Designer has a collection of frequently used form objects stored in a ready-to-use Library. Library objects may contain formatting, scripting and validation. The library that ships with LiveCycle Designer contains four groups:

  - **Standard library:** A complete set of basic form tools is available in LiveCycle Designer, including text fields, date fields, numeric fields, signature fields, drawing tools, and more.

  - **My favorites:** The most commonly used form tools are shown in a Large Icon view.

  - **Custom:** Complex Form Objects are made up of groups of individual fields, drop-down lists with stored values, and validation scripts.

  - **Barcodes:** You can choose from 45 different barcodes.

■ **Custom library objects:** You can customize and create additional objects and store them for future use, including formatting, scripting, and validation properties included with the object. A custom object also can be a group of individual objects stored together as a set. Add your custom objects to an existing library group, or create your own to keep things organized.

■ **Tables:** Designer has a table object in the library that you can easily customize to suit your needs. A table wizard helps you add tables quickly. Formatting tables is easily set with an alternating row property or to allow page breaks within the content.

■ **Subforms:** Using subforms to organize the layout of your form can help with alignment or general organization of related fields, and they are the basis of dynamic forms.

■ **Form fragments (available in LiveCycle Designer 8.1 and higher):** Form fragments are pieces of a form design that are used on multiple documents. They are stored in the fragment library as XDP files. Take a privacy disclaimer, for example; you may need to include it on many forms you design. By creating the disclaimer as a form fragment, you can store that text one time in the fragment library, reusing it as many times as needed and remaining confident that it contains the correct information. Then when that disclaimer has wording or formatting changes, you open the fragment library object to adjust it. Forms need to be stored in the native designer XDP format to take advantage of the fragments' updating abilities.

■ **Output formats:** When saving a LiveCycle Designer form, you can choose to save in XDP or PDF. If you deploy your forms using the LiveCycle Enterprise Suite, you also can choose HTML or Flash (LiveCycle Designer 8.1 or higher) as your desired output.

What you cannot do with LiveCycle Designer

Each of the PDF form design tools (Acrobat and LiveCycle Designer) has benefits and weaknesses. The following items are things that an AcroForm Designer may be accustomed to working with, but which do not behave the same way in LiveCycle Designer:

■ **Layers:** Designer does not support layers (Optional Content Groups) the way Acrobat does. Creating the appearance of layers requires creating subforms and then setting their visibility according to your needs.

■ **Limited color and graphic support:** LiveCycle Designer is not an Adobe native product; it was part of the acquisition of Accelio in 2001. RGB is the only color space supported. Graphics are limited to the following file types:

  ▪ BMP (Bitmap)

  ▪ EPS (Encapsulated PostScript)

  ▪ JPG (Joint Photographic Experts Group)

  ▪ GIF (Graphics Interchange Format, non-animated only)

  ▪ PNG (Portable Network Graphics)

  ▪ TIFF (Tagged Image File Format)

- **Page templates:** You cannot create Page Templates like you can with AcroForms. Designer forms can be made dynamic and spawn new elements on forms, but you cannot spawn a page from a template like you can in AcroForms.

- **Merge with other PDF documents into a single PDF:** PDF Packages (Acrobat 8) or PDF Portfolios (Acrobat 9) are required to combine a Designer form with other non-Designer PDF files. It is not possible to put a Designer form into an existing PDF as a single combined file.

- **Bookmarks and custom navigation require scripting:** In order to use bookmarks or custom navigation buttons in a Designer form, you need to write some JavaScript.

- **Initial view setting:** Some JavaScript is needed to control the Initial View of the PDF document.

- **Multimedia not supported:** LiveCycle Designer does not support movies or sounds the way Acrobat does. Using Multimedia with a Designer form could be accomplished by placing the Multimedia in a PDF and then combining those using PDF Packages (Acrobat 8) or PDF Portfolios (Acrobat 9).

As you can see, Acrobat form designers may need to adjust to some limitations. Most of these items have a workaround, so it becomes a matter of rather the long-term benefits outweighing the initial time investment. On the other hand, LiveCycle Designer offers significant enhancements over Acrobat forms with the data binding abilities, dynamic layouts, and reusable library objects. Weighing each of these items when deciding which product is right for you can help determine if one design tool offers more benefits for your project than the other.

We enjoy designing in both Acrobat and LiveCycle Designer and think the project requirements along with the audience expectations ought to be the determining factors in choosing the program used. We also realize that everyone has a certain comfort level with the two products, so when you have a limited amount of time, working in the product you are most comfortable with is sometimes the best option.

Using LiveCycle Designer and Acrobat

Both Acrobat and LiveCycle Designer create PDF forms, so both can open PDF forms. If you open an XML form in Acrobat, you can view and interact with the document. However, editing the actual form fields takes place in LiveCycle Designer. After you modify the document with LiveCycle Designer, going back to an AcroForm is not supported.

If you start a form design in Adobe Acrobat and then decide you want to work in LiveCycle Designer, you can. Opening an AcroForm in LiveCycle Designer causes the import wizard to open, asking you how you wish to import the document. Importing a PDF form has continued to improve in accuracy with each release of LiveCycle Designer.

CROSS-REF For more information on importing documents in LiveCycle Designer, see Chapter 23.

Editing XML forms in Acrobat

Adding security settings, distributing the form, and extending features in the free Adobe Reader are the only things Acrobat is allowed to modify on a Designer form. LiveCycle Designer must be used to edit the form fields on any forms that were opened and saved in LiveCycle Designer. Trying to modify a LiveCycle Designer form in Acrobat's Editing mode actually takes you to LiveCycle Designer.

TIP For static LCD forms, you can use convert to an Acrobat form by opening the Pages Panel and dragging the page icons to the desktop; the XML form opens in Acrobat with all Acrobat editing features, including editing and modifying fields. Dynamic forms, however, cannot be converted to Acrobat forms using this feature.

You may need to edit forms that were created by other people, but you may be unaware of the programs they used. If you want to check what product was used to create the form, you can open the Document Properties dialog box by choosing File ➪ Properties, as shown in Figure 21.3. The General tab lets you know if it was created by LiveCycle Designer or some other product.

FIGURE 21.3

The Document Properties dialog box indicates the authoring program used to create the form.

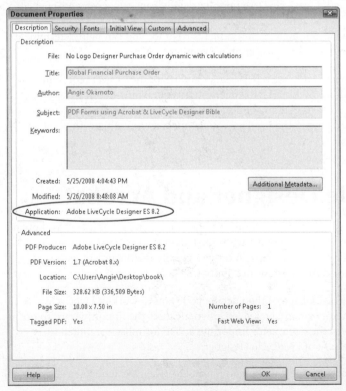

If you simply need to edit the form, and the authoring product doesn't matter to you, then opening the Acrobat Forms menu gives you enough information. The second choice in the Forms menu lets you edit forms. As shown in Figure 21.4, this menu item changes between *Add or Edit Forms Fields* for an Acrobat form and *Edit Form in Designer* if the form was built with LiveCycle Designer.

Enabling XML forms in Acrobat

LiveCycle Designer forms can be enabled in Acrobat the same way Acrobat forms can be. In order to start the process, you need to make sure the Designer form has been saved as a PDF.

STEPS: Enabling XML Designer Forms in Acrobat

1. Save your Designer form as a PDF.
2. Open the PDF in Adobe Acrobat.
3. Select Advanced ➪ Extend Features in Adobe Reader.
4. Click Save Now.

Remember that certain functions are restricted after enabling a document. If you didn't keep an original copy of the form and you open the enabled document in LiveCycle Designer to edit, you are prompted that doing so removes the special usage rights, as shown in Figure 21.5.

FIGURE 21.4

The second choice in the Forms menu changes depending on the document type opened in Acrobat.

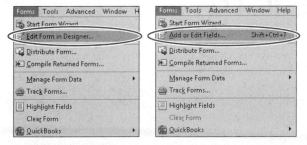

FIGURE 21.5

Opening an enabled form in LiveCycle Designer removes the special usage rights.

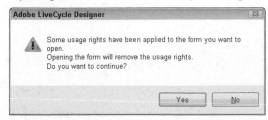

CROSS-REF **For more information on what usage rights are available and the limitations imposed by the Acrobat End User License Agreement (EULA), see Chapter 10.**

Distributing XML forms in Acrobat

After the form design has been finished and tested, you are ready to distribute your document to the form recipients. LiveCycle Designer has a Distribute Form button to facilitate the process, as shown in Figure 21.6. Clicking the Distribute Form button in LiveCycle Designer closes the form in LiveCycle Designer and opens it in Acrobat, displaying the Distribute Form wizard. Of course, you can open the form in Acrobat and start the distribute process from there. The button is simply a reminder that those features are available to an XML-based LiveCycle Designer form.

FIGURE 21.6

The Distribute Form button in LiveCycle Designer takes you to Acrobat to complete the process.

CROSS-REF **For more information on distributing forms, see Chapter 15.**

Looking at the Installed Files

LiveCycle Designer ships with a set of sample documents created to demonstrate the programs capabilities; these samples give you a resource to get started with. The sample files are stored in the program directory of your hard drive in the following location if English was chosen as the install language: *C:\Program Files\Adobe\Acrobat 9.0\Designer 8.2\EN\Samples*. If English was not the installed language, the EN folder is replaced with your language.

These files may initially seem buried and difficult to find, but they are certainly worth exploring. LiveCycle Designer provides you with their location in many places. The Welcome screen provides a link to the help files with detailed descriptions of the samples and their storage locations. The Help menu also provides a link to the Samples section of the help documentation. If you're searching the help file, you can find the sample files in the category "Sample Form Snippets and Forms."

Examining the sample files

Table 21.2 describes the sample files included with LiveCycle Designer.

TABLE 21.2	

LiveCycle Designer Sample Files

Folder Name	Description
Dunning Notice	This sample shows how a single design page adjusts when data is merged for printing. The resulting file is not an interactive form but demonstrates the ability to use multiple master pages.
E-Ticket	A dynamic form with six design pages that utilize two different master page layouts. Provides a great example of portrait and landscape orientations.
FormGuide	This folder contains three sample files: Immunization, Purchase Order, and TLA Life: • The immunization form shows a non-standard form design with sections rotated for folding. When rendered as Flash, this turns into a wizard driven document. • The purchase order is a dynamic sample that demonstrates how a repeating form section works when rendered as Flash. • The TLA Life form extends the standard options available with Form Guides utilizing customized panels built with Flex to demonstrate how damage to a car can be captured.
Grant Application	This interactive form does not have repeating sections. It has a dynamic field on the second page that allows it to flow onto additional pages if necessary.
Purchase Order	The purchase order folder contains multiple designs of the same document: an interactive form that is a static layout, a dynamic purchase order that adjusts the layout when data is merged with it, not to be completed by the form recipient, and a dynamic interactive version that is to be completed by the form recipient. The two interactive forms also have Form Guides setup to render them as Flash. The last sample contains a data connection to an XML Schema Definition file (XSD) to show how data can be mapped to the form design.
Scripting	A sample form designed to test script in both JavaScript and FormCalc. You don't need to open the script editor. Enter your script directly in the PDF form and click the buttons to test your skills.
Subform Set	Four samples to explore how you can use subform sets to display the same data in different ways. There are two sample XML data files that can be viewed with any of the four forms.
Tax Receipt	This dynamic form prints three copies of a donation receipt on a single page for tax reporting.

Let's look at some of these sample forms. The Dunning Notice is sent to the customer indicating that the payment for a receivable/debt is past due. When we open the form in Design view, it appears to be a one-page form. The main area of the document contains the following information: document number, document date, due date, days in arrears, level, and amount. This information is actually wrapped in a subform that repeats when populated with data.

To see the information change, select the Preview PDF tab at the top of the screen. The form is already designed to pull in a sample set of data, which contains three records, as shown in Figure 21.7. We can change the sample data file and watch the PDF grow to a second page with many records.

FIGURE 21.7

The Dunning Notice in the Preview PDF tab, with the Dunning Notice Level1 sample XML

To change the sample data on the Dunning Notice form installed with your LiveCycle Designer installation, follow these steps.

STEPS: Changing a Sample Data File Previewed in LiveCycle Designer

1. **Open the Form Properties dialog box.** Select File ➪ Form Properties.
2. **Select the Preview Tab.**
3. **Click the browse button to the right of the data path box, as shown in Figure 21.8**
4. **Open the XML file.** Select the *Dunning Notice Level3.xml* file in the directory, and choose open.

5. **Click OK in the Form Properties dialog box.**

6. **View the changes.** Select the Preview PDF tab to view the changes.

FIGURE 21.8

In the Preview tab of the Form Properties dialog box, click the browse button to select an alternate sample data file for previewing.

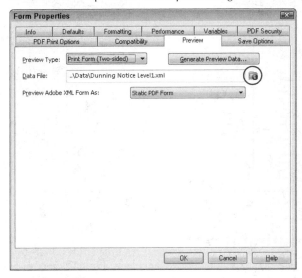

Changing the sample XML file associated with a LiveCycle form can be done as many times as necessary to verify that the form reacts to the data changes appropriately. Figure 21.9 shows the Dunning Notice with the *Dunning Notice Level3.xml* sample file.

TIP   If you are more interested in the end result of the alternate data sets and not as interested in the form design, then open the final results in the Outputs folder. The Outputs folder has a PDF stored with the results of each of the sample XML files.

Another Sample file, the E-Ticket, is a 6-page design with an output of 12 pages when viewed with the sample file. The E-Ticket is a wonderful example of how your form design can contain pages of different orientations and page requirements.

The help window has additional documentation to go with each of the numbered items in the E-Ticket sample file. Exploring these samples can give you a good overview of the program's ability to create complex dynamic form layouts. Many of the files also include scripting samples for your use.

FIGURE 21.9

The Dunning Notice changes to a two-page document when the sample XML file is changed.

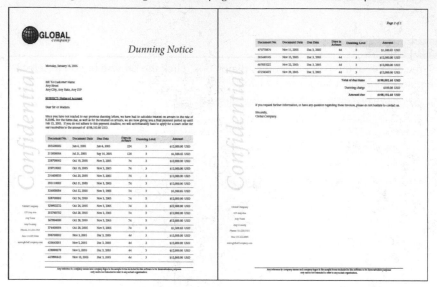

Using the scripting references

LiveCycle Designer allows scripting in one of two languages: FormCalc or JavaScript. The language you decide to write your script with affects how the form can be deployed. If you always save your Designer file as a PDF, then either language can safely be used. If you plan to deploy your forms using the LiveCycle Enterprise Suite servers as Flash or HTML, you need to use JavaScript, because FormCalc is not supported in browsers.

The scripting references in LiveCycle Designer are broken down into three categories:

- **Scripting using LiveCycle Designer ES:** This area gives you the overview of how scripting and calculations work. It explains where and how to place scripts in your form design. It shows you how to change the settings in LiveCycle Designer to suit your preferred scripting language. This area of the scripting guide has some very useful sections that compare JavaScript to FormCalc and list the comparable functions if one exists.

- **Scripting reference:** This area of the reference guide is for scripting with XFA and XML objects. This section provides the list of objects, properties, and methods available to the scripting languages. It lists both language syntax options if available.

- **FormCalc user reference summary:** This scripting reference lists the functions and formulas available in the FormCalc language. FormCalc is modeled after common spreadsheet formulas and was designed to be simple yet powerful.

Adobe maintains PDF versions of the scripting manuals on its Web site, which ensures that you have up-to-date information available. They can be downloaded and searched through normal PDF methods. For more information, check the following Web sites:

- `www.adobe.com/go/learn_lc_scriptingReference`
- `www.adobe.com/go/learn_lc_formCalc`
- `http://help.adobe.com/en_US/livecycle/es/LiveCycle_Designer_Scripting_Basics.pdf`
- `http://partners.adobe.com/public/developer/en/acrobat/sdk/AcroJS_DesignerJS.pdf`

CROSS-REF For more information on scripting using FormCalc and JavaScript, see Chapter 29.

Summary

- LiveCycle Designer creates PDF forms based on XML.
- LiveCycle Designer forms have Acrobat/Reader version dependencies, with the minimum being 6.02 to open the form.
- Acrobat Forms can be imported into LiveCycle Designer for editing.
- Designer form fields cannot be edited by Acrobat. Acrobat can only add security, enable usage rights in the free Reader, and distribute the Designer form.
- The Library palette contains a collection of frequently used form objects, many with formatting, script, and validation included.
- You can customize the Library by adding groups and custom objects for future use.
- Data bindings can be created to connect your LiveCycle form to a data source for additional data capabilities.
- Form fragments are frequently used pieces of information on multiple forms that can be updated easily when needed.
- Tables are easily created and fully supported by LiveCycle Designer.
- Subforms are used to organize related fields on the form and are the basis of dynamic flowing layouts.
- Designer forms do not support multimedia or layers.
- Some standard Acrobat settings like Initial View and Bookmarks require scripting to accomplish in Designer.
- Two scripting languages are available: FormCalc and JavaScript.
- Although either scripting language can be used in a PDF form, JavaScript is required if you leverage the LiveCycle Enterprise Suite to deploy as HTML or Flash.
- Templates are included with LiveCycle Designer to help you start using forms.
- Sample forms also are included for your use.

Chapter 22

Getting Familiar with the Designer Workspace

Adobe LiveCycle Designer is a powerful form design program, which becomes very apparent when you open the workspace. Designer makes extensive use of palettes that are loaded with all the tools and properties you need to create your forms.

As we have mentioned in previous chapters, when you create a form in LiveCycle Designer, you cannot edit the form in Acrobat. Now that we have covered the differences between Acrobat and Designer Forms, we are ready to start designing. Remember that unlike Acrobat, Designer allows you to do all the form design within the application. You don't need to use another authoring program to create your form background and labels. Just open Designer, and we'll discuss all the tools you'll need to build a new form.

In this chapter, we cover exploring the basic Designer workspace and descriptions for using tools, menus, and palettes.

IN THIS CHAPTER

The LiveCycle Designer welcome screen

Form Assistant options

Examining the palettes

Customizing the workspace

Getting Familiar with the LiveCycle Designer Environment

The first thing you see when you launch LiveCycle Designer is the Welcome to Adobe LiveCycle Designer window, as shown in Figure 22.1. The window is designed to help you get started using the program. It contains important links to sample files, new documents, existing documents, and the help files. Take a few moments to explore the options in the welcome window.

FIGURE 22.1

The Welcome to Adobe LiveCycle Designer window opens when you first launch LiveCycle Designer.

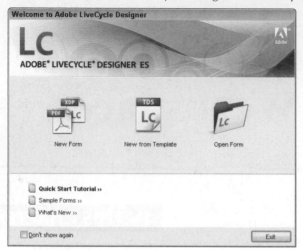

Navigating the welcome window

The welcome window contains three task buttons and three additional text links. The task buttons offer a quick way to work with your forms. They allow you to create new forms or open existing forms. The text links are provided for you to explore the sample forms installed with LiveCycle Designer, learn about new features, and create forms following a step-by-step tutorial.

The first task button in the welcome window is the New Form button. The icon contains two images: a PDF document and an XDP document. These are not your only options, but an indicator of the types that are available. Upon selecting this option, you are initially greeted by the New Form Assistant, as shown in Figure 22.2. The New Form Assistant can walk you through the process of creating your forms using a variety of methods.

TIP After you become more comfortable with the program, you may wish to bypass the welcome window when you open LiveCycle Designer. To bypass the window once, use the Exit button in the lower-right corner or the Esc key on your keyboard. The welcome window continues to appear each time you launch the program or begin a new form.

To stop the screen from opening on startup and each time you create a new form, check the Don't show again box in the lower-left corner. The next time you launch LiveCycle Designer, the welcome window doesn't open. If you want to reopen the welcome window, select Help ⇨ Welcome.

FIGURE 22.2

The New Form Assistant guides you through creating a form.

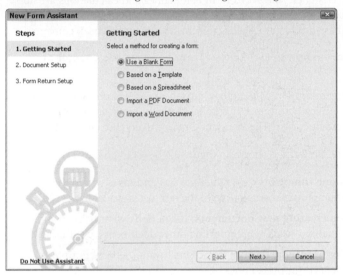

Creating forms with the New Form Assistant

You have these options for creating new forms using the New Form Assistant:

- **Use a Blank Form:** With this option, you can select the desired paper size, orientation, and number of blank pages to start your form. You then create the design of the document by adding the necessary text, graphics, and form fields using the tools in Designer.

- **Based on a Template:** There is no need to start from scratch, if one of these prebuilt templates has what you are looking for. This option allows you to create a new form from a variety of templates such as invoices, order forms, and purchase orders.

  Using the New Form Assistant, you can create a PDF form with interactive text fields based on the column headers in the Excel spreadsheet. The New Form Assistant creates one text field object for each column in the spreadsheet. Text field objects are positioned in the form from left to right and wrapped onto additional lines if needed. The caption and binding name of each text field object corresponds to the column header text in the spreadsheet.

- **Import a PDF Document:** You may already have forms built in another program. By converting them into PDF documents, you can then import them into Designer for further development. Or if you've already built a form in Acrobat, you'll want to use this method. When you import Acrobat forms with fields, Designer recognizes the fields and converts them to the equivalent Designer fields. You may use the PDF document as a static background image in the new LiveCycle Designer Form or convert it to a flowable layout as if it were created in LiveCycle Designer.

■ **Import a Word Document:** If you have forms created in Word, select this option to convert them. If the original Word document contains form fields, they are converted to form fields in LiveCycle Designer. The Word form field names and calculations are not maintained when converted to LiveCycle Designer. If the file contains only the labels on the form, then you need to add the form fields after the document has been converted.

CROSS-REF   For more information on how to use the New Form Assistant, see Chapter 23.

Each time you create a new document, import a document, or import a PDF from Acrobat, the New Form Assistant is launched. You can customize this behavior to suit your needs. Click the Do Not Use Assistant link in the lower-left corner. The Assistant Options dialog box appears.

These items appear in the Assistant Options, as shown in Figure 22.3:

■ **Skip the Assistant this one time:** This closes the Assistant and takes you to the New Dialog box to select a common paper size or one of the templates available.

■ **Skip the Assistant when creating new documents:** If you don't want help creating forms in LiveCycle Designer but want help importing other documents, use this setting.

■ **Don't show the New Form Assistant again:** If you don't want the New Form Assistant to help with new documents or imported ones, use this setting.

FIGURE 22.3

The Assistant Options dialog box allows you to control when you want the New Form Assistant to help.

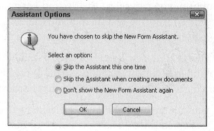

To change your New Form Assistant settings, open the options window by choosing Tools ⇨ Options and select the Wizards and Tips category on the left side of the window. The lower-right side displays the Form Wizard options, as shown in Figure 22.4.

When you choose not to use the Form Assistant, a different window appears when you select New Form. The New dialog box allows you to select a paper size to start a blank document or choose from one of the templates available, as shown in Figure 22.5.

FIGURE 22.4

The Options dialog box, where the Form Assistant settings are retained

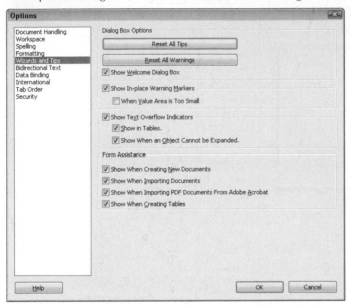

 TIP If you want to bypass both the Form Assistant and the New dialog box, you can do so by turning off the welcome window and turning off the Form Assistant. Each time you launch Designer after that, you have a blank gray interface screen. Clicking the New button on the toolbar starts a blank document based on your default template without needing to complete a dialog box.

The second task button in the welcome window is the New from Template button, which shows a LiveCycle TDS icon. Using this option starts the New Form Assistant described above (refer to Figure 22.2). It preselects the first step of the wizard and moves you to the second step to select the template. Open Form is the third task button in the welcome window, which launches a standard Open dialog box.

Quick Start Tutorial is the top link. This opens the LiveCycle Designer Help files and navigates to the Tutorial section. The Tutorial contains sample forms you can try, such as an office function survey and purchase order. These are step-by-step directions on how to create a form.

The Sample Forms option contains a variety of forms to explore and learn from. Click the link to open the Help window, where descriptions of each form are listed as well as the location of the document.

FIGURE 22.5

The New dialog box, where you can choose paper size for a blank document or start from a template

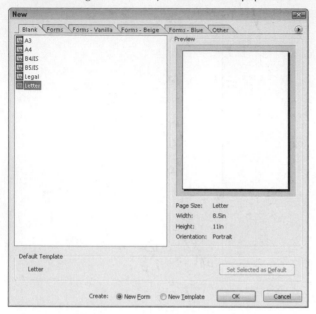

The last link in the welcome window is What's New. In each release of the program, new features are added and existing features enhanced. Trying to explore the program on your own and hoping to stumble upon each of these new features would be a difficult task. The Help file describes each of these new features or enhancements, so that you may start utilizing them. These are a few of our favorite new features in Designer:

- **Hyperlinks** (Version 8.2): You have the ability to change text into an interactive hyper-link. It's a long-awaited and much-welcomed feature.

- **Typography enhancements** (Version 8.2): Kerning, spacing, and tab leaders are available, to name a few. Check out the Font palette for more.

- **Tab order** (Version 8.2): With this enhancement, setting tab order can now be done in a list format via the new tab order palette. It is no longer necessary to click the objects on the page when changing to a custom order; you simply drag the items up or down in the list.

- **Form fragments** (Version 8.1): Form fragments are pieces of a form design that are used on multiple documents. They are stored in the fragment library as XDP files. Take a privacy disclaimer, for example; you may need to include it on many of the forms you design. By creating the disclaimer as a form fragment, you can store that text one time in the fragment library, reusing it as many times as needed and confident it contains the correct information. Then when that disclaimer has wording or formatting changes, you open the fragment library object to adjust it. Forms need to be stored in the native designer XDP format to take advantage of the fragments updating abilities.

Examining the workspace

One of the hardest things to adjust to in a new program is locating the tools you need. You may know what needs to be done to get your form ready; now you need to locate the appropriate tools to create it.

The Designer workspace offers menu commands, toolbars, palettes, and editors to help you accomplish your task. When you launch the program, you see many of these features already in the workspace, but others need to be turned on. As you grow more comfortable working in Designer, you'll notice that your own preferences affect how the workspace is arranged. As we explore the program in more depth, we discuss many of these items again in later chapters. Take some time to familiarize yourself with the terms used to describe the various areas of the Designer interface, as shown in Figure 22.6.

The title bar is located at the top of the program window. It contains the name of the program and the name of the document you are currently working on. The menu bar is just below the title bar and contains all the available commands.

The script editor

Smart forms require mathematical calculations or validation logic in order to collect the correct data. We don't want to depend on the form recipient having a calculator handy to complete complicated forms. The script editor allows you to write the code to make your form easier for the form recipient to complete. Scripting is permitted in JavaScript and FormCalc languages.

FIGURE 22.6

The Designer interface as it appears when you first launch the program

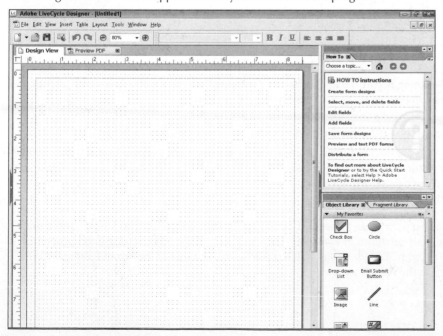

How Many Versions of LiveCycle Designer?

Some confusion surrounds the version numbers associated with LiveCycle Designer. This is because Designer is released with two product families: Adobe Acrobat Pro and Pro Extended (Windows Only) and LiveCycle Enterprise Suite (ES). Because these product families are on different release cycles, the currently available features are included at release time.

We hope this becomes less of an issue in future releases, by releasing the Acrobat and LiveCycle products on the same release cycle.

Did you realize that when you buy Acrobat Pro or Pro Extended, you receive a free copy of LiveCycle Designer? If you wanted to buy LiveCycle Designer, it would cost as much as Acrobat Pro. This is an important concept; because Adobe is giving you free software, the updates available are limited. When LiveCycle Designer is part of the Acrobat family, it receives only bug fixes. It does not receive updates with new feature enhancements.

Let's look at the last release of each product family in which Designer was included.

Product and Version	Date Released	Designer Version Number at Release	Designer Version Number after Updates*
Acrobat 8 Professional (Windows Only)	November 2006	8.0	8.05.X
LiveCycle Designer ES	July 2007	8.1	8.2
Acrobat 9 Pro and Pro Extended (Windows Only)	June 2008	8.2	No update yet

* at the time of this writing

CROSS-REF Scripting is covered in Chapter 29. Exploring the script editor is covered later in this chapter in the section "Opening the script editor."

Palettes, palette wells, and palette tabs

Three palette wells are docked to the workspace when you launch Designer. Two are open and visible on the right side of workspace: the How To palette and the Library palette. The third palette well, the Hierarchy palette, is hidden on the left side of the workspace. Hidden palettes can be turned on in the Window menu.

Palette wells have a palette bar, an expand button, a close button, and menus, and can hold more than one palette tab, as shown in Figure 22.7. Palettes contain the tools, settings, and properties available to work with. To hide or show all the palettes on one side of the layout editor, click the expand button on the palette border.

FIGURE 22.7

The Object Library palette well

While working in Designer and switching palettes, some items in the palette may not be visible. Because the palette well can be resized, information can get cut off the edges. When that occurs, a light gray bar with a double black arrow appears on the edge where information is not visible. To show the missing information, click the gray bar and the palette automatically resizes in that direction. Resizing the palette manually is also an option.

Many tools and settings are located within the palettes, and finding what you need may be challenging at first. Rest assured that this gets easier as you become more comfortable with Designer. You can create additional palette wells, reorganize the tabs within the palette wells, and even remove some palette wells if desired.

CROSS-REF For more information on changing palettes, see "Customizing the Workspace" later in this chapter.

Using the Hierarchy palette

The Hierarchy palette, shown in Figure 22.8, appears on the left side of the workspace. It is a structured view of each object in the form and is used for many purposes. We all know that objects can be very difficult to select sometimes. The Hierarchy tab makes selection easy; whatever you select in the Hierarchy palette is also selected in the active editor: Design View, Master Pages, or the XML source. The keyboard shortcut for the Hierarchy is Shift+F11.

TIP Keyboard shortcuts can be used to show or hide each of the palettes. If the palette is open, but not the active tab in the palette well, the shortcut activates it. When the palette is closed or when the palette well in which the tab appears is minimized, the shortcut opens it. When the palette is already open and is the active tab in the palette well, the shortcut closes the palette. Note that it does not close the palette well, only the palette tab, unless that palette tab is the only tab contained in the palette well.

FIGURE 22.8

The Hierarchy view of our purchase order form

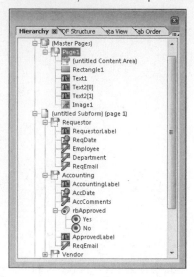

The hierarchy shows the objects placed on the form, in the order you placed them. It can be used to organize objects into logical groups of related items. The stacking order of objects displayed on the form can be altered in the hierarchy. Moving an item in the hierarchy does not affect its placement on the design page when the form is positioned content, as shown in Figure 22.9. The following methods work to select objects using the Hierarchy palette:

- **Single object:** Click the object.

- **Multiple adjacent objects:** Click the first object and then hold down the Shift key while clicking the last object. This selects all objects in between.

- **Multiple non-adjacent objects:** Click the first object and then hold down the Ctrl key while clicking each additional object.

- **Select a group:** If groups were created, you can select a group by clicking the group node in the hierarchy.

A clear understanding of the hierarchy is critical when we build dynamic forms with flowing layouts. The object's position in the hierarchy determines its layout on the design page when rendered. In a dynamic flowing layout, changing an object's position in the hierarchy changes the object's position in the design page, as shown in Figure 22.10.

FIGURE 22.9

The Hierarchy and Layout view of a positioned form. Notice that the order of objects in the hierarchy does not affect the position of objects on the design page.

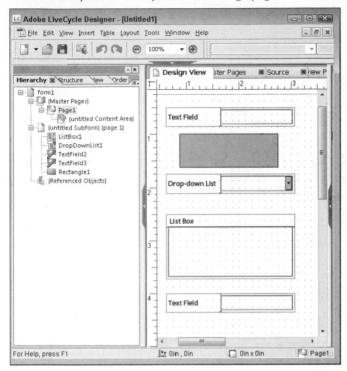

CROSS-REF **Designing dynamic forms is covered in Chapter 26.**

We recommend that you rename your objects and organize the hierarchy each time you design a form. It takes only a few minutes to complete, and you become more efficient when locating objects later. Objects can be renamed at any time during the design process. The object name can be edited in the Hierarchy palette, the Object palette, or the field editor.

FIGURE 22.10

The Hierarchy and Layout view of a flowed form. The objects' positions in the hierarchy caused them to move on the design page to match the order in the form template hierarchy.

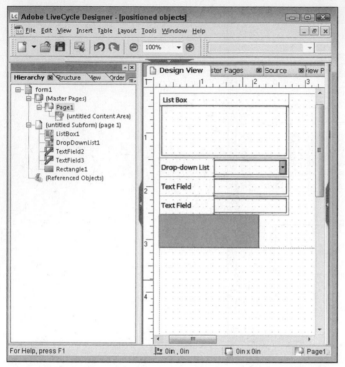

STEPS: Renaming an Object in the Hierarchy

1. **Right-click the object.** This displays the context menu.
2. **Choose Rename from the context menu.** The field name is highlighted in blue for you to replace.

   The keyboard shortcut to rename a field in the hierarchy is F2. Select the field, and press F2 on the keyboard to rename the field.
3. **Type the new field name.**
4. **Press Enter to save the new name.**

To organize the hierarchy, you simply drag the fields to the preferred locations. Dragging groups of fields is beneficial when portions of the form have already been organized.

Using the Data View palette

PDF forms are used to gather electronic data. What happens to that data after the form recipient completes the requested information? Does this data belong to an existing electronic file? Will someone rekey the data into that file?

A Designer form can have data bindings that allow you to exchange data between the form and another data source. If your form has a data connection established, the Data View palette displays the connection name and hierarchy of the data nodes, as shown in Figure 22.11. If no data connection is set up, this palette appears empty.

FIGURE 22.11

The Data View palette for a form bound to an XML sample data file

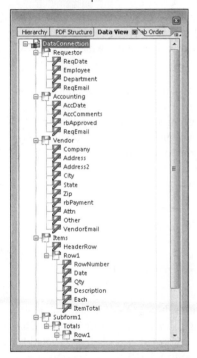

CROSS-REF See Chapter 31 for more information on data connections.

The Data View palette appears in the palette well docked on the left side of the workspace. Although no shortcut is designated for this palette, you can switch between palette tabs using the keyboard by pressing Ctrl+Tab. Keyboard shortcuts also can be assigned if desired.

CROSS-REF See "Customizing keyboard shortcuts" later in this chapter for details.

Using the PDF Structure palette

The PDF Structure palette is available only if the form was imported from a PDF file and set as a fixed background. If you import a structured PDF document as artwork, the PDF Structure tab displays tags and structural information about the background PDF. This information is used by assistive technologies to define the reading order and tabbing order in the document. If you import a PDF that is not tagged, or *not structured*, the PDF Structure palette allows you to add structure to the document. The palette gives a nice reminder on forms where the palette is unnecessary: "PDF Structure can only be used in PDF forms that contain artwork."

Using the Tab Order palette

Form recipients tabbing through a form when entering data is common practice. Although a few users still click the fields with the mouse, more users navigate using the keyboard. Tab Order is also very important when an assistive device is in use. The tab order determines which field is selected next in the navigation.

The Tab Order palette is new in Designer 8.2 and is used if the default tab order does not suit your needs. Tab order can be set in previous versions of Designer. However, no palette was available with which to alter the sequence. In any previous version of Designer, changing the tab order meant clicking each field in the order desired. This was a very tedious process for many users who were unaware of the shortcuts available to modify tab order in the middle of the sequence. Imagine the frustration of clicking the wrong field on a form with hundreds of fields. Using the palette to change tab order by dragging and dropping fields into the desired sequence is a great improvement over the previous method.

A number is displayed beside each object's name as shown in Figure 22.12. The number indicates the sequence of the objects within the tab order. To alter the current field's tab position, drag it to a new location in the Tab Order palette.

Using the Info palette

Metadata for the selected object can be found in the Info palette. If there is a <desc> tag included in the XML source for an object the Info palette displays the tag information. The form's metadata can be seen when the top level in the hierarchy is selected. This information is being populated by the form properties dialog box. To add or change information, go to File ➪ Form Properties and choose the Info tab.

The new Tab Order palette for setting custom tab sequences

Examining the Fields palettes

In Acrobat the field tools fit on a single toolbar. Designer offers many interactive field objects for you to use when creating forms. All those tools require more space to store them. The Library palette houses all of the form design objects.

Using the Library palette

Being able to store and reuse form field objects is one of best time-saving features when building forms in Designer. Unlike Acrobat where field object properties must be set or copied from an existing field each time, Designer stores your custom field preferences.

The Object Library palette is different than the other palettes in Designer, as shown in Figure 22.13. It has an accordion style appearance to the groups, with a triangle/arrow on the left side of the group name to indicate open or closed. The group is closed if the triangle is pointing toward the name. The group is open if the triangle is pointing down.

FIGURE 22.13

The Object Library palette

The Object Library palette contains all the different objects needed to create your forms. The Object Library is divided into four standard groups: My Favorites, Standard, Custom, and Barcodes. The Standard group contains each of the basic form field objects:

- **Button:** Use this when you want the form recipient to initiate an event such as submitting data, adding sections to a form, printing, and resetting form data.

- **Date/Time Field:** This is a specialized field with a data type set to date and/or time. The form recipient gets a pop-up calendar control to select the date. Customize the date format as needed for display as well as data collection.

- **Signature Field:** Digital signatures are used to authenticate users or attest to document contents. You can specify whether a signature covers the entire form or selected objects on the form. To use selected objects, you must create a collection and the signing party must use Acrobat or Adobe Reader version 8.0 or later.

- **Image Field:** An image field is used when the form recipient needs to attach an image to the form, or when the data being merged with the document contains record-specific images. For example, if the form is an employee emergency contact record, we may want to print the employee picture with the data.

- **Print Button:** Add a print button to your form as a reminder to the form recipient when a printed copy is needed. The print button opens the print dialog box to choose the print settings needed.

- **Reset Button:** A reset button can be used to clear data from all of the form fields back to their default values.

- **Submit Button:** When you want to submit the data via e-mail or the Internet, a submit button sends the data.

  - **Email Submit Button:** Clicking an e-mail submit button attaches either the form data or the entire form to an e-mail message for submission to the specified e-mail address. Be aware that this is not a secure process, which means the document can be opened by anyone who has access to that e-mail.

  - **HTTP Submit Button:** A Web site with a standard URL, which is able to process the incoming data, is required in order to use an HTTP submit button. When the form recipient clicks the button, the Acrobat viewer program sends the data using the Internet to the specified URL.

Understanding the Default Tab Order

Tab order in form fields can make your form user friendly or extremely frustrating to the form recipient. Making sure you take time to test this before distributing your form is imperative. Adobe realizes tab order is important and sets it up for you by default. Understanding how Designer sets the default tab order saves time and frustration when designing forms.

When building a form in Designer, the default tab order is determined by the position of the object in the form. Tabbing is set from top to bottom and left to right based on object position. In other words, the object with the smallest Y coordinate (vertical position) is first in the tab order. If multiple objects are aligned at the same Y coordinate, with different X coordinates (horizontal position), the leftmost object is first in the sequence.

Let's explore a form's tab order that is problematic and discuss what is causing the issues. Notice in the form below that the fields are organized into the applicant block on the left and the joint-applicant block on the right. The form with the incorrect tab order has trouble tabbing through the titles in the correct sequence. It also takes us to the co-applicant title before finishing the applicant block of data.

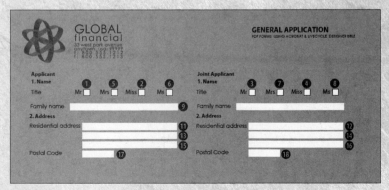

Form with wrong tab order

continued

continued

The problem with the titles tabbing out of sequence is caused by their Y coordinates not being identical. The author manually aligned the title fields. You can avoid this by using the alignment features.

Field Name	Y Coordinate Measurement	Incorrect Tab Position
Applicant Mr	1.7898 in	1
Applicant Mrs	1.795 in	5
Applicant Miss	1.7898 in	2
Applicant Ms	1.795 in	6
Joint Mr	1.7898 in	3
Joint Mrs	1.795 in	7
Joint Miss	1.7898 in	4
Joint Ms	1.795 in	8

To fix the titles, the fields must have the same Y coordinate. Once changed, the tab order of the title fields is fixed. However, the problem remains with the tab order jumping left to right through the fields. We want the applicant information filled in first and then the joint-applicant.

This can be achieved by wrapping the sections in a subform. A subform tells Designer that the fields are related and should be treated as a set. The tab order looks at the top-left handle of the subform for determining tab position. When the tab order reaches the first item in the subform, it tabs through all the subform items before going back to the main form. Below you'll find a form with the tab order set after the changes have been made.

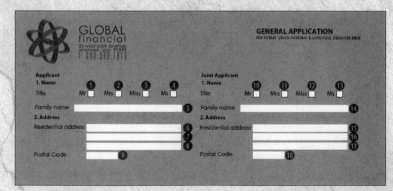

Form with correct tab order

CROSS-REF Distributing forms is covered in more detail in Chapter 30.

- **Numeric Field:** Use this when you need to collect floating decimal or integer data, including currency, use a Numeric field. Numeric fields are limited to two decimal places, so any additional data is rounded.

- **Password Field:** Placing a Password field on the form allows you to mask the entered characters displayed in the document.

- **Radio Button:** When you need to allow a single choice in a set of related options, use radio buttons. For example, if you ask form recipients for their gender, they should not be able to select both male and female.

- **Check Box:** When multiple choices are allowed in response to a question, use check boxes. For example, if you offer multiple services, form recipients should be able to select as many items as they are interested in.

- **Decimal Field:** A decimal field is very similar to a numeric field. Use a decimal field when you need to control the number of leading digits, or the number of decimal places.

- **Drop-down List:** When you want to provides the user with a list of choices for data entry, you can use a drop-down list. Only one choice is visible on the form until the button is clicked by the form recipient, and only one selection is allowed. You also can choose to allow a form recipient to enter custom text if the choice he needs is not included in the drop-down choices.

- **List Box:** A list box is similar to a drop-down list. A list box can show multiple lines on the form. The list box may accept multiple choices; however, custom entries are not allowed.

- **Table:** A table can be either a field or a static object. The standard table features are allowed, including header rows, body rows, and footer rows. If the table spans a page break, it is possible to define an overflow header and footer if desired. Tables also can be static in layout or dynamically adjusting based on user interaction or data merged with the form.

- **Text Field:** The text field is the most common form object and can accept multiple lines and formatting of the text if desired.

The Standard group of the Object Library also contains some static objects. Static objects do not allow user interaction:

- **Circle:** The circle object can be used for an ellipse, circle, or arc appearance and may include gradient fill effects.

- **Content Area:** Content areas reside on the master pages of the form. They control the layout of all other objects placed in the form design including subforms. Changing the content area size on the master page alters where objects can be placed on the design page.

- **Image:** This image object does not change based on user input or data merging. We use image fields to display company logos and graphics that remain consistent.

- **Line:** Drawn lines can be used for enhancing form design. Lines are available in a variety of dashed and dotted styles with custom sizes and colors.

- **Rectangle:** Drawn rectangles can include gradient fill effects, and you have four corner styles to choose from.

- **Subform:** A subform is a container used to organize objects in the form design. The subform also controls the objects positioning in the document.

- **Text:** Static text objects are used as labels, titles, and repeating header/footer information. Remember that these text objects do not allow user interaction in the form.

Exploring the Fragment Library

Adjacent to the Object Library palette, you will find the Fragment Library palette as shown in Figure 22.14. Many custom objects are used in multiple form designs, which of course is why we choose to store them as custom objects. We simply don't want to take the time to recreate the object each time it is used. Now consider that the custom object was something like a disclaimer, which every year gets reviewed by a committee. Worse yet, it gets reviewed every quarter. Now we need to locate every form that uses the custom object and replace it with the new one. Having the custom object certainly is better than having to copy and paste; however, this is exactly the type of thing that form fragments are good for.

FIGURE 22.14

The Fragment Library palette

Form fragments are custom objects that are stored in the file system as XDP files. When you place a form fragment in your design, a link to the fragment is created. When you make changes to that disclaimer, you only have one place that needs updated—the form fragment!

You also can create script fragments, if you have a script that is completely independent of an object, such as loop routine. Object-related scripts, such as validate and calculate, cannot be turned into script fragments.

CROSS-REF For information on how to create and use form fragments, see Chapter 24.

CAUTION A Designer form saved as an XDP automatically receives fragment updates. Any time the XDP is opened, or used in LiveCycle ES the fragment retrieves the current information available. A Designer form saved as a PDF file embeds the fragment at the time the document is saved. In order to update the fragment in the PDF file it must be opened in Designer and saved again.

Using the How To palette

This small palette usually docks on the right side of the design page. The How To palette contains a list of help topics for commonly used features. This feature does not open the complete help file; it provides you with the how-to steps directly in the palette.

There are seven main categories listed in the How To palette, as shown in Figure 22.15. Clicking a topic brings up additional choices to select from. Navigating the How To palette is very intuitive. A home link at the top takes you back to the main seven options. A drop-down menu lets you jump to another topic.

FIGURE 22.15

The How To palette showing the seven category options

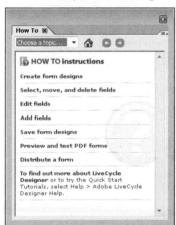

Using the Layout palette

The Layout palette contains the following settings regarding the selected object: size and position information, margins, and caption position as shown in Figure 22.16. The X/Y coordinates indicate where on the design page the object is currently placed. This measurement is usually based on the object's top-left handle, known as the anchor point. Changing the anchor point to any other handle or the center is possible. These additional options are located in the Anchor drop-down list. This is useful when selecting the Expand to fit option.

Objects in Designer forms can adjust in size based on content the form recipient provides or data that is merged to the form. Selecting the Expand to fit option is part of what allows that to occur. When the object size adjusts, it increases in height and width away from the anchor point. For a standard object with the top-left anchor, the object grows to the right and down.

FIGURE 22.16

The Layout palette

CROSS-REF For more information on dynamically expanding fields or forms, see Chapter 26.

Limited object rotation is also allowed. Buttons are available for the following settings: No Rotation/Remove Rotation, Rotate 90°, Rotate 180°, and Rotate 270°. Unfortunately, custom rotation is not supported in Designer.

Many field objects contain a caption. The caption can reside on any of the four sides of the field. Some form authors prefer captions on the left, while others prefer them below the object. An ongoing debate involves whether check boxes should have captions on the left or the right of the box. Changing the position is a simple click of the drop-down choices.

CROSS-REF For customizing captions and layout tips, see Chapter 25.

Using the Object palette

The Object palette contains sub-tabs. Which tabs are available depends on the selected object type. Static objects such as text or rectangles have only a sub-tab called Draw. You can set properties such as visible and locale as shown in Figure 22.17.

FIGURE 22.17

The Object palette

For fields, the Object palette contains three sub-tabs: Field, Value, and Binding. Some properties, such as name and data binding, are available for all object types. Many additional properties available here are specific to the currently selected field type:

- **Field:** The object tab properties change based on the object type. For example, a drop-down list is populated by the list items entered here, or you can change the style of a check mark.

- **Value:** If you want to have a preselected value when the form recipient opens your form, you can provide a default value on this tab. Validation rules also are set here.

- **Binding:** If you establish a data connection to your form, this tab stores the binding to the data.

CROSS-REF See Chapter 25 for details on using the Object palette to set properties.

Using the Border palette

The Border palette stores the settings for the border color, line weight, and fill effects as shown in Figure 22.18. Most objects have properties that can be set in the Border palette. However, four Library Objects do not have any properties in the Border palette: Line, Rectangle, Circle, and Content Area. The first three objects have borders available, but they are stored in the Object palette.

FIGURE 22.18

The Border palette

Currently, nine border styles, adjustable line weights, custom border colors, four corner styles with a customizable radius, solid colors, and gradient fills are available to choose from.

CROSS-REF   **Applying border properties is covered in Chapter 25.**

Using the Accessibility palette

Accessibility ensures that form recipients with disabilities can access electronic content and resources using assistive devices. LiveCycle Designer can create forms that comply with the U.S. federal code regulating accessibility for vision and mobility challenged persons. This code is generally referred to as Section 508. For more information, see www.section508.gov. Be aware that accessibility policies vary from country to country. Check your local policy as needed.

Just creating the form in Designer does not make it accessible. Some additional properties must be set to make it compliant. Because Designer forms are generally viewed as PDF files, many items discussed in Chapter 11 on making forms accessible apply to Designer created forms as well.

CROSS-REF   **See Chapter 11 for more details on accessibility.**

In the Accessibility palette, you can provide custom text for a screen reader as shown in Figure 22.19. A screen reader uses the following order when reading Designer created objects: custom text, tool tip, caption, and name. You can alter this order if necessary.

FIGURE 22.19

The Accessibility palette

Working with the tabs

The main portion of the program window is divided into four tabs. This area is known as the Layout Editor as shown in Figure 22.20. It is located between the palette wells in the center of the screen. When Designer is first launched, only the Design View and Preview PDF tabs are visible. To open the Master Pages tab in the editor, select View ⇨ Master Pages. Select View ⇨ XML Source to open the tab where changes can be made directly to the XML. Remember that if you close a tab, you can find them in the View menu.

FIGURE 22.20

The Layout Editor contains tabs for Design View, Master Pages, XML Source, and Preview PDF.

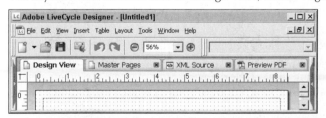

TIP Notice that the Master Pages, XML Source, and Preview PDF tabs have an X on the tab name to close them. You also can right-click the three editor tab names (Design View, Master Pages, and XML Source) at the top of the Layout Editor for a shortcut to turn the tabs on or off. When you right-click the PDF Preview tab it indicates whether the preview is static or dynamic as set in the form properties.

Using Design View

When working on a form design, much time is spent planning object placement and sequence of fields, colors, and other formats. You will spend most of your working time in LiveCycle Designer positioning and formatting fields on the Design View tab. Design View is the main layout area in LiveCycle Designer and is sometimes referred to as the Body Pages, as it was named in earlier versions.

Design View shows each page of your form as you continue to build it. Forms can be multiple page sizes and orientations. As you add objects to the design page, many visual properties can be set without using a palette. You can type captions, align objects with other objects, and more. The visible grid assists you with object placement and can be fine-tuned to suit your needs. Additional guides and drawing aid tools are available to make working in Design View easier.

CROSS-REF Working in Design View is covered in more depth in Chapters 24, 25, and 26.

Using master pages

Master pages control the layout and background of your form, including page size, orientation, and content areas. Every form has at least one master page. The Master Pages tab is hidden by default. To turn it on go to View ➪ Master Pages.

Although you could build a form without adding anything to the master pages, we don't recommend it. Does your form have elements that need to be consistent from page to page? Think of master pages in terms of headers and footers or page templates for your form design. A form can be designed with multiple page orientations, sizes, and layouts including columns. Subforms and flowed layout allow you to accomplish a column style form layout and just about any other you can conjure up.

CROSS-REF Master pages are explored in Chapter 25.

Using XML source

Designer forms are based on XML. Designer is a graphical user interface (GUI) for writing XML. Every object you add to the design page adds a new block of code to the source code. The XML can be edited directly on this tab if you are comfortable doing so. Most of us are not programmers and do not choose to work in the XML source view, but it has some very useful applications.

Suppose we have a form designed following all the corporate guidelines, except we forgot to change the font. All the objects on the form are the wrong font. Now we realize that selecting a field and changing the font is not a difficult task, but when a form has hundreds of fields on multiple pages, it gets very tedious. Using the hierarchy may be an option; you can select all the objects in the document and change the font. However, selecting any drawn objects and graphics causes the formatting toolbar to be disabled. Opening the XML source and running through Find and Replace can be much easier.

 **CAUTION** Be careful when editing the XML directly. Any flaw in the XML structure causes the document to not load or function properly.

 Working with XML is covered in more depth in Chapter 31.

Using the Preview PDF tab

Clicking the Preview PDF tab opens your form in Reader or Acrobat to test form functionality or simply to preview formats and layout. Previewing your form is required to test calculations and scripts, because scripts are not executed in Design View. Using the Preview PDF tab inside Designer prevents you from having to open an Acrobat viewer and open your file manually. After you're in the Preview PDF tab, the Acrobat viewer shortcuts become active.

NOTE The Preview PDF tab has a minimum requirement of Acrobat or Reader version 6.02 or higher to display. If you have loaded only LiveCycle Designer without loading Acrobat or Reader, the tab is not available. To preview a form in the Preview PDF tab, the Display PDF In Browser option must be selected in Acrobat or Reader. In the viewer program, verify that this is turned on by going to Edit ➪ Preferences ➪ Internet ➪ Display PDF in Browser. If the Display In Browser option is off, Acrobat or Reader is opened rather than using the Preview PDF tab in Designer.

Customizing the Workspace

The more we work in Designer, the more we open and close palettes, the more our preference for their location becomes apparent. In this section, we discuss how to move palette tabs into different palette wells. We explore how to adjust the design grid to suit our needs and insert guidelines for additional control when placing objects.

Customizing settings in the workspace can take a significant amount of time. We believe this to be time well spent, with the payoff showing in your day-to-day efficiency. Unfortunately, Designer does not have a setting to save customized workspace layouts. Designer retains the current workspace settings as long as it is properly shut down. If desired, you can easily reset the workspace to the default settings.

Using the Window menu

Controlling which palettes are currently visible and resetting them can all be found in the Window menu as shown in Figure 22.21. Turning palettes on and off is a simple click of the palette name in the Window menu. Any currently open Designer forms are located at the bottom of the menu. Various document arrangements become available when multiple files are open.

If no documents are currently open, Designer opens and creates new files maximized within the program window. If you choose to restore the document window to a smaller size, then Designer opens and creates documents arranged in the reduced area. To change this setting, select Window ➪ Arrange ➪ and then choose from Cascade, Tile, and Arrange. To reset palettes to their original locations, select Window ➪ Workspace ➪ Reset Palette Locations.

FIGURE 22.21

The Window menu

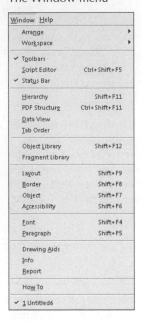

 **TIP** Sometimes options located in the Window menu are confused with the options in the View menu. Palettes are in the Window menu. Editor tabs are in the View menu.

Opening the Font and Paragraph palettes

Many of the font and paragraph settings can be found on the text formatting toolbar. However, every option is not available on the toolbar. To see the complete set of font and paragraph options, you need to open the palettes. To turn on the Font palette, select Window ⇨ Font. The palette well that opens also contains the paragraph palette. You can open the paragraph palette through the Window menu as well by selecting Window ⇨ Paragraph.

The Font palette contains settings for changing font styles, sizes, and colors. Some enhancements in version 8.2 are kerning, line spacing, and scaling, as shown in Figure 22.22

The Paragraph palette contains options for both vertical and horizontal alignment. You also can set indents, complete with first line and hanging styles as shown in Figure 22.23. The new feature on this tab is Hyphenate.

Notice at the top of both the font and paragraph palettes that a message appears: "Currently editing Caption and Value." This is an indicator of how much of the selected object is going to be formatted. You can set different fonts, sizes, colors, alignments, and margins for the caption and the field.

FIGURE 22.22

The Font palette

FIGURE 22.23

The Paragraph palette

CROSS-REF Formatting the field and caption independently is covered in Chapter 25.

Looking at drawing aids

A grid is visible when working in Design View and Master Pages. The grid is designed to help you align objects when placing them on the page. Objects are designed to snap to the dots of the grid. We recommend using the grid whenever possible. Adjusting the grid may be necessary to work efficiently with your own form designs. You also may want to insert some guidelines to simplify aligning multiple objects.

Any setting that affects the grid can be found in the Drawing Aids palette, as shown in Figure 22.24. Turn on the drawing aids by selecting Window ➪ Drawing Aids. Showing rulers and changing measurement units, grid line spacing, and guidelines are all controlled by the items you select here.

The rules and grid measurement units can be set to one of the following options: inches, centimeters, millimeters, and points.

FIGURE 22.24

The Drawing Aids palette

An often overlooked feature in Designer is the object border color and style when working in Design View and Master Pages View. Static objects have a solid blue border indicating they are non-interactive, whereas field objects have a solid orange border to indicate they are interactive. Subforms appear in the design page with a pink dashed border. Object border colors are a very helpful feature, which you can customize in the Drawing Aids palette. Each object type has a border color and style you can set by clicking the Styles button. We encourage you to try adjusting these settings; if you find that you prefer the defaults, a reset button is available.

TIP An easy way to tell if an object on the design page is static or interactive is to check the object's border color. Objects with solid blue borders are static, and objects with solid orange borders are interactive.

You may find you need to turn the Snap to Grid feature and the grid itself on and off at various stages of your form development. You can find those options and more in the View menu or use keyboard shortcuts if you prefer not to open the Drawing Aid palette. Use these Drawing Aid shortcuts:

- **Show/Hide Grid:** Ctrl+'
- **Snap to Grid:** Shift+Ctrl+'
- **Object Boundaries:** Ctrl+;

CROSS-REF See "Using the View menu" later in this chapter for more details.

Adding guidelines while you work can be extremely helpful and can be done from within the Drawing Aids palette or directly on the design pages. To set guidelines using the Drawing Aids palette, click the green plus sign (+) in either the vertical or horizontal area of the Guidelines Definitions section.

To set a guideline in the design page, locate the corner between the rulers. You'll see a small white area with cross hairs, as shown in Figure 22.25. Place your mouse in this area, and drag down and/or over into the design area. If you release your mouse while still in the vertical ruler, you set a horizontal guideline at that point on the vertical ruler. Likewise, you set a vertical guideline by releasing the mouse pointer while in the horizontal ruler. By releasing the mouse on the actual page, you are setting both a vertical and horizontal guide.

You can move a guide by dragging the blue triangle in the ruler to a new position. You also may make adjustments to the guidelines in the Drawing Aids palette.

Opening the script editor

The script editor is hidden by default in this version of Designer; select Window ➪ Script Editor to show it at the top of the workspace. The script editor shows a single line editor at first to maximize your design window. You can drag the editor window down to expose the multiline editor when you intend to work on scripting, as shown in Figure 22.26.

FIGURE 22.25

The design page after a 3-inch vertical guideline and a 1-inch horizontal guideline has been set

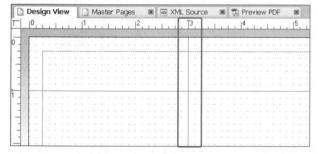

FIGURE 22.26

The multiline script editor

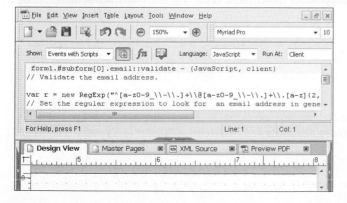

The Show box in the script editor is set to events with scripts by default. This allows you to see the selected object's code, regardless of the event the script is attached to. A numeric field may have a script written for both a calculate event and a validate event. The script editor shows both pieces of script separated by the events. Filtering the event list is certainly possible; just select the event you'd like from the drop-down list.

To the right of the Show box is a button called Show Events for Child Objects. The button is selected by default and allows you to see scripts for any child objects. Having this on allows you to select the top-level node in the hierarchy, and then the script editor shows all scripts contained in the form. It may contain more than you wish to see at times, so change the setting as needed.

The green FN button contains a list of functions available to the currently selected scripting language. The syntax checker looks at the all the scripts in the form for errors. Any errors found are reported in the Log tab of the Report palette.

Viewing the status bar

The status bar is an invaluable tool when designing forms. It's a shame the status bar is not visible by default, as it was in previous releases. To turn on the status bar, select Window ⇨ Status Bar. The status bar appears below the editors and palettes at the bottom of the workspace, as shown in Figure 22.27.

FIGURE 22.27

The Designer status bar

The status bar contains information regarding the currently selected object's position, size, and object name. These properties also can be found in various palettes, but this gives you a single, always visible, area to check settings. If you drag an object, the status bar updates the position information while dragging.

The form's current page number and total page count is indicated in the status bar. To the right of the page count indicator on the status bar are four editing icons. These are interactive buttons that you can turn on or off by clicking the icon.

 ■ **Lock Text:** When Lock Text is selected, clicking any object containing text selects the entire object frame. A single-click does not put you into Edit mode; a double-click is required. With Lock Text off, a single-click of an object containing text places your cursor in Edit mode.

 ■ **Lock Fields:** When Lock Fields is on, you cannot select the field objects in the design page, nor are they available in the hierarchy. No editing of the field objects is allowed.

■ **Lock Static Objects:** When Lock Static Objects is on, you cannot select the objects in the design page, nor are they available in the hierarchy. No editing of the objects is allowed.

 ■ **Lock Static Text Box:** This icon pertains only to Static Text Boxes with fixed dimensions that do not have auto-fit settings turned on. When Lock Static Text is on, typing or pasting information in a fixed-size static text box does not adjust the box size. With Lock Static Text off, the text box dimensions are allowed to adjust to the contents while typing or pasting information.

The first three of these icons can be found in Edit ➪ Lock. However the fourth icon regarding locking static text is not listed in the menus.

On the far right end of the status bar are three gray boxes that light up to indicate that one of the following keys on the keyboard is active:

■ CAP is for the Caps Lock key.

■ NUM is for the Number Lock key.

■ SCRL is for the Scroll Lock key.

The status bar is full of valuable information that can be seen at all times while editing. We recommend you turn the status bar on.

Changing palette views

As we've discussed many times before, the palette options in Designer are extensive. Turning them on and off as needed to set properties, access features, and maximize screen real estate seems to never end. The palette wells and tabs do not have to remain where they currently are located.

To move an entire palette well, including any tabs currently docked in that well, drag the palette bar. As you approach the center of the screen the palette begins to float and is not docked to the workspace side. To dock a palette well, drag the title bar toward the desired side of the workspace. The palette outline snaps to the side of the screen when you get close to the edge. Sometimes you don't want the palette well to dock to the sides, yet each time you try to drag the palette, it attempts to snap to an edge. You can prevent a palette well from docking by holding down the Ctrl key while you drag.

When dragging a palette away from a well, the palette outline changes shape. If the outline shows the tab with a palette well border, when dropped it creates a new palette well with only that tab inside. Dragging to the center of the design page is the easiest way to create a new floating palette well. If the outline shows only the tab name, then you are near an existing well, and a black frame surrounds that well. The black frame indicates that when you drop the palette it becomes docked in the surrounded palette well.

Enjoy customizing the workspace to your own liking. Experiment with different combinations of layouts, and see what works best for you.

Customizing keyboard shortcuts

Another time-saving technique is to use keyboard shortcuts. Many items have keyboard shortcuts already assigned to them, but others you need to assign yourself. The pull-down menus contain many commands. If the commands already have a keyboard shortcut assigned to them, the shortcut is shown to the right of the menu choice. If a command you use frequently does not have a shortcut, you can assign a custom keyboard shortcut. As shown in Figure 22.28, the keyboard shortcut window allows you to work with all the commands in the program, or you can filter the available list by selecting a product area from the drop-down list.

FIGURE 22.28

The Keyboard Shortcuts dialog box

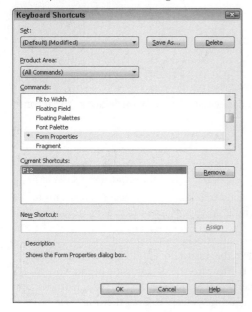

STEPS: Assigning a Keyboard Shortcut

1. **Select Tools ⇨ Keyboard Shortcuts.** This command opens the Keyboard Shortcuts dialog box.

2. **Select the desired command in the Commands list.**

3. **Click in the New Shortcut area.**

4. **Type the keys you want to assign as the shortcut.** If the shortcut is already assigned to another command, you receive a prompt regarding replacing the shortcut, as shown in Figure 22.29. If this happens, try to think of another shortcut. If you are sure the existing shortcut is one you do not use, then replace it.

FIGURE 22.29

The keyboard shortcut warning about replacing an existing shortcut

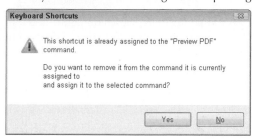

5. **Click the assign button.** After you have found a shortcut, click the Assign button. Clicking this button adds the shortcut to the dialog box.

6. **Save the shortcut.** You can save your custom shortcuts with a descriptive name for easy identification.

Resetting the keyboard shortcuts is as simple as choosing the default option from the top of the Keyboard Shortcut dialog box.

Adding tools and toolbars

Most of the toolbars are located below the menu bar and above the editors in the toolbar well. Toolbars can be docked to any of the four sides of your screen or allowed to float in the design space. For example, you may prefer to work with the layout tools near the selected objects on the page. Dragging a toolbar handle allows you to move a toolbar easily. The outline of the toolbar changes as you drag it. The outline appears as a thick, dotted border to indicate it's a floating position. As you approach an edge of the program window, the toolbar outline changes to a thin, black line indicating it can dock there. Follow these steps to move a toolbar.

STEPS: Moving a Toolbar to an Alternate Position

1. **Position the mouse cursor.** Place your mouse on the two dotted gray separator bars on the left edge of the toolbar. These gray bars are known as the toolbar handle.

2. **Click and drag the toolbar to an alternate location.**

3. **Drag the toolbar until it snaps back to the edge of the workspace.** If a toolbar is already floating and you want to move it or dock it, you may click and drag anywhere inside the title area of the toolbar.

 If a toolbar is floating and you want to put it back in its previously docked location, double-click anywhere in the title bar area of the toolbar.

These toolbars are available by default in Designer:

- **Standard:** The first toolbar in the interface, shown in Figure 22.30, contains options for New Document, Open File, Save, Distribute, Undo, Redo, Zoom Out, Zoom Percentage, and Zoom In.

- **Text Formatting:** The text formatting tools, shown in Figure 22.31, offer limited formatting choices, including Font, Size, Bold, Italic, Underline, and horizontal alignment options.

- **Layout:** This toolbar, shown in Figure 22.32, is for working with multiple objects. It contains tools for aligning, distributing, stacking, grouping, and merging.

- **Table:** The Table toolbar, shown in Figure 22.33, offers buttons for creating tables, inserting and deleting columns and rows, splitting and merging cells, and converting to and from tables.

- **Tools:** This toolbar, shown in Figure 22.34, offers additional basic tools for these tools: select object, hand, field edit, zoom, and tab order.

FIGURE 22.30

The Standard toolbar

FIGURE 22.31

The Text Formatting toolbar

FIGURE 22.32

The Layout toolbar

FIGURE 22.33

The Table toolbar

FIGURE 22.34

The Tools toolbar

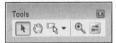

You can now create your own custom toolbars and add more tools to the existing toolbars in Designer. For example, if you frequently need to use the vertical alignment tools, you could add them to the existing Text Formatting toolbar or create a new toolbar. Customizing your toolbars begins by selecting Tools ⇨ Customize, as shown in Figure 22.35.

FIGURE 22.35

The Customize dialog box

To create a new toolbar, select the Toolbars tab and click New. Type a new name for your toolbar. To add additional tools to the toolbars, in the Customize window, select the Commands tab. Locate the desired tool, and drag it to an existing toolbar. We decided to make a new toolbar with all the buttons related to form fragments, as shown in Figure 22.36.

If you are trying to maximize your design space, you can close all the toolbars (floating and docked) by selecting Window ⇨ Toolbars. Just remember the same location to turn them back on.

FIGURE 22.36

A custom-made toolbar with options for form fragments

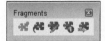

Using the View menu

The View menu, shown in Figure 22.37, contains commands for adjusting how you look at the design space and gives you access to the tab order. As mentioned previously, many Drawing Aids settings can be turned on and off from the View menu.

Changing zoom levels

When you first open Designer, the zoom level is set to maximize the available workspace. This setting is known as Fit Width, and it works the same way in the Acrobat viewers. The keyboard shortcut also is the same: Ctrl+2. You'll notice that if you expand or collapse a palette well on the left or right side of the screen, the design page adjusts automatically. However, if you need all the palettes open for settings, this leaves little room for working.

Many options are available for changing the zoom settings. Keyboard shortcuts are available for many common zoom settings, as shown in the View menu in Figure 22.36.

The Standard toolbar has zoom in, zoom out, and the zoom percentage options. The Tools toolbar has a zoom tool similar to Acrobat for clicking the design page in the desired location. No matter which method you choose for adjusting the zoom levels while working, make sure your zoom level is set appropriately for the task at hand.

Using the grid

The design grid is the dotted background on the Design View and Master Pages tabs. The spacing between the dots is controlled by the settings of the Drawing Aids palette. As you add objects to the design page, they snap to the grid dots to assist in layout and alignment. This is very helpful when your objects are consistent in size. However, when the objects vary in size, setting the spacing between objects can be difficult.

FIGURE 22.37

The View menu

With the Snap to Grid setting on, we tried to place three objects with different sizes below one another. We wanted the spacing between the objects to be equal. Notice in Figure 22.38 that this was not possible; the gap between the top two objects is smaller than the gap between the bottom two objects.

The Snap to Grid feature can be turned off temporarily to help you place, size, and align objects. Select View ⇨ Snap to Grid. Notice how we have much more control over the object placement with the Snap to Grid feature turned off, as shown in Figure 22.39.

FIGURE 22.38

With objects snapped to the grid, spacing between the objects is inconsistent.

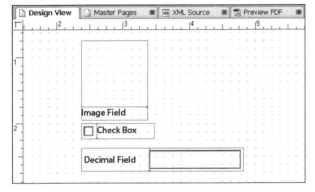

FIGURE 22.39

The Snap to Grid feature has been turned off, allowing more control over object placement.

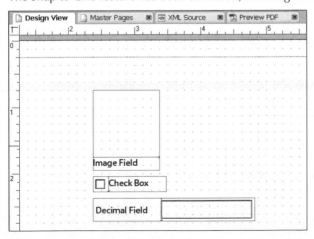

Perhaps you prefer ten dots per inch as opposed to the standard eight dots per inch. To customize the spacing of the dots on the grid, select Window ⇨ Drawing Aids. In the Drawing Aids palette, specify an interval of 10/in for X and for Y. Notice that the origin for the grid starts at 0. If you prefer the dots to begin where your margins are set, you can change the origin settings as well.

Summary

- Adobe LiveCycle Designer is a powerful form design program that creates forms based on XML.

- The main program window is divided into four areas: Design View, Master Pages, XML Source, and Preview PDF.

- Designer forms place a dependency on which specific versions of the Acrobat viewers can be used to interact with your form.

- Tasks are preformed through the use of menus, tools, and palettes.

- Palettes can be customized to your preferences. This includes showing or hiding palettes and rearranging palette positions.

- A limited set of tools is available on the default toolbars. Additional buttons can be added to the existing toolbars. You also can create new toolbars.

- Using keyboard shortcuts is another method of accessing tools and settings. If a keyboard shortcut is not assigned to a frequently used feature, you can add one.

- The design page has a dotted background. This design grid is used to snap objects into place. It can be customized to suit your needs.

- A New Form Assistant can help walk you through creating a new form.

- Forms can be imported from Microsoft Word, existing PDF files, and spreadsheets.

- The default tab order is based on the objects' positions on the design page. It starts at the top of the form and works top to bottom, left to right. The tab order can be adjusted easily by dragging fields up and down in a new palette, if the default tab order doesn't suit your needs.

- Form fragments are design pieces that are used in multiple form designs. Fragments are stored in the file system and can be updated easily.

- The Library palette contains all the basic form design objects necessary to create your forms. You can add custom objects to the library.

- The Hierarchy palette provides a structured view of your form design elements.

- Scripting is supported in both JavaScript and FormCalc.

Part VII

Creating XML Forms

After you're familiar with the Designer workspace it's time to jump in and create some forms and that's exactly what we do in Chapter 23. We talk about creating a form from a new blank page, importing a Microsoft Word form into Designer, importing cells from Excel spreadsheets, and working with PDF backgrounds. In Chapter 24 we examine all the field types, look at the Library palettes, adding custom Library objects, and how to work with form fragments. In Chapter 25 we talk about objects and cover assigning appearances, editing field attributes, working with patterns, and working with Master Page objects.

IN THIS PART

Chapter 23
Designing Forms in LiveCycle Designer ES

Chapter 24
Working with Designer's Form Fields and Objects

Chapter 25
Working with Objects

Chapter 23

Designing Forms in LiveCycle Designer ES

IN THIS CHAPTER

Getting familiar with forms standards

Designing for the form filler

Understanding form design basics

In Chapter 22 we provided a general overview of the LiveCycle Designer ES workspace and tried to give you an overview of various menu commands, palettes, and tools used to create forms. Coming up in Chapter 24 we talk about setting up libraries of objects, and in Chapter 25 we go into depth on formatting fields and objects. Think of these three chapters as reference chapters and bookmark them for reviewing the many commands and tools you have at your disposal for creating forms in Designer.

If you're reading this book in a linear fashion, you have some basics down after reviewing Chapter 22 and now you can look at creating some forms. Rather than provide you with all the foundations first, we want to mix it up a little and take you on a journey to quickly get into creating forms in Designer. By the time you get to Chapters 24 and 25, we hope that delving into more detail on adding form fields and objects to a page will make more sense after creating some forms by working through some steps in this chapter.

In this chapter we get to the basics of form design and look at examples for creating real-world forms by walking you through steps in using some of the tools, palettes, and menu commands. We make an effort in this chapter to help guide you through the many different options you have for creating a new form design. We walk you through creating forms from a blank new page, to forms based on templates, forms originating in programs like Microsoft Word, Microsoft Excel, Acrobat PDF documents, and how to create a custom template.

Back in the beginning of this book in Chapter 4 we talked about many of these types of original document formats converted to PDF and populated with form field objects in Acrobat's Form Editing Mode.

What you have available in Designer is neither better nor inferior to the options you have in Acrobat for creating forms. Basically, it's just *different* and sometimes the time in which you have to distribute a form and the requirements for managing the form data will dictate which program you use to create a new form.

After you finish this chapter go back and review Chapter 4 to develop your own personal preferences for what program is best to use for certain file types and forms needs, then take a careful look at Chapters 24 and 25 where we add some important details related to formatting fields and objects in LiveCycle Designer.

Remember there is no right or wrong in terms of what program you use to create a form. The choice is personal. What we can say is that for the serious forms author, knowing both programs equally and becoming familiar with the design characteristics of each program is to your advantage.

Creating New Forms from Blank Pages

For some time Adobe has been adding wonderful wizards to walk you through steps with various features in both Acrobat and LiveCycle Designer. Unlike Acrobat, Designer supports creating new documents from within the program, and one way to begin is by walking through the steps in the New Form Assistant wizard.

Choose File➪New and you are introduced to the New Form Assistant wizard shown in Figure 23.1. Each time you create a new file by using the File➪New menu command the New Form Assistant window opens. If you want to create a blank new page via the menu command, you can click the Do Not Use Assistant text in the lower-left corner of the New Form Assistant wizard. Doing so opens the Assistant Options dialog box shown in Figure 23.2.

When you click Do Not Use Assistant in the New Form Assistant wizard the Assistant Options dialog box offers you three choices. You can dismiss the New Form Assistant wizard one time when you create a new document, skip the assistant when always creating new documents, or choose not to show the assistant each time you create a form in Designer, whether staring from a blank document or otherwise.

When you start working with Designer it's a good idea to use the New Form Assistant so you can walk through steps in the wizard to begin working on a new form. If you later decide to disable the wizard from opening by choosing the Don't show the New Form Assistant again radio button in the Assistant Options dialog box, and at a later time you want to start using the New Form Assistant again, you can easily bring it back. Choose Tools➪Options to open the Options dialog box. In the left pane click Wizard and Tips and in the right pane you find a section for Form Assistant. When all the check boxes are checked as you see in Figure 23.3, the New Form Assistant opens when you create new documents, when you import documents, and when you import PDF documents.

FIGURE 23.1

Choose File ➪ New and the New Form Assistant wizard opens.

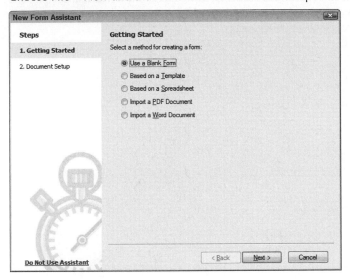

FIGURE 23.2

Click Do Not Use Assistant in the New Form Assistant wizard, and the Assistant Options dialog box opens.

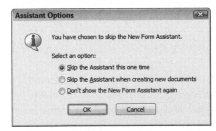

CROSS-REF The Show When Creating Tables check box has to do with showing the Table Assistant wizard. For more information on using the Table Assistant wizard, see Chapter 27.

For now, be aware of how you toggle on and off the New Form Assistant wizard. Later in this chapter we talk about using palettes and some menu commands.

FIGURE 23.3

Choose Tools ⇨ Options and check all check boxes in the Form Assistant area of the Wizard and Tips pane to bring back the default New Form Assistant wizard when creating new documents.

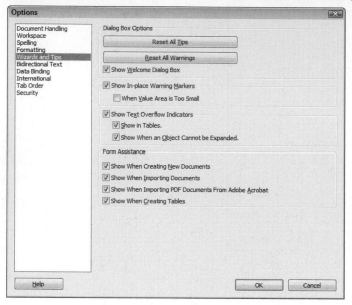

Setting up the environment

Before we begin using the New Form Assistant Wizard or any other method for creating a new form in Designer, let's continue where we left off in Chapter 22. In Chapter 22 we talked about examining tools, and later in Chapter 24 we add a little more to specifically review many options for field objects properties and changing field attributes. We won't go into depth in this chapter on defining fields and objects properties, but we want to set up the work environment to access tools we'll need to create a new design.

How you set up the Designer environment is a personal choice. As we mentioned in Chapter 22, you have many ways to produce the same results in regard to accessing tools and menus and adding objects to a page. As you begin working in Designer you may want to make some choices for how you access tools and commands. Rather than suggest a standard for forms authors, we want to describe the methods for customizing the environment. We'll leave the specifics for modifying the suggestions we make to you.

Among some of the items you might think about addressing when you start working on a new form are the following:

■ **New Form Assistant.** Ask yourself, "Do I want to use the New Form Assistant or not?" If you want to turn off the New Form Assistant, choose Tools ➪ Options and click Wizards and Tips in the left pane in Options dialog box. Under the Form Assistant area in the right pane remove the check marks for the first three items. Note that the last check mark has to do with the Table Assistant, which is unrelated to the New Form Assistant.

CROSS-REF For more information on using the Table Assistant, see Chapter 27.

■ **Organizing Palettes.** Another question to ask yourself is "Which palettes do I want to use?"

  ■ **How To palette.** By default the How To palette is loaded in the right palette bin. If you find yourself not using this palette often or you are experienced beyond the help information provided in the How To palette, dismiss it by clicking the *x* in the top-right corner of the palette. Dismissing this palette makes some room for more essential palettes such as the Object and Libraries palettes.

  ■ **Hierarchy.** The Hierarchy palette is essential to all forms authoring in Designer. You need access to this palette throughout the form design process. Because the additional default tabs for PDF Structure, Data View, and Tab Order don't take up any more room when the Hierarchy palette is open, it's best to leave the left side of the Designer window at the defaults.

  ■ **Object Library.** By default the Object Library palette is critical for your form design process. If you've set up a custom palette and a Fragment Library, it may be less essential to have this palette in view. Since all the Library palettes are nested together, open the Object Library and leave the other palettes assembled together in the same group.

  ■ **Object.** This palette is also essential for any form design and you should have the Field, Value, and Binding tabs loaded when an object is selected. By closing the How To palette, you have ample room to work comfortably by having the Object Library and Object palettes share the same palette bin on the right side of your workspace.

  ■ **Font.** Unless you set up a custom library with fields and objects you use consistently in your company, you'll need access to the Font palette. You have two choices to display font attribute options. You can open the palette (Window ➪ Font or press Shift+F4) and keep it open as a floating palette or docked in the panel bin on the right. Your other choice is to add the font options to a toolbar and keep it out of the palette bin to preserve the nice room you have for the Object Library and Object palettes. (See "Loading Tools" later in this list to learn how to add the font tools.)

  ■ **Paragraph.** The Paragraph palette is as important as the Font palette. You have the same choices for adding the palette to the palette bin or using a toolbar. Drag the Paragraph tools you want to use to the Toolbar Well. (Also see "Loading Tools" in this list.)

  ■ **Report.** The Report palette contains tabs for Warnings, Binding, and Log. Opening the palette takes very little room at the bottom of your workspace. As a default, keep it open.

- **Loading Tools.** Again we come to personal choices. When you launch Designer a limited set of tools are loaded in toolbars. You have a huge number of tool buttons you can add to toolbars to customize your workspace. To add new tool buttons to toolbars, choose Tools ⇨ Customize. When the Customize dialog box opens, click the Commands tab. In the left panel you see a list of Categories, and the right panel contains tool buttons as shown in Figure 23.4. To add a tool button to a toolbar, click an item in the right panel and drag it to a toolbar. When you release the mouse button the tool is dropped in the respective toolbar.

  - **File.** Some of the tools loaded by default may not be needed. You can handle tools such as Open, Save, Save As, and Print with keyboard shortcuts or menu choices you're already familiar with. These tools take up unnecessary space. If you want to remove them from the File toolbar drag each one from the toolbar back to the Customize dialog box.

  - **Edit.** The Edit toolbar also has some tools you're not like to use very much. The Undo and Redo tools have keyboard shortcut equivalents that are common to most programs. If you use keyboard shortcuts for these commands, remove the tools.

  - **View.** The Keep Drawing tool is handy so you may want to add it to the respective toolbar as well as the Page view tools for Actual Size, Fit to Page, and Fit to Width. These tools have similar icons and functions as Acrobat, so if you're used to using the tools, go ahead and add them to the View toolbar.

  - **Insert/Table.** For now, bypass these tools. We address working with tables in Chapter 27.

  - **Layout.** A number of alignment and sizing tools appear in the Layout list of tool buttons. Make sure all the layout tools for alignment and sizing are added to the toolbar.

  - **Fragments.** Bypass this toolbar for now. For more information on fragments, see Chapter 22.

  - **Text Formatting.** If you elected to not use the Font and Paragraph palettes, add the tools for formatting text and setting paragraph attributes.

  - **Settings.** These tools relate to customizing your workspace. Bypass this toolbar for now. We cover more on customizing your workspace in Chapter 22.

  - **Tools.** The Select Tool, Hand Tool, Field Edit Tool, and Zoom Tool are all handy tools. Make sure these tools are loaded. Click OK in the Customize dialog box and you return to the Designer workspace.

Making choices for what tools you want to load depends largely on the kinds of forms you design. You may find other tools helpful, such as tools for working with subforms that you may want accessible. For starters, if you load the tools we recommend here, you have an environment that will be helpful in creating forms we discuss in this chapter. As you move on to the chapters ahead, you should plan to revisit the Customize dialog box to add or remove tools. After you load the tools we recommend in this chapter your Designer workspace should look similar to Figure 23.5.

FIGURE 23.4

Click Commands in the Customize dialog box to view the tool buttons accessible in Designer.

FIGURE 23.5

The Designer workspace after customizing tools

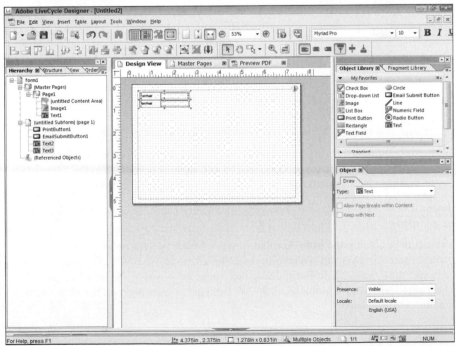

You have more customizing options by adding custom keyboard shortcuts. For example, if you want to set up a shortcut to use the F12 key to open the Form Properties dialog box, feel free to set up the shortcut or any others you feel will be helpful when designing forms.

CROSS-REF For learning how to set up custom keyboard shortcuts, see Chapter 22.

Creating blank new forms

After you get your workspace set up, it's time to start creating a form in Designer. We start this section by looking at creating blank new forms. When you create a blank form you need to use Designer as your layout program and add all assets (graphics and field objects) to the form.

You can create a blank new form in these three ways:

- **Click the New tool.** Click the New tool in the Designer File toolbar to create a blank new page at the current default size. You also can open the drop-down menu and choose a page size as shown in Figure 23.6.

FIGURE 23.6

Open the New drop-down menu and choose a page size for your blank new form.

TIP The default page sizes are contained in the Blank tab in the Template Manager. You can add to the list additional page sizes by adding new templates in the Template Manager. See "Creating a New Form Based on a Template" later in this chapter.

- **Choose File ⇨ New.** When you choose the menu command, the New Form Assistant wizard opens.

- **Create a new blank page from Acrobat.** If you're working in Acrobat, choose Forms ⇨ Start Form Wizard while in normal Viewer mode. After you choose the menu command the Create or Edit Form dialog box opens as shown in Figure 23.7. Click the No existing form radio button and click OK. Designer is launched and the New Form Assistant wizard opens.

FIGURE 23.7

Choose Forms ⇨ Start Form Wizard in Acrobat and when you click No existing form and click OK, Designer is launched,

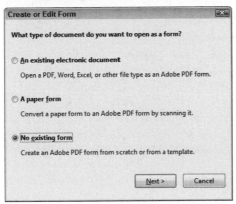

One difference between using the New tool and using the New Form Assistant wizard is that the New tool creates a blank page without providing you the options for choosing a page size, choosing an orientation, adding a Print button, or adding an Email button to the new form.

Using the New Form Assistant wizard

To begin creating a new form, we'll first look at starting with a blank form. When you begin with a blank form you have to add all graphic elements and form fields to the form. Unlike in Acrobat, you have the tools in Designer to add text and graphic objects to create a new design.

To begin working on a new form where you start with a blank page, follow these steps:

STEPS: Creating a New Form Using the New Form Assistant Wizard

1. **Choose File ⇨ New in Designer.** Making this menu selection opens the New Form Assistant wizard. We could click the New button in the File toolbar, but making that choice doesn't provide you with options for determining the page size, orientation, and adding Email and Print buttons.

2. **Click Next in the New Form Assistant wizard.** The New Form Assistant wizard opens with the first pane in view as shown earlier in Figure 23.1. Click the Next button and you arrive at the second pane shown in Figure 23.8.

3. **Choose a page size and orientation.** Open the Page Size drop-down menu, choose A5 for the page size, and click Landscape for the orientation. Click Next to open the last pane in the New Form Assistant wizard.

FIGURE 23.8

Choose a page size and orientation in the second wizard pane.

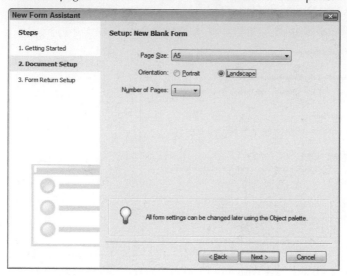

4. **Add Email and Print buttons.** By default the check boxes are enabled for adding an Email button and a Print button. Leave the check marks at the default and type a return e-mail address in the Return email address text box as shown in Figure 23.9.

5. **Click Finish.**

6. **Save the file.** You have a choice for saving the file. You can choose to save the file as an XDP file that can be opened only in Designer or as a PDF file in which case you can reopen the file in Designer or open it in Acrobat. For our purposes we'll save the file as XDP and later when we finish the form, we'll save it as a PDF document.

Keep this file open to follow additional steps in this chapter.

Adding objects to a blank page

In many workflows you have objects on a master page such as a header containing logo, a return address, or possibly the header objects and some footer items such as a form number, page number, and URL address.

When you add master page items these objects are generally placed outside the content area. By default the content area is sized to a full-page size with a margin when you create a blank new page. While working on a master page you can click the content area frame and size it to suit your design needs. As a matter of practice, it's a good idea to size the content area first while adding objects to the master page, and then move to the design page where you add the field objects.

FIGURE 23.9

Leave the default check boxes enabled and type an e-mail address in the Return email address check box.

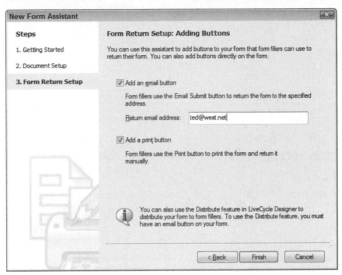

Setting up the master page

We'll continue using the form we created in the previous series of steps. To see how to add items to the master page, follow these steps:

ON the CD-ROM To follow these steps, you need a graphic object we'll place on a master page. Use the *globalLogo.tif* file from the Art folder in the Chapter23 folder on the book's CD-ROM.

STEPS: Designing a Master Page

1. **Open a form in Designer.** We continue using the form started from the last series of steps.

2. **Move the Print and Email buttons.** By default the Print and Email buttons appear at the top of the page. Move them to the bottom of the page to get them out of the way while we design the form.

3. **Click the Master Page tab to open the master page.**

4. **Resize the Content area.** Click the rectangle appearing on the master page and drag the center handle down to about the 1-inch mark (shown in the left ruler).

5. **Add an Image object.** With the Standard Library open, drag the Image object to the top of the form. Note that you have both an Image Field and an Image object. Be certain to drag the image object as shown in Figure 23.10.

FIGURE 23.10

Drag an Image object to the form on the master page.

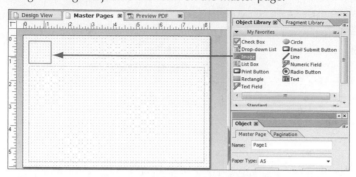

6. **Import an image.** Double-click the Image object and the Browse for Image dialog box opens. Locate the *globalLogo.tif* file from the book's CD-ROM and select it. Click Open to import the image.

NOTE When you save image files that you want to import into designer, be certain to not use CMYK color. You cannot import CMYK color files in Designer. Additionally, you are limited to certain file formats. Designer permits you to import BMP, EPS, JPG, GIF, PNG, and TIF image formats.

7. **Size the image.** Click the image and move the center right handle out to accommodate the size of the image. By default the image is sized proportionately.

8. **Embed the image.** If you do not embed the image, the image won't appear on your form when distributed. Open the Object palette if it is not open and check the Embed Image Data check box as shown in Figure 23.11.

9. **Add type to the master page.** Drag the Text object form the Standard Library to the area above the content frame. Note that you have a Text object and a Text Field object in the Standard Library. Be certain to drag the Text object.

FIGURE 23.11

Embed the image by clicking Embed Image Data in the Object palette.

10. **Set the type attributes and type new text.** If you loaded tools in the Toolbar Well this step should be very easy. In our example we typed *Request Transfer of Funds* for the text. We left the font at the default Myriad font choice and set the size to 18 point and aligned the text right by using the Text Formatting and custom toolbar we created for Paragraph settings to set the type attributes.

11. **Move the text to the top right corner.** Click the text object and drag it up to approximately the same vertical position as the top of the logo. (Look over Figure 12.13 later in this chapter to see the layout we used.)

12. **Add one more text object.** We'll add one more text object and place it below the Content area on the left side of the form. In our example we added the text *Form G101A • Revised 10/08* to the left side of the form. We continued using the Myriad font and sized the text to 8 points.

13. **Adding a bullet.** Keystrokes for creating special characters are easily forgotten when typing text. If you happen to forget how to add a special character like a bullet, place the cursor where you want the character to appear and open the Start menu. Choose All Programs> Accessories ➪ System Tools ➪ Character Map to open the Character Map dialog box. You can choose fonts from the Font drop-down menu and scroll the list of selected fonts. When you find the character you want to use, click it in the list and click Copy as shown in Figure 23.12. The character is placed on the clipboard. Close the Character Map dialog box and press Ctrl+V to paste the character at the cursor insertion point.

FIGURE 23.12

Open the Start menu and click All Programs ➪ Accessories ➪ System Tools ➪ Character Map. Click the character you want to use and click Copy. Paste the character at the cursor insertion point on your design.

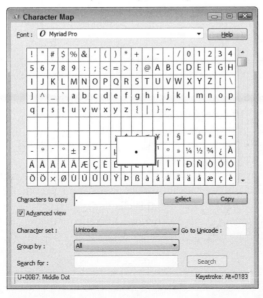

14. Add a page counter. Open the Custom Library palette and scroll down to find the *Page n of m* object. Drag this object to the lower-right corner. This object reports the current page out of the total pages on the form.

15. Save the file. In our example we keep the XDP format and choose File ⇨ Save to update our edits. The design we created up to this point appears in Figure 23.13.

FIGURE 23.13

The completed layout on the master page

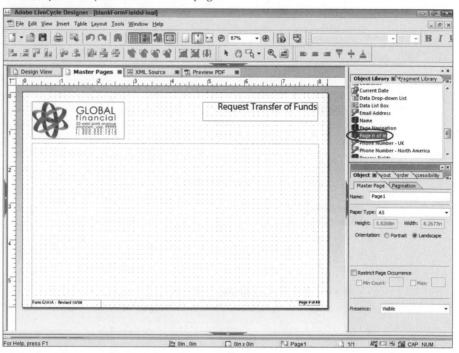

Adding field objects on the design page

When you're in a hurry it's easy to overlook switching from the master page to the design page. When you're ready to start adding field objects to a form, be certain to click the Design tab.

In Chapter 11 we used the *globalTransferLayers.pdf* document we created in Acrobat as shown in Figure 23.14. You can find samples of that file in the Chapter 11 folder on the book's CD-ROM. The form we started to create from a blank page in this chapter is just like the form we used in Chapter 11. When you're finished creating the form you can compare the results for the form created in Acrobat and the same form we create in Designer.

FIGURE 23.14

The form we created in Acrobat is the design we'll use to create the same form in Designer.

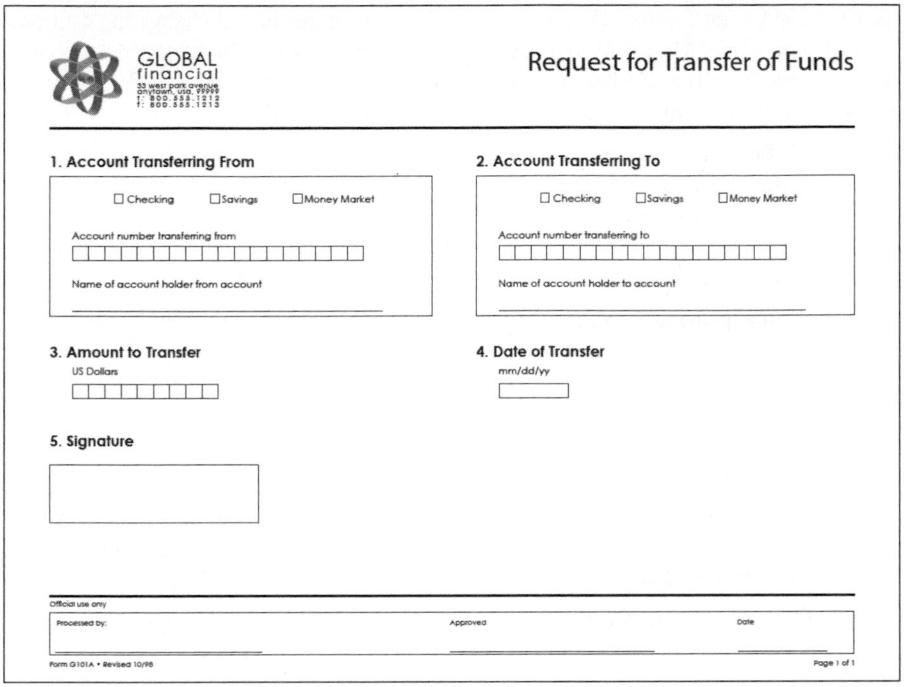
GLOBAL
financial
33 west park avenue
anytown, usa. 99999
t: 800.555.1212
f: 800.555.1213

Request for Transfer of Funds

1. Account Transferring From

☐ Checking ☐ Savings ☐ Money Market

Account number transferring from

Name of account holder from account

2. Account Transferring To

☐ Checking ☐ Savings ☐ Money Market

Account number transferring to

Name of account holder to account

3. Amount to Transfer

US Dollars

4. Date of Transfer

mm/dd/yy

5. Signature

Official use only

Processed by: Approved Date

Form G101A • Revised 10/98

Page 1 of 1

To continue working on the form we started in previous steps in this chapter, we'll look at adding field objects. To create the first block of fields where you see *1. Account Transferring From* in Figure 23.14, do the following:

ON the CD-ROM **If you missed anything from steps earlier in this chapter you can use the *blankForm MasterPage.xdp* file from the blankForm folder in the Chapter23 folder on the book's CD-ROM to continue following the steps below.**

STEPS: Adding Field Objects to a Blank Form

1. **Continue using the form from earlier steps in this chapter.** If you don't have the form saved, use the *blankFormMasterPage.xdp* from the book's CD-ROM.
2. **Add some text objects.** As you look at Figure 23.14 notice there are several text elements in the first block of fields. We begin by adding text for the title *1. Account Transferring From* and choose Myriad Pro Black for the font and set the point size to 10-point. You add the text on the design page just like adding text on the master page by dragging a Text object from the Standard Library palette. We continue adding the two lines of text below the check box fields and set the point size to 9-point. At this point, don't worry about the placement of the objects on the page. We can move them later.

3. **Add Radio Button fields.** Drag a Radio Button object to the area below the title. We leave the default appearance at Sunken Circle and change the default size from 10-point to 9-point in the Object palette Field tab. Double-click the default Radio Button text and type *Checking* for the caption. Drag two more radio button fields and change the captions to *Savings* and *Money Market*. When you observe the Fields tab in the Object palette you'll notice that the radio buttons belong to the same group as shown in Figure 23.15. This results in mutually exclusive choices for the radio buttons on the form.

4. **Add a comb field.** Drag the Text Field object from the Standard Library palette to the form below the text *Account number transferring from*. In the Field tab in the Object palette check the Comb of check box and type 18 in the characters text box as shown in Figure 23.16. Notice in Figure 23.16 you see the Appearance as Custom. We'll change the appearance to a custom look in the next step.

5. **Add a custom appearance.** We thought the default black color on the comb field was a little strong so we decided to make the border color a little more subtle by choosing a 25% gray. To change the border color to a custom color, open the Appearance drop-down menu and choose Custom to open the Custom Appearance dialog box. In the Custom Appearance dialog box click 25% gray as shown in Figure 23.17. After making the choice click OK and the borders for the comb field change to the custom color.

6. **Add a text field below the *Name of account holder from account* text object.** Drag a text field from the Standard Library palette and place it below the text. No special formatting is needed for this field.

7. **Add a line.** Click the Line object in the Standard Library palette and draw a line below the text field object you created in Step 6. This object is nestled up against the base of the text field.

8. **Draw a rectangle element around the objects.** To complete this group of text and field objects, click the Rectangle object in the Standard Library palette and draw a box around the objects as shown in the completed design in Figure 23.18.

FIGURE 23.15

The radio buttons added to the form belong to the same group.

FIGURE 23.16

Check Comb of and type 18 for the number of characters.

FIGURE 23.17

Choose Custom from the Appearance drop-down menu to open the Custom Appearance dialog box where custom colors can be selected for the text field border color.

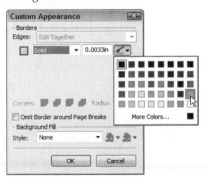

9. **Move the rectangle to the back.** While the rectangle is in front of the other objects you cannot easily select them. Moving the rectangle behind the objects makes selections of the objects much easier. Click the Select Tool and open a context menu on the Rectangle. Choose Send to Back from the menu options.

10. **Save the file.**

11. **Preview the file in Acrobat.** Click the Preview PDF tab and the file opens in Acrobat as shown in Figure 23.19. Check over the form to be sure all elements are positioned to your liking. Notice in Figures 23.18 and 23.19 you see the Email and Print buttons we moved to the bottom of the page earlier when setting up the master page elements.

FIGURE 23.18

The final set of objects shown in Designer

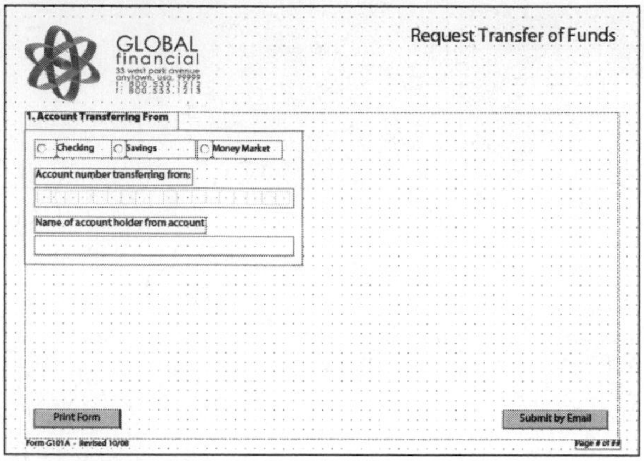

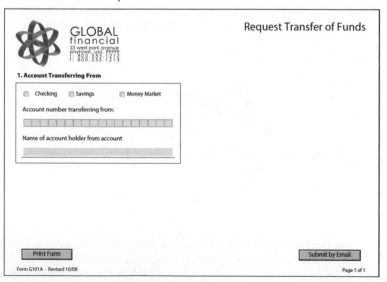

FIGURE 23.19

Click Preview PDF to preview the file in Acrobat

> **NOTE**   We presume you have Acrobat installed on your computer. If you do not have Acrobat installed, clicking the Preview PDF tab opens the PDF in another application such as a Web browser with a PDF Viewer plug-in. If the file doesn't open in an Acrobat viewer, open Acrobat if you have it installed or Adobe Reader and open the file.

Creating a Custom Library Group

The final form we want to create contains two almost identical blocks of text and field objects. Rather than start over and add new text and field objects to the form we created in the last series of steps, we can duplicate the first block and make the changes we need to make for the text objects. As we explained in Chapter 22, we don't need to worry about renaming the fields because all fields will have new instances after we duplicate them.

You can approach duplicating the fields in several ways as we explained in Chapter 22. You can use copy/paste, the Duplicate command, or press Ctrl after selecting all the objects and clicking on one of the objects and drag away. All these actions duplicate the first group of text and field objects on the form, adding new instances for all the objects.

If you want to design similar forms that use similar groups of fields, another method is to create a Custom Library Object comprised of all the objects in the group. To create a Custom Library object and duplicate the first group of fields on the form, do the following:

ON the CD-ROM **We'll continue using the same form created in steps up to this point in the chapter. If you haven't quite designed a form similar to Figure 23.18, you can use the *blankForm Fields01.xdp* file from the blankForm folder inside the Chapter23 folder on the book's CD-ROM.**

STEPS: Adding a Custom Library Group

1. **Continue with the form saved in the last series of steps.** If you haven't designed the form to appear similar to Figure 23.18, use the *blankFormFields01.xdp* file from the book's CD-ROM.

2. **Open the My Favorites Library palette.** Scroll the Standard Library palette up and collapse it by clicking the down-pointing arrow. You should see the My Favorites Library palette. Click the right-pointing arrow to expand the palette.

3. **Select all the text and field objects.** Draw a marquee around all the objects on the Design View page.

4. **Drag the objects to the My Favorites Library.** Note that you do not need to have the My Favorites Library palette open to add the elements to this library as shown in Figure 23.20. You can drag the elements to any library and choose the target library in the Add Library Object dialog box. We opened the My Favorites Library before dragging the elements to make it obvious where the objects ultimately are added.

5. **Type a name and description for the new library object.** After dragging objects to a library the Add Library Object dialog box opens as shown in Figure 23.21. Type a name for the objects item and type a description.

6. **Click OK.** By default the library object is targeted for the library you drag the elements to. However, you can choose another library group from the Tab Group drop-down menu. In our example we dragged the items to the My Library Group palette and that Tab Group appears as the default in the Add Library Group dialog box. After you click OK, the new item is added to the My Favorites Library palette as shown in Figure 23.22.

FIGURE 23.20

Drag the objects to the My Favorites Library.

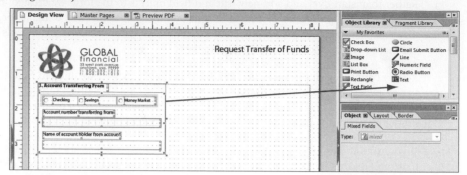

FIGURE 23.21

Type a name and description for the new library object.

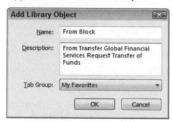

FIGURE 23.22

After you add an object to a library group, the object is listed according to the name you typed in the Add Library Object dialog box.

7. **Add the object to the form.** Click the new object you added to the My Favorites Library and drag to the form as shown in Figure 23.23.

8. **Change object attributes.** In our example we need to make three text changes. We need to change *from* to *to* in the three Text objects. The duplicated fields require no edits. Double-click a Text object and edit the text accordingly.

9. **Add additional objects.** The next two sections on the form each have a Text object and a Text Field object. Add the text *3. Amount to Transfer* on the left side of the form and below that add another Text object and type *US Dollars*. On the right side of the form add *Date of Transfer* and below the text add another Text object and type *mm/dd/yy*.

10. **Add a numeric and date field object.** Below the US Dollars text we need a numeric field. Drag the Numeric Field object from the Standard Library palette to the form below the *US Dollars* text. In the Object palette Field tab, choose None for the appearance. Click the Layout palette and for the Caption, choose None from the drop-down menu. Click the Right Justify tool in the Paragraph toolbar. Drag a Date Field to the form and position it under the *mm/yy/dd* text. Format the field the same using no appearance and no caption.

11. **Format a number field.** Click the Numeric Field object on the form and click Patterns in the Object palette Field tab. The Patterns – Numeric Field dialog box opens. Click the *$1,234.21* item in the left scrollable window and check the Allow Zero check box as shown in Figure 23.24. Click OK to apply the pattern and dismiss the dialog box.

12. **Format a date.** Click the Date Field and click Patterns in the Object palette Field tab to open the Patterns – Date Field as shown in Figure 23.25. Click 04/01/07 for the type and click the Allow Zero check box.

FIGURE 23.23

Drag the new object from the Library palette to the form.

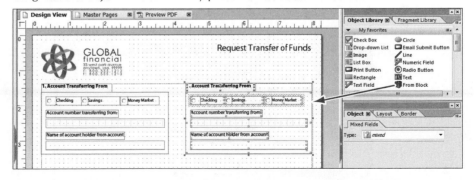

13. **Click OK to apply the pattern and dismiss the dialog box.** At this point your form should look similar to Figure 23.26.

14. **Preview the form.** Click Preview PDF to open the file in Acrobat. Examine the form to be sure all elements appear as you designed them. The form as it appears in Acrobat is shown in Figure 23.27.

FIGURE 23.24

Click the $1,234.21 pattern and check the Allow Zero check box.

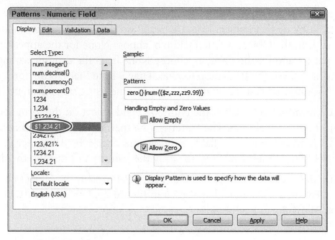

FIGURE 23.25

Click 04/01/07 for the type and check the Allow Zero check box.

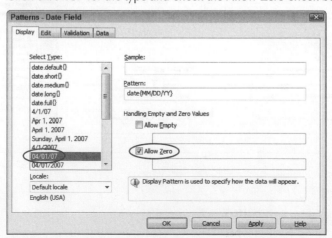

FIGURE 23.26

The form as it appears in Designer

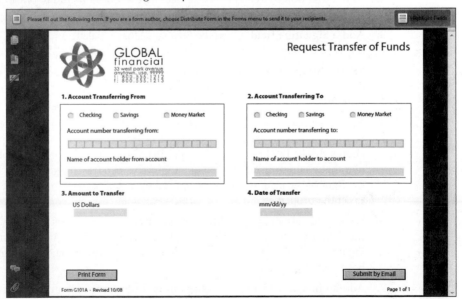

FIGURE 23.27

Click PDF Preview in Designer to preview the form in Acrobat.

Adding signatures and buttons

Up to now we've looked at field types that are used for user data entry. In a way, signature fields and buttons are similar in that, rather than deal with user data entry, they can execute some sort of action. This is most evident with button fields because we expect buttons to invoke some sort of action. The concept can be extended to signature fields where the action is to apply a digital signature and if desired execute an action to lock out fields.

On the original form we used in Chapter 11 we had a signature field and two button fields. For our current form, following the steps in this chapter, we'll use a signature field and three button fields.

To see how to add signatures and buttons to a form and set the properties to execute actions, follow these steps:

ON the CD-ROM We'll finish up the form we started from steps earlier in this chapter. If you haven't created a form similar to the one shown in Figure 23.26, use the *blankFormFields02.xdp* file from the blankForm folder in the Chapter23 Folder on the book's CD-ROM. For these steps we'll also use three image files from the Art folder in the Chapter23 folder: *resetForm.tif, submitByEmail.tif,* and *printForm.tif.*

STEPS: Adding a Signature and Button Fields

1. **Use the form saved from the last series of steps.** If you don't have a form that appears like the one saved from the last series of steps use the *blankFormFields02.xdp* form from the book's CD-ROM.

2. **Add a text object.** We have one remaining text object to add to our form. Add the text *5. Signature* below the field for US Dollars on the form.

3. **Add a Signature field.** Open the Standard Library palette and drag the Signature Field object to the form.

4. **Set the Signature field appearance properties.** Open the Field tab in the Object palette and choose None for the appearance. Click the Layout palette and choose None for the Caption.

5. **Set the signature handler.** Click the Signature tab in the Object palette and click Settings to open the Signature Settings dialog box. From the Name drop-down menu choose Adobe.PPKLite. The Adobe PPKLite choice uses the default Adobe signature handler that all users of Adobe Reader and Acrobat can use to sign a form. The check box to the right of the menu selection is enabled by default as shown in Figure 23.28. Click OK to set the properties.

6. **Lock fields after signing.** When you return to the Document pane the Signature tab in the Object palette should still be visible. Check Lock Fields After Signing as shown in Figure 23.29. This action locks all fields from any further data entry after the form has been digitally signed.

7. **Add an image.** Add an image object from the Standard Library palette. Double-click the object and import the *resetForm.tif* file from the Chapter 23 Folder on the book's CD-ROM. Size the object rectangle to a size similar to the default Print and Submit by Email buttons on the form.

8. **Set the image attributes.** In the Object palette's Draw tab check the Embed Image Data check box and choose Scale Image to Fit Rectangle as show in Figure 23.30.

FIGURE 23.28

Click Settings in the Signature tab in the Object Properties to open the Signature Settings dialog box.

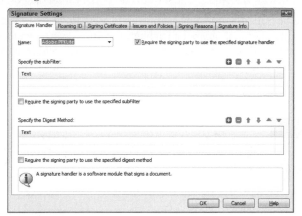

FIGURE 23.29

Click the Lock Fields After Signing check box in the Object palette's Signature tab.

FIGURE 23.30

Embed and size the image in the Draw tab.

9. **Add a button.** Currently we have two buttons on the form but neither button is used to reset the form. Therefore we need to add another button to the form. Open the Standard Library palette and drag the Reset Button object to the form. The Reset Form button has a script that comes with the object. The script is used to clear all data on the form.

10. **Format the appearance.** In the Object palette's Field tab remove the text where you see Reset Form for the Caption. Open the Highlighting drop-down menu and choose None as shown in Figure 23.31. Click the Border tab and choose Solid from the Edges drop-down menu and chose None for the Background Fill. We'll make this button appear transparent and place it over the graphic.

FIGURE 23.31

Delete the Caption text and choose None from the Highlight drop-down menu.

11. **Send the graphic object to the back.** Click the Image object where you imported the *resetForm.tif* file and open a context menu on the object. From the menu commands, choose Send to Back. By placing the graphic behind the button the button action can be executed with a mouse click.

12. **Group the objects.** Select both objects and click the Align Vertical Center and Align Horizontal Center commands in the Layout Align submenu. When aligned, keep both objects selected and choose Layout ➪ Group to group the selected objects.

13. **Move the objects to position.** Be careful when moving the objects. You need to move the cursor close to the gray border then click and drag. If you drag from the center, you'll drag the top button away from the graphic.

14. **Repeat the same steps for the Email Submit button and the Print button.** When you finish adding and positioning the objects, your Designer layout should look similar to Figure 23.32.

15. **Save the form.**

16. **Preview the form in Acrobat.** Click the PDF Preview tab and open the form in Acrobat. The final form should appear in Acrobat as you see in Figure 23.33.

Before deploying a form you should test the fields to be certain the data are added to field objects properly and the alignment and field formatting are correct.

FIGURE 23.32

The layout after adding the signature field and three buttons

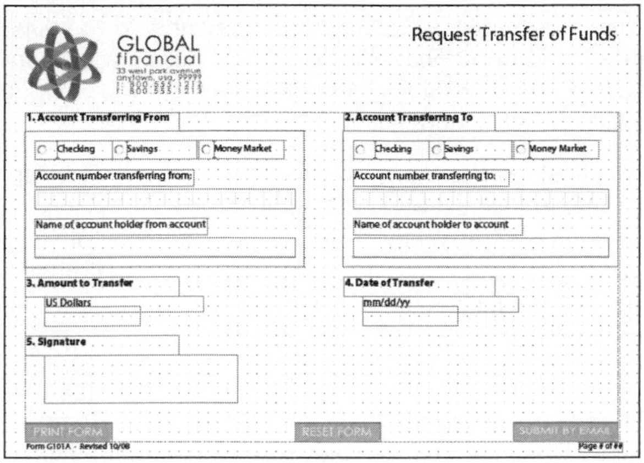

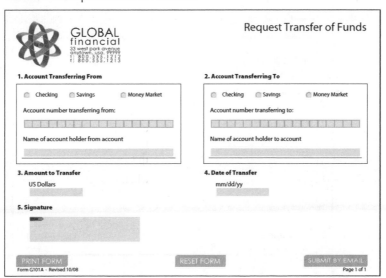

FIGURE 23.33

The final form previewed in Acrobat.

ON the CD-ROM You can review the final form on the CD-ROM in the blankForm folder in the Chapter23 Folder. The final designer file is *blankFormFieldsFinal.xdp* and the PDF form is *blankFormFieldsFinal.pdf*

Adding Objects to a Form

The steps used to produce the form shown in Figure 23.33 were an effort to duplicate as exactly as possible the form we designed in Acrobat using the same design appearance. We walked through the steps to produce a form to match an appearance of another form without regard to using design elements that would make the form more efficient.

If we didn't have a design to duplicate, our approach would have been a little different. Rather than using separate text objects for items such as the US Dollars and mm/dd/yy text, we would have used captions with the field objects. This method reduces the number of objects on a form. When you add a field with a caption you cut the number of objects in half, thereby reducing file size and making the form a little more efficient. If you have a form with static text and field objects where you need to add a caption you can select the objects and choose Merge As Caption from a context menu.

We also would eliminate the use of image objects for buttons on the form. The items used for Print Form, Reset Form, and Submit By Email used image objects as well as button field objects to duplicate the same look on the original form. Unless the design of your form demands this type of look, it would be best to eliminate the image objects. The total number of objects after adding the first block of fields would produce fewer objects as you can see in the Hierarchy palette.

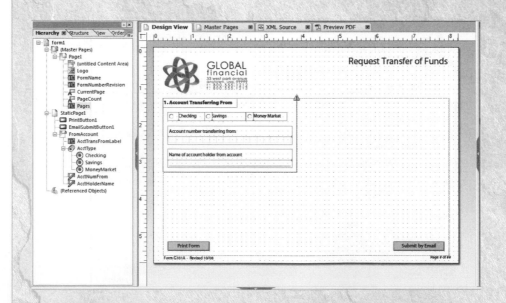

We would complete the form by wrapping the objects in a subform and assigning a black border to the subform, thereby eliminating a need to draw a rectangle object on the form. You can find out more about how to wrap objects in subforms in Chapter 28.

Using Microsoft Word documents

As you can see from all the previous steps we used to produce a simple design in LiveCycle Designer, it takes some time to create a form—especially if you're not familiar with the tools and commands in the program. Fortunately, you have many alternatives for laying out form designs.

The best design tool you can use for creating an initial form design is the program you're most familiar with. Designer supports creating forms from files originating from many different programs. Not all forms will benefit from original designs in other applications, but you will find a wealth of support when using application documents from a number of different programs.

If you happen to be an advanced user of Microsoft Word and you feel more comfortable creating forms designs in Word, you can use the program to not only set up the background design, but also add fields in Word. When the Word file is converted by Designer, the background elements and form fields convert nicely in Designer.

Setting up a Microsoft Word form

Word has a rich set of forms tools you can use to add form fields to a document. In addition to standard text and number fields you find check box fields, drop down lists, date and time fields, calculation fields, signature fields, barcodes, and more.

When you create a form in Microsoft Word and import the form into an XML form using Designer, the form fields are recognized by Designer. In Figure 23.34 we have a form we created in Microsoft Word. This form was created using Word's form features to populate the form with data fields.

The Word form has a header and footer and a table for the body composition. When you look over the fields in the Word file you can see many drop-down lists such as the one shown in Figure 23.35. All the attributes for fields like this are interpreted by Designer when you import the form.

Most of the elements in a Word form convert well in Designer. You may want to leave importing graphics to Designer rather than convert image files. Designer does a much better job of handling files like TIFF formats than converting the TIFF from a Word file. You also can experience some problems with forms having table cells and text colors for table cells. These are minor issues though because you can make changes in Designer relatively easily.

Converting a Word form to a Designer form

To convert Word files in Designer you use the same New Form Assistant wizard we've used several times in this chapter. One of the options you have when you first open the New Form Assistant wizard is a radio button choice to import a Word document.

To import a Word file in Designer, do the following.

FIGURE 23.34

A form designed in Microsoft Word

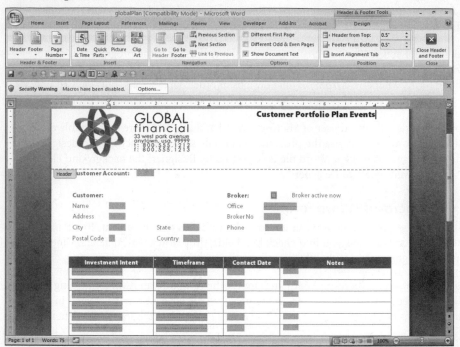

FIGURE 23.35

Form fields such as drop-down lists are converted by Designer with field attributes intact.

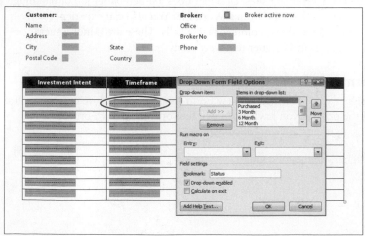

ON the CD-ROM To examine a Word file with form fields open the *globalPlan.doc* file in the Chapter23 Folder inside the globalPlan folder on the book's CD-ROM. The file is a Word 2003 file that can be opened in Word 2003 and Word 2007. We'll use this file with the following steps. In addition you'll need the *globalLogo.tif* file from the Art folder inside the Chapter23 folder.

NOTE Designer does support Word 2007 files for import. However, the results can be significantly different on import. The new form field tools for Word 2007 do not import well into Designer as of this writing. A regular Word document that does not have any fields will work fine in 2007 format, yet after importing the Word document the form is not a fillable form so you have to manually add field objects to the form. Until you find more support for Office 2007 files with Designer, we recommend saving your 2007 files in Word 2003 format.

STEPS: Importing a Word Document in Designer

1. **Be certain you have a Microsoft Word document saved as version 2003 available on your hard drive.** In our example we'll use the *globalPlan.doc* file from the book's CD-ROM.

2. **Open the New Form Assistant wizard.** Choose File ➪ New to open the wizard.

3. **Choose Import a Word Document in the Getting Started pane in the New Form Assistant.**

4. **Click Next and click the Browse button to open a Word document.** When the Open Word File dialog box opens, select the file to import and click Open. You return to the Setup: Import a Word Document pane in the wizard. Click Next.

5. **Add a print button.** Keep the Add a print button check box enabled and remove the check mark for Add an email button. Click Finish and the File Import Options dialog box opens.

6. **Choose file import options.** For our example we'll not use password security so leave the Security settings text boxes at the default as shown in Figure 23.36. Make sure the Ignore missing fonts and Convert Images check boxes are enabled. We'll replace the image on our form later but converting the image shows you how well the conversion worked on the logo image on our form.

7. **Click OK and the form opens in Designer.** As you can see in Figure 23.37, Designer did a very good job of converting the form fields as well as the text. We need to size the fields and do a little formatting as well as edit the text that was lost for the header row in the table, but these edits will take a fraction of the time compared to creating a similar form from scratch in Designer.

NOTE If you encounter a font problem when opening the Word file in Designer, click OK and accept the default substitution. We cover more on font substitution issues in Chapter 22.

FIGURE 23.36

Set the File Import Options and click OK.

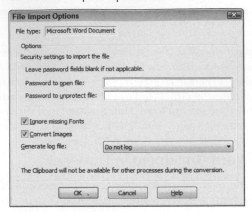

FIGURE 23.37

The converted form opened in Designer

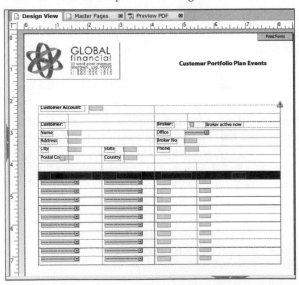

8. **Polish up the design.** We need to address the following edits to refine the form:

   ■ Open the master page and delete the logo. Add a new Image object and import the *global Logo.tif* file from the book's CD-ROM on the master page. Size and position the logo.

   ■ Return to Design View and move the Print button below the right side of the table.

- Size and align the field objects. Size all field objects on the form to fit within the table and in the areas above the table and align the objects. You can size one field, then select a column of fields or adjacent fields and choose Layout ⇨ Make Same Size ⇨ Both and use the Layout tools to align the objects.

- Change the table header row text to white. The header row text is not visible in the conversion. You need to select text and from the Text palette select White for the text color. When completed, your design should look similar to Figure 23.38.

 For more information on sizing and aligning fields, see Chapter 26.

FIGURE 23.38

The imported file after making some edits for sizing and positioning the fields

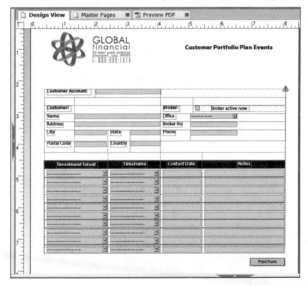

9. **Replace the State field.** Delete the field adjacent to the *State* text. Open the Custom Library palette and drag the U.S. States field object to the form. Format the field with None for the Caption and 0 (zero) for the Margins in the Object palette's Layout palette. Make sure None appears in the Border tab for the Edges and Background Fill.

10. **Replace the Country Field.** Delete the field object adjacent to the *Country* text and add the Countries field object from the Custom palette to the same location. Format the field identical to the formatting described in Step 9.

11. **Save the form.**

12. **Preview the form in Acrobat.** Click Preview PDF to display the finished form in Acrobat as shown in Figure 23.39.

FIGURE 23.39

The finished form as it appears in Acrobat

You don't need to create form fields in Word to convert a Word document in Designer. You can lay out the design elements in Word and import the Word file just like the form we imported in the previous steps. The important thing to note is that if you can quickly assemble a layout in Word, then feel free to use Word as your design application and Designer as the tool for adding field objects.

Using Microsoft Excel spreadsheets

Whereas Microsoft Word makes for a good design tool, Microsoft Excel, especially Excel 2007, falls far short of the ease for converting the native document to a Designer form. If you do a lot of work in Excel and you prefer to use it for designing forms with tables then you might be best served by opening the Excel file in Word and then importing the Word document in Designer. In Figure 23.40 you see a form we created in Microsoft Excel.

We used the New Form Assistant wizard to import the Excel file in Designer. When you work through the wizard, Designer prompts you to copy the cells you want to import so you need to return to Excel and copy the cells. When we pasted the clipboard data in Designer, the form appeared as you see in Figure 23.41.

FIGURE 23.40

FIGURE 23.40

A Microsoft Excel file

FIGURE 23.41

The form shown after importing the Excel file in Designer

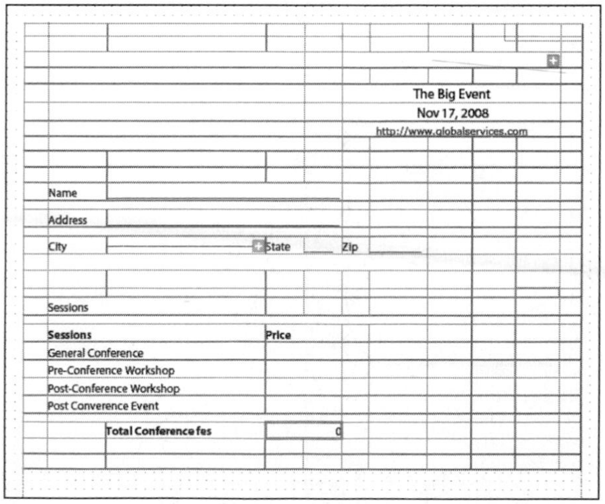

This form would take more work in Designer to polish it up than creating a new document. If Excel is your tool of trade be sure to pass the form through Word before importing into Designer. You can also convert Excel files to PDF and import the PDF document in Designer.

Creating a Form Based on a Template

Your alternative to creating new blank forms in Designer, when you want to use the program exclusively as a form design application, is to create a new form from a template. Designer is installed with a number of templates you can modify to suit many form needs. Rather than start from scratch with a new blank document, you can import a template and modify the form for your individual needs.

Examining the templates

All the available templates you have in Designer are visible in the Template Manager. To view the templates choose Tools ➪ Template manager and the Template Manager dialog box opens. This dialog box contains several tabs that include:

- **Blank.** Several sizes are shown in the Blank tab. The current assigned default page size is displayed for blank new forms in this tab.

- **Forms.** Click the Forms tab and you find all the preinstalled templates that come with Designer as shown in Figure 23.42. The layout of these forms uses a white background.

FIGURE 23.42

The Forms tab contains a list of preinstalled templates with white backgrounds.

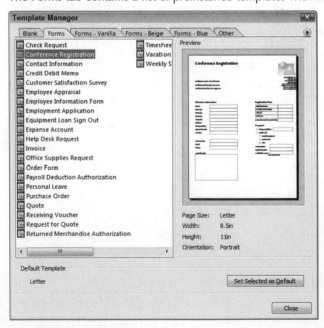

- **Forms – Vanilla/Forms – Beige/Forms-Blue.** These three separate tabs contain a list of identical templates as you find in the Forms tab except each tab lists templates with different colored backgrounds respective to the tab name.

- **Other.** By Default, the other category is empty. You use the Other category to add your own custom templates.

- **Flyout menu.** Click the right-pointing arrow in the top-right corner and you open a flyout menu with several menu commands used for managing templates as shown in Figure 23.43. You can add a new template to the Template Manager by clicking the Add Template menu item and choosing a template file. Template files are saved as an Adobe LiveCycle Designer Template (*.tds) file. Only a .TDS file can be selected to add as a template. When you add a template in the Template Manager the file appears in the Tab in view when you add the file. For example if you click the Forms – Beige tab and add a template, the template file is added to the Forms – Beige list.

FIGURE 23.43

Click the right-pointing arrow to open the flyout palette,

A template file is also added to the File menu. After adding a template, click the New tool to open the drop-down menu. Click Other and the submenu shows a list of your custom templates added in the Template Manager.

Adding a Category is a way for you to organize templates. You can add a new category, type a name for the category, and a new tab is added to the Template Manager dialog box. The Move Template menu item lets you move template files between the categories.

Creating a form from a template

You start creating a new form from a template by using the New Form Assistant wizard. After choosing File ➪ New click the Based on Template radio button in the first pane of the New Form Assistant wizard. Click Next, and the second pane is where you select the template to use for your new form as shown in Figure 23.44. From the scrollable list select the template you want to use.

FIGURE 23.44

Select the template you want to use from the scrollable list of templates.

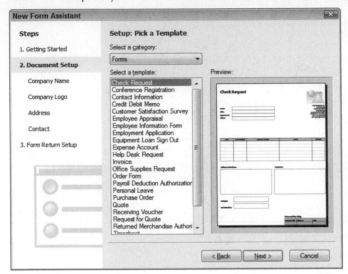

You step through the wizard answering questions related to importing an image, changing identifying information, and adding contact information. When you complete the steps in the wizard your form opens in Designer.

One of the nice things about some of the templates you have available is that some scripts are added to field objects on a few of the template forms. Use templates like the *Conference Registration, Credit Debit Memo, Expense Account,* and many others and you find scripts that produce calculation results.

Creating a custom template

A nice feature in Designer that we don't have in Acrobat is the ability to create custom templates. You might have a form that you use many times for different circumstances such as a purchase order form you use with a number of different vendors.

If you choose File ⇨ New and use the New Form Assistant wizard you can choose a purchase order form from a preset template that's installed with Designer. This is a generic form that enables you to customize the form to suit your company's needs. However, we believe the form is not designed well. When you open the template file, you see the top of the form appearing as shown in Figure 23.45.

FIGURE 23.45

The default Purchase Order form template file installed with Designer.

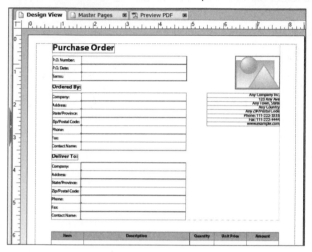

In the top-right corner of Figure 23.45 you see an Image Field. When you step through the New Form Assistant wizard you are prompted to identify your company logo. Since your company logo is not likely to change, this is a useless field. You don't want to keep looking for your logo image each time you fill in a purchase order.

If you look below the logo you see fields that are used to identify your company but the information isn't intuitive. You might think this area is used for the vendor information. When you step through the New Form Assistant wizard you are prompted to add information to fill in these fields with data that isn't likely to change.

On the left side of the form you find open-ended fields. These fields are used to identify a company location and shipping information. Each time you fill in the form you have to fill in information that again isn't likely to change often.

A much more useful design would be to use a static image for the logo. Add a title above the vendor data and use the fields you are prompted to fill in for the data that changes such as the vendor data. These changes will make it clear to anyone looking at the form that the fields on the right are for vendor information, and instead of having to fill in the fields on the left, we use static data that won't change for each form we fill out.

If you like the design of the form below the identifying information, you can edit this template and save it as a new custom template that can be used when filling in purchase order forms. To edit this template and make it available in the Template Manager, do the following.

We'll use a preinstalled template and edit the file. For the logo, you can use your own image. If you do not have an image file available use the *globalLogo.tif* file from the Art folder inside the Chapter23 folder on the book's CD-ROM.

STEPS: Editing a Template File

1. **Open a preinstalled template.** For these steps we use the *Purchase Order.tds* file. Choose File open and choose Adobe LiveCycle Designer Templates (*.tds) from the Files of type drop-down menu. Navigate to: Program Files/ /Adobe/Acrobat 9.0/Designer 8.2/EN/ Templates/Common Forms. Note that EN is for the English language files. If you have another language installation of Designer, locate the folder consistent with your language. Double-click the Purchase Order form.

2. **Choose Edit this template.** When you open a template file the Template Options dialog box opens. Click the Edit this template radio button and click OK to open the file as a template.

3. **Save the file.** Choose File ⇨ Save As and open the Other folder inside the Templates folder. By default the .TDS format appears in the Save as type drop-down menu. Click Save and you save a copy of the Purchase Order form. Be certain to complete this step before you edit the original form.

4. **Delete the Image Field object and replace it with an Image object.** Click the logo in the top-right corner of the form and delete it. Drag an Image object from the Standard Library palette to the same location as the default Image Field object. Double-click the new object and import your logo. In our example we import the *globalLogo.tif* file from the book's CD-ROM.

5. **Change the field types for the Ordered By fields.** Select the field objects below the *Ordered By* text but leave the Contact Name field deselected. Open the Layout palette and choose None from the Position drop-down menu. You need to individually change the object types beginning with the first field in the group. Right-click to open a context menu and chose Change Object Type ⇨ Text. We'll change all the Text Field objects to Text objects. Repeat the same steps for all fields and the form should look like Figure 23.46.

6. **Edit the Text objects.** Edit the Text objects to reflect information specific to your company. In our example we edited the text as shown in Figure 23.47.

7. **Delete the Deliver To items.** For this form, we'll assume the billing address and shipping address are the same. If you want to keep the Deliver To fields, follow Steps 5 and 6. If your shipping address varies you can leave the fields unedited.

8. **Add a Vendor title.** Click the *Ordered By:* text and press the Control key. When you see the cursor change to a + (plus) symbol drag to the right above the block of fields on the right side of the form. Change the text to *Vendor:*.

9. **Distribute the vendor fields.** The fields appear a little tight on the right so move them to distribute the fields similar to the fields on the left side of the form. You can select all but the first field and press the arrow key once. Then select all but the second field and press the arrow key once, and so on, to distribute the fields nicely on the form. After distributing the fields your form should appear similar to Figure 23.48.

FIGURE 23.46

Remove the caption and change the Text Field objects to Text objects.

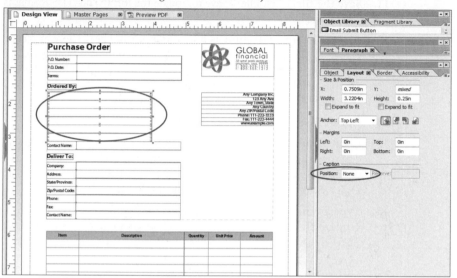

FIGURE 23.47

Edit the text to a default you want to appear for your company's identifying information.

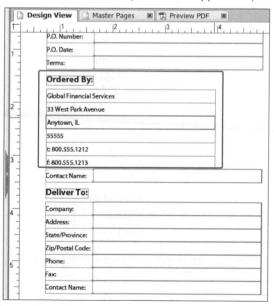

10. **Move the table up.** The table is located well below the fields. Select the table and move it up so the form appears similar to Figure 23.49 when viewed in a Fit to Page view.

11. **Save the file.** Click File ➪ Save to update the form. The .TDS format is used when you update the form.

12. **Close the form and add it as a template.** Click File ➪ Close and choose Tools ➪ Template Manager. Click the Other tab in the Template Manager and open the flyout menu. Choose Add Template and open the new template from the Other folder in the Templates folder. In our example we saved our new template as *Global Purchase Order.tds* and added it as a template as shown in Figure 23.50.

13. **Click Close in the Template Manager.**

14. **Create a new form based on a template.** Open the New drop-down menu (click the down-pointing arrow adjacent to the New icon in the File toolbar) and choose Other ➪ *<your template name>*. In our example we choose Other ➪ Global Purchase Order. Selecting the menu item opens the Template Assistant.

15. **Type a vendor name.** The first pane in the Template Assistant wizard prompts you for a vendor name. (Actually it says Please enter your company's name as shown in Figure 23.51 but we changed that to a vendor name.) Type a name and click Next.

FIGURE 23.48

The Deliver To fields are deleted, a new title has been added, and the fields on the right side of the form are redistributed.

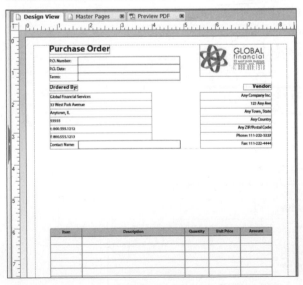

The final form after editing

Add the new template in the Other tab.

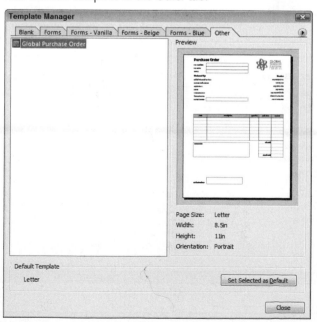

FIGURE 23.51

Type a vendor company name and click Next.

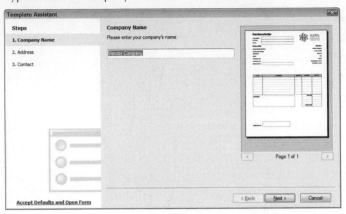

16. **Fill in the fields as you walk through the wizard.** Complete the fields in each tab in the wizard and click Finish after filling in the last pane.

17. **Preview the file.** After completing the wizard steps click the Preview PDF tab and open the form in Acrobat. The fields for the vendor information are populated from the data you supplied in the wizard as shown in Figure 23.52.

FIGURE 23.52

When you preview the PDF the vendor fields are populated with data from the Template Assistant wizard.

Purchase Order

GLOBAL
financial
33 west park avenue
anytown, usa. 99999
t: 800.555.1212
f: 800.555.1213

P.O. Number:

P.O. Date:

Terms:

Ordered By:

Global Financial Services

33 West Park Avenue

Anytown, IL

55555

t: 800.555.1212

f: 800.555.1213

Contact Name:

Vendor:

Rockwell Office Supplies

8768 North 11th Street

Boise, ID

USA

55555

Phone: 800.111.2222

Fax: 800.111.2223

Item	Description	Quantity	Unit Price	Amount

Preserving Field Attributes for the Template Assistant

If you edit a template and want to preserve the links to the Template Assistant wizard when creating a new form from the template, you have to exercise care and avoid actions that will break the links. You can copy and paste objects that are used in the wizard from one template to another or paste into a blank new page. You can modify default text and you can relocate objects on the page. You can delete objects without disturbing the other objects that appear in the Template Assistant.

You cannot, however, edit the paragraph attributes such as changing alignment for any item you want to appear in the Template Assistant. Nor can you change an object to another object type or edit object attributes, and you cannot create new objects or copy and paste objects on the same form if you want them to appear in the Template Assistant.

Importing a PDF Document

In Chapter 27 we use some examples for importing PDF files in a Designer form. You can import a PDF document to be used as a background for the form design and you can import forms with field objects created in Acrobat. When you import an Acrobat PDF form, Designer converts the Acrobat Form objects to XML form objects.

Some scripting is not translated from the Acrobat Form when you import the form in Designer. As we explain in Chapter 29, the JavaScript used in Acrobat varies from the JavaScript you use in Designer. In Chapter 35 we talk about some resources that help you understand more about translating scripts from Acrobat Forms to Designer forms.

In terms of designing forms, using PDF backgrounds provides you with some advantages and disadvantages. The advantages are, among other things, the fact that you can use your favorite design program to create the look of the form. Programs such as Adobe InDesign and Adobe Illustrator offer you much more advanced design opportunities than using Designer's layout tools or using Microsoft Word as a design tool. If you turn back to Chapter 9 and look over the *generalApplication.pdf* file or open the file from the book's CD-ROM in the Chapter 9 folder you find a form design that would be a challenge to produce in Microsoft Word. We designed this form in Adobe InDesign and used it for an Acrobat Form. We could easily import the same file in Designer and preserve the original design look.

The disadvantage you have with using PDF Backgrounds is that you don't have access to all of Designer's tools for creating objects. As we explain in Chapter 27, you cannot create tables when you use a PDF Background. Many of the automated types of features you have in Designer are not available to you so you have to manually add field objects.

If you have a design you want to use as something like a header, for example a masthead or a logo with text that is saved as a PDF file, you cannot import the PDF document in Designer. A portion of a PDF page cannot be introduced directly in Designer. Also, you cannot use a background that occupies a portion of a Designer page and have access to all the layout tools. PDF Backgrounds are imported in Designer via the New Form Assistant. If you want to use the Image object to import an object to occupy a header or some other element you need to save the PDF document from Acrobat in an image format supported by Designer such as TIF or JPEG.

Summary

- When creating a new form and using the File ➪ New menu command the New Form Assistant wizard opens. In the wizard you can choose from a number of documents to import in Designer.

- Creating a blank new page requires you to add all graphics and field objects to create a form.

- You can import Microsoft Word documents as a new form in Designer. If you have form fields in the original Word document, the field objects are recognized by Designer.

- When using Microsoft Word files, it is best to save the files as Word 2003 format if you want to import Word form fields.

- Microsoft Excel files are imported by copying cells in a spreadsheet and pasting them into a form. As a form design tool, Excel is not as powerful as Microsoft Word.

- You use the Template Manager to add new templates where you can create a new form based on a template.

- You can create custom templates and copy/paste objects from existing templates or modify existing templates and have fields recognized in the Template Assistant wizard.

- You can import PDF documents as PDF Backgrounds for preserving certain original designs.

- When using PDF Backgrounds you lose some of the layout tools features in Designer.

Chapter 24

Working with Designer's Form Fields and Objects

IN THIS CHAPTER

Adding objects

Aligning techniques

Creating custom library objects

Working with form fragments

L earning a new program can seem overwhelming. Many programs offer multiple ways to accomplish the same task. Designer is no exception. Why are there three ways to do exactly the same thing? Wouldn't it be easier if you had just one way to complete the task? Then you would have only one way to learn and remember. Fortunately, you don't have to remember every technique you learn, just the ones that work best for you.

If we polled a group of computer users for their favorite copy and paste method, we would receive different answers. Everyone has their own preferences, and no two users work exactly the same way.

In this chapter we explore many of the techniques available for adding, copying, moving, and aligning objects in Designer. By exploring them you can find the methods that work best for you. Even if you are not new to Designer, we hope to show you a new technique or two. After we cover the techniques for working with objects we'll examine the powerful features of the Object Library, form fragments, and master pages.

Adding Fields and Objects to a Form

Placing objects on the design page may seem like a straightforward task. A variety of techniques exist offering more efficient workflows depending on the task at hand. In this section we discuss the methods available for adding objects and some time-saving tips on when to use them.

When we place an object on the design page, Designer creates a new instance of that object. A new instance means that the object is an independent copy of the original. This instance has its own set of properties that you can set without affecting any other object on the form or in the Object Library.

Using the drag and drop metaphor

Many computer applications, including operating systems, use drag and drop. When you want to delete something, you drag it to the deleted items folder or the trash bin. You move files to new locations by dragging them from one folder to another. In LiveCycle Designer we frequently drag and drop objects to and from the design page and the palettes.

STEPS: Drag and Drop an Object to a New Location

1. **Open Designer and create a blank new page.** When you open the program, bypass the options for opening a file and choose File ➪ New or click the New tool to create a blank new page.

2. **Position you mouse over the object you want to move.** This can be an object on the page, an object in the library, or an object in the Hierarchy palette. In our example we use the Object Library palette. By Default the palette should be open. If you do not see the Library palette, choose Window ➪ Object Library.

3. **Click and hold the mouse button on the desired object.** This selects the object and begins the drag-and-drop process. Click the Button object as shown in Figure 24.1.

4. **With the mouse button held down, move the object to the new location.** This is the drag portion of the process. Dragging can occur within the same area of the workspace or between different areas of the workspace. Drag the Text Field object from the Object Library palette to the blank new page as shown in Figure 24.2.

FIGURE 24.1

Click an object in the Object Library palette.

Drag an object from the Object Library palette to the blank new page.

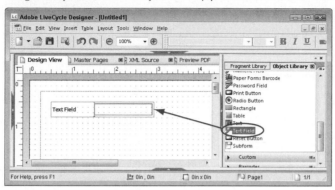

5. **Release the mouse button.** This is the drop action that releases the object in the new location. If you attempt to drag an object to a location that is not allowed, the mouse pointer changes to a no symbol.

In Designer we can use the drag-and-drop technique to drag objects from the Object Library onto the design page to create a new object. While you drag the object onto the design page, a dotted line appears showing the object's size and tentative location along with a screen tip listing the object's current X/Y coordinates as shown in Figure 24.3. When you release the mouse pointer the object is dropped on the design page and your mouse pointer returns to the regular selection arrow.

Drag and drop a text field.

When you use the drag-and-drop method, Designer creates a new instance of the object with a predetermined size. It also names the object according to the object type. If you create a standard object (non-customized), then Designer appends an incremental number to the end of the object name. For example, the first text field you drag onto the design page becomes TextField1, followed by TextField2, and so on, as shown in Figure 24.4. Each type of object has its own numbering sequence. The first numeric field is named NumericField1, regardless of how many other fields are already on the page.

FIGURE 24.4

The Hierarchy palette showing the unique field names

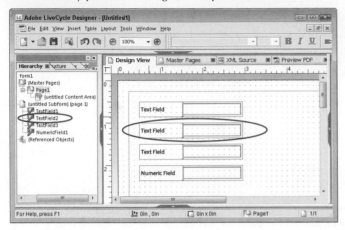

Stamping fields and objects

Acrobat and Designer both offer a stamping technique. When you stamp objects on the design page they are created using predetermined sizes. By selecting an object from the Object Library with a single click, you are now ready to stamp in the design page. Move your mouse pointer anywhere in the design page. The pointer is the same shape as the icon you selected in the Object Library, with a screen tip displaying the current X/Y coordinates. A single click stamps the object on the design page and returns your mouse pointer to the regular selection arrow.

Stamping fields can seem tricky the first couple of times. Unlike the drag-and-drop method, stamping provides no outline to show you where the object is going to be placed on the page, as shown in Figure 24.5. This method takes some practice. Remember, when you have a tool selected, the mouse pointer changes to that object's icon shape. Regardless of the shape, the coordinates are measured from the upper-left corner of the icon.

It may seem as if the object is dropped up and to the left of where you click. This is caused by the snap to grid setting, as shown in Figure 24.6. When you stamp the field on the page, the coordinates move up and left to the nearest dot on the grid if snap to grid is active. Test this by zooming in and dropping an object between the dots. You can drop them anywhere you'd like if you turn off the snap to grid feature.

FIGURE 24.5

Stamping a Text Field shows the screen tip measured from the top left of the mouse pointer, but no object outline.

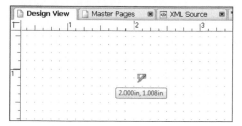

FIGURE 24.6

After stamping the text field, the object snaps to the nearest dot on the design grid.

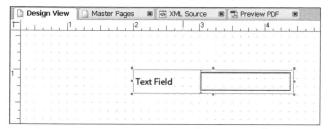

STEPS: Stamping Fields on the Design Page

1. Use the blank page opened in Designer from the preceding series of steps or create a new blank page.

2. **Click once on an object in the Object Library.** This selects the object and changes your mouse pointer into the object icon.

3. **Move your mouse over the design page.** Notice where the top-left corner of the mouse pointer is. This is where the top-left handle of the new object is placed.

4. **Click once to stamp the object.** A single click places one instance of the object on the design page. The first instance created is the object's default height and width. The mouse pointer returns to the normal selection arrow.

TIP You can continue stamping fields without having to reselect the object in the library again. The feature is called Keep Drawing and can be activated by right-clicking a tool in the Library.

Drawing fields and objects

If you do not want your fields created based on a predetermined size, you can draw a field. Drawing allows you to create any size objects you need. Rather than clicking and dragging an object from the Object Library, click the object one time in the Object Library to activate the tool. You can now move to anywhere in the design page to draw the object. Click and drag your mouse to determine the new object's location and size. As soon as you let go of the mouse, the regular mouse pointer returns to edit existing fields.

STEPS: Drawing Objects

1. **Click once on an object in the Object Library.** This selects the object and changes the mouse pointer into the object's icon.

2. **Move the mouse over the design page.** Notice where the top-left corner of the mouse pointer is. This is where the top-left handle of the new object is placed.

3. **Click and drag the mouse to draw the object until you reach the size desired.** By drawing the object you determine its height and width, as shown in Figure 24.7.

FIGURE 24.7

Drawing a text field

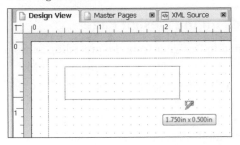

4. **Release the mouse pointer to finish drawing the object.** The mouse pointer icon changes back to the regular selection arrow.

You may find that when you begin adding fields to your form design, you want the tool to remain active to create multiples without having to reselect the tool each time from the Object Library. As we discussed in the stamping fields section previously, this feature is available in both Acrobat and Designer. In Acrobat this feature is called Keep Tool Selected. In Designer it is called Keep Drawing. The feature can be activated when a tool is active by selecting View ➪ Keep Drawing. Or, you can right-click the tool in the Object Library to turn Keep Drawing on from the context menu. Once selected, the Keep Drawing feature remains active until you turn it off again. To cancel the active object tool, press Esc.

> **TIP** To stamp a field in a custom size, turn on the Keep Drawing feature. Draw one field on the design page with the desired dimensions. Now the stamping feature will create objects with the same dimensions as the last drawn object. Every time you choose a tool from the library it resets to the default dimensions.

Copying fields and objects

Copying objects in Designer is just like copying items in other programs, with a variety of methods available. You may have already formatted the appearance of the object, set a calculation, or written a script that is simply easier to copy than to recreate. If you have a form with fields and layout that are similar to what you are building, copying fields can save significant design time.

You can make a copy of any object on the design page using your favorite copy technique. One of the more common methods to copy and paste, toolbar buttons, is missing in the Designer interface. Of course you can customize toolbars to add the cut, copy, and paste buttons if desired.

FIGURE 24.8

The Tools toolbar after adding the standard cut, copy, and paste options.

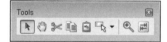

When you begin pasting in Designer, objects may not react the way you are accustomed to in other applications. In many applications such as word processors and e-mail programs we establish where the copy is to be located by placing the cursor in the desired location. In many graphics programs the copy is offset a small distance from the original. In Designer the copied location is determined by where the tip of the mouse pointer is located when you execute the paste command. This can work to your advantage when you become familiar with it. The first few times you paste in Designer it may seem a little odd. Try copying and pasting with various techniques to see if one method or another works better for you.

The copy and paste techniques available in Designer include:

- **The Edit menu:** Select the object you want to make a copy of. Select Edit ⇨ Copy and then select Edit ⇨ Paste.

- **Right-click:** Right-click the object you want to make a copy of. This opens the context menu. Select Copy from the context menu, right-click the design page approximately where you want the copy placed, and select Paste from the context menu.

- **Drag and drop:** Drag and drop normally moves an object. To make a copy (a duplicate) you need to hold down the Ctrl key when the mouse is released. Select the object you want to copy. Click and drag the object to the desired location then hold down the Ctrl key while you release the mouse.

- **Keyboard shortcuts.** The standard keyboard shortcuts for Cut (Ctrl + X), Copy (Ctrl + C), and Paste (Ctrl + V) work in Designer. Select the object you want to copy. Press Ctrl + C to copy it. Place your mouse pointer approximately where you want the copy placed, and then press Ctrl + V to paste it.

- **Duplicate:** You can find Duplicate in the Edit Menu. Select Edit ⇨ Duplicate from the menu bar or press Ctrl + D using the keyboard to duplicate the selected objects.

CROSS-REF For more details on the duplicate feature, see Duplicate Fields and Objects later in this chapter.

- **Copy and Paste buttons.** These buttons are not on the visible Designer toolbars unless you customize a toolbar and add them. Select the object you want to copy. Click the Copy button and then click the Paste button.

CROSS-REF For more information on customizing toolbars, see Chapter 22.

We have found that the right-click, paste method is the least efficient when placing objects. Using the right-click method requires you to move your mouse pointer to select the Paste command from the context menu. This also changes where the object is pasted accordingly.

Using the Insert menu to add objects

The Insert menu contains a choice for each of the library object groups with a cascading menu for each object contained in that group as shown in Figure 24.9. When you use the Insert menu, items are placed in the center of the design page. Inserting more than one object in a row stacks them on top of one another.

Adding objects with the menus can be useful when the palettes have been collapsed. However, we feel the other methods offer better workflows. Having the objects stacked in the center of the design page does not offer the most effective use of time.

Using the Tools toolbar to add objects

If you plan to create a large number of fields with standard settings and you need the design space more than the library palette, the Tools toolbar may be your best choice. The toolbar contains a button called the Field Edit tool. The drop-down Field Edit Tool allows you to choose one of the most common field types with default settings from the Standard Library. When you use the Field Edit tool you can stamp or draw fields. As shown in Figure 24.10, as soon as the field type is selected a checkmark is placed in the drop-down list and Keep Drawing is turned on.

FIGURE 24.9

The library groups in the Insert menu

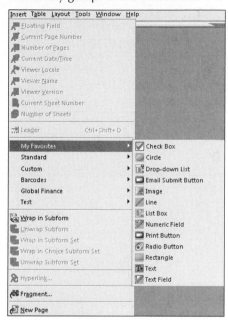

FIGURE 24.10

The Field Edit tool on the Tools toolbar

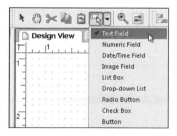

The Keep Drawing feature is automatically activated when you use the Field Edit tool in Designer 8.2. However, not all versions of Designer act this same way. In earlier Designer versions you may need to turn on the Keep Drawing feature. We like using the Field Edit tool when design space is limited to avoid having to open the right palette well. Unfortunately the Field Edit tool does not offer objects from other library groups.

Duplicating fields and objects

Duplicating fields is similar to copying a field. It makes a copy and then places the copy offset relative to the original object. The first time you duplicate an object, it is offset one point down from the original as shown in Figure 24.11. You can adjust the distance and direction of the offset placement by dragging the duplicated object. The next duplicate is offset in the same direction and the same relative distance as the one you dragged, as shown in Figure 24.12.

FIGURE 24.11

The first duplicated field is offset one point down on the design grid.

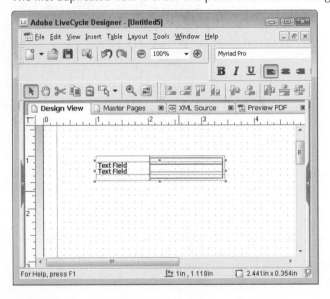

 **TIP**   You can easily make duplicates by using the keyboard shortcut of Ctrl+D.

STEPS: Duplicating an Object

1. **Choose File ⇨ New.** Create a new blank document.

2. **Drag a Text Field onto the upper-left corner of the design page.** This adds a text field object to the form. We dragged the text field from the Standard Group of the Object Library palette.

3. **With the text field selected, go to Edit ⇨ Duplicate (Ctrl + D).** This makes a copy of the text field one point down on the design grid.

FIGURE 24.12

The second duplicated field is offset the same relative distance as the first duplicate after dragging.

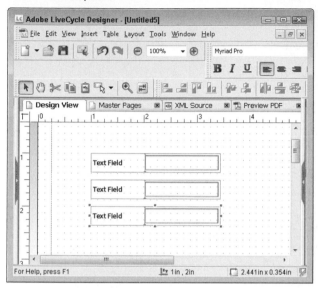

4. **Drag the duplicate text field down on the page, making sure they do not overlap.** This sets the direction and distance for the next Duplicate command. The Duplicate dialog box is shown in Figure 24.13.

5. **With the second text field selected, go to Edit ➪ Duplicate (Ctrl + D).** The third field is placed below the second, with equal spacing between the objects. Your screen should appear similar to Figure 24.12.

Creating duplicates of multiple objects is also possible. This works best if all the objects are offset the same distance and direction.

Using Copy Multiple

If you know in advance that you need to create more than one copy of an object or set of objects, Copy Multiple is another option. Acrobat has a similar feature called Place Multiple Fields, with some minor differences in terms and dialog box layout. One setting varies greatly between the two programs. When Acrobat asks for the number of times to copy the selected fields down or across, it wants a total number of fields desired, including the original. Designer requests the number of copies you want to create, not including the original.

FIGURE 24.13

Dragging the object sets the relative direction and distance for the new duplicate.

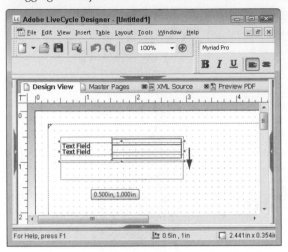

When you use Copy Multiple the dialog box prompts you for the desired number of copies, the offset direction, and the offset distance. It works just like duplicate, with a dialog box to control the settings as shown in Figure 24.14. Using Copy Multiple is recommended when the copied objects need to be equally spaced, or when they should have no spacing between them. They dialog box has a setting for touching that precisely aligns the objects without the need to measure the height and width of the objects.

In the Vertical Placement group you can place the copies above, below, or with no vertical movement relative to the original. Setting the Vertical Spacing to touching or offset by a measurement controls the distance between the objects. Keep in mind if you do not want the objects touching, then the offset measurement must be greater than the original object's height.

The Horizontal Placement group works in a similar way; you can place copies to the left, to the right, or with no horizontal movement relative to the original. Setting the Horizontal Spacing to touching or offset by a measurement controls the distance between the objects. If you do not want the objects touching, then the offset measurement must be greater than the original object's width.

Unless you are trying to achieve a stair step look to your fields, you probably shouldn't set the vertical and horizontal placement at the same time. The Copy Multiple dialog box retains your last setting.

The results of Copy Multiple and Duplicate can be identical; it is only a matter of preference in your workflow.

FIGURE 24.14

The Copy Multiple dialog box.

Selecting and aligning objects

How many hours have you spent trying to get things in exactly the right place? Have you ever thought there has to be an easier way? Many form designers use the "eyeball" technique. They rely on what they see on the page to determine object positions. For some users that means zooming in, placing a few objects, zooming back out, and checking to see if the position looks okay. For other users it means jotting down an object's coordinates and using them when placing other objects in the layout palette. These methods work, but they are not the most efficient workflows.

When placing objects in your form design, having things aligned makes a form neat and professional looking. It is worth the time required to align objects for a better overall form appearance. In this chapter we explore the many methods for aligning objects. Before we do, we need to discuss how to select more than one object.

Selecting multiple fields and objects on the design page

To align two or more fields using Designer's built-in techniques, you must first select the objects. Clicking an object selects that object. Clicking a second object deselects the first object. The methods available while working on the design page include:

- **Ctrl + Click:** To select multiple objects, hold down the Ctrl key while clicking additional objects. Using Ctrl allows you to be selective in which objects you grab. Ctrl key selects only the objects you click.

TIP Use caution when holding down the Ctrl key and clicking objects. If you hold the mouse pointer down too long, you may move the object(s) on the page, accidentally making copies of the selected objects. As we discussed previously, dragging and dropping an object with the Ctrl key down makes a copy.

- **Shift + Click:** The Shift key works just like Ctrl when selecting on the design page. The only difference is that although holding down the mouse too long moves the object(s) on the page, it does not create copies when using Shift.

- **Click and drag a selection marquee (lasso):** Use your mouse to click and drag a box around the desired objects to select them. You must fully enclose the object's handles inside your marquee for it to be included in the selection. Partially enclosing an object does not select it. Start with your mouse in a blank area of the design page, not over an object. Click and drag your mouse to draw a box around the objects. When you release the mouse button all objects fully enclosed by the marquee become selected.

- **Ctrl + A:** This keyboard shortcut selects all objects on the active page.

> **TIP** Acrobat and Designer differ when using the marquee method to select objects. In Acrobat you only need to touch the object to select it. In Designer, you must fully enclose the object's handles to select it.

When you have more than one object selected, the appearance of the object's handles becomes very important. When you select on the Design Page, the last object selected is the active object. The active object becomes the reference point that the other objects align to. The active object's handles are solid blue, as opposed to the other selected objects which have handles with a blue outline but no fill color, as shown in Figure 24.15. You can change the active object to any of the other selected objects by clicking the desired object. The solid blue handles move to the last selected object. Clicking an object outside of the selected objects selects the new object only and deselects the previous group.

FIGURE 24.15

The name field is the active object and has solid blue handles within a group of selected objects.

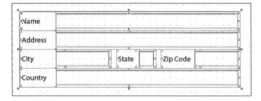

Selecting multiple fields and objects in the Hierarchy palette

If you have a tendency to hold the mouse pointer down too long when selecting multiple objects on the page, using the Hierarchy palette for selecting, as shown in Figure 24.16, may be a better choice for you.

FIGURE 24.16

Using the Hierarchy palette to select multiple objects

Using the Hierarchy palette also can be beneficial if objects are positioned very close to one another. The top object in the Hierarchy list is always the active object, regardless of the order selected. The selection methods in the Hierarchy palette include:

- **Ctrl + Click:** This works the same way in the Hierarchy palette as on the design page. Hold down the Ctrl key while clicking additional objects. Dragging and dropping with Ctrl does not make a copy in the Hierarchy palette.

- **Shift + Click:** The Shift key works differently in the Hierarchy palette than on the design page. Shift selects everything between the first object and the second object you click. Select the first object you want by clicking it, and then hold down Shift while you click the last object you want. All of the objects in between are also selected.

- **Shift + Arrow Key:** Holding down the Shift key while using either the up-arrow or down-arrow key selects the additional objects.

- **Ctrl + Arrow Key:** The Ctrl key takes a little more effort to use with the arrow keys. Holding down Ctrl while pressing the up-arrow or down-arrow key moves the focus to the next object. The object is not selected unless you press the spacebar.

- **Ctrl + A:** This keyboard shortcut selects all objects on the active page and works the same in the Hierarchy palette as on the design page.

No matter which method you use to select multiple objects, sometimes you get an extra object in the selection. You can remove an object from the selection as well, using the Ctrl key.

Aligning objects

Now that we have the selection techniques covered we can continue our discussion of alignment. As we discussed in Chapter 22, aligning objects does more than affect their appearance on the page. Alignment also affects the tab order the form recipient encounters when entering data in the form.

Remember that when multiple objects are selected the active object (noted by the solid blue handles) becomes the reference point for all other objects. Alignment choices affected by the active object include:

- **Edges:** Alignment can be to any of the four edges: left, right, top, and bottom.
- **Vertical Center:** The active object's vertical center becomes the alignment position.
- **Horizontal Center:** The active object's horizontal center becomes the alignment position.

The remaining alignment options are not affected by the active object:

- **To the Grid:** The objects are aligned to the dot on the grid nearest the upper-left selection handle. Each object is aligned to the grid independent of the other objects.
- **Center in Page Horizontally:** With a single object selected, this option places it centered between the left and right margins. If two or more objects are selected, the selected object's collective handles become the reference point. Selecting this option does not align the objects with each other. This method moves them as a set to the horizontal center of the page.
- **Center in Page Vertically:** With a single object selected, this option places it centered between the top and bottom margins. If two or more objects are selected, the selected object's collective handles become the reference point. Selecting this option does not align the objects with each other. This method moves them as a set to the vertical center of the page.

Methods for aligning objects include:

- **Layout Menu:** With the objects selected, use the Layout menu to choose an alignment from the available list:
  - **Layout ⇨ Align:** This submenu contains seven options: the four edges, vertical and horizontal centers, and to the grid as shown in Figure 24.17.
  - **Layout ⇨ Center in Page:** This submenu contains the two page-related options: Center in Page Vertically and Center in Page Horizontally, as shown in Figure 24.18.
- **Layout Toolbar:** The Layout toolbar contains six alignment choices: the four edges, vertical center, and horizontal center, as shown in Figure 24.19.
- **Keyboard:** Shortcuts exist for many of the alignment choices including:
  - **Ctrl + Right Arrow:** This shortcut aligns the selected objects on the right edge of the active object.
  - **Ctrl + Left Arrow:** This shortcut aligns the selected objects on the left edge of the active object.

- **Ctrl + Up Arrow:** This shortcut aligns the selected objects on the top edge of the active object.

- **Ctrl + Down Arrow:** This shortcut aligns the selected objects on the bottom edge of the active object.

- **Alt + Ctrl + Up Arrow:** This shortcut aligns the selected objects on the vertical center of the page.

- **Alt + Ctrl + Right Arrow:** This shortcut aligns the selected objects on the horizontal center of the page.

- **Alt + Ctrl + Left Arrow:** This shortcut aligns the selected objects to the grid.

Unfortunately, the alignment options are not available in the right-click context menus from either the design page or the Hierarchy palette.

FIGURE 24.17

The Layout ➪ Align menu

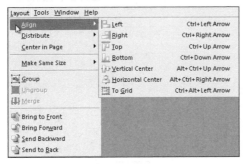

FIGURE 24.18

The Layout ➪ Center in Page menu

FIGURE 24.19

The Layout toolbar

Using guidelines

Creating a few guidelines before beginning your form design can significantly reduce the need to align objects. If we create a form with billing and mailing address blocks laid out left to right in a columnar style, adding the vertical guideline for the second column's position allows us to snap our objects to the line when adding them to the form, as shown in Figure 24.20. Adding a horizontal guideline for a row of various object types can save a significant amount of time.

FIGURE 24.20

A vertical guideline used in a columnar layout

CROSS-REF For details on using guidelines, see Chapter 22.

Distributing objects

In many form designs the fields may not have to be placed at a specific measurement; the intent is to space them out equally in the available design space. You don't need to do these calculations manually. Place the first and last objects in the desired position. Then use the Distribute feature to adjust the spacing between the objects equally. Distribution can be adjusted in either a vertical (down) or horizontal (across) direction.

Another distributing option called Rows and Columns aligns and distributes objects in both directions. Distribute Rows and Columns is recommended only when you have the same number of objects in each row and each column. Doing otherwise produces unexpected results.

STEPS: Distributing Objects

1. **Place the top or left-most object at the desired location.** Assuring this object is in the correct location alleviates the need to move the objects after distribution.

2. **Place the bottom or right-most object at the desired location.** The distributed distance is calculated by the total distance between the first and last object. Moving either of these objects closer or farther from the other objects changes the total calculated distance between objects.

3. **Select all objects to be distributed.**

4. **From the menu select Layout ➪ Distribute.** Figure 24.21 shows the Distribute submenu that appears. The submenu includes the following options:

   ■ **Across:** Choosing this option distributes the selected objects equally between the left-most object and the right-most object.

   ■ **Down:** Choosing this option distributes the selected objects equally between the top-most object and the bottom-most object.

   ■ **In Rows & Columns:** If the selected objects have equal quantities in each vertical area and equal quantities in each horizontal area, this option creates a table-like layout with the selected objects.

5. **Select the desired direction to distribute.** Objects are now equally spaced between the first and last selected object.

FIGURE 24.21

The Distribute menu contains options to assist in spacing out objects.

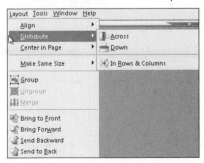

Grouping fields and objects

When objects are being moved and aligned frequently, sets of objects can become useful. Groups are used for formatting, aligning, and moving objects. Generally when we align objects in our form design we choose two objects we want to align on the same edge.

Sometimes you need to align a set of objects with another set that vary in type, size, and quantity of objects, as shown in figure 24.22. For example, you may have an address block on the left for billing information and another block on the right for shipping. The billing and shipping blocks of data do not always contain the same fields. You may have a contact phone number in the billing address and section for special notes in the shipping address. These fields may vary in size as well. Aligning the left and the right set can easily be done using a group.

To create a group, select the objects desired. Select Layout ⇨ Group. The Group button is also available on the Layout toolbar. Once the groups have been created, you can select both groups and align them the way you align regular objects. Keep in mind the combined boundary of the group is now treated as a single object that you are aligning with another object or group. The items within the group are not individually affected.

FIGURE 24.22

An example of two address blocks of different sizes grouped for alignment purposes

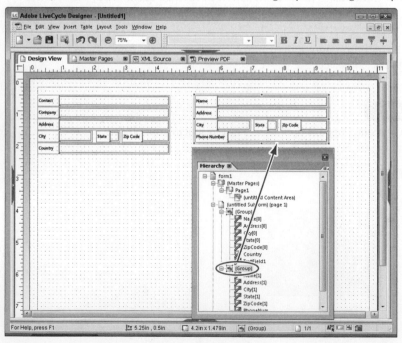

One more note about groups: They do not affect the objects' tab order. If your intent is to have the tab order go through a set of objects before moving on to any other area on the design page regardless of their position, you need to wrap the objects in a subform.

CROSS-REF   For information on how to create subforms and control tab order using subforms, see Chapter 27.

Examining the Object Library Palette

All the tools you need to create a form are contained in the Object Library. The Object Library is organized into groups that open and close in an accordion style with a triangle/arrow on the left side of the group name to indicate open or closed. The group is closed if the triangle is pointing toward the name. The group is open if the triangle is pointing down. By default the Object Library appears in the right palette well of the workspace.

The Object Library stores each of the objects with all their properties configured. The properties include font type, font size, object size, colors, borders, appearance, margins, and more. Placing an object on the design page creates a new instance of that object. This instance is a copy of the original object in the library. Any property settings you change in this instance do not affect the original.

The Object Library groups can be set to one of three views: Small Icons, Large Icons, and Sorted List. To change a group's view, you can right-click in the group, and select View from the context menu. It is also possible to change the group view by using the menu button on the Group tab and then selecting view from the menu.

Working with object types and default settings

Working with Designer Objects becomes easier as you become more familiar with the program interface. Many of the objects share default settings, while a few others have unique settings. To help with the alignment of captions between the object types we compiled the settings for each object in the standard library, as shown in Table 24.1.

TABLE 24.1   Standard Library Objects Default Properties

Object	Type	Font	Size	Width	Height	Left/Right Margins	Top/Bottom Margins	Reserve	Caption
Button	Interactive	Myriad Pro	10	1.125in	0.2362in	0	0	NA	NA
Check Box	Interactive	Myriad Pro	10	1.1024in	0.2362in	0.0394in	0	0.8268in	Right
Circle	Static	NA	NA	1in	1in	0	0	NA	NA
Content Area	Static	NA	NA	6.6929in	6.6929in	NA	NA	NA	NA
Date/Time Field	Interactive	Myriad Pro	10	2.4409in	0.3543in	0.0394in	0.0394in	0.9843in	Left
Decimal Field	Interactive	Myriad Pro	10	2.4409in	0.3543in	0.0394in	0.0394in	0.9843in	Left
Drop Down List	Interactive	Myriad Pro	10	2.4409in	0.3543in	0.0394in	0.0394in	0.9843in	Left
Email Submit	Interactive	Myriad Pro	10	1.375in	0.2362in	0	0	NA	NA
HTTP Submit Button	Interactive	Myriad Pro	10	1.125in	0.2362in	0	0	NA	NA
Image	Static	NA	NA	1in	1in	0	0	NA	NA
Image Field	Interactive	Myriad Pro	10	1in	1in	0	0	0.1969in	Bottom
Line	Static	NA	NA	1.5748in	0	0	0	NA	NA
List Box	Interactive	Myriad Pro	10	2.4409in	1.2205in	0.0394in	0.0394in	0.1969in	Top
Numeric Field	Interactive	Myriad Pro	10	2.4409in	0.3543in	0.0394in	0.0394in	0.9843in	Left
Paper Forms Barcode	Interactive	NA	NA	3.25in	1.75in	0	0	NA	NA

Object	Type	Font	Size	Width	Height	Left/Right Margins	Top/Bottom Margins	Reserve	Caption
Password Field	Interactive	Myriad Pro	10	2.4409in	0.3543in	0.0394in	0.0394in	0.9843in	Left
Print Button	Interactive	Myriad Pro	10	1.125in	0.2362in	0	0	NA	NA
Radio Button	Interactive	Myriad Pro	10	1.1024in	0.2362in	0.0394in	0	0.8661in	Right
Rectangle	Static	NA	NA	2in	1in	0	0	NA	NA
Reset Button	Interactive	Myriad Pro	10	1.125in	0.2362in	0	0	NA	NA
Signature Field	Interactive	Myriad Pro	10	2.4409in	0.3543in	0.0394in	0.0394in	0.9843in	Left
Subform	Static	NA	NA	3.937in	1.9685in	0	0	NA	NA
Table (one cell)	Static	Myriad Pro	10	1.1811in	0.3937in	0.0197in	0.0197in	NA	NA
Text	Static	Myriad Pro	10	1.153in	0.206in	0.0197in	0.0197in	NA	NA
Text Field	Interactive	Myriad Pro	10	2.4409in	0.3543in	0.0394in	0.0394in	0.9843in	Left

If you are wondering why the default objects have such strange measurements for their defaults, they were converted from metric measurements. For example 3.937 in is equal to 10 cm.

Exploring the Standard Group

The Standard Group of the Object Library contains one of each of the basic object types available in Designer. Because we discussed the basic object types in Chapter 22, we'll discuss more specifics here. All of the objects in the Standard group that have a font setting were created with Myriad Pro, 10 point font. Myriad Pro is one of the fonts that are always available in Acrobat and Adobe Reader. This eliminates the need to embed the fonts and reduces the overall file size.

Other settings such as height, width, caption, and margins vary by object type. Understanding these variations in settings makes aligning and spacing the objects consistently less daunting. The property variations cause objects to not align exactly, even when using the alignment features. The object boundaries are aligned, but the differences in margins or caption reserve cause the text within the object to not align as expected. The caption reserve is the amount of space in the composite object that is dedicated as the caption.

CROSS-REF   For a list of specific objects available, see Chapter 22.

For example, in a form with only a text field and a check box placed side by side, the captions of these fields do not appear at the same height even if the objects are aligned on the top edge as shown in Figure 24.23. Because the text in the caption is set to center vertically, the height of the objects causes them to not align. Altering the height of one object to match the other fixes this. Alignment issues caused by margins or caption reserve settings are not as obvious as height settings.

FIGURE 24.23

Aligned on the top, the captions do not align because of the objects' height.

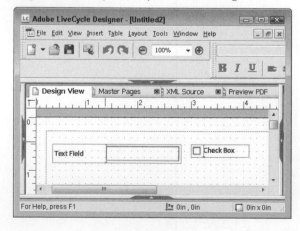

The default appearance of the field objects is set to sunken box. The sunken box appearance adds a shadowed border to the field area only, not the caption. This makes the fields stand out from the rest of the document text. Figure 24.24 shows the sunken box appearance of a text field compared to some other common appearances when opened in a viewer application.

FIGURE 24.24

The default sunken box appearance compared to other appearance settings

Exploring the My Favorites group

The My Favorites group of the library was set up for you to customize. Alter the existing objects or add custom library objects to the group as needed. It contains a few items to give you some ideas of what you might like to store. As shown in Figure 24.25, the objects in the My Favorites group are the most frequently used objects in the Standard group. They have exactly the same property settings as those in the Standard object group. This is one area we recommend changing to suit your needs because Myriad Pro fonts and sunken appearances do not work for everyone. Of course, you can create more groups in the Library as needed to store your custom objects.

CROSS-REF For more information on creating library groups, see "Creating Custom Library Objects" later in this chapter.

FIGURE 24.25

The My Favorites group of the Object Library palette

Exploring the Custom Group

The Custom Group of the Object Library contains specialized fields for your use. These specialized fields are one of the object types mentioned previously, with unique properties, and sometimes they include scripting. A custom object can be multiple fields stored together as a set. When stored in the library, all of the objects settings including their relative positions to one another are maintained. As shown in Figure 24.26, some of the custom objects included are:

- **Address Block:** This object set contains name and address fields organized as expected for addressing a letter or displaying billing information.

- **Countries:** This drop-down box is pre-populated with country names. You can customize the country choices if necessary.

- **Current Date:** A date field designed with script to populate the field with the current date.

- **Email Address:** This text field is designed to collect e-mail addresses. The script it contains validates against standard e-mail formats before allowing the user to continue.

- **U.S. States:** The 50 United States plus the District of Columbia are stored in this drop-down list. The list provides the form recipient a spelled-out state name, while the data being captured is the two-letter abbreviation.

- **Phone Number:** Formatted for either North America or the UK, these text fields allow numeric entries only in the appropriate format of the region selected.

- **U.S. Social Security Number:** This text field is formatted to require a nine-digit numeric entry that is formatted to include the dashes when the user exits the field.

- **Data Drop-down List:** A drop-down list with script attached that populates two columns of data from the data source connected to the form.

- **Signature – Print and Sign:** This object is a static text box with the words Signed By and a line for a wet signature.

FIGURE 24.26

The Custom Group of the Object Library palette

Many additional custom objects are available including page numbers, a data list box, and additional fields that are placed in the form when used with the additional LiveCycle ES components. We recommend you explore the custom objects so you are aware of these additional features. Don't spend the time creating one that already exists!

Exploring the Barcodes Group

Designer's Barcode Group contains an extensive set of supported barcodes as shown in Figure 24.27. Many businesses use barcodes on inventory. Forms that are scanned usually have a barcode to indicate which form is being processed. The data in a barcode is usually just a reference number and does not contain any identifying information. For example, the Universal Product Code (UPC) found on the items you purchase at the store does not contain the brand name, product name, price, or expiration date. It contains only a unique product number. When someone at the store scans the code, the store's central computer looks up the UPC number and returns the product information including the price. Most barcodes have two parts: the machine readable bars and the human readable text.

FIGURE 24.27

The Barcode Group of the Object Library palette

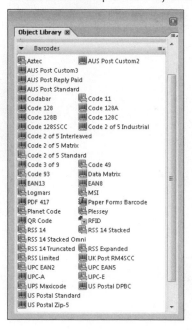

Barcodes use check digits to ensure the proper information was received when scanned. What happens if you take a black marker and add to the barcode? What if the barcode is torn, wrinkled, or wet? The scanner may not read the bar code correctly. Barcodes utilize error correction and check digits to minimize problems caused by minor flaws that otherwise render the barcode unusable. Check digits also prevent barcode tampering. The check digit is calculated by the scanning device each time a barcode is scanned. If the calculated check digit value does not match the printed check digit value the barcode is rejected and must be rescanned.

In Designer, barcode fields have data binding properties just like other field objects. Static barcodes usually contain the associated number stored in the barcode fields as the default value. Dynamic barcodes can be calculated values, such as a Make and Model when concatenated have a unique value that the barcode represents. All of the barcodes, except the Paper Forms Barcode, are generated only at specific points in the form rendering process. Those special processing events include when the form is initially rendered on the screen, just before it is printed, and just before it is saved.

Paper forms barcodes are unique in the way they work in Acrobat and Reader. They are the only barcode capable of changing as the form recipient completes a field and advances to the next field. You can watch the barcode adjust its contents as you fill in the form. Paper forms barcodes include the field names as well as the values those fields contain. To store both sets of data, they use a special two-dimension (2D) format that supports three encoding symbologies: PDF417, QR Code, and Data Matrix.

PDF417 is the default encoding, an open barcode standard developed by Symbol Technologies. The barcode data is stacked in two dimensions and is comprised of modules forming code words that are arranged in rows and columns. Because paper forms barcodes include multiple fields, you can set the barcode to accept all the form data, or only a collection of fields on the form.

 **Paper forms barcodes require an additional license for Adobe LiveCycle Barcoded Forms ES if the form is to be completed in Adobe Reader.**

Whichever barcode you decide to use on your form, careful testing is recommended to verify the barcode is readable by the intended scanning system.

Creating Custom Library Objects

Custom library objects are one of our favorite reasons for using Designer to create forms. Although not every company has a set of guidelines relating to creating forms, most large companies do. Think about generic documents that are presented to the public by your company. Do they have a consistent appearance in font, color, or layout? Documents produced by different departments may have different guidelines. Creating a number of forms that require a consistent appearance can be difficult without some documentation. If your company does not already have a set of guidelines or policies regarding form design, perhaps it is time to consider creating some.

The Standard and My Favorites groups of the Object Library are based on Myriad Pro fonts. What if the company requires Arial for all forms? What if the field's appearance must be underlined? Imagine if the company has policies regarding font size, color, alignment, logo use, and more. Constantly changing these properties each time you add a field to the form can be tedious, not to mention the potential for missing property settings, and having objects that do not comply with company guidelines.

Setting up a Custom Library Group with objects containing the desired settings helps improve form development and decrease design time. Working with Custom Objects also encourages compliance with company design policies.

Creating a new library group

Organizing your Object Library is like organizing your desk or file cabinet. If you throw everything on top of the desk, or just toss stuff in a drawer, you waste time trying to locate items the next time you want to use them. How you organize your custom groups is a personal choice. You can create the library groups to organize your custom objects before saving any objects. Or, you can add custom objects to the existing groups until you've had a chance to decide how you want to organize your custom objects. You can always reorganize the custom objects later if needed, moving or copying the object from one group to another when necessary.

If you have only a handful of customized objects, you probably can create a single group to store them all. If you can think of three or four different types of field formats you need in your forms then create a group for each style of document.

We strongly recommend that when storing custom objects you don't cut the object descriptions short. As you add more custom objects to the library, their variations become harder to detect. Using good descriptions helps you choose the desired object more quickly and helps when you reorganize.

STEPS: Creating a New Object Library group

1. **Open the Object Library palette, if necessary.** Select Window ➪ Object Library or use the keyboard shortcut Shift + F12.

2. **Click the Palette menu button in the upper-right corner.** This opens the Library palette menu as shown in Figure 24.28

3. **Select Add Group.** The Add Library Group dialog box opens as shown in Figure 24.29.

4. **Type a group name.** Enter a descriptive name for your group.

5. **Click OK.** This closes the Add Library Group dialog box and places the new group in the Object Library palette.

FIGURE 24.28

The Object Library palette menu

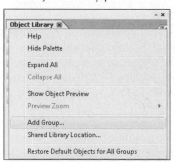

FIGURE 24.29

The Add Library Group dialog box

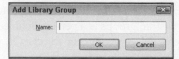

When you create a new group, it is immediately added to the Object Library. Because the newly created group is empty, the space dedicated to it is small. It is hard to see that the group is closed as indicated by the arrow to the left of the group name. When the group is opened a very small, white area becomes visible. When the group is active in the Object Library, a thin dotted border surrounds the group to indicate the groups' boundaries as shown in Figure 24.30. When adding a custom object to the group, drop the object within this dotted boundary. You should create the library group before adding custom objects to the library. You can't create a group during the Add process. You can move objects from one group to another, but this creates additional steps in the workflow.

FIGURE 24.30

A newly created custom library group, still empty

Adding a new library object

One of the best ways to create a collective set of custom library objects is to create a form from scratch. After you have added all of the objects to the form design and completed the formatting and design, look it over. How many of these objects would you recreate with the same settings for the next form you build?

Do you have a Designer form someone else created with the formatting you need? It doesn't matter who built the object or how long ago it was created. You can take any object on the design page or master pages and add it to the Object Library at any time.

STEPS: Adding a Custom Object to an Object Library Group

1. **Select the object(s) on the design page you want to add to the Object Library.** The object should already have its formatting and properties set.

2. **Place your mouse over the selected objects.** The mouse pointer shape changes to a black four-headed arrow:

3. **Drag and drop the object(s) on the desired group in the Object Library.** Don't worry if you dropped the object on the wrong group. This opens the Add Library Object dialog box, as shown in Figure 24.31, where you can change the storage group if necessary.

4. **Type a name for the custom object.** Object names should be short but descriptive.

FIGURE 24.31

The Add Library Object dialog box

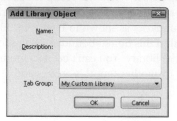

5. **Enter a description for the custom object.** We recommend the object's purpose, the object type(s), and any specific formatting or scripting you may have applied.

6. **Change the Tab Group, if necessary.** The tab group list contains all of the groups available in your Object Library.

7. **Click OK.** This closes the Add library Object dialog box and places the custom object in the group chosen in Step 7.

Your custom object has now been stored in the object library for future use. You can add, remove, and edit custom objects at any time. You also can set up a shared Object Library group.

Managing custom library objects

As you use custom objects over time you may need to adjust the objects you've created. You may need to change the object's fonts, appearances, or colors, for example. In a custom object made of multiple objects, you may need to add items or remove items from the set. You can modify, delete, or move objects to another library group after they are created. Perhaps a few objects were stored in an existing library group before the custom group was created. Managing custom objects includes:

- **Delete:** To delete an object from the library group, right-click the object and select Remove Object from Library in the context menu. The Delete key also deletes the selected object from the library group.

- **Move:** To Change the group where the custom object is stored, right-click the custom object. From the Context menu that appears select Move Object To. This displays a list of available library groups, as shown in Figure 24.32. Select the group desired from the list. Or, you can drag a library object from one group to another to move them.

- **Edit Object Description or Name:** To change the object's name or description, right-click and select Object Info from the context menu. The Edit Library Object Information dialog box opens for editing as shown in Figure 24.33.

- **Edit Objects or Object Properties:** To change the contents of the custom library object, drag an instance to the design page. Make the necessary changes to the object on the design page. Drag the objects back to the custom library. If you give the object the same name, Designer prompts you to replace the existing object as shown in Figure 24.34.

FIGURE 24.32

The Move Object To option in the context menu

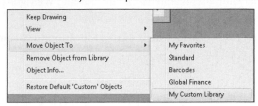

FIGURE 24.33

The Edit Library Object Information dialog box

FIGURE 24.34

Replace Existing Object warning

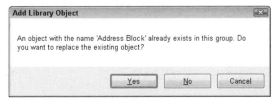

Sharing a custom library

Now that we have a custom library built, we want to share it with some coworkers. We want everyone to have the exact same set to use in their form designs. If we ask our coworkers to create the custom library from an existing form design, they may omit some objects or alter them before placing them in the library group. There is no sense in making everyone add the objects to their custom library groups and retype the descriptions since we can share our library groups.

STEPS: Setting up a Shared Library Group

1. **Create a folder in a network location all users have access to.** If necessary, ask someone in your IT department for assistance in locating or creating a shared folder with the proper permissions for each user. The name of this folder can be anything you choose. We recommend a generic name such as Designer Shared Libraries.

2. **Create a subfolder in this shared network location.** The name of this folder does not affect the Designer Library Name. However, naming it the same as the shared library group name in Designer simplifies maintenance and sharing. We right-clicked in the shared directory to create a new folder, as shown in Figure 24.35.

3. **Copy the custom library objects from their current location to the newly created folder.** It is best to open the library directly from the file system for this step. If you are unsure where the library objects are currently stored, you can check by opening the library group's properties from the library group menu. Figure 24.36 shows the library group properties where you can locate the path of the stored objects. Don't worry if you cannot read the entire path. We can copy it from the location box. Tab into the location box; this highlights the entire path. Right-click the path and choose Copy from the context menu. Now open an Explorer window and paste the copied address into the address bar.

4. **In Designer, if necessary create a new Library Group.** Name this group the same name as the shared folder you are connecting to. If you already have the custom group built, skip to Step 5.

CROSS-REF For more information on how to create a new Object Library Group see the section "Creating a New Object Library Group" earlier in this chapter.

FIGURE 24.35

Adding a subfolder to the network location for library objects

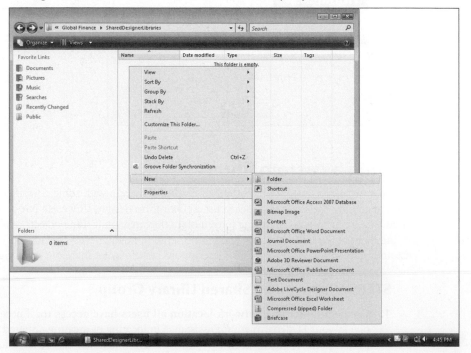

FIGURE 24.36

Opening the library group properties lists the current storage location in the file system.

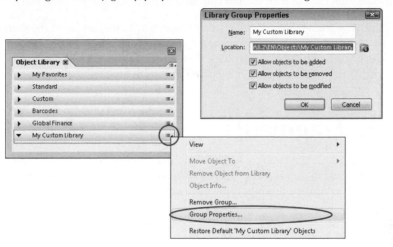

5. Using the shared Library Group menu, open the Group Properties dialog box.

6. **In the properties window, click the Browse button, as shown in Figure 24.37.** This opens the Browse For folder window.

FIGURE 24.37

Use the Browse button to select the library from a shared location.

7. **Navigate to the location of the shared folder on the network and click OK.** This sets the shared folder on the network as the new storage location for the library group.

8. **Click OK in the Group Properties dialog box to finish the process.** This stores the selected network folder as a new library group in designer.

9. **Repeat Steps 2 through 9 for any additional shared libraries.** Consider creating additional libraries for projects that have unique design requirements, departments that have special formatting requests, or any other specialized design needs.

When setting up shared library objects, you should have a select group of people manage the library. Without some restrictions placed on the library, anyone who has access to the shared library can add, edit, or remove objects from the shared library.

You can change these settings in the Group Properties in Designer, or in the shared network file. The settings available in Designer are there so that you don't accidentally remove or edit something. They can be turned on or off at any time. To truly secure the library from unwanted changes, talk with your IT department about configuring permissions on the shared network folder.

Form Fragments

Form fragments are similar to custom library objects. Form fragments are customized objects stored in the Fragment Library. Form fragments can be single or multiple objects with custom properties and scripts. You can create multiple fragment library groups to store your form fragments.

Some differences exist between form fragments and custom objects. While both a custom object and a form fragment create a new instance of an object on the form, the form fragment remains linked to the original object. When changes are made to the original form fragment, the changes can be updated anywhere the fragment was used. Updating happens automatically if the form was saved as an XDP file. If you saved your designer document as a PDF form, then you need to update the fragment.

Creating form fragments

Creating a form fragment is as easy as creating a custom object. What happens when you create the form fragment is a little different, however. Custom library objects can be single or multiple objects and are stored in the library the same way you created them on the design page. With a form fragment, you need to wrap the objects in a subform. If you already have the objects in a subform, you can use the existing subform. If you do not have a subform around your objects, then one is created before it is saved in the Fragment Library.

 For information on subforms, see Chapter 27.

STEPS: Creating a Form Fragment from Objects on the Design Page

1. **Select the object(s) on the design page you want to create the form fragment.** The objects should already have their formatting and properties set.

2. **Place your mouse over the selected objects.** The mouse pointer shape changes to a black four-headed arrow.

3. **Drag and drop the object(s) on the My Fragments group in the Fragment Library.** This opens the Create Fragment dialog box as shown in Figure 24.38.

   Or, right-click the selected objects and choose Fragments ➪ Create Fragment from the context menu.

FIGURE 24.38

The Create Fragment dialog box

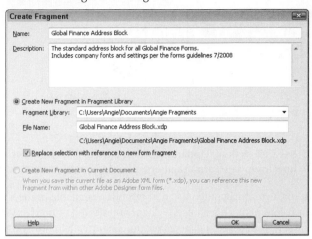

4. **Enter the Fragment Name.** This is the object name shown in the Fragment Library for future use.

5. **Enter a description for the fragment.** Enter information to describe the intended purpose of the fragment. You can find this information later by right-clicking a form fragment in the library and choosing Fragment Info.

6. **Click Create New Fragment in Fragment Library.** This is the default method for storing fragments that stores the fragments in your local file system. This makes using the fragment easy to find. We recommend this option. Any available Fragment Library appears in the drop-down list. You can create a new fragment library if necessary during this process.

CROSS-REF For more information on creating a new fragment library group, see the section "Creating Fragment Library groups" later in this chapter.

7. **Verify that the Replace selection with a reference to new form fragment check box is selected.** This creates the fragment and links the original in the form design file to the new fragment. This option is selected by default.

8. **Click OK to finish creating the fragment.** This saves the fragment in the library for future use as shown in Figure 24.39. Notice the objects are now in a purple shaded area. You can still see the individual objects in the Hierarchy palette and on the design page, but changing them is now restricted to altering the form fragment.

9. **Save the form.** Save the form as an XDP if you are going to continue design work, or if it is used with other LiveCycle products. This ensures that any changes to the form fragment automatically update in the XDP file. When the form is saved as a PDF the fragment becomes embedded in the document at the time the file is saved. You need to complete updates manually.

FIGURE 24.39

The Fragment Library palette

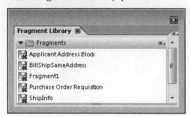

CROSS-REF   See the section "Updating form fragments" later in this chapter details on how to update form fragments.

Create New Fragment in Current Document is another option available in the Create Fragment dialog box. We do not recommend this choice. Designer files can be stored anywhere and have a tendency to be modified, renamed, and deleted over time. Not realizing the original fragment is stored inside a document causes links to be broken when the file is renamed or deleted. Accidental updates to other files can happen as well. The fragment objects appear and act like other objects in the document. Only a fragment indicator on the Hierarchy palette reminds you this is an original. When saving a fragment in the current document you must save as an XDP file or a Designer Template (TDS). A document already saved as a PDF disables the Create New Fragment in Current Document option.

Creating fragment library groups

The Fragment Library contains groups just like the Object Library. However, creating additional groups is different with fragments. Fragments are stored in a folder of your choice in the file system. Using the operating system, you can create as many folders in the file system you need to store fragments in. Adding them to the Fragment Library requires only that you open them through the Fragment palette menu.

Because Fragment Library groups can be made outside of the Designer interface, Designer allows you to quickly create multiple folders to organize the Fragment storage. When creating a new fragment Designer also allows the normal Browse dialog box to create a new folder during the save process if one does not already exist as shown in Figure 24.40.

Using form fragments

Once the form fragment is stored in the fragment library it is ready for use. Fragments are treated differently than other objects because they need to create a link to the original file. You can add form fragments to the design page using the following methods:

- **Drag and Drop:** This is the most common method and works the same as it does with any other object dragged from the library palette.

- **Insert Menu:** By selecting Insert ⇨ Fragment you browse for the desired fragment in the file system. Not as intuitive as using the Fragment Library palette.

- **Cut, Copy, and Paste:** Any existing instance of a fragment can be copied to another location and retain its fragment properties. The new copy is an instance of the fragment linked to the original in the fragment library.

- **Duplicate:** An existing fragment can be successfully duplicated if more than one copy is desired.

- **Copy Multiple:** The copy multiple dialog box can be used when many instances of a fragment are needed.

CROSS-REF For details on how to add an object using the above methods, refer to the section "Adding Fields and Objects to a Form" earlier in this chapter.

Two of the other methods are not available with fragments: stamping and drawing. Drawing fragments does not make much sense. The idea behind the fragment is that a single copy controls how objects look in any form design where they are placed. Drawing allows the creator to choose the object size. Unfortunately, stamping a fragment is also not available. We hope to see this feature in the future.

Once a form fragment is added to the design page the object has a purple dashed border as shown in Figure 24.41. When the mouse rolls over the fragment, or if the fragment is selected, a purple fill color appears over the objects with a fragment icon in the upper-left corner, as shown in Figure 24.42. The Hierarchy palette shows a fragment icon on top of the subform, as shown in Figure 24.43.

You can't select an individual object inside the fragment on the design page. This prevents changes to the fragment's contents. The individual objects can be seen in the Hierarchy palette, but they are a light gray color indicating they are disabled, as shown in Figure 24.44. You cannot select the disabled objects or resize the fragments. When you place the mouse pointer on a selection handle the icon changes to a NO symbol. Again, this is because the fragment controls the object's appearance. The fragment can be moved to another area on the design page, updated, removed, and placed inside other subforms or groups, but not altered.

FIGURE 24.40

Creating a new fragment library from the Create Fragment dialog box

Independent changes are one of the benefits to using custom objects, because they allow each instance to have different settings. Fragments do not offer this customization ability, and customizing defies the purpose of the fragment. If you find that a form that contains a fragment needs to be controlled independently, you can break the link and embed the objects into the current form design, as shown in Figure 24.45. This process disables all of the fragment's updating capabilities and cannot be undone. If you need the fragment object in the future, delete the existing objects and re-add the fragment object to the form design.

Are you still unsure where you can use a fragment? May we suggest an address block as a suitable place to start? How many forms do you have with an address block on them? You may have even stored the address block in your custom library with your formatting changes already. Any minor change to the layout position or font settings requires opening each of those forms and repeating the changes. Give fragments a try; when you start using them you'll wonder how you ever got along without them.

FIGURE 24.41

A fragment on the design page with purple outline

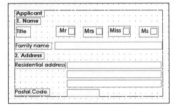

FIGURE 24.42

A selected fragment on the design page with purple fill color, and fragment icon

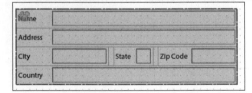

FIGURE 24.43

A fragment subform icon in the Hierarchy palette

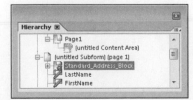

FIGURE 24.44

Disabled fragment objects in the Hierarchy palette

FIGURE 24.45

Breaking a fragment link

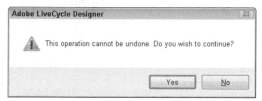

Updating form fragments

Fragments are great when multiple form designers need to use the same object on many form designs. The object is stored in a safe location, allowing the designers to place it on the form as needed. When a change occurs to the original fragment content, little work is required to update all of the forms that use the fragment.

Fragments placed in an XDP file receive the updates automatically. The updates are visible in the XDP files as soon as the altered fragment is saved. XDP files are used extensively with the LiveCycle servers and do not require the form to be edited by anyone for the fragment to be updated.

Fragments placed in a PDF file do not receive the update automatically. A form fragment contained in a PDF, when opened in Acrobat or Reader, appears exactly the same way as when it was last saved in Designer. In order for the PDF to get an updated fragment, it must be opened in Designer and resaved. This of course requires someone to resave every PDF form which contains fragments, and is not the most effective workflow.

Adding Fields and Objects to Master Pages

Master pages are the foundation for the design pages. The master pages control where in the form objects can be placed, what page size is used, the orientation, and more. A form design can have multiple master pages, allowing for various pages sizes, layouts, and orientations within the same form. Objects placed on the master pages appear on all body pages based on that master page.

If you have worked with a page layout program, then you are already familiar with how master pages work. If not, you might compare the master page to the header and footer of a word processing document. Page numbers, logos, and disclaimers are some common examples of items place on master pages. Master pages are much more than headers and footers though.

CROSS-REF For more details on configuring master pages, see Chapter 25.

Imagine a corporate stationary set. If the graphics, repeating text, fonts, and formats had to be recreated every time a page was added to the document, consistency would become a problem. In many stationary sets the first page is formal and the remaining pages have less content. When we lay out a letter with those properties we need the following:

- **Page 1 Master:** The company logo, name, address, phone numbers, and additional contact information are included on this page. This page is based on an 8½ × 11 inch page with a larger top margin for the company logo.

- **Page 2 Master:** Only selected contact information is provided on this page. This page is based on an 8½ × 11 inch page with reduced margins because the logo is not needed.

- **Page 3 Master:** The last page contains a business envelope with logo and address information. A standard number 10 business envelope is 4⅛ × 9½ inches. The third master page is based on these dimensions.

Creating three separate documents is unnecessary. One designer file can contain all three master pages. Even if the form results in a five-page letter, we restrict the master pages according to our needs. The page 1 master will only be used one time regardless of the total number of pages in the letter. The page 2 master will be used for all remaining pages in the letter. The envelope is an optional page that appears only if the user requests an envelope. As you can see, Designer offers extensive flexibility in laying out master pages in form designs.

By default the only object on the master page is a content area. The content area determines the boundaries of your body page and in many cases is equivalent to the page margins. Content areas can also be set up in other configurations such as columnar style or sections for newsletters. In this case they still control where the field objects can be placed but no longer reflect the page margins.

Every form has at least one content area. When the master pages are active, the content area has a pink dashed border as shown in Figure 24.46. Objects placed on the master page can be outside the content area. This is a recommend practice because by placing the objects outside of the content area, you ensure that objects added to the design pages do not overlap or run over the master page items. Page numbers and logos belong outside the content area. However, if you want to place a watermark style image behind the form contents, you can center it across the content area.

FIGURE 24.46

The Content area on a master page

How you add objects to the master pages is no different from adding them to body pages. You can add interactive field objects that you want to have appear on multiple pages. A customer name may be repeated at the top of each page of an order form. If you place the field in the master page you don't need to put another copy on each additional body page.

Using the Object Editor

When activated, the Object Editor appears as a blue frame around the selected object on the design page. You can turn on the Object Editor by selecting View ⇨ Object Editor from the menu. The editor appears only when working with a single field object at a time. If multiple objects are selected, the object editor does not appear. It also does not appear for static object types.

As shown in Figure 24.47, the selected field's name appears at the top of the Object Editor, where it can be renamed. Below the field on the left side of the Object Editor is a drop-down list to change the selected field to another field type. On the bottom right side of the field editor is a button to open the context menu. The context menu normally appears after right-clicking an object. Each of these items can be accessed other ways in designer. The Object Editor simply puts them in a single area for easy use. Using the Object Editor is a matter of personal preference.

New users should remember to rename objects as they are added to the design page. The blue frame can make moving and aligning objects difficult, so you may choose to turn this feature on and off while working.

FIGURE 24.47

The Object Editor

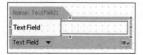

Although changing objects from one field type to another is possible, it is not generally recommended. Objects have different properties depending on the object type. Changing from a simple object type to a more complex object type is okay. However, when changing to a field type that doesn't utilize the same properties this additional information can stick to the new field and create unexpected results. Deleting undesired objects and recreating the correct object is safer if you are unsure what properties the two objects have in common.

> **TIP** The amount of random access memory (RAM) available on the computer plays a large part in object properties not being completely removed or added. Using an underpowered computer or attempting to run too many applications at the same time can intensify this problem. Verify the computer has met the minimum requirements for running LiveCycle Designer.

Summary

- Drag-and-drop is a common technique for moving items on the design page, changing palette configurations, and adding objects to the form design.

- When adding objects, using the stamping technique creates objects at their default size.

- Drawing objects allows you to determine the dimensions of the objects when they are created.

- You can continue to draw or stamp objects without going back to the Object Library palette for the tool by turning on the Keep Drawing feature. Using this feature in combination with stamping and drawing allows you to customize the stamped object's dimensions.

- Save formatting time by copying objects on the design page that already have the formatting desired.

- You can quickly make organized copies of an object that are offset the desired distance and direction by using the Duplicate feature.

- Copy Multiple is much like Duplicate but allows you to supply the total number of objects in a dialog box. Copy Multiple is extremely useful when you want the copied objects to touch with no space between them.

- Saving time when formatting and aligning requires selecting more than one object at a time. Many selection techniques are available.

- Aligning objects would be tedious if it required you to remember measurements or use visual cues only. Use the Alignment tools to increase productivity.

- Aligning sets of objects may require them to be grouped to produce the desired results.

- You can use subforms in place of groups to align objects. We recommend them when the objects can be logically organized into sections to clean up the form design. Subforms also allow you to control tab order.

■ You can add objects from the Library palette in many ways. If the objects in the Standard palette do not contain settings optimal for your form design, create your own custom library objects.

■ Form objects have extensive properties that you can set. To increase efficiency, create custom library objects with the properties you most frequently use. Use custom library groups to organize the custom objects created.

■ Designer supports a variety of barcode formats including 2D barcodes. The paper forms barcode included with Designer requires an additional license if the form is completed in Adobe Reader.

■ Objects that are used on multiple form designs that must be updated frequently should be stored as form fragments. Fragments can be updated easily and reduce editing time.

■ Sharing custom objects and fragments with coworkers ensures consistency between form designers. When you supply the objects to be placed on the form, less time is required to set properties.

■ Master pages are the basis of all forms. Every Designer document has at least one master page. Design pages can be restricted to a specified master page, including how many times that master page is used.

■ The Object Editor offers editing of field names on the design page.

Chapter 25

Working with Objects

I n Chapter 24 we introduced you to field objects and we talked about some of the formatting options you have for changing attributes. We expand our discussion on objects in this chapter to include text objects and look a little deeper into setting object attributes and using formatting controls.

Designer provides an abundant number of palette tabs to set attributes for all the objects you add to a form. Controlling font attributes, using paragraph formatting, setting stroke weights, binding data to objects, choosing patterns and similar types of controls require you to become familiar with the attributes and the tools you use to make edits on objects.

Think of this chapter as an extension of Chapter 24 and carefully examine the issues related to object formatting. Once you have an understanding for how to properly design objects and control the options associated with them, you'll be ready to move on to chapters ahead where we create some dynamic forms and work with form data.

IN THIS CHAPTER

Changing object appearances

Editing object properties

Changing tab orders

Formatting Field Objects Appearances

In Chapter 24 we talked about using the Libraries and dragging and dropping objects from a library palette to a form. You should be aware of the fact that when you drop an object on a form, you see a default view for an object in terms of the object's appearance.

The good folks at Adobe set up some default appearances for field objects using formatting attributes such as a sunken appearance, a caption, and a fixed size set between the caption and a field. In many cases you won't want to use the default appearances provided by Adobe and you'll want to change object attributes to meet your own design standards. If you don't know where to find an appearance option, it can be downright frustrating poking around the palettes to change an appearance.

Changing Appearance properties

Changing appearances for objects is handled in two palettes apart from the Font and Paragraph palettes used for formatting fonts and character alignments. Drag a Text Field object from the Standard Library palette to a blank new page and you see in the Object palette the default sunken box appearance with a caption and the caption aligned left as shown in Figure 25.1.

FIGURE 25.1

The default view of a Text Field object showing a caption aligned left and a sunken box appearance

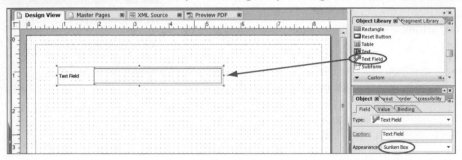

The Appearance attributes are assigned in the Field palette as shown in Figure 25.1 The caption arrangement however is controlled in another palette. Click the Layout panel in the Object palette and you find the Caption drop-down menu as shown in Figure 25.2.

Editing captions

When you create forms in Designer, it's a better choice for you to use captions than separate text and field objects. Captions associated with fields result in a single object that appears in the Hierarchy palette. If you add a field object and a text object you double the number of objects on your form. Keeping the number of objects to a minimum reduces file size, enables you to more easily edit objects when selecting them in the Hierarchy palette, reduces the number of data objects in associated data files, and generally makes the form much more efficient.

To change the location of the caption on an object such as a Text Field object make a choice from the menu items listed in the Caption drop-down menu in the Layout palette. The different choices you have for positioning captions are shown in Figure 25.3.

FIGURE 25.2

Click the Layout palette to locate options for editing captions.

FIGURE 25.3

Five choices for the caption positioning relative to the text field are selected from the Caption drop-down menu in the Layout palette.

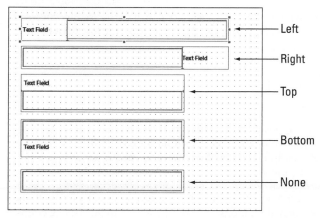

The Layout palette also provides options for positioning an object, controlling the size, and setting the margins. The items you can adjust in the Layout palette shown earlier in Figure 25.2 include:

- **X & Y Values:** The X text box holds a numeric value for the X (horizontal) position, and the Y value controls the vertical position on the page. You can drag objects on the page to a position or type values in the X and Y text boxes.

- **Width and Height:** The Width and Height text boxes hold numeric values for the size (width and height) of the object.

■ **Expand to fit:** Two check boxes appear below the Width/Height text boxes. When data are merged, you can have objects expand width, height, or both. The first Expand to fit check box controls width expansion. The second Expand to fit check box controls the height expansion.

■ **Anchor:** If you check one of the Expand to fit check boxes and merge data on a form, the expansion occurs from the Anchor point you choose from the Anchor drop-down menu shown in Figure 25.4. For example, if you choose the Middle Left, the object can grow from the middle left, to the right, top, and bottom.

FIGURE 25.4

Open the Anchor drop-down menu and choose an Anchor point for where expansion occurs.

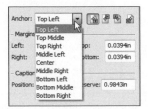

NOTE Changing the Anchor also changes the handle the X/Y coordinates are measured from. Unfortunately it does not change the handle that is used for the Snap to Grid setting. Snap to Grid always uses the top-left handle.

■ **Margins:** The ability to make margins choices offers you a lot of flexibility for polishing up a form design. You can inset the data from the border edges by making choices for the Left, Top, Right, and Bottom edges.

TIP If you're familiar with design applications you may be inclined to use point measurements like *0p36* for 36 points (or 1/2 inch). Designer behaves different than programs that support typographer's notations. In Designer, if you want to specify a measurement for points use something like *36 pt* (for 36 points).

■ **Rotations:** To the right of the Anchor drop-down menu you find four icons for rotations. The first item removes any preassigned rotations followed by Rotate to 90° (rotate counterclockwise), Rotate to 180°, and Rotate to 270° (rotate clockwise).

■ **Reserve:** Adjacent to the Caption drop-down menu you find the Reserve text box. The value typed in the text box determines the distance between the caption and the left side of the field box.

 **TIP** You can also change the Reserve amount by dragging the left side of the field box.

Editing appearances

Let's move back to the Field tab in the Object palette and notice the Appearance drop-down menu shown in Figure 25.5. The first four items are None, Underlined, Solid Box, and Sunken Box. These choices should be self-explanatory.

FIGURE 25.5

In the Field tab in the Object palette open the Appearance drop-down menu to make choices for an object's appearance.

If you choose Custom in the Appearance drop-down menu the Custom Appearance dialog box opens as shown in Figure 25.6. This dialog box provides a number of options to control the appearance of objects. Whereas appearance choices in Acrobat are limited to fixed border edges and fills using solid colors, Designer provides a number of choices for individually assigning values to each side of a border and adding gradient fills to objects.

FIGURE 25.6

Choose Custom in the Appearance drop-down menu and the Custom Appearance dialog box opens

The items you find in the Custom Appearance dialog box include:

- **Edges:** From the drop-down menu choose Edit Together or Edit Individually. If you choose Edit Individually, the dialog box expands to display the individual edges. Notice the solid bar on the side of the square for each of the four item choices below this drop-down menu. The bar shows you what side of the object rectangle applies to the choices you make from the line style drop-down menus. In Figure 25.6 notice that Solid appears for the left border edge followed by Dashed for the right edge, Dotted for the Top edge, and Dash dot for the bottom edge.

  To the right of the text boxes where the stroke values are specified, you find a down-pointing arrow adjacent to a pencil icon. Click the arrow and a drop-down menu opens where you can choose from preset colors or from your system custom color palette.

  In addition to the line style choices shown in Figure 25.6 you also have available some 3D styles, the results of which are shown in Figure 25.7. To use a 3D style you must choose Edit Together from the Edges drop-down menu.

FIGURE 25.7

Four different 3D styles applied to field objects

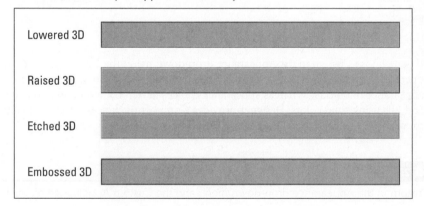

- **Corners:** Click one of the four icons to change a corner effect and in the Radius text box type a value for the corner radius amount you want applied.
- **Omit Border around Page Breaks:** Check this box to omit a border when an object spans multiple pages.
- **Background Fill:** Open the Style drop-down menu and you find a list of patterns and fill styles as shown in Figure 25.8. When using the Linear and Radial choices you can specify gradients to blend from one color to another by making choices from the down-pointing arrows adjacent to the paint bucket icons.

FIGURE 25.8

Open the Style drop-down menu and choose a Background Fill style.

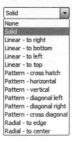

Changing object attributes

Moving down the Field tab in the Object palette, you find additional options for setting object properties as you can see in Figure 25.9. The choices you have relate more to the behavior of the fields than appearances. The items found under the Appearance drop-down menu include:

- **Allow Multiple Lines:** Check this box to allow multiple lines for a field object.

NOTE Even though a text field is tall enough for multiple lines to appear, it will not use the space allotted unless this setting is turned on.

- **Limit Length (Max Characters):** Check the check box and type a value for a maximum number of characters you want to occupy a field object.

- **Limit Length to Visible Area:** Choose this option when you want the number of characters to not exceed the visible size of the field object. This prevents overflow text from being hidden on a form with a static layout when printed.

- **Allow Page Breaks within Content:** You might use this option when you have a field object such as a comment box or area were you want a description added to a form. If the page breaks inside the content area the content is flowed to the next page.

- **Keep with Next:** Check this box to keep the object following it in the Hierarchy palette.

- **Comb of (characters):** Use this check box and specify the number of characters you want identified for comb fields. When the comb field is activated, each character is separated with a vertical bar. The widths of the vertically divided areas are determined by the width of the field object when equally divided by the number of characters specified.

CROSS-REF For more information on comb fields, see Chapters 3 and 4.

- **Field Format:** The default is Plain Text. You also can use RTF for the text formatting by making the choice from the drop-down menu.

- **Patterns:** See the section "Understanding pattern types" later in this chapter.

■ **Presence:** From the drop-down menu shown in Figure 25.9 you have a number of choices similar to many choices you have using the General Properties for field objects in Acrobat. Open the menu and you find:

FIGURE 25.9

Open the Presence drop-down menu in the Field tab in the Object palette for choices to display objects on screen and when printed.

■ **Visible:** By default this choice displays the object on the form.

■ **Visible (Screen Only):** This choice displays the object on screen when a recipient fills in a form. When the form is printed, the object does not appear on the printed output. You might use this option on a dynamic form where a form recipient can click a button to add new objects for completing a form. After completing the form, the button has no use when viewing the printed version of the form.

CROSS-REF For more information on using buttons with dynamic forms, see Chapter 28.

■ **Visible (Print Only):** When this choice is made, the object won't be visible to the form recipient when completing the form on a computer. When the form is printed, the object appears on the printed form. You might use this option to display an instruction to a form recipient as to what to do with the form after it's been printed such as adding a fax number or some description for routing the form manually.

■ **Hidden (Exclude from Layout):** Choosing this option hides an object from both screen viewing and when printed. You might design a form where a field is hidden, and on some action such as a button action, the object is made visible. Something like a response to a question about adding additional comments might show a field where comments can be added if a form recipient clicks a Yes button.

- One-sided Printing Only: The object is visible when the form is printed on one side only. You might use this option to show an object such as a page number like 1 of 2 pages.

- Two-sided Printing Only: The object is visible when the form is printed on two sides only. You might use this option to show an object such as text object indicating that something appears on the reverse side of the form.

- Locale: If you're a form author creating a form in an English-speaking country and the form recipients are filling in the form in another country such as El Salvador, you can choose from a number of different countries from the drop-down menu for a form recipient's geographic location.

NOTE **The default locale for the form has changed in recent releases of LiveCycle Designer. This also affects the default for each object placed on the form. The form default is currently set to the locale of the person who created the form. In previous versions this was set on the viewer's system locale, which meant that it would dynamically adjust based on the install language of the form filler's computer. Both settings have good merits. Just be sure you are aware of the settings in your forms. The form default can be seen by selecting File ⇨ Form Properties, then selecting the defaults tab.**

Changing font attributes

Font attributes are chosen from the Font palette that by default is not visible when you start up Designer. You have a number of options to choose from when accessing tools to change form attributes. You can open the Window ⇨ Font menu command or press Shift + F4 and the Font palette opens as a floating palette. You can then dock the palette in the palette bin on the left or right side of the Designer window (actually, docking on the right side makes more sense because you're likely to use the font choices in conjunction with the other palettes we've described in this chapter). Another option is to customize the toolbar and load tools for font attribute assignments and keep the tools at the top of the Designer window.

CROSS-REF **For more information about customizing toolbars and loading the Font and Paragraph tools in toolbars, see Chapter 23.**

When you choose Window ⇨ Font, by default both the Font and Paragraph palettes open in a floating palette as shown in Figure 25.10. In the palette, you find the following options:

A **Help options:** Click the icon in the top-right corner of the palette and you find three menu commands. Help opens the Help guide and takes you to the page where help information is found on fonts and font formatting. Choose Hide Palette and the palette disappears from view. The third option is List Font Names In Their Font. This menu item might be more appropriately named Show Font Styles In Their Font. Regardless, when the check box is enabled, you see the fonts as they will appear on the form page. When the check box is disabled, the fonts appear in name only without showing you the font appearances.

B   **Currently editing Caption and Value:** Click the right-pointing arrow below the Font tab title and a flyout menu displays three menu choices. The choices include:

■   **Edit Caption and Value:** This is the default setting from the flyout menu. This choice applies font changes to captions and field objects for the selected object.

■   **Edit Caption:** Making this choice applies changes only to captions.

■   **Edit Value:** Make this choice when you want to change font attributes to only the value in the field object.

C   **Font:** From the drop-down menu adjacent to Myriad Pro you see in Figure 25.10, you can choose from all the fonts installed in your system and accessible to Designer.

D   **Font Size:** Type a value in the text box or make a choice from the drop-down menu to change a font size.

E   **Style:** From left to right the font styles include Bold, Italic, Underline, and the last item has a drop-down menu to choose Strikethrough or Plain for the style. If you choose Strikethrough for the caption and not the field object, a third command shows you Mixed with a check mark. When a check mark appears adjacent to Mixed, a strikethrough is applied to either the caption or the object value or vice versa.

F   **Font Color:** Click the down-pointing arrow to choose a preset color or a custom color from the pop-up color palette.

G   **Baseline Shift:** Type a value in the text box to shift the text from the baseline upward. Use a negative value to move the text below the baseline. Note that when you enter values in any of the text boxes in the Font tab, the default unit of measure is in points.

H   **Vertical Scale:** Type a value in the text box to scale text vertically higher (above 100%) or lower (below 100%).

I   **Letter Spacing:** Increase the tracking for characters by typing a value in the text box. To tighten the tracking, use negative values.

J   **Horizontal Scale:** Type a value in the text box to scale text horizontally (stretched—above 100% or tighter—below 100%).

K   **Auto Kern:** Check the check box to apply auto kerning. Notice in Figure 25.11 you can see the effects of kerning (top text item) compared to text that wasn't auto-kerned (bottom text item).

FIGURE 25.10

The Font palette provides the options you need to change font attributes for objects.

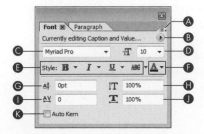

FIGURE 25.11

Text with Auto Kern enabled (top) compared to text without Auto Kern enabled (bottom)

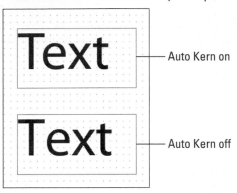

— Auto Kern on

— Auto Kern off

Setting paragraph attributes

You can access the Paragraph tools with the same options you have for accessing the Font tools. Choose Window ➪ Paragraph or press Shift + F5 to open the Paragraph palette shown in Figure 25.12. Likewise you can add tools to toolbars as we explained in the section "Changing font attributes" earlier in this chapter.

FIGURE 25.12

Choose Window ➪ Paragraph or press Shift + F5 to open the Paragraph palette.

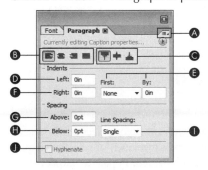

Options you have for making paragraph adjustments to objects text and values include:

A **Fly-out menu:** The menu provides options for accessing the Help guide with information on paragraph settings and a choice for hiding the palette.

B **Justification:** From left to right the four justification items justify text left, right, center, and full justification.

C **Vertical Justification:** Choose from (left to right) align top, center, and bottom.

D **Indents (Left):** Type a value to indent a line by the value entered. Use *n pt* to specify points.

E **Indents (First/By):** Choose from the drop-down menu None, First line, or Hanging for first line indents. If you choose First line, type a value in the By text box to indicate the value for the indentation. The same holds true for hanging indents.

F **Indents (Right):** Type a value for the right indentation within the field box.

G **Spacing (Above):** Type (in points) the amount of spacing you want preceding (Above) a paragraph.

H **Spacing (Below):** Type (in points) the amount of spacing you want following (Below) a paragraph.

I **Line Spacing:** Rather than having a leading value, Designer uses line spacing. Choose from the default Single or 1.5 lines, Double line, or Exactly. When you choose Exactly, a text box appears where you type in exact values for line spacing as shown in Figure 25.13.

FIGURE 25.13

When you choose Exactly, a text box appears where you can type the desired line spacing amount.

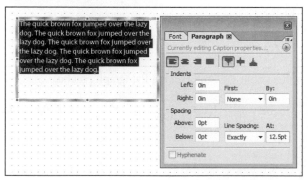

J **Hyphenate:** You'll find the Hyphenate check box disabled unless you select a field object. Click an object but don't select the text and the check box is available for selection. You can individually select hyphenation for captions using the Paragraph palette. However, when creating new forms, if you want hyphenation control for the entire form, choose Tools ⇨ Options and click the Formatting item. Make choices by checking check boxes for the items shown in Figure 25.14.

FIGURE 25.14

When creating new forms, select the hyphenation options you want by choosing
Tools ⇨ Options and click the Formatting item in the left pane. Check the boxes for the
hyphenation control you want in the right pane.

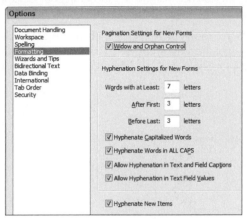

Editing strokes and fills

A number of geometric objects are available to you in the Standard Library palette. You can choose
from circle shapes, lines, and rectangles and each of the objects you add to a form utilize properties
options you find in the Draw tab in the Object palette shown in Figure 25.15.

FIGURE 25.15

From the Standard Library palette drag a Circle, Line, and/or Rectangle shape to the document page. Each
of the shapes has properties options edited in the Draw tab in the Object palette.

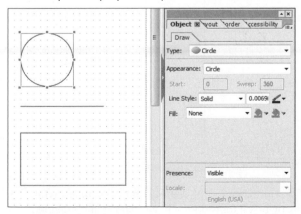

Embedding and Substituting Fonts in Forms

You'll notice that the Font palette and the Paragraph palette provide no options for font embedding when making type selections in Designer. Neither do the Object or Layout palettes offer you any switches for embedding fonts.

Font embedding is a global issue related to a form design and as such you might suspect the choices you have for font embedding is a function of the form properties. To enable font embedding, choose File ➪ Form Properties and click the Save Options tab. By default, Font embedding is turned on with the Embed Fonts check box enabled.

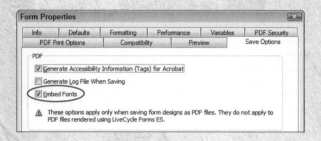

For just about any form design, you'll want to be certain to keep the check box enabled. Fonts are embedded in your forms only after saving the file.

You have further font control by opening the Options dialog box. Chose Tools ➪ Options and click the Document Handling item in the list in the left pane. If you want to modify font substitutions you do so in this dialog box by clicking the Modify Font Substitutions button. Another dialog box opens where you can choose what font substitutions you want to use for any fonts not installed in your system.

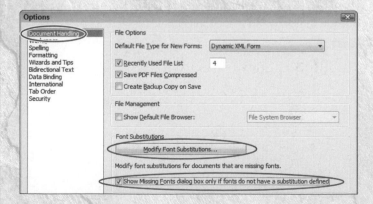

If you want to view fonts that are missing and do not have a font identified for substitution while editing a form, check the Show Missing Fonts dialog box if fonts do not have a substitution defined.

Working with elliptical shapes

Drag a Circle object from the Standard Library palette to the content area on a form and you can select from a number of properties options in the Draw tab shown in Figure 25.15. The Draw tab for the Circle object contains the following properties settings:

- **Appearance:** Open the Appearance drop-down menu and you find three choices that include:

  - **Ellipse:** When you choose Ellipse you may not see the object appearance change. Click one of the handles on the object and move it and then you'll see the object conform to an elliptical shape.

  - **Circle:** The Circle appearance differs from the Ellipse choice when you reshape the object. Dragging a handle to change the size constricts the object to a circle.

  - **Arc:** Choose Arc for the appearance and you see an arc drawn at 90°. In the Draw tab you have choices for the Start and the Sweep. If the Sweep remains a constant, changing the Start to 0°, 90°, 180°, and 270° moves the arc around the axis as shown in Figure 25.16. The Sweep value determines the length of the arc. Also in Figure 16.25 you can see the Start as a constant while the Sweep changed in values from 90° to 180°, 270°, and 45°.

FIGURE 25.16

Change the Start and Sweep values to change the rotation and size of an arc.

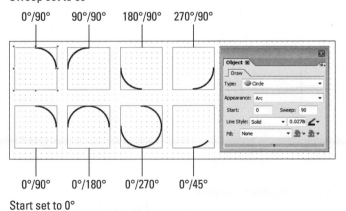

- **Line Style:** Line Style choices are the same for all geometric objects. Choose from None, Solid, Dashed, Dash Dot, or Dash Dot Dot. The size of the dashes and dots are determined in the text box adjacent to the Line Style drop-down menu. When typing values in the text box, use *n pt* for specifying stroke weights in points.

- **Color:** To the right of the stroke value text box is a drop-down menu where color choices are selected from the color pop-up palette. Choose a preset or custom color for the stroke value.

- **Fill:** You have the same choices for fills as you have with field objects. (See Figure 25.8 earlier in this chapter.)

Working with line shapes

Click the Line object in the Standard Library palette and click in the content area on a form. A line appears where you click the mouse button and the Draw tab changes to reflect properties options you have for lines.

The Appearance options in the Draw tab provide choices for Horizontal, Vertical, Line from left-bottom to top-right, and Line from left-top to bottom-right. If you have a line drawn in one direction, you can easily swap the direction with another choice by clicking another direction icon from the Appearance choices. For example, if you have a horizontal line drawn on a form and want to change direction to Line from left-top to bottom-right, click the Line from left-top to bottom-right icon and the line direction changes. When you want to draw lines on an arbitrary axis, drag the handle on one of the ends of the line and move the line around a 360° axis. A readout for the x,y coordinates of the line appears below the cursor as shown in Figure 25.17.

FIGURE 25.17

To draw a line with free rotation on an arbitrary axis, drag a handle around the page.

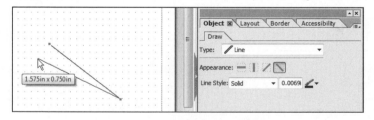

The line style and color choices are the same for lines as you have for elliptical objects explained in the section "Working with elliptical shapes."

Working with rectangular shapes

Drag a Rectangle object from the Standard Library palette to the content area on a form and the Draw tab changes to reflect properties choices for rectangle shapes. If you want to draw a square, resize the rectangle to a shape with equal dimensions for the sides and press the Shift key and drag to constrain additional resizing for a square.

The properties options for rectangles are the same as you find with circles with the exception of the Corners options. Click one of the four icons for Corners in the Draw tab as shown in Figure 25.18 to change the corner appearances. You edit the size of the corners by typing values in the Radius text box. By default the values typed in the text box are expressed in inches. Therefore, when specifying points use *n pt* for the amounts you type in the text box.

FIGURE 25.18

Rectangles have the same properties options as circles except for the Corner and Radius choices.

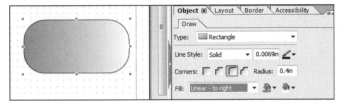

Setting Field Object Properties

Up to this point we've covered changing properties for objects in terms of an object's appearances. In regard to field objects you have many more options for properties adjustments when looking at formatting fields for handling data.

When we format fields for data handling we leave the Layout and Border palettes and work with the Field, Value, and Binding tabs.

Changing field attributes

To examine field attributes you need to select a data field. Objects such as Text Field, Numeric Field, Check Boxes, Radio Buttons, Drop-down Lists, Date/Time fields, and Signature fields all have different properties associated with the field types. For sake of simplicity we'll look at examining text and numeric fields.

Editing field attributes

Drag a Text Field from the Standard Library palette to the content area on a form. In the Field tab in the Object palette you find a number of options for appearance choices. In addition, you find a button to define a Pattern. Click the Patterns button and a dialog box opens where patterns are chosen for the field attributes.

CROSS-REF For a thorough explanation on working with Patterns see the section "Understanding pattern types" later in this chapter.

Other than the choice you have for Patterns, the Field tab for data fields provides you no options for data attribute settings. The real data assignments are handled in the Value and Binding tabs.

Editing value attributes

Click a field object on a form and click the Value tab in the Object palette. The first item to address is the Type choice you find at the top of the Value tab. Open the drop-down menu and you find a number of options for setting the field type in terms of the data entry as shown in Figure 25.19.

FIGURE 25.19

Click the Value tab and open the Type drop-down menu.

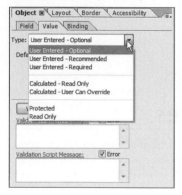

Choices you have for setting the Type options include:

- **User Entered – Optional:** Choose this option if a field is designed for user entry but filling in the field is an optional choice for the form recipient. Below the Type drop-down menu the Default text box is where you can type the default choice for the field. A form recipient can edit the default choice and change it.

- **User Entered – Recommended:** You can add a custom message in the Empty Message box after making this choice as shown in Figure 25.20. At runtime the message is displayed informing a recipient that you recommend the form filler add data to the field.

- **User Entered – Required:** If a form recipient tries to submit a form with a field marked as User Entered – Required and the field is left blank, the message you type in the Empty Message box is displayed and the recipient is prevented from submitting the form until the field is populated with data.

NOTE The Required property is not checked when printing forms, only when submitting electronically. This is by design, as a person may intend to print a blank or partially completed form and continue to complete the form on paper. If you need to control both required fields when printed, this requires some scripting.

FIGURE 25.20

Add a message to the Empty Message box that is displayed at runtime for recommended field types.

- **Calculated – Read Only:** When you have a field that is populated from a calculation formula and you don't want the form recipient to change the calculated value, choose this option.

- **Calculated – User Can Override:** Choosing this option places a calculated value in the field box but the form recipient can edit the value. Suppose you had a form where a form filler is choosing items for a new wardrobe. As items are selected the total value is reported in a total field. After making selections the amount total is reported at $615, but the form recipient doesn't want to spend more than $500. The form recipient edits the calculated total field and other fields can be instructed to automatically adjust so the total does not exceed $500.

- **Protected:** When you assign Protected to a field, the field value is not editable by a form recipient. You might have a form where you display fixed costs of items and you don't want the fixed costs edited. The form recipient merely chooses the quantity for items to be purchased and the total is automatically calculated. When you mark a field as protected and the form filler tabs through fields, the Protected fields are ignored in the tab order.

- **Read Only:** Fields marked as Read Only have similar attributes as Protected fields where the field data cannot be changed. However, when a form recipient tabs through the fields, the Read Only fields are not skipped—they are highlighted.

Binding data to fields

Later on in Chapters 26, 27, 28 and throughout Part IX we talk about binding data to forms and field objects. We won't go into the precise detail for binding data to forms and data fields in this chapter but we want to cover some basics that will make the chapters ahead more comprehensible.

Just as you have many options for setting properties for appearances and values, you also have a number of options when binding data to fields.

When a form is bound to a data source you associate the data element to a form source. This association is referred to as data binding. In more visual terms, you can see the illustration for binding data from an XML file to field objects in Figure 25.21.

FIGURE 25.21

An example of data binding from an XML file to form fields

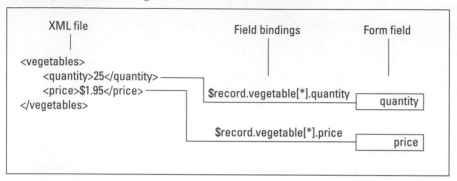

CROSS-REF For examples where data connections are bound to XML files see Chapters 27 and 31.

Designer needs to know when you bind data from data files to field objects exactly what data records are bound to what field objects and what type of binding are you associating to the objects. To make these choices you select from options in the Binding tab in the Object palette

Using Normal binding

To choose a binding option click a field you want to bind data to and click the Binding tab in the Object palette. Under the Default Binding (Open, Save, Submit) heading you find a text box and adjacent to the text box is an icon used for opening a pop-up menu. Click the options button and the menu appears as shown in Figure 25.22. The first option you see is Normal.

Normal binding enables data merging and saving options. Data values are stored *implicitly* according to Adobe data-merging rules. If you create a form and bind the data to an XML file using the Form Properties Preview tab, most of the fields on your form will default to Normal binding.

FIGURE 25.22

Open the pop-up menu in the Binding tab and click Normal for Normal binding.

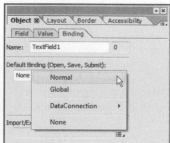

Normal binding is used for flowing data from imported data files when other options are set to determine data flow, and you use this binding option when creating dynamic forms. Typically you don't have to individually select each field and identify the binding when binding data to a form.

Using Global binding

Global binding is used when you have a field that contains data and the data are repeated in a form. You might have a form that is several pages and on page 1 you have a header row or some type of header on a master page. The same data is repetitive in the header for each page. All the fields in the header where the data are repeated would use a Global binding property.

To set a Global binding property to a set of fields, each field object must have the same exact name. When you bind to a data source using the Global binding property you only need to set the property on one of the fields having the same name. If you break the data connection for a Global binding property on one field, all fields with the same field name will also have the data connection broken.

Using a Data Connection

When you set up a data connection in the Data View palette, the data bindings default to the Normal binding property. If you make an edit on a form and you want to bind data from the data source to an edited field object where Normal binding is not connected to the data source you can open the Binding tab and from the pop-up menu chose Data Connection and select the item to bind to as shown in Figure 25.23.

The Data Connection submenu displays all the fields identified in the data source file that a form is bound to. Fortunately, when you create a data connection Normal binding usually takes care of all your binding associations and you rarely need to bind the data to individual data fields in the data file.

If you make choices for binding to specific nodes in a data source, then you are using Explicit binding. See the section later in this chapter on "Using Explicit binding."

FIGURE 25.23

To bind a field object to a specific record item in a data source file, select the source from the Data Connection submenu.

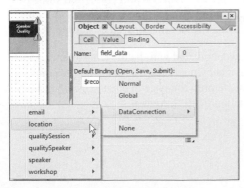

Using None for binding

Suppose you have a form that flows data spawning multiple fields when the data are imported into a form. You have a field on the form such as *Reviewed by* that is an open field where you type your name. This data is not part of the data being introduced in the form. As such, the binding for this field would have a choice of None in the Binding tab in the Object palette.

Using Explicit binding

Form designs use either *explicit* or *implicit* data bindings. Explicit binding refers to specific nodes within a record. Data references are used instead of object names to map nodes in the data source to objects in the form design. Explicit binding overrides automatic data matching just like Normal binding does.

Using Implicit binding

If you use Implicit binding, the names of the data nodes must match the corresponding containers and fields in the form and be presented in the same order as the form is filled in. This is automatic data matching and is the default choice when adding field objects from the Library palette. Implicit binding corresponds to the Normal binding option in the Binding tab.

Using Absolute binding expressions

An Absolute binding expression is a fully qualified SOM (Scripting Object Model) expression that describes an explicit data node. To create an Explicit binding with an absolute SOM expression, first create a data connection using the Data View palette.

To create a new data connection, open the flyout menu in the Data View palette and choose New Data Connection as shown in Figure 25.24. The New Data Connection dialog box opens. Choose a description from the radio button choices. If you have a sample XML file click the Sample XML Data radio button then click Next. Click the Browse icon and locate the file you want to bind to and click Finish.

CROSS-REF For more information on all the binding options available in Designer, see Chapter 31.

ON the CD-ROM We have a number of sample XML files contained on the book's CD-ROM. Look in the Chapter27 or Chapter31 folder on the book's CD-ROM and you'll find some sample XML files you can use to test this description. You can also use some of the sample files installed with Designer. For more information about using the sample files, see Chapter 32.

After creating a data connection, the Data View palette is populated with fields. Drag an individual node from the Data View palette onto the form design as shown in Figure 25.25. In our example, we dragged the @original node from the Data View palette onto the page to create a new form object. The default binding value is $.conferenceEvaluation.field[*].original.

FIGURE 25.24

Open the Data View palette and create a new data connection.

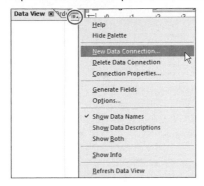

FIGUR 25.25

We dragged a node from the Data View palette to the form, and the binding was set as an Absolute binding expression.

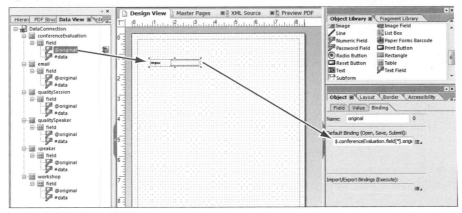

Using Relative binding expressions

A Relative binding expression is a partial binding expression. It is evaluated relative to the data node that is bound to the containing object. In Figure 25.26 we dragged a parent object (the *order* subform) to the form. The parent object is an Absolute binding expression, but all the children for this parent are Relative binding expressions. Using Relative binding provides better performance in large forms than using Absolute binding.

FIGURE 25.26

The parent node is an Absolute binding expression while all the children are Relative binding expressions.

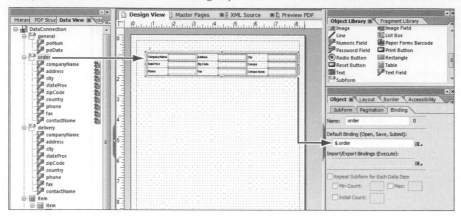

When you drag a parent node to a form, the parent is binding a value for the group. In our example the parent is $.order. The children for the group object automatically bind to the corresponding nodes in the data source.

Understanding pattern types

Patterns provide another field formatting opportunity—sometimes called masks in other applications. You might want a custom format for a date field or a telephone number. Rather than having to write scripting code to format fields, you can use one of the many different patterns Designer provides you for formatting field objects.

Designer goes one step further with patterns and also provides you with options for validating patterns as data are entered on a form. As you might suspect you find patterns accessible in the Field tab, and the validation options are logically placed in the Value tab.

Using Display Patterns

To access the options for Display Patterns, select a field object, click the Field tab in the Object palette, and click the Patterns button. The Patterns – <field type> dialog box opens. If you have a date field, the options appear differently than when using another field type such as a Text Field. When we selected a Text Field and clicked Patterns in the Field tab, the Patterns – Text Field dialog box opened as shown in Figure 25.27.

The Patterns dialog box has four tabs. They control the following:

- **Display:** In this pane you define how the data appears on a form. Click an item in the left pane and you see a sample display added to the Pattern text box in the right pane.

- **Edit:** The Edit tab displays the pattern used for how the data are entered.

- **Validation:** Click the Validation tab and you see the display for how the data must be described for it to be successfully formatted.

- **Data:** Click the Data tab and you find a display for how the data must be formatted for correct binding to a data source.

FIGURE 25.27

Click a field object and click Patterns in the Field tab in the Object palette to open the Patterns dialog box respective to the field type.

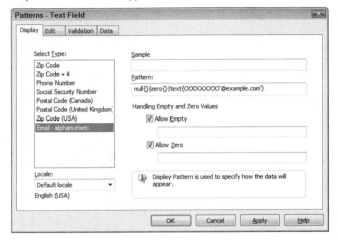

To experiment a little with using a pattern, follow these steps.

STEPS: Using a Pattern

1. **Create a blank new form in Designer.** Click the New tool in the File toolbar to create a blank new page.

2. **Add three field objects to the blank form.** Drag two Text Fields and a Date/Time Field to the blank page.

3. **Format the Patterns.** Click the first Text field object and open the Field tab in the Object palette. Click Patterns and choose Phone Number from the list in the left pane. Click OK and format the second Text field for an e-mail address and the third field for a Date. Note that you need to click OK after formatting each field, then select the field you want to edit and click Patterns to format an additional field.

4. **Preview the PDF.** Click Preview PDF.

5. **Add data to the fields.** Type the data corresponding to the field type. Your form should look similar to Figure 25.28.

FIGURE 25.28

Type data in the fields in a Preview PDF mode.

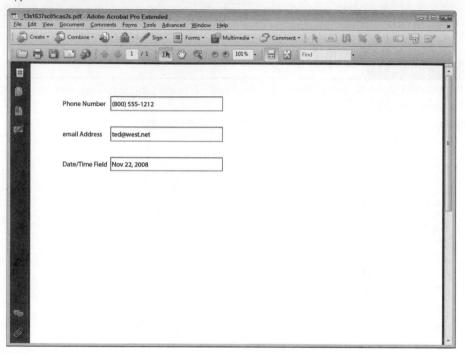

Creating a custom pattern

Suppose you have a need to modify a pattern or create a new pattern. For example, maybe you want to use an international phone number for the pattern. You need a country code using one, two, or three digits depending on the country, and you may have a phone number such as a cell phone number that uses 11 digits following the country code.

This kind of option is no problem for Designer. Add a Text Field and open the Patterns – Text Field dialog box by clicking Patterns in the Field tab in the Object palette. In the Display tab, add values that comprise the total digits you want for the pattern. Nines are wild card values; a 9 means any number typed in the field box is acceptable as long as the total digits do not exceed the number of digits defined in the pattern. For an international phone number with a country code having two digits followed by a cell phone number 99-9999-999-9999, the pattern would be edited as you see in Figure 25.29.

Using validation patterns

Following the example used for creating a custom pattern, you need to add a validation pattern. If you don't do this, an application alert dialog box opens when a recipient fills in the field, as shown in Figure 25.30.

FIGURE 25.29

A custom pattern edited in the Display tab in the Patterns – Text Field dialog box

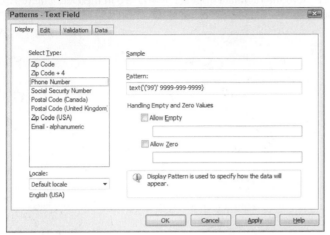

FIGURE 25.30

An application alert dialog box opens if the validation pattern doesn't match the Edit pattern.

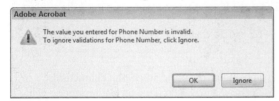

You can easily copy and paste patterns between the tabs. Copy the display pattern shown in Figure 25.29 and paste the data in the Pattern text boxes for the remaining three tabs. The Edit pattern accepts the data, the Validation pattern verifies the validity of the data, and the Data pattern describes how the data must be formatted if you want to bind the data to a data source.

When a form recipient completes a form, the data entered for our example field appears in the field box where you see Data Entered in Figure 25.31. The field formatted with the pattern is displayed as you see in the Phone Number field.

NOTE Figure 25.31 shows an example of how data are entered and the final display when a pattern has been applied. On a real form, you would only have the Phone Number field. The form filler would type the data as shown for the Data Entered field and upon pressing Enter or tabbing out of the field, the display would change to what you see for the Phone Number field.

FIGURE 25.31

When a form filler types data in a field with a pattern the raw data appears as you see in the Data Entered field. The actual display for our example appears as you see in the Phone Number field.

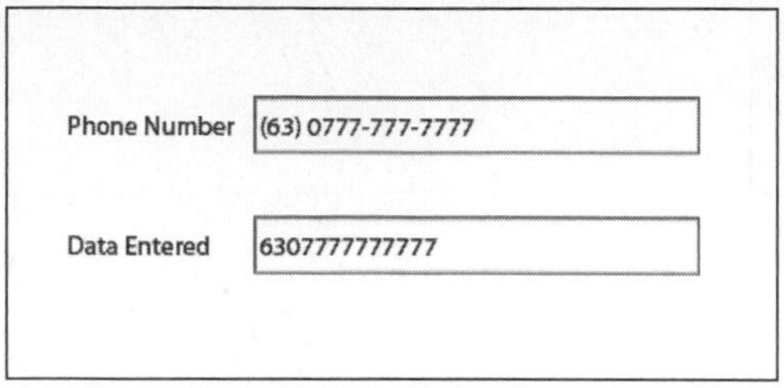

Phone Number	(63) 0777-777-7777
Data Entered	6307777777777

Creating an arbitrary mask

In Chapters 2 and 15 we talked about creating an arbitrary mask in Acrobat. You have the same options, and even more options, for defining custom patterns in Designer.

You might have a field where you want the form recipient to fill in unique values respective to a personal account number of some such condition and additional values are part of your own internal processing. Let's say you want a form filler to type four alpha characters and two numeric characters and you reserve the right to add your own four alpha characters at the end of the field. As an example, something like ABCD-65-ECHO, where *ECHO* is the fixed item you want as part of the pattern.

To create this type of pattern open the Patterns – Text Field dialog box and type the pattern as text {AAAA-99-'ECHO'} as shown in Figure 25.32.

In the above pattern, the character A is a wild card character meaning any alpha character is acceptable for the first four values. The number 9 is also a wild card character; any numeric value is acceptable for the second two values following the dash. The item in single quotes indicates that these four characters will precisely fall into the pattern.

When the form recipient fills in the form, the Data Entered item in Figure 25.33 is what needs to be typed in the field containing the pattern. When the form filler tabs out of the field the value appears as shown in the Arbitrary field in Figure 25.33.

CAUTION   It's critically important that you add the same pattern syntax to the Edit and Validation tabs in the Patterns – Text Field dialog box. Also, if binding data, you need the same pattern in the Data tab.

FIGURE 25.32

A custom pattern defined in the Patterns – Text Field dialog box

Sample	
Pattern:	
text{AAAA-99-'ECHO'}	

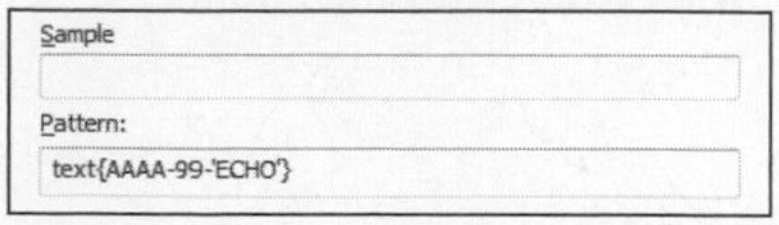

FIGURE 25.33

A custom pattern defined and applied from the data typed into a field using the characters shown in the Data Entered field

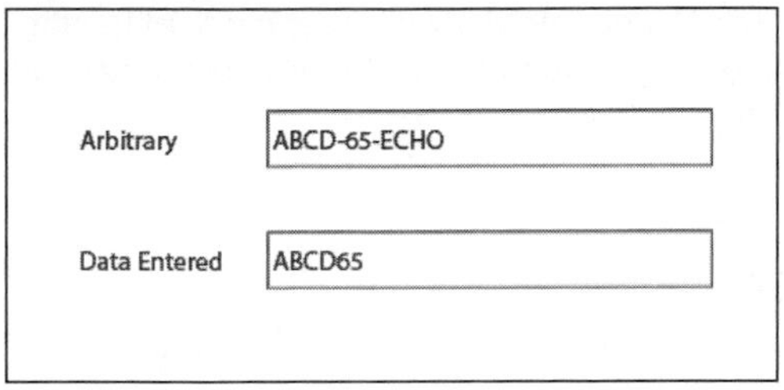

Arbitrary   ABCD-65-ECHO

Data Entered   ABCD65

Setting Tab Orders

In Chapter 7 we talked about setting tab orders in Acrobat and demonstrated how Acrobat 9 and greater uses a drag-and-drop metaphor to easily reorder the tabbing sequence on a form. You have several other options for letting Acrobat automatically determine a tab order based on rows and columns.

Acrobat uses the Fields panel where you apply changes to the tab order of fields on a form, but Designer has its own special Tab Order palette. Like Acrobat, Designer creates an automatic tab order for you based on the X/Y coordinate position of the objects. To get consistent tab results in your form is to properly align objects and wrap related objects in subforms. For the best results you can manually adjust the tab order after the objects are aligned and wrapped in subforms.

CROSS-REF For more information on the default tab order, see Chapter 22.

If you want to customize the tab order choose Window ⇨ Tab Order. A help document opens offering you some information related to setting tab orders in Designer. Review the document and click OK, and the Tab Order palette opens as shown in Figure 25.34.

Reordering fields

If you've worked in Acrobat and tried to manually change the tab order of fields on a form, you'll very much appreciate the marvelous opportunities you have in Designer to change a tab order.

When the Tab Order palette opens, click the Custom radio button at the top of the palette. In the list shown in the palette and in the Document pane you see the tab order numbers associated with fields. You can change a tab order through several means that include:

- **Drag and drop:** As in Acrobat 9 and greater, you can drag items in the list in the Tab Order palette up or down to reorder the tabs.
- **Click the arrows:** Click an item in the list and click either the down-pointing or up-pointing arrow at the top of the palette adjacent to the radio button options.

■ **Type a tab order number:** Click a number in the list and a text box opens as shown in Figure 25.35. Type the number you want for the new order and all the fields preceding the number change dynamically to fall into the new order.

> **TIP** You can also edit a tab number in the Tab Order palette by clicking the item to edit and pressing F2. The tab order number text is highlighted. Just type a new value and press the Enter key to change the tab order.

Changing the views

At times you may want to remain in the Tab Order palette but you may want to see the form without the tab numbers—especially when you have radio buttons and check boxes where the tab numbers obscure the field objects. To hide the numbers while remaining in the Tab Order palette click the Hide Order button at the top of the palette. The numbers on the form are hidden while the numbers in the Tab Order palette remain visible.

When you want to return to the same view on the form where the numbers are made visible again, click the Show Order button. When you click Hide Order the button changes its name to Show Order.

Another viewing option is viewing the form and tab order with the tab numbers only appearing for field objects. Notice in Figure 25.34 you see tab numbers appearing for the logo at the top of the page and the Purchase Order text below the logo. Objects such as these do not require fitting into the tab order. To observe just the fields with tab numbers, open the palette flyout menu (click the icon in the top-right corner of the Tab Order palette) and choose Show Fields Only. The view changes to what you see in Figure 25.36. Compare Figure 25.34 shown earlier with Figure 25.36 to see the difference in the display of the tab numbers.

FIGURE 25.34

Choose Window ⇨ Tab Order to open the Tab Order palette.

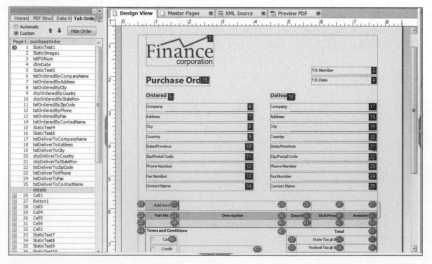

FIGURE 25.35

Click a number and type a new value in the text box to change the tab order

Returning to normal edit mode

To close the Tab Order palette and return to normal editing mode open the flyout menu in the Tab Order palette and choose Hide Palette. Alternately, you can open the Window menu and click the Tab Order command. Note that a check mark appears adjacent to the Tab Order menu command name. When you select the checked item, the Tab Order palette closes and the check mark is removed from the menu command.

You also can close the Tab Order palette by clicking one of the other tabs in the left palette bin such as the Hierarchy palette. This operation keeps the Tab Order palette tab open adjacent to the Data View tab where you can easily toggle between the tabs and reopen the Tab Order tab again by clicking on it.

FIGURE 25.36

Choose Show Fields Only from the flyout menu to hide tab numbers on non-field objects.

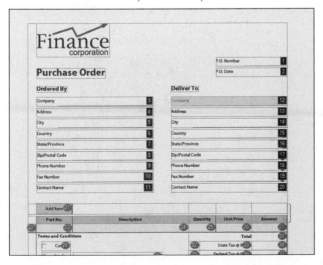

Summary

- Field appearances are assigned in the Object, Layout, and Border palettes.

- Adding captions to field objects helps reduce the number of objects needed to complete a form.

- Fields assigned with an Expand to fit property can be expanded to fit data flowed into a form at runtime.

- Fonts are edited in the Font palette accessible by choosing Window ⇨ Font.

- Paragraph formatting is handled in the Paragraph palette accessible by choosing Window ⇨ Paragraph.

- Font embedding is controlled in the Form Properties Dialog box in the Save Options tab.

- Modifying font substitutions is handled in the Options dialog box.

- Changing field Value attributes is handled in the Value tab in the Object palette.

- Binding data to field objects can be set for Normal or Global binding.

- When using Global binding you can have data entered or flowed into a form with the same data appearing for all fields with identical names.

- When using Implicit binding the names of the data nodes must match the corresponding containers and fields in the form.

- Explicit binding refers to specific nodes within a record.

- Patterns are used to format fields with special formatting characteristics.

- You can edit patterns and create your own custom field formatting.

- Tab Orders are set in the Tab Order palette accessible by choosing Window ⇨ Tab Orders.

- You can drag and drop fields listed in the Tab Order palette to change the order.

- You can edit the order numbers directly in the Tab Order palette.

Part VIII

Creating Dynamic Forms with LiveCycle Designer

This part deals with adding dynamic features to Designer forms. We begin by comparing static forms and dynamic forms, designing a dynamic form, adding instances, and using the Instance Manager in Chapter 26. In Chapter 27 we introduce tables and adding dynamic features to forms with tables. In Chapter 28 we cover all the things you need to know about using subforms.

IN THIS PART

Chapter 26
Creating Dynamic XML Forms

Chapter 27
Working with Tables

Chapter 28
Working with Subforms

Chapter 26

Creating Dynamic XML Forms

IN THIS CHAPTER

Working with static forms

Understanding dynamic forms

Working with text and field objects

Part VIII of this book is related to working with XML forms—particularly dynamic XML forms. We use the term dynamic throughout the second half of this book to refer to a certain type of form created in LiveCycle Designer that has what Adobe refers to as dynamic elements.

In Chapter 23, we talked about designing forms in LiveCycle Designer—both static and dynamic. In Chapters 24 and 25, we covered the essential tools, field and object properties, and commands that you need to become familiar with to create a form in Designer.

In Chapters 27 and 28, we talk about making forms dynamic using a number of methods you can employ in Designer to add dynamic characteristics to forms.

Before you embark on setting up a form containing dynamic elements, it is helpful to understand the differences between static forms and dynamic forms and when you need to plan for one type of form or another.

This chapter provides an initial exposure to the different form types and some introductory information you should know before moving on to the remaining chapters in this part.

Comparing Static and Dynamic Forms

Most of the forms we created in the chapters related to Adobe Acrobat are static forms. A static form contains a number of field objects that are fixed on the form and designed for user input as the form appears when opened in Acrobat. In some earlier chapters related to creating a form in Acrobat, we worked with forms similar to the one you see in Figure 26.1.

The form shown in Figure 26.1 is a static form. All the field objects on this form need to be planned ahead of time because the form recipient has no way to add field objects to the form. The ability to add field objects is one of the factors that make a form dynamic.

ON the CD-ROM **To examine the form shown in Figure 26.1, look in the Chapter 26 folder on the book's CD-ROM and open the *applicationDesignAcrobat.pdf* file.**

FIGURE 26.1

A static form created in Adobe Acrobat

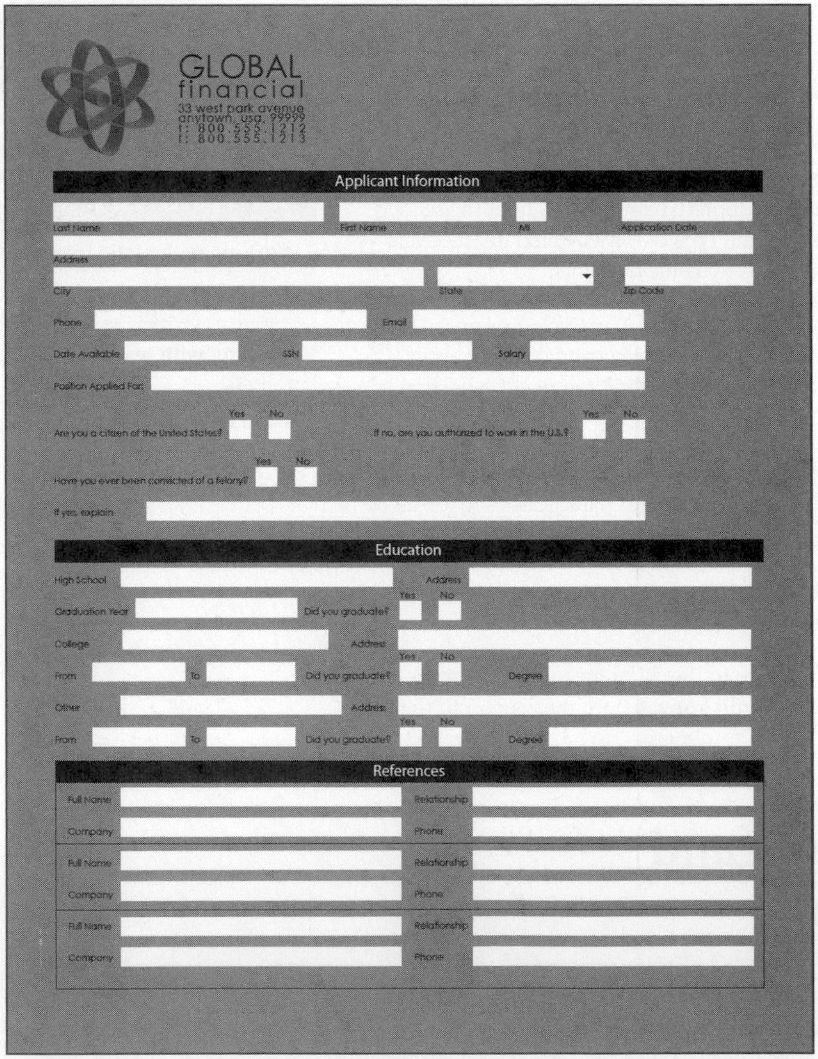
GLOBAL financial
33 west park avenue
anytown, usa, 99999
t: 800.555.1212
f: 800.555.1213

Applicant Information

Last Name | First Name | MI | Application Date
Address
City | State | Zip Code
Phone | Email
Date Available | SSN | Salary
Position Applied For:
Are you a citizen of the United States? Yes No | If no, are you authorized to work in the U.S.? Yes No
Have you ever been convicted of a felony? Yes No
If yes, explain

Education

High School | Address
Graduation Year | Did you graduate? Yes No
College | Address
From | To | Did you graduate? Yes No | Degree
Other | Address
From | To | Did you graduate? Yes No | Degree

References

Full Name | Relationship
Company | Phone
Full Name | Relationship
Company | Phone
Full Name | Relationship
Company | Phone

In Figure 26.2, you see a form created in LiveCycle Designer that is very similar to the form shown in Figure 26.1. However, on this form, notice the text where you see Add Reference and Remove this Reference. These objects are buttons that either add a new line to the table where the References section appears on the form or removes references from the form.

ON the CD-ROM **To examine the form shown in Figure 26.2, look in the Chapter 26 folder on the book's CD-ROM and open the *GFApplication.pdf* file.**

FIGURE 26.2

A dynamic form created in Adobe LiveCycle Designer

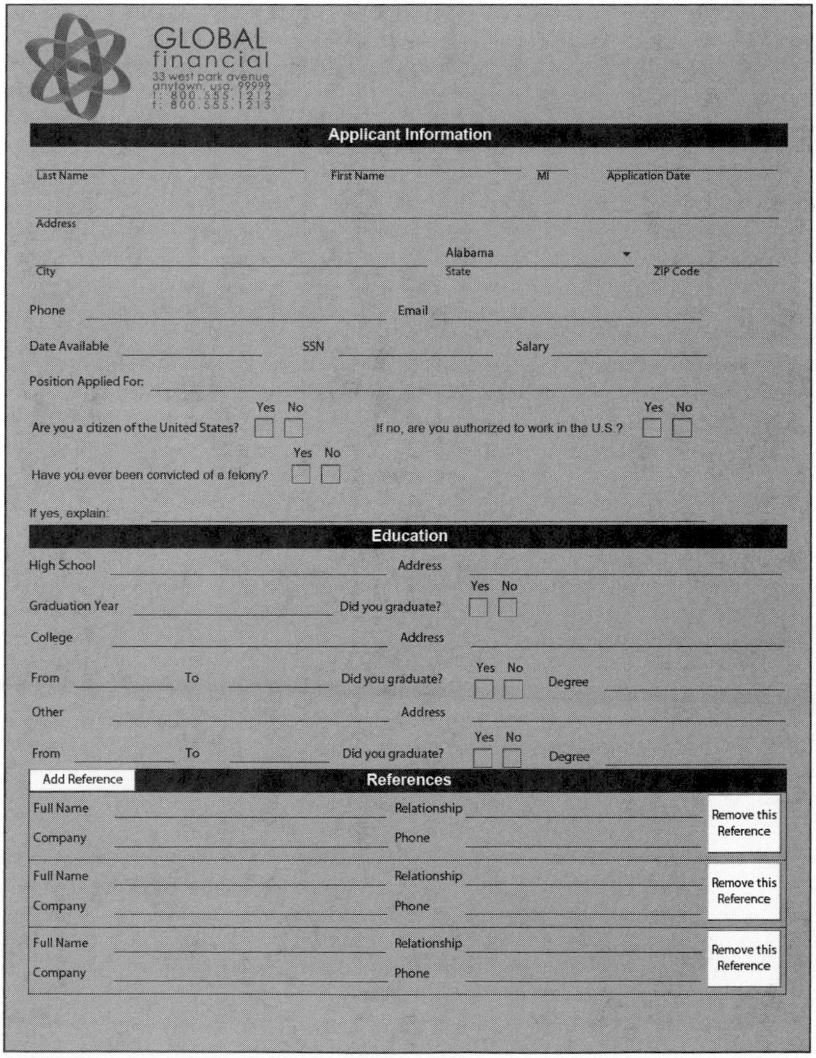

GLOBAL
financial
33 west park avenue
anytown, usa. 99999
t: 800.555.1212
f: 800.555.1213

Applicant Information

Last Name First Name MI Application Date

Address

City State Alabama ZIP Code

Phone Email

Date Available SSN Salary

Position Applied For:

Are you a citizen of the United States? Yes No If no, are you authorized to work in the U.S.? Yes No

Have you ever been convicted of a felony? Yes No

If yes, explain:

Education

High School Address

Graduation Year Did you graduate? Yes No

College Address

From To Did you graduate? Yes No Degree

Other Address

From To Did you graduate? Yes No Degree

Add Reference References

Full Name Relationship Remove this Reference
Company Phone

Full Name Relationship Remove this Reference
Company Phone

Full Name Relationship Remove this Reference
Company Phone

The form we created in Acrobat to demonstrate the comparison between static forms and dynamic forms is a single-page form. The form we created in LiveCycle Designer is a two-page form. When you open the second page of the form, you see more buttons that are designed to add and/or delete additional elements, as shown in Figure 26.3.

FIGURE 26.3

Page 2 of the dynamic form created in LiveCycle Designer

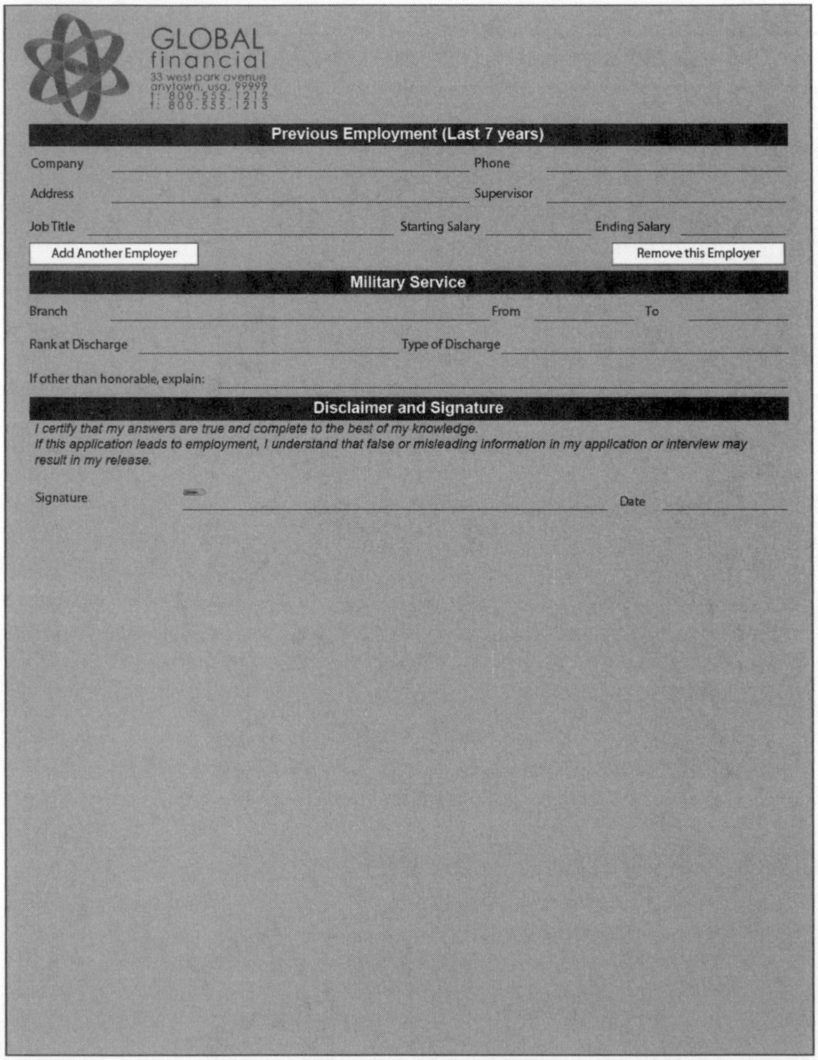
GLOBAL
financial
33 west park avenue
anytown, usa, 99999
t: 800.555.1212
f: 800.555.1213

Previous Employment (Last 7 years)

Company Phone
Address Supervisor
Job Title Starting Salary Ending Salary
Add Another Employer Remove this Employer

Military Service

Branch From To
Rank at Discharge Type of Discharge
If other than honorable, explain:

Disclaimer and Signature

I certify that my answers are true and complete to the best of my knowledge.
If this application leads to employment, I understand that false or misleading information in my application or interview may result in my release.

Signature Date

The button on page 2 where you see Add Another Employer is designed, as you might suspect, for adding fields for the form recipient to detail a work history. As a form filler clicks the button in either Acrobat or Adobe Reader, additional field objects are added to the form. Figure 26.4 shows the form after we clicked the Add Another Employer button several times.

FIGURE 26.4

After clicking the Add Another Employer button on the form, the form's dynamic components permitted adding new field objects.

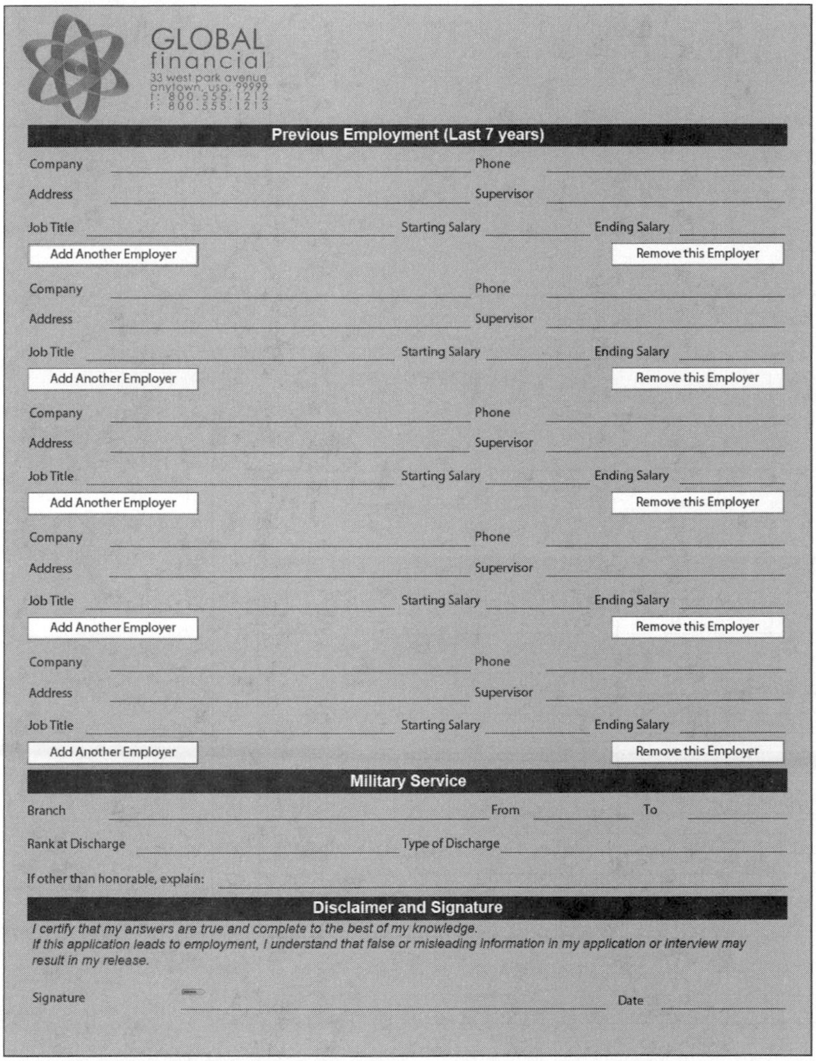

GLOBAL
financial
33 west park avenue
anytown, usa. 99999
t: 800.555.1212
f: 800.555.1213

Previous Employment (Last 7 years)

Company ____ Phone ____
Address ____ Supervisor ____
Job Title ____ Starting Salary ____ Ending Salary ____
Add Another Employer — Remove this Employer

Company ____ Phone ____
Address ____ Supervisor ____
Job Title ____ Starting Salary ____ Ending Salary ____
Add Another Employer — Remove this Employer

Company ____ Phone ____
Address ____ Supervisor ____
Job Title ____ Starting Salary ____ Ending Salary ____
Add Another Employer — Remove this Employer

Company ____ Phone ____
Address ____ Supervisor ____
Job Title ____ Starting Salary ____ Ending Salary ____
Add Another Employer — Remove this Employer

Company ____ Phone ____
Address ____ Supervisor ____
Job Title ____ Starting Salary ____ Ending Salary ____
Add Another Employer — Remove this Employer

Military Service

Branch ____ From ____ To ____
Rank at Discharge ____ Type of Discharge ____
If other than honorable, explain: ____

Disclaimer and Signature

I certify that my answers are true and complete to the best of my knowledge.
If this application leads to employment, I understand that false or misleading information in my application or interview may result in my release.

Signature ____ Date ____

Creating dynamic forms in Acrobat

Acrobat forms are not typically referred to as being dynamic forms. A PDF form created in Acrobat does not support tools and structures needed to create forms similar to the dynamic forms we create with Designer. However, you can add some dynamic elements to forms created in Acrobat.

The downside for creating Acrobat forms with dynamic elements is that many of the forms won't work in Adobe Reader. An Acrobat form that supports adding new elements or data is not something a user can use with the Adobe Reader software. Designer forms, however, can be constructed so new objects and data can be introduced into a form at runtime using the Adobe Reader software.

CROSS-REF **For more information on runtime, see the section "Understanding Runtime" later in this chapter.**

In Chapter 19, we created forms that were designed for Acrobat users only. On a form like the Attorney Worksheet we used in Chapter 19 and which is shown again here in Figure 26.5, we have several dynamic elements at work.

FIGURE 26.5

An Acrobat form containing JavaScripts that add dynamic interactivity to the form

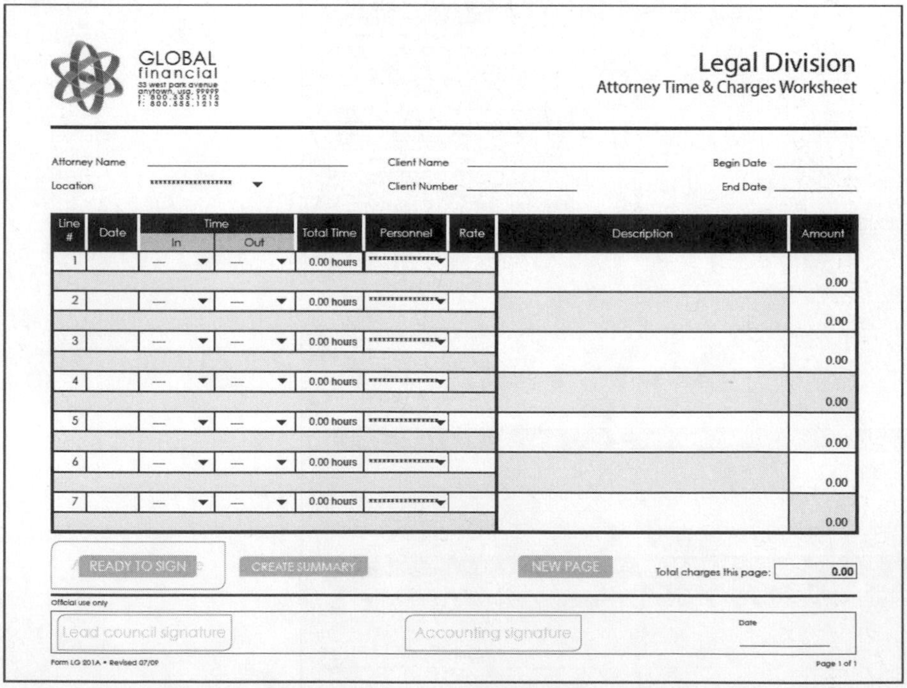
GLOBAL financial

Legal Division
Attorney Time & Charges Worksheet

Attorney Name | Client Name | Begin Date
Location | Client Number | End Date

Line #	Date	Time In	Time Out	Total Time	Personnel	Rate	Description	Amount
1		---	---	0.00 hours				0.00
2		---	---	0.00 hours				0.00
3		---	---	0.00 hours				0.00
4		---	---	0.00 hours				0.00
5		---	---	0.00 hours				0.00
6		---	---	0.00 hours				0.00
7		---	---	0.00 hours				0.00

READY TO SIGN | CREATE SUMMARY | NEW PAGE | Total charges this page: 0.00

Official use only

Lead council signature | Accounting signature | Date

Form LG 201A • Revised 07/09 | Page 1 of 1

A button on this form spawns a new page from a template. This action is a dynamic action that adds new pages according to the form filler's needs. Interestingly, spawning pages from templates is not supported in LiveCycle Designer. Designer, however, has its own method for creating new pages based on user demand or data flow.

The form shown in Figure 26.5 also has a button to send data from the form to another form where, through the use of JavaScript calculations, the data are summarized.

ON the CD-ROM To experiment with some dynamic features added to Acrobat forms, open the *globalAttorneySpawnRaw.pdf* file from the Chapter19 folder on the book's CD-ROM.

Using objects in Acrobat such as the docTemplate object and the addField object, you can add dynamic instances to PDF forms. However, you need to keep in mind that these dynamic features are supported only in Acrobat.

CROSS-REF For more information about using the docTemplate and addField objects in Acrobat, see Chapter 19.

Using dynamic elements in Designer

In Chapters 27 and 28, we provide several examples and a thorough understanding for creating dynamic forms in Designer. We won't go into the *hows* for creating dynamic forms in this chapter, but we want to introduce the concept so it will be a little clearer when you start creating dynamic forms in the chapters ahead.

Dynamic instances with forms occur under two basic conditions. One condition is related to data flow. When data are imported into a form, you can have the data flow create the necessary number of field objects and pages required to display all the data. If, for example, you have one data file containing 10 records, the rows of field objects are created to hold all 10 records. If you use the same form and import another data file containing 100 records of data, the rows of field objects are again created to hold all the data. This may require additional pages that are dynamically added to a form to accommodate all the data.

The other condition where dynamic elements are added to forms created in Designer is having new objects added to a form based on user control. You can add buttons to Designer forms that add data fields when a form filler needs to add rows (or columns) of data.

Understanding data binding

When you introduce data in an XML form, you are working with a file that has data binding to a data source, and the field objects are defined with various types of data binding. Designer needs to know where to place data on a form when you import data and when you want data to flow in a form.

In Acrobat, we need to be certain that the field names in a data file match exactly the field names in a form in order to import data. When introducing data in a LiveCycle Designer form, we have many more circumstances to control. We need to choose the type of binding, what kinds of expressions to use, and what kinds of files we are binding to. As you move through Chapters 27, 28, and 31, realize that you need to work with data connections and binding data to field objects.

Understanding Runtime

The dynamic features of some forms are apparent only when we use a form at what we call *runtime*. Runtime is related to either the use of the form by a form filler or when data are introduced in the form.

When data are imported, you see the dynamic features of a form realized, such as flowing data and populating the form with additional field objects. When a user clicks a button to add a new instance, it's a runtime event.

Changes that occur during the rendering process, or after the form has been rendered, are considered runtime changes and are not apparent at design time. To contrast the term, a Design Time change is any alteration made to the form while working in Design View or Master Page View of Designer.

Using the Hierarchy Palette

As we explain in Chapter 28, dynamic forms are made dynamic through the use of subforms. For now, don't be concerned about creating subforms; we cover that in much detail in Chapter 28. What you want to be aware of at this point is that subform elements, as well as all the objects on a form, appear in the Hierarchy palette, as shown in Figure 26.6.

FIGURE 26.6

The Hierarchy palette displays subforms and all the objects on a form.

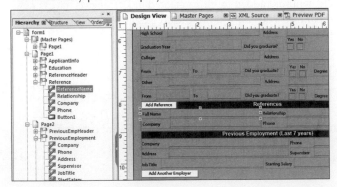

As you work with any type of form in Designer, and particularly forms with several subforms like the form shown in Figure 26.6, you'll want to locate and select objects and subforms in the Hierarchy palette. Poking around a form to select the right object where you want to change properties is much more difficult than clicking subforms and objects in the Hierarchy palette.

Understanding Dynamic Properties

Dynamic properties are properties assigned to form objects from a data source and updated at runtime. For example, we used the form shown in Figure 26.7 back in Chapter 18 when describing a JavaScript that adds data from one list box to another. The form is designed as a static form in Acrobat.

If we design a similar form using Designer and we populate the form from a data source, the dynamic properties of a drop-down list or list box object could be set to populate the field object at runtime. The dynamic properties of such a field object permit you to modify objects that are outside the original form design and rely on the data source to display the data.

A static form where the use of JavaScript populates one list box from selections made in another list box

Summary

- Static forms need to have all form field objects placed on a form during the design stage.

- Dynamic forms conform to the data added to a form. You can design forms where the form recipient adds new instances to populate the form with additional field objects or flow data into a form where field objects are dynamically created to accommodate the data.

- Some dynamic features can be added to Acrobat forms; however, using the forms is most often restricted to Acrobat only users.

- When importing data into a form, you must create data connections to field objects. These connections are referred to as data binding.

- Runtime is the term used when a form filler completes a form or data are flowed into the form.

- Dynamic features of forms are executed at runtime.

- When editing forms, use the Hierarchy palette to select subforms and objects.

- Dynamic properties of field objects are assigned from a data source file and updated at runtime.

Chapter 27

Working with Tables

Back in Chapter 8 we talked about creating tables in Acrobat. Here we are again talking about tables but now we look at tables as they relate to LiveCycle Designer ES. Because we have two chapters devoted to tables, you should get an idea for the level of significance we give to adding tables on forms.

To substantiate our belief that tables are an important part of creating forms, you need only look at Designer and see that the program has a special tool for creating and formatting tables. As a matter of fact, the table editor in Designer is almost on par with the table editors you find in programs like Adobe InDesign and Microsoft Word.

Tables really shine when we create dynamic forms and flow data into a table where we can watch Designer spawn new rows as the data are introduced. In Chapter 8 we talked about static tables in Acrobat and in Chapter 19 we talked about spawning new pages from templates that contain tables. However, the one thing Acrobat cannot do is create a form that dynamically extends a table design to accommodate data, either imported into a form, or by extending a user's need to spawn more rows or columns to add additional data.

The wonderful thing about the dynamic characteristics of an XML form is that the table expansion opportunities you provide to form recipients can be handled by both the Adobe Reader user and the Acrobat user when adding buttons to spawn new table rows.

In this chapter we look at designing both static tables and dynamic tables and how to work with table data.

IN THIS CHAPTER

Creating static and dynamic tables

Using XML data with tables

Adding sections to tables

Creating Tables in LiveCycle Designer ES

Let's start talking about tables with a basic understanding for static versus dynamic tables. If you remember the Workshop Summary form we used in Chapter 19, we created a static table in Acrobat. A modified version of the table from Chapter 19 when populated with data appears as you see in Figure 27.1. On this form we use a single table instead of the two tables we used in Chapter 19.

A static table created in Acrobat with data

Let's review this form again. The data you see in the table on the form in Figure 27.1 was summarized from other form data. The data could be from a database file you create in another program or in Acrobat sending data from one form to another form as we did in Chapter 19. When data are imported into a PDF form the table displays the data records and fields of data.

When we designed the form shown in Figure 27.1 in Acrobat we created the table to hold up to 15 records of data. Only eight records were imported into the form. If we have more than 15 records of data while using an Acrobat Form we need to create a template and spawn pages from a template to create additional data fields to hold the imported data or forget about any records in excess of 15. This means you need to anticipate ahead of time how much data you'll import on a form that you create in Acrobat.

As a comparison, take a look at Figure 27.2. This form was created in LiveCycle Designer. Notice that the form appears as though it can hold only one record of data.

FIGURE 27.2

A form having a dynamic table that was created in LiveCycle Designer

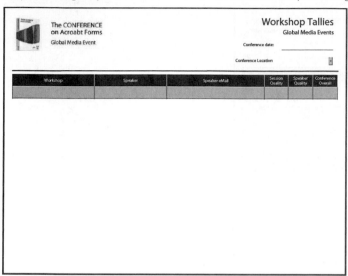

Using our Designer form when we import the same data into the form, the table on the form expands to accommodate all the records. Our new design for the form can hold up to 12 records on the form. If we use fewer than 12 records of data, the table conforms precisely to the amount of data we import, as shown in Figure 27.3. If we had substantially more data, the table could overflow to additional pages that are dynamically created to accommodate the data. This would require using a subform and constructing the file a little differently than the example file we use in this chapter.

CROSS-REF We limit our discussion on tables in this chapter to tables used for a single page form without getting into flowing data across multiple pages. For more on tables and adding more dynamic features that enable you to create new pages with tables, see Chapter 28.

If you worked through some of the exercises in Chapter 19 you know that we used many JavaScripts to calculate the data and send summary data to a slave document. The scripts weren't easy and they were quite complicated.

Now here's the nice surprise you find with creating a form like Figure 27.2 and importing the data resulting in a form like Figure 27.3. There are absolutely no programming steps you have to take to produce similar results. Everything is handled for you in the wonderful Table Assistant wizard. No FormCalc and no JavaScript code are necessary for you to write to create a dynamic table like you see in Figure 27.3.

FIGURE 27.3

When data are imported, the table expands to accommodate all records.

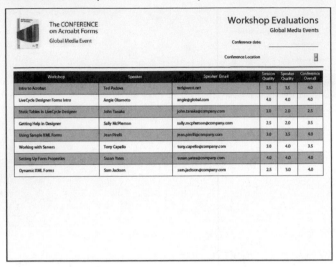

Creating a static table in Designer

We've added a little drama in this chapter to keep you on the edge and wanting to turn the page to read on. Just when you thought you were going to continue with Scene One, the authors decide to introduce a new scene. We're going to postpone Scene One regarding creating dynamic tables in Designer and begin by talking about a design similar to Figure 27.1 that is a flat form with no dynamic characteristics.

The reason we bother talking about static tables is that you may need to use design elements from other applications to create a form—something on the order of using a PDF background. If we open the form shown in Figure 27.1 in Designer, we cannot duplicate the background design if we want to dynamically create fields. A flat form like this requires you to set up a table very similar to the way you would create a table in Acrobat.

In addition to having no options for editing a background design, when you use a PDF background in Designer you cannot use the Insert Table command or the Table Assistant. Designer forces you to use manual methods for adding fields to a form when using backgrounds. If you have to adhere to a particular design created in another application and import the layout into Designer, you need to create a static table.

Fortunately Designer doesn't have the issues you find in Acrobat regarding field naming when you duplicate fields. If you remember some of the things we talked about in Chapter 8 regarding creating tables in Acrobat, you may remember how we had to copy fields to a temporary document, rename the fields, and paste different columns on our form using the fields we renamed in the temporary document. In Designer, each field you duplicate is automatically renamed in the Hierarchy palette. With this single difference for field naming, you'll find it easier to manually construct tables in Designer.

To see how we create a table that uses a PDF background, do the following.

ON the CD-ROM For the steps that follow we use the *workshopSummaryBackground.pdf* file from the Chapter27 folder on the book's CD-ROM.

STEPS: Creating a Static Table in LiveCycle Designer ES

1. **Open a PDF file with a table design in Designer.** For this example we use the *workshopSummaryBackground.pdf* form from the book's CD-ROM. Choose File ⇨ Open or click the Open tool, select the form to open, and click Open to display the New Form Assistant. In the New Form Assistant wizard click the Create an Interactive Form with Fixed Pages radio button as shown in Figure 27.4 and click Next.

2. **Disable the Return Setup options.** Uncheck the Add an email button and Add a print button in the second pane in the wizard as shown in Figure 27.5. Click Finish to open the document in Designer.

FIGURE 27.4

Leave the default radio button selection at Create an Interactive Form with Fixed Pages and click Next.

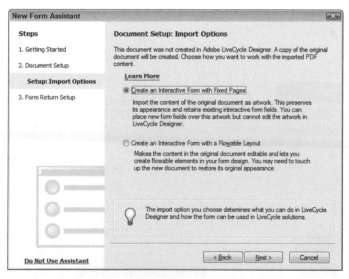

FIGURE 27.5

Uncheck the two check boxes and click Finish to open the form in Designer.

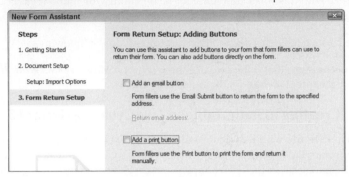

3. **Examine the Table menu.** Open the Table menu and notice that the Insert Table command is grayed out. If you open the Table ⇨ Insert menu, all the submenu commands are also grayed out as shown in Figure 27.6. Because we use a PDF background for this form, we do not have access to the Table commands in Designer. Notice also on Figure 27.6 that we hid the panels on the left side of the Designer window to make room for a larger view of our form and we have the Standard Library palette in view and ready to drag fields from the palette to the form.

4. **Add a field to the form.** We start populating this form by dragging a text field from the Standard Library palette and positioning the field in the first row and the first column of our table. In our example the field is the first *workshop* field. Size the field by dragging the corner handles so the field fits vertically and horizontally within the first row/first column in the table.

FIGURE 27.6

When using PDF backgrounds all the Table commands are not accessible.

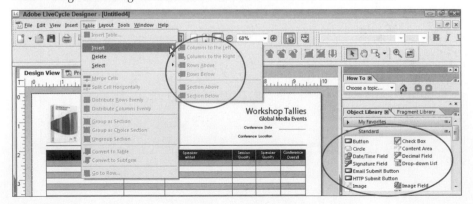

5. **Format the field.** We open the Hierarchy palette and click the default name, then type a field name for this first field. In our example we use *workshop* for the field name. We open the Object palette and choose None for the Appearance as shown in Figure 27.7.

6. **Close the right panels.** Because we have one field on the page with the formatting we'll use for the remaining fields, we can dismiss all the right panels from view. Click the vertical separator bar to collapse the panels.

7. **Duplicate the field.** Because we have this field formatted we can easily duplicate the field on our table for the field that we need added to the first row and second column. Click the first field, and then drag to the right to the spot where you want the new field added. Press Ctrl and release the mouse button. Size the field horizontally to fit the design.

8. **Rename the field.** The default name added by Designer is *workshop[1]*. Click the name and type *speaker*.

9. **Duplicate the remaining fields for the first row.** Continue with drag, position, and press Ctrl on a selected field to duplicate the field. As each field is duplicated, size the fields horizontally to fit the design. We'll worry about the vertical height later after creating all fields for the first row. For the remaining fields following the *speaker* field, we name the fields: *email, sessionQuality,* and *speakerQuality* as you can see in the Hierarchy palette in Figure 27.8.

10. **Size the first field to the exact vertical height and position on the page.**

11. **Select all the fields.** Be sure to drag the cursor around all the fields. Remember, in Designer you need to completely surround the fields with a marquee to select them.

FIGURE 27.7

Drag a text field from the Standard Library palette, change the field name in the Hierarchy palette, and set the Appearance properties to None.

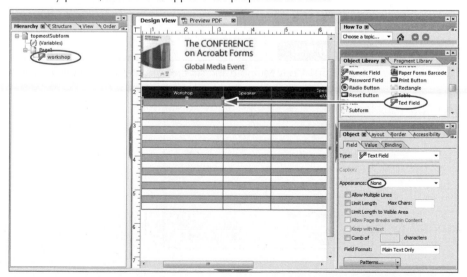

12. **Size the fields to the same height as the first field in the row.** Be certain the first field is your anchor field appearing with highlighted corner handles and choose Layout ➪ Make Same Size ➪ Height as shown in Figure 27.8.

13. **Align the fields.** With the fields still selected and the first field in the row highlighted with larger handles, choose Layout ➪ Align ➪ Top. Alternately, if the Layout toolbar is open you can click the Align Top tool.

14. **Copy multiple fields.** With the fields selected choose Edit ➪ Copy Multiple. The Copy Multiple dialog box opens as shown in Figure 27.9. In the Copy Multiple dialog box click the Place Below radio button and type the number of copies you want to place. On our example form we need nine copies. Type **9** for the number of copies, click the No Horizontal Movement radio button, and click OK to create the remaining nine rows of fields.

FIGURE 27.8

Select the fields and choose Layout ➪ Make Same Size ➪ Height.

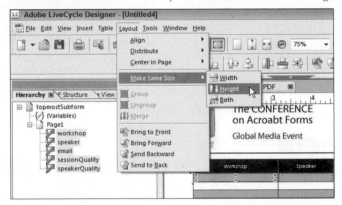

FIGURE 27.9

Chose Edit ➪ Copy Multiple and set the attributes for multiple copies in the Copy Multiple dialog box.

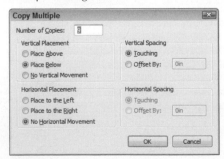

15. **Examine the form.** Notice in the Hierarchy palette all the fields have been named with different field names as you can see in Figure 27.10. Also notice that the fields on the table fit nicely on the design without you having to move the fields.

The Hierarchy palette lists the fields as an array.

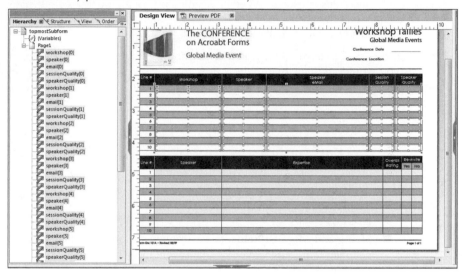

16. **Save the form.** Choose File ⇨ Save or click the Save tool. In the Save As dialog box that opens, notice that you only have the option to save the form as a Static Form. Type a name for the form and click Save.

CROSS-REF For more information on duplicating fields, setting field attributes, and sizing/aligning fields in LiveCycle Designer, see Chapter 24.

We won't bother populating the form because a much better solution for us is to create a dynamic form. We demonstrate the method here for creating a static form with a table to show you how to do it in the event you must use a PDF background to preserve the design of a form created in another application.

Things to note when comparing the methods for adding field objects in a table in Designer compared to Acrobat include the following:

- **Field naming.** In Acrobat you need to name fields in tables with unique field names. Designer automatically creates an array of field names when you duplicate a field.

Designer File Naming Conventions

In Acrobat we add fields to a form and name the fields with unique field names or we use hierarchical names such as item.0, item.1, item.2, and so on. When you duplicate names in Designer, Designer creates an array of field names such as item[0], item[1], item[2], etc. The names in Designer are not really unique field names but rather each instance of a field is treated as a unique field unless the binding for the fields is Global. When the binding is Global, the fields are treated the same way Acrobat treats the field names. The only difference is that the fields remain as separate instances unless you instruct Designer to make them different.

When you drag a field from a library palette to a form, Designer treats the fields as truly unique, much as you would add new field objects in Acrobat. However, if you add fields from a custom group, like the row fields we use as an example in this chapter, Designer creates an array.

- **Populating a table.** In Acrobat you use the Place Multiple Fields command and you need to copy the total number of fields pertaining to the rows (or columns) you want to duplicate. For example, if you have 10 rows as in our example, type **10** in the Create Multiple Copies of Fields dialog box. In Designer, specify the copies while excluding the selected fields. For example, when you have one row of selected fields, as in our example form, type **9** for the number of copies in the Copy Multiple dialog box.

- **Sizing and Aligning fields.** In Acrobat you size and align fields using a context menu command. In Designer you use the Layout tools in the Layout toolbar or use menu commands.

- **Duplicating fields.** In Acrobat you can duplicate fields using the Ctrl (or Option on the Mac) and click + drag (or use copy/paste keyboard shortcuts) a field or fields to duplicate them. All the duplicated fields have the same field name. You need to edit the field names in the Fields panel in Form Editing Mode, choose Rename Field from a menu command or context menu, or edit the field names in the field Properties window. In Designer, when you duplicate a field or fields by using either drag, position, Ctrl or copy/paste, the fields are automatically renamed.

Because of the renaming feature, manually creating tables is a much faster task in Designer than in Acrobat. The one advantage we believe Acrobat has over Designer is the use of a context menu to align and size fields. However, this is a minor issue because you can easily undock the Layout toolbar and keep it in a handy area for accessing the tools when aligning, sizing, and distributing fields.

CROSS-REF   For more information on designing tables in Acrobat, populating tables with fields, and setting field properties, see Chapter 8.

Creating static tables using Insert Table

If you want to start from scratch and create a table in Designer, you can use the Insert Table command. When you choose Table ⇨ Insert Table the Insert table dialog box opens. To create a simple table leave the radio button choice at the default as shown in Figure 27.11.

Choose table ⇨ Insert Table to open the Insert Table dialog box.

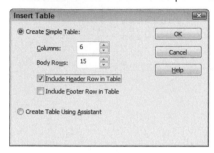

Identify the number of columns and rows you want to appear in the table and if you want a header (and/or footer) row make the choice(s) and click OK. In Figure 27.12 we added six columns and 15 rows and checked the Include Header Row in Table check box in the Insert Table dialog box. We then resized the columns by dragging the separator lines to set the cell sizes for each column and added a black solid fill in the Border palette for the header row.

You can format the table appearance by using the Border palette and choose from options for fills and border colors. In Figure 27.12 we chose Edit Individually for our Header row because we want a black border at the top of the table and white borders on the right and left sides and bottom of the header row.

When you design a table it's a good idea to periodically look over a PDF Preview in case you miss assigning colors and formatting cell appearances. In Figure 27.13 we clicked the PDF Preview tab and when the file appeared as a PDF Preview in Acrobat we noticed the type in the header row wasn't visible. Therefore we needed to return to Design View and set the type color to white in the Font palette. Frequent checks like this can help you make your design tweaks to get the appearances right before you start working with field objects.

You adjust column widths by moving the vertical lines left and right. Text for the table is handled by opening the Window ⇨ Font palette. In our example we want the type for the header row to be white against the black background. You can select the text for the first row in the Hierarchy palette and open the drop-down menu on a selection (for example, beside the A character) in the Font palette and choose a color from the pop-up color palette shown in Figure 27.12.

FIGRUE 27.12

Use the Border palette to change table cell fills and border colors.

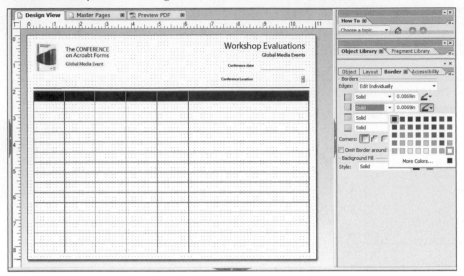

FIGURE 27.13

Frequently look at a PDF Preview as you design a table to be certain the appearance is correct.

So far the table design aspect of creating a static table is straightforward and easy. The next step is where you run into some problems. When data fields are added to a table, you need to individually drag the first row of fields to the table cells. For example, if you want to create a text field, open the Standard Library palette and drag a text field to the first cell in the first row. The field fits perfectly within the cell so you don't need to worry about sizing fields. You do have to adjust the field properties in the Object and Layout palettes. After you format the first row, you still need to manually add data cells to the table. Designer won't let you use the copy multiple command to populate the table.

The easiest way create a static table in Designer is to create only two rows (assuming you want a header row) in the Insert Table dialog box. Set up the header appearance and format the first row of data cells by adding text fields. Select all the data cells and drag them to the My Favorites in the Object Library. Designer prompts you to name the new Library item so type a name and click OK in the Add Library Object dialog box.

CROSS-REF For more information on creating custom library objects, see Chapter 24.

Once you have a complete row of fields in the My Favorites Library palette, drag a new row below the first row in the table. Designer won't let you use the Copy Multiple command so you need to drag each row individually; however, as the fields are added to your form, Designer renames the fields as shown in Figure 27.14.

We're not going to go into much more detail on creating static tables using the method described here because the method we used in the steps "Creating a Static Table in LiveCycle Designer" is a much faster solution.

Why does the Table Assistant exist? This may be your question if our claim is that Inserting a table for a number of rows and columns designed for handling data isn't the best way to approach the job. The answer is that using the Insert Table dialog box and choosing the Create Table Using Assistant option is where Designer excels at creating dynamic tables.

Working with dynamic tables

Dynamic tables can be designed for many uses and a few different models. For one model you can create a table that dynamically creates rows and/or columns on a single page, or for another model you can create tables that flow to additional pages along with any headers or footers assigned to the table.

In Figure 27.1 we're working with a known issue. The form is a summary of speaker evaluations at a conference event. The conference promoters know that there are a maximum of 12 workshops that will be held at any given event. No conference will have more than 12 workshop sessions. Since we can fit all 12 records of data on a single page, there is no need to set up the form to flow to additional pages. The dynamic aspects of the form create from one to 12 rows of data depending on the number of workshops held at any given event.

FIGURE 27.14

As new rows of fields are added to the form, the Hierarchy palette shows the fields as an array.

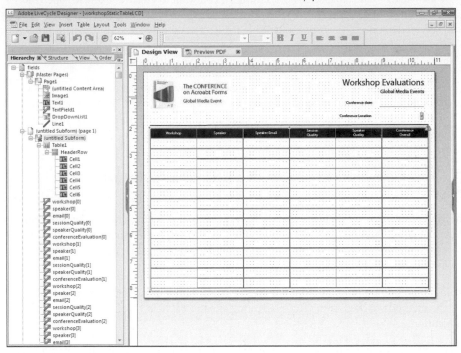

For other forms we may not have a known issue as it relates to the amount of data introduced on a form. If, for example, the conference promoters hold an event and collect evaluations data they want to aggregate on a form and the conference attendance varies between 100 and 500, the design of the form would be quite different. In this example we would create a form that dynamically spawns new pages as the data are introduced into the form.

CROSS-REF For our immediate purposes in regard to using the table features in Designer, we'll stick to designing tables on single page forms. For information related to flowing data across multiple pages see Chapter 28 where we talk about using subforms.

Designing the form

When we create a dynamic table like the original design shown earlier in Figure 27.2 and the populated form shown in Figure 27.3 we start with a blank new form in Designer we create by using the New Form Assistant. We can add graphic objects to the design using the Image tool from the Standard Library palette, but we cannot use a PDF background for the design of the table.

CROSS-REF For more information on creating new documents using the New Form Assistant, see Chapter 23.

ON the CD-ROM Check out the CD-ROM and look in the Chapter27 folder for the *workshopSumma-ryLCD.pdf* form. We use this form to explain the design we create in LiveCycle Designer. Additionally we use the *workshopSummaryLCD_data.xml* file to create the fields in Designer.

We created a new form U.S. letter size, landscape, and dismissed the e-mail tool and the print button in the New Form Assistant. We started on this form on the master page where we added an Image field to the form and imported the graphic in the top-left corner and added some text in the top-right corner. We also added two fields with captions in the top-right corner. One of the fields was Drop-down list where we added city names to the list in the List Items area in the Object palette Field panel as shown in Figure 27.15.

FIGURE 27.15

The first order of business for designing the form was adding elements in the Master Pages tab.

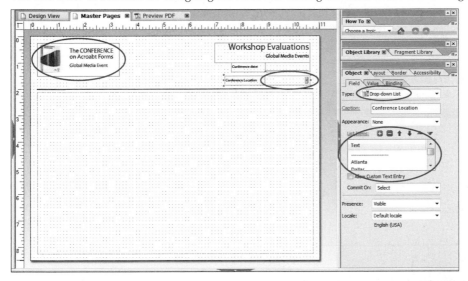

After adding a 2-point line horizontally across the page, we moved the content area frame just below the line.

Using the Table Assistant

After completing the master pages items, we're ready to design the form. The form design we use in this example is a table with a single header row and a single data row. Because the form will use a dynamic table we don't need to create all rows on the form as we did in the steps "Creating a Static Table in LiveCycle Designer" earlier in this chapter.

ON the CD-ROM   Use the *workshopSummaryLCD.pdf* form for the steps that follow. You can follow the steps by creating a table in a new form and then switch to the form on the CD-ROM to add the fields. Or, you can delete the table on the form from the CD-ROM to follow the steps.

We'll first look at creating the table design then later look at setting up field properties. To create a dynamic table, follow these steps.

STEPS: Creating Tables with the Table Assistant

1. **Create a new document in Designer.** We continue using the same file shown earlier in Figure 27.15. You can open the *workshopSummaryLCD.pdf* file from the book's CD-ROM, delete the table, and save the file under a new filename to follow the steps here.

2. **Insert a Table.** Choose Table ⇨ Insert Table to open the Insert table dialog box shown in Figure 27.16.

3. **Use the Table Assistant.** Click the Create Table Using Assistant radio button and click OK to open the Table Assistant wizard.

FIGURE 27.16

Click Create Table Using Assistant to open the Table Assistant wizard.

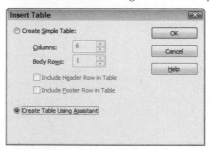

4. **Define the body layout.** In the first pane in the Table Assistant wizard you have two choices for the design of the table as shown in Figure 27.17. The first radio button choice is used when you want to create a static table like the table we designed earlier in Figure 27.12. The second radio button choice permits you to create a dynamic table. This radio button choice is your key to creating a table that sizes automatically to accommodate data. Click this radio button and type the number of columns you want for the table in the text box. In our example we used a table with six columns; therefore we typed 6 in the Number of Columns text box.

   Notice in Figure 27.17 that you do not have an option for choosing the number of body rows. Designer creates one body row for the form. Additional body rows are added when data are imported into the form.

FIGURE 27.17

Click Body Rows Vary Depending on Data and type the number of columns you want for the table.

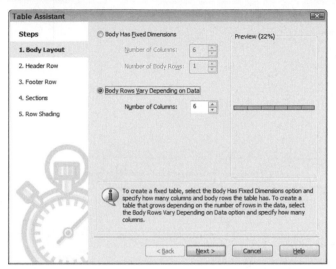

5. **Add a Header row.** Click Next and you arrive at the second pane in the Table Assistant wizard as shown in Figure 27.18. This pane provides choices for adding a header row. Click the Has Header Row radio button. Note that if you add a header row, Designer anticipates you'll flow headers across pages. When you create a data connection with a table containing a header, you'll see an error warning if the header isn't bound to the data file. We can get around this problem by not binding a header to a data connection as you'll see in the steps "Adding Fields to a Dynamic Table" later in this chapter. Also notice the Repeat Header Row for Each Page check box. You have to insert the table in a subform that is set up for flowed content for the check box to be active.

6. **Determine if you want a footer.** In our example we won't use a footer on the form. When you click Next in the wizard you arrive at the Footer Row panel. Bypass the options and click Next.

7. **Determine if you want sections added to the table.** The Sections pane shown in Figure 27.19 provides choices for adding table sections. You can add sections to a table with a new header and footer, and as sections are added move them up and down to organize the order. For our example we won't use sections so click Next when you arrive at this pane.

FIGURE 27.18

Add a Header Row and click Next.

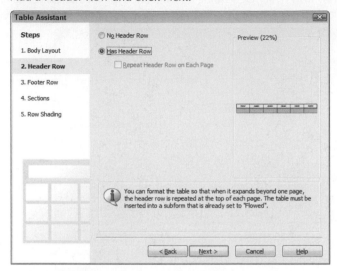

FIGURE 27.19

Leave the default at Has Body Rows And No Sections and click Next.

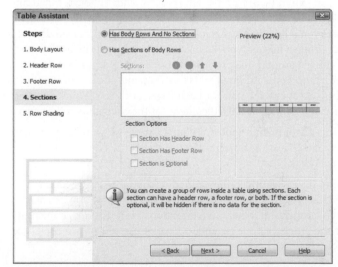

8. **Format the row colors.** The last pane in the Table Assistant wizard offers options for formatting row colors. Check the Alternating Row Colors check box shown in Figure 27.20 and click the down-pointing arrow adjacent to the First *n* Rows text box. Choose a color from the palette and make a similar choice for the Next row if you want two custom row colors. After setting up the row colors click Finish and your table appears on the form as shown in Figure 27.2.

FIGURE 27.20

Choose colors for the alternating rows and click Finish to add the table to the form.

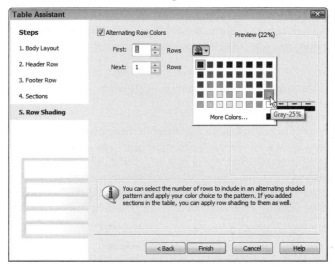

9. **Save the file.** Keep this file handy to follow additional steps in this chapter.

At this point we have the table designed for appearances but, as yet, we don't have any field objects on the form. To make this form a dynamic form, we'll bind the table cells to a data source.

Working with Table Data

You can add field objects to forms by dragging fields from the various Library palettes or by using a data source file and dragging fields from the Data View palette. When you drag fields from the Data View palette you are binding the field to the data source. When you add additional data to a dynamic form from a data file having the same file attributes you can flow the data into the form and Acrobat (where the data are imported) automatically creates additional field objects to accommodate the data.

When we set up our form, we use the Data View palette to drop field objects on the form. In order to see fields in the Data View palette you need to create a new Data Connection. Data connections are made to a variety of different file types. In this chapter we work with a simple solution to create a data file and then bind the data file to the form so you can drag and drop the fields on the form.

Creating an XML file

Oh horrors… you're going to have to read about XML and data files! Don't worry. If you're a beginner using LiveCycle Designer, we're going to make this section easy enough for you to create XML files and bind the data to your form.

ON the CD-ROM For this section and the steps that follow we use a sample XML file you can find in the Chapter 27 folder on the book's CD-ROM. When we import data into our form we'll use the *workshopSummaryLCD_data.xml* file.

Let's begin by looking at an XML file. In Figure 27.21 you can see an XML file opened in Microsoft XML Notepad. The file contains one record and six fields per record. This is enough data to create a data connection and add fields to our form.

The fields follow the root item *Row1* in the hierarchy in the left panel such as *workshop*, *speaker*, *email*, and so on. The data records appear in the right panel where you see sample data for the first record. You can edit a file like this by adding more records using simple copy/paste actions to copy the *Row1* item to create a duplicate. Using XML Notepad you press the Ctrl key drag-down to create another record. The name for the next group remains as *Row1*. Do not change this name. In the right panel you edit the data for each field while leaving the field names the same as shown in Figure 27.21.

FIGURE 27.21

A sample XML file opened in Microsoft XML Notepad

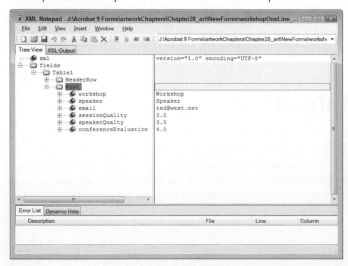

Using XML Editors

To create and edit XML files it's best to use an XML editor. These editors are designed to create and edit XML tags and data. You can find a number of free editors by searching the Internet for *XML Editors*. We chose XML Notepad from Microsoft to use for an external editor in this chapter. There are many editors and some much more sophisticated than XML Notepad. XML Notepad is easy to access from Microsoft's Web site and the download is less than a minute if you have a high-speed connection.

Microsoft Word is not the best XML editor but you can view XML data in Word. A quick launch of Word and viewing the XML data can inform you of the tag names and structure of the XML file.

This type of file is an example of a file you might use to create a data connection. If you use this file to create a data connection in Designer, the Data View palette shows the field names: *workshop speaker, email,* and so on. Each field shown in Figure 27.21 is included in the Data View palette with field names derived from the XML file.

The first thing we need to do is create an XML file. You could write the XML in an XML editor from scratch, but you may struggle to get the syntax right. The easiest way to create an XML file is to export data from the form you created in Designer. Since we don't have any fields on the form, we need to populate the form with field objects.

To create an XML file do the following.

To follow these steps you need a form created in Designer. Use the *workshopSummaryLCD.pdf* form from the Chapter27 folder from the book's CD-ROM. If you worked through steps earlier in this chapter for creating the summary form, you can use that form to follow the steps.

STEPS: Creating an XML Data File

1. **Open a form in Designer.** For our example we use the *workshopSummaryLCD.pdf* form from the book's CD-ROM.

2. **Open the Hierarchy palette and the panels on the right side of the Designer window.** We need the Object, Layout, Object Library, and Paragraph palettes to add fields and format the fields.

3. **Open the Object Library palette and drag a text field to the first cell in the row below the header.** The field fills the cell without a need to resize the field object.

4. **Name and format the field.** In the Hierarchy palette click the default name *TextField1* and rename the field to *workshop*. In the Layout palette choose None for the caption and set the margins as you like. In our example we used 0.125 for the left margin as shown in Figure 27.22.

FIGURE 27.22

Drag the Text Field object to the first table cell below the header and name the field in the Hierarchy palette.

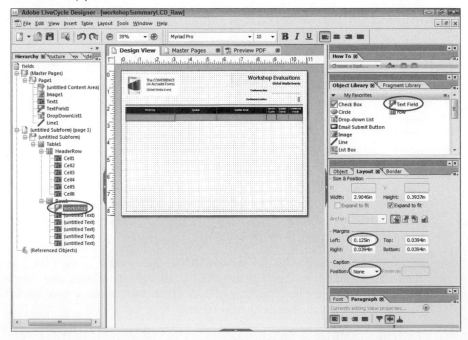

5. **Add the remaining fields.** Add text fields to all the cells in the table by dragging the Text Field object to each cell. Name the additional fields: *speaker, email, sessionQuality, speakerQuality*, and *conferenceEvaluation* in the Hierarchy palette. Open the Paragraph palette (Window⇨Paragraph) and click the Center icon for the last three cells in the row.

6. **Save the file.** Choose File⇨Save As and choose Adobe Dynamic XML Form (*.pdf) from the Save as type drop-down menu. Click Save to overwrite the file you opened.

7. **Populate the form with data.** Open the form in Acrobat and type data in the first row of fields. (Note that you cannot use PDF Preview in Designer. You need to open the PDF in Acrobat to add the data.)

8. **Export the data as XML.** Choose Forms⇨Manage Form Data⇨Export Data as shown in Figure 27.23. When you release the mouse button the Export Form Data As dialog box opens. Be certain to choose XML Files (*.xml) from the Save as type drop-down menu. Type a name for the file. In our example we used *workshopOneLine_data.xml* for the file name.

FIGURE 27.23

Add data to the six fields in the row and export the data as XML.

9. **Save the form.** Save the form with the data from Acrobat. We now have the data file we need to bind the fields using a data connection in our Designer form. We'll use this form in the next series of steps to populate our form with fields from the XML file.

If you want to look at the XML code you can open the data file in an XML editor. Pay particular attention to the tag names where you see items similar to Figure 27.21 earlier in this chapter. In the left panel in XML Notepad we find the tags *Table1, HeaderRow, and Row1*. These names are important because we want to use the same names in the Hierarchy palette in Designer in addition to the field names you see below the *Row1* tag shown in Figure 27.21.

Adding field objects from a data source file

At this point we have our form design populated with fields we created in Designer and the data file we created by adding data in Acrobat and exporting the data as XML. We'll now replace our original field objects with the fields we retrieve from the data file.

To follow these steps you need to continue using the file saved from the previous series of steps as well as the data source file we created.

STEPS: Adding Field Objects from a Data File

1. **Open the form in Designer.** Launch Designer and click File. From the menu options the form you last edited appears at the top of the list of recent files. Click the file you last edited to open in Designer. This filename should appear as *workshopSummaryLCD.pdf* or a name you used when you saved the file in Step 6 in the last series of steps.

2. **Delete the fields you added to the form.** Select the fields by clicking the first field inside the first cell in the row, press Shift, and click the last cell in the row. Press Delete to clear the fields. We don't need the fields now because we'll use the XML file to add new fields to the form.

3. **Open the Data View palette.** Click the Data View palette tab in the left panel area or choose Window ⇨ Data View.

4. **Create a data connection.** Click the icon in the top-right corner of the Data View palette to open the flyout menu and choose New Data Connection as shown in Figure 27.24. This action opens the Data Connection dialog box.

FIGURE 27.24

Choose New Data Connection from the flyout menu.

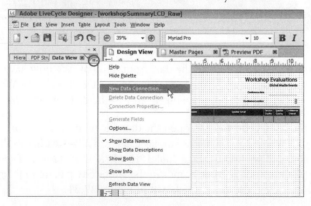

5. **Choose a data description.** When the New Data Connection dialog box opens, click Sample XML Data from the list of descriptions as shown in Figure 27.25.

FIGURE 27.25

Click the Sample XML Data radio button.

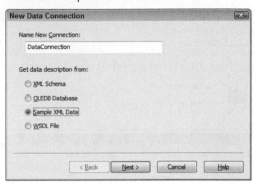

6. **Bind the data to a data source.** Click the folder icon to the right of the Select Sample XML Data File text box and the Open XML File dialog box opens. Locate the XML file you exported in Step 8 in the last series of steps, select it, and click Open. In our example we selected the *workshopOneLine_data.xml* file. After opening the file, Designer takes you back to the New Data Connection dialog box and your data connection appears in the text box as shown in Figure 27.26.

FIGURE 27.26

Select the XML file and the filename appears in the New Data Connection dialog box.

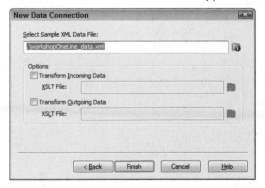

7. **Review the fields added to the form.** Click Finish and the Data View palette displays the fields bound to the data source as shown in Figure 27.27. These fields are the field objects you need to add to the first row in the table.

FIGURE 27.27

The fields from the XML file are added to the Data View palette.

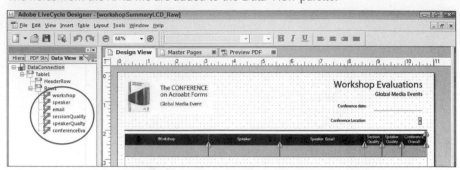

8. **Drag the first field in the Data View palette to the first cell in the row below the header.** In our example the first field is *workshop*. Drag the field to the first cell in the table below the header.

9. **Set the Binding Properties.** When you drag a field object to the form, the Binding Properties dialog box opens as shown in Figure 27.28. Update all properties by leaving the selection in the Binding Properties dialog box at the default and click OK.

FIGURE 27.28

Leave the settings at the default and click OK in the Binding Properties dialog box.

10. **Drag all fields individually to the form and click OK each time the Binding Properties dialog box opens.**

11. **Check for errors.** After adding fields from the Data View palette you'll find a few warning icons to the right of the header row. Designer wants to bind the header to the data file, but there are no data fields to bind to the form for the header row. We need to remove the data connection from the header on this form. To view the list of errors, open the Warnings palette by clicking the separator bar at the bottom of the Designer window.

If you don't see a separator bar at the bottom of the window, choose Window ⇨ Report and you'll see the three errors on this form as shown in Figure 27.29.

12. **Remove the binding from the objects shown in the Warnings palette.** Double-click the first item you see listed in the Warnings palette. In our example the item is *Row1*. The item is selected on your form. Open the Object palette and click the Bindings tab. In the Bindings tab open the Default Binding (Open, Save, Submit) drop-down menu. Note that the current binding for the object is Normal. We want to change it to None to remove the binding. Choose None from the menu as shown in Figure 27.29.

13. **Remove bindings from all the items reported in the Warnings tab.** Follow the same steps in Step 12 to remove the bindings from the remaining two items shown in the Warnings tab.

14. **Save the file.** Choose File ⇨ Save or click the Save tool and save the file under a new filename. On the CD-ROM in the Chapter 27 folder is the final file we created: *workshopSummaryLCD.pdf*.

FIGURE 27.29

Open the Warnings palette to review the errors found on the form. Change data binding for the head row cells to None.

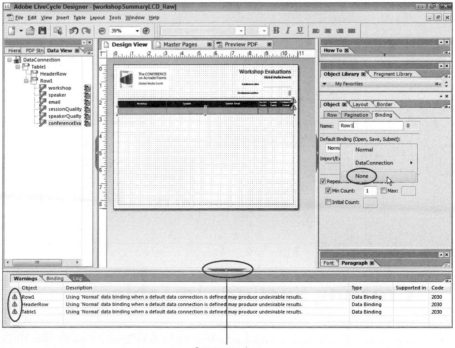

Separator bar

15. **Open the form in Acrobat.**
16. **Import data into the form.** Choose Forms ⇨ Manage Form Data ⇨ Import Data. Select the *workshopSummaryLCD_data.xml* file and import the data. The final file appears as shown in Figure 27.30.

NOTE **Your treatment for binding headers (see Steps 13 and 14) is handled differently when you create forms that flow across multiple pages. For more information on binding headers (and footers) to data sources, see Chapter 31.**

Do you need to have an XML form each time you create a table or a dynamic form? Quite simply, no you don't. The steps we used to create the form in Figure 27.30 could have been created even before you have a data file available. You can use other methods to create dynamic tables where you add field objects without a data source. We used the example to create the form shown in Figure 27.30 using field objects from the data source file. Next, we take a look at creating a similar table from scratch without using the field objects from a data file.

FIGURE 27.30

Import data and the table conforms to the amount of data imported.

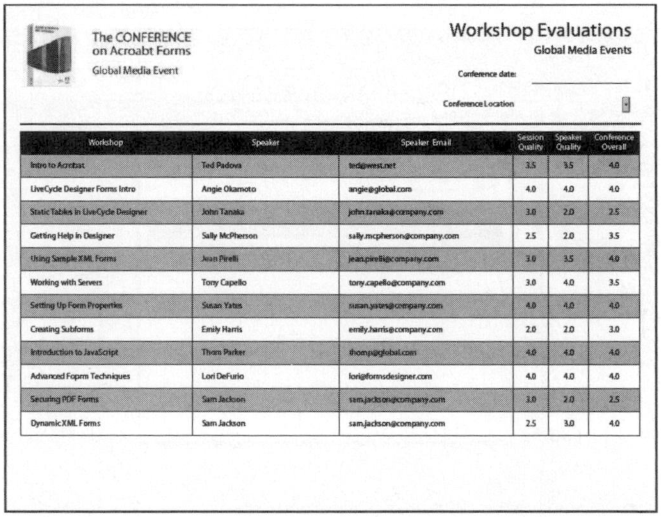
The CONFERENCE on Acroabt Forms
Global Media Event

Workshop Evaluations
Global Media Events

Conference date:

Conference Location

Workshop	Speaker	Speaker Email	Session Quality	Speaker Quality	Conference Overall
Intro to Acrobat	Ted Padova	ted@west.net	3.5	3.5	4.0
LiveCycle Designer Forms Intro	Angie Okamoto	angie@global.com	4.0	4.0	4.0
Static Tables in LiveCycle Designer	John Tanaka	john.tanaka@company.com	3.0	2.0	2.5
Getting Help in Designer	Sally McPherson	sally.mcpherson@company.com	2.5	2.0	3.5
Using Sample XML Forms	Jean Pirelli	jean.pirelli@company.com	3.0	3.5	4.0
Working with Servers	Tony Capello	tony.capello@company.com	3.0	4.0	3.5
Setting Up Form Properties	Susan Yates	susan.yates@company.com	4.0	4.0	4.0
Creating Subforms	Emily Harris	emily.harris@company.com	2.0	2.0	3.0
Introduction to JavaScript	Thom Parker	thomp@global.com	4.0	4.0	4.0
Advanced Foprm Techniques	Lori DeFurio	lori@formsdesigner.com	4.0	4.0	4.0
Securing PDF Forms	Sam Jackson	sam.jackson@company.com	3.0	2.0	2.5
DynamicXML Forms	Sam Jackson	sam.jackson@company.com	2.5	3.0	4.0

Creating Sections in Tables

We'll continue creating a form with a known number of maximum records that can fit on a single page form. In addition to creating a table as we've done in previous steps in this chapter, we'll add a section to our table. In our example we have some data that we'll add for a domestic (from the

United States) to one section of the table and data for an international section. We want to break up our data to appear with different header rows so the result appears as you see in Figure 27.31.

When we populate the table with data we want the domestic data to fall below the first header row and the international data to flow below the second header row. Our total amount of records will easily fall on a single page so we'll create a table with a section to divide the domestic data from the international data using dynamic properties that confine our results to a single page form.

Designing the form

The form shown in Figure 27.31 was created in Designer. Because we're not using a PDF Background we can use the Table Assistant to create the table with two sections. To follow steps to create the form you can use the *evenstLayout.xdp* file on the book's CD-ROM. When you open the file, you'll see the master page items have been added to the form as shown in Figure 27.32.

The following steps show you how to set up the form before we configure the fields for accepting data.

FIGURE 27.31

A dynamic table containing two sections

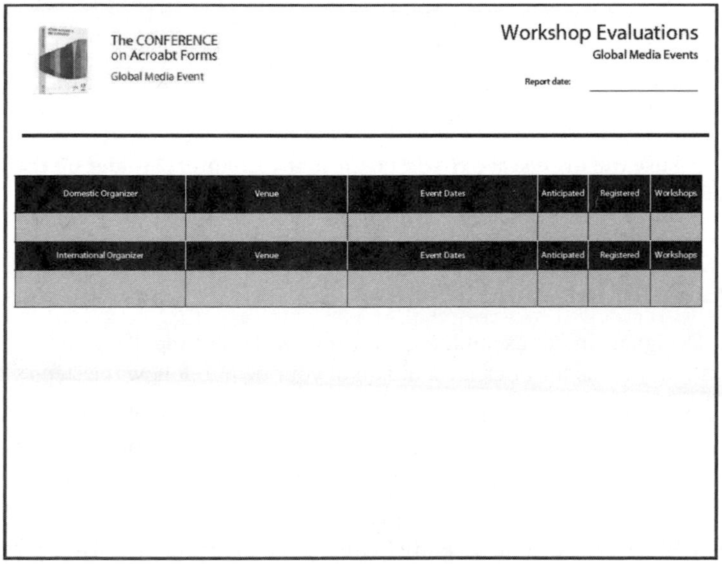

FIGURE 27.32

The sample file has master page items.

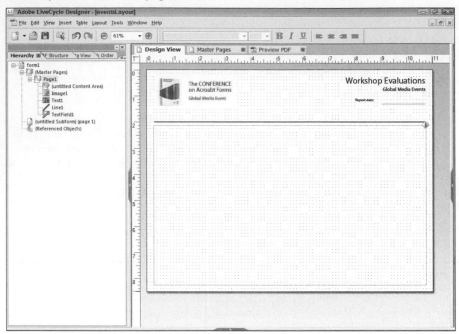

ON the CD-ROM For these steps we'll use the *eventsLayout.xdp* file from the Chapter27 folder on the CD-ROM. This file has the master page items placed on the form. The file can be opened only in Designer.

STEPS: Designing a Form for Table Sections

1. **Create a new file in Designer.** In our example we use the *eventsLayout.xdp* file from the book's CD-ROM. You can use this file or create a design of your own to follow the steps.

2. **Open the Table Assistant.** Be certain you are on the Design View page and choose Table ➪ Insert Table. When the Insert Table dialog box opens, type **6** for the number of columns and **1** for the number of rows and click the Create Table Using Assistant radio button to open the Table Assistant.

3. **Add a section to the table.** Click Next in the Body Layout pane, make sure Has Header Row is enabled in the second pane, and click Next. Click Next again without adding a footer and you arrive at the Sections pane. Click the Has Sections of Body Rows and click the Plus (+) icon to add a section to the table as you see in Figure 27.33. In the Table Selection dialog box you can add a name or click OK without adding a name for the section. Either choice is okay because we need to rename the section to the tag name used in our data file later. In our example we added *International* for the section name and clicked OK to return to the Sections pane in the Table Assistant.

FIGURE 27.33

Add a Section by clicking Has Sections of Body Rows and click the Plus (+) icon.

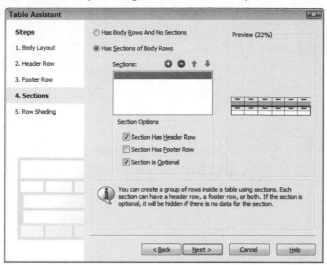

4. **Finish configuring the table.** Click Next and choose any colors you want for alternating row colors. In our example we used a light gray for the first row and white for the second row. After choosing the colors you want, click Finish and the table with two header rows is added to the form.

5. **Format the text cells.** Type headings for the six columns in both header rows as shown in Figure 27.34. Also move the column dividers to adjust the column sizes to the similar approximate sizes you see in Figure 27.34.

6. **Set the Fill color for the header rows and the header rows text.** In our example we filled the two header rows with black by selecting the rows, choosing Solid from the Background Fill Style drop-down menu in the Border palette, and choosing Black for the color. (Note that for the first cell we left the left side black, and the last cell in the row we left as black.) We adjusted the individual cell strokes by choosing White for the left and right sides of the cells. We then selected the cells in the first row and in the Text palette chose White for the color. We repeated the same steps to produce the same fills for the second header row as shown in Figure 27.35.

TIP
To easily select a row when you want to change the background fill color, first select the table and move the cursor to the far left of the row you want to edit—outside the table. When the cursor appears as a right-pointing arrow, click and the row is selected. When applying Border attributes you can apply changes to all cells within a selection. To change text color, click the cursor inside one cell and press Shift while clicking the last cell in a row. In the Text palette choose the text color you want to use.

FIGURE 27.34

Type names for the columns in each header row.

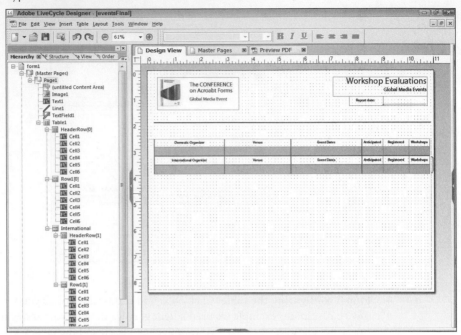

FIGURE 27.35

Fill the header rows black and fill the type with white.

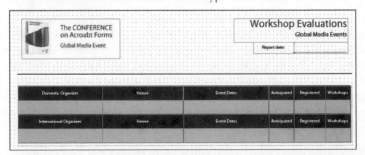

7. **Save the form.** Choose File ⇨ Save As. Type a new name for the file and from the Save as type drop-down menu be certain to choose Adobe Dynamic XML For (*.pdf) as shown in Figure 27.36.

FIGURE 27.36

Save the file as a dynamic form.

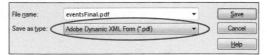

Adding fields

What we've accomplished up to this point is creating the basic layout for the form. We have a lot of flexibility and we can exercise freedom and artistic license for the appearance of the form. We can make our own personal choices by changing the attributes of the type and cells and other design elements. Other than setting up the initial table in the Table Assistant, you can make editing changes based on personal choices and don't need to worry about a rigid series of steps to be followed in a particular order.

Adding fields and adjusting field properties

What follows is completely different. Each step you perform to complete the table by adding data fields and setting up the form to accept data from a data file has to be performed with precision and in a more rigid order. If you miss one step, the form won't appear correctly in Acrobat and you won't be able to import data from the sample data file.

 **If you had any trouble creating the table from the previous series of steps you can use the *eventsFormRaw.pdf* file in the Chapter27 folder on the book's CD-ROM.**

To add fields and complete the form created in the previous series of steps, do the following.

STEPS: Adding Fields to a Table Containing Sections

1. **Open a form in Designer.** It's essential to use the form you saved in Step 7 in the previous series of steps or use the *eventsFormRaw.pdf* file from the book's CD-ROM to follow these steps.

2. **Add fields to the table.** Drag the Text Field object from the Standard Library palette to the cell rows for both rows following the headers. The field names for both rows beginning on the left side of the row are *organizer, venue, dates, anticipated, registered,* and *workshops.* Change the names from the default names to the names listed here in the Hierarchy palette.

   Later in these steps we'll import data into our form. The data form must use names precisely the same as the fields and elements contained in the data file. Be certain to name all the fields exactly as shown in Figure 27.37. Double check your work to make sure you typed the field names properly.

3. **Change the Table and Row names.** You may have names in the Hierarchy palette different from the tag names used in the data file. Be certain to change the names to match the names shown in Figure 27.38. Right below the *(untitled Subform) (page 1)* item in the Hierarchy palette you should see *Table1.*

Below Table1 in both areas of the Hierarchy palette, change the names of the header rows to *HeaderRow* and *HeaderRow2*.

Below the first row fields change the name from any other name you may find on your form to *Table1*. The first and second rows may have a name like *Row[0]* and *Row[1]*. Change *Row[1]* to *Row2*. The first row fields should change to *Row1*. If it does not change, be certain to change it to *Row1*.

Before you move on, carefully look over Figure 27.38 and be certain all the names in the Hierarchy palette match your form.

4. **Set up the binding for the Table.** We need to make sure all bindings are properly identified. We'll walk through each binding property in the Hierarchy palette to be sure they are properly set. Click the first *Table1* item in the Hierarchy palette. Open the Object palette and click the Binding tab. You should see the Default Binding appear as None. If it is not set to None, open the drop-down menu (click the icon to the right of the Default Binding text box to open the menu) and choose None as shown in Figure 27.39. The second *Table1* farther down the Hierarchy palette should automatically have no choice for setting the binding. You don't need to make any changes in the Binding tab for this item.

FIGURE 27.37

Change the field names in the Hierarchy palette.

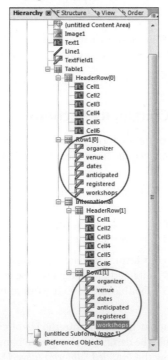

5.   **Set up the binding for the Header Rows.** Click *HeaderRow* in the Hierarchy palette. This item should appear under the first *Table1* item. Set the Binding to None in the Object palette Binding tab. Click the second header row labeled *HeaderRow2* in the Hierarchy palette. Change the binding to Normal.

6.   **Set up the binding for the fields.** Set the binding for the *Row1* ad *Row2* items to Normal. Under these headings click each field to be certain all the fields have the same Normal binding.

7.   **Repeat the rows for each data item.** Click *Row1* in the Hierarchy palette and in the Binding tab in the Object palette check Repeat Row for Each Data Item and check the Min Count check box as shown in Figure 27.40. By default 1 will appear in the text box. Leave the default and make the same change to the *Row2* item.

FIGURE 27.38

Edit the names in the Hierarchy palette.

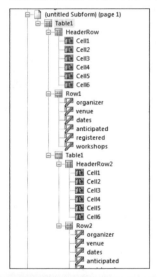

FIGURE 27.39

Be sure the binding for the first Table1 item is set to None.

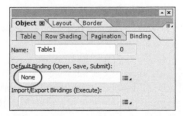

FIGURE 27.40

Check the Repeat Row for Each Data Item and Min Count check boxes.

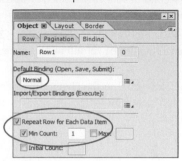

8. **Save the form.** Keep this file open to follow the remaining steps.

Setting some global properties

We have a few more steps to make our form a dynamic form. We need to set up some general global settings and adjust the subform properties. To complete the form, do the following.

 In addition to the file saved from the last series of steps, you need the *events_data. xml* file from the Chapter27 folder on the book's CD-ROM.

STEPS: Adjusting Form Properties

1. **Use the file saved from the last series of steps.**

2. **Adjust the subform properties.** Notice in the Hierarchy palette you see *(untitled Subform) (page 1)* at the top of the palette. Click this item and in the Object palette you find a new tab labeled *Subform*. Click the Subform tab and choose Flowed from the Content drop-down menu as shown in Figure 27.41. You must have this item set to Flowed in order to flow the data in the table.

FIGURE 27.41

Set the Subform Content properties to Flowed.

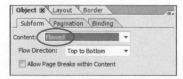

3. **Adjust the Default Form Properties.** Choose File ⇨ Form Properties. In the Form Properties window, click the Defaults tab. At the bottom of the window open the PDF Render Format drop-down menu and choose Dynamic XML Form as shown in Figure 27.42.

4. **Set the Preview properties.** Click Preview in the Form Properties window. From the Preview Type drop-down menu choose Interactive Form. This choice enables you to add and modify data on the form. Click the folder icon to display the Open XML File dialog box. We want to identify the data file we'll use for this form. Locate the *events_data.xml* file from the book's CD-ROM, select it, and click Open. When you return to the Form Properties window you'll see the file listed in the Data File text box as shown in Figure 27.43.

FIGURE 27.42

Set the PDF Render Format to Dynamic XML Form.

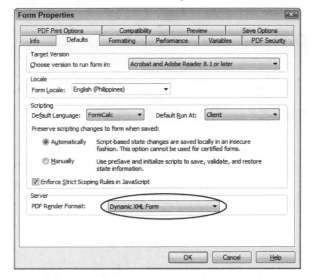

FIGURE 27.43

Choose Interactive Form and open the data file to use with this form.

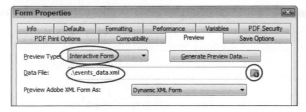

5. **Save the file.**

6. **Import the data.** Open the file in Acrobat and choose Forms ➪ Manage Form Data ➪ Import Data. Select the XML file from the book's CD-ROM and open it. If you performed all steps correctly your form should appear as you see in Figure 27.44.

FIGURE 27.44

The final form after importing data

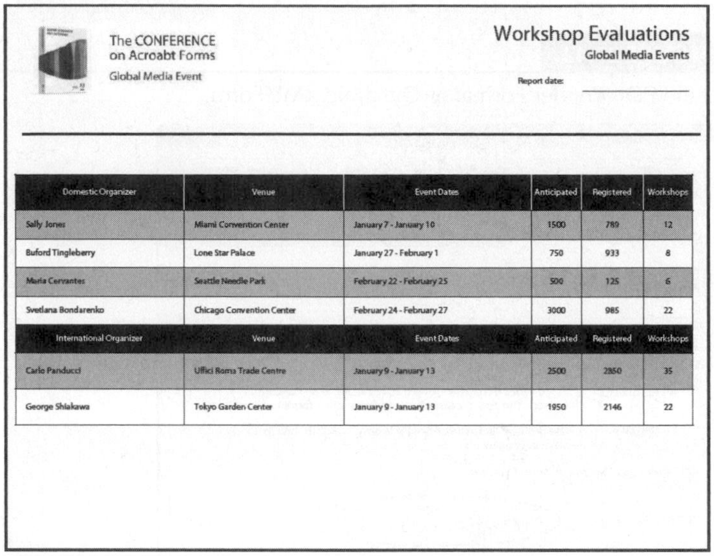
The CONFERENCE
on Acroabt Forms
Global Media Event

Workshop Evaluations
Global Media Events
Report date:

Domestic Organizer	Venue	Event Dates	Anticipated	Registered	Workshops
Sally Jones	Miami Convention Center	January 7 - January 10	1500	789	12
Buford Tingleberry	Lone Star Palace	January 27 - February 1	750	933	8
Maria Cervantes	Seattle Needle Park	February 22 - February 25	500	125	6
Svetlana Bondarenko	Chicago Convention Center	February 24 - February 27	3000	985	22
International Organizer	Venue	Event Dates	Anticipated	Registered	Workshops
Carlo Panducci	Uffici Roma Trade Centre	January 9 - January 13	2500	2850	35
George Shiakawa	Tokyo Garden Center	January 9 - January 13	1950	2146	22

NOTE **While in Designer you can click the PDF Preview tab to preview the form. In many cases the preview you see will be exactly the same as when opening the form in Acrobat. However, in some circumstances you won't see the exact same view when opening the file in Acrobat as when clicking the PDF Preview button. For your final test, be sure to open the file in Acrobat and test the data before you plan to use the final version of the form.**

Debugging problems

Every form author's dream is to get it all right the first time. Unfortunately, this is a rare occasion. We encounter problems designing complex forms in Designer about as often as you do. If you follow all the steps to create a form as shown in Figure 27.44 and you don't produce the same result, you need to diagnose the form for problems and double check the settings.

First, make a copy of the form in Designer by choosing File ➪ Save As and save the file under a new name. If you change a lot of items, you may want to return to the original form and start over or use some alternatives for making changes.

The most common problems you'll encounter with the form shown in Figure 27.44 are that you may see only one data row appearing under the first header row or you may find that the form looks okay when opened in Acrobat but the data don't import on the form. Another problem you may find is that when the data are imported only one section of data is imported under the first header row.

If these problems exist, the first items to check are the field and tag names. Open the data file in an XML editor like XML Notepad and look over the names used in the XML file. You need to be certain all the names for the Table item, the header rows, and the rows are the same as the same items in the Hierarchy palette. In addition, check all the field names and be certain they are identical to the field names in the Hierarchy palette.

The next area to examine is the Binding tab for all the items where we adjusted the binding properties. Be certain that the binding is set properly for all the fields. Table 27.1 provides a summary of the items we addressed in the Hierarchy palette.

TABLE 27.1

Properties Summary

Item	Palette	Tab	Properties Settings
(untitled Subform) (page 1)	Object	Subform	Flowed
Table 1 (first item below the untitled Subform)	Object	Binding	None
Table 1 (second Table1 in Hierarchy palette)	Object	Binding	Repeat check box off
HeaderRow	Object	Binding	None
HeaderRow2	Object	Binding	Normal
Row1 (and all fields nested below the heading)	Object	Binding	Normal
Row1 only	Object	Binding	Repeat Row for Each Data Item (checked) plus Min Count (checked)
Row2 (and all fields nested below the heading)	Object	Binding	Normal
Row2 only	Object	Binding	Repeat Row for Each Data Item (checked) plus Min Count (checked)

After you've checked the fields and tag names and verified all settings are as shown in Table 1, review the options we discussed related to setting the Form Properties. Review each property choice and make sure your settings match the steps in the section "Adjusting Form Properties."

If you still encounter problems, you may have just one field name misspelled, a tag name not spelled correctly, or maybe just one setting that makes you think that the Adobe engineers in Ottawa goofed up the program. Realize that the mistake is most likely yours, and perhaps one small oversight is the root of the problem. Step away from the situation, relax a little, and then come back and review your settings. When we first created the form shown in Figure 27.44 Ted contacted Angie in complete frustration because the data wasn't flowing into the form. Angie suggested reviewing the Form Properties but that didn't resolve the problem. What we both missed was that Ted saved the form as a Static Form on the first design. He forgot to save the form as a Dynamic Form. That one problem took quite a bit of time because neither of us thought that something so simple would be missed. Little oversights like this can be missed more often than the major changes you apply to field properties.

We reiterate that the form designs we created in this chapter were used for a known maximum number of records that can be added to a single page form. You have many more options available in Designer for flowing data across multiple pages, flowing headers and footers together with data on multiple pages, adding buttons to spawn new rows for something like a purchase order form, and other types of dynamic instances you want to add to your forms.

All of the options you have for creating tables to flow across multiple pages and adding buttons to spawn new fields are part of subforms, which is the subject of the next chapter. Turn the page to learn more about tables, subforms, and adding dynamic features to your forms.

Summary

- You use the Table ↪ Insert Table menu command to create a table in Designer.
- You open the Table Assistant by checking the Create Table Using Assistant check box in the Insert table dialog box.
- When using PDF backgrounds you are limited to creating static tables.
- Dynamic tables automatically add field objects according to the amount of data imported on a form.
- Field objects can be added to a form by binding the form to a data file and dragging the imported field objects from the Data View palette to the form.
- XML files can be edited in an XML Editor. You can view tags and field names in XML files by opening the files in an XML Editor, a text editor, a Web browser, or Microsoft Word.
- You add sections to tables in the Table Assistant.
- When creating dynamic tables without binding data to a form, you need to carefully review all the binding attributes as you add field objects to a form.
- You must set the binding attributes for tables, header rows, and rows to precise settings to flow data on a form.
- You must choose Flowed for the Content in a subform to flow data introduced in a dynamic form.
- You need to set certain Form Properties to make your form dynamic.
- Forms must be saved as Dynamic forms to import data from an XML file.

Chapter 28

Working with Subforms

IN THIS CHAPTER

Creating subforms

Understanding positioned and flowed content types

Using the Instance Manager

Testing and previewing dynamic forms

Most forms have groups of related items organized into sections to facilitate the form recipient completing the document. Grouping the related items visually is a good start. Physically creating subforms during the design process allows you to control many additional features.

Subforms are more than groups. In Designer groups are only used to format and align objects. Subforms are organizational containers that are useful for both static and dynamic forms. Subforms are used to create flowing dynamic layouts, control the tab sequence, and are used for data binding. Subforms properties specify if a page break is allowed within the subform area, which of the master pages content areas it is to be placed in, defining header and footer areas around the subform, and if the subform repeats, just to name a few.

Subforms are what make dynamic forms that grow and shrink possible in Designer. They are the containers that keep the objects inside them positioned correctly as the form adjusts. Subforms can be hidden until needed by the form recipient, creating a truly customized interactive experience for the user.

As we discussed in the previous Designer chapters, taking the time to name objects and organize them is vital to working efficiently in Designer. Each object must have a logical name and related objects are organized into subforms.

In this chapter we explore the benefits of using subforms in both static and dynamic form design. We discuss the subform properties necessary for effective subform use.

Creating Subforms

Every form has at least one subform. Designer creates this initial subform for you. It is the untitled page subform you see in the hierarchy each time you start a new form. The default subform size is set to match the content area of the master page. On a portrait letter size page the content measures 8 inches wide by 10.5 inches high, leaving you with a .25 inch margin on all four sides.

You can place a subform inside another subform and nest them. This is common practice. Usually the page subform is not altered in size and is left to match the content area. Additional subforms are added to control the position and flow of the remaining document. However, we don't want you to go overboard and add subforms where they aren't necessary. Having too many subforms can reduce a form's performance. Figure 28.1 shows the logical groups the form fits into. The form has been designed with section headings followed by the related form field objects.

An application form with section headings

Looking at the form hierarchy, as shown in Figure 28.2, we see all of the form's objects in a long list. We will not be very efficient finding objects in this disorganized list.

The hierarchy of the application form prior to adding subforms

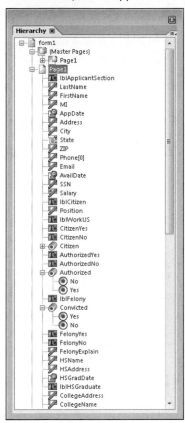

Some form designers create the subforms before placing any fields on the page. Other designers lay out the form and then decide which form objects belong together in subforms. Having an idea of how the form will look before you begin is helpful when adding subforms before adding the fields. If you are building a form from scratch and still determining how it is to be laid out, it is best to add the subforms after the design is set. Use the method that works best for you when adding subforms.

Placing subforms before adding content

The subform object is stored in the standard group of the Object Library. Adding a subform from the Standard library to the design page is just like adding other objects from the library. You can use your favorite technique including stamping, drag and drop, or drawing the subform.

CROSS-REF For details on how to add fields to the design page, see Chapter 24.

When you drag or stamp a subform on the design page its dimensions are set at 3.937 inches wide by 1.9685 inches high. You almost certainly need to resize this to suit your needs. Resize the subform using the layout palette or by dragging the handles on the design page.

When placing subforms before adding additional content to the form, pay close attention to the subform indicators as shown in Figure 28.3. The indicators appear as triangles when dragging objects into a subform, marking the four corners of the subform to assist in placing objects inside the boundaries.

FIGURE 28.3

The subform boundary indicators

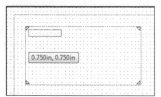

Compare the subform indicators in Figure 28.3 to Figure 28.4. Notice that the object is being placed below the nested subform, and the indicators appear in the corner of the page subform. Don't worry if you have difficulty placing objects inside a subform. The objects can be moved in or out of the subforms as necessary. Even the subforms can be removed and recreated if needed. Objects can also be repositioned using the Hierarchy palette. Drag a field and drop it on a subform name to place it inside that subform.

FIGURE 28.4

An object being placed in the outer subform

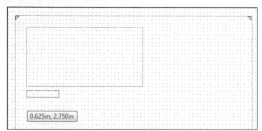

Adding subforms after adding content

After you have created the form design you are ready to organize the contents into subform containers. When adding subforms around existing objects, the process is called wrapping in a subform. When you wrap objects in a subform, the dimensions of the selected objects determine the subform size. This can be a huge time-saving feature if the intent is to tightly wrap the objects. If the form design is complete, this produces ideal results. However, if you are not finished with the form design and plan to add a few more objects, then resizing the subform may be necessary.

Let's look at how we might polish up the form shown earlier in Figure 28.2 by wrapping objects in a subform. To do so, follow these steps.

ON the CD-ROM The form you see in Figures 28.1 and 28.2 is included on the CD-ROM. For the following steps we use the GF*ApplicationNoSubforms.xdp* file from the Chapter28 folder on the book's CD-ROM.

STEPS: Wrapping Objects in a Subform

1. **Open a form.** We'll open the *GFApplicationNoSubforms.xdp* from the CD-ROM in Chapter 28.

2. **Select all objects to be grouped in to the subform.** If working with the *GFApplicationNoSubforms.xdp* file from the CD-ROM select all of the objects in the Applicant information section. Using the Hierarchy palette start the selection with the Section name (lblApplicantSection) and end with the text field for explaining a felony (FelonyExplain). Trying to select the objects on the design page with a marquee can be difficult because the objects are closely spaced together.

3. Right-click one of the selected objects. This opens the context menu of options.

TIP Wrap in Subform is found in the right-click menu when the mouse is over the selected objects in the design page or the hierarchy. It is also located in the Insert Menu and the Hierarchy palette menu.

4. **Choose Wrap in Subform.** As shown in Figure 28.5, this inserts a subform the same size as the collective object set and places the selected objects inside the new subform.

5. **Rename the subform.** Be sure to give the subform a name that makes sense to you. We named the new subform ApplicantInfo.

TIP Naming a subform follows the same rules as naming other objects. Objects must start with a letter, no spaces are allowed, and the name can contain numbers. Only a few special characters are allowed: a dash, an underscore, and a period. Special characters are highly discouraged because they have special meanings when scripting. Adding special characters in your field names complicates the script needed to refer to those objects.

FIGURE 28.5

The context menu when wrapping in a subform

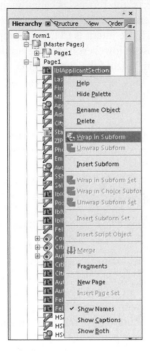

6. **Repeat these steps for the Education section.** Start with the HSName field and continue through the OtherDegree field.

7. **Save a copy of the form.** Save the form in a location of your choice on your computer. We continue to use this form in the next section. You may continue working on this copy of the file, or choose to open another sample from the CD-ROM for the next set of steps.

We have found that both methods are useful depending on the current layout. Wrapping in a subform is the method we choose to use most often, as it reduces the time needed to resize all of the subforms. Be careful when adding additional objects. If there is not enough empty space inside the subform boundaries, you need to resize it. Getting the subform handles selected when tightly wrapped around objects can be tricky. Therefore, using the Hierarchy palette to select the subform is the best practice to avoid accidentally selecting objects inside the subform.

Setting subform properties

Subforms properties affect how subforms are handled by Designer both at design time and runtime. The Object palette contains most of the settings we discuss in this section. Many of these properties apply to both static and dynamic forms, while a few apply only to dynamic layouts.

CROSS-REF For more information on design time versus runtime, see Chapter 29.

Understanding positioned and flowed content areas

One of the most important settings for subforms is the content type, as shown in Figure 28.6. Positioned and flowed layouts can be used in both static and dynamic forms. Flowed layouts are generally reserved for use with dynamic form design, but not always. The fact that the property has been changed to Flowed does not make your form dynamic. Many additional items must be properly configured before a document can change dynamically at runtime.

CROSS-REF For more information on creating dynamic forms, see Chapter 26.

FIGURE 28.6

The Subform tab of the Object palette shows the Content property.

The Content property determines how the objects in the subform are displayed, either positioned based on their coordinates or flowed by Designer into the next available location. When objects are added to the design page, they have coordinates that are stored in the Layout palette. The coordinates are subjective to the subform they are placed in. If a subform is set to Positioned, the coordinates are respected relative to the boundaries of the subform. If the subform position changes, the objects contained in the subform are also moved. Their new coordinates are determined by their relative position inside the subform.

In Figure 28.7 the three objects each have specific coordinates and are wrapped in a positioned subform. Let's focus on the Date/Time field coordinates: X = 2.125 in and Y = 1.25 in, which is where we placed them initially. When the subform is moved to a new location, the text field also moves but maintains its relative distance from the subform as shown in Figure 28.7.

FIGURE 28.7

The original Date/Time field coordinates in a positioned subform

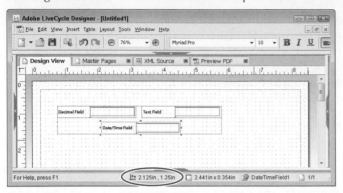

In Figure 28.8 the three objects were not moved individually to the new location; the subform was moved. The new coordinates of the Date/Time field are: X = 2.123 in and Y = 2.123 in.

FIGURE 28.8

The Date/Time field's new coordinates after the positioned subform was moved

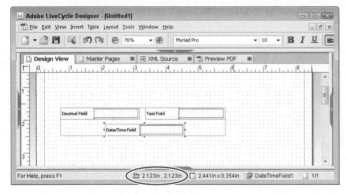

If a subform's Content property is set to Flowed, the coordinates are no longer utilized. Designer places each object in the next available position. Flowed documents can be top to bottom or Western Text. Top to bottom moves each object up and to the left until it touches the object above it. The objects flow in the form from top to bottom with no spaces between them. Figure 28.9 shows the same three objects' new locations after we set the Content property to Flowed with a top to bottom direction.

Notice how the objects all moved up and to the left within the subform. The subform height also changed to accommodate the objects' new positions. Opening the layout palette for any of the objects in the flowed subform gives the same results. They have height and width measurements but the coordinates are no longer stored, as shown in Figure 28.10.

FIGURE 28.9

The Date/Time field position after Flowed Top to Bottom

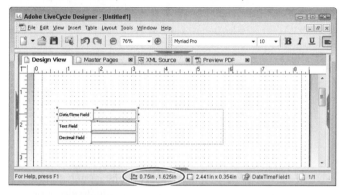

FIGURE 28.10

The Layout palette for an object in a flowed subform

It is important to point out that the Date/Time field was below the other two fields in the original positioned objects, as shown in Figure 28.7. In both of the flowed examples the Date/Time field is the first object in the subform, as shown in Figures 28.9 and 28.10. When using a positioned subform, the order in which the fields are listed in the hierarchy is irrelevant to their position on the page most of the time. However, a flowed form positions the objects based on their order in the hierarchy. This caused the date field to become the first field in the subform, as the hierarchy shows in Figure 28.11.

> **TIP**   The only situation where hierarchy position is a concern in a positioned form is when objects overlap each other and a stacking order must be determined. The object's position in the hierarchy determines the stacking order. The first object added is at the top of the hierarchy and is at the bottom of the stacking order.

FIGURE 28.11

The hierarchy determines the object order in a flowed subform.

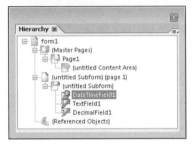

Western Text flows left to right. Designer takes each object and positions it immediately to the right of the previous object until it runs out of room in the content area on the right side. When no more room is available to the right, the objects continue below the existing objects and lay out in a left-to-right direction. The date field in our example is still the first object, but the other two objects move to new positions as shown in Figure 28.12 after the subform is set to Western Text.

FIGURE 28.12

The Date/Time field after flowing as Western Text

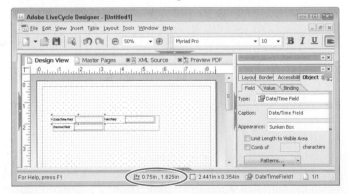

As we mentioned previously, flowed layouts are usually reserved for forms that are rendered in a dynamic layout. However, they can be used in a static layout as a shortcut to positioning objects. Have you ever needed to remove all of the spaces between a set of fields? Placing them in a subform with the correct flowed direction can do just that.

Setting the pagination options

When the subform is set to positioned content, many of the remaining properties are disabled in the Object palette. One that is still active seems to generate some confusion. The Subform tab provides a check box to allow page breaks within content, as shown in Figure 28.6. This may seem strange, so consider the following scenario: The subform is set to positioned, and we placed it where we wanted it on the page. There should be no question as to whether or not we want to allow a page break, right? Wrong. A positioned subform can be nested in a flowed subform. If the outer flowing subform pushes the positioned subform near a page break, should the content be allowed to split across two pages? Again, if your form is not designed to be dynamic you can safely ignore this option.

CROSS-REF For more information on nested subforms, see the section "Nesting Subforms" later in this chapter.

The remaining pagination options, as shown in Figure 28.13, can be found on the Pagination tab of the Object palette. These settings are restricted to a flowed subform or a positioned subform nested inside a flowed subform.

FIGURE 28.13

The Pagination tab of the Object palette

The options on the pagination tab of the object palette include:

- **Place:** This option determines where the initial subform will be laid out. Even though a subform is created in the design view of the form with other subforms above and/or below it, this does not mean it has to render in that position at runtime. Changing this setting allows you to customize the subform placement. Placement options are flexible in allowing you to choose either the content area (regardless of the page) or the page where you want the subform to be positioned as shown in Figure 28.14.

■ **Following Previous:** This is the default setting. It treats the subform just the way it was created on the design page. The subform follows the previous object in the parent subform of the hierarchy.

The Subform Place options

■ **In Content Area:** You must choose the content area by name. Use this setting when you want to place the subform within a specific content area. Remember that content areas are defined only on the master pages. Placing in a content area is very useful for columnar layouts. The subform is placed after any existing items already in the content area.

■ **Top of Next Content Area:** Without having to name the content area, you want Designer to find the next content area and place this subform at the top of it.

■ **Top of Content Area:** You must choose the content area by name. Use this option when you want the subform placed at the top of the content area instead of after the existing items.

■ **On Page:** You must specify the page number. This option places the subform on the specified page and creates a page break if one does not occur naturally.

■ **Top of Next Page:** Designer finds the top of the next page, without you specifying the specific number. This option also generates a page break if needed.

■ **Top of Page:** You specify the page number and Designer places the content at the top of the page, generating a page break if necessary.

The next four options are available only if the master page set has the printing property set to Print on Front Side Only, Print on Both Sides. Printing on the front side only or both sides is supported only in Acrobat 8.1 and later. The default setting for the master page set is Page Occurrence. Occurrence allows you to determine how many times a master page is used.

■ **On Odd Page:** Designer places the subform on pages that print on odd numbers only, with other content if any already exist.

■ **Top of Next Odd Page:** Designer places the subform on the top of the next odd-numbered page generating a page break and a blank page if needed.

■ **On Even Page:** Designer places the subform on pages that print on even numbers only, with other content if any already exist.

■ **Top of Next Even Page:** Designer places the subform on the top of the next even-numbered page generating a page break and a blank page if needed.

CROSS-REF For information on how to configure master pages to allow odd and even placement see Chapter 25.

■ **Keep With Previous:** Keep this subform together with the previous subform. Do not allow a page break between the two subforms. If one subform is pushed to the next page, they both move to the next page.

■ **Keep With Next:** Keep this subform together with the next subform. Do not allow a page break between the two subforms. If one subform is pushed to the next page, they both move to the next page.

■ **After:** After this subform has been placed in the form design, this setting determines what section should be filled next. Much like the options for setting initial placement, the after options include page area or content area choices as shown in Figure 28.15.

FIGURE 28.15

The subform After options

■ **Continue Filling Parent:** This is the default setting. It treats the remaining subforms just the way they were created on the design page. After this subform is placed Designer returns to the parent subform in the hierarchy to continue filling content. The subform's parent container is the next highest subform in the Hierarchy palette, as shown in Figure 28.16.

FIGURE 28.16

An example of parent/child relationships in the Hierarchy palette

Page 1 — Parent

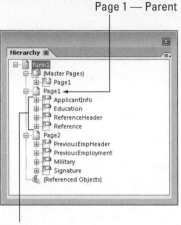

Children

- **Go to Next Content Area:** After this subform is placed, continue placing objects in the next content area.

- **Go to Content Area:** You must name the content area that is filled after this subform is placed.

- **Go to Next Page:** After this subform is placed, continue placing objects on the next page in the form.

- **Go to Page:** After this subform is placed, continue placing objects in the page you specified.

- **Go to Next Odd Page:** After this subform is placed, continue placing objects on the next odd page in the form. This option is available only if the master page set is configured for odd and even placement.

- **Go to Next Even Page:** After this subform is placed, continue placing objects on the next even page in the form. This option is available only if the master page set is configured for odd and even placement.

- **Conditional Breaks:** The number indicates how many conditional breaks are in the document. Set conditional breaks with the Edit button. Use this option to prevent widow and orphans in a table, for example. You can create a conditional break if there is only one body row on the first page of the table; insert a page break before the table header. Conditional breaks are also used to separate data by values in subform sets to manipulate the data set so it appears in a predetermined order. The Edit Conditional Break dialog box is shown in Figure 28.17.

FIGURE 28.17

The Edit Conditional Breaks dialog box

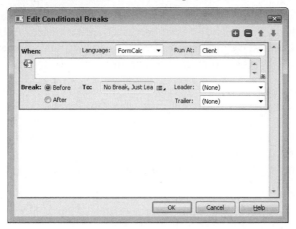

- **Overflow:** If the subform spans a page break, these settings determine how the remaining content is placed in the form:
  - **None:** Designer starts filling the next page because no overflow placement was specified.
  - **Go to Content Area:** Specify the content area name where you want the overflow information placed.
  - **Go To Page:** Specify the page where you want the overflow information placed.
- **Overflow Leader:** If the subform spans a page break, you can specify another subform as a repeating header (leader).
  - **Subform Name:** Specify the subform you want used as a repeating leader if the subform spans a page break.
  - **None:** No repeating leader is used.
  - **New:** Designer allows you to create a new subform and set it to be the repeating leader.
- **Overflow Trailer:** If the subform spans a page break, you can specify another subform as a repeating footer (trailer).
  - **Subform Name:** You specify the subform name you want to use as a repeating trailer if the subform spans a page break.
  - **None:** No repeating trailer is used.
  - **New:** Designer allows you to create a new subform and set it to be the repeating trailer.

Adding headers (overflow leaders) and footers (overflow trailers) to subforms

In a dynamic form, headers and footers are very important elements to consider when creating subforms. In Designer these are called overflow leaders and overflow trailers. If the form always remains static these are unnecessary. Overflow leaders and overflow trailers are used to specify what happens when the repeating subform spans a page break.

In the application we have been working on, the applicant information, education, and the signature sections have a limited amount of data being requested. However, in the remaining sections the amount of data input can vary according to the form recipient's personal history. To make these sections dynamic we should separate the section bar from the fields inside the section to allow the areas to be controlled independently. The shaded section bar becomes the overflow leader. It does not repeat every time we add a section, but it repeats if the section grows beyond the current page.

Compare the image in Figure 28.18 where the subform was not set up with overflow leaders and Figure 28.19 where the subform was set up with an overflow leader.

FIGURE 28.18

The colored section bar is repeating unnecessarily

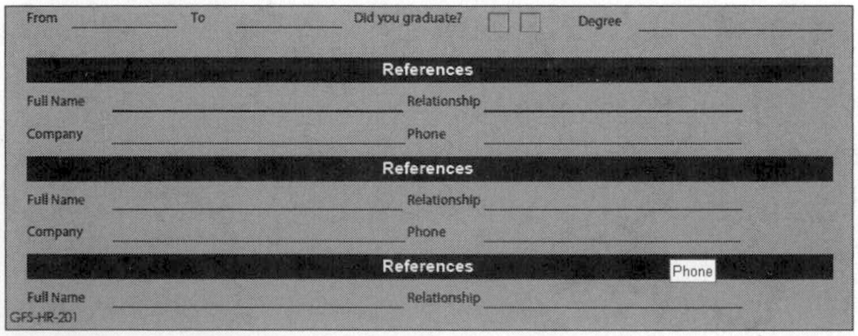

FIGURE 28.19

The colored section bar is appearing only once above the section

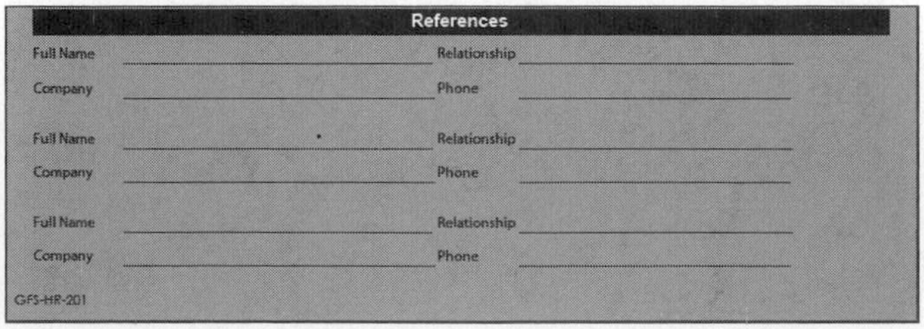

Setting up the overflow leaders and trailers requires changing only a few settings after the subforms have been created. The properties are stored in the Pagination Tab of the Object palette. We begin by creating the subforms for the reference sections and then adjust the overflow settings.

STEPS: Setting Up a Subform with an Overflow Leader

1. **Open a Form.** If you completed the steps Wrapping Objects in a Subform, you can continue using the file you saved. If not open the *GFApplicationOverflow.xdp* file from the Chapter28 folder on the book's CD-ROM.

2. **Select the References Section Bar.** The object name is lblReferenceSection in the hierarchy.

3. **Right-click the selected object.** This opens the context menu.

4. **Choose Wrap in Subform.** This inserts a subform the same size as the collective object set and places the selected objects inside the new subform.

5. **Rename the subform ReferenceHeader.** This name is how we refer to the overflow header.

6. **Select all the objects in the References section.** Start with the ReferenceName and continue through the Phone field. Notice there is only one set of fields in the form's References section. We need to set additional dynamic properties that allow this section to repeat as many times as we need.

7. **Right-click one of the selected objects.** This opens the context menu of options.

8. **Choose Wrap in Subform.** This inserts a subform the same size as the collective object set and places the selected objects inside the new subform. Notice the size of this subform does not extend the width of the page. The previous subforms extend to the page width because of the section name, which we did not include this time.

9. **Rename the subform Reference.** Notice that the remaining sections of the form have already been wrapped in subforms. This allows us to move on to the next step more quickly. If you'd like to build them yourself, right-click a subform and unwrap the subforms to proceed on your own. After you complete this step your form hierarchy should look similar to Figure 28.20.

10. **Resize the Reference subform.** We want the subform to be the width of the design page. Select the right handle and drag to the right edge. Or, select the Layout palette and increase the width to 9.5 inches.

11. **Save a copy of the form.** Save the form in a location of your choice on your computer. This step is very important. You always should save a copy of the form before changing the layout to flowed in case you encounter anything unusual and need to get back to the previous layout. Flowing the document can change far more than you realize. We recommend saving the form with a notation like GFApplicationbeforeFlowed. Even if you never need this extra file, it is better to know it is there.

FIGURE 28.20

The collapsed view of the application hierarchy

> **TIP**   All objects need to be wrapped in subforms prior to changing the main page form to flowed. Failing to do so results in objects moving extensively on the form design page. You can undo the flowed layout if you catch the misplaced objects soon enough. Double-check your form before changing the Content Type to Flowed.

12. **Select the Page1 subform.** Overflow leaders and trailers are allowed only in flowed documents. We need to change the Content Type of this subform to Flowed.

13. **Open the Subform Tab of the Object palette.** This is where the subform Content Type is stored.

14. **Change the Content Type to Flowed.** This causes any gaps between the subforms in the design page to be removed. The subforms now touch each other on the design page. If you need space between the subforms, add the blank space to a positioned subform.

15. **Verify the direction is Top to Bottom.** This is the default setting when changing the Content Type to Flowed.

16. **Select the Reference Subform.** We need to turn on the dynamics of this section. We start by setting the repeat for each data item then continue with setting the overflow leader properties.

17. **Open the Binding tab of the Object palette.** We need to allow the subform to repeat.

18. **Turn on Repeat Subform for Each Data Item.** Notice the minimum is set to 1 by default, but there are no maximum or initial numbers provided.

19. **Set the Minimum, Maximum, and Initial Values.** We want to prompt the form recipient to complete three references. We choose to not restrict them from adding a few more. Set the initial count of 3 and a maximum of 5. You also may choose to change the minimum number to 3 if desired. Our binding settings are shown in Figure 28.21.

CROSS-REF The settings we create here are fixed and don't allow the person filling in the form to change them. We create buttons later in this chapter to give control back to the form recipient. See the section "Creating User-Controlled Dynamic Forms" later in this chapter for details.

FIGURE 28.21

The Binding Tab properties of the Reference subform

20. **Open the Pagination Tab of the Object palette.** The Pagination tab allows you to decide where the subform should be placed initially and what to do if it spans a page break.

21. **Set the ReferenceHeader as the overflow leader.** If the references span a page break, this tells Designer to repeat the colored section bar at the top of the overflowed area. The Pagination tab should match Figure 28.22.

FIGURE 28.22

The Pagination Tab of the Object palette

22. **Select the Subform Tab of the Object palette.** We want the references to flow onto page 2 if necessary. However, we do not want a page break within a reference.

23. **Deselect Allow Page Breaks within Content.** This prevents page breaks within an instance of the References section. Because the page subform allows page breaks, this option allows a break to occur between instances of the references subform.

24. **Select the ReferenceHeader Section from the Hierarchy palette.** We want to ensure that if the content above the References sections grows or changes, a page break near the beginning of the References section does not cause the header bar to appear by itself at the bottom of a page. We always want the header bar to appear with the first reference.

25. **Open the Pagination Tab of the Object palette.** In the place settings we need to verify the ReferenceHeader is not separated from the References section.

26. **Select the Keep With Next option.** This ensures a page break does not occur between the header and first instance of the References section.

27. **Save a copy of the form.** Save the form in a location of your choice on your computer. We recommend naming it with the word flowed for clarity until after all the design work has been completed. We'll name our form *GFApplicationFlowed.xdp*. You may continue working on this copy of the file, or choose to open another sample from the CD-ROM for the next set of steps.

Previewing a dynamic form

Testing the form requires that we check a few additional settings before proceeding. Setting a form's Content Type to Flowed is only part of the process to making a dynamic form. Next we check the following form settings:

- **The form is saved either as an XDP or a dynamic XML form:** If the form has been saved as a static PDF, the flowing layout does not work properly. To check this setting select File ⇨ Save As from the menu. They keyboard shortcut for save as is Ctrl + Shift + S. Verify the form is either an XDP or a Dynamic XML form. The Save As window is shown in Figure 28.23.

NOTE   The Save As choices changed in each of the recent version updates of Designer. If your settings do not match the dialog box in Figure 28.23 you need to select a setting for a dynamic type form. For the purposes of this example, select any dynamic version number available in the Save As options.

- **The Preview Format allows dynamic content:** A form can be saved as a dynamic compatible type, but the preview still treats it as a static form. Check this setting by choosing File ⇨ Form Properties.
  - **Select the Preview Tab in the Properties window:** The Preview Type must be Interactive Form. Set Preview Adobe XML Form As to Dynamic XML Form if you save your files as XDP formats. Verify that your settings match Figure 28.24.

FIGURE 28.23

The Save As options in Designer 8.2

FIGURE 28.24

Preview tab settings

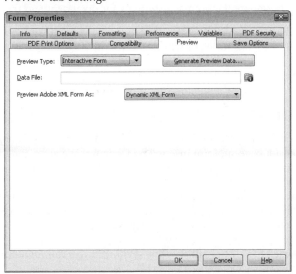

ON the CD-ROM The starting file (*GFApplicationFlowed.xdp*) and completed file (*GFApplication.xdp*) used in the "Preview a Dynamic Form" steps can be found in the Chapter28 folder on the CD-ROM.

STEPS: Verify Dynamic Properties and Preview a Dynamic Form

1. **Open a Form.** If you completed the steps "Setting Up a Subform with an Overflow Leader," you can continue using your saved file. If not, you can jump in here by opening the *GFApplicationFlowed.xdp* file in the Chapter28 folder on the CD-ROM.

2. **Go to File ⇨ Save As.** Verify the form is saved as Dynamic XML Form (*.pdf) or an XML Form (*.xdp) format. If necessary resave the file with one of these formats.

3. **Choose File ⇨ Form Properties and click the Preview Tab.** Because we are previewing from within Designer, we need to verify the preview performs dynamically:

   - Set the Preview Type to be Interactive Form.
   - Set the Preview Adobe XML As to Dynamic XML Form.

4. **Press OK to save the Form Properties.**

5. **Select the Preview PDF tab (F5).** If all the preceding settings have been correctly set, your form displays with three reference sections at the bottom of page 1. If the form does not have enough room for all three sections on page 1 and an instance of the references spills onto page 2, the page break is between references.

6. **Return to Design View.** If there were any unexpected results in the preview, then go back and double-check the steps above. If you continue to have trouble, try opening the sample files and compare the settings between your document and the samples.

7. **Save your form.** We'll save our form as *GFApplicationFlowed.xdp*. You may continue working on this copy of the file, or choose to open another sample from the CD-ROM when we continue working on this document in the steps for creating user-controlled dynamic buttons.

Nesting subforms

Technically we nested subforms in the previous section, because we wrapped objects in subforms and never altered the default page subform inserted by Designer. We are going to take a brief break from our application while we look at other documents that use nesting subforms.

Figure 28.25 shows a purchase order whose subforms are already set up with the fields grouped into logical sections. The sections across the top of the form are Requestor, Accounting, and Vendor; followed by the Items Table, Totals Table, and Signatures.

ON the CD-ROM The purchase order forms used in this section can be found in the Chapter28 folder of the CD-ROM.

This purchase order would not work well in a top-to-bottom flow with the current arrangement of subforms. The requestor information would be above the accounting information as shown in Figure 28.26. To get the form to respond the way we want it to, we need to either change the flowed direction or some additional subforms to control the position of some objects.

FIGURE 28.25

The Purchase Order form with a static layout

FIGURE 28.26

The existing purchase order design when changed to flowed layout

We do not want the top three sections to flow top to bottom, even though we want the rest of the form to do so. To prevent that from happening we need to wrap the top three subforms in another larger static subform. You might be wondering why we wrapped the three sections in smaller subforms to begin with. Why not take all of the objects at the top of the form and wrap them in a single subform to start? As we discussed in Chapter 22, default tab order works left to right then top to bottom. If we had a single subform at the top of this purchase order the tab sequence would not be logical for the person completing the form.

CROSS-REF   For more information on adjusting tab order in Designer, see Chapter 25. For default tab order behavior see Chapter 22.

Our intent is to create a form with flowed content, top-to-bottom direction, and the correct tab order maintained in the finished form. Once we have the top three subforms maintaining their respective positions we need to alter the single table row to become a dynamic table.

ON the CD-ROM   To follow these steps, use the *PurchaseOrder_Start.xdp* form from the Chapter28 folder on the book's CD-ROM.

STEPS: Nesting Subforms to Position Objects

1. **Open a form.** We opened the *GFPurchaseOrderStart.xdp* from the book's CD-ROM.

2. **Select the subforms to be nested in another subform.** We selected the Requestor, Accounting, and Vendor subforms in the Hierarchy palette. These are the objects we don't want moved when we flow the page subform.

CAUTION   Wrapping objects in another subform can cause calculations and scripts that have been written using relative syntax to fail. You need to double-check that all scripts and calculations work properly after adding subforms. The formulas in our purchase order were written with these changes in mind and continue to work.

CROSS-REF   For more information on using calculation scripts in Designer, see Chapter 29.

3. **Wrap the objects in a subform.** We right-clicked on a selected subform in the hierarchy and chose Wrap in Subform from the context menu. Notice in the Subform tab in the Object palette shows the content is positioned. This ensures the objects don't move inside the subform when the page subform is flowed. Also notice the subform width is the same size as the collective objects you selected. This subform is almost as wide as the design page and prevents the objects from shifting to the left.

CROSS-REF   For more details on other subform creation methods, see the section "Creating Subforms" earlier in this chapter.

4. **Rename the subform.** Always take the time to name objects logically. We named our new subform TopSection.

> **NOTE** We are not using the Wrap in Subform method for the next example. When wrapping objects in a subform the subform size is always equal to the size of the collective objects. When you adjust the subform size, the objects inside shift position. For this situation we recommend adding a subform object and then moving the desired objects inside the subform.

5. **Add a subform object to the design page below the Items table.** We need to prevent some additional objects from being repositioned when the page is flowed. We do not want the Totals below the table to move to the left side of the form.

6. **Rename the subform.** We called our subform LowerSection. We need to extend the width of the TableTotals subform to match the width of the content area to ensure they do not shift to the left.

7. **Change the subform width to match the content area width.** Verify the LowerSection subform starts at an X coordinate of .25 inches and the width is 9.5 inches. We selected the subform and used the Layout palette to make the changes. Don't worry about the height of the subform right now. Forgetting to alter the subform width causes totals to shift to the left when the document is flowed as shown in Figures 28.27 and 28.28.

FIGURE 28.27

The LowerSection subform is not as wide as the content area.

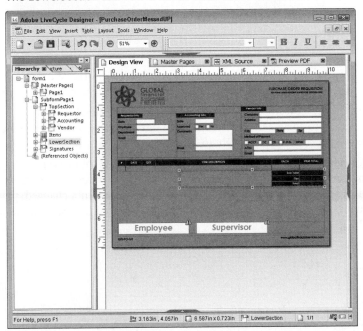

FIGURE 28.28

The Totals shifted to the left side because of the subform width.

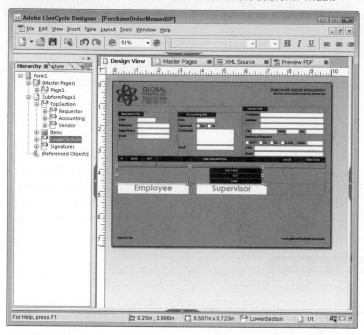

8. **Move the Totals Table into the LowerSection subform.** We used the Hierarchy palette to select the Totals Table and dragged it onto the LowerSection subform.

9. **Select the LowerSection subform and adjust the height.** Notice that the object height adjusted to enclose the table objects but did not reposition the table objects. We set the LowerSection subform height to .8 inches.

10. **Check the form hierarchy for subform order.** The subforms must be moved to the positions indicated in the Hierarchy palette. When we created the LowerSection subform, it was placed at the bottom of the Hierarchy palette. If not changed, the signatures appear above the LowerSection when the content is changed to flowed as shown in Figures 28.29 and 28.30.

FIGURE 28.29

The Hierarchy palette shows the Signature section above the LowerSection in our form.

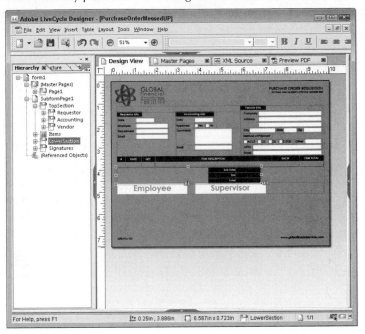

11. **Change the order of the subforms if necessary.** We needed to drag the LowerSection subform above the Signatures subform in the hierarchy.

12. **Save a copy of the form.** Always save your form before changing the subform Content Type to Flowed. Save the form in a location of your choice on your computer. We saved our form as *PurchaseOrderbeforeFlowed.xdp*.

13. **Set the Page subform to flowed content.** Select the SubformPage1 from the Hierarchy palette and open the Subform tab of the Object palette. Set the Content Type to Flowed. Leave the flow direction as Top to Bottom. Notice how the blank area between the subforms was removed, but the objects inside a positioned subform were not altered. Your form should look similar to Figure 28.31.

FIGURE 28.30

The form after flowing the document with the wrong order in the hierarchy

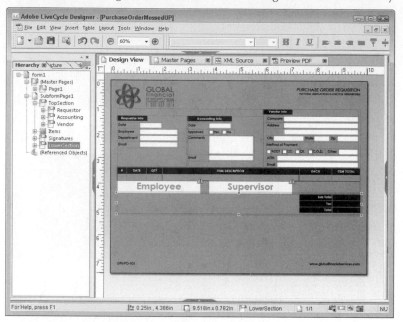

14. **Save a copy of the form.** Save the form in a location of your choice on your computer. We recommend naming it with the word *flowed* for clarity until after all the design work has been completed. We'll save our form as *GFPurchaseOrderFlowed.xdp*. We will continue to use this form in the next section. You may continue working on this copy of the file, or choose to open another sample from the CD-ROM for the next set of steps.

The Purchase Order form has been changed to a flowed content form. Why go to all that work, when we really don't want any of the objects to move? We are planning to turn Row1 of the table into a repeating subform that can adjust when we merge data with it, or when the form recipient is entering data they can adjust the number of desired rows.

The purchase order form after organizing in positioned and flowed subforms

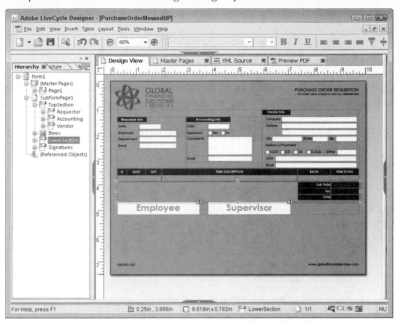

Using tables for dynamic subforms

Tables are frequently used in form design layouts because they provide structure and visual clarity to the form. In Designer tables are a specialized subform, which makes them ideal for repeating sections of a form. We will take the purchase order used in the previous section and allow the rows to repeat as needed for additional data. The process for making a table row repeat is the same as for a subform. Select the subform and change the binding to repeat for each data item.

CROSS-REF For more information on using tables in Designer, see Chapter 27.

By default a subform has a Content Type of Positioned, and the subform allows page breaks within the content area. We have already discussed those settings earlier in this chapter. It is important to understand that the table has those same default properties assigned to it. However, the rows within the table do not share those default properties. A table can have header rows, body rows, and footer rows. By default the setting to allow page breaks within the content area is not turned on for the rows within the table. These are optimal default settings, but worth noting before you begin to work with tables as repeating subforms.

ON the CD-ROM   To follow the next set of steps use the file saved from earlier steps or open the *PurchaseOrderFlowed.xdp* file from the Chapter28 folder on the book's CD-ROM.

STEPS: Setting a Table Row to Repeat

1. **Open a form.** We'll continue with the *GFPurchaseOrderFlowed.xdp* file from the previous steps. If you did not complete the previous set of steps you can open the *GFPurchaseOrderFlowed.xdp* form from the book's CD-ROM.

2. **Select the table row to be repeated.** We selected Row1 of the Items Table. Notice the Object palette already contains the Subform tab.

3. **Select the Binding Tab of the Object palette and turn on Repeat Row for Each Data Item.** Because our form was already set up for a flowed layout all we need to finish are the desired maximum value and initial counts.

4. **Set the Minimum, Maximum, and Initial Values.** We set an initial count of 5, left the minimum at 1, and did not specify a maximum value.

5. **Preview the Form.** Select the Preview PDF tab or press F5 on the keyboard to view your dynamic table. Verify that the form appears similar to Figure 28.32.

CROSS-REF   If your form does not show the additional table rows see the "Previewing a dynamic form" section earlier in this chapter.

6. **Save and close your form.**

We have created a form that is capable of adjusting dynamically based on data merged with the form. The form is also able to adjust the number of rows by changing the subform properties. We expand on this concept a little later in the chapter and give the user a button to adjust the number of rows while entering data.

FIGURE 28.32

The Purchase Order form with repeating table rows

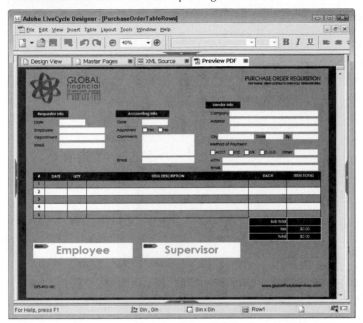

Creating dynamic expanding text fields

Having sections of a form that can grow and shrink dynamically (in both Acrobat and Adobe Reader) is one of the more powerful features and a big reason we enjoy designing forms in LiveCycle Designer. Sometimes a form is not as complicated as the samples used so far in this chapter. What if we need a comments page to attach several recipient comments to one of our forms? The comments page should use the same look and feel as our other forms. This means we need to include the header at the top, the form and page numbers at the bottom, and an area in the middle for comments, as shown in Figure 28.33.

ON the CD-ROM The Comments Page starting file and a completed version can be found in the Chapter29 folder on the book's CD-ROM.

FIGURE 28.33

A dynamic expanding text field

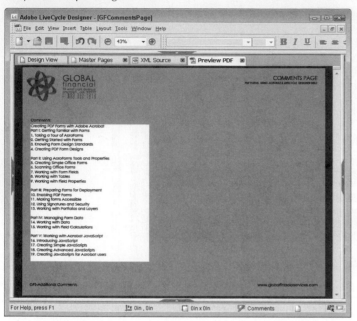

How do we create a form with a text field that grows instead of an entire subform? Although this example seems easier than the previous ones, it relies on the concepts covered earlier in this chapter. We begin with a basic Designer form with the default page subform set to positioned content and a regular text field as shown in Figure 28.34.

Notice the text field is not very tall. Without some property changes our comments form becomes a disaster. A default text field in Designer cannot handle more than a single line of text even if it is tall enough to hold many. As soon as the focus moves out of the text field, a plus sign appears in the lower-right corner to indicate that additional text cannot be displayed, as shown in Figure 28.35. The entire contents of the field are stored in the form data, but they cannot be displayed on the screen or in the printed document.

CROSS-REF For more information on formatting fields and setting field properties, see Chapter 25.

FIGURE 28.34

The beginning of our comments page

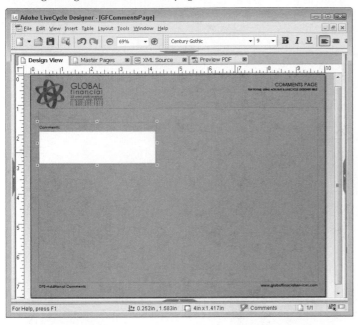

FIGURE 28.35

A text field clipping data in the display

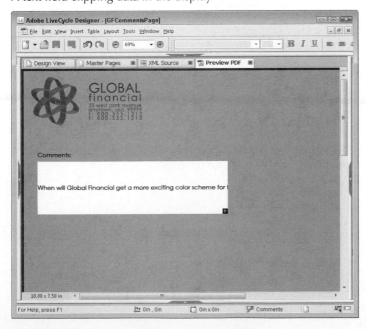

The first setting we need to discuss is the text field property: Allow Multiple Lines. Located in the Object palette, this check box allows the text to wrap within the available field space and produces a much better result for printed forms as shown in Figure 28.36.

A text field with Allow Multiple Lines selected

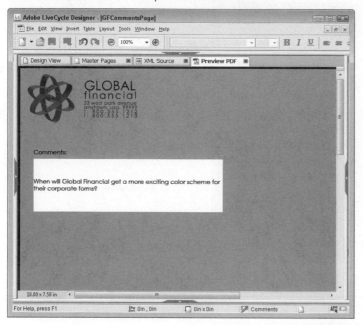

The problem remains when the form recipient enters more data than the field has room to display. The field reverts to showing the text field with the black plus sign in the lower-right corner of the field as shown in Figure 28.37. The improvement is apparent because we can see more than one line, but this solution does not meet our need for a growing text field for comments.

The second setting is the height of the field in the Layout palette. Turn on the Expand to fit check box and our form behaves more like what we wanted, as shown in Figure 28.38. Now our problem is at the bottom of the page where the content runs over the edge.

FIGURE 28.37

A text field with Allow Multiple Lines clipping data

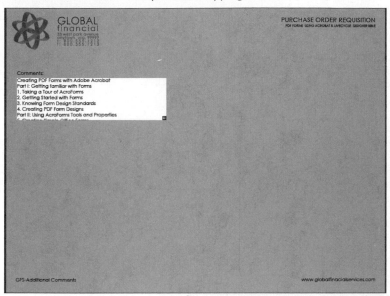

The third setting is the page subform type. It is still set to Positioned content (the default) and the text fields are set to Expand to fit. So the text field is spilling outside the subform area and covering the form number that was placed on the bottom of the master page.

CROSS-REF Subform content types are discussed in the section "Understanding positioned and flowed content areas" earlier in this chapter.

When we set the Content Type to Flowed and leave the flow direction set as Top to Bottom, we finally have all of the pieces together that we need to make our comments page work, as shown in Figure 28.39. The remaining items are a few aesthetic settings needed to finish the form. Because we are not working with a subform that can have a Leader set to repeat the comments label at the top of the second page, we should create that label as a static object in the master page and prevent the spillover from touching the logo.

FIGURE 28.38

A text field with Allow Multiple Lines and the height set to Expand to fit

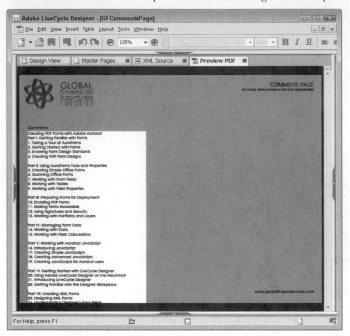

To add a comments page with an expanding text field, follow these steps.

ON the CD-ROM To follow the next set of steps, use the *GFCommentsPageStart.xdp* form from the Chapter28 folder on the book's CD-ROM.

STEPS: Creating a Comments Page with Expanding Text Field

1. **Open a form or create a new form with a text field on it.** We'll open the *GFCommentsPageStart.xdp* form from the Chapter28 folder on the book's CD-ROM.

2. **Select the Comments Text Field.** Open the Field tab of the Object palette.

3. **Turn on Allow Multiple Lines.** Figure 28.40 shows the check box setting. This setting allows the text to wrap within the available field area.

4. **Open the Layout palette and select Expand to fit under the height setting.** Figure 28.41 shows the Expand to fit option. This setting allows the text field to grow in height. However, if the page subform is still set to Positioned it spills out of the subform area and covers content below the page subform.

FIGURE 28.39

With the proper settings the text field spills over to page 2.

5. **Select the page subform and set the Content Type to Flowed.** Open the Subform tab of the Object palette to change the Content Type to Flowed.

6. **Remove the caption from the comments text field.** In the Layout palette set the caption property to None.

7. **Select the Master Page tab and insert a static text box above the comments field to be used as a caption.** Adjust the content area if necessary to make room. Your form should be similar to Figure 28.42.

8. **Save a copy of the form.** Save the form in a location of your choice on your computer.

9. **Preview and test the form.** Select the Preview PDF tab or Press F5. Enter enough text in the comment box to cause it to expand. Click outside the box to watch it adjust to the new contents.

FIGURE 28.40

The Allow Multiple Lines property in the Object palette

FIGURE 28.41

The Expand to fit property in the Layout palette

FIGURE 28.42

The master page after the caption changes

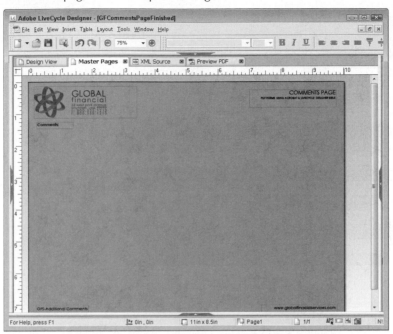

Creating a dynamic expanding text field requires an understanding of subforms and content areas to create a field that correctly spans more than one page. We want to expand these concepts of growing subforms and growing text fields together into another form example where both are used to complete the form design. The packing slip we are building is similar to the purchase order, as seen in Figure 28.43. This form has three subforms across the top of the page and a dynamic table below them.

The difference in the packing list is the field called Special Instructions. We need this area to be expandable, which in turn pushes down the table if needed. For this reason, we cannot wrap the shipping information area in a static subform. It must be a flowed subform.

FIGURE 28.43

A packing slip form

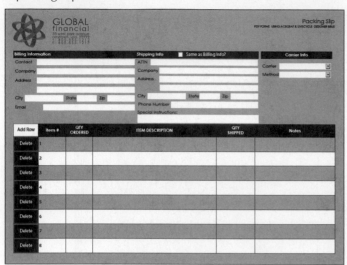

To create a flowing form with an expanding text field, follow these steps.

ON the CD-ROM To follow the next set of steps, use the *GFPackingSlipStart.xdp* form from the Chapter28 folder on the book's CD-ROM.

STEPS: Creating a Flowing Form with an Expanding Text Field

1. **Open a form.** We'll open the *GFPackingSlipStart.xdp* form from the book's CD-ROM.

2. **Open the Hierarchy palette.** Notice that the subforms have already been created and all subforms are positioned content types. Nothing is set up to flow yet.

3. **Select the Preview PDF tab.** Type a few characters followed by a return, and repeat until you have more than three lines of text in the Special Instructions field. When you tab out of the field, any text that didn't display in the first three lines is not visible on the form, as shown in Figure 28.44. We can't have the instructions cut off of the packing list when printed.

4. **Return to Design View.** We begin by setting the Special Instructions text field to expand properly.

5. **Select the Special Instructions field.** We need to set the text field to allow multiple lines.

6. **Open the Field tab of the Object palette, and select Allow Multiple Lines.** This setting allows the text to wrap within the currently available space. To have the field expand to accommodate additional text lines, we need to set the height of the field to expand to fit.

FIGURE 28.44

The special instructions field is being cut off.

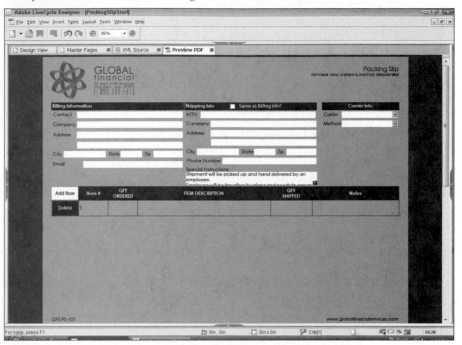

7. **Open the Layout palette and select the Expand to fit below the Height property.** When the form has been set to flow the contents, the height of the field adjusts as needed.

8. **Select the Preview PDF tab or press F5.** Type a few characters followed by a return, and repeat until you have more than three lines of text in the special instructions field. When you tab out of the field, any text that didn't display in the first three lines is not visible on the form. Notice that even though we have made the necessary adjustments to the text field, the field remains stationary in height. This is because the text field is inside a static subform that cannot adjust as needed.

9. **Return to Design View.** We need to change the subform properties to allow the section to adjust. We cannot set the subform to flow top to bottom, because it would change the layout of our fields in that area. We also cannot leave the subform on positioned content type.

10. **Select the Shipping subform from the Hierarchy palette.**

11. **Open the Subform tab of the Layout palette.**

12. **Change the Content Type from Positioned to Flowed.** This alters the layout of our subform and causes the fields to move to the left side of the subform.

13. **Change the Flowed Direction to Western Text.** This places the fields back into the proper layout for our needs. The text field cannot adjust yet because the page subform is still positioned content.

14. **Select the page1 subform from the Hierarchy palette.**

15. **Open the Subform tab of the Layout palette.**

16. **Change the Content Type from Positioned to Flowed.** This alters the layout of our subforms causing them to wrap down the left side of the page.

17. **Change the Flowed Direction to Western Text.** This places the subforms back into the proper layout for our needs.

18. **Select the Preview PDF tab or press F5.** Type a few characters followed by a return, and repeat until you have more than three lines of text in the Special Instructions field. When you tab out of the Special Instructions field, the size adjusts to your newly entered text and pushes the packing list table down the page as needed, as shown in Figure 28.45.

FIGURE 28.45

The Special Instructions field expanding as needed

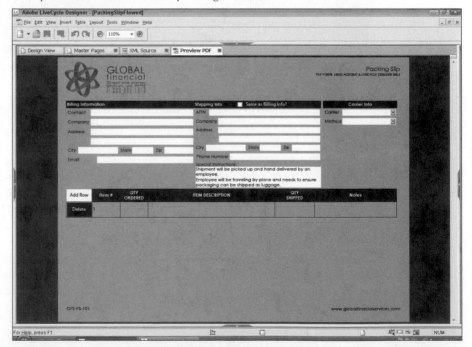

19. **Return to Design View.**

20. **Save a copy of the form.** Save the form in a location of your choice on your computer. We will save this form as *GFPackingSlipFlowed.xdp*.

In this example we took the concepts of dynamic subforms and dynamic text fields and combined them into a single form. We have found that when beginning to work with dynamic subforms and fields, designers tend to wrap objects in unnecessary extra layers of subforms.

For example, the fields in Shipping subform could have been split into two subforms, one for all of the static fields and another for the special instructions. By wrapping those two subforms in an additional subform (that makes three subforms for the shipping information section), we could have set the Shipping subform flow direction as Top to Bottom. This creates additional, unnecessary subform objects and can reduce your form's performance.

When you begin working with subforms we advise you to be creative with settings and explore other possible settings that may work with fewer objects on the form. Always save a copy of your form before setting the Content Type to Flowed so you can go back and adjust, or try different layout options.

Now we want to go back to our Purchase Order, Packing List, and Application forms to add the user-controlled buttons that complete our form designs.

Creating User-Controlled Dynamic Forms

The dynamic forms we built earlier in this chapter aren't quite finished. They don't allow the form recipient to control the form's dynamics. Creating buttons for the form recipient to adjust the form layout requires a little bit of script to finish. No need to panic—each button requires only two lines of code. Yes, we said two lines of code. You can even copy them from one of the forms on the CD-ROM if you'd like. If you went to look at the Table of Contents just now, it doesn't say anything about scripting in this chapter. We wanted you to keep reading so you would realize just how easy this can be.

CROSS-REF   **Understanding the differences between JavaScript and FormCalc, and writing calculation scripts, are covered in Chapter 29.**

We start by finishing our Purchase Order form that has all of the properties set to allow the dynamic table to grow. We just need to place two buttons to allow the user to add and remove rows of the table.

Understanding the Instance Manager

Designer has code built in to handle instances of subforms needed at runtime. This code, the Instance Manager, has the following methods available:

- **Add:** Use Add when you need an additional copy (instance) of a subform.

- **Remove:** Use Remove when you no longer need an existing copy (instance) of a subform.

- **Set:** Use Set to add or remove copies (instances) of a subform. Let's say we use the set method for four instances. If the form already contains two instances, the set method adds two more. If a form already contains five instances, the set method removes one. Set forces the number of subforms to appear.

- **Move:** Use Move to change the position of the subform instances already on the form.

Of the four methods available in the Instance Manager, we need only two for our example, Add and Remove. Let's move on to create the buttons so we can add our script.

Creating buttons to call the Instance Manager

Our Purchase Order form does not have any buttons. We need to adjust the table columns to give us room for a button in the header row and a button beside each row of the table to remove that row. When we have room for the buttons, we add the scripts to call the Instance Manager to adjust the rows.

ON the CD-ROM If you don't have the file saved from earlier steps handy, use the *GFPurchaseOrderIMStart.xdp* file from the Chapter28 folder on the book's CD-ROM.

STEPS: Adding Buttons to Call the Instance Manager

1. **Open a form.** If you completed the steps for setting a table row to repeat earlier in this chapter, you can continue to use your saved form. Or, you can open the *PurchaseOrderIMStart.xdp* file from the book's CD-ROM.

2. **Reduce the width of the Description column in the table by about .75 inches.** This gives us enough room to add a button next to the rows of the table. You can click and drag the width of the column on the design page, or use the Layout palette.

3. **Insert a new column to the left of the Item Number.** Right-click on the Item Number and select Insert ⇨ Columns to the Left from the context menu.

4. Adjust the new column to fill any remaining space in the table. Drag the column width until it fills the form.

CROSS-REF For details on working with tables, see Chapter 28.

5. **Add a button to the new column header area.** Drag the Button object from the Object Library to the untitled text area in the header row.

6. **Rename the button AddRow.** Using the Hierarchy palette, right-click the new button and select Rename from the context menu. Add a caption of Add Row to the button.

7. **Add a button to the new column in the body row.** Drag a Button object from the Object Library to the untitled text in the body row.

8. **Rename the button DeleteRow.** Using the Hierarchy palette, right-click the new button and select Rename from the context menu. Add a caption of Delete to the button. The new buttons should appear similar to the buttons in Figure 28.46.

FIGURE 28.46

The form design after the buttons have been added

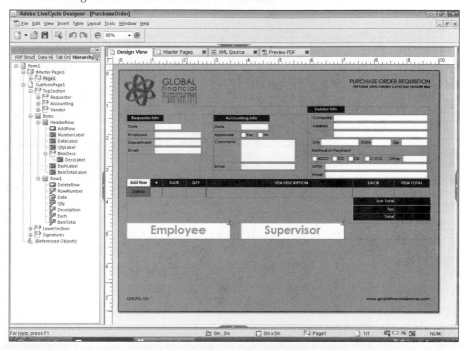

9. Format the two new buttons if desired.

10. **Open the script editor if necessary.** The script editor is located at the top of the screen above the Design View and Preview PDF tabs. To open or close the script editor, go to Window ➪ Script Editor. The keyboard shortcut for the Script Editor is Ctrl + Shift + F5.

11. **Select the AddRow button.**

12. **Select the click event from the Show drop-down list in the Script Editor.** The Show drop-down menu is located in the top-left corner of the Script Editor window; refer to Figure 28.47. The event determines when the script is run.

917

13. **Select JavaScript from the Language drop-down.** The Language drop-down list is located in the top-right corner of the Script Editor and specifies which of the scripting languages you are using as shown in Figure 28.47.

FIGURE 28.47

The Script Editor settings for the click event of the AddRow button

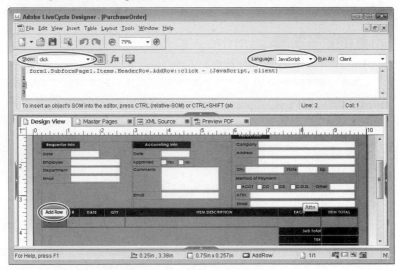

14. **Add the following two lines of code to the Script Editor.** The first line says locate Row1 in the form and set the addInstance method of the Instance Manager to true. The second line says find the top of the form and recalculate the entire form.

```
_Row1.addInstance(true);
xfa.form.recalculate(true);
```

> **TIP**   When typing in the Script Editor, code hinting pops up to help you. If the item you want is highlighted, you can press Enter to select it. Then continue typing your code. Scripting in Designer is case-sensitive. You must enter the code exactly as you see it here.

> **NOTE**   When first selecting an event from the Show drop-down list, only the event name is listed. After code has been written the Show list contains an asterisk after the event name. When working with scripts you can tell which events have scripts associated with them by selecting the Show drop-down list and looking for the asterisks.

15. **Save a copy of the form.** Save the form in a location of your choice on your computer.

16. **Select the DeleteRow button.**

17. **Select the click event from the Show drop-down list in the Script Editor.** The Show box is located in the top left corner of the Script Editor window; refer to Figure 28.47. The event determines when the script is run.

18. **Select JavaScript from the Language drop-down.** The Language drop-down list is located in the top-right corner of the Script Editor, as shown in Figure 28.47, and specifies which of the scripting languages you are using.

19. **Add the following two lines of code to the Script Editor.** The first line says locate Row1 and call the removeInstance method of the Instance Manager to remove this row of the table. The second line says find the top of the form and tell the form to recalculate.

```
_Row1.removeInstance(this.parent.index);
xfa.form.recalculate(true);
```

20. **Select the HeaderRow from the Hierarchy.** We want to repeat this header information if enough rows are added to the table to cause a page break.

21. **Open the Pagination Tab of the Object palette.** Select Include Header Row in Subsequent Pages option.

NOTE You can write the same script in multiple ways. For example, you can rewrite the "xfa.form. recalculate(true)" statement and the "_Row1.addInstance(true)" using a number *1* in place of the word *true*. Most of the Designer help documentation uses the numeric version of the scripting. We chose to use the word for clarity in this chapter.

22. **Save the form.**

23. **Select the Preview PDF tab or press F5.** The form already contains five rows in the table because of the section we completed earlier in this chapter. Click Add to add a row. Click Delete to remove a row.

24. **Return to Design View.** If your code is not working correctly, double-check that it is entered exactly as shown here. A letter in the wrong case causes the code to not work. Also check each line of your code for a semicolon on the end. If you still have trouble, open the completed form on the CD-ROM and compare your document.

We created buttons so the form recipient can add and remove rows from a table while they are entering data into the form. To use the preceding code again for another form, you need to have the correct reference to the table row you wish to dynamically change.

CROSS-REF For details on referencing objects in scripts, see Chapter 29. For help with comparing FormCalc scripts to JavaScripts, see Chapter 32.

Testing Forms and Previewing XML Data in Dynamic Forms

Forms are not only for collecting data; you also can use them to display data. When testing a form's functionality, entering data each time you want to test takes a long time. Wouldn't it be easier if you could import some sample data? You can, and you don't have to understand XML files to do so.

We talked a little bit about Extensible Markup Language (XML) in Chapter 21. XML is an industry standard format designed to structure, store, transport, and exchange data. Many files can read and write XML including Acrobat and Designer.

If you are comfortable with XML and have some sample files to work with, you are ready to move on to importing XML data. If you need a sample XML file, let's create one.

Creating some sample XML data

We need to use Acrobat to complete the following steps. Opening a form in Acrobat (Standard, Pro, or Pro Extended) enables you to extract data from the form. We are going to open Acrobat, fill out the form one time, and save that form data as an XML file to use each time we test the form. Sounds easy enough, don't you think? To try it, follow these steps.

ON the CD-ROM Use the *GFPackingSlipFinished.pdf* form from the Chapter28 folder on the book's CD-ROM to follow these steps.

STEPS: Creating a Sample XML Data File from an Acrobat Form or Designer Form

1. **Open the form in Acrobat.** We opened the *GFPackingSlipFinished.pdf* file from the book's CD-ROM.

2. **Enter some sample data into the form.** As shown in Figure 28.48, make sure you enter realistic sample information. One of the best ways to test a form is by completing it just as the form recipient is expected to. Take your time, you won't have to do this each time you test the form in the future unless you want to. If you encounter anything that you don't like, make a note about it so you can modify the form.

3. **Once the form has been completed, select Forms ⇨ Manage Form Data ⇨ Export Data.** The Forms menu is shown in Figure 28.49.

4. **In the Export Form Data as Dialog box, name the file and leave the save as type set to XML files.** Make sure the file location is easy to locate again for the next set of steps.

5. **Close Acrobat.** You do not need to save the form. Because the data has already been exported you can import the data again in the future.

CROSS-REF For more information in importing and exporting data from Acrobat, see Chapter 14. For more information on editing XML data, see Chapter 27.

When importing data into a form in Acrobat, you can save the form with the completed data contained in the document. When importing sample data in Designer the data is only used for previewing and testing purposes. You still need Acrobat to import or export data from the PDF form.

FIGURE 28.48

Sample data entered in Acrobat

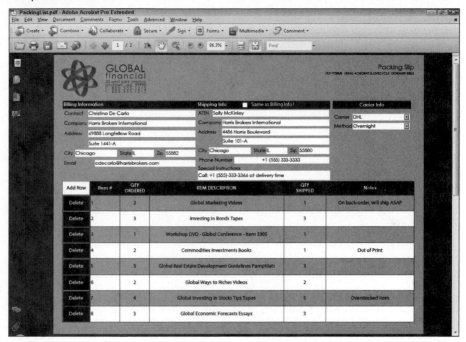

FIGURE 28.49

The Export Data menu in Acrobat

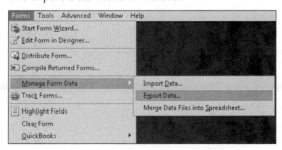

Importing sample XML data

Now that we have a sample XML file, we would like to be able to utilize it each time we preview our Designer form. We recommend you create a few different sample XML files to test your forms with. Having a sample file with too little data does not push the form to the limit and verify all settings are working properly. A form with too much data can cause you to miss problems. Using sample XML data in Designer requires only setting a few form properties.

By creating our own sample XML file directly from the form we can rest assured that the data populates the form again in the proper fields. If your sample XML file came from a different source, you may need to match the fields in the XML data with the field names in the Designer form. Designer is excellent at handling data from various sources and correctly displaying it in the form.

 **For more information in creating data bindings in Designer, see Chapters 27 and 31.**

Using form properties

We discussed several form properties necessary for previewing dynamic forms correctly inside Designer. The Form Properties are also where we set up the sample XML file we wish to use when testing and previewing our form in Designer. Open the Form Properties dialog box by choosing File ➪ Form Properties.

To test a file using XML data and binding the data to the form, follow these steps.

 **To follow these steps use the *GFPackingSlipFinished.pdf* form from the Chapter28 folder of the CD-ROM and the data file you exported from the last series of steps.**

STEPS: Importing Sample XML Data in Designer

1. **Open the form in Designer.** We opened the *GFPackingSlipFinished.pdf* form from the book's CD-ROM.

2. **Select Row1, and in the Repeat Row for Each Data Item, set the initial count to 1.** Because we are going to use this form to print packing slips, we don't need the extra blank lines in the form.

3. **Select the Preview PDF tab to verify that only one row of the table appears.**

4. **Return to Design View.**

5. **Choose File ➪ Form Properties and click the Preview tab.** As we mentioned in the previewing dynamic forms section, it is important to verify that the Preview Type is set to Interactive Form, and the Preview Adobe XML Form As Dynamic Form is also set.

6. **In the Data File area, click the Browse button on the right as indicated in Figure 28.50.** Navigate to where you stored the XML file and press Open to return to the Form Properties Dialog box.

FIGURE 28.50

The Form Properties dialog box with a sample XML file set

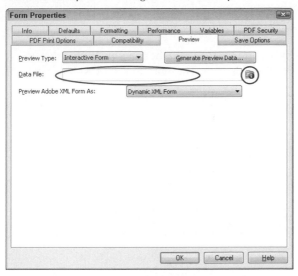

7. **Select the Preview PDF tab or press F5 to test the form data.** Once the file has been selected in the Preview tab, it appears each time you preview the form. You can repeat Steps 5 through 7 to see various amounts of data.

Taking the time to locate or create a few sample XML files the first time you need them can greatly reduce the testing time used again in the future. We recommend using two or three sample XML files to test the forms during production. If you are unfamiliar with the form data, then ask someone who uses the form to do the initial testing and have them save the file in Acrobat for you to export.

Troubleshooting dynamic forms

Dynamic forms don't always work exactly the way we want them to. Some very common settings to double-check include:

- The form is saved either as an XDP or a Dynamic XML form (*.pdf).
- The Preview Adobe XML Form property is set to allow dynamic content in the Preview tab of the Form Properties dialog box.
- At least one subform has the Content Type set to Flowed.

- Repeat Subform for Each Data Item is selected for the repeating subform, or Repeat Row for Each Data Items is selected for a table row.

- Scripts used in buttons to add and remove subforms have no typographical mistakes.

- The Acrobat viewer is a supported version for dynamic content.

We hope you agree that when you have grasped the concepts behind dynamic forms, turning them on and making them work is not difficult. The more you work with dynamic forms the easier it becomes.

Summary

- Subforms are a key part of building flowed document layouts.

- Subforms also control tab order.

- You can add subforms before or after adding content.

- Coordinates of objects are respected and maintained on positioned content areas.

- Coordinates of objects in flowed content areas are relative to the container's coordinates.

- You can nest subforms to create optimal layouts.

- Subforms can flow in Top to Bottom or Western Text (left to right) directions.

- Tables are specialized subforms with additional properties for easy formatting.

- Dynamic forms can adjust based on user input or merged data.

- You can add buttons to a form design to allow the form recipient to control the subforms.

- Use the Instance Manager when scripting changes to the number of subforms.

- Use sample data for previewing and testing form designs.

- Troubleshoot dynamic form issues by checking basic form properties and file type settings.

Part IX

Working with Data and Scripts

We finish up in the last part talking about XML data and scripting using FormCalc and JavaScript. In Chapter 29 we begin this part covering the two scripting languages you use in Designer, using the Script Editor, and comparing scripting languages. In Chapter 30 we talk about distributing forms, saving templates, and using Form Guides. In Chapter 31 we cover working with data, creating new data connections, and binding data to data connections.

In Chapter 32 we examine some sample forms and demonstrate how the sample forms installed with Designer can be modified for your own personal use. In Chapter 33 we talk about databases and getting data out of Designer and into a data base file and vice versa.

In Chapter 34 we introduce you to working with LiveCycle ES servers. For industrial strength forms use, this chapter offers you information on how servers manage form data and the kinds of server products that are available to support data from Designer forms.

We threw in Chapter 35 to finish up the book by offering you some guidelines and recommendations for learning more about Designer. The program is complex and a single book won't provide you solutions for all your forms needs. In this chapter we offer a number of URL links and recommended resources to expand your learning.

IN THIS PART

Chapter 29
Introducing LiveCycle Designer Scripting

Chapter 30
Deploying Forms

Chapter 31
Working with Data

Chapter 32
Examining Some Sample Dynamic Forms

Chapter 33
Working with Databases

Chapter 34
Introducing LiveCycle Enterprise Suite

Chapter 35
Getting More Help with LiveCycle Designer

Chapter 29

Introducing LiveCycle Designer Scripting

In Chapter 15 we covered field calculations for Acrobat Forms using Simplified Field Notation. In Section V we discussed JavaScript for Acrobat Forms. Acrobat and Designer both offer two scripting languages. Designer uses FormCalc and JavaScript. FormCalc is similar to Simplified Field Notation but is more powerful. FormCalc has some built-in functions such as a spreadsheet program to help you write formulas. You don't need to pick a single scripting language in Designer. A form can have script using either of the languages.

Scripting is not required to create a form. Scripting enhances forms and allows you to control their behavior at runtime. A form with script allows a more customized user experience than a form without script. Scripting also can be used for controlling data entry, ensuring the form captures the intended data from the form filler.

You may not wish to become a programmer, but understand that scripting is possible in Designer forms. Knowing what the program is capable of doing is half the battle in learning a new program. It may be some time down the road before you decide you are ready to try scripting. It may be the result of a division of job duties where you work. The form designer builds the forms and then sends the form to the programming department to have scripts added. In this case you need to be able to express your intentions to the programming department so they understand what you want the scripts to do.

We begin this chapter with the advantages of scripting, and then discuss where scripting goes in a Designer form. We explore the Script Editor and some shortcuts to writing scripts. We discuss the differences and similarities between the two languages to help you decide when to use one scripting language over the other.

IN THIS CHAPTER

Scripting basics

Locating scripts

Creating scripts in FormCalc and JavaScript

Comparing the scripting languages

Debugging scripts

Scripting Advantages

LiveCycle Designer's built-in form design capabilities are fantastic. When you add the ability to script, the capabilities become phenomenal. Scripting can enhance a form design and turn an ordinary form into a smart form with a better user experience.

We create forms to collect electronic information from the form filler. Lots of time and planning goes into this process. Have you looked at your form from the perspective of the person completing it? Have you asked them to enter the same information more than once? Have you asked them to perform mathematical calculations? These are only a few reasons we add scripts to a form. Many form fillers expect smart forms these days, we are inclined to agree. Nothing is more aggravating then being asked to complete a form, only to find out it is non-interactive. The longer we work with forms, the more we expect our forms to do.

Scripts can be used for automating form entries that repeat, such as billing and shipping information. You can handle this situation in many ways. One solution is to copy the billing information into the shipping information. Another solution is shown in Figures 29.1 and 29.2. The repeated information is simply removed from the layout to give more space to other fields.

FIGURE 29.1

A packing slip with both the billing and shipping address fields showing

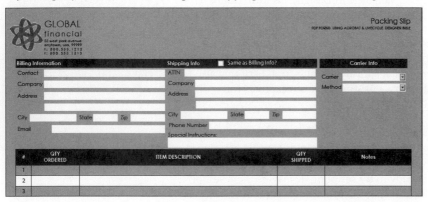

ON the CD-ROM The packing slip shown in Figures 29.1 and 29.2 can be found in the Chapter29 folder of the CD-ROM. This file is a dynamic that adjusts the field layout based on the same as billing info check box. The Purchase Order shown in Figure 29.3 has two copies of the file on the CD-ROM. *PurchaseOrderJS.pdf* contains the completed calculations from this chapter done in JavaScript. *PurchaseOrderFC.pdf* contains the completed calculations from this chapter done in FormCalc.

FIGURE 29.2

The packing slip with hidden information

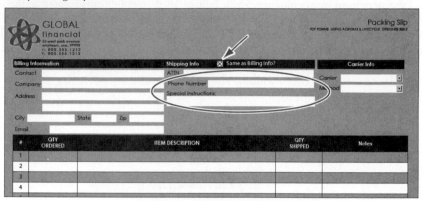

Creating calculations for multiplying the line items in an order form, totaling those lines, and adding the tax for the user is another common example of scripting, as shown in Figure 29.3. How you use the scripting capabilities in your forms is limited only by your ability to come up with creative uses for them.

FIGURE 29.3

A purchase order form with calculations

#	DATE	QTY	ITEM DESCRIPTION	EACH	ITEM TOTAL
1	Aug 1, 2008	3	GFS-PS-101, Pkg of 100	$5.50	$16.50
2	Aug 1, 2008	5	GFS-HR-201, Pkg of 100	$5.50	$27.50
3					
4					
5					
6					
7					
8					
9					
10					
				Sub Total	$44.00
				Tax	$2.86
				Total	$46.86

GFS-PO-101

www.globalfinacialservices.com

Consider who enters the information into your form. How do they work through the form, and what can we do to make that experience better? Our challenge to you is to locate or create the scripts that can make your forms easier to use and then make those improvements to your forms.

Using the Script Editor

To write scripts in Designer, begin by opening the Script Editor. The Script Editor is located in the palette well above the design window but is hidden by default. The Window menu contains the option to open the Script Editor, Window ⇨ Script Editor. Or, you can use the keyboard shortcut Ctrl + Shift + F5 to open the editor. The first time the Script Editor is opened, it opens with a single script line visible, as shown in Figure 29.4. We refer to this as the single-line Script Editor. We recommend that you extend the Script Editor window into a multiline editor by dragging the palette well border down, as shown in Figure 29.5

FIGURE 29.4

The single-line Script Editor

FIGURE 29.5

The multiline Script Editor

The Script Editor shows script for the selected object in the form. In the top left area of the Script Editor is a Show drop-down list, as shown in Figure 29.6. By default the Show list is set to events with scripts. The Script Editor displays a continuous list of scripts for any events. An event that is unavailable to the active object appears dimmed in the list. Any event in the list with an asterisk contains scripting. Choosing an event from the Show list changes the Script Editor window accordingly.

 To the right of the Show box is a button to show events for child objects. This button is on by default and allows you to select a subform and see all of the scripts contained in the objects in the subform. It also makes it possible to select the top level of the form from the Hierarchy palette and see all of the script contained in the form. Deselecting the Show events for child objects button changes the Script Editor to show only the active object. Leaving this button selected can reduce performance if you are working on a form with an excessive number of scripts or if the computer is low on resources.

 The green fn button is a function button. When selected it opens a list of built-in functions available based on the currently selected scripting language. To use a function from the list and place it in your code, highlight the function and either double-click your mouse, or press Enter on the keyboard.

FIGURE 29.6

The show box of the Script Editor

Checking the script in your form for syntax errors is only a click away. This button checks all of the scripts in your form for syntax errors. Any errors found are shown in the Log tab of the Reports palette. Checking for syntax errors is a good idea, but it does not catch all of your scripting problems.

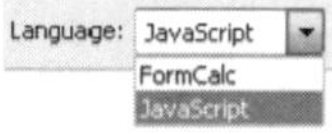

The Language drop-down list on the right side of the Script Editor window changes the language for the current script session only.

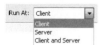 **CAUTION** If you have multiple objects selected, or the show events for child objects selected, changing the scripting language affects all visible scripts.

 **TIP** If you wish to change a single script when multiple scripts are in the Script Editor, right-click. Choosing a script language from the context menu is limited to the script where you right-clicked.

The Run At drop-down list allows you to change the location where the script executes.

 Changing the Run At location while multiple scripts are visible changes all scripts. To change a single script, right-click and select the Run at option from the context menu.

Setting Scripting Language Preferences

Each time you create a new blank document in Designer, a template controls many of the form properties such as the page size, margins, fonts, and more. That template includes the scripting language that becomes the default in the document. Changing the scripting language can be done at many places in the form. When you write each script, you can choose the scripting language. Setting the scripting language for multiple scripts is also an option. If you seem to be changing the scripting language most of the time, then you should change the document default.

The scripting preferences used in the current form are stored in the Defaults tab of the Form Properties dialog box (File ➪ Form Properties) as shown in Figure 29.7. Unfortunately, no default keyboard shortcut exists for accessing the form properties. We encourage you to create one if you use this window as frequently as we do.

FIGURE 29.7

The Form Properties dialog box

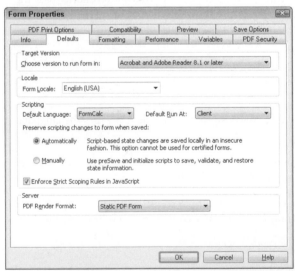

CROSS-REF Customizing keyboard shortcuts is discussed in Chapter 22.

In addition to the scripting language, other preference settings affect each script you create in Designer. The scripting preferences include:

- **Language:** The preferred scripting language for the current form.
  - FormCalc is the default language. Working in FormCalc is similar to writing a spreadsheet formula.
  - JavaScript is also available and provides more flexibility in coding.
- **Run At:** Where scripts are executed for processing.
  - **Client:** This is the default setting. Any script you put into your designer form is executed on the form filler's computer by the viewing application.
  - **Server:** Use this setting if you want the LiveCycle ES components to do the processing of lengthy scripts that may take lots of time or need access to resources only available on the server. The results are returned to the form in the browser.
  - **Client and Server:** The scripts are made available to both the client and the server for processing.
- **Preserve Scripting changes to form when saved:** Specifies how scripting changes are saved.
  - **Automatically:** This is the default setting. Each time a form is saved the scripting changes are preserved. This setting cannot be used with certified forms.
  - **Manually:** This setting is mainly used for certified forms and requires additional scripting using the delta script object to function properly.
- **Enforce Strict Scoping Rules in JavaScript:** This setting is on by default when the selected target version supports the setting. It is recommended only if the target output is Acrobat/Reader version 8.1 or higher and is automatically deselected when lower than 8.1. Strict scoping rules affect how long a variable can be referred to. This length of time is called the variable scope. A form designed to open in the browser as HTML may need altered script to function properly when strict scoping is enforced.

Changing these settings alters the scripting preferences that are set when the Script Editor opens in the current document only.

STEPS: Changing the Scripting Preferences for the Current Document

1. **Work with the open document.** If necessary start a new file by selecting File ➪ New.
2. **Select File ➪ Form Properties.** This opens the Form Properties dialog box. The settings found in this window apply only to the active document.
3. **Select the Defaults tab.** The scripting section of the Defaults tab stores the scripting language preference for the active document as shown in Figure 29.8.

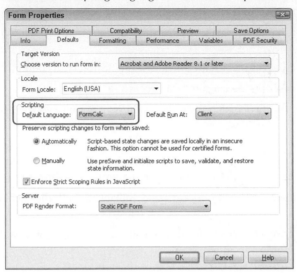

FIGURE 29.8

The default scripting language in the Form Properties dialog box

4. **Choose JavaScript or FormCalc from the Default Language drop-down.** The default setting is FormCalc.

5. **Press OK.** Save your changes and close the dialog box.

 To make the scripting language a permanent change, alter the default template used to build new documents.

 For information on creating or modifying templates see Chapter 23.

Writing Scripts

Deciding which scripting language to use is a personal choice. Being comfortable with formula writing in a spreadsheet program such as Microsoft Excel gives you an edge with FormCalc. Existing knowledge of scripting on the Web suggests you'd be comfortable with JavaScript in Designer. The functionality desired and the ease of writing the script are also considerations.

A factor to consider when choosing a scripting language is how the form will be deployed. Forms rendered using LiveCycle Forms ES can be represented as PDF, HTML, or Flash. These options are shown in Figures 29.9 through 29.13. HTML and Flash require the scripting language to be set as JavaScript. The Flash rendering appears in the form recipient's browser like a wizard with Next buttons to navigate. The data is all captured in the PDF in the background, which allows the user to print the original PDF version while completing the form.

FIGURE 29.9

The first panel of the purchase order form rendered as Flash in the browser using LiveCycle Forms ES

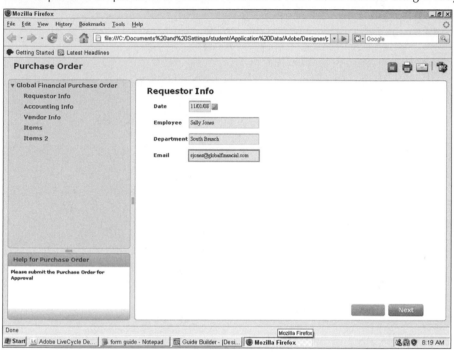

The first panel of the form is the section for requestor information. Notice the Next button on the lower-right area of the screen. Navigational links are also provided on the left side of the form. The remaining screens in Figures 29.10 through 29.12 have been cropped to show the right side of the form. This is the area that changes.

FIGURE 29.10

The second panel of the purchase order form rendered as Flash

FIGURE 29.11

The third panel of the purchase order form rendered as Flash

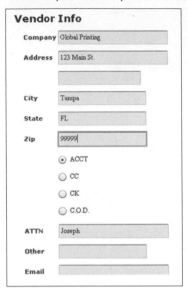

FIGURE 29.12

The fourth panel of the purchase order form rendered as Flash

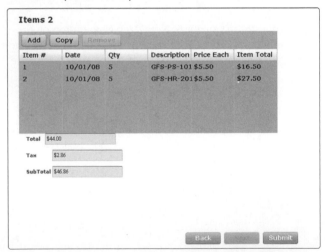

FIGURE 29.13

The PDF view of the purchase order form when completed in the Flash form

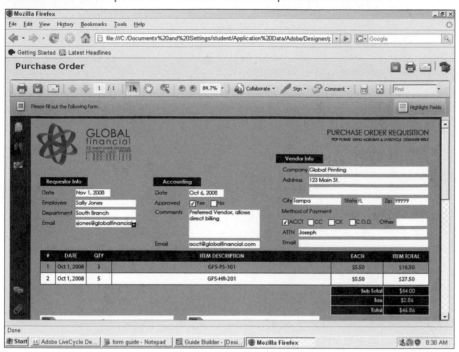

CROSS-REF For an overview of LiveCycle Enterprise Suite (ES), see Chapter 34.

A form rendered in PDF format supports both of the scripting languages, even allowing both to be used within the same form. For forms rendered as HTML or Flash, JavaScript must be used because they do not support FormCalc. FormCalc is an Adobe proprietary language and should not be used when rendering forms in formats other than PDF.

Both FormCalc and JavaScript are case-sensitive languages. Be extremely careful when entering code. A single character typed in the wrong case can cause your script to fail. Finding these typos is one of the most tedious tasks in long scripts, especially when you are first learning to script. It is difficult to determine if you typed something incorrectly or if something else is causing the problem.

A shortcut exists for entering the object name in the script window. You can place your cursor in the Script Editor, and then hold down the Ctrl key while clicking an object on the design page to add it to the script window, as shown in Figure 29.14. This enters the relative path to the object. If you need to start at the top of the form hierarchy and work your way down then you need the absolute path. To get the absolute path, hold down Ctrl + Shift while clicking an object.

FIGURE 29.14

The mouse pointer appears as a V while adding relative or absolute references to the Script Editor. Holding down Ctrl while mousing over the Each field shows the V symbol. Clicking returns the object's relative syntax.

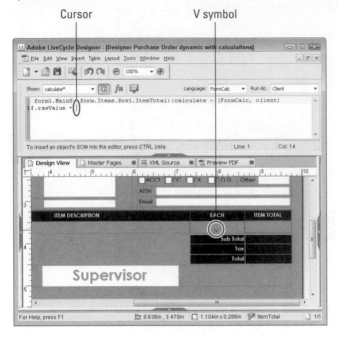

Scripts can become lengthy and hard to read. Adding comments to the code can help you decipher the intent or provide clues for someone who is learning to script. Comments can be added to either scripting language by preceding them with two forward slashes (//) as shown in Figure 29.15. In the Script Editor any comment appears in green text indicating it is not executed with the other code.

Keywords, function names, and operators appear as blue text in the script editor. Fields, variables, strings, and numbers appear in black text. These color coding features are designed to help you write your code. If you type the keyword Sum in your script but it remains black, make sure the first letter is uppercase.

TIP   The Script Editor color coding may appear to stop working on occasion. Although we are unsure of the exact cause, running low on system resources exaggerates the problem. Try closing unnecessary applications before continuing. Opening and closing the Script Editor also may restore the color coding.

FIGURE 29.15

Comments, keyword color coding, and line numbers help when scripting

Comments in green

Line numbers   Keywords and operators in blue: if, then, else, endif, =

Features like showing the line numbers in the Script Editor and statement completion options can be turned on or off according to your preferences. You also can change syntax formatting options in the Script Editor. FormCalc and JavaScript use the same color setting in the Script Editor. We recommend that you change the blue settings in one language to an alternate color as another visual indicator when you switch between the scripting languages. The Script Editor formatting is stored in the Options window. Select the Workspace category from Tools ➪ Options to select the FormCalc or JavaScript editor settings you would like.

STEPS: Changing the Script Editor Formatting Settings

1. **Select Tools ➪ Options.** This opens the Options dialog box.

2. **Select the Workspace category from the left side.** The Workspace category dialog box appears, as shown in Figure 29.16 The workspace options include settings for the Design View/Master Pages, the Script Editor, XML, and whether or not Designer is the default design program.

3. **Select the FormCalc Syntax Formatting button.** As shown in Figure 29.17 the font, size, color, and background color can be set for each of the syntax types.

4. **Select the Keyword option from the color setting list.** Set the formatting options to your preferences.

Referencing objects

You can refer to an object using multiple methods in either language. All of the examples in this section refer to the value of the ItemTotal in our purchase order form, as shown in Figure 29.18.

FIGURE 29.16

The Workspace category of the Options dialog box.

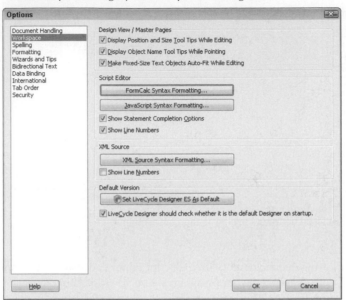

FIGURE 29.17

The FormCalc Syntax Formatting dialog box

The fully qualified syntax works from any point on the form. This means the form starts at the top level of the hierarchy and works down through the tree to find the desired object. An example of the fully qualified syntax for the value of the ItemTotal Field in our Purchase Order form follows:

```
form1.MainSubform.Items.Row1.ItemTotal.rawValue; //FormCalc
form1.MainSubform.Items.Row1.ItemTotal.rawValue; //JavaScript
```

FIGURE 29.18

The ItemTotal field in the purchase order form shown in the Hierarchy palette

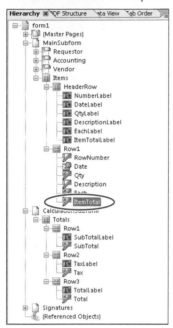

Notice how the fully qualified version is the same in both languages. Some syntax shortcuts are available. The .rawValue property is the default property in FormCalc and is assumed by Designer if omitted. FormCalc also does not require the end of the statement character (;) to be placed in the script. Each new line in the Script Editor is considered a new statement. The following shortened FormCalc script is equivalent to the preceding fully qualified line and can be used anywhere in the form:

```
form1.MainSubform.Items.Row1.ItemTotal //FormCalc
```

If two objects exist in different containers of the hierarchy you can use relative reference syntax. Relative references start based on the current location and work their way up the tree to locate the desired object. The syntax must begin with the name of the highest level container object that the two objects do not have in common. See Figure 29.19 for an expanded view of the hierarchy.

FIGURE 29.19

The purchase order form hierarchy expanded

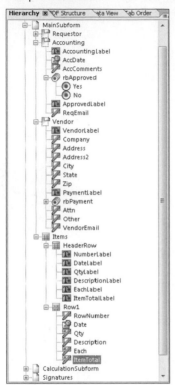

If you think about the ItemTotal field in terms of human relationships, we can form an analogy. The MainSubform is a parent, with four children: Requestor, Accounting, Vendor, and Items as shown in Figure 29.20. Any object contained in one of the four children can talk to a sibling's object without going to the parent first. It simply requires that they talk to the sibling who holds the object. Although going up to the parent level and then back down won't hurt anything, it is unnecessary. Any object in the MainSubform could use the following syntax to reach the value of the ItemTotal.

```
Items.Row1.ItemTotal //FormCalc
Items.Row1.ItemTotal.rawValue; //JavaScript
```

If two objects exist in the same container of the hierarchy, they are referred to as sharing the same context. This means the shortened reference syntax is directly to the object name and property desired. Any Object in the Row1 container can refer to the value of the ItemTotal with the following syntax:

```
ItemTotal //FormCalc
ItemTotal.rawValue; //JavaScript
```

The parent/child relationship of items in the MainSubform

MainSubform — Parent   Children

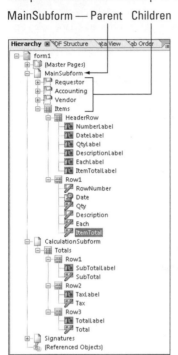

Both scripting languages offer a unique shortcut to refer to the active object and reduce the size of the reference syntax. Although it is possible to always refer to the object with relative or absolute syntax, it is not necessary and makes the scripts longer and more difficult to read. The following lines refer to the value of the ItemTotal when referring to the active object:

```
$.rawValue; //FormCalc
$ //Shortened FormCalc
this.rawValue; //JavaScript
```

> **TIP**   When you are unsure what syntax you need to reach the desired object, try using the shortcut for adding the relative (Ctrl + Click Object) or absolute path (Ctrl + Shift + Click Object) to your script. You may need to add the desired property to the end, but it helps you find the correct syntax to reach the object.

When setting the value of a field equal to an expression, again some shortcuts are available. If the object you are setting the value of is omitted the active field is assumed. All of the following examples set the value of the LineTotal equal to the product of the Qty and Each fields as shown in Figure 29.21:

```
$.rawValue = Qty.rawValue * Each.rawValue; // FormCalc
$ = Qty * Each //FormCalc shortened
Qty * Each //FormCalc omitting active object
this.rawValue = Qty.rawValue * Each.rawValue; //JavaScript
Qty.rawValue * Each.rawValue; //JavaScript omitting the active object
```

FIGURE 29.21

The LineTotal calculation options

#	DATE	QTY	ITEM DESCRIPTION	EACH	ITEM TOTAL
1	Aug 1, 2008	3	GFS-PS-101, Pkg of 100	$5.50	$16.50
2	Aug 1, 2008	5	GFS-HR-201, Pkg of 100	$5.50	$27.50
3					
4					
5					
6					
7					
8					
9					
10					

Sub Total	$44.00
Tax	$2.86
Total	$46.86

GFS-PO-101

www.globalfinancialservices.com

Although it is possible to set the value of the active object while omitting the active object reference in both scripting languages, all of our examples show the field whose value we are setting. We choose to show this to maintain clarity about what the script is designed to do. Whether you choose to use scripting shortcuts or the more explicit statements in your code is a personal preference. The reason we discuss all the options is to help you understand the scripts you find in other locations and interpret them effectively.

Choosing the right scripting event

Each time you write a script in Designer you attach it to an event. This determines when the code should execute. The event that we focus on in this chapter is the calculate event. There are many additional events that offer the functionality you may need. The event you choose is the initialization point of the code execution. The events are broken down into the following three categories:

■ **Process Events:** Process events occur automatically because of an internal process or form action. For example, a dynamic form contains an Add button. When the user clicks the button, the additional section is created and the remaining portion of the document must be laid out. This triggers other process events. The process events include:

   ■ **calculate:** When the form design and data are merged, when any field used in a calculation changes in value, and when a field loses focus. Losing focus means exiting the field by clicking or tabbing in another area of the form.

- **form:ready:** After the form design and data are merged. The document has not yet been presented to the user on the screen. It is still stored in memory, and the initialize, calculate, and validate events are complete.

- **indexChange:** Any time a subform section is added or removed from the document the number of subforms has changed and so has the index which refers to them.

- **initialize:** After the form design is merged with data. The initialize event occurs for each object on the form. This event fires any time additional fields are added to the form during runtime such as adding subforms.

- **layout:ready:** After the form design and data are merged the layout is applied. This is when pagination occurs.

- **validate:** Any time a field loses focus, and when the form design and data merge, and upon submission of data.

- **Interactive Events:** These events occur as a direct result of the user's actions. Interactive events include:

  - **change:** Any time a content of a field is altered. This includes typing, pasting, cutting, using drop-down lists, and more.

  - **click:** When the mouse is clicked within the scripted region. The region may be a button, a field, and so on. The region's boundaries are determined by the size of the object.

  - **enter:** Any time the object receives focus, and becomes active. Focus means the object was tabbed to on the keyboard or clicked by the mouse.

  - **exit:** Any time the object loses focus by tabbing out or clicking away from the object.

  - **mouseDown:** When the mouse button is held down over the object, but not yet released.

  - **mouseEnter:** When the user moves the mouse over the object but has not clicked yet.

  - **mouseExit:** When the user moves the mouse out of the boundary of the object. Usually this is when you roll over something, then roll off again without doing anything. It also occurs if you roll over, click but not release the mouse button and roll off again.

  - **mouseUp:** When the mouse button is released within the boundary of the object.

  - **postOpen:** When a drop-down list is opened.

  - **postSign:** After a digital signature is applied.

  - **preOpen:** Before a drop-down list is opened.

  - **preSign:** Before a digital signature is applied.

- **Application Events:** Application events are the result of the actions that the application performs. Application events include:

  - **docClose:** The very end of the form processing, after all validations complete.

  - **docReady:** After the form is opened in Acrobat or Reader.

- **postPrint:** After the document prints.
- **postSave:** After the document saves.
- **postSubmit:** After the form is submitted.
- **prePrint:** Before the document prints.
- **preSave:** Before the document saves.
- **preSubmit:** Before the form is submitted.

Although we focus on the calculate event in this chapter, we frequently use other events as well. Think about when you want your script to be executed, and locate that event. It is most common to script against the calculate, validate, and interactive events when first learning.

CROSS-REF More complicated scripts are explored in Chapter 32. We also explore subform scripts in Chapter 27.

Using FormCalc

FormCalc is an Adobe proprietary language, available in the LiveCycle ES components, Designer, Acrobat, and Reader. FormCalc is generally used for simpler formulas and because of the shortened syntax available requires less code to execute. FormCalc usually provides better performance than JavaScript because it executes simple calculations and validations more quickly.

Writing a script in FormCalc is similar to writing a formula in Microsoft Excel. Predefined functions exist to simplify the work needed to use common formulas. FormCalc has more than 60 predefined functions currently in the built-in function list. They are categorized into the following groups:

- **Arithmetic:** Standard mathematical formulas for items such as:
  - **Abs:** The absolute value of the expression.
  - **Avg:** The average of the non-null elements in the expression.
  - **Ceil:** The whole number greater than or equal to a given number.
  - **Count:** The number of non-null elements in the expression.
  - **Floor:** The largest whole number less than or equal to a given number.
  - **Max:** The largest value in the expression.
  - **Min:** The smallest value in the expression.
  - **Mod:** The modulus (remainder) of a division expression.
  - **Round:** Rounds an expression to the given number of decimal places.
  - **Sum:** Adds the numbers in the expression.
- **Date and Time:** Date and time functions based on the epoch date. Epoch is an instant in time chosen as the origin. These calculations are based on a midnight, January 1, 1900 start date.

- **Time2Num:** Number of milliseconds based on a time string.
- **Date:** The current system date in the number of days.
- **Date2Num:** The number of days based on a date string.
- **DateFmt:** A date formatted string given a date format style.
- **IsoDate2Num:** The number of days given a valid date string.
- **IsoTime2Num:** The number of milliseconds given a valid time string.
- **LocalDateFmt:** A localized date formatted string given a date format style.
- **LocalTimeFmt:** A localized time formatted string given a date format style.
- **Num2Date:** A date string given the number of days.
- **Num2GMTime:** A Greenwich Mean Time (GMT) time string given a number of milliseconds.
- **Num2Time:** A time string given the number of milliseconds.
- **Time:** Current system time as a number of milliseconds.
- **TimeFmt:** A time format given a time format style.

- **Financial:** Common financial calculations including:
  - **Apr:** Annual percentage rate for a loan.
  - **CTerm:** Number of periods needed for a compound term.
  - **FV:** Future value based on consistent payment amounts and intervals at a fixed APR.
  - **IPmt:** Interest paid on a loan over a set period of time.
  - **NPV:** Net present value of an investment based on a discount amount rate and future cash flows.
  - **Pmt:** Payment for a loan based on constant payments and interest rate.
  - **PPmt:** Principal paid on a loan over a set period of time.
  - **PV:** Present value of an investment based on constant payments and rates.
  - **Rate:** Compound interest rate per period.
  - **Term:** The number of periods needed.

- **Logical:** Logical functions including:
  - **Choose:** Select a value from a given list.
  - **Exists:** Whether a given parameter is an accessor to an existing object. An accessor is a method called in scripting to access the contents of an object but does not modify that object.
  - **HasValue:** Rather a given parameter is an accessor with a value. Null, empty, and blank are not considered values.
  - **Oneof:** If a value is in a given set.
  - **Within:** If a value is within a given range.

- **Miscellaneous:** Functions that don't fit into the other categories including:
  - **Eval:** The value of a given form calculation.
  - **Null:** Returns a null value, meaning no value, empty.
  - **Ref:** A reference to an existing object.
  - **UnitType:** Returns the units of a unitspan. A unitspan is a string consisting of a number followed by a unit name.
  - **UnitValue:** Returns the numeric value of a measurement with its associated unitspan, after an optional unit conversion.
- **String:** Formulas dedicated to working with text.
  - **At:** Locates the starting character position of a string within another string.
  - **Concat:** Joining two or more character strings end to end (concatenation).
  - **Decode:** The decoded version of a text string.
  - **Encode:** The encoded version of a text string.
  - **Format:** Formats according to the specified picture format string.
  - **Left:** Extracts the specified number of characters, starting from first character on the left.
  - **Len:** The number of characters in a string (length).
  - **Lower:** Converts the string to lowercase characters.
  - **Ltrim:** Returns the string, trimming all spaces from the left or front of the string.
  - **Parse:** Analyses according to the specified picture format string.
  - **Replace:** Replaces all occurrences of the specified string with a replacement string.
  - **Right:** Extracts the specified number of characters, starting from first character on the right.
  - **Rtrim:** Returns the string, trimming all spaces from the right or end of the string.
  - **Space:** A string consisting of a given number of blank spaces.
  - **Str:** Converts a number to a string, formats and rounds decimals to specified number of digits.
  - **Stuff:** Inserts a string into another string.
  - **Substr:** Extracts a portion of a string.
  - **Upper:** Converts the string to uppercase characters.
  - **Uuid:** A Universally Unique Identifier (UUID).
  - **WordNum:** Returns the English text of a given number.
- **URL:** Functions for use with Uniform Resource Locators, a global address on the World Wide Web.

- **Get:** Downloads the contents of the URL.
- **Post:** Posts data to the URL.
- **Put:** Uploads data to the URL.

Putting the FormCalc script into the fields only takes a few minutes. We will take the dynamic purchase order from we created in a previous chapter and add the necessary mathematical calculations to complete the form.

ON the CD-ROM The *StartingPurchaseOrder.xdp* form can be found on the CD-ROM in the Chapter29 folder. If you have any difficulty completing the steps in this section, the finished file is included on the CD-ROM. You can open it and explore these scripts in *PurchaseOrderFC.pdf*.

STEPS: Calculating a Line Total

1. **Open a Designer file.** Be sure to open the *StartingPurchaseOrder.xdp* in Chapter29 on the CD-ROM.

2. **Select the Preview PDF tab.** Fill in a few fields in the purchase order table. Notice there are no calculations in this form.

3. **Return to Design View.** Select the Design View tab to start creating the needed calculations.

4. **Select the ItemTotal Field.** We will create a formula that multiplies the quantity times the price per item to calculate the item total.

5. **Open the Script Editor.** Select Window ⇨ Script Editor or press Ctrl + Shift + F5 if necessary to open the script editor.

6. **Expand to the multiline Script Editor.** If necessary drag the palette border down to open the multiline Script Editor for more editing room.

7. **Change the Show drop-down to calculate.** Select calculate from the drop-down list in the Show box to set the event the calculation occurs on. We don't want the form filler to have to take extra steps to get the calculation to appear. By placing our script in the calculate event, any time a field value changes the line totals recalculate.

8. **Verify the Calculation Language is set to FormCalc.** Use the Language drop-down list on the right side of the Script Editor to select FormCalc if necessary.

9. **Verify the Run At is set to Client.** Use the Run At drop-down on the right side of the Script Editor to select Client if necessary. This allows the script to execute in the viewer application on the computer where the form is being completed.

10. **Turn on the Line Numbers in the Script Editor.** If desired, you can turn on line numbers in the Script Editor to match the line numbers in our code sample. To turn on the line numbers, right-click in the Script Editor and select Show Line Numbers from the context menu. You do not need to type the line numbers in our code samples; they are for reference only.

11. **Type the code in the Script Editor.** Type the following code into the Script Editor. Remember that FormCalc is a case-sensitive scripting language. We can use the field names directly because they both reside in the same node of the hierarchy. The $.raw-Value refers to the active form field, in our case the ItemTotal. We are setting its value equal to the Qty field times the Each field. Your code should match the screenshot in Figure 29.22 after this step.

    1. $.rawValue = Qty * Each;

FIGURE 29.22

The ItemTotal script, multiplying the quantity field times the Each field.

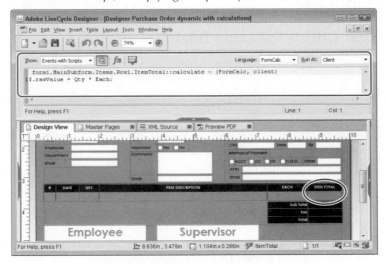

12. **Test your script.** Select the Preview PDF tab fill in a few quantities and prices in the each column. The line totals should now be calculating. Also notice that since the line totals are a calculated value, you aren't allowed to change them.

13. **Return to Design View.** Return to Design View to continue editing your form.

14. **Save a copy of the form.** Save the form in a location of your choice on your computer.

That wasn't as difficult as you thought, was it? We will continue by adding a few more calculations to our Purchase Order form. We need calculations for the subtotal at the bottom of the table, the tax amount, and the grand total. Taking the scripts in the order of difficulty to write, we save the subtotal calculation for last because this table is a dynamic table. The script we write must be able to adjust for the changing number of rows it may contain.

STEPS: Calculating the Tax Amount

1. **Open a Designer file.** We continue using the *StartingPurchaseOrder.xdp* from the previous steps.

2. **Select the Tax Field.** We will create a formula that multiplies the subtotal amount times the local tax rate to calculate the tax due.

3. **Open the Script Editor.** Select Window ⇨ Script Editor or press Ctrl + Shift + F5 if necessary to open the Script Editor. This time the Script Editor should open to the size you had previously left it.

4. **Change the Show drop-down to calculate.** Select calculate from the drop-down list in the show box to set the event the calculation occurs on.

5. **Verify the Calculation Language is set to FormCalc.** Use the Language drop-down list on the right side of the Script Editor to select FormCalc if necessary.

6. **Verify the Run At is set to Client.** Use the Run At drop-down on the right side of the Script Editor to select Client if necessary. This allows the script to execute in the viewer application on the computer where the form is being completed.

7. **Type the code in the Script Editor.** Type the following code into the Script Editor. Remember that FormCalc is a case-sensitive scripting language. Because the tax field we are calculating is in a different node of the hierarchy than the subtotal, we need to access them from the branch of the hierarchy they have in common, the rows of the Totals table. We start at the node they have in common and work our way down the hierarchy until we reach the desired field. Your script should appear like the screenshot in Figure 29.23 when finished.

```
1. $.rawValue = Row1.SubTotal*.065;
```

TIP You can use a shortcut to get the proper object name into the Script Editor without typing it. Ensure your cursor is in the Script Editor at the proper location. Hold down the Ctrl key and click the desired object on the design page. This enters the relative path to the object. If you need the absolute path, hold down Ctrl + Shift while clicking the object.

8. **Test the script.** Select the Preview PDF tab. Fill in a subtotal amount (we will calculate this shortly). The tax amount should be calculating now.

9. **Return to Design View.** Return to Design View to continue editing your form.

10. **Save a copy of the form.** Save the form in a location of your choice on your computer.

Creating the Total calculation by adding the subtotal and the tax amount together is very similar to creating the sales tax calculation. By selecting the Total field you can enter the following into the calculate event of the Script Editor, as shown in Figure 29.24:

```
1. $.rawValue = Row1.SubTotal + Row2.Tax;
```

FIGURE 29.23

The FormCalc script in the editor to calculate sales tax

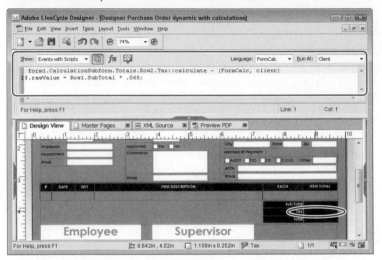

FIGURE 29.24

The Total field script

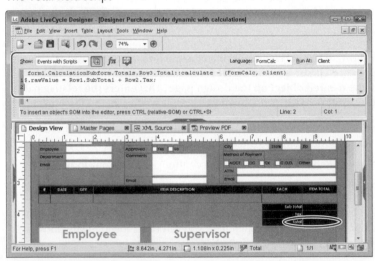

If you have any trouble, follow the steps for entering the tax amount again. The same formula could be written using the Sum function instead of manually adding the fields as indicated in the following code, and shown in Figure 29.25:

```
1. $.rawValue = Sum(Row1.SubTotal,Row2.Tax);
```

FIGURE 29.25

An alternate total field script, using the Sum function

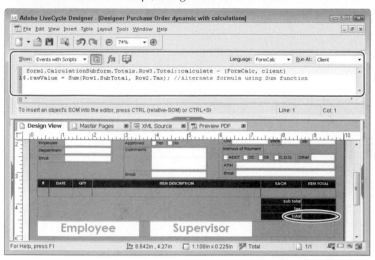

Either formula produces the same results. Using the Sum function over the manual addition is preferable in this case. Creating the subtotal script to add the table rows will be a little different. Since the table is dynamic, it is capable of growing or shrinking. We want our calculation to work regardless of the number of rows contained in the table.

Because the additional rows added to the table create objects with the same name, Designer creates an array of objects. An array is an ordered list of related objects. Each item contained in the array is known as an element. The elements are indexed starting with 0. Accessing that array makes summing the table a simple formula without the need to know exactly how many rows it contains.

STEPS: Calculating the SubTotal

1. **Open a Designer file.** We continue using the *StartingPurchaseOrder.xdp* from the previous steps.

2. **Select the SubTotal Field.** We will create a formula that sums the Item Total for each row of the table.

3. **Open the Script Editor.** Select Window ➪ Script Editor, or press Ctrl + Shift + F5 if necessary to open the Script Editor. This time the Script Editor should open to the size you had previously left it.

4. **Change the Show drop-down to calculate.** Select calculate from the drop-down list in the show box if necessary.

5. **Verify the Calculation Language is set to FormCalc.** Use the Language drop-down list on the right side of the Script Editor to select FormCalc if necessary.

6. **Verify the Run At is set to Client.** Use the Run At drop-down on the right side of the Script Editor to select Client if necessary. This allows the script to execute in the viewer application on the computer where the form is being completed.

7. **Type the code in the Script Editor.** The beginning of this formula is exactly like the others. The Sum function also hasn't changed. We add a set of brackets with an asterisk inside after the object name that repeats in the form. The asterisk allows us to get all of the objects contained in the array. Your script should appear like the screenshot in Figure 29.26 when finished.

```
1. $.rawValue = Sum(MainSubform.Items.Row1[*].ItemTotal);
```

FIGURE 29.26

The total field script using FormCalc

8. **Test your script.** Select the Preview PDF tab. Fill in a subtotal amount (we will calculate this shortly). The tax amount should be calculating now.

9. **Return to Design View.** Return to Design View to continue editing your form.

10. **Save a copy of the form.** Save the form in a location of your choice on your computer.

We have discussed the need to clean and organize your field objects by renaming them and putting them into subform containers. The next code sample is the same script that is necessary if the subform objects are not renamed. The pound sign (#) in the script is an indicator of an untitled object. The brackets with the zero ([0]) indicate there is an array of those untitled objects. Because the subform is untitled, we have to go up another level to establish where it resides in the hierarchy.

```
$.rawValue = Sum(form1.#subform[0].Items.Row1[*].ItemTotal);
```

Scripting with FormCalc is like writing formulas in a spreadsheet program. Once you become familiar with the events available for scripting and the formula names, the rest is simply typing. Exploring the sample forms on the CD-ROM and the forms loaded with Designer gives you a great start to writing your own. Remember, you can borrow the code from one of those existing forms until you are ready to write them on your own. Let's see what it would take to recreate these purchase order scripts in JavaScript.

Using JavaScript

JavaScript is an open source, object-based, platform independent scripting language that is used to add interactivity to forms on Web sites. The Designer implementation of JavaScript is different from JavaScripts written in Acrobat or HTML code. Object-oriented languages depend on the object models of the environment they reside in. Each of these three environments has a unique object model to script against. When searching the Web for scripting samples, be sure to include the keywords *Designer* and/or *LiveCycle* to limit the results to scripts that work in Designer.

If we use the same purchase order file used in the FormCalc section, we'll have a direct comparison between the two languages when we finish. Learning to script in another language is no more difficult than the first language; it only has different syntax rules. Once you've grasped the key concepts of objects and events it is only a matter of learning the differences in syntax.

Let's discuss the Purchase Order form. We need to add only four calculations to the document to complete the form design. The ItemTotal field in each row, the SubTotal, the Tax, and the Total fields each need a script. If we are going to write the forms calculations in JavaScript, then we should change the default scripting language in the form to save a few steps each time we open the script editor.

CROSS-REF   See "Changing the Scripting Preferences for the Current Document" section earlier in this chapter for details.

 The *StartingPurchaseOrder.xdp* form can be found on the CD-ROM in the Chapter29 folder. The finished file is also included on the CD-ROM. You can open it and explore these scripts in *PurchaseOrderJS.pdf*.

STEPS: Adding JavaScript Calculations to the Purchase Order

1. **Open a Designer file.** We opened the *StartingPurchaseOrder.xdp* from the CD-ROM.

2. **Change the default scripting language for the document.** Select File ⇨ Form Properties. On the Defaults tab, change the default language in the scripting section to JavaScript. Press OK to save the changes.

3. **Select the ItemTotal Field.** We will create a formula that multiplies the quantity times the price per item to calculate the item total.

4. **Open the Script Editor.** Select Window ⇨ Script Editor or press Ctrl + Shift + F5 if necessary to open the Script Editor.

5. **Change the Show drop-down to calculate.** Select calculate from the drop-down list in the show box if necessary.

6. **Verify the Calculation Language is set to JavaScript.** The Language drop-down list is on the right side of the Script Editor. Because we changed the default scripting language for this document, we assume this was already set in the following steps and do not remind you to check each time.

7. **Type the code in the Script Editor.** The keyword *this* refers to the active object, the ItemTotal field. We are setting the rawValue of the active field equal to the value of the Qty field times the value of the Each field. The JavaScript version of this formula requires only a little more text because the rawValue property is not assumed in JavaScript. Your script should match Figure 29.27:

```
1. this.rawValue = Qty.rawValue * Each.rawValue;
```

FIGURE 29.27

ItemTotal formula in JavaScript

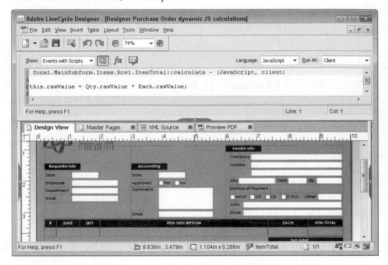

8. **Test the script.** Select the Preview PDF tab. Enter some numbers in the Qty and Each fields to test your calculations.

9. **Return to Design View.** Return to Design View to continue editing your form.

10. **Save a copy of the form.** Save the form in a location of your choice on your computer. We continue to create our form calculations by moving on to the Tax field.

11. **Select the Tax Field.** We will create a formula that multiplies the SubTotal times the current tax rate of 6.5 percent.

12. **Open the Script Editor.** Select Window ➪ Script Editor, or press Ctrl + Shift + F5 if necessary to open the Script Editor.

13. **Change the Show drop-down to calculate.** Select calculate from the drop-down list in the show box if necessary.

14. **Type the code in the Script Editor.** The keyword *this* refers to the active object, the Tax field. We are setting the rawValue of the active field equal to the value of the SubTotal * .065. Because the Tax field and the SubTotal are both inside the Totals Table (container) but not in the same subcontainer we use a relative path to reach it. After entering the following code, your script should match Figure 29.28.

```
this.rawValue = Row1.SubTotal.rawValue * .065;
```

FIGURE 29.28

Tax field calculation in JavaScript

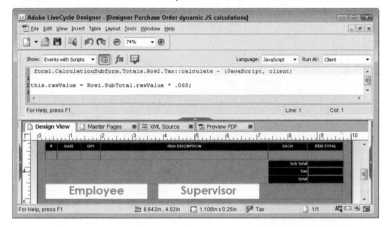

15. **Test the script.** Select the Preview PDF tab. Enter a number in the SubTotal field to test your calculation.

16. **Return to Design View.** Return to Design View to continue editing your form.

17. **Select the Total Field.** We will create a formula that adds the SubTotal and Tax fields.

18. **Open the Script Editor.** Select Window ⇨ Script Editor, or press Ctrl + Shift + F5 if necessary to open the Script Editor.

19. **Change the Show drop-down to calculate.** Select calculate from the drop-down list in the show box if necessary.

20. **Type the code in the Script Editor.** The keyword *this* refers to the active object, the Total field. We are setting the rawValue of the active field equal to the sum of the SubTotal and Tax Fields. After this step your script should match Figure 29.29. Again due to their positions we use a relative path to reach them:

```
1. this.rawValue = Row1.SubTotal.rawValue + Row2.Tax.rawValue;
```

FIGURE 29.29

Total calculation using JavaScript

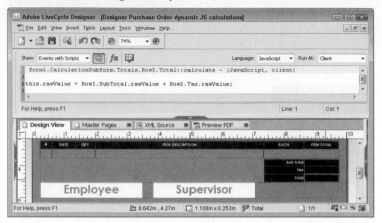

21. **Test your script.** Select the Preview PDF tab. Enter a number in the SubTotal field to test your calculation.

22. **Return to Design View.** Return to Design View to continue editing your form.

23. **Save the form.**

To finish the SubTotal field in JavaScript we need to discuss a few more concepts. We can't use a function to add the elements of the Row1.ItemTotal array. This requires us to loop through the elements and add the values together manually. We need a temporary storage facility to hold the value of our calculation while we work our way through the array. We also need to figure out how many items are in the array and instruct the loop to continue through the array until all items have been added.

A for loop structure consists of the following pieces:

```
for (var=startvalue;var<=endvalue;var=var+increment) {
    statement
    }
```

Use the for loop when you know how many times the script should run. It loops through the code the specified number of times. The three arguments are:

- **A Start value:** A variable is declared and given a starting value.
- **The ending value:** When the variable reaches this ending value, the loop stops.
- **Increment:** How much the variable increments with each time through the loop.

A variable is a temporary storage facility, defined with the var keyword. Variables can be declared in a formula, such as the one we are using, which makes its value available in the current formula only. Or a variable can be defined in a more broad location such as the form, or a script object that changes the objects that have access to the value stored in the variable.

We need three variables to write this formula. The first variable we declare holds all of the ItemTotal fields. This variable is named fields, and the contents are an array of fields.

The second variable holds the total we are calculating. This variable is named total and is initially set to a value of zero.

The third variable is a counter to determine when we have looped through all of the elements in the fields array. This variable is named i and initially set to a value of zero. The letter i is commonly chosen for this purpose as an abbreviation for integer. An integer is a whole number. We need to take the counter and increment it by one each time it goes through the loop. This can be done by taking the variable i and adding one to it each time. Typing i = i +1 accomplishes that. Another scripting shortcut is to shorten that statement into: i++. Our *for* loop continues as long as the counter is less than or equal to the number of elements in the fields array.

24. **Select the SubTotal Field.** We will create a formula that adds all the ItemTotal fields together.

25. **Open the Script Editor.** Select Window ⇨ Script Editor, or press Ctrl + Shift + F5 if necessary to open the Script Editor.

26. **Change the Show drop-down to calculate.** Select calculate from the drop-down list in the show box if necessary.

27. **Type the code in the Script Editor.** The keyword *this* refers to the active object, the SubTotal field. We are setting the rawValue of the active field equal to the sum of the ItemTotal in each row of the table. Because JavaScript doesn't contain a sum function that allows us to add items stored in the array, we need to create a loop to add the items in the array one at a time. Check your script with Figure 29.30 when finished with this step.

```
1. var fields = xfa.resolveNodes("MainSubform.Items.Row1[*].
   ItemTotal");
2. var total = 0;
3.
4. for (var i=0; i < fields.length; i++) {
5.   total = total + fields.item(i).rawValue;
6.   }
7.
8. this.rawValue = total;
```

■ **Line 1:** Defines the fields variable and sets it equal to the array of the Row1 ItemTotal Fields.

- **Line 2:** Defines the total variable and sets it equal to zero. By setting the variable at zero, the counter remains one number lower than the field count; we can simply say as long as the counter is less than the number of fields. If we started at one, we would need to test as long as the counter is less than or equal to the field count.

- **Line 3:** Is for readability and could be removed.

- **Line 4:** Is the beginning of the *for* loop. The three arguments are set here.

- **Line 5:** Sets the total variable equal to whatever it currently contains plus the value of the current element in the array.

- **Line 6:** The closing bracket of the for loop

- **Line 7:** Is for readability and could be removed.

- **Line 8:** Sets the value of the active field, the SubTotal equal to the amount in the total variable.

FIGURE 29.30

The for loop used to calculate the SubTotal field in JavaScript

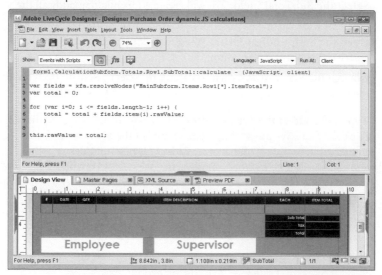

28. **Test the script.** Select the Preview PDF tab. Enter a few numbers in the Qty and Each fields to test your calculation.

29. **Return to Design View.** Return to Design View to save your form.

30. **Save the form.**

Congratulations, you completed the calculations in the Purchase Order form using JavaScript. Learning to write loops is a necessity when learning scripting. Loops are useful in many situations. However, as you can see from the previous example the FormCalc Sum function is much easier in this situation. We chose to explore it here to accomplish two tasks: Exposure to a simple loop structure, and to be able to compare the two languages functionality.

Debugging Scripts

What do you do when you have written a script and everything looks correct, but the script does not produce the desired results? Where do you start to troubleshoot? Our first recommendation is to reread your script and double-check the case of each word, as shown in Figures 29.31 and 29.32. Both scripting languages are case-sensitive and are the cause of much frustration for beginners. Functions, fields, and properties must all be typed exactly the way they are defined.

FIGURE 29.31

Locate the typographical error that is preventing this script from running.

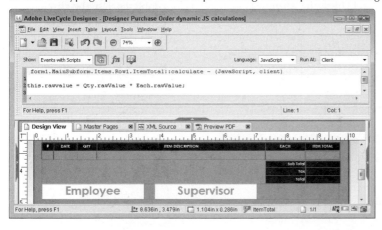

If that doesn't seem to be the problem, did you remember to set the scripting language to the type you were writing? The best JavaScript code won't function if the language is still set to FormCalc. Of course the opposite produces the same problem.

FIGURE 29.32

The error has been corrected in this script.

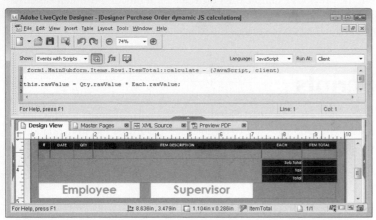

Turn on the Report palette, and check the warnings and log tabs for problems. Use the check scripts button of the Script Editor to generate these warnings. Although allowed in FormCalc, removing the .rawValue property from a JavaScript function generates a message in the Warning tab of the Report palette, as shown in Figure 29.33.

FIGURE 29.33

The Warning tab of the Report palette

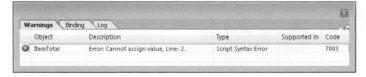

Clicking the palette menu and selecting Help opens the help window with Report palette topic open. A link there takes us to the About warning messages help topic where we follow another link to the Addressing scripting error messages topic. Here we find a link to the syntax checking help PDF document on the Web site http://help.adobe.com/en_US/livecycle/8.2/lcdesigner_syntaxchecking.pdf where error number 7003 is explained as a "Syntax Script Error: An assignment attempts to access a constant such as a number, string, or XML."

Sometimes a little detective work on our own is a faster solution. Double-clicking the item in the Warnings tab opens the Script Editor and takes you to the line of code that generated the error, as shown in Figure 29.34. After a little thought we would probably realize that we forgot the .rawValue property on each of the fields.

FIGURE 29.34

The Script Editor with a highlighted line of code, indicating an error

Take a look at the Log tab of the Report palette. The message generated here, as shown in Figure 29.35, is a little more descriptive and maybe would have pointed us in the right direction.

FIGURE 29.35

The Log tab of the Report palette, with errors

Another great tool is the JavaScript Debugger in Acrobat. In the Preview PDF tab, you can turn on the JavaScript Debugger by pressing Ctrl + J. With the same error still in the form the console window shows multiple errors as seen in Figure 29.36.

FIGURE 29.36

The JavaScript Debugger console window with errors

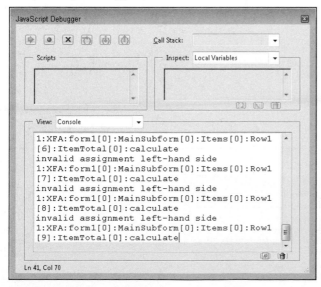

The error appears in the console window ten times because the calculation error is in the repeating row of the dynamic table that has ten rows. The console is telling us that there is an error due to an invalid assignment on the left side of the formula. Again after some checking we realize the .rawValue properties are missing.

Both the JavaScript Debugger and the Log tab of the Report palette can have the existing errors cleared to verify the errors you see are current, and not an old problem already corrected. As indicated by Figure 29.37, click the trash can in the lower-right corner of the JavaScript Debugger to clear the console window. To clear the Log tab in the Report palette, select the Palette menu and choose Clear Warning, as shown in Figure 29.38. To clear the console window, press the trash can button in the lower-right corner. The only way to clear an item from the Warnings tab of the Report palette is to fix the error that generates the message.

FIGURE 29.37

The JavaScript Debugger clear console button

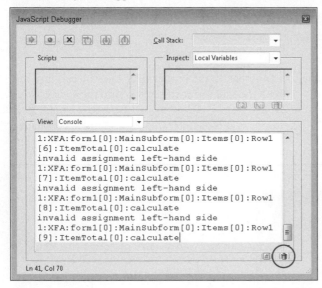

FIGURE 29.38

The Report palette clear warnings option

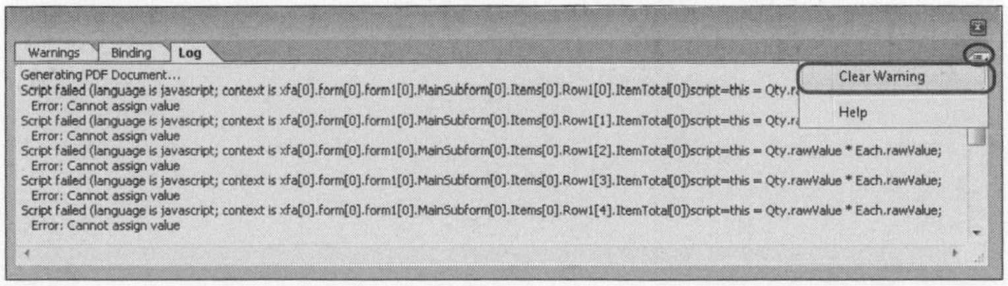

Many tools exist to help you find and fix the errors in scripts. Don't give up, keep looking. If you have a similar script in another location you can try copying and pasting the good code into the Script Editor where the broken script is. Sometimes comparing this way helps troubleshoot a problem.

Getting Help

Writing script is not something you perfect overnight. This book is not a FormCalc or a JavaScript reference book. Each of those topics deserves a book of its own. Our goal is to expose you to the scripting languages in the hope that you become interested and want to learn more. We want to provide you with some basic information that helps you decipher the scripts you find, and some samples to explore.

When searching for scripts on the Internet be sure to use keywords like *Designer, LiveCycle, FormCalc, JavaScript, Forms,* and *Scripts.* The results contain sample code, tips, and cautionary notes others have collected while scripting. As we mentioned in the Acrobat JavaScript chapters, bookmark your favorite sites and make frequent visits to check for updates.

Some of the best documentation available comes straight from Adobe, the reference manuals available from their Web site. Many are available as PDF files you can download, search, add to your library collection, and even make comments on for future use.

CROSS-REF For more information regarding your own library collection of help documentation see the section "Adding the JavaScript Manual to Your Organizer" in Chapter 16.

You can find more information about scripting languages and resources for LiveCycle Designer 8.x on Adobe's Web site at `http://kb.adobe.com/selfservice/viewContent.do?externalId=333249`. This page contains links to many of the resources listed in this section and always offers the most current version of the resources.

There is a specific reference guide for Acrobat users migrating to LiveCycle Designer to help convert existing JavaScripts. You can find the reference for Converting Acrobat® JavaScript for Use in LiveCycle™ Designer Forms at `http://www.adobe.com/devnet/livecycle/articles/AcroJS_DesignerJS.pdf`.

Documentation regarding the Adobe XML Forms Architecture (XFA) specification can be found at `http://partners.adobe.com/public/developer/xml/index_arch.html`.

The FormCalc Specification Version 2.0 is a PDF available from Adobe's Web site, and can be found at `http://partners.adobe.com/public/developer/en/xml/formcalc_2.0.pdf`.

CROSS-REF For more information see the section "Using online services" in Chapter 16.

The Designer help file offers many resources that include both FormCalc and JavaScript. It is titled Scripting Using LiveCycle Designer ES and includes the following topics:

- **About scripting in LiveCycle Designer ES:** An introduction to how scripting works, calculations, and what objects can contain scripts.

- **Configuring LiveCycle Designer ES Workspace for Scripting:** Describes how to use the Script Editor and setting your scripting preferences.

- **Creating Calculations and Scripts:** Deciding when and where to place your scripts, the statement completion options, how to view scripts, the debugger, and more.

- **Events:** An alphabetical list of events, the event types, and diagrams explaining the event order.

- **Scripting Languages:** The differences between FormCalc and JavaScript functions, the basics for using each language.

- **Referencing Objects in Calculations and Scripts:** How to reference objects using absolute and relative syntax and any additional syntax shortcuts.

- **Variables:** Naming, defining, and using variables.

- **Debugging Calculations and Scripts:** How to turn on, use, and troubleshoot with the tabs in the report palette. How to use the Acrobat JavaScript Debugger with LiveCycle Designer.

- **Working with a Host Application:** LiveCycle ES Forms, Acrobat, Adobe Reader, or an HTML browser are hosts you can work with.

- **Working with the Event Model:** Using the event object properties and methods, you can retrieve information that otherwise is not accessible through scripts.

- **Creating and Reusing JavaScript Functions:** How to create a script object, custom JavaScript functions, and use them in other scripts.

- **Using Script Fragments:** How to create a reusable script object, stored in the fragment library.

- **Moving from Scripting in Acrobat to LiveCycle Designer ES:** The differences between scripting in Acrobat and Designer are discussed, determining how much is supported and what needs to be converted.

- **Examples of Common Scripting Tasks:** Specific examples for common items such as calculating totals in tables, changing visual properties, using the Instance Manager in dynamic forms, and more.

Using the FormCalc user reference

Contained in the LiveCycle Designer help file is a FormCalc user reference. The reference is broken down into the following areas:

- **Introducing FormCalc:** This area explains what FormCalc is, why there are two scripting languages in Designer, and an alphabetical function list.

- **Language Reference:** Provides an explanation of the building blocks used in the FormCalc language such as keywords, operators, comments, identifiers, and more. Putting those building blocks together to form expressions is also explained.

- **Functions:** Help for each category of functions, including a link to each function within the categories:
  - **Arithmetic Functions**
  - **Date and Time Functions**
  - **Financial Functions**
  - **Logical Functions**
  - **Miscellaneous Functions**
  - **String Functions**
  - **URL Functions**

Using the LiveCycle Designer Scripting Reference

The LiveCycle® Designer ES Scripting Reference, Version 8.2 is available from the Adobe Web site at http://help.adobe.com/en_US/livecycle/8.2/lcdesigner_scripting_reference.pdf. This file can also be accessed using the help file in Designer: Help ⇨ Scripting Reference. The help window that follows contains a topic called About the Object Scripting Reference that contains a direct link to the previously mentioned scripting reference on Adobe's Web site.

In the Designer help files are several resources on scripting:

- **About the Object Scripting Reference:** Information regarding the objects, properties, and methods that you can use in LiveCycle Designer.

- **Version mapping to XFA:** This document explains how each release of the XML Form Architecture Maps to a version of LiveCycle Designer. It helps explain when features become available.

- **XML Form Object Model Class Hierarchy:** Explains the XML Form Object Model Classes, and whether or not they inherit properties and methods from their parent classes.

- **Scripting Objects:** An alphabetical list of all objects supported in the scripting environment including the parent-child hierarchy relationships.

- **Scripting Properties:** An alphabetical list of all properties supported.

- **Scripting Methods:** An alphabetical list of all methods supported.

Using a combination of all of the resources listed here provides the most well-rounded resource guide we can think of. Open a form that already contains scripts, make a backup copy, and tear apart the script it contains. Can you improve the existing code to reduce the number of lines of code? Try changing the existing code from the current scripting language to the other. Explore the sample files and try your own code!

Comparing Scripting Languages

As we found by creating our calculations in the Purchase Order form in both languages, you can do many of the same things in both languages. One language may be better suited than another for a particular task. Table 29.1 lists JavaScript methods and comparable FormCalc functions

As shown in Figure 29.36, we found that creating the SubTotal formula was much less complicated when using the Sum function in FormCalc than writing a for loop in JavaScript. Yes, sometimes that exact JavaScript loop is needed in a Designer form because it is rendered as HTML and browsers don't understand FormCalc.

TABLE 29.1

JavaScript Methods with the Comparable FormCalc Function

JavaScript Method	FormCalc Function	Description
Math.abs	Abs	Absolute Value
String.search	At	Locates the starting character position of a string within another string.
Math.ceil	Ceil	The whole number greater than or equal to a given number.
String.concat	Concat	Joining two or more character strings end to end (concatenation).
Date.getDate	Date	Current Date. JS does not use the Epoch date the way FormCalc does.
eval	Eval	The value of a given form calculation.
Math.floor	Floor	The largest whole number less than or equal to a given number.
String.substring	Left	Extracts the specified number of characters, starting from first character on the left.
String.length	Len	The number of characters in a string (length).
String.toLowerCase	Lower	Converts the string to lowercase characters.
Math.max	Max	The largest value in the expression.
Math.min	Min	The smallest value in the expression.
modulo (%) operator	Mod	The modulus (remainder) of a division expression.
String.replace	Replace	Replaces all occurrences of the specified string with a replacement string.
String.substring	Right	Extracts the specified number of characters, starting from first character on the right.
Math.round	Round	Rounds an expression to the given number of decimal places.
String or Number. toString	Str	Converts a number to a string, format and round decimals to specified number of digits.

JavaScript Method	FormCalc Function	Description
String.substring	Substr	Extracts a portion of a string.
Date.getTime	Time	Current Time. JS does not use the Epoch date the way FormCalc does.
String.toUpperCase	Upper	Converts the string to uppercase characters.
String.search	Within	If a value is within a given range.

Summary

- Scripting enhances form design for a more customized user experience.

- FormCalc is the default scripting language in Designer and is an Adobe proprietary language.

- JavaScript is the alternate scripting language.

- FormCalc contains more than 60 predefined functions to work with.

- Functions automate common mathematical expressions.

- Changing the scripting preferences can include the default language for the current form and where the code executes.

- The Script Editor formatting can be changed to create visual differences in the scripting languages.

- Entering references to other objects can be relative or absolute.

- The keyword *this* refers to the active object in JavaScript, whereas in FormCalc we use $.

- Debugging scripts using the Report palette and the JavaScript Debugger tools can help you troubleshoot your scripts.

- To change the scripting language for all new designer forms, you need to customize the default template.

- Adobe offers many resources for learning FormCalc and JavaScript. Check the Adobe Web site for the most current reference manuals available.

Chapter 30

Deploying Forms

IN THIS CHAPTER

Preparing forms for deployment

Saving static or dynamic designer forms

Distributing forms

Viewer version requirements

Form deployment is a critical piece of any form workflow. Before forms are deployed for use, they must be properly designed, tested, and saved. We have already covered how to create the forms and set the necessary properties to have your form ready for deployment.

Knowing how to do something and remembering to do all those things are two completely different matters. Many things should be considered before deployment.

The form design and added functionality must convey the intended message. Tab sequence, formulas, and scripting all need to be tested for a user-friendly experience. Sometimes, we all need a gentle reminder that a built-in spell-checking program is not a replacement for human proofreading.

After we complete the checklist for testing and proofing our forms, we are ready to distribute them to the people who need to use them. Whether the form will be used by a few or by many people, we need to deploy it properly.

Preparing for Deployment

The number of people involved in deploying a form varies by organization. The form designer may be the one responsible for the entire process in a smaller company. In larger companies, many people are involved. How a form is prepared for deployment can vary as greatly as who is responsible for doing so.

Poorly developed forms can be caused by a lack of communication between departments, undefined procedures, time constraints, and inexperienced designers. Most often it is simply because the appropriate person was unaware a problem existed.

No matter which situation you find yourself in, consider adding the following items to your form deployment checklist:

- **Content:** The form contains all the elements necessary to meet the business requirements of the form and conveys the intended information. The form has been proofed for typographical errors, correct fonts, images, and other items. It is important to double-check that the company guidelines and policies were followed during the form design process.

- **Fields:** The correct field types have been utilized in the form design to collect the required information. Any validation rules or masks needed have been set to ensure the correct data is collected from the form recipient. A field that allows erroneous information to be collected can cause delays in the workflow.

  The best way to check the form for correct field types is to enter data into each and every field during the testing phase. Do not skip fields when testing. As a second test, merge a sample file with the form. Using both methods improves the likelihood of finding potential problems.

CROSS-REF Acrobat field types are discussed in Chapter 7. For more information on Designer field types, see Chapter 24. Designer properties such as validation and masks can be found in Chapter 25.

- **Calculations and scripts:** Any scripts placed in the form have been tested for accuracy and usability in the appropriate viewer applications. The viewer application and the file type can both affect scripting. If a problem is found, check to see if the viewer application supports the scripting in question, in addition to checking the syntax of the script.

CROSS-REF For more information on scripting in Acrobat forms, see Chapters 15 through 18. Designer scripting is discussed in Chapters 28 and 29.

- **Tab order:** The tab sequence is logical, and not erratic, for completing the form. Acrobat and Designer determine the default tab order in different ways. Both programs offer an easy-to-use tab order palette to reorder the fields.

  Acrobat relies on the order in which you placed the fields on the form to determine the default tab order. Manually changing the tab order in Acrobat is more common than in Designer because of this.

  Designer uses the field coordinates from left to right and then top to bottom to set the default tab order. The best way to fix tab order in Designer is to correctly align the fields and use subforms to wrap related items together. Setting the tab order manually is useful in some situations, but some minor adjustments in alignment produce the same results in Designer.

CROSS-REF For more information on tab order in Acrobat forms, see Chapter 7. Designer tab order is discussed in Chapters 24 and 25.

■ **Save:** Choose the best file format for the form requirements. Embedding unnecessary fonts increases file size. Maintaining compatibility with older viewer versions also increases file size. A form saved in the wrong file format may cause compatibility issues and unexpected script failures.

CROSS-REF See the section "Saving LiveCycle Designer Forms" later in this chapter for more information. More information on optimizing Designer files is in Chapter 34.

■ **Security:** Protect the form design from unauthorized edits using password protection or certified documents. Use digital signatures to lock the fields after the form is completed to ensure the received data has not been altered.

CROSS-REF For more information on security, see Chapter 12 and the "Adding Security" section later in this chapter.

■ **Extend features:** If the form is to be enabled for extended usage in Adobe Reader, make sure it is the last step of the deployment process. Any additional changes to the form require removing the special extended features. The form can be extended using the Advanced menu in Acrobat or the Distribute Form wizard. We recommend that you test the form both before the features are extended and after.

CROSS-REF For more information on extended usage in Adobe Reader, see Chapter 10.

■ **Data collection:** Discuss the available options with other people involved in the form workflow. Verify that the process for collecting this form data has been established and tested.

CROSS-REF For more information on data collection options, see Chapters 14 and 34 and the "Distributing Forms" section later in this Chapter.

■ **Test the form:** Thoroughly test the form by completing it several times as if you are the form recipient. Be creative; a great way to test the form is by attempting to enter incorrect data. What happens when the unexpected data is received is just as important as what happens when the correct data is received. Do not assume that the form recipient is paying attention to the requirements of the form or the field they are working on. As the form tester, your job is to try to break it. Deploying a form with errors can be extremely embarrassing and appears unprofessional.

Start testing the form in the viewer most form recipients are expected to have. The form should be tested in all the viewing applications in which the form will be deployed. At the very least, the form should be tested in at least one version of Acrobat and one version of Adobe Reader.

Saving LiveCycle Designer Forms

We've all saved files before and can select File ➪ Save without any difficulty. However, saving forms in Designer offers some different formats to choose from. While this may seem like no big deal, it makes the difference between a form working the way it was intended and a form failing. Understanding the form types available in LiveCycle Designer combined with the version of the viewer affects how we save our Designer forms. When you save a form the first time, or when using Save As, you see the dialog box shown in Figure 30.1.

FIGURE 30.1

The Save As dialog box in Designer 8.2

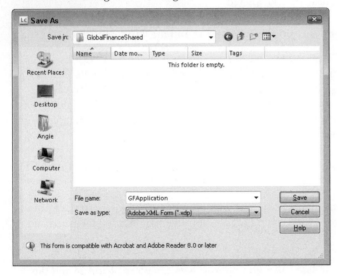

Notice in the lower-left corner of the Save As window that a message displays to indicate what version of Acrobat and Reader the form is currently compatible with. When designing, you can set the version you need to be compatible with, known as the *target version*. The message in the Save As window is for your information.

CROSS-REF For more information on checking compatibility with viewers, see the section "Setting the target version" later in this chapter.

The Save As choices have changed in each of the recent version updates of Designer. Some settings that were formerly located in the Save As dialog box have now moved to the Form Properties dialog box, as shown in Figure 30.2. The Save options can be located by selecting File ⇨ Form Properties and then choosing the Save Options tab.

FIGURE 30.2

The Save Options tab of the Form Properties dialog box

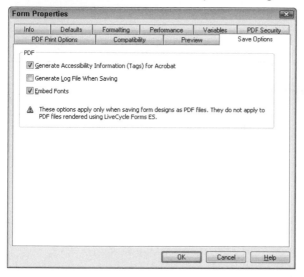

The Save Options located in the Form Properties dialog box apply only when saving a file as a PDF format that does *not* use the LiveCycle Forms ES for rendering. When rendering using LiveCycle Forms ES, the Save Option settings are ignored. These options include:

- **Generate Accessibility Information (Tags) for Acrobat:** Tags embed accessibility information for screen readers (text-to-speech devices) into the PDF to ensure that it is rendered properly.

CROSS-REF For more information on accessibility, see Chapter 11.

- **Generate Log File when Saving:** The log file is given the same name and placed in the same directory as the saved PDF.

- **Embed Fonts:** Choosing to embed the fonts ensures that the document always displays and prints using the fonts it was designed with. This also causes the file size to increase as a result and can affect the performance of the form.

CROSS-REF For more information on optimizing Designer forms, see Chapter 34.

After we have checked that the form properties are set correctly, we are ready to save our form. Saving the form in Designer offers many format choices, as shown in Figure 30.3. The format chosen may affect form functionality.

FIGURE 30.3

The Save As formats available in Designer 8.2

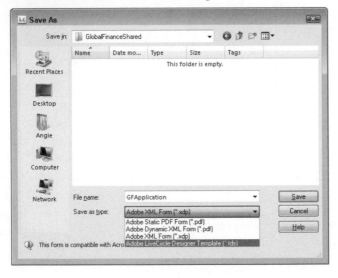

The default Save As format in LiveCycle Designer is Static PDF. You can change the default behavior according to your own preferences. You can change the default setting by selecting Tools ➪ Options ➪ Document Handling ➪ Default File Type for New Forms, as shown in Figure 30.4.

Saving static forms

Static forms do not change in layout or number of pages. Many Acrobat forms are static forms, and paper forms also are static. The space dedicated to the object is reserved, even if the object is not needed by the form recipient or the data being merged with the form. Select the Save as type option Adobe Static PDF Form (*.pdf) in these cases, as shown in Figure 30.5.

Saving a Designer form as static gives us the best backwards compatibility with the viewer applications. Remember that Acrobat forms have been available for much longer than Designer forms, all the way back to Acrobat and Reader 4. However, PDF forms based on XML did not exist then. The first version of Acrobat or Reader that can open a Designer form is version 6.02. The version required to open your specific form depends on what additional functionality you add to the form.

FIGURE 30.4

The default file type for new forms setting

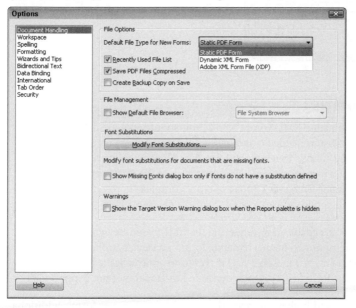

FIGURE 30.5

The Save As window with a static PDF form selected

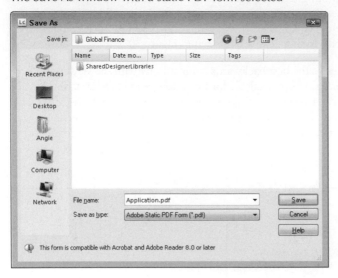

Saving dynamic forms

When saving a file as an Adobe Dynamic XML Form (*.pdf), you should include dynamic features. Dynamic forms are designed to adjust as needed by adjusting the layout when merging data with form. Another reason dynamics are used is to allow the form recipient the ability to alter the form by adding or removing sections of a form as needed. This changing of the document layout is called flowing the content in Designer. Dynamic forms are more complex than static forms, requiring a higher version of the viewing applications.

The first version of the viewers that is capable of re-rendering the XML-based Designer forms when changes occur is version 7.05. Attempting to open a dynamic form in a viewer application between 6.02 and 7.03 opens the form with an error message stating this form appears to be a newer format. The viewer application supports the form fields, but the dynamic functionality is not supported.

Although any viewer versions 6.02 and higher can open the XML-based Designer forms, additional features and functions have been introduced over the years. As the new functions become available, the viewing applications receive updates to be able to utilize these abilities.

In Designer 8.1 and earlier, the target version was part of the Save As feature. Each version number had its own Save As option, as shown in Figure 30.6. This was confusing to many users, and as a result these are now separate properties. Choosing which version number you want to deploy your forms with is called the target version and is covered in the next section of this chapter.

FIGURE 30.6

The Save As options in Designer 8.0-8.1

When you create a dynamic form design that is incorrectly saved as a static form, the dynamic elements do not function. The viewer application does not re-render the form, which is required when dynamic changes to the form occur.

CAUTION A dynamic form saved as a static form opens and allows the user to fill in the data of any fields that were displayed initially. Buttons scripted to allow dynamic interaction still appear, but they do not function properly when clicked. Clicking the buttons generally results in nothing happening at all, including no error messages. This causes a great amount of frustration for experienced users and confusion for inexperienced users.

CROSS-REF For more troubleshooting ideas, see Chapter 28.

Setting the target version

When designing a form, you can specify the viewer version you think most of the form recipients have when working with the form. This allows you to test functionality and see warnings when trying to utilize features that are not supported. The target version is stored in the Form Properties dialog box. To change the target version settings, select File ➪ Form Properties and then choose the Defaults tab, as shown in Figure 30.7.

The Defaults tab of the Form Properties dialog box shows the Target Version options.

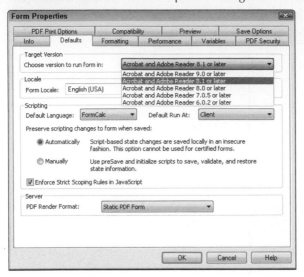

While working on a form design and testing, you can right-click the Preview PDF tab to see which format is currently selected, as shown in Figure 30.8.

Right-clicking the Preview PDF tab shows the current setting.

You should have the same viewer loaded on your computer as you have set in the target version. Doing otherwise may cause errors to appear because the Preview PDF tab uses the target version of the saved form.

When a feature is used in the form design that is not supported by the target version, a message appears in the Warnings tab of the Report palette. If the feature is important to the form design functionality, then the target version must be updated accordingly. If the feature is not required for the form design, changing some settings may allow the form to render correctly in the currently selected target version. For information on troubleshooting target version errors, see the "Addressing target warning messages" topic in the Designer Help files.

Saving XDP forms

When working in LiveCycle Designer making constant edits, be sure to leave the file in a Designer native format. This ensures that, when the file is double-clicked from its storage location, it opens directly in Designer. The Save as type is Adobe XML Form (*.xdp).

An XDP form with embedded images is generally larger than the PDF counterpart. Our tendency is to store in XDP format for the majority of the design phase and save as PDF files after most of the design and testing have been completed.

The XDP format also is required if you are using Adobe LiveCycle Forms ES to render the form as HTML.

CROSS-REF For more information on the LiveCycle ES solution components for servers, see Chapter 34.

Rendering HTML forms

LiveCycle Designer creates XML-based forms. When you put this power together with the LiveCycle Forms ES, you can render in additional formats, including HTML, as shown in Figure 30.9.

FIGURE 30.9

A Designer form rendered as HTML using LiveCycle Forms ES

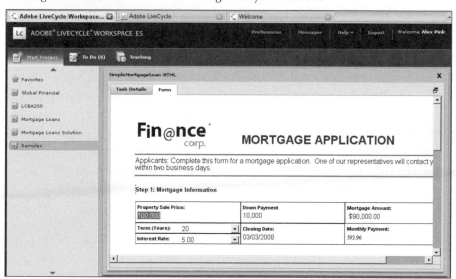

Forms that are to be rendered as HTML need to follow some additional guidelines. Because a browser is the viewing application, the limitations of the browser may affect your form. A browser does not understand the FormCalc scripting language, so all scripting must be done using JavaScript. Any object type may be placed in your form design except signature fields. HTML forms require that all objects have a unique name, even across different object types. For example, you cannot name a text field and a subform with the same name.

LC Forms ES takes the XDP file that Designer creates and renders the form in a browser-compatible HTML format instead. Forms ES renders the Designer page subforms as the HTML pages in a wizard-style document that contains next and previous buttons to reach the additional pages.

Rendering form guides

Form guides are another way to display your Designer form in a wizard-style environment using Flash Player inside a browser window. Any existing Designer form can be made into a Form Guide. It doesn't matter if the form was saved as a PDF or an XDP. LiveCycle Designer has another tool called the Guide Builder to help you create the Flash rending of the form. However, you cannot deploy the form as a Flash file (.SWF) unless you render it using Adobe LiveCycle ES.

The Guide Builder is located in Tools ➪ Create or Edit Form Guide. After the basic form design has been created, you need to make sure the field naming has been completed and any calculations that were created use JavaScript. The Guide Builder offers several layout choices for your Flash form, as well as the ability to customize it, as shown in Figure 30.10.

When you preview the form guide, the form is rendered as a .SWF file and displayed in the default browser. In order to preview the form guide as Flash when working with Guide Builder, you need Flash Player 9 or higher for the default browser you are working with.

A form guide has many pieces that make up the layout:

- **The form guide layout:** The outer container that holds all the panels is called the Form Guide layout. It also contains some standard buttons for Save, Print, and Email.
  - **The navigation panel:** The navigation panel lists the sections in the Form Guide in a hierarchy structure and provides them as links to the other areas in the Flash file.
  - **The data entry panel:** This panel contains the areas where fields are placed for user interaction. These panels allow you to choose from a variety of layout options.

■ **The guide help panel:** If help is associated with a navigation panel, it appears in the help panel.

■ **Navigation controls:** The Guide Builder automatically creates the Next, Back, and Submit buttons for the navigation controls.

The Guide Builder is worthy of its own chapter; it has many features that we could discuss. However, because rendering the form guide as Flash requires the LiveCycle ES Components to deploy them, we restrict our content to this brief overview with Figures 30.11, 30.12, and 30.13 to show how the Global Finance Purchase Order form appears in Flash.

FIGURE 30.10

The Guide Builder layout with the purchase order form

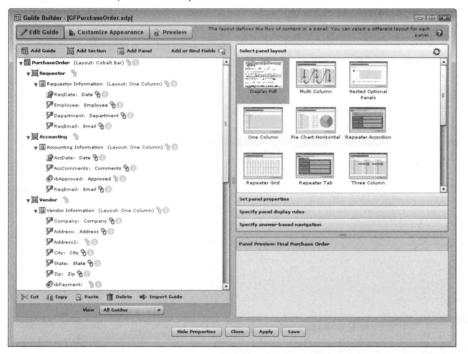

FIGURE 30.11

The purchase order requestor information panel

FIGURE 30.12

The purchase order items repeating information panel

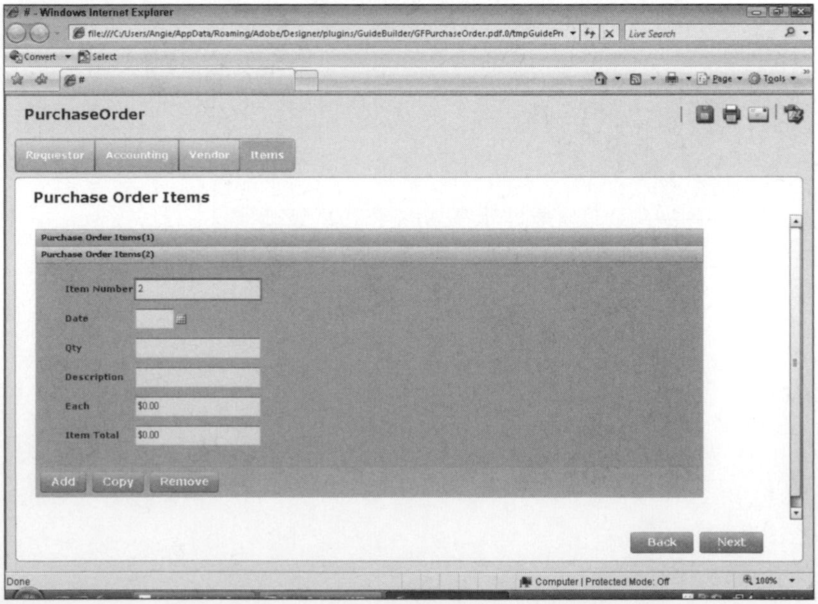

FIGURE 30.13

The purchase order viewed as a PDF in the Flash Player

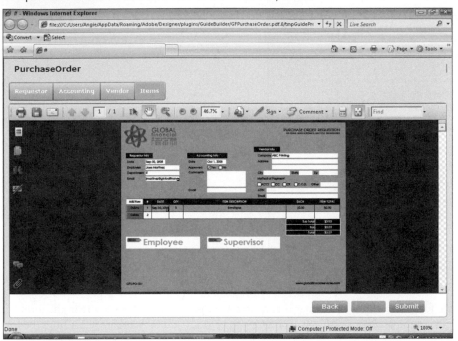

CROSS-REF For more information on the LiveCycle ES Components, see Chapter 34.

Adding Security

The Portable Document Format is excellent for sharing files. What many people forget is that anyone with Acrobat can open and modify a PDF file. To ensure the file is not altered after deploying it, the file must be secured. By adding password security to the PDF file, we can allow the form fields to be filled in without allowing other document changes.

Password security can be added in either Acrobat or Designer. In Designer, select File ➪ Form Properties ➪ PDF Security to set a password on the PDF file. When you enable the option to use a password to restrict printing and editing of the document and its security settings, the options available include all the same settings as Acrobat files, as shown in Figure 30.14.

FIGURE 30.14

The PDF Security tab of the Form Properties dialog box

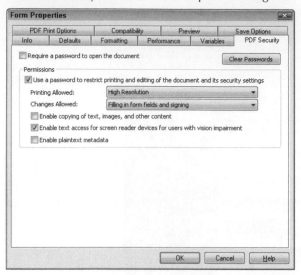

Editing a PDF form created with Designer is restricted because of the XML structure in the form template. Some of the security settings will continue to be restricted in Acrobat. Select from the following settings:

- **Printing Allowed:** Printing can be prevented, allowed at low resolution, or allowed at a high resolution. When a permission password is set on the file, printing is set to None by default. We recommend changing the setting to allow printing when working with forms.

- **Changes Allowed:** Select from the following options:

    - **None:** No changes are allowed to the file unless the password is entered.

    - **Inserting, deleting, and rotating pages:** Acrobat cannot edit these items in a PDF form created with Designer. Acrobat can only temporarily rotate the view of the page.

    - **Filling in form fields and signing:** Allow the form recipient to complete the form fields and sign the signature fields.

    - **Commenting, filling in form fields, and signing:** In addition to the form field option above, commenting may be allowed. If you save the document as Static PDF, then commenting works. If you save as Dynamic PDF, then comments are not allowed.

- ■ **Any except extracting pages:** Extracting pages is not allowed on a PDF form created with Designer. This setting is equivalent to no security on a form created with Designer.

- ■ **Enable copying of text, images, and other content:** If the setting is enabled, then by selecting information in the PDF file, it can be copied to other applications. The setting is turned off by default.

- ■ **Enable text access for screen reader devices for users with vision impairment:** When a file is protected, this setting must remain enabled for accessibility devices to read the document properly.

Signature fields provide a different level of security to the form. As discussed in Chapter 12, a signature field can be used to lock the form fields from any additional changes. They also can be set to lock a limited set of fields. Designer has the same capabilities, but it implements them in a slightly different way.

The settings are contained on the Signature tab of the Object palette. Signature options allow locking all the fields, none of the fields, or based on a collection of fields, as shown in Figure 30.15. Collections provide the ability to create sets of fields and name them for the purposes of signature fields and paper forms barcodes.

FIGURE 30.15

Signature settings in the Object palette

Creating and modifying collections is similar to selecting the fields you wish to lock in Acrobat. To create a new collection or manage an existing one, select the New/Manage Collection from the Signature tab of the Object palette, or select File ➪ Form Object Collections from the menu. The Collection List dialog box displays to work with any existing collections and provides tools for creating new collections, as shown in Figure 30.16.

FIGURE 30.16

The Collection List dialog box

To create a collection of fields, select the New Button and give the collection a name. With the name selected, press the modify button to open the Collection Editor, as shown in Figure 30.17. In the Collection Editor, select the appropriate fields. Selecting a page or a subform check box selects all the objects within that container. An individual field can be selected or deselected with the individual check boxes. As we discussed, in Acrobat selecting all the fields and removing a few from the selection may provide a more efficient method of selection. Non-supported objects are hidden by default, such as static text and drawn objects.

After the collection has been created, the Signature tab properties display the collections in the drop-down list. The collection may be used to select the fields to lock or to exclude them from all the other fields being locked. Many additional security features are available, including certificates and policies.

CROSS-REF For more information on security, see Chapter 14.

FIGURE 30.17

The Collection Editor showing the available fields

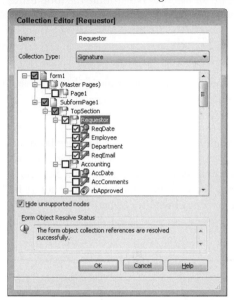

Distributing Forms

The distribution method you select is affected by many factors, including the number of form recipients, their location, the intended purpose of the collected data, which viewing application is used, and the form requirements. Each form deserves the independent analysis of deciding what is best for this form and the recipients. Because so many variables factor into the decision, there is not a single best choice.

A shared network folder works well for a form that is aimed at an internal audience. Acrobat.com is a great option for a small-to-medium public audience. E-mail distribution works for either internal or external audiences, but it requires the data collector to process that incoming mail. In situations where the number of responses is large, the LiveCycle ES products are best suited to handle the data.

In Chapter 14, we covered distributing Acrobat forms extensively. Distributing Designer forms really is no different. A Designer form must first be saved as a PDF in order to distribute it. You can begin the distribution process from either Acrobat or LiveCycle Designer. If you are working in

LiveCycle Designer, select File ⇨ Distribute Form or use the Distribute button on the standard tool-bar. Clicking the Distribute button closes the form in Designer and opens the PDF form in Acrobat, launching the Distribute Form wizard. The wizard allows you to distribute the form using e-mail, Acrobat.com, or a network folder.

CROSS-REF   For specifics on how to distribute a form, see Chapter 14.

When you open LiveCycle Designer by starting a new form or editing an existing form in Acrobat, LiveCycle Designer prompts you to distribute it when you close the form, as shown in Figure 30.18. This prompt does not occur if you open LiveCycle Designer directly.

The LiveCycle ES Components are designed to deploy, route, and collect form data. They keep the form data and the form presentation separate, allowing you to remerge the data with a form at any point in the workflow process. A form completed by an employee can be merged with a different form template when viewed by accounting for processing. The form may contain information that is not relevant for everyone to see; the servers allow you to control who sees what.

FIGURE 30.18

Designer prompts you to distribute a form when closing a form.

CROSS-REF   For more information on working with servers, see Chapter 34.

Many additional methods can be used for deploying your forms. We hope to have covered enough here to give you the tools you need to decide which deployment process works best for your organization.

Summary

- Designer forms saved as static PDF forms do not adjust in layout.

- Static Designer forms require an Acrobat viewer version 6.02 or higher to open them.

- Designer forms saved as dynamic PDF forms do adjust in layout based on data merged with the form or user interaction.

- Dynamic Designer forms require an Acrobat viewer version 7.05 or higher to work correctly.

- The target version is the viewer you plan to deploy your Designer form in.

- Setting the target version offers warnings while designing and testing your form.

- XDP files are the native Designer format.

- To render as HTML or Flash form guides, you need to use a LiveCycle ES Component.

- To render a Designer form as HTML, you must save it as an XDP file.

- Distributing forms in Designer is the same process as in Acrobat. The form must be saved as a PDF format to begin the distribution process.

Chapter 31

Working with Data

As we previously discussed in Chapter 14, data is a very important part of form development and all too often it is overlooked or written off at development time. We've all encountered the mentality of "one thing at a time"; we'll consider implementing that in the next phase; we can't do everything at once, anything will be better than what we had.

As we previously discussed in Chapter 14, data is a very important part of form development and all too often it is overlooked or written off at development time. We've all encountered the mentality of "one thing at a time"; we'll consider implementing that in the next phase; we can't do everything at once, anything will be better than what we had.

If we design the form, only to expect the form recipient to mail or fax back a printed copy of that information, we have solved only a minute piece of the overall form collection problem, the readability of the returned data. What about the need to enter that data into an electronic system, or sharing that data with interested parties in our organization?

Mailing or faxing requires the form recipient to take additional steps that rely on them to follow through with the process. What if they lose the fax number, or don't have access to a fax machine? The Postal Service does a wonderful job of delivering mail as long as it is legible, has a valid address, and proper postage. These are just a few of the items that can cause a delay in data collection. Even worse, we may never receive the data. Capturing data electronically is the real value in creating fillable forms.

In this chapter we focus on working with XML form data in a Designer form. After we discuss how XML is structured, we explore creating data connections in Designer to streamline testing and extracting data.

IN THIS CHAPTER

XML file structure

Creating data connections in Designer

XML editing programs

Data connections restricted in Reader

Creating an XML File

Extensible Markup Language (XML) is an open-source industry standard document markup language designed to structure, store, and transport data. Data in the XML file is stored as plain text. This allows for software and hardware independent data storage. The data is stored in the XML file with self-descriptive tags. The tags are not predetermined by the XML specification; they are defined by the author of the XML file. An XML data file can store any data where the structure can be represented as a tree. A sample XML file from our Purchase Order form developed in Chapter 28 is shown in Figure 31.1.

FIGURE 31.1

The Purchase Order Sample XML

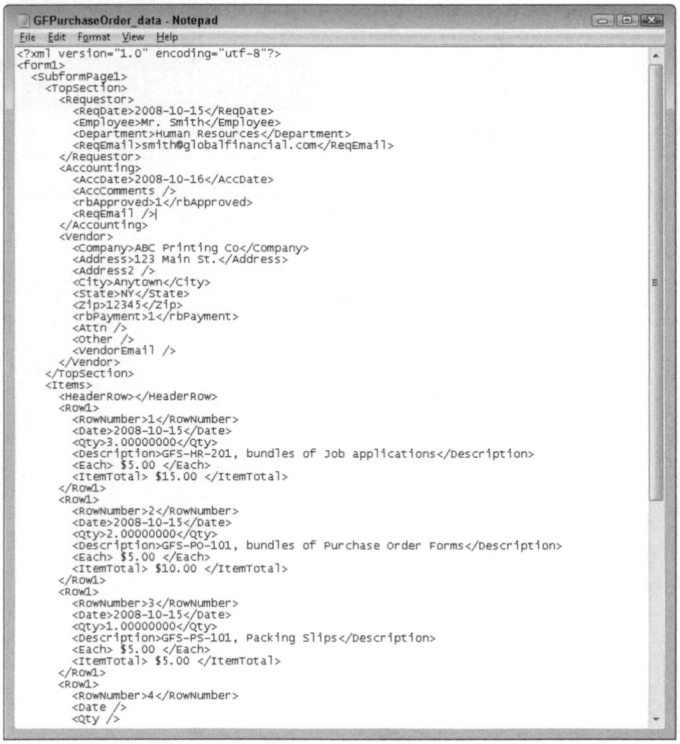


```
<?xml version="1.0" encoding="utf-8"?>
<form1>
  <SubformPage1>
    <TopSection>
      <Requestor>
        <ReqDate>2008-10-15</ReqDate>
        <Employee>Mr. Smith</Employee>
        <Department>Human Resources</Department>
        <ReqEmail>smith@globalfinancial.com</ReqEmail>
      </Requestor>
      <Accounting>
        <AccDate>2008-10-16</AccDate>
        <AccComments />
        <rbApproved>1</rbApproved>
        <ReqEmail />
      </Accounting>
      <Vendor>
        <Company>ABC Printing Co</Company>
        <Address>123 Main St.</Address>
        <Address2 />
        <City>Anytown</City>
        <State>NY</State>
        <Zip>12345</Zip>
        <rbPayment>1</rbPayment>
        <Attn />
        <Other />
        <VendorEmail />
      </Vendor>
    </TopSection>
    <Items>
      <HeaderRow></HeaderRow>
      <Row1>
        <RowNumber>1</RowNumber>
        <Date>2008-10-15</Date>
        <Qty>3.00000000</Qty>
        <Description>GFS-HR-201, bundles of Job applications</Description>
        <Each> $5.00 </Each>
        <ItemTotal> $15.00 </ItemTotal>
      </Row1>
      <Row1>
        <RowNumber>2</RowNumber>
        <Date>2008-10-15</Date>
        <Qty>2.00000000</Qty>
        <Description>GFS-PO-101, bundles of Purchase Order Forms</Description>
        <Each> $5.00 </Each>
        <ItemTotal> $10.00 </ItemTotal>
      </Row1>
      <Row1>
        <RowNumber>3</RowNumber>
        <Date>2008-10-15</Date>
        <Qty>1.00000000</Qty>
        <Description>GFS-PS-101, Packing Slips</Description>
        <Each> $5.00 </Each>
        <ItemTotal> $5.00 </ItemTotal>
      </Row1>
      <Row1>
        <RowNumber>4</RowNumber>
        <Date />
        <Qty />
```

You can use many different applications to create a sample XML file. When and how the XML file is created depends on your preferred workflow. Some possible options include:

■ **An existing data source.** Use one of these options when a database, spreadsheet, or other data file already exists and the Designer form needs to collect or present data that is stored in those existing fields:

   ■ **Use the data source.** An existing data source can be used to create the XML file and then connected to a form to create the necessary data bindings. Most database programs allow you to export the data set as an XML file, and many include the option for exporting the schema as well.

   ■ **Use XSLT.** If the form and the data source have already been created, changing either can be difficult. It may be best to use an Extensible Stylesheet Language Transformation file to transform the form data to match the data source. The XSLT can be applied to either the form or the data source.

■ **No existing data source.** Use one of these options when there is not an existing data file designed to store the information:

   ■ **Create a new XML file.** Using an XML editor, the data structure can be designed before the form or the data source is created.

   ■ **Create the XML from the Form.** Use the existing Designer form, or create a new form, and use it to generate the sample XML file.

   ■ **Create the data source.** Continue with the preceding options in the existing data source section.

In situations where a data source is managed by another department, it is best to coordinate the sharing of data before the form design takes place. This can save a large amount of design time by allowing us to generate the data bindings while building the form. Do not underestimate the importance of collecting the data into a useful format. Explore the documentation of the programs you use for information on exporting to XML.

Keep in mind that the XML the form generates for efficient field use in Designer is not equivalent to an XML file that would be efficient for a spreadsheet or a database. How you decide to store the data for easy retrieval and reporting depends on many factors: your comfort level with the computer programs available, the complexity of the data, and the intended use of the collected data.

In static forms where no items repeat, the data can be stored easily in a flat file. Think of a flat file as a row in a spreadsheet where each column contains a unique heading, and a single row contains the information the form contained. Using the form to generate the sample XML followed by importing that information into a spreadsheet works well for flat files.

CROSS-REF For instructions on how to use the form to generate a sample XML file, see Chapter 28.

Taking our sample XML file we can simply open it in a spreadsheet program such as Microsoft Excel and continue to append additional data through the import external data process. We also can use the distribute features of Acrobat to collect the form data into a response file that can be exported to a spreadsheet after all of the responses have been collected. The exported data also can be imported into a database program.

CROSS-REF For information on distributing forms and collecting responses, see Chapters 14 and 30.

When dynamic forms use repeating sections, a database that can handle relational data is better suited to store the data. Trying to store relational data in a spreadsheet program causes some common problems: repeating data in multiple rows to store the relational components as separate lines; and repeating columns to store data in a single row. A relational database program can store the information in multiple related tables to eliminate storing repeating data and optimize data retrieval.

When using a relational database, we recommend that the database be constructed first, and the XML schema be created from the database and used in the form development.

Understanding XML structure

XML is stored in a structured tree format. The following list introduces many of the XML terms we use in this chapter:

- **Attribute**. An attribute is part of an element that provides additional descriptive information regarding that element. Attributes appear inside the element tag, and the attribute value must always be quoted.

NOTE Attributes can be better expressed as a nested child element in many cases. Elements have more functionality than attributes. Attributes cannot contain multiple values, cannot describe structure, are not expandable, and are more difficult to manipulate with code.

- **Child**. An element contained within another element is considered a child element. This is also known as nesting elements.

- **Document prolog**. The document prolog resides outside of the root element and is usually the first thing in the XML file. The prolog contains up to three pieces of information:

  ```
  <?xml version="1.0" encoding="utf-8"?>
  ```

  - **The XML declaration**. The declaration states the version of XML in use in the document.

  - **The character encoding**. If this is omitted, it is assumed that Unicode Transformation Format (UTF-8) or UTF-16 is in use.

  - **Document Type Declaration**. The Document Type Declaration may be included in the document prolog and contains a link to the Document Type Definition (DTD) file if one is in use. A Document Type Definition provides the documentation regarding the elements and attributes contained in the XML file, including their relationships. DTD are not used very frequently because XML Schema Definition files are the current preferred method for describing XML files.

- **Element**. The elements make up the majority of the XML file. Elements include the starting tag of the element, the closing tag of the element, and everything in between. This means an element may contain attributes, other elements, or text. In the following example element, the element is all of the text including the tags:

  ```
  <form> This is the content inside the form tags. </form>
  ```

- **Nesting**. The process of placing one element inside another creates a nested element. The outer element is known as the parent and the inner element is known as the child.

- **Parent**. The outer element of a nested pair of elements is considered the parent. This is also known as nesting elements.

- **Root element**. Only one root element is allowed, and is alternatively called the document element. All other elements are nested inside the root element.

- **Tag**. Tags come in pairs. The first tag is the starting tag and defines the beginning of the element. The second tag is the closing tag and indicates the end of the element. The tags include the characters that indicate the start or end of an element, but not the element content itself. An example element appears as follows:

  ```
  <message> These contents are not tags. </message>
  ```

  The tags contain the word "message" and are always enclosed in < and > symbols

- **Valid**. An XML file is valid when it is both well formed and conforms to some semantic rules that are user-defined. The XML is validated against the DTD or the XML Schema associated with the file.

- **Well-formed**. An XML file is well formed when it conforms to all of the XML syntax rules.

The XML syntax rules are:

- **XML documents must have a root element.** Only one root element is allowed and all other elements must be nested inside the root element.

- **All XML elements must have a closing tag.** Missing tags cause malformed XML to be unreadable. The following data fails because of the missing </Employee> tag.

  ```
  </Form>
  <ReqDate>2008-10-15</ReqDate>
  <Employee>Mr. Smith
  <Department>Human Resources</Department> <ReqEmail>smith@
      globalfinancial.com</ReqEmail>
  </Form>
  ```

- **XML elements must be properly nested.** Elements must be closed in the opposite order from the order in which they are started. The following data from our purchase order file is improperly nested and fails because the employee tag was not properly closed before the department data was introduced:

```
</Form>
<ReqDate>2008-10-15</ReqDate>
<Employee>Mr. Smith
<Department>Human Resources</Department></Employee>
<ReqEmail>smith@globalfinancial.com</ReqEmail>
</Form>
```

- **XML Schema Definition**. An XML Schema Definition (XSD) is an XML-based alternative to a DTD file. The XSD describes the structure of the XML document. XML Schemas are more powerful than DTDs; they support data types and name spaces.

- **XML tags are case sensitive.** You must open and close a tag using the same case. A good example is:

```
<Department>Human Resources</Department>
```

A bad example is indicated by the lowercase letter d in the closing tag that does not match the opening tag case:

```
<Department>Human Resources</department>
```

- **XML attribute values must be quoted.** If you choose to use attributes in your XML file the values must be enclosed in quotes. In the following variation of our purchase order information, the date of the request has become an attribute of the form tag:

```
<Form ReqDate="2008-10-15">
<Employee>Mr. Smith</Employee>
<Department>Human Resources</Department>
<ReqEmail>smith@globalfinancial.com</ReqEmail>
</Form>
```

- **Entity references are required.** Only the following five entity references are built into the XML specification:

  - &amp. Used for the ampersand symbol (&).

  - &lt. Used for the less than symbol (<).

  - &gt. Used for the greater than symbol (>).

  - &quot. Used for a quotation mark symbol (").

  - &apos. Used for the apostrophe symbol (').

Some additional notes regarding XML files:

- **Comments**. In XML, comments are enclosed between the following symbols:

  <!-- and -->. An example of a comment is the following:

```
<!-- Form revision reviewed 6/1/08 with team. -->
```

- **White space.** White space is preserved in XML files. Extra spaces appear just as they are stored in the XML.

- **Empty elements**. A special shorthand is allowed for empty elements in XML files that do not break the rule that all elements must have a closing tag. The following two lines of code are equivalent:

```
<ReqEmail></ReqEmail>
<ReqEmail/>
```

■ **New line.** XML Stores a new line as LF.

Becoming more familiar with these terms makes working with XML data files easier. You can find additional information regarding XML and XML Schema files on the W3Schools Web site at: `www.w3schools.com`.

Using XML editors

When you choose to work with the XML data file directly we recommend using another program. The XML source tab in Designer is for the form design, not the sample XML data. Many editors exist for this purpose. Because XML is raw text, if you are comfortable editing on your own any text editing tool will work including Notepad, Wordpad, and Microsoft Word.

Programs that are designed specifically for working with XML give you additional tools such as color-coordinating objects, statement completion, and graphical representation of the XML data. Two of the free XML editing programs are:

■ **XML Notepad 2007**. This is a free Microsoft product. Our Purchase Order XML file exported from the PDF form is shown in Figure 31.2 as opened in XML Notepad 2007.

FIGURE 31.2

The purchase order XML file opened in XML Notepad 2007

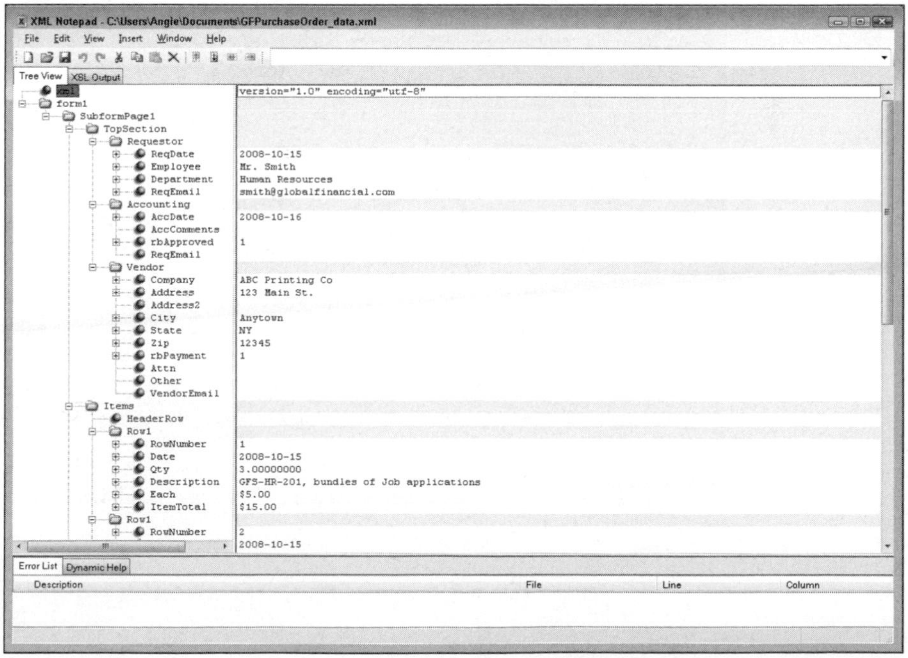

CROSS-REF   **For more information on using XML Notepad, see Chapter 27.**

■ **Liquid XML Studio 2008.** This product is from Liquid-Technologies and is available in a free community edition or a purchased edition. The same purchase order XML file is shown open in Liquid XML in Figure 31.3.

As you can see from Figures 31.2 and 31.3 the XML editors vary greatly in appearance. Another view of the same XML data appears in Figure 31.4 when opened in Windows Notepad.

All of the available tools, whether purchased or free, offer editing capabilities for modifying the structure of the XML by adding elements, attributes, and data values. How you edit the XML varies in each product, as do the features they offer. Some of the XML editors offer Schema editing tools.

Choosing an XML editor is a personal preference. Take the time to find an XML editor you are comfortable with to modify your data files. Most of the purchase products also offer trial downloads to test the software before purchasing.

FIGURE 31.3

The purchase order XML file opened in Liquid XML Studio 2008

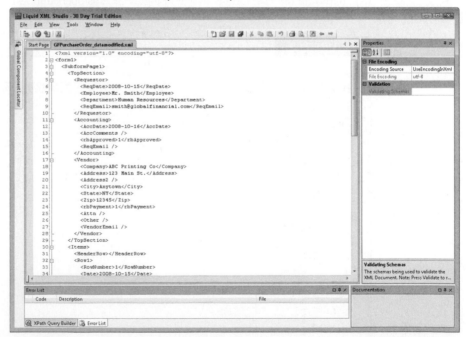

FIGURE 31.4

The purchase order XML file opened in Windows Notepad

Don't overlook the tools you already own. If you purchased Acrobat Pro or Pro Extended as part of an Adobe Creative Suite bundle, you may already own Adobe Dreamweaver, which is a great XML editor as well.

Creating New Data Connection

Regardless of which data type you decide to work with, you need to create the data connection in the Designer form to ensure the fields bind correctly to the data source. All of the data connection types have pros and cons. In this section we explore each type and explain why you may want to use or avoid a particular data connection for your form.

Creating a new Data Connection ties the form to the available data source. It does not explicitly set any field bindings. Implicit binding can occur once the Data Connection is established. We cover field binding later in the "Setting Field Bindings" section of this chapter.

CROSS-REF For more information on data binding terms, see Chapter 25. For specifics on creating field bindings to a data connection see the section "Setting Field Bindings" later in this chapter.

Getting started with a new data connection begins the same way for all four connection types. You can create a new data connection in three ways:

- **File Menu**. Select File ➪ New Data Connection from the menu to create a new data connection.

- **Right-click in the Data View palette**. Open the Data View palette by selecting Window ➪ Data View. Right-click in the palette area and select New Data Connection from the context menu.

- **The Data View palette Menu**. Open the Data View palette by selecting Window ➪ Data View. Select the palette menu in the upper-right corner of the palette and choose New Data Connection from the menu as shown in Figure 31.5.

FIGURE 31.5

The New Data Connection option in the Data View palette menu

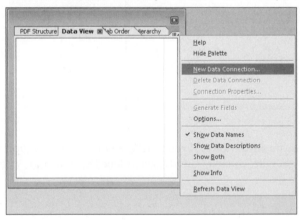

When you've opened the New Data Connection dialog box, the first decision is what type of data connection to make. A form may have more than one data connection established, but the form can use only one XML sample file or one XML schema file. We discuss the specifics of each of the connection types in the next section.

Binding to an XML schema

XML schema files are more powerful as a data connection in Designer than XML sample data files. The schema describes the elements in the XML data so that additional properties can be determined in the Designer form. A schema file that includes data types, field sizes, and occurrence information can set those properties for you in your form design.

Schema are imperative to working with the LiveCycle ES components in order to be able to use the built-in XPath formula windows. Without the schema all formulas must be manually created by typing the equivalent to branch of the XML tree each time you wish to use an element.

CROSS-REF For more information on the LiveCycle ES components, see Chapter 34.

ON the CD-ROM For the following steps we use the *POSchema.xsd* file from the Chapter 31 folder on the book's CD-ROM.

STEPS: Binding to an XML Schema

1. **Open a form, or create a new one.** We choose to start with a new form design.

2. **Open the Data View palette.** Select Window ➪ Data View if necessary to show the Data View palette.

3. **Right-click in the Data View palette and select New Data Connection.** Right-clicking in the Data View palette opens the context menu options where you can find the New Data Connection option.

4. **Give the Data Connection a name.** We typed POSchema as our Data Connection name. This name does not have to be the same name as the file you are connecting to. It should be descriptive enough to indicate what the form is using as a data source. The Connection name cannot contain spaces, nor start with a number.

5. **Select the XML Schema radio button.** This sets the data connection type to be an XML Schema Definition (XSD). The dialog box should match Figure 31.6.

6. **Browse for the XSD file.** As shown in Figure 31.7, use the browse button to find the XSD file you wish to use.

7. **If desired, select the Embed XML Schema option.** This increases the file size, but adds extensive drill-down capabilities when writing XPath formulas in the LiveCycle ES components and reusing the data later

8. **If desired, select the Transform options.** When connecting a form to a data source that uses different XML elements, an Extensible Stylesheet Language Transformation (XSLT) can be used to convert the XML from one format to the other. An XSLT can be applied to the incoming data, the outgoing data, or both if needed.

FIGURE 31.6

The first step in connecting to an XML Schema Definition

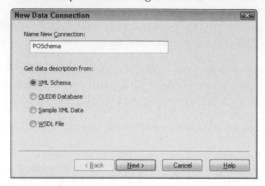

FIGURE 31.7

Use the browse button to select the XSD file.

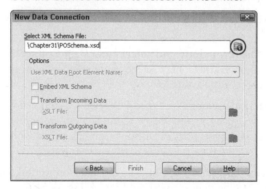

9. **Select Finish to establish your data connection.** Once the dialog box has closed, the Data View palette is populated with the Schema information as shown in Figure 31.8.

Once the data connection has been established, you can bind your schema file to the existing fields in the form even if they do not share the same name. Or, if you are starting from scratch with a new form the XML schema can be used to generate the form fields, including the data type and field size if specified in the schema.

FIGURE 31.8

The Data View palette connected to the POSchema file

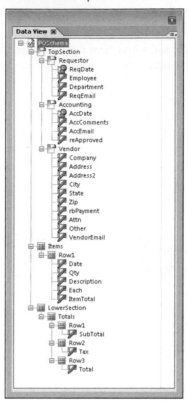

Binding to an XML sample file

If no XML schema is available, binding to an XML sample file is the next best option. A sample XML file allows you to bind fields on the form with fields in the sample XML file even if they don't have the same name. However, the sample XML file knows only the field names. It knows nothing about the data type, field size, or any attributes. If you use the sample XML file to create your form fields, all fields are text data types until you alter them.

ON the CD-ROM For the following steps we use the GFPurchaseOrder_data.*xml* file from the Chapter 31 folder on the book's CD-ROM.

STEPS: Binding to an XML Sample File

1. **Open a form, or create a new one.** We choose to start with a new form design.

2. **Open the Data View palette.** Select Window ➪ Data View if necessary to show the Data View palette.

3. **Right-click in the Data View palette and select New Data Connection.** Right-clicking in the Data View palette opens the context menu options where you can find the New Data Connection option.

4. **Give the Data Connection a name.** We typed *POSampleXML* as our Data Connection name. This name does not need to match the name of the file you are connecting to. It should be descriptive enough to indicate what the form is using as a data source. The connection name cannot contain spaces, nor start with a number.

5. **Select the Sample XML Data radio button.** This sets the data connection type to be a sample XML file. The dialog box should match Figure 31.9.

FIGURE 31.9

The first step in connecting to a sample XML file

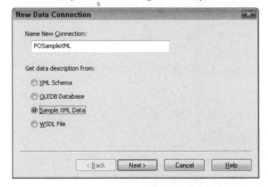

6. **Browse for the sample XML File.** Use the browse button to find the XML file you wish to use.

7. **If desired, select the Transform options needed.** When connecting a form to a data source that uses different XML elements an Extensible Stylesheet Language Transformation (XSLT) can be used to convert the XML from one format to the other. A XSLT can be applied to the incoming data, the outgoing data, or both if needed.

8. **Select Finish to establish your data connection.** Once the dialog box has closed, the Data View palette is populated with the sample XML information as shown in Figure 31.10.

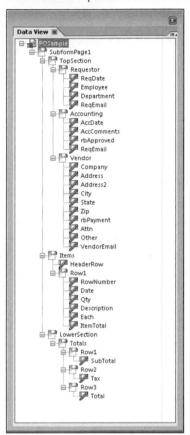

FIGURE 31.10

The Data View palette connected to the POSample file

Binding to an OLEDB database

Binding to a database is another connection option. Using a database tied directly to a form requires scripting to control when records can be inserted, updated, and deleted and to perform the record navigation capabilities for the records in the database. Without the necessary script, form recipients may be able to alter database records they should only be viewing.

A form can be connected to more than one database connection. OLEDB is the only database connection allowed with LiveCycle Designer ES. By using Microsoft OLEDB, an integration standard, for your ODBC drivers you can also access other databases by using a Data Source Name (DSN).

Security concerns in Acrobat specify that the client computer must have a DSN configured for each ODBC connection to function. External data connections are restricted in the free Adobe Reader unless the form has extended usage rights from LiveCycle Reader Extensions.

 **CAUTION** Binding directly to a database is restricted in the free Adobe Reader and requires that the form have extended usage rights from LiveCycle Reader Extensions.

The preferred method of binding data to a database is by using another process or product to control the processing of the form data. This may be done by LiveCycle Forms ES, a Web service, or other data solution provider. If you still wish to connect directly to the database you need to set up a Data Source Name (DSN) for each database connection on every machine that needs to connect to that file. On a Windows machine the settings can be found in the Administrative Tools of the Control Panel.

STEPS: Creating a Data Source Name (DSN) on Windows

1. **Open the Control Panel.** You can find this in the Start menu as a link for most Windows machines. It also can be opened from a Run command by typing **control.exe** and pressing Enter.

2. **Open the Administrative Tools.** The Administrative Tools are located in the System and Maintenance category when working in Category view. Or, Administrative Tools can be found alphabetically listed in the Classic view.

3. **Open Data Sources (ODBC).** This opens the ODBC Database Administrator.

4. **Select the System DSN tab.** The DSN window appears showing any existing system Data Source Names, and allows you to create new Data Source Names as shown in Figure 31.11.

FIGURE 31.11

The ODBC Database Administrator System DSN tab

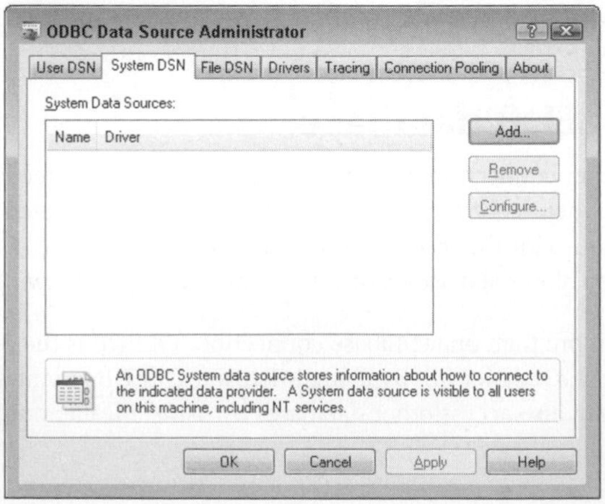

5. **Select the Add button to create a new data source connection.** Figure 31.12 shows the dialog box where the driver type of the data source is selected.

FIGURE 31.12

The Create New Data Source dialog box

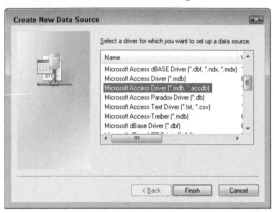

6. **Select the appropriate driver type for the data source and select Finish.** This opens the Connection window for the driver type selected. Figure 31.13 shows the Microsoft Access Setup window.

FIGURE 31.13

The ODBC Microsoft Access Setup Dialog box

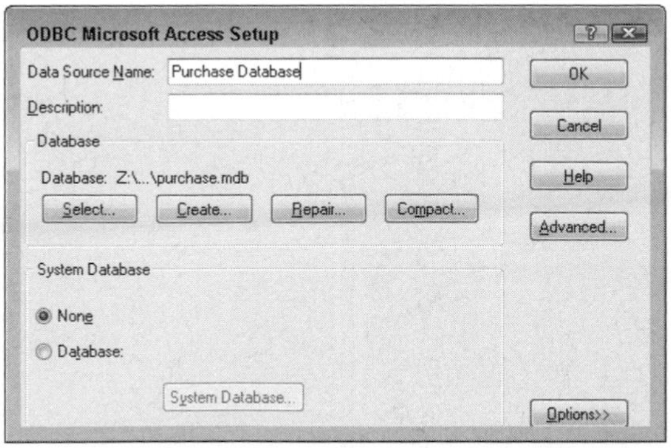

7. **Type in a Data Source Name (required) and supply a description (optional).** The data source name does not have to match the database name.

8. **Use the Select button to browse for the database file.** Figure 31.14 shows the Select Database dialog box used to browse for the data source.

FIGURE 31.14

The Select Database dialog box

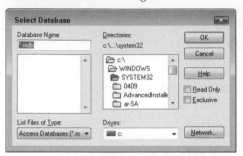

9. **Select the database and press OK.** This returns you to the setup dialog box shown in Figure 31.14.

10. **Set additional options as needed.** If the database requires a password, you may supply it using the Advanced button as shown in Figure 31.15. It is also possible to set the database to open in Read Only mode or Exclusive Mode by expanding the options as shown in Figure 31.16.

FIGURE 31.15

The Set Advanced Options dialog box for login and password

FIGURE 31.16

The expanded Options for Exclusive or Read Only modes

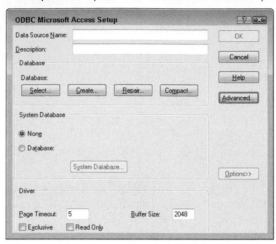

11. **Select OK to finish the Access setup window.** The System DSN tab now shows the System Data Source Name you defined as shown in Figure 31.17.

FIGURE 31.17

The saved Data Source Name

Be sure to use the same settings on all of the computers that connect to the data source so as not to cause naming conflicts. Once the Data Source Name has been created on the form recipient's computer the Designer form can be configured to use the data source as long as the form recipient uses Acrobat (Standard, Pro, or Pro Extended) to complete the form, or if the form has been given extended usage rights by LiveCycle Reader Extensions to work in the free Adobe Reader.

 For the following steps we use the *Purchase.mdb* file from the Chapter31 folder on the book's CD-ROM.

STEPS: Binding to OLEDB

1. **Open a form, or create a new one.** We choose to start with a new form design.

2. **Open the Data View palette.** Select Window ➪ Data View to show the Data View palette.

3. **Right-click in the Data View palette and select New Data Connection.** Right-clicking in the Data View palette opens the context menu options where you can find the New Data Connection option.

4. **Give the Data Connection a name.** We typed *PurchaseDB* as our Data Connection name. This name does not have to match the name of the file you are connecting to. It should be descriptive enough to indicate what the form is using as a data source. The Connection name cannot contain spaces, nor start with a number.

5. **Select the OLEDB Data radio button.** This sets the data connection type to be a database connection. The dialog box should match Figure 31.18.

FIGURE 31.18

The first step in connecting to a database

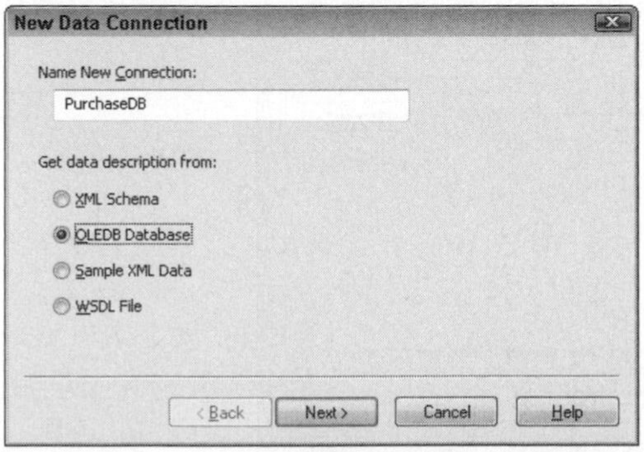

New Data Connection
Name New Connection:
PurchaseDB
Get data description from:
○ XML Schema
● OLEDB Database
○ Sample XML Data
○ WSDL File
< Back   Next >   Cancel   Help

6. **Select the Build Button.** Use the Build button to find the database name you created in previous steps "Creating a Data Source Name (DSN) on Windows" in the Data Link Properties dialog box.

7. **Select the Connection Tab of the Data Link Properties window.**

8. **Choose the DSN name from the drop-down list.** The DSN name previously set up appears in the drop-down list. Figure 31.19 shows the Connection Tab with the DSN name selected.

FIGURE 31.19

The Connection Tab with the data source name selected

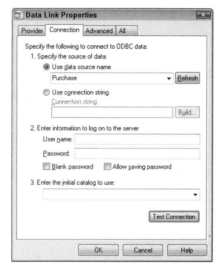

9. **Select the Test Connection Button.** Verify your database connection is set up properly by testing the connection.

10. **Select OK to return to the OLEDB connection window.** Even though the connection string appears in the window, as shown in Figure 31.20, by connecting to the DSN, Acrobat is allowed to connect to the data source.

11. **Select the Table, Stored Procedure or SQL Query you wish to use for your form and select Next.** This entire process may be repeated as many times as needed to connect to all of the objects in the database you wish to use.

FIGURE 31.20

The OLEDB Connection window showing the connection string

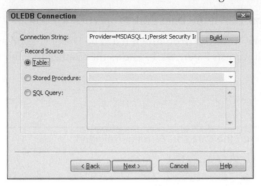

12. If the database requires authentication, enter the username and password or other options. Figure 31.21 shows the additional options available in the ADO Properties window.

FIGURE 31.21

ADO Properties allow username/password and additional options

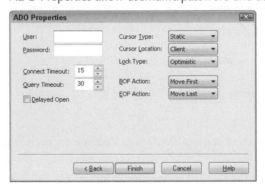

13. **Select Finish to create your data connection.** Once the dialog box has closed the Data View palette is populated with the database information as shown in Figure 31.22.

Be very cautious when setting up OLEDB connections directly to a database without another buffer between the form and data in the database. It is very easy for the form recipient to add and remove data. We highly recommend that you utilize another tool such as the Adobe LiveCycle ES components to help manage the data between the form and the database.

FIGURE 31.22

The Data View palette after connecting to multiple tables in a database

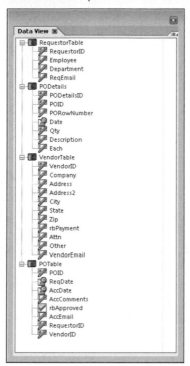

Binding to a WSDL file

A Web Service Definition Language (WSDL) file is an XML-based language for describing Web services. A program connecting to a Web service can read the WSDL to determine what functions are available on the server, and request an available service. A Designer form can have multiple WSDL connections. The Web services offered vary greatly in what they are and what they can do. Some examples include:

- **Conversions**. Currency, temperature, units of measure, pressure, power, angles, languages, and more.

- **Look up Utilities**. ZIP codes, weather, sunrise/sunset time, IP addresses, area codes, ISBN numbers, verify e-mail addresses, and verify mailing addresses, for example.

- **Graphics**. Barcodes and Braille.

- **Communications**. Text or fax messages.

- **Business**. Mortgage rates, validate credit cards, gold and silver rates, validate bank routing information, stock quotes, and more.

Connecting a Designer form to a WSDL to perform these services is available if the form will be completed in Acrobat (Standard, Pro, or Pro Extended). WSDL calls are restricted in the free Adobe Reader program. Extended rights would be required from LiveCycle Reader Extensions for Reader to be able to utilize the Web services.

STEPS: Binding to an WSDL

1. **Open a form, or create a new one.** We choose to start with a new form design.

2. **Open the Data View palette.** Select Window ⇨ Data View if necessary to show the Data View palette.

3. **Right-click in the Data View palette and select New Data Connection.** Right-clicking in the Data View palette opens the context menu options where you can find the New Data Connection option.

4. **Give the Data Connection a name.** We typed in CurrencyConvertor as our Data Connection name. This name does not have to match the name of the file you are connecting to. It should be descriptive enough to indicate what the form is using as a data source. The Connection name cannot contain spaces, nor start with a number.

5. **Select the WSDL File radio button and choose next.** This sets the data connection type to be Web Service Definition Language file.

6. **Type in the URL of the WSDL.** If you are unsure of the URL it is recommended that you open a browser window and locate the WSDL file, then copy and paste the URL into the dialog box in Designer. Figure 31.23 shows the URL of a currency convertor used in our file.

FIGURE 31.23

The WSDL URL

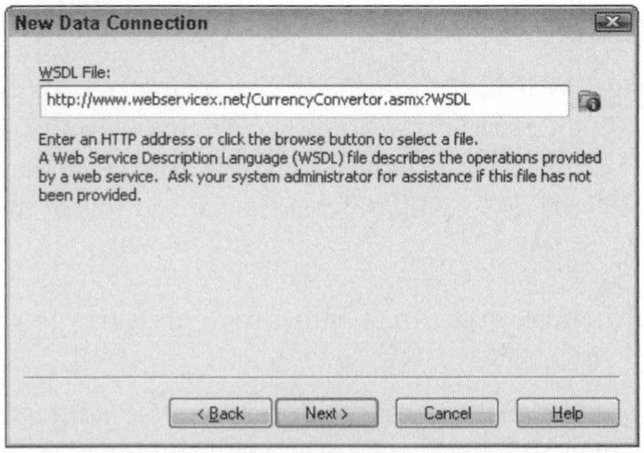

If the WSDL connection cannot be established the error shown in Figure 31.24 appears. Many different things can cause this error including mistyping the URL, the Web service is not currently available, no Internet connection is available, attempting with Adobe Reader or an unsupported version of Adobe Acrobat (prior to 7.05).

FIGURE 31.24

An error when the WSDL connection cannot be established

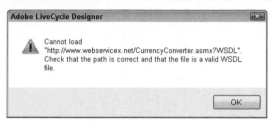

7. **Select the Connection Properties.** Once the WSDL has been successfully connected, a property window appears showing the available options. Normally a SOAP request or Post/Get request is what you find here as shown in Figure 31.25.

FIGURE 31.25

The WSDL Connection Properties dialog box

8. **Specify any additional Connection properties as needed.** Not all WSDL files allow public connections. If using a secure WSDL connection, you need to specify additional properties as shown in Figure 31.26.

9. **Select Finish to establish your data connection.** Once the dialog box has closed, the Data View palette is populated with the WSDL services as shown in Figure 31.27.

After you have created the WSDL connection you can integrate the available WSDL services with the rest of the form functionality. We decided to expand the Purchase Order by adding a currency convertor to the price. Use the Web service to take the vendor's currency format and convert it to our currency format. Use the returned currency conversion rate to adjust the total on the Purchase Order accordingly.

FIGURE 31.26

The additional WSDL Connection Properties dialog box

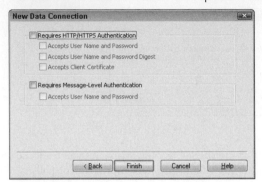

FIGURE 31.27

The Data View palette after a WSDL connection has been established

   For a list of a number of WSDL services you can find on the Internet, visit `http://www.xmethods.net`.

   For the following steps we use the **GF*PurchaseOrder_Start*.xdp** file from the **Chapter31 folder on the book's CD-ROM.**

STEPS: Adding a Currency Convertor WSDL to the Purchase Order Form

1. **Open a form.** We'll open the GF*PurchaseOrder_Start*.xdp from the CD-ROM in Chapter 31.
2. **Open the Data View palette.** Select Window⇨Data View to show the Data View palette.

3. **Right-click in the Data View palette and select New Data Connection.** Right-clicking in the Data View palette opens the context menu options where you can find the New Data Connection option.

4. **Give the Data Connection a name.** We typed *CurrencyConvertor* as our Data Connection name.

5. **Select the WSDL File radio button and choose Next.** This sets the data connection type to Web Service Definition Language file.

6. **Type in the URL of the WSDL and choose next.** We typed in:

   `http://www.webservicex.net/CurrencyConvertor.asmx?wsdl`

7. **Select the top operation from the Connection Properties and choose Next.** The top choice in the three conversion rate operations is the service we can connect to as shown in Figure 31.28. The other two operations did not allow any connections, as indicated by the description when selected. Another indicator that the operation is not a supported type is that the Next button is not active.

FIGURE 31.28

The currency convertor operation choices

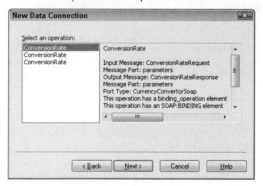

8. **No additional properties are needed, so choose Finish.** The Web service we are connecting to is a free service and does not require any additional properties to connect to it.

9. **Explore the Data View palette.** Expand the data view palette to see the available services.

10. **Drag the four currency convertor objects to the form from the Data View palette.** Place the currency convertor fields in the blank area of the LowerSection subform. The four objects are FromCurrency, ToCurrency, ConversionRateResponse, and ConversionRateBtn.

CROSS-REF For more information on creating fields from Data Connections see the section "Setting Field Bindings" later in this chapter.

11. **Arrange the fields and adjust the captions as needed.** Take a few minutes to arrange the new fields in the available space. Leave enough room for one additional field.

12. **Add a new Numeric Field to the LowerSection Subform and name it ConvertedTotal.** We will perform the calculation using the Web service results to alter the existing total to the converted total. Your form should appear similar to Figure 31.29.

FIGURE 31.29

The LowerSection of the Purchase Order with the new currency convertor fields

13. **Select the ConvertedTotal field and open the script editor.** If necessary select Window ⇨ Script Editor (Ctrl + Shift + F5) to open the Script Editor.

14. **Select the Calculate Event from the show drop-down, and set FormCalc as the scripting language.** For a simple multiplication problem, FormCalc is shorter syntax to write.

15. **Enter the Calculation to multiply the ConversionRateResult and the Total Field.** We entered the following calculation script:

```
Totals.Row3.Total * ConversionRateResult;
```

The Script Editor for the ConvertedTotal field should appear similar to Figure 31.30.

CROSS-REF For more information on syntax rules and variations available when writing scripts, see Chapter 29.

FIGURE 31.30

The calculation script to multiply the conversion rate times the total field

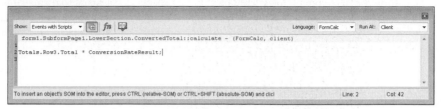

16. **Save the Form and test it in the Preview PDF tab.** Enter some data into the quantity and each fields.

17. **Select a From Currency and To Currency, then click the Currency Convertor button.**

18. **Verify the results are correct.** Verify the Conversion Rate Response was returned, and the Converted total correctly used the Conversion Rate. Your form should appear similar to Figure 31.31.

FIGURE 31.31

The completed Currency Convertor additions to our purchase order form

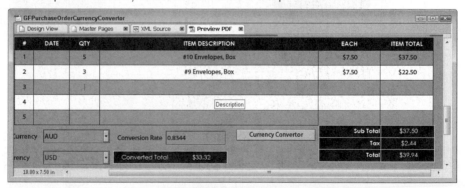

19. **Return to Design View and close the form.**

As you can see, in many applications Web services can be utilized for form enhancements. Remember that WSDL calls are restricted in the free Adobe Reader unless enabled by LiveCycle Reader Extensions.

Setting Field Data Bindings

Creating the data connection is only part of the process to get fields to display and map properly to the data source. Normal binding is the default setting in Designer and uses implicit binding to work. As we discussed in Chapter 25, implicit binding takes the data file and compares it to the form for exact field name matches. When the data file and the form fields don't match another binding method is necessary.

CROSS-REF For more information on Binding types see Chapter 25.

Setting bindings to existing fields

Once a data connection has been established we can bind the fields to the data source. You can bind existing fields to the data source in these two basic ways:

- **Using the Data View palette.** Drag the fields in the Data View palette directly to objects in the design page to create absolute bindings between the data nodes and the form objects. Figure 31.32 shows the Requestor Info Date (ReqDate) field being bound by dragging the element from the Data View palette and dropping it on the field.

FIGURE 31.32

Drag and Drop a data element from the Data View palette to a form object to create data bindings.

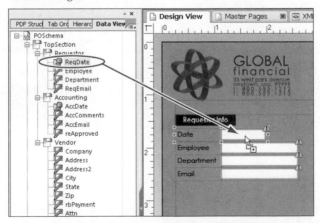

Dragging and dropping an element on the form object opens a properties window to offer additional options. In the case of an XML sample file, the only information available is the name of the field. With a Schema file, additional properties such as field size, data type, caption, and more can be retrieved. Figure 31.33 shows the property window. You may want the same settings for each field in this form; by making the appropriate choices and selecting Don't Show Again, the settings will be retained until you change them. To return to the properties window after it has been hidden, select the Data View palette Menu and choose Options to change your settings as shown in Figure 31.34.

FIGURE 31.33

The Binding Properties dialog box opens when dragging from the Data View palette

FIGURE 31.34

The Binding Options dialog box

- **Using the Binding Tab of the Object palette.** With the object selected in the form design, open the binding tab of the object palette to select the data node to bind to. Figure 31.35 shows the flyout data binding options when setting the binding for the Employee field using the Object palette.

Once a binding has been specified for a field, the Data View palette updates with an icon to show which fields have been bound as shown in Figure 31.36. The red and green arrows indicate import (green) and export (red) data bindings.

FIGURE 31.35

The data source structure appears in the binding tab to define a connection between fields and the data source

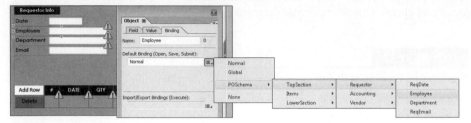

FIGURE 31.36

Data View palette Binding Icon

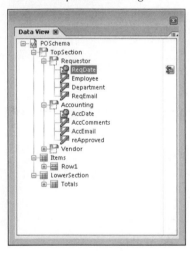

Another other way to check data bindings is to view the Binding tab of the Report palette, and select Window➪Report to open the palette if necessary. Figure 31.37 shows the palette menu offers filters for the different types of bindings to help you isolate specific binding settings more quickly.

When binding a field to a data element with the Data View palette or in the Object palette, Designer establishes an explicit binding. With explicit bindings a reference to the data element becomes embedded in the form design and ignores the automatic data matching. An explicit binding can be either relative or absolute. Absolute bindings ensure the exact data element can be found regardless of the object name. We recommend using the drag-and-drop method from the Data View palette as the preferred method.

FIGURE 31.37

The Binding Tab filters in the Menu button

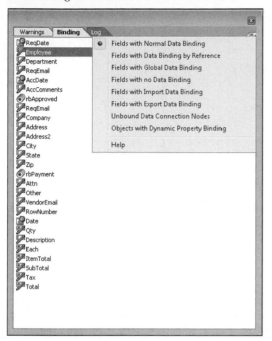

When binding to a dynamic form with repeating sections, relative binding is generally required to correctly bind the contents. In addition, relative binding expressions require less processing when merging data with a form design. Absolute bindings are not recommended with repeating sections unless the intent is to filter the repeating data. In order to set a relative reference for an existing subform, you will need to use the Binding Tab of the Object palette. Once the subform binding is established, dragging the elements from the Data View palette to the fields inside the subform sets relative bindings.

Setting bindings while creating new fields

If the data connection is established at the beginning of the form design process, you can take advantage of the information the data file has when creating your fields. Rather than building each of the field objects and then setting the bindings, you can simply drag the data elements to the design page to create the objects and establish their bindings all in one step as shown in Figure 31.38.

Dragging a complex container from the Data View palette creates the container object and all of the child objects it contains. This can be a huge time-saving feature if you have either a sample XML data file or better yet a Schema file to work with.

FIGURE 31.38

Dragging a data element onto a new form design creates the object and sets the binding

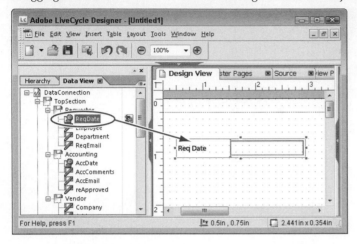

Summary

- Extensible Markup Language (XML) is used for data storage and transfer.

- Designer can use a Sample XML data file, XML Schema, OLEDB, or WSDL files to create data bindings.

- An XML Schema defines the data set, which can include data types and additional properties.

- Database and WSDL connections are restricted in the free Adobe Reader.

- The default binding type in Designer is Normal. Normal is implicit binding.

- Explicit bindings can be relative or absolute when connected to a data source.

- Bindings can be added to existing fields by dragging from the Data View palette or using the Data tab of the Object palette.

Chapter 32

Examining Some Dynamic Forms

Adobe has made an effort to assist you as much as possible in learning to use Designer to create forms both static and dynamic. The Designer Help document is a reference guide as well as an instructive tutorial.

You also have at your disposal some sample forms that came with your Acrobat installation. Several forms are designed as examples of static and dynamic forms. You can browse the form contents and see how they were constructed. The scripts are available in the Script Editor where you can copy and paste scripts to achieve similar results on your own forms or modify the existing forms to suit your own company's needs.

In this chapter we begin by looking at the tutorials in the LiveCycle Designer Help document and then move on to examine the forms samples.

IN THIS CHAPTER

Using the tutorials

Using the sample forms

Finding sample forms on the Internet

Working with Designer's Tutorials

Open the Help file by choosing Help ⇨ Adobe LiveCycle Designer Help or pressing F1. The Help file contains more than 900 pages of help information. In addition to the help resources in this file, a section is devoted to tutorials. The Help document's Quick Start Tutorial section lists the tutorials available in the guide. Open the Help guide (Help ⇨ Adobe LiveCycle Designer Help), click Contents, and then expand the Quick Start Tutorials list to see the separate tutorial items as shown in Figure 32.1.

FIGURE 32.1

Open the Help document and expand the list of Quick Start Tutorials to see the tutorial samples.

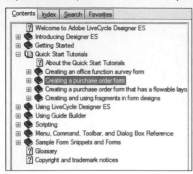

The Quick Start Tutorials area in the Help document provides these four tutorial files:

- **Creating an office function survey form.** This tutorial walks you through creating a static form with a Submit By Email button. You use the New Form Assistant to create the form and add the Submit By Email button in the New Form Assistant wizard. The tutorial details each step in the process for adding objects.

- **Creating a purchase order form.** This tutorial walks you through steps to create a static form with a print button. Again you follow steps to add objects and format fields. The tutorial also introduces adding scripts to produce calculation results.

- **Creating a purchase order form that has a flowable layout.** This tutorial introduces creating a dynamic form as shown in Figure 32.2. As you import data from a companion data file, the number of rows in the table expands to accommodate the data. If you've read many chapters up to this point in the book, this tutorial will have greater value than creating the static forms. The tutorial walks you through steps to create a document where the form's fixed layout is converted to a flowable layout by adding subforms. This tutorial is a great resource to accompany Chapter 28, where we introduce subforms.

- **Creating and using fragments in form designs.** This tutorial walks you through steps to work with the fragment library and use fragments for a collection of forms. This tutorial expands upon Chapter 24, where we introduced form fragments.

If you have a basic understanding for creating static forms, using the Library palettes to add objects to a form, and using the Object palette for editing an object's properties, look over the flowable purchase order tutorial and the form fragments tutorial to learn more about some of Designer's advanced features.

FIGURE 32.2

The form with flowable content is a dynamic form.

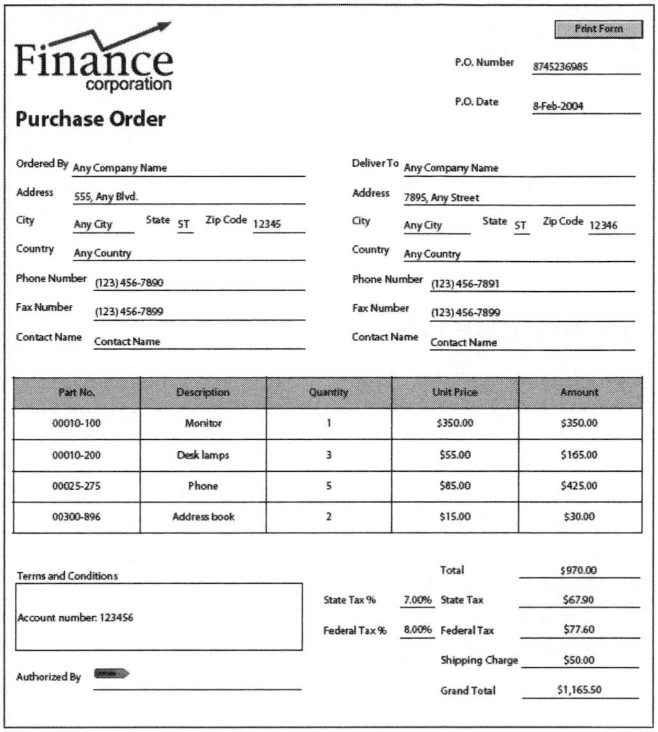

Print Form

Finance corporation

Purchase Order

P.O. Number 8745236985

P.O. Date 8-Feb-2004

Ordered By Any Company Name
Address 555, Any Blvd.
City Any City State ST Zip Code 12345
Country Any Country
Phone Number (123) 456-7890
Fax Number (123) 456-7899
Contact Name Contact Name

Deliver To Any Company Name
Address 7895, Any Street
City Any City State ST Zip Code 12346
Country Any Country
Phone Number (123) 456-7891
Fax Number (123) 456-7899
Contact Name Contact Name

Part No.	Description	Quantity	Unit Price	Amount
00010-100	Monitor	1	$350.00	$350.00
00010-200	Desk lamps	3	$55.00	$165.00
00025-275	Phone	5	$85.00	$425.00
00300-896	Address book	2	$15.00	$30.00

Terms and Conditions

Account number: 123456

Authorized By

Total $970.00
State Tax % 7.00% State Tax $67.90
Federal Tax % 8.00% Federal Tax $77.60
Shipping Charge $50.00
Grand Total $1,165.50

Examining the Sample Forms

The Help guide contains a description of the sample files installed with Designer. For a quick look at the descriptions of these files, choose Help ➪ Samples. The Help guide opens in the section of the guide related to the samples files descriptions and how to use them.

The sample forms are contained in the Acrobat 9.0\Designer 8.2\<*language installation*>\Samples folder (<*language installation*> is respective to the language you use with Designer). For the English language forms use the Acrobat 9.0\Designer 8.2\EN\Samples\Forms folder. Inside the Forms folder you find these eight subfolders:

- **Dunning Notice**
- **E-Ticket**

- FormGuide
- Grant Application
- Purchase Order
- Scripting
- SubformSet
- Tax Receipt

The sample files are designed to help you become more familiar with various features in Designer for creating forms. Several subfolders also contain Data folders for using XML data with the respective forms.

Copying the Sample files

The first thing you should do is open the Acrobat 9.0\Designer 8.2\EN\Samples folder and copy the folder. Locate another area on your hard drive where you keep documentation on Designer and paste the Samples folder in this location. If you make edits on the copied forms, you can always return to the original forms.

Another reason to consider copying the files is that if you make comment notes on forms or create edited versions of the forms and save them to the original Samples folder, all your Samples files are lost if you deinstall Designer or upgrade to a newer version. Designer keeps some original files when you upgrade the program (see User Log-on\AppData\Roaming\Adobe\Designer). If you upgraded from an earlier version of Designer you'll find an 8.2 folder and another folder (such as 8.0) inside the Designer folder. If you open a folder for an earlier version of Designer, you'll find an Objects and Templates folder. What you won't find however, is a Samples folder.

Examining the Dunning Notice form

Inside the Designer 8.2 folder in the \EN\Samples\Forms\Dunning Notice\ folder you find these four subfolders:

- **Data.** This folder contains three XML data files used to populate the Dunning Notice form.
- **Forms.** A single form appears in this folder.
- **Images.** An image file in this folder is used for the Global Company logo (not appearing on the form in Designer but rendered when the form is converted to PDF).
- **Outputs.** This folder contains three rendered forms that were created by using the three data files.

Let's look at the form first, and later we'll look at how the form is used. Follow these steps to examine the form.

STEPS: Examining the Dunning Notice Form

1. **Open the Dunning Notice form in Designer.** Choose File ⇨ Open and navigate to Acrobat 9.0\Designer 8.2\EN\Samples\Forms\Dunning Notice\Forms. Select the Dunning Notice.xdp form and click Open.

2. **Open the Hierarchy palette (if the palette bin on the right is open, close it by clicking the separator bar).** As you look over the Hierarchy palette, notice the number of subforms contained in the document as shown in Figure 32.3.

3. **View the Master Pages items.** Click the Master Pages tab and click the object in the top-left corner. Notice in the Object palette this item is an Image field as shown in Figure 32.4. When the form is rendered an image is added to this field.

4. **Render the form.** Click Preview PDF in Designer to display the form in Acrobat. When the form opens in Acrobat you see data added to the form and the logo appearing in the top-left corner as shown in Figure 32.5.

FIGURE 32.3

Open the Dunning Notice form and open the Hierarchy palette.

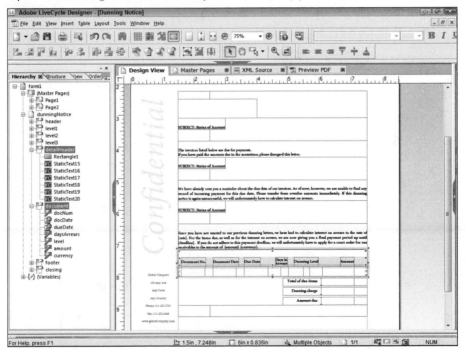

FIGURE 32.4

The master page contains an Image field.

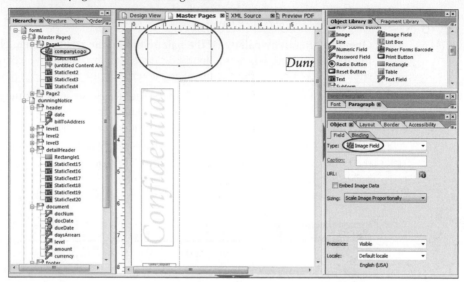

FIGURE 32.5

Click Preview PDF to open the form in Acrobat.

Without examining anything else on the Dunning Notice form you know that some data binding obviously was added to the form. In the form design shown in Figure 32.4 you see a single row in a table where data are added in the form. There is no button to spawn new rows on the form, so the result you see in Figure 32.5, where three rows of data appear on the rendered form, had to pick up that data somewhere.

This sample file was designed for you to make data connections and observe the results. If you open the Data folder inside the Dunning Notice folder you see three XML data files. The default file used when you open the form and render it uses the Dunning Notice Level1.xml file, where this file is chosen for binding to the fields is in the Form Properties.

Choose File ⇨ Form Properties to open the Form Properties dialog box. Click Preview and here is where you find the data file identified for binding to the field objects as shown in Figure 32.6. If you want to use another data file, click the Browse icon (Folder with the i symbol adjacent to the Date File text box). Browse your hard drive and locate the Dunning Notice\Data folder. Select another data file and open it. When you render the form, you see more data introduced in the table.

The Preview tab in the Form Properties informs you of what file is used to bind to the data fields.

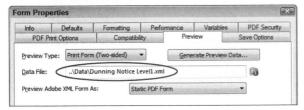

Examining the E-ticket form

The E-Ticket form is a multi-page form of 12 pages. When you open the E-Ticket form from the Samples\Forms\E-Ticket\Forms folder you find the coverPage appearing as shown in Figure 32.7. Following the coverPage you find a page for the itinerary (including pages for flight header and flight number), customs, medical, accommodation (including a hotel header and hotel page), and a boarding pass.

This form has a number of subforms as shown in Figure 32.7. Notice you also have two master pages used with this form. One master page is designed to print a portrait page and the other is designed to print a landscape page. Click the Master Page tab and you can see the two pages used for the form.

You find the data binding again in the Form Properties dialog box to a single file available in the Samples\Forms\E-Ticket\Data folder. When you open the Form Properties dialog box, click the Preview tab and locate the data file and load it in the Data File text box. This form is designed to be printed two-sided so you make an additional choice in the Preview tab for Print Form (two-sided) from the Preview Type drop-down menu.

FIGURE 32.7

The E-Ticket form opens showing the coverPage.

The form uses a few JavaScripts to concatenate names for the hotel accommodation. To view the JavaScripts, click the hotelHeader subform in the Hierarchy palette and open the Script Editor (CTRL/Shift + F5). The JavaScript is shown in the Script Editor as you see in Figure 32.8.

FIGURE 32.8

Click the hotelHeader subform in the Hierarchy palette and open the Script Editor to show the JavaScript.

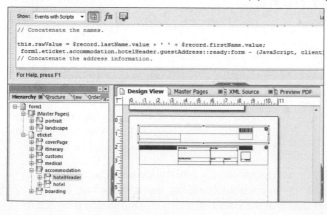

You'll notice that many fields on this form use a Global binding. The data from the XML form is reused on several pages. To examine the form thoroughly click the fields in the Hierarchy palette and open the Object palette. Click the Binding tab to observe how the data are used with the pages on this form.

Examining the Form Guide

The FormGuide folder contains three files: Immunization, Purchase Order, and TLALife. The Immunization form is designed to be printed and folded to a size that fits neatly in a passport passbook. By using the form guide the sample form demonstrates how a form designed for print can be filled in electronically online in an alternate view. If you render the form and attempt to fill in the form electronically you'll soon notice that the form would be a challenge to complete in Acrobat. By using a form guide, the form recipient has a much easier time completing this form.

The Purchase Order form is a version of the same Purchase Order form contained in another folder (see the section "Examining the Purchase Order form" later in this chapter). This form uses a form guide to present an alternative view that helps the form recipient to fill in the form.

The TLA Life sample form guide demonstrates advanced uses in form guides. The form is designed for a recipient to fill in the form to report an accident and uses images that the form guide displays relative to a damaged vehicle. As with the other forms in this folder you need the LiveCycle Forms ES server to use the form guides.

CROSS-REF For more information on Form Guides, see Chapter 30.

The sample forms provide you an opportunity to view the alternative views in a Web browser using Adobe's server. We won't display all the from guides here, but let's use the Purchase Order form as an example to show how form guides are used with these sample Designer forms.

To display the alternative view using form guides, do the following.

STEPS: Using Form Guides

1. **Open the Purchase Order.xdp form.** In Designer choose File ➪ Open and navigate to the \Program Files\Adobe\Acrobat 9.0\Designer 8.2\EN\Samples\Forms\FormGuide\ PurchaseOrder\Forms folder and open the PurchaseOrder.xdp file. The file opens in Designer as shown in Figure 32.9.

2. **Open the Guide Builder.** Choose Tools ➪ Create or Edit Form Guide to open the Guide Builder shown in Figure 32.10. In this panel you see the layout and design for the guide style. You can click the Customize Appearance tab and edit the style for different appearances if you like. For our example we'll use the default settings.

FIGURE 32.9

Open the Purchase Order form from the FormGuide samples folder.

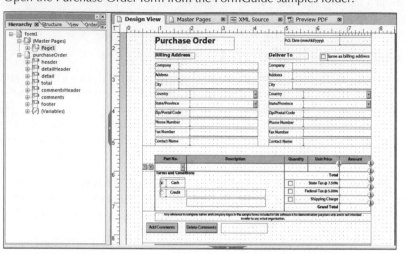

FIGURE 32.10

Choose Tools ⇨ Create or Edit Form Guide to open the Guide Builder.

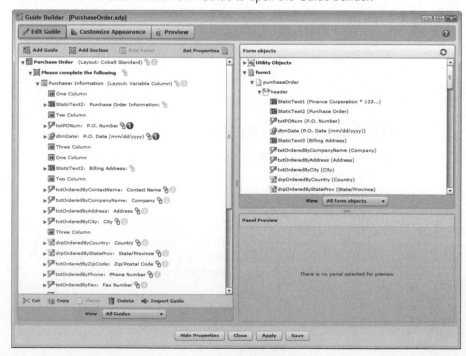

3. **Click the Preview tab.** When you click Preview another panel opens as shown in Figure 32.11. You can view the various content items by clicking the bars in the lower portion of the Guide Builder window. The default view showing the copyright information is shown in Figure 32.11.

4. **Check Include PDF preview and click the Preview button.** Designer pauses momentarily displaying a progress bar as the preview is rendered. Wait until the rendering is complete and your default Web browser opens.

5. **Allow the blocked content.** Your Web browser may display a warning indicating that the security setting in your browser is blocking the Active X controls to view the page. If you see an alert, click the text or open a context menu and choose Allow Blocked Content.

6. **Observe the form in your browser.** After enabling the content to be displayed, your Web browser loads the first guide page as shown in Figure 32.12.

FIGURE 32.11

Click the Preview tab to open the Preview panel.

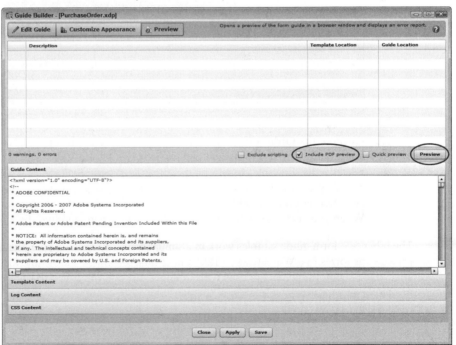

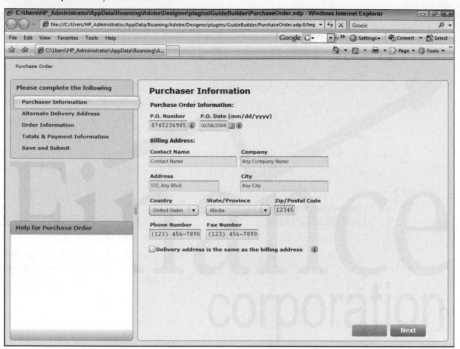

FIGURE 32.12

The form opens in your Web browser.

7. **Observe the Order information page.** Click the Next button and click Next again to arrive at the Order Information page as shown in Figure 32.13. Here you add data that relates to the flowable content on the form. To experiment, make a choice from the Part No. drop-down menu and type a number in the Quantity text box. Click the Add button and another option is added where you can add more part numbers and quantities. When you click Next you arrive at the last panel where you find the Submit button.

The other two form guide samples work in a similar way. You need to open the Guide Builder and preview the forms in a Web browser. Take a little time to explore the sample files and you can get an idea for how form guides are used with Designer. Keep in mind that to use form guides you need a server product as we explain in Chapter 30.

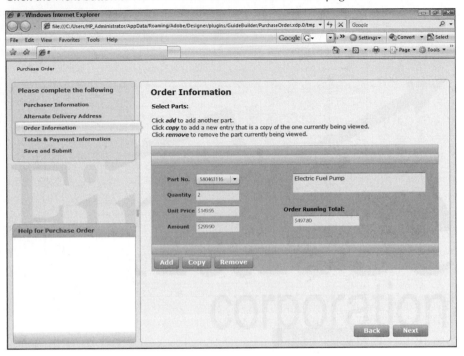

FIGURE 32.13

Click the Next button twice to arrive at the Order Information page.

Examining the Grant Application form

The Grant Application form found in the \Samples\Forms\Grant Application\Forms folder is a static PDF file. When you open the form you find a two-page document as shown in Figure 32.14. This form has no companion data file or form guides. The only asset is the static PDF document.

This form demonstrates the following:

- **Page numbering.** Page numbers are calculated at runtime by inserting runtime properties into a Text object. Notice the JavaScript for calculating the PageCount in Figure 32.14.

- **Maximum characters per field.** Click a field in the Hierarchy palette and you find the Field tab in the Object palette showing a limit length for the fields as shown in Figure 32.15.

FIGURE 32.14

Open the Grant Application form from the Samples folder.

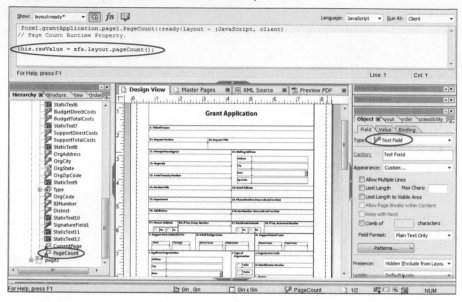

FIGURE 32.15

The fields are defined with maximum character limits.

- **Multi-line fields.** In Figure 32.15 you see the check box unchecked for the selected field for Allow Multiple Lines. On page 2 in the form there is a large field designed for a form recipient to fill in a description. This field uses the Allow Multiple Lines option in the Field tab in the Object palette.

- **Picture patterns.** Several picture patterns are used for field objects on the form. Click the items such as BudgetDirectCosts, BudgetTotalCosts, SupportDirectCosts, or SupportTotalCosts and you find these fields identified with patterns in the Object palette's Field tab. The patterns demand the form recipient use the correct values when adding data to these fields. If the correct data are not supplied, a dialog box appears as shown in Figure 32.16 when the form is completed in Acrobat/Reader.

FIGURE 32.16

The picture patterns are used to force the form recipient to supply data in the correct format. If the data are not supplied in the correct format a dialog box opens displaying the acceptable format.

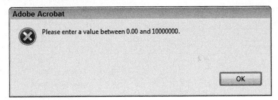

In addition to these items you find fields using the US States Custom library object and the tab order for the document we set up using a columnar order.

Examining the Purchase Order form

When you open the \Samples\Forms\Purchase Order folder you find three different forms with several subfolders. The three individual folders for Dynamic, Dynamic Interactive, and Interactive are the same forms designed differently. The designs are:

- **Interactive.** This form is a static form having a fixed number of rows in a table where the form recipient specifies items for a purchase order.
- **Dynamic.** This form is bound to a data file that resides in the Purchase Order\Data file. When the form is rendered, the data from the Purchase Order.xml file are flowed into the document.
- **Dynamic Interactive.** This form can be used in a couple of ways. You can choose to add data from the Purchase Order.xml file by adding the connection in the Preview tab in the Form Properties dialog box; in which case, when the form is rendered, the form is populated with data from the XML file as shown in Figure 32.17. The other way you can use this form is to avoid a data connection and render the form. The form can be opened directly in Acrobat/Reader where the data are typed by the form recipient. You'll see the form appear with dynamic elements where a form recipient can add and delete rows from the table as shown in Figure 32.18.

FIGURE 32.17

A form rendered using a data connection

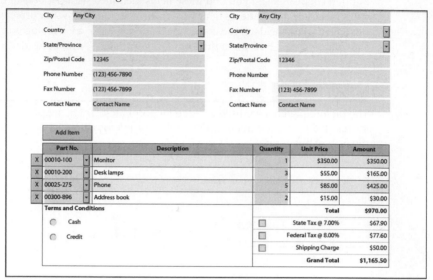

City	Any City		City	Any City
Country	▾		Country	▾
State/Province	▾		State/Province	▾
Zip/Postal Code	12345		Zip/Postal Code	12346
Phone Number	(123) 456-7890		Phone Number	
Fax Number	(123) 456-7899		Fax Number	(123) 456-7899
Contact Name	Contact Name		Contact Name	Contact Name

Add Item

	Part No.		Description	Quantity	Unit Price	Amount
X	00010-100	▾	Monitor	1	$350.00	$350.00
X	00010-200	▾	Desk lamps	3	$55.00	$165.00
X	00025-275	▾	Phone	5	$85.00	$425.00
X	00300-896	▾	Address book	2	$15.00	$30.00

Terms and Conditions			Total	$970.00
○ Cash		☐	State Tax @ 7.00%	$67.90
○ Credit		☐	Federal Tax @ 8.00%	$77.60
		☐	Shipping Charge	$50.00
			Grand Total	$1,165.50

FIGURE 32.18

A form rendered without a data connection

Phone Number		Phone Number	
Fax Number		Fax Number	
Contact Name		Contact Name	

Add Item

	Part No.		Description	Quantity	Unit Price	Amount
X		▾				
X		▾				
X		▾				

Terms and Conditions			Total	
○ Cash		☐	State Tax @ 0.00%	$0.00
○ Credit		☐	Federal Tax @ 0.00%	$0.00
		☐	Shipping Charge	
			Grand Total	$0.00

Add Comments

email Purchase Order

Authorized By

In addition to the three forms found in the three separate folders from the \Forms\Purchase Order folder, you can open the \Forms\Purchase Order\Form Fragments folder and find another Forms folder where the same three forms use form fragments. In the Form Fragments folder you find a number of form fragments used in the forms. The Data folder contains two XML files to bind data to the forms.

CROSS-REF For more information on using form fragments, see Chapter 24.

The last folder in the Purchase Order folder contains a folder titled Schema. You find a single Purchase Order form in the Forms folder and two data folders. One folder is titled Data and the other is titled Schema. The data folder contains a sample XML file and the Schema folder contains an .xsd file for binding to an XML Schema. You can view the data files by opening them in an XML editor.

CROSS-REF For more information on viewing and exiting XML files in an XML Editor, see Chapter 27.

The Purchase Order folder provides a wealth of sample files demonstrating a number of design types and data handling methods. It's worth spending time exploring the files in the subfolders. One of our favorites among these samples is the dynamic interactive form. This form has a good use of subforms, dynamic flowing elements, some scripting to calculate various field results, and an option to bind data to the sample data file. If you tear this form apart you can learn much about how dynamic forms are created.

Examining the Scripting form

The Scripting form found in the \Forms\Scripting folder is designed to test your JavaScript and FormCalc code. The form has several fields where you supply data including text boxes, a list box, a drop-down list, two radio buttons, and a check box as shown in Figure 32.19. You can test scripts for behaviors assigned to any of the field objects. This form is very handy if you write scripts and encounter problems with the execution of the scripts. Although not quite as powerful as the JavaScript Debugger in Acrobat, this form can be a useful tool.

CROSS-REF For more information on using the JavaScript Debugger, look over the chapters in Part V.

FIGURE 32.19

The Scripting.pdf document has a number of field types used for testing code in FormCalc and JavaScript.

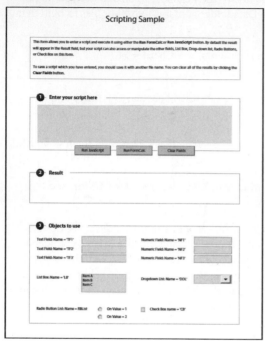

To see how this form is used to check scripts, do the following.

STEPS: Using the Scripting Form

1. **Open the Scripting.pdf form in Acrobat.** Alternately, you can open the form in LiveCycle Designer and click Preview PDF. The form is found at: \Program Files\Adobe\ Acrobat 9.0\Designer 8.2\EN\Samples\Forms\Scripting\Forms. A single folder appears in the Scripting folder and a single form appears in the \Scripting\Forms folder.

2. **Add some data to the NF1 and NF2 fields.** In our example we add 75 to the FN1 field and 6 to the NF2 field as shown in Figure 32.20.

3. **Clear the form.** Click the Clear Fields button just in case you've played with the form. All the field values are cleared after clicking the button.

4. Add a FormCalc script to test the code. In the item *1. Test your script here text box* type a FormCalc Script. In our example we want to test a script that multiplies the values of the NF1 and NF2 fields and adds 12 percent to the total. We also check to see if the NF2 is larger than the NF1 field. If it is, we calculate the total to be zero. If it is not, we run the calculation script. The script would be written as follows:

```
1. if (NF1 < NF2) then
2.    NF3 = 0
3. else
4.    NF3 = (NF1 * NF2) + ((NF1 * NF2) * .12)
5. endif
```

FIGURE 32.20

Type values in the NF1 and NF2 fields.

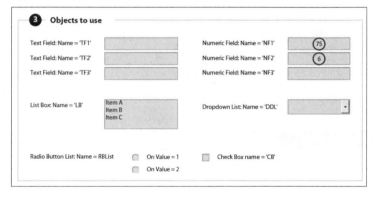

5. Click the Run FormCalc button. The results are shown in the item 2. Result window and the NF3 field box as shown in Figure 32.21.

6. Clear the form. Click the Clear Fields button.

7. Test a JavaScript. Type a JavaScript in the item 1. Test your script here text box. In our example we use a JavaScript to produce the same results as the FormCalc script as shown in Figure 32.22. We used following script:

```
1. if (NF1.rawValue < NF2.rawValue)
2.    NF3.rawValue = 0
3. else
4.    NF3.rawValue = NF1.rawValue * NF2.rawValue + ((NF1.rawValue *
   NF2.rawValue) * .12)
```

FIGURE 32.21

Type the code for a FormCalc script and click Run FormCalc to see the results.

FIGURE 32.22

A sample JavaScript executed in the Scripting.pdf file

8. **Run the script.** Click the Run JavaScript button. The result shown in the 2. Result field shows the same result we calculated with the FormCalc script.

 The numbers in the code are used here only as a reference. When you type the code in the Scripting document do not use the line numbers.

For the scripts used with both scripting languages we look at the NF1 and NF2 fields at the bottom of the page in the 3. Object to use area. We first added 75 to the NF1 field and 6 to the NF2 field. In line 1 of the code for both code samples we check to see if NF1 is less than NF2. If NF1 is less then NF2, the result for the NF3 field is zero as determined in the second line of code. If NF1 is not less than zero we move to line 4, multiply NF1 * NF2, and then add (NF1 * NF2) * .12 which results in 12 percent of the product of the NF1 and NF2 fields.

This form can be a useful tool when you want to write scripts on your forms and when you want to compare scripts written in FormCalc to JavaScripts.

Examining the SubformSet forms

The SubFormSet folder contains a SubformSet Sample file as shown in Figure 32.23. This form has three subforms. Two data files are contained in the Data folder. The form is designed to bind the data from one of the sample data files and examine the subform set when the form is rendered.

FIGURE 32.23

The SubformSet form

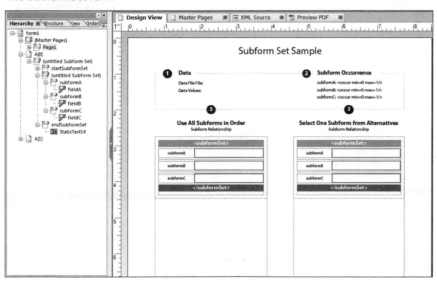

You can open the XML data files in an XML editor and examine the arrangement of the data. In Figure 32.24 we opened the DataA.XML file from the Data folder in the SubformSet folder. Notice the arrangement of the data to be introduced in the subforms in this file.

FIGURE 32.24

The DataA.XML file opened in an XML editor

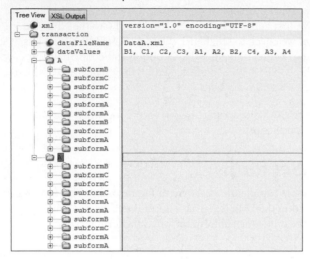

We created a data connection in the Form Properties to the DataA.xml file and rendered the form. When the form opened in Acrobat, the subforms were arranged as you see in Figure 32.25.

FIGURE 32.25

The form using the DataA file rendered in Acrobat

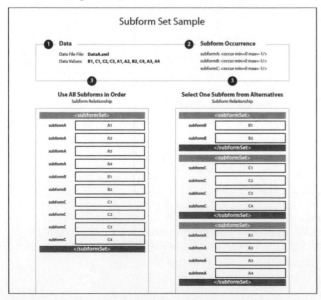

When we opened the DataB file in an XML editor the subform data arrangement appeared as shown in Figure 32.26. When we created a data connection to the DataB file and rendered the form, the SubformSets appeared as shown in Figure 32.27.

FIGURE 32.26

The DataB.XML file opened in an XML editor

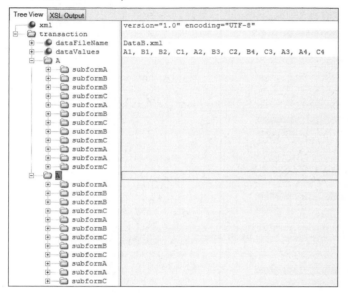

You can examine the Outputs folder and see the differences for the layouts of the subform sets according to some choices made in the Binding tab and the Subform Sets tab in the Object palette. Study these differences to gain a little more understanding for how subform layout properties affect the rendered forms.

Examining the Tax Receipt form

The Tax Receipt form in the Samples\Forms\Tax Receipt\Forms folder is another form that uses a data file from a Data folder. A single block of fields is wrapped in a subform identified with flowed content. The data file contains three records so when the form is rendered three sets of the same block of fields appear on the form.

FIGURE 32.27

The form using the DataB file rendered in Acrobat

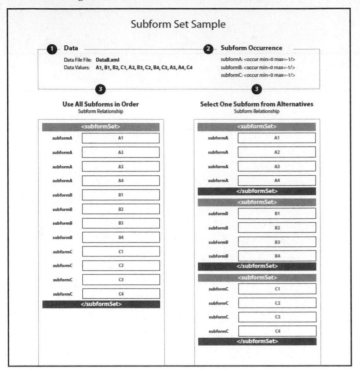

This form has several items to demonstrate that include:

- **Form hierarchy structure.** The form is based on the data structure to take advantage of the data binding.

- **Master page.** A footer is added as a master page item.

- **Flowed content.** As shown in Figure 32.28, the form uses a subform (taxReceipt) set up for flowed content with the direction set to Top to Bottom.

- **Subform occurrence.** Notice in Figure 32.28 you see a subform for receipt. The form is designed to have three copies printed. Therefore the subform occurrence is set to three in the Subform tab in the Object palette as shown in Figure 32.29.

FIGURE 32.28

The Tax Receipt form uses a subform with flowed content to flow data from several records.

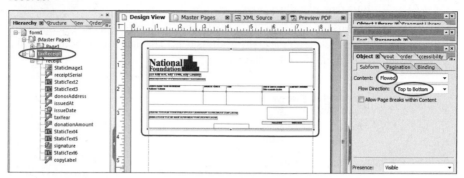

FIGURE 32.29

When the form is rendered, three copies of the receipt appear on each page.

- **Global fields.** A number of fields are duplicated for the receipt. The data are the same for all three copies of the receipt so these fields have a Global binding set up in the Object palette Binding tab.

- **Image field.** The signature used on the form is a scan of a wet signature. Therefore, an Image field was used to import the image and the binding was set to Global to repeat the image on the three copies of the receipt. This design affords you the ability to easily change the image when a new signatory becomes the responsible party to sign a receipt. All that's needed is to replace the image file with the same filename and in the same location as the original image.

- **Max Characters/Multiple lines.** Some fields are set to maximum number of characters and a few formatted for Allow Multiple Lines.

- **Picture patterns.** Some fields on this form use picture patterns. The Date fields use a long date identified as a pattern.

- **Scripting.** A JavaScript is contained in this form. Open the Script Editor CRTL + Shift + F5 and click on the donorAddress field. The data for the address field is concatenated using a JavaScript as shown in Figure 32.30.

FIGURE 32.30

Open the Script Editor and click the donorAddress field to see the JavaScript used to concatenate the fields.

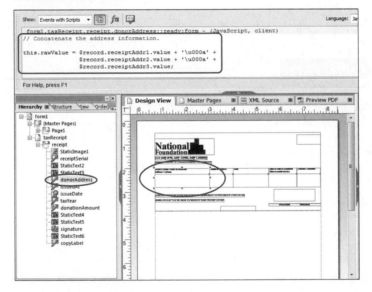

When you add a data connection in the Form Properties to the XML file in the Data folder and render the form you see the results of creating three copies of the receipt on a single page as shown in Figure 32.31.

This sample form doesn't have many fields but it is a great example for demonstrating setting field attributes, working with subforms, creating multiple copies of a form, and binding data.

FIGURE 32.31

When the form is rendered, three copies of the receipt are shown on a single page.

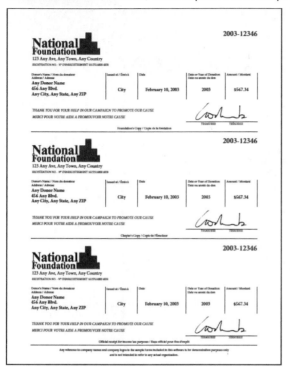

Exploring Sample Forms Online

A number of LiveCycle Designer forms appear on Adobe's Web site and are uploaded with tutorials explaining how a form was constructed. Log on to `http://www.adobe.com/devnet/livecycle/` and you find a list of support services as shown in Figure 32.32.

This site changes frequently because of contributions made by Designer gurus, so we won't demonstrate examples here. You might want to make a frequent visit to the Web site to search for new content and sample forms along with a downloadable tutorial.

FIGURE 32.32

A number of sample forms and tutorial guides are available at Adobe's Web site.

Summary

- The Designer Help guide Quick Start Tutorial sections contain tutorials that walk you through steps to design a number of different forms.

- You should copy the Samples folder installed with your Acrobat installation to a new folder location so that you can return to the original sample files.

- A collection of eight sample files is installed with Designer to help you understand more about designing static and dynamic forms.

- Additional sample forms can be found on Adobe's Web site at http://www.adobe.com/devnet/livecycle/.

Chapter 33

Working with Databases

IN THIS CHAPTER

Using a form to create a database

Exporting database records

Using a database to store form data

O ur form design is complete. The data is ready to be collected, but where are we going to put it? Leaving the form data in the PDF file looks nice but is not an efficient way to store the information. The design elements of the form take a significant amount of the file size. Each time we store another copy we are wasting additional storage space needed for the form itself. If we extract the information from the form design and store only the data, the amount of space needed is greatly reduced. Having all of the data in a single location also allows us to analyze the collected information.

After all the time and effort we put into designing our forms it would be a shame to not have a well-designed storage facility to house the data. A database provides a permanent organized storage facility to place all of our form data for easy retrieval and reporting.

Database programs, like other software programs, are available from a variety of vendors and range in capabilities. The enterprise-level databases reside on a server and are usually managed by an IT department. The smaller desktop database programs are run on a single machine. The database program selected to store the data normally depends on the available resources.

Getting data from the form to the database for storage can be achieved with an export /import process or a direct connection to the form. For security reasons, we will use the export/import features. Most database administrators do not allow a form direct access to the database without some additional safeguards in place to protect the data. This chapter focuses on Microsoft Access as the database tool.

Working with a Database

The purpose of a database is to store the raw data and provide efficient data retrieval. A well-designed database minimizes data redundancy while ensuring that the data remains consistent when you insert, update, or delete a record. A database is capable of storing relational information while maintaining the data integrity of the related pieces.

Not all databases are designed equally. A well-designed database is considered normalized. Normalization is a technique for designing related tables that prevents data problems from occurring. Figure 33.1 shows a normalized table designed to store applicant information. When a database has not been normalized a table can contain multiple instances of a given piece of data. The more often this occurs, the more likely inconsistencies exist in the data.

The ApplicantInfo table of the applications database

When data is stored in a single table the database is being underutilized and is considered denormalized. A spreadsheet or other flat file format could store the data. The power of a database resides in its relational capabilities. Normalization is used to break the original large table into multiple smaller tables. The smaller tables are more specialized topics that, if they were combined, would convey the same information as the original table as shown in Figure 33.2.

It is rare for the fields in a form design structure to match a pre-existing database structure. You can map the fields in Designer based on a sample XML data file or an XML Schema file. In the database, you can do field mapping when importing the data. Another method is to incorporate an XML Style Transfer Sheet (XSLT) during the import/export process from the form and the database. The XSLT would alter the data hierarchy to match the desired output, saving the step of mapping the fields while importing and exporting.

FIGURE 33.2

The normalized tables joined as a form to show all of the original fields contained in the original form

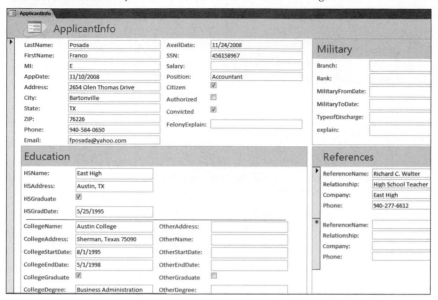

Exploring a database design

If you are unfamiliar with building a database, we recommend that you enlist the help of someone well versed in database design. Be prepared with samples of forms, data sets, and some ideas for what you wish to do with the data before meeting to discuss building the database.

Database design is a broad topic with some general guidelines that designers choose to interpret in their own ways. We designed a database to store our job applicant information. Keep in mind in a real-world situation the applicant data is a small part of a bigger process. The Applicant database included in the Chapter33 folder on the CD-ROM is over-simplified to demonstrate how a form and a database can work together. This database is not intended to be put into production.

 **The applications.mdb file is included in the Chapter33 folder on the CD-ROM.**

Our application form contains five main areas: applicant information, education, military, previous employment, and references as shown in Figure 33.3. To optimize storage and prevent inconsistencies, we should store each piece of information only once. Then we refer to that piece of information again when we need it. This requires us to approach the form from a new perspective.

FIGURE 33.3

The Designer application form

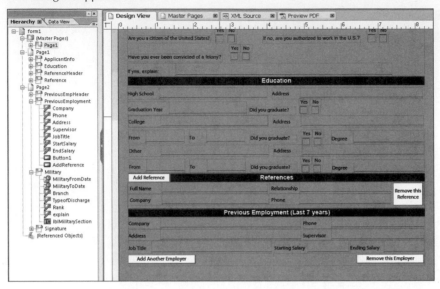

When the individual pieces of the data are pulled apart to be stored separately, the smaller groups of data have nothing in common to connect the applicant to the appropriate history. We need to add a field to each of the related sections as a connecting field to help us maintain the data integrity in the database. In database terminology this common field is known as a primary key and a foreign key. The primary key is a unique identifying field in the applicant information table. For other tables related to the applicant information that unique piece of information is included to determine the related records. In the related tables the shared field is called the foreign key.

Many databases use a unique number assigned to each main record to keep related information connected properly. We intend to use the form to collect the information, so we want to use a field that is collected in the form and does not need database connectivity to be generated. For our application we have two pieces of information that are unique to each applicant, their Social Security number and their e-mail address. We chose to use the e-mail address to avoid unnecessary use of the Social Security number. This required us to add a hidden field to each of the sections of the form below the applicant information.

The file GFApplication_DB.pdf in the Chapter 33 folder on the CD-ROM has already been modified, as shown in Figure 33.4. The AppEmail field was added to each section except the applicant info section. The AppEmail fields also have a script that sets their value equal to the value of the Email field in the Applicant Info section. The visibility property of the AppEmail fields is set to invisible.

Another change we made to the application revolves around extra subform sections that were used for organization. The data bindings were modified so that any section that does not contain fields was set to none. This prevents the exported data from having extra data nodes when importing them into the database.

FIGURE 33.4

The modified Designer Application form with a hidden field named AppEmail

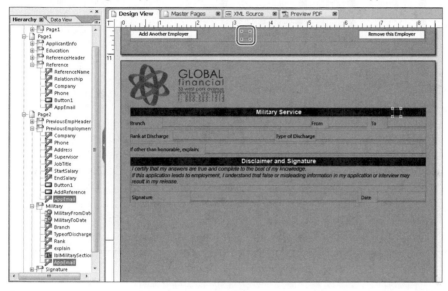

Redesigning a form to better fit with a database is common when the form and the database are not built at the same time. Since the database ultimately holds all of the collected data, it is easier to change the form to match the database design than to try to adjust the extracted data from each form.

Database design is subjective and you need to consider the entire process when setting up the database. One could argue that the education section should contain multiple tables, or the position applied for should not be stored with the applicant's demographic information. Having only five tables in our database gives us a good idea of how fields can be broken down while keeping the content manageable for discussion. Our applicant database diagram appears in Figure 33.5.

A form in the database looks similar to our Designer form as shown in Figure 33.6. You may need to map the fields from one to the other to ensure the information is stored and displayed in the correct fields. The more complex the database, the more likely you need to map the fields with data bindings.

FIGURE 33.5

The applicant database diagram

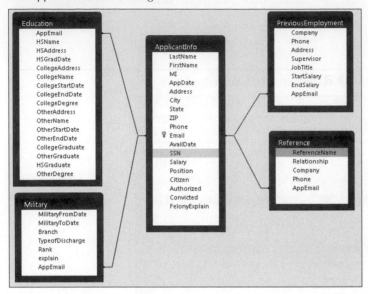

FIGURE 33.6

The applicant form in an Access database

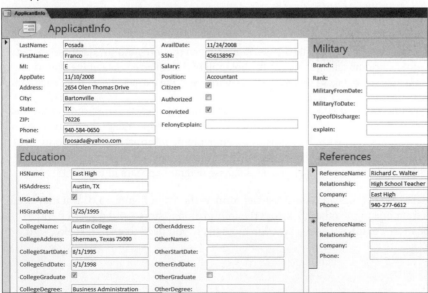

The steps required to create a table in Microsoft Access depend on the version of the software you have loaded. Our database was created by exporting an XML sample data set from the Designer application form, imported into Microsoft Access and then modified to suit our needs.

CROSS-REF For information on exporting data from a form, see Chapters 14 and 31.

Importing data into an Access database

Armed with a sample XML file from our Designer application form, we are ready to import the data into a blank database or to append data to tables in an existing database. In Microsoft Access 2007 importing an XML file is an option located in the External Data ribbon. In Microsoft Access 2002 or 2003 the import XML option is located in the file menu. The following steps focus on using Access 2007.

ON the CD-ROM The applications.mdb file is included in the Chapter33 folder on the CD-ROM. You can use this file or create your own for the following steps.

STEPS: Importing XML Data into the Database

1. **Open the database or create a new one in Microsoft Access.** We opened the applications.mdb file in the Chapter33 folder on the CD-ROM.

2. **Select the External Data tab in the Ribbon.** This is where the import and export options are located in Access. Figure 33.7 shows the Import XML File button.

FIGURE 33.7

The XML File button in the Import group of the External Data tab

3. **Select the XML File option from the Import group.** Clicking the XML file button opens the dialog box to locate your XML file.

4. **Click the Browse button to locate your XML data file.** Navigate to where the XML file is located and click Open to return to the dialog box. You can create your own sample XML file by filling in the GFApplication_DB.pdf and exporting the data using Acrobat. Or you can use the Application_SampleData.XML in the Chapter33 folder on the CD-ROM.

5. **Select the Import Options and click OK.** The Import XML dialog box appears showing the tables that are going to be built based on the XML file you are importing, as shown in Figure 33.8. The first time we built the database file, we selected the Structure and Data option. Now that the database is built, we selected the Append Data to Existing Tables option.

FIGURE 33.8

The Import XML tables and options

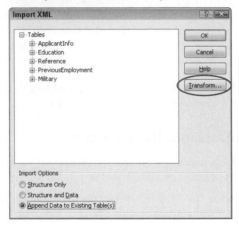

NOTE There is no way to exclude a table from this step of the process. However, you can change the data binding in the Designer form to none to stop the data node from being created in the first place.

   a. **Structure Only:** If this is a blank database and you are going to create the tables from the XML file but are not ready for the data to be imported choose this option.

   b. **Structure and Data:** Select this option if you wish to build the tables, and include the data at the same time.

   c. **Append Data to Existing Table(s):** If the tables already exist, and match the node names of the XML file you can add the data to the existing tables.

6. **Click OK.** The confirmation window appears indicating whether the import was successful or not. It also allows you to save the import steps for reuse.

7. **Close the confirmation window.** If you imported to the applications.mdb file you are now ready to work with the data in Access. If the import created a new database the tables most likely need some adjustments to be used as a permanent storage facility.

The more complex the database, the more helpful an XSLT file can be. Our database is very simple, which allows us to import and export directly to the tables without the need to transform the data. The database can be used for reports, queries, and exporting data back to an XML file for remerging with the form when needed.

Exporting data from the Access database

In order to export a single file that contains all of the applicant's original information, you need to create a query, form, or report that remerges all of the related information into a single location for export. Our application.mdb file contains a form that puts all five tables back together for you to export data from. The Applicant Info form is considered the main form, with four related subforms that share the AppEmail field with the ApplicantInfo table.

STEPS: Exporting XML Data from the Database

1. **Open the database object that reconnects all of the pieces.** We opened the Applicant Info form in the applications.mdb file in the Chapter33 folder on the CD-ROM.

2. **Navigate to the record that contains the information you wish to export.** We selected the first record in the database.

3. **Select the External Data tab in the Ribbon.** The XML options for importing and exporting are contained in this area.

4. **Click More in the Export group.** Four additional options appear in the drop-down list as shown in Figure 33.9.

FIGURE 33.9

The More button in the External Data Tab's Export group

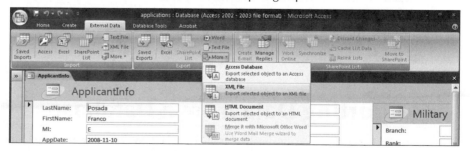

5. **Select the XML File option.** In order to import the data back into a designer form we need a format that Designer understands.

6. **Browse for the location where you want the XML data file placed.** Navigate to the desired location and name the exported data. We named the file ApplicantInfoDB.xml.

7. **Click More.** We need to change the settings to include the additional subforms data in the export process. As shown in Figure 33.10, select the subforms under the Applicant Info. On the right we set the Records to Export to the current record.

The Export XML Data options dialog box

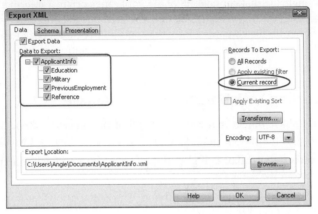

8. **Select each of the subform check boxes.** Be sure to check the Education, Military, PreviousEmployment, and Reference boxes to include the subform data in the export.

9. **Export the current record.** Select the current record from the Records to Export section on the top right of the export window.

10. **Click OK.** This finishes the export process.

Now that the data has been exported from the database, we need to import it into the Designer form. There are many reasons to put the data back into the original form. We may need to reprint the original information or share it with someone who does not have access to the database program.

Importing Data from a Database

Even though we created the database from a sample XML file extracted from our application form, that does not mean the exported database file will import correctly in the Designer form. The original form did not contain any data connections. This means the field bindings are implicit and data binds with a field only when the name and order of the data nodes match the corresponding subforms and when the field names match exactly.

The database object that was used to export the information may contain the same fields, but if they are grouped into different subform sets the implicit binding cannot locate the fields. Because many database objects can be used to export data and many different methods can be used to create those objects, it is always a good idea to test the process of returning the data to the original form.

Testing the exported database data in the original form

The form we created in Access to look like the original Designer form contains all of the fields we need. It is organized with the applicant information in the main form with other table information being part of the subforms. This creates a different data node sequence when we export the data. We also could build a query that joins the tables and results in another sequence. To test the database-exported information in the Designer form, we attach it as the sample XML file for previewing. This is one of the quickest ways to see which fields bind correctly to the sample file.

STEPS: Attach the Exported Database XML File to the Designer Form as a Sample File for Preview

1. **Open the original designer form.** We opened the GFApplication_DB.pdf file in the Chapter33 folder from the book's CD-ROM.

2. **Open the Form Properties.** Select File ➪ Form Properties to open the Form Properties dialog box.

3. **Select the Preview Tab.** This is where the sample data file is selected for preview.

4. **Browse for the exported database file.** Using the Browse button navigate to the location where you stored the exported XML file we named ApplicantInfoDB.xml as shown in Figure 33.11.

FIGURE 33.11

The Preview tab of the Form Properties window with the data file selected

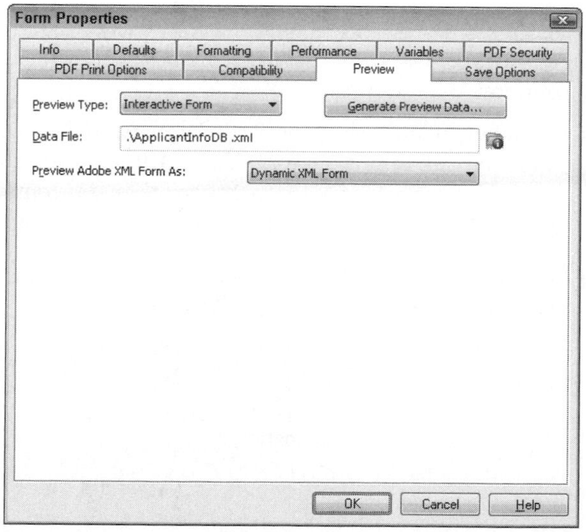

5. **Click OK to save your settings.**

6. **Preview the form.** Select the Preview PDF tab to see the sample file merged with the form. If you used the GFApplication_DB.pdf form contained in the Chapter33 folder on the book's CD-ROM you will see that the first section of the form data merged correctly. All other sections appear empty, as shown in Figure 33.12, because the XML data nodes do not match the form hierarchy.

FIGURE 33.12

The Preview PDF shows the applicant section data merged properly while the other sections appear empty.

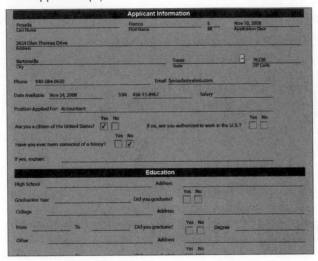

7. **Return to Design View.** Because the form does not bind all of the fields correctly we need to evaluate our options.

8. **Save the form with a new name.** Select File ⇨ Save As to open the Save As dialog box. Give the form a new name; we named our form TestingGFApplication_DB.pdf. We recommend that you save the original form design until all testing is completed and the form is working as desired in case you need to revert to the clean copy.

Either we need to modify one of the database objects to match the form data nodes or the form can be modified to match the database structure. The form can use data bindings to map the fields to the proper data nodes. An alternative solution is to use an XSLT applied to the data to transform it into the same structure as the form. We chose to modify the form to use data bindings in the form.

Modifying a form for importing data

The Designer form will be used to collect the applicant information we need to store in the Microsoft Access database. Changing the form's hierarchy to match the database would cause our repeating subform sections not to function properly. Changing the database object to match the form hierarchy may be possible but would require changing and testing until things matched. Attempting to fix the database object is not the most effective use of time.

By creating some simple data bindings we can change the form to match the database and use the new form for both importing data to the form and exporting data from the form. We need to create a data connection to something from the database: a direct connection, a sample XML file, or a schema. We choose to use the sample XML file we already created.

STEPS: Setting up Data Binding for Importing and Exporting

1. **Open the form.** If you completed the previous set of steps, open the file saved in Step 8. If not, you can open the TestingGFApplication_DB.pdf from the Chapter33 folder on the book's CD-ROM.

2. **Open the Data View palette.** Select Window ⇨ Data View to show the Data View palette.

3. **Right-click in the Data View palette and select New Data Connection.** Right-clicking in the Data View palette opens the context menu options where you can find the New Data Connection option.

4. **Give the Data Connection a name.** We typed in ApplicantDB_XML as our Data Connection name. This name does not have to match the name of the file you are connecting to.

> **CROSS-REF** For more information on Data Connections, see Chapter 31.

5. **Select the Sample XML Data radio button.** This sets the data connection type to be a sample XML file.

6. **Browse for the Sample XML File.** Use the Browse button to find the XML file you wish to use. We selected the ApplicantInfoDB.xml we exported earlier from the database, or use the one in the Chapter33 folder.

7. **Select Finish to establish your data connection.** Once the dialog box has closed the Data View palette is populated with the sample XML information as shown in Figure 33.13.

8. **Create Relative Bindings for the repeating subforms.** Select the Reference subform from the Hierarchy palette. Open the Binding Tab of the Object palette. Open the data binding option button. Follow the data connection until you locate the Reference subform and select it. The binding should appear as:

```
$.ApplicantInfo.Reference[*]
```

FIGURE 33.13

The Data View palette connected to the sample XML file from the database export

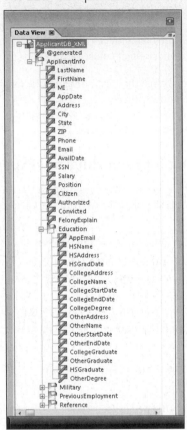

CROSS-REF For details on how to create the data bindings, see Chapter 31.

Repeat for the PreviousEmployment section, its binding should appear as

```
$.ApplicantInfo.PreviousEmployment[*]
```

9. **Create the explicit bindings.** The form fields have to be tied to the XML data nodes explicitly because the data nodes do not match the form hierarchy. We recommend starting at the top of the Data View palette and dragging each field on to the matching designer form object. After the binding is complete, the Data View palette appears as shown in Figure 33.14.

FIGURE 33.14

The Data View palette after all bindings have been created

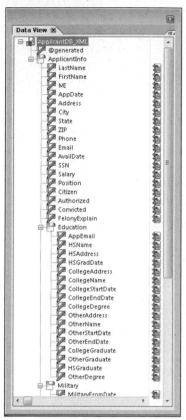

10. **Verify that a sample XML file is attached for previewing.** Open the Form Properties and select the Preview tab. If necessary, browse for a sample XML file from the database to test with.

11. **Preview the form.** Select the Preview PDF tab to carefully check each section of the form for the correct data. It is very easy to create a connection from a data node to the wrong field when dragging and dropping in Step 8.

12. **Return to Design View.** Correct any missing or incorrect data bindings, repeating Steps 8 through 12 until all fields appear correctly in the preview.

13. **Save the form.**

> **TIP** To troubleshoot and double-check data bindings, open the Report palette. The Binding tab shows fields with normal binding by default. If this area is empty, all fields have been explicitly bound by reference. Using the palette menu, change to the Fields with Data Binding by Reference or the Fields with No Data Binding to ensure you have set each type to the correct fields.

Once you have established and tested the data connection, we recommend that you export a set of form data to import into the database again. Thus verifying the process works from both directions. You can use the new form to collect data that is stored in the database and as a template for remerging data from the database later.

Summary

- You can use a Designer form to collect information to be stored in a database.

- Database designs do not organize the data the same way a form does.

- The Designer form may require changes to bind properly with the database and maintain data integrity.

- A normalized database reduces data redundancy and stores individual pieces of information one time.

- Importing and exporting data from the database prevents unintentional changes from being made to the database records.

- Because database tables store the information in smaller subsets than the original form, create another database object to combine the smaller pieces back into a complete set.

- Data bindings are important when exporting to a database. Verify that all fields are bound to the correct data node.

- Test the import and export process after any change has been made to either the form or the database to ensure both continue to work together.

- The Binding tab of the Report palette is a great tool for troubleshooting data connections.

Chapter 34

Introducing LiveCycle Enterprise Suite

IN THIS CHAPTER

Learning about LiveCycle ES components

Customizing the Workspace

Using the Workbench

Improving performance

Businesses have procedures in place that use a variety of software programs to help them achieve their business goals. Every organization has its own customized implementation of the hardware and software needed to reach those goals. The inherent problem with most systems is that the products from different vendors don't integrate well with one another. Usually this translates into additional data entry work for employees or some migration work for information services.

What if we could collect the necessary information from an employee or customer one time and have it populate each of those appropriate products as needed? What if we could rout that information to the next person in the chain of command for approval, if necessary, without the need for us to fill out additional forms or computer screens? This is exactly the type of thing that LiveCycle ES can do.

Perhaps you have only heard of LiveCycle ES, and wondered what people were talking about. You may even work with a component of LiveCycle ES but wondered what else it could do. If you are asking yourself, "What is LiveCycle ES?" that is the question we hope to answer in this chapter.

This chapter is not intended to teach you how to work with the components in LiveCycle Enterprise Suite (ES). Several books this size would be needed to cover all of the solution components available. We are going to introduce the LiveCycle Enterprise Suite and explore its capabilities.

Examining a Process

Global Finance is the company we have utilized for most of our form designs throughout this book. We continue to explore their business needs here in the LiveCycle ES chapter as well. We built many forms for Global Finance in the preceding chapters, one of which was a Purchase Order form that dynamically adjusts with buttons to add and remove rows of data.

Global Finance requires that all purchase orders be submitted to the employee's manager for approval. If the amount of the purchase order is less than $500 the manager's approval is sufficient for accounting to process the request. If the purchase order amount is more than $500 then the director of the department is required to review the PO before sending it to accounting for processing. Accounting then assigns an authorization number to the PO and notifies the vendor. If either the manager or the department head denies the PO, the employee who completed the original PO is to be notified. If the accounting department receives the PO with all of the appropriate approvals, a PO number is assigned and sent to the vendor and the employee receives notification.

Looking at the paper workflow

Let's first examine the paper-centric process to discuss the potential for delays or problems. An employee submits a PO for $515 to the manager for review on Monday. The manager should review the PO and submit it to the department director for approval. How many of these situations are common enough to cause a delay in that workflow?

- **The manager submits directly to accounting:** The manager assumes because the amount is only $15 over their approval threshold, accounting will approve it without needing approval from the department director.

- **The manager, director, or accounting personnel are out on vacation:** The PO sits pending approval until the following Monday when they return.

- **The employee bypasses the supervisor:** The employee submits it directly to the director or accounting department without getting initial approval from the manager.

- **The PO is completed but forgotten in a pile of paperwork on someone's desk.**

- **The data is incomplete:** Lacking the appropriate information, the form must be returned to the employee for more information to resume processing.

When any delay occurs in the paper process the only way to know where the paperwork is hung up is to begin asking questions. This, of course, relies on the fact that someone has noticed they didn't receive the approval or denial notification in a timely fashion. Worse yet, the requested items on the purchase order items aren't missed until the first time they are needed. Now the delay in the paper process is delaying other employees' work.

Comparing a paper process to the LiveCycle ES workflow

When this same process is deployed through LiveCycle ES we can address and prevent many common delays to the workflow. The business process design has built-in rules that employees cannot ignore or circumvent. Using the preceding example from above for a purchase order of $515, what happens to each of those same problem scenarios?

- **The manager cannot submit directly to accounting:** The business process dynamically chooses the appropriate person to route the PO based on the dollar amount it contains. No guessing or skipping of any step in the process takes place because the dollar amount is near the approval threshold. If the amount is under $500 it goes to accounting, and if it is over $500 it goes to the department director, with no exceptions.

- **Someone on vacation does not cause delays:** Two potential solutions are available to remedy this problem. Both would be implemented because one requires human interaction, and the other does not.

  - **The vacationing party sets their out-of-office status in LiveCycle ES:** This alerts the system to route to an alternate manager or director who can process the PO in their absence.

  - **The vacationing party forgets to set their out-of-office status in LiveCycle ES:** The business process waits the allotted amount of time, 48 hours in this case, and then routes to an alternate for approval. When a process is escalated, such as in this situation, the action the process takes can vary greatly. A reminder e-mail may be sent, or the supervisor may be notified or asked to complete the approval.

- **The employee cannot bypass the manager.** Because the Submit button is controlled by the business process, the employee has no way to circumvent the system.

- **The PO cannot be forgotten in a pile of papers:** Using LiveCycle ES you have no paperwork to lose. The information is all routed electronically. If an employee would like to know where the PO is delayed, they can track their own PO to see where it is in the process pending approval.

- **The data cannot be submitted if it is incomplete:** Using an electronic form with required fields prevents the document from beginning the workflow if it is incomplete.

Taking the time to create an effective electronic workflow may cost a little more up front with the purchase of the server components and licensing, but the return on that investment can save you even more time and money in the long run.

Justifying the need for electronic processes

We know, it sounds great but justifying an electronic workflow to management generates many questions. How much training do my employees need to use the new process? How complicated is it to document and explain to the employees who are not computer savvy? The paper form we currently use is self explanatory and everyone likes what we have. We don't experience any major delays with the current PO system so why change it?

Our purchase order example is only one form. How many forms does your business use every day? How much time is spent walking that form from one office to another for approval? How much additional time is wasted because the employee waits for that approver to finish a phone call so they can discuss the request? What about the hand-written paper form that can't be entered into the accounting system because it's illegible? We are sure that if you look at your existing paper-based processes with a little bit of objectivity you can find room for improvement.

CROSS-REF For more information on the costs associated with paper workflows, see Chapter 2.

Exploring the LiveCycle ES solution

Beginning with the employee who needs to submit a purchase order we walk though the LiveCycle process step by step to show you how easy and efficient it is for the form recipient. We provide information to fuel that conversation with management on how easy the process can be.

STEPS: Exploring the Purchase Order Process in LiveCycle ES

1. **Alex logs into the LiveCycle ES Workspace to create a purchase order.** The employee needs to have access to all of their forms in one convenient and secure location. Figure 34.1 shows the login page.

FIGURE 34.1

The LiveCycle ES Workspace login page

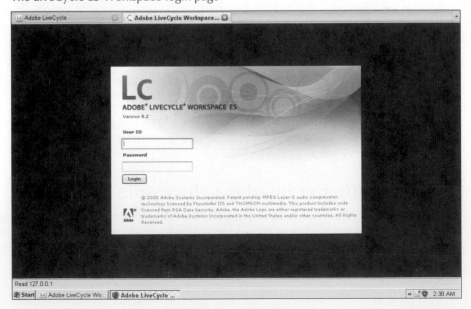

2. **The welcome page displays.** As Figure 34.2 shows the employee is allowed to Start a Process, Look at their To Do List, Track items they participated in, Change Preferences or Read Messages. The Workspace is an easy-to-use Web page, even for individuals who use the system only occasionally.

FIGURE 34.2

The Workspace welcome page

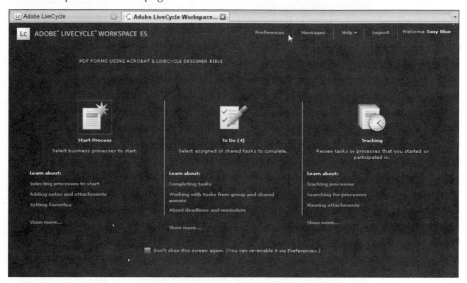

3. **Alex selects the Start Process icon.** The categories appear on the left side of the screen, with process cards available on the right as shown in Figure 34.3.

4. **Alex selects the PO process card to begin filling in the form.** The PDF form loads on the right side of the screen for the employee to complete as shown in Figure 34.4. The form design contains all the calculations necessary to complete the form. Data validation exists to prevent incorrect data entries, and required fields must be filled in before submitting the form.

5. **Alex completes the form by clicking Complete.** Clicking Complete in the lower-right corner of the workspace screen returns Alex to the Category view. This routes the form to Alex's manager for review. Alex can track the PO progress by looking at the tracking information available in the workspace.

FIGURE 34.3

The Category view with process cards

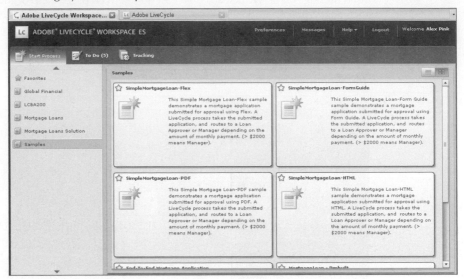

FIGURE 34.4

The PDF form loaded into the workspace

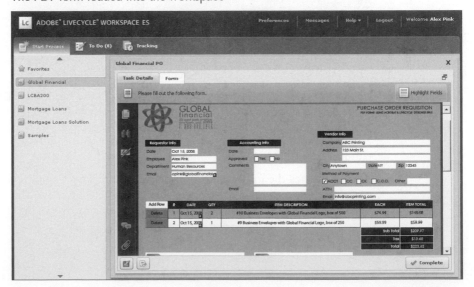

6. **Tony (Alex's manager) logs into the workspace to look for documents pending approval.** Any process started by another employee that needs Tony's approval appears as an item in the To Do list.

   Tony's To Do List shows the number of pending items on the welcome page. Figure 34.5 shows that Tony has five items to attend to.

FIGURE 34.5

Tony's welcome page shows five To Do items.

7. **Tony selects the To Do Icon.** The To Do list opens with cards for each of the tasks with instructions and other information available.

8. **Tony selects a task by clicking it.** The PDF form opens for review. Tony adds any necessary information to the form, then approves or denies it using the buttons in the lower-right corner of the workspace as shown in Figure 34.6.

9. **The LiveCycle ES Server routes the PO for the next step.** If the amount is under $500 the purchase order appears in the accounting department's To Do list. If the amount is over $500, it appears in the department director's To Do list.

10. **Alex wonders how the PO is progressing.** Alex logs into the workspace and selects the tracking link. Next Alex selects the category from the left, and if necessary changes the date range to filter the list as shown in Figure 34.7.

FIGURE 34.6

Tony can approve or reject the PO.

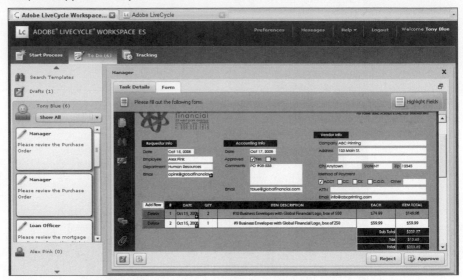

FIGURE 34.7

The items in the Tracking List for the selected category within the specified date range

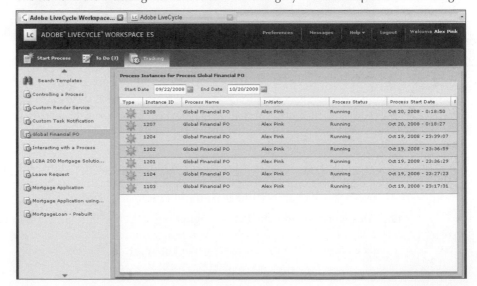

11. **Alex selects the task she is concerned with.** The tracking information shows which steps of the process have been completed and their status as shown in Figure 34.8.

Alex tracks the PO.

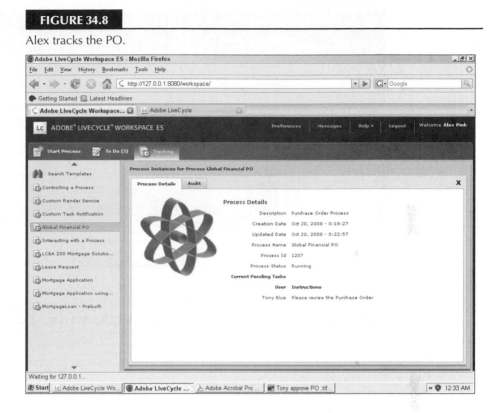

12. **Accounting approves the Purchase Order.** LiveCycle ES e-mails the vendor with the purchase order attached and notifies Alex of the approval and the PO number that was assigned. The accounting system is updated with the transaction information.

13. **Alex views the approval notification.** Alex receives a To Do item indicating the approval and showing the PO number that was assigned as shown in Figure 34.9.

LiveCycle ES makes working with forms easier to manage than paper-based workflows. The process is sure to follow business rules, and you can avoid common pitfalls in the electronic routing. Form designs also can change over time. With LiveCycle ES the forms that are currently in process are allowed to finish, while any new processes are immediately deployed with the newest version of the form. You don't need to gather and destroy the old printed documents or worry about missed paper copies appearing in the workflow months after a change has occurred. Now that you have a good understanding of how LiveCycle ES can work, we will get into what LiveCycle ES is.

FIGURE 34.9

Alex reviews the PO approval.

Getting an Overview of LiveCycle ES

LiveCycle ES (LCES) is an enterprise server platform based on Java 2 Platform Enterprise Edition (J2EE) for developing, building and deploying Web-based enterprise applications. LCES runs as a J2EE service on a J2EE application server using a Service Oriented Architecture (SOA) that allows this platform to lie on top of the existing infrastructure. SOA is an architecture style intended to define how two services interact, allowing one service to perform a function on behalf of the other. Each service is self-contained and loosely coupled so they remain independent of one another.

LCES is designed to automate and streamline complex business processes that involve multiple departments, intricate business rules, and back-end systems. LCES is not a replacement for current systems. It is a complementary set of services that enable straight-through processing, affording you the ability to manage information more accurately, improve quality of service, and decrease costly cycle times. LiveCycle ES can separate the data from the presentation in a process, thus allowing independent storage of both the forms and the data at any point in the workflow. The data can then be remerged with the existing form or another form if needed later in the workflow.

LCES provides all the tools needed to design, implement, and automate the documents and processes both inside and outside the firewall. LiveCycle ES combines PDF, Flex, Flash, and HTML technologies to provide a unified developer experience.

LiveCycle ES clients

A benefit to using LiveCycle ES is that the end user does not need any additional purchased software to participate in a deployed process. The client software applications available to deploy your LCES applications are readily available client applications.

The hardest decision may be which client your application should be deployed in. You may find the answer varies in different phases of the process. Luckily LCES happily obliges your indecisiveness. If you build forms using LiveCycle Designer you can use the same basic form design with some adjustments when rendering in the following client applications:

- **Adobe Reader:** The freely distributed Adobe PDF viewer application intended for users who need to view and print PDF files. Adobe Reader is available for an ever-increasing number of platforms and languages.

- **Adobe Flash Player:** The freely distributed Adobe Flash viewer application is designed for playing SWF files built with Flash, Flex, and other third-party products. The Flash Player is built into some Web browsers and is available as a plug-in for many others. Forms designed with Form Guides can be rendered as Flash content as shown in Figure 34.10.

FIGURE 34.10

A form deployed as Flash

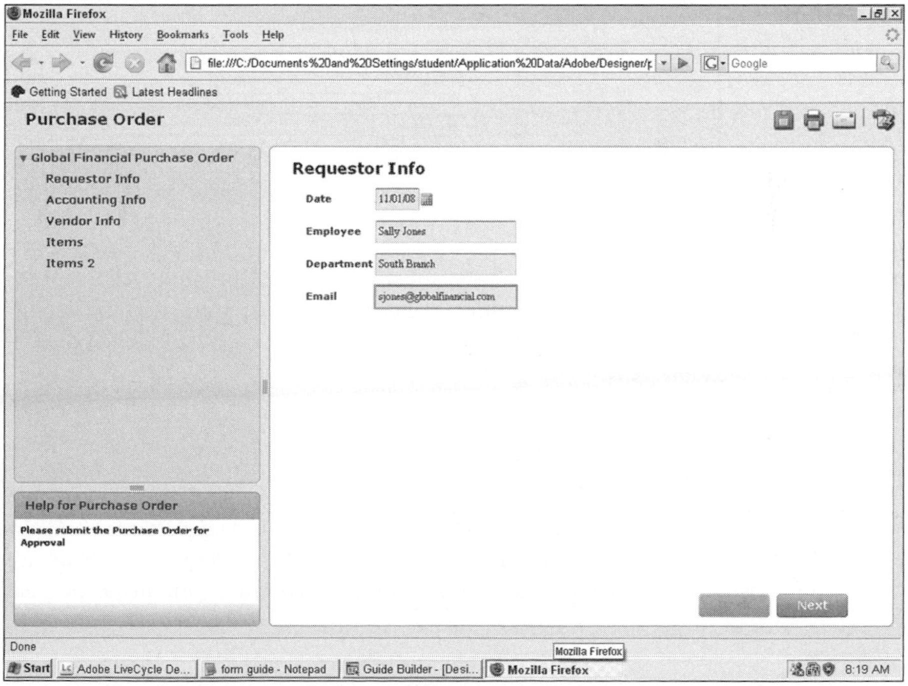

CROSS-REF | For more information on Adobe Reader, see Chapter 2.

■ **HTML browser:** Web browsers are available from a variety of vendors, designed to display pages written in Hyper Text Markup Language (HTML). The browser enables interaction with text, images, and multimedia made available from a Web page. An XDP form can be rendered as HTML using LiveCycle ES Forms as shown in Figure 34.11.

FIGURE 34.11

A form deployed as HTML

■ **Adobe AIR:** The newest member in the ES Client group, Adobe AIR is a cross-platform runtime environment for rich Internet applications that can be deployed as a desktop application. Content originally developed for the Web can be ported to the desktop using Adobe AIR.

LiveCycle ES Foundation

The LCES Foundation is included with the purchase of any of the LCES solution components. It includes the underlying server capabilities that support the deployment and management of your applications. The Foundation allows integration with the company's existing infrastructure. The Foundation also provides exception handling, orchestration, and invocation methods.

Service container

The common architectural foundation or runtime environment is the service container. It supports the solution components and services. The service container enables linking multiple solution components in a process. You can easily add, remove, and update. services The service container provides flexibility, extensibility and simplified deployment. How a service is invoked becomes transparent to the service container; it always provides a consistent way to interact with the services.

Foundation services

You can enable integration with common IT infrastructures. Some of the services included are: e-mail, file utilities, LDAP, Web services, FTP, JDBC, and more. Some examples of the foundation integration include looking up employee information in LDAP or placing files in a network folder for automated processing.

Administration tools

The administration tools offer a Web interface for the LiveCycle ES Administration Console as shown in Figure 34.12. The Administration Console offers endpoint, archive, and user management. Other administration tools allow you to configure server settings including port numbers, and apply service packs and patches to LiveCycle ES. You also can track stalled processes with the administration tools.

FIGURE 34.12

The LiveCycle ES Administration Console home page

Items in the LiveCycle ES Administration Console are logically grouped into one of two categories: Services or Settings. The Services page gives you access to any of the solution components installed, as shown in Figure 34.13. The Settings page provides access to items that affect the entire LiveCycle ES Server installation, rather than a specific component. You can change items such as users, ports, and credentials in the Settings page as shown in Figure 34.14.

FIGURE 34.13

The LiveCycle ES Administration Console Services page

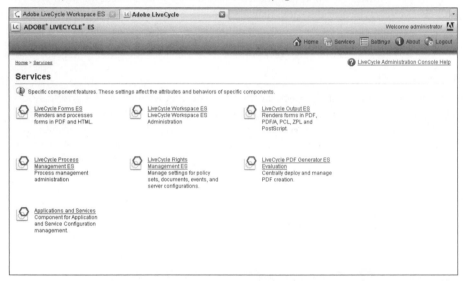

The About link in the upper-right corner of the Administration Console provides specific information as to the version of LiveCycle you are running as shown in Figure 34.15. This page includes any patches, service packs, and specific components that are installed.

Central repository

The Central repository is where forms, process diagrams, images, fragments, policies, and other assets are stored for retrieval when needed. The Central repository also handles version control as items are updated. Any dependencies between a process and assets are tracked by LCES for assembly into the application or an archive.

FIGURE 34.14

The LiveCycle ES Administration Console Settings page

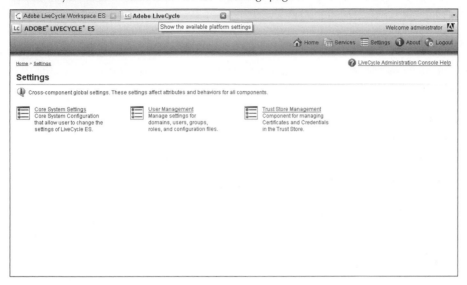

FIGURE 34.15

The LiveCycle ES Administration About page

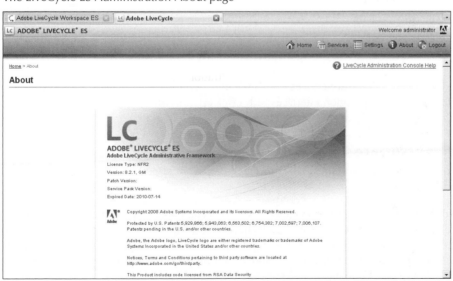

LiveCycle ES solution components

The solution components are not programs; they are set of related operations that are deployed as services. A program is a standalone piece of software that can run independently of other software programs. The solution components share the Foundation, allowing you to activate only the components necessary to achieve the goals of your application.

Unlike in some previous releases, components can be easily added later by running the configuration manager. The components are categorized into the following groups.

Data capture

This group of components offers options to capture enterprise data with interactive form fields. They may be utilized together or independently in the business process:

■ **Adobe LiveCycle Forms ES:** LiveCycle Forms ES can render XDP forms as PDF in Reader, as a Flash-based Form Guide, or an HTML Web page. It assembles PDF forms into packages. Form fragments are retrieved and placed into forms at runtime. This component creates Flash-based forms at runtime from form guides defined in XDP templates. It can handle file attachments for PDF and HTML forms. This component includes LiveCycle Data Services to retrieve data and allow merging with form templates at runtime.

■ **Adobe LiveCycle Reader® Extensions ES:** Adobe Reader has some additional functionality that allows filling in form fields, digital signatures, and comments, and the ability to save. These features are disabled for normal PDF documents. When Reader extensions are applied to a document, Reader turns the appropriate functionality on for use with the enabled document.

■ **Adobe LiveCycle Barcoded Forms ES:** With this component you can capture form data using 2D barcodes that can be decoded and extracted to XML format for automated processing. Barcodes can help bridge the gap between paper and electronic forms if you're still using fax or mail.

■ **Adobe LiveCycle Data Services ES:** This component promotes data exchange between Flex and AJAX application interfaces with LiveCycle ES and backend systems. Data Services allows RIAs to generate PDF files.

Information assurance

Security is often overlooked with digital documents. Protect your electronic files using the information assurance components:

■ **Adobe LiveCycle Rights Management ES:** This component was formerly known as Policy Server. It applies persistent protection to a document regardless of file distribution method or storage location. Permission settings and policy changes are dynamic. You can use this component to watermark confidential information with usernames to ensure compliance with company policies or enable document auditing to track viewing and printing. You can revoke an outdated file and replace it with a link to the new document, and apply rights management to documents in PDF, Microsoft Office, or CAD formats.

- **Adobe LiveCycle Digital Signatures ES:** With this component you can certify forms for authenticity and security. You can add blank signature fields to documents, apply digital signatures, and verify and clear signature fields in automated processes.

Document output

For documents that do not require interactive form fields this group of solution components can be used to create your files:

- **Adobe LiveCycle PDF Generator ES:** This component automates the creation and assembly of PDF documents from most native formats. The server-side PDF creation tool supports PDF/X and PDF/A formats. You can assemble files into PDF packages, renumber pages, add headers and footers, watermarks, and metadata. You also can convert PDF files to PostScript, TIFF, or JPEG formats and create searchable PDF files from image formats using OCR.

- **Adobe LiveCycle PDF Generator 3D ES:** You can create and assemble PDF documents from engineering product data rendered in 3D format.

- **Adobe LiveCycle Output ES:** With this component you can populate forms with XML data to dynamically generate personalized documents on demand in print or electronic formats. You can convert PDF to postscript, multipage TIFF files, and JPEG formats. Output ES allows control of printer-specific settings such as paper tray selection, duplex, stapling, sorting, and collating.

- **Adobe LiveCycle Production Print ES:** This component populates forms with XML to dynamically generate personalized documents for high-volume production environments. Some examples include statements, bill production, and enrollment forms. Production Print can process thousands of pages per minute. Post processing includes batch sorting, batch splitting, printing multiple pages on a single piece of paper (imposition), and marking for insertion machines.

Process management

The workflow tools in the process management group help you automate human centric business processes. Monitor active processes and gather real time event information using these tools:

- **Adobe LiveCycle Process Management ES:** This component was previously known as LiveCycle Workflow. Process Management allows you to design workflows that mirror existing business processes. In addition to setting the business logic needed at each decision point you can assign tasks to users, specify the type of form to be rendered, provide task instructions, set up rules for reminders, escalate an unfinished task to supervisors to handle, and set deadlines.

- **Adobe LiveCycle Business Activity Monitoring ES:** You can monitor, analyze, and tune your LCES applications. Turn on this component to receive real-time event and data integration information for a deployed process.

Content services

Content management systems to help organize your forms, data files, and other assets used a business process. Version control and file locking prevent editing by multiple users with these tools:

- **Adobe LiveCycle Content Services ES:** Store, manage, and collaborate on the content used in your LCES applications. Content Services offers check-in and check-out services for documents, versioning, auditing, metadata extraction, and searches. Three interfaces are offered to work with Content Services: LiveCycle Contentspace ES (Web interface), Microsoft Office plug-in, and shared folders.

- **Adobe LiveCycle ES Connectors for ECM:** Extend your LCES applications to integrate with existing enterprise content management systems. Currently components are available for IBM File Net, EMC Documentum, and IBM Content Manager. Processes defined in LiveCycle can utilize content stored in the external ECM system.

LiveCycle ES development tools

The development tools available for LiveCycle ES include: Adobe LiveCycle ES Workbench, Adobe Flex Builder, Adobe LiveCycle Designer ES, and the LiveCycle ES Software Development Kit (SDK). We focus on Adobe LiveCycle ES Workbench and Adobe LiveCycle Designer ES because they are included with most of the solution components. Flex Builder is available as a separate purchased tool.

LiveCycle Workbench ES

LiveCycle Workbench ES, as shown in Figure 34.16, is an integrated Development Environment (IDE) based on Eclipse.

FIGURE 34.16

LiveCycle ES Workbench showing a process

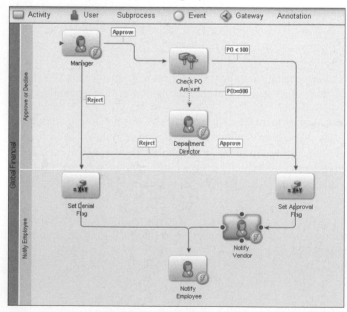

Originally supported by a group of software vendors, the Eclipse Project was created by IBM in November 2001. In January 2004 the Eclipse Foundation was created as an independent not-for-profit corporation to allow a vendor-neutral, open community to develop around Eclipse. The open source community focuses on creating an open development platform.

Workbench is the process diagram development tool. With Workbench you can use modeling components to visually create a business process diagram, set routes, and set conditions to control the business logic. Workbench is divided into three main tools:

- **Editors:** Use the Editors to create or edit objects such as form designs or workflow diagrams as shown in Figure 34.16. Below Figure 34.17 shows a form design open in the Workbench using LiveCycle Designer as the editor.

FIGURE 34.17

LiveCycle Designer opened inside the workbench to edit a form

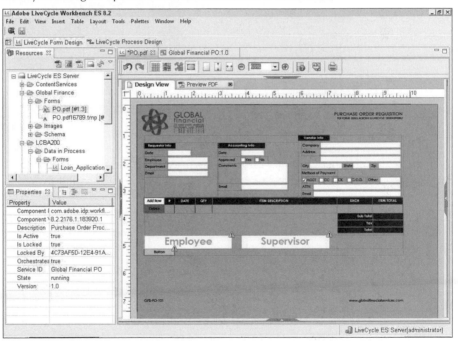

- **Views:** Views are tabs within a window containing supporting elements for work done in the editor. Figure 34.18 shows the workbench with Processes and Services open on the left side of the Workbench area.

FIGURE 34.18

Workbench showing the Processes and Services views on the left of the editor

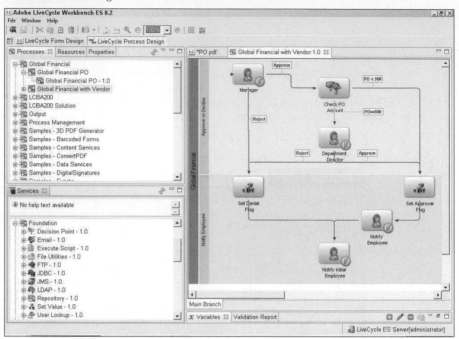

Views can be moved to any of the four sides of the workbench. If a side already contains another view, they can share the space and dock the tabs in the same window space as shown in Figure 34.19. Or they can split the available window area and stack on top of each other as shown in Figure 34.20.

When a view does not have enough space allocated to work effectively you can double-click the tab name to maximize any view. Double-clicking the tab again returns it to its previous location. Some of the views available in Workbench include:

- **Processes:** As you create your business processes you name them and organize them into categories. These categories appear in a hierarchical view with each process nested under the category it belongs to.

- **Variables:** The variables view is displays all defined variables in the currently selected process.

■ **Components:** A hierarchy view of all of the services available within each of the solution components you have installed in your development environment.

■ **Resources:** The directories, images, forms, and archives you have stored in the repository.

FIGURE 34.19

Views with the Resources and Components docked in the same window sharing the available area

NOTE It is important to point out some variances in terminology between the development tools on the server and the desktop tools of Acrobat and Designer. In Designer we call the area where items like the Library and Hierarchy are located palettes and those palettes reside in palette wells. In Acrobat we call these areas Navigation Panels. In LiveCycle Workbench these areas are called views. They contain objects and properties we need when working in the environment.

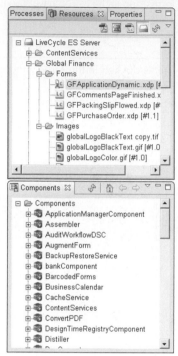

FIGURE 34.20

Views with the Resources and Components stacked in the available space

- **Perspectives:** Perspectives are a named, organized collection of editors and views designed to optimize your work area for a particular task. Adobe LiveCycle Workbench ES contains two built-in perspectives:

  - **LiveCycle Form Design Perspective:** Optimizes the views for form design using LiveCycle Designer as the form design editor inside the workbench, surrounded by the Resources and Properties views. When you work with LiveCycle Designer inside Workbench, the additional views around designer limit the work area as shown in Figure 34.21.

FIGURE 34.21

The LiveCycle Form Design Perspective

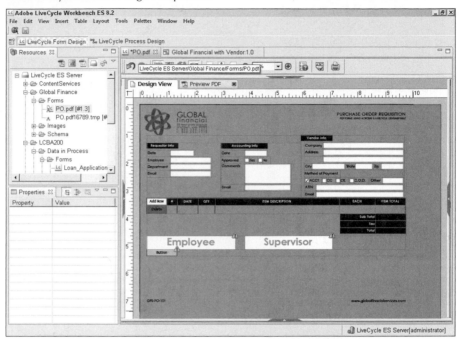

■ **LiveCycle Process Design Perspective**. This view optimizes the interface for designing workflow or process diagrams. The editor window allows you to add modeling elements to the canvas. You define routes for your process diagram by connecting the modeling elements. You can change the views on the left to more process design-related items as shown in Figure 34.22.

LiveCycle Designer ES

LiveCycle Designer is the form design tool that creates Extensible Markup Language (XML)-based forms that can be stored as an XML Data Package (XDP) or a Portable Document Format (PDF) file. Designer is a graphical design interface that allows drag and drop field creation. Form designs can include tables and subforms that dynamically adjust their contents based on user interaction or data merged with the form.

FIGURE 34.22

The LiveCycle Process Design Perspective

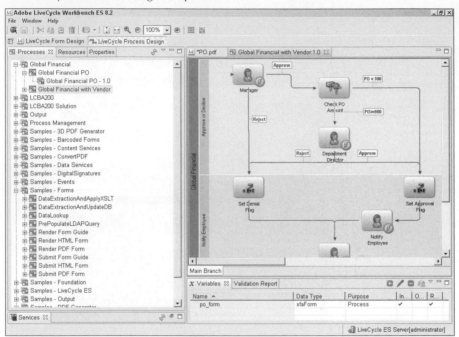

CROSS-REF   **For more information on using LiveCycle Designer, see Parts VI through IX.**

Adobe Flex Builder

Another Eclipse based development tool, Adobe Flex Builder contains editors for working with MXML, ActionScript, and Cascading Style Sheets (CSS). Flex Builder is designed to optimize the resources needed to write Flex code more quickly and efficiently and offers features such as statement completion, debugging, and syntax coloring. Visually design the layout, appearance, and behavior of your Flex application. You also can work with the new datagrid to create interactive data analysis.

Taking a Tour of LiveCycle Workspace ES

Workspace is a Flex-based application, rendered in a browser window, that can be completely customized using Flex builder. Customization allows companies to provide branding for their LiveCycle Workspace that is consistent with other corporate content. View a LiveCycle ES Workspace requires that the client machines have Flash Player 9.01 or higher loaded.

What is the Workspace?

The LiveCycle Workspace ES is the central point for users involved in form-related processes in LiveCycle ES. It becomes the User Interface (UI) for LiveCycle ES deployed processes. A user can log in to start a new process, look at their to-do list, and track where in a process their form is currently located.

To see the interface you need to have a login provided by your LiveCycle Server administrator. The login page is the first page you see when opening the Workspace, as shown in figure 34.23.

FIGURE 34.23

The Workspace login page

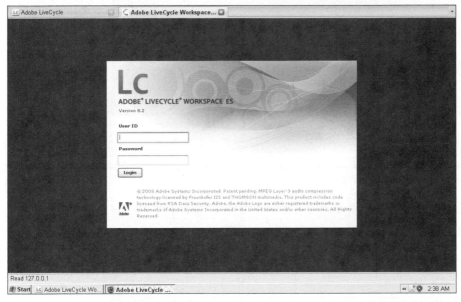

Overview of the interface

Once you have logged into the Workspace the welcome page gives you shortcuts to the three main areas, plus links to change preferences, read messages, get help, and log out as shown in Figure 34.24. The administrator can display a message of the day for users to read on the welcome page.

Start Process

Selecting the Start Process icon opens the Category view of the process cards. The Favorites Category appears at the top of the list, followed by the remaining categories in alphabetical order. The LiveCycle administrator defines the categories that become the organizational containers seen in the Workspace as shown in Figure 34.25.

FIGURE 34.24

The Workspace welcome page

FIGURE 34.25

The Start Process favorites and other categories

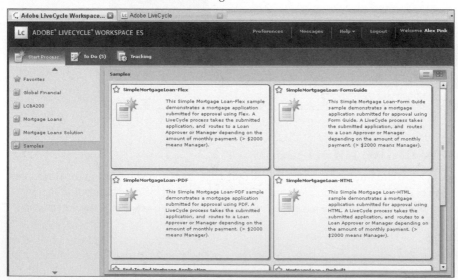

Within a category you'll find each of the related processes assigned to that category. If the company has an extensive list of categories and processes the employee is encouraged to add the ones they use most frequently to their favorites category for easier retrieval. A process card is added to the Favorites category by clicking the star icon in the upper-left corner of the process card.

Process cards take lots of screen space as shown in Figure 32.26 and can be changed to a List view at your option, as shown in Figure 32.27. Change the view using the view buttons in the upper-right corner of the workspace. The List button shows four horizontal bars. The Card button shows a grid of four rectangles. The view changes affect both the Start Process and To Do areas of the Workspace.

FIGURE 34.26

Card View takes lots of space.

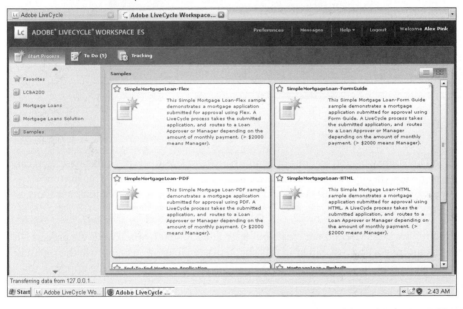

Starting a new instance of a process only requires a single click on the process card or a double-click anywhere in the row of the List view.

FIGURE 34.27

List view of processes

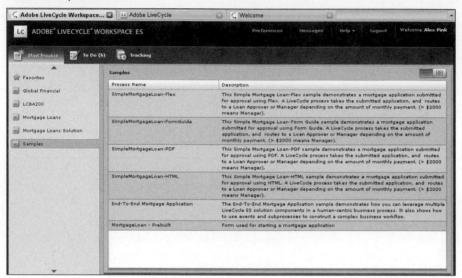

To Do

Items in the To Do list may be notifications of pending processes you began. In that case, you can open the task to review the information. The item contains a Complete button. This button removes the task from your To Do list. You can go back and review this information later if necessary using the tracking feature.

Other To Do items are tasks you did not create but are routed to you by the LiveCycle process. In our example "Examining a Process" earlier in this chapter the manager must approve the purchase order before it can be sent on to accounting. The employee's manager becomes the approver for the purchase order.

If the manager is on vacation, the purchase order may have to be necessary routed to another manager. The alternate person may be a specific individual or the entire group of managers. In the case of a group assignment, the first manager who has the opportunity to take care of the task can claim it and continue the process. If you are a member of a group that is responsible for reviewing items, you may see the pool of tasks that have been assigned to the group in addition to your own tasks.

The tasks in the To Do show everything assigned to the logged-in user. This list can be filtered down into the categories they belong to. The drop-down list is next to username of the person logged in, as shown in Figure 34.28, or the group name the tasks were assigned to. Filtering allows you to prioritize the tasks without sorting through them manually.

FIGURE 34.28

The To Do list category filter

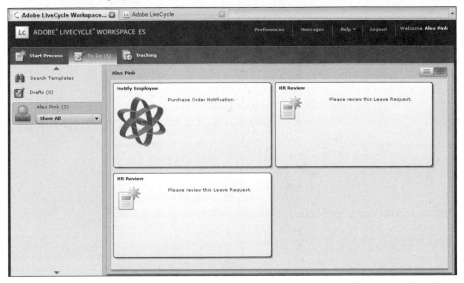

Tracking

Tracking allows the user to search for a process they have participated in. The process can be currently running or a completed process. The window is grouped by the process name and filtered by a start date and end date. Tracking provides many pieces of information from the tracking window, as shown in Figure 32.29.

If you need additional information, double-click the task to open the process details, as shown in Figure 34.30, and audit information as shown in Figure 34.31. In the audit information you can see the tasks associated with the process, who was assigned each task, and if you are the initiator of the process, the completed form as well.

Preferences

The Workspace preferences, as shown in Figure 34.32, allow you to set your Out of Office Status, assign tasks to another user while out of the office, share your task queue as well as request access to another queue. You also can change the columns that appear for the To Do List view and Tracking view.

FIGURE 34.29

The Tracking Page filtered by process name and date range

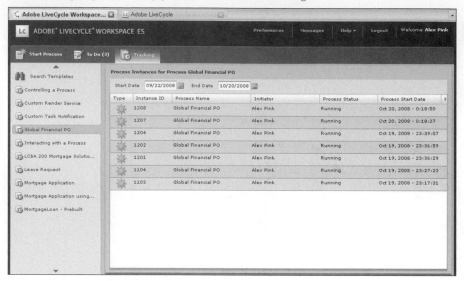

FIGURE 34.30

The process details of a tracking request

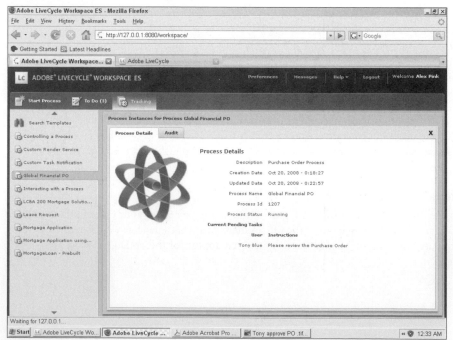

FIGURE 34.31

The audit details of the tracking request

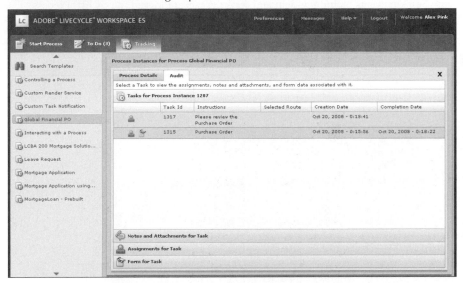

FIGURE 34.32

The Preferences page

Messages

The Messages link, as shown in Figure 34.33, provides notices of events that occur during your current session. Session events including login and server errors are logged in this list. Process events notifying you of new tasks arriving are also logged here.

The Messages page

Optimizing Designer Forms–Server Deployment

Most of this book talks about designing forms in one way or another. Now we shift the focus from the form design to optimizing the forms for use with LiveCycle Server. How you optimize a file varies between Acrobat and Designer. The following list pertains to Designer forms, although many of these points apply to Acrobat Forms as well. Although many things influence a form's performance, file size is one of the most important factors to watch. The following are general considerations to keep in mind when designing forms to reduce the overall file size:

- **Use compressed graphic types.** JPEG or GIF formats provide good image quality while maintaining a reasonable file size.

- **Use embedded images rather than linked images.** Having the image readily available reduces the time required to render the form. With linked images, you need time to gather the image information and render the image. The PDF format is very good at reducing the size of graphics even further.

- **Minimize the number of objects on your form.** Designer forms can have a reduced file size when fewer objects are used on the design page. Use the built-in caption properties of the objects rather than creating a field with second static text object as its caption. If the form was built his way, take the time to merge the field with the static text object.

  To merge a static text object with a field as a caption, select both objects. Right-click and select Merge as Caption from the context menu as shown in Figure 34.34.

FIGURE 34.34

Merging a static text object with a field as a caption to reduce the number of objects

- **Reduce or avoid using embedded fonts.** Do not embed fonts unless the font appearance is more important than the increase in file size.

  One solution is to use a font available to all versions of Reader and Acrobat so embedding fonts, or font substitutions, are not necessary. The following fonts are included with Acrobat and Reader and display without substitutions:

  - Courier Std, Courier Std Bold, Courier Std Bold Oblique, Courier Std Oblique
  - Minion Pro Bold, Minion Pro Bold It, Minion Pro It, Minion Pro Regular

- Myriad Pro Bold, Myriad Pro Bold It, Myriad Pro It, Myriad Pro Regular
- Symbol (Type 1)

To ensure that a form design looks the same when viewed on screen or printed using PCL print drivers, and PostScript print drivers, you should use one of these fonts:

- Courier
- Arial
- Times New Roman

- **Examine the need for accessibility.** While accessibility is necessary in many areas, accessible forms take longer to process.

- **Consider different templates for the interactive form version and the printed form version.** Removing all the interactivity from a document intended for print can improve performance considerably.

The remaining recommendations relate to form processing when using LiveCycle ES Solution components and don't have as much impact in a standalone form:

- **When submitting form data, select XML as the file format to reduce the transfer time of the data file.**

- **When rendering the form using LiveCycle Server, allow the form to be cached or use a SeedPDF.** When a form is cached, the data is merged into a pre-generated version of the form and is always available to dynamic form designs. Some limitations exist when using static form designs. A SeedPDF is a customized PDF document (it contains only fonts) that is appended with a form design and data at runtime.

- **When running batches of the same form using LiveCycle Server, gather all of the data into a single file before merging to individual documents.**

- **When running multiple batches using LiveCycle Server, group all of the instances of the same forms together, and then run the next group.** Alternating between two or more forms slows the performance.

- **When fields or subforms are not needed for data binding, set the binding property to none.** Failure to do so causes the program to search for a matching data node in the correlating XML file each time.

Scripting considerations

When you write script to handle calculations, validations, and other processing, by default all script runs on the client machine. The form recipient's viewer application (Acrobat, Reader, or the browser) is responsible for the script contained in the form. Knowing how that form is going to be rendered influences your scripting language choice because FormCalc is not supported in HTML. Using scripts increases the processing time required to render forms. Patterns (masks) offer better performance than scripts, with the same results, and you should explore them first.

FormCalc is the default scripting language in LiveCycle Designer. You can use it for any XDP or PDF form as long as it is not rendered as HTML. FormCalc script can be executed on the client or the server. FormCalc is similar to common spreadsheet formulas, which makes this an easy transition for many users. One of the benefits to using FormCalc is that the calculation engine is small and therefore quick to process the request.

JavaScript is the alternative scripting language in LiveCycle Designer and you can use it for any Designer form deployment. It also can be executed on the client or the server. JavaScript provides more robust scripting options, but can cause performance issues on long, complex scripts.

Choosing whether the script should execute on the client or server machine depends on the functionality desired and the complexity of the code. Changing where they execute influences their performance. For example, a calculation script designed to run on the client machine is executed in real time while the form recipient enters data. Furthermore, scripts that declare variables when run on the client retain values for the duration set by the scope of the variable declaration.

With script executed on the server, the calculation occurs on the server, the data is remerged with the form, and is presented back to the viewer application. This can add significant transfer time to a form, but it is necessary when the client application is incapable of running the script. Variables are available only while the script is executing. As soon as the form is presented to the viewer application, they no longer exist.

Setting a form to both client and server can cause both the client and the server to attempt to execute the script. If a form is using LiveCycle Forms and the client is incapable of executing the script, LiveCycle Forms attempts to process the script anyway.

Scripting a form rendered in HTML requires a few additional notes of consideration:

- **JavaScript must be used as the scripting language.**
- **Client-side script for HTML forms must use the JavaScript resolveNode expression to locate objects in the hierarchy.** Fully qualified notation that walks through the hierarchy fails in HTML rendered forms.
- **The browser application must be a supported version: Microsoft Internet Explorer 5.x, Netscape 6.0 or later, or Opera 5 or later.**
- **The browser must have client side JavaScript enabled for any scripts to execute.**

File type considerations

PDF or XDP formats are allowed most of the time with the LiveCycle ES Solution components. When choosing your file format, remember that file size is crucial to form performance. To improve performance, use PDF files whenever possible because they are usually smaller than their XDP counterparts.

Use PDF files in these situations:

- **When using static form design.** If the form design will not change in layout, then PDF is the better choice.

- **If the form will be viewed only in Acrobat or Reader.** If there is no need to alter the format, use the smallest format possible—PDF.

- **If digital signatures are required in the rendered form.** Saving digital signatures requires the entire PDF to be saved.

Use XDP in these situations:

- **When you expect server-side processing.**

- **When rendering the form as an HTML page or as a Flash based Form Guide.** LiveCycle ES solution components are very powerful when given an XDP file with the proper instructions. The same file form design can be rendered as HTML or Flash.

Additional server-required objects

When you place forms into the LiveCycle ES Process Management workflow, the server expects certain fields on the form. These fields are stored as a custom object for you to use at design time in LiveCycle Designer. In the Custom Library group is a custom object called Process Fields. The process fields contain nine objects, as shown in Figure 34.35, that provide the necessary connection to the Process Management workflow.

FIGURE 34.35

The Process Fields custom group object in LiveCycle Designer

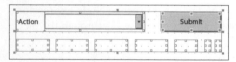

You don't need to customize these objects in the form design or provide them static values at design time. The fields are merged with the necessary information at runtime to allow the form to participate with the workflow.

If a form design does not contain these additional fields, you may be able to add them using a form bridge as part of the process design in LiveCycle Process Management.

Summary

- LiveCycle ES runs as a J2EE service on a J2EE application.
- The LiveCycle ES Foundation provides loosely coupled services that allow the components to work with one another and integrate with existing systems.
- The Central Repository manages form versions, graphics, and other assets needed in a process.
- Many solution components are available for LiveCycle ES. Components are not products; they are services deployed on a J2EE application.
- LiveCycle ES is known for its ability to extract data from the presentation layer of a process and remerge them at any point later.
- Components are available for: data capture, information assurance, document output, process management, and content services.
- The LiveCycle Workbench is where process design takes place.
- LiveCycle Designer is used to create XML base forms that are utilized by LiveCycle ES.
- Workspace is the GUI for deployed processes.
- Adobe Flex Builder can be used to customize the Workspace to allow corporate branding.
- Forms should be optimized for performance before deploying them in a process.
- File size is one of the most important considerations in optimizing a form.
- Number of objects included in the form design and the complexity of the form design impact the performance at runtime.
- Script may need to be altered when forms are rendered in different formats.
- Special field objects are required for processing forms in LiveCycle ES.
- LiveCycle ES is a powerful set of solution components for electronic business processes inside and outside the enterprise firewall.

Chapter 35

Getting More Help with LiveCycle Designer

IN THIS CHAPTER

Finding help sources

Exploring help on the Web

Using manuals and references

Keeping up to date with RSS feeds

Let's face it. LiveCycle Designer is not a very intuitive program, and it's quite complicated. Anyone telling you differently thinks in code and complex tasks. For the rest of us, the learning curve is steep, and becoming proficient requires much patience and dedicated study.

With this book, we've tried to expose you to many of Designer's methods and how to use the program from the ground up. However, we cannot hope to satisfy everyone's needs and special circumstances. To become a LiveCycle Designer advanced user, you need to go beyond this book and research other sources to help you learn more about the program and more easily create forms in Designer.

In this chapter, we point you to some places to start your research and advanced learning for more knowledge as it relates to LiveCycle Designer.

Using Some Help Guidelines

If you have a background in programming and database logic, you may find much of working with LiveCycle Designer to be intuitive and easy to learn. If you don't have skills in programming and understanding database management, you are likely to have much difficulty getting up to speed in the program. Some people say that Designer is easy and intuitive. We define easy as something a child or an elderly grandparent can learn in 30 minutes. This program doesn't fall into that category. If someone tells you it's easy to learn, don't believe it! Adobe LiveCycle Designer is complex and tough to learn—especially if you're trying to learn the program from the online guide. You won't become a Designer expert by reading a single book on the subject. Many users need some sort of formal training.

If you intend to spend a good part of your workday designing interactive dynamic forms, you may want to look at a framework for learning the program in detail. Here are some of our recommendations for getting the most out of Adobe LiveCycle Designer:

- **Practice with the program.** Nothing beats diving into a software program and starting to use it. But before you attempt to create some sophisticated forms, try to design static forms. Don't jump into adding subforms and trying to create dynamic forms, and don't worry about database connections. The more you can become familiar with the different field types and setting field properties, the better off you'll be when it comes time to design more complex forms.

  Be sure you understand the Library palette, the Object palette and its Value tab, and the Border palette thoroughly. Practice so they become very intuitive and you know exactly where you want to go to change properties for objects and fields. Like any other kind of learning, starting with the basics helps you trim some time off the learning curve. Be sure you understand Chapters 22 through 24. The foundation for creating forms is comprehensive in these chapters.

- **Attend a class.** Some type of formal training is always best when working with a program as complex as LiveCycle Designer. Search out your local community colleges, universities, and private training centers that offer classes on Designer. But be certain to carefully review the class content before you enroll in a class. If you see classes advertised as "Creating PDF Forms" or "Learning Adobe LiveCycle Designer," make sure that the class instructor and the contents of the class cover creating dynamic forms. An overview of working with fields and creating static PDF forms isn't going to do much more for you than what you can learn by reading through the chapters in this book.

  Some private training centers may boast about having credentialed instructors who are Adobe Certified Experts in Photoshop, Illustrator, InDesign, Dreamweaver, Acrobat, Flash, and a few other programs. My guess is you won't find anyone claiming to have all these certificates who knows Designer in depth, at least to the level you need. Look for people who live in the program and do some sort of professional forms design work or are celebrated speakers frequently talking at conferences and expos.

  Adobe has a full-blown certification program in Designer, and learning from a certified LiveCycle Designer trainer is your best avenue. You can find certified LiveCycle Designer trainers by logging on to `http://partners.adobe.com` and selecting Training Providers from the "Find products and services" list on the home page.

- **Get a video.** Check regularly online to see if a video or DVD is released as an instructional tutorial. Videos and DVDs can cover much more territory in less time than reading the online guide.

■ **Attend a conference.** One of the best ways to learn features, tips, and workarounds about a program is to attend a conference. You get some special benefits from attending a conference. You can attend sessions and sometimes find pre- or post-conference workshops that offer full-day courses on Designer. The added benefit is you can gather some e-mail addresses for Adobe employees, speakers, and other conference participants. There's probably not a more valuable asset than having someone to call when you really get stuck on a problem.

■ **Be patient.** Learning Designer for the average person is like learning a foreign language. You have to start with basics, add continual reinforcement, and keep practicing. Don't try to create complex forms too quickly. Take your time, and learn a little each day. Try to devote some time to concepts, and practice many times over so the steps in a process become intuitive and second nature. When you get frustrated, move away from the program and come back the next day. Sometimes a good night's rest can help you solve a problem in a matter of a few minutes that was an all-day burden the day before.

Using Internet Resources

A wealth of information on LiveCycle Designer can be found online. Many Web pages are found on Adobe's Web site—some in a few obscure locations. You need to search in your Web browser and poke around a little to find some valuable resources. What you can find are helpful guides, user forums, instructional materials, training programs, templates, forms samples, and other information.

The Web is continually changing, so it's a good idea to make some periodic visits to your search engine and explore the search results from time to time. Some of the staples for Web information on Designer stays relatively fixed in the same location on Adobe's Web site—or at least you are automatically forwarded to a new area where the material you want to return to can be found. Inasmuch as the Web sites remain in static locations, the URLs are often long and difficult to remember.

You may want to create links in Acrobat to some of the more valuable Web sites to browse periodically. You can easily bookmark Web site URLs, but that means you need to be working in your Web browser. When you have instant access from within Acrobat, it's easy to click a menu item or button to search for an answer when you're stumped about some aspect of working in Designer (or Acrobat).

In Chapter 19, we talked about adding menu commands in Acrobat and we used JavaScript to add menu items in the top-level menu bar. You also have an option for creating toolbar buttons using JavaScript. Unfortunately, the *addToolButton* object is not available with LiveCycle Designer, so you need to add the new tool buttons in Acrobat. Because you're likely to have Acrobat open during most Designer editing sessions, you'll find it convenient to add tools that launch some important URLs.

ON the CD-ROM We added several JavaScripts that you can add to your Acrobat JavaScript folder in the Chapter35 folder inside the *jsFolder* on the book's CD-ROM. Copy the files to your Acrobat JavaScript folder, and the tool buttons are added to an Add-on toolbar. For locating the JavaScript folder where you need to copy the files, see Chapter 19.

We have several files you can add to the JavaScript folder on the book's CD-ROM with different URLs. We could have added all the JavaScript in a single routine, but we wanted to keep it simple in case you want to modify some scripts to delete some from the JavaScripts folder after you've had a look at them. Each file contains code similar to the following and shown in Figure 35.1:

```
1. app.addToolButton({
2.    cName: "Designer Home",
3.    cExec: "app.launchURL('http://adobe.com/products/livecycle/
      designer/');",
4.    cLabel: "Designer Home",
5.    cToolText: "Adobe Designer Home Page",
6.    cEnable: "event.rc = true",
7.    nPos: 0}
8. );
```

FIGURE 35.1

The code written in a text editor

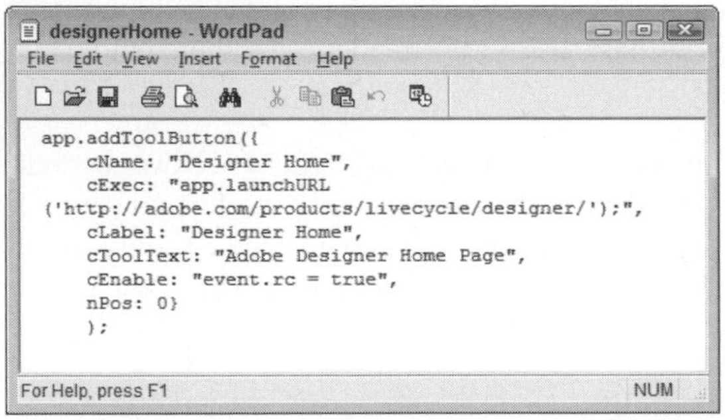

```
designerHome - WordPad
File  Edit  View  Insert  Format  Help

app.addToolButton({
    cName: "Designer Home",
    cExec: "app.launchURL
('http://adobe.com/products/livecycle/designer/');",
    cLabel: "Designer Home",
    cToolText: "Adobe Designer Home Page",
    cEnable: "event.rc = true",
    nPos: 0}
    );

For Help, press F1                                      NUM
```

NOTE **The code is written in a simple text editor as explained in Chapter 19. Be sure to use a text editor and not a word processor when writing the code and save the file as text only with a *.js* extension.**

In line 1, we use the *addToolButton* object to add a tool to the Add-ins toolbar shown in Figure 35.2. Line 2 is the name of the tool. You need to be certain that each tool you add to the Add-ins toolbar has a unique name. In line 3, we execute the action. In this case, we launch a URL. When you click the tool, your default Web browser opens and takes you to the URL specified in this line of code. If you want to modify the URL launch, just edit the text in the line between the single quote marks.

FIGURE 35.2

A custom toolbar in Acrobat with tools created with JavaScript that launch URLs

In line 4, we add a label for the tool. You can add icons to the tool button faces with a few more lines of code, but we wanted to keep this simple so you can easily modify the target location to suit your personal needs. In line 5, we added the tooltip, and line 6 makes the tool active. In line 7, we identify the position of the tool in the toolbar. The 0 (zero) position is the first location of the tool in the toolbar.

TIP **The code in the sample files is intentionally kept very simple to help you easily make edits in the scripts to customize the toolbar buttons for your own personal use. You can get fancier by adding icon images to the toolbar using JavaScript. For code samples for how to add icons to toolbars, see the JavaScript Specification guide that you can download from Adobe's Web site.**

The links you find using the JavaScripts in the CD-ROM folder include:

- http://adobe.com/products/livecycle/designer (Adobe LiveCycle Designer ES Home page): Here you find information provided by Adobe on Designer, getting support, and many links to solutions providers.

- http://www.adobe.com/devnet/livecycle/designing_forms.html (Adobe Developer Connection): This site provides a wealth of information on LiveCycle Designer. You find tips and tutorials for using the program, links to references such as FormCalc, LiveCycle Designer ES Scripting Reference, and many different developer links.

- `http://www.adobe.com/devnet/acrobat/` (the Developer Connection for Acrobat): You find similar information here related to Acrobat as you find in the LiveCycle ES Developer Connection.

- `http://kb.adobe.com/selfservice/viewContent.do?externalId=333249` (Scripting Languages and Resources): Here you find information related to scripting languages supported by Designer, links to sample forms, help with converting JavaScript from Acrobat Forms to Designer forms, scripting reference guides, and more.

- `http://www.adobeforums.com/webx/.3bb7d189/` (LiveCycle Designer User-to-User Forums): This site is a user forum where you can post questions and review responses from questions posted by professionals in the Designer user community.

- `http://www.adobe.com/devnet/acrobat/javascript` (Acrobat Development Center–JavaScript for Acrobat): This site is dedicated to providing information on Acrobat JavaScript. You'll find links to reference guides, debuggers, information on converting Acrobat JavaScript to Designer JavaScript, and more.

- `http://www.pdfscripting.com` (Tutorials, Tools, Scripts, and Samples for scripting Acrobat and PDF): This site is primarily related to Acrobat JavaScript, but you'll also find some Designer scripting available. Thom Parker of Windjack Solutions, an Acrobat solutions developer, has created a Web site with six hours of video training, copy/paste JavaScript routines, tutorials, a library of scripted PDF examples, and automation tools such as the buttons we talk about adding to Acrobat in this chapter. You'll find a huge amount of information related to JavaScript and detailed explanations for the novice as well as advanced users.

Using the Reference Manuals

Let's face it, reference manuals are a necessary evil for most of us. With the exception of a few, no one really likes sitting down and reading a reference manual from cover to cover. But even the most advanced users live by reference manuals and couldn't do without them.

The operative here is *reference*. These manuals are your right-hand assistants and not intended for you to digest them in entirety. It's like the book you're reading. We add lots of cross-references in this book because we expect people to jump around, locate some information on getting a solution to a problem, and then put the book aside and be on your way to work on your forms. Reference manuals are exactly that. They are there for you to focus on solutions and get the kind of information you need quickly to resolve problems. A number of resources are available to you, and you'll want to keep them handy to make frequent visits.

LiveCycle Designer Help Guide

One of the best references you can find on Designer is always available when you're in the program. Choose Help ⇨ Adobe LiveCycle Designer Help, or press F1 on your keyboard. The Adobe LiveCycle Designer Help file opens, as shown in Figure 35.3. In the Help Guide, you have several options for viewing and searching help information.

The Contents section of the Help Guide opens by default. Here you see a topical listing of all the help information contained in the guide. Click the plus (+) icons to expand a section and browse content by topical listings. The Index tab displays an index of the guide. Click the Index tab, and the panel changes as shown in Figure 35.4. At the top of the Index panel, you see a text box where you can type search criteria to search the Index panel.

FIGURE 35.3

Choose Help ⇨ Adobe LiveCycle Designer Help, or press F1 to open the Help Guide.

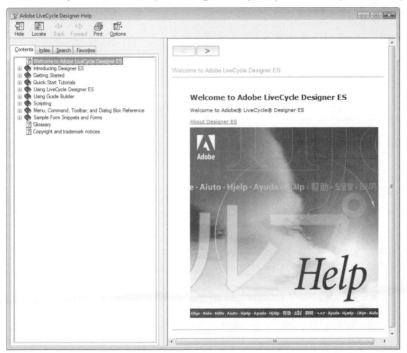

Click Index, and the Index panel opens.

The Search tab offers you options for searching the Guide and using Boolean expressions in your search criteria. Type text in the text box and open the fly-away menu, as shown in Figure 35.5. Choose from Boolean AND, OR, NEAR (proximity), and NOT, and then type additional text in the text box. Press Enter, and the search results are reported in the Search Panel.

The Favorites panel is an area where you can mark pages to return to. Double-click an item in the left panel to place the respective page in view in the right panel, and click Add at the bottom of the Favorites panel to add a new favorite.

Click the right-pointing arrow to open the fly-away palette and choose a Boolean expression.

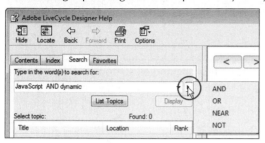

The Help Guide is always available when you're in Designer, but unfortunately the Help Guide doesn't come in the form a PDF document that you can browse while not working in the program. In addition, Designer offers no option to create comment notes in the Help Guide. If you want to carry a PDF around with you on a laptop where you don't have Designer installed, add comment notes for remarks and code listings, or print the entire help document at a copy shop to produce a printed version of the guide, you can create your own PDF version of the Help document.

To create a PDF version of the Help document you need to convert the Help document to several PDF files and then combine the files into a single PDF document. To learn how to perform the conversion and document assembly, follow these steps.

STEPS: Creating a PDF Version of the LiveCycle Designer Help Guide

1. **Open the Help Guide.** Open Designer, and press F1 on your keyboard.
2. **Click a topic in the Contents panel.** Click the root name on one of the items in the Contents panel, as shown in Figure 35.6.

Click a root name of an item in the Contents panel.

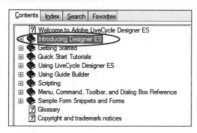

3. **Click the Print tool.** The Print Topics dialog box opens, as shown in Figure 35.7.

4. **Print the heading and subtopics.** In the Print Topics dialog box, choose Print the selected heading and all subtopics, as shown in Figure 35.7.

FIGURE 35.7

Click the radio button beside Print the selected heading and all subtopics.

5. **Identify the Printer.** Click OK in the Print Topics dialog box, and the Print dialog box opens. Choose Adobe PDF for the printer driver, and click Print. When you print a topic, you may have to wait some time for the file to print to PDF. There are more than 900 pages in the complete Help Guide, and some topics will take quite a while to print. Wait for the resultant file to open in Acrobat before proceeding.

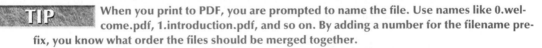

TIP When you print to PDF, you are prompted to name the file. Use names like 0.welcome.pdf, 1.introduction.pdf, and so on. By adding a number for the filename prefix, you know what order the files should be merged together.

6. **Click all the items individually, and repeat Steps 2 through 5.**

7. **Open Acrobat.**

8. **Choose File ➪ Combine ➪ Merge Files into a Single PDF.** In the Combine Files wizard, click the Add Files button and add all the files that you printed to PDF, as shown in Figure 35.8.

9. **Combine the files.** Click Combine Files, and Acrobat merges the PDF files together in a single PDF document. After merging the files, click Save when prompted and save the merged documents under a new filename. At this point, you can delete the original individual files.

10. **Add an index.** Choose Advanced ➪ Document Processing ➪ Manage Embedded Index. The Manage Embedded Index dialog box opens, as shown in Figure 35.9. Click the Embed Index button, and an index is embedded in the file. Acrobat automatically saves the file after embedding an index.

FIGURE 35.8

Add the PDF files in the Combine Files wizard.

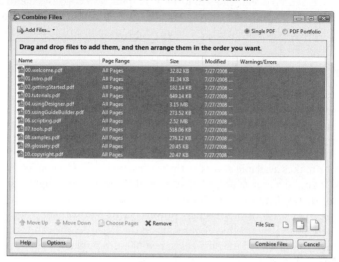

FIGURE 35.9

Choose Advanced ⇨ Document Processing ⇨ Manage Embedded Index, and click Embed Index in the Manage Embedded Index dialog box.

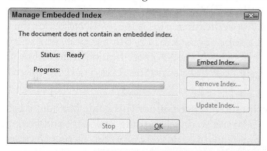

Copy the final file to a folder where you keep reference documents on your computer. Be sure to keep the documents outside your Acrobat application folder. When you upgrade Acrobat and LiveCycle Designer, all folders are lost inside the application folders.

The final file you create from the Help Guide is a PDF document. You can add comment notes to the document, keep it open on another monitor in Acrobat if you work on two monitors, search the file using Acrobat Search, create links to forms examples, and copy the file to a computer where you can read it using Adobe Reader. If you want to add comments in Adobe Reader, you can enable the PDF with Reader usage rights using Acrobat Pro or Pro Extended.

Using scripting guides

Scripting guides are essential documents when you want to write code using either FormCalc or JavaScript in Designer and when you want to write JavaScripts in Acrobat. Some of the top JavaScript programmers we know keep the guide open whenever they add new routines to forms and JavaScripts at the folder level.

Fortunately, Adobe makes available several scripting resources to help you learn to write code and debug problems. If you're a user of an earlier version of Designer, you might start looking in the Designer folder inside the Acrobat folder for the FormCalc manual. This manual was installed on your computer in earlier versions of Designer. However with Acrobat 9 and above, all reference documents are Web hosted. By hosting documents on the Web, Adobe can routinely update manuals after they are developed. And in some cases, manuals are published after a product release, so hosting these types of documents on the Web makes sense.

Some of the more important reference documents you'll want to download include:

- **Acrobat JavaScript Reference:** This manual is the primary reference for Acrobat JavaScript and writing JavaScript code. `http://www.adobe.com/devnet/acrobat/pdfs/js_api_reference.pdf`.

- **Adobe XML forms 2.7 specification:** This is the specification for the XFA architecture. `http://partners.adobe.com/public/developer/en/xml/xfa_spec_2_7.pdf`. There are several versions of the XFA specification architecture. You'll find several other manuals at `http://partners.adobe.com/public/developer/xml/index_arch.html`.

- **Calculations and Scripts Reference Guide:** This guide provides a basic understanding of objects, events, models, and so on when using JavaScript and FormCalc. `http://partners.adobe.com/public/developer/en/tips/CalcScripts.pdf`.

- **Converting Acrobat JavaScript for Use in LiveCycle Designer:** This guide helps you understand more about converting Acrobat JavaScript to JavaScripts that can be used in Designer. `http://partners.adobe.com/public/developer/en/acrobat/sdk/AcroJS_DesignerJS.pdf`.

- **FormCalc specification, version 2.0:** You'll need this FormCalc specification manual to write scripts using FormCalc in Designer. `http://partners.adobe.com/public/developer/en/xml/formcalc_2.0.pdf`.

- **LiveCycle Designer ES Scripting Errors:** Use this guide (which we mentioned in Chapter 29) to understand error messages related to JavaScript and FormCalc. `http://help.adobe.com/en_US/livecycle/8.2/lcdesigner_syntaxchecking.pdf`.

- **Scripting Object Model expression specification (SOM), v2.0:** This reference guide describes the syntax used in form objects, values, properties, and methods. `http://partners.adobe.com/public/developer/en/xml/som_2.0.pdf`.

- **Scripting Samples:** Nothing beats seeing examples of scripts used in actual forms. Visit the Adobe Web site for sample documents containing scripts. `http://www.adobe.com/devnet/livecycle/designer_scripting_samples.html`.

Other guides and documents are found on Adobe's Web pages. Start with looking at `http://partners.adobe.com/public/developer/xml/index_arch.html` for links to many other documents.

Monitoring RSS Feeds

You can find a number of RSS feeds on Adobe's Web site to keep up to date with recently published articles and information right in Acrobat. One of the best sources for scripting is found at Thom Parker's JavaScript Corner on Acrobat Users (`www.acrobatusers.com`). Thom frequently writes articles related to JavaScript and LiveCycle Designer scripting on his blog site (`www.acrobatusers.com/blogs/thomp`).

If you want to monitor new additions to Thom's contributions or another area on Adobe's Web site where blogs and RSS feeds are found, you can add RSS feeds in the Tracker. To add an RSS feed in the Tracker, follow these steps.

STEPS: Adding an RSS Feed to the Tracker

1. **Open the Preferences dialog box.** By default, Acrobat 9 and greater has RSS feeds turned off in the Tracker. You need to enable RSS feeds in the Tracker Preferences before you can add a new feed to the Tracker. Press Ctrl/⌘+K to open the Preferences dialog box, and click Tracker in the left pane.

2. **Enable RSS feeds.** Check the Enable RSS feeds in Tracker in the right pane, as shown in Figure 35.10.

FIGURE 35.10

Check Enable RSS feeds in Tracker in the Tracker Preferences.

3. **Locate an RSS feed in your Web browser.** In our example, we'll use Thom's JavaScript Corner blog site. When you visit `www.acrobatusers.com`, you'll find RSS Feeds listed under the News item in the red banner, as shown in Figure 35.11. Click RSS Feeds, and a Web page listing all the RSS feeds on Acrobat Users opens.

FIGURE 35.11

Locate an RSS feed in your Web browser.

4. **Copy a feed.** On the second page in our example shown in Figure 35.12, we located the feed we wanted, right-clicked (Control+click on the Macintosh), and chose Copy Shortcut (Copy Link on the Macintosh) to copy the RSS feed link.

FIGURE 35.12

Copy the RSS link.

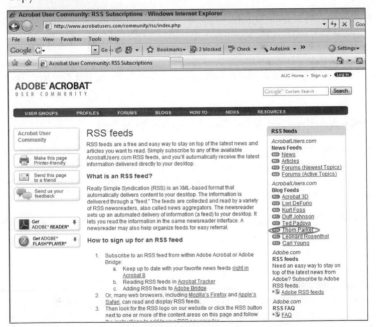

5. **Open the Tracker.** Choose Forms ⇨ Track Forms to open the Tracker.

6. **Click RSS in the left panel.** When the Tracker opens, you'll see RSS in the left panel, as shown in Figure 35.13, if you enabled the preference choice in the Tracker Preferences.

Click RSS in the left panel in the Tracker.

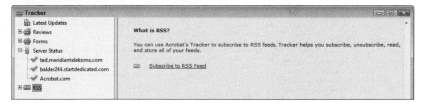

7. **Subscribe to a feed.** Click Subscribe to RSS Feed in the right panel. This action opens the Add Subscription dialog box shown in Figure 35.14.

8. **Paste the feed link in the Add Subscription dialog box.** Press Ctrl/⌘+V to paste the copied link on the clipboard to the Add Subscription text box.

Paste the RSS link in the Add Subscription text box.

9. **Delete the *feed//* text.** By default, you'll find a URL containing text such as *feed//http:*... You need to delete the *feed//* text in the Add Subscription text box. The URL should begin with *http://*. Delete the text, and press OK.

10. **Open the feed in the Tracker.** Expand the RSS heading so you can see the items nested below the heading, and you'll find the feed you added to the Tracker. One nice thing about using the Tracker as an RSS reader is that you can convert the entire list from a feed in the Tracker to a PDF document by opening a context menu and choosing Convert To PDF, as shown in Figure 35.15.

You can convert a list in the tracker from the RSS feed to PDF by opening a context menu and choosing Convert To PDF.

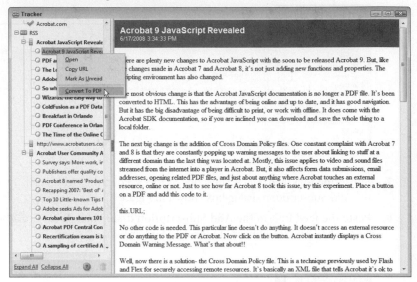

In these steps, we used a blog site on Acrobat Users to monitor the blog posts. You can monitor a number of other sites for frequent information updates. Search for RSS feeds on Adobe's Web site, and you'll find a number of different products and forums that you can keep in touch with. When you open the Tracker, your feeds are updated in Acrobat.

Summary

- Among other things, attending workshops and conferences are good means for learning a program like LiveCycle Designer.

- An abundant amount of information, training resources, and help guides can be found on Adobe's Web site.

- Adobe provides a wealth of reference manuals you can download from the Internet.

- You can add RSS feeds to the Tracker and keep up to date with blogs and other RSS type posts in the Tracker window.

Appendix

Using the CD-ROM

This appendix provides information on the contents and system requirements of the CD-ROM that accompanies this book.

System Requirements

The CD is a cross-platform CD and can be read by both Macintosh and Windows computers. Macintosh users need System 10.2 or above. Windows users need Windows XP Service Pack 2 or above or Windows Vista.

Installation Instructions

To install the items from the CD to your hard drive, follow these steps.

1. **Insert the CD into your computer's CD-ROM drive.**

   The license agreement appears.

   Note to Windows users: The interface won't launch if you have auto-run disabled. In that case, choose Start ➪ Run. (For Windows Vista, choose Start ➪ All Programs ➪ Accessories ➪ Run.) In the dialog box that appears, type *D:\Start.exe*. (Replace *D* with the proper letter if your CD drive uses a different letter. If you don't know the letter, see how your CD drive is listed under My Computer.) Click OK.

   Note for Mac Users: When the CD icon appears on your desktop, double-click the icon to open the CD and double-click the Start icon.

System requirements

Installation instructions

CD-ROM contents

Troubleshooting

Check your CD build to verify the name of this icon.

2. **Read through the license agreement and then click the Accept button if you want to use the CD.**

   The CD interface appears. The interface allows you to browse the contents and install the programs with just a click of a button (or two).

Contents

The CD contains the following:

- Adobe Reader 9.0 software
- The entire text of this book as a PDF document with an embedded index
- Author-created forms and sample files
- Author-created eBook on PDF forms tips

Adobe Reader 9.0

Double-click the Adobe Reader installer and install the Reader software from the book's CD. Adobe Reader is coded separately for PowerPC Macs and Intel Macs, so be sure to choose the installer appropriate for your computer.

NOTE **Before you install Adobe Reader 9 on your computer, check out Adobe's Web site at www.adobe.com/products/acrobat/readermain.html to see if there's a newer version of the Reader software than Adobe Reader 9.0, as you may have purchased this book after Adobe has updated the Reader software. If you find a version later than 9.0 on Adobe's Web site, download that version.**

PDF version of the book

The entire text of the *PDF Forms Using Acrobat and LiveCycle Designer Bible* is available on the CD as a PDF document. Any Acrobat viewer 7.0 or above can open the PDF file and view the contents.

To search the embedded index, open the Search panel by pressing Ctrl/⌘+Shift+F. When the Search panel opens, type a word in the first text box. Acrobat automatically uses the embedded index to find searched words.

Author-created PDF documents

The Chapters folder contains forms and sample files to help you through most of the steps in the text of the book. All chapters that support companion files with work-through steps are identified by chapter number. Open a chapter and the text in the book covers steps to follow to create the form(s) respective to the chapter number where the files are found.

You'll also find a folder titled *SampleForm*. This folder contains a sample dynamic form contributed by Carlo M. Arellano. We liked this form so much Carlo granted permission to include the form on the CD-ROM. Look over this form to see a fine example for using subforms in LiveCycle Designer.

PDF forms eBook

An author-created eBook on 101 forms tips is included in the Chapter16 folder. The file is a PDF Portfolio containing tips and many easy to copy and paste JavaScripts. Any Acrobat viewer version 7.0 or above can view the file.

Troubleshooting

If you have difficulty installing or using any of the materials on the companion CD, try the following solutions:

- **Turn off any anti-virus software that you may have running.** Installers sometimes mimic virus activity and can make your computer incorrectly believe that it is being infected by a virus. (Be sure to turn the anti-virus software back on later.)

- **Close all running programs.** The more programs you're running, the less memory is available to other programs. Installers also typically update files and programs; if you keep other programs running, installation may not work properly.

- **Refer to the ReadMe:** Please refer to the ReadMe file located at the root of the CD-ROM for the latest product information at the time of publication.

Customer Care

If you have trouble with the CD-ROM, please call the Wiley Product Technical Support phone number at (800) 762-2974. Outside the United States, call 1(317) 572-3994. You can also contact Wiley Product Technical Support at `http://support.wiley.com`. John Wiley & Sons will provide technical support only for installation and other general quality control items. For technical support on the applications themselves, consult the program's vendor or author.

To place additional orders or to request information about other Wiley products, please call (877) 762-2974.

Index

Symbols and Numerics

% (modulo) operator method, 968

&amp entity reference, 998

&apos entity reference, 998

&gt entity reference, 998

&lt entity reference, 998

&quot entity reference, 998

[1]/1 tool, 86

2D (two-dimension) format, 771

101AcroFormsTips_A9.pdf document, 511

A

Abs function, 946

Absolute binding expressions, 810–812

Accelio, 632

Access databases
    exporting data from, 1063–1064
    importing data into, 1061–1063
    look of form in, 1060

Access Level menu, 430

accessibility
    assistive devices
        Accessibility Setup Assistant, 295
        preferences, setting, 293–294
    designing forms for
        elements, editing, 312–319
        fields, 311–312
        languages, 310–311
        overview, 305–310
    overview, 291–292
    tagged PDF files
        status of, checking, 297–302
        tags, creating, 302–305
    workflow for authoring accessible forms, 296–297

Accessibility Full Check dialog box, 300–301

Accessibility options, 293–294

Accessibility palette, 678–679

Accessibility Report panel, 301, 304–305

Accessibility Setup Assistant, 295

Accessible layer, 309

Account number transferring from field, 535

Acrobat
    forms
        aggregating data, 11–12
        cost effectiveness of, 17
        dynamic, 828–829
        editing, 7–10
        e-mailing, 412–413
        fillable, 20–21
        hosted on Web servers, 21–29
        populating with field objects, 5–6
        scanning, 18, 131–133
        static, 18–20
    LCD, using with
        distributing XML forms, 648
        editing XML forms, 646–647
        enabling XML forms, 647–648
        overview, 645
    PDF documents
        converting files to, 62–64
        overview, 3–4
        special features, adding to, 10
    versions of
        Acrobat 6, 30–31
        Acrobat 7, 30–31, 268
        Acrobat 8, 30–31, 268, 662
        Acrobat 9, 29–31, 82, 267, 268, 662

Acrobat 9 PDF Bible, 55

Acrobat ConnectNow, 428

Acrobat Distiller
    overview, 59, 65
    PostScript files
        converting to PDF, 66–67
        printing, 66

Acrobat JavaScript Reference manual, 1120

Acrobat PDF Maker dialog box, 60

Acrobat Scan
  overview, 113
  presets
    custom scans, 119–120
    editing, 117–118
    overview, 116–117
  scanner drivers
    Photoshop plug-in software, 114–115
    TWAIN software, 114
    WIA scan drivers, 115–116
  setting options, 120
Acrobat Scan dialog box, 125, 129, 131
Acrobat Standard Forms Editing feature, 30
Acrobat Standard on Mac feature, 30
Acrobat tab, 3, 59
Acrobat User Data folder, 626
Acrobat Users Community Web site, 511
Acrobat Users Forum Web page, 511
Acrobat.com
  logging into
    Adobe IDs, creating, 425–426
    Preferences dialog box, adding information to,
      426–427
  overview, 424
  services, using, 427–428
  submitting forms to, 429–431
  viewing files on, 432–433
actions
  adding to buttons, 261–263
  comment text boxes, creating, 551–553
  document
    alerts, adding to, 523–524
    JavaScript, 496
    overview, 491
  Execute menu item, 233
  Go to a page view, 233, 235
  Import form data, 233, 235
  Multimedia operation, 233, 235
  Open a file, 233, 235
  Open a Web link, 233, 235
  overview, 230–232
  page, 233, 491, 495–496
  Play a sound, 234
  removing, 108
  Reset a form, 105, 234
  Run a JavaScript, 234–235, 491–492, 551, 578

  Set layer visibility, 234, 395–396
  Show/hide a field, 234
  Submit a form, 8–9, 235, 388
  Up button, 226, 232, 575
Actions tab. See also actions
  assigning multiple actions, 262
  availability of, 209, 236, 244–245
Actions window, 232
Acumen Journal, 511
Add a print button, 329
Add an email button, 329
Add another button to group option, 145
Add Another Employer button, 827
Add button, 232, 574
Add Contacts button, 351
Add Digital ID dialog box, 339
Add Digital ID wizard, 338
Add File button, 451
Add Files pull-down menu, 126–127
Add Filter button, 442
Add Library Group dialog box, 715, 772, 774
Add Library Object dialog box, 715–716, 773
Add method, 916
Add New Field pull-down menu
  Button tool, 7
  overview, 85–86, 107
  Show Tools on Toolbar option, 138
  Text Field tool, 102
Add option, 224, 439
Add or Edit Fields command, 84, 91
Add or Edit Fields dialog box, 98–99, 133
Add Printer Marks tool, 52
Add Returned Forms dialog box, 453
Add Row button, 641
Add Subscription dialog box, 1123
Add to Collection menu command, 508–509
Add Welcome & Header panel, 371, 374
addField object, 594–597, 829
addMenuItem object, 624
Address Block object, 768
addToolButton object, 1112–1113
Administration About page, 1085
Administration Console home page, 1083–1084
Administration Console Services page, 1084–1085
Adobe Acrobat
  forms
    aggregating data, 11–12
    cost effectiveness of, 17

dynamic, 828–829
editing, 7–10
e-mailing, 412–413
fillable, 20–21
hosted on Web servers, 21–29
populating with field objects, 5–6
scanning, 18, 131–133
static, 18–20
LCD, using with
distributing XML forms, 648
editing XML forms, 646–647
enabling XML forms, 647–648
overview, 645
PDF documents
converting files to, 62–64
overview, 3–4
special features, adding to, 10
versions of
Acrobat 6, 30–31
Acrobat 7, 30–31, 268
Acrobat 8, 30–31, 268, 662
Acrobat 9, 29–31, 82, 267, 268, 662
Adobe Acrobat ConnectNow, 428
Adobe Acrobat Distiller
overview, 59, 65
PostScript files
converting to PDF, 66–67
printing, 66
Adobe Acrobat Scan
overview, 113
presets
custom scans, 119–120
editing, 117–118
overview, 116–117
scanner drivers
Photoshop plug-in software, 114–115
TWAIN software, 114
WIA scan drivers, 115–116
setting options, 120
Adobe AIR, 1082
Adobe Buzzword, 428
Adobe Designer XML Forms, 268
Adobe Dynamic XML Form option, 855, 978
Adobe Flash Player
form guides, 982, 986
LCD, 1081
LiveCycle Workspace ES, 1094

Adobe Flash videos
alternate text descriptions, 314
converting to PDF, 84
including in PDF forms, 234–235
Adobe Flex Builder, 1094
Adobe Form Server, 632
Adobe IDs, 425–427
Adobe Illustrator
designing forms with, 58
editing objects with, 70–72
Adobe InDesign, 44, 65
Adobe LCES Foundation
administration tools, 1083–1084
Central repository, 1084–1085
overview, 1082
service container, 1083
services, 1083
Adobe LiveCycle Barcoded Forms ES, 148, 1086
Adobe LiveCycle Business Activity Monitoring ES, 1087
Adobe LiveCycle Content Services ES, 1088
Adobe LiveCycle Data Services ES, 1086
Adobe LiveCycle Designer (LCD)
accessibility, 296
advantages of, 643–644
Custom Library objects
adding, 773–774
groups of, 771–773
managing, 774–775
sharing, 775–778
deploying forms
distribution, 990–991
preparing for, 971–973
security, 986–990
designing forms
based on templates, 732–741
from blank pages, 698–731
importing PDF documents, 741–742
overview, 697–698
dynamic forms, 640–642, 829
enabling forms, 278
environment
fields palettes, 669–679
New Form Assistant, 657–660
overview, 655–656
tabs, 679–681
welcome window, 656–657
workspace, 661–669, 681–694

Adobe LiveCycle Designer (LCD) *(continued)*
fields
adding to master pages, 784–785
copying, 749–750
drawing, 748–749
duplicating, 752–753
grouping, 761–763
overview, 743–744
stamping, 746–748
form fragments
creating, 778–780
groups of, 780
updating, 783
using, 780–783
help resources
guidelines for, 1109–1111
Internet resources, 1111–1114
reference manuals, 1114–1121
RSS feeds, 1121–1124
installed files
sample files, 648–652
scripting references, 652–653
launching, 83
limitations of, 644–645
Object Editor, 785–786
Object Library palette
Barcodes Group, 769–771
Custom Group, 768–769
default settings, 763–771
My Favorites group, 767–768
object types, 763–766
Standard Group, 766–767
objects
adding to master pages, 784–785
aligning, 757–760
Copy Multiple option, 753–755
copying, 749–750
distributing, 760–761
dragging and dropping, 744–746
drawing, 748–749
duplicating, 752–753
grouping, 761–763
Insert menu, 750
overview, 670–671, 673–674, 743–744
selecting multiple, 755–757

stamping, 746–748
Tools toolbar, 750–751
versus OpenOffice.org Writer, 56
overview, 17–18, 639–640, 1093–1094
rendering
form guides, 982–986
HTML forms, 981–982
sample forms
copying, 1030
Dunning Notice, 1030–1033
E-ticket, 1033–1035
FormGuide, 1035–1039
Grant Application, 1039–1041
online, 1053–1054
overview, 1029–1030
Purchase Order, 1041–1043
Scripting, 1043–1047
SubformSet, 1047–1049
Tax Receipt, 1049–1053
saving forms
dynamic, 978–979
overview, 974–976
setting target version, 979–980
static, 977–978
XDP, 981
scanning forms for, 128, 133–134
scripts
advantages of, 928–929
debugging, 961–965
help resources, 965–967
versus other languages, 968–969
overview, 927
preferences, 932–934
Script Editor, 930–932
writing, 934–961
spawning pages, 269
system requirements, 642–643
tutorials, 1027–1029
using on Macintosh
development history of, 632–633
editing XML files, 636–638
overview, 631–632
setting up, 633–635
using with Acrobat
distributing XML forms, 648
editing XML forms, 646–647

enabling XML forms, 647–648

overview, 645

versions of, 662

Adobe LiveCycle Designer ES Scripting Errors guide, 1120

Adobe LiveCycle Designer Help Guide, 1115–1120

Adobe LiveCycle Designer Scripting Reference, 967, 1113

Adobe LiveCycle Digital Signatures ES, 1087

Adobe LiveCycle Enterprise Suite (LCES)

  clients, 1081–1082

  components of

    content services, 1087–1088

    data capture, 1086

    document output, 1087

    information assurance, 1086–1087

    process management, 1087

  development tools

    Flex Builder, 1094

    LCD, 1093–1094

    Workbench, 1088–1093

  form deployment, 644

  interface

    To Do list, 1098–1099

    Messages link, 1102

    overview, 1094–1095

    Preferences page, 1099–1101

    Start Process icon, 1095–1098

    Tracking page, 1099

  LCES Foundation

    administration tools, 1083–1084

    Central repository, 1084–1085

    overview, 1082

    service container, 1083

    services, 1083

  overview, 1071, 1080

  process

    electronic, 1073

    justifying, 1073–1074

    paper, 1072

    solution, 1074–1080

  scripting, 652

  server deployment

    file type considerations, 1105–1106

    overview, 1102–1104

    scripting considerations, 1104–1105

    server-required objects, 1106

  versions of, 662

Adobe LiveCycle ES Connectors for ECM, 1088

Adobe LiveCycle ES Developer Connection, 1114

Adobe LiveCycle ES Workspace, 1074

Adobe LiveCycle Form Design Perspective, 1092–1093

Adobe LiveCycle Forms ES, 1086

Adobe LiveCycle Output ES, 1087

Adobe LiveCycle PDF Generator 3D ES, 1087

Adobe LiveCycle PDF Generator ES, 1087

Adobe LiveCycle Process Design Perspective, 1093

Adobe LiveCycle Process Management ES, 1087

Adobe LiveCycle Production Print ES, 1087

Adobe LiveCycle Reader Extensions Server (LCRE), 267, 270, 1086

Adobe LiveCycle Rights Management ES, 359, 1086

Adobe LiveCycle Rights Management Servers option, 333

Adobe LiveCycle Workbench ES, 1088–1093

Adobe PDF Layers

  converting layers to, 65

  creating layered documents, 391–392

  exporting support, 308–309, 395

Adobe PDF Settings for supported documents dialog box, 63, 65

Adobe Photoshop

  custom colors, 533

  editing

    images, 72

    scanned forms, 114

    scanned signatures, 323–324, 326

  plug-ins, 114–115

  stamps, using images as, 277

Adobe Photoshop Acquire plug-ins, 114–115

Adobe Photoshop Elements

  custom colors, 533

  editing

    images, 72

    scanned forms, 129

  plug-ins, 114–115

Adobe Pi font, 216

Adobe Presenter, 30

Adobe Reader

  batch sequences

    creating, 282–283

    custom, 287–289

    overview, 281–282

    preset, 284–287

  capabilities of, 17, 268

Adobe Reader (continued)
  enabling features
    comments, 272–277
    digital signatures, 270–271
    editing enabled forms, 278–281
    form server products, 269–270
    LCD forms, 278
    licensing limitations, 268–269
    overview, 267–268
    Save form data feature, 270–271
    with wizards, 277–278
  LCD forms, 1081
  overcoming limitations of, 10
  overview, 29
  versions of, 520, 642
Adobe Reader dialog box, 270–271
Adobe Static PDF Form option, 977–978
Adobe XML forms 2.7 specification, 1120
Advanced attribute, 229
Advanced Auto-Complete feature, 176
Advanced Editing toolbar
  alternative to, 7, 104
  Crop tool, 55
  grayed out, 346
  opening, 386
  Preview mode, 381
  Select Object tool, 92
  TouchUp Object tool, 70–72
  TouchUp Text tool, 68
Advanced menu, 92, 331–332
Advanced Preferences dialog box, 335
Advanced tab, 310–311, 350
aggregating data
  from legacy files, 452–454
  overview, 11–12
  when responses file does not exist, 454–456
agree button, 396–399
agreeButton.pdf file, 393, 395
.ai files, 65
AIR, 1082
alerts, application
  adding to document actions, 523–524
  application beeps, 524–525
  assessing
    viewer types, 522–523
    viewer versions, 520–522
  message alerts, 518–519

Align Horizontal Center command, 722
Align Top tool, 840
Align Vertical Center command, 722
aligning
  fields, 158–159
  objects, 757–760
Alignment pull-down menu, 217
All Marks check box, 53
Allow Multiple Lines check box, 795, 906–907, 910, 1040
Allow Page Breaks within Content check box, 795
Allow Rich Text Formatting check box, 218
Allow Zero check box, 717–718
alternate text, 314–317
Alternate Text box, 315, 317
Alternating Row Colors check box, 851
Always hide forms document message bar check box, 173
An existing electronic document radio button, 95
analog signatures, scanning, 323–324
Anchor drop-down menu, 792
anchor field, 158–160, 186, 188, 840
anchor point, 675–676, 792
annotations
  coordinates, assessing, 548–550
  overview, 547–548
  text box comments, 550–553
anti-virus software, 1127
app.addSubMenu item, 625
Appearance attributes, for objects, 790
Appearance drop-down menu
  Draw tab, 803–804
  Field tab, 793, 795
  Sign Document dialog box, 341
Appearance tab
  availability of, 236, 244
  Button Properties dialog box, 8
  Check Box Properties dialog box, 256–257
  Text Field Properties dialog box, 102–103, 209, 213–216
AppEmail field, 1058
app.fs.backgroundColor = color.ltGray script, 546
app.fs.clickAdvances = false script, 545
app.fs.cursor = cursor.visible script, 545
app.fs.escapeExits = true script, 546
app.fs.isFullScreen = true script, 546
Apple Boot Camp, 633
applicant database diagram, 1059–1060
applicant form, 1059–1060
ApplicantInfo table, 1056, 1063

Application Alert dialog box, 521
application alerts
    adding to document actions, 523–524
    application beeps, 524–525
    assessing
        viewer types, 522–523
        viewer versions, 520–522
    message alerts, 518–519
application beeps, 524–525
application events
    docClose, 945
    docReady, 945
    postPrint, 946
    postSave, 946
    postSubmit, 946
    prePrint, 946
    preSave, 946
    preSubmit, 946
application response dialog boxes
    for credit card numbers, 580–582
    for name fields, 577–580
`applicationDesignAcrobat.pdf` file, 824
`applicationDetail.pdf` file, 253, 255
`applicationGuidelines.pdf` document, 379
Applications directory, 506
applications.mdb file, 1057, 1063
Apr function, 947
Arbitrary Mask feature, 30, 237, 460, 816–817
arbitrary masks, 30, 237, 253–255, 460, 816–817
Archive Data dialog box, 449
Archive tool, 439, 449
archiving response data, 439, 449–450
Arellano, Carlo M., 1127
Assemble Forms in PDF Collections feature, 30
assessing
    coordinates, 548–550
    viewer types, 522–523
    viewer versions, 520–522
Assistant Options dialog box, 658, 698–699
assistive devices
    Accessibility Setup Assistant, 295
    preferences, setting, 293–294
At function, 948
`attorneyName` variable, 594
`attributeList` list box, 576
attributes, XML, 996

auto field detection
    batch sequence preset for, 286–287
    columns, 465
    comb fields, 47
    editing results, 184–189
    naming fields, 151
    one-step operation, 95
    overview, 48
    tables, 183–184
    troubleshooting, 109–110
Auto Font Size option, 214
Auto Kern option, 798
Auto Tab Order via Page Properties feature, 30
Auto-Complete Entry List dialog box, 175
Auto-Complete features, 174–176
Auto-Complete pull-down menu, 175
Auto-Fill feature, 176
automatic field detection
    batch sequence preset for, 286–287
    columns, 465
    comb fields, 47
    editing results, 184–189
    naming fields, 151
    one-step operation, 95
    overview, 48
    tables, 183–184
    troubleshooting, 109–110
averaging data, 462–466
Avg function, 946

B

Background Fill option, 794
Background Fill Style drop-down menu, 863
backing up forms, 278–279
Barcode Field Properties window, 229
barcode fields
    multiple, 245
    overview, 148–149
    properties, setting, 229–230, 241–243
    support for in Acrobat versions, 30
    tab options, 210
Barcode tool, 141, 148
Barcoded Forms ES, 148, 1086
Barcodes Group, 643, 769–771
Based on a Template radio button, 657, 733
Baseline Shift option, 798

Basic Auto-Complete feature, 176
Basic Layouts panel, 369
batch sequences
    creating, 282–283
    custom, 287–289
    overview, 281–282
    preset
        automatic field detection, 286–287
        OCR, 286–287
        PDF Optimizer, 284–286
        scanned file optimization, 286
        tab order, 287
    setting up, 610–612
Batch Sequences dialog box
    Detect Form Fields item, 286–287
    enabling PDF forms, 281–283
    JavaScript, 610–612
    scanning forms, 134–135
begins with option, 443
Behavior attribute, 227
behaviors, field
    check boxes
        designing, 537
        JavaScripts, adding to, 537–539
        overview, 536–537
    hiding fields, 525–529
    highlight color, 530–531
    locking fields, 529–530
    radio buttons, 536–537
    showing fields, 525–529
    text colors
        changing, 531–533
        custom, 533–536
BFMA (Business Forms Management Association) standards,
    35–36
binding data
    Absolute binding expressions, 810–811
    Data Connection option, 809
    Explicit binding, 810
    Global binding, 809
    Implicit binding, 810
    LCD, 643
    None option, 810
    Normal binding, 808–809
    objects, 829–830
    to OLEDB databases, 1007–1015
    overview, 807–808, 1001–1002

Relative binding expressions, 811–812
setting bindings
    to existing fields, 1022–1025
    while creating new fields, 1025–1026
    to WSDL files, 1015–1021
    to XML sample files, 1005–1007
    to XML schema, 1003–1005
binding expressions
    Absolute, 810–812
    Relative, 811–812
Binding Options dialog box, 1023
Binding Properties dialog box, 858, 1023
Binding tab
    bindings, setting to existing fields, 1022–1025
    Normal binding, 808
    overview, 677
    subforms
        layout properties, 1049
        setting up with overflow leader, 890–891
    table rows, setting to repeat, 902
black-and-white paper forms, 33–34. *See also* scanning forms
Blank tab, 732
`blankFormFields01.xdp` file, 715
`blankFormFields02.xdp` file, 720
`blankFormFieldsFinal.xdp` file, 723
`blankFormMasterPage.xdp` file, 711
`blankPage.pdf` file, 164
Bleed Marks check box, 52–53
Bookmark Properties dialog box, 494, 603
bookmarks, 494, 645
Bookmarks panel, 76–77, 491
Boot Camp, 633
Border palette, 677–678, 843–844
`bOverlay` flag, 601, 607, 617
`bRename` flag, 601, 607
`Broker score` text field, 462–463
Browse For folder window, 777
Business Activity Monitoring ES, 1087
Business Forms Management Association (BFMA) standards,
    35–36
button faces, 257–260
Button Field Appearance Properties, 551
Button Field Properties window
    date stamping, 563
    fields
        adding, 596–597
        resetting, 544
        showing hidden, 528

JavaScript actions, adding, 503
Submit Form buttons, customizing, 418–419
Button is checked by default check box, 219–220
Button Labels submenu, 141
button objects
actions
copying script from Console and pasting into, 502–503
to create comment text boxes, 551–553
adding, 84, 719–724
for calling Instance Manager, 916–919
multiple, 245
for navigating in PDF Portfolios, 385–389
overview, 103–104, 142–143, 670
properties
actions, adding to, 261–263
button faces, 257–260
options, 226–229
overview, 764
Reset Form, 104–107
Submit Form
adding, 7–10
creating, 107–109
e-mailing forms with, 407
hacking, 416–421
tab options, 210
Button Properties dialog box
button faces, adding, 258, 260
buttons
adding to documents in portfolios, 386–387
Reset Form, 105–106
Submit Form, 7–8, 108
layer visibility, changing, 395–397
templates, spawning new pages from, 601
Button Style drop-down menu, 219–220, 245
Button tool
buttons
Reset Form, 104
Submit Form, 7
keyboard shortcut for, 93, 142
Button Value option, 144–145, 220, 245
Buttons with the same name and value are selected in unison check box, 220
Buzzword, 428

C

Calculate button, 615
calculate event, 944
Calculate tab
availability of, 236
averaging data fields, 463
calculations formulas, 249–250
field scripts, 493
functions, creating, 573
overview, 239, 460–461
summing
columns of fields, 555
data, 469–470
text fields, 209
time calculations, 484
Calculated Fields dialog box, 479
Calculated – Read Only option, 807
Calculated – User Can Override option, 807
calculating fields
overview, 249–251
preset formulas
averaging data, 462–466, 470–479
formatting fields, 458–460
overview, 457–458, 460–462
products, 466–469
setting orders, 479–480
summing data, 469–479
SFN
naming fields for, 481
overview, 480–481
performing math calculations with, 481–482
time, 482–485
using names from spawned pages, 588–591
Calculation formulas field, 183, 446
calculation scripts
date stamps, 561–564
sales tax
with fixed tax rates, 557
overview, 556
with user-supplied tax rates, 557–558
shipping charges, 559–561
summing columns and rows, 553–556
Calculations and Scripts Reference Guide, 1120
Calendar pop-up window button, 442
Caption drop-down menu, 790

captions, editing, 790–792
Cascading Style Sheets (CSS), 1094
case sensitivity, 153
CD-ROM
   contents of
      Adobe Reader 9.0, 1126
      author-created PDF documents, 1126–1127
      PDF forms eBook, 1127
      PDF version of book, 1126
   customer care, 1127
   installation instructions, 1125–1126
   system requirements, 1125
   troubleshooting, 1127
Ceil function, 946
Center window, 77
Central repository, 1084–1085
Certificate Viewer dialog box, 349, 353
certificates
   acquiring via e-mail attachments, 347–348
   exporting from signed documents, 348–350
   levels of trust, adding to, 350–353
change event, 945
Change Permissions Password option, 358
Changes Allowed drop-down menu, 358, 362, 987
Character Map dialog box, 709
Characters text box, 219
check box fields
   adding to tables, 191
   averaging data
      overview, 464–466
      preparing for, 471–474
      process of, 477–479
   behaviors
      adding JavaScripts to, 537–539
      designing, 537
      overview, 536–537
   BFMA standards, 35
   calculating
      shipping charges, 560–561
      sums, 474–477
   fonts with box characters, 47, 99
   hierarchical names, 183
   multiple, 245
   overview, 143–144, 673
   properties, 219–222, 255–257, 764
   tab options, 210
Check box is checked by default check box, 219–220

Check Box Properties dialog box
   JavaScripts, adding to check boxes, 538
   mutually exclusive check boxes
      adding to tables, 194
      creating, 256
   preparing check boxes for averaging data, 472–473
   shipping fees, calculating, 560
Check Box Style drop-down menu, 219–220, 245
Check Box tool, 143, 221, 255
Check spelling option, 218, 225
Checking check box field, 536
Choose Contacts to Import dialog box, 351
Choose function, 947
Choose Icon button, 228, 258
Circle Button Style, 220–222
Circle object, 673, 764
Clear all Guides command, 166
Clear all option, 442
Clear button, 228, 575
Clear Fields button, 1044
Clear Form command, 92
ClearScan technology, 113, 122–123
click event, 945
clipboard, 195–196, 198–199, 432–433
Close button, 213
Close Form Editing button
   availability of, 91
   overview, 87
   pasting fields, 156
   point size, determining, 215
   toggling views, 89
Collaborate submenu, 425
Collapse button, 87
Collapse/Expand Fields panel, 87
Collection Editor, 989
Collection List dialog box, 989
Color drop-down menu, 804
color mode, 129
colors
   highlight, 530–531
   text
      changing, 531–533
      custom, 533–536
columns
   automatic field detection, 465
   File Details view, 378–381

summing, 470, 553–556
vertical guidelines, 760
comb fields, 23, 30, 47, 251–255
Comb of [ ] characters check box, 219, 252, 795
Combine Files wizard, 64, 368, 1119
Combo Box Field properties window, 481
Combo Box Properties window, 460
Combo Box tool, 141, 146
combo boxes
automatic detection of, 183
defaults for, setting, 226
multiple, 245
overview, 146–147
properties of, setting, 222–226
tab options, 210
Commands tab, 702
Comment & Markup toolbar
annotation comment coordinates, locating, 549
fields, adding using JavaScript, 595
stamps, creating, 273–274
text box comments, creating, 551
wet signatures, applying, 325
Comment task button, 549
comments
custom stamps
adding, 276–277
creating, 273–275
overview, 271
text box, 550–553
using with forms, 272–273
Comments panel, 85, 171, 425
Commit selected value immediately check box, 224
Company score text field, 462
Compatibility option, 357
Compile Data dialog box, 450–451, 453
Compile Returned Forms command, 90–91, 450–451
completedForms folder, 11
Components view, 1091
Concat function, 948
Configure Presets dialog box, 117–118, 120–121
Configure Signature Appearance dialog box, 336, 341
Confirm Password text box, 339
Connection tab, 1013
ConnectNow, 428
Console, JavaScript
copying script from, 502–503
overview, 500
writing script in, 500–502

contains option, 443
Content Area object, 673, 764, 785
Content property, 879, 880
Content Services ES, 1088
Contents folder, 115, 626
context menus, 94
Conversion Rate Response, 1021
Convert document information check box, 60
Convert Images check box, 727
ConvertedTotal field, 1020
converting
files to PDF
with Acrobat, 62–64
with Distiller, 65–67
exporting, 64–65
with PDFMaker, 59–61
scanned forms, 128–134
with wizards, 95–99
image files to text
in Macintosh, 125–126
in Windows, 123–124
LCD forms to Acrobat forms, 636–638
tables to application documents
in Excel, 200–201
overview, 199–200
in Word, 202–203
Word forms to LCD forms, 725–730
Converting Acrobat JavaScript for Use in LiveCycle Designer
guide, 1120
coordinates, assessing, 548–550
Copy as Table option, 203
Copy Multiple dialog box, 753–755, 840, 842
copying
fields, 156, 749–750
JavaScript, 502–503
non-table data, 197–199
objects, 749–750
sample forms, LCD, 1030
CorelDraw, 58, 64, 70
Corners option, 794, 805
costs
of forms, comparing, 16–17
of using LCD, 635
Count function, 946
Countries drop-down box, 768
Create Accessible (Tagged) PDF file check box, 60
Create Acrobat Layers check box, 65, 309
Create Adobe ID link, 425–426

Create Adobe PDF button, 4
Create an Interactive Form with Fixed Pages radio button, 837
Create bookmarks check box, 60
Create Custom Stamp dialog box, 274
Create Dataset File feature, 30
Create Fragment dialog box, 778–781
Create Go to View dialog box, 383–385
Create Link dialog box, 383–385
Create Multiple Copies of Fields dialog box
    field names, 193
    multiple fields, creating, 162
    overview, 30
    populating
        rows, 191
        tables, 842
    preparing check boxes for averaging data, 473
Create New Collection dialog box, 509
Create New Data Source dialog box, 1009
Create or Edit Form Guide option, 1035–1036
Create or Edit Form wizard
    converting
        native Word documents to PDF forms, 95
        Office forms to PDF documents, 42
    forms
        creating, 704–705
        scanning, 131, 133
    overview, 82–83
Create PDF button, 4, 59, 428, 589
Create PDF Compatible File check box, 65
Create PDF From File command, 126
Create PDF From Scanner dialog box, 123
Create PDF From Tracker Details command, 436–437
Create Summary button, 586, 598
Create Table Using Assistant radio button, 845, 848, 862
Credit Card field, 580
credit card numbers, 580–582
crop mark, 51
Crop Pages tool, 52–53, 55
Crop tool, 55, 72
cropping pages, 51–54
CrossOver Mac, 634
CSS (Cascading Style Sheets), 1094
CTerm function, 947
Ctrl + A selection method, 757
Ctrl + Arrow Key selection method, 757
Ctrl + Click selection method, 757

Ctrl key, 755
Currency Convertor button, 1021
Current Date field, 768
Currently editing Caption and Value options, 798
`currentValueIndices` object, 592
cursors
    unloading, 141
    using loaded, 107
Custom Appearance dialog box, 712–713, 793–794
Custom calculation script radio button
    barcode properties, 243
    Calculate tab, 239, 461
    Format tab, 564
    functions, creating, 573
    null values, adding to fields, 565
    sales tax, calculating, 558
    summing columns of fields, 555
Custom Format Script window, 493, 532–533
Custom Format Scripts, 460, 564, 567
Custom Group, 643, 768–769
Custom Keystroke Script window, 493
Custom Keystroke Scripts, 460, 567, 573
Custom Library Group, 715–719, 771
Custom Library objects
    adding, 773–774
    groups of, 715–719, 771–773
    managing, 774–775
    overview, 644
    sharing, 775–778
Custom Library palette, 710, 729
custom navigation button, 645
Custom option, 238, 460
Custom Page Sizes dialog box, 50
Custom radio button, 817
Custom Scan dialog box, 117, 119–121
custom stamps
    adding, 276–277
    creating, 273–275
`customerSatisfactionFieldsAuto.pdf` file, 471, 474
`customerSatisfactionSimplePopulated.pdf` form, 462, 465
Customize dialog box, 691, 702–703
Customize Toolbars feature, 30

D

data
    Acrobat.com
        logging into, 425–427
        overview, 424
        submitting forms to, 429–431
        using services, 427–428
        viewing files on, 432–433
    binding
        Absolute binding expressions, 810–811
        Data Connection option, 809
        Explicit binding, 810
        Global binding, 809
        Implicit binding, 810
        LCD, 643
        None option, 810
        Normal binding, 808–809
        objects, 829–830
        to OLEDB databases, 1007–1015
        overview, 807–808, 1001–1002
        Relative binding expressions, 811–812
        setting bindings, 1022–1026
        to WSDL files, 1015–1021
        to XML sample files, 1005–1007
        to XML schema, 1003–1005
    collection of, 30, 438–439
    deploying forms
        e-mailing, 406–416
        hacking Submit Form button, 416–421
        hosting on Web sites, 404–406
    LCD
        data connections, 1001–1021
        overview, 993
        setting bindings, 1022–1026
        XML files, 994–1001
    managing
        manually distributed forms, 450–456
        responses, 437–450
        Tracker, 434–437
    network servers, 422–424
    overview, 403–404
Data Connection submenu, 809
Data Drop-down List Box item, 769
Data Entered field, 815–817
Data Exchange File – Export Options dialog box, 347

Data Exchange File – Exporting Certificate dialog box, 349–350
Data File text box, 1033
Data Services ES, 1086
data source files, 856–860, 995
Data Source Name (DSN), 1007–1008, 1013
Data tab, 813, 815
Data View palette
    data bindings, setting, 1022, 1024
    data connections, setting, 809–810, 1002–1007, 1015–1016, 1019
    overview, 667–668
    table data, 851–852, 856
    testing exported database data, 1066
DataA.XML file, 1047–1049
databases
    Access
        exporting data from, 1063–1064
        importing data into, 1061–1063
        look of form in, 1060
    design of, 1057–1061
    importing data from
        modifying form for, 1067–1070
        overview, 1064–1065
        testing exported data in original form, 1065–1066
    overview, 1055–1057
Date function, 947
Date option, 237, 460
Date received field, 420
date stamps, 561–564
Date2Num function, 947
DateFmt function, 947
Date.getDate method, 968
Date.getTime method, 969
Date/Time Field object, 670, 764
Deactivate Read Out Loud command, 318
Debugger
    opening, 499–500
    overview, 963–964
    preferences, setting, 498–499
debugging
    dynamic forms, 870–872
    LCD scripts, 961–965
Decimal Field object, 673, 764
Decode function, 948
Default button, 48

Default Language drop-down menu, 934
Default Layout and Zoom section, 75
Default Settings drop-down menu, 67
Default state drop-down menu, 398
default tab order, 671–672
Default Tab Order option, 178
Default User Space, 548
Default Value text box, 218, 252
default zeros, eliminating
adding null values to fields, 564–566
overview, 469
replacing with null values, 566–569
Defaults tab, 932-933, 979–980
Delete All Comments command, 282
Delete button, 232, 575
Delete the filter item, 442
Delete option, 224, 439
deleting fields, 158, 598
Delrina, 632
deploying forms
e-mailing
manually collecting responses in inbox, 407–412
overview, 406
receiving and filling in distributed forms, 414–416
using Acrobat, 412–413
using Submit Form buttons, 407
hacking Submit Form button
editing properties, 416–420
JavaScript functions, 420–421
overview, 416–417
hosting on Web sites
instructions for downloading, 405–406
overview, 404
site design, 405
LCD
adding security, 986–990
distributing forms, 990–991
preparing for, 971–973
via server
file type considerations, 1105–1106
overview, 1102–1104
scripting considerations, 1104–1105
server-required objects, 1106
<desc> tag, 668
Description combo box, 570

design pages
adding field objects to, 710–714
selecting multiple objects on, 755–756
Design View tab, 679–680, 683–684
Designer application (LCD)
accessibility, 296
advantages of, 643–644
Custom Library objects
adding, 773–774
groups of, 771–773
managing, 774–775
sharing, 775–778
deploying forms
distribution, 990–991
preparing for, 971–973
security, 986–990
designing forms
based on templates, 732–741
from blank pages, 698–731
importing PDF documents, 741–742
overview, 697–698
dynamic forms, 640–642, 829
enabling forms, 278
environment
fields palettes, 669–679
New Form Assistant, 657–660
overview, 655–656
tabs, 679–681
welcome window, 656–657
workspace, 661–669, 681–694
fields
adding to master pages, 784–785
copying, 749–750
drawing, 748–749
duplicating, 752–753
grouping, 761–763
overview, 743–744
stamping, 746–748
form fragments
creating, 778–780
groups of, 780
updating, 783
using, 780–783
help resources
guidelines for, 1109–1111
Internet resources, 1111–1114

reference manuals, 1114–1121
RSS feeds, 1121–1124
installed files
sample files, 648–652
scripting references, 652–653
launching, 83
limitations of, 644–645
Object Editor, 785–786
Object Library palette
Barcodes Group, 769–771
Custom Group, 768–769
default settings, 763–771
My Favorites group, 767–768
object types, 763–766
Standard Group, 766–767
objects
adding to master pages, 784–785
aligning, 757–760
Copy Multiple option, 753–755
copying, 749–750
distributing, 760–761
dragging and dropping, 744–746
drawing, 748–749
duplicating, 752–753
grouping, 761–763
Insert menu, 750
overview, 670–671, 673–674, 743–744
selecting multiple, 755–757
stamping, 746–748
Tools toolbar, 750–751
versus OpenOffice.org Writer, 56
overview, 17–18, 639–640, 1093–1094
rendering
form guides, 982–986
HTML forms, 981–982
sample forms
copying, 1030
Dunning Notice, 1030–1033
E-ticket, 1033–1035
FormGuide, 1035–1039
Grant Application, 1039–1041
online, 1053–1054
overview, 1029–1030
Purchase Order, 1041–1043
Scripting, 1043–1047
SubformSet, 1047–1049
Tax Receipt, 1049–1053

saving forms
dynamic, 978–979
overview, 974–976
setting target version, 979–980
static, 977–978
XDP, 981
scanning forms for, 128, 133–134
scripts
advantages of, 928–929
debugging, 961–965
help resources, 965–967
versus other languages, 968–969
overview, 927
preferences, 932–934
Script Editor, 930–932
writing, 934–961
spawning pages, 269
system requirements, 642–643
tutorials, 1027–1029
using with Acrobat
distributing XML forms, 648
editing XML forms, 646–647
enabling XML forms, 647–648
overview, 645
using on Macintosh
development history of, 632–633
editing XML files, 636–638
overview, 631–632
setting up, 633–635
versions of, 662
Designer File toolbar, 704
Designer Template (TDS), 736, 780
designing forms
for accessibility
elements, editing, 312–319
fields, 311–312
languages, 310–311
overview, 305–310
converting to PDF
with Acrobat, 62–64
with Distiller, 65–67
with PDFMaker, 59–61
editing
images, 72
objects, 70–72
overview, 67–68
text, 68–69

designing forms *(continued)*
  exporting to PDF, 64–65
  initial views
    layout, adjusting, 76–77
    magnification, adjusting, 76–77
    overview, 75–76
    user interface options, 77–78
    Window options, 77
  in LCD
    based on templates, 732–741
    from blank pages, 698–731
    importing PDF documents, 741–742
    overview, 697–698
  PDF forms, 41–43
  replacing pages, 73–74
  standards for
    BFMA, 35–36
    individual, 36
    overview, 33–34
    PDF forms, 36–39
    W3C, 36
  tools for
    Excel, 54–55
    illustration programs, 58
    layout programs, 57
    OpenOffice.org Writer, 56
    other programs, 58–59
    overview, 43
    PowerPoint, 55–56
    Word, 44–54
Desktop Email Application, 415–416
Detect Form Fields item, 134–135, 286–287
Deubert, John, 511
digital IDs
  creating, 337–341
  custom appearance, 334–336
  overview, 321–322, 332–334
Digital IDs option, 333
Digital Signature Properties window, 147, 529
Digital Signature tool
  applying multiple signatures, 345
  digital signature fields
    adding, 147
    properties, setting, 240–241
  labels, 141

digital signatures
  applying multiple, 345–346
  digital IDs
    creating, 337–341
    custom appearance, 334–336
    overview, 332–334
  enabling files for, 270–271
  JavaScripts, assigning to, 493–494
  locking fields, 342–345
  overview, 30, 147, 321–322
  properties, setting, 240–241
  signing, 341–342
  tab options, 210
  third-party signature handlers, 323
  validating
    certificates, 347–353
    overview, 346
    with Trusted Identities, 354
  wet signatures
    adding in Reader, 324–326
    overview, 37
    preparing files for using LCD, 328–331
    scanning analog, 323–324
    using with Acrobat recipients, 326–328
Digital Signatures and Data Encryption item, 339
Digital Signatures ES, 1087
Digital Signatures Properties Signed tab, 344, 530
Digitally sign the document on the page feature, 271
Direct Selection tool, 72
Directory Servers option, 333
disabilities. *See* accessibility
Discard Objects pane, 285
Display drop-down menu, 351
Display PDF in Browser check box, 405
Display tab, 812–815
Distiller
  overview, 59, 65
  PostScript files
    converting to PDF, 66–67
    printing, 66
Distribute command, 163, 454
Distribute Form button, 98, 104, 648
Distribute Form command, 31, 91, 277–278, 404
Distribute Form logon dialog box, 425–426
Distribute Form tool, 37, 278

Distribute Form wizard
  Acrobat.com, 425, 429–430
  data management, 434, 450
  distributing forms
    via e-mail, 406–409, 412, 414
    XML, 648
  enabling forms, 277–278
  hacking Submit Form button, 417–418
  LCD, 990
  network servers, 422
  overview, 87
Distribute menu, 760–761
distribute_collectForms folder, 451–452
distributed.pdf file, 417, 420, 423
distributing
  forms
    via e-mail, 406–412
    with LCD, 989–991
    XML in Acrobat, 648
  objects, 760–761
doAmountCalcs function, 592
doAmountTotals( ) function, 593
docTemplate object, 829
document actions
  alerts, adding to, 523–524
  JavaScript, 496
  overview, 491
Document Actions dialog box, 496–497, 523
document language, 296
Document Level JavaScript, 603, 618
Document menu, 636–637
Document Message Bar feature, 31, 104, 174, 307
Document pane
  context menus, 94
  editing
    enabled PDF files, 279–280
    objects using Illustrator, 71
  multiple fields, creating, 162
  overview, 82, 84, 86–88
  scanning forms, 113
  signatures, 720
document prolog, 996
Document Properties dialog box
  digital signatures, 331
  embedded fonts, 215
  Initial View settings, 75–76

  languages, choosing, 310
  security settings, 358–359, 364
  status of tagged PDF files, checking, 297–298
  XML forms, editing, 646
Document Properties Security pane, 359
Document Property metadata, 22, 39
Document Restrictions Summary, 364
Document Type Definition (DTD), 996
document viewing scripts
  full screen scripts, 545–546
  navigating pages, 545
  resetting fields
    with JavaScript, 543–544
    preserving default values, 544
    separate fields for, 542–543
  zooming views, 544–545
document-level scripts
  JavaScript, 495
  message alerts, adding to, 518–519
  overview, 491
  viewer versions, assessing, 520–522
does not contain option, 443
does not equal option, 443
Don't show the New Form Assistant again radio button, 658
Don't show Welcome Page again check box, 373
doSession( ) function, 619
doSpeaker( ) function, 619
Down button, 232, 575
Download Linked File As check box, 406
downloading forms, 405–406
Downsample Images drop-down menu, 122
Drag and Drop Tab Order in Fields Panel feature, 31
dragging and dropping objects, 744–746
Draw tab, 801, 803
Drawing Aids palette, 683, 692
drawing fields and objects, 748–749
drop-down lists, 673, 764
DSN (Data Source Name), 1007–1008, 1013
DTD (Document Type Definition), 996
Dunning Notice folder, 649–650
Dunning Notice form, 1030–1033
Dunning Notice Level3.xml file, 650
Duplicate command, 715, 753
Duplicate context menu command, 157
Duplicate dialog box, 753
Duplicate Field dialog box, 157, 605

duplicating fields and objects, 752–753
duplicating text fields, 183
dynamic expanding text fields, 903–915
dynamic forms
    Acrobat/Reader minimum version requirements, 642
    binding data, 829–830
    creating
        with Acrobat, 828–829
        with LCD, 643
    Hierarchy palette, 830–831
    overview, 20
    properties, 831
    runtime, 830
    \Samples\Forms\Purchase Order folder, 1041
    saving, 872
    versus static, 823–830
    using in LCD, 829
Dynamic Interactive form, 1041
Dynamic LiveCycle Designer Document, 642
dynamic tables
    creating, 845–846
    designing, 846–847
    Table Assistant wizard, 847–851

E

Edges option, 794
Edit Batch Sequence dialog box, 282–283, 286–287, 610
Edit button, 232, 492
Edit Conditional Break dialog box, 886–887
Edit Entry List button, 175
Edit Fields command, 91–92
Edit Image option, 72
Edit Layout button, 89, 97, 103
Edit Layout mode, 148
Edit Library Object Information dialog box, 775
Edit Object option, 72
Edit pattern, 815
Edit PDF Portfolio panel, 369–370, 373–374, 378
Edit Portfolio view, 377, 379
Edit Sequence dialog box
    batch sequences, creating, 282, 287, 610–611
    preparing forms for editing, 134
Edit tab, 812
Edit toolbar, 702
editing
    automatic field detection results, 184–189
    captions, 790–792
    enabled forms, 278–281

field names
    in Fields panel, 151–152
    in Properties dialog box, 153–154
    in Viewer mode, 153
fills, 801–805
form elements for accessibility
    alternate text, 314–317
    reading form aloud, 318–319
    reading order, 312–314
    reading preferences, 317–318
images, 72
objects, 70–72, 793–795
overview, 7–10
strokes, 801–805
Submit Form button properties, 416–420
text, 68–69
in Viewer mode, 92–94
WIA scan driver presets, 117–118
XML files in Acrobat, 636–638, 646–647
Editing mode, 646
editors, JavaScript, 504–505
Editors tool, 1089
electronic workflow, 47
elements, XML, 997
eliminating default zeros
    adding null values to fields, 564–566
    overview, 469
    replacing with null values, 566–569
elliptical shapes, 803–804
e-mail
    attachments, acquiring certificates via, 347–348
    form distribution via
        with Acrobat, 412–413
        manually collecting responses, 407–412
        overview, 406
        receiving and filling in distributed forms, 414–416
        with Submit Form buttons, 407
Email All Recipients option, 435–436
Email Recipients Who Haven't Responded option, 435
Email Submit object, 764
Embed Fonts check box, 802, 976
Embed Image Data command, 708, 720
embedded fonts, 68–69, 215, 802, 1103–1104
embedded images, 981, 1103
employee-ApplicationExtract.pdf document, 109–110
employee.signature field, 343
employee.submitForm field, 529

Empty Message box, 807
Enable Commenting in Adobe Reader command, 278
Enable copying of text, images, and other content option, 358, 987
Enable for Commenting and Analysis in Adobe Reader option, 31, 272
Enable for Forms Saving and Digital Signatures in Adobe Reader feature, 31
Enable JavaScript debugger after Acrobat is restarted check box, 499
Enable text access for screen reader devices for the visually impaired check box, 358
Enable text access for screen reader devices for users with vision impairment check box, 988
Enable Unicode Support check box, 339
Enable Usage Rights in Adobe Reader dialog box
    enabling
        form saving and digital signatures, 270
        forms in PDF Portfolios, 390
        LCD forms, 278
    special features, adding to PDF documents, 10
enabling
    comments, 272–277
    digital signatures, 270–271
    editing enabled forms, 278–281
    form server products, 269–270
    forms in PDF Portfolios, 390
    LCD forms, 278
    licensing limitations, 268–269
    overview, 10, 267–268
    Save form data feature, 270–271
    with wizards, 277–278
    XML forms in Acrobat, 647–648
Encode function, 948
encoding symbologies, 771
Encryption level option, 357–358
End User License Agreement (EULA)
    form servers, 270
    licensing limitations, 268–269
    usage rights, 37
ends with option, 443
enter event, 945
Enterprise Suite (LCES)
    clients, 1081–1082
    components of
        content services, 1087–1088
        data capture, 1086
        document output, 1087

information assurance, 1086–1087
process management, 1087
development tools
    Flex Builder, 1094
    LCD, 1093–1094
    Workbench, 1088–1093
form deployment, 644
interface
    To Do list, 1098–1099
    Messages link, 1102
    overview, 1094–1095
    Preferences page, 1099–1101
    Start Process icon, 1095–1098
    Tracking page, 1099
LCES Foundation
    administration tools, 1083–1084
    Central repository, 1084–1085
    overview, 1082
    service container, 1083
    services, 1083
overview, 1071, 1080
process
    electronic, 1073
    justifying, 1073–1074
    paper, 1072
    solution, 1074–1080
scripting, 652
server deployment
    file type considerations, 1105–1106
    overview, 1102–1104
    scripting considerations, 1104–1105
    server-required objects, 1106
versions of, 662
equals option, 443
E-ticket folder, 1029, 1033
E-ticket form, 649, 651, 1033–1035
EULA (End User License Agreement)
    form servers, 270
    licensing limitations, 268–269
    usage rights, 37
Eval function, 948, 968
evenstLayout.xdp file, 861
event model, 966
event.changeEx parameter, 572
events
    application
        docClose, 945
        docReady, 945

events *(continued)*
    application *(continued)*
        postPrint, 946
        postSave, 946
        postSubmit, 946
        prePrint, 946
        preSave, 946
        preSubmit, 946
    interactive
        change, 945
        click, 945
        enter, 945
        exit, 945
        mouseDown, 945
        mouseEnter, 945
        mouseExit, 945
        mouseUp, 945
        postOpen, 945
        postSign, 945
        preOpen, 945
        preSign, 945
    process
        calculate, 944
        form:ready, 945
        indexChange, 945
        initialize, 945
        layout:ready, 945
        validate, 945
`event.target` object, 533
`event.willCommit` parameter, 572
Excel
    aggregating form data, 11
    designing forms with, 43, 54–55, 730–731
    exporting tables to, 200–201
    viewing data in, 12
Execute JavaScript command, 288
Execute menu item action, 233, 235
Exists function, 947
exit event, 945
Expand to fit check box, 792, 910, 913
explicit data binding, 810
Export Adobe PDF dialog box, 64–65, 309
Export button, 347
Export command, 202–203
Export Data As dialog box, 347
Export Data From Multiple Files dialog box, 454–455

Export Data From Multiple Forms dialog box, 11, 204
Export Data menu, 31, 438, 444, 921
Export Form Data As dialog box, 855, 920
Export Progress dialog box, 12, 455
Export Value option, 220, 224, 245
Export Value text box, 194, 472–474
exporting
    certificates
        to files, 347–348
        from signed documents, 348–350
    data from Access databases, 1063–1064
    to PDF, 64–65
    table data, 204
    tables
        to Excel, 200–201
        to Word, 202–203
expressions, binding
    Absolute, 810–812
    Relative, 811–812
Extend Usage Rights in Adobe Reader dialog box, 330
Extensible Markup Language (XML)
    binding data to
        sample files, 1005–1007
        schema, 1003–1005
    creating
        data, 852–855, 920–921
        files, 994–996
    distributing forms, 648
    editing
        files, 636–638
        forms, 646–647
    editors for, 999–1001
    enabling forms, 647–648
    exporting, 31
    importing, 447–448, 922–924
    overview, 640
    structure of, 996–999
    syntax rules, 997–998
Extensible Stylesheet Language Transformation (XSLT), 995, 1003, 1006, 1056
External Data tab, 1061, 1063
Extract Pages command, 110, 637

F

Field Edit tool, 750–751
Field Format check box, 795

Field is used for file selection option, 218
Field Name text box
  fields, adding, 102
  overview, 140
  Reset Form buttons, 104
  Submit Form buttons, 7
Field Properties dialog box, 490
field scripts, 490–494
Field Selection dialog box
  automatic field detection, 465
  averaging data, 464, 477
  barcode properties, 241, 243
  calculating products, 468
  calculation formulas, 250–251, 461–462
  locking fields, 530
  signature fields, 343
  summing columns and rows, 553
Field tab, 677, 813, 1039
fields
  adding
    from data source files, 856–860
    manually, 190–199
    overview, 101–103
    via JavaScript, 586–597
  appearance of
    changing, 790–795
    fills, 801–805
    font attributes, 797–799
    object attributes, 795–797
    overview, 789–790
    paragraph attributes, 799–801
    strokes, 801–805
  automatic detection of
    batch sequence preset for, 286–287
    editing results, 184–189
    overview, 45, 183–184
  binding data to
    Absolute binding expressions, 810–811
    Data Connection option, 809
    Explicit binding, 810
    Global binding, 809
    Implicit binding, 810
    None option, 810
    Normal binding, 808–809
    overview, 807–808
    Relative binding expressions, 811–812

buttons, adding
  overview, 103–104
  Reset Form, 104–107
  Submit Form, 107–109
calculating
  overview, 249–251
  preset formulas, 457–480
  SFN, 480–482
  time, 482–485
configuration rules, 38
deleting, 598
eliminating from print, 541–542
filling in
  Auto-Complete features, 174–176
  with Typewriter tool, 169–171
Form tools
  common features for, 140–142
  loading, 138
  overview, 149–150
grids
  overview, 166
  setting up, 167–169
  snapping to, 169
hierarchy structure, 643
locking, 343, 529–530
multiple copies of, creating, 161–163
naming
  automatically, 151
  conventions for, 153
  editing names, 151–154
  hierarchical names, 154–155
  overview, 150
  for SFN, 481
  text, 246–248
navigating between, 171–172
organizing
  aligning, 158–159
  copying, 156
  deleting, 158
  moving, 157–158
  overview, 155
  pasting, 156
  placing multiple, 156–157
  setting attribute defaults, 159–160
  sizing, 159
populating forms with, 5–6

fields (*continued*)
 properties of. *See also* Properties window
  binding data to fields, 807–812
  buttons, 257–263
  check boxes, 255–257
  editing, 244–245
  field attributes, 805–806
  patterns, 812–817
  Properties bar, 243–244
  text fields, 246
  value attributes, 806–807
 reordering, 817–818
 resetting
  with JavaScript, 543–544
  preserving default values, 544
  separate fields for, 542–543
 rulers
  drawing guidelines, 166
  overview, 165–166
  snapping fields to guidelines, 166
 selecting, 160
 showing, 525–529
 tab orders, 176–179
 types of
  barcode, 148–149
  button, 142–143
  check box, 143–144
  combo boxes, 146–147
  digital signature, 147
  list boxes, 145–146
  overview, 137
  radio button, 144–145
  text, 139–140
 Viewer mode
  creating in, 163–165
  editing in, 92–94
 viewing, 172–174
 visibility of, 38
Fields drop-down menu, 442
fields palettes
 Accessibility, 678–679
 Border, 677–678, 843–844
 Fragment Library, 674–675, 778–780
 How To, 675, 701
 Layout
  captions, editing, 791–792
  comments pages, creating with expanding text
   fields, 908

flowing forms, creating with expanding text fields, 913
 height of field setting, 906
 numeric and date field objects, adding, 717
 object coordinates, 879
 objects in flowed subforms, 881
 Ordered By fields, changing field types for, 736
 overview, 675–676
 XML data files, creating, 854
Library
 help guidelines, 1110
 overview, 669–674
 table data, 851–852
 workspace, 662
Object
 appearance properties, 790
 appearances, editing, 793
 binding fields to data elements, 1024
 display patterns, 813
 help guidelines, 1110
 master pages, designing, 708
 organizing palettes, 701
 overview, 676–677
 pagination options, 882
 properties, 677
 signature settings, 988
 strokes and fills, editing, 801
 subform properties, 878
 Subform tab, 879
Fields panel
 field names, editing, 151–152
 formatting fields, 247–248
 forms, creating for spawning pages, 590
 mutually exclusive check boxes, adding to tables, 195
 overview, 87
 reading order, 312–313
 tab order, 178, 817
`fieldsTemplate.pdf` file, 164
File Details tool, 377, 379
File Details view
 columns, adding, 378–381
 overview, 376–378
File Import Options dialog box, 727–728
File toolbar, 508, 702
`filename_responses.pdf` file, 429
filing scripts, 512–516
Fill Color option, 243
Fill Color swatch, 105
Fill drop-down menu, 31, 804

Fill swatch, 8
fillable forms. *See also* scanning forms
    converting scanned forms to, 131–133
    overview, 20–21
filling in
    distributed forms, 414–416
    fields
        Auto-Complete features, 174–176
        navigating, 171–172
        with Typewriter tool, 169–171
        viewing, 172–174
fills, editing, 801–805
Filter definition drop-down menu, 442–444
Filter option, 438
Filter Settings panel, 441–442
filtering response data, 441–444
Find Element dialog box, 126
Fit Page view, 77, 544
Fit Page zoom level, 463
fixed response options
    functions, creating, 571–573
    overview, 569–570
    programmer's notes, 570
Flash Player
    form guides, 982, 986
    LCD, 1081
    LiveCycle Workspace ES, 1094
Flash videos
    alternate text descriptions, 314
    converting to PDF, 84
    including in PDF forms, 234–235
flatbed scanners, 19. *See also* scanning forms
Flatten Form Fields feature, 31
Flatten Layers command, 310
Flex Builder, 1094
Floor function, 946
flowed content areas, 879–882
folder level JavaScript, 626
Font Color option, 798
Font drop-down menu, 69
Font option, 244, 797–798
Font palette
    embedding fonts, 802
    font attributes, 797–798
    overview, 682–683, 701
    substituting fonts, 802
Font pull-down menu, 215

Font Size pull-down menu, 102, 798
Font Size text box, 102, 798
fonts
    attributes, 797–799
    BFMA standards, 35
    editing text when not available, 69
    embedded, 68–69, 215, 802, 1103–1104
footers, 888–892
Form Editing mode
    Acrobat versions, 31
    Add or Edit Fields menu command, 84
    automatic field detection, 48, 184–185, 308
    browsing, 84–88
    button faces, adding, 258
    button fields, 142
    converting LCD static forms to Acrobat forms, 636
    distributing forms on Acrobat.com, 429
    duplicating tables, 475
    editing fields in, 92–94
    field objects, adding, 5–6
    formatting fields, 247
    loading Form tools, 138
    OCR, 121
    overview, 81–82
    returned forms, compiling, 450
    scanning forms, 131
    Start Forms Wizard menu command, 82–83
    toggling views, 88–92
Form Editing toolbar
    Form tools, 137–138, 141–143
    overview, 85–86
Form Field drop-down menu
    button faces, adding, 260
    buttons, adding, 387
    date stamping, 563
    layer visibility, changing, 397
    overview, 211
    resetting forms, 543
form fragments
    creating, 778–780
    groups of, 780
    overview, 644, 660
    updating, 783
    using, 780–783
form guide layout, 982–983
form name_distributed.pdf file, 417
form name_responses.pdf file, 417

Form Properties dialog box
  Dunning Notice forms, 1033
  exported database XML files, attaching, 1065
  keyboard shortcut for, 704
  sample data files, changing, 651
  sample XML data, importing, 922–923
  saving LCD forms, 975, 979
  scripting language preferences, 932–934
  security, 987
  Tax Receipt forms, 1052
Form Server, 632
form server products, 269–270, 632
Form thumbnail preview option, 439
Form tools
  adding fields with, 101
  common features for
    cursors, unloading, 141
    labels, 141
    sizing, 140
    tooltips, 141–142
  loading, 138
  overview, 91
Format function, 948
Format tab
  arbitrary masks, formatting, 253
  date stamping, 563–564
  field scripts, 493
  formatting fields, 247, 458–460
  overview, 236–238
  replacing zeros with null values, 566
  text colors, changing, 532, 535
  time calculations, 484
FormCalc
  calculating taxes, 951–952
  case sensitivity, 937
  functions, 946–949
  overview, 927, 1104–1105
  scripts, checking, 1045
  summary forms, creating, 446
  user reference, 652, 966–967
  writing scripts in, 946–954
FormCalc specification, version 2.0 manual, 1120
FormCalc Syntax Formatting button, 939
FormCalc Syntax Formatting dialog box, 940
FormGuide folder, 649
FormGuide forms, 1035–1039
form:ready event, 945

forms
  Acrobat
    aggregating data, 11–12
    cost effectiveness of, 17
    dynamic, 828–829
    editing, 7–10
    e-mailing, 412–413
    fillable, 20–21
    hosted on Web servers, 21–29
    populating with field objects, 5–6
    scanning, 18, 131–133
    static, 18–20
  backing up, 278–279
  converting
    LCD to Acrobat, 636–638
    to PDF, 59–67
    Word to LCD, 725–730
  copying sample, 1030
  deploying
    e-mailing, 406–416
    hacking Submit Form button, 416–421
    hosting on Web sites, 404–406
    LCD, 971–973, 986–991
    via server, 1102–1106
  designing
    for accessibility, 305–319
    converting to PDF, 59–67
    editing, 67–72
    exporting to PDF, 64–65
    initial views, 75–78
    in LCD, 697–742
    PDF forms, 41–43
    replacing pages, 73–74
    standards for, 33–39
    tools for, 43–59
  dynamic
    Acrobat/Reader minimum version requirements, 642
    binding data, 829–830
    creating, 643, 828–829
    Hierarchy palette, 830–831
    overview, 20
    properties, 831
    runtime, 830
    \Samples\Forms\Purchase Order folder, 1041
    saving, 872
    versus static, 823–830
    using in LCD, 829

enabling
    editing enabled forms, 278–281
    form server products, 269–270
    LCD, 278
    in PDF Portfolios, 390
    Save form data feature, 270–271
    XML in Acrobat, 647–648
hosting
    instructions for downloading, 405–406
    overview, 21–29, 404
    site design, 405
reading
    aloud, 318–319
    order for, 312–314
    preferences for, 317–318
sample, LCD
    copying, 1030
    Dunning Notice form, 1030–1033
    E-ticket form, 1033–1035
    FormGuide forms, 1035–1039
    Grant Application form, 1039–1041
    online, 1053–1054
    overview, 1029–1030
    Purchase Order form, 1041–1043
    Scripting form, 1043–1047
    SubformSet forms, 1047–1049
    Tax Receipt form, 1049–1053
scanning
    Acrobat Scan, 113–120
    Batch Sequences command, 134–135
    converting to PDF, 128–134
    OCR, 120–128
    optimizing, 286
    overview, 603–605
    paper, 18
    setting up batch sequence, 610–612
    splitting files, 612–613
    summarizing data with, 617–623
    using in single file, 605–607
    using individual, 607–610
subforms
    dynamic expanding text fields, 903–915
    headers and footers, 888–892
    LCD, 644
    nesting, 894–901
    overview, 873–875

placing, 875–878
previewing, 892–894
properties, setting, 879–887
testing forms, 919–924
troubleshooting dynamic forms, 923–924
user-controlled dynamic forms, 915–919
using tables for, 901–903
XML
    distributing, 648
    editing, 646–647
    enabling, 647–648
Forms Document Message bar, 172–173
forms industry
    comparing costs, 16–17
    cost effectiveness of Acrobat forms, 17
    overview, 15–16
Forms menu, 31, 90–91, 647
Forms option, 435
Forms tab, 732–733
Forms toolbar, 31, 81, 278
Forms-Beige tab, 733
Forms-Blue tab, 733
Forms-Vanilla tab, 733
Fragment Library palette, 674–675, 778–780
fragment link, 782
fragment subform icon, 782
Fragments toolbar, 702
From Blank Page command, 589
Fujitsu Scansnap 510 scanner, 116
Full Screen mode, 37, 77, 233
full screen scripts, 545–546
functions
    adding to menus, 624–626
    FormCalc, 946–949
FV function, 947

G

General field properties window, 562
General tab
    default view, 208–209
    eliminating fields from print, 541
    fields, adding, 103
    multiple fields, editing properties, 244
    overview, 211–213, 236
    preparing check boxes for averaging data, 472
    Read Only check box, 471

General tab (*continued*)
    Required check box, 464
    status of tagged PDF files, checking, 297–298
    Submit Form buttons, 108
`generalApplcation_populated.pdf` file, 382
`generalApplication.pdf` document, 247, 249, 251, 258, 261, 276, 741
Generate Accessibility Information (Tags) for Acrobat check box, 975
Generate Log File when Saving check box, 975
Get Annotation Coordinates menu command, 624, 626
Get Field Names menu command, 626
Get function, 949
Get Started button, 439
Getting Started pane, 727
`GFApplication_DB.pdf` file, 1065
`GFApplicationFlowed.xdp` file, 894
`GFApplicationNoSubforms.xdp` file, 877
`GFApplicationOverflow.xdp` file, 889
`GFApplication.pdf` file, 825
`GFCommentsPageStart.xdp` form, 908
`GFPackingSlipFinished.pdf` form, 920, 922
`GFPackingSlipStart.xdp` form, 912
`GFPurchaseOrder_data.xml` file, 1005
`GFPurchaseOrderFlowed.xdp` file, 900
`GFPurchaseOrderIMStart.xdp` file, 916
`GFPurchaseOrder_Start.xdp` file, 1018
Global binding, 809
Global Finance Purchase Order forms, 983
Global Stamp option, 276
`globalApplicationDesign.pdf` file, 73
`globalApplicationRawPopulated.pdf` file, 73
`globalAttorneySpawnCalcTape.pdf` file, 603
`globalAttorneySpawnPopulated.pdf` file, 594, 614, 615
`globalAttorneySpawnRaw.pdf` document, 591, 594–595, 598, 600–602, 613, 829
`globalAttorneySummary.pdf` file, 614
`globalAttorneyTime.pdf` file, 485
`globalBlankForm.pdf` document, 452
`globalBrokerChaptersFirst.pdf` file, 191
`globalCommitteeMembership.pdf` file, 84
`globalCreditApp.pdf` document, 138, 149–150, 198
`globalEmploymentApplicationRaw.pdf` file, 184
`globalLogo.jpg` file, 371, 373
`globalLogo.tif` file, 707, 727
`globalPerformanceList.pdf` form, 573, 576, 578

`globalPerformanceReview.pdf` form, 526, 529, 542, 545, 573
`globalPicnic_responses.pdf` file, 437
`globalPicnicRawLCD.pdf` file, 636
`globalPicnicRaw.pdf` file, 407, 417, 429
`globalPicnicSummary.pdf` form, 445, 447
`globalPlan.doc` file, 727
`globalServicesPortfolio.pdf` file, 389
`globalTransferAgree.pdf` file, 393
`globalTransferAltText.pdf` file, 317–318
`globalTransferFields.pdf` form, 393, 395, 518, 520, 522–523, 531, 535, 537–538
`globalTransferFinal.pdf` document, 398
`globalTransferFundsFields.pdf` file, 312, 314
`globalTransferFundsLayers.pdf` file, 310
`globalTransferLayers.pdf` document, 710
`globalTransferTerms.pdf` file, 393
Go to a page view action, 233, 235
Grant Application folder, 649
Grant Application forms, 1039–1041
Grid command, 166
grids
    LCD, 692–694
    overview, 166
    setting up, 167–169
    snapping to, 169
Group Properties dialog box, 777
grouping
    fields, 761–763
    objects, 761–763
Guide Builder, 982–983
Guide color swatch, 167
guidelines
    aligning objects with, 760
    drawing, 166
    snapping fields to, 166
Guidelines Definitions section, 684–685
`guidelinesButton.pdf` file, 258
`guidelinesMessage.pdf` document, 258, 260

H

Hand tool
    navigating fields, 171
    pasting fields, 156, 513
    toggling views, 88
HasValue function, 947

headers
    adding to PDF Portfolios, 374–376
    adding to subforms, 888–892
Height text box, 49, 791
`Hello World` message, 518
help resources
    Acrobat, 55, 1028
    LCD
        fonts, 797
        guidelines for, 1109–1111
        Internet resources, 1111–1114
        reference manuals, 1114–1121
        RSS feeds, 1121–1124
helpClose button, 262
`helpMenu.js` file, 627
helpMessage button, 262
Hidden (Exclude from Layout) check box, 796
Hide palette option, 797
Hide radio button, 261
Hide Rulers option, 166
Hide Tape button, 603
Hide window controls box, 77–78
Hierarchy palette
    buttons for calling Instance Manager, 917
    debugging, 871
    dynamic forms, 830–831
    field properties, 865–867
    flowing forms with expanding text fields, creating, 912
    form fragments, 781–783
    JavaScripts, viewing, 1034
    objects
        dragging and dropping, 746
        nesting subforms to position, 898–899
        repositioning, 876
        selecting multiple, 756–757
        wrapping in subforms, 878
    overview, 663–666, 701
    parent/child relationships, 886
    static tables, creating, 839, 841
    XML data files, creating, 854
highlight colors, 530–531
Highlight Content option, 315
Highlight Fields button, 88, 92, 97, 172–173
Home view, 376, 381
Horizontal Placement group, 754
Horizontal Scale option, 798
Horizontal Spacing feature, 754

hosting forms
    instructions for downloading, 405–406
    overview, 21–29, 404
    site design, 405
hotelHeader subform, 1034
How To palette, 675, 701
HTML (Hyper Text Markup Language), 1082
HTTP Submit Button object, 671, 764
Hyperlinks feature, 660
Hyphenate check box, 800

I

Icon and Label State attribute, 227
Icon Placement dialog box, 258, 388
IDE (Integrated Development Environment), 1089
IDs
    Adobe, 425–427
    digital
        creating, 337–341
        custom appearance, 334–336
        overview, 321–322, 332–334
`if` statement, 520, 541
Illustrator
    designing forms with, 58
    editing objects with, 70–72
Image & Text option, 372
Image Field button, 330–331
Image Field object
    default properties, 764
    editing template files, 736
    Standard group, 670
images
    converting to text
        in Macintosh, 125–126
        in Windows, 123–124
    editing, 72
    embedded, 981, 1103
    Object Library palette, 673
    Standard Library palette, 764
    text, 296
Implicit binding, 810
Import a file from file system radio button, 95
Import a PDF Document option, 133, 657–658
Import as Layer dialog box, 393–394
Import Contact Settings dialog box, 351, 353
Import form data action, 233, 235

importing
  data from databases
    modifying form for, 1067–1070
    overview, 1064–1065
    testing exported data in original form, 1065–1066
  data into Access databases, 1061–1063
  PDF documents in LCD, 741–742
  XML data in PDF forms, 447–448
Include field names text box, 241
Include Header Row in Table check box, 843
Indents (First/By) menu, 800
Indents (Left) menu, 800
Indents (Right) menu, 800
InDesign, 44, 65
Index tab, 1115–1116
indexChange event, 945
Info palette, 668
Initial View tab
  LCD, 28
  settings, 22
  zoom levels, 544
initial views
  layout, adjusting, 76–77
  LCD, 645
  magnification, adjusting, 76–77
  overview, 75–76
  user interface options, 77–78
  window options, 77
initialize event, 945
Insert menu
  adding objects with, 750
  library groups, 751
Insert Table command, 836, 838, 843–845
Insert table dialog box, 843, 845
Insert/Table toolbar, 702
installing
  Acrobat on Windows, 634–635
  CD-ROM, 1125–1126
Instance Manager
  creating buttons for calling, 916–919
  methods, 916
  overview, 916
Integrated Development Environment (IDE), 1089
Interactive design, 1041
Interactive Elements option, 65
interactive events
  change, 945
  click, 945

enter, 945
exit, 945
mouseDown, 945
mouseEnter, 945
mouseExit, 945
mouseUp, 945
postOpen, 945
postSign, 945
preOpen, 945
preSign, 945
Interface mode, 91–92
internal forms, 45
Internal Revenue Service, 21
Internet Email application, 415–416
Internet protocol, 36
Internet resources, 1111–1114
interpolated resolution, 129
Invert Black and White Images check box, 120
Invisible Rectangle option, 383
IPmt function, 947
is after option, 444
is before option, 443
is blank option, 443
is exactly option, 444
is greater than option, 443
is less than option, 443
is not blank option, 443
is not option, 443
is option, 443
is today option, 444
is within last 30 days option, 444
is within last 7 days option, 444
is yesterday option, 444
IsoDate2Num function, 947
IsoTime2Num function, 947
Item List option, 224
Item option, 224
Item Total column, 468
Item Total field, 559, 949
ItemTotal formula, 950, 956

J

Java 2 Platform Enterprise Edition (J2EE), 1080
JavaScript Console
  copying script from, 502–503
  overview, 500
  writing script in, 500–502

JavaScript Debugger
   opening, 499–500
   overview, 963–964
   preferences, setting, 498–499
JavaScript Editor, 419
JavaScript Editor dialog box, 234, 492
JavaScript for Acrobat API Reference, 505–511
JavaScript Functions dialog box
   alert messages, 519
   calculating time, 593
   creating functions, 571–572
   document-level JavaScripts, 495
   viewer versions, assessing, 522
   zoom levels, 545
JavaScripts
   annotations
      coordinates, assessing, 548–550
      overview, 547–548
      text box comments, 550–553
   application alerts
      adding to document actions, 523–524
      application beeps, 524–525
      message alerts, creating, 518–519
      viewer types, assessing, 522–523
      viewer versions, assessing, 520–522
   application response dialog boxes
      for credit card numbers, 580–582
      for name fields, 577–580
   calculation scripts
      date stamps, 561–564
      sales tax, 556–558
      shipping charges, 559–561
      summing columns and rows, 553–556
   copying and pasting, 502–503
   custom formatting
      eliminating zeros, 564–569
      fixed response options, 569–573
      moving items between lists, 573–577
   document viewing scripts
      full screen scripts, 545–546
      navigating pages, 545
      resetting fields, 542–544
      zooming views, 544–545
   editors, 504–505
   field behaviors
      check boxes, 536–539
      hiding fields, 525–529

      highlight colors, 530–531
      locking fields, 529–530
      radio buttons, 536–537
      showing fields, 525–529
      text colors, 531–536
   fields
      `addField` object, 594–597
      calculating time, 591–594
      calculating using names from spawned pages,
         588–591
      deleting, 598
      overview, 586–587
      spawned, 588
   filing, 512–516
   finding, 494
      bookmarks, 494
      document actions, 496
      document-level scripts, 495
      field scripts, 491–494
      overview, 490–491
      page actions, 495–496
      page templates, 496–498
   links, 1113
   manuals
      `101AcroFormsTips_A9.pdf` document, 511
      JavaScript for Acrobat API reference, 505–511
   menus
      functions, adding to, 624–626
      overview, 623–624
      URLs, adding to, 627–628
   methods with comparable FormCalc functions, 968–969
   online services
      non-subscription, 511–512
      subscription, 512
   optional content groups, 582–584
   overview, 31, 489, 517, 585
   printing forms
      documents, 541
      eliminating fields from print, 541–542
      pages, 541
   searching for, 505
   secondary forms
      overview, 613–614
      sending data to summary forms, 615–617
      setting up, 614–615
      summarizing data, 617–623

JavaScripts (*continued*)
   submission scripts
      submitting form data, 540
      submitting forms, 539–540
   Submit Form button, 420–421
   summary, 628
   templates
      appending pages to documents, 600–602
      creating, 599–600
      overlaying on form pages, 602–603
      overview, 598
      scanned forms, 603–613
   writing LCD scripts with, 955–961
JavaScripts folder, 626
JetForm, 632
johnDoe-Solid.pdf file, 324
johnDoeTrans.png file
   creating digital IDs, 335
   wet signatures
      with Acrobat Audience, 327
      using LCD, 329
.js files, 625, 627
Justification menu, 799

K

Keep Drawing feature, 702, 748–749, 751
Keep Tool Selected feature, 748
Keep with Next check box, 795
key algorithm, 339
Keyboard method, 758–759
keyboard shortcuts
   for Button tool, 93, 142
   for Form Properties dialog box, 704
   LCD, 688–689
   for navigating between fields, 172

L

Label attribute, 228
labels, 141
Language drop-down list, 918, 931, 953
Layer Options drop-down menu, 398
Layer Properties dialog box, 398
layers
   adding, 393–394
   adjusting, 130
   default states, 397–399

LCD and, 644
   locking, 398–399
   overview, 391–393
   visibility of, 395–397
Layers panel
   eye icon, 309–310
   Trash icon, 326
Layout attribute, 227
Layout Menu method, 758
Layout palette
   captions, editing, 791–792
   expanding text fields
      comments pages with, 908
      flowing forms with, 913
   height of field setting, 906
   objects
      coordinates of, 879
      in flowed subforms, 881
      numeric and date field, 717
   Ordered By fields, changing field types for, 736
   overview, 675–676
   XML data files, creating, 854
layout programs, 57
Layout toolbar
   alignment options, 758, 760, 840
   overview, 690
   tools, adding to, 702
layout:ready event, 945
lblReferenceSection object, 889
LCD (Adobe LiveCycle Designer)
   accessibility, 296
   advantages of, 643–644
   Custom Library objects
      adding, 773–774
      groups of, 771–773
      managing, 774–775
      sharing, 775–778
   deploying forms
      distribution, 990–991
      preparing for, 971–973
      security, 986–990
   designing forms
      based on templates, 732–741
      from blank pages, 698–731
      importing PDF documents, 741–742
      overview, 697–698
   dynamic forms, 640–642, 829

enabling forms, 278
environment
    fields palettes, 669–679
    New Form Assistant, 657–660
    overview, 655–656
    tabs, 679–681
    welcome window, 656–657
    workspace, 661–669, 681–694
fields
    adding to master pages, 784–785
    copying, 749–750
    drawing, 748–749
    duplicating, 752–753
    grouping, 761–763
    overview, 743–744
    stamping, 746–748
form fragments
    creating, 778–780
    groups of, 780
    updating, 783
    using, 780–783
help resources
    guidelines for, 1109–1111
    Internet resources, 1111–1114
    reference manuals, 1114–1121
    RSS feeds, 1121–1124
installed files
    sample files, 648–652
    scripting references, 652–653
launching, 83
limitations of, 644–645
Object Editor, 785–786
Object Library palette
    Barcodes Group, 769–771
    Custom Group, 768–769
    default settings, 763–771
    My Favorites group, 767–768
    object types, 763–766
    Standard Group, 766–767
objects
    adding to master pages, 784–785
    aligning, 757–760
    Copy Multiple option, 753–755
    copying, 749–750
    distributing, 760–761
    dragging and dropping, 744–746
    drawing, 748–749
    duplicating, 752–753
    grouping, 761–763
    Insert menu, 750
    overview, 670–671, 673–674, 743–744
    selecting multiple, 755–757
    stamping, 746–748
    Tools toolbar, 750–751
versus OpenOffice.org Writer, 56
overview, 17–18, 639–640, 1093–1094
rendering
    form guides, 982–986
    HTML forms, 981–982
sample forms
    copying, 1030
    Dunning Notice, 1030–1033
    E-ticket, 1033–1035
    FormGuide, 1035–1039
    Grant Application, 1039–1041
    online, 1053–1054
    overview, 1029–1030
    Purchase Order, 1041–1043
    Scripting, 1043–1047
    SubformSet, 1047–1049
    Tax Receipt, 1049–1053
saving forms
    dynamic, 978–979
    overview, 974–976
    setting target version, 979–980
    static, 977–978
    XDP, 981
scanning forms for, 128, 133–134
scripts
    advantages of, 928–929
    debugging, 961–965
    help resources, 965–967
    versus other languages, 968–969
    overview, 927
    preferences, 932–934
    Script Editor, 930–932
    writing, 934–961
spawning pages, 269
system requirements, 642–643
tutorials, 1027–1029
using with Acrobat
    distributing XML forms, 648
    editing XML forms, 646–647
    enabling XML forms, 647–648
    overview, 645

LCD (Adobe LiveCycle Designer) *(continued)*
  using on Macintosh
    development history of, 632–633
    editing XML files, 636–638
    overview, 631–632
    setting up, 633–635
  versions of, 662
LCES (Adobe LiveCycle Enterprise Suite)
  clients, 1081–1082
  components of
    content services, 1087–1088
    data capture, 1086
    document output, 1087
    information assurance, 1086–1087
    process management, 1087
  development tools
    Flex Builder, 1094
    LCD, 1093–1094
    Workbench, 1088–1093
  form deployment, 644
  interface
    To Do list, 1098–1099
    Messages link, 1102
    overview, 1094–1095
    Preferences page, 1099–1101
    Start Process icon, 1095–1098
    Tracking page, 1099
  LCES Foundation
    administration tools, 1083–1084
    Central repository, 1084–1085
    overview, 1082
    service container, 1083
    services, 1083
  overview, 1071, 1080
  process
    electronic, 1073
    justifying, 1073–1074
    paper, 1072
    solution, 1074–1080
  scripting, 652
  server deployment
    file type considerations, 1105–1106
    overview, 1102–1104
    scripting considerations, 1104–1105
    server-required objects, 1106
  versions of, 662

LCES Foundation
  administration tools, 1083–1084
  Central repository, 1084–1085
  overview, 1082
  service container, 1083
  services, 1083
LCRE (Adobe LiveCycle Reader Extensions Server),
    267, 270, 1086
leaveRequestEnabled.pdf file, 324
leaveRequestLCDenabled.pdf file, 329
leaveRequest.pdf file, 327, 329, 359
leaveRequestSignatures.pdf file, 348, 350
leaveSignaturesLock.pdf file, 341, 343, 345
leaveSignaturesNoLock.pdf file, 343
Left function, 948
legacy files
  aggregating data from, 452–454
  compiling data from, 451–454
Len function, 948
Less Discount field, 559
Letter Spacing option, 798
Levels dialog box, 130
Library folder, 626
Library Group menu, 777
Library palette
  help guidelines, 1110
  overview, 669–674
  working with Table Data, 851–852
  workspace and, 662
license agreement, 1125
licensing, 68, 268–269
Limit Length check box, 795
Limit Length to Visible Area check box, 795
Limit of [ ] characters option, 218
Limited Execute Menu Items feature, 31
Line Color option, 243
Line object
  Object Library palette, 674
  Standard Library palette, 764, 804
line shapes, 804
Line Spacing menu, 800
Line Style drop-down menu, 803
Line Style option, 244
Line Thickness option, 244
LineTotal calculation, 944
link attribute, 383

Link Properties dialog box, 494
Link tool, 381–382
Link Type drop-down menu, 383
links, 491, 494
Liquid XML Studio 2008, 1000
List Box Properties dialog box, 146
List Box Properties Options tab, 576
List Box tool, 141, 146
list boxes
    default properties, 764
    field detection, 183
    Object Library palette, 673
    overview, 145–146
    properties, setting, 222–226, 245
    tab options, 210
List Field Names command, 624
List view icon, 440
lists, moving items between, 573–577
LiveCycle Barcoded Forms ES, 148, 1086
LiveCycle Business Activity Monitoring ES, 1087
LiveCycle Content Services ES, 1088
LiveCycle Data Services ES, 1086
LiveCycle Designer (LCD)
    accessibility, 296
    advantages of, 643–644
    Custom Library objects
        adding, 773–774
        groups of, 771–773
        managing, 774–775
        sharing, 775–778
    deploying forms
        distribution, 990–991
        preparing for, 971–973
        security, 986–990
    designing forms
        based on templates, 732–741
        from blank pages, 698–731
        importing PDF documents, 741–742
        overview, 697–698
    dynamic forms, 640–642, 829
    enabling forms, 278
    environment
        fields palettes, 669–679
        New Form Assistant, 657–660
        overview, 655–656
        tabs, 679–681
        welcome window, 656–657
        workspace, 661–669, 681–694

fields
    adding to master pages, 784–785
    copying, 749–750
    drawing, 748–749
    duplicating, 752–753
    grouping, 761–763
    overview, 743–744
    stamping, 746–748
form fragments
    creating, 778–780
    groups of, 780
    updating, 783
    using, 780–783
help resources
    guidelines for, 1109–1111
    Internet resources, 1111–1114
    reference manuals, 1114–1121
    RSS feeds, 1121–1124
installed files
    sample files, 648–652
    scripting references, 652–653
launching, 83
limitations of, 644–645
Object Editor, 785–786
Object Library palette
    Barcodes Group, 769–771
    Custom Group, 768–769
    default settings, 763–771
    My Favorites group, 767–768
    object types, 763–766
    Standard Group, 766–767
objects
    adding to master pages, 784–785
    aligning, 757–760
    Copy Multiple option, 753–755
    copying, 749–750
    distributing, 760–761
    dragging and dropping, 744–746
    drawing, 748–749
    duplicating, 752–753
    grouping, 761–763
    Insert menu, 750
    overview, 670–671, 673–674, 743–744
    selecting multiple, 755–757
    stamping, 746–748
    Tools toolbar, 750–751
versus OpenOffice.org Writer, 56
overview, 17–18, 639–640, 1093–1094

LiveCycle Designer (LCD) *(continued)*
  rendering
    form guides, 982–986
    HTML forms, 981–982
  sample forms
    copying, 1030
    Dunning Notice, 1030–1033
    E-ticket, 1033–1035
    FormGuide, 1035–1039
    Grant Application, 1039–1041
    online, 1053–1054
    overview, 1029–1030
    Purchase Order, 1041–1043
    Scripting, 1043–1047
    SubformSet, 1047–1049
    Tax Receipt, 1049–1053
  saving forms
    dynamic, 978–979
    overview, 974–976
    setting target version, 979–980
    static, 977–978
    XDP, 981
  scanning forms for, 128, 133–134
  scripts
    advantages of, 928–929
    debugging, 961–965
    help resources, 965–967
    versus other languages, 968–969
    overview, 927
    preferences, 932–934
    Script Editor, 930–932
    writing, 934–961
  spawning pages, 269
  system requirements, 642–643
  tutorials, 1027–1029
  using with Acrobat
    distributing XML forms, 648
    editing XML forms, 646–647
    enabling XML forms, 647–648
    overview, 645
  using on Macintosh
    development history of, 632–633
    editing XML files, 636–638
    overview, 631–632
    setting up, 633–635
  versions of, 662
LiveCycle Designer Scripting Reference, 967, 1113
LiveCycle Digital Signatures ES, 1087

LiveCycle Enterprise Suite (LCES)
  clients, 1081–1082
  components of
    content services, 1087–1088
    data capture, 1086
    document output, 1087
    information assurance, 1086–1087
    process management, 1087
  development tools
    Flex Builder, 1094
    LCD, 1093–1094
    Workbench, 1088–1093
  form deployment, 644
  interface
    To Do list, 1098–1099
    Messages link, 1102
    overview, 1094–1095
    Preferences page, 1099–1101
    Start Process icon, 1095–1098
    Tracking page, 1099
  LCES Foundation
    administration tools, 1083–1084
    Central repository, 1084–1085
    overview, 1082
    service container, 1083
    services, 1083
  overview, 1071, 1080
  process
    electronic, 1073
    justifying, 1073–1074
    paper, 1072
    solution, 1074–1080
  scripting, 652
  server deployment
    file type considerations, 1105–1106
    overview, 1102–1104
    scripting considerations, 1104–1105
    server-required objects, 1106
  versions of, 662
LiveCycle Designer ES Scripting Errors guide, 1120
LiveCycle Designer Help Guide, 1115–1120
LiveCycle ES Connectors for ECM, 1088
LiveCycle ES Developer Connection, 1114
LiveCycle ES Workspace, 1074
LiveCycle Form Design Perspective, 1092–1093
LiveCycle Forms ES, 1086
LiveCycle Output ES, 1087
LiveCycle PDF Generator 3D ES, 1087

LiveCycle PDF Generator ES, 1087
LiveCycle Process Design Perspective, 1093
LiveCycle Process Management ES, 1087
LiveCycle Production Print ES, 1087
LiveCycle Reader Extensions Server (LCRE), 267, 270, 1086
LiveCycle Rights Management ES, 359, 1086
LiveCycle Workbench ES, 1088–1093
loaded cursors, 107
LocalDateFmt function, 947
Locale check box, 797
LocalTimeFmt function, 947
Location field, 483
Lock Fields After Signing check box, 721
Lock Fields button, 686
Lock Static Objects button, 687
Lock Static Text Box button, 687
Lock Text button, 686
Locked check box, 158, 212
locking
    fields, 342–345, 529–530
    layers, 398–399
Log tab, 931
logging into Acrobat.com
    adding information to Preferences dialog box, 426–427
    creating Adobe IDs, 425–426
Logo & Structured Text style, 374, 375
Lower function, 948
LowerSection subform, 897–898
Ltrim function, 948

M

MacOS folder, 626
Magic Wand tool, 326
magnification, zoom, 76–77
Magnification tool, 86
MainSubform field, 942
Make Searchable (Run OCR) box, 125, 129
Manage Custom Sizes option, 50
Manage Embedded Index dialog box, 1118–1119
Manage Form Data command, 90, 92
Manage Trusted Identities dialog box, 350, 353
Management options, 438–439
Managing Security Policies dialog box, 360, 362
Managing Security Policies wizard, 360–361
MAPI (Messaging Application Programming Interface)
    checking for compliance, 412
    receiving and filling in distributed forms, 416

Margins drop-down menu, 792
Mark as read-only option, 240
master pages
    fields, adding to, 784–785
    objects, adding to, 784–785
    setting up, 707–710
Master Pages tab
    comments pages, creating with expanding text fields, 909
    design grid, 692
    drawing aids, 683–684
    elements, adding in, 847
    E-ticket form, 1033
    Layout Editor, 679
    master pages
        designing, 707
        viewing items, 1031–1032
    turning on, 680
Math.abs method, 968
Math.ceil method, 968
Math.floor method, 968
Math.max method, 968
Math.min method, 968
Math.round method, 968
Max function, 946
MediaBox, 55
Menu bar, 85
Merge As Caption command, 724
Merge Data into Spreadsheet command, 613
Merge Files into Spreadsheet command, 455
mergedFiles.pdf document, 605
merging data into spreadsheets, 11–12
message alerts, 518–519
Message Bar, 88
Messages link, 1102
Messaging Application Programming Interface (MAPI)
    checking for compliance, 412
    receiving and filling in distributed forms, 416
methods
    Instance Manager
        Add, 916
        Move, 916
        Remove, 916
        Set, 916
    JavaScript
        % (modulo) operator, 968
        Date.getDate, 968
        Date.getTime, 969
        Math.abs, 968

methods (*continued*)
    JavaScript (*continued*)
        Math.ceil, 968
        Math.floor, 968
        Math.max, 968
        Math.min, 968
        Math.round, 968
        modulo (%) operator, 968
        Number.toString, 968
        String, 968
        String.concat, 968
        String.length, 968
        String.replace, 968
        String.search, 968–969
        String.substring, 968–969
        String.toLowerCase, 968
        String.toUpperCase, 969
    selection
        Ctrl + A, 757
        Ctrl + Arrow Key, 757
        Ctrl + Click, 757
        Shift + Arrow Key, 757
        Shift + Click, 757
Microsoft Excel
    aggregating form data, 11
    designing forms with, 43, 54–55, 730–731
    exporting tables to, 200–201
    viewing data in, 12
Microsoft Office, 3, 42
Microsoft PowerPoint, 43, 55–56
Microsoft Windows Notepad, 58
Microsoft Windows WordPad, 58
Microsoft Word
    converting documents to PDF files, 95–99
    converting to LCD forms, 725–730
    design elements, 45–47
    exporting tables to
        with Copy as Table option, 203
        with Export command, 202–203
    form design and, 43
    overview, 44–45
    page sizes
        Macintosh, 50
        overview, 47–48
        Windows, 48–50
    preparing forms for print
        cropping, 51–54
        overview, 50–51
        trim marks, adding, 51–54
    setting up forms, 725

Min function, 946
mini Properties window, 139
Mod function, 946
modulo (%) operator method, 968
More option, 244
More Page Options option, 49
More Tools window, 325
Mouse Triggers, 232, 560, 581
Mouse Up text, 108
mouseDown event, 945
mouseEnter event, 945
mouseExit event, 945
mouseUp event, 945
Move method, 916
Move Object To option, 775
moving
    fields, 157–158
    items between lists, 573–577
msg statement, 522
Multi-line text field, 218
Multimedia operation action, 233, 235
Multiple selection option, 224
My Favorites group
    creating custom library objects, 771
    overview, 643, 767–768
My Favorites Library palette
    adding Custom Library Group, 715–716
    creating static tables, 845
My Files icon, 428
Myriad Pro font, 766, 771

N

Name Field text, 140
Name property, 211
Name Sequence dialog box, 282, 287, 610
Name text box, 153
naming conventions
    for fields, 38, 153
    for files, 842
naming fields
    application response dialog boxes for, 577–580
    automatically, 151
    conventions for, 38, 153
    editing, 151–154
    hierarchical names, 154–155
    overview, 150
    for SFN, 481
    text, 246–248

navigating
    LCD welcome window, 656–657
    pages, 545
    in PDF Portfolios
        buttons for, adding, 385–389
        navigation links, adding, 382–385
        preview options, 381–382
navigation links, 296, 382–385
Navigation pane
    accessibility, checking, 298–299
    Accessibility Report, 301–302, 304
    alternate text, adding to objects, 314
    reading order, setting, 313
    Tags panel, 314–315, 316
Navigation tab, 76
nested elements, 997
nesting subforms, 894–901
network servers, 422–424
New Assistant Form wizard, 83
New Collection button, 509
New Data Connection dialog box
    data connections, choosing, 1002
    field objects, adding from data files, 856–857
New Data Connection option
    binding data
        setting up for importing and exporting, 1067
        to XML sample files, 1006
    Data View palette, 1002
New dialog box, 659–660
New Document toolbar, 513
New Document window, 48
New drop-down menu, 704
New Form Assistant wizard
    default, 700
    Do Not Use Assistant option, 698–699
    Excel, 730
    forms
        converting Word to LCD, 725
        creating, 657–660, 733–735
        scanning, 133
    importing PDF documents, 742
    overview, 705–706
    settings, 658
    static tables, creating, 837
New Form button, 656
New Object Library group, 772
New Page button
    deleting fields, 598
    designing forms, 586

New Security Policy wizard, 360–361
New Sequence button, 610
New tool, 744, 813
New Window view, 381–382
Next Page tool, 86
No Line option, 244
None option
    Binding tab, 810
    Format tab, 459
    Select format category menu, 236
Normal binding
    compared to Explicit and Implicit, 810
    overview, 808–809
Notepad, 58
Nothing happens when signed option, 240
NPV function, 947
Null function, 948
null values
    adding to fields, 564–566
    replacing zeros with, 566–569
Num Pad Enter key
    application alert dialog boxes, 521
    functions, adding to menus, 624
    JavaScript Console, 500, 502, 550
    renaming fields, 152
Num2Date function, 947
Num2GMTime function, 947
Num2Time function, 947
Number attending field, 100
Number option
    Format tab, 459
    Select format category menu, 236–237
Number.toString method, 968
Numeric Field object, 673, 717, 764

O

Object Editor, 785–786
Object Library palette
    Barcodes Group, 643, 769–771
    buttons for calling Instance Manager, 916
    Custom Group, 643, 768–769
    default settings, 763–771
    drag and drop technique, 744–745
    list boxes, 673
    My Favorites group, 643, 767–768
    objects
        drawing, 768
        Image, 673

Object Library palette *(continued)*
  objects *(continued)*
    Line, 674
    Rectangle, 674
    stamping, 746
    static, 673–674
    types of, 763–766
  organizing palettes, 701
  overview, 670–673
  Palette menu button, 772
  preparing forms for wet signatures, 329
  Standard Group, 643, 766–767
  XML data files, creating, 854
Object palette
  appearance properties, changing, 790, 793
  binding fields to data elements, 1024
  display patterns, 813
  help guidelines, 1110
  master pages, designing, 708
  organizing palettes, 701
  overview, 676–677
  pagination options, setting, 882
  properties, 677
  signature settings, 988
  strokes and fills, editing, 801
  subform properties, setting, 878
  Subform tab, 879
Object Scripting Reference, 967
objects. *See also* fields
  adding
    to forms, 724
    with Insert menu, 750
    to master pages, 784–785
  editing, 70–72
  LCD
    adding to master pages, 784–785
    aligning, 757–760
    Copy Multiple option, 753–755
    copying, 749–750
    distributing, 760–761
    dragging and dropping, 744–746
    drawing, 748–749
    duplicating, 752–753
    grouping, 761–763
    Insert menu, 750
    overview, 670–671, 673–674, 743–744
    selecting multiple, 755–757

    stamping, 746–748
    Tools toolbar, 750–751
  multiple, selecting, 755–757
  stamping, 746–748
  text, 296
Objects layer, 309
OCR (Optical Character Recognition)
  batch sequence preset for, 286–287
  converting image files to text
    in Macintosh, 125–126
    in Windows, 123–124
  features of, 121–123
  overview, 120–121, 129
  recognizing text in multiple files, 126–128
  workflow for authoring accessible PDF forms, 296
ODBC Database Administrator System DSN tab, 1008
ODBC Microsoft Access Setup dialog box, 1009
Office application, 3, 42
OLEDB Connection window, 1013–1014
OLEDB Data radio button, 1012
OLEDB databases, 1007–1015
Omit Border around Page Breaks option, 794
On Blur option, 396
On Focus Mouse Trigger, 581
One Full Page tool, 86–87
Oneof function, 947
online sample forms, 1053–1054
Open a file action, 233, 235
Open a Web link action, 233, 235
Open dialog box, 327
Open in Full Screen mode option, 77
Open Original Form option, 435
Open Table in Spreadsheet command, 200, 203
Open tool, Toolbar Well, 279
openDoc ( ) object, 616
OpenOffice.org Writer, 56, 64
Optical Character Recognition (OCR)
  batch sequence preset for, 286–287
  converting image files to text
    in Macintosh, 125–126
    in Windows, 123–124
  features of, 121–123
  overview, 120–121, 129
  recognizing text in multiple files, 126–128
  workflow for authoring accessible PDF forms, 296
optical resolution, 129
Optimize Scanned PDF item, 286–287

Options dialog box, 659, 939
Options drop-down menu, 310
Options Properties dialog box, 193
Options tab
    barcode fields, 229–230
    buttons, 226–229, 387
    check boxes, 219–222, 256–257
    combo boxes, 222–226
    font attributes, 215
    list boxes, 222–226
    radio buttons, 209, 219–222
    text fields, 217–219
Order Form Fields item, 287
Order panel
    accessibility
        checking, 298–299
        designing forms for, 306
    reading order, setting, 313
    tags, adding to untagged PDF documents, 304
Order Tabs by Column option, 178
Order Tabs by Row option, 178
Order Tabs Manually option, 178
Organizer tool, 508, 510, 514
organizing fields
    aligning, 158–159
    attribute defaults, setting, 159–160
    copying, 156
    deleting, 158
    moving, 157–158
    overview, 155
    pasting, 156
    placing multiple, 156–157
    sizing, 159
Orientation property, 212
oSessScroreFld variable, 619
Other Accessibility Options option, 294
Other tab, 733
output format, 644
Output Options dialog box
    batch sequences, creating, 283, 611
    making choices in, 128
    PDF Optimizer, 284
    splitting files, 613
Overall Rating field, 623
overflow leaders, 888–892
overflow trailers, 888–892
Override Page Display option, 294

P

packing slip form, 912
Page & Ruler Units option, 167
page actions, 233, 491, 495–496
Page Layout drop-down menu, 76–77
Page Layout tab, 48
Page panel, 76
Page Properties dialog box, 495
Page Setup dialog box, 48, 50
Page Size drop-down menu, 705
page size, in Microsoft Word
    Macintosh, 50
    overview, 47–48
    Windows, 48–50
Page templates
    JavaScript, 496–498
    LCD, 645
Page Templates dialog box
    forms for spawning pages, 589
    PDF documents, 497
    Viewer mode, 599
Pages panel
    converting files to PDF using Acrobat, 64
    pages
        adding to formulas document, 514
        replacing, 73–74
    tab order, setting, 177
Pages tab, 495
pagination, 882–887
Pagination Tab
    buttons for calling Instance Manager, 919
    Object palette, 891–892
Palette menu button, 772
palette wells, 662–663, 687
palettes
    Accessibility, 678–679
    Border, 677–678, 843–844
    Data View
        data connections, setting, 809–810, 1002–1007,
            1015–1016, 1019
        field data bindings, setting, 1022, 1024
        overview, 667–668
        table data, 851–852, 856
        testing exported database data, 1066
    Font
        embedding fonts, 802
        font attributes, changing, 797–798

palettes *(continued)*
  Font *(continued)*
    overview, 682–683, 701
    substituting fonts, 802
  Fragment Library, 674–675, 778–780
  Hierarchy
    buttons for calling Instance Manager, 917
    debugging, 871
    dragging and dropping objects, 746
    dynamic forms, 830–831
    field properties, 865–867
    flowing forms with expanding text fields, 912
    form fragments, 781–783
    JavaScripts, viewing, 1034
    nesting subforms to position objects, 898–899
    overview, 663–666, 701
    parent/child relationships, 886
    repositioning objects, 876
    selecting multiple objects in, 756–757
    static tables, creating, 839, 841
    wrapping objects in subforms, 878
    XML data files, creating, 854
  How To, 675, 701
  Info, 668
  Layout
    captions, editing, 791–792
    comments pages with expanding text fields, 908
    flowed subforms, 881
    flowing forms with expanding text fields, 913
    height of field setting, 906
    numeric and date field objects, 717
    object coordinates, 879
    Ordered By fields, changing field types for, 736
    overview, 675–676
    XML data files, creating, 854
  Library
    help guidelines, 1110
    overview, 669–674
    table data, 851–852
    workspace, 662
  Object
    appearance properties, 790, 793
    binding fields to data elements, 1024
    display patterns, 813
    help guidelines, 1110
    master pages, designing, 708
    organizing palettes, 701
    overview, 676–677

    pagination options, setting, 882
    properties, 677
    signature settings, 988
    strokes and fills, editing, 801
    subform properties, setting, 878
    Subform tab, 879
  Object Library
    Barcodes Group, 643, 769–771
    buttons for calling Instance Manager, 916
    Custom Group, 643, 768–769
    default settings, 763–771
    drag and drop technique, 744–745
    drawing fields and objects, 768
    Image object, 673
    Line object, 674
    list boxes, 673
    My Favorites group, 643, 767–768
    object types, 763–766
    organizing palettes, 701
    overview, 670–673
    Palette menu button, 772
    Rectangle object, 674
    stamping fields and objects, 746
    Standard Group, 643, 766–767
    static object, 673–674
    wet signatures, preparing forms for, 329
    XML data files, creating, 854
  overview, 662–663
  Paragraph
    embedding and substituting fonts, 802
    opening, 682–683
    organizing palettes, 701
    paragraph attributes, setting, 799
  PDF Structure, 668
  Tab Order, 668, 817–819
  tabs, 662–663
  views
    keyboard shortcuts, 688–689
    overview, 687
    tools and toolbars, 689–691
Paper Capture Multiple Files dialog box, 126, 127
Paper Forms Barcode object, Standard Library palette, 764, 770
paper forms design
  check boxes, 35
  flow of, 36
  fonts, 35
  grouping form elements, 35

language, 35
positioning, 35
radio buttons, 35
Reset buttons, 36
signatures, 36
Submit buttons, 36
white space, 35
PaperCapture.acroplugin folder, 115
paperless office, 15
paragraph attributes, 799–801
Paragraph palette
embedding and substituting fonts, 802
opening, 682–683
organizing palettes, 701
paragraph attributes, setting, 799
Paragraph toolbar, 717
Parallels Desktop, 634
parent element, 997
Parker, Thom, 511–512
Parse function, 948
Password Field object, 673, 765
Password option, 218
Password Security – Settings dialog box, 356–357, 361
Password text box, 339
passwords
overview, 354
security policies, 359–364
settings options, 355–359
Paste Clipboard Image as Stamp tool, 325
pasting
fields, 156
JavaScript into button actions, 502–503
non-table data, 197–199
patterns
arbitrary masks, 816–817
custom, 814
Display Patterns, 812–814
validation, 814–816
Patterns dialog box, 812–813
Patterns – <field type> dialog box, 812
Patterns – Numeric Field dialog box, 717
Patterns – Text Field dialog box, 814, 816
Patterns check box, 795
PDF (Portable Document Format)
converting files to
with Acrobat, 62–64
with Distiller, 65–67
exporting, 64–65

with PDFMaker, 59–61
scanned forms, 128–134
with wizards, 95–99
creating forms from, 99
documents
author-created on CD-ROM, 1126–1127
converting files to, 62–64
importing into LCD, 741–742
overview, 3–4
special features, adding to, 10
exporting files to, 64–65
fillable forms, 20–21
LCD, 1093
PDFMaker, 59–61, 99
scanned paper forms, 18
security, 986
static forms, 18–20
tagged files
checking status of, 297–302
creating tags, 302–305
PDF drop-down menu, 66
PDF From File menu command, 124
PDF Generator 3D ES, 1087
PDF Generator ES, 1087
PDF Layers
converting layers to, 65
exporting support, 308–309, 395
layered documents, creating, 391–392
PDF Optimizer, 109, 284–286
PDF Output Style pull-down menu, 122, 124
PDF Packages, 280, 645
PDF Portfolio document pane, 439
PDF Portfolio interface, 369
PDF Portfolio toolbar, 440
PDF Portfolios
creating
headers, adding, 374–376
overview, 368–371
welcome pages, adding, 371–373
enabling forms, 271, 280–281, 390
File Details view
columns, adding, 378–381
overview, 376–378
navigating in
buttons for, adding, 385–389
navigation links, adding, 382–385
preview options, 381–382

PDF Portfolios (*continued*)
    overview, 367
    submitting forms from, 390
    tools, 376
PDF Preview button, 870
PDF Security tab, 987
PDF Structure palette, 668
PDFMaker
    converting files to PDF using
        in Macintosh, 61
        in Windows, 59–60
    creating forms from PDF files, 99
Percentage option, 237
Personnel field, 483
Perspectives view, 1092
Phone Number field, 768, 815–816
Photoshop
    custom colors, 533
    editing
        images, 72
        scanned forms, 114
        scanned signatures, 323–324, 326
    plug-ins, 114–115
    stamps, using images as, 277
Photoshop Acquire plug-ins, 114–115
Photoshop Color Picker dialog box, 533
Photoshop Elements
    custom colors, 533
    editing
        images, 72
        scanned forms, 129
    plug-ins, 114–115
Pi font, 216
Pick button
    barcode properties, 241
    calculations formulas, 250, 461
picture pattern, 1041
Place Below radio button, 840
Place Multiple Fields command
    columns, adding, 191
    designing forms, 467
    eliminating zeros, 567
    field names, 475
    formatting fields in tables, 247–248
    JavaScript and, 556
    multiple copies of fields, creating, 161
    organizing fields, 156

populating tables, 842
preparing check boxes for averaging data, 472–473
radio buttons and check boxes, 193
time calculations, 483
Planet PDF Web site, 512
Play a sound action, 234
Plug-ins folder, 115
Pmt function, 947
PNG images, 327
point size, determining, 215
Portable Document Format (PDF)
    converting files to
        with Acrobat, 62–64
        with Distiller, 65–67
        exporting, 64–65
        with PDFMaker, 59–61
        scanned forms, 128–134
        with wizards, 95–99
    creating forms from, 99
    documents
        author-created on CD-ROM, 1126–1127
        converting files to, 62–64
        importing into LCD, 741–742
        overview, 3–4
        special features, adding to, 10
    exporting files to, 64–65
    fillable forms, 20–21
    LCD, 1093
    PDFMaker, 59–61, 99
    scanned paper forms, 18
    security, 986
    static forms, 18–20
    tagged files
        checking status of, 297–302
        creating tags, 302–305
Portfolio Editing mode, 374
POSchema.xsd file, 1003
positioned content areas, 879–882
Post function, 949
postOpen event, 945
PostScript files
    converting to PDF, 66–67
    printing, 66
postSign event, 945
powerAttorney.pdf file, 384
PowerPoint, 43, 55–56
PPmt function, 947

Preferences category, Ribbon, 59
Preferences dialog box
    accessibility preferences, setting, 293
    Acrobat.com, 426–427
    editing fields in Viewer mode, 93
    file types supported by Acrobat for conversion to PDF, 62
    RSS feeds, adding to Tracker, 1121
    viewing locations, 424
    writing and executing scripts in JavaScript Console, 500
Preferences page, 1099–1101
Preflight window, 393
preOpen event, 945
Presence check box, 796
Presence drop-down menu, 796
Presenter, 30
Presets pull-down menu, 118
preSign event, 945
Preview PDF tab
    calculating line total, 949
    checking forms, 1069
    Dunning Notice forms, 650
    editing template files, 740
    expanding text fields
        comments pages with, 909
        flowing forms with, 912
    JavaScript Debugger, 963
    Layout Editor, 679
    overview, 681
    testing scripts, 950–951, 954
Preview Tab
    binding to data fields, 1033
    dynamic forms, 892–893
    exported database XML files, attaching to LCD forms, 1065
    sample data files, changing, 651
    viewing Preview panel, 1037
Preview tool, 86, 381
Preview Type drop-down menu, 869
previewing
    subforms, 892–894
    XML data, 919–924
Previous Page tool, 86
Print Button object, 670, 765
Print command, 61
Print dialog box, 61, 66, 541
Print Production tool, 51, 55
Print tool, 1118

Print Topics dialog box, 1118
printing
    JavaScripts for
        documents, 541
        eliminating fields from print, 541–542
        pages, 541
    PostScript files, 66
    Word
        cropping, 51–54
        overview, 50–51
        trim marks, adding, 51–54
Printing Allowed option, 358
Printing Allowed setting, Designer, 987
process card, 1097
Process Design Perspective, 1093
process events
    calculate, 944
    form:ready, 945
    indexChange, 945
    initialize, 945
    layout:ready, 945
    validate, 945
Process Management ES, 1087
Process Management workflow, 1106
Processes view, 1089
Production Print ES, 1087
`productOrder.pdf` form, 549, 559, 562
Program Files directory, 506
Properties bar, 31, 243–244
Properties dialog box
    dropping fields on form, 139
    editing field names in, 153–154
    properties, setting, 99
    Select Object tool, 89
Properties mini window, 386
Properties window
    default views of, 208–209
    overview, 207–208
    tabs
        Actions, 230–235
        Appearance, 213–216
        Calculate, 239
        Format, 236–238
        General properties, 211–213
        Options, 217–230
        overview, 209–210
        Selection Change, 240

Properties window (*continued*)
   tabs (*continued*)
      Signed, 240–241
      Validate, 238
      Value, 241–243
Protected option, 807
public key certificate, 359
Purchase Order folder, 649, 1043
Purchase Order form
   designs in, 1041–1043
   FormGuide folder, 1035
   with static layout, 895
Purchase Order Requisition form, 467, 469
Purchase.mdb file, 1012
PurchaseOrder_Start.xdp form, 896
PurchaseOrderbeforeFlowed.xdp file, 899
PurchaseOrderFC.pdf file, 928
PurchaseOrderFlowed.xdp file, 902
PurchaseOrderJS.pdf file, 955
purchaseOrder.pdf file, 161
purchaseOrder.pdf form, 553, 558, 567
purchaseOrderSimpleCalc.pdf form, 468–470, 471
Put function, 949
PV function, 947

Q

QuarkXPress, 44, 64, 395
Quick Access to Forms feature, 31
Quick Check menu command, 298
Quick Start Tutorials, 659, 1027–1028
QuickBooks, 90, 92
QuickLook, 64

R

radio button fields
   adding
      to blank forms, 712
      to tables, 194–197
   automatic field detection, 183, 186–187
   averaging data with, 464–466
   behaviors, 536–537
   BFMA standards, 35
   fonts, 47, 99
   Library palette, 673
   multiple fields, editing properties, 245
   overview, 144–145

properties
   default, 765
   setting, 219–222
  tab options, 210
Radio Button Style option, 219
Radio Button tool, 186, 221
Radio Group Name option, 145, 186
Radio Group Name pull-down menu, 145
random access memory (RAM), 786
Rate function, 947
.rawValue property, 941
Read Only check box, 103, 212, 563
Read Only option, 807
Read Out Loud section, 318–319
Reader
   batch sequences
      creating, 282–283
      custom, 287–289
      overview, 281–282
      preset, 284–287
   capabilities of, 17, 268
   enabling features
      comments, 272–277
      digital signatures, 270–271
      editing enabled forms, 278–281
      form server products, 269–270
      LCD forms, 278
      licensing limitations, 268–269
      overview, 267–268
      Save form data feature, 270–271
      with wizards, 277–278
   LCD forms, 1081
   overcoming limitations of, 10
   overview, 29
   versions of, 520, 642
Reader Enable Document for Commenting dialog box, 272
Reader Extensions Server (LCRE), 267, 270, 1086
reading forms
   aloud, 318–319
   order for, 312–314
   preferences for, 317–318
Reading Preferences settings, 317
ReadMe file, 1127
Ready to Sign button, 587, 595, 598
Recipient list option, 435
Recognize Text dialog box, 124
Recognize Text in Multiple Files Using OCR command,
      126, 135

Recognize Text – Settings dialog box, 122
Recognize Text Using OCR command
    batch sequences, 134–135
    converting documents with, 123
    detecting fields, 287
Rectangle comment, 551
Rectangle object
    Object Library palette, 674
    Standard Library palette, 765, 804
Rectangle tool, 549
rectangular shapes, 804–805
redundancy, 19
Ref function, 948
References Section Bar, 889
Registration Mark, 53
Relative binding expressions, 811–812
Remember me check box, 427
Remember numerical data check box, 175
Remove method, 916
removeField object, 598
Rename Field option, 195, 249
renaming objects and fields, 152, 543, 666
reordering fields, 817–818
Replace Document Colors option, 294
Replace Existing Object warning, 775
Replace function, 948
Replace Pages command, 73, 171
replacing pages, 73–74
Report palette
    Binding tab, 1024, 1070
    clear warnings option, 964
    Log tab, 931
    organizing palettes, 701
    Warning tab, 962–963
Require a password to open the document option, 358
Required check box, 464
Required field option, 145
Required field text box, 140
Required property, 212
Reserve drop-down menu, 792
Reset a form action, 105, 234
Reset a Form dialog box, 106, 235, 542
Reset Button object, 670, 765
Reset Form button
    adding to forms, 104–107
    attributes, 542
    script, 722

resetForm.pdf file, 385
resetting fields
    with JavaScript, 543–544
    preserving default values, 544
    separate fields for, 542–543
Resize window, 77
resolution, 129
resolveNode expression, 1105
Resources view, 1091
responses
    aggregating data, 454–456
    archiving data, 449–450
    exporting data, 444–445
    filtering data, 441–444
    manually adding data to file, 450–451
    manually collecting in e-mail inbox, 407–412
    overview, 437–440
    summary files, 445–448
    viewing data, 440
Responses option, 435
responses.pdf file
    Distribute Form wizard, 423, 434
    editing Submit Form button properties, 417
    JavaScript functions, 420
Restrict editing and printing of the document. A password
        will be required in order to change these
        permission settings check box, 358
Retain Page Layout radio button, 202
Reviews option, 435
Ribbon, 3, 1061
Right function, 948
Rights Management ES, 359, 1086
Risk Disclosure Statement, 382
riskDisclosure.pdf file, 384
root element, 997
Rotated User Space, 548
Rotations drop-down menu, 792
Round function, 946
rows, summing, 553–556
RSS feeds, 1121–1124
Rtrim function, 948
rulers
    drawing guidelines, 166
    overview, 165–166
    snapping fields to guidelines, 166
Rulers option, 88
Run a JavaScript action, 234–235, 491–492, 551, 578

Run At drop-down list, 931, 954
Run custom validation script radio button, 238
Run Form Field Recognition feature, 48, 98
Run FormCalc button, 1045–1046
Run Sequence button, 283
runtime, 830

S

sales tax, calculating
    with fixed tax rates, 557
    overview, 556
    with user-supplied tax rates, 557–558
sample files
    LCD, 648–652
    XML, 1005–1007
sample forms, LCD
    copying, 1030
    Dunning Notice, 1030–1033
    E-ticket, 1033–1035
    FormGuide, 1035–1039
    Grant Application, 1039–1041
    online, 1053–1054
    overview, 1029–1030
    Purchase Order, 1041–1043
    Scripting, 1043–1047
    SubformSet, 1047–1049
    Tax Receipt, 1049–1053
Sample Forms option, 659
Sample XML Data radio button, 857
SampleForm folder, 1127
Save a Copy dialog box, 279
Save Adobe PDF File As dialog box, 60
Save As dialog box, 974
Save As DOC Settings dialog box, 202
Save as PDF option, 66
Save command, 110
Save dialog box, 61
Save File dialog box, 444
Save form data feature, 270–271
Save Options tab, 802, 975
Save Target As check box, 406
saving forms
    LCD
        dynamic, 978–979
        overview, 974–976
        setting target version, 979–980

static, 977–978
        XDP, 981
    overview, 110–111
Scan feature
    overview, 113
    presets
        custom scans, 119–120
        editing, 117–118
        overview, 116–117
    scanner drivers
        Photoshop plug-in software, 114–115
        TWAIN software, 114
        WIA scan drivers, 115–116
    setting options, 120
scannedForms folder, 605, 608, 610
scanner drivers
    Photoshop plug-in software, 114–115
    TWAIN software, 114
    WIA, 115–116
Scanner Options dialog box, 120
Scanner pull-down menu, 117, 120
Scanners and Cameras dialog box, 115
scanning forms
    Acrobat Scan
        overview, 113
        presets, 116–120
        scanner drivers, 114–116
        setting options, 120
    Batch Sequences command, 134–135
    converting to PDF
        fillable forms, 131–133
        LCD, 133–134
        overview, 128–130
    OCR
        converting image files to text, 123–126
        features of, 121–123
        overview, 120–121
        recognizing text in multiple files, 126–128
    optimizing, 286
    overview, 603–605
    paper, 18
    setting up batch sequence, 610–612
    splitting files, 612–613
    summarizing data with
        adding fields to, 617–619
        reusing JavaScripts, 623
        sending data to summary files, 619–623
    using in single file, 605–607
    using individual, 607–610

Script Editor
    calculating line total, 949
    formatting, 939
    formulas and, 447
    LCD workspace, 661–662
    multiline, 930
    opening, 685–686
    overview, 930–932
    settings, 918
    single-line, 930
Script Editor window, 917
script fragment, 966
Script Name text box, 495, 518, 571
scripting
    bookmarks and custom navigation, 645
    debugging, 966
    guides, 1120–1121
    language, 934
    preferences, 933
    reference, 652–653, 967
    tasks, 966
Scripting folder, 649
Scripting form, 1043–1047
Scripting Object Model (SOM), 810, 1121
Scripting.pdf form, 1044, 1046
Scrolling long text check box, 218
Scrolling Pages tool, 86
SDK (Software Development Kit), 1088
Search tab, 1116
Searchable Image (Exact) option, 122–123
Searchable Image option, 122–123
searchable text
    assistive devices, 296
    converting image files to, 124
secondary forms
    overview, 613–614
    sending data to, 615–617
    setting up, 614–615
    summarizing data
        adding new fields to scanned forms, 617–619
        reusing JavaScripts, 623
        sending data to summary files, 619–623
sections, table
    designing, 861–865
    fields
        adjusting properties, 865–868
        debugging problems, 870–872
        setting global properties, 868–870
    overview, 860–861

Secure task button, 332, 360
security
    adding to LCD forms, 986–990
    creating policies, 360–364
    overview, 38, 359
Security Method drop-down menu, 355–356
Security Preferences dialog box, 335
Security Settings dialog box, 322, 337–340, 347
Security Settings window, 332–333
Security Settings wizard, 337
Security tab, 331, 357
Select & Zoom toolbar, 325
Select Action drop-down menu
    actions, adding to buttons, 262
    Actions properties, 230
    application response dialog boxes, 578
    buttons, adding to documents within portfolios, 388
    calculating shipping fees, 560
    check box and radio button behaviors, 536
    copying script from Console and pasting into button
        action, 503
    fields, adding to forms using JavaScript, 596
    Reset Form buttons, 105–106
    resetting fields using JavaScript, 544
    showing hidden fields in forms, 527
    Submit Form buttons, 108
    submitting forms, 235
Select Commands button, 282, 610
Select Database dialog box, 1010
Select Email Client dialog box, 416
Select File Containing Form Data dialog box, 11, 448, 454
Select File to Replace Pages dialog box, 73
Select Folder to Save File dialog box, 447
Select format category drop-down menu, 236, 463, 484, 532
Select Icon dialog box, 258–259, 387–388
Select Image for Custom Stamp dialog box, 274
Select Object tool
    Advanced Editing toolbar, 92–93
    arrow keys, 157
    averaging data, 463, 472
    calculating shipping fees, 559
    fillable forms, 20
    Form Editing Mode, 85
    JavaScripts
        adding to check box fields, 538
        finding, 491
        reference document, creating, 513
    locking fields, 529
    overview, 89

Select Object tool *(continued)*
    properties, setting, 99
    renaming fields, 543
    Submit Form buttons, customizing, 418
    text colors, changing, 532, 535
    unloading cursors, 141
Select output location options pull-down menu, 283
Select Source File dialog box, 393
Select Trigger pull-down menu, 231–232, 396, 578
selecting multiple objects
    on design page, 755–756
    in Hierarchy palette, 756–757
Selection Change tab, 240
seminarGlobal.doc file, 95, 99
seminarGlobal.pdf file, 95
seminarGlobalPopulated.pdf file, 101–102
seminarLayered.pdf file, 393
seminar.pdf file, 5
Send Form dialog box, 415
servers, deploying forms on
    file type considerations, 1105–1106
    overview, 1102–1104
    scripting considerations, 1104–1105
    server-required objects, 1106
service container, 1083
Service Oriented Architecture (SOA), 1080
Set Advanced Options dialog box, 1010
Set Field Calculation Order dialog box, 479–480
Set layer visibility action, 234–235, 395–396
Set method, 916
SetDescriptionEntries( ) function, 572
SetEachValue( ) function, 572
Settings toolbar, 702
SFN (Simplified Field Notation)
    Acrobat versions, 31
    averaging data from placeholder fields, 479
    calculation properties, 239
    naming fields for, 481
    overview, 461, 480–481
    performing math calculations with, 481–482
    scripts, 482
    writing calculation scripts, 553
Share option, 428
SharePoint Portal Server, 424
SharePoint Workspaces, 422, 424
sharing Custom Library objects, 775–778
Shift + Arrow Key selection method, 757

Shift + Click selection method, 757
shipping charges, calculating, 559–561
Shipping subform, 913, 915
Show All Properties button, 147
Show All Properties text box, 140
Show Certificate button, 349
Show Comment & Markup toolbar, 273
Show drop-down list, 918
Show Events for Child Objects button, 686
Show Field Properties command, 92, 155, 208
Show Navigation Panel Buttons option, 78
Show Package Contents option, 115
Show Tab Numbers option, 178
Show Tools on Toolbar menu command, 85, 138
Show When Creating Tables check box, 699
Show/hide a field action, 234–235
Show/Hide Field dialog box, 261–262, 396
showing fields, 525–529
Sign an existing signature field feature, 271
Sign Document dialog box, 341–342, 345
Sign task button, 331–332
Signature Field Properties window, 343
signature fields
    adding, 719–724
    automatic field detection, 47
    configuring for locking fields, 343–345
    designing forms for recipients, 37
    editing multiple, 245
    hiding, 399
    Object Library palette, 670
    signing in, 341–342
    Standard Library palette, 765
Signature – Print and Sign object, 769
Signature Properties dialog box, 346, 349
Signature Settings dialog box, 721
Signature tab, 720, 988
Signature Validation dialog box, 348
Signature Validation Status dialog box, 348
signatures, digital
    applying multiple, 345–346
    digital IDs
        creating, 337–341
        custom appearance, 334–336
        overview, 332–334
    enabling files for, 270–271
    JavaScripts, assigning to, 493–494
    locking fields, 342–345

overview, 30, 147, 321–322
properties, setting, 240–241
signing, 341–342
tab options, 210
third-party signature handlers, 323
validating
   certificates, 347–353
   overview, 346
   with Trusted Identities, 354
wet signatures
   adding in Reader, 324–326
   overview, 37
   preparing files for using LCD, 328–331
   scanning analog, 323–324
   using with Acrobat recipients, 326–328
Signatures panel, 354
Signatures panel drop-down menu, 354
Signed tab, 240–241, 343
Simplified Field Notation (SFN)
   Acrobat versions, 31
   averaging data from placeholder fields, 479
   calculation properties, 239
   naming fields for, 481
   overview, 461, 480–481
   performing math calculations with, 481–482
   scripts, 482
   writing calculation scripts, 553
Simplified Field Notation text box, 481
Single Page Continuous menu command, 76
Single Page menu command, 76
Size drop-down menu, 49
Size option, 244
sizing fields, 140, 159
Skip the Assistant this one time option, 658
Skip the Assistant when creating new documents option, 658
Sliding Row layout, 369–370
smart forms, 21
Snap to Grid setting, 169, 683, 693, 792
snapping
   fields to guidelines, 166
   to grids, 169
Snapshot tool, 325
SOA (Service Oriented Architecture), 1080
Software Development Kit (SDK), 1088
SOM (Scripting Object Model), 810, 1121
Sort drop-down menu, 380
Sort items option, 224
Sort pull-down menu, 88, 196

Space function, 948
Spacing (Above) menu, 800
Spacing (Below) menu, 800
spawn object, 601
spawned fields, 588
spawning pages from templates
   appending pages to documents, 600–602
   creating, 599–600
   overlaying on form pages, 602–603
   overview, 598
   scanned forms, 603–613
spawnPageFromTemplate object, 588
Special Instructions field, 912
Special option, 237, 460
Specify File Details panel, 377–379
Split Document dialog box, 612–613
splitting files, 612–613
spreadsheets, 11–12, 200
Stamp comment, 288
Stamp pull-down menu, 273, 276
stamping
   fields, 746–748
   objects, 746–748
Standard Business Stamps file, 289
Standard Group, 643, 766–767, 771
Standard Library palette
   Custom library group, 715, 717
   default properties, 764–765
   designing forms, 846
   elliptical shapes, 803
   Field Edit tool, 750
   field objects, adding to blank forms, 711
   Line object, 804
   Paper Forms Barcode object, 770
   Radio Button object, 712
   signature and button fields, 720–722
   static table, creating in LCD, 838
   strokes and fills, editing, 801
   template files, editing, 736
   Text Field object, 790, 865
   text fields, creating, 845
Standard Library tab, 707–708
Standard toolbar, 690, 692
Start Form wizard, 82, 95, 131
Start Form Wizard command
   blank forms, creating, 704–705
   converting
     documents, 4
     Office forms to PDF documents, 42

Start Form Wizard command *(continued)*
    Form Editing Mode, 90–91
    overview, 82–83
    Viewer Mode, 91
Start Process icon, 1095–1098
Start the Program radio button, 115
StartingPurchaseOrder.xdp form, 949, 953, 955
static barcodes, 770
static forms, 18–20, 646, 872
Static LiveCycle Designer Document, 642
static objects, 673–674, 1103
static tables
    creating, 836–842
    Insert Table command, 843–845
status bar, 686–687
Sticky Note, 432
Str function, 948
String method, 968
String.concat method, 968
String.length method, 968
String.replace method, 968
String.search method, 968–969
String.substring method, 968–969
String.toLowerCase method, 968
String.toUpperCase method, 969
strokes
    editing, 801–805
    weight of, 47
Stuff function, 948
Style drop-down menu, 795, 798
Sub Total field, 559
Subform object
    Object Library palette, 674
    Standard Library palette, 765
Subform Place option, 884
Subform Set folder, 649
Subform Sets tab, 1049
Subform tab
    comments pages, creating with expanding text fields, 909
    Layout palette, 913–914
    pagination options, setting, 882
    positioned and flowed content areas, 879
    subforms, setting up with overflow leaders, 890, 892
subforms
    dynamic expanding text fields, 903–915
    headers and footers, 888–892
    LCD, 644
    nesting, 894–901

    overview, 873–875
    placing
        before adding content, 875–876
        after adding content, 877–878
    previewing, 892–894
    properties, setting
        overview, 878
        pagination options, 882–887
        positioned and flowed content areas, 879–882
    testing forms, 919–924
    troubleshooting dynamic forms, 923–924
    user-controlled dynamic forms
        Instance Manager, 916–919
        overview, 915
    using tables for, 901–903
SubformSet forms, 1047–1049
submission scripts
    submitting form data, 540
    submitting forms, 539–540
Submit a form action, 8–9, 235, 388
Submit Form Actions tab, 528
Submit Form button
    adding to forms, 7–10, 107–109
    Distribute Form button, 104
    distributed forms
        managing manually, 450
        receiving and filling in, 414
    e-mailing forms with, 407
    hacking
        editing properties, 416–420
        JavaScript functions, 420–421
        overview, 416–417
    overview, 671
    showing hidden fields on form, 527
    submitting forms to Acrobat.com, 429
Submit Form Button Field Properties window, 527–528
Submit Form Selections dialog box
    editing forms, 8
    enabling forms in PDF Portfolios, 390
    opening, 389
    submission scripts, creating, 539
    Submit Form buttons, 108
submitFormButton.pdf file, 385
submitting forms
    to Acrobat.com, 429–431
    overview, 539–540
    from PDF Portfolios, 390
Substr function, 948

Sum function, 946, 953, 961
summarizing data with scanned forms
    adding fields, 617–619
    reusing JavaScripts, 623
    sending data to summary files, 619–623
summary files, 445–448
summary forms
    sending data to, 615–617
    summarizing data with, 619–623
Summary pane, 363
summing data
    columns and rows, 553–556
    overview, 469–479
sunken text field box, 767
Symantec, 632
Symbol Technologies, 771
syntax checker, 686
System DSN tab, 1011
system requirements
    CD-ROM, 1125
    LCD, 642–643
System\Library\Image Capture\TWAIN Data Sources
        folder, 113

T

Tab key, 38, 171
tab order
    batch sequence preset for, 287
    changing views, 818–819
    overview, 660
    reordering fields, 817–818
    returning to normal edit mode, 819
    rules, 38
    setting, 176–179
Tab Order option, 294
Tab Order palette, 668, 817–819
Tab Order pane, 176–178
Tab Order pull-down menu, 88
tabbing, 671
Table Assistant wizard, 699, 835, 847–851
Table toolbar, 690
tables
    adding fields manually
        columns, 191–193
        mutually exclusive fields, 194–197
        non-table data, 197–199

overview, 190
    rows, 191
    auto-detecting fields in
        editing results, 184–189
        overview, 183–184
    converting to application documents
        Excel, 200–201
        overview, 199–200
        Word, 202–203
    default properties, 765
    duplicating, 475
    exporting data, 204
    LCD
        data, 851–860
        dynamic, 845–851
        objects, 833–835
        overview, 644
        sections, 860–872
        static, 836–845
    Object Library palette, 673
    overview, 181–182
    using for subforms, 901–903
TableTotals subform, 897
tagged PDF files
    checking status of
        full accessibility check, 300–302
        overview, 297–298
        quick accessibility check, 298–300
    creating tags, 302–305
    overview, 296
tags, XML, 996, 997
Tags panel, 304, 314–316
Tax Field, 951
Tax field calculation, 957
Tax Receipt folder, 649
Tax Receipt form, 1049–1053
TDS (Designer Template), 736, 780
Technology With An Important Name (TWAIN) software,
        114, 131
Template Assistant wizard, 738, 741
Template Manager dialog box, 732–733, 735, 738
Template Options dialog box, 736
template.pdf document, 605
templates
    creating forms from, 733–734
    custom, 734–741
    LCD, 643

templates *(continued)*
overview, 732–733
spawning pages from
appending pages to documents, 600–602
creating templates, 599–600
overlaying templates on form pages, 602–603
overview, 598
scanned forms, 603–613
Term function, 947
Test Connection button, 1013
testing forms, 919–924
`TestingGFApplication_DB.pdf` file, 1066
text
alternate, 314–317
colors
changing, 531–533
custom, 533–536
editing, 68–69
OCR
converting image files to text, 123–126
features of, 121–123
overview, 120–121
recognizing text in multiple files, 126–128
text box comments, 550–553
Text Box Field properties window, 481
Text Color option, 244
text extraction, 297
Text Field dialog box, 812
Text Field menu, 805
Text Field Properties dialog box
application response dialog boxes, 578, 580
calculating
sales tax, 558
sums for check box fields, 476
calculation formulas, 250–251
fields
adding, 102–103
editing names, 153
formatting, 247, 252, 458–460
font attributes, changing, 215
layer visibility, changing, 396
null values, 565
overview, 209
properties, setting, 100
summing
columns of fields, 555
data in columns, 470

tab options, 210
text colors, 532, 535
Text Field Properties Format tab, 591
Text Field tool
adding fields, 102
formatting
arbitrary masks, 253
comb fields, 251
fields, 458
organizing fields, 155
setting text options, 217
tooltips, 141–142
text fields
default properties, 765
editing multiple, 245
loaded cursors, 107
Object Library palette, 673
overview, 139–140
properties, setting
arbitrary mask fields, 253–255
calculating, 249–251
comb fields, 251–255
naming, 246–248
overview, 217–219
stamping, 747
tab options, 210
Text Formatting toolbar, 690–691, 702, 709
Text object, 674, 717, 765
Text palette, 371, 729, 864
TextEdit, 58
third-party signature handlers, 323
This script executes when the field is signed option, 241
this.numPages script, 545
`this.pageNum` object, 590
this.pageNum script, 545
this.pageNum-- script, 545
this.pageNum++ script, 545
this.pageNum=1 script, 545
TIFF format, 725
time, calculating, 482–485, 591–594
Time function, 947
Time option, 237, 460
Time Stamp Servers option, 333
Time2Num function, 947
TimeFmt function, 947
To Do Icon, 1077
To Do list, 1098–1099

toggling views, 88–92
Toolbar Well
    Acrobat versions, 138
    enabled PDF files, editing, 279
    fields, editing in Viewer mode, 92
    labels, 141
    Typewriter tool, 170
    wet signatures, applying, 325
toolbars, adding to workspace, 689–691
Toolbars tab, 691
Tools menu, 381
Tools toolbar, 690–691, 702, 750–751
Tooltip property, 211
tooltips, 141–142, 154
Total field script, 952
Total Fields command, 624
Total Templates command, 624
Total Time column, 485, 591
TouchUp Object tool, 70–72, 327–328
TouchUp Properties dialog box, 68–69, 315
TouchUp Text tool, 68–70
Track Forms command, 31, 92
Tracker, 409–410, 418, 431, 434–437, 453, 1123
Tracker Preferences dialog box, 424, 436, 1121
Tracking page, 1099–1100
Transfer Method, 120
transferNotTagged.pdf file, 303–304
transferTagged.pdf file, 303
Transparency check box, 326
travelExpenseSample.pdf file, 512
trim marks, 51–54
troubleshooting
    automatic field detection, 109–110
    CD-ROM, 1127
    dynamic forms, 923–924
Trusted Identities
    adding levels of trust to certificates, 350–353
    validating signatures, 354
tutorials, LCD, 1027–1029
TWAIN (Technology With An Important Name) software,
        114, 131
two-dimension (2D) format, 771
Type drop-down menu, 806–807
type font, 297
Type tool, 72
Typewriter tool, 19, 31, 169–171
Typography enhancements feature, 660

U

UltraForms, 24
Unicode Transformation Format (UTF-8), 996
unit of measure, 166
Units & Guides option, 167
UnitType function, 948
UnitValue function, 948
Universal Product Code (UPC), 769
unloading cursors, 141
Unspecified option, 177
Up button action, 226, 232, 575
UPC (Universal Product Code), 769
Update option, 438
updating form fragments, 783
Up/Down option, 224
Upper function, 948
URLs, adding to menus, 627–628
U.S. Federal Government, 17
U.S. Social Security Number field, 769
U.S. States drop-down box, 768
Usage Options drop-down menu, 339
USC Google Groups, 512
Use a Blank Form option, 657
Use Column Order option, 177
Use Current Properties as New Defaults option
    appearances, setting current as default, 106
    attribute defaults, setting, 159
    defining defaults for button fields, 260
    formatting fields, 458
    sizing forms, 189
Use Document Structure option, 177
Use Row Order option, 177
User Entered – Optional option, 806
User Entered – Recommended option, 806
User Entered – Required option, 806
user reference summary, 652
User Space, 548
user-controlled dynamic forms
    Instance Manager
        creating buttons for calling, 916–919
        overview, 916
    overview, 915
UTF-8 (Unicode Transformation Format), 996
Uuid function, 948

V

Validate properties, 493
Validate Signature option, 354
Validate tab, 236, 238
validating signatures
   certificates
      acquiring via e-mail attachments, 347–348
      exporting from signed documents, 348–350
      levels of trust, adding to, 350–353
   overview, 346
   with Trusted Identities, 354
validation patterns, 814–816
Validation tab, 813
Value is the...of the following fields drop-down menu,
      461, 468
Value property, 677
Value tab, 241–243, 806
Variables view, 1090
version mapping, 967
vertical guideline, 760
Vertical Justification menu, 800
Vertical Placement group, 754
Vertical Scale option, 798
Vertical Spacing feature, 754
videos, Flash
   alternate text descriptions, 314
   converting to PDF, 84
   including in PDF forms, 234–235
View File Now button, 455
View menu
   Editor tabs, 682
   grid, 692–694
   zoom levels, 692
View Responses option, 435
View Responses text link, 437
View toolbar, 702
Viewer mode
   Acrobat 8, 81
   automatic field detection, 48
   button fields, 142
   Button tool, accessing, 93
   editing forms, 7
   examining Forms menu, 90
   fields
      creating, 163–165
      editing, 92–94
      editing names of, 153

   versus Form Editing Mode, 94
   toggling views, 89
viewers
   accessing, 520–521
   Adobe
      Acrobat 9 Pro, 29–30
      Acrobat 9 Pro Extended, 30
      Acrobat 9 Standard, 29
      Reader, 29
   considerations when choosing, 37
   types of, 522–523
   versions of
      setting target, 979–980
      using different, 30–31
viewing
   fields, 172–174
   files on Acrobat.com, 432–433
   response data, 440
Viewing toolbar, 86
views
   changing, 818–819
   initial
      layout, adjusting, 76–77
      magnification, adjusting, 76–77
      overview, 75–76
      user interface options, 77–78
      Window Options, 77
   palettes
      adding tools and toolbars, 689–691
      keyboard shortcuts, 688–689
      overview, 687
   toggling, 88–92
   zooming, 544–545
Views tool, 1089
VirtualBox, 634
virtualization software, 633–634
visibility layer, 395–397
visibility property, 1058
Visible (Print Only) check box, 796
Visible (Screen Only) check box, 796
Visible check box, 796
VMWare Fusion, 634

W

W3C (World Wide Web Consortium) standards, 36
Warning tab, 962
Warnings palette, 858–859

Web servers, forms hosted on, 21–29
Web Service Definition Language (WSDL) files, 1015–1021
welcome pages, 371–373, 438
Welcome to Form Editing Mode dialog box, 95
welcome window, LCD, 656–657
wet signatures
    adding in Reader, 324–326
    overview, 37
    preparing files for using LCD, 328–331
    scanning, 323–324
    using with Acrobat recipients, 326–328
white space, 35
WIA (Windows Imaging Architecture) scan drivers
    overview, 115–116
    presets
        custom scans, 119–120
        editing, 117–118
        overview, 116–117
Width text box, 49, 791
Wiley Product Technical Support phone number, 1127
WindJack Solutions, 623
Window menu
    drawing aids, 683–685
    Font palette, 682–683
    overview, 681
    Paragraph palette, 682–683
    script editor, 685–686
    status bar, 686–687
Window options, 77
Windows Imaging Architecture (WIA) scan drivers
    overview, 115–116
    presets
        custom scans, 119–120
        editing, 117–118
        overview, 116–117
Windows Notepad, 58
Windows WordPad, 58
Wingding font, 47, 99
Within function, 947
wizards
    Combine Files, 64, 368, 1119
    converting to PDF files with, 95–99
    Create or Edit Form
        converting Office forms to PDF documents, 42
        converting Word documents to PDF forms, 95
        creating forms, 704–705
        overview, 82–83
        scanning forms, 131, 133

creating forms from PDF files with, 99
Distribute Form
    Acrobat.com, 425, 429–430
    data management, 434, 450
    distributing forms, 406–409, 412, 414, 648
    enabling forms, 277–278
    hacking Submit Form button, 417–418
    LCD, 990
    network servers, 422
    overview, 87
enabling features with, 277–278
Managing Security Policies, 360–361
New Assistant Form, 83
    converting Word forms to LCD, 725
    creating forms, 657–660, 733–735
    default, 700
    Do Not Use Assistant option, 698–699
    Excel, 730
    importing PDF documents, 742
    overview, 705–706
    scanning forms, 133
    settings, 658
    static tables, creating, 837
New Security Policy, 360–361
overview, 94
properties, setting, 99–101
Start Form, 82, 95, 131
Table Assistant, 699, 835, 847–851
Template Assistant, 738, 741
Word application
    converting documents to PDF files, 95–99
    converting to LCD forms, 725–730
    design elements, 45–47
    exporting tables to
        with Copy as Table option, 203
        with Export command, 202–203
    form design and, 43
    overview, 44–45
    page sizes
        Macintosh, 50
        overview, 47–48
        Windows, 48–50
    preparing forms for print
        cropping, 51–54
        overview, 50–51
        trim marks, adding, 51–54
    setting up forms, 725
WordNum function, 948

WordPad, 58
Workbench, 1089
Workbench ES, 1088–1093
workshop name check box, 620
workshop name field, 620
Workshop Summary form, 834
`workshopForms.pdf` file, 617, 619
`workshopFormsPopulated.pdf` file, 617
`workshopOneLine_data.xml` file, 857
`workshopSummaryBackground.pdf` file, 837
`workshopSummaryLCD_data.xml` file, 847, 852
`workshopSummaryLCD.pdf` form, 847–848, 854
`workshopSummary.pdf` form, 617
workspace, LCD
    palette tabs, 662–663
    palette views, 687–691
    palette wells, 662–663
    palettes, 662–668
    script editor, 661–662
    View menu, 692–694
    Window menu, 681–687
Workspace category dialog box, 939–940
Workspace login page, 1074, 1095
Workspace welcome page, 1075, 1096
World Wide Web Consortium (W3C) standards, 36
WSDL (Web Service Definition Language) files, 1015–1021
WSDL Connection Properties dialog box, 1017–1018

X

X Value text box, 791
XDP (XML Data Package) forms, 981, 1093
XFA (XML Form Architecture), 640, 965
XML (Extensible Markup Language)
    binding data to
        sample files, 1005–1007
        schema, 1003–1005
    creating
        data, 852–855, 920–921
        files, 994–996

distributing forms, 648
editing
    files, 636–638
    forms, 646–647
editors for, 999–1001
enabling forms, 647–648
exporting, 31
importing, 447–448, 922–924
overview, 640
structure of, 996–999
syntax rules, 997–998
XML Data Package (XDP) forms, 981, 1093
XML File button, 1061
XML Form Architecture (XFA), 640, 965
XML Form Object Model Class Hierarchy, 967
XML Notepad 2007, 999
XML Schema Definition (XSD), 998, 1003
XML Schema radio button, 1003
XML Source tab, 680–681
XSD (XML Schema Definition), 998, 1003
XSLT (Extensible Stylesheet Language Transformation), 995, 1003, 1006, 1056

Y

Y Value text box, 791

Z

Zapf Dignbat font, 47, 99
zeros, eliminating
    adding null values to fields, 564–566
    overview, 469
    replacing with null values, 566–569
Zoom In tool, 86, 185
zoom levels, 692
Zoom Out tool, 86
zooming views, 544–545

Wiley Publishing, Inc.
End-User License Agreement

READ THIS. You should carefully read these terms and conditions before opening the software packet(s) included with this book "Book". This is a license agreement "Agreement" between you and Wiley Publishing, Inc. "WPI". By opening the accompanying software packet(s), you acknowledge that you have read and accept the following terms and conditions. If you do not agree and do not want to be bound by such terms and conditions, promptly return the Book and the unopened software packet(s) to the place you obtained them for a full refund.

1. **License Grant.** WPI grants to you (either an individual or entity) a nonexclusive license to use one copy of the enclosed software program(s) (collectively, the "Software" solely for your own personal or business purposes on a single computer (whether a standard computer or a workstation component of a multi-user network). The Software is in use on a computer when it is loaded into temporary memory (RAM) or installed into permanent memory (hard disk, CD-ROM, or other storage device). WPI reserves all rights not expressly granted herein.

2. **Ownership.** WPI is the owner of all right, title, and interest, including copyright, in and to the compilation of the Software recorded on the disk(s) or CD-ROM "Software Media". Copyright to the individual programs recorded on the Software Media is owned by the author or other authorized copyright owner of each program. Ownership of the Software and all proprietary rights relating thereto remain with WPI and its licensers.

3. **Restrictions On Use and Transfer.**

    (a) You may only (i) make one copy of the Software for backup or archival purposes, or (ii) transfer the Software to a single hard disk, provided that you keep the original for backup or archival purposes. You may not (i) rent or lease the Software, (ii) copy or reproduce the Software through a LAN or other network system or through any computer subscriber system or bulletin-board system, or (iii) modify, adapt, or create derivative works based on the Software.

    (b) You may not reverse engineer, decompile, or disassemble the Software. You may transfer the Software and user documentation on a permanent basis, provided that the transferee agrees to accept the terms and conditions of this Agreement and you retain no copies. If the Software is an update or has been updated, any transfer must include the most recent update and all prior versions.

4. **Restrictions on Use of Individual Programs.** You must follow the individual requirements and restrictions detailed for each individual program in the "What's on the DVD" appendix of this Book. These limitations are also contained in the individual license agreements recorded on the Software Media. These limitations may include a requirement that after using the program for a specified period of time, the user must pay a registration fee or discontinue use. By opening the Software packet(s), you will be agreeing to abide by the licenses and restrictions for these individual programs that are detailed in the "Using the CD-ROM" appendix and on the Software Media. None of the material on this Software Media or listed in this Book may ever be redistributed, in original or modified form, for commercial purposes.

5. **Limited Warranty.**

   (a) WPI warrants that the Software and Software Media are free from defects in materials and workmanship under normal use for a period of sixty (60) days from the date of purchase of this Book. If WPI receives notification within the warranty period of defects in materials or workmanship, WPI will replace the defective Software Media.

   (b) WPI AND THE AUTHOR OF THE BOOK DISCLAIM ALL OTHER WARRANTIES, EXPRESS OR IMPLIED, INCLUDING WITHOUT LIMITATION IMPLIED WARRANTIES OF MERCHANTABILITY AND FITNESS FOR A PARTICULAR PURPOSE, WITH RESPECT TO THE SOFTWARE, THE PROGRAMS, THE SOURCE CODE CONTAINED THEREIN, AND/OR THE TECHNIQUES DESCRIBED IN THIS BOOK. WPI DOES NOT WARRANT THAT THE FUNCTIONS CONTAINED IN THE SOFTWARE WILL MEET YOUR REQUIREMENTS OR THAT THE OPERATION OF THE SOFTWARE WILL BE ERROR FREE.

   (c) This limited warranty gives you specific legal rights, and you may have other rights that vary from jurisdiction to jurisdiction.

6. **Remedies.**

   (a) WPI's entire liability and your exclusive remedy for defects in materials and workmanship shall be limited to replacement of the Software Media, which may be returned to WPI with a copy of your receipt at the following address: Software Media Fulfillment Department, Attn.: PDF Forms Using Acrobat and LiveCycle Designer Bible, Wiley Publishing, Inc., 10475 Crosspoint Blvd., Indianapolis, IN 46256, or call 1-800-762-2974. Please allow four to six weeks for delivery. This Limited Warranty is void if failure of the Software Media has resulted from accident, abuse, or misapplication. Any replacement Software Media will be warranted for the remainder of the original warranty period or thirty (30) days, whichever is longer.

   (b) In no event shall WPI or the author be liable for any damages whatsoever (including without limitation damages for loss of business profits, business interruption, loss of business information, or any other pecuniary loss) arising from the use of or inability to use the Book or the Software, even if WPI has been advised of the possibility of such damages.

   (c) Because some jurisdictions do not allow the exclusion or limitation of liability for consequential or incidental damages, the above limitation or exclusion may not apply to you.

7. **U.S. Government Restricted Rights.** Use, duplication, or disclosure of the Software for or on behalf of the United States of America, its agencies and/or instrumentalities "U.S. Government" is subject to restrictions as stated in paragraph (c)(1)(ii) of the Rights in Technical Data and Computer Software clause of DFARS 252.227-7013, or subparagraphs (c) (1) and (2) of the Commercial Computer Software - Restricted Rights clause at FAR 52.227-19, and in similar clauses in the NASA FAR supplement, as applicable.

8. **General.** This Agreement constitutes the entire understanding of the parties and revokes and supersedes all prior agreements, oral or written, between them and may not be modified or amended except in a writing signed by both parties hereto that specifically refers to this Agreement. This Agreement shall take precedence over any other documents that may be in conflict herewith. If any one or more provisions contained in this Agreement are held by any court or tribunal to be invalid, illegal, or otherwise unenforceable, each and every other provision shall remain in full force and effect.

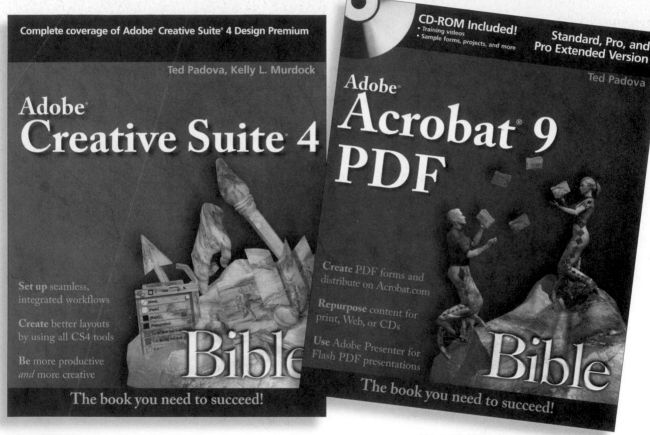